1000
CHOCOLATE
BAKING &
DESSERT RECIPES

1000
CHOCOLATE
BAKING &
DESSERT RECIPES

This is a Parragon Book
First published in 2003

Parragon
Queen Street House
4 Queen Street
Bath BA1 1HE, UK

ISBN: 1-40541-651-3

Printed in Indonesia

Produced by The Bridgewater Book Company Ltd, Lewes, East Sussex

Thanks to the following contributors Sarah Banbery, Linda Doeser,
Stephanie Horner, Tom Kitch, Lesley Mackley, Gina Steer, Susanna Tee

New photography Ian Parsons
Home economists Richard Green, Brian Wilson

NOTE

This book uses imperial and metric measurements. Follow the same units
of measurement throughout; do not mix imperial and metric.
All spoon measurements are level: teaspoons are assumed to be 5 ml and
tablespoons are assumed to be 15 ml.
Unless otherwise stated, milk is assumed to be whole milk,
eggs and individual vegetables such as potatoes are medium
and pepper is freshly ground black pepper.

The nutritional information provided for each recipe is per serving or per person.
Optional ingredients, variations or serving suggestions have
not been included in the calculations. The times given for each recipe are an approximate
guide only because the preparation times may differ according to the techniques used by
different people and the cooking times may vary as a result of the type of oven used.

Recipes using raw or very lightly cooked eggs should be
avoided by infants, the elderly, pregnant women, convalescents
and anyone suffering from an illness.

contents

INTRODUCTION

Enjoy the delicious delights of the 1,000 chocolate, baking and dessert recipes in this collection. Find old favourites and numerous new and utterly tempting sweet dishes to try out. Whenever you are preparing a family meal, a filling and tasty treat for children's lunchboxes, a slice or biscuit for coffee or teatime with friends or a rich dessert or petit four to round off a dinner party or festive meal – you will find yourself reaching again and again for this book.

Children need little encouragement to eat biscuits or muffins, and will enjoy helping to make and decorate many of the small cakes and slices in this book. Each recipe contains the following information: preparation and cooking times, number of portions and level of difficulty (one chef's hat for an easy recipe, rising to five chef's hats for a difficult one). There are plenty of cook's tips and variations for you to follow.

Since all the recipes in this book are sweet, you may wish to use unsalted butter. Unsalted butter is specified for any recipe where salted would impair the taste, as in many of the cold desserts and gâteaux, petits fours and confectionery. In less rich recipes – tea breads, pancakes, cakes or biscuits, for example – either salted or unsalted butter may be used.

Chocolate features in the majority of recipes in this collection. For many of us, chocolate is sheer indulgence. Delicious as a taste in its own right, chocolate is particularly versatile in the kitchen as it pairs so well with all manner of other ingredients: spices, cream, fruit, nuts, liqueurs – and, as a sauce or filling, it transforms the simple into the sumptuous. Few can resist a slice of rich chocolate cake or a biscuit, a chocolate-covered petit four or a comforting bedtime drink. There are decadent smoothies and chocolate cocktails to try, too.

Types and styles of chocolate

Today there is an impressive range of styles and qualities of chocolate, readily available in our stores, from the basic cooking chocolate to the finest, cocoa-rich varieties. The most suitable variety for each recipe is not necessarily the most expensive: the texture of the different chocolates varies with the amount of cocoa they contain. Mousses, for example, can become much too heavy if the chocolate contains too much cocoa solid, because it acts in the same way as adding too much flour. The recipes only specify good-quality chocolate where its superior flavour enhances the result. In these cases, chocolate containing over 50 per cent cocoa is considered to be good quality, with 70 per cent-plus indicating the finest chocolate of all, which is probably better for eating rather than cooking.

chocolate-flavoured cake covering

This product has an inferior flavour because it contains vegetable fat instead of cocoa butter, but it is useful for making decorations because of the high fat content. As a compromise, add a few squares to a good-quality chocolate.

white chocolate

For colour contrast, especially for cake decoration, white chocolate is unbeatable. However, white chocolate has a lower content of cocoa butter, so choose a luxury cooking variety and take care not to overheat it when melting. There is also a vanilla-flavoured variety.

plain or continental plain chocolate

These styles of chocolate contain a minimum of 34 per cent cocoa solids and are generally around 50 per cent. They are ideal for most everyday cooking purposes. For special recipes, choose a luxury chocolate with a cocoa solid content of 70–75 per cent for a richer, more intense flavour, but do be aware that the higher the cocoa content, the denser the texture of your dessert or gâteau.

milk chocolate

As the name implies, this chocolate has a milder, creamier flavour, which makes it more popular with children than the plain variety. It is also useful for decorations. It must contain a minimum of 10 per cent cocoa mass and 12 per cent milk solids. Extra care must be taken when melting milk chocolate, because its milk content makes it more sensitive to heat than the plain variety.

chocolate chips

Available in plain, milk or white chocolate, these chips are useful for baking and decoration. They are especially good in biscuits, as well as sweets and a whole range of delicious confections. Chocolate buttons (usually milk) are also good for decorating cakes and small cakes and slices intended for children.

cocoa powder

This powder tastes bitter, and gives a good, strong chocolate flavour in cooking. It is mostly used in cakes. Do not use drinking chocolate powder unless a recipe specifically calls for it.

Storage

Most chocolate, including cocoa powder, can be stored for up to a year if it is kept in a cool, dry place away from direct heat or sunlight.

Preparing chocolate

Many recipes require chocolate to be melted before it is added with the other ingredients. One of the easiest ways to melt chocolate is on the hob:

1 Break the chocolate into small, equal-sized pieces and put into a heatproof bowl.

2 Place the bowl over a saucepan of gently simmering water, making sure the base of the bowl does not come into contact with the water. Do not allow any hot water to get into the chocolate, or it will harden rather than melt.

3 Once the chocolate starts to melt, stir gently until smooth, then remove from the heat.

This hob method is the one suggested in most of the recipes. Never melt chocolate over direct heat (unless melting with other ingredients, such as cream or butter, and in this case keep the heat very low). You can also melt chocolate in a low oven (160°C/325°F/Gas Mark 3). Break up the chocolate into pieces and place in an ovenproof bowl in the centre of the oven for about 10–15 minutes.

microwave method

To melt chocolate in a microwave oven:

1 Break chocolate into small pieces and place in a microwave-proof bowl.

2 Put the bowl into the microwave oven and melt. As a guide, melt 125 g/ 4$\frac{1}{2}$ oz plain chocolate on High for 2 minutes, and white or milk chocolate on Medium for 2–3 minutes.

3 Stir the chocolate, leave to stand for a few minutes, then stir again. If necessary, return it to the microwave for a further 30 seconds (different brands melt at different rates).

Note: As microwave oven temperatures and settings vary, you should consult the manufacturer's instructions first.

basic recipes

rich chocolate pastry

makes: 1 x 20-cm/8-inch flan case
preparation time: 10 minutes,
plus 30 minutes chilling

4 tbsp cocoa powder

200 g/7 oz plain flour, plus extra for dusting

100 g/3½ oz butter, softened

4 tbsp caster sugar

2 egg yolks

few drops of vanilla essence

1–2 tbsp cold water

1 Sift the cocoa powder and flour into a large bowl. Add the butter and rub it in with your fingertips until the mixture resembles fine breadcrumbs. Stir in the caster sugar. Add the egg yolks, vanilla essence and enough water to mix to the consistency of a dough.

2 Cover the pastry in clingfilm and leave to chill in the refrigerator for about 30 minutes. Roll out the pastry on a lightly floured work surface. It will line a 20-cm/8-inch flan tin or cake tin.

shortcrust pastry

makes: 1 x 15-cm/6-inch flan case
preparation time: 10 minutes,
plus 30 minutes chilling

115 g/4 oz plain flour

2 tbsp butter

2 tbsp lard or white vegetable fat

2 tbsp cold water

1 Sift the flour into a mixing bowl. Cut the butter and fat into small cubes and add them to the flour. Using your fingertips, gently rub the fats and flour together until the fat breaks down into tiny pieces and the mixture resembles fine breadcrumbs.

2 Use a round-bladed knife to stir in enough water to make the consistency of a dough. Gather into a ball and knead briefly. If it feels sticky, sprinkle over a little flour. Cover the pastry in clingfilm and leave to chill in the refrigerator for about 30 minutes. Roll out the pastry on a lightly floured work surface. It will line a 20-cm/8-inch flan case or cake tin.

sweet shortcrust pastry

makes: 1 x 20-cm/8-inch flan case
preparation time: 10 minutes,
plus 30 minutes chilling

225 g/8 oz plain flour

115 g/4 oz butter

2 tbsp lard or white vegetable fat

55 g/2 oz golden caster sugar

6 tbsp cold milk

Make in the same way as the shortcrust pastry, above, stirring in the sugar after you have rubbed the butter and fat into the flour and using milk instead of water.

pâte sucrée

makes: 1 x 20-cm/8-inch flan case
preparation time: 10 minutes,
plus 30 minutes chilling

225 g/8 oz plain flour

115 g/4 oz butter, chilled and cubed

55 g/2 oz golden caster sugar

1 egg yolk

1 tsp vanilla essence

a little water

Make in the same way as the shortcrust pastry, left, stirring in the sugar after you have rubbed the butter into the flour. Stir in the egg yolk and vanilla essence, with a little water if necessary, to make a smooth dough.

rich shortcrust pastry

makes: 1 x 20-cm/8-inch flan case
preparation time: 10 minutes,
plus 30 minutes chilling

175 g/6 oz plain flour, plus extra for dusting

100 g/3½ oz butter, diced

1 tbsp golden caster sugar

1 egg yolk, beaten with 1 tbsp water

1 Sift the flour into a large bowl. Add the butter and rub it in with your fingertips until the mixture resembles fine breadcrumbs, then stir in the sugar. Stir in the beaten egg yolk.

2 Knead lightly to form a firm dough. Cover with clingfilm and leave to chill in the refrigerator for 30 minutes.

3 Roll out the dough on a lightly floured work surface and use to line a 20-cm/8-inch flan tin.

Chocolate Decorations

Decorations add a special touch to a cake or dessert. They can be interleaved with baking paper and stored in airtight containers. Decorations made with plain chocolate will keep for 4 weeks, and with milk or white chocolate for 2 weeks.

chocolate curls

1 Choose a thick bar of chocolate, and keep it at room temperature.

2 Using a sharp vegetable peeler, scrape lightly along the chocolate to form fine curls, or more firmly to form thicker ones.

chocolate caraque

It takes a little practice to achieve the professional look of caraque as a decoration for cakes and desserts, although the technique is in itself not difficult.

1 Break a bar of chocolate into pieces and put in a heatproof bowl set over a saucepan of gently simmering water, stirring until it melts. Spread the melted chocolate over a clean acrylic chopping board or, preferably, a marble slab and leave to set.

2 When the chocolate has set, hold the board firmly, position a large, smooth-bladed knife on the chocolate and pull the blade towards you at an angle of 45°, scraping along the chocolate to form the caraque. You should end up with irregularly shaped long scrolls (see below).

3 Using the knife blade, lift the caraque off the board.

chocolate leaves

You need first to select some freshly picked leaves with well-defined veins that are clean, dry and pliable. Rose leaves and bay leaves are particularly suitable.

1 Holding a leaf by its stem, paint a smooth layer of melted chocolate on to the underside with a small paintbrush or pastry brush.

2 Repeat with the remaining leaves, then place, chocolate side up, on a baking sheet lined with greaseproof paper.

3 Refrigerate for at least an hour until set. When set, peel each leaf away from its chocolate coating.

chocolate sauce

Many dessert recipes include their own version of a chocolate sauce. Here is a basic chocolate sauce, which you can prepare very quickly. A tablespoon of brandy may be added, if preferred.

serves: 4
preparation time: 10 minutes

85 g/3 oz continental plain chocolate

150 ml/5 fl oz single cream

1 Break the chocolate into small pieces and place in a heavy-based saucepan with the cream. Heat very gently over a low heat, stirring constantly, until a smooth sauce is formed.

2 Transfer to a heatproof jug and serve warm.

chocolate icing

115 g/4 oz best-quality plain chocolate

115 g/4 oz unsalted butter

2 tbsp cold water or dark rum

Melt the chocolate with the water or rum in a heatproof bowl set over a saucepan of gently simmering water and stir until the chocolate is melted. Whisk in the butter a tablespoon at a time. Leave to cool, whisking occasionally, before use.

homemade crème fraîche

2 tbsp buttermilk

300 ml/10 fl oz double cream

Put the buttermilk in a preserving jar or a jar with a screw top. Add the cream, then close securely and shake to blend. Leave to set at warm room temperature for 6–8 hours, then refrigerate for at least 8 hours and up to 4 days. It will develop a slightly tangy flavour. Beat lightly before using.

Small Cakes, Slices & Biscuits

Who can resist the smell or taste of fresh-baked biscuits,

cookies and muffins? You will be spoilt for choice in this

chapter, which includes such tempting treats as Lemon

Chocolate Pinwheels, Chocolate Pretzels, Spiced Almond

Biscuits, White Chocolate Cookies,

Chocolate & Nut Crescents and Double

Chocolate Muffins. You can satisfy

hungry children with healthy treats

such as Coconut Flapjacks or Chocolate & Apple Oaties, or

offer indulgent morsels like Vanilla Hearts or Lavender

Biscuits during a mid-morning break

shared with family or friends.

Chocolate Chip Oat Cookies

Cookies expand during cooking, so it is best to bake them in several batches. Store these chocolate chip cookies in an airtight container for up to a week.

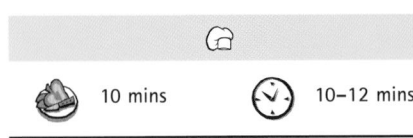

🐚 10 mins   🕐 10–12 mins

MAKES 24

INGREDIENTS

115 g/4 oz butter or margarine, plus extra for greasing

115 g/4 oz demerara sugar

1 egg

1 tbsp golden syrup

1 tbsp water

1 tsp vanilla essence

½ tsp almond essence

150 g/5½ oz plain flour, unsifted

½ tsp bicarbonate of soda

pinch of salt

2 tbsp boiling water

85 g/3 oz rolled oats

85 g/3 oz plain chocolate chips

85 g/3 oz white chocolate chips

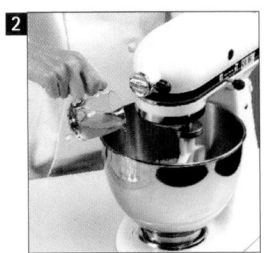

1 Preheat the oven to 180°C/350°F/Gas Mark 4. Grease 2 large baking sheets.

2 Put the butter, sugar, eggs, golden syrup, water and vanilla and almond essences in a large bowl or free-standing mixer and beat.

3 In a separate bowl, mix together the flour, bicarbonate of soda, salt, boiling water and oats, and then add to the egg mixture. Beat together thoroughly.

4 Stir in the plain and white chocolate chips, trying to incorporate them evenly, then put rounded teaspoonfuls of the mixture on to the greased baking sheets, allowing room for the cookies to expand. Transfer the sheets to the preheated oven and bake for 10–12 minutes.

5 Remove the cookies from the oven, then transfer to a wire rack and leave them to cool completely.

White Chocolate Cookies

These chunky cookies reveal a secret as you bite into them and discover the white chocolate chips scattered through them.

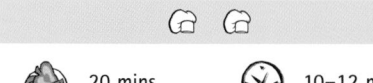

20 mins   10–12 mins

MAKES 24

INGREDIENTS

115 g/4 oz butter, softened, plus extra for greasing

115 g/4 oz soft brown sugar

1 egg, beaten

250 g/9 oz self-raising flour

pinch of salt

125 g/4½ oz white chocolate, chopped

50 g/1¾ oz chopped Brazil nuts

1 Preheat the oven to 190°C/375°F/Gas Mark 5. Grease several baking sheets lightly with a little butter.

2 In a large mixing bowl, cream together the butter and sugar until light and fluffy.

3 Gradually add the beaten egg to the creamed mixture, beating well after each addition.

4 Sift the flour and salt into the creamed mixture and blend well.

5 Stir in the white chocolate chunks and the chopped Brazil nuts.

6 Place heaped teaspoonfuls of the mixture on the prepared baking sheets. Put no more than 6 on each sheet because the cookies will spread during cooking.

7 Bake in the oven for 10–12 minutes, or until just golden brown.

8 Transfer the cookies to wire racks and leave until completely cold.

VARIATION
Use plain or milk chocolate instead of white chocolate, if you prefer.

Walnut & Chocolate Cookies

These delicious cookies will not be in the biscuit tin for long! They are too good, served with a cup of coffee, to resist.

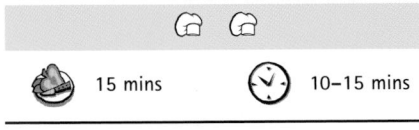

🕐 15 mins   🕐 10–15 mins

MAKES 24

INGREDIENTS

115 g/4 oz butter, softened, plus extra for greasing

55 g/2 oz golden granulated sugar

55 g/2 oz light muscovado sugar

1 egg, beaten

½ tsp vanilla essence

115 g/4 oz plain flour

2 tbsp cocoa powder

½ tsp bicarbonate of soda

115 g/4 oz milk chocolate chips

55 g/2 oz walnuts, chopped coarsely

1 Preheat the oven to 180°C/350°F/Gas Mark 4. Grease 2 large baking sheets. Put the butter, granulated sugar and muscovado sugar in a bowl and beat until light and fluffy. Gradually beat in the egg and vanilla essence.

2 Sift the flour, cocoa and bicarbonate of soda into the mixture and stir in carefully. Stir in the chocolate chips and walnuts. Drop spoonfuls of the mixture, well apart, on greased baking sheets.

3 Bake in the preheated oven for 10–15 minutes, until the mixture has spread and the cookies are starting to feel firm. Leave on the baking sheets for 2 minutes, then transfer to wire racks to cool completely.

COOK'S TIP
The minimum cooking time will give cookies that are soft and chewy in the middle. The longer cooking time will produce crisper cookies.

Double Chocolate Chip Cookies

Boasting both white and plain chocolate chips, these cookies are the ultimate treat for chocolate lovers.

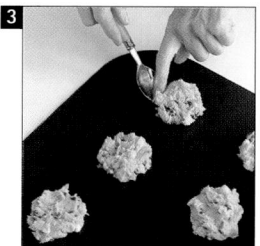

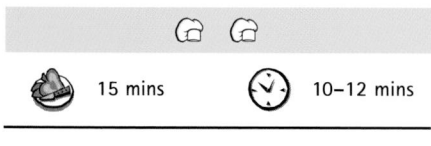 15 mins   10–12 mins

MAKES ABOUT 24

INGREDIENTS

200 g/7 oz butter, softened, plus extra for greasing

200 g/7 oz golden caster sugar

½ tsp vanilla essence

1 large egg

225 g/8 oz plain flour

pinch of salt

1 tsp bicarbonate of soda

115 g/4 oz white chocolate chips

115 g/4 oz plain chocolate chips

1 Preheat the oven to 180°C/350°F/ Gas Mark 4. Grease 2 baking sheets with butter. Place the butter, sugar and vanilla essence in a large bowl and beat together. Gradually beat in the egg until the mixture is light and fluffy.

2 Sift the flour, salt and bicarbonate of soda over the mixture and fold in. Fold in the chocolate chips.

3 Drop heaped teaspoonfuls of the mixture on to the prepared baking sheets, allowing room for the cookies to spread during cooking. Bake in the oven for 10–12 minutes, or until crisp outside but still soft inside. Leave to cool on the baking sheets for 2 minutes, then transfer to wire racks to cool completely.

COOK'S TIP
If you prefer crisp cookies, rather than soft, cook them for a little longer, about 13–15 minutes, then proceed as in the recipe.

Viennese Chocolate Fingers

These biscuits have a fabulously light, melting texture. You can leave them plain, but for real indulgence, dip them in chocolate to decorate.

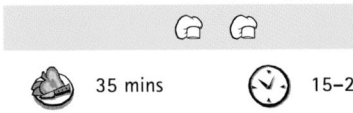

35 mins

15–20 mins

MAKES 18

INGREDIENTS

115 g/4 oz unsalted butter, plus extra
  for greasing

6 tbsp icing sugar

225 g/8 oz self-raising flour, sifted

3 tbsp cornflour

200 g/7 oz plain chocolate,
  broken into pieces

1 Preheat the oven to 190°C/375°F/Gas Mark 5. Lightly grease 2 baking sheets. Beat the butter and sugar in a mixing bowl until light and fluffy. Gradually beat in the flour and cornflour.

2 Put 75 g/2¾ oz of the plain chocolate in a heatproof bowl set over a saucepan of gently simmering water and stir until melted. Beat the melted chocolate into the mixture.

3 Place in a piping bag fitted with a large star nozzle and pipe fingers about 5 cm/2 inches long on to the baking sheets, allowing room for the biscuits to spread during cooking.

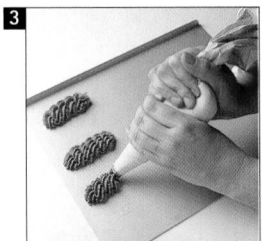

4 Bake in the preheated oven for 12–15 minutes. Leave to cool slightly on the baking sheets, then transfer to a wire rack and leave to cool completely.

5 Melt the remaining chocolate as in step 2. Dip one end of each biscuit in the chocolate, allowing the excess to drip back into the bowl.

6 Place the biscuits on a sheet of baking paper and leave the chocolate to set before serving.

COOK'S TIP
If the mixture is too thick
to pipe, beat in a little milk to
thin it down.

Chocolate Chip Cookies

No chocolate cook's repertoire would be complete without a chocolate chip cookie recipe. This recipe can be used to make several variations.

35 mins   10–12 mins

MAKES 18

INGREDIENTS

115 g/4 oz soft margarine, plus extra for greasing

225 g/8 oz plain flour

1 tsp baking powder

115 g/4 oz soft brown sugar

50 g/1¾ oz caster sugar

½ tsp vanilla essence

1 egg

115 g/4 oz plain chocolate chips

1 Preheat the oven to 190°C/375°F/ Gas Mark 5. Lightly grease 2 baking sheets. Place all of the ingredients in a large mixing bowl and beat until they are thoroughly combined.

2 Place tablespoonfuls of the mixture on to the prepared baking sheets, allowing room for the cookies to spread during cooking.

3 Bake in the preheated oven for 10–12 minutes, or until the cookies are golden brown.

4 Using a palette knife, transfer the cookies to a wire rack and leave until completely cool.

VARIATIONS

For Choc & Nut Cookies, add 55 g/2 oz chopped hazelnuts to the basic mixture. For Double Choc Cookies, beat in 40 g/1½ oz melted plain chocolate. For White Chocolate Chip Cookies, use white chocolate chips instead of the plain chocolate chips.

Chocolate & Coconut Biscuits

These delicious, melt-in-the-mouth biscuits are finished off with a simple icing and a generous sprinkling of coconut.

 40 mins   15–20 mins

MAKES 24

INGREDIENTS

115 g/4 oz soft margarine, plus extra for greasing

1 tsp vanilla essence

55 g/2 oz icing sugar, sifted

140 g/5 oz plain flour

2 tbsp cocoa powder

100 g/3½ oz desiccated coconut

2 tbsp butter

100 g/3½ oz white marshmallows

grated white chocolate, to decorate

1 Preheat the oven to 180°C/350°F/Gas Mark 4. Lightly grease a baking sheet. Beat together the margarine, vanilla and icing sugar in a bowl until fluffy. Sift together the flour and cocoa and beat it into the mixture with 60 g/2¼ oz coconut.

2 Roll rounded teaspoons of the mixture into balls and place on the prepared baking sheet, allowing room for the biscuits to spread during cooking.

3 Flatten the balls slightly with a palette knife and bake in the preheated oven for 12–15 minutes, until just firm.

4 Leave to cool on the baking sheet for a few minutes before transferring to a wire rack to cool completely.

5 Place the butter and marshmallows in a small saucepan and heat gently, stirring until melted. Spread a little of the icing over each biscuit and dip in the remaining coconut. Leave to set. Decorate with grated white chocolate before serving.

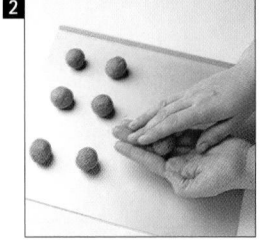

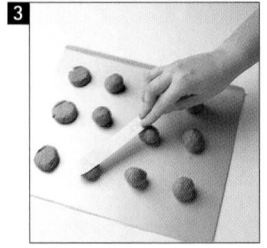

Chocolate Vanilla Pinwheels

These two-tone spiral biscuits look impressive, but they are easy to make. Presented in a pretty box, they make an ideal gift.

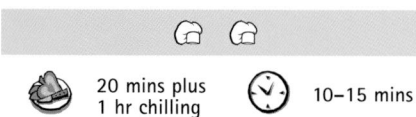

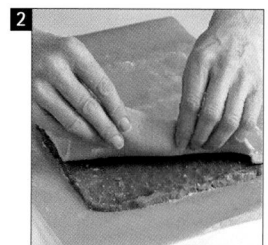

20 mins plus 1 hr chilling · 10–15 mins

MAKES ABOUT 36

INGREDIENTS

225 g/8 oz butter, softened, plus extra for greasing

115 g/4 oz golden caster sugar

325 g/11½ oz plain flour, plus extra for dusting

1 tbsp cocoa powder

1 tsp vanilla essence

1 Put the butter and sugar in a bowl and beat until light and fluffy. Transfer half the mixture to another bowl and add 175 g/6 oz of the flour and the cocoa. Stir the vanilla essence into the other half of the mixture and sift in the remaining flour. Stir both mixtures to make firm pliable doughs.

2 On a floured work surface, roll out each dough piece to a rectangle measuring 20 x 28 cm/8 x 11 inches. Place the chocolate dough on a piece of greaseproof paper and carefully place the vanilla dough on top. Roll up firmly from a long side, using the paper to guide the rolling. Wrap the roll in the paper and chill in the refrigerator for 1 hour, or until firm.

3 Preheat the oven to 180°C/350°F/Gas Mark 4. Grease 2 or 3 baking sheets. Unwrap the dough and cut into thin slices. Place the biscuits on the prepared baking sheets and bake in the preheated oven for 10–15 minutes, until golden. Cool on the baking sheets for 2 minutes, then transfer to wire racks to cool completely.

COOK'S TIP
Roll up the dough firmly or the biscuits will crack.

Chocolate & Apricot Biscuits

White chocolate and apricots make a very flavourful combination.
Serve these biscuits as an afternoon treat or after dinner with coffee.

15 mins plus
1 hr to chill

10 mins

MAKES 24

INGREDIENTS

425 g/15 oz white chocolate, chopped into
small pieces

140 g/5 oz plain flour, sifted, plus extra
for dusting

½ tsp baking powder

½ tsp bicarbonate of soda

pinch of salt

4 tbsp butter, plus extra for greasing

5 tbsp granulated sugar

1 tsp vanilla essence

1 egg

85 g/3 oz ready-to-eat dried apricots,
chopped, plus 3–4 extra, cut into thin
slices, to decorate

1 Put 85 g/3 oz of the white chocolate
pieces into a heatproof bowl set over
a saucepan of gently simmering water; stir
until melted. Remove from the heat. Sift
the flour, baking powder, bicarbonate of
soda and salt into a separate bowl. In
another bowl, cream the butter, sugar and
vanilla. Beat in the egg. Add the apricots,
melted chocolate and 175 g/6 oz of the
remaining chocolate pieces.

2 Add the flour mixture and beat well.
Using your hands, form the mixture
into a ball. Cover the bowl with clingfilm
and chill in the refrigerator for at least 1
hour. Preheat the oven to 180°C/350°F/
Gas Mark 4. Grease 1–2 large baking sheets.

3 Roll out the mixture into an oblong
2 mm/$\frac{1}{16}$ inch thick. Using biscuit
cutters, make 24 circles. Put on the baking
sheets, place in the preheated oven and
bake for 10 minutes. Transfer to a wire
rack to cool. Melt the remaining chocolate
(see step 1) and dip the biscuits in it. Put
each one on greaseproof paper, decorate
with apricot slices and leave to set. Store
in an airtight container in the refrigerator.

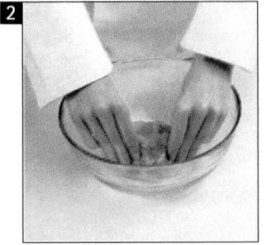

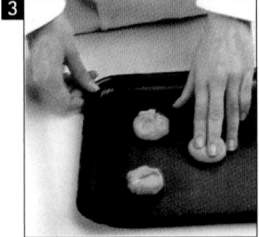

Lemon Chocolate Pinwheels

These stunning biscuits will have your guests guessing what are the mystery ingredients that give the pinwheels their exotic flavour!

15 mins plus 1 hr chilling

10–12 mins

MAKES 40

INGREDIENTS

175 g/6 oz butter, softened, plus extra for greasing

350 g/12 oz plain flour, plus extra for dusting

250 g/9 oz caster sugar

1 egg, beaten

25 g/1 oz plain chocolate, broken into pieces

grated rind of 1 lemon

 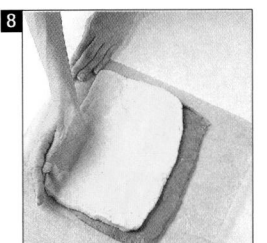 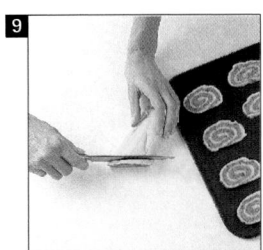

1 Grease and flour several baking sheets.

2 In a large mixing bowl, cream together the butter and sugar until light and fluffy.

3 Gradually add the beaten egg to the creamed mixture, beating well after each addition.

4 Sift the flour into the creamed mixture and mix thoroughly until a soft dough forms.

5 Transfer half of the dough to another bowl. Put the chocolate in a heatproof bowl set over a saucepan of gently simmering water until melted. Cool slightly. Beat in the chocolate.

6 Stir the grated lemon rind into the other half of the plain dough.

7 On a lightly floured work surface, roll out the dough to form 2 rectangles.

8 Lay the lemon dough on top of the chocolate dough. Roll up tightly, using a sheet of baking paper to guide you. Chill the dough for 1 hour.

9 Preheat the oven to 190°C/375°F/ Gas Mark 5. Cut the roll into 40 slices, place on the baking sheets and bake in the oven for 10–12 minutes, or until lightly golden. Transfer to a wire rack and leave to cool completely before serving.

COOK'S TIP
To make rolling out easier, place each piece of dough between 2 sheets of baking paper.

Molten Chocolate Biscuits

The ultimate biscuits – chocolate hazelnut spread, from a jar, packed inside a chocolate biscuit to produce an irresistible soft chocolate centre.

20 mins plus
30 mins chilling

15 mins

MAKES 12–14

INGREDIENTS

115 g/4 oz butter, plus extra for greasing

225 g/8 oz self-raising flour

2 tbsp cocoa powder

115 g/4 oz caster sugar

1 egg, beaten

plain flour, for dusting

200 g/7 oz chocolate hazelnut spread

milk, for brushing

icing sugar, for dusting

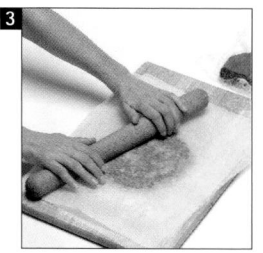

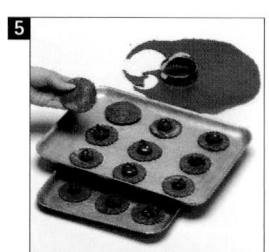

1 Preheat the oven to 190°C/375°F/ Gas Mark 5. Grease 2 large baking sheets. Sift the flour and cocoa together.

2 Beat the butter and caster sugar together until soft and fluffy. Gradually beat in the egg, then the sifted flour. Place the dough on a lightly floured work surface and knead for a short time until smooth. Chill in the refrigerator for 30 minutes.

3 Place the dough between 2 sheets of floured baking paper, thinly roll out half of it and cut into circles using a 5.5-cm/2¼-inch plain biscuit cutter.

4 Place the circles on the prepared baking sheets and place heaped teaspoons of the chocolate hazelnut spread on each. Brush the edges with a little milk.

5 Roll out the remaining dough and cut into circles using a 7-cm/2¾-inch plain biscuit cutter. Place on top of the chocolate hazelnut spread and seal the edges well.

6 Bake the biscuits in the oven for about 15 minutes, until firm. Transfer to a wire rack and leave to cool. When cold, dust with sifted icing sugar.

Chocolate Butter Biscuits

Topping these simple chocolate biscuits with a spoonful of chocolate and half a walnut turns them into something quite sophisticated.

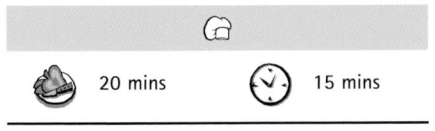

20 mins   15 mins

MAKES 24

I N G R E D I E N T S

115 g/4 oz butter, plus extra for greasing

175 g/6 oz plain flour

35 g/1¼ oz cocoa powder

115 g/4 oz caster sugar

1 egg, beaten

175 g/6 oz plain chocolate, broken into pieces

24 walnut halves

1 Preheat the oven to 180°C/350°F/Gas Mark 4. Grease 2–3 large baking sheets. Sift the flour and cocoa together into a large bowl.

2 Add the butter to the flour mixture and rub in until the mixture resembles fine breadcrumbs. Stir in the sugar, then add enough of the beaten egg to form a soft dough.

3 On a lightly floured work surface, roll out the dough to 3-mm/⅛-inch thickness, then cut into circles, using a 6-cm/2½-inch plain biscuit cutter. Place the circles on the prepared baking sheets, allowing room for the biscuits to spread during cooking.

4 Bake the biscuits in the oven for about 15 minutes, until firm. Transfer to a wire rack and leave to cool.

5 When the biscuits have cooled, melt the chocolate in a heatproof bowl set over a saucepan of gently simmering water. Spoon a little of the melted chocolate on to the centre of each biscuit, then top with a walnut half. Leave to set before serving.

Chocolate Orange Biscuits

These delicious chocolate biscuits have a tangy orange icing.
Children love them cut into animal shapes.

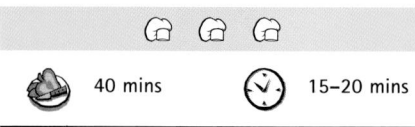

🧈 40 mins ⏱ 15–20 mins

MAKES 30

I N G R E D I E N T S

90 g/3¼ oz butter, softened

60 g/2¼ oz caster sugar

1 egg

1 tbsp milk

280 g/10 oz plain flour, plus extra
   for dusting

2 tbsp cocoa powder

I C I N G

175 g/6 oz icing sugar, sifted

3 tbsp orange juice

a little plain chocolate,
   broken into pieces

1 Preheat the oven to 180°C/350°F/
Gas Mark 4. Line 2 baking sheets with
sheets of baking paper.

2 Beat together the butter and sugar
until the mixture is light and fluffy.
Beat in the egg and milk until well
combined. Sift the flour and cocoa into the
bowl and gradually mix together to form a
soft dough. Use your fingers to incorporate
the last of the flour and bring the dough
together.

3 Roll out the dough on a lightly floured
work surface until 5 mm/¼ inch thick.
Cut out circles using a 5-cm/2-inch fluted
round biscuit cutter.

4 Place the circles on the prepared
baking sheets and bake in the
preheated oven for 10–12 minutes, or
until golden.

5 Let the biscuits cool on the baking
sheet for a few minutes before
transferring them to a wire rack to cool
completely and become crisp.

6 To make the icing, put the icing sugar
in a bowl and stir in enough orange
juice to form a thin icing that will coat
the back of the spoon. Put a spoonful of
icing in the centre of each biscuit and
leave to set. Place the plain chocolate in a
heatproof bowl set over a saucepan of
gently simmering water and stir until
melted. Drizzle thin lines of melted
chocolate over the biscuits and leave to
set before serving.

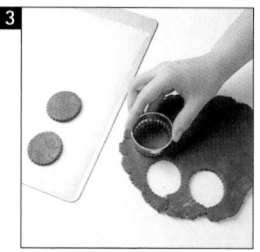

Chocolate & Apple Oaties

Apple sauce and apple juice add a pleasing sweetness to these biscuits.
They can be stored in an airtight container for several days.

🍰 45 mins   🕐 15 mins

MAKES 24

INGREDIENTS

115 g/4 oz butter or margarine, plus extra
   for greasing

70 g/2½ oz apple sauce

2 tbsp apple juice

100 g/3½ oz demerara sugar

1 tsp bicarbonate of soda

1 tsp almond essence

4 tbsp boiling water

115 g/4 oz rolled oats

280 g/10 oz plain flour, unsifted

pinch of salt

55 g/2 oz plain chocolate chips

1 Preheat the oven to 200°C/400°F/
Gas Mark 6. Grease a large baking
sheet.

2 Blend the butter (or margarine) and
sugar in a food processor until a
fluffy consistency is reached. Blend in the
apple sauce and apple juice.

3 In a separate bowl, mix together the
bicarbonate of soda, almond essence
and water, then add to the food processor
and mix with the apple mixture. In
another bowl, mix together the oats, flour
and salt, then gradually stir into the apple
mixture and beat well. Stir in the
chocolate chips.

4 Put 24 rounded tablespoonfuls of the
mixture on to the baking sheet,
allowing room for the biscuits to spread
during cooking. Transfer to the preheated
oven and bake for 15 minutes, or until
golden brown.

5 Remove the biscuits from the oven,
then transfer to a wire rack and leave
them to cool completely before serving.

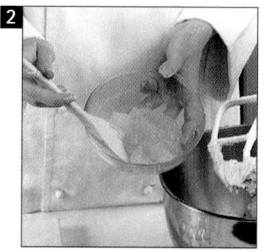

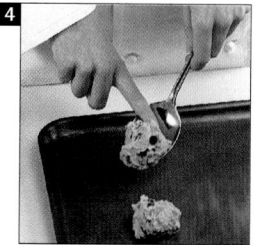

Hazelnut Bites

Toasted hazelnuts and chocolate partner each other very successfully. Use milk or white chocolate if preferred.

45 mins   10–15 mins

MAKES 24

INGREDIENTS

115 g/4 oz butter, plus extra for greasing

140 g/5 oz demerara sugar

1 egg

1 tbsp almond essence

140 g/5 oz plain flour

¾ tsp baking powder

pinch of salt

175 g/6 oz rolled oats

85 g/3 oz plain chocolate chips

100 g/3½ oz hazelnuts, toasted and chopped

300 g/10½ oz plain chocolate pieces

1 Preheat the oven to 180°C/350°F/ Gas Mark 4. Grease a large baking sheet. Cream the butter and sugar together in a bowl. Add the egg and almond essence and beat well. In a separate bowl, sift together the flour, baking powder and salt. Beat in the egg mixture. Stir in the oats, chocolate chips and half of the hazelnuts.

2 Divide the mixture into 24 teaspoonfuls of dough and place on a baking sheet or sheets. Flatten with a rolling pin. Transfer to the preheated oven and bake for 10 minutes, or until the biscuits are golden brown.

3 Remove the biscuits from the oven, then transfer to a wire rack and leave to cool completely. Put the chocolate pieces into a heatproof bowl set over a saucepan of gently simmering water and stir until melted. Cover the tops of the biscuits with melted chocolate, then top with a sprinkling of the remaining hazelnuts. Leave to cool on greaseproof paper before serving. Store the biscuits in an airtight container in the refrigerator.

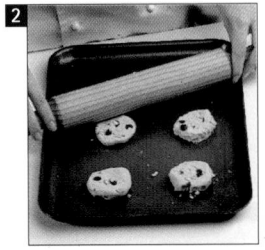

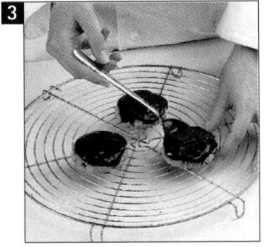

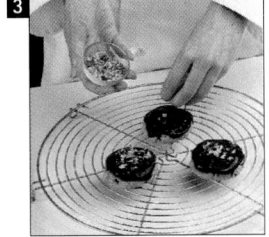

Mocha Walnut Cookies

These cookies have a lovely chewy texture. Serve with a cup of coffee for a delicious mid-morning snack.

🍰 20 mins   🕐 10–15 mins

MAKES ABOUT 16

INGREDIENTS

115 g/4 oz butter, softened, plus extra for greasing

115 g/4 oz light muscovado sugar

85 g/3 oz golden granulated sugar

1 tsp vanilla essence

1 tbsp instant coffee granules, dissolved in 1 tbsp hot water

1 egg

175 g/6 oz plain flour

½ tsp baking powder

¼ tsp bicarbonate of soda

55 g/2 oz milk chocolate chips

55 g/2 oz walnuts, chopped coarsely

1 Preheat the oven to 180°C/350°F/ Gas Mark 4. Grease 2 baking sheets. Put the butter, light muscovado sugar and granulated sugar in a bowl and beat until light and fluffy. Put the vanilla essence, coffee and egg in a separate bowl and whisk together.

2 Gradually add to the butter and sugar, beating until fluffy. Sift the flour, baking powder and bicarbonate of soda into the mixture and fold in carefully. Fold in the chocolate chips and walnuts.

3 Spoon heaped teaspoonfuls of the mixture on to the prepared baking sheets, allowing room for the cookies to spread. Bake for 10–15 minutes, until crisp on the outside but still soft inside. Leave to cool on the sheets for 2 minutes, then transfer to wire racks to cool completely.

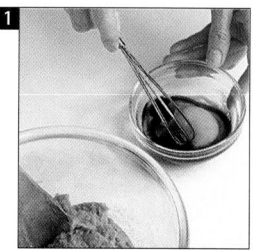 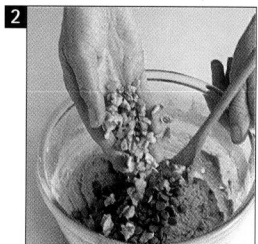 

COOK'S TIP
Muscovado sugar has a tendency to be lumpy, so it is a good idea to sift it before use.

Chocolate & Nut Crescents

These crisp little biscuits are a variation on a biscuit that is served in Greece for festivals and on special occasions.

20 mins   20–25 mins

MAKES 40

INGREDIENTS

225 g/8 oz butter, softened, plus extra
    for greasing

85 g/3 oz golden caster sugar

1 egg yolk

1 tsp dark rum

55 g/2 oz shelled walnuts, ground

225 g/8 oz plain flour, plus extra
    for shaping

55 g/2 oz cornflour

1 tbsp cocoa powder

sifted icing sugar, for dusting

1 Preheat the oven to 180°C/350°F/ Gas Mark 4. Grease several baking sheets. Place the butter and sugar in a bowl and beat together until pale and fluffy. Beat in the egg yolk and rum. Stir in the ground walnuts. Sift the flour, cornflour and cocoa over the mixture and stir, adding a little more flour, if necessary, to make a firm dough.

2 With lightly floured hands, break off walnut-size pieces of dough and roll into 7.5-cm/3-inch lengths, thick in the centre and tapering into pointed ends. Shape into crescents and place on the prepared baking sheets.

3 Bake in the preheated oven for 20–25 minutes, or until firm. Leave to cool on the baking sheets for 2 minutes, then transfer to wire racks to cool completely. Lightly dust the biscuits with icing sugar before serving.

COOK'S TIP
Do not use ready-ground walnuts as they are too fine. Prepare your own in a food processor if possible, taking care not to over-grind them.

Nutty Chocolate Drizzles

Drizzling a little melted chocolate over these biscuits makes a very quick yet attractive decoration.

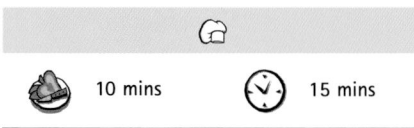

10 mins   15 mins

MAKES 24

INGREDIENTS

200 g/7 oz butter or margarine, plus extra for greasing

275 g/9½ oz demerara sugar

1 egg

140 g/5 oz plain flour, sifted

1 tsp baking powder

1 tsp bicarbonate of soda

125 g/4½ oz rolled oats

1 tbsp bran

1 tbsp wheatgerm

115 g/4 oz mixed nuts, toasted and chopped coarsely

200 g/7 oz plain chocolate chips

115 g/4 oz raisins and sultanas

175 g/6 oz plain chocolate, chopped coarsely

1 Preheat the oven to 180°C/350°F/ Gas Mark 4. Grease a large baking sheet. In a large bowl, cream together the butter, sugar and egg. Add the flour, baking powder, bicarbonate of soda, oats, bran and wheatgerm and mix together until well combined. Finally, stir in the nuts, chocolate chips and dried fruit.

2 Put 24 rounded tablespoonfuls of the mixture on to the greased baking sheet. Transfer to the preheated oven and bake for 12 minutes, or until the biscuits are golden brown.

3 Remove the biscuits from the oven, then transfer to a wire rack and leave to cool. Meanwhile, put the chocolate pieces in a heatproof bowl set over a saucepan of gently simmering water until melted. Stir the chocolate, then leave to cool slightly. Use a spoon to drizzle the chocolate in waves over the biscuits, or spoon it into a piping bag and pipe zig-zag lines over the biscuits. Store in an airtight container in the refrigerator before serving.

Chocolate Nut Crunchies

If you are a fan of Brazil nuts, these are the biscuits for you. Use milk chocolate chips instead of the plain chocolate chips if preferred.

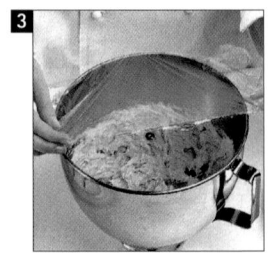

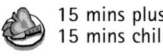

15 mins plus
15 mins chilling   15 mins

MAKES 30

INGREDIENTS

3 tbsp butter or margarine, plus extra
  for greasing

55 g/2 oz lard or white vegetable fat

125 g/4½ oz demerara sugar

1 egg

1 tsp vanilla essence

1 tbsp milk

90 g/3¼ oz plain flour, unsifted

115 g/4 oz rolled oats

1 tsp bicarbonate of soda

pinch of salt

175g/6 oz plain chocolate chips

55 g/2 oz chopped Brazil nuts

1 Preheat the oven to 180°C/350°F/Gas Mark 4. Grease a large baking sheet.

2 Put the butter, lard, sugar, egg, vanilla essence and milk in a free-standing mixer and beat for at least 3 minutes, or until a fluffy consistency is reached.

3 In a separate bowl, combine the flour, oats, bicarbonate of soda and salt. Stir into the egg mixture, then add the chocolate chips and Brazil nuts, and mix thoroughly. Cover the bowl with clingfilm. Chill in the refrigerator for 30 minutes.

4 Put 30 rounded tablespoonfuls of the mixture on to the greased baking sheet, allowing room for the biscuits to spread during cooking. Transfer to the preheated oven and bake for 15 minutes, or until the biscuits are golden brown.

5 Remove the biscuits from the oven, then transfer to a wire rack and leave to cool before serving.

Coffee Wholemeal Bakes

These delicious, dark biscuits, flavoured with coffee and toasted chopped hazelnuts, are perfect served with coffee.

🍰 20 mins   🕐 16–18 mins

MAKES 24

INGREDIENTS

175 g/6 oz butter or margarine, plus extra for greasing

200 g/7 oz soft brown sugar

1 egg

70 g/2½ oz plain flour

1 tsp bicarbonate of soda

pinch of salt

70 g/2½ oz wholemeal flour

1 tbsp bran

225 g/8 oz plain chocolate chips

185 g/6½ oz rolled oats

1 tbsp strong coffee

100 g/3½ oz hazelnuts, toasted and chopped coarsely

1 Preheat the oven to 190°C/375°F/ Gas Mark 5. Grease a large baking sheet. Cream the butter and sugar together in a bowl. Add the egg and beat well, using a hand whisk if preferred.

2 In a separate bowl, sift together the plain flour, bicarbonate of soda and salt, then add in the wholemeal flour and bran. Mix in the egg mixture, then stir in the chocolate chips, oats, coffee and hazelnuts. Mix well, with an electric whisk if preferred.

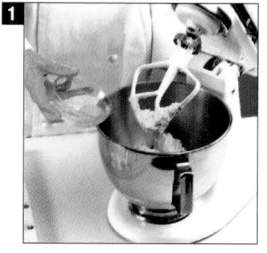  

3 Put 24 rounded tablespoonfuls of the mixture on to the prepared baking sheet, allowing room for the biscuits to spread during cooking. Alternatively, with lightly floured hands, break off pieces of the mixture and roll into balls (about 25 g/1 oz each), place on the baking sheet and flatten them with the back of a teaspoon. Transfer the baking sheet to the preheated oven and bake for 16–18 minutes, or until the biscuits are golden brown.

4 Transfer the biscuits to a wire rack and leave to cool before serving.

Chocolate Wheatmeals

These biscuits will keep well in an airtight container for at least 1 week. Dip them in white, milk or plain chocolate.

1 hr   15–20 mins

MAKES 20

INGREDIENTS

75 g/2¾ oz butter, plus extra for greasing

125 g/4½ oz demerara sugar

1 egg

1 tbsp wheatgerm

150 g/5½ oz wholewheat self-raising flour

70 g/2½ oz self-raising flour, sifted

125 g/4½ oz chocolate, broken into pieces

1 Preheat the oven to 180°C/350°F/ Gas Mark 4. Lightly grease a baking sheet. Beat the butter and sugar until fluffy. Add the egg and beat well. Stir in the wheatgerm and flours. Bring the mixture together with your hands.

2 Roll rounded teaspoonfuls of the mixture into balls and place on the prepared baking sheet, allowing room for the biscuits to spread during cooking.

3 Flatten the biscuits slightly with the tines of a fork. Bake in the preheated oven for 15–20 minutes, until golden. Leave to cool on the baking sheet for a few minutes before transferring to a wire rack to cool completely.

COOK'S TIP
These biscuits can be frozen very successfully. Freeze them at the end of step 3 for up to 3 months. Defrost and then dip them in melted chocolate.

4 Put the chocolate in a heatproof bowl set over a saucepan of gently simmering water until melted. Dip each biscuit in the chocolate to cover the flat side and a little way around the edges. Let the excess drip back into the bowl.

5 Place the biscuits on a sheet of baking paper in a cool place and leave the chocolate to set before serving.

Chocolate Temptations

Piping white chocolate lines over these biscuits gives them a touch of elegance and sophistication.

🍰 15–20 mins   🕐 20 mins

MAKES 24

I N G R E D I E N T S

90 g/3¼ oz unsalted butter, plus extra
   for greasing

365 g/12½ oz plain chocolate

1 tsp strong coffee

2 eggs

140 g/5 oz soft brown sugar

185 g/6½ oz plain flour

¼ tsp baking powder

pinch of salt

2 tsp almond essence

85 g/3 oz chopped Brazil nuts

85 g/3 oz chopped hazelnuts

40 g/1½ oz white chocolate

1 Preheat the oven to 180°C/350°F/ Gas Mark 4. Grease a large baking sheet. Put 225 g/8 oz of the plain chocolate with the butter and coffee into a heatproof bowl set over a saucepan of gently simmering water and heat until the chocolate is almost melted.

2 Meanwhile, beat the eggs in a bowl until fluffy. Whisk in the sugar gradually until thick. Remove the chocolate from the heat and stir until smooth. Add to the egg mixture and stir until combined.

3 Sift the flour, baking powder and salt into a bowl and stir into the chocolate mixture. Chop 85 g/3 oz of the plain chocolate into pieces and stir into the mixture. Stir in the almond essence and chopped nuts.

4 Put 24 tablespoonfuls of the mixture on to the baking sheet, transfer to the preheated oven and bake for 16 minutes. Transfer the biscuits to a wire rack to cool.

To decorate, melt the remaining chocolate (plain and white) in turn as in step 1, then spoon into a piping bag and pipe lines on to the biscuits.

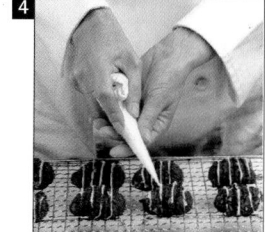

Chocolate Pretzels

If you thought of pretzels as exclusively salted, then think again.
Store these pretzels in an airtight container for up to 1 week.

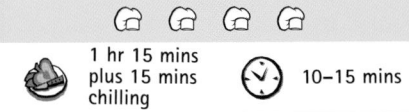

1 hr 15 mins
plus 15 mins
chilling

10–15 mins

MAKES 30

INGREDIENTS

75 g/2¾ oz unsalted butter, plus extra
for greasing

100 g/3½ oz caster sugar

1 egg

280 g/10 oz plain flour

25 g/1 oz cocoa powder

TO FINISH

1 tbsp butter

100 g/3½ oz plain chocolate

icing sugar, for dusting

1 Preheat the oven to 190°C/375°F/
Gas Mark 5. Lightly grease a baking
sheet. Beat together the butter and sugar
in a mixing bowl until light and fluffy. Beat
in the egg.

2 Sift together the flour and cocoa and
gradually beat in to form a soft
dough. Use your fingers to incorporate the
last of the flour and bring the dough
together. Chill for 15 minutes.

3 Break pieces from the dough and roll
into thin sausage shapes about
10 cm/4 inches long and 5 mm/¼ inch
thick. Twist into pretzel shapes by making
a circle, then twist the ends through each
other to form a letter 'B'.

4 Place on the baking sheet, allowing
room for the pretzels to spread.

5 Bake in the preheated oven for
8–12 minutes. Leave the pretzels to
cool slightly on the baking sheet, then
transfer to a wire rack to cool completely.

6 Put the butter and chocolate in
a heatproof bowl set over a saucepan
of gently simmering water until the
chocolate has melted. Stir to combine.

7 Dip half of each pretzel into the
chocolate and allow the excess
chocolate to drip back into the bowl. Place
the pretzels on a sheet of baking paper and
leave to set.

8 When set, dust the non-chocolate-
coated side of each pretzel with icing
sugar before serving.

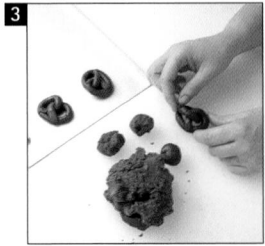

Chocolate Roundels

Irresistibly flavoured with Amaretto, plain chocolate chips, hazelnuts and raisins, these biscuits are simple to make.

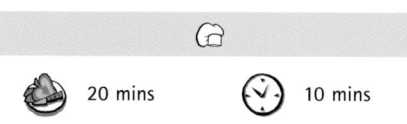

20 mins   10 mins

MAKES 24

INGREDIENTS

225 g/8 oz butter or margarine, plus extra for greasing

225 g/8 oz demerara sugar

1 tbsp milk

1 egg

1 tsp almond essence

1 tbsp Amaretto

225 g/8 oz plain flour, sifted, plus extra for rolling

1 tsp bicarbonate of soda

pinch of salt

175 g/6 oz plain chocolate chips

70 g/2½ oz hazelnuts, chopped finely

75 g/2¾ oz raisins

icing sugar, to decorate

1 Preheat the oven to 180°C/350°F/ Gas Mark 4. Grease a large baking sheet. Mix the butter, sugar and milk together in a bowl. Add the egg, almond essence and Amaretto and beat well.

2 In a separate bowl, sift together the flour, bicarbonate of soda and salt. Then mix in the egg mixture, along with the chocolate chips, nuts and raisins. Mix together thoroughly.

3 Sprinkle flour on a work surface or cutting board. Using your hands, roll the mixture into balls, then put them on to the greased baking sheet, allowing room for them to spread during cooking. Flatten them into roundels with a rolling pin and trim the edges with a cutter if needed.

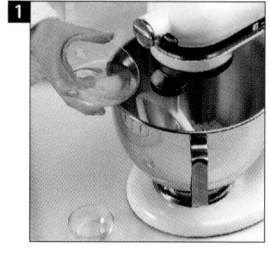
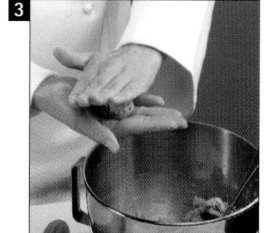

4 Transfer the biscuits to the preheated oven and bake for 10 minutes, or until golden brown. Transfer to a wire rack and leave to cool. Sprinkle over icing sugar before serving.

Chocolate Almond Snowballs

These tasty little biscuits are an ideal choice at Christmas. The 'snow' on them is simply a generous sprinkling of icing sugar.

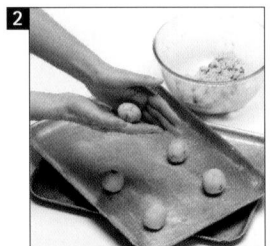

20 mins

15–20 mins

MAKES 25

INGREDIENTS

85 g/3 oz butter, plus extra for greasing

200 g/7 oz plain flour

pinch of baking powder

55 g/2 oz caster sugar

1 egg yolk

few drops almond essence

40 g/1½ oz milk chocolate chips

25 g/1 oz icing sugar

1 Preheat the oven to 160°C/325°F/ Gas Mark 3. Grease 1–2 large baking sheets. Sift the flour and baking powder together.

2 Beat the butter and caster sugar together until soft and fluffy. Beat in the egg yolk and almond essence, then the flour. Stir in the chocolate chips. Shape the mixture into 2.5-cm/1-inch balls and place on the baking sheets, allowing room for the biscuits to spread during cooking.

3 Bake the biscuits in the oven for 15–20 minutes, until firm. Transfer to a wire rack and leave to cool slightly.

4 Put the icing sugar in a large polythene bag, add a few warm biscuits and shake gently until coated. Return to the wire rack and repeat with the remaining cookies. Leave to cool on the wire rack until cold.

Chocolate Snow Flurries

As their name suggests, these little domes of soft, fudge-like biscuits are coated with coconut to give them the appearance of sprinkled snow.

10 mins plus
3 hrs chilling

15 mins

MAKES 32

INGREDIENTS

175 g/6 oz plain flour

55 g/2 oz cocoa powder

1 tsp baking powder

5 tbsp sunflower oil

225 g/8 oz caster sugar

2 eggs

1 tsp vanilla essence

40 g/1½ oz desiccated coconut

1 Sift the flour, cocoa and baking powder together. In a large bowl, whisk the oil, sugar, eggs and vanilla essence together until well blended, then fold in the flour mixture. Cover the bowl and leave to chill in the refrigerator for at least 3 hours.

2 Preheat the oven to 180°C/350°F/ Gas Mark 4. Line 2–3 large baking sheets with baking paper. Shape heaped teaspoonfuls of the mixture into balls using your hands, then roll in the coconut. Place on the prepared baking sheets, allowing room for the biscuits to spread during cooking.

3 Bake the biscuits in the preheated oven for 15 minutes, until firm. Transfer to a wire rack and leave to cool.

Chocolate Macaroons

Classic macaroons are always a favourite for coffee-time: they are made even better by the addition of rich dark chocolate.

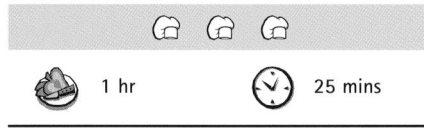

🍰 1 hr   🕐 25 mins

MAKES 18

INGREDIENTS

butter, for greasing

75 g/2¾ oz plain chocolate, broken into pieces

2 egg whites

pinch of salt

200 g/7 oz caster sugar

125 g/4½ oz ground almonds

grated coconut, for sprinkling (optional)

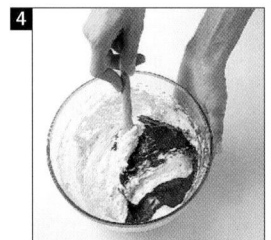
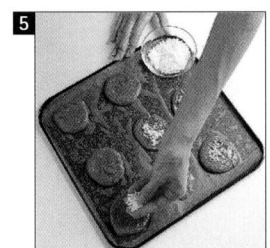

1 Preheat the oven to 150°C/300°F/Gas Mark 2. Grease 2 baking sheets and line with baking paper or rice paper.

2 Melt the plain chocolate in a small heatproof bowl set over a saucepan of gently simmering water. Leave to cool slightly.

3 Whisk the egg whites with the salt until soft peaks form.

4 Gradually whisk the caster sugar into the egg whites, then fold in the almonds and cooled melted chocolate.

5 Place heaped teaspoons of the mixture spaced well apart on the prepared baking sheets and spread into circles about 6 cm/2½ inches across. Sprinkle with grated coconut (if using).

6 Bake in the preheated oven for about 25 minutes, or until they are firm.

7 Leave to cool before carefully lifting from the baking sheets. Transfer the macaroons to a wire rack and leave to cool completely before serving.

VARIATION

For a traditional finish, top each macaroon with half a glacé cherry before baking.

Biscuit & Cream Sandwiches

Delicious chocolate shortbread biscuits, with a delicate hint of spice, are sandwiched together with chocolate cream. Assemble just before serving.

	25 mins plus 2 hrs chilling		20 mins

SERVES 4

INGREDIENTS

125 g/4½ oz butter, softened

75 g/2¾ oz golden icing sugar

115 g/4 oz plain flour

40 g/1½ oz cocoa powder

½ tsp ground cinnamon

FILLING

125 g/4½ oz plain chocolate, broken into pieces

50 ml/2 fl oz double cream

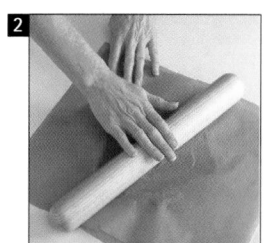

1 Preheat the oven to 160°C/325°F/ Gas Mark 3. Line a baking sheet with non-stick baking paper. Place the butter and sugar in a large bowl and beat together until light and fluffy. Sift the flour, cocoa and ground cinnamon into the bowl and mix to form a dough.

2 Place the dough between 2 sheets of non-stick baking paper and roll out to 3 mm/⅛ inch thick. Cut out 6-cm/2½- inch circles and place on the prepared baking sheet. Bake in the preheated oven for 15 minutes, or until firm to the touch. Leave to cool for 2 minutes, then transfer to wire racks to cool completely.

3 Meanwhile, make the filling. Place the chocolate and cream in a saucepan and heat gently until the chocolate has melted. Stir until smooth. Leave to cool, then leave to chill in the refrigerator for 2 hours, or until firm. Sandwich the biscuits together in pairs with a spoonful of chocolate cream and serve.

COOK'S TIP
Do not sandwich the biscuits together too long before serving, otherwise they will go soft. Store unsandwiched biscuits in an airtight container for up to 3 days.

Dutch Macaroons

These unusual biscuit treats are delicious served with coffee. They also make an ideal dessert biscuit to serve with ice cream.

40 mins   20–25 mins

MAKES 20

INGREDIENTS

rice paper

2 egg whites

200 g/7 oz caster sugar

175 g/6 oz ground almonds

225 g/8 oz plain chocolate

1 Preheat the oven to 180°C/350°F/ Gas Mark 4. Cover 2 baking sheets with rice paper. Whisk the egg whites in a large mixing bowl until stiff, then fold in the sugar and ground almonds.

2 Place the mixture in a large piping bag fitted with a 1-cm/½-inch plain nozzle and pipe fingers, about 7.5 cm/ 3 inches long, allowing room for the biscuits to spread during cooking.

3 Bake in the preheated oven for 15–20 minutes, until golden. Transfer to a wire rack and leave to cool. Remove the excess rice paper from around the edges.

4 Melt the chocolate and dip the bottom of each biscuit into the chocolate. Place the macaroons on a sheet of baking paper and leave to set.

5 Drizzle any remaining chocolate over the top of the biscuits (you may need to reheat the chocolate in order to do this). Leave it to set before serving.

COOK'S TIP
Rice paper is edible, so you can just break off the excess from around the edge of the biscuits. Remove it completely before dipping in the chocolate, if you prefer.

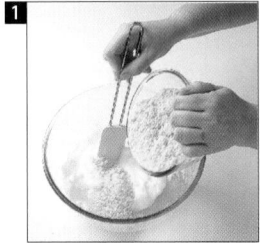
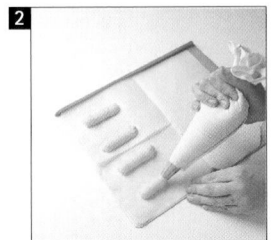

Chocolate Peanut Cookies

Made with peanut butter, chopped peanuts and chocolate chips, these cookies are always a hit with children.

 10 mins plus 1 hr to chill   20 mins

MAKES 24

INGREDIENTS

200 g/7 oz butter or margarine, plus extra for greasing

275 g/9½ oz soft brown sugar

350 g/12 oz crunchy peanut butter

1 egg

2 tsp almond essence

280 g/10 oz plain flour

1 tsp bicarbonate of soda

85 g/3 oz plain chocolate chips

50 g/1¾ oz peanuts

1 Preheat the oven to 180°C/350°F/Gas Mark 4. Grease a large baking sheet. Chop the peanuts and set aside. Cream the butter and sugar together in a bowl until fluffy. Add the peanut butter, egg and almond essence and mix thoroughly.

2 In a separate bowl, fold in the flour and bicarbonate of soda; add gradually to the peanut butter mixture. Stir in the chocolate chips and peanuts and mix thoroughly. Cover the bowl with clingfilm and leave to chill in the refrigerator for 1 hour, or until the dough is firm.

3 Put 24 rounded balls of the dough on to the greased baking sheet, then flatten with a palette knife. Ensure that they are well spaced because they may expand during cooking. Transfer to the preheated oven and bake for 20 minutes, or until the cookies are golden brown.

4 Remove the cookies from the oven, then transfer to a wire rack and leave them to cool before serving.

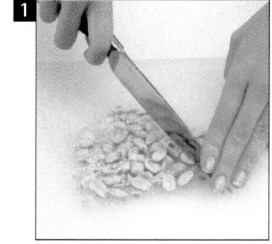

Chocolate Peanut Biscuits

These delicious biscuits contain two popular ingredients: peanuts and chocolate. The rice flour gives them an original twist.

🍰 40 mins   🕐 10 mins

MAKES 50

INGREDIENTS

200 g/7 oz plain flour

175 g/6 oz rice flour

2 tbsp cocoa powder

1 tsp baking powder

pinch of salt

140 g/5 oz white vegetable fat

200 g/7 oz caster sugar

1 tsp vanilla essence

150 g/5½ oz raisins, chopped

115 g/4 oz unsalted peanuts, chopped finely

175 g/6 oz continental plain chocolate, broken into pieces

1 Preheat the oven to 180°C/350°F/ Gas Mark 4. Line several baking sheets with sheets of baking paper.

2 Sift the flours, cocoa, baking powder and salt into a bowl and stir well.

3 Using an electric whisk, beat the fat and sugar in a large bowl for about 2 minutes until light and creamy. Blend in the vanilla essence and the flour mixture to form a soft dough. Stir in the raisins.

4 Put the chopped peanuts on a plate. Pinch off walnut-size pieces of the dough and roll into balls. Drop into the peanuts and roll to coat, pressing them lightly to stick. Place the balls well apart on the prepared baking sheets.

5 Using the base of a drinking glass dipped in flour, gently flatten each ball to a circle about 5 mm/¼ inch thick.

6 Bake in the preheated oven for about 10 minutes, until golden and lightly set; do not over-bake. Cool on the sheets for about 1 minute, then, using a palette knife, transfer to a wire rack to cool.

7 Put the chocolate in a heatproof bowl set over a saucepan of gently simmering water until melted. Drizzle the tops of the biscuits with the chocolate when they have cooled. Leave to set before transferring to an airtight container with greaseproof paper between the layers.

Chocolate Raisin Biscuits

These delicious biscuits, flavoured with chocolate, raisins and almonds, are especially hard to resist.

15–20 mins | 16 mins

MAKES 55

I N G R E D I E N T S

200 g/7 oz butter, plus extra for greasing

400 g/14 oz demerara sugar

2 eggs

1 tsp almond essence

280 g/10 oz plain flour, sifted

pinch of salt

1 tsp bicarbonate of soda

1 tsp baking powder

250 g/9 oz rolled oats

325 g/11½ oz raisins

115 g/4 oz plain chocolate

225 g/8 oz almonds, chopped finely

1 Preheat the oven to 190°C/375°F/Gas Mark 5. Grease several large baking sheets. Finely chop the chocolate. Cream the butter and sugar together in a bowl until fluffy. Mix in the eggs and almond essence.

2 In a separate bowl, sift together the flour, salt, bicarbonate of soda and baking powder. Add the egg mixture with the rolled oats, raisins, chopped chocolate and almonds, and mix together thoroughly.

3 With lightly floured hands, shape the mixture into small balls (each about 25 g/1 oz) and place on the baking sheets, allowing room for the biscuits to spread during cooking. Use a palette knife or the bottom of a glass to press lightly down on the biscuits to flatten slightly. Transfer to the oven and bake for 16 minutes, or until the biscuits are golden brown.

4 Remove the biscuits from the oven, then transfer to a wire rack and leave to cool before serving.

Easter Biscuits

Despite their name, these biscuits are good to eat at any time of year! They will be popular with adults and children alike.

40 mins   15 mins

MAKES 20

INGREDIENTS

150 g/5½ oz butter, softened, plus extra for greasing

150 g/5½ oz golden caster sugar

1 egg, beaten

2 tbsp milk

40 g/1½ oz chopped candied peel

115 g/4 oz currants

350 g/12 oz plain flour, plus extra for dusting

1 tsp ground mixed spice

GLAZE

1 egg white, lightly beaten

2 tbsp golden caster sugar

1 Preheat the oven to 180°C/350°F/Gas Mark 4. Grease 2 large baking sheets. Place the butter and sugar in a bowl and beat until light and fluffy. Gradually beat in the egg and milk. Stir in the candied peel and currants, then sift in the flour and mixed spice. Mix together to make a firm dough. Knead lightly until smooth.

2 On a floured work surface, roll out the dough to 5 mm/¼ inch thick and use a 5-cm/2-inch round biscuit cutter to stamp out the biscuits. Re-roll the dough trimmings and stamp out more biscuits until the dough is used up. Place the biscuits on the prepared baking sheets and bake in the preheated oven for 10 minutes.

3 Remove from the oven to glaze. Brush with the egg white and sprinkle with the caster sugar, then return to the oven for an additional 5 minutes, or until lightly browned. Leave to cool on the baking sheets for 2 minutes, then transfer to wire racks to cool completely.

VARIATION
If you do not like candied peel, you can substitute another 1 oz of extra currants instead.

Chocolate Chip Oaties

Rolled oats give a light texture and a nutty flavour to these biscuits.
They are superb served with a cup of fresh coffee.

15 mins   15 mins

MAKES ABOUT 20

I N G R E D I E N T S

115 g/4 oz butter, softened,
  plus extra for greasing

100 g/3½ oz soft brown sugar

1 egg

85 g/3 oz rolled oats

1 tbsp milk

1 tsp vanilla essence

115 g/4 oz plain flour

1 tbsp cocoa powder

½ tsp baking powder

175 g/6 oz plain chocolate,
  broken into pieces

175 g/6 oz milk chocolate, broken
  into pieces

1 Preheat the oven to 180°C/350°F/
Gas Mark 4. Grease 2 baking sheets.
Place the butter and sugar in a bowl and
beat together until light and fluffy.

2 Beat in the egg, then add the oats,
milk and vanilla essence. Beat
together until well blended. Sift the flour,
cocoa and baking powder into the mixture
and stir. Stir in the plain and milk
chocolate pieces.

3 Place tablespoonfuls of the mixture on
the prepared baking sheets and flatten
slightly with a fork. Bake in the preheated
oven for 15 minutes, or until slightly risen
and firm. Leave to cool on the baking
sheets for 2 minutes, then transfer to wire
racks to cool completely.

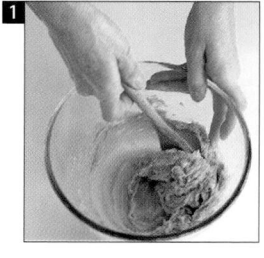

Zebra Biscuits

These tempting biscuits are topped with milk and white chocolate buttons, making them a favourite with children. Leave to cool before serving.

15 mins plus
3 hrs chilling   15 mins

MAKES 18–20

INGREDIENTS

55 g/2 oz plain chocolate,
  broken into pieces

140 g/5 oz plain flour

1 tsp baking powder

1 egg

140 g/5 oz caster sugar

50 ml/2 fl oz sunflower oil, plus extra
  for oiling

½ tsp vanilla essence

2 tbsp icing sugar

1 small packet milk chocolate buttons

1 small packet white chocolate buttons

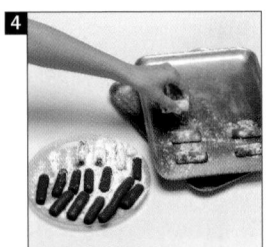

1 Melt the chocolate in a heatproof bowl set over a saucepan of gently simmering water. Leave to cool. Sift the flour and baking powder together.

2 Meanwhile, in a large bowl, whisk the egg, sugar, oil and vanilla essence together. Whisk in the cooled, melted chocolate until well blended, then gradually stir in the sifted flour. Cover the bowl and leave to chill for at least 3 hours.

3 Preheat the oven to 190°C/375°F/Gas Mark 5. Oil 1–2 large baking sheets. Shape tablespoonfuls of the mixture into log shapes using your hands, each measuring about 5 cm/2 inches.

4 Roll the logs generously in the icing sugar, then place on the prepared baking sheets, allowing room for the biscuits to spread during cooking.

5 Bake the biscuits in the preheated oven for about 15 minutes, until firm. As soon as the biscuits are done, place 3 chocolate buttons down the centre of each, alternating the colours. Transfer to a wire rack and leave to cool.

Chocolate Ribbon Biscuits

Enlist the help of children when you make these biscuits, for they will be impressed with the results – both their taste and appearance.

20 mins plus
4 hrs chilling

15 mins

MAKES 50

I N G R E D I E N T S

2 tbsp cocoa powder

2 tbsp water

225 g/8 oz butter, plus extra for greasing

115 g/4 oz caster sugar

350 g/12 oz plain flour, plus extra
for dusting

1 tsp vanilla essence

1 Line the bottom of a 22 x 11-cm/ 8¹/₂ x 4¹/₂-inch loaf tin with baking paper. Mix the cocoa with the water to form a paste.

2 Whisk the butter, sugar and flour together until the mixture resembles fine breadcrumbs. Divide the mixture in half and add the cocoa paste to one portion. Knead with your hands until the mixture is evenly coloured and forms a smooth dough.

3 Add the vanilla essence to the remaining mixture, knead to form a smooth dough and divide it in half.

4 Using your fingertips, evenly press out each piece of dough on a lightly floured work surface to the size of the prepared tin.

5 Layer the flattened pieces of dough in the tin, starting with a chocolate layer. Press well together to remove any trapped air. Cover and leave to chill in the refrigerator for at least 4 hours.

6 Preheat the oven to 190°C/375°F/Gas Mark 5. Grease 3–4 large baking sheets. Turn out the dough and cut widthways into thirds, then slice each third widthways into 5-mm/¹/₄-inch slices. Place on the baking sheets, allowing room for the biscuits to spread during cooking.

7 Bake the biscuits in the preheated oven for 15 minutes, or until firm. Transfer to a wire rack and leave to cool.

Peanut Butter Cookies

These crunchy cookies will be popular with children of all ages as they contain their favourite food – peanut butter.

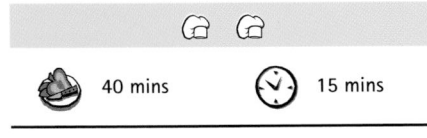

🥄 40 mins   🕐 15 mins

MAKES 20

I N G R E D I E N T S

115 g/4 oz butter, softened, plus extra for greasing

115 g/4 oz crunchy peanut butter

225 g/8 oz granulated sugar

1 egg, beaten lightly

150 g/5½ oz plain flour

½ tsp baking powder

pinch of salt

75 g/2¾ oz chopped unsalted peanuts

1 Preheat the oven to 180°C/350°F/ Gas Mark 4. Lightly grease 2 baking sheets with a little butter.

2 In a large mixing bowl, beat together the butter and peanut butter.

3 Gradually add the granulated sugar and beat well.

4 Add the beaten egg, a little at a time, beating after each addition until it is thoroughly combined.

5 Sift the flour, baking powder and salt into the peanut butter mixture.

6 Add the peanuts and bring all of the ingredients together to form a soft dough. Wrap and chill for 30 minutes.

7 Form the dough into 20 balls and place them on the prepared baking sheets about 5 cm/2 inches apart to allow room for the cookies to spread during cooking. Flatten them slightly with your hand.

8 Bake in the oven for 15 minutes, until golden brown. Transfer the cookies to a wire rack and leave to cool.

COOK'S TIP

For extra crunch and a sparkling appearance, sprinkle the cookies with demerara sugar before baking.

Peanut Butter Oat Cookies

These are easy for children to make because they require no shaping or rolling out and all the ingredients are mixed together in one bowl.

 40 mins ⊙ 12 mins

MAKES 26

I N G R E D I E N T S

115 g/4 oz butter, softened

115 g/4 oz crunchy peanut butter

115 g/4 oz golden caster sugar

115 g/4 oz light muscovado sugar

1 egg, beaten

½ tsp vanilla essence

85 g/3 oz plain flour

½ tsp bicarbonate of soda

½ tsp baking powder

pinch of salt

115 g/4 oz rolled oats

1 Preheat the oven to 180°C/350°F/ Gas Mark 4. Put the butter and peanut butter in a bowl and beat together. Beat in the caster and muscovado sugars, then gradually beat in the egg and vanilla essence.

2 Sift the flour, bicarbonate of soda, baking powder and salt into a bowl and stir in with the oats. Drop teaspoonfuls of the mixture, well apart, on to greased baking sheets. Flatten slightly with a fork.

3 Bake in the preheated oven for 12 minutes, or until lightly browned. Leave to cool on the baking sheets for 2 minutes, then transfer to wire racks to cool completely.

VARIATION
Smooth peanut butter
can be used if preferred.

Lavender Hearts

Lavender covers the Provençal landscape during summer, and local bakers incorporate its distinctive flavour into their sweet recipes.

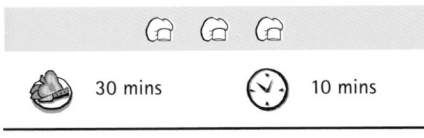

30 mins   10 mins

MAKES 48

INGREDIENTS

280 g/10 oz plain flour, plus extra for dusting

100 g/3½ oz chilled butter, diced

6 tbsp caster sugar

1 large egg

1 tbsp dried lavender flowers, chopped very finely

TO DECORATE

4 tbsp icing sugar

1 tsp water

2 tbsp fresh lavender flowers

1 Preheat the oven to 180°C/350°F/ Gas Mark 4. Line 2 baking sheets with baking paper. Put the flour in a bowl, add the diced butter and lightly rub in with your fingertips until the mixture resembles fine breadcrumbs.

2 Stir in the sugar. Lightly beat the egg, then add to the flour and butter mixture with the lavender flowers. Stir to form a stiff dough.

3 Turn out the dough on to a lightly floured work surface and roll out until about 5 mm/¼ inch thick.

4 Using a 5-cm/2-inch heart-shaped biscuit cutter, press out 48 hearts, occasionally dipping the cutter into extra flour, and re-rolling the trimmings as necessary. Transfer the pastry hearts to the baking sheets.

5 Prick the surface of each heart with a fork. Place in the preheated oven and bake for 10 minutes, or until the biscuits are lightly browned. Transfer to a wire rack set over a sheet of baking paper to cool.

6 Sift the icing sugar into a bowl. Add 1 teaspoon of cold water and stir until a smooth icing forms, adding a little extra water if necessary.

7 Drizzle the icing from the tip of a metal spoon over the cooled biscuits in a random pattern. Immediately sprinkle with the fresh lavender flowers while the icing is still soft so they stick in place.

8 Leave the biscuits to stand for at least 15 minutes, until the icing has set. Store the biscuits for up to 4 days in an airtight container.

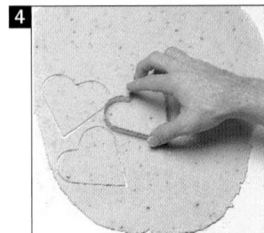

Lavender Biscuits

Guests will be surprised and delighted by these original and unusual fragrant biscuits.

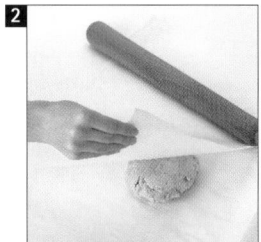

15 mins

12 mins

MAKES 10-12

INGREDIENTS

115 g/4 oz butter, softened,
  plus extra for greasing

55 g/2 oz golden caster sugar,
  plus extra for dusting

1 tsp chopped lavender leaves

finely grated rind of 1 lemon

175 g/6 oz plain flour

1 Preheat the oven to 150°C/300°F/ Gas Mark 2. Grease a large baking sheet. Place the caster sugar and lavender leaves in a food processor. Process until the lavender is very finely chopped, then add the butter and lemon rind and process until light and fluffy. Transfer to a large bowl. Sift in the flour and beat until the mixture forms a stiff dough.

2 Place the dough on a sheet of baking paper and place another sheet on top. Gently press down with a rolling pin and roll out to 3–5 mm/$^1/_8$–$^1/_2$ inch thick. Remove the top sheet of paper and stamp out circles from the dough using a 7-cm/2$^3/_4$-inch round biscuit cutter. Re-knead and re-roll the dough trimmings and stamp out more biscuits.

3 Using a palette knife, carefully transfer the biscuits to the prepared baking sheet. Prick the biscuits with a fork and bake in the preheated oven for 12 minutes, or until pale brown. Leave to cool on the baking sheet for 2 minutes, then transfer to a wire rack and leave to cool completely.

COOK'S TIP
If you do not have a food processor, you can mix the dough by hand. Knead it into a ball before rolling out in step 2.

Rosemary Biscuits

Do not be put off by the idea of herbs being used in these crisp biscuits – try them, and you will be pleasantly surprised.

40 mins plus 30 mins chilling

15 mins

MAKES 25

INGREDIENTS

4 tbsp butter, softened, plus extra for greasing

4 tbsp caster sugar

grated rind of 1 lemon

4 tbsp lemon juice

1 egg, separated

2 tsp finely chopped fresh rosemary

200 g/7 oz plain flour, sifted, plus extra for dusting

caster sugar, for sprinkling (optional)

1 Preheat the oven to 180°C/350°F/ Gas Mark 4. Lightly grease 2 baking sheets with a little butter.

2 In a large mixing bowl, cream together the butter and sugar until pale and fluffy.

3 Add the lemon rind and juice, then the egg yolk, and beat until they are thoroughly combined. Stir in the chopped fresh rosemary.

4 Add the sifted flour, mixing well until a soft dough is formed. Wrap in clingfilm and chill in the refrigerator for 30 minutes.

5 On a lightly floured work surface, roll out the dough thinly and stamp out about 25 circles with a 6-cm/2½-inch biscuit cutter. Arrange the dough circles on the prepared baking sheets.

6 In a bowl, lightly whisk the egg white. Gently brush the egg white over the surface of each biscuit, then sprinkle with a little caster sugar, if liked.

7 Bake in the preheated oven for about 15 minutes.

8 Transfer the biscuits to a wire rack and leave to cool before serving.

VARIATION

In place of the fresh rosemary, use 1½ teaspoons of dried rosemary, if you prefer.

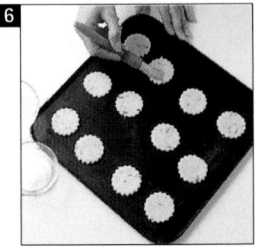

Walnut & Cinnamon Blondies

Blondies are brownies without the chocolate! They taste just as delicious served with a cup of coffee.

20 mins   20–25 mins

MAKES 9

INGREDIENTS

115 g/4 oz butter, plus extra for greasing

225 g/8 oz soft brown sugar

1 egg

1 egg yolk

140 g/5 oz self-raising flour

1 tsp ground cinnamon

85 g/3 oz coarsely chopped walnuts

1 Preheat the oven to 180°C/350°F/ Gas Mark 4. Grease and line the bottom of a 18-cm/7-inch square cake tin. Place the butter and sugar in a saucepan over a low heat and stir until the sugar has dissolved. Cook, stirring, for an additional 1 minute. The mixture will bubble slightly, but do not let it boil. Leave to cool for 10 minutes.

2 Stir the egg and egg yolk into the mixture. Sift in the flour and cinnamon, add the nuts and stir until just blended. Pour the cake mixture into the prepared tin, then bake in the preheated oven for 20–25 minutes, or until springy in the centre and a skewer inserted into the centre of the cake comes out clean.

3 Leave to cool in the tin for a few minutes, then run a knife around the edge of the cake to loosen it. Turn the cake out on to a wire rack and peel off the paper. Leave to cool completely. When cold, cut into squares.

COOK'S TIP
Do not chop the walnuts too finely, as the blondies should have a good texture and a slight crunch to them.

Ranger Cookies

These large cookies are ideal for children when they go off on an adventure trail – even if it is only to the bottom of the garden!

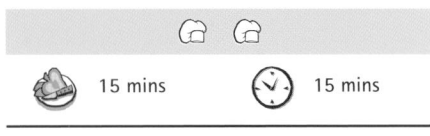
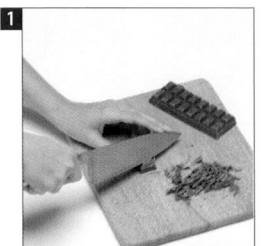

🕐 15 mins 🕐 15 mins

MAKES 12

I N G R E D I E N T S

115 g/4 oz butter, plus extra for greasing

150 g/5½ oz milk chocolate

175 g/6 oz plain flour

½ tsp baking powder

115 g/4 oz caster sugar

115 g/4 oz soft brown sugar

2 eggs, beaten

½ tsp vanilla essence

85 g/3 oz rolled oats

85 g/3 oz sultanas

1 Preheat the oven to 190°C/375°F/Gas Mark 5. Grease 3 large baking sheets. Coarsely chop the chocolate into 8-mm/¼-inch pieces. Sift the flour and baking powder together.

2 Beat the butter, caster sugar and brown sugar together until soft and fluffy. Gradually beat in the eggs, then the vanilla essence and sifted flour. Stir in the oats, sultanas and chocolate pieces.

3 Place heaped tablespoons of the mixture on the prepared baking sheets, allowing room for the cookies to spread during cooking.

4 Bake the cookies in the preheated oven for about 15 minutes, until lightly browned. Leave to stand for 5 minutes, then transfer the cookies to a wire rack and leave to cool.

Spicy Chocolate Chip Cookies

Chocolate and spices are the perfect marriage, so the addition of nutmeg, cinnamon and cloves turns these popular cookies into something special.

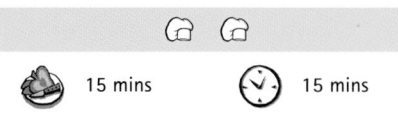

🍰 15 mins   🕐 15 mins

MAKES 10

INGREDIENTS

115 g/4 oz butter, plus extra for greasing

140 g/5 oz self-raising flour

3 tbsp cocoa powder

½ tsp ground cinnamon

¼ tsp ground cloves

¼ tsp grated nutmeg

85 g/3 oz caster sugar

85 g/3 oz soft brown sugar

1 egg, beaten

100 g/3½ oz plain chocolate chips

1 Preheat the oven to 180°C/350°F/ Gas Mark 4. Grease 2 large baking sheets. Sift the flour, cocoa, cinnamon, cloves and nutmeg together.

2 Beat the butter, caster sugar and brown sugar together until soft and fluffy. Gradually beat in the egg, then the flour mixture. Stir in the chocolate chips.

3 Place 10 tablespoonfuls of the mixture on the prepared baking sheets, allowing room for the cookies to spread during baking. Press each one down using the back of a wet spoon.

4 Bake the cookies in the preheated oven for 15–20 minutes, until lightly browned. Leave for 1 minute, then transfer the cookies to a wire rack and leave to cool.

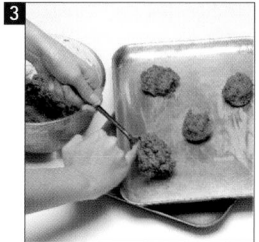
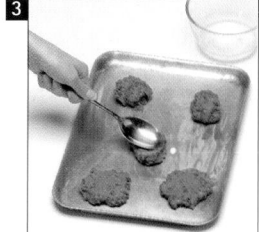

Chewy Golden Biscuits

A little glacé icing drizzled over these biscuits makes for a highly effective decoration.

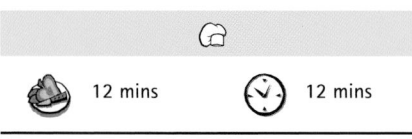

12 mins		12 mins

MAKES 30

INGREDIENTS

175 g/6 oz butter or margarine, plus extra for greasing

250 g/9 oz soft brown sugar

350 g/12 oz golden syrup

3 egg whites

250 g/9 oz rolled oats

280 g/10 oz plain flour

pinch of salt

1 tsp baking powder

icing sugar, to decorate

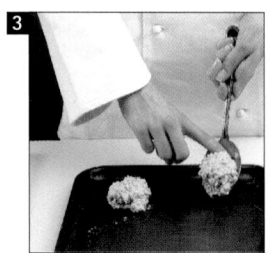

1 Preheat the oven to 180°C/350°F/ Gas Mark 4 and grease a large baking sheet.

2 In a large mixing bowl, blend the butter, sugar, golden syrup and egg whites together. Gradually add the oats, flour, salt and baking powder and mix thoroughly.

3 Drop 30 rounded tablespoonfuls of the mixture on to the baking sheet and transfer to the preheated oven.

4 Bake for 12 minutes, or until the biscuits are light brown.

5 Remove from the oven and leave to cool on a wire rack. To make the icing, combine a little sifted icing sugar with water, drizzle over the biscuits and leave to set. Alternatively, sprinkle over sifted icing sugar and serve.

Caraway Biscuits

The caraway seed is best known for its appearance in rye bread. Here, caraway seeds give these biscuits a distinctive flavour.

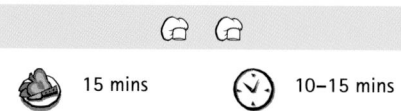

15 mins   10–15 mins

MAKES 36

INGREDIENTS

85 g/3 oz butter, cut into small pieces, plus extra for greasing

280 g/10 oz plain flour

pinch of salt

225 g/8 oz caster sugar

1 egg, beaten

2 tbsp caraway seeds

demerara sugar, for sprinkling

1 Preheat the oven to 160°C/325°F/Gas Mark 3. Grease 2 baking sheets lightly.

2 Sift the flour and salt into a mixing bowl. Rub in the butter with your fingertips until the mixture resembles fine breadcrumbs. Stir in the sugar.

3 Reserve 1 tablespoon of the beaten egg for brushing the biscuits. Add the rest of the egg to the mixture along with the caraway seeds and bring together to form a soft dough.

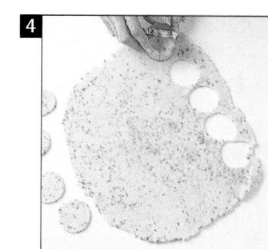

4 On a lightly floured work surface, roll out the dough thinly and then cut out about 36 circles with a 6-cm/2½-inch biscuit cutter.

5 Transfer the circles to the prepared baking sheets, brush with the reserved egg and sprinkle with demerara sugar.

6 Bake in the preheated oven for 10–15 minutes, until the biscuits are lightly golden and crisp.

7 Leave to cool on a wire rack and store in an airtight container.

VARIATION
Caraway seeds have a nutty, delicate anise flavour. If you don't like this, replace them with poppy seeds.

Jamaican Rum Biscuits

Dark rum and coconut lend a deliciously exotic flavour to these biscuits. They are ideal for serving after dinner with coffee.

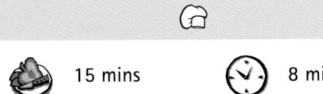

15 mins   8 mins

MAKES 36

INGREDIENTS

175 g/6 oz butter or margarine, plus extra for greasing

55 g/2 oz sesame seeds

55 g/2 oz chopped mixed nuts

140 g/5 oz plain flour

¼ tsp baking powder

pinch of salt

275 g/9½ oz demerara sugar

1 egg

1 tsp dark rum

2 tbsp coconut flakes, to decorate

1 Preheat the oven to 180°C/350°F/Gas Mark 4. Grease a large baking sheet.

2 Spread the sesame seeds and chopped nuts out on an ungreased baking sheet and toast them for about 10 minutes, or until slightly browned. Remove from the oven and set aside. Leave the oven on.

3 Sift together the flour, baking powder and salt in a large mixing bowl. Add the sugar, egg and rum and beat together well.

4 Put 36 rounded teaspoonfuls of the mixture on to the greased baking sheet, allowing room for them to spread during cooking. Transfer to the preheated oven and bake for about 8 minutes, or until golden brown.

5 Remove from the oven and leave to cool on a wire rack. Decorate with the coconut flakes and serve.

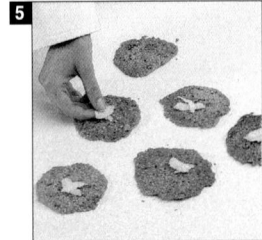

Caribbean Cookies

Flavoured with banana, fruit juice and coconut, these cookies simply melt in the mouth.

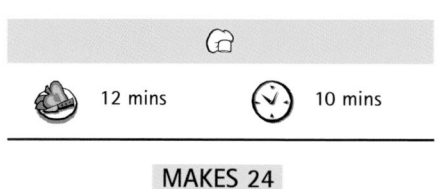

12 mins   10 mins

MAKES 24

I N G R E D I E N T S

butter, for greasing

25 g/1 oz mashed banana

1 tbsp pineapple juice

1 tbsp orange juice

4 tbsp peanut oil

1 egg

1 tbsp milk

140 g/5 oz plain flour

¼ tsp bicarbonate of soda

75 g/2¾ oz desiccated coconut

demerara sugar, for sprinkling

 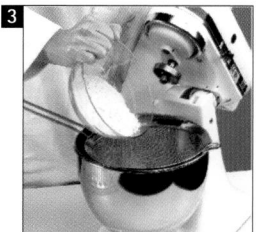 

1 Preheat the oven to 180°C/350°F/Gas Mark 4. Grease a large baking sheet.

2 In a large bowl, cream together the banana, fruit juices, oil, egg and milk. Transfer to a food mixer.

3 With the machine running, sift in the flour and bicarbonate of soda, beating constantly. Add in the desiccated coconut and mix well.

4 Drop rounded teaspoonfuls on to the greased baking sheet, allowing room for the cookies to spread during cooking. Sprinkle with the demerara sugar. Transfer to the preheated oven and bake for 10 minutes, or until the cookies are golden brown.

5 Remove the cookies from the oven and transfer to a wire rack to cool before serving.

Chocolate Drop Cookies

These cookies get their name from the method with which they are made – spoonfuls of the mixture are dropped on to the baking sheets.

  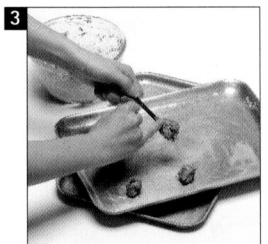

🍳 10 mins   🕐 15–20 mins

MAKES 20

INGREDIENTS

115 g/4 oz butter, plus extra for greasing

90 g/3¼ oz plain flour

2 tbsp cocoa powder

55 g/2 oz caster sugar

½ tsp vanilla essence

1 Preheat the oven to 190°C/375°F/Gas Mark 5. Grease 2–3 large baking sheets. Sift the flour and cocoa together.

2 Beat the butter, caster sugar and vanilla essence together in a large bowl until soft and fluffy. Stir in the flour mixture until well blended.

3 Drop teaspoonfuls of the mixture on to the prepared baking sheets, allowing room for the cookies to spread during cooking.

4 Bake the cookies in the preheated oven for 15–20 minutes, until firm. Leave for 1 minute, then transfer to a wire rack and leave to cool.

Mocha Biscuits

The word mocha, which describes a combination of chocolate and coffee, comes from the name of a port in Yemen where coffee was first grown.

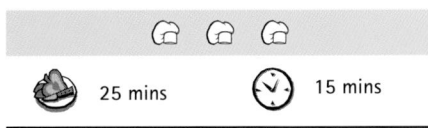

🍰 25 mins   🕐 15 mins

MAKES 18

I N G R E D I E N T S

4 tbsp butter, plus extra for greasing

225 g/8 oz plain flour

3 tbsp cocoa powder

½ tsp baking powder

100 g/3½ oz plain chocolate chips

1 tbsp instant coffee granules

70 g/2½ oz caster sugar

70 g/2½ oz soft brown sugar

1 egg, beaten

1 Preheat the oven to 180°C/350°F/Gas Mark 4. Grease 3 large baking sheets. Sift the flour, cocoa and baking powder together in a large bowl.

2 Put 40 g/1½ oz of the chocolate chips and the butter in a saucepan and heat gently until melted. Add the coffee granules and stir until dissolved, then leave to cool slightly.

3 When the chocolate mixture has cooled, stir in the caster sugar, brown sugar and egg. Stir into the flour mixture, then stir in the remaining chocolate chips.

4 Knead the mixture to combine, then drop heaped tablespoons of the dough on to the prepared baking sheets, allowing room for the biscuits to spread during cooking.

5 Bake in the preheated oven for about 15 minutes, until firm. Leave for 5 minutes, then transfer to a wire rack and leave to cool.

Fruit Morsels

Serve these cookies with coffee or tea, or after dinner to accompany a special-occasion dessert.

  12 mins   10 mins

MAKES 36

INGREDIENTS

125 g/4½ oz butter or margarine, plus extra for greasing

175 g/6 oz ready-to-eat dried apricots

85 g/3 oz dried dates

140 g/5 oz plain flour

75 g/2¾ oz rolled oats

90 g/3½ oz wheat flakes

½ tsp bicarbonate of soda

pinch of salt

140 g/5 oz soft brown sugar, plus extra for dusting

2 eggs

1 tsp almond essence

1 Preheat the oven to 190°C/375°F/Gas Mark 5. Grease a large baking sheet. Chop the dried apricots and dates.

2 Sift the flour into a large bowl and mix in the oats, wheat flakes, bicarbonate of soda and salt.

3 Blend the sugar and butter. Beat in the eggs until the mixture is light and fluffy. Add the flour mixture gradually, stirring. Blend in the almond essence and fruit. Mix well.

4 Drop 36 teaspoonfuls of the mixture on to the baking sheet, allowing room for the biscuits to spread. Dust with sugar. Bake for 10 minutes, or until golden brown.

5 Remove the biscuits from the oven, place on a wire rack and leave them to cool before serving.

Crystallized Fruit Biscuits

A flavourful addition to any biscuit tin, these biscuits are delicious at any time of the day. Store for up to a week.

 12 mins   20 mins

MAKES 20

INGREDIENTS

2 egg whites

225 g/8 oz almonds, ground finely

140 g/5 oz caster sugar

1 tsp finely grated orange rind

½ tsp ground cinnamon

2 tbsp crystallized fruit

demerara sugar, for sprinkling

1 Preheat the oven to 180°C/350°F/ Gas Mark 4. Line 2 large baking sheets with baking paper, greasing if necessary.

2 In a large mixing bowl, beat the egg whites until stiff. Using a knife, gently fold in the almonds, sugar, orange rind, cinnamon and fruit.

3 When the mixture is smooth, transfer to a piping bag with a large nozzle (at least 1 cm/½ inch in diameter) and pipe filled circles of the mixture on to the baking paper, each about 7.5 cm/3 inches in diameter. Allow room for the biscuits to spread during cooking.

4 Sprinkle with the demerara sugar. Transfer to the preheated oven and bake for 20 minutes, or until the biscuits are light brown.

5 Remove from the oven and transfer to a wire rack. Decorate with candied fruit and allow to cool completely before serving.

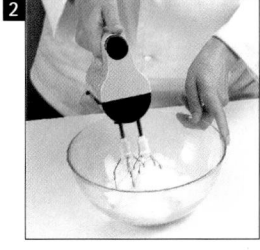

Citrus Crescents

For a sweet treat, try these pretty crescent-shaped biscuits, which have a lovely citrus tang to them.

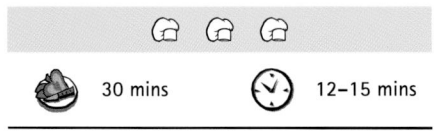

30 mins   12–15 mins

MAKES 25

INGREDIENTS

75 g/2¾ oz butter, softened, plus extra for greasing

70 g/2½ oz caster sugar, plus extra for sprinkling (optional)

1 egg, separated

200 g/7 oz plain flour, plus extra for dusting

grated rind of 1 orange

grated rind of 1 lemon

grated rind of 1 lime

2–3 tbsp orange juice

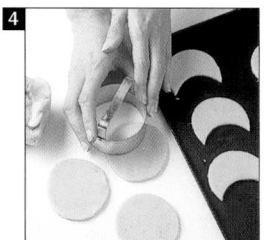

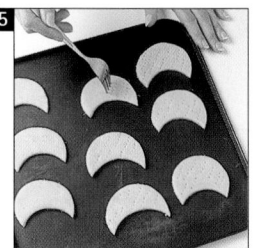

1 Preheat the oven to 200°C/400°F/ Gas Mark 6. Lightly grease 2 baking sheets with a little butter.

2 In a mixing bowl, cream together the butter and sugar until light and fluffy, then gradually beat in the egg yolk.

COOK'S TIP
Store the citrus crescents in an airtight container. Alternatively, they can be frozen for up to 1 month.

3 Sift the flour into the creamed mixture and mix until evenly combined. Add the orange, lemon and lime rind to the mixture, with enough of the orange juice to form a soft dough.

4 Roll out the dough on a lightly floured work surface. Stamp out circles using a 7.5-cm/3-inch biscuit cutter. Make crescent shapes by cutting away one-quarter of each circle. Re-roll the trimmings to make 25 crescents.

5 Place the crescents on the prepared baking sheets, spacing them apart to allow room for the biscuits to spread during cooking. Prick each one with a fork.

6 Lightly whisk the egg white in a small bowl and brush it over the biscuits. Dust with extra caster sugar, if using.

7 Bake in the oven for 12–15 minutes. Transfer the biscuits to a wire rack to cool and crispen before serving.

Lemon Disks

Simple but elegant, these biscuits combine the sharpness of lemon with the flavour of spices.

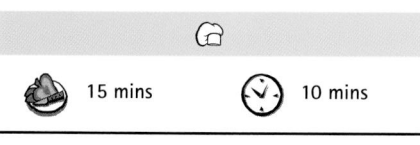 15 mins   🕐 10 mins

MAKES 30

I N G R E D I E N T S

175 g/6 oz butter or margarine, plus extra for greasing

200 g/7 oz soft brown sugar, plus extra for dusting

2 tbsp golden syrup

1 egg

350 g/12 oz plain flour

pinch of salt

1 tsp bicarbonate of soda

1 tsp ground ginger

1 tsp ground mixed spice

1 tsp grated lemon rind

demerara sugar, or cinnamon for dusting

1 Preheat the oven to 190°C/375°F/Gas Mark 5. Grease a large baking sheet.

2 Cream the butter, sugar and syrup in a large mixing bowl. Beat in the egg.

3 Gradually sift the flour, salt, bicarbonate of soda, ginger and mixed spice into the creamed mixture, stirring constantly. Add the lemon rind and mix thoroughly.

4 Form the mixture into 30 or so balls (about 1 rounded tablespoon each). Space the balls about 2.5 cm/1 inch apart on the greased baking sheet and flatten slightly with a palette knife. Dust the balls with demerara sugar. Transfer to the preheated oven and cook for 10 minutes, or until the biscuits are light brown.

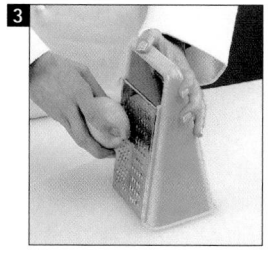

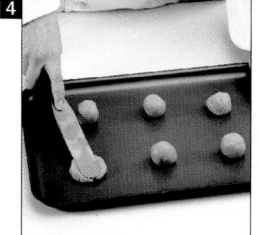

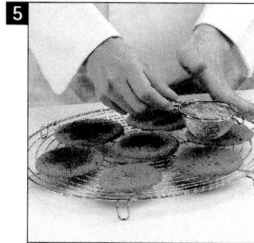

5 Transfer the biscuits from the oven to a wire rack and leave them to cool completely. One option is to sprinkle with demerara sugar or cinnamon. Alternatively, leave plain and serve only with grated lemon rind.

Lemon Drops

Serve these with lemon tea, sweetened with a little honey if liked. They also make a delicious dessert.

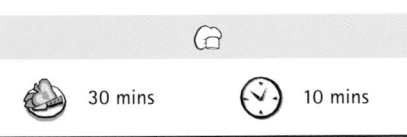
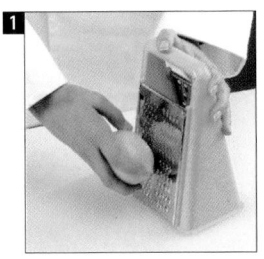
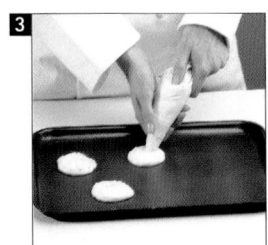

30 mins

10 mins

MAKES 24

INGREDIENTS

115 g/4 oz butter or margarine, plus extra for greasing

200 g/7 oz caster sugar

2 tbsp lemon juice

1 tbsp finely grated lemon rind

2 tbsp water

225 g/8 oz plain flour, sifted

1 tsp bicarbonate of soda

½ tsp cream of tartar

TO DECORATE

icing sugar

crystallized fruit, chopped finely (optional)

1 Preheat the oven to 180°C/350°F/Gas Mark 4. Grease a large baking sheet. Beat together the butter, caster sugar, lemon juice, lemon rind and water.

2 In a separate bowl, mix together the flour, bicarbonate of soda and cream of tartar. Add the butter mixture and blend together well.

3 Spoon the mixture into a piping bag fitted with a star-shaped nozzle. Pipe 24 fancy drops, about the size of a tablespoon, on to the greased baking sheet, allowing room for the biscuits to spread during cooking. Transfer to the preheated oven and bake for 10 minutes, or until the lemon drops are golden brown.

4 Remove from the oven, then transfer to a wire rack and leave to cool completely. Dust with icing sugar and sprinkle over the crystallized fruit, if liked.

Lemon Jumbles

These melt-in-the-mouth biscuits are made extra special by dredging them with icing sugar just before serving.

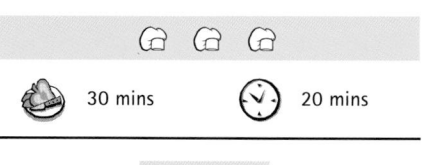

🍰 30 mins   🕐 20 mins

MAKES 50

INGREDIENTS

75 g/2¾ oz butter, softened, plus extra for greasing

115 g/4 oz caster sugar

grated rind of 1 lemon

1 egg, beaten lightly

4 tbsp lemon juice

350 g/12 oz plain flour

1 tsp baking powder

1 tbsp milk

icing sugar, for dredging

1 Preheat the oven to 160°C/325°F/Gas Mark 3. Lightly grease several baking sheets with a little butter.

2 In a mixing bowl, cream together the butter, caster sugar and lemon rind, until pale and fluffy.

3 Add the beaten egg and lemon juice, a little at a time, beating well after each addition.

4 Sift the flour and baking powder into the creamed mixture and blend together. Add the milk, mixing to form a firm dough.

5 Turn the dough out on to a lightly floured work surface and divide into about 50 equal-sized pieces.

6 Roll each piece into a sausage shape with your hands and twist in the middle to make an 'S' shape.

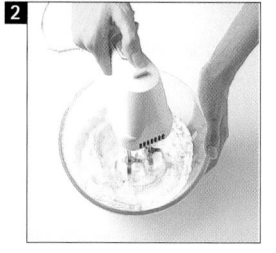

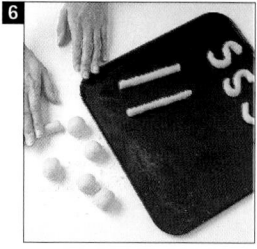

7 Place the biscuits on the prepared baking sheets and bake in the oven for 15–20 minutes. Leave to cool completely on a wire rack. Dredge generously with icing sugar before serving.

VARIATION
If you prefer, shape the dough into other shapes – letters of the alphabet or geometric shapes – or just make into round biscuits.

Sugared Orange Diamonds

Wrapped in cellophane and tied with ribbon, these Cointreau-flavoured biscuits would make an attractive gift.

30 mins plus 2 hrs chilling   15 mins

MAKES 24

INGREDIENTS

115 g/4 oz butter or margarine, plus extra for greasing

140 g/5 oz demerara sugar

2 tbsp orange juice

1 tbsp Cointreau

350 g/12 oz plain flour, sifted, plus extra for dusting

175 g/6 oz walnuts, chopped coarsely

1 tbsp finely grated orange rind

icing sugar, for dusting

1 Put the butter, sugar, orange juice and Cointreau in a bowl and beat together until a fluffy consistency is reached.

2 In a separate bowl, mix together the flour, walnuts and orange rind. Add the butter mixture and mix until thoroughly combined. Cover with clingfilm and leave to chill in the refrigerator for 2 hours.

3 When ready to use, preheat the oven to 180°C/350°F/Gas Mark 4. Grease a large baking sheet.

4 Lightly flour a board or work surface. Roll out the dough into an oblong about 3 mm/⅛ inch thick, then use a sharp knife or biscuit cutter to cut out 24 diamond shapes. Put the diamonds on to the greased baking sheet. Transfer to the oven and bake for 15 minutes, or until the biscuits are golden brown.

5 Remove from the oven, transfer to a wire rack and leave to cool. Dust with icing sugar before serving.

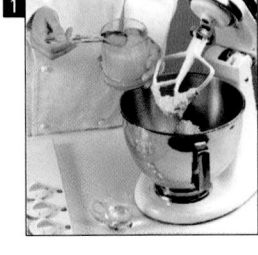

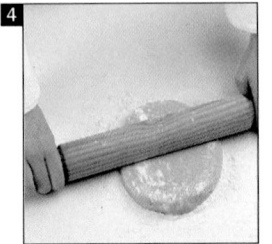

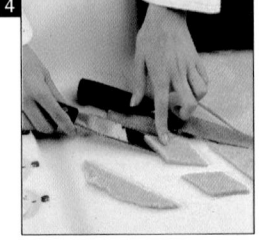

Banana Biscuits

Bananas lend a natural sweetness to these biscuits. For optimum flavour, use over-ripe bananas in this recipe.

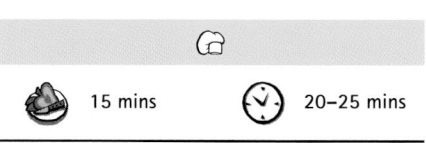

15 mins   20–25 mins

MAKES 20

I N G R E D I E N T S

butter, for greasing

115 g/4 oz plain flour

1 tsp baking powder

pinch of salt

1 tsp ground mixed spice

1½ bananas

175 g/6 oz apple sauce

1 tsp brandy

250 g/9 oz golden syrup

100 g/3½ oz rolled oats

2 tbsp sultanas

T O   D E C O R A T E

1 tbsp chopped crystallized mixed fruit

1 tbsp chopped dried banana chips

1 Preheat the oven to 180°C/350°F/Gas Mark 4. Grease a large baking sheet. Sift together the flour, baking powder, salt and mixed spice into a large bowl.

2 Coarsely chop the banana and place with the apple sauce, brandy and golden syrup in a food mixer and blend together until smooth. Stir in the oats and sultanas. Add the banana mixture to the spiced flour and beat together thoroughly.

3 Put 20 rounded tablespoonfuls of the mixture on to the greased baking sheet, allowing room for the biscuits to spread during cooking. Transfer to the preheated oven and bake for 20–25 minutes, or until golden brown.

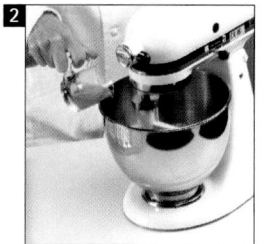
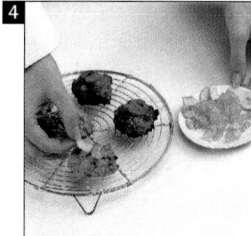

4 Remove the biscuits from the oven and place on a wire rack to cool. Before serving, decorate with the chopped crystallized fruit and the banana chips.

Banana Pecan Cookies

The mashed banana makes these cookies really moist, while the toasted nuts give them a crunchy texture.

12 mins

15 mins

MAKES 20

INGREDIENTS

150 g/5½ oz butter or margarine, plus extra for greasing

125 g/4½ oz soft brown sugar

1 egg

225 g/8 oz plain flour

1 tbsp baking powder

¼ tsp bicarbonate of soda

pinch of salt

2 tsp ground mixed spice

4 tbsp milk

2 bananas

250 g/9 oz rolled oats

70 g/2½ oz pecan nuts, toasted and chopped coarsely

1 Preheat the oven to 190°C/375°F/Gas Mark 5. Grease a large baking sheet. Mash the banana and set aside. Cream the butter and sugar in a large mixing bowl, then beat in the egg.

2 Gradually sift the flour, baking powder, bicarbonate of soda, salt and mixed spice into the creamed mixture and mix thoroughly. Stir in the milk and the mashed banana. Finally, add the oats and chopped pecan nuts and mix well.

3 Drop 20 rounded tablespoonfuls of the mixture on to the baking sheet, allowing room for the cookies to spread. Transfer to the preheated oven and bake for 15 minutes, or until light brown.

4 Transfer from the oven to a wire rack and leave them to cool before serving.

Ginger Chocolate Chip Squares

These moist squares are gently spiced with cinnamon, cloves and nutmeg. Leave to cool completely, then serve as a dessert or with coffee.

10 mins   30 mins

MAKES 15

INGREDIENTS

4 pieces stem ginger in syrup

225 g/8 oz plain flour

1½ tsp ground ginger

1 tsp ground cinnamon

¼ tsp ground cloves

¼ tsp grated nutmeg

115 g/4 oz soft brown sugar

115 g/4 oz butter

115 g/4 oz golden syrup

100 g/3½ oz plain chocolate chips

1 Preheat the oven to 150°C/300°F/ Gas Mark 2. Finely chop the stem ginger. Sift the flour, ground ginger, cinnamon, cloves and nutmeg into a large bowl. Stir in the chopped stem ginger and sugar.

2 Put the butter and the syrup into a saucepan and heat gently until melted. Bring to the boil, then pour the mixture into the flour mixture, stirring all the time. Beat until the mixture is cool enough to handle.

3 Add the chocolate chips to the mixture. Press evenly into a 20 x 30-cm/ 8 x 12-inch Swiss roll tin.

4 Transfer to the oven and bake for 30 minutes. Cut into squares, then leave to cool in the tin.

Banana & Chocolate Biscuits

Adding mashed banana to the mixture for these biscuits makes for a really moist texture somewhere between a cake and a biscuit.

10 mins   15 mins

MAKES 30

INGREDIENTS

115 g/4 oz butter, plus extra for greasing

350 g/12 oz plain flour

½ tsp baking powder

1 small banana

60 g/2¼ oz caster sugar

60 g/2¼ oz soft brown sugar

1 egg, beaten

½ tsp vanilla essence

85 g/3 oz milk chocolate chips

1 Preheat the oven to 190°C/375°F/ Gas Mark 5. Grease 2–3 large baking sheets. Sift the flour and baking powder together. Mash the banana.

2 Beat together the butter, caster sugar and brown sugar until soft and fluffy. Gradually beat in the egg, then beat in the banana and vanilla essence until well mixed. Beat in the flour mixture, then stir in the chocolate chips.

3 Place heaped tablespoons of the mixture on the prepared baking sheets, allowing room for the biscuits to spread during cooking.

4 Bake the biscuits in the preheated oven for about 15 minutes, until lightly browned. Transfer to a wire rack and leave to cool.

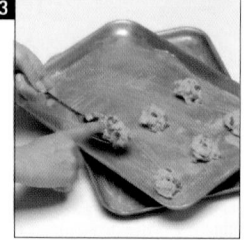

Apricot & Chocolate Biscuits

The apricots in these deliciously moist biscuits give them a lovely fruity flavour. If there are any left, store in an airtight container.

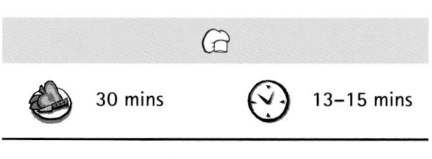

30 mins   13–15 mins

SERVES 4

INGREDIENTS

85 g/3 oz butter, softened, plus extra
  for greasing

2 tbsp golden granulated sugar

4 tbsp soft brown sugar

½ tsp vanilla essence

1 egg

150 g/5½ oz self-raising flour

115 g/4 oz plain chocolate,
  chopped coarsely

115 g/4 oz ready-to-eat dried apricots,
  chopped coarsely

1 Preheat the oven to 180°C/350°F/ Gas Mark 4. Grease 2 baking sheets. Place the butter, granulated sugar, brown sugar and vanilla essence in a bowl and beat together. Add in the egg and beat until light and fluffy.

2 Sift the flour over the mixture and fold in, then fold in the chocolate and chopped apricots.

VARIATION
As an alternative to dried apricots, try other dried fruit such as dried cranberries, cherries or raisins.

3 Put tablespoonfuls of the mixture on to the prepared baking sheets, allowing room for the biscuits to spread during cooking. Bake in the preheated oven for 13–15 minutes, or until crisp on the outside but still soft inside. Leave to cool on the baking sheets for 2 minutes, then transfer the biscuits to wire racks to cool completely.

Persian Rice Crescents

These little biscuits, made with rice flour, have a fine texture and a delicate flavour. They are excellent with strong black coffee.

30 mins, plus 1 hr resting

15 mins

MAKES 60

INGREDIENTS

200 g/7 oz butter, unsalted for preference, softened, plus extra for greasing

115 g/4 oz icing sugar, sifted, plus extra for dusting

2 egg yolks

½–1 tsp ground cardamom or 1 tbsp rosewater

175 g/6 oz rice flour, sifted

1 egg white, beaten lightly

75 g/2¾ oz finely chopped pistachio nuts or almonds

1 Grease several baking sheets.

2 Using an electric whisk, beat the butter in a large bowl until light and creamy. Gradually add the icing sugar and beat for 2 minutes until light and fluffy. Gradually add the egg yolks, beating well after each addition. Add the cardamom and the rice flour and mix to a soft dough.

3 Turn the dough on to a lightly floured work surface and knead lightly. Turn the mixing bowl over the dough and leave to rest for about 1 hour.

4 When ready to use, preheat the oven to 180°C/350°F/Gas Mark 4. Roll heaped teaspoonfuls of the dough into balls, then form into crescent shapes. Place 5 cm/2 inches apart on the prepared baking sheets. Mark a pattern on the tops with a spoon.

5 Brush each crescent with a little beaten egg white and sprinkle with the chopped nuts.

6 Bake in the preheated oven for about 15 minutes, or until the bases start to colour; the tops should remain very pale. Reduce the heat if the tops start to colour.

7 Cool on the baking sheets for about 2 minutes, then transfer the biscuits to wire racks to cool completely. Dust with icing sugar before serving.

 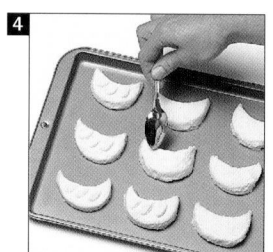 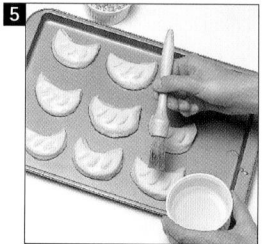

COOK'S TIP
Cooking-oil sprays are ideal for lightly greasing baking sheets when making biscuits.

Melting Hearts

Serve these little heart-shaped biscuits with a cup of coffee, or to round off a romantic Valentine's Day dinner.

10 mins plus
8 hrs chilling

15 mins

MAKES 24

INGREDIENTS

140 g/5 oz plain flour, plus extra
  for dusting

1½ tsp ground mixed spice

½ tsp ground ginger

pinch of salt

½ tsp bicarbonate of soda

115 g/4 oz butter or margarine, plus extra
  for greasing

100 g/3½ oz soft brown sugar

2 small eggs

1 tsp cocoa powder

½ tsp Kahlua

35 g/1¼ oz hazelnuts, toasted and
  chopped coarsely

12 fresh mint leaves, to decorate

125 ml/4 fl oz double cream or
  soured cream, to serve

1 In a large bowl, sift together the flour, spices, salt and bicarbonate of soda. In a separate bowl, cream together the butter and sugar. Beat in the eggs, then add the cocoa, Kahlua and flour mixture gradually and continue beating until smooth. Cover with clingfilm and leave to chill in the refrigerator for at least 8 hours or overnight if possible.

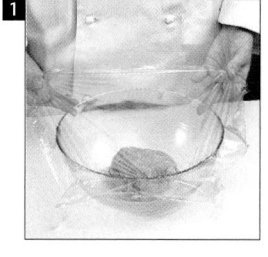

2 When ready to use, preheat the oven to 180°C/350°F/Gas Mark 4 and grease a baking sheet. Lightly flour a board or work surface. Roll out the dough into an oblong about 3 mm/⅛ inch thick, then cut

out 24 heart shapes using a biscuit cutter or a sharp knife. Place the hearts on to the greased baking sheet. Transfer to the preheated oven and bake for 15 minutes, or until the biscuits are golden brown.

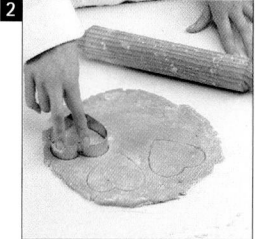

3 Remove from the oven, then transfer to a wire rack and sprinkle over the hazelnuts. When cool, serve with double cream or soured cream topped with fresh mint leaves.

Pistachio & Cardamom Tuiles

These wafer-thin, crisp, nutty biscuits are ideal for serving with fresh fruit desserts or as a delicious alternative to ordinary wafers for ice cream.

30 mins   8-10 mins

MAKES 18

INGREDIENTS

6 cardamom pods

55 g/2 oz butter, melted and cooled, plus extra for greasing

2 egg whites

115 g/4 oz golden caster sugar

115 g/4 oz plain flour

25 g/1 oz chopped pistachio nuts

1 Preheat the oven to 180°C/350°F/Gas Mark 4. Crush the cardamom pods and remove the husks. Grind the black seeds using a pestle and mortar and set aside. Grease 2-3 baking sheets and a rolling pin. Place the egg whites and caster sugar in a bowl. Whisk together with a fork until frothy.

2 Sift the flour into the bowl. Add the pistachio nuts and ground cardamom and mix with a fork. Add the butter and mix together thoroughly. Drop teaspoonfuls of the mixture on to the baking sheets, allowing room for the biscuits to spread during cooking. Using a palette knife, spread each one out slightly.

3 Bake in the preheated oven, 1 sheet at a time, for 8-10 minutes, or until the edges are firm. Lift the biscuits off carefully with a palette knife and place over the rolling pin while still warm. Leave to set for 1-2 minutes, then lift off carefully and transfer to a wire rack to cool. Store in an airtight container.

COOK'S TIP
Do not be tempted to bake more than one tray of biscuits at a time, otherwise the second batch will become too firm before you have time to shape them.

Amaretti

Traditionally, these moreish little Italian macaroons are made with apricot kernels, but almonds are used here.

30 mins   30 mins

MAKES ABOUT 40

INGREDIENTS

150 g/5½ oz blanched almonds

150 g/5½ oz caster sugar

1 large egg white

icing sugar, for dusting

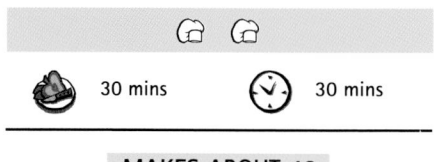
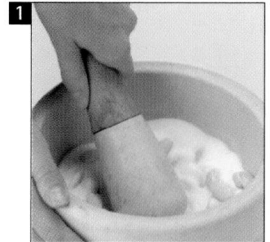
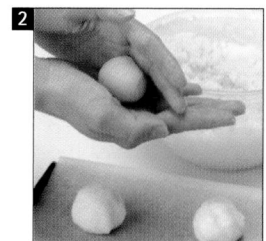

1 Preheat the oven to 120°C/250°F/ Gas Mark ½. Crush the almonds with the caster sugar using a pestle and mortar, or finely chop the almonds and then combine with the sugar in a bowl.

2 Lightly beat the egg white, then stir it into the almond mixture to form a firm dough. Line 2 baking sheets with baking paper and place walnut-sized portions of the dough on them, allowing plenty of room for the biscuits to spread during cooking. Dust with icing sugar.

3 Bake in the preheated oven for 30 minutes. Transfer to wire racks to cool completely.

Almond Biscuits

Almond trees grow in abundance all over the Mediterranean region, so the slightly sweet nut appears frequently in regional dishes.

🍰 25 mins   🕐 20–25 mins

MAKES 32

INGREDIENTS

175 g/6 oz blanched almonds

200 g/7 oz butter, softened

6 tbsp icing sugar, plus extra
for sifting

325 g/11½ oz plain flour

2 tsp vanilla essence

½ tsp almond essence

1 Line 2 baking sheets with baking paper. Using a sharp knife, finely chop the almonds, or process them in a food processor, taking care not to let them turn into a paste. Set aside. Preheat the oven to 180°C/350°F/Gas Mark 4.

2 Put the butter in a bowl and beat with an electric whisk until smooth. Sift in the icing sugar and continue beating until creamed and smooth.

3 Sift in the flour from above the bowl and beat it in until blended. Add the vanilla and almond essences and beat the mixture again to form a soft dough. Stir in the chopped almonds.

4 Using a teaspoon, shape the dough into 32 walnut-sized round balls. Place on the prepared baking sheets, allowing room for the biscuits to spread during cooking. Bake in the preheated oven for 20–25 minutes, until the biscuits are set and just starting to turn brown.

5 Leave the biscuits to stand on the baking sheets for 2 minutes to firm up. Sift a thick layer of icing sugar over them. Then transfer them to a wire rack and leave to cool completely.

6 Lightly dust with more icing sugar, just before serving. They can be stored in an airtight container for up to 1 week.

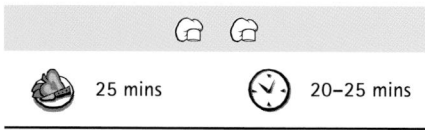

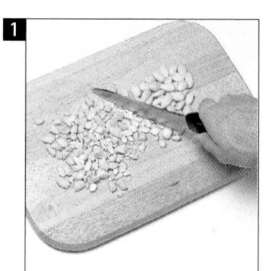

VARIATIONS
Pecan nuts can be used instead of the almonds. If liked, 2 teaspoons finely grated orange rind can be added to the dough in step 3.

Spiced Almond Biscuits

These almond biscuits are delicately spiced with ground mixed spice. Serve with a cup of tea for a delicious mid-afternoon treat.

12 mins plus
30 mins chilling   15 mins

MAKES 30

INGREDIENTS

175 g/6 oz butter or margarine, plus extra for greasing

100 g/3½ oz caster sugar

25 g/1 oz almonds, chopped finely

½ tsp ground mixed spice

pinch of salt

1 tsp vanilla essence

250 g/9 oz plain flour, plus extra for dusting

1 egg white, beaten lightly

chopped almonds, to decorate

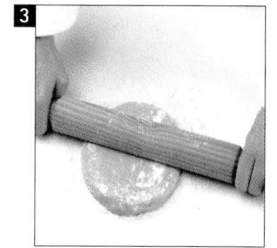
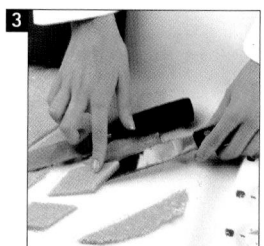

1 Preheat the oven to 160°C/325°F/ Gas Mark 3 and grease 2 large baking sheets. Mix half the sugar with the almonds and mixed spice and set aside.

2 In a mixing bowl, cream the butter and half the sugar with the salt and vanilla essence. Sift in the flour and mix well. Cover the bowl with clingfilm and transfer to the refrigerator to chill for 30 minutes.

3 Sprinkle flour on a work surface or cutting board and roll out the dough to 1-cm/½-inch thickness. Cut the dough into circles 5 cm/2 inches in diameter or cut into diamonds. Transfer to the baking sheets. Brush lightly with egg white and prick with a fork.

4 Sprinkle with the sugar and almond mixture. Transfer to the oven and bake for 15 minutes, or until the biscuits are golden. Remove from the oven and sprinkle with chopped almonds before serving.

Spiced Biscuits

These spicy biscuits are perfect to serve with fruit salad or ice cream for a very easy instant dessert.

35 mins   10–12 mins

SERVES 12

INGREDIENTS

175 g/6 oz butter, unsalted for preference, plus extra for greasing

185 g/6½ oz soft brown sugar

250 g/9 oz plain flour

pinch of salt

½ tsp bicarbonate of soda

1 tsp ground cinnamon

½ tsp ground coriander

½ tsp ground nutmeg

¼ tsp ground cloves

2 tbsp dark rum

1 Preheat the oven to 180°C/350°F/Gas Mark 4. Grease 2 baking sheets with a little butter.

2 Cream together the butter and sugar and whisk until light and fluffy.

3 Sift the flour, salt, bicarbonate of soda, cinnamon, coriander, nutmeg and cloves into the creamed mixture.

4 Add the dark rum and stir it into the creamed mixture.

5 Using 2 teaspoons, place small mounds of the mixture on the prepared baking sheets, allowing room for the biscuits to spread during cooking.

6 Bake in the preheated oven for 10–12 minutes, until golden brown in colour.

7 Transfer the biscuits to wire racks to cool and crispen before serving.

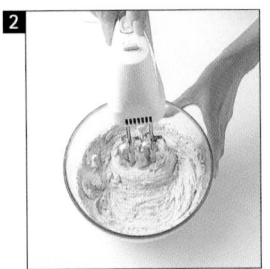

COOK'S TIP

Use the back of a fork or spoon to flatten the cookies slightly before baking.

Chocolate Walnut Biscuits

These chocolate and walnut biscuits are moreish, but topped with a fudge icing they are divine! Choose a plain or milk chocolate topping.

25 mins plus
30 mins chilling

20 mins

MAKES 18–20

INGREDIENTS

COOKIES

butter, for greasing

85 g/3 oz plain chocolate

115 g/4 oz walnut pieces

1 egg, separated

115 g/4 oz caster sugar

40 g/1½ oz plain flour

TOPPING

85 g/3 oz plain or milk chocolate, broken into pieces

4 tbsp butter

55 g/2 oz soft brown sugar

2 tbsp milk

200 g/7 oz icing sugar

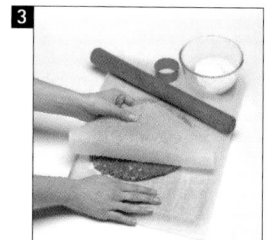

1 Grease 2 large baking sheets. To make the biscuits, coarsely grate the chocolate. Finely chop the walnut pieces.

2 Whisk the egg white until stiff, then fold in the caster sugar. Stir in the grated chocolate, walnuts, flour and egg yolk. Knead in the bowl for a short time until smooth. Wrap the dough in greaseproof paper and leave to chill in the refrigerator for 30 minutes.

3 Preheat the oven to 190°C/375°F/Gas Mark 5. Place the dough between 2 sheets of floured baking paper and roll out to 8-mm/¼-inch thickness, then cut into circles using a 5-cm/2-inch biscuit cutter. Place on the prepared baking sheets.

4 Bake the biscuits in the oven for about 20 minutes, until golden brown. Transfer to a wire rack and leave to cool.

5 When cold, make the topping. Put the chocolate, butter, brown sugar and milk in a saucepan and heat gently until the sugar has dissolved. Bring to the boil, then boil rapidly for 3 minutes.

6 Remove the saucepan from the heat and gradually sift in the icing sugar. Beat with a wooden spoon until smooth, then beat for an additional 2 minutes, until the topping is thick enough to spread.

7 Using a wet palette knife, spread the chocolate fudge topping immediately over the top of each biscuit. Leave to set.

Spiced Fruit & Nut Biscuits

Bananas, dates and walnuts make up these delicious biscuits, spiced with a little ground mixed spice. Store in an airtight container for several days.

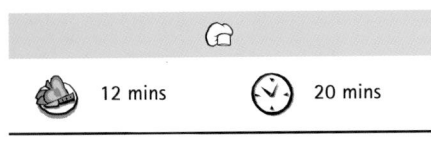

🔥 12 mins   🕐 20 mins

MAKES 20

I N G R E D I E N T S

butter, for greasing

300 g/10½ oz mashed bananas

5 tbsp vegetable oil

1 tsp almond essence

1 egg, beaten

1 tsp ground mixed spice

pinch of salt

250 g/9 oz rolled oats

75 g/2¾ oz raisins

75 g/2¾ oz sultanas

85 g/3 oz dates, chopped finely

40g/1½ oz walnuts, chopped finely

1 Preheat the oven to 180°C/350°F/Gas Mark 4. Grease a large baking sheet.

2 Blend the bananas, vegetable oil, almond essence, egg, mixed spice and salt together in a large mixing bowl. Add the oats and mix well. Finally, stir in the dried fruit and walnuts until evenly distributed.

3 Drop 20 rounded tablespoonfuls of the mixture on to the greased baking sheet, allowing room for the biscuits to spread during cooking.

4 Bake in the preheated oven for 20 minutes, or until the biscuits are golden brown.

5 Transfer the biscuits from the oven to a wire rack and leave them to cool completely before serving.

Traditional Spiced Biscuits

These spicy biscuits are delicious served with either coffee or tea. You can replace the sultanas with chopped mixed nuts if you prefer.

🍰 15 mins plus 1 hr chilling   🕐 12 mins

MAKES 36

INGREDIENTS

225 g/8 oz plain flour

2 tsp ground mixed spice

1 tsp salt

1 tsp bicarbonate of soda

175 g/6 oz butter or margarine, plus extra for greasing

100 g/3½ oz granulated sugar

200 g/7 oz soft brown sugar, plus extra for dusting

2 eggs

4 tbsp milk

300 g/10½ oz rolled oats

75 g/2¾ oz raisins

75 g/2¾ oz sultanas

1 Mix the flour, mixed spice, salt and bicarbonate of soda together and sift into a large mixing bowl.

2 One at a time, mix in the butter, both sugars, the eggs and the milk. Beat the mixture until it is smooth.

3 Stir in the oats and dried fruit. Cover the bowl with clingfilm and chill in the refrigerator for 1 hour.

4 Preheat the oven to 190°C/375°F/Gas Mark 5. Grease a large baking sheet.

5 Put 36 tablespoonfuls of the mixture on to the greased baking sheet, allowing room for the biscuits to spread during cooking. Dust lightly with brown sugar. Transfer to the preheated oven and bake for 12 minutes, or until the biscuits are golden brown.

6 Remove the biscuits from the oven and place on a wire rack to cool completely before serving.

Classic Oatmeal Biscuits

A no-fuss biscuit to enjoy with a morning cup of coffee. These easy-to-make biscuits can be stored in airtight containers for several days.

 10 mins   15 mins

MAKES 30

I N G R E D I E N T S

175 g/6 oz butter or margarine, plus extra for greasing

250 g/9 oz demerara sugar

1 egg

4 tbsp water

1 tsp vanilla essence

375 g/13 oz rolled oats

140 g/5 oz plain flour

1 tsp salt

½ tsp bicarbonate of soda

1 Preheat the oven to 180°C/350°F/ Gas Mark 4 and grease a large baking sheet.

2 Cream the butter and sugar together in a large mixing bowl or free-standing mixer. Beat in the egg, water and vanilla essence until the mixture is smooth.

3 In a separate bowl, mix the oats, flour, salt and bicarbonate of soda. Gradually stir the oat mixture into the butter mixture until thoroughly combined.

4 Put 30 rounded tablespoonfuls of the mixture on to the greased baking sheet, making sure they are well spaced. Transfer to the preheated oven and bake for 15 minutes, or until the biscuits are golden brown.

5 Remove from the oven and place on a wire rack to cool before serving.

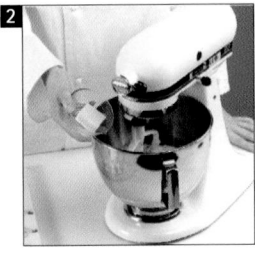

Oat & Raisin Biscuits

These oaty, fruity biscuits couldn't be easier to make and are delicious served with a creamy rum and raisin ice cream.

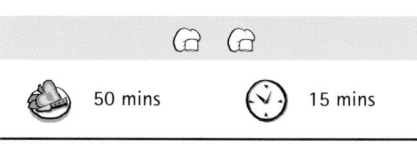

50 mins   15 mins

SERVES 4

INGREDIENTS

4 tbsp butter, plus extra for greasing

125 g/4½ oz caster sugar

1 egg, beaten

70 g/2½ oz plain flour

½ tsp salt

½ tsp baking powder

150 g/5½ oz rolled oats

140 g/5 oz raisins

2 tbsp sesame seeds

1 Preheat the oven to 180°C/350°F/Gas Mark 4. Lightly grease 2 baking sheets.

2 In a large mixing bowl, cream together the butter and sugar until light and fluffy.

3 Gradually add the beaten egg, beating well after each addition, until thoroughly combined.

4 Sift the flour, salt and baking powder into the creamed mixture. Mix gently to combine. Add the rolled oats, raisins and sesame seeds and mix together until thoroughly combined.

5 Place tablespoonfuls of the mixture on the prepared baking sheets, allowing room for the biscuits to spread during cooking, and flatten them slightly with the back of a spoon.

6 Bake the biscuits in the preheated oven for 15 minutes.

7 Let the biscuits cool slightly on the baking sheets.

8 Carefully transfer the biscuits to a wire rack and leave to cool completely before serving.

COOK'S TIP
To enjoy these biscuits at their best, store them in an airtight container.

Oat & Hazelnut Morsels

Try these delicious biscuits with a refreshing cup of mint tea in the afternoon, or give them to hungry children as a healthy snack.

10 mins   12–15 mins

MAKES 30

I N G R E D I E N T S

175 g/6 oz butter or margarine, plus extra for greasing

225 g/8 oz demerara sugar

1 egg, beaten

4 tbsp milk

1 tsp vanilla essence

½ tsp almond essence

115 g/4 oz hazelnuts

140 g/5 oz plain flour

1½ tsp ground mixed spice

¼ tsp bicarbonate of soda

pinch of salt

300 g/10½ oz rolled oats

150 g/5½ oz sultanas

1 Preheat the oven to 190°C/375°F/Gas Mark 5. Grease 2 large baking sheets.

2 Cream the butter and sugar together in a large mixing bowl. Blend in the egg, milk and vanilla and almond essences until thoroughly combined. Chop the hazelnuts finely.

3 In a separate bowl, sift the flour, mixed spice, bicarbonate of soda and salt together. Add to the creamed mixture slowly, stirring continuously. Mix in the oats, sultanas and hazelnuts.

4 Put 30 rounded tablespoonfuls of the mixture on to the greased baking sheets, making sure they are well spaced.

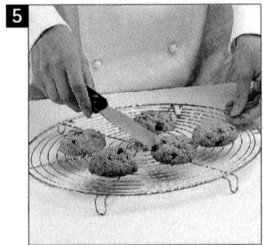

Transfer to the preheated oven and bake for 12–15 minutes, or until the biscuits are golden brown.

5 Remove the biscuits from the oven and place on a wire rack to cool before serving.

Hazelnut & Almond Oaties

These biscuits are made with a delectable combination of rolled oats, coarsely chopped nuts and plain chocolate chips.

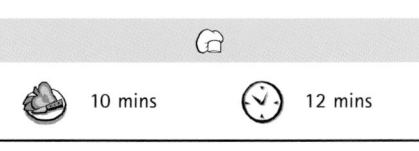

10 mins   12 mins

MAKES 36

INGREDIENTS

175 g/6 oz butter or margarine, plus extra for greasing

140 g/5 oz demerara sugar

1 egg

90 g/3¼ oz plain flour

½ tsp salt

1 tsp bicarbonate of soda

¼ tsp almond essence

125 g/4½ oz rolled oats

40 g/1½ oz hazelnuts, chopped coarsely

40 g/1½ oz almonds, chopped coarsely

175 g/6 oz plain chocolate chips

1 Preheat the oven to 190°C/375°F/ Gas Mark 5 and grease a large baking sheet.

2 Cream the butter and sugar together in a large mixing bowl. Then beat in the egg.

3 In a separate bowl, sift the flour, salt and bicarbonate of soda, then stir into the butter mixture.

4 Add the almond essence and oats and beat thoroughly. Finally, mix in the nuts and chocolate chips.

5 Put 36 teaspoonfuls of the mixture on to the greased baking sheet, making sure they are well spaced. Transfer to the preheated oven and bake for 12 minutes, or until the biscuits are golden brown.

6 Remove the biscuits from the oven, then place on a wire rack and leave them to cool before serving.

Fig & Walnut Biscuits

Figs and walnuts make a flavourful combination, here complemented by dried dates. These biscuits are delicious served with coffee.

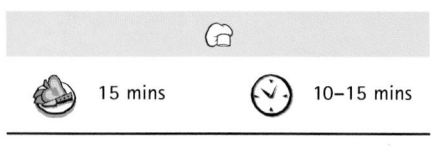

15 mins   10–15 mins

MAKES 20

INGREDIENTS

225 g/8 oz butter or margarine, plus extra for greasing

75 g/2¾ oz dried figs

115 g/4oz honey

4 tbsp demerara sugar

2 eggs, beaten

pinch of salt

1 tsp ground mixed spice

1 tsp bicarbonate of soda

½ tsp vanilla essence

2 tbsp dried dates, chopped finely

225 g/8 oz plain flour

175 g/6 oz rolled oats

40 g/1½ oz walnuts, chopped finely

fig pieces, to decorate (optional)

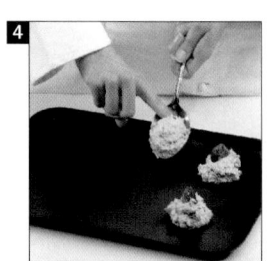

1 Preheat the oven to 180°C/350°F/Gas Mark 4. Grease a large baking sheet.

2 Finely chop the figs. Mix the butter, honey, figs and sugar together in a large bowl. Beat in the eggs and mix thoroughly.

3 Combine the salt, mixed spice, bicarbonate of soda, vanilla essence and dates, stirring constantly. Add them to the creamed mixture gradually. Sift the flour into the mixture, stirring constantly. Finally, mix in the oats and walnuts.

4 Drop 20 rounded tablespoonfuls of the mixture on to the greased baking sheet, allowing room for the biscuits to spread. Decorate with fig pieces, if desired.

Bake in the preheated oven for 10–15 minutes, or until the biscuits are golden brown.

5 Transfer the biscuits from the oven to a wire rack and leave to cool before serving.

Oaty Pecan Biscuits

These light, crisp biscuits are delicious just as they are, but they are also good served with cheese. Let them cool completely before serving.

10 mins   15 mins

MAKES 15

INGREDIENTS

115 g/4 oz butter, softened, plus extra for greasing

85 g/3 oz light muscovado sugar

1 egg, beaten

85 g/3 oz plain flour

½ tsp baking powder

55 g/2 oz rolled oats

55 g/2 oz pecan nuts, chopped

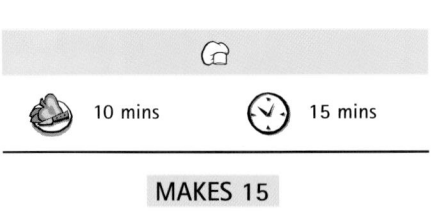

1 Preheat the oven to 180°C/350°F/ Gas Mark 4 and grease several baking sheets. Put the butter and sugar in a bowl and beat until light and fluffy. Gradually beat in the egg.

2 Sift the flour and baking powder into the mixture. Add the oats and pecan nuts. Stir together until well combined. Drop tablespoonfuls of the mixture on to the baking sheets, allowing room for the biscuits to spread during cooking.

3 Bake in the oven for 15 minutes, or until pale golden. Leave to cool on the baking sheets for 2 minutes, then transfer to wire racks to cool completely.

COOK'S TIP
To save a lot of hard work, beat the butter and sugar together with an electric whisk, or use a food processor.

Oat & Walnut Spice Biscuits

These delicately spiced biscuits are quick and easy to make and are delicious served with either coffee or tea at any time of the day.

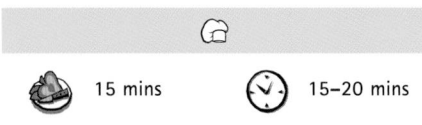
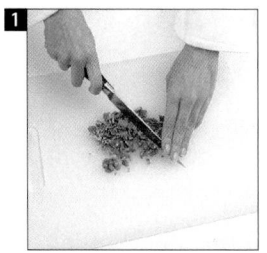
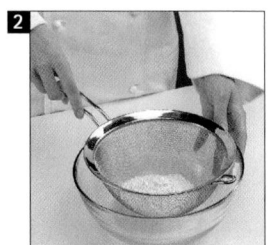

15 mins   15–20 mins

MAKES 20

INGREDIENTS

2 tbsp butter or margarine, plus extra for greasing

200 g/7 oz soft brown sugar

85 g/3 oz walnuts

140 g/5 oz plain flour

2 tsp bicarbonate of soda

pinch of salt

1¼ tsp ground mixed spice

2 eggs, beaten

2 tsp vanilla essence

175 g/6 oz rolled oats

150 g/5½ oz raisins

150 g/5½ oz sultanas

1 Preheat the oven to 180°C/350°F/Gas Mark 4 and grease 2 large baking sheets. Cream the butter and sugar together in a large mixing bowl. Chop the walnuts coarsely.

2 In a separate bowl, sift together the flour, bicarbonate of soda, salt and mixed spice, then stir into the butter mixture. Blend in the eggs, vanilla essence and oats until they are thoroughly combined. Finally, add the dried fruit and nuts and mix well.

3 Put 10 rounded tablespoonfuls of the mixture on to each greased baking sheet, allowing room for the biscuits to spread during cooking. Bake for 15–20 minutes, or until the biscuits are firm.

4 Remove the biscuits from the oven and cool before serving.

Cherry & Walnut Biscuits

Using slightly bitter maraschino cherries adds an interesting dimension to these biscuits. An excellent alternative to after-dinner chocolates.

12 mins   10 mins

MAKES 30

INGREDIENTS

175 g/6 oz butter or margarine, plus extra for greasing

200 g/7 oz soft brown sugar

2 eggs

350 g/12 oz plain flour

pinch of salt

2 tsp baking powder

2 tbsp milk

1 tsp almond essence

150 g/5½ oz chopped walnuts

75 g/2¾ oz raisins

75 g/2¾ oz sultanas

100 g/3½ oz maraschino cherries

200 g/7 oz wheat flakes, crushed

15 maraschino cherries, to decorate

1 Preheat the oven to 190°C/375°F/ Gas Mark 5. Grease a large baking sheet. Halve the 15 maraschino cherries and set aside.

2 Cream the butter and sugar in a large bowl until a fluffy consistency is reached. Beat in the eggs.

3 Gradually sift the flour, salt and baking powder into the creamed mixture. Add the milk and almond essence and mix thoroughly. Stir in the walnuts, dried fruit and maraschino cherries.

4 Form the dough into 30 balls (about 1 rounded tablespoon each) and roll in the crushed wheat flakes. Space the dough balls about 2 cm/1 inch apart on the greased baking sheet. Place half a maraschino cherry on the top of each dough ball, if desired. Transfer to the preheated oven and cook for 10 minutes, or until the biscuits are light brown.

5 Transfer from the oven to a wire rack and leave to cool.

Prepare-Ahead Biscuits

Make the dough for these biscuits, then slice and bake it as and when required. The dough keeps in the refrigerator for up to one week.

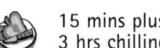

15 mins plus 3 hrs chilling   10 mins

MAKES 25

INGREDIENTS

200 g/7 oz plain flour, plus extra for dusting

25 g/1 oz cocoa powder

1 tsp baking powder

115 g/4 oz butter, plus extra for greasing

175 g/6 oz caster sugar

55 g/2 oz plain chocolate chips

1 egg, beaten

1 Sift the flour, cocoa and baking powder into a large mixing bowl. Add the butter and rub in until the mixture resembles fine breadcrumbs. Stir in the sugar, chocolate chips and egg and mix together to form a dough.

2 Turn the dough on to a lightly floured work surface and knead for 1 minute, then shape into a 5-cm/2-inch long roll. Wrap the dough roll in foil and store in the refrigerator for at least 3 hours, or place in the freezer.

3 When ready to use, preheat the oven to 190°C/375°F/Gas Mark 5. Grease 1–2 baking sheets. Unwrap the dough roll and cut into 1-cm/¹/₂-inch thick slices. Place on the baking sheets and bake in the oven for about 10 minutes, until firm. Leave for 1 minute, then transfer the biscuits to a wire rack and leave to cool.

VARIATIONS
Replace the chocolate chips with sultanas, dried apricots or raisins, or add a combination of chopped hazelnuts, almonds or walnuts and chocolate chips.

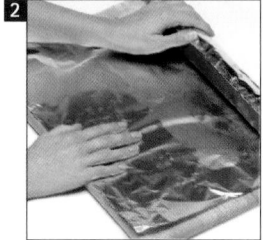

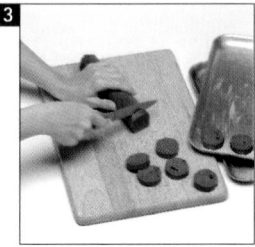

Milk Chocolate Chunk Cookies

The dough for these large, soft cookies is rich and bursting with chunks of milk chocolate. Serve with tea for a delicious mid-afternoon treat.

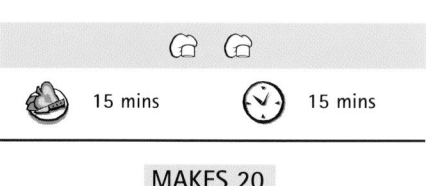

15 mins   15 mins

MAKES 20

INGREDIENTS

175 g/6 oz butter, plus extra for greasing

300 g/10½ oz milk chocolate

175 g/6 oz rolled oats

140 g/5 oz plain flour

1 tsp baking powder

175 g/6 oz caster sugar

175 g/6 oz soft brown sugar

2 eggs, beaten

½ tsp vanilla essence

1 Preheat the oven to 180°C/350°F/Gas Mark 4. Grease 4 large baking sheets. Coarsely chop the chocolate into 8-mm/¼-inch pieces. Put the oats into a food processor and blend until ground to a powder. Sift the flour and baking powder together.

2 Beat the butter, caster sugar and brown sugar together until soft and fluffy. Gradually beat in the eggs, then beat in the vanilla essence and sifted flour. Stir in the oats and chocolate pieces.

3 Place 20 teaspoonfuls of the mixture on the prepared baking sheets, allowing room for the cookies to spread during cooking. Press each one down using the back of a wet spoon.

4 Bake the cookies in the preheated oven for about 15 minutes, until lightly browned. Leave for 5 minutes, then transfer to a wire rack and leave to cool.

Mixed Nut Biscuits

If you are a lover of nuts, these biscuits are a real treat, and will be very hard to resist. Try to leave them to cool completely before eating.

🕓 12 mins　🕐 12–14 mins

MAKES 36

I N G R E D I E N T S

115 g/4 oz butter or margarine, plus extra for greasing

35 g/1¼ oz mixed nuts

100 g/3½ oz caster sugar

100 g/3½ oz soft brown sugar

pinch of salt

1 tsp almond essence

2 egg whites, beaten lightly

3 tsp water

140 g/5 oz plain flour

½ tsp baking powder

½ tsp bicarbonate of soda

175 g/6 oz rolled oats

icing sugar, for dusting (optional)

1　Preheat the oven to 190°C/375°F/Gas Mark 5. Grease 2 large baking sheets.

2　Finely chop the nuts and set aside. In a large mixing bowl, cream the butter, sugars, salt and almond essence until light and fluffy. Beat in the egg whites and water. Sift the flour, baking powder and bicarbonate of soda together and add to the mixture. Blend in the oats and nuts.

3　Drop 36 rounded tablespoonfuls of the mixture on to the greased baking sheets, allowing room for the biscuits to spread during cooking. Transfer to the oven and bake for 12–14 minutes.

4　Transfer the biscuits to a wire rack, dust with icing sugar, if liked, and leave to cool completely.

Orange Cream Cheese Biscuits

Using cream cheese in these biscuits adds lightness and texture to the basic dough. They look particularly attractive decorated with orange rind.

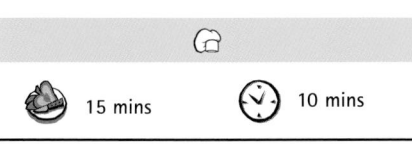

🍮 15 mins   🕐 10 mins

MAKES 30

I N G R E D I E N T S

225 g/8 oz butter or margarine, plus extra for greasing

200 g/7 oz soft brown sugar

6 tbsp cream cheese

1 egg, beaten lightly

325 g/11½ oz plain flour

1 tsp bicarbonate of soda

1 tbsp orange juice

1 tsp finely grated orange rind

demerara sugar, to sprinkle

fine strips of orange rind, to decorate (optional)

1 Preheat the oven to 190°C/375°F/Gas Mark 5. Grease a large baking sheet. In a large mixing bowl, cream together the butter, sugar and cream cheese until light and fluffy. Mix in the egg and sift in the flour and bicarbonate of soda. Add the orange juice and rind and mix well.

2 Drop about 30 rounded tablespoonfuls on to the greased baking sheet, allowing room for the biscuits to spread during cooking. Sprinkle with demerara sugar.

3 Transfer to the preheated oven and bake for 10 minutes, or until the biscuits are light brown at the edges.

4 Remove the biscuits from the oven and leave to cool on a wire rack before serving. Decorate with a few strips of orange rind, if desired.

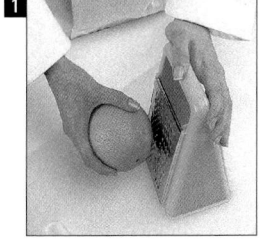

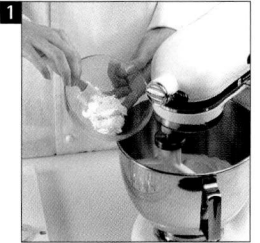

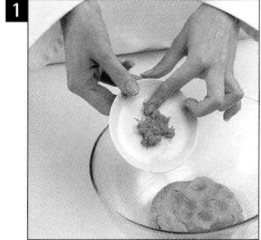

Carrot Biscuits

Grated carrot adds a natural sweetness to these delicious biscuits, which complements the ground mixed spice perfectly.

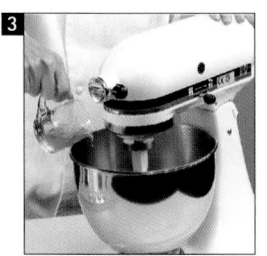
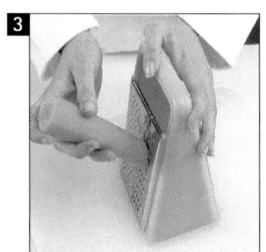

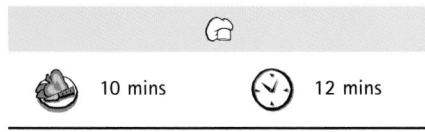

10 mins   12 mins

MAKES 24

INGREDIENTS

4 tbsp butter or margarine, plus extra for greasing

140 g/5 oz plain flour

½ tsp ground mixed spice

25 g/1 oz low-fat milk powder

¼ tsp bicarbonate of soda

1 tsp baking powder

pinch of salt

55 g/2 oz soft brown sugar, plus extra for dusting

250 g/9 oz golden syrup

1 egg

300 g/10½ oz grated carrots

1 tsp vanilla essence

225 g/8 oz rolled oats

1 Preheat the oven to 190°C/375°F/ Gas Mark 5 and grease a large baking sheet.

2 In a bowl, sift together the flour, mixed spice, milk powder, bicarbonate of soda, baking powder and salt.

3 Blend the butter, sugar and golden syrup together in a large bowl. Beat in the egg thoroughly. Add the dry ingredients gradually, stirring continuously. Blend in the carrots with the vanilla essence and oats.

4 Put 24 tablespoonfuls of the mixture on to the baking sheet, allowing room for the biscuits to spread during cooking.

Dust with brown sugar. Transfer to the preheated oven and bake for 12 minutes, or until the biscuits are golden brown.

5 Remove the biscuits from the oven, then place on a wire rack and leave them to cool completely before serving.

Orange Horns

It is much easier to shape these biscuits into horn shapes while they are still warm from the oven. Leave them to cool before serving.

10 mins   7 mins

MAKES 30

I N G R E D I E N T S

115 g/4 oz butter or margarine, plus extra for greasing

1 orange

125 g/4½ oz soft brown sugar

pinch of salt

1 egg white, beaten lightly

½ tsp baking powder

85 g/3 oz oatmeal

150 g/5½ oz finely chopped Brazil nuts (or hazelnuts)

1 tbsp milk

1 tsp orange juice

1 Preheat the oven to 160°C/325°F/Gas Mark 3. Grease a large baking sheet.

2 Grate the orange and set aside. Blend the butter and sugar together in a bowl until the mixture is fluffy. Add the remaining ingredients and mix thoroughly.

3 Drop 30 rounded teaspoonfuls of the mixture on to the baking sheet and flatten into small circles using the bottom of a glass. Transfer to the preheated oven and bake for 7 minutes, then remove from the oven.

4 Leave to cool slightly. Place each biscuit in turn on a rolling pin to help start the desired curve, completing the horn shape by hand, while the biscuit is still warm.

5 Leave the biscuits to cool on a wire rack before serving.

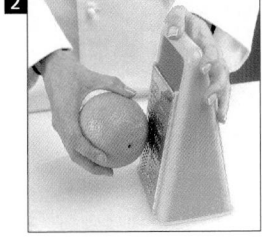

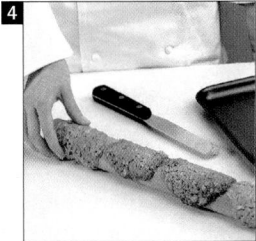

Party Biscuits

These biscuits are studded with colourful sugar-coated chocolate beans, and are ideal for children's birthday parties.

 10 mins   10–12 mins

MAKES 16

INGREDIENTS

115 g/4 oz butter, softened, plus extra
    for greasing

115 g/4 oz soft brown sugar

1 tbsp golden syrup

½ tsp vanilla essence

175 g/6 oz self-raising flour

85 g/3 oz sugar-coated chocolate beans

1 Preheat the oven to 180°C/350°F/ Gas Mark 4, then grease 2 baking sheets. Place the butter and sugar in a bowl and beat together with an electric whisk until light and fluffy, then beat in the syrup and vanilla essence.

2 Sift in half the flour and work it into the mixture. Stir in the chocolate beans and the remaining flour and work the dough together with your fingers.

3 Using your fingers, roll the dough into 16 balls and place them on the prepared baking sheets, allowing room for the biscuits to spread during cooking.

COOK'S TIP
To make a slightly less sweet version of these biscuits, you could use chocolate chips, cherries or chopped dried apricots instead of the chocolate beans.

Do not flatten them. Bake in the preheated oven for 10–12 minutes, or until pale golden at the edges.

4 Remove from the oven. Leave to cool on the baking sheets for 2 minutes, then transfer to wire racks to cool completely.

Christmas Biscuits

These festive biscuits will quickly become part of your holiday baking repertoire. Store in an airtight container for up to a week.

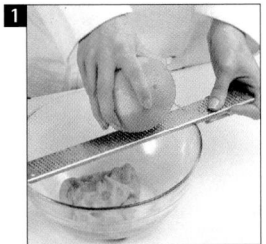

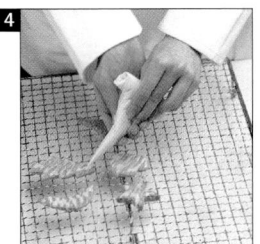

30 mins plus 4 hrs chilling

10 mins

MAKES 24

INGREDIENTS

900 g/2 lb plain flour, plus extra for dusting

1 tbsp bicarbonate of soda

1 tbsp ground ginger

3 tsp ground mixed spice

pinch of salt

225 g/8 oz butter or margarine, plus extra for greasing

500 g/1 lb 2 oz golden syrup

200 g/7 oz demerara sugar

125 ml/4 fl oz water

1 egg

1 tsp brandy

1 tsp very finely grated orange rind

55 g/2 oz icing sugar, plus extra to decorate

1 In a large bowl, sift together the flour, bicarbonate of soda, ginger, mixed spice and salt. In a separate bowl, beat together the butter, golden syrup, sugar, water, egg and brandy until thoroughly combined. Gradually stir in the grated orange rind, then the flour mixture.

2 Halve the dough, wrap in clingfilm and refrigerate for at least 4 hours (it will keep for up to 6 days). When ready to use, preheat the oven to 180°C/350°F/ Gas Mark 4 and grease a baking sheet.

3 Flour a board or work surface. Roll each half of dough into a ball, then roll it to a thickness of 3 mm/⅛ inch. Using Christmas biscuit cutters or a knife, cut

festive shapes such as stars and trees. Put the biscuits on to the baking sheet, then transfer to the preheated oven and bake for 10 minutes, or until golden brown. Remove the biscuits from the oven and transfer to a wire rack, then set aside.

4 When the biscuits have cooled, mix the icing sugar with a little water to make a glacé icing. Drizzle this icing over some of the biscuits, and decorate the remainder with sifted icing sugar.

Ginger Oat Biscuits

These mouthwatering squares are delicately flavoured with ground cinnamon, nutmeg and ginger. They are ideal to serve for dessert.

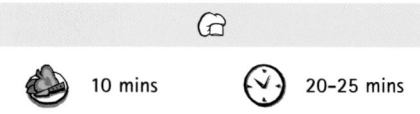

10 mins   20-25 mins

MAKES 24

INGREDIENTS

115 g/4 oz butter or margarine, plus extra for greasing

140 g/5 oz soft brown sugar

225 g/8 oz plain flour, plus extra for dusting

85 g/3 oz rolled oats

55 g/2 oz bran

½ tsp ground cinnamon

½ tsp ground nutmeg

1 tsp ground ginger

150 ml/5 fl oz cold water

1 Preheat the oven to 180°C/350°F/ Gas Mark 4 and grease a large baking sheet.

2 In a large mixing bowl, combine the sugar, flour, oats, bran and spices. Add the butter and mix with your fingers until the mixture resembles breadcrumbs. Gradually add the water, mixing with your fingers, until the dough is stiff.

3 Sprinkle flour on to a cutting board or work surface. Roll out the dough until 1 cm/½ inch thick. Cut into 5-cm/2-inch squares and place on the baking sheet.

4 Transfer to the preheated oven and bake for 20–25 minutes, or until the biscuits are golden brown. Remove the biscuits from the oven and place on a wire rack to cool before serving.

Gingersnaps

Nothing compares with the taste of these freshly baked authentic gingersnaps, which have a lovely hint of orange flavour.

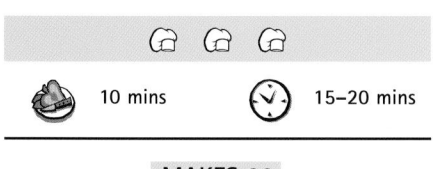

10 mins

15–20 mins

MAKES 30

INGREDIENTS

115 g/4 oz butter, plus extra for greasing

350 g/12 oz self-raising flour

pinch of salt

200 g/7 oz caster sugar

1 tbsp ground ginger

1 tsp bicarbonate of soda

85 g/3 oz golden syrup

1 egg, beaten lightly

1 tsp grated orange rind

1 Preheat the oven to 160°C/325°F/ Gas Mark 3. Lightly grease several baking sheets.

2 Sift the flour, salt, sugar, ground ginger and bicarbonate of soda into a large mixing bowl.

3 Heat the butter and golden syrup together in a saucepan over a very low heat until the butter has melted.

4 Leave the butter mixture to cool slightly, then pour it on to the dry ingredients. Add the egg and orange rind and mix together thoroughly.

5 Using your hands, carefully shape the dough into 30 even-sized balls.

6 Place the balls on the prepared baking sheets, allowing room for the biscuits to spread during cooking, then flatten them slightly with your fingers.

7 Bake in the preheated oven for 15–20 minutes. Carefully transfer the biscuits to a wire rack to cool and become crisp.

COOK'S TIP

Store these biscuits in an airtight container and eat them within 1 week.

Gingerbread People

This is a favourite with children, who love to make the gingerbread shapes. The recipe makes a pliable dough that is very easy to handle.

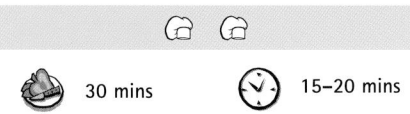

30 mins   15–20 mins

MAKES 20

INGREDIENTS

115 g/4 oz butter, plus extra
    for greasing

450 g/1 lb plain flour, plus extra
    for dusting

2 tsp ground ginger

1 tsp ground mixed spice

2 tsp bicarbonate of soda

100 g/3½ oz golden syrup

115 g/4 oz light muscovado sugar

1 egg, beaten

TO DECORATE

currants

glacé cherries

85 g/3 oz icing sugar

3–4 tsp water

1 Preheat the oven to 160°C/325°F/Gas Mark 3, then grease 3 large baking sheets. Sift the flour, ginger, mixed spice and bicarbonate of soda into a large bowl. Place the butter, syrup and sugar in a saucepan over a low heat and stir until melted. Pour on to the dry ingredients and add the egg. Mix together to make a dough. The dough will be sticky to start with, but will become firmer as it cools.

2 On a lightly floured work surface, roll out the dough to about 3 mm/ ⅛ inch thick and stamp out gingerbread people shapes. Place on the prepared baking sheets. Re-knead and re-roll the trimmings and cut out more shapes until the dough is used up. Decorate with currants for eyes and pieces of cherry for mouths. Bake for 15–20 minutes, or until firm and lightly browned.

3 Remove from the oven and leave to cool on the baking sheets for a few minutes, then transfer to wire racks to cool completely. Mix the icing sugar with the water to a thick consistency. Place the icing in a small plastic bag and cut a tiny hole in one corner. Use the icing to pipe buttons or bows on to the cooled biscuits.

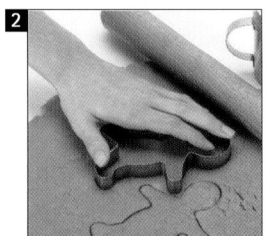

COOK'S TIP
At Christmas, cut out star and bell shapes. When the biscuits come out of the oven, gently pierce a hole in each one with a skewer. Thread ribbons through and hang on the Christmas tree.

Ginger-Topped Fingers

A delicious sticky ginger topping turns these shortbread fingers into a real treat. To decorate, pipe lines of white icing on the tops.

15 mins

40 mins

MAKES 16

INGREDIENTS

175 g/6 oz butter, plus extra for greasing

225 g/8 oz plain flour

1 tsp ground ginger

85 g/3 oz caster sugar

GINGER TOPPING

1 tbsp golden syrup

55 g/2 oz butter

2 tbsp icing sugar

1 tsp ground ginger

1 Preheat the oven to 180°C/350°F/Gas Mark 4. Grease a 28 x 18-cm/11 x 7-inch oblong cake tin. Sift the flour and ginger into a bowl and stir in the sugar. Rub in the butter until the mixture starts to stick together.

2 Press the mixture into the prepared tin and smooth the top with a palette knife. Bake in the preheated oven for 40 minutes, or until very lightly browned.

3 To make the topping, place the syrup and butter in a small saucepan over a low heat and stir until melted. Stir in the icing sugar and ginger. Remove the shortbread from the oven and pour the topping over it while both are still hot. Leave to cool slightly in the tin, then cut into 16 fingers. Transfer the fingers to wire racks to cool.

COOK'S TIP
The shortbread will be quite soft when it first comes out of the oven, but it will become firm as it cools. Leave these fingers to cool completely before serving.

Apple Shortcakes

These freshly baked biscuits are split and filled with sliced apples and whipped cream. The shortcakes can be eaten either warm or cold.

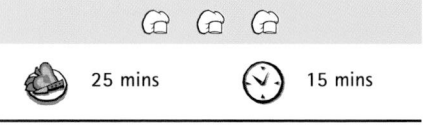

25 mins | 15 mins

MAKES 4

I N G R E D I E N T S

2 tbsp butter, cut into small pieces, plus extra for greasing

175 g/6 oz plain flour

½ tsp salt

1 tsp baking powder

1 tbsp caster sugar

50 ml/2 fl oz milk

icing sugar, for dusting

FILLING

3 eating apples, peeled, cored and sliced

100 g/3½ oz caster sugar

1 tbsp lemon juice

1 tsp ground cinnamon

300 ml/10 fl oz water

150 ml/5 fl oz double cream, whipped lightly

1 Preheat the oven to 220°C/425°F/Gas Mark 7. Lightly grease a baking sheet with a little butter.

2 Sift the flour, salt and baking powder into a mixing bowl. Stir in the sugar, then rub in the butter with your fingertips until the mixture resembles fine breadcrumbs.

3 Pour in the milk and mix to a soft dough. On a lightly floured work surface, knead the dough lightly, then roll out to 1 cm/½ inch thick. Stamp out 4 circles, using a 5-cm/2-inch cutter. Transfer the circles to the baking sheet.

4 Bake in the preheated oven for about 15 minutes, until risen and lightly browned. Leave to cool.

5 To make the filling, place the apple slices with the sugar, lemon juice and cinnamon in a saucepan. Add the water, bring to the boil and simmer, uncovered, for 5–10 minutes, until the apples are tender. Leave to cool a little, then remove the apples.

6 Split the shortcakes in half. Place each bottom half on an individual serving plate and spoon on a quarter of the apple slices, then the cream. Place the other half of the shortcake on top. Serve dusted with icing sugar.

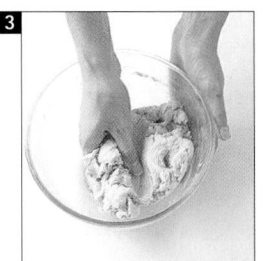

Christmas Shortbread

Make this wonderful shortbread and then give it the Christmas touch by cutting it into different shapes with seasonal cookie cutters.

30 mins plus 10–15 mins chilling

10–15 mins

MAKES 24

INGREDIENTS

125 g/4½ oz caster sugar

225 g/8 oz butter, plus extra for greasing

350 g/12 oz plain flour, sifted, plus extra for dusting

pinch of salt

TO DECORATE

55 g/2 oz icing sugar

silver balls

glacé cherries

angelica

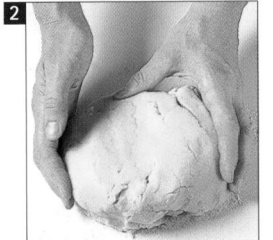

1 Beat the sugar and butter together in a large bowl until combined (thorough creaming is not necessary).

2 Sift in the flour and salt and work together to form a stiff dough. Turn out on to a lightly floured work surface. Knead lightly for a few moments until smooth, but avoid over-handling. Chill in the refrigerator for 10–15 minutes. Preheat the oven to 180°C/350°F/Gas Mark 4. Grease several baking sheets.

3 Roll out the dough on a lightly floured work surface and cut into shapes with small Christmas cutters, such as trees, bells, stars and angels. Place on greased baking sheets.

4 Bake in the oven for 10–15 minutes, until pale golden brown. Leave to cool on the baking sheets for 10 minutes, then transfer to wire racks to cool completely.

5 Mix the icing sugar with a little water to make a glacé icing, and use to ice the biscuits. Before the icing sets, decorate with silver balls, tiny pieces of glacé cherries and angelica. Store in an airtight container or wrap the biscuits individually in cellophane, tie with coloured ribbon or string, then hang them on the Christmas tree as edible decorations.

Scottish Shortbread

Many traditional recipes for shortbread contain a small amount of rice flour, which gives each wedge a delicate, crisp texture.

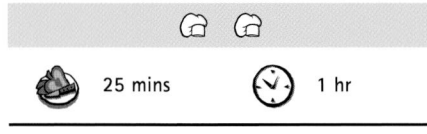

🍰 25 mins ⏲ 1 hr

MAKES 16

INGREDIENTS

175 g/6 oz butter, unsalted for preference, at room temperature, plus extra for greasing

280 g/10 oz plain flour, plus extra for dusting

40 g/1½ oz rice flour

¼ tsp salt

50 g/1¾ oz caster sugar

50 g/1¾ oz icing sugar, sifted

¼ tsp vanilla essence (optional)

caster sugar, for sprinkling

1 Preheat the oven to 120°C/250°F/ Gas Mark ½. Grease 2 x 20-cm/8-inch cake or flan tins with removable bottoms. Sift the plain flour, rice flour and salt into a bowl; set aside.

2 Using an electric whisk, beat the butter for about 1 minute in a large bowl until creamy. Add the sugars and continue beating for 1–2 minutes until very light and fluffy. If using, beat in the vanilla essence.

3 Using a wooden spoon, stir the flour mixture into the creamed butter and sugar until well blended. Turn on to a lightly floured work surface. Divide the dough into 2 pieces, knead each lightly and press into a circle.

4 Press a dough circle into each tin, smoothing the surface. Lightly sprinkle the surfaces of each dough round with a little caster sugar.

5 Using a sharp knife, mark each dough round into 8 wedges. Prick with a fork and bake in the preheated oven for 50–60 minutes, until the shortbread is pale golden and crisp. Cool in the tins on a wire rack for about 5 minutes.

6 Carefully remove the side of each tin and slide the bottoms on to a heatproof surface. Using the knife marks as a guide, cut each shortbread into 8 wedges while still warm. Cool completely on the wire rack, then store in airtight containers.

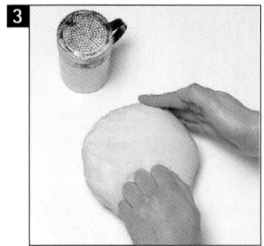

Shortbread Fantails

These biscuits are perfect for afternoon tea, or they can be served with vanilla or chocolate ice cream for a really delicious dessert.

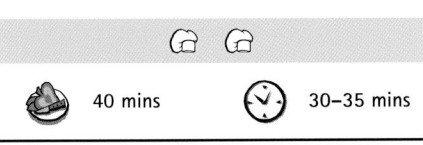

40 mins 30–35 mins

SERVES 8

INGREDIENTS

115 g/4 oz butter, softened, plus extra for greasing

40 g/1½ oz granulated sugar

2 tbsp icing sugar

225 g/8 oz plain flour, plus extra for dusting

pinch of salt

2 tsp orange flower water

caster sugar, for sprinkling

1 Preheat the oven to 160°C/325°F/Gas Mark 3. Lightly grease a shallow 20-cm/8-inch round cake tin.

2 In a large mixing bowl, cream together the butter, the granulated sugar and the icing sugar until light and fluffy.

3 Sift the flour and salt into the creamed mixture. Add the orange flower water and bring everything together to form a soft dough.

4 On a lightly floured work surface, roll out the dough to an 20-cm/8-inch circle. Place in the prepared tin. Use a fork to press neatly around the edge. Score 8 triangles with a knife then prick the surface.

5 Transfer the shortbread to the preheated oven and bake for 30–35 minutes, or until the shortbread is crisp and the top is pale golden.

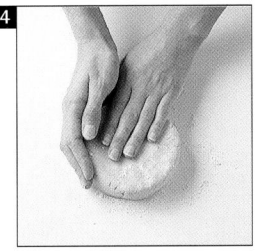

6 Sprinkle with caster sugar, then cut along the marked lines to make the fantails.

7 Leave the shortbread to cool before removing the pieces from the tin. Store in an airtight container.

COOK'S TIP
For a crunchy addition, sprinkle 2 tablespoons chopped mixed nuts over the top of the fantails before baking.

Chocolate Shortbread

This delicious buttery chocolate shortbread is the perfect addition to the biscuit tin of any chocoholic. Leave it to cool completely before eating.

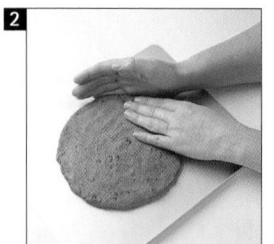

40 mins   40 mins

MAKES 12

INGREDIENTS

175 g/6 oz butter, softened, plus extra for greasing

225 g/8 oz plain flour

1 tbsp cocoa powder

4 tbsp caster sugar

50 g/1¾ oz plain chocolate, chopped finely

1 Preheat the oven to 160°C/325°F/ Gas Mark 3. Lightly grease a baking sheet. Place all the ingredients in a large mixing bowl and beat together until they form a dough. Knead the dough lightly.

2 Place the dough on the baking sheet and roll out to form a 20-cm/ 8-inch circle.

3 Pinch the edges of the dough with your fingertips to form a decorative edge. Prick the dough all over with a fork and mark into 12 wedges, using a knife.

4 Bake in the oven for 40 minutes, until firm and golden. Leave to cool slightly before cutting into wedges. Transfer to a wire rack to cool completely.

VARIATION

To make small shortbread biscuits, roll out the dough on a lightly floured work surface to 8 mm/ ¾ inch thick. Cut out 7.5-cm/3-inch circles with a biscuit cutter. Transfer to a greased baking sheet and bake as above. If liked, coat half the biscuit in melted chocolate.

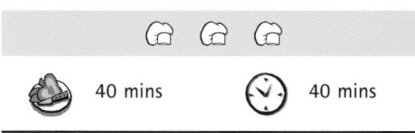

Chocolate Chip Shortbread

Buttery shortbread sprinkled with chocolate chips – nothing could be simpler or more delicious! Store in an airtight jar for several days.

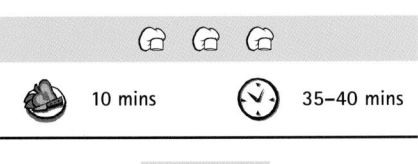

10 mins

35–40 mins

MAKES 10

INGREDIENTS

115 g/4 oz butter, diced, plus extra for greasing

115 g/4 oz plain flour

55 g/2 oz cornflour

55 g/2 oz golden caster sugar

40 g/1½ oz plain chocolate chips

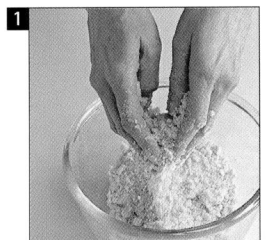

1 Preheat the oven to 160°C/325°F/Gas Mark 3. Grease a 23-cm/9-inch loose-bottom fluted flan tin. Sift the flour and cornflour into a large bowl. Stir in the sugar, then add the butter and rub it in until the mixture starts to bind together.

2 Turn into the prepared flan tin and press evenly over the bottom. Prick the surface with a fork. Sprinkle with the chocolate chips and press lightly into the surface.

3 Bake in the preheated oven for 35–40 minutes, or until cooked but not browned. Mark into 8 portions with a sharp knife. Leave to cool in the tin for 10 minutes, then transfer to a wire rack to cool completely.

VARIATION
To give the shortbread a crunchier texture, use semolina as a substitute for the cornflour. Use milk or white chocolate chips in place of plain.

Millionaire's Shortbread

These rich squares of shortbread are topped with caramel and finished with chocolate to make a very special treat for both adults and children!

🍰 55 mins   🕐 30 mins

MAKES 4

INGREDIENTS

115 g/4 oz butter, cut into small pieces, plus extra for greasing

225 g/8 oz plain flour

60 g/2¼ oz soft brown sugar, sifted

TOPPING

4 tbsp butter

60 g/2¼ oz soft brown sugar

500 ml/18 fl oz condensed milk

150 g/5½ oz milk chocolate

1 Preheat the oven to 190°C/375°F/Gas Mark 5. Lightly grease a 23-cm/9-inch square cake tin.

2 Sift the flour into a mixing bowl and rub in the butter with your fingers until the mixture resembles fine breadcrumbs. Add the sugar and mix to form a firm dough.

3 Press the dough into the bottom of the prepared tin and prick the bottom with a fork.

4 Bake in the preheated oven for 20 minutes, until lightly golden. Leave to cool in the tin.

5 To make the topping, place the butter, sugar and condensed milk in a non-stick saucepan and cook over gentle heat, stirring constantly, until the mixture comes to the boil.

6 Reduce the heat and cook for 4–5 minutes, until the caramel is pale golden and thick and is coming away from the sides of the saucepan. Pour the topping over the shortbread layer and leave to cool.

7 When the caramel topping is firm, melt the milk chocolate in a heatproof bowl set over a saucepan of gently simmering water. Spread the melted chocolate over the topping. Leave to set in a cool place, then cut the shortbread into squares or fingers to serve.

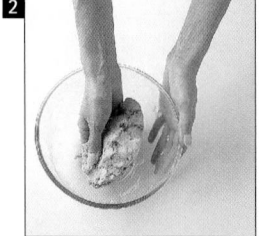
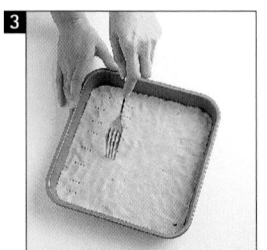

COOK'S TIP
Ensure the caramel layer is completely cool and set before coating it with the melted chocolate, otherwise they will mix together.

Vanilla Hearts

This is a classic shortbread biscuit which melts in the mouth. Here, the biscuits are made in pretty heart shapes.

 30 mins   15–20 mins

MAKES 16

INGREDIENTS

175 g/6 oz butter, cut into small pieces, plus extra for greasing

280 g/10 oz plain flour, plus extra for dusting

100 g/3½ oz caster sugar, plus extra for dusting

1 tsp vanilla essence

1 Preheat the oven to 180°C/350°F/Gas Mark 4. Lightly grease a baking sheet.

2 Sift the flour into a large mixing bowl and rub in the butter with your fingertips until the mixture resembles fine breadcrumbs.

3 Stir in the caster sugar and vanilla essence and bring the mixture together with your hands to make a smooth, firm dough.

4 On a lightly floured work surface, roll out the dough to a thickness of 2.5 cm/1 inch. Stamp out 12 hearts with a heart-shaped biscuit cutter measuring about 5 cm/2 inches across and 2.5 cm/1 inch deep.

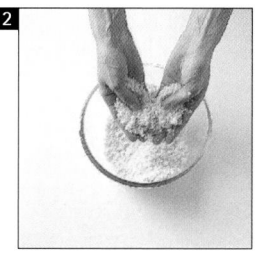 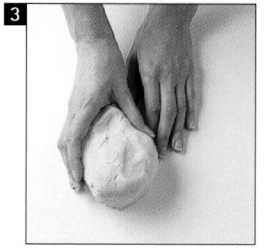 

5 Arrange the hearts on the prepared baking sheet. Bake in the preheated oven for 15–20 minutes, until the hearts are a light golden colour.

6 Transfer the vanilla hearts to a wire rack and leave to cool.

7 Dust the biscuits with a little caster sugar just before serving.

COOK'S TIP
Place a fresh vanilla pod in your caster sugar and keep it in a storage jar for several weeks to give the sugar a delicious vanilla flavour.

Chocolate Peanut Butter Slices

Children in particular will love these slices made with crunchy peanut butter and condensed milk. Store in airtight containers.

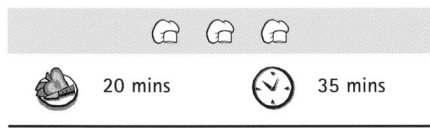

20 mins   35 mins

MAKES 25

INGREDIENTS

300 g/10½ oz milk chocolate

350 g/12 oz plain flour

1 tsp baking powder

225 g/8 oz butter

350 g/12 oz soft brown sugar

175 g/6 oz rolled oats

70 g/2½ oz chopped mixed nuts

1 egg, beaten

400 g/14 oz condensed milk

70 g/2½ oz crunchy peanut butter

1 Preheat the oven to 180°C/350°F/ Gas Mark 4. Finely chop the chocolate. Sift the flour and baking powder into a large bowl.

2 Add the butter to the flour and rub in until the mixture resembles breadcrumbs. Stir in the sugar, oats and chopped nuts.

3 Put a quarter of the mixture into a bowl and stir in the chopped chocolate. Set aside.

4 Stir the egg into the remaining mixture, then press into the bottom of a 30 x 20-cm/12 x 8-inch roasting tin.

5 Bake the base in the preheated oven for 15 minutes. Meanwhile, mix the condensed milk and peanut butter together. Pour the mixture over the base and spread evenly, then sprinkle the reserved chocolate mixture on top and press down lightly.

6 Return to the oven and bake the slices for an additional 20 minutes, until golden brown. Leave to cool in the tin, then cut into slices.

Chocolate Chip & Walnut Slices

Although these slices can be made in a matter of moments, the result is truly delicious and they will disappear in moments too!

 10 mins   25–30 mins

MAKES 18

INGREDIENTS

225 g/8 oz butter, plus extra for greasing

115 g/4 oz walnut pieces

200 g/7 oz plain chocolate chips

175 g/6 oz caster sugar

few drops vanilla essence

225 g/8 oz plain flour

1 Preheat the oven to 180°C/350°F/ Gas Mark 4. Grease a 20 x 30-cm/8 x 12-inch Swiss roll tin. Coarsely chop the walnut pieces to about the same size as the chocolate chips.

2 Beat the butter and sugar together until pale and fluffy. Add the vanilla essence, then stir in the flour. Stir in the walnuts and chocolate chips. Press the mixture into the prepared tin.

3 Bake the mixture in the preheated oven for 20–25 minutes, until golden brown. Leave to cool in the tin, then cut into slices.

Mincemeat Crumble Bars

These crumble bars make a change from traditional mince pies, but they are bound to be popular at any time of the year!

40 mins plus 20 mins chilling

32–35 mins

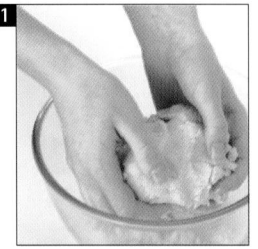 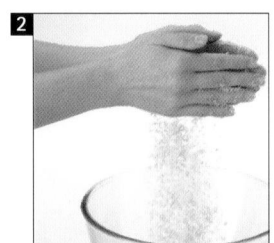 

MAKES 12

INGREDIENTS

400 g/14 oz mincemeat

icing sugar, for dusting

BOTTOM LAYER

140 g/5 oz butter, plus extra for greasing

85 g/3 oz golden caster sugar

140 g/5 oz plain flour

85 g/3 oz cornflour

TOPPING

115 g/4 oz self-raising flour

6 tbsp butter, cut into pieces

85 g/3 oz golden caster sugar

25 g/1 oz flaked almonds

1 Grease a shallow 28 x 20-cm/11 x 8-inch cake tin. To make the bottom layer, place the butter and sugar in a bowl and cream together until light and fluffy. Sift in the flour and cornflour and, with your hands, bring the mixture together to form a ball. Push the dough into the cake tin, flattening it out and pressing it into the corners, then chill in the refrigerator for 20 minutes. Meanwhile, preheat the oven to 200°C/400°F/Gas Mark 6. Bake the bottom layer in the oven for 12–15 minutes, or until puffed and golden.

2 To make the crumble topping, place the flour, butter and sugar in a bowl and rub together into coarse crumbs. Stir in the almonds.

3 Spread the mincemeat over the bottom layer and scatter the crumbs on top. Bake in the oven for an additional 20 minutes, or until golden. Leave to cool slightly, then cut into 12 pieces and leave to cool completely. Dust with sifted icing sugar, then serve.

COOK'S TIP
Make sure that you bake the bottom layer thoroughly. If it is undercooked, it will not be crisp enough.

Almond Slices

A mouthwatering dessert that is sure to impress your guests, especially if it is served with a spoonful of whipped cream.

🍰 10 mins   🕐 45 mins

SERVES 8

INGREDIENTS

3 eggs

60 g/2¼ oz ground almonds

140 g/5 oz milk powder

200 g/7 oz granulated sugar

½ tsp saffron strands

115 g/4 oz butter, unsalted for preference

1 tbsp flaked almonds, to decorate

1 Preheat the oven to 160°C/325°F/ Gas Mark 3. Heat the eggs together in a mixing bowl and set aside.

2 Place the ground almonds, milk powder, sugar and saffron in a large mixing bowl and stir to mix well.

3 Melt the butter in a small saucepan over a low heat. Pour the melted butter over the dry ingredients and mix well until thoroughly combined.

4 Add the reserved beaten eggs to the mixture and stir to blend well.

5 Spread the cake mixture evenly in a shallow 20-cm/8-inch ovenproof dish and bake in the preheated oven for 45 minutes, or until a skewer inserted into the centre comes out clean.

6 Cut the almond cake into slices. Decorate the almond slices with flaked almonds, and transfer to serving plates. Serve hot or cold.

COOK'S TIP
These almond slices are best eaten hot, but they may also be served cold. They can be made a day or even a week in advance and reheated. They also freeze beautifully.

Apricot Slices

These vegan slices are ideal for children's lunchboxes. They are full of flavour and made with healthy ingredients.

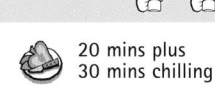 

20 mins plus
30 mins chilling

1 hr

MAKES 12

INGREDIENTS

PASTRY

100 g/3½ oz margarine, cut into small
   pieces, plus extra for greasing

350 g/10½ oz plain wholemeal flour

50g/1¾ oz finely ground mixed nuts

4 tbsp water

soya milk, to glaze

FILLING

175 g/6 oz dried apricots

grated rind of 1 orange

350 ml/12 fl oz apple juice

1 tsp ground cinnamon

55 g/2 oz raisins

1 Preheat the oven to 200°C/400°F/Gas Mark 6. Lightly grease a 23-cm/9-inch square cake tin. To make the dough, place the flour and nuts in a mixing bowl and rub in the margarine with your fingers until the mixture resembles breadcrumbs. Stir in the water and bring together to form a dough. Wrap and leave to chill for 30 minutes.

2 To make the filling, place the apricots, orange rind and apple juice in a saucepan and bring to the boil. Simmer for 30 minutes until the apricots are mushy. Cool slightly, then process in a food processor or blender to a purée. Alternatively, press the mixture through a fine sieve. Stir in the cinnamon and raisins.

3 Divide the dough in half, roll out 1 half and use to line the bottom of the tin. Spread the apricot purée over the top and brush the edges of the dough with water. Roll out the rest of the dough to fit over the top of the apricot purée. Press down and seal the edges.

4 Prick the top of the dough with a fork and brush with soya milk. Bake in the preheated oven for 20–25 minutes, until the pastry is golden. Leave to cool slightly before cutting into 12 bars. Serve the slices either warm or cold.

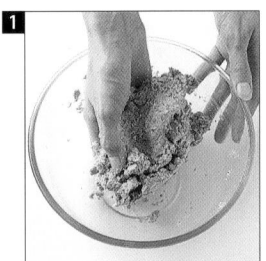

COOK'S TIP
These slices will keep in an airtight container for 3–4 days.

Mexican Pastelitos

These little cookies are traditionally served at Mexican weddings, their icing sugar coating reflecting the white of the bridal gown.

20 mins

30–40 mins

MAKES 40-50

INGREDIENTS

225 g/8 oz butter, softened, plus extra for greasing

55 g/2 oz caster sugar

225 g/8 oz plain flour

115 g/4 oz cornflour

1 tsp ground cinnamon

55 g/2 oz icing sugar, sifted, to decorate

1 Preheat the oven to 160°C/325°F/ Gas Mark 3. Grease 2 baking sheets. Place the butter and caster sugar in a bowl and beat until light and fluffy. Sift the flour, cornflour and cinnamon into a separate bowl, then gradually work them into the creamed mixture with a wooden spoon. When well mixed, knead until smooth.

2 Take 1 teaspoonful of the dough at a time and roll into a ball. Place the little balls on the prepared baking sheets. Bake in the preheated oven for 30–40 minutes, or until pale golden.

3 Place the icing sugar in a shallow dish and toss the pastelitos in it while they are still warm. Leave to cool on wire racks.

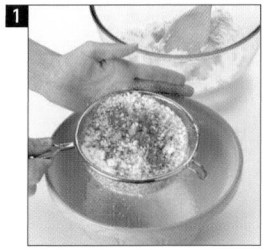
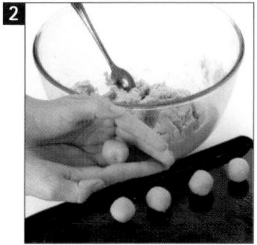

Gingerbread Squares

Gingerbread is delicious either on its own or served with a spoonful or two of vanilla ice cream as a quick and easy dessert.

40 mins

10 mins

MAKES 24

INGREDIENTS

175 g/6 oz butter, plus extra for greasing

50 g/1¾ oz soft brown sugar

5 tbsp molasses

1 egg white

1 tsp almond essence

200 g/7 oz plain flour

¼ tsp bicarbonate of soda

¼ tsp baking powder

pinch of salt

½ tsp ground mixed spice

½ tsp ground ginger

55 g/2 oz eating apples, cooked

1 Preheat the oven to 180°C/350°F/Gas Mark 4. Grease a large cake tin and line it with baking paper. Chop the apple and set aside. Put the butter, sugar, molasses, egg white and almond essence in a food processor and beat until smooth.

2 In a separate bowl, sift together the flour, bicarbonate of soda, baking powder, salt, mixed spice and ginger. Add to the creamed mixture and beat together well. Stir the apples into the mixture, then pour the mixture into the lined cake tin.

3 Transfer to the preheated oven and bake for 10 minutes, or until golden brown. Remove from the oven and cut into 24 pieces. Transfer the gingerbread to a wire rack and leave to cool completely before serving.

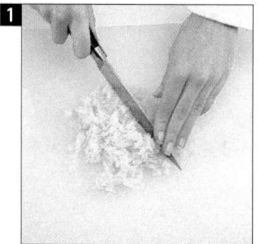
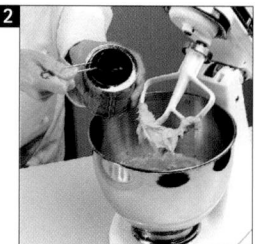

Gingerbread

This spicy gingerbread is made even more moist and flavourful by the addition of chopped fresh apples. Serve as a mid-afternoon snack.

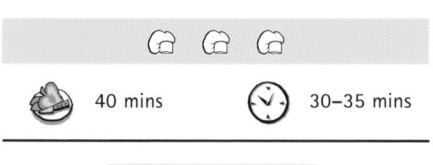

40 mins   30–35 mins

MAKES 12 BARS

INGREDIENTS

175 g/6 oz butter, plus extra for greasing

175 g/6 oz soft brown sugar

2 tbsp molasses

225 g/8 oz plain flour

1 tsp baking powder

2 tsp bicarbonate of soda

2 tsp ground ginger

150 ml/5 fl oz milk

1 egg, beaten lightly

2 eating apples, peeled, chopped and coated with 1 tbsp lemon juice

1 Preheat the oven to 160°C/325°F/Gas Mark 3. Grease a 23-cm/9-inch square cake tin and line with baking paper.

2 Melt the butter, sugar and molasses in a saucepan over a low heat. Remove the saucepan from the heat. Leave to cool.

3 Sift the flour, baking powder, bicarbonate of soda and ginger together into a large mixing bowl.

4 Stir in the milk, beaten egg and the cooled buttery liquid, followed by the chopped apples coated with the lemon juice.

5 Mix together gently, then pour the mixture into the prepared tin.

6 Bake in the preheated oven for 30–35 minutes, until the cake has risen and a skewer inserted into the centre comes out clean.

7 Leave the cake to cool in the tin before turning out and cutting into 12 bars.

VARIATION

If you enjoy the flavour of ginger, try adding 1 tablespoon finely chopped stem ginger to the mixture in step 3.

Cinnamon Squares

These moist, cakelike squares have a lovely spicy flavour. Sunflower seeds give them a nutty texture. Leave to cool before cutting into squares.

🍰 1 hr   🕐 45 mins

MAKES 12

INGREDIENTS

225 g/8 oz butter, softened, plus extra
  for greasing

225 g/8 oz caster sugar

3 eggs, beaten lightly

225 g/8 oz self-raising flour

½ tsp bicarbonate of soda

1 tbsp ground cinnamon

150 ml/5 fl oz soured cream

55 g/2 oz sunflower seeds

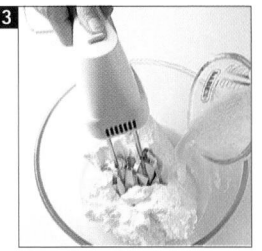
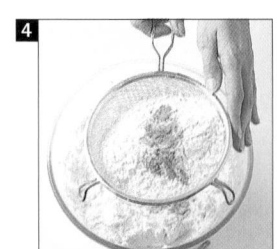

1 Preheat the oven to 180°C/350°F/
Gas Mark 4. Grease a 23-cm/9-inch
square cake tin with a little butter and
line the bottom with baking paper.

2 In a large mixing bowl, cream
together the butter and caster sugar
until the mixture is light and fluffy.

3 Gradually add the beaten eggs to the
mixture, beating thoroughly after
each addition.

4 Sift the flour, bicarbonate of soda and
cinnamon together into the creamed
mixture and fold in, using a metal spoon
in a figure-of-eight movement.

5 Spoon in the soured cream and
sunflower seeds and mix gently until
well combined.

6 Spoon the mixture into the prepared
cake tin and smooth the surface with
the back of a spoon or a knife.

7 Bake in the preheated oven for about
45 minutes, until the mixture is firm
to the touch when pressed with a finger.

8 Loosen the edges with a round-
bladed knife, then turn out on to
a wire rack to cool completely. Slice into
12 squares before serving.

COOK'S TIP

These moist squares will
freeze well and will keep
for up to 1 month.

Hazelnut Squares

These can be made quickly and easily for an afternoon tea-time treat. The hazelnuts can be replaced by any other nut if preferred.

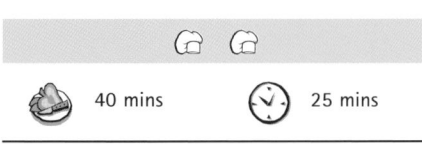

40 mins   25 mins

MAKES 16

INGREDIENTS

75 g/2¾ oz butter, cut into small pieces, plus extra for greasing

150 g/5½ oz plain flour

pinch of salt

1 tsp baking powder

150 g/5½ oz soft brown sugar

1 egg, beaten lightly

4 tbsp milk

150 g/5½ oz halved hazelnuts

demerara sugar, for sprinkling (optional)

1 Preheat the oven to 180°C/350°F/Gas Mark 4. Grease a 23-cm/9-inch square cake tin and line with baking paper.

2 Sift the flour, salt and baking powder into a large bowl.

3 Rub in the butter with your fingertips until the mixture resembles fine breadcrumbs. Stir in the soft brown sugar.

4 Add the beaten egg, milk and nuts to the mixture and stir well until thoroughly combined.

5 Spoon the mixture into the prepared cake tin, spreading it out evenly, and smooth the surface. Sprinkle with demerara sugar (if using).

6 Bake in the preheated oven for about 25 minutes, or until the mixture is firm to the touch when pressed gently with a finger.

7 Leave to cool for 10 minutes in the tin, then loosen the edges with a round-bladed knife and turn out on to a wire rack. Cut into squares and leave to cool completely before serving.

VARIATION
For a coffee-time square, replace the milk with the same amount of cold, strong black coffee – the stronger the better.

Mocha Brownies

A hint of coffee gives these brownies a sophisticated flavour and will quickly become a firm family favourite.

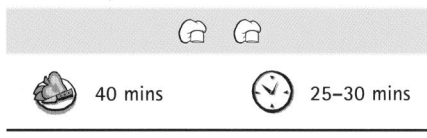

40 mins   25–30 mins

MAKES 16

INGREDIENTS

4 tbsp butter, plus extra for greasing

115 g/4 oz plain chocolate, broken into pieces

55 g/2 oz pecan nuts

175 g/6 oz dark muscovado sugar

2 eggs

1 tbsp instant coffee granules dissolved in 1 tbsp hot water

85 g/3 oz plain flour

½ tsp baking powder

1 Preheat the oven to 180°C/350°F/Gas Mark 4. Grease and line the bottom of a 20-cm/8-inch square cake tin. Put the chocolate and butter into a saucepan and heat very gently until melted. Stir and leave to cool.

2 Coarsely chop the pecan nuts and set aside. Put the sugar and eggs into a bowl and cream together until light and fluffy. Fold in the chocolate and cooled coffee and mix thoroughly. Sift in the flour and baking powder and lightly fold into the mixture. Carefully fold in the chopped nuts. Pour the mixture into the prepared tin and bake in the preheated oven for 25–30 minutes, until firm and a skewer inserted into the centre comes out clean.

3 Leave to cool in the tin for a few minutes, then run a knife around the edge of the cake to loosen it. Turn the cake out and peel off the paper. Place the cake on a wire rack to cool completely. When cold, cut into squares.

COOK'S TIP
The brownies will sink slightly and crack as they cool.

Pecan Brownies

Pecan nuts and chocolate complement each other very successfully in this version of brownies. Dust with icing sugar, if liked.

40 mins   30 mins

MAKES 20

INGREDIENTS

225 g/8 oz butter, unsalted for preference, plus extra for greasing

70 g/2½ oz plain chocolate

125 g/4½ oz plain flour

¾ tsp bicarbonate of soda

¼ tsp baking powder

55 g/2 oz pecan nuts

100 g/3½ oz demerara sugar

½ tsp almond essence

1 egg

1 tsp milk

1 Preheat the oven to 180°C/350°F/ Gas Mark 4. Grease a large baking sheet and line it with baking paper.

2 Put the chocolate in a heatproof bowl set over a saucepan of gently simmering water and heat until it is melted. Meanwhile, sift together the flour, bicarbonate of soda and baking powder in a large bowl.

3 Finely chop the pecan nuts and set aside. In a separate bowl, cream together the butter and sugar, then mix in the almond essence and the egg. Remove the chocolate from the heat and stir into the butter mixture. Add the flour mixture, milk and chopped nuts to the bowl and stir until well combined.

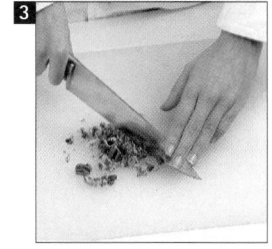 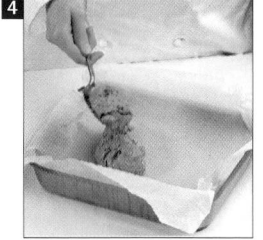 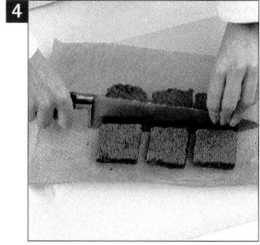

4 Spoon the mixture on to the greased baking sheet and smooth it. Transfer to the preheated oven and cook for 30 minutes, or until firm to the touch (it should still be a little soft in the centre). Remove from the oven and leave to cool completely. Cut into 20 squares and serve.

Cappuccino Squares

These cakes are made by the all-in-one method and baked in one tin, so they are very easy to put together. Store in airtight containers.

50 mins

40–45 mins

MAKES 15

INGREDIENTS

225 g/8 oz butter, softened, plus extra for greasing

225 g/8 oz self-raising flour

1 tsp baking powder

1 tsp cocoa powder, plus extra for dusting

225 g/8 oz golden caster sugar

4 eggs, beaten

3 tbsp instant coffee powder dissolved in 2 tbsp hot water

ICING

115 g/4 oz white chocolate, broken into pieces

4 tbsp butter, softened

3 tbsp milk

175 g/6 oz icing sugar

cocoa powder, to decorate

1 Preheat the oven to 180°C/350°F/Gas Mark 4. Grease and line the bottom of a shallow oblong 28 x 18-cm/11 x 7-inch tin. Sift the flour, baking powder and cocoa into a bowl. Add the butter, caster sugar, eggs and coffee. Beat well, by hand or with an electric whisk, until smooth. Spoon into the tin and smooth the top.

2 Bake in the preheated oven for 35–40 minutes, or until risen and firm. Leave to cool in the tin for 10 minutes, then turn out on to a wire rack and peel off the lining paper. Leave to cool completely. To make the icing, place the chocolate, butter and milk in a heatproof bowl set over a saucepan of simmering water and stir until the chocolate has melted.

3 Remove the bowl from the saucepan and sift in the icing sugar. Beat until smooth, then spread over the cake. Dust the top of the cake with sifted cocoa, then cut into squares.

COOK'S TIP
When melting the icing ingredients, make sure that the bottom of the bowl does not touch the simmering water, otherwise the chocolate will seize and become unusable.

Almond Biscotti

These hard Italian biscuits are traditionally served at the end of a meal for dipping into a sweet white wine. Try them with coffee or ice cream.

30 mins | 25 mins

SERVES 4

INGREDIENTS

250 g/9 oz plain flour, plus extra for dusting

1 tsp baking powder

pinch of salt

140 g/5 oz caster sugar

2 eggs, beaten

finely grated rind of 1 unwaxed orange

100 g/3½ oz whole blanched almonds, toasted lightly

1 Preheat the oven to 180°C/350°F/Gas Mark 4. Lightly dust a baking sheet with flour. Sift the flour, baking powder and salt into a bowl. Add the sugar, eggs and orange rind and mix to a dough, then knead in the toasted almonds.

2 Roll out the dough into a ball, cut in half and roll out each portion into a log about 4 cm/1½ inches in diameter. Place on the floured baking sheet and bake in the oven for 10 minutes. Remove from the oven and leave to cool for 5 minutes.

3 Using a serrated knife, cut the logs into 1-cm/½-inch thick diagonal slices. Arrange the slices on the baking sheet and return to the oven for an additional 15 minutes, or until slightly golden. Transfer to a wire rack to cool and become crisp.

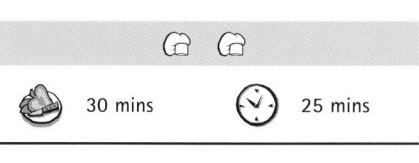

Chocolate Biscotti

Italian-style dry biscuits are a traditional accompaniment to black coffee after dinner, but you may find yourself nibbling them the morning after.

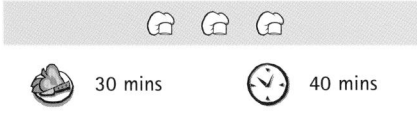

30 mins   40 mins

MAKES 16

INGREDIENTS

butter, for greasing

1 egg

100 g/3½ oz caster sugar

1 tsp vanilla essence

150 g/5½ oz plain flour

½ tsp baking powder

1 tsp ground cinnamon

50 g/1¾ oz continental plain chocolate, chopped coarsely

55 g/2 oz toasted flaked almonds

55 g/2 oz pine nuts

1 Preheat the oven to 180°C/350°F/Gas Mark 4. Lightly grease a large baking sheet with a little butter.

2 Whisk the egg, sugar and vanilla essence in a mixing bowl with an electric mixer until thick and pale – the mixture should leave a trail when the whisk is lifted.

3 Sift the flour, baking powder and cinnamon into a separate bowl, then sift the ingredients into the egg mixture and fold in gently. Stir in the chocolate, almonds and pine nuts.

4 Turn on to a lightly floured work surface and shape into a flat log, measuring 23 cm/9 inches long and 2 cm/¾ inch wide. Transfer to the prepared baking sheet.

5 Bake the biscotti in the preheated oven for 20–25 minutes, or until golden. Remove from the oven and leave to cool for 5 minutes, or until firm.

6 Transfer the log to a cutting board. Using a serrated bread knife, cut the log on the diagonal into slices about 1 cm/½ inch thick and arrange them on the baking sheet. Return to the oven for 10–15 minutes, turning the biscotti on to the other side halfway through the cooking time to bake evenly.

7 Leave to cool for about 5 minutes, then transfer the biscotti to a wire rack to cool completely.

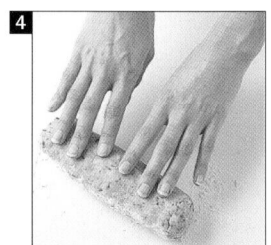

Chocolate Pistachio Biscuits

These crisp Italian biscotti are made with fine cornmeal as well as flour, to give them an interesting texture. They are perfect served with coffee.

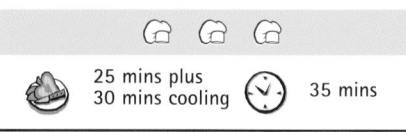

25 mins plus
30 mins cooling   35 mins

MAKES 24

INGREDIENTS

2 tbsp butter, unsalted for preference, plus extra for greasing

175 g/6 oz plain chocolate, broken into pieces

350 g/12 oz self-raising flour, plus extra for dusting

1½ tsp baking powder

85 g/3 oz caster sugar

70 g/2½ oz cornmeal

finely grated rind of 1 lemon

2 tsp Amaretto

1 egg, beaten lightly

115 g/4 oz coarsely chopped pistachio nuts

2 tbsp icing sugar, for dusting

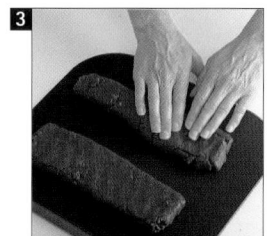

1 Preheat the oven to 160°C/325°F/ Gas Mark 3. Grease a baking sheet with butter. Put the chocolate and 2 tablespoons of butter in a heatproof bowl set over a saucepan of gently simmering water. Stir over a low heat until melted and smooth. Remove from the heat and cool slightly.

2 Sift the flour and baking powder into a bowl and mix in the caster sugar, cornmeal, lemon rind, Amaretto, egg and pistachio nuts. Stir in the chocolate mixture and mix to a soft dough.

3 Lightly dust your hands with flour, divide the dough in half and shape each piece into a 28-cm/11-inch long cylinder. Transfer the cylinders to the prepared baking sheet and flatten, with the palm of your hand, to about 2 cm/ ¾ inch thick. Bake the biscuits in the preheated oven for about 20 minutes, until firm to the touch.

4 Remove the baking sheet from the oven and leave the cooked pieces to cool. When cool, put the cooked pieces on a cutting board and slice them diagonally into thin biscuits. Return them to the baking sheet and bake for an additional 10 minutes, until crisp. Remove from the oven and transfer to a wire rack to cool. Dust lightly with icing sugar.

Chocolate Marshmallow Fingers

These rich slices are packed with crunchy pieces of digestive biscuits, mini marshmallows and lots of white chocolate chips.

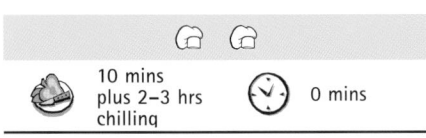

10 mins
plus 2–3 hrs
chilling

0 mins

MAKES 18

INGREDIENTS

350 g/12 oz digestive biscuits

125 g/4½ oz plain chocolate, broken into pieces

225 g/8 oz butter

25 g/1 oz caster sugar

2 tbsp cocoa powder

2 tbsp honey

55 g/2 oz mini marshmallows

100 g/3½ oz white chocolate chips

1 Put the digestive biscuits in a polythene bag and, using a rolling pin, crush into small pieces.

2 Put the chocolate, butter, sugar, cocoa and honey in a saucepan and heat gently until melted. Remove from the heat and leave to cool slightly.

3 Stir the crushed biscuits into the chocolate mixture until well mixed. Add the marshmallows and mix well, then finally stir in the chocolate chips.

4 Turn the mixture into a 20-cm/ 8-inch square cake tin and lightly smooth the top. Put in the refrigerator and leave to chill for 2–3 hours, until set. Cut into fingers before serving.

Macadamia Nut Caramel Bars

These delicious caramel biscuit bars are bursting with macadamia nuts and topped with a layer of chocolate. Store in airtight containers.

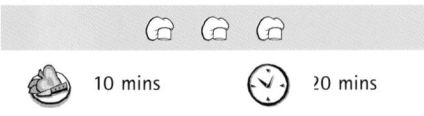

10 mins   20 mins

MAKES 16

INGREDIENTS

BASE

115 g/4 oz macadamia nuts

280 g/10 oz plain flour

175 g/6 oz soft brown sugar

115 g/4 oz butter

TOPPING

115 g/4 oz butter

100 g/3½ oz soft brown sugar

200 g/7 oz milk chocolate chips

1 Preheat the oven to 180°C/350°F/ Gas Mark 4. Coarsely chop the macadamia nuts. To make the base, beat together the flour, sugar and butter until the mixture resembles fine breadcrumbs.

2 Press the mixture into the bottom of a 30 x 20-cm/12 x 8-inch Swiss roll tin. Sprinkle over the chopped nuts.

3 To make the topping, put the butter and sugar in a saucepan and, stirring constantly, slowly bring the mixture to the boil. Boil for 1 minute, stirring constantly, then carefully pour the mixture over the macadamia nuts.

4 Bake in the preheated oven for about 20 minutes, until the caramel topping is bubbling. Remove from the oven and immediately sprinkle the chocolate chips evenly on top. Leave for 2–3 minutes, until the chocolate chips start to melt then, using the blade of a knife, swirl the chocolate over the top. Leave to cool in the tin, then cut into bars.

VARIATIONS
Walnuts or pecan nuts could be used if preferred.

Chocolate & Apricot Squares

These squares are made with white chocolate, which makes them extremely rich, so keep them quite small, or slice them thinly to serve.

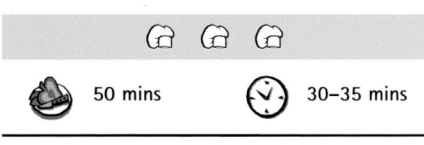

50 mins

30–35 mins

MAKES 12

INGREDIENTS

125 g/4½ oz butter, plus extra for greasing

175 g/6 oz white chocolate, chopped

4 eggs

100 g/3½ oz caster sugar

250 g/9 oz plain flour, sifted

1 tsp baking powder

pinch of salt

100 g/3½ oz ready-to-eat dried apricots, chopped

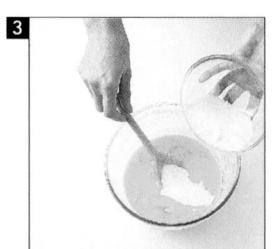

1 Preheat the oven to 180°C/350°F/Gas Mark 4. Lightly grease a 20-cm/ 8-inch square cake tin and line the bottom with a sheet of baking paper.

2 Melt the butter and chocolate in a heatproof bowl set over a saucepan of gently simmering water. Stir frequently with a wooden spoon until the mixture is smooth and glossy. Leave the mixture to cool slightly.

3 Beat the eggs and caster sugar into the butter and chocolate mixture until well combined.

4 Fold in the flour, baking powder, salt and chopped dried apricots and mix thoroughly.

5 Pour the mixture into the tin and bake in the preheated oven for about 25–30 minutes.

6 The centre of the cake may not be completely firm, but it will set as it cools. Leave in the tin to cool.

7 When the cake is completely cold, turn it out carefully and slice into bars or small squares.

Chocolate Coconut Layers

These biscuits consist of a chewy coconut layer resting on a crisp chocolate biscuit base. Leave to cool, then cut into squares to serve.

1 hr   35 mins

MAKES 9

INGREDIENTS

75 g/2¾ oz butter or margarine, plus extra for greasing

225 g/8 oz plain chocolate digestive biscuits

200 ml/7 fl oz canned evaporated milk

1 egg, beaten

1 tsp vanilla essence

2 tbsp caster sugar

40 g/1½ oz self-raising flour, sifted

125 g/4½ oz grated coconut

50 g/1¾ oz plain chocolate (optional)

1 Preheat the oven to 190°C/375°F/ Gas Mark 5. Grease a shallow 20-cm/ 8-inch square cake tin and line the bottom.

2 Crush the biscuits in a polythene bag with a rolling pin or process them in a food processor.

3 Melt the butter in a saucepan and stir in the crushed biscuits thoroughly.

4 Press the mixture into the bottom of the cake tin.

5 Beat together the evaporated milk, egg, vanilla and sugar until smooth. Stir in the flour and grated coconut. Pour over the biscuit layer and use a palette knife to smooth the top.

6 Bake in the preheated oven for 30 minutes, or until the coconut topping has become firm and just golden.

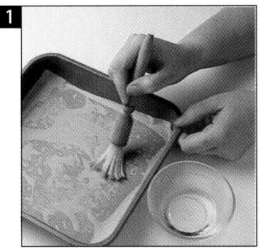

7 Leave to cool in the cake tin for about 5 minutes, then cut into squares. Leave to cool completely in the tin.

8 Carefully remove the squares from the tin and place them on a cutting board. Melt the plain chocolate (if using) and drizzle it over the squares to decorate them. Leave the chocolate to set before serving.

VARIATION
Store the squares in an airtight container for up to 4 days. They can be frozen, undecorated, for up to 2 months. Defrost at room temperature.

Chocolate Caramel Squares

It is hard to resist these wonderfully rich biscuits, which consist of a crunchy oat layer, a creamy caramel filling and a chocolate topping.

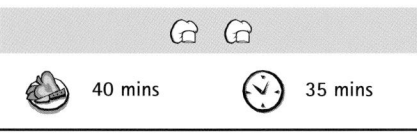
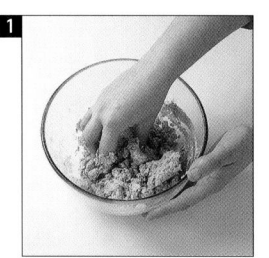
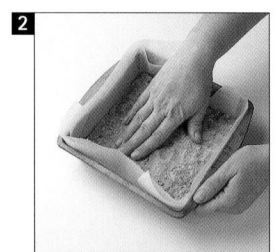

40 mins   35 mins

MAKES 16

INGREDIENTS

75 g/2¾ oz soft margarine

60 g/2¼ oz soft brown sugar

140 g/5 oz plain flour

40 g/1½ oz rolled oats

CARAMEL FILLING

2 tbsp butter

2 tbsp soft brown sugar

225 ml/8 fl oz condensed milk

TOPPING

100 g/3½ oz plain chocolate

25 g/1 oz white chocolate (optional)

1 Preheat the oven to 180°C/350°F/ Gas Mark 4. Beat together the margarine and brown sugar in a bowl until light and fluffy. Beat in the flour and the rolled oats. Use your fingertips to bring the mixture together, if necessary.

COOK'S TIP

If liked, you can line the tin with baking paper so that the oat layer can be lifted out before cutting it into pieces.

2 Press the mixture into the base of a shallow 20-cm/8-inch square cake tin.

3 Bake the biscuits in the preheated oven for 25 minutes, or until just golden and firm. Cool in the tin.

4 Place the ingredients for the caramel filling in a saucepan and heat gently, stirring until the sugar has dissolved. Bring slowly to the boil over a very low heat, then boil very gently for 3–4 minutes, stirring constantly, until thickened.

5 Pour the caramel filling over the oat layer in the tin and leave to set.

6 Melt the plain chocolate and spread it over the caramel. If using the white chocolate, place in a heatproof bowl set over a saucepan of gently simmering water until melted. Pipe lines of white chocolate over the plain chocolate. Using a cocktail stick, feather the white chocolate into the plain chocolate. Leave to set, then cut into squares to serve.

Sticky Chocolate Brownies

Everyone loves chocolate brownies and these are particularly moist and delicious. Serve as a mid-afternoon treat or as an instant dessert.

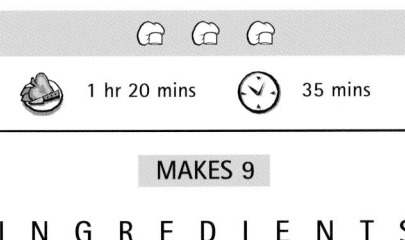

1 hr 20 mins   35 mins

MAKES 9

INGREDIENTS

85 g/3 oz butter, unsalted for preference, plus extra for greasing

140 g/5 oz caster sugar

100 g/3½ oz soft brown sugar

125 g/4½ oz plain chocolate

1 tbsp golden syrup

2 eggs

1 tsp chocolate or vanilla essence

100 g/3½ oz plain flour

2 tbsp cocoa powder

½ tsp baking powder

1 Preheat the oven to 180°C/350°F/Gas Mark 4. Lightly grease a 20-cm/8-inch shallow square cake tin and line the bottom with baking paper.

2 Place the butter, sugars, chocolate and golden syrup in a heavy-based saucepan and heat gently, stirring until the mixture is well blended and smooth. Remove from the heat and leave to cool.

3 Beat together the eggs and chocolate or vanilla extract. Whisk in the cooled chocolate mixture.

4 Sift together the flour, cocoa and baking powder and fold carefully into the egg and chocolate mixture using a metal spoon or palette knife.

5 Spoon the cake mixture into the prepared tin and bake in the preheated oven for 25 minutes, until the top is crisp and the edge of the cake is starting to shrink away from the tin. The inside of the cake will still be quite stodgy and soft to the touch.

6 Leave the cake to cool completely in the tin, then cut it into squares to serve.

Double Chocolate Brownies

Plain chocolate, cocoa powder and white chocolate chips make these delicious brownies a chocolate-lover's dream.

25 mins   55–60 mins

MAKES 9 LARGE OR 16 SMALL

INGREDIENTS

115 g/4 oz butter, plus extra for greasing

115 g/4 oz plain chocolate, broken into pieces

300 g/10½ oz golden caster sugar

pinch of salt

1 tsp vanilla essence

2 large eggs

140 g/5 oz plain flour

2 tbsp cocoa powder

100 g/3½ oz white chocolate chips

FUDGE SAUCE

4 tbsp butter

225 g/8 oz golden caster sugar

150 ml/5 fl oz milk

250 ml/9 fl oz double cream

225 g/8 oz golden syrup

200 g/7 oz plain chocolate, broken into pieces

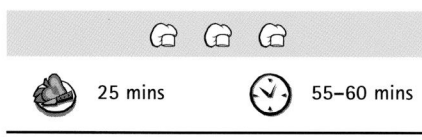

1 Preheat the oven to 180°C/350°F/ Gas Mark 4. Grease and line the bottom of a 18-cm/7-inch square cake tin. Place the butter and chocolate in a small heatproof bowl set over a saucepan of gently simmering water until melted. Stir until smooth. Leave to cool slightly. Stir in the sugar, salt and vanilla essence. Add the eggs, one at a time, until blended.

2 Sift the flour and cocoa powder into the mixture and beat until smooth. Stir in the chocolate chips, then pour the mixture into the tin. Bake in the preheated oven for 35–40 minutes, or until the top is evenly coloured and a cocktail stick inserted into the centre comes out almost clean. Leave to cool slightly while preparing the sauce.

3 To make the sauce, place the butter, sugar, milk, cream and syrup in a small saucepan and heat gently until the sugar has dissolved. Bring to the boil and stir for 10 minutes, or until the mixture is caramel-coloured. Remove from the heat and add the chocolate. Stir until smooth. Cut the brownies into squares and serve immediately with the sauce.

Chocolate Brownies

You really can have a low-fat chocolate treat. These moist bars contain a dried fruit paste, which enables you to bake without adding any fat.

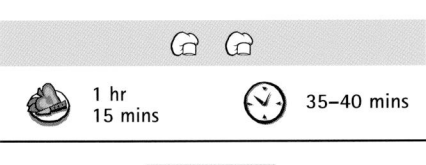

1 hr 15 mins

35–40 mins

MAKES 12

INGREDIENTS

butter, for greasing

55 g/2 oz unsweetened stoned dates, chopped

55 g/2 oz ready-to-eat dried prunes, chopped

6 tbsp unsweetened apple juice

4 medium eggs, beaten

400 g/14 oz soft brown sugar

1 tsp vanilla essence

4 tbsp low-fat drinking chocolate powder, plus extra for dusting

2 tbsp cocoa powder

225 g/8 oz plain flour

85 g/3 oz plain chocolate chips

ICING

85 g/3 oz icing sugar

1–2 tsp water

1 tsp vanilla essence

1 Preheat the oven to 180°C/350°F/ Gas Mark 4. Grease and line a 18 x 28-cm/7 x 11-inch cake tin with baking paper. Place the dates and prunes in a small saucepan and add the apple juice. Bring to the boil, cover and simmer for 10 minutes until soft. Beat to form a smooth paste, then set aside to cool.

2 Place the cooled fruit in a large mixing bowl and stir in the eggs, sugar and vanilla essence. Sift in 4 tablespoons of drinking chocolate powder, the cocoa and the flour, and fold in with the chocolate chips until thoroughly incorporated.

3 Spoon the mixture into the prepared tin and smooth over the top. Bake for 25–30 minutes, until firm to the touch or until a skewer inserted into the centre comes out clean. Cut into 12 bars and leave to cool in the tin for 10 minutes. Transfer to a wire rack to cool completely.

4 To make the icing, sift the sugar into a bowl and mix with sufficient water and the vanilla essence to form a soft, but not too runny, icing.

5 Drizzle the icing over the chocolate brownies and leave to set. Dust with the extra chocolate powder before serving.

COOK'S TIP
Make double the amount, cut one of the cakes into bars and open-freeze, then store in polythene bags. Take out pieces of cake as and when you need them – they'll take no time at all to defrost.

Chocolate Chip Brownies

Choose a good-quality plain chocolate for these chocolate chip brownies to give them a rich flavour that is not too sweet.

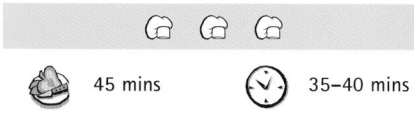
45 mins   35–40 mins

MAKES 12

INGREDIENTS

225 g/8 oz butter, softened, plus extra
 for greasing

150 g/5½ oz plain chocolate,
 broken into pieces

280 g/10 oz plain flour

100 g/3½ oz caster sugar

4 eggs, beaten

75 g/2¾ oz chopped pistachio nuts

100 g/3½ oz white chocolate,
 chopped coarsely

icing sugar, for dusting

1 Preheat the oven to 180°C/350°F/Gas Mark 4. Lightly grease a 23-cm/9-inch baking tin and line with greaseproof paper.

2 Melt the plain chocolate and butter in a heatproof bowl set over a saucepan of gently simmering water. Leave to cool slightly.

3 Sift the flour into a separate mixing bowl and stir in the caster sugar.

4 Stir the eggs into the melted chocolate mixture, then pour this mixture into the flour and sugar mixture, beating well. Stir in the pistachio nuts and white chocolate, then pour the mixture into the tin, spreading it evenly into the corners.

5 Bake in the preheated oven for 30–35 minutes, until firm to the touch. Leave to cool in the tin for 20 minutes, then turn out on to a wire rack.

6 Leave to cool completely, then cut into 12 pieces and dust with icing sugar.

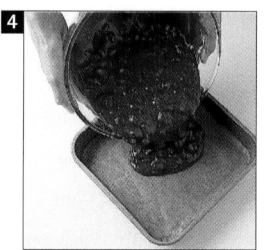

COOK'S TIP
The brownie won't be completely firm in the centre when it is removed from the oven, but it will set when it has cooled.

Soured Cream Brownies

Soured cream in the topping gives these brownies a more sophisticated flavour. They make a fabulous dessert.

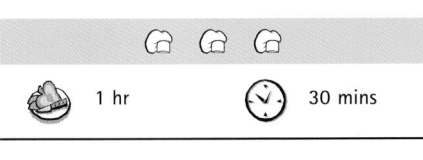

1 hr   30 mins

MAKES 9 LARGE OR 16 SMALL

I N G R E D I E N T S

55 g/2 oz butter, plus extra for greasing

115 g/4 oz plain chocolate,
   broken into pieces

175 g/6 oz soft brown sugar

2 eggs

2 tbsp strong coffee, cooled

85 g/3 oz plain flour

½ tsp baking powder

pinch of salt

55 g/2 oz walnuts, chopped

I C I N G

115 g/4 oz plain chocolate,
   broken into pieces

150 ml/5 fl oz soured cream

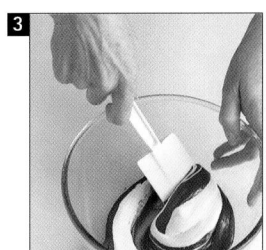

1 Preheat the oven to 180°C 350°F/ Gas Mark 4. Grease a 20-cm/8-inch square cake tin with butter and line with baking paper. Place the chocolate and butter in a small heatproof bowl and set over a saucepan of gently simmering water until melted. Stir until smooth. Remove from the heat and leave to cool.

2 Beat the sugar and eggs together until pale and thick. Fold in the chocolate mixture and coffee. Mix well. Sift the flour, baking powder and salt into the mixture and fold in. Fold in the walnuts. Pour the mixture into the tin and bake in the oven for 20–25 minutes, or until set. Leave to cool in the tin.

3 To make the icing, melt the chocolate in a heatproof bowl set over a saucepan of gently simmering water until melted. Stir in the soured cream and beat until evenly blended. Spoon the topping over the brownies and make a swirling pattern with a palette knife. Leave to set in a cool place. Cut into squares, then remove from the tin and serve.

VARIATION
These brownies can be made without the icing and served warm with vanilla ice cream or whipped cream.

Chocolate Fudge Brownies

Here, a traditional brownie mixture has a cream cheese ribbon through the centre and is topped with a delicious chocolate fudge icing.

 1 hr 20 mins 45–50 mins

MAKES 16

I N G R E D I E N T S

75 g/2¾ oz butter, plus extra for greasing

200 g/7 oz low-fat soft cheese

½ tsp vanilla essence

2 eggs

225 g/8 oz caster sugar

3 tbsp cocoa powder

100 g/3½ oz self-raising flour, sifted

50 g/1¾ oz chopped pecan nuts

F U D G E   I C I N G

4 tbsp butter

1 tbsp milk

75 g/2¾ oz icing sugar

2 tbsp cocoa powder

pecan nuts, to decorate (optional)

1 Preheat the oven to 180°C/350°F/ Gas Mark 4. Lightly grease a 20-cm/ 8-inch square shallow cake tin and line the bottom.

2 Beat together the cheese, vanilla essence and 5 teaspoons of caster sugar until smooth, then set aside.

3 Beat the eggs and remaining caster sugar together until light and fluffy. Place the butter and cocoa in a small saucepan and heat gently, stirring, until the butter melts and the mixture combines, then stir it into the egg mixture. Fold in the flour and nuts.

4 Pour half of the mixture into the tin and smooth the top. Carefully spread the soft cheese over it, then cover it with the remaining mixture. Bake in the preheated oven for 40–45 minutes. Leave to cool in the tin.

5 To make the icing, melt the butter in the milk. Stir in the icing sugar and cocoa. Spread the icing over the brownies and decorate with pecan nuts (if using). Leave the icing to set, then cut into squares to serve.

VARIATION
Omit the cheese layer if preferred. Use walnuts in place of the pecan nuts.

White Chocolate Brownies

Made with white chocolate and walnut pieces, these moist brownies make a pleasant change from the more usual plain chocolate ones.

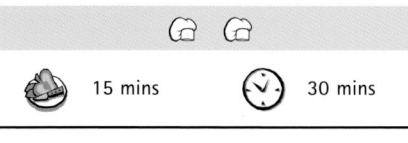

15 mins   30 mins

MAKES 9

INGREDIENTS

115 g/4 oz butter, plus extra for greasing

225 g/8 oz white chocolate

75 g/2¾ oz walnut pieces

2 eggs

115 g/4 oz soft brown sugar

115 g/4 oz self-raising flour

1 Preheat the oven to 180°C/350°F/ Gas Mark 4. Lightly grease a 18-cm/ 7-inch square cake tin.

2 Coarsely chop 175 g/6 oz of the chocolate and all the walnuts. Put the remaining chocolate and the butter in a heatproof bowl set over a saucepan of gently simmering water. When melted, stir together, then set aside to cool slightly.

3 Whisk the eggs and sugar together, then beat in the cooled chocolate mixture until well mixed. Fold in the flour, chopped chocolate and the walnuts. Turn the mixture into the prepared tin and smooth the surface.

4 Transfer the tin to the preheated oven and bake the brownies for about 30 minutes, until just set. The mixture should still be a little soft in the centre. Leave to cool in the tin, then cut into 9 squares before serving.

VARIATIONS
You can vary the nuts by using almonds, pecan nuts or hazelnuts instead of the walnuts.

Chequerboard Biscuits

Children will love eating these two-tone chocolate biscuits. If you do not mind a little mess, let them help put the biscuits together.

   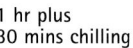

1 hr plus
30 mins chilling   10 mins

SERVES 18

INGREDIENTS

175 g/6 oz butter, softened, plus extra
for greasing

6 tbsp icing sugar

1 teaspoon vanilla essence or grated rind
of ½ orange

300 g/10½ oz plain flour

25 g/1 oz plain chocolate, melted

1 egg white, beaten

1 Preheat the oven to 180°C/350°F/ Gas Mark 4. Lightly grease a baking sheet. Beat the butter and icing sugar in a mixing bowl until light and fluffy. Beat in the vanilla essence.

2 Gradually beat in the flour to form a soft dough. Use your fingers to incorporate the last of the flour and bring the dough together.

3 Divide the dough in half and beat the melted chocolate into one half. Keeping each dough half separate, cover and leave to chill for about 30 minutes.

4 Roll out each piece of dough to a rectangle measuring 7.5 x 20 cm/3 x 8 inches and 4 cm/1½ inches thick. Brush one piece of dough with a little egg white and place the other on top.

5 Cut the block of dough in half lengthways and turn over one half. Brush the side of one strip with egg white and butt the other up to it, so that it resembles a chequerboard.

6 Cut the block into thin slices and place each slice flat on the baking sheet, allowing enough room for them to spread a little during cooking.

7 Bake in the oven for about 10 minutes, until just firm. Leave to cool on the baking sheet for a few minutes, then carefully transfer to a wire rack with a palette knife. Leave to cool completely.

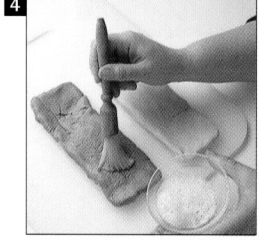

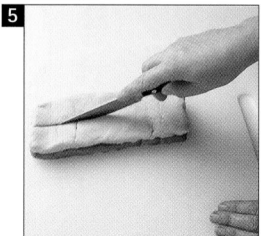

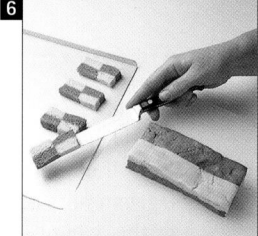

Chocolate Crispy Bites

A favourite with children, this version of crispy bites has been given a new twist, which is sure to be extremely popular.

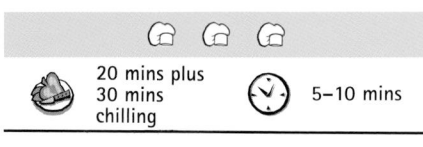

20 mins plus
30 mins
chilling

5–10 mins

MAKES 16

INGREDIENTS

WHITE LAYER

4 tbsp butter, plus extra for greasing

1 tbsp golden syrup

150 g/5½ oz white chocolate

50 g/1¾ oz toasted rice cereal

DARK LAYER

4 tbsp butter

2 tbsp golden syrup

125 g/4½ oz plain chocolate,
   broken into small pieces

75 g/2¾ oz toasted rice cereal

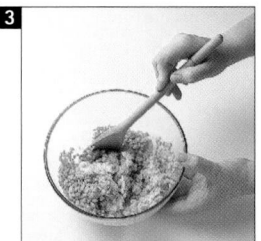

1 Grease a 20-cm/8-inch square cake tin and line with baking paper.

2 To make the white chocolate layer, melt the butter, golden syrup and chocolate in a bowl set over a saucepan of gently simmering water.

3 Remove from the heat and stir in the rice cereal until it is well combined.

4 Press into the prepared tin and smooth the surface.

5 To make the plain chocolate layer, melt the butter, golden syrup and plain chocolate in a bowl set over a saucepan of gently simmering water.

6 Remove from the heat and stir in the rice cereal. Pour the plain chocolate over the hardened white chocolate layer, leave to cool, then leave to chill until hardened.

7 Turn out of the cake tin and cut into small squares, using a sharp knife.

COOK'S TIP
These bites can be made up to 4 days ahead. Keep them covered in the refrigerator until ready to use.

No-Bake Chocolate Squares

Combining chocolate, cereal, nuts and cherries, these little treats not only taste delicious but look fantastic.

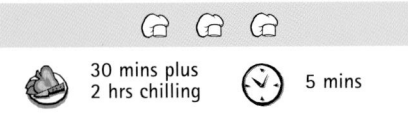

30 mins plus
2 hrs chilling   5 mins

MAKES 16

I N G R E D I E N T S

275 g/9½ oz plain chocolate,
broken into pieces

175 g/6 oz butter

4 tbsp golden syrup

2 tbsp dark rum, optional

175 g/6 oz plain biscuits

25 g/1 oz toasted rice cereal

75 g/2¾ oz chopped walnuts or pecan nuts

100 g/3½ oz glacé cherries,
    chopped coarsely

25 g/1 oz white chocolate, to decorate

1 Place the plain chocolate in a large mixing bowl with the butter, syrup and dark rum (if using) and set over a saucepan of gently simmering water until melted, stirring until blended.

2 Break the biscuits into small pieces and stir into the chocolate mixture along with the toasted rice cereal, nuts and cherries.

3 Line an 18-cm/7-inch square cake tin with baking paper. Pour the mixture into the tin and smooth the top, pressing down well with the back of a spoon. Leave to chill for 2 hours.

4 To decorate, melt the white chocolate and drizzle it over the top of the cake randomly. Leave it to set. To serve, carefully turn out of the tin and remove the baking paper. Cut the cake into 16 squares.

VARIATION
Brandy or Cointreau can be used instead of the rum if you prefer. Cherry brandy also works well.

Chocolate Slices

Packed with cherries, digestive biscuits, chocolate and almonds, these slices make a popular after-school snack for children.

15 mins plus 2 hrs chilling   0 mins

MAKES 16

INGREDIENTS

225 g/8 oz digestive biscuits

8 glacé cherries

225 g/8 oz plain chocolate, broken into pieces

225 g/8 oz butter

2 tbsp golden syrup

4 tbsp sultanas

115 g/4 oz flaked almonds

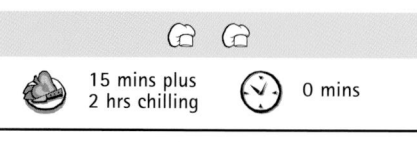
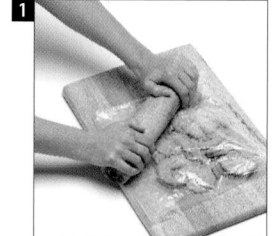

1 Put the digestive biscuits into a polythene bag and, using a rolling pin, crush into small pieces. Slice the cherries into quarters.

2 Put the chocolate, butter and golden syrup in a saucepan and heat gently until melted. Remove from the heat and leave to cool slightly. Stir in the crushed biscuits, cherries, sultanas and almonds until well mixed.

3 Turn the mixture into a 20 x 30-cm/ 8 x 12-inch Swiss roll tin and lightly spread over the bottom. Put in the refrigerator and leave to chill for 2–3 hours, until set. Cut into slices before serving.

Chocolate Madeleines

These tasty little French cakes are baked in ribbed oval moulds, which give them their delicate shell-like appearance.

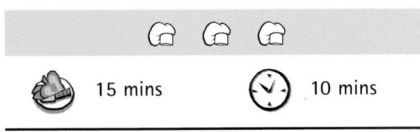

15 mins   10 mins

MAKES 12

INGREDIENTS

4 tbsp butter, plus extra for greasing

55 g/2 oz plain flour, plus extra for dusting

2 tbsp cocoa powder

1 egg

½ tsp vanilla essence

70 g/2½ oz icing sugar

icing sugar, for dusting

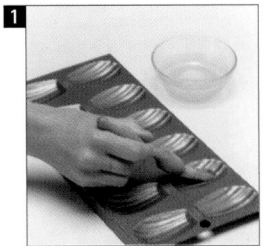

1 Grease and flour a 12-mould madeleine sheet, then leave to chill. Preheat the oven to 190°C/375°F/Gas Mark 5.

2 Melt the butter, then leave to cool. Sift the flour and cocoa together. In a large bowl, whisk the egg and vanilla essence for 2 minutes. Sift in the icing sugar, then whisk for an additional 3 minutes, until thick and smooth. Gradually fold in the flour mixture, then fold in the butter, being careful not to knock out any air. Spoon a little of the mixture equally into the prepared moulds.

COOK'S TIP
Don't be tempted to dust the madeleines with icing sugar before they have cooled or it will soak into them.

3 Bake the madeleines in the oven for about 10 minutes, until just firm to the touch. Carefully ease them out of the moulds, transfer to a wire rack, moulded-side uppermost, and leave to cool. When cold, dust with sifted icing sugar.

Chocolate Chip Flapjacks

Turn flapjacks into something special with the addition of chocolate chips. Use white rather than plain chocolate chips if preferred.

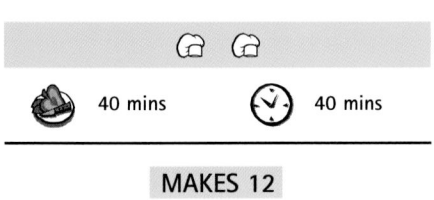

🍮 40 mins   🕐 40 mins

MAKES 12

INGREDIENTS

115 g/4 oz butter, plus extra for greasing

60 g/2¼ oz caster sugar

1 tbsp golden syrup

350 g/12 oz rolled oats

85 g/3 oz plain chocolate chips

85 g/3 oz sultanas

1 Preheat the oven to 180°C/350°F/ Gas Mark 4. Lightly grease a shallow 20-cm/8-inch square cake tin.

2 Place the butter, caster sugar and golden syrup in a saucepan and cook over a low heat, stirring constantly until the butter and sugar melt and the mixture is well combined.

3 Remove the saucepan from the heat and stir in the rolled oats until they are well coated. Add the chocolate chips and the sultanas and mix well to combine everything.

4 Turn into the prepared tin and press down well.

5 Bake in the preheated oven for 30 minutes. Cool slightly, then mark into fingers. When almost cold, cut into bars or squares and transfer to a wire rack to cool completely.

COOK'S TIP
The flapjacks will keep in an airtight container for up to 1 week, but they are so delicious they are unlikely to last that long!

Hazelnut Chocolate Crunch

These chewy, nutty oat crunch bars are very filling, so they are great for a snack at any time of the day or for packing into a lunchbox.

30 mins   25-30 mins

MAKES 12

INGREDIENTS

115 g/4 oz butter, plus extra for greasing

200 g/7 oz rolled oats

55 g/2 oz hazelnuts, lightly toasted and chopped

55 g/2 oz plain flour

85 g/3 oz light muscovado sugar

2 tbsp golden syrup

55 g/2 oz plain chocolate chips

1 Preheat the oven to 180°C/350°F/Gas Mark 4. Grease a 23-cm/9-inch shallow square tin. Place the oats, nuts and flour in a large bowl and mix.

2 Place the butter, sugar and syrup in a large saucepan and heat gently until the sugar has dissolved. Pour in the dry ingredients and mix well. Stir in the chocolate chips.

3 Turn the mixture into the prepared tin and bake in the preheated oven for 20-25 minutes, or until golden brown and firm to the touch. Mark into 12 rectangles using a knife and leave to cool in the tin. Cut the oat crunch bars with a sharp knife before removing from the tin.

COOK'S TIP
Instead of using a saucepan, heat the butter, sugar and syrup in a microwave oven on Medium for 2½ minutes.

Nutty Oat Squares

These delicious oat squares are really quick and easy to make, and have a delightful texture that is irresistible.

30 mins

30–35 mins

MAKES 16 PIECES

INGREDIENTS

115 g/4 oz butter, plus extra for greasing

200 g/7 oz rolled oats

115 g/4 oz chopped hazelnuts

55 g/2 oz plain flour

2 tbsp golden syrup

85 g/3 oz light muscovado sugar

1 Preheat the oven to 180°C/350°F/Gas Mark 4. Lightly grease a 23-cm/9-inch square ovenproof dish or cake tin. Place the rolled oats, chopped hazelnuts and flour in a large mixing bowl and stir together.

2 Place the butter, syrup and sugar in a saucepan over a low heat and stir until melted. Pour on to the dry ingredients and mix well. Turn into the prepared ovenproof dish and smooth the surface with the back of a spoon.

3 Bake in the preheated oven for 20–25 minutes, or until golden and firm to the touch. Mark into 16 pieces and leave to cool in the tin. When completely cold, cut through with a sharp knife and remove from the dish.

Coconut Flapjacks

Ever-popular, freshly baked, chewy flapjacks are just the thing to serve with a fresh cup of coffee, or as an after-school snack.

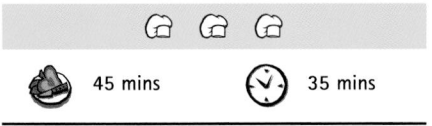

45 mins   35 mins

MAKES 16

INGREDIENTS

200 g/7 oz butter, plus extra for greasing

200 g/7 oz demerara sugar

2 tbsp golden syrup

300 g/10½ oz rolled oats

100 g/3½ oz grated coconut

70 g/2½ oz chopped glacé cherries

1 Preheat the oven to 180°C/350°F/Gas Mark 4. Lightly grease a 30 x 23-cm/12 x 9-inch baking sheet and set aside.

2 Heat the butter, sugar and golden syrup in a large saucepan over a low heat until just melted.

3 Stir in the oats, coconut and glacé cherries and mix well until evenly combined.

4 Spread the mixture evenly on to the prepared baking sheet and gently press down with the back of a palette knife to form a smooth surface.

5 Bake the flapjack in the preheated oven for about 30 minutes, until golden.

6 Remove from the oven and leave to cool on the baking sheet for 10 minutes.

7 Cut the mixture into squares using a sharp knife.

8 Carefully transfer the flapjack squares to a wire rack and leave to cool completely.

COOK'S TIP
The flapjacks are best stored in an airtight container and eaten within 1 week. They can also be frozen for up to 1 month.

Fruity Flapjacks

Great favourites with children and popular with parents, too, these tasty cereal bars are healthy, inexpensive and very easy to make.

🍯 45 mins ⏱ 15–20 mins

MAKES 14

INGREDIENTS

sunflower oil, for brushing

140 g/5 oz rolled oats

115 g/4 oz demerara sugar

85 g/3 oz raisins

115 g/4 oz low-fat sunflower margarine, melted

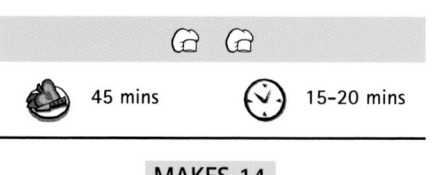
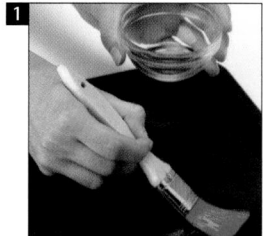

1 Preheat the oven to 190°C/375°F/Gas Mark 5. Lightly brush a 28 x 18-cm/ 11 x 7-inch shallow rectangular cake tin with oil. Combine the oats, sugar and raisins with the margarine, stirring well.

2 Spoon the oat mixture into the tin and press down firmly with the back of a spoon. Bake in the preheated oven for 15–20 minutes, or until golden.

3 Using a sharp knife, score lines to mark out 14 bars, then leave the flapjack to cool in the tin for 10 minutes. Carefully transfer the bars to a wire rack to cool completely.

VARIATION
Substitute the same quantity of dried cranberries for the raisins.

Fruity Muffins

The perfect choice for people on a low-fat diet, these little muffins contain no butter, just a little sunflower oil. Serve while still warm.

 20 mins 25–30 mins

MAKES 10

INGREDIENTS

280 g/10 oz self-raising wholemeal flour

2 tsp baking powder

2 tbsp molasses sugar

100 g/3½ oz ready-to-eat dried apricots, chopped finely

1 medium banana, mashed with 1 tbsp orange juice

1 tsp finely grated orange rind

300 ml/10 fl oz skimmed milk

1 egg, beaten

3 tbsp sunflower oil

2 tbsp rolled oats

fruit spread, honey or maple syrup, to serve

1 Preheat the oven to 200°C/400°F/Gas Mark 6. Place 10 muffin paper cases in a muffin tin. Sift the flour and baking powder into a mixing bowl, adding any husks that remain in the sieve. Stir in the sugar and chopped apricots.

2 Make a well in the centre and add the banana, orange rind, milk, beaten egg and oil. Mix together well to form a thick batter and divide among the muffin cases.

3 Sprinkle with a few rolled oats and bake in the oven for 25–30 minutes, until well risen and firm to the touch, or until a cocktail stick inserted into the centre comes out clean.

4 Transfer the muffins to a wire rack to cool slightly. Serve the muffins while still warm with a little fruit spread, honey or maple syrup.

VARIATION

If you like dried figs, they make a deliciously crunchy alternative to the apricots; they also go very well with the flavour of orange. Other ready-to-eat dried fruit, chopped finely, can be used as well.

Cranberry Muffins

These flavourful muffins make a nice change from sweet cakes for serving with coffee. Leave to cool completely before serving.

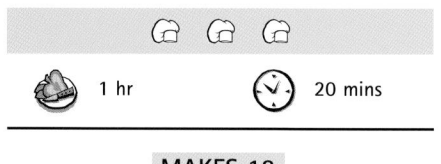

1 hr   20 mins

MAKES 18

INGREDIENTS

butter, for greasing

225 g/8 oz plain flour

2 tsp baking powder

½ tsp salt

50 g/1¾ oz caster sugar

4 tbsp butter, melted

2 eggs, beaten lightly

175 ml/6 fl oz milk

115 g/4 oz fresh cranberries

50 g/1¾ oz freshly grated
   Parmesan cheese

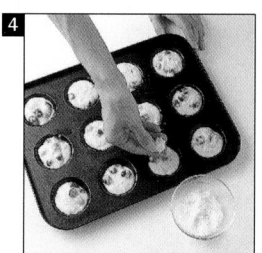

1 Preheat the oven to 200°C/400°F/ Gas Mark 6. Lightly grease 2 muffin tins with a little butter.

2 Sift the flour, baking powder and salt into a mixing bowl. Stir in the caster sugar.

3 In a separate bowl, combine the butter, beaten eggs and milk, then pour into the bowl of dry ingredients. Mix lightly together until all of the ingredients are evenly combined, then stir in the fresh cranberries.

4 Divide the mixture between the prepared tins. Sprinkle the grated Parmesan cheese over the top.

5 Bake in the preheated oven for about 20 minutes, or until the muffins are well risen and a golden brown colour.

6 Leave the muffins to cool slightly in the tins. Transfer the muffins to a wire rack and leave to cool completely.

VARIATION
For a sweeter alternative, replace the Parmesan cheese with demerara sugar in step 4 if you prefer.

Apple & Cinnamon Muffins

These spicy muffins are quick and easy to make with a few stock ingredients and two small apples. The crunchy sugar topping is a treat.

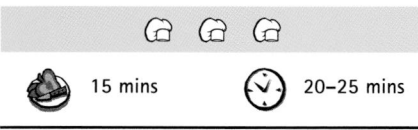

15 mins

20–25 mins

MAKES 6

INGREDIENTS

85 g/3 oz plain wholemeal flour

70 g/2½ oz plain white flour

1½ tsp baking powder

pinch of salt

1 tsp ground cinnamon

40 g/1½ oz golden caster sugar

2 small eating apples, peeled, cored and finely chopped

125 ml/4 fl oz milk

1 egg, beaten

4 tbsp butter, melted

TOPPING

12 brown sugar lumps, crushed coarsely

½ tsp ground cinnamon

1 Preheat the oven to 200°C/400°F/ Gas Mark 6. Place 6 muffin paper cases in a muffin tin.

2 Sift the 2 flours, baking powder, salt and cinnamon into a large bowl and stir in the sugar and chopped apples. Place the milk, egg and butter in a separate bowl and mix. Add the wet ingredients to the dry ingredients and gently stir until just combined.

3 Divide the mixture between the paper cases. To make the topping, mix together the crushed sugar lumps and cinnamon and sprinkle over the muffins. Bake in the preheated oven for 20–25 minutes, or until risen and golden. Serve the muffins warm or cold.

VARIATION

If you like, you can split this mixture into 12 portions to make small muffins.

Banana Pecan Muffins

This is a good way of using up ripe bananas. Do not over-mix the mixture or the muffins will be tough. Try hazelnuts instead of pecan nuts.

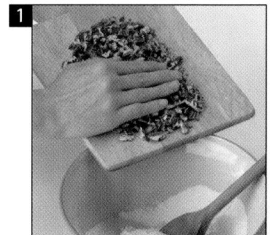

🍳 15 mins   🕐 20–25 mins

MAKES 8

I N G R E D I E N T S

150 g/5½ oz plain flour

60 g/2¼ oz golden caster sugar

1½ tsp baking powder

pinch of salt

115 g/4 oz cup pecan nuts, chopped coarsely

2 large ripe bananas, mashed

75 ml/2½ fl oz milk

2 tbsp butter, melted

1 egg, beaten

½ tsp vanilla essence

1 Preheat the oven to 190°C/375°F/ Gas Mark 5. Place 8 muffin paper cases in a muffin tin. Sift the flour, baking powder and salt into a bowl, add the sugar and pecan nuts and stir to combine.

2 Put the mashed bananas, milk, butter, egg and vanilla essence in another bowl and mix together. Add the wet ingredients to the dry ingredients and gently stir until just combined.

3 Divide the mixture between the paper cases and bake in the preheated oven for 20–25 minutes, or until risen and golden. Transfer to a wire rack to cool.

Rice Muffins with Amaretto

Italian rice gives these delicate muffins an interesting texture. The amaretti biscuits complement the flavours and add a crunchy topping.

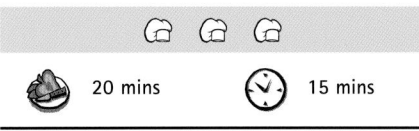

20 mins   15 mins

MAKES 12

INGREDIENTS

butter, for greasing

140 g/5 oz plain flour

1 tbsp baking powder

½ tsp bicarbonate of soda

½ tsp salt

1 egg

4 tbsp honey

125 ml/4 fl oz milk

2 tbsp sunflower oil

½ tsp almond essence

175 g/6 oz cooked risotto rice

2–3 amaretti cookies, crushed coarsely

AMARETTO BUTTER

115 g/4 oz butter, unsalted for preference, at room temperature

1 tbsp honey

1–2 tbsp Amaretto

1–2 tbsp mascarpone cheese

1 Preheat the oven to 200°C/400°F/Gas Mark 6. Grease a 12-cup muffin tin or 2 x 6-cup tins. Sift the flour, baking powder, bicarbonate of soda and salt into a large bowl and stir. Make a well in the centre.

2 In another bowl, beat the egg, honey, milk, oil and almond essence with an electric whisk for about 2 minutes, or until light and foamy. Gradually beat in the rice. Pour into the well and, using a fork, stir lightly until just combined. Do not beat too long or the mixture can become lumpy.

3 Spoon the mixture into the prepared muffin tins. Sprinkle each with some of the amaretti crumbs and bake in the preheated oven for 15 minutes, or until risen and golden. The tops should spring back lightly when pressed.

4 Cool in the tins on a wire rack for about 1 minute. Carefully remove the muffins and leave to cool slightly.

5 To make the Amaretto butter, put the butter and honey in a small bowl and beat until creamy. Add the Amaretto and mascarpone and beat together. Spoon into a small serving bowl and serve with the warm muffins.

COOK'S TIP
Line the muffin tin with muffin paper cases to avoid sticking.

Fudge Nut Muffins

Chewy pieces of fudge give these muffins a lovely texture and contrast with the crunchiness of the nuts. Store in airtight containers.

🐻 🐻 🐻

30 mins   🕐 20–25 mins

MAKES 12

INGREDIENTS

250 g/9 oz plain flour

4 tsp baking powder

85 g/3 oz caster sugar

6 tbsp crunchy peanut butter

1 egg, beaten

4 tbsp butter, melted

175 ml/6 fl oz milk

150 g/5½ oz vanilla fudge, cut into small pieces

3 tbsp coarsely chopped unsalted peanuts

1 Preheat the oven to 200°C/400°F/ Gas Mark 6. Line a 12-hole muffin tin with double muffin paper cases. Sift the flour and baking powder into a bowl. Stir in the sugar. Add the peanut butter and stir until the mixture resembles breadcrumbs.

2 Place the egg, butter and milk in a separate bowl and beat until blended, then stir into the dry ingredients until just blended. Lightly stir in the fudge pieces. Spoon the mixture into the muffin cases.

3 Sprinkle the chopped peanuts on top and bake in the preheated oven for 20–25 minutes, or until well risen and firm to the touch. Leave to cool for 2 minutes, then remove the muffins to a wire rack to cool completely.

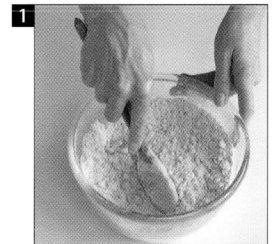

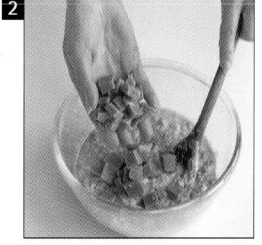

Chocolate Chip Muffins

Muffins are always popular and are so simple to make. Mini muffins are fabulous bite-sized treats for young children – and perfect for parties.

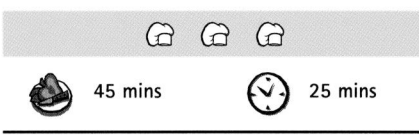

45 mins 25 mins

MAKES 12

INGREDIENTS

3 tbsp soft margarine

200 g/7 oz caster sugar

2 large eggs

150 ml/5 fl oz whole milk natural yogurt

5 tbsp milk

280 g/10 oz plain flour

1 tsp bicarbonate of soda

175 g/6 oz plain chocolate chips

VARIATION
The mixture can also be used to make 6 large or 24 mini muffins. Bake mini muffins for 10 minutes, or until springy to the touch.

1 Preheat the oven to 200°C/400°F/ Gas Mark 6. Line a muffin tin with 12 paper cases.

2 Place the margarine and sugar in a mixing bowl and beat with a wooden spoon until light and fluffy. Beat in the eggs, yogurt and milk until combined.

3 Sift the flour and bicarbonate of soda into the mixture. Stir until just blended.

4 Stir in the chocolate chips, then spoon the mixture into the paper cases and bake in the preheated oven for 25 minutes, or until a fine skewer inserted into the centre comes out clean. Leave the muffins to cool in the tin for 5 minutes, then turn out on to a wire rack to cool completely.

Double Chocolate Muffins

Chocolate-flavoured muffins with a white chocolate icing are sure to please children and adults alike.

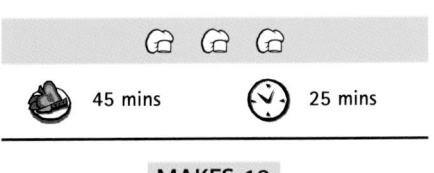

45 mins   25 mins

MAKES 12

INGREDIENTS

200 g/7 oz plain flour

25 g/1 oz cocoa powder,
   plus extra for dusting

1 tbsp baking powder

1 tsp ground cinnamon

115 g/4 oz golden caster sugar

185 g/6½ oz white chocolate,
   broken into pieces

2 eggs

100 ml/3½ fl oz sunflower oil

225 ml/8 fl oz milk

1 Preheat the oven to 200°C/400°F/ Gas Mark 6. Line a 12-hole muffin tin with muffin paper cases. Sift the flour, cocoa, baking powder and cinnamon into a large mixing bowl. Stir in the sugar and 125 g/4½ oz of the white chocolate.

2 Place the eggs and oil in a separate bowl and whisk until frothy, then gradually whisk in the milk. Stir into the dry ingredients until just blended. Spoon the mixture into the paper cases, filling each three-quarters full. Bake in the preheated oven for 20 minutes, or until well risen and springy to the touch. Leave to cool for 2 minutes, then remove the muffins and transfer to a wire rack to cool them completely.

3 Melt the remaining white chocolate in a heatproof bowl set over a saucepan of gently simmering water until melted and spread over the top of the muffins. Leave to set, then dust the tops with a little cocoa and serve.

COOK'S TIP
When stirring the muffin mixture together, do not over-stir or the muffins will be tough. The mixture should be quite lumpy.

Triple Chocolate Muffins

Packed with melting plain and white chocolate, these creamy muffins are a chocoholic's delight. Serve with coffee for a real treat.

15 mins   20 mins

MAKES 11

INGREDIENTS

250 g/9 oz plain flour

25 g/1 oz cocoa powder

2 tsp baking powder

½ tsp bicarbonate of soda

100 g/3½ oz plain chocolate chips

100 g/3½ oz white chocolate chips

2 eggs, beaten

300 ml/10 fl oz soured cream

85 g/3 oz light muscovado sugar

85 g/3 oz butter, melted

1 Preheat the oven to 200°C/400°F/Gas Mark 6. Line 11 cups of 1 or 2 muffin tins with muffin paper cases. Sift the flour, cocoa, baking powder and bicarbonate of soda into a large bowl, add the plain and white chocolate chips and stir.

2 Place the eggs, soured cream, sugar and butter in a separate mixing bowl and mix well. Add the wet ingredients to the dry ingredients and stir gently until just combined.

3 Using 2 spoons, divide the mixture between the paper cases and bake in the preheated oven for 20 minutes, or until well risen and firm to the touch. Serve warm or cold.

COOK'S TIP
As with all muffins, these chocolate delights taste best if they are eaten fresh, on the day they are made.

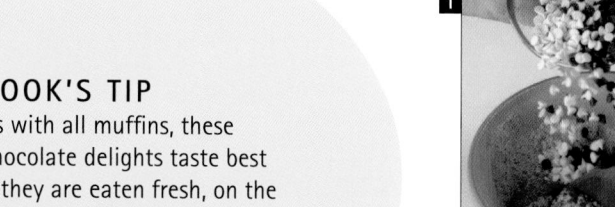

Marshmallow Muffins

Children adore these muffins filled with mini marshmallows and chocolate chips and will no doubt enjoy making them, too.

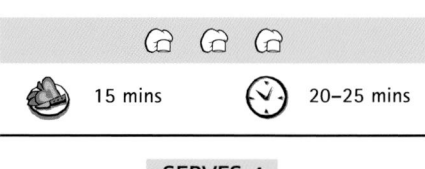

🥄 15 mins   🕐 20–25 mins

SERVES 4

INGREDIENTS

70 g/2½ oz butter

280 g/10 oz plain flour

6 tbsp cocoa powder

3 tsp baking powder

85 g/3 oz caster sugar

100 g/3½ oz milk chocolate chips

55 g/2 oz white mini marshmallows

1 egg, beaten

300 ml/10 fl oz milk

1 Preheat the oven to 190°C/375°F/ Gas Mark 5. Place 12 muffin paper cases in a muffin tin. Melt the butter.

2 Sift the flour, cocoa and baking powder together into a large bowl, Stir in the sugar, chocolate chips and marshmallows until well mixed.

3 Whisk the egg, milk and melted butter together, then gently stir into the flour to form a stiff batter. Gently stir in the chocolate chips and marshmallows. Spoon the mixture into the muffin cases.

4 Bake the muffins in the preheated oven for 20–25 minutes, until well risen and golden brown. Leave to cool in the tin for 5 minutes, then transfer to a wire rack and leave to cool completely.

COOK'S TIP
Don't over-beat the mixture (there should still be a few lumps of flour) or the muffins will be crusty.

Chocolate Orange Muffins

These muffins are a favourite with children of all ages. They are best served warm and are particularly good served for breakfast.

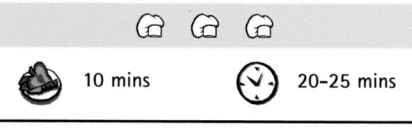

10 mins

20–25 mins

MAKES 8–10

INGREDIENTS

sunflower oil, for oiling

125 g/4½ oz self-raising flour

125 g/4½ oz self-raising wholemeal flour

25 g/1 oz ground almonds

55 g/2 oz soft brown sugar

55 g/2 oz plain chocolate chips

rind and juice of 1 orange

175 g/6 oz cream cheese

2 eggs

1 Preheat the oven to 190°C/375°F/Gas Mark 5. Thoroughly oil the muffin tins.

2 Sift the flours in a mixing bowl and add the ground almonds and sugar.

3 Mix together the orange rind and juice, the cream cheese and the eggs. Make a well in the centre of the flour mixture and stir in the liquid, then add the chocolate chips. Beat well to combine all the ingredients.

4 Spoon the mixture into the muffin tins, filling them no more than three-quarters full.

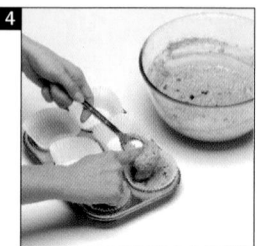

VARIATION
Use 25 g/1 oz desiccated coconut instead of the ground almonds.

5 Bake in the centre of the preheated oven for 20–25 minutes, or until well risen and golden brown.

6 Leave to cool slightly on a wire rack, but eat them as fresh from the oven as possible.

Potato & Raisin Muffins

Using potatoes in sweet dishes may seem an odd idea, but, in fact, they add a lightness and lift to all kinds of baked goods.

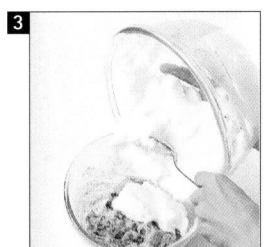

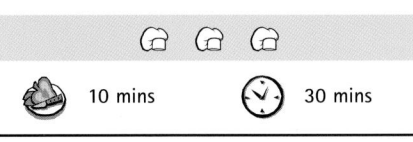

🍲 10 mins   🕐 30 mins

MAKES 12

INGREDIENTS

butter, for greasing

125 g/4½ oz self-raising flour, plus extra for dusting

175 g/6 oz floury potatoes, diced

2 tbsp soft brown sugar

1 tsp baking powder

140 g/5 oz raisins

4 eggs, separated

1 Preheat the oven to 200°C/400°F/ Gas Mark 6. Lightly grease and flour 12 muffin tins. Cook the diced potatoes in a saucepan of boiling water for 10 minutes, or until tender. Drain well and mash until smooth.

2 Transfer the mashed potatoes to a mixing bowl and add the flour, sugar, baking powder, raisins and egg yolks. Stir well to mix thoroughly.

3 In a clean, greasefree bowl, whisk the egg whites until they are standing in peaks. Using a metal spoon, gently fold them into the potato mixture until fully incorporated.

4 Divide the mixture between the prepared tins.

5 Cook the muffins in the preheated oven for 10 minutes. Reduce the oven temperature to 160°C/325°F/Gas Mark 3 and cook the muffins for 7–10 minutes, or until risen.

6 Remove the muffins from the tins and serve warm, buttered, if liked.

COOK'S TIP
Instead of spreading the muffins with plain butter, serve them with cinnamon butter made by blending 5 tablespoons of butter with a large pinch of ground cinnamon.

New Orleans Rice Cakes

This classic New Orleans breakfast dish is a cross between a doughnut and a fritter. Serve the cakes hot, sprinkled with icing sugar.

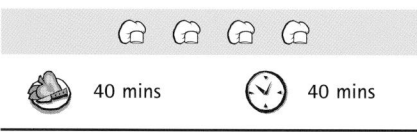
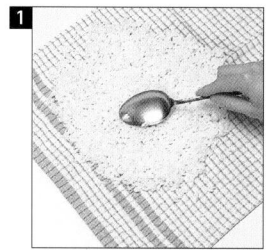

40 mins   40 mins

MAKES ABOUT 12 CAKES

I N G R E D I E N T S

100 g/3½ oz long-grain white rice

1 egg

2–3 tbsp sugar

1½ tsp baking powder

½ tsp ground cinnamon

¼ tsp salt

2 tsp vanilla essence

75 g/2¾ oz plain flour

vegetable oil, for frying

icing sugar, for dusting

1 Bring a saucepan of water to the boil. Sprinkle in the rice and return to the boil, stirring once or twice. Reduce the heat and simmer for 15–20 minutes, or until the rice is tender. Drain, rinse and drain again. Spread the rice on to a dry tea towel to dry completely.

2 Using an electric whisk, beat the egg for about 2 minutes until light and frothy. Add the sugar, baking powder, cinnamon and salt and continue beating until well blended; beat in the vanilla. Add the flour and stir until well blended, then gently fold in the rice. Cover the bowl with clingfilm and leave to rest at room temperature for about 20 minutes.

3 Meanwhile, heat 10 cm/4 inches of oil in a deep-fat fryer to 190°C/375°F, or until a cube of bread browns in about 25–30 seconds.

4 Drop rounded tablespoons of the batter into the oil, about 3 or 4 at a time. Cook for 4–5 minutes, turning gently, until puffed and golden and cooked through.

5 Using a slotted spoon, transfer to double-thickness kitchen paper to drain, then transfer to a low oven to keep warm while frying the rest. Continue with the remaining batter until it is used up. Dust the rice cakes with icing sugar to serve.

Rock Drops

These fruit rock drops are more substantial than a crisp biscuit. Serve them fresh from the oven to enjoy them at their best.

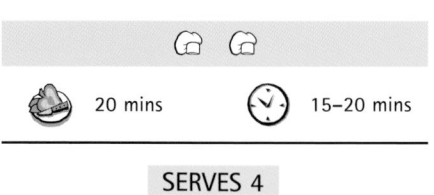

🥮 20 mins   🕐 15–20 mins

SERVES 4

INGREDIENTS

4 tbsp butter, cut into small pieces, plus extra for greasing

200 g/7 oz plain flour

2 tsp baking powder

60 g/2¼ oz demerara sugar

75 g/2¾ oz sultanas

2 tbsp glacé cherries, chopped finely

1 egg, beaten lightly

2 tbsp milk

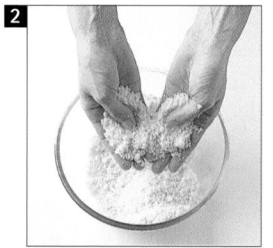

1 Preheat the oven to 200°C/400°F/Gas Mark 6. Lightly grease a baking sheet with a little butter and set aside.

2 Sift the flour and baking powder together into a mixing bowl. Rub in the butter with your fingertips until the mixture resembles breadcrumbs.

3 Stir in the sugar, sultanas and glacé cherries.

4 Add the egg and the milk to the mixture. Mix to form a soft dough.

5 Spoon 8 mounds of the dough on to the prepared baking sheet, allowing room for the biscuits to spread during cooking.

6 Bake in the preheated oven for about 15–20 minutes, until firm to the touch when pressed with a finger.

7 Remove the rock drops from the baking sheet. Either serve piping hot from the oven or transfer to a wire rack and leave to cool before serving.

COOK'S TIP

For convenience, prepare the dry ingredients in advance and stir in the liquid just before cooking,

Cherry & Sultana Rockies

Rock cakes are always popular and they are very quick and easy to make. To be at their best they should be eaten the day they are made.

40 mins   10–15 mins

MAKES 10–12

I N G R E D I E N T S

85 g/3 oz butter, plus extra for greasing

250 g/9 oz self-raising flour

1 tsp ground mixed spice

85 g/3 oz golden caster sugar

55 g/2 oz glacé cherries, quartered

55 g/2 oz sultanas

1 egg

2 tbsp milk

demerara sugar, for sprinkling

1 Preheat the oven to 200°C/400°F/Gas Mark 6. Lightly grease a baking sheet. Sift the flour and mixed spice into a bowl. Add the butter and rub in until the mixture resembles breadcrumbs. Stir in the sugar, cherries and sultanas.

2 Break the egg into a bowl and whisk in the milk. Pour most of the egg mixture into the dry ingredients and mix with a fork to make a stiff, coarse dough, adding the rest of the egg and milk, if necessary.

3 Using 2 forks, pile the dough into 10 rocky heaps on the prepared baking sheet. Sprinkle with demerara sugar. Bake in the preheated oven for 10–15 minutes, or until golden and firm to the touch. Leave to cool on the baking sheet for 2 minutes, then transfer to a wire rack to cool completely.

VARIATION
Mixed dried fruit could be used as an alternative to the cherries and sultanas in these rock cakes.

Coconut & Cherry Cakes

Coconut and glacé cherries make these little cakes really moist, and give them a sweet flavour that will make them a hit with children.

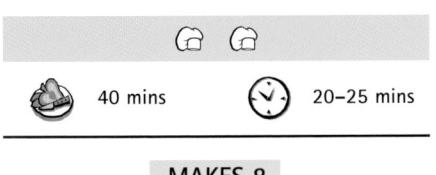

40 mins   20–25 mins

MAKES 8

INGREDIENTS

115 g/4 oz butter, softened

115 g/4 oz golden caster sugar

2 tbsp milk

2 eggs, beaten

85 g/3 oz self-raising flour

½ tsp baking powder

85 g/3 oz desiccated coconut

115 g/4 oz glacé cherries, quartered

1 Preheat the oven to 180°C/350°F/ Gas Mark 4. Line 1 or 2 muffin tins with 8 muffin paper cases. Place the butter and sugar in a bowl and cream together until light and fluffy, then stir in the milk.

2 Gradually beat in the eggs. Sift in the flour and baking powder and fold in with the coconut. Gently fold in most of the cherries. Spoon the mixture into the paper cases and scatter the remaining cherries on top.

3 Bake in the preheated oven for 20–25 minutes, or until well risen, golden and firm to the touch. Transfer to a wire rack to cool.

Mini Orange Rice Cakes

These mini rice cakes, fragrant with orange or sometimes lemon rind, are found in many of the bakeries and coffee shops in Florence.

1 hr 30 mins 40 mins

MAKES ABOUT 16

INGREDIENTS

700 ml/1¼ pints milk

pinch of salt

1 vanilla pod, split, seeds removed and reserved

200 g/7 oz risotto rice

100 g/3½ oz sugar

2 tbsp butter

grated rind of 2 oranges

2 eggs, separated

2 tbsp Cointreau or rum

1 tbsp freshly squeezed orange juice

1 orange, cut into small wedges, to decorate

icing sugar, for dusting

1 Bring the milk to the boil in a large saucepan over a medium-high heat. Add the salt and vanilla pod and seeds, and sprinkle in the rice. Return to the boil, stirring once or twice. Reduce the heat and simmer, stirring frequently, for about 10 minutes.

2 Add the sugar and butter and simmer for about 10 minutes, stirring frequently, until the mixture is thick and creamy. Pour into a bowl and stir in the orange rind. Remove the vanilla pod. Leave to cool to room temperature, stirring occasionally. Meanwhile, preheat the oven to 190°C/375°F/Gas Mark 5.

3 Beat the egg yolks with the Cointreau and orange juice, then beat into the cooled rice mixture.

4 Beat the egg whites until almost stiff, but not too dry. Stir a spoonful into the rice mixture to lighten it, then gently fold in the remaining whites.

5 Line a muffin tin with 16 muffin paper cases. Spoon the batter into the paper cases, filling them to the brim. Bake in the preheated oven for 20 minutes, until golden and cooked through. Place on a wire rack to cool for 2 minutes, then remove the liners. Leave to cool completely.

6 Decorate with tiny wedges of orange and dust with icing sugar just before serving.

Lemon Butterfly Cakes

Butterfly cakes may remind you of children's birthday parties, but these attractive, creamy, miniature delights are for adults, too!

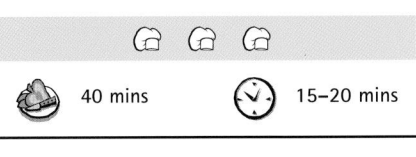

40 mins   15–20 mins

MAKES 12

INGREDIENTS

115 g/4 oz self-raising flour

½ tsp baking powder

115 g/4 oz butter, softened

115 g/4 oz golden caster sugar

2 eggs, beaten

finely grated rind of ½ lemon

2–4 tbsp milk

icing sugar, for dusting

FILLING

55 g/2 oz butter

115 g/4 oz icing sugar

1 tbsp lemon juice

1 Preheat the oven to 190°C/375°F/ Gas Mark 5. Place 12 paper cases in a muffin tin.

2 Sift the flour and baking powder into a bowl. Add the butter, sugar, eggs, lemon rind and enough milk to give a medium-soft consistency. Beat thoroughly until smooth. Divide the mixture between the paper cases and bake in the preheated oven for 15–20 minutes, or until well risen and golden. Transfer to wire racks to cool.

3 To make the filling, place the butter in a bowl, then sift in the icing sugar and add the lemon juice. Beat well until smooth and creamy. When the cakes are quite cold, use a sharp-pointed vegetable knife to cut a circle from the top of each cake, then cut each circle in half.

4 Spoon a little of the buttercream into the centre of each cake and press the 2 semi-circular pieces into it to resemble wings. Dust the cakes with sifted icing sugar before serving.

Chocolate Butterfly Cakes

Filled with a tangy lemon buttercream, these appealing little cakes will become an all-time favourite with both adults and children.

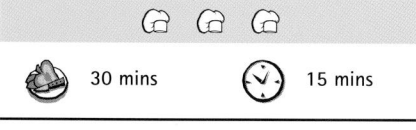

30 mins   15 mins

MAKES 12

INGREDIENTS

115 g/4 oz soft margarine

100 g/3½ oz caster sugar

225 g/8 oz self-raising flour

2 large eggs

2 tbsp cocoa powder

25 g/1 oz plain chocolate, melted

icing sugar, for dusting

LEMON BUTTERCREAM

85 g/3 oz butter, unsalted for preference, softened

150 g/5½ oz icing sugar, sifted

grated rind of ½ lemon

1 tbsp lemon juice

1 Preheat the oven to 180°C/350°F/Gas Mark 4. Line a shallow muffin tin with 12 muffin paper cases. Place all of the ingredients for the cakes, except for the melted chocolate, in a large bowl, and beat with an electric whisk until the mixture is just smooth. Beat in the melted chocolate.

2 Spoon equal amounts of the mixture into each paper case, filling them three-quarters full. Bake in the preheated oven for 15 minutes, or until springy to the touch. Transfer to a wire rack and leave to cool.

3 Meanwhile, make the lemon buttercream. Place the butter in a mixing bowl and beat until fluffy, then gradually beat in the icing sugar. Beat in the lemon rind and gradually add the lemon juice, beating well.

4 When cold, cut the top off each cake, using a serrated knife. Cut each cake top in half.

5 Spread or pipe the buttercream icing over the cut surface of each cake and push the 2 cut pieces of cake top into the icing to form wings. Dust with icing sugar.

VARIATION

For a chocolate buttercream, beat the butter and icing sugar together, then beat in 25 g/1 oz melted plain chocolate.

Chocolate Parfait Sandwiches

This is a novel way of serving a creamy white chocolate parfait in a crisp pastry 'sandwich'. It is the perfect finale to any dinner-party meal.

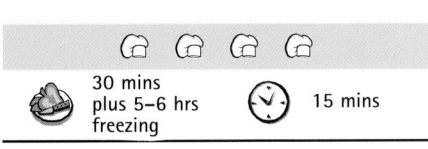

30 mins plus 5–6 hrs freezing

15 mins

SERVES 4

INGREDIENTS

3 large egg whites

140 g/5 oz caster sugar

400 ml/14 fl oz whipping cream, whipped

140 g/5 oz white chocolate, grated

350 g/12 oz ready-rolled puff pastry

1 To make the parfait, beat the egg whites and the sugar together in a heatproof bowl, then set the bowl over a saucepan of gently simmering water. Using an electric whisk, beat the whites over the heat until you have a light and fluffy meringue. This will take up to 10 minutes. Remove from the heat, add the chocolate and keep whisking to cool. Fold in the whipping cream.

2 Spoon the parfait into a shallow rectangular freezerproof container and freeze for 5–6 hours.

3 Meanwhile, preheat the oven to 180°C/350°F/Gas Mark 4 and line a baking sheet with baking paper. Cut the pastry into regular-sized rectangles to accommodate a slice of the parfait. Place the pastry rectangles on the baking sheet and top with another baking sheet, which will keep the pastry flat but crisp. Bake in the oven for 15 minutes, transfer to a wire rack and leave to cool.

4 About 20 minutes before you are ready to serve, remove the parfait from the freezer. When it has softened, cut the parfait into slices and put each slice between 2 pieces of pastry to make a 'sandwich'.

COOK'S TIP
For a more elegant version, drizzle a little melted plain chocolate over the sandwiches or sprinkle with a little sifted icing sugar.

Chocolate Rum Babas

A little fiddly to make, but well worth the effort. Indulge in these tasty cakes with coffee, or serve them as a dessert with summer fruit.

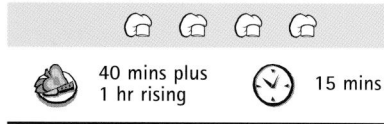

40 mins plus 1 hr rising | **15 mins**

SERVES 4

INGREDIENTS

2 tsp melted butter, for greasing

100 g/3½ oz white bread flour

2 tbsp cocoa powder

5 g/⅛ oz easy-blend dried yeast

pinch of salt

1 tbsp caster sugar

40 g/1½ oz plain chocolate, grated

2 eggs

3 tbsp tepid milk

4 tbsp butter, melted

SYRUP

4 tbsp honey

2 tbsp water

4 tbsp rum

TO SERVE

whipped cream

cocoa powder, for dusting

fresh fruit (optional)

1 Preheat the oven to 200°C/400°F/Gas Mark 6. Lightly grease 4 individual ring tins. Sift the flour and cocoa into a large, warmed mixing bowl. Stir in the yeast, salt, sugar and chocolate. In a separate bowl, beat the eggs, add the milk and butter and beat until mixed.

2 Make a well in the centre of the dry ingredients and pour in the egg mixture, beating to mix to a batter. Beat the batter for 10 minutes, ideally in a food processor with a dough hook. Divide the batter between the tins – it should come halfway up the sides of the tins.

3 Place the tins on a baking sheet and cover with a damp tea towel. Set aside in a warm place until the mixture rises almost to the tops of the tins. Bake in the preheated oven for 15 minutes.

4 To make the syrup, gently heat all of the ingredients in a small saucepan. Turn out the babas and put on a wire rack placed above a tray to catch the syrup.

Drizzle the syrup over the babas and leave for at least 2 hours to let the syrup soak in. From time to time, spoon the syrup that has collected in the tray back over the babas.

5 Fill the centre of the babas with whipped cream and sprinkle a little cocoa over the top. Serve the babas with fresh fruit, if desired.

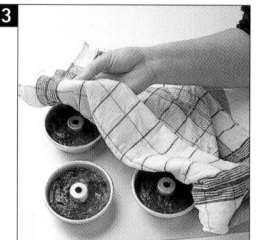

Malted Chocolate Wedges

These tasty malted biscuit wedges are perfect with a bedtime drink, although you can enjoy them at any time of the day.

  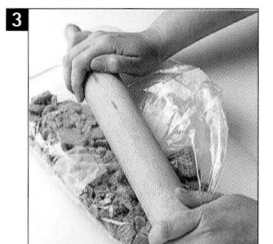 

45 mins   5 mins

MAKES 16

INGREDIENTS

85 g/3 oz butter, plus extra for greasing

2 tbsp golden syrup

2 tbsp malted chocolate drink

225 g/8 oz malted milk biscuits

75 g/2¾ oz milk or plain chocolate, broken into pieces

2 tbsp icing sugar

2 tbsp milk

1 Grease and line the bottom of a shallow 18-cm/7-inch round cake tin or flan tin.

2 Place the butter, golden syrup and malted chocolate drink in a small saucepan and heat gently, stirring all the time until the butter has melted and the mixture is well combined.

3 Crush the biscuits in a polythene bag with a rolling pin, or process them in a food processor. Stir the biscuit crumbs into the chocolate mixture and mix well.

4 Press the mixture into the prepared tin and then chill in the refrigerator until firm.

5 Place the chocolate pieces in a small heatproof bowl with the sugar and the milk. Place the bowl over a saucepan of gently simmering water and stir until the chocolate melts and the mixture is combined.

6 Spread the chocolate icing over the biscuit base and let the icing set in the tin. Using a sharp knife, cut into wedges to serve.

VARIATION
Add chopped pecan nuts to the biscuit crumb mixture in step 3, if liked.

Chocolate Cup Cakes

A variation on an old favourite, these delicious little cakes will appeal to both kids and grown-ups. Leave the cakes to chill before serving.

 20 mins plus 1 hr chilling 20 mins

MAKES 18

INGREDIENTS

85 g/3 oz butter, softened

100 g/3½ oz caster sugar

2 eggs, lightly beaten

2 tbsp milk

55 g/2 oz plain chocolate chips

225 g/8 oz self-raising flour

25 g/1 oz cocoa powder

ICING

225 g/8 oz white chocolate

150 g/5½ oz low-fat cream cheese

1 Preheat the oven to 200°C/400°F/ Gas Mark 6. Line a shallow muffin tin with 18 muffin paper cases.

2 Beat together the butter and sugar until pale and fluffy. Gradually add the eggs, beating well after each addition. Add a little of the flour if the mixture starts to curdle. Add the milk, then fold in the chocolate chips.

3 Sift together the flour and cocoa and fold into the mixture with a metal spoon or palette knife. Divide the batter equally between the muffin paper cases and smooth the tops.

4 Bake in the preheated oven for 20 minutes, or until well risen and springy to the touch. Cool on a wire rack.

5 To make the icing, melt the chocolate in a heatproof bowl set over a saucepan of gently simmering water. Cool slightly. Beat the cream cheese until softened, then beat in the chocolate. Spread a little of the icing over each cake and leave to chill for 1 hour before serving.

VARIATION

Add white chocolate chips or chopped pecan nuts to the mixture instead of the plain chocolate chips if you prefer. You can also add the finely grated rind of 1 orange for a chocolate and orange flavour.

Cup Cakes

These pretty little cakes are light and moist, with a tempting fudgy chocolate topping – perfect for serving at any time of the day.

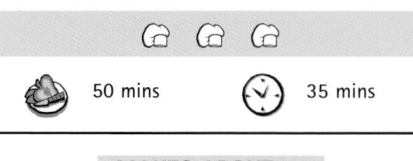

50 mins   35 mins

MAKES ABOUT 20

INGREDIENTS

200 ml/7 fl oz water

85 g/3 oz butter

85 g/3 oz caster sugar

1 tbsp golden syrup

3 tbsp milk

1 tsp vanilla essence

1 tsp bicarbonate of soda

2 tbsp cocoa powder

225 g/8 oz plain flour

ICING

50 g/1¾ oz plain chocolate, broken into pieces

4 tbsp water

50 g/1¾ oz butter

50 g/1¾ oz white chocolate, broken into pieces

350 g/12 oz icing sugar

TO DECORATE

crystallized rose petals

crystallized violets

1 Preheat the oven to 180°C/350°F/ Gas Mark 3. Line 2 muffin tins with 20 muffin paper cases.

2 Place the water, butter, sugar and syrup in a saucepan. Heat gently, stirring, until the sugar has dissolved, then bring to the boil. Reduce the heat and cook gently for 5 minutes. Remove from the heat and leave to cool. Place the milk and vanilla essence in a bowl. Add the bicarbonate of soda and stir to dissolve. Sift the cocoa and flour into a separate bowl and add the syrup mixture. Stir in the milk and beat until smooth.

3 Carefully spoon the mixture into the paper cases to come within two-thirds of the tops. Bake in the preheated oven for 20 minutes, or until well risen and firm to the touch. Leave to cool on a wire rack. To make the icing, place the plain chocolate in a small heatproof bowl with half the water and half the butter and set the bowl over a saucepan of gently simmering water until melted. Stir until smooth and leave to stand over the water. Repeat with the white chocolate and remaining water and butter.

4 Stir half the icing sugar into each bowl and beat until smooth and fudgy. Divide the icings between the cakes, filling to the top of the paper cases. Leave to cool, then place a rose petal on each of the plain chocolate-iced cakes and a violet on each white chocolate-iced cake. Leave to set before serving.

VARIATION
Instead of the crystallized flower petals, the cakes could be decorated with chocolate curls or chopped hazelnuts.

White Chocolate Florentines

These attractive jewelled biscuits are coated with white chocolate to give them a delicious flavour. They make particularly attractive gifts.

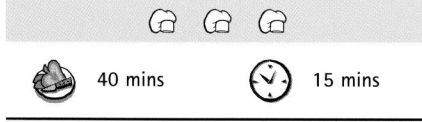

40 mins   15 mins

MAKES 24

INGREDIENTS

200 g/7 oz butter

125 g/4½ oz caster sugar

125 g/4½ oz walnuts, chopped

generous 1 cup almonds, chopped

55 g/2 oz sultanas, chopped

25 g/1 oz glacé cherries, chopped

25 g/1 oz mixed candied peel, chopped finely

2 tbsp single cream

225 g/8 oz white chocolate

1 Preheat the oven to 180°C/350°F/ Gas Mark 4. Line 3–4 baking sheets with non-stick baking paper.

2 Melt the butter over low heat and then add the sugar, stirring until it has dissolved. Boil the mixture for exactly 1 minute. Remove from the heat.

3 Add the walnuts, almonds, sultanas, glacé cherries, candied peel and cream to the saucepan, stirring well to mix.

4 Drop heaped teaspoonfuls of the mixture on to the baking sheets, allowing plenty of room for them to spread during cooking. Bake in the preheated oven for 10 minutes, or until golden brown.

5 Remove the biscuits from the oven and neaten the edges with a knife while they are still warm. Leave to cool slightly, and then transfer them to a wire rack to cool completely.

6 Melt the chocolate in a heatproof bowl placed over a saucepan of gently simmering water. Spread the underside of the biscuits with chocolate and use a fork to make wavy lines across the surface. Leave to cool completely.

7 Store the florentines in an airtight container, kept in a cool place.

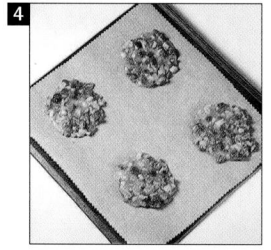

COOK'S TIP

A combination of white and plain chocolate florentines looks very attractive, especially if you are making them as gifts. Pack them in pretty boxes, lined with tissue paper and tied with some ribbon.

Florentine Twists

These famous and delicious florentine biscuits are twisted into curls or cones before the ends are dipped in a little chocolate.

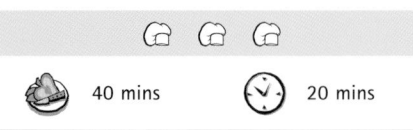

🍰 40 mins   🕐 20 mins

MAKES 20

I N G R E D I E N T S

85 g/3 oz butter, plus extra for greasing

125 g/4½ oz caster sugar

55 g/2 oz blanched or flaked almonds, chopped coarsely

3 tbsp raisins, chopped

40 g/1½ oz chopped mixed candied peel

40 g/1½ oz glacé cherries, chopped

3 tbsp dried apricots, chopped finely

finely grated rind of ½ lemon or ½ small orange

115 g/4 oz plain or white chocolate

1 Preheat the oven to 180°C/350°F/ Gas Mark 4. Line 2–3 baking sheets with non-stick baking paper; then grease 4–6 cream horn moulds, or a fairly thin rolling pin or wooden spoon handles.

2 Melt the butter and sugar together gently in a large heavy-based saucepan, then bring to the boil for 1 minute. Remove the saucepan from the heat and stir in all the remaining ingredients, except for the chocolate. Leave to cool.

3 Put heaped teaspoonfuls of the mixture on to the baking sheets, allowing plenty of room for the biscuits to spread during cooking (perhaps only 3–4 biscuits per sheet) and flatten slightly.

4 Bake in the preheated oven for 10–12 minutes, or until golden. Leave to cool until they start to firm up. As they cool, press the edges back to form a neat shape. Remove each one with a palette knife and wrap quickly around a cream horn mould, or lay over the rolling pin or spoon handles. If they become too firm to bend, return to the oven for a few minutes to soften.

5 Leave until cold and crisp and then slip carefully off the horn moulds or remove from the rolling pin or spoons.

6 Melt the chocolate in a heatproof bowl set over a saucepan of gently simmering water and stir until smooth. Either dip the end of each florentine twist into the chocolate or, using a pastry brush, paint chocolate to come about halfway up the twist. As the chocolate sets, it can be marked into wavy lines with a fork. Leave to set before serving.

Pineapple Florentines

These florentines combine candied pineapple, angelica and almond in a delicate, crisp biscuit with a delicious chocolate coating.

🦐 🦐 🦐

🍯 45 mins   🕐 10–12 mins

MAKES ABOUT 14

I N G R E D I E N T S

85 g/3 oz butter

85 g/3 oz demerara sugar

1 tbsp golden syrup

25 g/1 oz plain flour, sifted

2 tbsp angelica, chopped coarsely

25 g/1 oz glacé cherries, chopped coarsely

55 g/2 oz flaked almonds, chopped coarsely

55 g/2 oz glacé pineapple, chopped coarsely

1 tsp lemon juice

115 g/4 oz plain chocolate, broken into pieces

1 Preheat the oven to 180°C/350°F/ Gas Mark 4. Line several baking sheets with baking paper. Place the butter, sugar and syrup in a saucepan and heat gently until melted, then stir in the flour, angelica, cherries, almonds, pineapple and lemon juice.

2 Place walnut-sized mounds of the mixture well apart on the baking sheets and flatten with a fork. Bake in the oven for 8–10 minutes, or until golden. Use a palette knife to neaten the ragged edges. Leave to cool for 1 minute, then transfer to a wire rack to cool completely.

3 Melt the chocolate in a heatproof bowl set over a saucepan of gently simmering water. Spread melted chocolate over the bottom of each biscuit, placing them, chocolate side up, on a wire rack. Use a fork to mark the chocolate into wavy lines. Leave to stand until set.

COOK'S TIP
Try serving these with vanilla ice cream for an instant dessert.

Florentines

These luxury biscuits will be popular at any time of the year, but they make a particularly wonderful treat at Christmas.

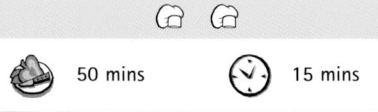

50 mins   15 mins

MAKES 10

INGREDIENTS

55 g/2 oz butter

50 g/1¾ oz caster sugar

25 g/1 oz plain flour, sifted

50 g/1¾ oz almonds, chopped

35 g/1¼ oz chopped mixed candied peel

50 g/1¾ oz raisins, chopped

2 tbsp chopped glacé cherries

finely grated rind of ½ lemon

125 g/4½ oz plain chocolate, broken into pieces

1 Preheat the oven to 180°C/350°F/ Gas Mark 4. Line 2 large baking sheets with baking paper.

2 Heat the butter and sugar in a small saucepan until the butter has just melted and the sugar dissolved. Remove from the heat.

3 Stir in the flour and mix well. Stir in the chopped almonds, candied peel, raisins, cherries and lemon rind. Place teaspoonfuls of the mixture well apart on the baking sheets.

4 Bake in the preheated oven for about 10 minutes, or until the florentines are lightly golden.

5 As soon as the florentines are removed from the oven, press the edges into neat shapes while still on the baking sheets, using a biscuit cutter. Leave to cool on the sheets until firm, then transfer to a wire rack to cool completely.

6 Melt the chocolate in a heatproof bowl set over a saucepan of gently simmering water. Spread the melted chocolate over the smooth side of each florentine. As the chocolate starts to set, mark wavy lines in it with a fork. Leave the florentines to set, chocolate side up.

VARIATION
Replace the plain chocolate with white chocolate or cover half of the florentines in plain chocolate and half in white.

Ladies' Kisses

These melt-in-the-mouth biscuits, sandwiched together with chocolate, are divine at coffee-time or served as petits fours after dinner.

1 hr plus
2 hrs chilling

30–35 mins

SERVES 20

INGREDIENTS

175 g/6 oz butter, unsalted for preference

115 g/4 oz caster sugar

1 egg yolk

100 g/3½ oz ground almonds

175 g/6 oz plain flour

55 g/2 oz plain chocolate,
    broken into pieces

2 tbsp icing sugar, for dusting

2 tbsp cocoa powder, for dusting

1 Line 3 baking sheets with baking paper, or use 3 non-stick sheets. Cream the butter and sugar together until pale and fluffy. Beat in the egg yolk, then beat in the almonds and flour. Continue beating until thoroughly mixed. Shape the dough into a ball, wrap in clingfilm and chill in the refrigerator for 1½–2 hours.

2 Preheat the oven to 160°C/325°F/Gas Mark 3. Unwrap the dough, break off walnut-sized pieces and roll them into balls between the palms of your hands. Place the dough balls on the prepared baking sheets, allowing space for the biscuits to spread during cooking. You may need to cook them in batches. Bake in the preheated oven for 20–25 minutes, until golden. Carefully transfer the biscuits, still on the baking paper (if using), to wire racks to cool.

3 Melt the chocolate in a heatproof bowl set over a saucepan of gently simmering water. Remove the biscuits from the baking paper (if using). Spread the melted chocolate on the flat sides and sandwich them together in pairs. Return to the wire racks to cool. Lightly dust with a mixture of icing sugar and cocoa powder.

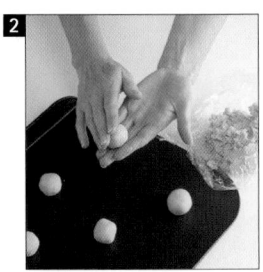

Chocolate Crinkles

These chocolate biscuits are popular at Christmas. Children enjoy shaping the mixture into balls, so invite them to help you.

30 mins plus 3 hrs chilling

15 mins

MAKES 24

INGREDIENTS

140 g/5 oz plain flour

1 tsp baking powder

25 g/1 oz walnut pieces

25 g/1 oz plain chocolate, broken into pieces

55 g/2 oz butter, plus extra for greasing

60 g/2¼ oz caster sugar

1 tsp vanilla essence

1 egg, beaten

2 tbsp milk

25 g/1 oz icing sugar

1 Sift the flour and baking powder together. Finely chop the walnuts. Melt the chocolate in a heatproof bowl set over a saucepan of gently simmering water, then set aside to cool slightly.

2 Meanwhile, whisk the butter, caster sugar and vanilla essence together until soft and fluffy. Gradually whisk in the egg, then whisk in the melted chocolate.

3 Whisk in the flour mixture alternatively with the milk. Stir in the chopped walnuts. Chill the mixture in the refrigerator for at least 3 hours.

4 Preheat the oven to 180°C/350°F/ Gas Mark 4. Grease 2–3 large baking sheets. Put the icing sugar into a large polythene bag.

5 Shape the mixture into 2.5-cm/1-inch balls, then roll each one in the icing sugar. Place on the prepared baking sheets, allowing room for the biscuits to spread during cooking.

6 Bake the biscuits in the preheated oven for about 15 minutes, until firm. Transfer to a wire rack and leave to cool.

VARIATION
Pecan nuts could be used instead of the walnuts.

Raspberry Chocolate Eclairs

These small éclairs are perfect for serving at a summer tea party. They look particularly appealing arranged on a pretty serving plate.

🍰 🍰 🍰 🍰 🍰

⏲ 30 mins   🕐 40 mins

MAKES 20–24

INGREDIENTS

55 g/2 oz butter

150 ml/5 fl oz water

70 g/2½ oz plain flour, sifted

2 eggs, beaten

FILLING AND TOPPING

175 ml/6 fl oz double cream

1 tbsp icing sugar

175 g/6 oz fresh raspberries

85 g/3 oz plain chocolate,
   broken into pieces

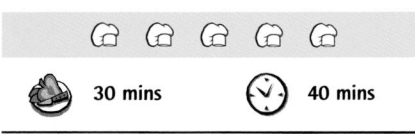

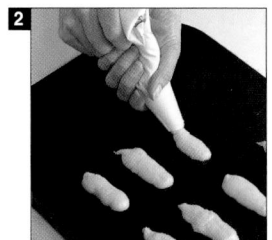

1 Preheat the oven to 220°C/425°F/ Gas Mark 7. To make the choux pastry, place the butter and water in a heavy-based saucepan and bring to the boil over a low heat. Add the flour, all at once, and beat thoroughly until the mixture leaves the side of the saucepan. Leave to cool slightly, then vigorously beat in the eggs, a little at a time.

2 Spoon the mixture into a piping bag fitted with a 1-cm/½-inch nozzle and pipe 20–24 x 7.5-cm/3-inch lengths on to dampened baking sheets. Bake in the preheated oven for 10 minutes, then reduce the oven temperature to 190°C/375°F/Gas Mark 5 and bake for an additional 20 minutes, or until crisp and golden brown. Split the side of each éclair to let the steam escape, and transfer to a wire rack to cool completely.

3 To make the filling, place the cream and icing sugar in a bowl and whip until thick. Spoon into the éclairs. Place a few raspberries in each éclair.

4 Melt the chocolate in a heatproof bowl set over a saucepan of gently simmering water. Spread a little on each éclair. Leave to set, then serve.

COOK'S TIP

The raw piped choux mixture can be made a few days ahead and frozen, then baked directly from the freezer for 5 minutes longer than usual.

Chocolate Eclairs

Pastry cream (crème pâtissière) is the traditional filling for éclairs, but if time is short, you can fill them with whipped cream.

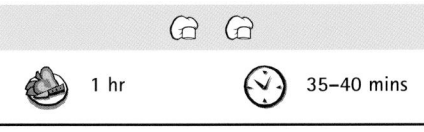

🧈 1 hr   🕐 35–40 mins

MAKES 10

INGREDIENTS

DOUGH

70 g/2½ oz butter, cut into small pieces, plus extra for greasing

150 ml/5 fl oz water

100 g/3½ oz plain flour, sifted

2 eggs

PASTRY CREAM

2 eggs, beaten lightly

4 tbsp caster sugar

2 tbsp cornflour

300 ml/10 fl oz milk

¼ tsp vanilla essence

ICING

2 tbsp butter

1 tbsp milk

1 tbsp cocoa powder

55 g/2 oz icing sugar

white chocolate, broken into pieces

1 Preheat the oven to 200°C/400°F/ Gas Mark 6. Lightly grease a baking sheet. Place the water in a saucepan, add the butter and heat gently until the butter melts. Bring to a rolling boil, then remove the saucepan from the heat and add the flour all at once, beating well until the mixture leaves the sides of the saucepan and forms a ball. Leave to cool slightly, then gradually beat in the eggs to form a smooth, glossy mixture. Spoon into a large piping bag fitted with a 1-cm/½-inch plain nozzle.

2 Sprinkle the baking sheet with a little water. Pipe éclairs 7.5 cm/3 inches long, spaced well apart. Bake in the preheated oven for 30–35 minutes, or until crisp and golden. Make a small slit in the side of each éclair to let the steam escape. Leave to cool on a wire rack.

3 Meanwhile, make the pastry cream. Whisk the eggs and sugar until thick and creamy, then fold in the cornflour. Heat the milk until almost boiling and pour on to the eggs, whisking. Transfer to the saucepan and cook over a low heat, stirring until thick. Remove the saucepan from the heat and stir in the vanilla essence. Cover with baking paper and leave to cool.

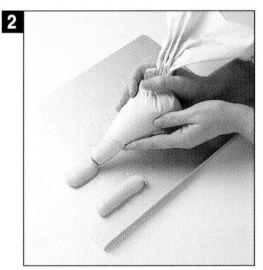

4 To make the icing, melt the butter with the milk in a saucepan, remove from the heat and stir in the cocoa and sugar. Split the éclairs lengthways and pipe in the pastry cream. Spread the icing over the top of the éclair. Melt a little white chocolate in a heatproof bowl set over a saucepan of gently simmering water, then spoon over the chocolate icing, swirl in and leave to set.

Chestnut Cream Squares

These little cakes look wonderful, and are well worth the preparation time. The magical combination of flavours is out of this world.

45 mins plus
11–11 hrs 30 mins
freezing/standing

55–60 mins

MAKES 30

INGREDIENTS

BOTTOM LAYER

85 g/3 oz plain chocolate, broken into pieces

85 g/3 oz butter, unsalted for preference

4 tbsp icing sugar

4 eggs, separated

100 g/3½ oz caster sugar

100 g/3½ oz plain flour

5 tbsp sour cherry jam

3 tbsp kirsch

DARK LAYER

100 g/3½ oz plain chocolate

85 ml/3 fl oz milk

4 tsp caster sugar

¼ tsp vanilla essence

1 egg yolk

1 tbsp cornflour

generous 2 tbsp icing sugar

300 ml/10 fl oz double cream

WHITE LAYER

450 ml/16 fl oz double cream

1 tbsp icing sugar

CHESTNUT LAYER

350 g/12 oz chestnut purée

4 tsp dark rum

2 tsp caster sugar

30 cherries, to decorate

1 Preheat the oven to 180°C/350°F/Gas Mark 4. Line a 30 x 25 x 5-cm/12 x 10 x 2-inch cake tin with baking paper. Melt the chocolate in a heatproof bowl set over a saucepan of gently simmering water, then cool slightly. Mix the butter, icing sugar and chocolate together. Beat in the egg yolks, 1 at a time.

2 Whisk the egg whites in a separate bowl until soft peaks form, whisk in the caster sugar until stiff, then fold into the chocolate mixture. Sift the flour, then fold into the mixture. Spoon into the tin and smooth the surface. Bake for 30 minutes.

3 Remove from the oven, leave to cool, then cut around the edges with a knife. Invert on to a flat surface. Wash and dry the cake tin and line with baking paper. Return the bottom layer to the tin. Bring the jam to the boil in a small saucepan, sieve and leave to cool. Sprinkle the kirsch over the bottom layer, then spread with the cherry jam.

4 Melt the chocolate in a heatproof bowl set over a saucepan of gently simmering water. Remove from the heat. Put the milk, caster sugar and vanilla essence into a saucepan and bring to the boil. Remove from the heat. Mix the egg yolk, cornflour and 2 tablespoons of the hot milk in a bowl, add to the milk in the saucepan and return to a medium heat. Cook, stirring, for 3–5 minutes until thickened. Stir in the icing sugar and melted chocolate. Remove from the heat. Beat the cream until thick, then stir it into the chocolate mixture. Spread over the layer in the tin, cover and freeze for 1½–2 hours.

5 When the dark layer is half frozen, make the white layer. Whisk the cream with the sugar until thick, then spread over the dark layer. Cover and freeze for 8 hours.

6 Remove the cake from the tin, with the white layer uppermost. Beat together the chestnut purée, rum and sugar. Pipe or press through a garlic press and spread over the white layer. Cut the cake into 30 squares and top each one with a cherry. Leave to chill for 30 minutes before serving.

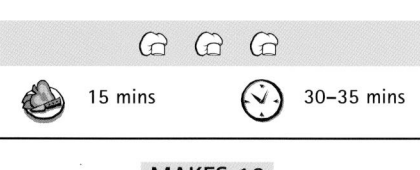

Chocolate Strawberry Slices

Here, strawberry jam and plain chocolate chips are sandwiched between an oat crumble mixture to make delicious biscuit slices.

15 mins 30–35 mins

MAKES 16

INGREDIENTS

225 g/8 oz plain flour

1 tsp baking powder

100 g/3½ oz caster sugar

85 g/3 oz soft brown sugar

225 g/8 oz butter

150 g/5½ oz rolled oats

225 g/8 oz strawberry jam

100 g/3½ oz plain chocolate chips

25 g/1 oz chopped almonds

1 Preheat the oven to 190°C/375°F/ Gas Mark 5. Line a 30 x 12-cm/12 x 8-inch deep-sided Swiss roll tin with baking paper. Sift the flour and baking powder into a large bowl.

2 Add the caster sugar and brown sugar to the flour and mix well. Add the butter and rub in until the mixture resembles breadcrumbs. Stir in the oats.

3 Press three-quarters of the mixture into the bottom of a 23-cm/9-inch square cake tin. Bake in the preheated oven for 10 minutes.

4 Spread the jam over the cooked base, then sprinkle over the chocolate chips. Mix the remaining flour mixture and almonds together. Sprinkle over the chocolate chips and press down gently.

5 Return to the oven and bake for an additional 20–25 minutes, until golden brown. Leave to cool in the tin, then cut into slices.

VARIATION
Seedless raspberry jam would work equally well in this recipe.

Mocha Rolls

Plain and white chocolate are combined with coffee and Kahlúa in these attractive sponge-cake rolls.

 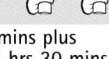

35 mins plus
1–2 hrs 30 mins
chilling/setting

50–55 mins

MAKES 16

INGREDIENTS

150 ml/5 fl oz cold, strong, black coffee

1 tbsp gelatine

1 tsp Kahlúa or other coffee-flavoured liqueur

225 g/8 oz ricotta cheese

280 g/10 oz white chocolate, broken into pieces

25 g/1 oz plain chocolate

SPONGE CAKE

3 eggs, plus 1 egg white

85 g/3 oz caster sugar

100 g/3½ oz plain flour

2 tbsp butter, melted

1 Preheat the oven to 180°C/350°F/Gas Mark 4. For the sponge cake, base-line a 30 x 20 x 4-cm/12 x 8 x 1½-inch cake tin with baking paper. Put the eggs, egg white and sugar in a heatproof bowl set over a saucepan of gently simmering water. Whisk until pale and thickened.

2 Remove the mixture from the heat, then whisk until cool. Sift the flour over the mixture and fold in. Fold in the melted butter, a little at a time. Pour the mixture into the prepared tin and bake for 25–30 minutes, until the cake is firm to the touch and has shrunk slightly from the sides of the tin. Remove from the oven and transfer to a wire rack, still standing on the baking paper, to cool.

3 Meanwhile, put 2 tablespoons of the coffee into a small heatproof bowl and sprinkle the gelatine on the surface.

Leave to soften for 2 minutes, then set the bowl over a saucepan of gently simmering water and stir until the gelatine has dissolved. Remove from the heat. Put the remaining coffee, liqueur and ricotta in a food processor and process until smooth. Add the gelatine mixture in a single stream and process briefly. Scrape the mixture into a bowl, cover with clingfilm and chill in the refrigerator for 1–1½ hours, until set.

4 Peel the baking paper from the cooled cake. Using a knife, cut horizontally through the cake. Trim off any dried edges. Cut each piece of cake in half lengthways. Place each piece between 2 sheets of baking paper and roll with a rolling pin to make it more flexible.

5 Spread the cut side of each cake piece with an even 5-mm/¼-inch thick layer of the coffee filling, leaving a 5-mm/¼-inch margin all round. Cut each strip across into 4 pieces, to give a total of 16. Roll up each piece from the short end, like a Swiss roll.

6 Melt the white chocolate in a heatproof bowl set over a saucepan of barely simmering water. Remove from the heat. Place 1 roll, seam-side down, on a metal palette knife and hold it over the bowl of melted chocolate. Spoon the chocolate over the roll to coat. Transfer the roll to a sheet of baking paper and repeat with the remaining rolls.

7 Put the plain chocolate in a heatproof bowl set over a saucepan of gently simmering water. Remove from the heat. Spoon it into a greaseproof paper piping bag fitted with a small, plain nozzle and pipe zig-zags along the rolls. Leave to set completely before serving.

 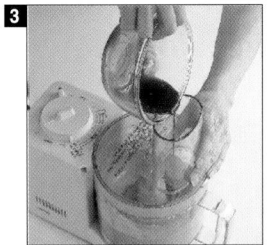 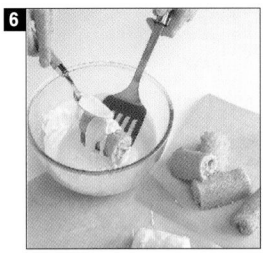

Meringues

These are just as meringues should be – as light as air and at the same time crisp and melt-in-the-mouth. Store in an airtight container.

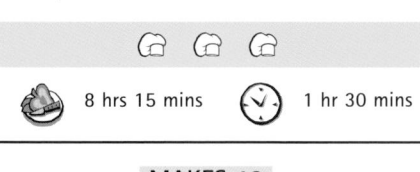

8 hrs 15 mins   1 hr 30 mins

MAKES 13

INGREDIENTS

4 egg whites

115 g/4 oz granulated sugar

115 g/4 oz caster sugar

300 ml/10 fl oz double cream, whipped lightly

salt

1 Preheat the oven to 120°C/250°F/ Gas Mark ½. Line 3 baking sheets with sheets of baking paper.

2 In a large clean bowl, whisk the egg whites with a pinch of salt until stiff, using an electric hand-held whisk or a balloon whisk. You should be able to turn the bowl upside down without any movement from the egg whites.

3 Whisk in the granulated sugar, a little at a time; the meringue should start to look glossy at this stage.

4 Sprinkle in the caster sugar, a little at a time, and continue whisking until all the sugar has been incorporated and the meringue is thick, white, and stands in tall peaks.

5 Transfer the meringue mixture to a piping bag fitted with a 2-cm/¾-inch star nozzle. Pipe about 26 small whirls on to the prepared baking sheets.

6 Bake in the preheated oven for 1½ hours, or until the meringues are pale golden in colour and can be easily lifted off the paper. Leave to cool in the turned-off oven overnight.

7 Just before serving, sandwich the meringues together in pairs with the whipped cream and arrange them on a serving plate.

VARIATION
For a finer texture, replace the granulated sugar with caster sugar.

Chocolate Meringues

These delicate meringues are an ideal choice for an extra-special occasion – pile them high in a pyramid for pure, bite-sized magic.

1 hr 25 mins   1 hr

MAKES 8

INGREDIENTS

4 egg whites

200 g/7 oz caster sugar

1 tsp cornflour

40 g/1½ oz plain chocolate, grated

TO FINISH

100 g/3½ oz plain chocolate

150 ml/5 fl oz double cream

1 tbsp icing sugar

1 tbsp brandy (optional)

1 Preheat the oven to 140°C/275°F/ Gas Mark 1. Line 2 baking sheets with baking paper. Whisk the egg whites until soft peaks form, then gradually whisk in half of the sugar. Continue whisking until the mixture is very stiff and glossy.

2 Carefully fold in the remaining sugar, cornflour and grated chocolate with a metal spoon or palette knife.

3 Spoon the mixture into a piping bag fitted with a large star or plain nozzle. Pipe 16 large rosettes or mounds on the lined baking sheets.

4 Bake in the oven for about 1 hour, changing the position of the baking sheets after 30 minutes. Without opening the oven door, turn off the oven and leave the meringues to cool in the oven. Once cold, carefully peel off the baking paper.

5 Melt the plain chocolate in a heatproof bowl set over a saucepan of gently simmering water and carefully spread it over the bottom of the meringues. Stand them upside down on a wire rack until the chocolate has set. Whip the cream, icing sugar and brandy (if using) until the cream holds its shape. Spoon into a piping bag and use to sandwich the chocolate-coated meringues together in pairs.

VARIATION
To make mini meringues, use a star-shape nozzle and pipe about 24 small rosettes. Bake for about 40 minutes until crisp.

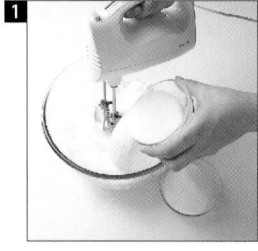

Mexican Meringues

The Mexican name for these delicate meringues is *suspiros*, meaning 'sighs' – supposedly the contented sighs of the nuns who created them.

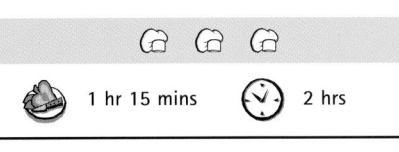

🍓 1 hr 15 mins 🕐 2 hrs

MAKES 25

INGREDIENTS

4–5 egg whites, at room temperature

pinch of salt

¼ tsp cream of tartar

¼–½ tsp vanilla essence

140–200 g/5–7 oz caster sugar

⅛–¼ tsp ground cinnamon

115 g/4 oz plain or continental plain chocolate, grated

TO SERVE

ground cinnamon, for dusting

115 g/4 oz strawberries

chocolate-flavoured cream (see Cook's Tip)

1 Preheat the oven to 150°C/300°F/ Gas Mark 2. Whisk the egg whites until they are foamy, then add the salt and cream of tartar and beat until very stiff. Whisk in the vanilla, then slowly whisk in the sugar, a small amount at a time, until the meringue is shiny and stiff. This should take about 3 minutes by hand, and under 1 minute with an electric whisk.

2 Whisk in the ground cinnamon and grated chocolate. Spoon mounds of about 2 tablespoons on to an ungreased, non-stick baking sheet. Space the mounds out well.

3 Place in the preheated oven and cook for 2 hours, until set.

4 Carefully remove from the baking sheet. If the meringues are too moist and soft, return them to the oven to firm up and dry out. Leave to cool completely.

5 Serve the meringues dusted with cinnamon and accompanied by strawberries and the chocolate-flavoured cream (see Cook's Tip).

COOK'S TIP
To make the flavoured cream, simply stir half-melted chocolate pieces into stiffly whipped cream, then chill until solid.

Chocolate Ginger Meringues

These meringues are flecked with plain chocolate and sandwiched together with a delicious ginger cream. Assemble just before serving.

1 hr | 1 hr 40 mins

MAKES 8 PAIRS

INGREDIENTS

225 g/8 oz plain chocolate

4 egg whites

225 g/8 oz golden caster sugar

FILLING

300 ml/10 fl oz double cream

1 tbsp syrup from the stem ginger jar

3 pieces stem ginger, chopped finely

1 Preheat the oven to 120°C/250°F/Gas Mark ½. Line 2 baking sheets with non-stick baking paper. Grate half the plain chocolate. Put the egg whites in a clean, greasefree bowl and whisk until stiff. Whisk in half the remaining sugar with the grated chocolate.

2 Pipe or spoon 16 tablespoons of the meringue mixture on to the prepared baking sheets. Bake in the oven for 1½ hours, or until dry. Transfer to wire racks to cool. Put the remaining chocolate in a heatproof bowl set over a saucepan of gently simmering water until melted. Spread a little melted chocolate over the base of each meringue. Leave to set.

3 To make the filling, put the cream in a bowl and whisk until thick. Stir in the ginger syrup, then add the chopped ginger and stir gently to incorporate. Sandwich the meringues together in pairs with the ginger cream before serving.

COOK'S TIP
Take care not to over-whisk the meringue mixture after adding the grated chocolate.

Chocolate Peppermint Slices

A fresh mint-flavoured icing, sandwiched between a shortbread biscuit base and a chocolate coating, make these slices deliciously different.

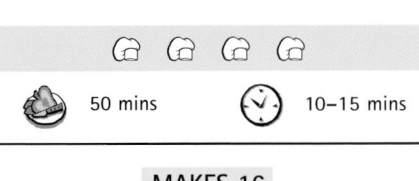

50 mins   10–15 mins

MAKES 16

INGREDIENTS

55 g/2 oz butter, plus extra for greasing

55 g/2 oz caster sugar

115 g/4 oz plain flour

175 g/6 oz icing sugar

½ tsp peppermint essence

175 g/6 oz plain chocolate, broken into pieces

1–2 tbsp warm water

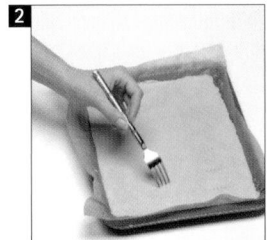
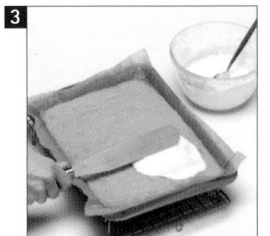

1 Preheat the oven to 180°C/350°F/ Gas Mark 4. Grease and line a 20 x 30-cm/8 x 12-inch Swiss roll tin with baking paper. Whisk the butter and sugar together until pale and fluffy. Stir in the flour until the mixture binds together.

2 Knead the mixture to form a smooth dough, then press into the prepared tin. Prick the surface all over with a fork. Bake in the preheated oven for 10–15 minutes, until lightly browned and just firm to the touch. Leave to cool in the tin.

3 Sift the icing sugar into a bowl. Gradually add the water, then add the peppermint essence. Spread the icing over the base, then leave to set.

4 Melt the chocolate in a heatproof bowl set over a saucepan of gently simmering water, then spread over the peppermint icing. Leave to set, then cut into slices.

Christmas Tree Clusters

Popcorn is the perfect nibble to have around at Christmas. Wrapped in cellophane, these clusters make ideal decorations for the Christmas tree.

🔥 10 mins   🕐 20 mins

MAKES 16

I N G R E D I E N T S

1 tbsp vegetable oil

25 g/1 oz unpopped corn

2 tbsp butter

4 tbsp soft brown sugar

4 tbsp golden syrup

25 g/1 oz glacé cherries, chopped

55 g/2 oz sultanas or raisins

25 g/1 oz ground almonds

2 tbsp flaked almonds

½ tsp ground mixed spice

1 To pop the corn, heat the oil in a large saucepan or in a popcorn pan. The oil is hot enough when a kernel spins around in the pan. Add the unpopped corn, cover tightly and pop the corn over medium-high heat, shaking the saucepan frequently.

2 Remove the saucepan from the heat and wait until the popping sound subsides.

3 Put the butter, sugar and syrup into a separate saucepan and heat, stirring frequently, to dissolve the sugar. Do not boil. Remove from the heat once the sugar is dissolved.

4 Add the popped corn, glacé cherries, sultanas or raisins, ground and flaked almonds and mixed spice to the syrup mixture, stirring well. Leave to cool for a few minutes.

5 Shape the mixture into small balls. Leave to cool completely. Wrap in cellophane and tie with coloured ribbon or string and hang from the Christmas tree.

VARIATION

Omit the cherries, sultanas, ground almonds and mixed spice and replace with 75 g/2¾ oz coarsely chopped pecan nuts and ½ teaspoon ground cinnamon to make pecan clusters.

Lebkuchen

These spicy biscuits are traditionally eaten in Germany on the feast day of St Nicholas, but they are good to eat at any time of the year!

25 mins   15–20 mins

MAKES ABOUT 60

INGREDIENTS

3 eggs

200 g/7 oz golden caster sugar

55 g/2 oz plain flour

2 tsp cocoa powder

1 tsp ground cinnamon

½ tsp ground cardamom

¼ tsp ground cloves

¼ tsp ground nutmeg

175 g/6 oz ground almonds

55 g/2 oz mixed candied peel, chopped finely

TO DECORATE

115 g/4 oz plain chocolate

115 g/4 oz white chocolate

sugar crystals

1 Preheat the oven to 180°C/350°F/Gas Mark 4. Line several baking sheets with non-stick baking paper. Put the eggs and sugar in a heatproof bowl set over a saucepan of gently simmering water. Whisk until thick and foamy. Remove the bowl from the saucepan and continue to whisk for 2 minutes.

2 Sift the flour, cocoa, cinnamon, cardamom, cloves and nutmeg into the bowl and stir in with the ground almonds and chopped peel. Drop heaped teaspoonfuls of the mixture on to the prepared baking sheets, spreading them gently into smooth mounds.

3 Bake in the oven for 15–20 minutes, until light brown and slightly soft to the touch. Cool on the baking sheets for 10 minutes, then transfer to wire racks to cool completely. Put the plain and white chocolate in 2 separate heatproof bowls set over 2 saucepans of gently simmering water until melted. Dip half the biscuits in melted plain chocolate and half in white. Sprinkle with sugar crystals and leave to set.

Cakes
& Gâteaux

There are those dull days or quiet weekends that make us

want to retreat to the warmth and comfort of the kitchen

and what better way to spend an afternoon than to

indulge in some baking? Few things culinary can lift jaded

spirits in quite the same way as a

tempting slice of homemade cake.

Here are everyday cakes and gâteaux

for special occasions, from spicy rich

fruit cakes to sumptuous creamy cheesecakes. Favourites

include Mississippi Mud Cake, Double Chocolate Roulade

and Tropical Fruit Vacherin. Unleash

your creative genius and get baking.

Chocolate Ganache Cake

Ganache – a divine mixture of chocolate and cream – is used to fill and decorate this rich chocolate cake, making it a chocolate lover's dream.

🍰🍰

🥣 1 hr plus
2 hrs chilling   🕐 40 mins

SERVES 10

I N G R E D I E N T S

175 g/6 oz butter plus extra for greasing

175 g/6 oz caster sugar

4 eggs, beaten lightly

250 g/9 oz self-raising flour

1 tbsp cocoa powder

50 g/1¾ oz plain chocolate, melted

G A N A C H E

450 ml/16 fl oz cream

375 g/13 oz plain chocolate,
   broken into pieces

T O   F I N I S H

200 g/7 oz chocolate-flavoured
   cake covering

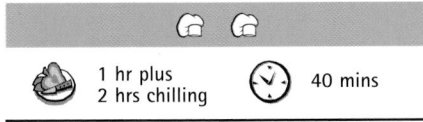

1 Preheat the oven to 180°C/350°F/ Gas Mark 4. Lightly grease and base-line a 20-cm/8-inch springform cake tin. Beat the butter and sugar until light and fluffy. Gradually add the eggs, beating well after each addition. Sift the flour and cocoa together. Fold into the cake mixture. Fold in the melted chocolate.

2 Pour into the prepared tin and smooth the top. Bake in the preheated oven for 40 minutes, or until springy to the touch. Leave the cake to cool for 5 minutes in the tin, then turn out on to a wire rack and leave to cool completely. Cut the cake into 2 layers.

3 To make the ganache, place the cream in a saucepan and bring to the boil, stirring. Add the chocolate and stir until melted. Pour into a bowl, cool, then chill for 2 hours, or until set and firm. Whisk the mixture until light and fluffy.

4 Reserve one-third of the ganache. Use the remaining ganache to sandwich the cake together and spread over the top and sides of the cake.

5 Melt the cake covering and spread it over a large sheet of baking paper. Leave to cool until just set. Cut into strips a little wider than the height of the cake. Place the strips around the edge of the cake, overlapping them slightly.

6 Pipe the reserved ganache in tear drops or shells to cover the top of the cake. Leave to chill for 1 hour.

Swedish Chocolate Cake

This is the ideal snack to eat with a mid-morning cup of coffee.
Serve with whipped cream for a special treat.

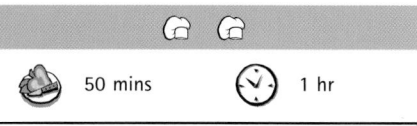

🍰 50 mins   🕐 1 hr

MAKES 23-CM/9-INCH CAKE

INGREDIENTS

90 g/3¼ oz butter, unsalted for preference,
   plus extra for greasing

40 g/1½ oz dry white breadcrumbs

85 g/3 oz plain chocolate,
   broken into pieces

175 g/6 oz caster sugar

2 eggs, separated

1 tsp vanilla essence

225 g/8 oz plain flour

1 tsp baking powder

125 ml/4 fl oz single cream

1 Preheat the oven to 150°C/300°F/Gas Mark 2. Grease a deep 23-cm/9-inch round cake tin with butter. Sprinkle the breadcrumbs into the tin and press them on to the base and sides.

2 Put the chocolate in a heatproof bowl set over a saucepan of gently simmering water. Stir over low heat until melted, then remove from the heat.

3 Cream the butter with the sugar until pale and fluffy. Beat in the egg yolks, one at a time, and add the vanilla.

4 Sift one-third of the flour with the baking powder, then beat into the egg mixture. Mix together the cream and melted chocolate, then beat one-third of this mixture into the egg mixture. Continue adding the flour and the chocolate mixture alternately, beating well after each addition.

5 Whisk the egg whites in a separate bowl until stiff peaks form. Fold the egg whites into the chocolate mixture.

6 Pour into the prepared tin and bake in the preheated oven for about 50 minutes, until a skewer inserted into the centre of the cake comes out clean. Turn the cake out on to a wire rack to cool before serving.

Chocolate Battenberg Cake

Although this cake requires care and patience to prepare, the result is well worth the effort.

25 mins · 25–30 mins

SERVES 8–10

INGREDIENTS

1 tsp sunflower oil, for oiling

175 g/6 oz butter or margarine, softened

175 g/6 oz caster sugar, plus extra for rolling and sprinkling

3 eggs, beaten

175 g/6 oz self-raising flour

1 tsp vanilla essence

55 g/2 oz plain chocolate

6 tbsp apricot jam

1 tbsp lemon juice

450 g/1 lb ready-made white marzipan

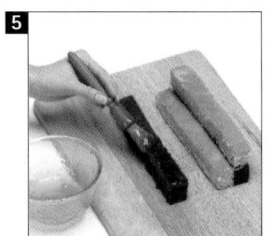

1 Preheat the oven to 190°C/375°F/ Gas Mark 5. Lightly oil and line a 26 x 20-cm/10 x 8-inch oblong baking tin with non-stick baking paper. Make a partition down the centre of the tin with the paper.

2 Cream the butter with the sugar until light and fluffy. Gradually beat in the eggs, adding a little flour after each addition. When all the eggs have been added stir in the remaining flour. Spoon half the mixture into a separate bowl.

3 Add the vanilla essence to one bowl with 1–2 tablespoons of cooled boiled water and mix to form a smooth dropping consistency. Set aside. Melt the chocolate in a heatproof bowl set over a saucepan of gently simmering water. Stir until smooth, then add to the second bowl together with 1–2 tablespoons of cooled boiled water and mix to achieve the same consistency as the vanilla mixture.

4 Spoon both mixtures into the prepared cake tin, placing the vanilla mixture down one side of the tin and the chocolate mixture down the other side. Smooth and level the top, then bake in the preheated oven for 25–30 minutes, or until a skewer inserted into the centre comes out clean. Remove and leave until cold before removing from the tin and discarding the lining paper.

5 Heat the jam and lemon juice, then rub through a sieve. Cut both cakes in half lengthways and trim to an even shape. Brush the sides with apricot glaze and place the cakes together to form a chequerboard effect. Press together firmly.

6 Roll the marzipan out on a lightly sugared work surface or cutting board to form a 30 x 23-cm/12 x 9-inch oblong. Brush the base of the cake with the apricot glaze and place in the centre of the marzipan. Brush all the sides of the cake, then bring the marzipan up and around the cake, pressing firmly into the sides and top. Use your forefinger and thumb to make a decorative edge down both sides of the cake. Mark a pattern down the centre and sprinkle with a little extra caster sugar.

Apricot & Cherry Cake

This chocolate cake has a really moist texture and is filled with plump apricots and cherries.

15 mins   50–60 mins

SERVES 8–10

INGREDIENTS

1 tsp sunflower oil, for oiling

175 g/6 oz ready-to-eat dried apricots, chopped

115 g/4 oz glacé cherries, chopped

175 g/6 oz butter, softened

175 g/6 oz caster sugar

115 g/4 oz plain chocolate

½ tsp almond essence

3 eggs, beaten

175 g/6 oz self-raising flour

25 g/1 oz ground almonds

4–6 white sugar lumps

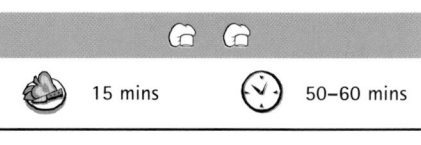
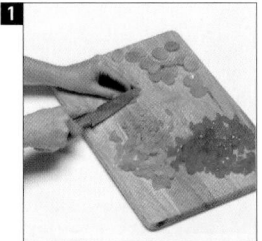

1 Preheat the oven to 180°C/350°F/Gas Mark 4. Lightly oil and line the base of a 20-cm/8-inch cake tin with non-stick baking paper. Ensure the apricots and cherries are chopped to an even size. Cream the butter with the sugar until light and fluffy. Melt the chocolate in a heatproof bowl set over a saucepan of gently simmering water, then add to the creamed mixture with the almond essence. Stir well.

2 Gradually beat in the eggs, a little at a time and beating well after each addition and adding a little flour after each addition. When all the eggs have been added, stir in the remaining flour with the ground almonds and the apricots. Mix to form a soft dropping consistency, adding 1–2 tablespoons of cooled boiled water, then stir in the glacé cherries.

3 Turn into the prepared cake tin and smooth the top. Lightly crush the sugar lumps and scatter over the top of the cake. Bake in the preheated oven for 50–60 minutes, or until a skewer inserted into the centre comes out clean. Remove from the oven and leave to cool in the tin before turning out on to a wire rack and discarding the lining paper. Store in an airtight container.

COOK'S TIP
Ground almonds not only help to keep this cake moist, but also improve its keeping qualities.

Date & Chocolate Cake

Moist and moreish, this fruity chocolate cake will prove to be a popular after-school snack.

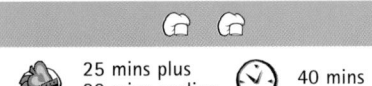

25 mins plus
20 mins cooling   40 mins

MAKES 18-CM/7-INCH CAKE

INGREDIENTS

115 g/4 oz unsalted butter, plus extra
  for greasing

115 g/4 oz self-raising flour, plus 1 tbsp
  extra for dusting

115 g/4 oz plain chocolate,
  broken into pieces

1 tbsp grenadine

1 tbsp golden syrup

4 tbsp caster sugar

2 large eggs

2 tbsp ground rice

1 tbsp icing sugar, to decorate

FILLING

115 g/4 oz chopped dried dates

1 tbsp lemon juice

1 tbsp orange juice

1 tbsp demerara sugar

55 g/2 oz chopped blanched almonds

2 tbsp apricot jam

1 Preheat the oven to 180°C/350°F/Gas Mark 4. Grease and flour 2 x 18-cm/7-inch sandwich tins. Put the chocolate, grenadine and syrup in a heatproof bowl set over a saucepan of gently simmering water. Stir over low heat until the chocolate has melted and the mixture is smooth. Remove from the heat and leave to cool.

2 Cream the butter and caster sugar together until pale and fluffy. Gradually beat in the eggs, then the cooled chocolate mixture.

3 Sift the flour into another bowl and stir in the ground rice. Fold the flour mixture into the creamed mixture.

4 Divide the cake mixture between the prepared tins and smooth the surface. Bake in the preheated oven for 20–25 minutes, until golden and firm to the touch. Turn out on to a wire rack to cool.

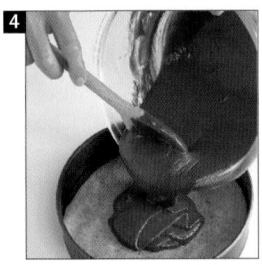

5 To make the filling, put all the ingredients into a saucepan and stir over low heat for 4–5 minutes, until fully incorporated. Remove from the heat, leave to cool, then use it to sandwich the cakes together. Dust the top of the cake with icing sugar to decorate.

Chocolate Tray Bake

This is a good family cake that keeps well. Baked in a shallow rectangular cake tin, the squares are ideal for serving with morning coffee.

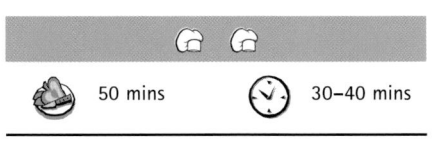

50 mins 30–40 mins

SERVES 15

INGREDIENTS

butter, for greasing

400 g/14 oz self-raising flour, sifted

3 tbsp cocoa powder, sifted

200 g/7 oz caster sugar

200 g/7 oz soft margarine

4 eggs, beaten

4 tbsp milk

55 g/2 oz milk chocolate chips

55 g/2 oz plain chocolate chips

55 g/2 oz white chocolate chips

icing sugar, for dusting

1 Preheat the oven to 180°C/350°F/ Gas Mark 4. Grease a 33 x 23 x 5-cm/ 13 x 9 x 2-inch cake tin with a little butter.

2 Place all of the ingredients except for the chocolate chips and icing sugar in a large mixing bowl and beat together until smooth.

3 Beat in the milk, plain and white chocolate chips.

4 Spoon the cake mixture into the prepared cake tin and smooth the top. Bake in the preheated oven for 30–40 minutes, until risen and springy to the touch. Leave to cool in the tin.

5 Once cool, dust with icing sugar. Cut into squares to serve.

VARIATION
For an attractive finish, cut thin strips of paper and lay in a criss-cross pattern on top of the cake. Dust with icing sugar, then remove the paper strips.

Chocolate Truffle Cake

Soft chocolate sponge topped with a rich chocolate truffle mixture makes a cake that chocoholics will die for.

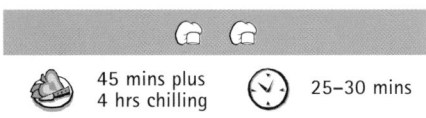

45 mins plus
4 hrs chilling

25–30 mins

SERVES 12

INGREDIENTS

75 g/2¾ oz butter plus extra for greasing

75 g/2¾ oz caster sugar

2 eggs, beaten lightly

75 g/2¾ oz self-raising flour

½ tsp baking powder

85 g/3 oz cocoa powder

50 g/1¾ oz ground almonds

TRUFFLE TOPPING

350 g/12 oz plain chocolate

115 g/4 oz butter

300 ml/10 fl oz double cream

70 g/2½ oz plain cake crumbs

3 tbsp dark rum

TO DECORATE

50 g/1¾ oz plain chocolate,
broken into pieces

cape gooseberries

1 Preheat the oven to 180°C/350°F/ Gas Mark 4. Lightly grease and base-line an 20-cm/8-inch round springform tin. Beat the butter and sugar together until light and fluffy. Gradually add the eggs, beating well after each addition.

2 Sift the flour, baking powder and cocoa together and fold into the cake mixture along with the ground almonds. Pour into the prepared tin and bake in the preheated oven for 20–25 minutes, or until springy to the touch. Leave the cake to cool slightly in the tin, then transfer to a wire rack to cool completely. Wash and dry the tin and return the cooled cake to the tin.

3 To make the topping, heat the chocolate, butter and cream in a heavy-based saucepan over low heat and stir until smooth. Cool, then chill for 30 minutes. Beat well with a wooden spoon and chill for an additional 30 minutes. Beat the mixture again, then add the cake crumbs and rum, beating until well combined. Spoon over the sponge cake and leave to chill for 3 hours.

4 Meanwhile, put the chocolate in a heatproof bowl set over a saucepan of gently simmering water until melted. Dip the cape gooseberries in the melted chocolate until partially covered. Leave to set on baking paper. Transfer the cake to a serving plate; decorate with the cape gooseberries.

Chocolate Truffle Torte

Chocolate and cream on a thin sponge base make this a wickedly rich cake – a good choice for a party.

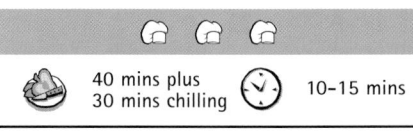
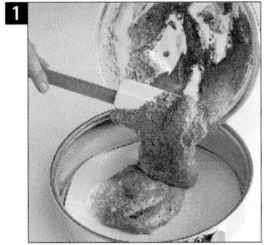

40 mins plus
30 mins chilling   10–15 mins

SERVES 10

INGREDIENTS

SPONGE
butter, for greasing

50 g/1¾ oz golden caster sugar

2 eggs

40 g/1¼ oz plain flour

25 g/1 oz cocoa powder

4 tbsp strong black coffee

2 tbsp brandy

TRUFFLE FILLING
600 ml/1 pint whipping cream

425 g/15 oz plain chocolate,
broken into pieces

TO DECORATE
cocoa powder

icing sugar

1 Preheat the oven to 220°C/425°F/Gas Mark 7. Grease and line a 23-cm/9-inch springform cake tin. Put the sugar and eggs in a heatproof bowl set over a saucepan of gently simmering water. Whisk together until pale and mousselike. Sift in the flour and cocoa and fold gently into the mixture. Pour into the prepared tin and bake in the oven for 7–10 minutes, or until risen and firm to the touch.

2 Transfer to a wire rack to cool. Wash and dry the tin and replace the cooled cake in the tin. Mix together the coffee and brandy and brush over the cake. To make the truffle filling, put the cream in a bowl and whisk until just holding very soft peaks. Put the chocolate in a heatproof bowl set over a saucepan of gently simmering water until melted. Carefully fold the cooled melted chocolate into the cream. Pour the chocolate mixture over the sponge. Chill until set.

3 To decorate the torte, sift cocoa over the top and remove carefully from the tin. Using strips of card or greaseproof paper, sift bands of icing sugar over the torte to create a striped pattern. Cut into slices with a hot knife, to serve.

COOK'S TIP
It is important that the cream is only whipped lightly because it thickens when the chocolate is added.

White Truffle Cake

A light white sponge, topped with a rich creamy-white chocolate truffle mixture, makes an out-of-this-world treat.

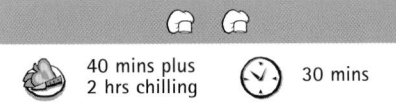

40 mins plus
2 hrs chilling

30 mins

SERVES 12

INGREDIENTS

butter, for greasing

50 g/1¾ oz white chocolate

2 eggs

50 g/1¾ oz caster sugar

70 g/2½ oz plain flour

TRUFFLE TOPPING

300 ml/10 fl oz double cream

350 g/12 oz white chocolate, broken into pieces

250 g/9 oz mascarpone cheese

TO DECORATE

350 g/12 oz plain, milk or white chocolate curls (see page 9)

cocoa powder, for dusting

1 Preheat the oven to 180°/350°F/Gas Mark 4. Grease and base-line a round 20-cm/8-inch springform cake tin. Put the white chocolate in a heatproof bowl set over a saucepan of gently simmering water until melted.

2 Whisk the eggs and caster sugar in a mixing bowl for 10 minutes, or until very light and foamy, and a trail is left when the whisk is dragged across the surface. Sift the flour and fold into the eggs with a metal spoon. Add the melted white chocolate. Pour the mixture into the tin and bake in the preheated oven for 25 minutes, or until springy to the touch. Leave to cool slightly, then transfer to a wire rack until completely cold. Return the cold cake to the tin.

3 To make the topping, place the cream in a saucepan and bring to the boil, stirring constantly. Leave to cool slightly, then add the white chocolate and stir until melted and combined. Remove from the heat and set aside until almost cool, stirring, then mix in the mascarpone cheese. Pour on top of the cake and leave to chill for 2 hours.

4 Decorate with chocolate curls (see page 9) and sprinkle with cocoa.

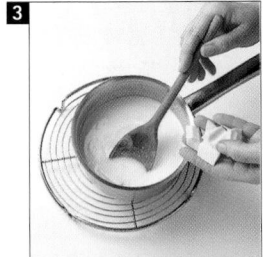

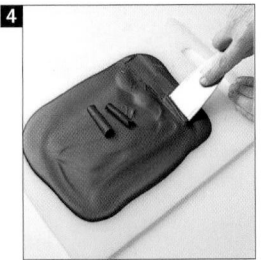

Chocolate Fudge Cake

This rich chocolate cake with soft fudge icing makes a perfect birthday cake for a chocolate lover.

25 mins plus 1 hr chilling

35–45 mins

SERVES 8

INGREDIENTS

175 g/6 oz butter, unsalted for preference, softened, plus extra for greasing

175 g/6 oz golden caster sugar

3 eggs, beaten

3 tbsp golden syrup

3 tbsp ground almonds

225 g/8 oz self-raising flour

pinch of salt

40 g/1½ oz cocoa powder

ICING

225 g/8 oz plain chocolate, broken into pieces

100 g/3½ oz dark muscovado sugar

225 g/8 oz butter, unsalted for preference, diced

5 tbsp evaporated milk

½ tsp vanilla essence

1 To make the icing, put the chocolate, sugar, butter, evaporated milk and vanilla essence in a heavy-based saucepan. Heat gently, stirring constantly, until melted. Pour into a bowl and leave to cool. Cover with clingfilm and leave to chill for 1 hour, or until spreadable. Preheat the oven to 180°C/350°F/Gas Mark 4. Grease and base-line 2 x 20-cm/8-inch cake tins.

2 To make the cake, put the butter and sugar in a bowl and beat until light and fluffy. Gradually beat in the eggs. Stir in the syrup and ground almonds. Sift the flour, salt and cocoa into a bowl, then fold it into the mixture. Add a little water if necessary to make a dropping consistency. Spoon the mixture into the prepared tins and bake in the oven for 30–35 minutes, until springy to the touch and a skewer inserted into the centre comes out clean.

3 Leave in the tins for 5 minutes, then transfer to wire racks to cool. When the cakes are completely cold, sandwich them together with half of the icing. Spread the remaining icing over the top and sides of the cake, swirling it to give a frosted appearance.

COOK'S TIP
If the cake mixture starts to curdle while you are adding the eggs, beat in a little of the flour.

Chocolate & Orange Cake

A classic favourite combination of flavours makes this cake ideal for a treat. Omit the icing if preferred, and sprinkle with icing sugar.

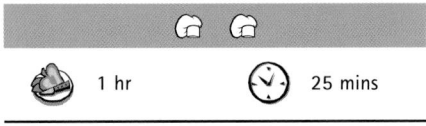

🍰 1 hr   🕙 25 mins

SERVES 8

INGREDIENTS

175 g/6 oz butter, plus extra for greasing

175 g/6 oz caster sugar

3 eggs, beaten

225 g/8 oz self-raising flour, sifted

2 tbsp cocoa powder, sifted

2 tbsp milk

3 tbsp orange juice

grated rind of ½ orange

ICING

175 g/6 oz icing sugar

2 tbsp orange juice

a little plain chocolate, to decorate

1 Preheat the oven to 190°C/375°F/Gas Mark 5. Lightly grease a 20-cm/8-inch deep round cake tin.

2 Beat the sugar and butter together in a bowl until light and fluffy. Gradually add the eggs, beating well after each addition. Carefully fold in the flour.

3 Divide the mixture in half. Add the cocoa and milk to half, stirring until well combined. Add the orange juice and rind to the other half.

4 Place tablespoonfuls of each mixture into the prepared tin and swirl together with a skewer, to create a marbled effect. Bake in the preheated oven for 25 minutes, or until the cake is springy to the touch. Leave to cool in the tin for a few minutes before transferring to a wire rack to cool completely.

5 To make the icing, sift the icing sugar into a mixing bowl and mix in enough of the orange juice to form a smooth icing. Spread the icing over the top of the cake. Melt the chocolate in a heatproof bowl set over a saucepan of gently simmering water. Pipe thin lines of chocolate over the icing, then feather the pattern by dragging a clean cocktail stick across the lines. You need to drag the cocktail stick alternately from left to right, then right to left to create the desired feathered effect.

VARIATION

Add 2 tablespoons rum or brandy to the chocolate mixture instead of the milk. The cake also works well when flavoured with grated lemon rind and juice instead of the orange.

Chocolate & Pear Sponge

Fresh pear slices are placed on top of a moist chocolate sponge, making an ingenious combination of flavours for a dessert or snack.

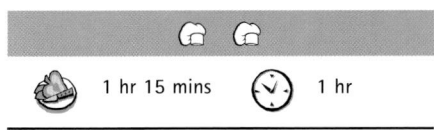

1 hr 15 mins   1 hr

SERVES 6

INGREDIENTS

175 g/6 oz butter, softened, plus extra
   for greasing

175 g/6 oz soft light brown sugar

3 eggs, beaten

175 g/6 oz self-raising flour

2 tbsp cocoa powder

2 tbsp milk

2 small pears, peeled, cored and sliced

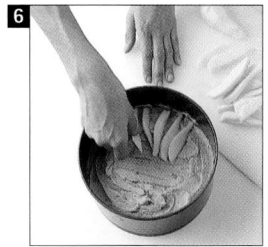

1 Preheat the oven to 180°C/350°F/Gas Mark 4. Grease a 20-cm/8-inch loose-based cake tin and line the base with baking paper.

2 In a large mixing bowl, cream together the butter and brown sugar until the mixture is pale and fluffy.

3 Gradually add the beaten eggs to the creamed mixture, beating well after each addition to make sure the mixture is blended smoothly and does not curdle.

4 Sift the flour and cocoa into the creamed mixture and fold in gently with the milk until combined.

5 Spoon the mixture into the prepared tin. Smooth the surface with the back of the spoon.

6 Lay the pear slices on top of the cake mixture, arranging them in a radiating pattern.

7 Bake in the preheated oven for about 1 hour, until the cake is just firm to the touch.

8 Leave the cake to cool in the tin, then transfer to a wire rack to cool completely before serving.

COOK'S TIP
Serve the cake with melted chocolate drizzled over the top for a delicious dessert.

Chocolate Fudge Gâteau

This gâteau is absolutely delicious and combines all of the most wickedly delectable ingredients.

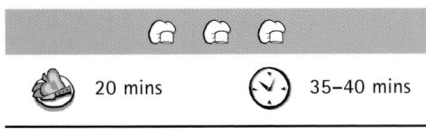

20 mins   35–40 mins

SERVES 10

INGREDIENTS

1 tsp sunflower oil, for oiling

85 g/3 oz plain chocolate

225 g/8 oz butter, softened

225 g/8 oz light muscovado sugar

4 eggs, beaten

225 g/8 oz self-raising flour

55 g/2 oz ground almonds

115 g/4 oz soft vanilla fudge, chopped small

ICING

175 g/6 oz butter, softened

280 g/10 oz icing sugar, sifted

3–4 tbsp single cream

55 g/2 oz light muscovado sugar

1 tbsp cocoa powder, sifted

TO DECORATE

55 g/2 oz plain chocolate, grated

cocoa-dusted truffles

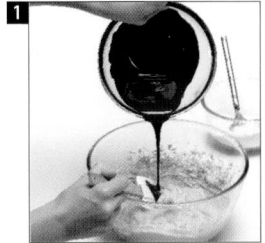  

1 Preheat the oven to 180°C/350°F/Gas Mark 4. Lightly oil and line the base of 2 x 20-cm/8-inch shallow cake tins with non-stick baking paper. Melt the chocolate in a heatproof bowl set over a saucepan of gently simmering water. Cream the butter and sugar together until light and fluffy, then gradually add the eggs, beating well between each addition and adding a little flour after each addition. When all the eggs have been added, stir in the melted chocolate and then the remaining flour and mix lightly together.

2 Stir in the ground almonds together with 1–2 tablespoons of cooled boiled water. Mix to form a soft dropping consistency. Stir in the fudge pieces, then divide between the 2 lined cake tins and smooth the tops. Bake in the preheated oven for 35–40 minutes, or until the tops spring back when touched lightly with a finger. Remove and leave to cool before turning out on to wire racks and discarding the lining paper. Leave until cold.

3 Beat the butter for the icing until soft and creamy, then gradually beat in the icing sugar, adding a little cream as the mixture becomes stiff. Add the muscovado sugar with the cocoa and stir lightly. Stir in sufficient of the remaining cream to give a soft spreadable icing.

4 Place the grated chocolate on a sheet of non-stick baking paper. Split the cakes in half horizontally and sandwich together with a third of the prepared icing. Spread another third around the sides, then roll the cake in the grated chocolate. Place on a serving plate. Spread the top with the remaining icing, piping rosettes around the outside edge for an attractive finish. Decorate with the truffles before serving the gâteau.

Praline & Fruit Gâteau

With its chocolate ganache and sponge base, this cake would be ideal to serve at a formal dinner party or a family gathering.

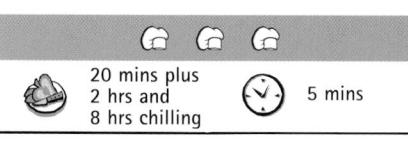

20 mins plus 2 hrs and 8 hrs chilling

5 mins

SERVES 8

INGREDIENTS

1 tsp sunflower oil, for oiling

600 ml/1 pint double cream

225 g/8 oz plain chocolate

6–8 tbsp Cointreau or Grand Marnier

115 g/4 oz granulated sugar

4 tbsp water

115 g/4 oz whole blanched almonds

300 g/10½ oz fresh fruit such as strawberries (sliced if large), blueberries and raspberries

12 trifle sponge cakes

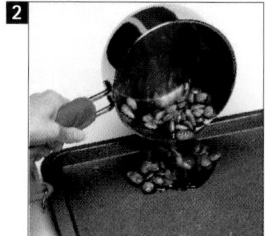

1 Lightly oil and line the base of a 900-g/2-lb loaf tin with non-stick baking paper. To make the ganache, pour 225 ml/8 fl oz of the double cream into a heavy-based saucepan. Break the chocolate into small pieces and add to the saucepan together with 2 tablespoons of the liqueur. Heat gently, stirring until the chocolate has melted and the mixture is smooth. Pour into a bowl, cool, then chill for 2 hours, or until set and firm. Whisk the mixture until light and fluffy.

2 Place the sugar with the water into a clean heavy-based saucepan and heat gently until the sugar has dissolved, stirring occasionally. Bring to the boil and boil steadily for 10 minutes, or until a light golden caramel forms. Remove from the heat and add the almonds. Pour on to a lightly oiled baking sheet and leave until cold and set. Place in 1 or 2 thick polythene bags and pound lightly with a rolling pin or mallet until crushed. Set aside. Clean the fruit and set aside.

3 Cut the trifle sponges into thin fingers and place a layer in the base of the loaf tin. Sprinkle with a little of the remaining liqueur. Set aside some pieces of praline for decoration, then scatter over half of the remaining crushed praline and spoon over half of the chocolate ganache. Set aside a few soft fruits for decoration, then top with half the prepared fruit. Repeat the layers again, finishing with a layer of sponge. Cover the top layer with

some clingfilm and weigh down with either clean weights or cans. Leave overnight in the refrigerator.

4 When ready to serve, remove the weights and clingfilm, then invert and turn out. Whip the remaining cream until soft peaks form, then use to cover the top and sides of the gâteau. Using a fork, make swirls over the cream and decorate with the remaining praline and fruit.

Mincemeat Cake

Use a mincemeat that is suitable for vegetarians so everyone can enjoy this fruity cake.

15 mins

1 hr 45 mins– 2 hrs

SERVES 10–12

INGREDIENTS

1 tsp sunflower oil, for oiling

225 g/8 oz butter or margarine, softened

225 g/8 oz light muscovado sugar

1 tbsp grated orange rind

4 eggs, beaten

300 g/10½ oz plain flour

85 g/3 oz plain chocolate

85 g/3 oz ground almonds

175 g/6 oz chopped dried dates

115 g/4 oz glacé cherries, chopped

115 g/4 oz glacé fruit, such as mandarins, pineapple and pears, chopped

400 g/14 oz mincemeat

175 g/6 oz whole pieces of glacé fruit, to decorate

1 Preheat the oven to 160°C/325°F/Gas Mark 3. Lightly oil and line the base and sides of a 23-cm/9-inch cake tin with non-stick baking paper. Cream the butter with the sugar and orange rind until light and fluffy. Gradually beat in the eggs, a little at a time, adding a little flour after each addition. Melt the chocolate in a heatproof bowl set over a saucepan of gently simmering water.

2 When all the eggs have been added, stir in the remaining flour together with the ground almonds and mix lightly, then add the chopped dates, glacé cherries and glacé fruit. Mix lightly.

3 Stir the melted chocolate until smooth, then add to the mixture and stir lightly. Finally, add in the mincemeat and mix well, then spoon into the prepared cake tin. Smooth the top.

4 Bake in the preheated oven for 25 minutes, or until the top is slightly firm. Remove and arrange the whole pieces of glacé fruit on top. Return to the oven and continue to bake for 1 hour 45 minutes–2 hours, or until cooked. (Cover the top with foil if the cake browns too quickly.) Remove and leave the cake to become cold before removing from the tin and discarding the lining paper. Store in an airtight container.

COOK'S TIP

When using melted chocolate in cakes, make sure that the chocolate is thoroughly melted and is cool before adding to the cake mixture.

Caribbean Chocolate Cake

Chocolate and spice are combined in this light cake with a stem ginger topping.

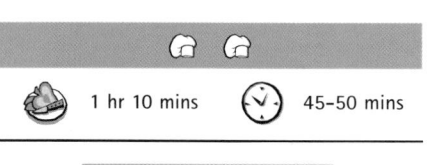

1 hr 10 mins   45–50 mins

MAKES 12 SQUARES

INGREDIENTS

115 g/4 oz butter, plus extra for greasing

250 g/9 oz self-raising flour

25 g/1 oz cocoa powder

1 tbsp ground ginger

1 tsp ground cinnamon

½ tsp bicarbonate of soda

140 g/5 oz light muscovado sugar

2 eggs

1½ tbsp golden syrup

1½ tbsp milk

TOPPING

6 pieces stem ginger

85 g/3 oz icing sugar

1 tbsp dark rum

a little syrup from the stem ginger jar

1 Preheat the oven to 160°C/325°F/Gas Mark 3. Grease and base-line a shallow 18-cm/7-inch square cake tin. Sift the flour, cocoa, ginger, cinnamon and bicarbonate of soda into a bowl. Rub in the butter, then stir in the sugar. Make a well in the centre.

2 Put the eggs in a bowl with the syrup and milk. Whisk together, then pour into the dry ingredients and beat until smooth and glossy. Spoon the mixture into the prepared tin and bake in the preheated oven for 45–50 minutes, until well risen and firm to the touch. Leave in the tin for 30 minutes, then transfer to a wire rack to cool completely.

3 For the topping, cut each piece of stem ginger into quarters and arrange on top of the cake. Sift the icing sugar into a bowl and stir in the rum and enough of the ginger syrup to make a smooth icing. Drizzle the icing over the cake and leave to set. Cut the cake into squares to serve.

COOK'S TIP
This cake benefits from being kept in an airtight container for a day before eating.

Chocolate & Walnut Cake

This walnut-studded chocolate cake has a creamy butter icing. It is perfect for entertaining because it can be made the day before.

🍰 1 hr   🕐 45 mins

SERVES 8

INGREDIENTS

2 tsp melted butter, for greasing

4 eggs

125 g/4½ oz caster sugar

75 g/2¾ oz plain chocolate, broken into pieces

125 g/4½ oz plain flour

1 tbsp cocoa powder

2 tbsp butter, melted

115 g/4 oz walnuts, chopped finely

ICING

75 g/2¾ oz plain chocolate

115 g/4 oz butter

175 g/6 oz icing sugar

2 tbsp milk

walnut halves, to decorate

1 Preheat the oven to 160°C/325°F/Gas Mark 3. Grease and line a deep, round, 18-cm/7-inch cake tin. Place the eggs and caster sugar in a bowl and whisk with an electric whisk for 10 minutes, or until foamy and a trail is left when the whisk is dragged across the surface. Put the chocolate in a heatproof bowl set over a saucepan of gently simmering water until melted.

2 Sift the flour and cocoa together and fold into the eggs and sugar with a spoon or a palette knife. Fold in the melted butter, melted chocolate and chopped walnuts. Pour into the tin and bake in the preheated oven for 30–35 minutes, or until springy to the touch.

3 Leave to cool in the tin for 5 minutes, then transfer to a wire rack and leave to cool completely.

4 To make the icing, melt the chocolate and leave to cool slightly. Beat together the butter, icing sugar and milk until the mixture is pale and fluffy. Whisk in the melted chocolate.

5 Cut the cake into 2 layers of equal thickness. Place the bottom half on a serving plate, spread with some of the icing and put the other half on top. Smooth the remaining icing over the top of the cake with a palette knife, swirling it slightly as you do so for a decorative effect. Decorate the cake with walnut halves, and serve.

German Chocolate Cake

This is a classic German cake, made with chocolate and hazelnuts, which is lovely served with a cup of coffee or tea.

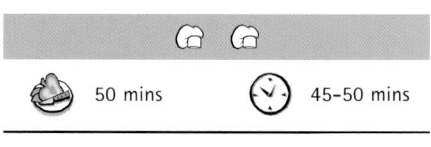

50 mins   45–50 mins

SERVES 8

INGREDIENTS

175 g/6 oz butter, unsalted for preference, softened, plus extra for greasing

plain flour, for dusting

225 g/8 oz dark muscovado sugar

140 g/5 oz self-raising flour

1 tbsp cocoa powder

1 tsp ground mixed spice

3 eggs, beaten

100 g/3½ oz ground hazelnuts

2 tbsp black coffee

sifted icing sugar, to decorate

1 Preheat the oven to 180°C/350°F/Gas Mark 4. Grease and flour a 19-cm/7½-in kugelhopf tin. Put the butter and sugar in a bowl and beat until light and fluffy. Sift the flour, cocoa and mixed spice into a bowl.

2 Beat the eggs into the creamed mixture, one at a time, adding 1 tablespoon of the flour mixture with the second and third eggs. Fold in the remaining flour, cocoa, ground hazelnuts and coffee.

3 Turn into the prepared tin and bake in the preheated oven for 45–50 minutes, until the cake springs back when the top is lightly pressed. Leave in the tin for 10 minutes, then turn out on to a wire rack to cool. Dust generously with icing sugar before serving.

COOK'S NOTE
A kugelhopf tin is a special fluted ring tin. If you do not have one, use a 23-cm/9-inch ring mould instead.

Chocolate Almond Cake

Chocolate and almonds complement each other perfectly in this delicious cake. Be warned though – one slice will never be enough!

2 hrs plus 30 mins chilling   40 mins

SERVES 8

INGREDIENTS

175 g/6 oz butter, plus extra for greasing

175 g/6 oz plain chocolate

100 g/3½ oz caster sugar

4 eggs, separated

¼ tsp cream of tartar

40 g/1½ oz self-raising flour

125 g/4½ oz ground almonds

1 tsp almond essence

TOPPING

125 g/4½ oz milk chocolate

2 tbsp butter

4 tbsp double cream

TO DECORATE

25 g/1 oz plain chocolate

2 tbsp toasted flaked almonds

1 Preheat the oven to 190°C/375°F/Gas Mark 5. Lightly grease and base-line a 23-cm/9-inch round springform tin. Break the chocolate into small pieces and place in a small saucepan with the butter. Heat gently, stirring until melted and well combined.

2 Place half of the caster sugar in a bowl with the egg yolks and whisk until pale and creamy. Add the melted chocolate and butter mixture, beating until well combined.

3 Sift the cream of tartar and flour together and fold into the chocolate mixture with the ground almonds and almond essence.

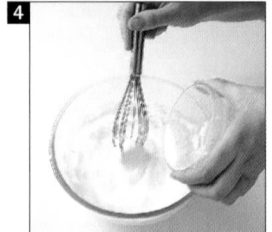

4 Whisk the egg whites in a bowl until soft peaks form. Add the remaining caster sugar and whisk for about 2 minutes by hand, or 45–60 seconds if using an electric whisk, until thick and glossy. Fold the egg whites into the chocolate mixture and spoon into the tin. Bake in the preheated oven for 40 minutes, until just springy to the touch. Leave to cool.

5 To make the topping, heat the ingredients in a heatproof bowl set over a saucepan of gently simmering water. Remove from the heat and beat for 2 minutes. Leave to chill for 30 minutes. Transfer the cake to a serving plate and spread with the topping. Melt the plain chocolate in a heatproof bowl set over a saucepan of gently simmering water. Scatter the cake with the flaked almonds and drizzle with the chocolate. Leave the topping to set for 2 hours before serving.

Family Chocolate Cake

An easy-to-make cake, ideal for a family treat. Keep the decoration simple – you could use a shop-bought icing or filling, if liked.

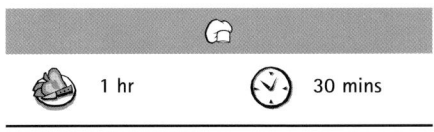

1 hr   30 mins

SERVES 8

INGREDIENTS

115 g/4 oz soft margarine, plus extra
   for greasing

100 g/3½ oz caster sugar

2 eggs

1 tbsp golden syrup

140 g/5 oz self-raising flour, sifted

2 tbsp cocoa powder, sifted

FILLING AND TOPPING

4 tbsp icing sugar, sifted

2 tbsp butter

100 g/3½ oz white or milk cooking
   chocolate

a little milk or white chocolate, for melting

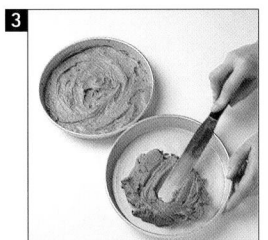

1 Preheat the oven to 190°C/375°F/Gas Mark 5. Lightly grease 2 x 18-cm/7-inch sandwich tins.

2 Place all of the ingredients for the cake in a large mixing bowl and beat with an electric whisk until smooth.

3 Divide the mixture between the prepared tins and smooth the tops. Bake in the oven for 20 minutes, or until springy to the touch. Leave to cool for a few minutes in the tins, then transfer to a wire rack to cool completely.

4 To make the filling, beat the icing sugar and butter together until light and fluffy. Melt the cooking chocolate in a heatproof bowl set over a saucepan of gently simmering water. Beat half into the icing mixture and use to sandwich the cakes together.

5 Spread the remaining melted cooking chocolate over the top of the cake. In a separate heatproof bowl, melt a little milk or white chocolate (see step 4). Pipe circles of contrasting melted milk or white chocolate and feather into the cooking chocolate by dragging lines through the circles using a clean cocktail stick. Leave to set before serving.

COOK'S TIP
Ensure that you eat this cake on the day of baking, because it does not keep well.

Chocolate Slab Cake

This chocolate slab cake gets its moist texture from the soured cream, which is stirred into the beaten mixture.

55 mins | 50 mins

SERVES 4

INGREDIENTS

200 g/7 oz butter, plus extra for greasing

100 g/3½ oz continental plain chocolate, broken into pieces

75 ml/2½ fl oz water

350 g/12 oz plain flour

2 tsp baking powder

250 g/9 oz soft light brown sugar

75 ml/2½ fl oz soured cream

2 eggs, beaten

ICING

200 g/7 oz plain chocolate

6 tbsp water

3 tbsp single cream

1 tbsp butter, chilled

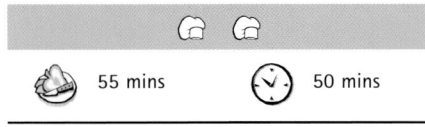

1 Preheat the oven to 190°C/375°F/Gas Mark 5. Grease a 33 x 20-cm/13 x 8-inch square cake tin and line the bottom with baking paper. Melt the butter and chocolate with the water in a saucepan over low heat, stirring frequently.

2 Sift the flour and baking powder into a mixing bowl and stir in the sugar.

3 Pour the hot chocolate liquid into the bowl and then beat well until all of the ingredients are evenly mixed. Stir in the soured cream, followed by the eggs.

4 Pour the mixture into the cake tin and bake in the preheated oven for 40–45 minutes, until springy to the touch.

5 Leave the cake to cool slightly in the tin before turning it out on to a wire rack. Leave to cool completely.

6 To make the icing, melt the chocolate with the water in a saucepan over very low heat, stir in the cream and remove from the heat. Stir in the chilled butter, then pour the icing over the cooled cake, using a palette knife to spread it evenly over the top of the cake.

COOK'S TIP

Put the cake on the wire rack to ice it, and place a large baking sheet underneath to catch any drips.

Chilled Rum Chocolate Cake

Apart from melting the chocolate, this delicious refrigerator cake requires no cooking at all!

10 mins
plus 8 hrs
soaking/chilling

2 mins

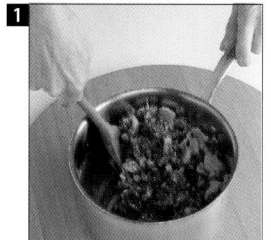

SERVES 10–12

INGREDIENTS

2 tbsp dark rum

50 g/1¾ oz raisins

85 g/3 oz butter, unsalted for preference

3 tbsp golden syrup

175 g/6 oz plain chocolate

225 g/8 oz digestive biscuits, crushed

60 g/2¼ oz glacé cherries, halved

50 g/1¾ oz macadamia nuts, chopped coarsely

grated rind of 1 orange

TOPPING

55 g/2 oz plain chocolate, broken into pieces

2 tbsp butter, unsalted for preference

a little white chocolate, to decorate

1 Put the rum and raisins in a bowl and leave to soak for several hours, or preferably overnight. Line a 450-g/1-lb loaf tin with clingfilm. Put the butter, golden syrup and chocolate in a saucepan and heat gently until the chocolate has melted. Remove from the heat and stir in the raisins, crushed digestive biscuits, cherries, nuts and grated orange rind.

2 Transfer the mixture to the prepared tin. Leave to chill until firm. Turn the cake out on to a serving plate and remove the clingfilm.

3 To make the topping, put the plain chocolate and butter in a heatproof bowl set over a saucepan of gently simmering water and heat until melted. Stir until smooth, then spread over the top and sides of the cake. In a separate bowl, melt the white chocolate and drizzle over the top of the cake. Leave to chill until the topping has set. Serve cut into thin slices.

COOK'S TIP
If you omit the chocolate topping, this cake is perfect for cutting into small pieces to serve with coffee after dinner.

No-Bake Refrigerator Cake

Ideal for children to make, with help to melt the chocolate, this cake needs no baking and is quickly prepared – but requires chilling overnight.

20 mins plus
12 hrs chilling

5–8 mins

MAKES 22 x 11–CM/8½ x 4¼–INCH CAKE

INGREDIENTS

200 g/7 oz butter, unsalted for preference, diced

225 g/8 oz plain chocolate, broken into pieces

70 g/2½ oz chopped glacé cherries

50 g/1¾ oz chopped walnuts

12 rectangular plain chocolate biscuits

1 Line a 450-g/1-lb loaf tin with greaseproof paper or baking paper.

2 Put the butter and chocolate in a heatproof bowl set over a saucepan of gently simmering water. Stir constantly over low heat until they have melted and the mixture is smooth. Remove from the heat and cool slightly.

3 In a separate bowl, mix together the cherries and walnuts. Spoon one-third of the chocolate mixture into the prepared tin, cover with a layer of biscuits and top with half the cherries and walnuts. Make further layers, ending with the chocolate mixture. Cover with clingfilm and leave to chill in the refrigerator for at least 12 hours. When chilled, turn the cake out on to a serving dish.

Chocolate Cake with Syrup

An intensely flavoured chocolate cake that is particularly good served slightly warm, with soured cream, as a dessert.

15 mins   50 mins

SERVES 12

INGREDIENTS

115 g/4 oz unsalted butter,
  plus extra for greasing

225 g/8 oz plain chocolate,
  broken into pieces

1 tbsp strong black coffee

4 large eggs

2 egg yolks

115 g/4 oz golden caster sugar

40 g/1½ oz plain flour

2 tsp ground cinnamon

85 g/3 oz ground almonds

chocolate-covered coffee beans,
  to decorate

SYRUP

300 ml/10 fl oz strong black coffee

115 g/4 oz golden caster sugar

1 cinnamon stick

1 Preheat the oven to 190°C/375°F/Gas Mark 5. Grease and line the bottom of a deep 20-cm/8-inch round cake tin. Place the chocolate, butter and coffee in a heatproof bowl and set over a saucepan of gently simmering water until melted. Stir to blend, then remove from the heat and leave to cool slightly.

2 Place the whole eggs, egg yolks and sugar in a separate bowl and whisk together until thick and pale. Sift the flour and cinnamon over the egg mixture. Add the almonds and the chocolate mixture and fold in carefully. Spoon the mixture into the prepared tin. Bake in the preheated oven for 35 minutes, or until the tip of a knife inserted into the centre comes out clean. Leave to cool slightly before turning out on to a serving plate.

3 Meanwhile, make the syrup. Place the coffee, sugar and cinnamon stick in a heavy-based saucepan and heat gently, stirring, until the sugar has dissolved. Increase the heat and boil for 5 minutes, or until reduced and thickened slightly. Keep warm. Pierce the surface of the cake with a cocktail stick, then drizzle over half the coffee syrup. Decorate with chocolate-covered coffee beans and serve, cut into wedges, with the remaining coffee syrup.

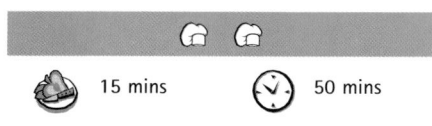

Chocolate & Mango Layer

Canned peaches can be used instead of mangoes for this deliciously moist cake if you prefer.

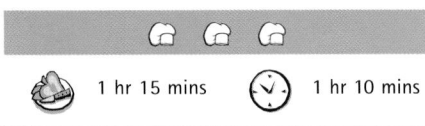

1 hr 15 mins   1 hr 10 mins

SERVES 12

INGREDIENTS

butter, for greasing

55 g/2 oz cocoa powder

150 ml/5 fl oz boiling water

6 large eggs

275 g/9½ oz caster sugar

350 g/12 oz self-raising flour

800 g/1 lb 12 oz canned mangoes

1 tsp cornflour

400 ml/14 fl oz double cream

75 g/2¾ oz grated plain chocolate

1 Preheat the oven to 160°C/325°F/Gas Mark 3. Grease a deep 23-cm/9-inch round cake tin and base-line with baking paper.

2 Place the cocoa in a small bowl and gradually add the boiling water; blend to form a smooth paste.

3 Place the eggs and caster sugar in a mixing bowl and whisk until the mixture is very thick and creamy. Fold in the cocoa mixture. Sift the flour and fold into the cake mixture.

4 Pour the mixture into the tin and smooth the top. Bake in the preheated oven for about 1 hour, or until springy to the touch.

5 Leave the cake to cool in the tin for a few minutes, then turn out and cool completely on a wire rack. Peel off the lining paper and cut the cake into 3 layers.

6 Drain the mangoes, reserving the juice, and put a quarter of them in a food processor and blend until smooth. Mix the cornflour with about 3 tablespoons of the mango juice to form a smooth paste. Add to the blended mangoes. Transfer to a small pan and heat gently, stirring until the paste thickens. Leave to cool.

7 Chop the remaining mango. Whip the cream and reserve about one quarter. Fold the mango into the remaining cream and use to sandwich the layers of cake together. Place on a serving plate. Spread some of the remaining cream around the side of the cake. Press the grated chocolate lightly into the cream. Spread the mango paste over the centre and pipe cream rosettes to form a decorative edge.

Devil's Food Cake

This classic melt-in-the-mouth chocolate cake, is given a tangy citrus-flavoured icing in this recipe.

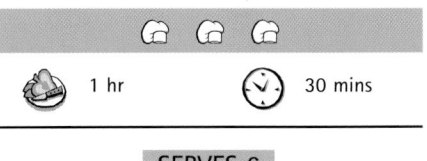

🍰 1 hr   🕐 30 mins

SERVES 6

I N G R E D I E N T S

butter, for greasing

100 g/3½ oz plain chocolate, broken into pieces

325 g/11½ oz self-raising flour

1 tsp bicarbonate of soda

225 g/8 oz butter

500 g/1 lb 2 oz soft light brown sugar

1 tsp vanilla essence

3 eggs

125 ml/4 fl oz buttermilk

200 ml/7 fl oz boiling water

I C I N G

225 g/8 oz caster sugar

2 egg whites

1 tbsp lemon juice

3 tbsp orange juice

candied orange rind, to decorate

1 Preheat the oven to 190°C/375°F/Gas Mark 5. Grease and base-line 2 x 20-cm/8-inch sandwich tins. Put the chocolate in a heatproof bowl set over a saucepan of gently simmering water until melted. Sift the flour and bicarbonate of soda together.

2 Beat the butter and sugar in a bowl until pale and fluffy. Beat in the vanilla essence and the eggs one at a time, beating well after each addition. Add a little flour if the mixture starts to curdle.

3 Fold the melted chocolate into the mixture until well blended. Gradually fold in the remaining flour, then stir in the buttermilk and boiling water.

4 Divide the mixture between the tins and smooth the tops. Bake in the preheated oven for 30 minutes, until springy to the touch. Leave the cakes to cool in the tins for 5 minutes, then transfer to a wire rack to cool completely.

5 Place the icing ingredients in a large heatproof bowl set over a saucepan of gently simmering water. Whisk until thickened and forming soft peaks. Remove from the heat and whisk until the mixture is cool.

6 Sandwich the 2 cakes together with some icing. Spread the remainder over the sides and top of the cake, swirling it as you do so. Decorate with candied orange rind.

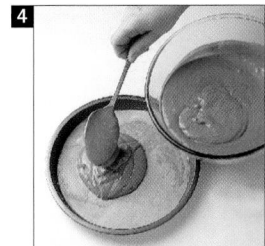

Chocolate & Pineapple Cake

Decorated with thick yogurt and canned pineapple, this is a low-fat cake, but it is by no means lacking in flavour.

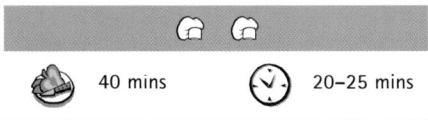

🍰 40 mins   🕐 20–25 mins

SERVES 9

I N G R E D I E N T S

175 g/6 oz low-fat spread, plus extra
   for greasing

175 g/6 oz caster sugar

115 g/4 oz self-raising flour, sifted

3 tbsp cocoa powder, sifted

1½ tsp baking powder

2 eggs

225 g/8 oz canned pineapple pieces in
   natural juice

125 ml/4 fl oz low-fat thick natural yogurt

about 1 tbsp icing sugar

grated chocolate, to decorate

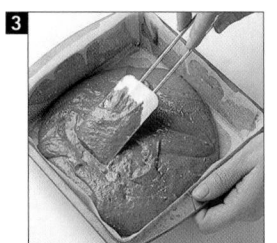

1 Preheat the oven to 190°C/375°F/Gas Mark 5. Lightly grease a 20-cm/ 8-inch square cake tin with low-fat spread.

2 Place the low-fat spread, caster sugar, flour, cocoa, baking powder and eggs in a large mixing bowl. Beat with a wooden spoon or electric whisk until smooth.

3 Pour the mixture into the prepared tin and smooth the surface. Bake in the preheated oven for 20–25 minutes, or until springy to the touch. Leave to cool slightly in the tin before transferring to a wire rack to cool completely.

4 Drain the pineapple, chop the pineapple pieces and drain again. Reserve some of the pineapple pieces for the decoration, then stir the remainder into the yogurt and sweeten to taste with icing sugar.

5 Spread the pineapple and yogurt mixture over the cake and decorate with the reserved pineapple pieces. Sprinkle with the grated chocolate.

Raspberry Dessert Cake

The raspberries in this cake give it a fresh tangy flavour. Serve with fresh raspberries and whipped cream.

35 mins   40–50 mins

SERVES 8–10

INGREDIENTS

225 g/8 oz butter, plus extra for greasing

250 g/9 oz plain chocolate

1 tbsp strong black coffee

5 medium eggs

90 g/3¼ oz golden caster sugar

90 g/3¼ oz plain flour, sifted

1 tsp ground cinnamon

150 g/5½ oz fresh raspberries

icing sugar, for dusting

TO SERVE

fresh raspberries

whipped cream

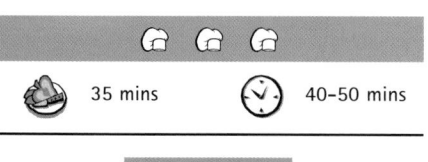

1 Preheat the oven to 160°C/325°F/ Gas Mark 3. Grease and base-line a 23-cm/9-inch cake tin. Put the chocolate, butter and coffee in a heatproof bowl set over a saucepan of gently simmering water and heat until melted. Stir and leave to cool slightly.

2 Put the eggs and sugar in a bowl and beat until thick and pale. Gently fold in the chocolate. Sift the flour and cinnamon into a bowl, then fold into the chocolate mixture. Pour into the prepared tin and sprinkle the raspberries evenly over the top.

3 Bake in the preheated oven for 35–45 minutes, until the cake is well risen and springy to the touch. Leave to cool in the tin for 15 minutes before turning out on to a large plate. Dust with icing sugar and serve with raspberries and cream.

VARIATION
Frozen raspberries may be used if fresh are not available. Thaw thoroughly and drain off any excess juice before using.

Chocolate Tropical Fruit Cake

This cake is ideal for a summer lunch party, an informal tea or an elegant dinner party. You can, of course, vary the fruit.

25 mins plus 2 hrs chilling

20–25 mins

SERVES 10

INGREDIENTS

1 tsp sunflower oil, for oiling

85 g/3 oz plain flour

2 tbsp cocoa powder

3 large eggs

115 g/4 oz caster sugar

40 g/1½ oz unsalted butter, melted

1 small mango, peeled, stoned and chopped

1 papaya, seeded, stoned and chopped

1 kiwi, peeled and sliced

fresh coconut shavings, to decorate

ICING

225 g/8 oz plain chocolate

225 ml/8 fl oz double cream

1 tbsp framboise or brandy

40 g/1½ oz toasted chopped hazelnuts

1 Preheat the oven to 190°C/375°F/Gas Mark 5. Sift the flour and cocoa together twice and set aside. Lightly oil and line the base of a 23-cm/9-inch cake tin with non-stick baking paper.

2 Place the eggs and sugar in a heatproof bowl set over a saucepan of gently simmering water. Whisk until very thick and creamy and doubled in volume. Remove the bowl from the saucepan and continue to whisk until the mixture has cooled.

3 Gently stir in the sifted flour and then the butter in a figure-of-eight action, taking care not to over-mix. Pour the mixture into the prepared tin and bake in the centre of the preheated oven for 20–25 minutes, or until the top springs back when touched lightly with a finger. Remove from the oven and leave to cool for 10 minutes. Turn out on to a wire rack and discard the lining paper. Leave until cold before decorating.

4 Meanwhile, make the icing. Break the chocolate into small pieces and place in a heavy-based saucepan together with the cream and framboise. Heat gently, stirring frequently until smooth. Pour into a bowl, large enough to accommodate a whisk. Leave to cool, then chill until completely cold. When ready to use, whisk the icing until light and fluffy.

5 Split the cooled cake in half and sandwich together with one-third of the icing, pressing the halves lightly together.

6 Spread half of the remaining icing over the sides of the cake and press on the nuts. Spread the remaining icing over the top, swirling to give a decorative effect. Decorate with the chopped fruit and serve. Store in the refrigerator and use within 2–3 days.

Chocolate & Prune Gâteau

Using prunes in place of any butter may sound a little strange but in fact it works extremely well, giving a very moist, rich cake.

20 mins plus 2 hrs marinating

30–35 mins

SERVES 10–12

INGREDIENTS

1 tsp sunflower oil, for oiling

225 g/8 oz ready-to-eat dried prunes

4 tbsp brandy

175 g/6 oz caster sugar

3 eggs, beaten

85 g/3 oz plain chocolate

115 g/4 oz ground almonds

55 g/2 oz plain flour, sifted

1 tsp baking powder, sifted

TOPPING

115 g/4 oz plain chocolate

1 tbsp butter

1 tbsp golden syrup

150 ml/5 fl oz double cream

dragees, to decorate

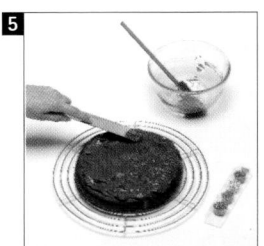

1 Preheat the oven to 190°C/375°F/Gas Mark 5. Lightly oil and line the base of a 23-cm/9-inch cake tin. Snip the prunes into small pieces and place in a bowl. Pour over the brandy and leave for up to 2 hours, or until the brandy has been absorbed. Place in a food processor or blender and process to form a purée.

2 Place the prune purée in the bowl of a free-standing mixer or in a bowl set over a saucepan of gently simmering water. Add the sugar and whisk until well incorporated. Add the eggs and continue to whisk until the mixture is very thick and creamy. (Remove from the heat, if applicable, and continue to whisk until cool.)

3 Melt the chocolate in a heatproof bowl set over a saucepan of gently simmering water. Stir until smooth and gently mix into the mixture. Add the ground almonds, flour and baking powder, then, stirring very lightly, mix until thoroughly incorporated, adding 2–3 tablespoons of cooled boiled water to give a soft dropping consistency. Turn into the prepared cake tin, tap lightly on the work surface to remove any air bubbles and level the surface. Bake in the preheated oven for 30–35 minutes, or until the top springs back when touched lightly with a clean finger. Remove from

the oven and leave to cool. Remove from the tin and discard the lining paper.

4 Break the chocolate into small pieces and place in a heavy-based saucepan and add the butter, syrup and cream. Heat gently, stirring frequently until the mixture is smooth. Remove from the heat and leave to cool until thickened, stirring occasionally.

5 Spoon the cooled chocolate icing over the top and sides of the cake, swirling to give a decorative effect. Leave to set before decorating with the dragees.

Chocolate Passion Cake

What could be nicer than passion cake with added chocolate? Rich and moist, this cake is fabulous with afternoon tea.

55 mins   55 mins

SERVES 6

INGREDIENTS

butter, for greasing

5 eggs

125 g/4½ oz caster sugar

175 g/6 oz plain flour

40 g/1½ oz cocoa powder

2 carrots, peeled, grated finely
   and squeezed until dry

50 g/1¾ oz chopped walnuts

2 tbsp sunflower oil

350 g/12 oz medium-fat cream cheese

175 g/6 oz icing sugar

175 g/6 oz milk or plain
   chocolate, melted

1 Preheat the oven to 190°C/375°F/Gas Mark 5. Lightly grease and base-line a 20-cm/8-inch deep round cake tin.

2 Place the eggs and sugar in a large mixing bowl set over a saucepan of gently simmering water and whisk until very thick. Lift the whisk up and let the mixture drizzle back – it will leave a trail for a few seconds when thick enough.

3 Remove the bowl from the heat. Sift the flour and cocoa into the bowl and carefully fold in. Fold in the grated carrots, walnuts and oil until they are just combined.

4 Pour into the prepared tin and bake in the preheated oven for 45 minutes. Leave the cake to cool slightly, then turn out on to a wire rack to cool completely.

5 Beat together the cream cheese and icing sugar until combined. Beat in the melted chocolate. Split the cake in half and sandwich together again with half of the chocolate mixture. Cover the top of the cake with the remainder of the chocolate mixture, swirling it with a knife. Leave to chill, or serve at once.

COOK'S TIP
The undecorated cake can be frozen for up to 2 months. Thaw at room temperature for 3 hours or overnight in the refrigerator.

Marble Cake

This cake looks impressive but is easy to make. Just drag a skewer through two contrasting cake mixtures to create a marbled effect.

45 mins   60–70 mins

MAKES 10 SLICES

INGREDIENTS

225 g/8 oz butter, softened, plus extra for greasing

55 g/2 oz plain chocolate

1 tbsp strong black coffee

280 g/10 oz self-raising flour

1 tsp baking powder

225 g/8 oz golden caster sugar

4 eggs, beaten

50 g/1¾ oz ground almonds

2 tbsp milk

1 tsp vanilla essence

ICING

125 g/4½ oz plain chocolate

2 tbsp butter

2 tbsp water

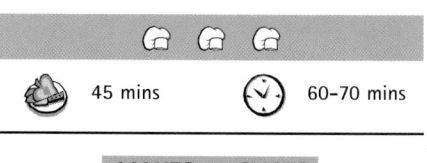
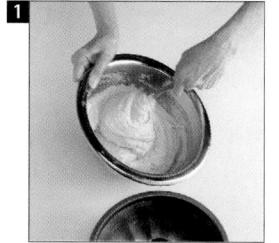
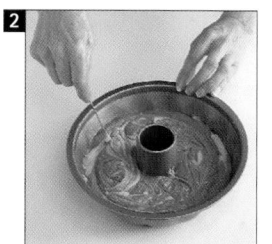

1 Preheat the oven to 180°C/350°F/Gas Mark 4. Grease a 1.7-litre/3-pint ring mould. Put the chocolate and coffee in a heatproof bowl set over a saucepan of gently simmering water. Heat until melted. Leave to cool. Sift the flour and baking powder into a bowl. Add the butter, sugar, eggs, ground almonds and milk. Beat well until smooth.

2 Transfer one half of the mixture to another bowl and stir in the vanilla essence. Stir the cooled soft chocolate into the other half of the mixture. Place spoonfuls of the 2 mixtures alternately into the ring mould, then drag a skewer through to create a marbled effect. Smooth the top. Bake in the preheated oven for 50–60 minutes, until risen and a skewer inserted into the centre comes out clean. Leave in the mould for 5 minutes, then turn out on to a wire rack to cool.

3 To make the icing, put the chocolate, butter and water into a heatproof bowl set over a saucepan of simmering water. Heat until melted. Stir and pour over the cake, working quickly to coat the top and sides. Leave to set before serving.

COOK'S TIP
If you prefer a plain cake, omit the icing and simply dust the top of the cake with sifted icing sugar.

Orange Marble Cake

Separate chocolate and orange cake mixtures are combined in a ring mould to achieve the marbled effect in this light sponge.

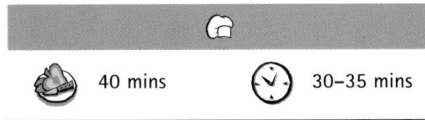

40 mins   30–35 mins

SERVES 8

INGREDIENTS

175 g/6 oz butter, softened, plus extra for greasing

175 g/6 oz caster sugar

3 eggs, beaten

175 g/6 oz self-raising flour, sifted

25 g/1 oz cocoa powder, sifted

5–6 tbsp orange juice

grated rind of 1 orange

1 Preheat the oven to 180°C/350°F/ Gas Mark 4. Lightly grease a 25-cm/ 10-inch ring mould.

2 In a mixing bowl, cream together the butter and sugar with an electric whisk for about 5 minutes.

3 Add the beaten eggs a little at a time, whisking well after each addition.

4 Using a metal spoon, fold the flour into the creamed mixture carefully, then spoon half of the mixture into a separate mixing bowl.

5 Fold the cocoa and half of the orange juice into the mixture in one of the bowls and mix gently.

6 Fold the remaining orange juice and orange rind into the mixture in the other bowl and mix gently.

7 Place alternate spoonfuls of each mixture around the mould, then drag a skewer through them to create a marbled effect.

8 Bake in the preheated oven for 30–35 minutes, until well risen and a skewer inserted into the centre comes out clean.

9 Leave the cake to cool in the mould before turning out on to a wire rack.

VARIATION

For a richer chocolate flavour, add 40 g/1½ oz chocolate chips to the cocoa mixture.

Moist Chocolate Cake

The sweetness of whipped marshmallow icing complements the mouthwatering flavour of this moist plain chocolate sponge.

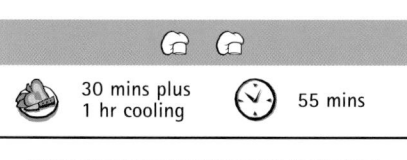

30 mins plus
1 hr cooling

55 mins

MAKES 15-CM/6-INCH CAKE

I N G R E D I E N T S

90 g/3¼ oz butter, unsalted for preference, plus extra for greasing

225 g/8 oz caster sugar

½ tsp vanilla essence

2 eggs, beaten lightly

85 g/3 oz plain chocolate, broken into pieces

75 ml/2½ fl oz buttermilk

175 g/6 oz self-raising flour

½ tsp bicarbonate of soda

pinch of salt

55 g/2oz milk chocolate, grated, to decorate

I C I N G

175 g/6 oz white marshmallows

1 tbsp milk

2 egg whites

2 tbsp caster sugar

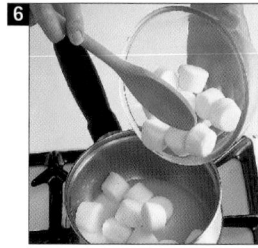

1 Preheat the oven to 160°C/325°F/Gas Mark 3. Grease an 850 ml/1½-pint pudding basin. Cream the butter, sugar and vanilla together until pale and fluffy, then gradually beat in the eggs.

2 Melt the plain chocolate in a heatproof bowl over a saucepan of gently simmering water. Stir in the buttermilk gradually, until well combined. Remove the saucepan from the heat and leave to cool slightly.

3 Sift the flour, bicarbonate of soda and salt into a separate bowl.

4 Add the chocolate mixture alternately with the flour mixture to the creamed mixture, a little at a time. Spoon the cake mixture into the pudding basin and smooth the surface.

5 Bake in the preheated oven for about 50 minutes, until a skewer inserted into the centre of the cake comes out clean. Turn out on to a wire rack to cool.

6 Meanwhile, make the icing. Put the marshmallows and milk in a small saucepan and heat very gently until the marshmallows have melted. Remove the saucepan from the heat and leave to cool.

7 Whisk the egg whites until soft peaks form, then add the sugar and continue whisking, until stiff peaks form. Fold the egg white into the cooled marshmallow mixture and set aside for 10 minutes.

8 When the cake is cool, cover the top and sides with the marshmallow icing. Top with grated milk chocolate.

Rippled Chocolate Gâteau

The icing on this gâteau has a wonderfully crunchy texture because it includes muscovado sugar, which does not completely dissolve.

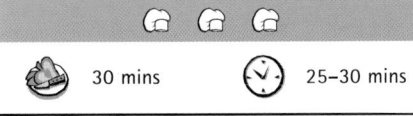

30 mins   25–30 mins

SERVES 10

INGREDIENTS

1 tsp sunflower oil, for oiling

175 g/6 oz butter or margarine, softened

175 g/6 oz caster sugar

1 tsp vanilla essence

3 eggs, beaten

175 g/6 oz self-raising flour

25 g/1 oz ground almonds

25 g/1 oz plain chocolate

ICING

225 g/8 oz plain chocolate, broken into pieces

5 tbsp butter

2 tbsp maple or golden syrup

70 g/2½ oz dark muscovado sugar

TO DECORATE

40 g/1½ oz flaked almonds, toasted

chocolate shavings

1 Preheat the oven to 190°C/375°F/Gas Mark 5. Oil and line the bases of 2 x 18-cm/7-inch shallow cake tins with baking paper. Cream the butter, sugar and vanilla until light and fluffy. Add the eggs a little at a time, adding a little flour after each addition. When all the eggs have been added, stir in the remaining flour and the ground almonds. Add 1–2 tablespoons of cooled boiled water and mix lightly to form a smooth dropping consistency.

2 Melt the 25 g/1 oz of chocolate in a heatproof bowl set over a saucepan of gently simmering water. Stir until smooth, then pour over the cake mixture.

Gently mix in a figure-of-eight action. Take care not to over-mix or the rippled effect will be lost. Divide between the 2 cake tins and smooth the tops. Tap lightly on the work surface to remove any air bubbles.

3 Bake in the preheated oven for 25–30 minutes, or until golden and the top springs back when touched lightly with a finger. Remove from the oven and leave for 10 minutes before transferring to a wire rack and discarding the lining paper. Leave until cold before icing.

4 To make the icing, break the chocolate into small pieces and place in a heavy-based saucepan and add the butter and maple syrup. Heat gently, stirring frequently, until the chocolate has melted and the mixture is smooth. Add the sugar and stir gently until the mixture is well blended. Leave until cool and beginning to thicken. Beat occasionally during this time.

5 Split each cake in half and use one-third of the icing to sandwich the 4 layers together. Spread an additional third round the sides of the cake and roll in the flaked almonds. Spoon the remaining icing on top and spread with a swirling action to give a decorative effect. Sprinkle with the chocolate shavings to serve. Store in an airtight container.

Chocolate Chiffon Cake

This delicious cake has a thick layer of crushed praline in the centre and on the top which provides a delicious crunch.

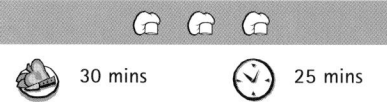

30 mins   25 mins

SERVES 8–10

INGREDIENTS

1 tsp sunflower oil, for oiling

3 large eggs, separated

175 g/6 oz caster sugar

4 tbsp sunflower oil

40 g/1½ oz plain chocolate

1 tbsp cocoa powder

85 g/3 oz plain flour

1 tsp cream of tartar

PRALINE

115 g/4 oz granulated sugar

50 ml/2 fl oz water

85 g/3 oz blanched almonds

ICING AND DECORATION

115 g/4 oz butter or margarine, softened

225 g/8 oz icing sugar, sifted

1 tbsp cocoa powder, sifted

1–2 tbsp strong black coffee

55 g/2 oz toasted flaked almonds

few whole almonds

1 Preheat the oven to 180°C/350°F/Gas Mark 4. Lightly oil and line the bases of 2 x 18-cm/7-inch shallow cake tins and 1 x baking sheet.

2 To make the praline, heat the sugar and water together in a heavy-based saucepan, stirring frequently until the sugar has dissolved. Bring to the boil and boil steadily for 10 minutes, or until a golden caramel is formed. Remove from the heat and add the almonds. Pour the

praline onto the oiled baking sheet and leave until cold. Place in a polythene bag and pound with a rolling pin until crushed.

3 Place the egg yolks with the sugar in a heatproof bowl set over a saucepan of gently simmering water. Whisk until very thick and creamy and a trail is left when the whisk is dragged across the surface. (Alternatively, whisk the egg yolks and sugar in the bowl of a free-standing mixer.) Remove from the heat and whisk until cool.

4 Whisk in the sunflower oil together with 2 tablespoons of cooled boiled water. Melt the chocolate in a heatproof bowl set over a saucepan of gently simmering water. Gently stir in the melted chocolate. Sift the cocoa with the flour and cream of tartar and stir into the egg mixture. Whisk the egg whites until stiff peaks form, then fold into the mixture and stir lightly. Spoon into the prepared cake

tins and bake in the preheated oven for 25 minutes or until the top springs back when touched lightly with a finger. Remove and leave to cool before removing from the tins and discarding the lining paper. Leave until cold.

5 To make the icing, cream the butter until soft, then gradually beat in the icing sugar together with the cocoa and the strong black coffee to give a soft spreading consistency. Spread over one cake and scatter with most of the crushed praline. Place the second cake on top and press lightly together.

6 Spread half the remaining icing round the sides of the cake, then roll in the flaked almonds and transfer to a serving plate. Spread the remaining icing over the top and sprinkle with the remaining praline. Arrange a few whole almonds on top and serve.

Orange Mousse Cake

With a plain chocolate sponge sandwiched together with a light, creamy orange mousse, this spectacular cake is irresistible.

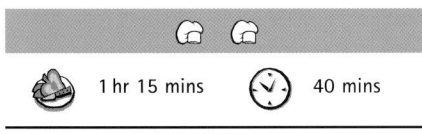

1 hr 15 mins   40 mins

SERVES 12

INGREDIENTS

175 g/6 oz butter, plus extra for greasing

175 g/6 oz caster sugar

4 eggs, beaten lightly

1 tbsp cocoa powder

250 g/9 oz self-raising flour

50 g/1¾ oz plain, orange-flavoured chocolate, melted

ORANGE MOUSSE

2 eggs, separated

4 tbsp caster sugar

200 ml/7 fl oz freshly squeezed orange juice

2 tsp powdered gelatine

3 tbsp water

300 ml/10 fl oz double cream

peeled orange slices, to decorate

1 Preheat the oven to 180°C/350°F/Gas Mark 4. Grease and base-line a 20-cm/8-inch springform cake tin. Beat the butter and sugar in a bowl until light and fluffy. Gradually add the eggs, beating well after each addition. Sift the cocoa and flour together and fold into the mixture. Fold in the chocolate.

2 Pour into the prepared tin and smooth the top. Bake in the preheated oven for 40 minutes, or until springy to the touch. Leave the cake to cool for 5 minutes in the tin, then turn out and cool completely on a wire rack.

3 Meanwhile, make the mousse. Beat the egg yolks and sugar until light. Whisk in the orange juice. Sprinkle the gelatine over the water in a small bowl and leave it to go spongy. Place over a saucepan of hot water and stir until the gelatine has dissolved. Stir into the mousse.

4 Whip the cream until holding its shape, reserve a little for decoration and fold the rest into the mousse. Whisk the egg whites until soft peaks form, then fold in. Leave in a cool place until starting to set, stirring occasionally.

5 Halve the cold cake and place one half in the tin. Pour in the mousse and press the second half on top. Chill until set. Transfer to a dish, pipe cream rosettes on the top and arrange orange slices in the centre.

Chocolate Yogurt Cake

Adding yogurt to the cake mixture gives the finished cake a deliciously moist texture.

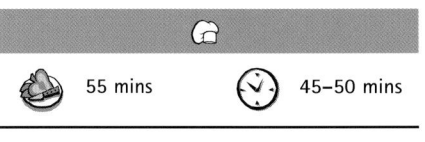

55 mins   45–50 mins

SERVES 8

INGREDIENTS

butter, for greasing

150 ml/5 fl oz vegetable oil

150 ml/5 fl oz whole milk natural yogurt

225 g/8 oz soft light brown sugar

3 eggs, beaten

140 g/5 oz self-raising wholemeal flour

140 g/5 oz self-raising flour, sifted

2 tbsp unsweetened cocoa

1 tsp bicarbonate of soda

50 g/1¾ oz plain chocolate, broken into pieces

FILLING AND TOPPING

150 ml/5 fl oz whole milk natural yogurt

150 ml/5 fl oz double cream

140 g/5 oz fresh soft fruit, such as strawberries or raspberries

1 Preheat the oven to 180°C/350°F/Gas Mark 4. Grease a deep 23-cm/9-inch round cake tin and line the bottom with baking paper.

2 Place the oil, yogurt, sugar and beaten eggs in a large mixing bowl and beat together until well combined. Sift the flours, cocoa and bicarbonate of soda together and beat into the bowl until well combined. Put the chocolate in a heatproof bowl set over a saucepan of gently simmering water until melted. Beat the melted chocolate and stir into the mixture.

3 Pour into the prepared tin and bake in the preheated oven for 45–50 minutes, or until a fine skewer inserted into the centre of the cake comes out clean. Leave the cake to cool in the tin for 5 minutes, then turn out on to a wire rack to cool completely. When cold, split the cake into 3 layers.

4 To make the filling, place the yogurt and cream in a large mixing bowl and whisk well until the mixture stands in soft peaks.

5 Place one layer of cake on to a serving plate and spread with some of the cream. Top with a little of the fruit (slicing larger fruit such as strawberries). Repeat with the next layer. Top with the final layer of cake and spread with the rest of the cream. Arrange more fruit on top and cut the cake into wedges to serve.

Lemon & Yogurt Cake

This cake is served with a rich chocolate sauce but it can be also be served with cream or a fruit coulis.

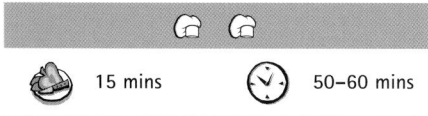

15 mins

50–60 mins

SERVES 10

INGREDIENTS

1 tsp sunflower oil, for oiling

175 g/6 oz butter or margarine, softened

175 g/6 oz caster sugar

1 tbsp finely grated lemon rind, preferably from an unwaxed lemon

3 eggs, separated

225 g/8 oz self-raising flour

35 g/1¼ oz ground almonds

125 ml/4 fl oz natural yogurt

85 g/3 oz white chocolate, grated

1½–2 tbsp lemon juice

3 tbsp icing sugar, sifted

SAUCE

175 g/6 oz plain chocolate

1 tbsp butter

125 ml/4 fl oz milk

2 tbsp natural yogurt

1 Preheat the oven to 160°C/325°F/Gas Mark 3. Lightly oil and line the base of a 23-cm/9-inch cake tin with non-stick baking paper. Cream the butter with the sugar and lemon rind until light and fluffy.

2 Add the egg yolks one at a time, beating well between each addition and adding a little flour after each addition. When all the egg yolks have been added, stir in the remaining flour together with the almonds and yogurt and 1–2 tablespoons cooled boiled water. Mix to form a soft dropping consistency. Add the grated chocolate and stir in carefully.

3 Whisk the egg whites until stiff but not dry, then stir into the cake mixture. Turn into the prepared tin and bake on the middle shelf of the preheated oven for 50–60 minutes, or until it is well risen and the top feels firm when touched with a finger.

4 Meanwhile, blend the lemon juice with the icing sugar until smooth. Once the cake is cooked, remove from the oven and pour the lemon icing over the top. Leave until cold before removing from the tin and discarding the lining paper.

5 To make the sauce, put all the ingredients except the yogurt in a heavy-based saucepan and heat gently, stirring until smooth. Stir in the yogurt and serve with the cake.

Chocolate Blackcurrant Cake

You can vary the chocolate and fruit in this cake. Try using grated milk or plain chocolate and use either summer berries or redcurrants.

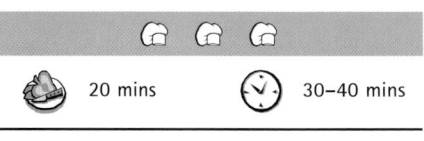

20 mins   30–40 mins

SERVES 10

INGREDIENTS

1 tsp sunflower oil, for oiling

175 g/6 oz butter, softened

175 g/6 oz sugar

3 eggs, separated

175 g/6 oz self-raising flour

150 ml/5 fl oz buttermilk

50 g/1¾ oz ground almonds

55 g/2 oz white chocolate, grated

TOPPING

200 ml/7 fl oz double cream

2 tbsp framboise liqueur or Cointreau

300 g/10 oz fresh ripe blackcurrants, or other berries of your choice, cleaned

55 g/2 oz toasted flaked almonds

chocolate curls, to decorate (see page 9)

1 Preheat the oven to 180°C/350°F/Gas Mark 4. Lightly oil and line the base and sides of a 23-cm/9-inch cake tin. Beat the butter and sugar until light and creamy, then beat in the egg yolks one at a time, adding a little flour after each yolk. When all the yolks have been added, stir in the remaining flour together with the buttermilk and stir gently until well mixed.

2 Gradually stir in the ground almonds and then the grated chocolate. Whisk the egg whites until soft peaks form, then fold into the mixture a spoonful at a time. Turn into the prepared tin and bake in the preheated oven for 30–40 minutes, or until the top feels firm and springs back when touched lightly with a finger. Remove from

the oven and leave in the tin until almost cold before turning out and discarding the lining paper. Leave until cold.

3 Whip the cream with the liqueur. Place the flaked almonds on to a large sheet of non-stick baking paper. Use

half the cream to cover the sides of the cake, then roll in the nuts. Spread the remaining cream on top, then decorate with the fruit and chocolate curls. Store, lightly covered, in the refrigerator.

Mississippi Mud Cake

Mud cake is a dense chocolate cake, perfect for a special occasion. Keep your portions small as it is very rich.

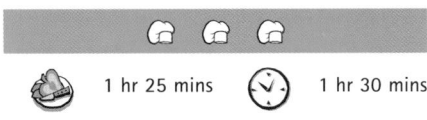

1 hr 25 mins   1 hr 30 mins

SERVES 16

INGREDIENTS

250 g/9 oz butter, cut into pieces, plus extra for greasing

150 g/5½ oz plain chocolate, broken into pieces

400 g/14 oz golden caster sugar

250 ml/9 fl oz hot water

3 tbsp Tia Maria or brandy

325 g/11½ oz plain flour

1 tsp baking powder

25 g/1 oz cocoa powder

2 eggs, beaten

1 Preheat the oven to 160°C/325°F/ Gas Mark 3. Grease and base-line a 20-cm/8-inch round cake tin. Put the butter, chocolate, sugar, hot water and Tia Maria in a heavy-based saucepan over low heat and heat gently until the chocolate melts.

2 Stir until smooth, transfer the mixture to a large bowl and leave to cool for 15 minutes. Sift in the flour, baking powder and cocoa and whisk in, then whisk in the eggs. Pour the mixture into the prepared tin.

3 Bake in the preheated oven for 1½ hours, or until risen and firm to the touch. Leave in the tin for 30 minutes, then turn out and remove the paper. Place on a wire rack to cool completely. Decorate with chocolate curls and serve with raspberries.

COOK'S TIP
Cover the cake loosely with foil if it starts to over-brown.

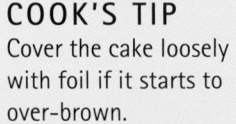

Layered Meringue Gateau

Surprisingly easy, but somewhat time-consuming to make, this magnificent gâteau makes a wonderfully impressive dinner-party dessert.

 1 hr 40 mins   6 hrs, or overnight

SERVES 6

I N G R E D I E N T S

6 egg whites

175 g/6 oz caster sugar

175 g/6 oz icing sugar

2 tbsp cornflour

F I L L I N G

225 ml/8 fl oz double cream

140 g/5 oz plain chocolate, broken into pieces

4 tsp dark rum

T O   D E C O R A T E

150 ml/5 fl oz double cream

4 tsp caster sugar

1–2 tsp cocoa powder, for dusting

1 Preheat the oven to 120°C/250°F/Gas Mark ½. Prepare 5 sheets of baking paper by drawing an 18-cm/7-inch circle on each; use to line baking sheets.

2 Whisk the egg whites until soft peaks form. Mix the sugars and cornflour together and sift it into the egg whites, a little at a time, whisking constantly until firm peaks form.

3 Spoon the meringue mixture into a piping bag fitted with a round nozzle. Starting from the centre, pipe 5 spirals, measuring 18 cm/7 inches, on each of the prepared pieces of baking paper.

4 Bake in a preheated oven, at the lowest possible temperature with the door slightly ajar, for 6 hours, or overnight.

5 After baking, carefully peel the meringue spirals from the baking paper and place on wire racks to cool.

6 To make the filling, pour the cream into a small saucepan and place over low heat. Add the chocolate and stir until melted. Remove the saucepan from the heat and beat the mixture with an electric whisk. Beat in the dark rum, then cover with clingfilm and chill overnight or for as long as the meringues are baking.

7 To assemble the gâteau, beat the filling with an electric whisk until thick and smooth. Place 3 of the meringue layers on the work surface and spread the filling over them. Stack the 3 layers, one on top of the other, and place an uncovered meringue layer on top. Crush the fifth meringue into crumbs and set aside.

8 To make the decoration, whisk the cream with the sugar until thick. Carefully spread the mixture over the top of the gâteau. Sprinkle the meringue crumbs over the cream and dust the top of the gâteau with cocoa. Serve within 2 hours.

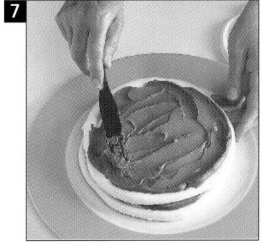

Mocha Walnut Meringue

Walnuts, plain chocolate, coffee and brandy complement each other perfectly in this easy-to-make gâteau.

50 mins   1 hr 35 mins

SERVES 8

INGREDIENTS

MERINGUE

4 egg whites

225 g/8 oz golden caster sugar

125 g/4¼ oz walnuts, chopped finely

FILLING

175 g/6 oz plain chocolate

3 tbsp butter, unsalted for preference

2 tbsp strong black coffee

2 tbsp brandy

175 ml/6 fl oz whipping cream

icing sugar, or a little plain chocolate,
    if liked, to decorate

1 Preheat the oven to 140°C/275°F/ Gas Mark 1. Line 2 baking sheets with baking paper. Put the egg whites into a large bowl and whisk until stiff peaks form, then whisk in half the sugar. Add the walnuts to the remaining sugar and mix together. Fold into the meringue mixture.

2 Spread the meringue in 2 x 20-cm/ 8-inch circles on the prepared baking sheets. Bake in the oven for about 1½ hours, until completely dry. Leave to cool in the oven.

3 To make the filling, break the chocolate into pieces and put into a bowl with the butter, coffee and brandy. Set over a saucepan of gently simmering water until melted. Stir and leave to cool.

Put the cream in a bowl and whip lightly, then stir in the chocolate mixture. Sandwich the meringue circles together with the chocolate cream. Dust with icing sugar or drizzle with a little plain chocolate, melted in a heatproof bowl over a saucepan of gently simmering water, just before serving.

VARIATION
Instead of walnuts, chopped toasted hazelnuts or ground almonds may be added to the meringue.

Mocha Layer Cake

Chocolate cake and a creamy coffee-flavoured filling are combined in this delicious mocha cake, perfect for any occasion.

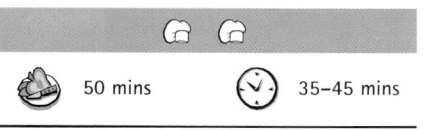

50 mins   35–45 mins

SERVES 8

INGREDIENTS

butter, for greasing

250 g/9 oz self-raising flour

¼ tsp baking powder

4 tbsp cocoa powder

115 g/4 oz caster sugar

2 eggs

2 tbsp golden syrup

150 ml/5 fl oz sunflower oil

150 ml/5 fl oz milk

FILLING

1 tsp instant coffee powder

1 tbsp boiling water

300 ml/10 fl oz double cream

2 tbsp icing sugar

TO DECORATE

50 g/1¾ oz chocolate shavings

chocolate caraque (see page 9)

icing sugar, for dusting

1 Preheat the oven to 180°C/350°F/Gas Mark 4. Lightly grease 3 x 18-cm/ 7-inch sandwich tins.

2 Sift the flour, baking powder and cocoa into a large mixing bowl. Stir in the sugar. Make a well in the centre and stir in the eggs, syrup, oil and milk. Beat with a wooden spoon, gradually mixing in the dry ingredients to make a smooth mixture. Divide the mixture between the prepared tins.

3 Bake in the preheated oven for 35–45 minutes, or until springy to the touch. Leave to cool in the tins for 5 minutes, then turn out on to a wire rack to cool completely.

4 Dissolve the instant coffee in the boiling water and place in a bowl with the cream and icing sugar. Whip until the cream is just holding its shape. Use half of the cream to sandwich the 3 cakes together. Spread the remaining cream over the top and sides of the cake. Lightly press the chocolate shavings into the cream around the edge of the cake.

5 Transfer to a serving plate. Lay the caraque over the top of the cake. Cut a few thin strips of baking paper and place on top of the caraque. Dust lightly with icing sugar, then carefully remove the paper. Serve.

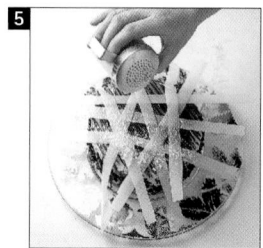

Black & White Chocolate Cake

This splendidly dramatic-looking cake should be eaten within 2 or 3 days – if it will last that long!

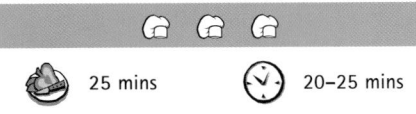

🍰 25 mins   🕐 20–25 mins

SERVES 12–14

INGREDIENTS

1 tsp sunflower oil, for oiling

3 large eggs

115 g/4 oz caster sugar

115 g/4 oz plain flour, sifted

55 g/2 oz white chocolate, grated

white and plain chocolate curls to decorate

ICING

175 g/6 oz plain chocolate

4 tbsp unsalted butter

1 tbsp golden syrup

2 tbsp brandy or Cointreau

4 tbsp raspberry jam

2 tbsp lemon juice

1 Preheat the oven to 190°C/375°F/ Gas Mark 5. Lightly oil and base-line a 23-cm/9-inch shallow cake or flan tin. Place the eggs and sugar in a heatproof bowl set over a saucepan of gently simmering water. Whisk until very thick and creamy and doubled in volume. Remove the bowl from the saucepan and continue to whisk until the mixture is cool.

2 Add the chocolate and very gently stir into the mixture, then stir in the sifted flour. Spoon into the lined cake or flan tin and tap lightly on the work surface to level. Bake in the preheated oven for 20–25 minutes, or until golden and the top springs back when touched lightly with a finger. Remove from the oven and leave to cool before turning out on to a wire rack and discarding the lining paper. Leave until cold.

3 Break the chocolate into small pieces and place in a heavy-based saucepan. Add the butter, syrup and brandy and heat gently, stirring frequently until the mixture is smooth and blended. Leave to cool, stirring occasionally until the mixture has thickened.

4 Heat the jam and lemon juice together until blended, then rub through a sieve and use to coat the top and sides of the cake. Spoon the cooled and thickened icing over the top and sides and decorate with white and plain chocolate curls.

COOK'S TIP

With this cake it is very important to ensure that the egg and sugar mixture is very thick and creamy.

Chocolate Brownie Cake

This moist cake, full of dried cranberries and toasted flaked almonds, and with an intense chocolate flavour, is a taste of chocolate heaven.

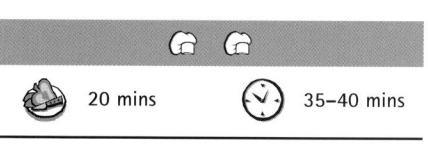

🍰 20 mins 🕐 35–40 mins

SERVES 10

INGREDIENTS

200 g/7 oz butter

115 g/4 oz plain chocolate

280 g/10 oz granulated sugar

115 g/4 oz light muscovado sugar

4 eggs

175 g/6 oz plain flour

1 tsp vanilla essence

pinch of salt

75 g/2¾ oz dried cranberries

75 g/2¾ oz flaked almonds, toasted

almonds, to decorate

FOR THE ICING

115 g/4 oz plain chocolate

2 tbsp butter

225 g/8 oz icing sugar

3–4 tbsp milk

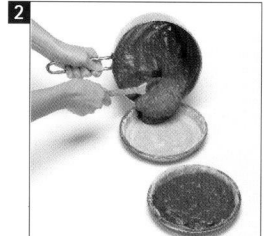

1 Preheat the oven to 180°C/350°F/Gas Mark 4 and base-line 2 x 18-cm/7-inch shallow cake tins with non-stick baking paper. Place the butter in a heavy-based saucepan, break the chocolate into small pieces and add to the saucepan. Heat gently, stirring frequently until the mixture has melted. Remove from the heat and stir until smooth. Add the sugars, stir well, then leave to cool for 10 minutes.

2 Beat the eggs, then gradually add to the cooled mixture, beating well after each addition. Stir in the flour, vanilla essence and salt. Stir in the cranberries and nuts, mix, then divide between the prepared cake tins.

3 Bake in the preheated oven for 25–30 minutes, or until the tops feel firm but spring back when touched lightly with a finger. Remove from the oven and leave to cool. Turn out on to a wire rack and leave until cold. Discard the lining paper.

4 To make the icing, melt the chocolate and butter in a heavy-based saucepan and stir until smooth. Gradually beat in the icing sugar with sufficient milk to give a smooth spreading consistency. Use to sandwich the two cakes together, then spread the top and sides with the remaining icing, swirling the top to give a decorative effect. Arrange a few almonds on top. Leave the icing to set before serving the cake.

Sunken Drunken Cake

This dense rich cake contains no flour and will sink and crack slightly when you take it out of the oven. Leave until cold before decorating.

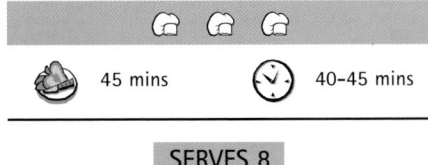

🍰 45 mins   🕐 40–45 mins

SERVES 8

INGREDIENTS

115 g/4 oz butter, diced, plus extra for greasing

flour, for dusting

140 g/5 oz plain chocolate, broken into pieces

2 tbsp brandy

175 g/6 oz golden caster sugar

6 eggs, separated

125 g/4½ oz ground almonds

400 ml/14 fl oz whipped cream, to decorate

ground cinnamon, for dusting

1 Preheat the oven to 160°C/325°F/ Gas Mark 3. Grease a 23-cm/9-inch springform cake tin and line the base with non-stick baking paper. Dust the sides with flour. Place the chocolate and brandy in a heatproof bowl and set over a saucepan of gently simmering water until the chocolate has melted. Stir until smooth, then leave to cool slightly.

2 Place the butter in a separate bowl, add the sugar and beat until light and creamy. Add the egg yolks, one at a time, beating well after each addition, then stir in the melted chocolate. Add the ground almonds and beat in. Place the egg whites in a large, spotlessly clean, greasefree bowl and whisk until stiff but not dry. Stir 2 tablespoons of the whisked egg whites into the chocolate mixture, then carefully fold in the remainder.

3 Spoon the mixture into the prepared tin and bake in the preheated oven for 35–40 minutes, or until well risen and just firm to the touch. Leave to stand in the tin to cool completely. When cold, remove the cake from the tin and peel away the lining paper, then transfer to a serving plate. Spoon whipped cream over the top to decorate and dust with a little cinnamon. Serve, cut into slices.

COOK'S TIP

This cake is very fragile and benefits from being chilled for at least 10 minutes in the refrigerator before serving. Any uneaten cake should be covered with foil and stored in the refrigerator.

Double Chocolate Gâteau

A chocolate sponge layered with white chocolate cream and covered in plain chocolate icing. Ideal as a celebration cake or a dessert.

1 hr plus
2 hrs chilling

55–65 mins

SERVES 10

INGREDIENTS

225 g/8 oz butter, softened, plus extra for greasing

225 g/8 oz golden caster sugar

4 eggs, beaten

225 g/8 oz self-raising flour

55 g/2 oz cocoa powder

a little milk (optional)

FILLING

250 ml/9 fl oz whipping cream

225 g/8 oz white chocolate, broken into pieces

ICING

350 g/12 oz plain chocolate, broken into pieces

115 g/4 oz butter

100 ml/3½ fl oz double cream

TO DECORATE

115 g/4 oz plain chocolate curls (see page 9)

2 tsp icing sugar and cocoa powder, mixed

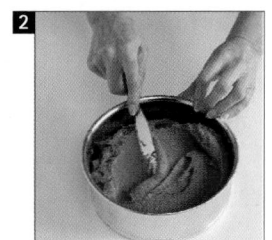

1 To make the filling, put the cream in a saucepan and heat to almost boiling. Put the white chocolate in a food processor and chop. With the motor running, pour the hot cream through the feed tube and process for 10–15 seconds until smooth. Transfer to a bowl, leave to cool, then cover with clingfilm and chill in the refrigerator for 2 hours, or until firm. Whisk until just starting to hold soft peaks.

2 Preheat the oven to 180°C/350°F/ Gas Mark 4. Grease and base-line a 20-cm/8-inch deep round cake tin. Put the butter and sugar in a bowl and beat until light and fluffy. Gradually beat in the eggs. Sift the flour and cocoa into a bowl, then fold into the mixture, adding milk, if necessary, to make a dropping consistency. Spoon into the prepared tin and bake in the oven for 45–50 minutes, until a skewer inserted into the centre comes out clean. Leave to stand in the tin for 5 minutes. Transfer to a wire rack to cool completely.

3 To make the icing, put the chocolate in a heatproof bowl set over a saucepan of gently simmering water until melted. Stir in the butter and cream. Leave to cool, stirring occasionally until the mixture is a thick spreading consistency. Slice the cake horizontally into 3 layers. Sandwich the layers together with the white chocolate filling. Cover the top and sides of the cake with the icing and arrange the chocolate curls over the top. Sift the mixed icing sugar and cocoa over the cake.

Chocolate Cognac Torte

A crumbly ginger chocolate case topped with velvety smooth chocolate brandy cream makes this a blissful treat, ideal if served with coffee.

40 mins plus 2 hrs chilling

5 mins

SERVES 12

INGREDIENTS

CASE

250 g/9 oz gingernut biscuits

75 g/2¾ oz plain chocolate

85 g/3 oz butter

FILLING

225 g/8 oz plain chocolate

250 g/9 oz mascarpone cheese

2 eggs, separated

3 tbsp brandy

300 ml/10 fl oz double cream

4 tbsp caster sugar

TO DECORATE

100 ml/3½ fl oz double cream

chocolate-coated coffee beans

1 Crush the gingernut biscuits in a bag with a rolling pin or in a food processor. Melt the chocolate and butter together and pour over the biscuits. Mix well, then use to line the base and sides of a 23-cm/9-inch loose-based fluted flan tin or springform tin. Leave to chill while preparing the filling.

2 To make the filling, melt the chocolate in a bowl set over boiling water. Remove from the heat and beat in the mascarpone cheese, egg yolks and brandy.

3 Lightly whip the cream until just holding its shape and fold in the chocolate mixture.

4 Whisk the egg whites in a greasefree bowl until standing in soft peaks.

Add the caster sugar a little at a time and whisk until thick and glossy. Fold into the chocolate mixture, in 2 batches, until just mixed.

5 Spoon the mixture into the prepared gingernut case and leave to chill for at least 2 hours. Carefully transfer to a serving plate. To decorate, whip the cream and pipe on to the torte and add the chocolate-coated coffee beans.

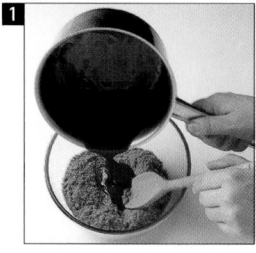  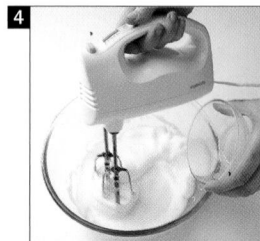

VARIATION
If chocolate-coated coffee beans are unavailable, use chocolate-coated raisins to decorate.

Almond & Apricot Torte

This torte is very moist, so it is best stored, lightly covered, in the refrigerator. It should be eaten within 2 days.

25 mins | 30 mins

SERVES 10

INGREDIENTS

1 tsp sunflower oil, for oiling

115 g/4 oz butter, softened

115 g/4 oz caster sugar

1 tbsp finely grated orange rind

1 tbsp finely grated lemon rind

4 eggs, separated

55 g/2 oz self-raising flour

115 g/4 oz ground almonds

115 g/4 oz ricotta cheese

2 tbsp Amaretto

175–225 g/6–8 oz plain chocolate, grated

4 tbsp apricot jam

1 tbsp lemon juice

few fresh apricots, halved and stoned, or ready-to-eat dried apricots, to decorate

TO SERVE

mascarpone cheese

2 tbsp Amaretto

summer berries or extra fresh apricots

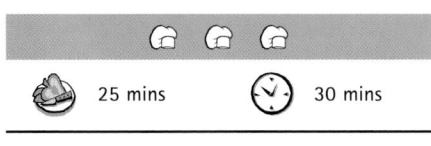
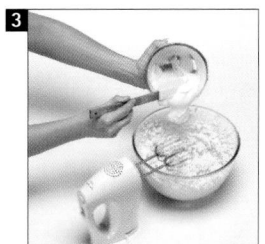

1 Preheat the oven to 180°C/350°F/Gas Mark 4. Lightly oil and base-line a 23-cm/9-inch loose-based cake or flan tin. Cream the butter, sugar and orange and lemon rind together until light and fluffy. Gradually beat in the egg yolks, adding a little of the flour after each addition. When all the egg yolk has been added, stir in the remaining flour together with the ground almonds.

2 Beat the ricotta cheese with the Amaretto until soft and creamy and stir into the cake mixture until well mixed. Add 55 g/2 oz of the grated chocolate to the mixture and stir lightly.

3 Whisk the egg whites until soft peaks form and stir into the mixture. Spoon into the prepared cake or flan tin and smooth the top. Bake in the preheated oven for 30 minutes, or until the top is golden and firm to the touch. Remove from the oven and leave to cool before removing from the cake tin and discarding the lining paper. Leave until cold.

4 Heat the apricot jam and lemon juice together, then rub through a sieve. Brush the jam all over the cake, then sprinkle over the remaining grated chocolate, pressing the chocolate lightly into the sides and top. Beat the mascarpone cheese with the Amaretto and place in a serving bowl.

5 Decorate the torte with the fresh or dried apricots and serve with mascarpone cheese and fresh summer berries or more apricots.

Chocolate & Almond Torte

This torte is perfect for serving on a hot, sunny day with a spoonful of whipped cream and a selection of fresh summer berries.

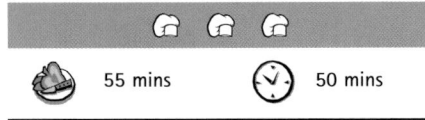

55 mins   50 mins

SERVES 10

INGREDIENTS

175 g/6 oz butter, softened, plus extra for greasing

225 g/8 oz continental plain chocolate, broken into pieces

3 tbsp water

175 g/6 oz soft light brown sugar

25 g/1 oz ground almonds

3 tbsp self-raising flour

5 eggs, separated

115 g/4 oz finely chopped blanched almonds

icing sugar, for dusting

double cream, to serve (optional)

1 Preheat the oven to 180°C/350°F/Gas Mark 4. Grease a 23-cm/9-inch loose-based cake tin and line the base with baking paper.

2 Put the chocolate and water in a heatproof bowl set over a saucepan of gently simmering water until melted, stirring until smooth. Add the sugar and stir until dissolved. Remove from the heat.

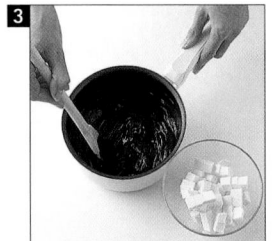

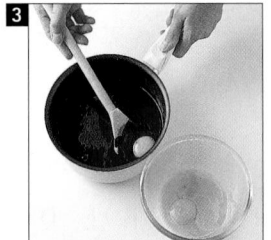

3 Add the butter in small amounts until it has melted into the chocolate. Lightly stir in the ground almonds and flour. Add the egg yolks one at a time, beating well after each addition.

4 Whisk the egg whites until soft peaks form, then fold into the chocolate mixture with a metal spoon. Stir in the chopped almonds. Pour the mixture into the cake tin and smooth the surface.

5 Bake in the preheated oven for 40–45 minutes, until well risen and firm (the cake will crack on the surface during cooking).

6 Leave to cool in the tin for 30–40 minutes. Turn out on to a wire rack to cool completely. Dust with icing sugar and serve with cream, or fresh fruit for a lighter option.

COOK'S TIP

For a nuttier flavour, toast the chopped almonds in a dry frying pan over medium heat for 2 minutes until lightly golden.

Iced Chocolate Torte

If you can't decide whether you prefer dark chocolate or rich, creamy white chocolate, then this gâteau is definitely for you.

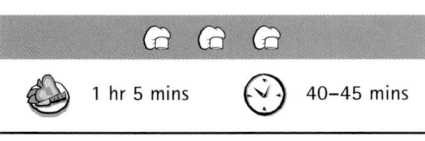

🍰 1 hr 5 mins   🕐 40–45 mins

SERVES 6

INGREDIENTS

butter, for greasing

4 eggs

115 g/4 oz caster sugar

115 g/4 oz plain flour

DARK CHOCOLATE CREAM

150 ml/5 fl oz double cream

150 g/5½ oz continental plain chocolate, broken into small pieces

FROSTING

75 g/2¾ oz white chocolate

1 tbsp butter

1 tbsp milk

4 tbsp icing sugar, sifted

chocolate caraque (see page 9), to decorate

1 Preheat the oven to 180°C/350°F/ Gas Mark 4. Grease and base-line a 20-cm/8-inch round springform tin. Beat the eggs and caster sugar in a large mixing bowl with an electric whisk for about 10 minutes, or until the mixture is very light and foamy and a trail is left when the whisk is dragged across the surface.

2 Sift the flour and fold in with a metal spoon or palette knife. Pour into the prepared tin and bake in the oven for 35–40 minutes, or until springy to the touch. Leave the cake to cool slightly, then transfer to a wire rack to cool completely.

3 While the cake is cooling, make the chocolate cream. Place the cream in a saucepan and bring to the boil, stirring.

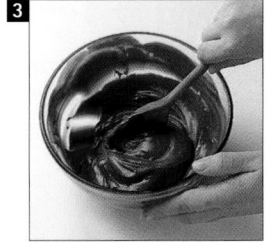

Add the dark chocolate and stir until melted and well combined. Remove from the heat, transfer to a bowl and leave to cool. Beat with a wooden spoon until thick.

4 When the cake is cold, cut it in half horizontally. Sandwich the layers with the chocolate cream, then place on a wire rack.

5 To make the icing, melt the chocolate and butter together and stir until blended. Whisk in the milk and icing sugar, and continue whisking until cool. Pour over the cake and spread with a palette knife to coat the top and sides. Decorate with chocolate caraque and leave the icing to set.

Chocolate Marquise Alice

The smooth filling is delicately flavoured with orange, surrounded with crisp chocolate finger biscuits, and topped with orange segments and kumquats.

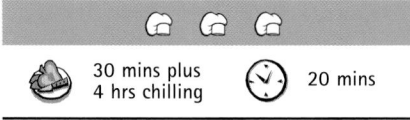

30 mins plus
4 hrs chilling

20 mins

SERVES 8

INGREDIENTS

SPONGE

1 tsp sunflower oil, for oiling

2 eggs

55 g/2 oz caster sugar

55 g/2 oz plain flour, plus 1 tsp for dusting

FILLING AND DECORATION

3 eggs, separated

55 g/2 oz caster sugar

1 tbsp finely grated orange rind

115 g/4 oz plain chocolate

3 tbsp orange juice

2 tsp gelatine

450 ml/16 fl oz double cream

4 tbsp Cointreau or Grand Marnier

2–3 oranges, peeled and segmented

44 plain chocolate finger biscuits

kumquats, to decorate

1 Preheat the oven to 200°C/400°F/Gas Mark 6 and lightly oil an 18-cm/ 7-inch flan tin and dust with a teaspoon of flour. Whisk the eggs with the sugar until very thick and creamy, then stir in the flour in a figure-of-eight action. Pour into the flan tin and bake in the oven for 12–15 minutes, or until well risen and the top feels firm when lightly touched with a finger. Remove and cool slightly before turning out from the flan tin. Set aside.

2 Put the egg yolks with the sugar and orange rind either in the bowl of a free-standing mixer or in a large mixing bowl placed over a saucepan of gently simmering water. Whisk until thick and creamy. If applicable, remove the bowl from the pan and continue to whisk until the mixture is cool. Melt the chocolate in a heatproof bowl set over a saucepan of gently simmering water. Stir until smooth, then stir into the whisked egg mixture.

3 Heat the orange juice until almost boiling, then sprinkle in the gelatine and stir until dissolved. Cool slightly, then fold into the mixture, stirring throughout. Whip 150 ml/5 fl oz of the cream until softly peaking, then stir into the egg mixture together with half the Cointreau or Grand Marnier. Whisk the egg whites in a clean bowl until stiff, then gently fold into the mixture a little at a time.

4 Place the cake in the base of a 20-cm/ 8-inch loose-based cake tin or springform tin. Set aside a few orange segments for decoration, then place the rest in the base and sprinkle over the remaining liqueur. Spoon over the prepared chocolate mixture, smooth the top and leave in the refrigerator for 4 hours, or until set.

5 When ready to serve, whip the remaining cream until softly peaking. Remove the gâteau from the cake tin and spread the sides with the cream. Press the chocolate finger biscuits into the sides and place on a serving plate. Decorate the top with a little cream, arrange a few orange segments and kumquats on top and serve.

Chocolate Berry Dacquoise

An excellent choice to serve in the summer when home-grown berries are at their best.

25 mins plus
4 hrs chilling

1–1½ hrs

SERVES 10

INGREDIENTS

4 egg whites

225 g/8 oz caster sugar

55 g/2 oz ground hazelnuts

225 g/8 oz plain chocolate

350 ml/12 fl oz double cream

2 tbsp kirsch

350 g/12 oz mixed summer berries, such as baby strawberries, raspberries and blueberries

1 Preheat the oven to 140°C/275°F/ Gas Mark 1. Line 3 baking sheets with non-stick baking paper and mark 3 x 18-cm/7-inch rounds on each. Whisk the egg whites until very stiff, then gradually add the sugar, whisking well after each addition. When all the sugar has been added, stir in the ground hazelnuts. Mix lightly until thoroughly incorporated.

2 Divide the meringue between the 3 baking sheets and then spread evenly within the circles. Bake in the preheated oven for 1 hour–1 hour 30 minutes, or until the meringues feel firm to the touch. Leave to cool, then remove from the baking sheets. Leave until cold.

3 Break the chocolate into small pieces and place in a heavy-based saucepan and add 225 ml/8 fl oz of the cream and kirsch. Heat gently, stirring until melted and smooth. Remove, pour into a bowl, cool, then chill for at least 2 hours, or until set. Once set, whisk until light and fluffy.

4 Spread two-thirds of the chocolate filling over 2 of the meringues and spread to the edges. Arrange most of the fruit over the chocolate filling, reserving the remaining fruit for decoration. Place the meringues one on top of the other, ending with a plain meringue.

5 Whip the remaining cream until stiff, then reserve a little for decoration and use the remainder to spread round the sides of the meringues. Spread the remaining chocolate on the top meringue and swirl with the tines of a fork. Decorate the top with the remaining cream and fruit and chill for 2 hours before serving.

Sachertorte

Do make sure you have a steady hand when writing the name on the top and leave the chocolate to harden before serving.

3 hrs 30 mins

1–1 hr 15mins

SERVES 10

INGREDIENTS

140 g/5 oz butter, unsalted for preference, plus extra for greasing

175 g/6 oz continental plain chocolate, broken into pieces

140 g/5 oz caster sugar

6 eggs, separated

175 g/6 oz plain flour

ICING & FILLING

175 g/6 oz continental plain chocolate

5 tbsp strong black coffee

115 g/4 oz icing sugar

6 tbsp good-quality apricot jam

50 g/1¾ oz continental plain chocolate, melted

1 Preheat the oven to 150°C/300°F/ Gas Mark 2. Grease and base-line a 23-cm/9-inch springform cake tin. Put the chocolate in a heatproof bowl set over a saucepan of gently simmering water until melted. Beat the butter and 70 g/2½ oz of the sugar until pale and fluffy. Add the egg yolks and beat well. Add the chocolate in a thin stream, beating well. Sift the flour; fold it into the mixture. Whisk the egg whites until they stand in soft peaks. Add the remaining sugar and whisk for 2 minutes by hand, or 45–60 seconds if using an electric whisk, until glossy. Fold half into the chocolate mixture, then fold in the remainder.

2 Spoon into the prepared tin and smooth the top. Bake in the preheated oven for 1–1¼ hours, until a skewer inserted into the centre comes out clean.

Cool in the tin for 5 minutes, then transfer to a wire rack to cool completely.

3 To make the icing, melt the chocolate and beat in the coffee until smooth. Sift the icing sugar into a bowl. Whisk in the melted chocolate mixture to give a thick icing. Halve the cake. Warm the apricot jam, spread over one half of the cake and sandwich together. Invert the cake on a wire rack. Spoon the icing over the cake and spread to coat the top and sides. Leave to set for 5 minutes, letting any excess drop through the rack. Transfer to a serving plate and leave to set for at least 2 hours.

4 To decorate, spoon the melted chocolate into a small piping bag and, with a fine plain nozzle, pipe the word 'Sacher' or 'Sachertorte' on the top of the cake. Leave to harden before serving.

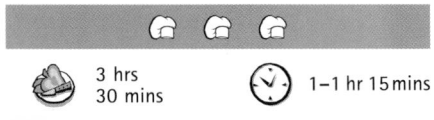

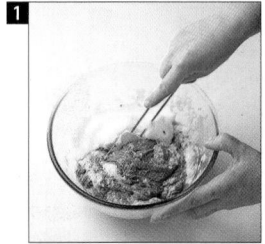

Bistvitny Torte

This is a Russian chocolate marble cake that is soaked in a delicious flavoured syrup and decorated with chocolate and cream.

1 hr 10 mins   35 mins

SERVES 10

INGREDIENTS

CHOCOLATE TRIANGLES
25 g/1 oz continental plain chocolate, broken into pieces

25 g/1 oz white chocolate, broken into pieces

CAKE
butter, for greasing

175 g/6 oz soft margarine

175 g/6 oz caster sugar

½ tsp vanilla essence

3 eggs, beaten lightly

280 g/10 oz self-raising flour

50 g/1¾ oz continental plain chocolate

SYRUP
115 g/4 oz granulated sugar

6 tbsp water

3 tbsp brandy or sherry

150 ml/5 fl oz double cream

1 Preheat the oven to 190°C/375°F/Gas Mark 5. To make the triangles, place a sheet of baking paper on to a baking sheet. Put the plain and white chocolate in 2 separate heatproof bowls set over saucepans of gently simmering water until melted. Place alternate spoonfuls of the melted plain and white chocolate on to the paper. Spread together to form a thick marbled layer, then leave the chocolate to set. Cut into squares, then into triangles.

2 To make the cake, grease a 23-cm/9-inch ring tin. Beat the margarine and sugar until light and fluffy. Beat in the

vanilla essence. Gradually add the eggs, beating well after each addition. Fold in the flour. Divide the mixture in half. Melt the plain chocolate and stir into one half.

3 Place spoonfuls of each mixture into the prepared tin and swirl together with a skewer to create a marbled effect.

4 Bake in the preheated oven for 30 minutes, or until the cake is springy to the touch. Leave to cool in the

tin for a few minutes, then transfer to a wire rack to cool completely.

5 To make the syrup, place the sugar in a small saucepan with the water and heat until the sugar has dissolved. Boil for 1–2 minutes. Remove from the heat and stir in the brandy. Leave the syrup to cool slightly, then spoon it slowly over the cake, letting it soak into the sponge. Whip the cream and pipe swirls of it on top of the cake. Decorate with the marbled chocolate triangles.

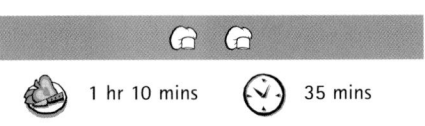

Torta del Cielo

This Italian almond-flavoured sponge cake has a dense, moist texture.
It makes the perfect accompaniment to a good strong cup of coffee.

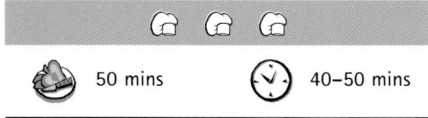

🍰 50 mins   🕐 40–50 mins

SERVES 4–6

INGREDIENTS

225 g/8 oz butter, unsalted for preference, at room temperature, plus extra for greasing

175 g/6 oz almonds in their skins

225 g/8 oz sugar

3 eggs, beaten lightly

1 tsp almond essence

1 tsp vanilla essence

70 g/2½ oz plain flour

pinch of salt

TO SERVE

icing sugar, for dusting

toasted flaked almonds

1 Preheat the oven to 180°C/350°F/Gas Mark 4. Lightly grease a round or square 20-cm/8-inch cake tin and line with baking paper.

2 Place the almonds in a food processor and grind until a crumbly mixture.

3 In a bowl, beat together the butter and sugar until smooth and fluffy. Beat in the almonds, eggs and almond and vanilla essences. Blend well.

4 Stir in the flour and salt, and mix together briefly, until the flour is just incorporated.

5 Pour or spoon the cake mixture into the greased tin and smooth the surface. Bake in the preheated oven for 40–50 minutes, or until the cake feels spongy when pressed.

6 Remove the cake from the oven and transfer to a wire rack to cool completely. To serve, lightly dust the cold cake with icing sugar and decorate with the toasted flaked almonds.

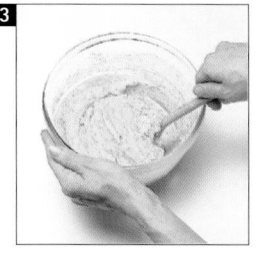

Dobos Torte

This wonderful cake originates from Hungary and consists of thin layers of light sponge topped with a crunchy caramel layer.

40 mins   10–16 mins

SERVES 8

INGREDIENTS

3 eggs

115 g/4 oz caster sugar

1 tsp vanilla essence

115 g/4 oz plain flour

FILLING

175 g/6 oz plain chocolate, broken into pieces

175 g/6 oz butter

2 tbsp milk

350 g/12 oz icing sugar

CARAMEL

115 g/4 oz granulated sugar

4 tbsp water

1 Preheat the oven to 200°C/400°F/Gas Mark 6. Draw 4 x 18-cm/7-inch circles on sheets of baking paper. Place 2 of them upside down on 2 baking sheets.

2 Beat the eggs and caster sugar in a large mixing bowl with an electric whisk for 10 minutes, or until the mixture is light and foamy and a trail is left when the whisk is dragged across the surface. Fold in the vanilla essence. Sift the flour and fold in with a metal spoon.

3 Spoon a quarter of the mixture on to one of the baking sheets and spread out to the size of the circle. Repeat with the other circle. Bake in the preheated oven for 5–8 minutes, or until golden brown. Cool on wire racks. Repeat with the remaining mixture.

4 To make the filling, put the chocolate in a heatproof bowl set over a saucepan of gently simmering water. Cool slightly. Beat the butter, milk and icing sugar until pale and fluffy. Whisk in the melted chocolate.

5 Place the sugar and water for the caramel in a heavy-based saucepan. Heat gently, stirring, to dissolve the sugar. Boil gently until pale golden in colour.

Remove from the heat. Pour over one cake layer as a topping. Leave to harden slightly. Mark into 8 portions with an oiled knife.

6 Remove the cakes from the baking paper. Trim the edges. Sandwich the layers together with some of the filling, finishing with the caramel-topped cake. Place on a serving plate, spread the sides with the filling mixture and pipe rosettes on the top of the cake.

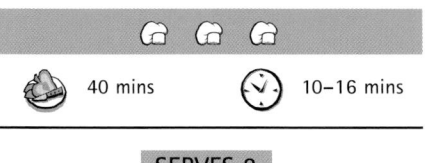
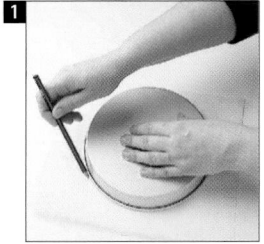
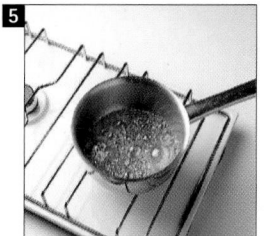

Strawberry Chocolate Cake

Strawberries and cream and chocolate cake make the perfect treat for a hot summer's day. Store in the refrigerator for up to 24 hours.

50 mins   30–40 mins

SERVES 8

INGREDIENTS

CHOCOLATE SPONGE

butter, for greasing

3 eggs

115 g/4 oz golden caster sugar

115 g/4 oz plain flour

2 tbsp cocoa powder

TO FINISH

150 g/5½ oz strawberries

300 ml/10 fl oz double cream

½ tsp vanilla essence

1 tbsp icing sugar

2 tbsp kirsch

chocolate curls (see page 9)

1 Preheat the oven to 190°C/375°F/Gas Mark 5. Grease and line a 22-cm/8½-inch cake tin. Put the eggs and sugar in a bowl and whisk together with an electric whisk, until thick and mousselike and a trail is left when the whisk is dragged across the surface. Sift the flour and cocoa together into a bowl, then carefully fold in to the whisked mixture. Turn into the prepared tin and bake in the oven for 30–40 minutes, until the cake springs back when lightly pressed in the centre. Leave to stand for 5 minutes, then turn out on to a wire rack to cool.

2 Meanwhile, prepare the filling. Set aside 4 strawberries and slice the rest. Put the cream, vanilla essence and icing sugar in a bowl and whisk until thick. Set aside two-thirds of the cream and fold the sliced strawberries into the remainder. Slice the chocolate sponge across into 2 layers and sprinkle each layer with 1 tablespoon of kirsch. Place 1 layer on a serving plate and spread over the strawberry cream mixture. Place the other sponge layer on top.

3 Put some of the reserved cream in a piping bag fitted with a fluted nozzle and spread the remainder over the top and sides of the cake. Coat the side with chocolate curls. Pipe the cream round the top of the gâteau. Cut the reserved strawberries in half, keeping the stalks intact, and arrange on top of the cream.

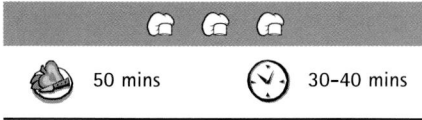

COOK'S TIP

If you do not want to make the chocolate curls, decorate the side of the cake with crushed chocolate flake bars.

Chocolate Cherry Gâteau

Chocolate and cherries are a classic combination. It is the perfect cake for all special occasions.

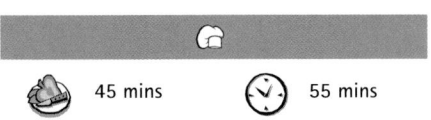

🍰 45 mins   🕐 55 mins

MAKES 23-CM/9-INCH CAKE

I N G R E D I E N T S

3 tbsp butter, unsalted for preference, melted, plus extra butter for greasing

1 kg/2 lb 4 oz fresh cherries, stoned and halved

225 g/8 oz caster sugar

100 ml/3½ fl oz cherry brandy

125 g/4½ oz plain flour

55 g/2 oz cocoa powder

½ tsp baking powder

4 eggs

1 litre/1¾ pints double cream

TO DECORATE

grated continental plain chocolate

whole fresh cherries

1 Preheat the oven to 180°C/350°F/Gas Mark 4. Grease and line a 23-cm/9-inch springform cake tin. Put the cherries in a saucepan and add 3 tablespoons of the sugar and the cherry brandy. Simmer for 5 minutes. Drain and set aside the syrup. In another bowl, sift together the flour, cocoa and baking powder.

2 Put the eggs in a heatproof bowl and beat in all but 2 tablespoons of the remaining sugar. Place the bowl over a saucepan of gently simmering water and whisk for 6 minutes until thickened. Remove from the heat, then gradually fold in the flour mixture and the melted butter. Spoon into the cake tin. Bake for 40 minutes. Remove from the oven and leave to cool.

3 Turn out the cake and cut in half horizontally. Mix the cream with the last of the sugar and whisk until peaking. Spread the syrup over the cut sides of the cake. Arrange the cherries on top of one of the cut sides, cover with cream and then add more cherries on top.

4 Place the other cake half on top of the cherries, cream side-down, then cover the top and sides of the cake with cream. Press grated chocolate over the top and sides. Decorate with whole cherries and serve.

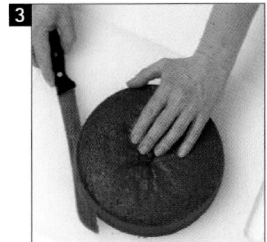

Chocolate Marmalade Cake

This cake will keep for up to 1 week if stored in an airtight container, because the addition of marmalade makes it really moist.

15 mins   1 hr 5 mins

SERVES 12–14

INGREDIENTS

1 tsp sunflower oil, for oiling

225 g/8 oz butter or margarine, softened

225 g/8 oz caster sugar

5 tbsp Seville orange marmalade

4 eggs, beaten

225 g/8 oz self-raising flour

55 g/2 oz ground almonds

115 g/4 oz plain chocolate, grated

few pieces candied orange peel, to decorate

1 tsp icing sugar, sifted, to serve

1 Preheat the oven to 180°C/350°F/ Gas Mark 4. Lightly oil and line the base of a 20-cm/8-inch cake tin with non-stick baking paper. Cream the butter and sugar together until light and fluffy then stir in the marmalade.

2 Gradually beat in the eggs a little at a time, beating well between each addition and adding a little flour after each addition. When all the eggs have been added, stir in the remaining flour together with the ground almonds and finally stir in the grated chocolate.

3 Spoon into the prepared cake tin and smooth the top. Bake in the preheated oven on the middle shelf for 45 minutes, then remove from the oven and arrange the candied peel on the top of the cake. Return to the oven and continue to bake for an additional 15–20 minutes or until a skewer inserted into the centre of the cake comes out clean. Remove and leave to cool before removing from the tin and discarding the lining paper. Decorate with the candied orange peel, and sprinkle with the icing sugar to serve.

COOK'S TIP

For a change, chop the chocolate rather than grating it or substitute best-quality white chocolate for the plain chocolate. If you cannot find Seville orange marmalade, use another one of your choice.

Giggle Cake

It's a mystery how this cake got its name – perhaps it's because it's easy to make and fun to eat.

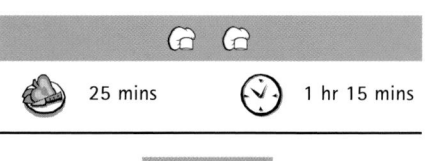

25 mins   1 hr 15 mins

SERVES 8

INGREDIENTS

350 g/12 oz mixed dried fruit

150 g/5½ oz butter or margarine, plus extra for greasing

175 g/6 oz soft light brown sugar

280 g/10 oz self-raising flour

pinch of salt

2 eggs, beaten

225 g/8 oz canned chopped pineapple, drained

140 g/5 oz glacé cherries, halved

1 Preheat the oven to 180°C/350°F/ Gas Mark 4. Put the mixed dried fruit into a large bowl and cover with boiling water. Set aside to soak for 10–15 minutes, then drain well.

2 Put the butter or margarine and sugar into a large saucepan and heat gently until melted. Add the drained mixed dried fruit and cook over low heat, stirring frequently, for 4–5 minutes. Remove from the heat and transfer to a mixing bowl. Set aside to cool.

3 Sift together the flour and salt into the dried fruit mixture and stir well. Add the eggs, mixing until the ingredients are thoroughly incorporated.

4 Add the pineapple and cherries to the cake mixture and stir to combine. Transfer to a greased and lined 900-g/ 2-lb loaf tin and smooth the surface.

5 Bake in preheated oven for about 1 hour, or until a skewer inserted into the centre comes out clean. If not, return to the oven for a few more minutes. Transfer the cake to a wire rack to cool completely before serving.

VARIATION
If you wish, add 1 teaspoon ground mixed spice to the cake mixture, sifting it in with the flour. Bake the cake in an 18-cm/7-inch round cake tin if you don't have a loaf tin of the right size. Remember to grease and line it first.

Chocolate Ring

This light cake has a delicate hint of chocolate and vanilla. In summer, decorate it with edible rose petals, but remember to rinse them first.

🍰 25 mins   🕐 30–35 mins

SERVES 10

I N G R E D I E N T S

1 tsp sunflower oil, for oiling

85 g/3 oz plain flour, plus extra for dusting

175 g/6 oz caster sugar

5 egg whites

½ tsp cream of tartar

salt

1 tsp vanilla essence

55 g/2 oz white chocolate, grated

I C I N G

175 g/6 oz plain chocolate

55 g/2 oz butter

225 g/8 oz icing sugar

2 egg yolks

white and milk chocolate buttons or rose petals, to decorate

1 Preheat the oven to 180°C/350°F/ Gas Mark. Lightly oil a 1.2-litre/2-pint ring mould, dust with the flour and set aside. Sift the flour with half the caster sugar at least 4 times. Set aside.

2 Place the egg whites in a large mixing bowl and whisk until soft peaks form. Add the cream of tartar, salt and vanilla essence and whisk for an additional 1 minute. Gradually whisk in all the remaining sugar, whisking well between each addition. Carefully fold in the sifted flour and then the grated chocolate.

3 Turn the mixture into the prepared tin and tap lightly on the work surface to remove any air bubbles. Bake in the preheated oven for 25–30 minutes, or until the top feels firm and springs back when touched lightly with a finger.

4 Remove the tin from the oven and invert on to a wire rack. Leave to stand until cold, then remove the tin.

5 Break the chocolate for the icing into small pieces and place in a large heatproof bowl set over a saucepan of gently simmering water and add the butter. Heat, stirring frequently, until melted and smooth. Remove from the heat and stir in 3 tablespoons of the icing sugar. Beat the egg yolks with 2 tablespoons of water, then gradually beat into the icing. Continue to add the icing sugar, beating well until a smooth, spreadable icing is formed. Use to cover the entire cake, then decorate with white and milk chocolate buttons or rose petals and leave to set before serving.

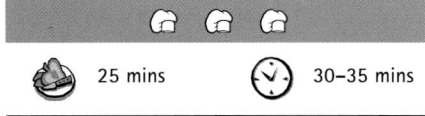

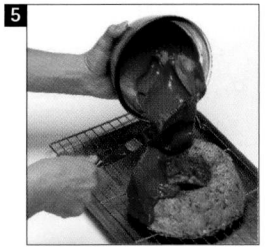

COOK'S TIP
Placing a small circle of baking paper in the base of the tin will make the cake easier to remove.
Ease the sides of the cake with a round-bladed knife.

Orange Chocolate Ring Cake

The addition of fresh oranges makes this cake very fruity and moist.
The flavour is complemented by the orange and chocolate icings.

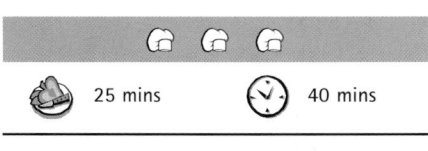

25 mins   40 mins

MAKES 8-10 SLICES

INGREDIENTS

175 g/6 oz butter, softened, plus extra
  for greasing

2 small oranges

85 g/3 oz plain chocolate

250 g/9 oz self-raising flour

1½ tsp baking powder

200 g/7 oz caster sugar

3 eggs, beaten

ICING

175 g/6 oz icing sugar

2 tbsp orange juice

55 g/2 oz plain chocolate, broken
  into pieces

1 Preheat the oven to 160°C/325°F/Gas Mark 3. Grease an 850 ml/1½-pint fluted or plain ring mould. Grate the rind from one of the oranges and set aside. Pare the rind from the other orange and set aside. Cut the skin and pith from the oranges, then cut them into segments by cutting down between the membranes with a sharp knife. Chop the segments into small pieces, reserving as much juice as possible. Grate the chocolate coarsely.

2 Sift the flour and baking powder into a bowl. Add the butter, sugar, eggs, grated orange rind and any reserved juice. Beat until the mixture is smooth. Fold in the chopped oranges and grated chocolate. Spoon the mixture into the prepared tin and bake for 40 minutes, or until well risen and golden brown. Leave in the tin for 5 minutes, then turn out on to a wire rack to cool completely.

3 To make the icing, sift the icing sugar into a bowl and stir in enough orange juice to make a coating consistency. Using a spoon, drizzle the icing over the cake. Put the chocolate in a heatproof bowl set over a saucepan of gently simmering water until melted. Drizzle the melted chocolate over the cake. Scatter the reserved strips of rind on top. Leave to set before serving.

COOK'S TIP
You do not need to be skilful at cake decorating to ice a cake as described above. The more untidy it looks, the better!

Apricot & Chocolate Ring

A tasty fruit bread in the shape of a ring. You could use sultanas instead of the dried apricots if preferred.

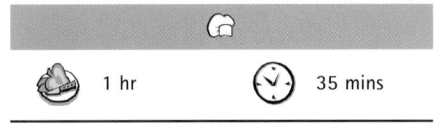

1 hr   35 mins

SERVES 12

INGREDIENTS

85 g/3 oz butter, cut into pieces, plus extra for greasing

450 g/1 lb self-raising flour, sifted

4 tbsp caster sugar

2 eggs, beaten

150 ml/5 fl oz milk

plain flour, for dusting

FILLING AND DECORATION

2 tbsp butter, melted

125 g/4½ oz ready-to-eat dried apricots, chopped

85 g/3 oz plain chocolate chips

1–2 tbsp milk, for glazing

25 g/1 oz plain chocolate, broken into pieces

1 Preheat the oven to 180°C/350°F/Gas Mark 4. Grease a 25-cm/10-inch cake tin and base-line with baking paper.

2 Rub the butter into the flour until the mixture resembles fine breadcrumbs. Stir in the caster sugar, eggs and milk to form a soft dough.

3 Roll out the dough on a lightly floured work surface to form a 35-cm/14-inch square.

4 Brush the melted butter over the surface of the dough. Mix together the apricots and chocolate chips and spread them over the dough to within 2.5 cm/1 inch of the top and bottom.

5 Roll up the dough tightly, like a Swiss roll, and cut it into 2.5-cm/1-inch slices. Stand the slices in a ring around the edge of the prepared tin at a slight tilt. Brush with a little milk.

6 Bake in the preheated oven for 30 minutes, or until cooked and golden. Leave the bread to cool in the tin for about 15 minutes, then transfer to a wire rack to cool.

7 Put the chocolate in a heatproof bowl set over a saucepan of gently simmering water until melted. Drizzle the chocolate over the ring, to decorate.

COOK'S TIP

This cake is best served very fresh, ideally on the day it is made. It is fabulous served slightly warm.

Calypso Fruit Cake

Here's a rich, spicy fruit cake with good keeping qualities which has a moist dense flavour.

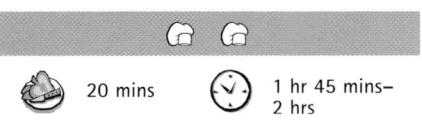

20 mins

1 hr 45 mins–2 hrs

SERVES 14–16

INGREDIENTS

1 tsp sunflower oil, for oiling

225 g/8 oz ready-to-eat dried prunes

5 tbsp water

115 g/4 oz plain chocolate

225 g/8 oz butter, softened

225 g/8 oz dark muscovado sugar

1 tsp ground cinnamon

1 tsp ground ginger

½ tsp mixed spice

4 eggs, beaten

280 g/10 oz plain flour

55 g/2 oz ground almonds

225 g/8 oz sultanas

175 g/6 oz raisins

85 g/3 oz dried cranberries

225 g/8 oz glacé cherries, chopped

85 g/3 oz angelica, chopped

225 g/8 oz chopped mixed nuts

2 tbsp dark rum or brandy

4–6 crushed brown sugar lumps or 2 tbsp demerara sugar

COOK'S TIP

This cake keeps really well. If you want to serve it for a special occasion, prick the bottom lightly and pour over 2 tablespoons of rum before using.

1 Preheat the oven to 160°C/325°F/Gas Mark 3. Oil and line a 23-cm/9-inch cake tin with baking paper. Place the prunes in a saucepan with 5 tablespoons water and place over moderate heat. Bring to the boil. Simmer for 5–8 minutes, or until the water has been absorbed and the prunes are plump. Leave to cool, then purée in a food processor or blender. Melt the chocolate in a heatproof bowl set over a saucepan of gently simmering water. Stir until smooth. Stir into the prune purée.

2 Cream the butter with the sugar and spices until light and fluffy, then beat in the prune and chocolate mixture. Add the eggs a little at a time, beating well between each addition and adding a little flour after each addition.

3 When all the eggs have been added, stir in the remaining flour together with the ground almonds. Add all the fruit and nuts and stir lightly, then add the rum and mix to form a soft dropping consistency. Turn into the prepared cake tin and smooth the top. Sprinkle with the crushed sugar lumps.

4 Bake in the preheated oven for 1 hour 45 minutes–2 hours, or until a skewer inserted into the centre of the cake comes out clean. Remove from the oven and leave to cool before removing from the tin and discarding the lining paper. Leave to stand until cold before cutting. Store in an airtight container or wrap well in greaseproof paper and cover in foil.

Nutty Chocolate Ring

This cake also makes a delicious dessert with the centre filled with soft fruit and served with lightly whipped cream.

15 mins

30–40 mins

SERVES 8–10

INGREDIENTS

1 tsp sunflower oil, for oiling

1 tbsp plain flour, for dusting

115 g/4 oz butter or margarine, softened

115 g/4 oz caster sugar

1 tsp ground cinnamon

2 eggs, separated

25 g/1 oz plain flour

½ tsp baking powder

115 g/4 oz milk chocolate

85 g/3 oz ground almonds

2–3 tbsp cooled boiled water

55 g/2 oz toasted flaked almonds, plus a few extra to decorate

25 g/1 oz white chocolate

1 Preheat the oven to 180°C/350°F/Gas Mark 4. Lightly oil a 1.2-litre/2-pint ring mould and line the base with a circle of baking paper. Dust lightly with flour. Cream the butter with the sugar and cinnamon until light and fluffy. Add the egg yolks, adding a little flour after each addition. Sift the remaining flour and baking powder together. When all the egg yolks have been added, stir in the flour and baking powder.

2 Melt the chocolate in a heatproof bowl set over a saucepan of gently simmering water. Stir until smooth, then stir into the mixture and mix in the ground almonds with the cooled boiled water to give a soft dropping consistency. Add the flaked almonds and stir lightly. Whisk the egg whites until stiff, add to the mixture and stir lightly, then spoon the mixture into the prepared cake tin.

3 Bake in the preheated oven for 25–35 minutes, or until a skewer inserted into the centre comes out clean. Remove from the oven and leave to cool for a few minutes before turning out on to a wire rack. Leave until cold. Melt the white chocolate in a heatproof bowl set over a saucepan of gently simmering water and drizzle over the cold cake, then sprinkle with a few extra flaked almonds.

COOK'S TIP
The easiest way to toast flaked almonds is to spread them on a baking sheet and place in the oven at 190°C/375°F/Gas Mark 5 for 5–7 minutes.

Tropical Fruit Vacherin

Meringue layers are sandwiched with a rich chocolate cream and topped with tropical fruit. Prepare in advance and make up just before required.

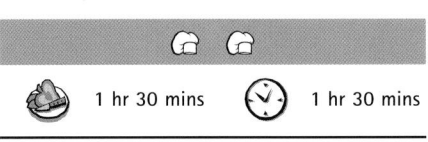
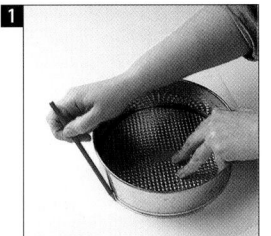

1 hr 30 mins   1 hr 30 mins

SERVES 10

INGREDIENTS

6 egg whites

275 g/9½ oz caster sugar

85 g/3 oz grated coconut

FILLING AND TOPPING

85 g/3 oz plain chocolate, broken
  into pieces

3 egg yolks

3 tbsp water

1 tbsp dark rum (optional)

4 tbsp caster sugar

450 ml/16 fl oz double cream

selection of tropical fruit, sliced or cut into
  bite-sized pieces

1 Preheat the oven to 140°C/275°F/Gas Mark 1. Draw 3 x 20-cm/8-inch circles on baking paper and place on baking sheets.

2 Whisk the egg whites until soft peaks form, then gradually whisk in half of the sugar and continue whisking until the mixture is very stiff and glossy. Carefully fold in the remaining sugar and the coconut.

3 Spoon the mixture into a piping bag fitted with a star nozzle and cover the circles with piped swirls. Bake in the preheated oven for 1½ hours, changing the position of the baking sheets halfway through. Without opening the oven door, turn off the oven and leave the meringues to cool inside the oven, then peel away the baking paper.

4 While the meringues are cooling, make the filling. Place the chocolate pieces, egg yolks, water, rum (if using) and sugar in a small heatproof bowl and place it over a saucepan of gently simmering water. Cook over low heat, stirring, until the chocolate has melted and the mixture has thickened. Cover with a disc of baking paper and set aside until cold.

5 Whip the cream and fold two-thirds of it into the chocolate mixture. Sandwich the meringue layers together with the chocolate mixture. Place the remaining cream in a piping bag fitted with a star nozzle and pipe around the edge of the meringue. Arrange the tropical fruit in the centre.

Raspberry Vacherin

A vacherin is made of layers of crisp meringue sandwiched together with fruit and cream. It makes a fabulous gâteau for special occasions.

1hr 45 mins   1hr 30 mins

SERVES 10

INGREDIENTS

3 egg whites

175 g/6 oz caster sugar

1 tsp cornflour

25 g/1 oz plain chocolate, grated

FILLING

175 g/6 oz plain chocolate

450 ml/16 fl oz double cream, whipped

300 g/10½ oz fresh raspberries

a little melted chocolate, to decorate

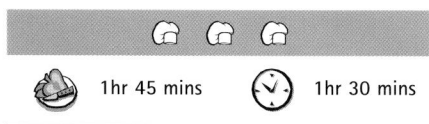

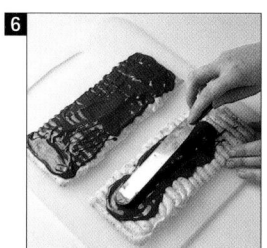

1 Preheat the oven to 140°C/275°F/Gas Mark 1. Draw 3 rectangles, 10 x 25 cm/4 x 10 inches, on sheets of baking paper and place on 2 baking sheets.

2 Whisk the egg whites in a mixing bowl until soft peaks form, then gradually whisk in half of the sugar and continue whisking until the mixture is very stiff and glossy.

3 Carefully fold in the rest of the sugar, the cornflour and the grated chocolate with a metal spoon or a palette knife.

4 Spoon the meringue mixture into a piping bag fitted with a 1-cm/½-inch plain nozzle and pipe lines across the rectangles.

5 Bake in the preheated oven for 1½ hours, changing the position of the baking sheets halfway through. Without opening the oven door, turn off the oven and leave the meringues to cool inside the oven, then peel away the baking paper.

6 To make the filling, melt the chocolate and spread it over 2 of the meringue layers. Leave to harden.

7 Place 1 chocolate-coated meringue on a plate and top with about one-third of the cream and raspberries. Gently place the second chocolate-coated meringue on top and spread with half of the remaining cream and raspberries. Place the last meringue on the top and decorate with the remaining cream and raspberries.

8 Put a few pieces of plain chocolate in a heatproof bowl set over a saucepan of gently simmering water until melted. Drizzle a little melted chocolate over the top of the vacherin and serve.

Chocolate Layer Log

This unusual chocolate cake is very popular with children, who love the appearance of the layers when it is sliced.

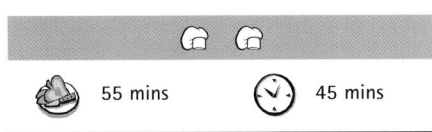

55 mins   45 mins

SERVES 8

INGREDIENTS

115 g/4 oz soft margarine, plus extra for greasing

115 g/4 oz caster sugar

2 eggs

115 g/4 oz self-raising flour

25 g/1 oz cocoa powder

2 tbsp milk

WHITE CHOCOLATE BUTTERCREAM

75 g/2¾ oz white chocolate

2 tbsp milk

150 g/5½ oz butter

85 g/3 oz icing sugar

2 tbsp orange-flavoured liqueur

chocolate curls (see page 9), to decorate

1 Preheat the oven to 180°C/350°F/ Gas Mark 4. Grease and line the sides of 2 x 400-g/14-oz food cans.

2 Beat together the margarine and sugar in a bowl until light and fluffy. Gradually add the eggs, beating well after each addition. Sift the flour and cocoa together and fold into the mixture. Fold in the milk.

3 Divide the mixture between the 2 prepared cans. Stand the cans on a baking sheet and bake in the preheated oven for 40 minutes, or until springy to the touch. Leave to cool for about 5 minutes in the cans, then turn out and cool completely on a wire rack.

4 Meanwhile, make the buttercream. Put the chocolate and milk in a saucepan and heat gently until the chocolate has melted, stirring until well combined. Leave to cool slightly. Beat together the butter and icing sugar until light and fluffy. Beat in the orange liqueur. Gradually beat in the chocolate mixture.

5 Cut both cakes into 1-cm/½-inch thick slices, then sandwich together with some of the buttercream.

6 Place the cake on a serving plate and spread the remaining buttercream over the top and sides. Decorate with the chocolate curls, then serve the cake cut diagonally into slices.

Rich Chocolate Loaf

This chocolate dessert is made without baking, simply by combining its rich ingredients, and then chilling them.

30 mins, plus 1 hr chilling   0 mins

MAKES 15 SLICES

INGREDIENTS

1 tsp melted butter, for greasing

85 g/3 oz almonds

150 g/5½ oz plain chocolate

6 tbsp butter, unsalted for preference

225 ml/8 fl oz canned condensed milk

2 tsp ground cinnamon

75 g/2¾ oz amaretti biscuits, crushed

55 g/2 oz ready-to-eat dried apricots, chopped coarsely

1 Line a 650-g/1 lb 7-oz loaf tin with foil and grease very lightly.

2 Using a sharp knife, coarsely chop the almonds.

3 Place the chocolate, butter, condensed milk and cinnamon in a heavy-based saucepan.

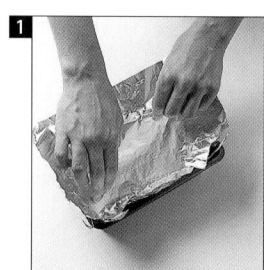

4 Heat the mixture over low heat for 3–4 minutes, stirring constantly with a wooden spoon, until the chocolate has melted. Beat thoroughly.

5 Using a wooden spoon, stir the almonds, crushed amaretti biscuits and apricots into the chocolate mixture, until completely incorporated.

6 Pour the mixture into the prepared tin and leave to chill in the refrigerator for about 1 hour, or until set.

7 Cut the loaf into slices to serve.

COOK'S TIP
To melt chocolate, break it into manageable pieces. The smaller the pieces, the quicker it will melt.

Chocolate Lamington Cake

This cake is based on an Australian cake named after Lord Lamington, a former Governor of Queensland.

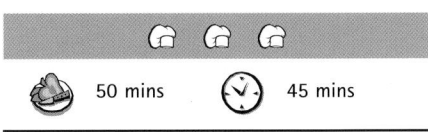

🍰 50 mins 🕐 45 mins

SERVES 8

INGREDIENTS

175 g/6 oz butter or margarine, plus extra for greasing

175 g/6 oz caster sugar

3 eggs, beaten lightly

175 g/6 oz self-raising flour

2 tbsp cocoa powder

50 g/1¾ oz plain chocolate, broken into pieces

5 tbsp milk

1 tsp butter

85 g/3 oz icing sugar

about 8 tbsp desiccated coconut

150 ml/5 fl oz double cream, whipped

1 Preheat the oven to 180°C/350°F/Gas Mark 4. Lightly grease a 450-g/1-lb loaf tin – preferably a long, thin tin measuring about 7.5 x 25 cm/3 x 10 inches.

2 Cream together the butter or margarine and sugar in a bowl until light and fluffy. Gradually add the eggs, beating well after each addition. Sift the flour and cocoa together. Fold into the mixture.

3 Pour the mixture into the prepared tin and level the top. Bake in the preheated oven for 40 minutes, or until springy to the touch. Leave to cool for 5 minutes in the tin, then turn out on to a wire rack to cool completely.

4 Place the chocolate, milk and butter in a heatproof bowl set over a saucepan of gently simmering water. Stir until the chocolate has melted. Add the icing sugar and beat until smooth. Leave the icing to cool until it is thick enough to spread, then spread it all over the cake. Sprinkle with the desiccated coconut and leave to stand until the icing has set.

5 Cut a V-shape wedge from the top of the cake. Put the cream in a piping bag fitted with a plain or star nozzle. Pipe the cream down the centre of the channel and replace the wedge of cake on top of the cream. Pipe cream down either side of the wedge of cake. Serve.

Chocolate & Vanilla Loaf

An old-fashioned favourite, this cake will keep well if stored in an airtight container or wrapped in a piece of foil in a cool place.

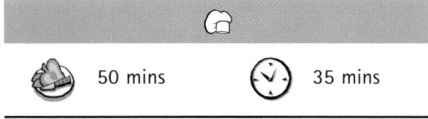

50 mins   35 mins

SERVES 10

INGREDIENTS

175 g/6 oz caster sugar

175 g/6 oz soft margarine, plus extra for greasing

½ tsp vanilla essence

3 eggs

280 g/10 oz self-raising flour, sifted

50 g/1¾ oz plain chocolate, broken into pieces

icing sugar, for dusting

1 Preheat the oven to 190°C/375°F/Gas Mark 5. Lightly grease a 450-g/1-lb loaf tin.

2 Beat the sugar and soft margarine together in a bowl until the mixture is light and fluffy.

3 Beat in the vanilla essence. Gradually add the eggs, beating well after each addition. Carefully fold the self-raising flour into the mixture.

4 Divide the mixture in half. Put the plain chocolate in a heatproof bowl set over a saucepan of gently simmering water until melted. Stir the melted chocolate into one half of the mixture until well combined.

5 Place the vanilla mixture in the tin and smooth the top. Spread the chocolate mixture over the vanilla layer.

6 Bake in the preheated oven for 30 minutes, or until springy to the touch.

7 Leave the loaf to cool in the tin for a few minutes before transferring to a wire rack to cool completely.

8 Serve the loaf lightly dusted with icing sugar.

COOK'S TIP
Freeze the loaf undecorated for up to 2 months. Thaw at room temperature.

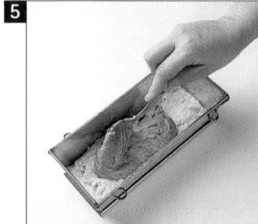

Christmas Cake

Christmas would not be the same without a traditional fruit cake. This one is decorated with a delicious lemony white icing.

🍰 45 mins plus 8 hrs to soak 🕐 3 hrs

MAKES 20-CM/8-INCH CAKE

INGREDIENTS

125 g/4½ oz raisins

125 g/4½ oz stoned dates, chopped

125 g/4½ oz sultanas

125 g/4½ oz glacé cherries, rinsed and drained

125 ml/4 fl oz brandy

225 g/8 oz butter, plus extra for greasing

225 g/8 oz caster sugar

4 eggs

grated rind of 1 orange and 1 lemon

1 tbsp black treacle

280 g/10 oz plain flour

½ tsp salt

½ tsp baking powder

1 tsp mixed spice

2 tbsp toasted almonds, chopped

2 tbsp toasted hazelnuts, chopped

ICING

350 g/12 oz icing sugar

1 egg white

juice of 1 lemon

1 tsp vanilla essence

holly leaves, to decorate

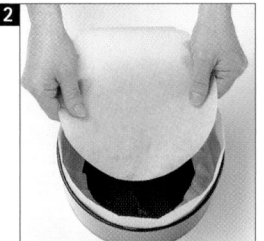

1 Make this cake at least 3 weeks in advance. Put all the fruit in a bowl, pour over the brandy and soak overnight.

2 Preheat the oven to 110°C/225°F/Gas Mark ¼. Grease and line a 20-cm/8-inch cake tin with greaseproof paper. In a bowl, cream together the butter and sugar until fluffy. Gradually beat in the eggs, then stir in the citrus rind and treacle. In a separate bowl, sift together the flour, salt, baking powder and mixed spice, then fold it into the egg mixture. Fold in the soaked fruit and brandy, and the chopped nuts. Spoon the mixture into the prepared cake tin and bake for at least 3 hours. If it starts to brown too quickly, cover with foil. The cake is cooked when a skewer inserted into the centre comes out clean. Remove from the oven and leave to cool on a wire rack. Store in an airtight container until required.

3 To make the icing, put the icing sugar, egg white, lemon juice and vanilla into a bowl and mix until smooth. Spread it over the top and sides of the cake, using a fork to give a textured finish. Decorate with holly leaves.

Easy Christmas Cake

This is an easy way of making a Christmas cake because there is no creaming required. Boiling the fruit mixture first makes a very moist cake.

45 mins

2 hrs 10 mins–
2 hrs 40 mins

MAKES 20-CM/8-INCH CAKE

INGREDIENTS

250 g/9 oz butter, cut into pieces, plus extra for greasing

400 g/14 oz dark muscovado sugar

2 tbsp molasses

1.5 kg/3 lb 5 oz luxury mixed dried fruit

finely grated rind and juice of
    1 large orange

6 tbsp brandy

5 eggs, beaten

250 g/9 oz mixed nuts, chopped coarsely

50 g/1¾ oz ground almonds

375 g/13 oz plain flour

½ tsp baking powder

1 tbsp mixed spice

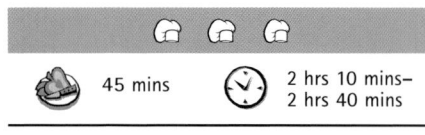

1 Preheat the oven to 150°C/300°F/Gas Mark 2. Put the butter, sugar, molasses, dried fruit, orange rind and juice and brandy in a large saucepan. Bring slowly to the boil, then simmer gently for 10 minutes, stirring occasionally. Remove from the heat and leave to cool.

2 Grease and base-line a 20-cm/8-inch deep round cake tin and wrap a double layer of paper round the outside of the tin. Stir the eggs, mixed nuts and ground almonds into the fruit mixture and mix well. Sift in the flour, baking powder and mixed spice. Stir in gently but thoroughly. Spoon into the prepared tin and smooth the top.

3 Bake in the preheated oven for 1 hour, then reduce the heat to 140°C/275°F/ Gas Mark 1 and bake for 2–2½ hours, until a skewer inserted into the centre comes out clean. Cool in the tin, then turn out and store, wrapped in greaseproof paper and foil, until ready to decorate.

COOK'S TIP

Cover the cake with marzipan and icing or simply top with nuts and fruit.

Yule Log

A chocolate yule log is a popular alternative to a traditional Christmas cake and is an eye-catching centrepiece on a festive tea table.

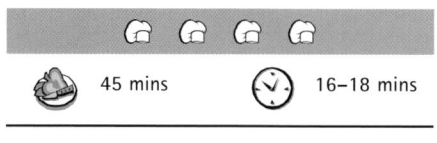

45 mins   16–18 mins

SERVES 8

INGREDIENTS

CHOCOLATE SPONGE

butter, for greasing

3 eggs

175 g/6 oz caster sugar

70 g/2½ oz plain flour

25 g/1 oz cocoa powder

caster sugar, for sprinkling

SYRUP

85 g/3 oz golden caster sugar

4 tbsp Cointreau

ORANGE BUTTERCREAM

4 tbsp butter, softened

85 g/3 oz icing sugar, sifted

grated rind of 1 orange

1 tbsp Cointreau

CHOCO BUTTERCREAM

1 tbsp cocoa powder

85 g/3 oz butter

140 g/5 oz icing sugar, sifted

coarse chocolate caraque (see page 9)

cocoa powder and icing sugar, for dusting

1 Preheat the oven to 200°C/400°F/ Gas Mark 6. Grease and line a 20 x 30-cm/8 x 12-inch Swiss roll tin. Put the eggs and sugar in a bowl and whisk together with an electric whisk, until thick and mousselike and a trail is left when the whisk is dragged across the surface. Sift the flour and cocoa together into a bowl, then fold into the whisked mixture. Turn into the prepared tin and bake in the oven

for 8–10 minutes, until the cake springs back when lightly pressed. Wring out a clean tea towel in hot water and place on a work surface. Put a sheet of greaseproof paper on top and sprinkle with caster sugar. Turn the sponge on to the paper, peel off the lining paper and trim the edges of the cake. Roll up the sponge from a long side, with the paper inside. Hold in position for a few seconds, then cool on a wire rack with the join underneath.

2 To make the syrup, put the sugar in a small saucepan with a generous 150 ml/5 fl oz water. Heat gently until the sugar dissolves, then boil for 2 minutes until syrupy. Stir in the Cointreau and leave to cool. Unroll the Swiss roll and remove the paper. Sprinkle with the syrup. To make the orange buttercream, put the

butter in a bowl and beat until creamy. Gradually beat in the icing sugar, then the orange rind and Cointreau. Beat until smooth. Spread over the sponge and roll up again.

3 To make the chocolate buttercream, put the cocoa in a small bowl and stir in 1 tablespoon boiling water. Leave to cool. Put the butter in a bowl and beat until creamy. Gradually beat in the icing sugar, then beat in the cooled cocoa until smooth. Cut off a quarter of the roll diagonally and attach to the side of the roll with chocolate buttercream. Cover the roll with the remaining buttercream and use a palette knife to mark lines to represent bark. Cover the cake with chocolate caraque and sift cocoa over. Finish with a dusting of icing sugar.

White Chocolate Yule Log

This log is delicious at Christmas – and can easily be adapted for other occasions! Decorate with marzipan holly berries and leaves if you like.

45 mins   8–10 mins

SERVES 8–10

INGREDIENTS

1 tsp sunflower oil, for oiling

3 eggs

115 g/4 oz caster sugar, plus extra for sprinkling

115 g/4 oz self-raising flour

55 g/2 oz white chocolate, grated

ICING

175 g/6 oz butter, softened

350 g/12 oz icing sugar

1–2 tbsp milk

1 tsp vanilla essence

115 g/4 oz white chocolate, melted

TO DECORATE

½–1 tsp cocoa powder

marzipan holly berries and leaves

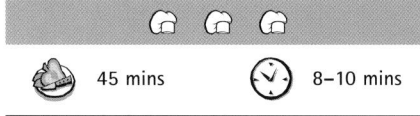

1 Preheat the oven to 220°C/425°F/Gas Mark 7. Lightly oil and line a Swiss roll tin with 1 whole sheet of non-stick baking paper. Place the eggs and sugar in a heatproof bowl set over a saucepan of gently simmering water. Whisk until very thick and creamy, then remove from the water and continue to whisk until cool. (Alternatively, place the eggs and sugar in the bowl of a free-standing mixer and whisk until thick and creamy.)

2 Sift the flour into the whisked mixture and stir lightly together with 1 tablespoon of cooled boiled water. Melt the chocolate in a heatproof bowl set over a saucepan of gently simmering water. Stir until smooth, then stir into the mixture. Pour into the lined Swiss roll tin.

3 Tap the tin lightly on the work surface to smooth the top. Bake in the preheated oven for 8–10 minutes, or until the top springs back when touched lightly with a finger. Remove from the oven and invert on to a sheet of baking paper sprinkled with caster sugar. Roll up and leave until cold.

4 Cream the butter with the icing sugar, adding sufficient milk to give a smooth spreadable consistency. Stir in the vanilla essence and the melted white chocolate.

5 Unroll the cold cake and trim all the edges. Spread one-third of the prepared icing to within 5 mm/¼ inch of the edges, and roll up as tightly as possible. Cut the Swiss roll diagonally in half and arrange in a log shape. Use the remaining icing to cover the cake completely. Mark the icing with the tines of a fork to give a bark effect and decorate with a sprinkle of cocoa and the marzipan holly berries and leaves.

Panforte di Siena

This famous Tuscan honey and nut cake is a Christmas speciality.
In Italy it is sold in pretty boxes, and served in very thin slices.

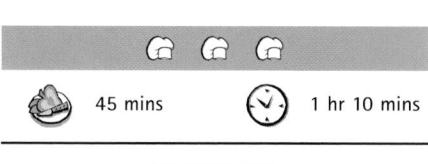

🍰 45 mins 🕐 1 hr 10 mins

SERVES 12

INGREDIENTS

150 g/5½ oz whole almonds, split

115 g/4 oz hazelnuts

85 g/3 oz mixed candied peel, chopped

55 g/2 oz ready-to-eat dried apricots

55 g/2 oz candied pineapple

grated rind of 1 large orange

70 g/2½ oz plain flour

2 tbsp cocoa powder

2 tsp ground cinnamon

115 g/4 oz caster sugar

175 g/6 oz honey

icing sugar, for dusting

1 Preheat the oven to 150°C/300°F/Gas Mark 2. Toast the almonds under the grill until lightly browned, and then place in a bowl.

2 Toast the hazelnuts until the skins split. Place on a dry tea towel and rub off the skins. Coarsely chop the hazelnuts and add them to the almonds, together with the candied peel.

3 Chop the apricots and pineapple fairly finely and add to the nuts, together with the orange rind. Mix well.

4 Sift the flour, cocoa and cinnamon into the nut mixture and mix well.

5 Line a round 20-cm/8-inch cake tin or deep, loose-bottomed flan tin with baking paper.

6 Put the sugar and honey into a saucepan and heat until the sugar dissolves. Boil gently for about 5 minutes, or until the mixture thickens and starts to turn a deeper shade of brown. Quickly add to the nut mixture and mix thoroughly. Turn into the prepared tin and smooth the top using the back of a damp spoon.

7 Cook in the preheated oven for 1 hour. Remove the cake from the oven and leave in the tin until completely cool. Take out of the tin and carefully peel off the paper. Before serving, decorate the cake by dredging with sifted icing sugar.

Bûche de Noël

This is the traditional French Christmas cake. It consists of a chocolate cake roll filled with and encased in a delicious rich chocolate icing.

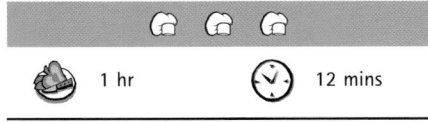

🍰 1 hr   🕐 12 mins

SERVES 10

INGREDIENTS

CAKE

butter, for greasing

4 eggs

115 g/4 oz caster sugar

100 g/3½ oz self-raising flour

2 tbsp cocoa powder

ICING

150 g/5½ oz plain chocolate, broken into pieces

2 egg yolks

150 ml/5 fl oz milk

115 g/4 oz butter

4 tbsp icing sugar

2 tbsp dark rum (optional)

TO DECORATE

a little white glacé or royal icing

icing sugar, for dusting

holly leaves

1 Preheat the oven to 200°C/400°F/Gas Mark 6. Grease and line a 30 x 23-cm/12 x 9-inch Swiss roll tin.

2 Beat the eggs and sugar in a bowl with an electric whisk for 10 minutes, or until the mixture is light and foamy and a trail is left when the whisk is lifted off the surface. Fold in the flour and cocoa. Pour into the tin and bake in the preheated oven for 12 minutes, or until springy to the touch. Turn out on to baking paper sprinkled with caster sugar. Peel off the lining paper and trim the edges. Cut a small slit halfway into the cake 1 cm/½ inch from one of the short ends. Roll up tightly, enclosing the baking paper. Place on a wire rack to cool.

3 To make the icing, put the chocolate in a heatproof bowl set over a saucepan of gently simmering water. Beat in the egg yolks, whisk in the milk and cook, stirring all the time, until the custard thickens enough to coat the back of a wooden spoon. Cover with dampened greaseproof paper and cool. Beat the butter and sugar until pale. Beat in the custard and rum (if using).

4 Unroll the sponge, spread with one-third of the icing and roll up. Place on a serving plate. Spread the remaining icing over the cake and mark with a fork to give the effect of bark. Leave to set. Pipe glacé icing to form the rings of the log. Sprinkle the cake with sugar and decorate with holly leaves.

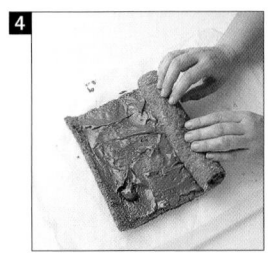

Black Forest Roulade

Do not worry if the roulade cracks when it is rolled up. It has a tendency to do this – and it does not detract from the luscious taste.

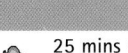

 25 mins plus overnight standing   🕐 25 mins

SERVES 8–10

INGREDIENTS

1 tsp sunflower oil, for oiling

175 g/6 oz plain chocolate

2–3 tbsp kirsch or brandy

5 eggs

225 g/8 oz caster sugar

2 tbsp icing sugar, sifted

FILLING AND DECORATION

350 ml/12 fl oz double cream

1 tbsp kirsch or brandy

350 g/12 oz fresh black cherries, stoned, or 400 g/14 oz canned morello cherries, drained and stoned

chocolate squares, to decorate

1 Preheat the oven to 190°C/375°F/ Gas Mark 5. Line a Swiss roll tin with 1 whole sheet of non-stick baking paper. Break the chocolate into small pieces and place in a heatproof bowl set over a saucepan of gently simmering water. Add the kirsch and heat gently, stirring until the mixture is smooth. Remove from the pan and set aside.

2 Place the eggs and sugar in a large heatproof bowl and set over the saucepan of gently simmering water. (Alternatively, place in the bowl of a free-standing mixer and use a balloon whisk.) Whisk the eggs and sugar until very thick and creamy and the whisk leaves a trail when dragged across the surface. Remove the bowl from the heat and whisk in the cooled chocolate.

3 Spoon into the prepared Swiss roll tin, then tap the tin lightly on the work surface to smooth the top. Bake in the preheated oven for 20 minutes, or until the top feels firm to the touch. Remove from the oven and immediately invert on to a whole sheet of baking paper which is sprinkled with the icing sugar. Lift off the tin and lining paper, then roll up, encasing the baking paper in the roulade. Leave until cold.

4 Whip the cream until soft peaks form, then stir in the kirsch, reserving 1–2 tablespoons. Unroll the roulade and spread the cream to within 5 mm/¼ inch of the edges. Set aside a few of the cherries for decoration and scatter the remainder over the cream. Carefully roll up the roulade again and place on a serving platter. Decorate the top with small rosettes or small spoonfuls of the reserved cream, the reserved cherries and squares of chocolate.

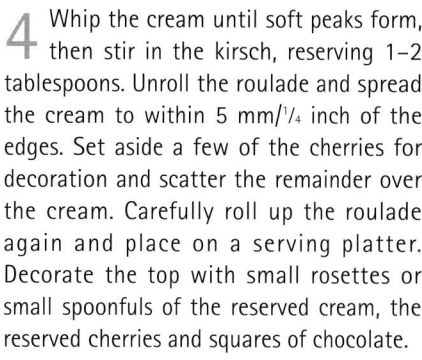

Chocolate Roulade

Don't worry if the cake cracks when rolled – this is quite normal. If it doesn't crack, consider yourself a real chocolate wizard in the kitchen!

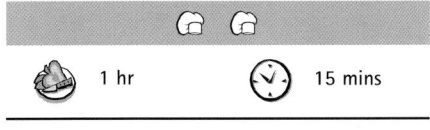

🍰 1 hr   🕐 15 mins

SERVES 6

INGREDIENTS

150 g/5½ oz plain chocolate,
 broken into pieces

2 tbsp water

6 eggs

175 g/6 oz caster sugar

4 tbsp plain flour

1 tbsp cocoa powder

FILLING

300 ml/10 fl oz double cream

175 g/6 oz sliced strawberries

TO DECORATE

icing sugar, for dusting

chocolate leaves (see page 9)

1 Preheat the oven to 200°C/400°F/Gas Mark 6. Line a 38 x 25-cm/15 x 10-inch Swiss roll tin. Put the chocolate and water in a heatproof bowl set over a saucepan of gently simmering water until melted. Leave to cool.

2 Place the eggs and sugar in a bowl and whisk for 10 minutes, or until the mixture is pale and foamy and a trail is left when the whisk is lifted off the surface. Whisk in the chocolate. Sift the flour and cocoa and fold into the mixture. Pour into the tin and smooth the top.

3 Bake in the preheated oven for 12 minutes. Dust a sheet of baking paper with icing sugar. Turn out the roulade and remove the lining paper. Roll the roulade with the fresh baking paper inside. Place on a wire rack, cover with a damp tea towel and leave to cool.

4 Whip the cream. Unroll the roulade and scatter over the fruit. Spread the cream over the roulade and re-roll. Dust with icing sugar.

5 Place the roulade on a plate. Make the chocolate leaves and use them to decorate the roulade.

Double Chocolate Roulade

A plain chocolate mousse is rolled round white chocolate cream to make a luscious dessert, perfect as a finale to any special-occasion meal.

30 mins plus standing and chilling

20-25 mins

SERVES 8

INGREDIENTS

ROULADE

115 g/4 oz plain chocolate, broken into pieces

4 eggs, separated

115 g/4 oz golden caster sugar

1 tsp instant coffee granules dissolved in 2 tbsp hot water, cooled

FILLING

225 ml/8 fl oz whipping cream

140 g/5 oz white chocolate

3 tbsp Tia Maria

TO DECORATE

sifted icing sugar

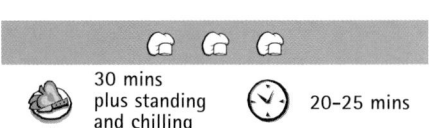

1 Preheat the oven to 180°C/350°F/Gas Mark 4. Line a 23 x 33-cm/9 x 13-inch Swiss roll tin with baking paper. To make the roulade, put the chocolate in a heatproof bowl set over a saucepan of gently simmering water until melted. Leave to cool. Put the egg yolks and sugar in a bowl and whisk together until pale and mousselike. Gently fold in the cooled melted chocolate followed by the cooled coffee. Put the egg whites in another bowl and whisk until stiff but not dry. Stir a little of the egg white into the chocolate mixture and carefully fold in the rest. Pour the mixture into the prepared tin and bake in the oven for 15–20 minutes, until firm. Cover with a clean damp tea towel and leave in the tin overnight.

2 To make the filling, put the cream in a saucepan and heat until almost boiling. Put the white chocolate in a food processor and chop coarsely. With the motor running, pour the hot cream through the feed tube. Process for 10–15 seconds, until smooth. Stir in the Tia Maria. Transfer to a bowl and leave to cool. Cover and chill overnight. When you are ready to assemble the roulade, whisk the chocolate cream until it starts to form soft peaks.

3 Cut a sheet of greaseproof paper slightly larger than the roulade, place on the work surface and sift icing sugar over it. Turn the roulade out on to the paper and carefully peel away the lining paper. Spread the white chocolate cream over the roulade and roll up, starting at a short side nearest to you and pushing away from you with the paper. Transfer seam-side down to a serving dish. Chill for 2 hours.

COOK'S TIP

If you do not have time, it is not essential to chill the roulade for 2 hours before serving. However, the roulade firms up in this time and becomes easier to slice.

Chocolate Coconut Roulade

Here, a coconut-flavoured roulade is encased in a rich chocolate coating.
It is served with fresh raspberry coulis, which provides a piquant contrast.

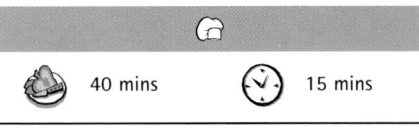

40 mins   15 mins

SERVES 8

I N G R E D I E N T S

butter, for greasing

3 eggs

70 g/2½ oz caster sugar,
    plus extra for sprinkling

70 g/2½ oz self-raising flour

1 tbsp block creamed coconut, softened
    with 1 tbsp boiling water

35 g/1¼ oz desiccated coconut

6 tbsp good-quality raspberry jam

CHOCOLATE COATING

200 g/7 oz plain chocolate

5 tbsp butter

2 tbsp golden syrup

RASPBERRY COULIS

300 g/10½ oz fresh or frozen raspberries,
    thawed if frozen

2 tbsp water

4 tbsp icing sugar

1 Preheat the oven to 200°C/400°F/Gas Mark 6. Grease and line a 23 x 30-cm/9 x 12-inch Swiss roll tin with baking paper. Whisk the eggs and caster sugar in a large mixing bowl (with a hand or electric whisk) for about 10 minutes, or until the mixture is very light and foamy and a trail is left when the whisk is dragged across the surface.

2 Sift the flour and fold in with a metal spoon or a palette knife. Fold in the creamed coconut and desiccated coconut. Pour the cake mixture into the prepared tin and bake in the preheated oven for 10–12 minutes, or until springy to the touch.

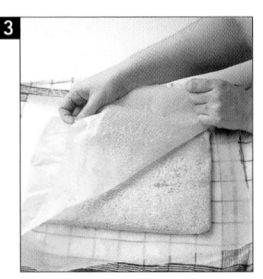

3 Sprinkle a sheet of baking paper with a little caster sugar and place on top of a damp tea towel. Turn the cake out on to the baking paper and carefully peel away the lining paper. Spread the jam over the sponge and roll up from the short end, using the tea towel to help you. Place seam-side down on a wire rack and leave the roulade to cool completely.

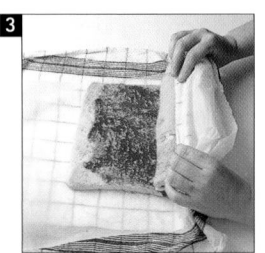

4 Meanwhile, make the coating. Melt the chocolate and butter, stirring. Stir in the golden syrup; leave to cool for 5 minutes. Spread it over the cooled roulade and leave to set. To make the coulis, purée the fruit in a food processor with the water and sugar; sieve to remove the seeds. Cut the roulade into slices and serve with the coulis.

Strawberry Roulade

Serve this moist, light sponge cake rolled up with a creamy almond and strawberry filling for a delicious tea-time treat.

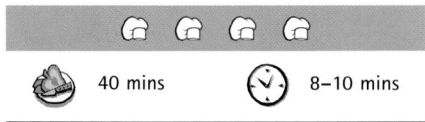

🧊 40 mins   🕐 8–10 mins

SERVES 8

I N G R E D I E N T S

3 large eggs

115 g/4 oz caster sugar

115 g/4 oz plain flour

1 tbsp hot water

F I L L I N G

175 g/6 oz low-fat mascarpone cheese

1 tsp almond essence

225 g/8 oz small strawberries

T O D E C O R A T E

1 tbsp flaked almonds, toasted

1 tsp icing sugar

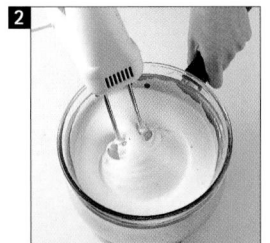
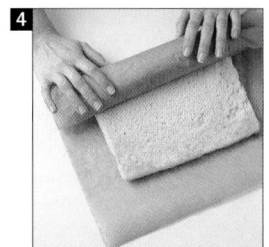
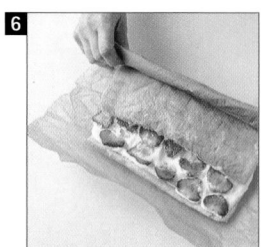

1 Preheat the oven to 220°C/425°F/Gas Mark 7. Line a 35 x 25-cm/14 x 10-inch Swiss roll tin with baking paper.

2 Place the eggs in a heatproof bowl with the caster sugar. Place the bowl over a saucepan of gently simmering water and whisk until pale and thick.

3 Remove the bowl from the saucepan. Sift in the flour and fold into the eggs along with the hot water. Pour the mixture into the prepared tin and bake in the preheated oven for 8–10 minutes, until golden and set.

4 Turn out the cake on to a sheet of baking paper. Peel off the lining paper and roll up the sponge cake tightly along with the baking paper. Wrap in a tea towel and leave to cool.

5 Mix together the mascarpone cheese and the almond essence. Reserving a few strawberries for decoration, wash, hull and slice the rest. Chill the mascarpone mixture and the strawberries in the refrigerator until required.

6 Unroll the cake, spread the mascarpone mixture over the surface and sprinkle with sliced strawberries. Roll the cake up again and transfer to a serving plate. Sprinkle with almonds and lightly dust with icing sugar. Decorate with the reserved strawberries.

Victoria Sandwich

This cake is extremely versatile, and lends itself to a number of treatments, such as filling with whipped cream and halved strawberries.

40 mins   25–30 mins

SERVES 8

INGREDIENTS

175 g/6 oz self-raising flour

1 tsp baking powder

175 g/6 oz butter, softened, plus extra for greasing

175 g/6 oz golden caster sugar

3 eggs

TO FINISH

3 tbsp raspberry jam

225 ml/8 fl oz double cream, whipped

caster sugar, for dusting

1 Preheat the oven to 180°C/350°F/ Gas Mark 4. Grease and base-line 2 x 20-cm/8-inch sandwich tins. Sift the flour and baking powder into a bowl and add the butter, sugar and eggs. Mix together, then beat well until smooth.

2 Divide the mixture evenly between the prepared tins and spread smooth. Bake in the oven for 25–30 minutes, until well risen and golden brown, and the cakes feel springy to the touch.

3 Leave in the tins for 5 minutes, then turn out and remove the paper. Place on wire racks to cool completely. Sandwich the cakes with the raspberry jam and whipped cream and sprinkle the caster sugar on top.

VARIATION

Coffee sandwich cake: Blend 1 tablespoon instant coffee granules with a little hot water and add to the ingredients before mixing. Sandwich with coffee buttercream.

Lemon Syrup Cake

The lovely light and tangy flavour of the sponge cake is balanced by the lemony syrup poured over the top.

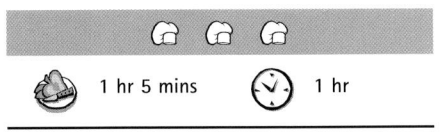

1 hr 5 mins   1 hr

SERVES 6–8

INGREDIENTS

butter, for greasing

225 g/8 oz plain flour

2 tsp baking powder

225 g/8 oz caster sugar

4 eggs

150 ml/5 fl oz soured cream

grated rind of 1 large lemon

4 tbsp lemon juice

150 ml/5 fl oz sunflower oil

SYRUP

4 tbsp icing sugar

3 tbsp lemon juice

1 Preheat the oven to 180°C/350°F/ Gas Mark 4. Lightly grease a 20-cm/ 8-inch loose-based round cake tin and line the base with baking paper.

2 Sift the flour and baking powder together into a mixing bowl and stir in the sugar.

3 In a separate bowl, whisk the eggs, soured cream, lemon rind, lemon juice and oil together. Pour the egg mixture into the dry ingredients and mix well until evenly combined.

4 Pour the mixture into the prepared tin and bake in the preheated oven for 45–60 minutes, until risen and golden brown.

5 Meanwhile, to make the syrup, combine the icing sugar and lemon juice in a small saucepan. Stir over low heat until just starting to bubble and turn syrupy.

6 As soon as the cake comes out of the oven, prick the surface with a fine skewer, then brush the syrup over the top. Leave the cake to cool completely in the tin before turning out and serving.

COOK'S TIP
Pricking the surface of the hot cake with a skewer ensures that the syrup seeps right into the cake and the full flavour is absorbed.

Eggless Sponge

This is a healthy, but still absolutely delicious, variation of the classic sponge layer cake and is suitable for vegans.

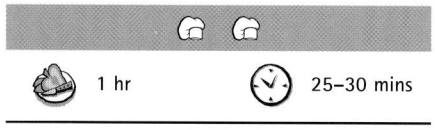

🍰 1 hr   🕐 25–30 mins

SERVES 6

INGREDIENTS

vegan margarine, for greasing

250 g/9 oz self-raising wholemeal flour

2 tsp baking powder

175 g/6 oz caster sugar

6 tbsp sunflower oil

225 ml/8 fl oz water

1 tsp vanilla essence

4 tbsp strawberry or raspberry reduced-sugar spread

caster sugar, for dusting

1 Preheat the oven to 180°C/350°F/ Gas Mark 4. Grease 2 x 20-cm/ 8-inch sandwich tins and line them with baking paper.

2 Sift the self-raising flour and baking powder into a large mixing bowl, stirring in any bran remaining in the sieve. Stir in the caster sugar.

3 Pour in the sunflower oil, water and vanilla essence. Mix well with a wooden spoon for about 1 minute, until the mixture is smooth, then divide between the prepared tins.

VARIATIONS
Replace 2 tablespoons of the flour with cocoa, or replace 2 teaspoons of flour with instant coffee powder. For a citrus-flavoured sponge, add the grated rind of ½ lemon or orange to the flour in step 2.

4 Bake in the preheated oven for about 25–30 minutes, or until the centre of each cake springs back when lightly touched.

5 Leave the sponge cakes to cool slightly in the tins before turning them out and transferring to a wire rack to cool completely.

6 Remove the baking paper and place one sponge cake on a serving plate. Cover with the reduced-sugar spread and place the other sponge on top. Dust the eggless sponge cake with a little caster sugar before serving.

Chocolate & Mandarin Gâteau

The sharp tang of the mandarins, especially if you use fresh fruit, helps cut the richness of this gâteau.

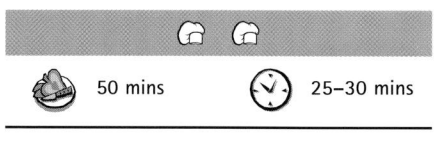

🍰 50 mins   🕐 25–30 mins

SERVES 4–6

INGREDIENTS

1 tsp sunflower oil, for oiling

3 eggs

115 g/4 oz caster sugar

1 tbsp finely grated orange rind

115 g/4 oz plain chocolate, grated

115 g/4 oz plain flour

4 tbsp butter, melted

200 ml/7 fl oz double cream

2 tbsp Cointreau or Grand Marnier

300 g/10 oz canned mandarins or 3 fresh mandarins, peeled and segmented

few maraschino cherries, to decorate

1 Preheat the oven to 180°C/350°F/Gas Mark 4. Lightly oil and line the base of a 23-cm/9-inch cake tin. Place the eggs, sugar and orange rind in a heatproof bowl set over a saucepan of gently simmering water or in the bowl of a free-standing mixer. Whisk until very thick and creamy and a trail is left when the whisk is dragged across the surface.

2 Remove from the heat, if applicable, and continue to whisk until cool. Carefully stir in 55 g/2 oz of the grated chocolate and then the flour, taking care not to over-mix. Continue to mix gently, then stir in the melted butter. Turn the mixture into the prepared cake tin and bake in the preheated oven for 25–30 minutes, or until the top springs back when touched with a finger. Remove and leave to cool before removing from the tin and discarding the lining paper.

3 Whip the cream and liqueur until thick and spread half round the sides of the cake. Place the remaining grated chocolate on a sheet of greaseproof paper and roll the sides of the cake in the chocolate. Place on a serving platter. Use the remaining cream to spread over the top and to decorate. Arrange the mandarin segments and cherries attractively over the cream and serve. Store in the refrigerator and eat within 2 days.

COOK'S TIP
If you use canned fruit for decoration, choose fruit in natural syrup. Drain thoroughly and pat dry on kitchen paper.

Chocolate Chestnut Gâteau

This spectacular cake tastes as good as it looks and is ideal to serve when entertaining family and friends.

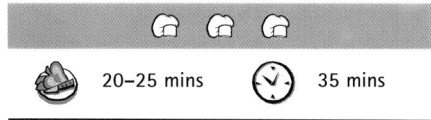

🍰 20–25 mins　🕐 35 mins

SERVES 8

INGREDIENTS

1 tsp sunflower oil, for oiling

225 g/8 oz butter, softened

225 g/8 oz caster sugar

4 eggs, beaten

225 g/8 oz self-raising flour

55 g/2 oz white chocolate, grated

CHESTNUT FROSTING

115 g/4 oz canned or fresh sweetened chestnut purée

4 tbsp butter, softened

350 g/12 oz icing sugar, sifted

1–2 tbsp milk

55 g/2 oz plain chocolate

1 tsp vanilla essence

TO DECORATE

55 g/2 oz chopped hazelnuts, toasted

55 g/2 oz plain chocolate

1 tbsp butter

2 tsp golden syrup

few marrons glacés (optional)

1　Preheat the oven to 180°C/350°F/Gas Mark 4. Lightly oil and line the base of 2 x 20-cm/8-inch shallow cake tins with non-stick baking paper. Cream the butter and sugar together until light and fluffy, then add the eggs a little at a time, beating well between each addition and adding a little flour after each addition. When all the eggs have been added, stir in the remaining flour together with 1–2 tablespoons of cooled boiled water to give a smooth dropping consistency.

2　Stir in the grated chocolate, mix lightly and divide between the prepared tins. Smooth the tops and bake in the preheated oven for 25 minutes, or until the top springs back when touched lightly with a finger. Remove from the oven and leave to cool before turning out and discarding the lining paper. Leave until cold, then split each cake horizontally in half.

3　Cream the chestnut purée and butter together until smooth, then gradually beat in the sifted icing sugar with a little milk to give a spreadable consistency. Melt the chocolate in a heatproof bowl set over a saucepan of gently simmering water. Stir the vanilla essence and the melted chocolate into the purée. Set aside 2–3

tablespoons of the icing, then use half the icing to sandwich the cakes together. Place the hazelnuts on a sheet of baking paper. Spread the remaining icing round the sides of the cake and roll in the nuts. Place on a serving plate. Place the reserved icing in a piping bag fitted with a star nozzle and pipe small rosettes round the top edge of the cake.

4　Place the remaining ingredients in a heavy-based saucepan and heat gently, stirring until the chocolate and butter have melted. Leave to cool until starting to thicken, then spoon over the top of the cake. Decorate with marrons glacés (if using) and serve.

Chocolate Madeira Cake

This light cake will certainly become a firm favourite because it has a delicious, velvety chocolate taste without being too rich.

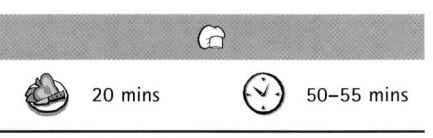

🍰 20 mins   🕐 50–55 mins

SERVES 8–10

INGREDIENTS

1 tsp sunflower oil, for oiling

55 g/2 oz self-raising flour

1 tsp baking powder

115 g/4 oz butter or margarine, softened

115 g/4 oz caster sugar

3 eggs, beaten

25 g/1 oz ground almonds

115 g/4 oz drinking chocolate powder

1 tbsp icing sugar, to decorate

ICING

225 g/8 oz icing sugar

1½ tbsp cocoa powder

2 tbsp butter

3–4 tbsp hot water

1 Preheat the oven to 180°C/350°F/Gas Mark 4. Lightly oil and line the base of an 18-cm/7-inch cake tin with non-stick baking paper. Sift the flour and baking powder together and set aside.

2 Cream the butter with the sugar until light and fluffy, then gradually beat in the eggs, adding a little of the flour after each addition. When all the eggs have been added, stir in the remaining flour together with the ground almonds. Sift the drinking chocolate powder into the mixture and stir lightly.

3 Spoon the mixture into the prepared cake tin and smooth the top. Bake in the preheated oven for 50–55 minutes, or until a skewer inserted into the centre of the cake comes out clean. Remove from the oven and leave to cool before removing from the tin and discarding the lining paper. Leave until cold.

4 Sift the icing sugar and cocoa together into a mixing bowl and make a hollow in the centre. Place the butter in the centre. Mix with with sufficient hot water to form a smooth spreadable icing. Coat the top and sides of the cake with icing, swirling it to give a decorative effect. Dust with icing sugar.

Jewel-Topped Madeira Cake

Brightly coloured glacé fruit make a stunning topping for this classic Madeira cake.

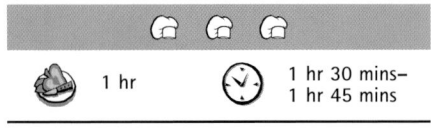

1 hr

1 hr 30 mins–
1 hr 45 mins

SERVES 8-10

INGREDIENTS

225 g/8 oz butter, softened, plus extra for greasing

225 g/8 oz golden caster sugar

finely grated rind of 1 lemon

4 eggs, beaten

350 g/12 oz self-raising flour, sifted

2–3 tbsp milk

FRUIT TOPPING

2½ tbsp honey

300 g/10½ oz glacé fruit

1 Preheat the oven to 160°C/325°F/ Gas Mark 3. Grease and base-line a 20-cm/8-inch deep round cake tin. Put the butter, sugar and lemon rind in a bowl and beat together until light and fluffy. Gradually beat in the eggs. Gently fold in the flour, alternately with enough milk to give a soft dropping consistency.

2 Spoon the mixture into the prepared tin and bake in the preheated oven for 1½–1¾ hours, until risen and golden and a skewer inserted into the centre comes out clean.

3 Leave in the tin for 10 minutes, then turn out, remove the paper and place on a wire rack to cool. To make the topping, brush the honey over the cake and arrange the fruit on top.

VARIATION
Traditionally, a Madeira cake is simply decorated with a slice of candied peel on top. This should be placed on the cake after it has been cooking for 1 hour.

Caraway Madeira

This is a classic Madeira cake made in the traditional way with caraway seeds. If you do not like their flavour, they can be omitted.

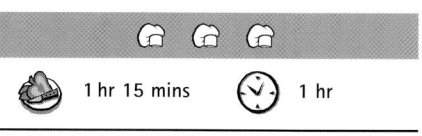

🍰 1 hr 15 mins   ⏲ 1 hr

SERVES 8

INGREDIENTS

200 g/7 oz butter, softened, plus extra for greasing

200 g/7 oz soft light brown sugar

3 eggs, beaten lightly

350 g/12 oz self-raising flour

1 tbsp caraway seeds

grated rind of 1 lemon

6 tbsp milk

1 or 2 strips citron rind

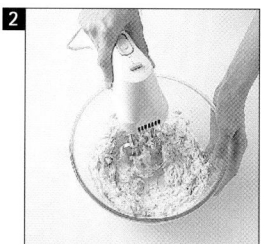

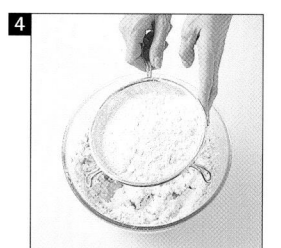

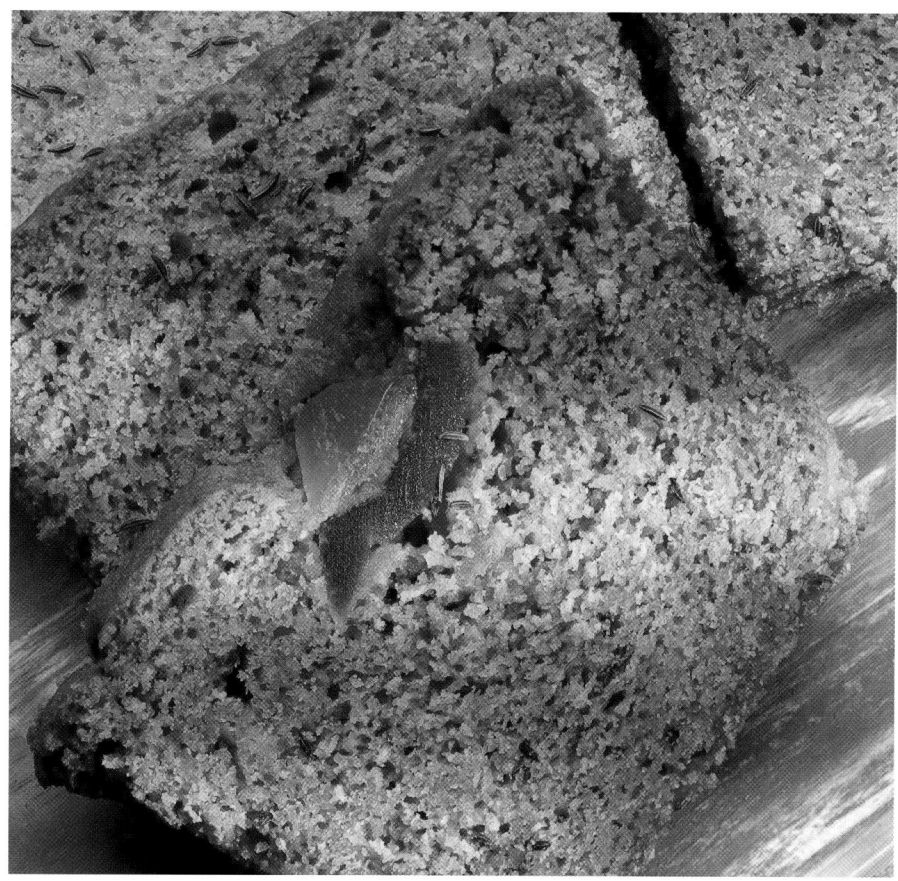

1 Preheat the oven to 160°C/325°F/Gas Mark 3. Grease and line a 900-g/2-lb loaf tin.

2 In a bowl, cream together the butter and brown sugar until pale and fluffy.

3 Gradually add the beaten eggs to the creamed mixture, beating well after each addition.

4 Sift the flour into the bowl and gently fold into the creamed mixture with a figure-of-eight movement.

5 Add the caraway seeds, lemon rind and milk, and gently fold in until thoroughly blended.

6 Spoon the mixture into the prepared tin and smooth the surface.

7 Bake in the preheated oven for 20 minutes.

8 Remove the cake from the oven and gently place the strips of citron rind on top of the cake. Return it to the oven and bake for an additional 40 minutes, or until the cake is well risen, golden brown and a fine skewer inserted into the centre comes out clean.

9 Leave the cake to cool in the tin before turning out and transferring to a wire rack to cool completely.

COOK'S TIP
Citron rind is available in the baking section of large stores. If it is unavailable, you can substitute candied peel.

Caraway Kugelhopf

Kugelhopf is a traditional German speciality which is a cross between a bread and a cake. Caraway seeds add an unusual flavour.

 15 mins plus 1 hr 30 mins rising

 30 mins

SERVES 8–10

INGREDIENTS

280 g/10 oz white bread flour

55 g/2 oz golden caster sugar

2 tsp easy-blend dried yeast

4 tsp caraway seeds

50 ml/2 fl oz tepid water

115 g/4 oz butter, melted, plus extra for greasing

3 eggs, beaten

icing sugar, for dusting

1 Sift the flour into a warmed bowl and stir in the sugar, yeast and caraway seeds. Make a well in the centre. In another bowl, mix together the water, butter and eggs and pour into the dry ingredients. Beat vigorously until smooth. Cover the bowl with clingfilm and leave in a warm place until the mixture has doubled in size.

2 Grease a 20-cm/8-inch kugelhopf tin. Stir the mixture and turn into the mould. Cover with clingfilm and leave to prove again until doubled in size. Preheat the oven to 200°C/400°F/Gas Mark 6.

COOK'S TIP

If you do not have a kugelhopf tin, use an ordinary ring mould. Because a kugelhopf tin has a lot of detailed indentations, it is important to grease it thoroughly so that the cake turns out easily.

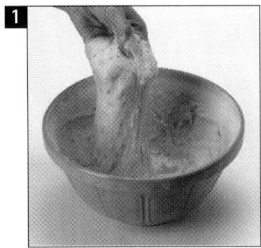

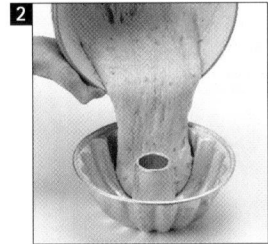

3 Remove the clingfilm and bake the kugelhopf in the oven for 20 minutes. Reduce the oven temperature to 190°C/375°F/Gas Mark 5 and bake for an additional 10 minutes, until well risen and golden brown. Leave in the tin for 10 minutes, then turn out and place on a wire rack to cool. Sift icing sugar over. Serve with butter while slightly warm.

Fruity Potato Cake

Sweet potatoes mix beautifully with fruit and brown sugar in this unusual cake. Add a few drops of rum or brandy if you like.

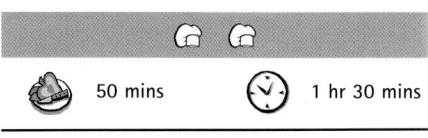

50 mins

1 hr 30 mins

SERVES 6

INGREDIENTS

1 tbsp butter, melted, plus extra for greasing

675 g/1 lb 8 oz sweet potatoes, peeled and diced

115 g/4 oz demerara sugar

3 eggs

3 tbsp skimmed milk

1 tbsp lemon juice

grated rind of 1 lemon

1 tsp caraway seeds

175 g/6 oz chopped dried fruit, such as apple, pear or mango

2 tsp baking powder

whipped cream, to decorate

1 Preheat the oven to 160°C/325°F/Gas Mark 3. Lightly grease an 18-cm/7-inch square cake tin.

2 Bring a large saucepan of water to the boil. Add the sweet potatoes, bring back to the boil and cook for 10 minutes or until soft. Drain and mash until smooth.

3 Transfer the mashed sweet potatoes to a mixing bowl while still hot and add the butter and sugar, mixing thoroughly to dissolve.

4 Beat in the eggs, skimmed milk, lemon juice and half the rind, caraway seeds and chopped dried fruit. Add the baking powder and mix well.

5 Pour the mixture into the prepared cake tin and smooth the top. Cook in the preheated oven for about 1-1¼ hours, or until a skewer inserted into the centre comes out clean.

6 Remove the cake from the tin and transfer to a wire rack to cool. Cut into thick slices, top each slice with whipped cream and the remaining lemon rind and serve.

Carrot & Ginger Cake

This melt-in-the-mouth version of a favourite cake has a fraction of the fat of the traditional cake.

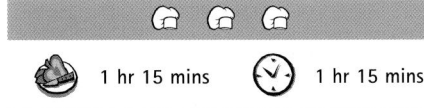

🕐 1 hr 15 mins   🕐 1 hr 15 mins

SERVES 10

INGREDIENTS

butter, for greasing

280 g/10 oz plain flour

1 tsp baking powder

1 tsp bicarbonate of soda

2 tsp ground ginger

½ tsp salt

175 g/6 oz dark muscovado sugar

325 g/11½ oz grated carrots

2 pieces chopped stem ginger

1 tbsp grated fresh root ginger

55 g/2 oz raisins

2 eggs, beaten

3 tbsp sunflower oil

juice of 1 orange

ICING

225 g/8 oz low-fat cream cheese

4 tbsp icing sugar

1 tsp vanilla essence

TO DECORATE

grated carrot

finely chopped stem ginger

ground ginger

1 Preheat the oven to 180°C/350°F/Gas Mark 4. Grease and line a 20-cm/ 8-inch round cake tin with baking paper.

2 Sift the flour, baking powder, bicarbonate of soda, ground ginger and salt into a bowl. Stir in the sugar, carrots, stem ginger, root ginger and raisins. Beat together the eggs, oil and orange juice, then pour into the bowl. Mix the ingredients together well.

3 Spoon the mixture into the tin and bake in the oven for 1–1¼ hours, until firm to the touch or until a skewer inserted into the centre of the cake comes out clean. Leave to cool in the tin.

4 To make the icing, place the cream cheese in a bowl and beat to soften. Sift in the icing sugar and add the vanilla essence. Mix well.

5 Remove the cake from the tin and spread the icing over the top. Decorate the cake and serve.

Carrot Cake

This classic favourite is always popular with children and adults alike when it is served for afternoon tea. It is also good served as a dessert.

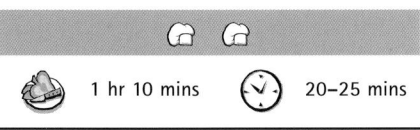

1 hr 10 mins   20–25 mins

MAKES 12 BARS

INGREDIENTS

butter, for greasing

125 g/4½ oz self-raising flour

pinch of salt

1 tsp ground cinnamon

125 g/4½ oz soft light brown sugar

2 eggs

100 ml/3½ fl oz sunflower oil

175 g/6 oz finely grated carrot

25 g/1 oz grated coconut

2 tbsp chopped walnuts

walnut pieces, to decorate

ICING

4 tbsp butter, softened

55 g/2 oz cream cheese

140 g/5 oz icing sugar, sifted

1 tsp lemon juice

1 Preheat the oven to 180°C/350°F/Gas Mark 4. Lightly grease a 20-cm/ 8-inch square cake tin with a little butter and line with baking paper.

2 Sift the flour, salt and ground cinnamon into a large bowl and stir in the brown sugar. Add the eggs and oil to the dry ingredients and mix well.

3 Stir in the grated carrot, coconut and chopped walnuts.

4 Pour the mixture into the prepared tin and bake in the preheated oven for 20–25 minutes, or until just firm to the touch. Leave to cool in the tin.

5 Meanwhile, make the cream cheese icing. In a bowl, beat together the butter, cream cheese, icing sugar and lemon juice until the mixture is light, fluffy and creamy.

6 Turn the cake out of the tin. Spread the cake with the icing and decorate with a few walnut pieces. Cut into 12 bars or slices.

VARIATION
For a moister cake, replace the coconut with 1 coarsely mashed banana.

Pear & Ginger Cake

This deliciously buttery pear and ginger cake is ideal with a cup of coffee, or you can serve it with cream for a delicious dessert.

15 mins   40 mins

SERVES 6

INGREDIENTS

200 g/7 oz butter, unsalted for preference, softened, plus extra for greasing

200 g/7 oz caster sugar

200 g/7 oz self-raising flour, sifted

1 tbsp ground ginger

3 eggs, beaten lightly

450 g/1 lb dessert pears, peeled, cored and sliced thinly

1 tbsp soft light brown sugar

ice cream or cream, to serve (optional)

1 Preheat the oven to 180°C/350°F/Gas Mark 4. Lightly grease a deep 20-cm/8-inch cake tin with butter and base-line with baking paper.

2 Using a whisk, combine all but 2 tablespoons of the butter with the sugar, flour, ginger and eggs, and mix to form a smooth consistency.

3 Spoon the cake mixture into the prepared tin, smoothing out the surface.

4 Arrange the pear slices over the cake mixture. Sprinkle with the brown sugar and dot with the remaining butter.

5 Bake in the preheated oven for 35–40 minutes, or until the cake is golden on top and feels springy to the touch.

6 Serve the pear and ginger cake warm, with ice cream or cream, if you wish.

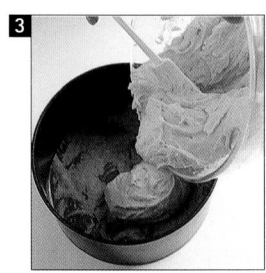

COOK'S TIP
Store ground ginger in an airtight jar, preferably made of coloured glass, or store in a clear glass jar in a cool, dark place.

Candied Ginger Cake

Ground ginger, stem ginger and ginger syrup make this a wonderfully gingery cake!

🍰 1 hr 🕐 45–50 mins

SERVES 12

INGREDIENTS

butter, for greasing

225 g/8 oz self-raising flour

1 tbsp ground ginger

1 tsp ground cinnamon

½ tsp bicarbonate of soda

115 g/4 oz butter

140 g/5 oz light muscovado sugar

grated rind of ½ lemon

2 eggs

1½ tbsp golden syrup

1½ tbsp milk

TOPPING

6 pieces stem ginger

85 g/3 oz icing sugar

4 tbsp syrup from the stem ginger jar

lemon juice

1 Preheat the oven to 160°C/325°F/ Gas Mark 3. Grease and base-line an 18-cm/7-inch square cake tin. Sift the flour, ginger, cinnamon and bicarbonate of soda into a bowl. Rub in the butter, then stir in the sugar and lemon rind. Make a well in the centre. Put the eggs, syrup and milk in a bowl and whisk together. Pour into the dry ingredients. Beat until smooth.

2 Spoon the mixture into the prepared tin and bake in the preheated oven for 45–50 minutes, until well risen and firm to the touch. Leave in the pan for 30 minutes, then turn out and remove the paper. Leave on a wire rack to cool completely.

3 Cut each piece of stem ginger into quarters and arrange the pieces on top of the cake. Sift the icing sugar into a bowl and stir in the ginger syrup and enough lemon juice to make a smooth icing. Put the icing in a polythene bag and cut a tiny hole in one corner. Drizzle the icing over the cake. Leave to set and then cut the cake into squares.

COOK'S TIP
This cake is better if it is kept in an airtight container for 1 day before eating.

Chocolate Banana Cake

The addition of bananas to this cake gives a wonderful moist texture with a subtle hint of banana.

1 hr   50–60 mins

SERVES 10–12

INGREDIENTS

1 tsp sunflower oil, for oiling

2 ripe bananas (about 225 g/8 oz in weight after peeling)

2 tbsp lemon juice

175 g/6 oz butter or margarine, softened

175 g/6 oz light muscovado sugar

2 eggs, beaten

225 g/8 oz self-raising flour

85 g/3 oz pecan nuts, chopped coarsely

55 g/2 oz plain chocolate

TOPPING

25 g/1 oz white chocolate

few pecan nuts

1 Preheat the oven to 180°C/350°F/Gas Mark 4. Lightly oil and line the base of a 900-g/2-lb loaf tin with non-stick baking paper. Cut the bananas into pieces, add the lemon juice and mash to form a purée. Set aside.

2 Cream the butter with the sugar until light and fluffy, then gradually beat in the eggs, adding a little flour after each addition. When all the eggs have been added, stir in the banana purée and then the remaining flour. Add the chopped pecan nuts. Melt the chocolate in a heatproof bowl set over a saucepan of gently simmering water. Stir until smooth, then stir lightly into the cake mixture.

3 Spoon the cake mixture into the prepared tin and bake in the preheated oven for 45–55 minutes, or until a skewer inserted into the centre comes out clean. Remove from the oven and leave until cool before removing from the tin and discarding the lining paper. Leave until cold.

4 Melt the chocolate in a heatproof bowl set over a saucepan of gently simmering water. Stir until smooth, then drizzle over the cooled cake. Arrange the pecan nuts on top, fixing with melted chocolate, and serve once the chocolate has set. Store in an airtight container and eat within 3 days of making.

COOK'S TIP

Make sure that this cake is eaten quickly. With the addition of bananas it does not last as long as some cakes.

Pear Cake

This is a really moist cake, deliciously flavoured with chopped pears and cinnamon and drizzled with lots of honey.

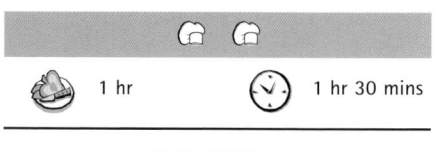

1 hr   1 hr 30 mins

SERVES 8

INGREDIENTS

margarine, for greasing

4 pears, peeled and cored

2 tbsp water

250 g/9 oz plain flour

2 tsp baking powder

85 g/3 oz soft light brown sugar

4 tbsp milk

2 tbsp honey, plus extra for drizzling

2 tsp ground cinnamon

2 egg whites

1 Preheat the oven to 150°C/300°F/ Gas Mark 2. Grease and base-line a 20-cm/8-inch cake tin.

2 Put 1 pear in a food processor with the water and process until almost smooth. Transfer to a mixing bowl.

3 Sift in the flour and baking powder. Beat in the sugar, milk, honey and cinnamon and mix with your fingers.

4 Chop all but 1 of the remaining pears and add to the mixture.

5 Whisk the egg whites until stiff peaks form and gently fold into the mixture until fully blended.

6 Slice the remaining pear and arrange it in a fan pattern on the base of the prepared tin.

7 Spoon the cake mixture into the tin and cook in the preheated oven for 1¼–1½ hours, or until cooked through and golden.

8 Remove from the oven and leave to cool in the tin for 10 minutes. Turn the cake out on to a wire rack and drizzle with honey. Set aside to cool completely, then cut into slices to serve.

COOK'S TIP

To test if the cake is cooked through, insert a skewer into the centre – if it comes out clean, the cake is cooked. If not, return the cake to the oven and test at frequent intervals.

Fresh Pear & Cinnamon Cake

This cake smells wonderful while it is baking and the combination of pear and cinnamon is divine.

1 hr 15 mins   1 hr 30 mins

SERVES 8

INGREDIENTS

3–4 firm pears, depending on the size

1 vanilla pod

200 g/7 oz golden caster sugar

2 large eggs

200 g/7 oz butter, melted and cooled

300 g/10½ oz plain flour

1 tbsp ground cinnamon

½ tsp bicarbonate of soda

4 tbsp golden icing sugar

1 Preheat the oven to 180°C/350°F Gas Mark 4. Thoroughly grease a 20-cm/8-inch springform cake tin. Peel and quarter the pears and remove the cores. Cut the pears into small cubes, place in a saucepan and cover with water. Split the vanilla pod to expose the seeds and add to the saucepan. Bring to the boil and simmer gently until the pears are tender. Leave in the saucepan to cool. Drain the pears, reserving their cooking liquid, and pat dry with kitchen paper.

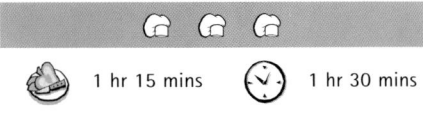

2 Put the sugar, eggs and butter in a bowl and whisk together. Sift the flour, cinnamon and bicarbonate of soda into another bowl. Fold the flour into the sugar and egg mixture, one-third at a time. Carefully fold in the pears. Transfer the mixture to the prepared mould and bake in the oven for 50–55 minutes, until a skewer inserted into the centre comes out clean. Leave in the mould to cool for 20 minutes, then turn out on to a wire rack to cool completely.

3 To make the icing, sift the icing sugar into a bowl and add enough of the reserved pear juice to give a pouring consistency. Drizzle the icing over the cake and leave to set before serving.

VARIATION
As an alternative to fresh pears, canned pears could be used.

Coffee Caramel Cake

This intensely flavoured coffee cake is complemented perfectly with a delicious caramel icing, decorated with chocolate-coated coffee beans.

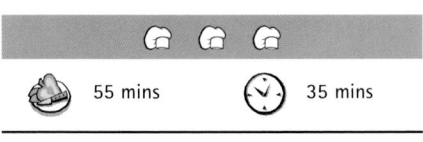

55 mins   35 mins

SERVES 8–10

INGREDIENTS

175 g/6 oz butter, softened, plus extra for greasing

175 g/6 oz golden caster sugar

3 eggs, beaten

280 g/10 oz self-raising flour, sifted

100 ml/3½ fl oz strong black coffee

ICING

125 ml/4 fl oz whole milk

125 g/4½ oz butter

3 tbsp golden caster sugar

575 g/1lb 4 oz icing sugar

chocolate-coated coffee beans, to decorate

1 Preheat the oven to 180°C/350°F/ Gas Mark 4. Grease and base-line 2 x 20-cm/8-inch sandwich tins. Put the butter and sugar in a bowl and beat together until light and fluffy. Gradually beat in the eggs, then fold in the flour and coffee. Divide the mixture between the prepared tins and bake in the oven for 30 minutes, until well risen and springy to the touch. Leave in the tins for 5 minutes, then turn out and remove the paper. Place on wire racks to cool completely.

2 To make the icing, put the milk and butter in a saucepan and heat gently until the butter has melted. Remove from the heat and set aside. Put the caster sugar in a heavy-based saucepan and heat gently until the sugar dissolves and turns a golden caramel. Remove from the heat and stir in the warm milk. Return to the heat and stir until the caramel dissolves.

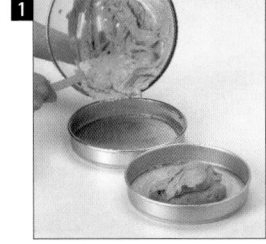

3 Remove from the heat and gradually stir in the icing sugar, beating until the icing is a smooth spreading consistency. Sandwich the cakes together with some of the icing and spread the rest over the top and sides. Decorate with chocolate-coated coffee beans and serve.

Coffee Streusel Cake

This cake has a moist coffee sponge cake on the bottom, covered with a crisp crunchy, spicy topping.

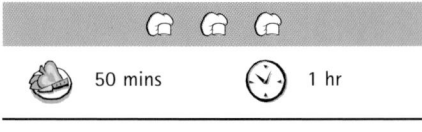

50 mins   1 hr

SERVES 8

INGREDIENTS

butter, for greasing

225 g/8 oz plain flour

1 tbsp baking powder

70 g/2½ oz caster sugar

150 ml/5 fl oz milk

2 eggs

115 g/4 oz butter, melted and cooled

2 tbsp instant coffee powder mixed with 1 tbsp boiling water

50 g/1¾ oz chopped almonds

icing sugar, for dusting

TOPPING

70 g/2½ oz self-raising flour

70 g/2½ oz demerara sugar

2 tbsp butter, cut into small pieces

1 tsp ground mixed spice

1 tbsp water

1 Preheat the oven to 190°C/375°F/Gas Mark 5. Grease and line a 23-cm/ 9-inch loose-based cake tin.

2 Sift the flour and baking powder into a mixing bowl, then stir in the caster sugar.

3 Whisk the milk, eggs, melted butter and coffee mixture together and pour on to the dry ingredients. Add the chopped almonds and mix lightly together. Spoon the mixture into the prepared tin.

4 To make the topping, mix the flour and sugar together in a bowl.

5 Rub in the butter with your fingertips until the mixture resembles breadcrumbs. Sprinkle in the mixed spice and water and bring the mixture together in loose crumbs. Sprinkle the topping evenly over the cake.

6 Bake in the preheated oven for 50 minutes–1 hour. Cover loosely with foil if the topping starts to brown too quickly.

7 Leave to cool in the tin. Dust with icing sugar just before serving.

Almond Cake

Glazing with a honey syrup after baking gives this cake a lovely moist texture, but it can be eaten without the glaze if preferred.

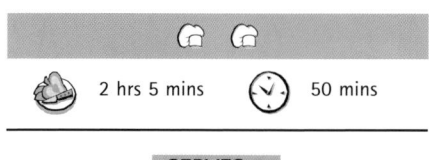

2 hrs 5 mins   50 mins

SERVES 8

INGREDIENTS

75 g/2¾ oz soft margarine, plus extra for greasing

75 g/2¾ oz soft light brown sugar

2 eggs

175 g/6 oz self-raising flour

1 tsp baking powder

4 tbsp milk

2 tbsp clear honey

50 g/1¾ oz flaked almonds

SYRUP

225 g/8 oz honey

2 tbsp lemon juice

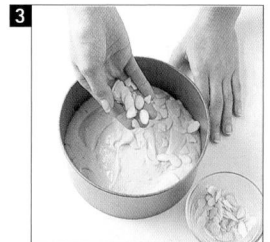

1 Preheat the oven to 180°C/350°F/Gas Mark 4. Grease an 18-cm/7-inch round cake tin and line with baking paper.

2 Place the margarine, brown sugar, eggs, flour, baking powder, milk and honey in a large mixing bowl and beat well with a wooden spoon for about 1 minute, or until all of the ingredients are thoroughly mixed together.

3 Spoon into the prepared tin, smooth the surface with the back of a spoon or a knife and sprinkle with the almonds.

4 Bake in the preheated oven for about 50 minutes, or until the cake is well risen and a fine skewer inserted into the centre of the cake comes out clean.

5 Meanwhile, make the syrup. Combine the honey and lemon juice in a small saucepan and simmer over low heat for about 5 minutes, or until the syrup starts to coat the back of a spoon.

6 As soon as the cake comes out of the oven, pour the syrup over it, letting it seep into the middle of the cake.

7 Leave the cake to cool for at least 2 hours before slicing.

COOK'S TIP
Experiment with different flavoured honeys for the syrup glaze until you find the one that you like best.

Almond & Hazelnut Gâteau

This is a light, nutty cake made with a rich chocolate cream. Simple to create, it is a gâteau you are sure to make again and again.

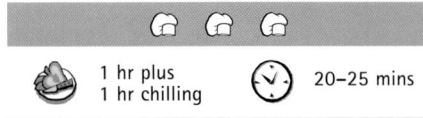

1 hr plus
1 hr chilling

20–25 mins

SERVES 8

INGREDIENTS

butter, for greasing

4 eggs

115 g/4 oz caster sugar

50 g/1¾ oz ground almonds

50 g/1¾ oz ground hazelnuts

50 g/1¾ oz plain flour

70 g/2¾ oz flaked almonds

FILLING

100 g/3½ oz plain chocolate

1 tbsp butter

300 ml/10 fl oz double cream

icing sugar, for dusting

1 Preheat the oven to 190°C/375°F/Gas Mark 5. Grease 2 x 18-cm/7-inch sandwich tins. Base-line with baking paper.

2 Whisk the eggs and caster sugar in a large mixing bowl with an electric whisk for about 10 minutes, or until the mixture is very light and foamy and a trail is left when the whisk is dragged across the surface.

3 Fold in the ground nuts, sift the flour and fold in with a metal spoon or palette knife. Pour into the prepared tins.

4 Scatter the flaked almonds over the top of one of the cakes. Bake both of the cakes in the preheated oven for 15–20 minutes, or until springy to the touch.

5 Leave to cool slightly in the tins. Remove the cakes from the tins and transfer to a wire rack to cool completely.

6 Meanwhile, make the filling. Melt the chocolate, remove from the heat and stir in the butter. Leave the mixture to cool slightly. Whip the cream until just holding its shape, then fold in the melted chocolate until mixed.

7 Place the cake without the extra almonds on a serving plate and spread the filling over it. Leave the filling to set slightly, then place the almond-topped cake on top and chill for about 1 hour. Dust with icing sugar and serve.

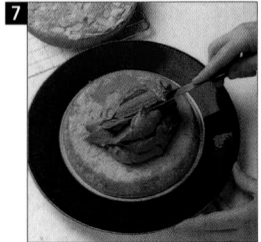

Cherry & Almond Cake

Ground almonds add richness to the cake and help its keeping qualities. It is good served at any time of day.

50 mins | 1 hr 30 mins–1 hr 45 mins

SERVES 8

INGREDIENTS

175 g/6 oz butter, softened, plus extra for greasing

300 g/10½ oz glacé cherries

175 g/6 oz golden caster sugar

3 eggs

40 g/1½ oz ground almonds

280 g/10 oz plain flour

1½ tsp baking powder

70g/2½ oz flaked almonds, to decorate

1 Preheat the oven to 160°C/325°F/ Gas Mark 3. Grease and base-line an 18-cm/7-inch deep square cake tin. Cut the cherries in half, then put them in a strainer and rinse to remove all the syrup. Pat dry with kitchen paper and set aside.

2 Put the butter, caster sugar, eggs and ground almonds in a bowl. Sift in the flour and baking powder. Beat thoroughly until smooth, then stir in the cherries. Spoon the mixture into the prepared tin and smooth the top.

3 Sprinkle the flaked almonds over the cake. Bake in the preheated oven for 1½–1¾ hours, until well risen and a skewer inserted into the centre of the cake comes out clean. Leave in the tin for 10 minutes, then turn out, remove the paper and place on a wire rack to cool.

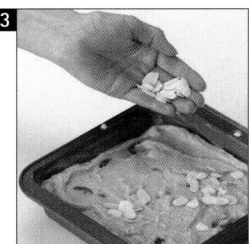

COOK'S TIP

Washing and drying the cherries before use helps prevent them sinking.

Orange & Almond Cake

This light and tangy citrus cake is better eaten as a dessert than as a cake. It is especially good served at the end of a large meal.

50 mins

35–40 mins

SERVES 8

INGREDIENTS

butter, for greasing

4 eggs, separated

125 g/4½ oz caster sugar, plus 2 tsp for the cream

finely grated rind and juice of 2 oranges

finely grated rind and juice of 1 lemon

100 g/3½ oz ground almonds

4 tbsp self-raising flour

200 ml/7 fl oz whipping cream

1 tsp ground cinnamon

4 tbsp flaked almonds, toasted

icing sugar, for dusting

1 Preheat the oven to 180°C/350°F/ Gas Mark 4. Grease and base-line an 18-cm/7-inch round deep cake tin.

2 Blend the egg yolks with the sugar until the mixture is thick and creamy. Whisk half of the orange rind and all of the lemon rind into the egg yolks. Combine the orange and lemon juice with the ground almonds and stir into the egg yolks. Fold in the flour. Whisk the egg whites until stiff and gently fold in.

3 Pour the mixture into the tin and smooth the surface. Bake in the preheated oven for 35–40 minutes, or until golden and springy to the touch. Set aside to cool in the tin for 10 minutes and then turn out on to a rack to cool completely.

4 Whip the cream to form soft peaks. Stir in the remaining orange rind, cinnamon and sugar.

5 Cover the cake with the almonds, dust with icing sugar and serve with the cream.

VARIATION
To serve with a syrup, boil the juice and finely grated rind of 2 oranges, 85 g/3 oz caster sugar and 2 tablespoons water for 5–6 minutes. Stir in 1 tablespoon orange flavoured liqueur just before serving.

Sicilian Citrus Cake

Serve this delicious fragrant cake after dinner, with a small glass of limoncello or Cointreau if you like.

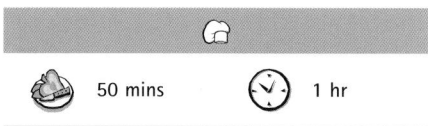

50 mins   1 hr

SERVES 4

INGREDIENTS

1 tsp olive oil, for oiling

175 g/6 oz plain flour

1 tsp baking powder

1 tsp bicarbonate of soda

pinch of salt

175 g/6 oz caster sugar

2 eggs

finely grated rind and juice of 1 orange

2 tbsp limoncello (lemon liqueur) or orange-flavoured liqueur, such as Cointreau

TOPPING

225 ml/8 fl oz double cream, whipped

3 tbsp icing sugar

1 tbsp grated orange rind

strips of candied orange and lemon peel, to decorate

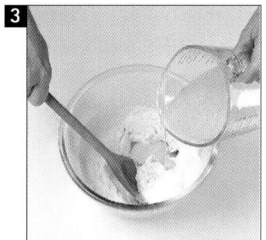

1 Preheat the oven to 180°C/350°F/Gas Mark 4. Oil a 20-cm/8-inch cake tin and line it with baking paper.

2 Sift the flour, baking powder, bicarbonate of soda and salt into a large mixing bowl, then stir in the caster sugar.

3 In a separate bowl, mix the eggs with the orange rind and juice. Stir in the limoncello or orange liqueur, then pour the mixture into the flour and stir well.

4 Transfer the mixture to the prepared cake tin, smooth the surface and bake in the centre of the preheated oven for at least 1 hour, until firm and golden. Remove from the oven and leave to cool, then turn out the cake on to a serving plate.

5 To make the topping, put the cream into a bowl and add the icing sugar and grated orange rind. Mix well, then spread over the top of the cake. Decorate with strips of candied orange and lemon peel and serve.

Orange Kugelhopf Cake

Baking in a deep, fluted kugelhopf tin ensures that you create a cake with a stunning shape. The moist cake is full of fresh orange flavour.

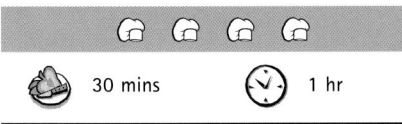

30 mins   1 hr

SERVES 6–8

INGREDIENTS

200 g/7 oz butter, softened, plus extra for greasing

200 g/7 oz caster sugar

4 eggs, separated

425 g/15 oz plain flour

pinch of salt

3 tsp baking powder

300 ml/10 fl oz fresh orange juice

1 tbsp orange flower water

1 tsp grated orange rind

SYRUP

175 ml/6 fl oz orange juice

200 g/7 oz granulated sugar

1 Preheat the oven to 180°C/350°F/Gas Mark 4. Grease and flour a 25-cm/ 10-inch kugelhopf tin or deep ring mould.

2 In a bowl, cream together the butter and caster sugar until light and fluffy. Add the egg yolks, 1 at a time, whisking well after each addition.

3 Sift the flour, a pinch of salt and the baking powder together into a separate bowl. Fold the dry ingredients and the orange juice alternately into the creamed mixture with a metal spoon, working as lightly as possible. Stir in the orange flower water and orange rind.

4 Whisk the egg whites until they form soft peaks and gently fold them into the mixture.

5 Pour into the prepared tin or mould and bake in the preheated oven for 50–55 minutes, or until a metal skewer inserted into the centre of the cake comes out clean.

6 Bring the orange juice and sugar to the boil in a small saucepan over low heat, then simmer gently for 5 minutes until the sugar has dissolved.

7 Remove the cake from the oven and leave to cool in the tin for 10 minutes.

8 Prick the top of the cake with a fine skewer and brush over half of the syrup. Leave the cake to cool, still in the tin, for an additional 10 minutes.

9 Invert the cake on to a wire rack placed over a deep plate and brush the syrup over the cake until it is entirely covered. Serve warm or cold.

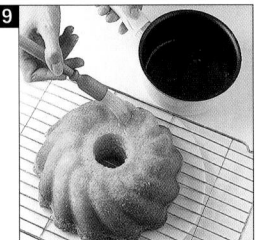

Clementine Cake

This cake is flavoured with clementine rind and juice, creating a rich buttery cake bursting with fruit flavour. Orange would also work well.

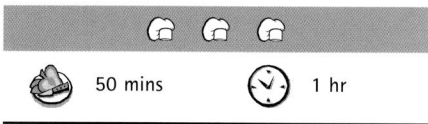

50 mins   1 hr

SERVES 8

INGREDIENTS

175 g/6 oz butter, softened, plus extra for greasing

2 clementines

175 g/6 oz caster sugar

3 eggs, beaten lightly

175 g/6 oz self-raising flour

3 tbsp ground almonds

3 tbsp single cream

GLAZE AND TOPPING

6 tbsp clementine juice

2 tbsp caster sugar

3 white sugar lumps, crushed

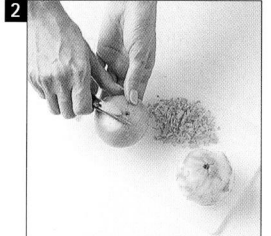

1 Preheat the oven to 180°C/350°F/Gas Mark 4. Grease an 18-cm/7-inch tin and base-line with baking paper.

2 Pare the rind from the clementines and chop it finely. In a bowl, cream the butter, sugar and clementine rind together until pale and fluffy.

3 Gradually add the beaten eggs to the mixture, beating thoroughly after each addition.

4 Gently fold in the flour, ground almonds and cream. Spoon the mixture into the prepared tin.

5 Bake in the preheated oven for about 55–60 minutes, or until a fine skewer inserted into the centre comes out clean. Leave to cool slightly.

6 Meanwhile, make the glaze. Put the clementine juice into a small saucepan with the caster sugar. Bring to the boil over a low heat and simmer for 5 minutes.

7 Turn out the cake on to a wire rack. Drizzle the glaze over the cake until it has been absorbed and sprinkle with the crushed sugar lumps. Leave to cool completely before serving.

COOK'S TIP
If you prefer, chop the rind from the clementines in a food processor or blender along with the sugar in step 2. Tip the mixture into a bowl with the butter and start to cream the mixture.

Caribbean Coconut Cake

Desiccated coconut and coconut cream make this moist cake rich and delicious, and are complemented by the pineapple jam.

50 mins | 25 mins

SERVES 8

INGREDIENTS

280 g/10 oz butter, softened, plus extra for greasing

200 g/7 oz golden caster sugar

3 eggs

200 g/7 oz self-raising flour

1½ tsp baking powder

½ tsp freshly grated nutmeg

70 g/2½ oz desiccated coconut

5 tbsp coconut cream

200 g/7 oz icing sugar

5 tbsp pineapple jam

desiccated coconut, toasted, to decorate

1 Preheat the oven to 180°C/350°F/Gas Mark 4. Grease and line the bases of 2 x 20-cm/8-inch sponge cake tins. Place 175 g/6 oz of the butter in a bowl with the sugar and eggs. Sift in the flour, baking powder and nutmeg. Beat together until smooth, then stir in the coconut and 2 tablespoons of coconut cream.

2 Divide the mixture between the prepared tins and carefully smooth over the tops. Bake in the preheated oven for 25 minutes, or until golden and firm to the touch. Leave to cool in the tins for 5 minutes, then turn out on to a wire rack, peel off the lining paper and leave to cool completely.

3 Sift the icing sugar into a bowl and add the remaining butter and coconut cream. Beat together until smooth. Spread the pineapple jam on one of the cakes and top with just under half of the buttercream. Place the other cake on top. Spread the remaining buttercream on top of the cake and scatter with the toasted desiccated coconut.

COOK'S TIP
Coconut cream comes in small cartons. What remains after making this cake can be used in custards, soups or curries, or can be poured over fresh fruit in place of cream.

Italian Lemon Rice Cake

This lemony cake should have a crisp crust with a soft moist centre. Soaking the currants in dark rum brings out their fruitiness.

🍰 1 hr 15 mins   🕐 1 hr 15 mins

SERVES 8–10

I N G R E D I E N T S

1 litre/1¾ pints milk

pinch of salt

350 g/12 oz risotto rice

1 vanilla pod, split

40 g/1½ oz currants

50 ml/2 fl oz dark rum or water

2 tsp melted butter, for greasing

cornmeal, for dusting

175 g/6 oz sugar

grated rind of 1 large lemon

4 tbsp butter, cut into pieces

3 eggs

2–3 tbsp lemon juice (optional)

icing sugar

TO SERVE

175 g/6 oz mascarpone cheese

2 tbsp dark rum

2 tbsp whipping cream

1 Bring the milk to the boil. Sprinkle in the salt and rice and bring back to the boil. Add the vanilla pod and seeds. Reduce the heat and simmer, stirring occasionally, for 30 minutes.

2 Meanwhile, bring the currants and rum to the boil, then set aside.

3 Preheat the oven to 160°C/325°F/Gas Mark 3. Brush the bases and sides of a 25-cm/10-inch loose-based cake tin with butter. Dust with about 2–3 tablespoons of cornmeal and shake out any excess.

4 Remove the rice from the heat and remove the vanilla pod. Stir in all but 1 tablespoon of sugar, with the lemon rind and butter, until the sugar has dissolved. Place in ice-cold water to cool. Stir in the soaked currants and remaining rum.

5 Beat the eggs with an electric whisk, for about 2 minutes, until light and foamy. Gradually beat in about half the rice mixture, then stir in the rest. If using, stir in the lemon juice.

6 Pour into the prepared tin and smooth the top. Sprinkle with the reserved sugar and bake in the preheated oven for about 40 minutes, or until risen, golden and slightly firm. Cool in the tin on a wire rack.

7 Turn out and dust with icing sugar. Transfer the cake to a serving plate. Whisk the mascarpone with the rum and cream and serve with the cake.

Citrus Honey Cake

This light-textured cake is drizzled with honey and lemon juice while it is still warm from the oven, giving it a rich and zesty flavour.

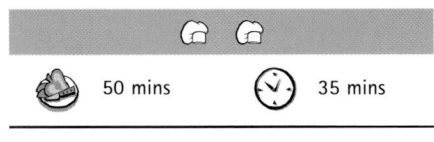
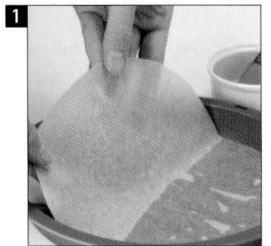

50 mins | 35 mins

MAKES 23-CM/9-INCH CAKE

INGREDIENTS

sunflower or corn oil, for brushing

40 g/1½ oz reduced-fat sunflower margarine

4 tbsp honey

finely grated rind and juice of 1 lemon

150 ml/5 fl oz skimmed milk

175 g/6 oz plain flour

1½ tsp baking powder

½ teaspoon mixed spice

6 tbsp semolina

2 egg whites

2 tsp sesame seeds

1 Preheat the oven to 200°C/400°F/Gas Mark 6. Lightly brush a 23-cm/9-inch round cake tin with oil and line the base with baking paper. Put the margarine and 3 tablespoons of the honey in a heavy-based saucepan and melt over very low heat. Remove the saucepan from the heat. Reserve 1 tablespoon of the lemon juice and stir the remainder into the honey mixture with the lemon rind and milk.

2 Sift the flour, baking powder and mixed spice into a bowl, then tip the mixture into the saucepan, together with the semolina, and beat. Whisk the egg whites until soft peaks form, then gently fold them into the mixture. Spoon into the prepared tin and smooth the surface. Sprinkle the sesame seeds evenly on top.

3 Bake in the preheated oven for about 30 minutes, or until golden brown and springy to the touch. Combine the remaining honey and lemon juice in a small jug and pour it over the cake. Set aside in the tin to cool before serving.

VARIATION

For a change, flavour this cake with orange rind and juice instead of the lemon.

Honey Spice Cake

This cake benefits from being kept for a day before eating, so it is best made in advance and stored in an airtight container.

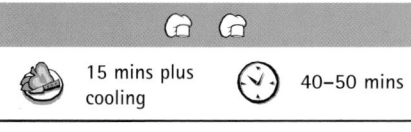

15 mins plus cooling

40–50 mins

SERVES 8–10

INGREDIENTS

150 g/5½ oz butter, plus extra for greasing

175 g/6 oz light muscovado sugar

250 g/9 oz honey

225 g/8 oz self-raising flour

½ tsp ground ginger

½ tsp ground cinnamon

½ tsp caraway seeds

the seeds from 8 cardamom pods, ground

2 eggs, beaten

ICING

280 g/10 oz icing sugar

warm water

1 Preheat the oven to 180°C/350°F/Gas Mark 4. Grease a 23-cm/9-inch round cake tin. Put the butter, sugar, honey and 1 tablespoon water into a saucepan. Heat gently until the butter has melted and the sugar has dissolved. Remove from the heat and leave to cool for 10 minutes.

2 Sift the flour into a bowl and mix in the ginger, cinnamon, caraway seeds and cardamom. Make a well in the centre. Pour in the honey mixture and the eggs and beat well until smooth. Pour the mixture into the prepared tin and bake in the oven for 40–50 minutes, until well risen and a skewer inserted into the centre comes out clean. Leave in the tin for 5 minutes, then transfer to a wire rack to cool.

3 To make the icing, sift the icing sugar into a bowl. Stir in enough warm water to make a smooth flowing icing. Spoon over the cake, letting it flow down the sides. Leave to set before serving.

COOK'S TIP
Choose a strongly flavoured honey so that it is not overpowered by the spices.

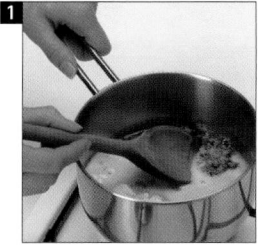

Passion Fruit Angel Cake

Angel cake is wonderfully light and airy. A passion fruit icing makes it even more delicious.

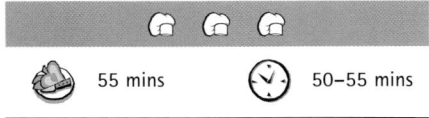

🍰🍰🍰

🍰 55 mins   ⏱ 50–55 mins

SERVES 8

INGREDIENTS

90 g/3¼ oz plain flour

280 g/10 oz caster sugar

8 large egg whites

1 tsp cream of tartar

pinch of salt

1 tsp vanilla essence

2 tbsp warm water

ICING

4 passion fruit

175 g/6 oz icing sugar

1 Preheat the oven to 180°C/350°F/ Gas Mark 4. Sift the flour and 2 tablespoons of sugar on to a sheet of greaseproof paper. Put the egg whites in a large clean bowl and whisk until frothy, then stir in the cream of tartar and salt. Sprinkle in the vanilla essence and warm water and continue whisking until the egg whites are stiff but not dry. Sift in the remaining sugar, 2 tablespoons at a time, whisking between each addition until the mixture forms soft peaks.

2 Gently fold in the flour and sugar mixture, in several batches. Pour the mixture into a non-stick angel cake tin with a funnel. It should be about two-thirds full. Bake in the oven for 50–55 minutes, until the top is brown and dry to the touch. Turn the tin upside down and leave until the cake is completely cold. Ease the cake out of the tin with a palette knife and place on a serving plate.

3 To make the icing, halve the passion fruit and scoop out the pulp into a sieve set over a bowl. Press the juice from the pulp with a wooden spoon. Stir in enough icing sugar to make an icing with the consistency of double cream. Pour the icing over the cake and leave to set.

COOK'S TIP

If you do not have an angel cake tin, any other tin can be used.

Coconut Cake

This is a great, all-time family favourite. Serve cut into slices with a cup of coffee for an afternoon snack.

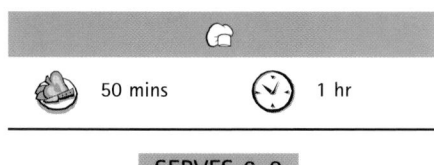

🧈 50 mins 🕐 1 hr

SERVES 6-8

INGREDIENTS

115 g/4 oz butter, cut into small pieces, plus extra for greasing

225 g/8 oz self-raising flour

pinch of salt

115 g/4 oz demerara sugar

100 g/3½ oz grated coconut, plus extra for sprinkling

2 eggs, beaten lightly

4 tbsp milk

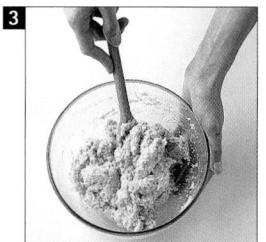

1 Preheat the oven to 160°C/325°F/Gas Mark 3. Grease a 900-g/2-lb loaf tin and line the base with baking paper.

2 Sift the flour and salt into a mixing bowl and rub in the butter with your fingertips until the mixture resembles fine breadcrumbs.

3 Stir in the sugar, coconut, eggs and milk and mix to a soft dropping consistency.

4 Spoon the mixture into the tin and smooth the surface with a palette knife. Bake in the oven for 30 minutes.

COOK'S TIP
The flavour of this cake is enhanced by storing it in a cool dry place for a few days before eating.

5 Remove the cake from the oven and sprinkle with the extra coconut. Return the cake to the oven and bake for an additional 30 minutes, until well risen and golden and a fine skewer inserted into the centre comes out clean.

6 Leave the cake to cool slightly in the tin before turning out and transferring to a wire rack to cool completely. Serve cut into slices.

Sicilian Cassata

This rich cake with its filling of ricotta cheese, candied peel, almonds and plain chocolate is a speciality of Sicily.

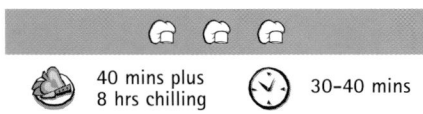

🦪 🦪 🦪

🍰 40 mins plus 8 hrs chilling   🕐 30–40 mins

SERVES 8

INGREDIENTS

CAKE

175 g/6 oz butter, softened, plus extra for greasing

175 g/6 oz self-raising flour

2–3 tbsp cocoa powder

1 tsp baking powder

175 g/6 oz golden caster sugar

3 eggs

FILLING

450 g/1 lb ricotta cheese

100 g/3½ oz plain chocolate, grated

115 g/4 oz golden caster sugar

3 tbsp Marsala

70 g/2½ oz chopped candied peel

40 g/1½ oz chopped almonds

TO DECORATE

sifted icing sugar

chocolate curls (see page 9)

1 Preheat the oven to 190°C/375°F/ Gas Mark 5. Grease and base-line an 18-cm/7-inch loose-based cake tin. Sift the flour, cocoa and baking powder into a large bowl. Add the butter, sugar and eggs and beat well until smooth. Pour the mixture into the prepared tin and bake in the oven for 30–40 minutes, until well risen and firm to the touch. Leave in the tin for 5 minutes, then turn out on to a wire rack to cool.

2 Wash and dry the cake tin and grease and line it again. To make the filling, rub the ricotta cheese through a sieve into a bowl. Add the chocolate, sugar and Marsala and beat thoroughly until the mixture is light and fluffy. Stir in the candied peel and chopped almonds.

3 Cut the thin crust off the top of the cake and discard. Cut the cake horizontally into 3 layers. Place the first slice in the prepared tin and cover with half the ricotta mixture. Repeat the layers, finishing with a cake layer. Press down lightly, cover with a weight and chill overnight. To serve, turn the cake out on to a serving plate. Sift icing sugar over and decorate the top with chocolate curls.

Nutty Polenta Cake

It is important to use the instant polenta in this recipe, otherwise the texture will be very gritty. Use plain or milk chocolate if preferred.

1 hr   1 hr

SERVES 10–12

INGREDIENTS

1 tsp sunflower oil, for oiling

115 g/4 oz mixed nuts, such as hazelnuts, almonds and pistachio nuts

175 g/6 oz butter, softened

175 g/6 oz light muscovado sugar

1 tbsp grated orange rind

3 eggs, beaten

115 g/4 oz self-raising flour

1½ tsp ground cinnamon

85 g/3 oz milk chocolate, chopped

85 g/3 oz instant polenta

2 tbsp orange juice

25 g/1 oz white chocolate

few whole nuts, to decorate

1 Preheat the oven to 180°C/350°F/Gas Mark 4. Lightly oil and base-line a 900-g/2-lb loaf tin with non-stick baking paper. Place the nuts in a food processor and process until finely chopped. Set aside.

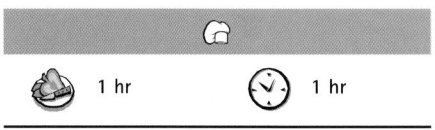

2 Cream the butter with the sugar and orange rind until light and fluffy. Gradually beat in the eggs, adding a little flour after each addition. When all the eggs have been added, stir in the remaining flour together with the ground cinnamon, the chopped chocolate and the polenta. Stir lightly, adding sufficient orange juice to give a soft dropping consistency.

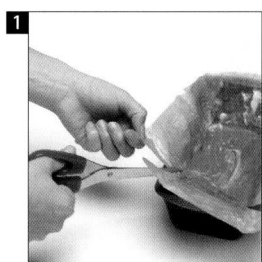

3 Turn into the prepared loaf tin and smooth the top. Bake in the preheated oven for 50–60 minutes, or until a skewer inserted into the centre comes out clean. Remove from the oven and leave to cool before turning out on a wire rack and discarding the lining paper.

4 Melt the white chocolate in a small heatproof bowl set over a saucepan of gently simmering water. Stir until smooth, then use to drizzle over the top of the cake. Press the whole nuts into the melted chocolate and leave to set before serving.

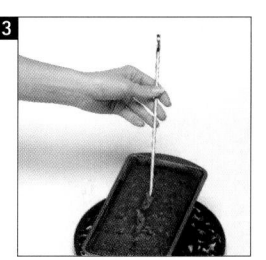

COOK'S TIP
If you cannot find instant polenta, use ground almonds.

Golden Polenta Cake

Polenta makes an extremely moist cake with a good colour. Its texture is quite dense, compared to one made with all wheat flour.

40 mins   1 hr

SERVES 4–6

INGREDIENTS

100 g/3½ oz butter, plus extra for greasing

100 g/3½ oz caster sugar

2 eggs, beaten

6 tbsp self-raising flour

1 tsp baking powder

100 g/3½ oz instant polenta

150 g/5½ oz sultanas

50 g/1¾ oz chopped almonds

grated rind and juice of 1 orange

TO DECORATE

icing sugar

toasted flaked almonds

mascarpone cheese, to serve

1 Preheat the oven to 180°C/350°F/Gas Mark 4. Grease a 20-cm/8-inch cake tin and line it with baking paper.

2 Cream together the butter and caster sugar in a bowl, then gradually whisk in the beaten eggs. Fold in the flour, baking powder and polenta. Add the sultanas, almonds and the orange rind and juice, and stir together well.

3 Transfer the mixture to the prepared cake tin and smooth the surface. Bake in the centre of the preheated oven for 1 hour, until firm and golden. Remove from the oven and leave to cool, then turn out the cake on to a serving plate.

4 Sprinkle over the icing sugar and flaked almonds and serve with generous spoonfuls of mascarpone.

Crispy-Topped Fruit Bake

The crushed sugar lumps give a lovely crunchy texture to this very easy-to-make blackberry and apple dessert.

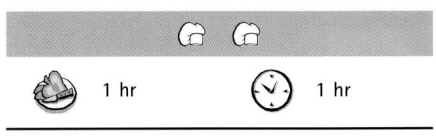

🍰 1 hr   🕐 1 hr

SERVES 10

INGREDIENTS

butter or margarine, for greasing

350 g/12 oz cooking apples

3 tbsp lemon juice

350 g/12 oz self-raising wholemeal flour

½ tsp baking powder

1 tsp ground cinnamon, plus extra for dusting

115 g/4 oz prepared blackberries, thawed if frozen, plus extra to decorate

115 g/4 oz light muscovado sugar

1 egg, beaten

200 ml/7fl oz low-fat natural yogurt

55 g/2 oz white or brown sugar lumps, crushed lightly

sliced eating apple, to decorate

1 Preheat the oven to 190°C/375°F/Gas Mark 5. Grease and line a 900-g/2-lb loaf tin with a little butter. Core, peel and finely dice the apples. Place them in a saucepan with the lemon juice, bring to the boil, cover and simmer for about 10 minutes until soft and pulpy. Beat well and set aside to cool.

VARIATION
Try replacing the blackberries with blueberries. Use the canned or frozen variety if fresh blueberries are unavailable.

2 Sift the flour, baking powder and cinnamon into a bowl, adding any husks that remain in the sieve. Stir in 70 g/2½ oz of the blackberries and the sugar.

3 Make a well in the centre of the ingredients and add the egg, yogurt and cooled apple purée. Mix well to incorporate thoroughly. Spoon the mixture into the loaf tin and smooth the top.

4 Sprinkle with the remaining blackberries, pressing them down into the cake mixture, and top with the crushed sugar lumps. Bake in the preheated oven for 40–45 minutes. Remove from the oven and set aside in the tin to cool.

5 Remove the cake from the tin and peel away the lining paper. Serve dusted with cinnamon and decorated with extra blackberries and apple slices.

Blueberry & Lemon Drizzle

The lemon syrup, which is poured over this cake, gives it a wonderful fresh tangy flavour. Leave to cool completely before cutting into squares.

50 mins   1 hr

SERVES 12

INGREDIENTS

225 g/8 oz butter, softened, plus extra for greasing

225 g/8 oz golden caster sugar

4 eggs, beaten

finely grated rind of 1 lemon

325 g/11½ oz self-raising flour, sifted

25 g/1 oz ground almonds

juice of 1 lemon

90 g/3¼ oz fresh blueberries

FOR THE TOPPING

juice of 2 lemons

115 g/4 oz golden caster sugar

55 g/2 oz icing sugar, to decorate (optional)

1 Preheat the oven to 180°C/350°F/Gas Mark 4. Grease and base-line a 20-cm/8-inch square cake tin. Put the butter and sugar in a bowl and beat together until light and fluffy. Gradually beat in the eggs, adding a little flour towards the end to prevent curdling. Beat in the lemon rind, then fold in the flour and almonds with enough lemon juice to give a dropping consistency.

2 Fold in three-quarters of the blueberries and turn into the prepared tin. Smooth the surface, then scatter the remaining blueberries on top. Bake for about 1 hour, until firm to the touch and a skewer inserted into the centre comes out clean.

3 Meanwhile, make the topping. Put the lemon juice and caster sugar in bowl and mix together. As soon as the cake comes out of the oven, prick it all over with a fine skewer and pour the lemon mixture over. Leave in the tin until completely cold, and decorate with a little drizzled icing if desired. Then cut into 12 squares.

COOK'S TIP
If you warm a lemon in the microwave for a few seconds on Full Power, it will yield more juice.

Sticky Date Cake

The toffee topping on this sticky cake makes it particularly moreish.
An ideal midweek dessert.

1 hr

1hr 10 mins–
1hr 25 mins

SERVES 8

INGREDIENTS

175 g/6 oz stoned dates, chopped

300 ml/10 fl oz boiling water

115 g/4 oz butter, softened, plus extra
   for greasing

175 g/6 oz golden caster sugar

3 eggs, beaten

280 g/10 oz self-raising flour, sifted

½ tsp ground cinnamon

1 tsp bicarbonate of soda

FOR THE TOPPING

175 g/6 oz light muscovado sugar

4 tbsp butter

3 tbsp double cream

1 Put the dates in a bowl and cover with the boiling water. Preheat the oven to 180°C/350°F/Gas Mark 4. Grease a 23-cm/9-inch springform cake tin. Put the butter and sugar in a bowl and beat until light and fluffy. Gradually beat in the eggs, then fold in the flour and cinnamon.

2 Add the bicarbonate of soda to the dates and water, then pour on to the creamed mixture. Mix well. Pour into the tin. Bake in the oven for 1–1¼ hours, until well risen and firm to the touch.

3 To make the topping, put the sugar, butter and cream in a pan. Heat gently until the sugar has melted. Bring to the boil, simmer for 3 minutes, then pour over the cake. Put under the grill until bubbling. Leave to cool in the tin, then transfer to a wire rack to cool completely.

Apricot Cake

The moist, fruity layer of filling makes this lovely light cake a welcome treat with a cup of mid-morning coffee or as a dessert.

50 mins plus
30 mins chilling

1 hr 15 mins

MAKES 25-CM/10-INCH CAKE

INGREDIENTS

BASE

225 g/8 oz plain flour, plus extra
for dusting

pinch of salt

35 g/1¼ oz caster sugar

grated rind of ½ lemon

4 tbsp water

90 g/3¼ oz butter, unsalted for preference,
softened

FILLING

250 g/9 oz short-grain rice

450 ml/16 fl oz skimmed milk

90 g/3¼ oz caster sugar

grated rind and juice of ½ lemon

1 tbsp apricot jam

3 eggs, separated

800 g/1 lb 12 oz apricots, peeled, halved
and stoned

icing sugar, for dusting

1 Sift the flour with a pinch of salt into a bowl and add the sugar, lemon rind, water and butter. Mix well, using an electric whisk or fork, until crumbly. Turn out on to a lightly floured work surface and knead lightly until smooth. Roll out and use to line the base and about 3 cm/1¼ inches of the sides of a 25-cm/10-cm springform cake tin. Chill in the refrigerator for 30 minutes, then bake blind (see Cook's Tip) in a preheated oven, 200°C/400°F/Gas Mark 6, for 10 minutes.

2 Meanwhile, make the filling. Put the rice, milk, sugar and lemon rind in a heavy-based saucepan and bring to the boil. Reduce the heat and simmer for 30 minutes. Remove the saucepan from the heat, stir in the lemon rind and juice and apricot jam and set aside to cool.

3 Stir the egg yolks into the cooled rice mixture. Whisk the egg whites until stiff, then fold gently into the rice mixture. Remove the cooked base from the oven, discard the baking beans and lining paper and reduce the oven temperature to 180°C/350°F/Gas Mark 4. Arrange the apricot halves, flat-side uppermost, over the cooked base. Spoon the rice mixture over the top, spreading it out evenly. Bake for 45 minutes, or until a skewer inserted into the centre of the cake comes out clean. Cool on a wire rack and dust with icing sugar before serving.

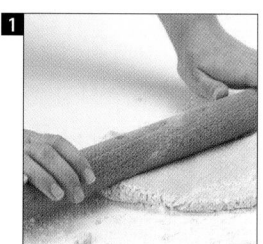
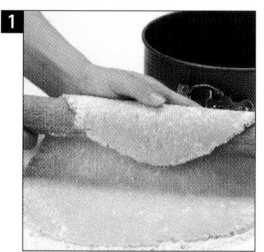

COOK'S TIP

To bake blind, prick the base all over with a fork and then line with baking paper or greaseproof paper. Partially fill with baking beans – either shop-bought ceramic or metal beans, or haricot beans kept specially for the purpose.

Banana & Lime Cake

A substantial cake that is ideal served for tea. The mashed bananas help to keep the cake moist, and the lime icing gives it extra zing and zest.

45 mins   40–45 mins

SERVES 8–10

INGREDIENTS

butter, for greasing

300 g/10½ oz plain flour

1 tsp salt

1½ tsp baking powder

175 g/6 oz soft light brown sugar

1 tsp grated lime rind

1 egg, beaten lightly

1 banana, mashed with 1 tbsp lime juice

150 ml/5 fl oz low-fat natural yogurt

115 g/4 oz sultanas

TOPPING

125 g/4½ oz icing sugar

1–2 tsp lime juice

½ tsp finely grated lime rind

TO DECORATE

banana chips

finely grated lime rind

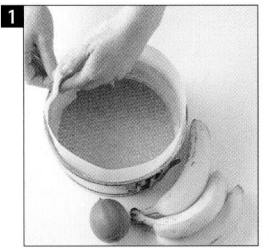

1 Preheat the oven to 180°C/350°F/Gas Mark 4. Grease a deep, round 18-cm/7-inch cake tin with butter and line with baking paper.

2 Sift the flour, salt and baking powder into a mixing bowl and stir in the sugar and lime rind.

3 Make a well in the centre of the dry ingredients and add the egg, banana, yogurt and sultanas. Mix well until thoroughly incorporated.

4 Spoon the mixture into the tin and smooth the surface. Bake in the preheated oven for 40–45 minutes, until firm to the touch or until a skewer inserted into the centre comes out clean. Leave to cool in the tin for 10 minutes, then turn out on to a wire rack.

5 To make the topping, sift the icing sugar into a small bowl and mix with the lime juice to form a soft, but not too runny icing. Stir in the grated lime rind. Drizzle the lime icing over the cake, letting it run down the sides.

6 Decorate with banana chips and lime rind. Leave to set for 15 minutes.

VARIATION

For a delicious alternative, replace the lime rind and juice with orange and the sultanas with chopped apricots.

Rich Fruit Cake

Serve this moist, fruit-laden cake for a special occasion. It would also make an excellent Christmas cake.

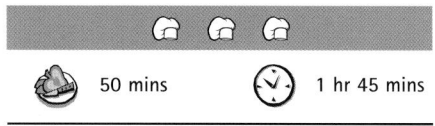

50 mins   1 hr 45 mins

SERVES 8–10

INGREDIENTS

butter or margarine, for greasing

125 g/4½ oz stoned dates

100 g/3½ oz ready-to-eat dried prunes

200 ml/7 fl oz unsweetened orange juice

2 tbsp molasses

1 tsp finely grated lemon rind

1 tsp finely grated orange rind

300 g/10½ oz self-raising wholemeal flour

1 tsp mixed spice

150 g/5½ oz raisins

150 g/5½ oz sultanas

75 g/2¾ oz currants

150 g/5½ oz dried cranberries

3 large eggs, separated

TO DECORATE

1 tbsp apricot jam, softened

icing sugar, for dusting

175 g/6 oz fondant icing

strips of orange rind

strips of lemon rind

1 Preheat the oven to 160°C/325°F/ Gas Mark 3. Grease and line a deep 20-cm/8-inch round cake tin. Chop the dates and prunes and place in a saucepan. Pour over the orange juice, gently bring to the boil, then simmer for 10 minutes. Remove the saucepan from the heat and beat the fruit mixture until puréed. Add the molasses and lemon and orange rinds. Set aside to cool.

2 Sift the flour and mixed spice into a bowl and add the dried fruit. When the date and prune mixture is cool, whisk in the egg yolks. In a clean bowl, whisk the egg whites until stiff peaks form. Spoon the fruit mixture into the dry ingredients and mix together.

3 Gently fold in the egg whites. Transfer to the prepared tin and bake in the preheated oven for 1½ hours. Leave to cool.

4 Remove the cake from the tin and brush the top with jam. Dust the work surface with icing sugar and roll out the fondant icing thinly. Lay it over the top of the cake and trim the edges. Decorate with orange and lemon rind and serve.

Vanilla Tea Cake

Slices of juicy fruit soaked in sugar syrup are one of the great delicacies of Provence and southern Italy. Serve as a delicious afternoon treat.

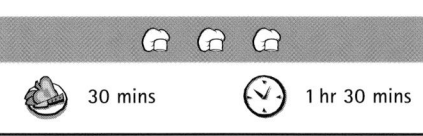

30 mins   1 hr 30 mins

SERVES 8

INGREDIENTS

175 g/6 oz butter, softened, plus extra for greasing

300 g/10½ oz good-quality glacé fruit, such as cherries, and candied orange, lemon and lime rind

75 g/2¾ oz ground almonds

finely grated rind of ½ lemon

85 g/3 oz plain flour

85 g/3 oz self-raising flour

175 g/6 oz plus 2 tbsp vanilla-flavoured sugar (see Cook's Tip)

½ tsp vanilla essence

3 large eggs, beaten lightly

pinch of salt

glacé fruit, to decorate

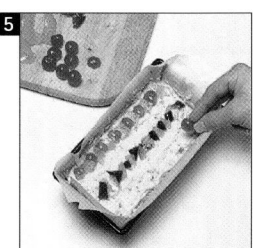

1 Preheat the oven to 180°C/350°F/Gas Mark 4. Grease a 22 x 12 x 5-cm/8 x 4 x 2-inch loaf tin, then line the base with a piece of baking paper.

2 Chop the fruit into even-sized small pieces, reserving a few larger slices for the top. Place in a bowl with the ground almonds, lemon rind and 2 tablespoons of the plain flour, and stir together. Set aside.

3 Beat the butter and vanilla-flavoured sugar together until fluffy and creamy. Beat in the vanilla essence and eggs, a little at a time.

4 Sift both flours and the salt into the creamed mixture, then fold in. Fold in the fruit and ground almonds.

5 Spoon into the tin and smooth the surface. Arrange the reserved fruit on the top. Loosely cover the tin with foil, making sure it does not touch the cake mixture. Bake in the preheated oven for about 1½ hours, until risen and a skewer inserted into the centre comes out clean.

6 Cool in the tin on a wire rack for 5 minutes, then turn out and remove the lining. Cool completely on a wire rack. Wrap in foil and store in an airtight container for up to 4 days. Serve decorated with glacé fruit.

COOK'S TIP
Make your own vanilla-flavoured sugar by storing a sliced vanilla pod in a closed jar of caster sugar.

Glacé Fruit Cake

This cake is extremely colourful; you can choose any mixture of glacé fruit, or stick to just one type if you prefer.

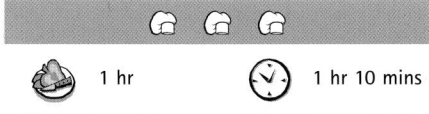

1 hr   1 hr 10 mins

SERVES 8

INGREDIENTS

175 g/6 oz butter, softened, plus extra for greasing

175 g/6 oz caster sugar

3 eggs, beaten lightly

175 g/6 oz self-raising flour, sifted

2½ tbsp ground rice

finely grated rind of 1 lemon

4 tbsp lemon juice

125 g/4½ oz glacé fruit, chopped

icing sugar, for dusting (optional)

1 Preheat the oven to 180°C/350°F/Gas Mark 4. Lightly grease an 18-cm/ 7-inch cake tin with a little butter and line with baking paper.

2 In a bowl, whisk together the butter and caster sugar until the mixture is light and fluffy.

3 Add the beaten eggs, a little at a time. Using a metal spoon, gently fold in the flour and ground rice.

4 Add the grated lemon rind and lemon juice, followed by the chopped glacé fruit. Lightly mix all the ingredients together.

5 Spoon the mixture into the prepared tin and smooth the surface with the back of a spoon or a knife.

6 Bake in the preheated oven for 1 hour–1 hour 10 minutes, until well risen or until a skewer inserted into the centre of the cake comes out clean.

7 Leave the cake to cool in the tin for 5 minutes, then turn out on to a wire rack to cool completely.

8 Dust well with icing sugar (if using) before serving.

COOK'S TIP
Wash and dry the glacé fruits before chopping them. This will prevent them sinking to the bottom of the cake during cooking.

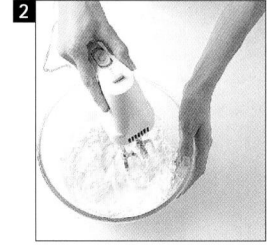

Crunchy Fruit Cake

Cornmeal adds texture to this cake, flavoured with dried fruit and pine kernels, as well as a golden yellow colour.

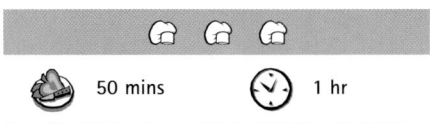

🍰 50 mins   🕐 1 hr

SERVES 8

INGREDIENTS

125 g/4½ oz butter, softened, plus extra for greasing

115 g/4 oz caster sugar

2 eggs, beaten

55 g/2 oz self-raising flour, sifted

1 tsp baking powder

100 g/3½ oz cornmeal

250 g/9 oz mixed dried fruit

25 g/1 oz pine kernels

grated rind of 1 lemon

4 tbsp lemon juice

2 tbsp milk

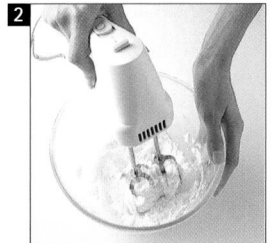

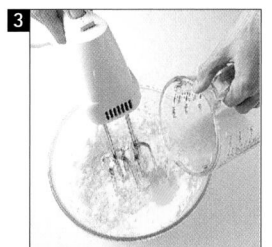

1 Preheat the oven to 180°C/350°F/Gas Mark 4. Grease an 18-cm/7-inch cake tin with a little butter and line the base with baking paper.

2 In a bowl, whisk together the butter and sugar until light and fluffy.

3 Whisk in the beaten eggs, a little at a time, whisking thoroughly after each addition.

4 Gently fold the flour, baking powder and cornmeal into the mixture until totally incorporated.

5 Stir in the mixed dried fruit, pine kernels, grated lemon rind, lemon juice and milk.

6 Spoon the mixture into the prepared tin and smooth the surface.

7 Bake in the preheated oven for about 1 hour, or until a skewer inserted into the centre of the cake comes out clean.

8 Leave the cake to cool in the tin before turning out.

VARIATION
For a crumblier cake, omit the cornmeal and use 175 g/6 oz self-raising flour instead.

Sugar-Free Fruit Cake

This cake is full of flavour from the mixed fruit. The fruit gives the cake its sweetness, so there is no need for extra sugar.

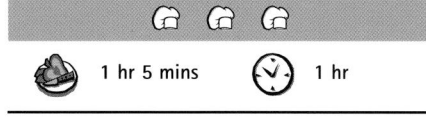

🔥 1 hr 5 mins   🕐 1 hr

SERVES 8

INGREDIENTS

125 g/4½ oz butter, cut into small pieces, plus extra for greasing

350 g/12 oz plain flour

2 tsp baking powder

1 tsp ground mixed spice

55 g/2 oz ready-to-eat dried apricots, chopped

85 g/3 oz chopped stoned dates

70 g/2½ oz glacé cherries, chopped

100 g/3½ oz raisins

125 ml/4 fl oz milk

2 eggs, beaten lightly

grated rind of 1 orange

5–6 tbsp orange juice

3 tbsp honey

1 Preheat the oven to 180°C/350°F/Gas Mark 4. Grease a 20-cm/8-inch round cake tin with a little butter and line the base with baking paper.

2 Sift the flour, baking powder and mixed spice together into a large mixing bowl.

3 Add the butter and rub it in with your fingertips until the mixture resembles fine breadcrumbs.

4 Carefully stir in the apricots, dates, glacé cherries and raisins with the milk, beaten eggs, grated orange rind and orange juice.

5 Stir in the honey and mix everything together to form a soft dropping consistency. Spoon into the prepared cake tin and smooth the surface.

6 Bake in the preheated oven for 1 hour, until a fine skewer inserted into the centre of the cake comes out clean.

7 Leave the cake to cool in the tin before turning out.

VARIATION
For a fruity alternative, replace the honey with 1 mashed ripe banana, if you prefer.

Olive Oil, Fruit & Nut Cake

It is worth using a good-quality olive oil for this cake because this will determine its flavour. The cake will keep well in an airtight container.

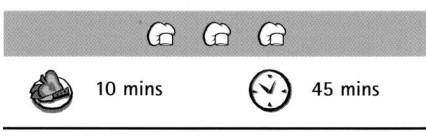

10 mins   45 mins

SERVES 8

INGREDIENTS

butter, for greasing

280 g/10 oz self-raising flour

50 g/1¾ oz caster sugar

125 ml/4 fl oz milk

50 ml/2 fl oz orange juice

150 ml/5 fl oz olive oil

115 g/4 oz mixed dried fruit

25 g/1 oz pine kernels

1 Preheat the oven to 180°C/350°F/Gas Mark 4. Grease an 18-cm/7-inch cake tin and line with baking paper.

2 Sift the flour into a mixing bowl and stir in the caster sugar.

3 Make a well in the centre of the dry ingredients and pour in the milk and orange juice. Stir the mixture with a wooden spoon, gradually beating in the flour and sugar.

4 Pour in the olive oil, stirring well so that all of the ingredients are thoroughly mixed.

5 Stir the mixed dried fruit and pine kernels into the mixture and spoon into the prepared tin. Gently smooth the top with a palette knife.

6 Bake the cake in the preheated oven for about 45 minutes, until it is golden brown and just firm to the touch.

7 Leave the cake to cool in the tin for a few minutes before transferring to a wire rack to cool completely.

8 Serve the cake warm or cold and cut into slices.

COOK'S TIP
Pine kernels are best known as the flavouring ingredient in the classic Italian pesto, but here they give a delicate, slightly resinous flavour to this cake.

Spiced Fruit Cake

The addition of cardamom pods gives a wonderful aromatic flavour and smell to this cake. Store in an airtight container for several days.

🔥 🔥

🍰 20 mins   🕐 50–60 mins

SERVES 12

I N G R E D I E N T S

1 tsp sunflower oil, for oiling

6 cardamom pods

175 g/6 oz butter or margarine

175 g/6 oz light muscovado sugar

1 tsp ground cinnamon

½ tsp ground ginger

3 eggs, beaten

225 g/8 oz self-raising flour

85 g/3 oz dried cranberries

generous 85 g/3 oz ready-to-eat dried apricots, chopped, plus extra, to decorate

85 g/3 oz sultanas

I C I N G

175 g/6 oz plain chocolate

2 tbsp butter

2 tbsp golden syrup

2 tbsp milk

1 Preheat the oven to 160°C/325°F/Gas Mark 3. Lightly oil and line the base of a 20-cm/8-inch cake tin with non-stick baking paper. Lightly pound the cardamom pods until cracked open. Scrape out the seeds.

2 Cream the butter with the sugar and spices until light and fluffy. Gradually beat in the eggs adding in a little flour after each addition. When all the eggs have been added, stir in the remaining flour.

3 Add the cardamom seeds, dried cranberries, apricots and sultanas and stir lightly, adding 1–2 tablespoons of cooled boiled water to give a soft consistency. Spoon into the prepared cake tin and smooth the top. Bake in the preheated oven for 50–60 minutes, or until a skewer inserted into the centre comes out clean. Remove and leave to cool in the cake tin before removing from the tin and discarding the lining paper. Leave until cold before icing.

4 Break the chocolate into small pieces and place in a heavy-based saucepan together with the butter. Heat gently, stirring frequently, until the chocolate and butter have melted and the mixture is smooth. Remove from the heat and stir in the syrup and milk. Beat until the icing is smooth, then use to coat the top of the cake, swirling to give a decorative effect. Pipe 12 icing rosettes around the edge of the cake and top with extra apricots.

Caribbean Chocolate Cake

This cake can be stored for a week. Simply let the cake cool completely, then wrap in non-stick baking paper and foil and leave in a cool place.

2 hrs 30 mins

1 hr 45 mins– 2 hrs

SERVES 12–14

INGREDIENTS

225 g/8 oz butter, softened, plus extra for greasing

85 g/3 oz ready-to-eat dried apricots

115 g/4 oz ready-to-eat dried papaya

175 g/6 oz ready-to-eat dried mango

115 g/4 oz ready-to-eat dried pineapple

25 g/1 oz stem ginger

1 tsp ground ginger

1 tsp ground cinnamon

½ tsp ground cloves

225 g/8 oz dark muscovado sugar

4 eggs, beaten

225 g/8 oz plain flour

generous 55 g/2 oz ground almonds

115 g/4 oz plain chocolate

115 g/4 oz self-raising wholemeal flour

2–3 tbsp rum, brandy or orange juice

TOPPING

4 tbsp apricot jam

1 tbsp lemon juice

225 g/8 oz assorted glacé fruit

115 g/4 oz mixed nuts

1 Preheat the oven to 160°C/325°F/Gas Mark 3. Lightly grease and line a 23-cm/9-inch cake tin with non-stick baking paper. Chop the dried fruit and ginger. Beat the butter with the spices and sugar until light and creamy. Gradually beat in the eggs, adding a little flour after each addition. When all the eggs have been added, stir in the remaining flour and the ground almonds. Melt the chocolate in a heatproof bowl set over a saucepan of gently simmering water. Stir the chocolate until smooth, then stir into the mixture.

2 Add all the fruit and stem ginger and stir lightly. Sift the wholemeal flour into the bowl, then add the husks remaining in the sieve to the bowl. Mix lightly, adding sufficient rum, brandy or orange juice to form a soft dropping consistency. Turn into the tin and smooth the top.

3 Bake in the preheated oven for 1 hr 45 mins–2 hours. Cover the top with foil if it browns too much. Remove from the oven and leave in the tin until almost cold before removing from the tin and discarding the lining paper.

4 Heat the apricot jam and lemon juice together, then rub through a sieve. Brush over the top of the cake. Arrange the assorted glacé fruit and nuts over the top. Brush the fruit and nuts with the remaining apricot glaze and leave for 2 hours to leave the jam to set before serving.

COOK'S TIP

For a different topping, brush the cooked cake with 1–2 tablespoons of apricot glaze, then top with a circle of marzipan and decorate with the glacé fruit and nuts if liked.

Apple Cake with Hard Cider

This can be warmed through and served with cream for a dessert or eaten as a snack with a morning cup of coffee, if preferred.

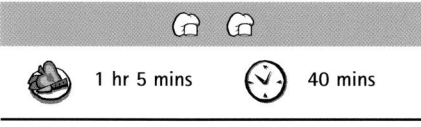

🔔 1 hr 5 mins   🕐 40 mins

SERVES 8

INGREDIENTS

85 g/3 oz butter, cut into small pieces, plus extra for greasing

280 g/10 oz self-raising flour

1 tsp baking powder

85 g/3 oz caster sugar

450 g/1 lb chopped dried apple

100 g/3½ oz raisins

150 ml/5 fl oz cider

1 egg, beaten

140 g/5 oz raspberries

1 Preheat the oven to 190°C/375°F/Gas Mark 5. Grease a 20-cm/8-inch cake tin and line with baking paper.

2 Sift the flour and baking powder into a mixing bowl and rub in the butter with your fingertips until the mixture resembles fine breadcrumbs.

3 Stir in the caster sugar, chopped dried apple and raisins.

4 Pour in the cider and egg and mix together until thoroughly blended. Stir in the raspberries very gently so they do not break up.

5 Pour the cake mixture into the prepared cake tin.

6 Bake in the preheated oven for about 40 minutes, or until risen and lightly golden.

7 Set the cake aside to cool in the tin, then turn out on to a wire rack. Set aside until completely cold before serving.

VARIATION

If you don't want to use cider or you are making the cake for children, replace it with clear apple juice.

Spiced Apple Ring

Adding grated fresh apple and crunchy almonds to the cake mixture makes this ring beautifully moist yet with a crunch to it.

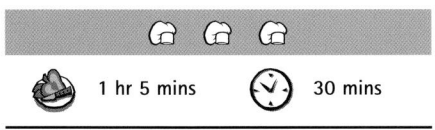

1 hr 5 mins · 30 mins

SERVES 8

INGREDIENTS

175 g/6 oz butter, softened, plus extra for greasing

175 g/6 oz caster sugar

3 eggs, beaten lightly

175 g/6 oz self-raising flour

1 tsp ground cinnamon

1 tsp ground mixed spice

2 eating apples, cored and grated

2 tbsp apple juice or milk

25 g/1 oz flaked almonds

1 Preheat the oven to 180°C/350°F/Gas Mark 4. Lightly grease a 10-inch/25-cm ovenproof ring mould.

2 In a mixing bowl, cream together the butter and sugar until light and fluffy. Gradually add the beaten eggs, beating well after each addition.

3 Sift the flour and spices, then carefully fold them into the creamed mixture with a figure-of-eight movement.

4 Stir in the grated apples and the apple juice or milk and mix to a soft dropping consistency.

5 Sprinkle the flaked almonds around the base of the mould and spoon the cake mixture on top. Smooth the surface with the back of the spoon.

6 Bake in the preheated oven for about 30 minutes, until well risen and a fine skewer inserted into the centre comes out clean.

7 Leave the cake to cool in the tin before turning out and transferring to a wire rack to cool completely. Serve the apple ring cut into slices.

COOK'S TIP
This cake can also be made in an 18-cm/7-inch round cake tin if you do not have an ovenproof ring mould.

Sweet Risotto Cake

Served with your favourite summer berries and a scented mascarpone cream, this baked sweet risotto makes an unusual dessert.

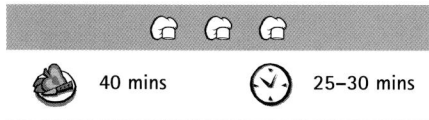

🍳 40 mins 🕐 25–30 mins

SERVES 6–8

INGREDIENTS

2 tbsp melted butter, for greasing

70 g/2½ oz risotto rice

300 ml/10 fl oz milk

3–4 tbsp sugar

½ tsp freshly grated nutmeg

½ tsp salt, plus a pinch for the almond mixture

200 g/7 oz plain flour

1½ tsp baking powder

1 tsp bicarbonate of soda

1–2 tbsp caster sugar

1 egg

175 ml/6 fl oz milk

125 ml/4 fl oz soured cream or natural yogurt

1 tbsp butter, melted

2 tbsp honey

½ tsp almond essence

2 tbsp toasted flaked almonds

icing sugar, for dusting (optional)

MUSCAT BERRIES

350 g/12 oz mixed summer berries, such as strawberries (halved), raspberries and blueberries

1–2 tbsp sugar

50 ml/2 fl oz Muscat wine

MASCARPONE CREAM

225 g/8 oz mascarpone cheese

2 tbsp Muscat wine

1 tbsp honey

½ tsp almond essence

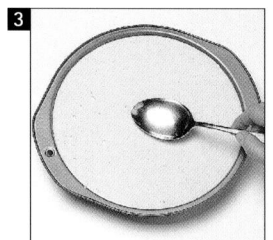

1 Preheat the oven to 160°C/325°F/ Gas Mark 3. Grease a 23–25-cm/ 9–10-inch loose-bottomed cake tin. Put the rice, milk, sugar, nutmeg and ½ teaspoon of salt in a heavy-based saucepan. Bring to the boil, reduce the heat slightly and cook, stirring constantly, until the rice is tender and the milk is almost absorbed. Leave to cool.

2 Combine the flour, baking powder, bicarbonate of soda, pinch of salt and the caster sugar. In a bowl, beat the egg, milk, soured cream, butter, honey and almond essence with an electric whisk until smooth. Gradually beat in the cooled rice. Stir in the flour mixture and the almonds.

3 Spoon the rice and almond mixture gently into the prepared cake tin, smoothing the top evenly. Bake in the preheated oven for about 20 minutes, or until golden. Cool in the tin on a wire rack.

4 While the cake is cooking, put the berries in a bowl and add the sugar and wine. To make the mascarpone cream, stir all the ingredients together and chill.

5 Remove the sides of the tin and slide the cake gently on to a serving plate. Dust the cake with icing sugar and serve warm with the Muscat berries and mascarpone cream piped on top of the cake.

Passion Cake

Decorating this moist, rich carrot cake with sugared flowers lifts it into the celebration class. It is a perfect choice for Easter.

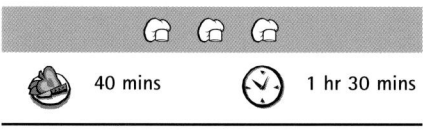

40 mins   1 hr 30 mins

SERVES 10

INGREDIENTS

butter, for greasing

150 ml/5 fl oz sunflower or corn oil

175 g/6 oz golden caster sugar

4 tbsp natural yogurt

3 eggs, plus 1 extra yolk

1 tsp vanilla essence

115 g/4 oz walnut pieces, chopped

175 g/6 oz carrots, grated

1 banana, mashed

225 g/8 oz flour

85 g/3 oz fine oatmeal

1 tsp bicarbonate of soda

1 tsp baking powder

1 tsp ground cinnamon

½ tsp salt

ICING

125 g/4½ oz cream cheese

4 tbsp natural yogurt

85 g/3 oz icing sugar

1 tsp grated lemon rind

2 tsp lemon juice

TO DECORATE

primroses and violets

1 egg white, beaten lightly

3 tbsp caster sugar

1 Preheat the oven to 180°C/350°F/Gas Mark 4. Grease and line a 23-cm/9-inch round cake tin. Beat the oil, sugar, yogurt, eggs, egg yolk and vanilla essence. Beat in the chopped walnuts, grated carrot and banana.

2 Sift together the remaining ingredients and gradually beat into the mixture.

3 Pour the mixture into the tin and level the surface. Bake in the preheated oven for 1½ hours, or until firm, and a fine skewer inserted into the centre comes out clean. Leave to cool in the tin for 15 minutes, then turn out on to a wire rack.

4 To make the icing, beat together the cheese and yogurt. Sift in the icing sugar and stir in the lemon rind and juice. Spread over the top and sides of the cake.

5 To prepare the decoration, dip the flowers quickly in the beaten egg white, then sprinkle with caster sugar to cover the surface completely. Place well apart on baking paper. Leave in a warm, dry place for several hours, until they are dry and crisp. Arrange the flowers in a pattern on top of the cake.

Simnel Cake

Simnel is a traditional English cake, baked at Easter; this version includes Amaretto, which intensifies its almond flavour and keeps it very moist.

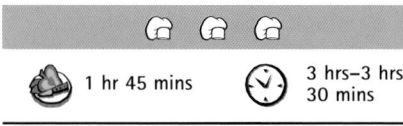

1 hr 45 mins   3 hrs–3 hrs 30 mins

SERVES 8–10

INGREDIENTS

225 g/8 oz unsalted butter, plus extra for greasing

115 g/4 oz glacé cherries

55 g/2 oz whole, blanched almonds

350 g/12 oz sultanas

350 g/12 oz currants

350 g/12 oz raisins

115 g/4 oz candied peel

55 g/2 oz ground almonds

grated rind of 1 lemon

grated rind of 1 orange

75 ml/2½ fl oz Amaretto

225 g/8 oz soft brown sugar

6 eggs

1 kg/2 lb 4 oz ready-made marzipan

1½ tsp baking powder

1 tsp ground cinnamon

280 g/10 oz plain flour

lightly beaten egg white, for brushing

1 Line a 23-cm/9-inch round cake tin with greaseproof paper and grease it thoroughly.

2 Wash the cherries and pat dry, then halve them. Finely chop the almonds. Mix the dried fruit, nuts, ground almonds and the lemon and orange rind. Add half the Amaretto, and set aside for 1 hour.

3 Preheat the oven to 180°C/350°F/ Gas Mark 4.

4 Cream the butter until soft, then add the sugar and beat until pale and fluffy. Whisk the eggs and add little by little, beating well to avoid the mixture curdling. Measure off 115 g/4 oz of marzipan and grate it coarsely using a grater. Add this and the soaked fruit to the cake mixture. Sift the baking powder and ground cinnamon with the flour and fold in gently.

5 Put half of the mixture in the prepared cake tin and smooth over. Roll out half of the remaining marzipan into a 20-cm/8-inch circle and put into the cake tin. Cover with the remaining mixture. Smooth over, making a slight dip in the centre.

6 Cook in the preheated oven for 1 hour, then reduce the temperature to 160°C/325°F/Gas Mark 3. Cook for an additional 2 hours, then test with a skewer inserted into the centre. If the skewer does not come out clean, cook for an additional 30–45 minutes.

7 Remove the cake from the oven and prick the surface lightly with a fork or skewer. Pour over the remaining Amaretto and leave to cool completely before removing from the cake tin. Keep the cake covered in greaseproof paper with a layer of foil until required.

8 Brush the cake surface with a little egg white. Use the remaining marzipan to make decorations, such as flowers, leaves, and twisted strands around the base of the cake.

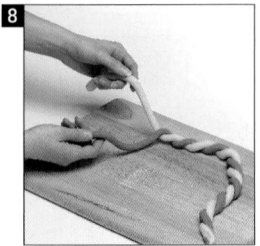

Chestnut Slab Cake

This quick and simple dessert is a favourite at Christmas in France. It can be made in advance and will keep for up to 1 week in the refrigerator.

20 mins plus 2–3 hrs chilling | 5 mins

SERVES 6–8

INGREDIENTS

300 g/10½ oz unsalted butter, cubed, plus extra for greasing

850 g/1 lb 14 oz canned unsweetened chestnut purée

4 tbsp icing sugar

200 g/7 oz continental plain chocolate, grated

3 tsp kirsch

TOPPING

115 g/4 oz continental plain chocolate

1–2 tbsp warm milk

marrons glacés, to decorate

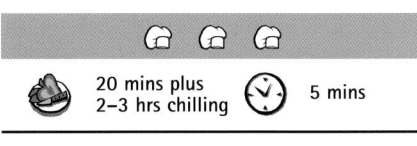

1 Grease and line a 900-g/2-lb loaf tin. Tip the chestnut purée into a heavy-based saucepan and heat gently. When it is hot, remove from the heat and add the butter, sugar, grated chocolate and kirsch. Stir thoroughly. Pour into the prepared loaf tin, smooth the top and chill in the refrigerator for 2–3 hours.

2 To make the topping, break the chocolate into pieces and place in a heatproof bowl set over a saucepan of gently simmering water with 1 tablespoon of milk and stir until the chocolate has melted. Add an additional tablespoon of milk if needed to make a smooth, glossy topping.

3 Turn the cake out of the loaf tin on to a serving plate. Cover with the topping, letting it trickle down the sides. Decorate with marrons glacés and cut into slices to serve.

COOK'S TIP
This cake is very rich, so keep your slices thin. It is delicious with tiny cups of black coffee or perhaps a liqueur.

Plum-Topped Chocolate Cake

You can use any type of plums for this recipe, but make sure that they are not too ripe or they will not hold their shape during cooking.

15 mins   30–40 mins

SERVES 12

INGREDIENTS

1 tsp sunflower oil, for oiling

175 g/6 oz butter or margarine, softened

175 g/6 oz caster sugar

few drops of almond essence

3 eggs, beaten

55 g/2 oz self-raising flour

115 g/4 oz ground almonds

85 g/3 oz white chocolate, grated

300 g/10½ oz red plums

2 tbsp apricot or raspberry jam

1 tbsp lemon juice

1 tbsp flaked almonds

1 Preheat the oven to 190°C/375°F/Gas Mark 5. Lightly oil and line the base of a 20-cm/8-inch square cake tin with non-stick baking paper. Cream the butter with the sugar and almond essence until light and fluffy. Gradually beat in the eggs, adding a little flour after each addition. When all the eggs have been added, stir in the remaining flour.

2 Add the ground almonds with 1–2 tablespoons of cooled boiled water and mix to form a smooth dropping consistency. Add the grated chocolate and stir lightly. Spoon into the prepared tin and smooth the top.

3 Rinse the plums, cut in half, stone and slice thickly. Arrange the plum slices over the cake. Heat the jam and lemon juice together and brush or spoon over the plums and sprinkle with the flaked almonds.

4 Bake in the preheated oven for 30–40 minutes, or until a skewer inserted into the centre of the cake comes out clean. Remove from the oven and leave to cool before removing from the tin and discarding the lining paper. Cut into squares to serve.

COOK'S TIP
Cover the cake with foil if the top browns too quickly as it cooks.

Raspberry Refrigerator Cake

This is quite the most decadent special-occasion dessert. The rich chocolate filling combines well with the cherries.

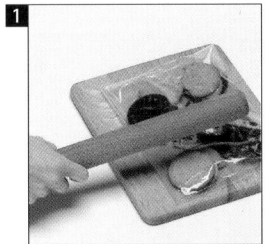

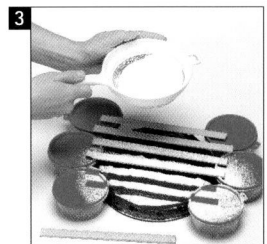

15–20 mins plus 2–3 hrs chilling

10 mins

SERVES 4

INGREDIENTS

225 g/8 oz half-coated chocolate biscuits

6 tbsp butter

2 tbsp golden syrup

300 g/10½ oz plain chocolate

300 ml/10 fl oz double cream

4 tbsp brandy

275 g/9½ oz fresh raspberries, strawberries or fruit of your choice

TO DECORATE

175 ml/6 fl oz double cream, whipped

fresh cherries or other fruit and
    1 tsp icing sugar

1 Place the biscuits in a polythene bag and pound lightly until crushed. Alternatively, place in a food processor and process for 1 minute. Heat the butter and syrup together until blended, then stir in the crushed biscuits and mix in lightly. Press the biscuits into the sides and base of a 20-cm/8-inch springform tin. Leave in the refrigerator while preparing the filling.

2 Break the chocolate into small pieces and place in a heavy-based saucepan. Add the cream and brandy and heat gently until smooth. Remove from the heat and cool, stirring occasionally. Leave to cool.

3 Pick over the fruit, cutting large ones in half, then arrange over the chocolate biscuit base. Stir the chocolate and cream mixture, then pour over the fruit. Leave in the refrigerator until set. Decorate with the whipped cream, cherries and icing sugar. Store in the refrigerator.

COOK'S TIP
Use only best-quality chocolate for this recipe.

Crêpes, Loaves, Pastries & Cheescakes

Breakfast, lunch and teatime are amply catered for in the

delights of this chapter. Here you will find some classic

and some entirely new ideas for baking,

from Scotch Pancakes to Balinese

Banana Crêpes, from traditional

Teacakes and Hot Cross Buns to

Chocolate Nut Soda Bread, along with individual Apricot

Tartes Tatin, Fruity Filo Nests and Maple Pecan Tarts.

Scotch Pancakes

Traditional Scotch pancakes are sometimes known as drop scones.
Either way they will always be a very welcome sight on the tea table.

25 mins   20 mins

SERVES 4

INGREDIENTS

225 g/8 oz self-raising flour

2 tsp baking powder

pinch of salt

2 tbsp golden caster sugar

1 egg

200 ml/7 fl oz milk

butter, for greasing

ORANGE BUTTER

175 g/6 oz butter

25 g/1 oz icing sugar, sifted

finely grated rind of 1 orange and 2 tbsp orange juice

1 To make the orange butter, place all of the ingredients in a bowl and beat together until light and fluffy. Chill in the refrigerator while making the pancakes.

2 To make the pancakes, sift the flour, baking powder and salt into a bowl. Stir in the sugar and make a well in the centre. Place the egg and milk in a separate bowl, whisk together and pour into the well. Gradually draw the flour into the liquid by stirring with a wooden spoon, then beat thoroughly to make a smooth batter.

3 Grease a griddle or heavy-based frying pan and set over medium-high heat. Drop spoonfuls of the batter into the pan and cook for 2–3 minutes, or until bubbles burst on the surface and the underside is golden. Turn over with a palette knife and cook for an additional 1 minute, or until golden on the other side. Keep warm in a clean tea towel until all the pancakes are cooked. Serve with the orange butter.

COOK'S TIP
Heat up the griddle or frying pan gently and check it is ready by dropping a small amount of pancake batter on to the surface, which should sizzle.

Chocolate Crêpes

Serve these sweet soufflé-filled, golden chocolate crêpes with flambéed summer berries for a superb contrast if you like.

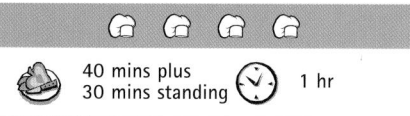

🍰 40 mins plus 30 mins standing 🕐 1 hr

SERVES 6

I N G R E D I E N T S

115 g/4 oz plain flour

1 tbsp cocoa powder

1 tsp caster sugar

2 eggs, beaten lightly

175 ml/6 fl oz milk

2 tsp dark rum

85 g/3 oz butter, unsalted for preference

icing sugar, for dusting

FILLING

5 tbsp double cream

225 g/8 oz plain chocolate

3 eggs, separated

2 tbsp caster sugar

BERRY SAUCE

2 tbsp butter

4 tbsp caster sugar

150 ml/5 fl oz orange juice

300 g/10½ oz mixed berries, such as raspberries, blackberries and strawberries

3 tbsp white rum

1 To make the crêpes, sift the flour, cocoa and caster sugar into a bowl. Make a well in the centre and add the eggs, beating them in a little at a time. Add the milk and beat until smooth. Stir in the dark rum.

2 Melt the butter and stir 2 tablespoonfuls into the batter. Cover with clingfilm and leave to stand for 30 minutes.

3 To cook the crêpes, brush the bottom of an 18-cm/7-inch crêpe pan or non-stick frying pan with melted butter and set over medium heat. Stir the batter and pour 3 tablespoonfuls into the pan, swirling it to cover the base. Cook for 2 minutes, or until the underside is golden, flip over, cook for 30 seconds, then slide on to a plate. Cook another 11 crêpes in the same way. Stack them interleaved with greaseproof paper.

4 For the filling, pour the cream into a heavy-based saucepan, add the chocolate and melt over low heat, stirring. Remove from the heat. In a heatproof bowl, beat the egg yolks with half of the caster sugar until creamy, beat in the chocolate cream and leave to cool.

5 In a separate bowl, whisk the egg whites until soft peaks form, add the rest of the caster sugar and beat until stiff peaks form. Stir a spoonful of the whites into the chocolate mixture, then fold the mixture into the remaining egg whites with a spoon.

6 Preheat the oven to 200°C/400°F/Gas Mark 6. Brush a baking sheet with melted butter. Spread 1 crêpe with 1 tablespoon of the filling, then fold it in half and in half again to make a triangle. Place on the baking sheet. Repeat with the remaining crêpes. Brush the tops with the remaining melted butter and bake for 20 minutes.

7 For the berry sauce, melt the butter in a heavy-based frying pan over low heat, stir in the sugar and cook until golden. Stir in the orange juice and cook until syrupy. Add the berries and warm through, stirring gently. Add the white rum, heat gently for 1 minute, then ignite. Shake the frying pan until the flames have died down. Transfer the crêpes to serving plates with the sauce and serve.

Apple Pancakes

If you cannot wait to get your first chocolate 'fix' of the day, serve these pancakes for breakfast. They also make a perfect family dessert.

15 mins   45 mins

SERVES 4

INGREDIENTS

280 g/10 oz plain flour

1½ tsp baking powder

4 tbsp caster sugar

1 egg

1 tbsp butter, melted, plus extra for greasing

300 ml/10 fl oz milk

1 eating apple

40 g/1½ oz plain chocolate chips

chocolate sauce or maple syrup, to serve

1 Sift the flour and baking powder into a mixing bowl. Stir in the caster sugar. Make a well in the centre and add the egg and melted butter. Gradually whisk in the milk to form a smooth batter.

2 Peel, core and grate the apple and stir it into the batter with the chocolate chips.

3 Heat a griddle pan or heavy-based frying pan over medium heat and grease it lightly. For each pancake, place about 2 tablespoons of the batter on to the griddle or frying pan and spread to make a 7.5-cm/3-inch circle.

4 Cook for a few minutes until you see bubbles appear on the surface of the pancake. Turn over and cook for an additional 1 minute. Remove from the pan and keep warm. Repeat with the remaining batter to make about 12 pancakes.

5 To serve, stack 2 or 3 pancakes on an individual serving plate and serve them with hot chocolate sauce or maple syrup.

COOK'S TIP

To keep the cooked pancakes warm, pile them on top of each other with greaseproof paper in between to prevent them sticking to one another.

Crêpes with Apples

The sharpness of the apples contrasts with the sweetness of the butterscotch sauce in this mouthwatering crêpe recipe.

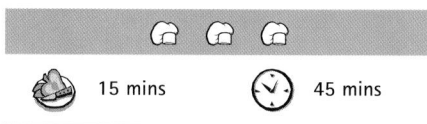

15 mins   45 mins

SERVES 4

I N G R E D I E N T S

150 g/5½ oz plain flour

pinch of salt

1 tsp finely grated lemon rind

1 egg

300 ml/10 fl oz milk

1–2 tbsp vegetable oil, plus extra for greasing

strips of pared lemon rind, to garnish

FILLING

225 g/8 oz cooking apples, peeled, cored and sliced

2 tbsp sultanas

SAUCE

6 tbsp butter

3 tbsp golden syrup

60 g/2¼ oz light muscovado sugar

1 tbsp dark rum or brandy (optional)

1 tbsp lemon juice

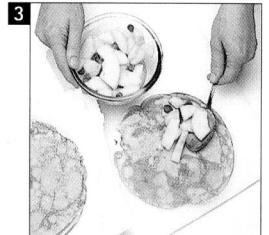

1 Preheat the oven to 160°C/325°F/Gas Mark 3. Sift the flour and salt into a bowl. Add the lemon rind, egg and milk and whisk to form a smooth batter.

2 Heat a little oil in a heavy-based frying pan. Make 8 thin crêpes, using extra oil as required. Stack the cooked crêpes, layering them with greaseproof paper or baking paper and keep warm.

3 To make the filling, cook the apples with the sultanas in a little water over low heat until soft. Divide the mixture evenly among the crêpes and roll up or fold into triangles. Brush an ovenproof dish with a little oil and arrange the crêpes in it. Bake in the preheated oven for about 15 minutes, until warmed through.

4 To make the sauce, melt the butter, syrup and sugar together in a saucepan, stirring well. Add the rum or brandy (if using) and the lemon juice. Do not let the mixture boil.

5 Serve the crêpes on warm plates, with a little sauce poured over, and garnished with strips of lemon rind.

Mango & Strawberry Crêpes

Everybody loves crêpes, and when they are filled with exotic fruit, they are irresistible. Dust with icing sugar and serve immediately.

20 mins plus
20 mins standing   15 mins

SERVES 4

INGREDIENTS

FILLING

100 g/3½ oz Greek-style natural yogurt

225 g/8 oz mascarpone cheese

icing sugar (optional)

1 mango, peeled and diced

225 g/8 oz strawberries, hulled and quartered

2 passion fruit

CREPES

100 g/3½ oz plain flour

2 tbsp cocoa powder

pinch of salt

1 egg, beaten

300 ml/10 fl oz milk

oil, for frying

icing sugar, for dusting

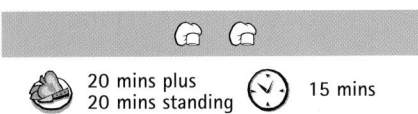

1 Prepare the filling. Put the yogurt and mascarpone cheese in a bowl and sweeten with icing sugar, if desired. Stir in the mango and strawberries. Cut the passion fruit in half and scoop out the pulp and seeds. Stir into the fruit mixture

2 Make the crêpes. Sift the flour, cocoa and salt into a bowl and make a well in the centre. Add the egg and whisk well with a balloon whisk. Gradually beat in the milk, drawing in the flour from the sides to form a smooth batter. Cover and, if possible, leave to rest for 20 minutes. Heat a small amount of oil in an 18-cm/ 7-inch crêpe pan or non-stick frying pan. Pour in just enough batter to thinly coat the base of the pan. Cook over moderately high heat for about 1 minute, then turn and cook the other side for ½–1 minute, until cooked through.

3 Transfer the crêpe to a plate and keep hot. Repeat with the remaining batter, stacking the cooked crêpes on top of each other with greaseproof paper in between each one. Keep warm in the oven while cooking the remainder. Divide the filling among the crêpes, roll up and dust with icing sugar. Serve at once.

Chocolate Banana Pancakes

Pancakes are given the chocolate treatment here to make a fabulous dinner-party dessert. Prepare ahead of time for easy entertaining.

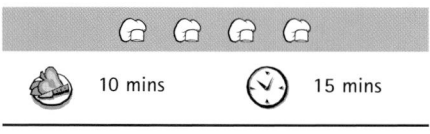

10 mins   15 mins

SERVES 4

INGREDIENTS

3 large bananas

6 tbsp orange juice

grated rind of 1 orange

2 tbsp orange- or banana-flavoured liqueur

HOT CHOCOLATE SAUCE

1 tbsp cocoa powder

2 tsp cornflour

3 tbsp milk

40 g/1½ oz plain chocolate, broken into pieces

1 tbsp butter

175 g/6 oz golden syrup

¼ tsp vanilla essence

PANCAKES

115 g/4 oz plain flour

1 tbsp cocoa powder

1 egg

1 tsp sunflower oil

300 ml/10 fl oz milk

oil, for frying

1 Peel and slice the bananas and arrange them in a dish with the orange juice and rind and the liqueur. Set aside.

2 Mix the cocoa and cornflour in a bowl, then stir in the milk. Put the chocolate in a saucepan with the butter and golden syrup. Heat gently, stirring until well blended. Add the cocoa mixture and bring to the boil over gentle heat, stirring. Simmer for 1 minute, then remove from the heat and stir in the vanilla essence.

3 To make the pancakes, sift the flour and cocoa into a mixing bowl and make a well in the centre. Add the egg and oil. Gradually whisk in the milk to form a smooth batter. Heat a little oil in a heavy-based frying pan and pour off any excess. Pour in a little batter and tilt the frying pan to coat the base. Cook over medium heat until the underside is browned. Flip over and cook the other side. Slide the pancake out of the frying pan and keep warm. Repeat until all the batter has been used.

4 To serve, reheat the chocolate sauce for 1–2 minutes. Fill the pancakes with the bananas and fold in half or into triangles. Pour over a little chocolate sauce and serve.

Balinese Banana Crêpes

These little stacks of rich banana crêpes, drizzled with fragrant lime juice, are quite irresistible at any time of the day.

15 mins plus 1 hr chilling

20 mins

SERVES 6

INGREDIENTS

225 g/8 oz plain flour

pinch of salt

4 eggs, beaten

2 large, ripe bananas, peeled and mashed

300 ml/10 fl oz coconut milk

vegetable oil, for frying

TO DECORATE

sliced banana

6 tbsp lime juice

icing sugar

coconut cream

1 Place the flour, salt, eggs, bananas and coconut milk in a food processor or blender and process to a smooth batter. Alternatively, if you don't have a food processor, sift the flour and salt into a large mixing bowl and make a well in the centre, then add the remaining ingredients and beat well until smooth.

2 Chill the batter for 1 hour. Remove from the refrigerator and beat briefly again. Heat a small amount of oil in a small frying pan until very hot.

3 Drop tablespoonfuls of batter into the frying pan. Cook until the crêpes are golden underneath.

4 Flip over and cook the other side until golden brown. Cook in batches until you have used up all the batter, making about 36 crêpes. Remove and drain thoroughly on kitchen paper.

5 Serve the crêpes in a stack, decorated with sliced bananas, sprinkled with lime juice and sugar and topped with coconut cream.

COOK'S TIP

These little crêpes are best eaten hot and freshly cooked, so keep them hot in a slow oven while the others are cooking.

Pear Crêpes with Chocolate

Chocolate and pears go well together in these crêpes. They are at their best when served immediately.

15 mins plus
30 mins chilling

30 mins

SERVES 4

INGREDIENTS

CREPES

125 g/4½ oz plain flour

pinch of salt

3 eggs

250 ml/9 fl oz milk

2 tbsp lemon oil or vegetable oil

FILLING

250 g/9 oz pears

8 cloves

3 tbsp currants

pinch of mixed spice

CHOCOLATE SAUCE

125 g/4½ oz plain chocolate, broken into small pieces

35 g/1¼ oz butter

6 tbsp water

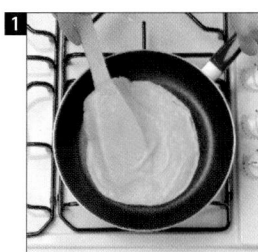

1 To make the crêpes, sift the flour and salt into a bowl. Whisk in the eggs and milk. Cover with clingfilm and chill for 30 minutes. Preheat the oven to 160°C/325°F/Gas Mark 3. Heat a little oil in a frying pan until hot. Add a large spoonful of the batter and cook over high heat until golden. Turn over and cook briefly on the other side. Cook the other crêpes in the same way, stacking them on a plate.

2 To make the filling, bring a saucepan of water to the boil. Peel and slice the pears, then add to the saucepan with the cloves and currants. Reduce the heat and simmer for 5 minutes. Remove from the heat, drain and discard the cloves. Cool a little. Brush an ovenproof dish with oil.

Stir the mixed spice into the fruit, then divide between the crêpes. Fold into triangles or roll into horns. Arrange in the dish and bake for 15 minutes.

3 To make the sauce, gently melt the chocolate, butter and water together in a small saucepan, stirring constantly. Serve the crêpes with the sauce.

Cherry Pancakes

This dish can be made with either fresh stoned cherries or, if your time is very short, you can use canned cherries for extra speed.

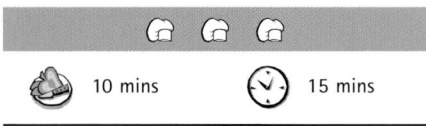

10 mins   15 mins

SERVES 4

INGREDIENTS

FILLING

400 g/14 oz canned stoned cherries

½ tsp almond essence

½ tsp mixed spice

2 tbsp cornflour

PANCAKES

115 g/4 oz plain flour

pinch of salt

2 tbsp chopped fresh mint

1 egg

300 ml/10 fl oz milk

vegetable oil, for frying

icing sugar and toasted flaked almonds, to decorate

1 Put the cherries and 300 ml/10 fl oz of the can juice in a saucepan with the almond essence and mixed spice. Stir in the cornflour and bring to the boil, stirring until thickened and clear. Set aside.

2 To make the pancakes, sift the flour and salt into a bowl. Add the mint. Make a well in the centre. Gradually beat in the egg and milk to form a smooth batter.

3 Heat 1 tablespoon of oil in an 18-cm/ 7-inch frying pan and pour off the oil when hot. Add just enough batter to coat the base of the pan. Cook for 1–2 minutes, or until the underside is cooked. Flip the pancake over and cook for 1 minute. Remove from the pan and keep warm. Heat 1 tablespoon of the oil in the frying pan again and repeat to use up all the batter.

4 Spoon a quarter of the cherry filling on to a quarter of each pancake and fold the pancake into a cone shape. Dust with icing sugar and sprinkle the toasted flaked almonds over the top. Serve the pancakes immediately.

Fruit Pancakes

Serve these pancakes with a spoonful of whipped cream to make the perfect finale to a summer barbecue or dinner party.

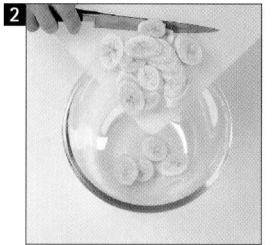

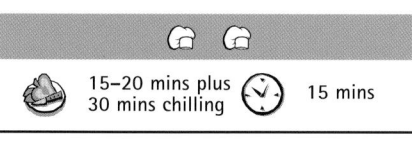

15–20 mins plus 30 mins chilling   15 mins

SERVES 4

INGREDIENTS

125 g/4¼ oz plain flour

pinch of salt

2 eggs

300 ml/10 fl oz milk

2–3 tbsp vegetable oil

FILLING

1 banana

1 tbsp lemon juice

2 nectarines, stoned and cut into small pieces

1 mango, peeled, stoned and cut into small pieces

3 kiwi fruit, peeled and cut into small pieces

2 tbsp maple syrup

icing sugar, to decorate

whipped cream, to serve

1 To make the pancakes, sift the flour and salt into a bowl. Whisk in the eggs and milk. Cover with clingfilm and chill for 30 minutes.

2 To make the filling, peel and slice the banana and put into a large bowl. Pour over the lemon juice and stir gently until coated. Add the nectarines, mango, kiwi fruit and maple syrup and stir together gently until mixed.

3 Heat a little oil in a frying pan until hot. Remove the batter from the refrigerator and add a large spoonful to the frying pan. Cook over high heat until golden, then turn it over and cook briefly on the other side. Remove from the frying pan and keep warm. Cook the other pancakes in the same way, stacking them as more are cooked. Keep warm. Divide the fruit filling between the pancakes and fold into triangles or roll into horns. Dust with icing sugar and serve with whipped cream.

Exotic Fruit Pancakes

These pancakes are filled with an exotic array of tropical fruit. Decorate lavishly with tropical flowers or mint sprigs.

10 mins plus
30 mins chilling

35 mins

SERVES 4

INGREDIENTS

BATTER

150 g/5½ oz plain flour

pinch of salt

1 egg

1 egg yolk

300 ml/10 fl oz coconut milk

4 tsp vegetable oil, plus extra for frying

FILLING

1 banana

1 papaya

juice of 1 lime

2 passion fruit

1 mango, peeled, stoned and sliced

4 lychees, stoned and halved

1–2 tbsp honey

flowers or fresh mint sprigs, to decorate

1 Sift the flour and salt into a bowl. Make a well in the centre and add the egg, egg yolk and a little of the coconut milk. Gradually draw the flour into the egg mixture, beating well and gradually adding the remaining coconut milk to form a smooth batter. Stir in the oil. Cover and chill for 30 minutes.

2 Peel and slice the banana and place in a bowl. Peel and slice the papaya, discarding the seeds. Add to the banana with the lime juice and mix well. Cut the passion fruit in half and scoop out the flesh and seeds into the fruit bowl. Stir in the mango, lychees and honey.

3 Heat a little oil in a 15-cm/6-inch frying pan. Pour in just enough of the batter to cover the base of the frying pan and tilt so that it spreads thinly and evenly. Cook until the pancake is just set and the underside is lightly browned, turn and briefly cook the other side. Remove from the frying pan and keep warm. Repeat with the remaining batter to make a total of 8 pancakes.

4 To serve, place a little of the prepared fruit filling along the centre of each pancake and then roll it into a cone shape. Lay on warmed serving plates, decorate with flowers or mint sprigs and serve.

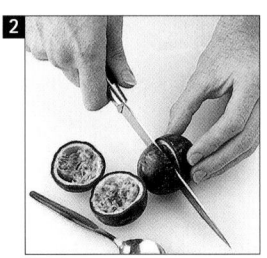

Lemon & Ricotta Pancakes

These thick soft pancakes can be served for breakfast, tea or even as a delicious dessert. Perfect served with a little cherry or blueberry jam.

10 mins   20–30 mins

MAKES 15

INGREDIENTS

250 g/9 oz ricotta cheese

5 tbsp golden caster sugar

3 large eggs, separated

finely grated rind of 1 lemon

2 tbsp melted butter

55 g/2 oz plain flour

warmed cherry or blueberry conserve, to serve

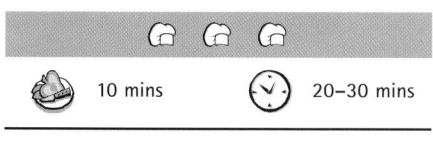
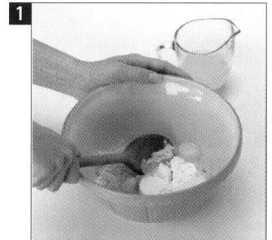

1 Put the ricotta cheese, sugar and egg yolks in a large bowl and mix together. Stir in the lemon rind and melted butter. Sift in the flour and fold in. Put the egg whites in another bowl and whisk until soft peaks form. Gently fold the egg whites into the ricotta mixture.

2 Heat a large non-stick frying pan over medium heat. Add heaped tablespoonfuls of batter, allowing room for them to spread. Cook for 1–2 minutes, until the underside is coloured, then turn over and cook on the other side for an additional 2 minutes.

3 Keep warm, wrapped in a clean tea towel, until all the pancakes are cooked. Serve with the warmed jam.

Sicilian Crêpes

These rich crêpes resemble a sweet cannelloni stuffed with sweetened ricotta and are served with a chocolate sauce.

30 mins plus
10 mins resting

30 mins

SERVES 4

INGREDIENTS

125 g/4½ oz plain flour

1 tsp baking powder

250 ml/9 fl oz milk

2 eggs, beaten

4 tbsp unsalted butter, melted

finely grated rind 1 lemon

finely grated rind 1 orange

CHOCOLATE SAUCE

140 g/5 oz plain chocolate, chopped

125 ml/4 fl oz double cream

1 tbsp Amaretto (optional)

FILLING

250 g/9 oz ricotta cheese

1 tsp vanilla essence

115 g/4 oz shelled pistachio nuts, chopped

115 g/4 oz blanched almonds, chopped

140 g/5 oz plain chocolate, chopped

1 tbsp orange flower water or orange juice

55 g/2 oz icing sugar, sifted

75 g/3 oz sultanas

15 g/1 oz mixed candied peel, chopped

1 First, make the filling. Beat the ricotta cheese with the vanilla essence and stir in the other ingredients. Chill the mixture in the refrigerator.

2 To make the sauce, melt the chocolate in a heatproof bowl set over a saucepan of gently simmering water, cool slightly and stir in the cream and Amaretto (if using). Set aside.

3 To make the crêpe batter, sift the flour with the baking powder and whisk in the milk, eggs and butter, stir in the lemon and orange rinds and whisk. Leave to rest for 10 minutes.

4 Heat a 20-cm/8-inch non-stick frying pan and add a spoonful of batter. Cook for 1–2 minutes, then flip over and cook for an additional minute or so.

Repeat until all the batter is used, keeping the prepared crêpes warm in a slow oven until they are all cooked.

5 To assemble, put a spoonful of the ricotta mixture along one side of each crêpe and roll up. Put 3 crêpes on each plate and drizzle with the chocolate sauce to serve immediately.

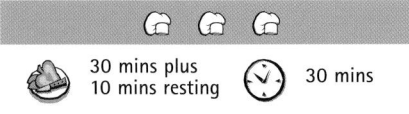

Walnut Crêpes & Chocolate

These fluffy crêpes are easy to make and could be served with sliced bananas and cream instead of the chocolate brandy sauce.

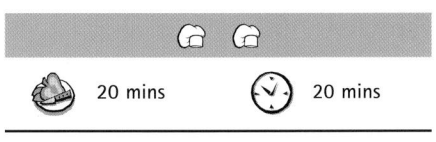   

🕐 20 mins 🕐 20 mins

SERVES 4

INGREDIENTS

325 g/11½ oz ricotta cheese

175 ml/6 fl oz milk

4 eggs, separated

125 g/4½ oz flour

1 tsp baking powder

pinch of salt

55 g/2 oz chopped walnuts

4 tbsp butter

CHOCOLATE BRANDY SAUCE

150 ml/5 fl oz double cream

140 g/5 oz milk chocolate, chopped

1 tbsp brandy (optional)

1 To make the chocolate brandy sauce, heat the cream until almost boiling, then pour over the chocolate and stir until melted and smooth. Stir in the brandy (if using) and set aside.

2 To make the crêpes, put the ricotta cheese, milk and egg yolks in a mixing bowl and stir well. Sift in the flour, baking powder, salt and walnuts and mix well.

3 Whisk the egg whites until stiff, then fold into the ricotta mixture.

4 Heat a non-stick frying pan and wipe with a little of the butter, pour a ladleful of batter into the frying pan and cook for 2–3 minutes, until bubbles appear. Flip over and cook for an additional 2–3 minutes. Repeat, using a little more butter each time, until you have 8 crêpes.

5 Serve with the chocolate brandy sauce poured over.

Polenta Crêpes with Compôte

Polenta gives these crêpes a delicious nutty flavour and the chocolate chips melt into little pools of hot sauce. Serve with soured cream.

 30 mins plus 30 mins standing   20 mins

MAKES 12–15

INGREDIENTS

55 g/2 oz plain flour

55 g/2 oz instant polenta

1 tsp baking powder

25 g/1 oz caster sugar

1 egg, plus 1 egg yolk

300 ml/10 fl oz milk

1 tsp vanilla essence

1 tbsp melted butter

sunflower oil, for greasing

55 g/2 oz plain chocolate chips

BERRY COMPOTE

450g/1 lb mixed berries, such as strawberries, raspberries, blackcurrants and redcurrants

115 g/4 oz icing sugar

125 ml/4 fl oz soured cream, to serve

1 First, prepare the crêpe batter. Sift the flours and baking powder together in a large bowl and make a well in the centre. Mix the sugar, egg, egg yolk, half the milk and the vanilla essence together and add to the well in the flour. Whisk the ingredients, gradually drawing in the flour, then beat well to form a smooth thick batter. Add the remaining milk and set aside for at least 30 minutes.

2 Meanwhile, make the berry compôte. Put the fruit and sugar into a heavy-based saucepan and heat over very gentle heat until the sugar has melted and the berries have popped, releasing their juice. Remove from the heat and keep warm.

3 Stir the melted butter into the crêpe batter. Heat a very small amount of oil in a heavy-based frying pan, then use kitchen paper to wipe out any excess. When the frying pan is smoking hot, reduce the heat to medium, then use a ladle to pour batter into the frying pan to make 2 crêpes. Do not tip the frying pan, as these crêpes are meant to be quite small and thick. Sprinkle a few chocolate chips on the surface. Cook until bubbles appear in the crêpes, then quickly flip each crêpe over, then remove. Repeat the process with the remaining batter and chocolate, interleaving the crêpes with greaseproof paper and keeping them warm in a moderate oven or between 2 plates set over a saucepan of simmering water.

4 Serve 2 or 3 crêpes per person, arranged overlapping on individual plates, with the warm berries spooned over them, and a generous helping of soured cream.

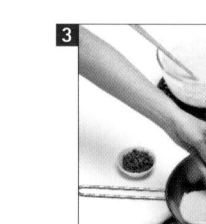

Chocolate Chip Pancakes

For an impressive dessert, serve these rich pancakes stacked one on top of the other with the toffee sauce poured over.

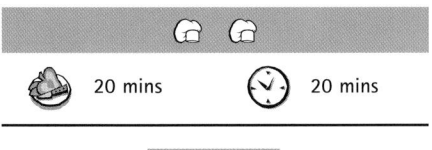

20 mins   **20 mins**

SERVES 4

INGREDIENTS

325 g/11½ oz ricotta cheese

175 ml/6 fl oz milk

4 eggs, separated

125 g/4½ oz flour

1 tsp baking powder

pinch of salt

55 g/2 oz milk chocolate, grated

2 tbsp butter

TOFFEE ORANGE SAUCE

4 tbsp unsalted butter

85 g/3 oz soft light brown sugar

150 ml/5 fl oz double cream

2–3 tbsp orange juice or Cointreau

1 To make the toffee orange sauce, melt the butter with the sugar in a saucepan over low heat until the sugar has melted, stir in the cream and bring to the boil. Simmer for 3–4 minutes. Remove from the heat and stir in the orange juice or Cointreau. Set aside.

2 To make the pancakes, put the ricotta cheese, milk and egg yolks in a mixing bowl and stir well. Sift in the flour, baking powder and salt, add the chocolate and mix well.

3 Whisk the egg whites until stiff, then fold into the ricotta mixture.

4 Heat a non-stick frying pan and wipe with a little of the butter. Spoon in 2 tablespoons of the batter and cook for 2–3 minutes, until bubbles appear, then flip the pancake over and cook for an additional 2–3 minutes. Repeat with a little more butter each time until you have 8 pancakes. Serve topped with the sauce.

Pancake Pieces

This is a cheap and cheerful, easy-to-make and filling dessert that is perfect for midweek family suppers.

10 mins 15 mins

SERVES 4

INGREDIENTS

2 tbsp caster sugar

1 tsp ground cinnamon

125 g/4½ oz plain flour

pinch of salt

2 eggs, beaten lightly

125 ml/4 fl oz milk

400 g/14 oz canned apricot halves in syrup

sunflower oil, for frying

1 Combine the sugar and cinnamon in a small bowl and set aside. Sift the flour and salt into a bowl. Whisk in the eggs and milk and continue whisking until smooth. Drain the apricots and stir the syrup into the batter. Coarsely chop the apricots and set aside.

2 Heat a large crêpe pan or heavy-based frying pan and brush with oil. Pour in all the batter and cook over medium heat for 4–5 minutes, until the underside is golden brown. Turn over using a palette knife or fish slice and cook the second side for 4 minutes, until golden. Tear the pancake into bite-sized pieces with 2 spoons or forks.

3 Add the apricots to the frying pan and heat through briefly. Divide the pancake pieces and apricots between individual plates, sprinkle with the sugar mixture and serve immediately.

VARIATION

These pancake pieces are also delicious mixed with 400 g/14 oz canned morello cherries in syrup instead of apricots.

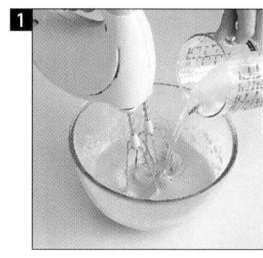

Fruity Pancake Bundles

This unusual pancake is filled with a sweet cream flavoured with ginger, nuts and apricots and served with a raspberry and orange sauce.

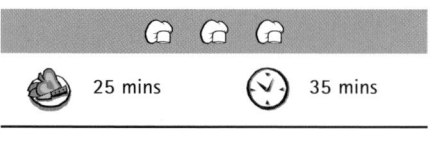

🍰 25 mins   🕐 35 mins

SERVES 2

INGREDIENTS

BATTER

55 g/2 oz plain flour

pinch of salt

¼ tsp ground cinnamon

1 egg

125 ml/4 fl oz milk

lard or white vegetable fat, for cooking

FILLING

1½ tsp plain flour, sifted

1½ tsp cornflour

1 tbsp caster sugar

1 egg

150 ml/5 fl oz milk

4 tbsp chopped nuts

55 g/2 oz ready-to-eat dried apricots, chopped

1 piece stem or crystallized ginger, chopped finely

SAUCE

3 tbsp raspberry jam

4½ tsp orange juice

finely grated rind of ¼ orange

1 Preheat the oven to 180°C/350°F/Gas Mark 4. To make the batter, sift the flour, salt and cinnamon into a bowl and make a well in the centre. Add the egg and milk and gradually beat in until smooth.

2 Melt a little fat in a medium frying pan. Pour in half the batter. Cook for 2 minutes until golden, then turn and cook the other side for 1 minute, until browned. Set aside and make a second pancake.

3 For the filling, beat the flour with the cornflour, sugar and egg. Gently heat the milk in a saucepan, then beat 2 tablespoons of it into the flour mixture. Transfer to the saucepan and cook gently, stirring constantly until thick. Remove from the heat, cover with baking paper to prevent a skin forming and leave to cool.

4 Beat the nuts, apricots and ginger into the cooled mixture and put a heaped tablespoonful in the centre of each pancake. Gather and squeeze the edges together to make a bundle. Place in an ovenproof dish and bake in the preheated oven for 15–20 minutes, until hot and golden, but not too brown.

5 To make the sauce, melt the jam gently with the orange juice, then sieve. Return to a clean saucepan with the orange rind and heat through. Serve with the pancakes.

Christmas Rice Pancakes

These delicious pancakes are almost like little rice puddings scented with Christmas mincemeat. They make an elegant festive dessert.

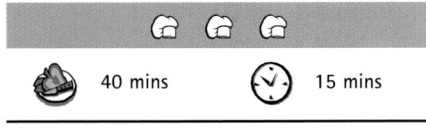

🍰 40 mins   🕐 15 mins

MAKES ABOUT 24 CREPES

I N G R E D I E N T S

700 ml/1¼ pints milk

salt

100 g/3½ oz long-grain white rice

1 cinnamon stick

50 g/1¾ oz sugar

50 g/1¾ oz plain flour

1 tsp baking powder

¾ tsp bicarbonate of soda

2 eggs, beaten

125 ml/4 fl oz soured cream

2 tbsp dark rum

1 tsp vanilla essence

½ tsp almond essence

2 tbsp butter, melted

350 g/12 oz mincemeat

melted butter, for frying

ground cinnamon, for dusting

1 To make the pancakes, bring the milk to the boil in a saucepan. Add a pinch of salt and sprinkle in the rice. Add the cinnamon stick and simmer gently for about 35 minutes, until the rice is tender and the milk almost absorbed.

2 Remove from the heat, add the sugar and stir until dissolved. Discard the cinnamon stick and pour into a large bowl. Cool, stirring occasionally, for about 30 minutes.

3 Combine the flour, baking powder, bicarbonate of soda and a pinch of salt; set aside. Beat the eggs with the soured cream, rum, vanilla and almond essences and the melted butter. Whisk the egg mixture into the rice, then stir in the flour mixture until just blended; do not over-mix. Fold in the mincemeat.

4 Heat a large frying pan or griddle pan and brush with butter. Stir the batter and drop 2–3 tablespoons into the pan. Cook for about 2 minutes, until the undersides are golden and the tops covered with bubbles that burst open. Gently turn and cook for an additional minute. Keep warm.

5 Dust the pancakes with cinnamon and serve. A chilled rum and raisin custard goes well with these pancakes (see Cook's Tip).

COOK'S TIP

Soak 150 g/5½ oz raisins in boiling water. Bring 350 ml/12 fl oz milk with a vanilla pod and seeds to the boil. Cool for 10 minutes. Beat 5 eggs with a little sugar; beat in half the milk and return all to the saucepan. Cook, without boiling, until thick. Add drained raisins and 2–3 tbsp dark rum.

Lace Crêpes with Fruit

These super-light crêpes melt in your mouth. They are filled with a gingered fruit salad of melon, grapes and lychees.

10 mins   5 mins

SERVES 4

I N G R E D I E N T S

3 egg whites

4 tbsp cornflour

3 tbsp cold water

1 tsp vegetable oil

F R U I T   F I L L I N G

350 g/12 oz fresh lychees

¼ Ogen or Charentais melon

175 g/6 oz seedless green grapes

1-cm/½-inch piece fresh root ginger

2 pieces stem ginger in syrup

2 tbsp ginger wine or dry sherry

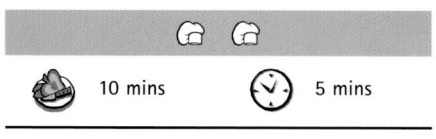

1 To make the fruit filling, peel the lychees and remove the stones. Place the lychees in a bowl. Scoop out the seeds from the melon and remove the skin. Cut the melon flesh into small pieces and place in the bowl.

2 Wash and dry the grapes, remove the stalks and add to the bowl. Peel the root ginger and cut into thin shreds or grate finely. Drain the stem ginger pieces, reserving the syrup, and chop the ginger pieces finely.

3 Stir the root ginger and stem ginger into the bowl with the ginger wine or sherry and the stem ginger syrup. Cover with clingfilm and set aside.

4 Meanwhile, prepare the crêpes. In a small jug, combine the egg whites, cornflour and cold water, stirring until very smooth.

5 Brush a small non-stick crêpe pan with oil and heat until hot. Drizzle the surface of the pan with a quarter of the cornflour mixture to give a lacy effect. Cook for a few seconds until set, then carefully lift out and transfer to kitchen paper to drain. Set aside and keep warm.

Repeat with the remaining mixture to make 4 crêpes in total.

6 To serve, place a crêpe on each of 4 serving plates, put the fruit filling on one half of each crêpe and fold the crêpes over. Serve immediately.

Thai Crêpes & Tropical Fruits

Coconut milk, papayas and passion fruit give these delicate little crêpes an exotic flavour.

🐻 🐻

🍲 15 mins   🕐 20 mins

SERVES 4

INGREDIENTS

2 eggs

125 ml/4 fl oz coconut milk

175 ml/6 fl oz milk

140 g/5 oz plain flour

½ tsp salt

1 tbsp caster sugar

1 tbsp butter, melted

oil, for frying

sifted icing sugar, for dusting

FILLING

2 papayas

3 passion fruit

juice of 1 lime

2 tbsp icing sugar

1 In a bowl, whisk the eggs, coconut milk and milk together. Sift the flour and salt into a large bowl. Stir in the sugar. Make a well in the flour and gradually beat in the egg mixture to form a smooth batter. Stir in the melted butter.

2 Heat a 20–23-cm/8-9-inch non-stick frying pan and brush with oil. Pour in enough batter to coat the base of the frying pan. Tip the frying pan as you pour it in, so the base is evenly coated. Cook until browned on the underside and set on top, then turn the crêpe over and cook the other side. Place on a plate, then cover with foil and keep warm while you make the remaining crêpes.

3 Peel the papayas and halve, then scoop out the seeds, reserving a few. Cut into chunks and place in a bowl. Cut the passion fruit in half. Scoop the seeds and pulp into the bowl. Stir in the lime juice and icing sugar. Put a little filling on a quarter of each crêpe. Fold in half and then into quarters. Dust with sifted icing sugar. Scatter over the reserved papaya seeds and serve.

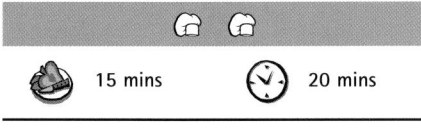

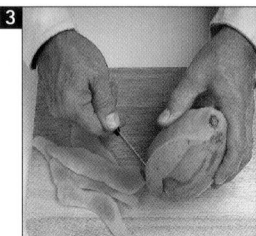

Coconut Crêpes

These pretty, lacy-thin crêpes, which are often coloured a delicate pale-pink or tinted green, are sold by Thai street vendors.

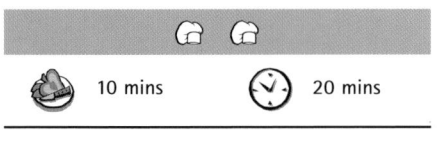
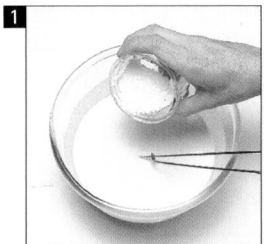

10 mins   20 mins

SERVES 4

INGREDIENTS

90 g/3¼ oz rice flour

3 tbsp caster sugar

pinch of salt

2 eggs

600 ml/1 pint coconut milk

4 tbsp grated coconut

vegetable oil, for frying

2 tbsp palm sugar, to decorate

fresh mango or banana, to serve

1 Place the rice flour, sugar and salt in a bowl and add the eggs and coconut milk, whisking until a smooth batter forms. Alternatively, place all the ingredients in a food processor or blender and process to a smooth batter. Beat in half the coconut.

2 Heat a small amount of oil in a wide, heavy-based frying pan. Pour in a little batter, swirling the frying pan to cover the surface thinly and evenly. Cook until pale golden underneath.

3 Turn or toss the crêpe and cook the other side until light golden brown.

4 Turn out the crêpe and keep hot while using the remaining batter to make a total of 8 crêpes.

5 Serve the crêpes folded or loosely rolled, with slices of mango or banana and sprinkled with palm sugar and the remaining coconut, toasted.

COOK'S TIP
Rice flour gives the crêpes a light, smooth texture, but if it's not available, use ordinary plain flour instead.

Chocolate Rum & Raisin Crêpes

These sophisticated crêpes are filled with rum-soaked fruit and smothered in a rich chocolate sauce.

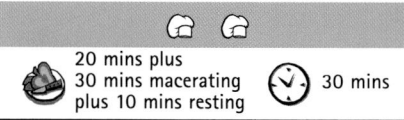

20 mins plus
30 mins macerating
plus 10 mins resting

30 mins

SERVES 4

INGREDIENTS

1 tsp icing sugar

5 tbsp raisins or sultanas

2 tbsp dark rum

125 g/4½ oz plain flour

1 tsp baking powder

225 ml/8 fl oz milk

2 eggs, beaten

4 tbsp unsalted butter, melted

CHOCOLATE SAUCE

150 ml/5 fl oz double cream

140 g/5 oz plain chocolate, chopped

1 Put the sugar, raisins, sultanas and dark rum in a bowl and mix well. Leave to soak for at least 30 minutes.

2 To make the sauce, heat the cream until almost boiling, then pour over the chocolate. Whisk until the chocolate is melted and smooth. Set aside.

3 To make the crêpes, sift the flour and baking powder together in a large bowl. Whisk the milk, eggs and butter together and pour into the flour. Whisk until smooth. Leave the mixture to rest for 10 minutes.

4 Heat a 20-cm/8-inch non-stick frying pan and add a spoonful of the batter, swirling to cover the base of the frying pan. Cook the crêpe for 1–2 minutes, until brown, then flip over and cook for an additional minute or so. Remove the crêpe and keep warm. Repeat until you have used up all the batter.

5 Sprinkle each crêpe with a teaspoonful of raisins, then fold in 4 or roll it up. Put any spare raisins in the chocolate sauce and drizzle over the crêpes to serve.

Crêpes with Honeycomb Butter

These light crêpes are delicious with the rich honeycomb butter but are equally good served with maple syrup and blueberries.

20 mins plus 10 mins standing

20 mins

SERVES 4

I N G R E D I E N T S

125 ml/4 fl oz buttermilk or natural yogurt

125 ml/4 fl oz milk

2 eggs, separated

2 tbsp caster sugar

2 tbsp unsalted butter, melted

175 g/6 oz plain flour

1 tsp baking powder

CHOCOLATE HONEYCOMB BUTTER

55 g/2 oz chocolate-covered honeycomb

4 tbsp unsalted butter, softened

1 To make the chocolate honeycomb butter, crush the honeycomb in a polythene bag until it resembles rough breadcrumbs and mix thoroughly with the butter. Chill until ready to serve.

2 To make the crêpes, whisk the buttermilk, milk, egg yolks, sugar and melted butter together in a large bowl. Sift the flour and baking powder together and whisk into the buttermilk mixture until smooth. Leave the mixture to stand for 10 minutes.

3 Whisk the egg whites until soft peaks form, then fold into the batter.

4 Heat a non-stick frying pan over a medium heat and add 1 tablespoon of batter. Cook the crêpe for 2–3 minutes, until small bubbles appear on the surface, then flip over and cook for an additional 2–3 minutes. Repeat until you have 8 crêpes.

5 Serve the crêpes hot with the cold butter melting on to them.

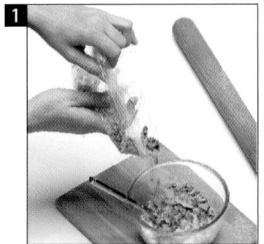

COOK'S TIP

If you cannot find chocolate-covered honeycomb, use chopped chocolate instead.

Pecan & Chocolate Crêpes

American-style crêpes studded with nuts and chocolate are popular at any time of the day.

10 mins   40 mins

SERVES 12

INGREDIENTS

225 g/8 oz self-raising flour

1 tsp baking powder

pinch of salt

1 egg

300 ml/10 fl oz milk

1 tbsp butter, melted

½ tsp vanilla essence

2 tbsp golden caster sugar

55 g/2 oz plain chocolate chips

40 g/1½ oz shelled pecan nuts, chopped

corn or sunflower oil, for frying

butter, to serve (optional)

1 Sift the flour, baking powder and salt into a large bowl and make a well in the centre. Place the egg and milk in a small bowl and mix, pour into the well in the dry ingredients and whisk to make a thick, smooth batter.

2 Beat in the melted butter and vanilla essence, then stir in the caster sugar, chocolate chips and chopped nuts. Heat a teaspoon of oil in a large frying pan or flat griddle pan. Drop large tablespoonfuls of the batter into the hot pan to make crêpes 7.5-cm/3-inches across. Cook over medium heat for 3 minutes, or until small bubbles appear on the surface of each crêpe.

3 Turn with a palette knife and cook for an additional 2–3 minutes, or until golden. Keep the crêpes warm by wrapping in foil or kitchen paper while cooking the remainder of the batter. Serve with butter.

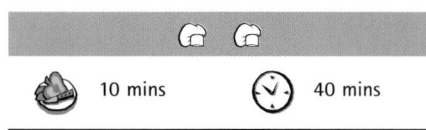

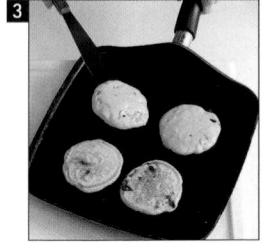

Sweet Potato Bread

This is a great-tasting loaf, coloured light orange by the sweet potato. Added sweetness from the honey is offset by the tangy orange rind.

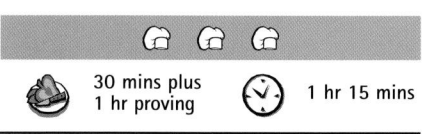

30 mins plus 1 hr proving

1 hr 15 mins

SERVES 8

INGREDIENTS

90 g/3¼ oz butter, plus extra for greasing

225 g/8 oz sweet potatoes, diced

150 ml/5 fl oz tepid water

2 tbsp honey

2 tbsp vegetable oil

3 tbsp orange juice

85 g/3 oz semolina

280 g/10 oz white bread flour

2½ tsp easy-blend dried yeast

1 tsp ground cinnamon

grated rind of 1 orange

1 Lightly grease a 675-g/1 lb 8-oz loaf tin. Cook the sweet potatoes in a saucepan of boiling water for about 10 minutes, or until soft. Drain thoroughly and mash until smooth.

2 Meanwhile, mix the water, honey, oil and orange juice together in a large mixing bowl.

3 Add the mashed sweet potatoes, semolina, three-quarters of the flour, the yeast, ground cinnamon and grated orange rind and mix thoroughly to form a dough. Set aside for about 10 minutes.

4 Dice the butter and knead it into the dough with the remaining flour. Knead for about 5 minutes until smooth.

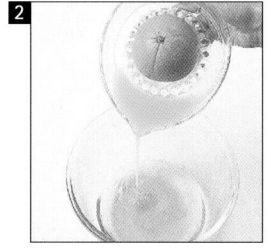

5 Place the dough in the prepared loaf tin. Cover and set aside in a warm place for 1 hour, or until doubled in size.

6 Preheat the oven to 190°C/375°F/Gas Mark 5. Cook the loaf for 45–60 minutes, or until the bottom sounds hollow when tapped. Serve warm.

Spicy Carrot-Rice Loaf

Rice flour gives this delicious loaf a tender crumb, while the cooked rice adds a chewy texture. Use any kind of cooked rice.

1 hr 30 mins

1–1 hr 15 mins

SERVES 8–10

INGREDIENTS

115 g/4 oz butter, melted and cooled, plus extra for greasing

280 g/10 oz plain flour, plus extra for dusting

60 g/2¼ oz rice flour

2 tsp baking powder

½ tsp bicarbonate of soda

½ tsp salt

1 tsp ground cinnamon

½ tsp grated nutmeg

½ tsp ground ginger

⅓ cup cooked risotto or long-grain white rice

75 g/2¾ oz chopped pecan nuts

100 g/3½ oz sultanas or raisins

3 eggs

1 cup sugar

115 g/4 oz soft light brown sugar

2 carrots, grated

icing sugar, for dusting

1 Preheat the oven to 180°C/350°F/Gas Mark 4. Lightly grease a 23 x 12.5-cm/9 x 5-inch loaf tin. Line with non-stick baking paper and grease with a little butter. Dust lightly with flour.

2 Sift the flour, rice flour, baking powder, bicarbonate of soda, salt and spices into a bowl. Add the rice, nuts and sultanas or raisins and toss well to coat. Make a well in the centre of the dry ingredients and set aside.

3 Using an electric whisk, beat the eggs for about 2 minutes, until light and foaming. Add the sugars and continue beating for an additional 2 minutes. Beat in the melted butter, then stir in the grated carrots until blended.

4 Pour the egg and carrot mixture into the well and, using a fork, stir until a soft batter forms. Do not over-mix; the batter should be slightly lumpy.

5 Pour into the prepared tin and smooth the top. Bake in the preheated oven for 1–1¼ hours, or until risen and golden. Cover the loaf with foil if it colours too quickly.

6 Cool the loaf in the tin on a wire rack for about 10 minutes. Carefully turn out and leave to cool completely. Dust with a little icing sugar and cut into thin slices to serve.

Apricot & Walnut Bread

Serve this fruit bread freshly made, sliced and buttered with a cup of tea in the afternoon, or try it for breakfast.

25 mins plus 1 hr 30 mins proving

30 mins

SERVES 12

INGREDIENTS

4 tbsp butter, plus extra for greasing

plain flour, for dusting

350 g/12 oz white bread flour

½ tsp salt

1 tsp golden caster sugar

2 tsp easy-blend dried yeast

115 g/4 oz ready-to-eat dried apricots, chopped

55 g/2 oz walnuts, chopped

150 ml/5 fl oz tepid milk

75 ml/2½ fl oz tepid water

1 egg, beaten

TOPPING

85 g/3 oz icing sugar

walnut halves

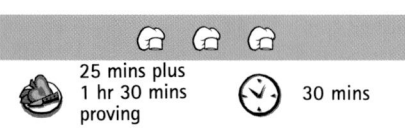

1 Grease and flour a baking sheet. Sift the flour and salt into a warm bowl and stir in the sugar and yeast. Rub in the butter and add the apricots and walnuts. Make a well in the centre. In another bowl, mix together the milk, water and egg. Pour into the dry ingredients and mix to a soft dough. Turn on to a floured work surface and knead for 10 minutes until smooth. Put in an oiled bowl, cover with oiled clingfilm and leave in a warm place until doubled in size.

2 Turn the dough on to a floured work surface and knead lightly for 1 minute. Divide into 5 equal pieces and roll each piece into a rope 30 cm/ 12 inches long. Plait 3 ropes together, pinching the ends to seal, and place on the prepared baking sheet. Twist the remaining two ropes together and place on top. Cover lightly with oiled clingfilm and leave in a warm place until doubled in size.

3 Preheat the oven to 220°C/425°F/Gas Mark 7. Bake the bread in the oven for 10 minutes, then reduce the heat to 190°C/375°F/Gas Mark 5 and bake for an additional 20 minutes. Transfer to a wire rack to cool. To make the topping, sift the icing sugar into a bowl and stir in enough water to make a thin icing. Drizzle the icing over the loaf and decorate the top with walnut halves.

VARIATION
As an alternative to apricots, use glacé cherries, dried cranberries or dates.

Barm Brack

This Irish bread was traditionally baked with a wedding ring in the mixture in the belief that whoever received it would be married within the year.

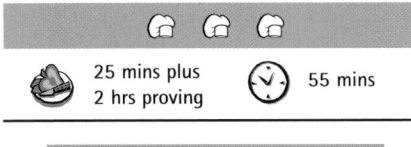

25 mins plus
2 hrs proving

55 mins

MAKES A 23-CM/9-INCH LOAF

INGREDIENTS

650 g/1 lb 7 oz white bread flour, plus extra for dusting

1 tsp mixed spice

1 tsp salt

2 tsp easy-blend dried yeast

55 g/2 oz golden caster sugar

300 ml/10 fl oz tepid milk

150 ml/5 fl oz tepid water

4 tbsp butter, softened

325 g/11½ oz mixed dried fruit

milk, for glazing

1 Sift the flour, mixed spice and salt into a warmed bowl. Stir in the yeast and the caster sugar. Make a well in the centre and pour in the milk and water. Mix well to make a sticky dough. Place on a lightly floured work surface and knead the dough until no longer sticky. Put into a clean oiled bowl, cover with clingfilm and leave in a warm place for 1 hour, until doubled in size.

2 Turn the dough out on to a floured work surface and knead lightly for 1 minute. Add the butter and dried fruit to the dough and work them in until completely incorporated. Return the dough to the bowl, replace the clingfilm and leave to prove for 30 minutes. Grease a 23-cm/9-inch round cake tin. Pat the dough to a neat round and fit in the tin. Cover and leave in a warm place until it has risen to the top of the tin. Preheat the oven to 200°C/400°F/Gas Mark 6.

3 Brush the top of the loaf lightly with milk and bake in the oven for 15 minutes. Cover the loaf with foil, reduce the oven temperature to 180°C/350°F/Gas Mark 4 and bake for 45 minutes, until the bread is golden and sounds hollow when tapped underneath. Leave on a wire rack to cool.

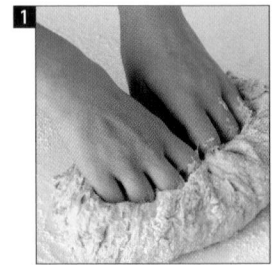

COOK'S TIP
Letting the bread prove 3 times gives it its particular open texture, but if time is short, you can omit the second proving.

Chocolate & Nut Soda Bread

This is a delicious sweet version of traditional Irish soda bread which is every bit as good as the original.

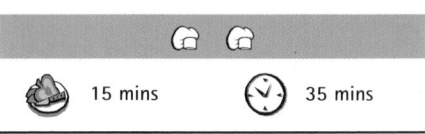

🍰 15 mins   🕐 35 mins

SERVES 6

INGREDIENTS

450 g/1 lb plain flour, plus extra for dusting

3 tsp caster sugar

1 tsp salt

1 tsp bicarbonate of soda

140 g/5 oz milk chocolate, chopped

150 g/5½ oz mixed nuts, chopped

1 egg, beaten

300 ml/10 fl oz buttermilk

1 Sift the flour into a large bowl and mix in the sugar, salt, bicarbonate of soda, chocolate and nuts.

2 Make a well in the centre and pour in the beaten egg and buttermilk. Gradually incorporate the flour, a little at a time, until you have a soft dough.

3 Turn on to a floured board and gently knead for a minute or two. Add a little more flour if the dough is too wet.

4 Preheat the oven to 220°C/425°F/Gas Mark 7.

5 Shape the dough into a circle and score the top with a cross. Place the loaf on a lightly floured baking sheet and bake for 15 minutes, then reduce the oven temperature to 200°C/400°F/Gas Mark 6 for an additional 20 minutes.

6 Cool the loaf on a wire rack.

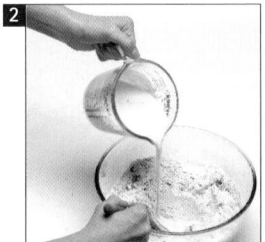

COOK'S TIP

A mixture of walnuts, pecan nuts and hazelnuts works well, but you could also use Brazil nuts, almonds and macadamia nuts.

Date & Honey Loaf

This bread is full of good things – chopped dates, sesame seeds and honey. Toast thick slices and spread with cream cheese for a light snack.

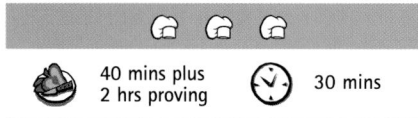

40 mins plus
2 hrs proving

30 mins

1 LOAF

INGREDIENTS

butter, for greasing

250 g/9 oz white bread flour, plus extra for dusting

70 g/2½ oz wholemeal bread flour

½ tsp salt

7 g/¼ oz easy-blend dried yeast

200 ml/7 fl oz tepid water

3 tbsp sunflower oil

3 tbsp honey

85 g/3 oz chopped stoned dates

2 tbsp sesame seeds

1 Grease a 900-g/2 lb loaf tin with a little butter.

2 Sift both types of flour into a large mixing bowl, and stir in the salt and yeast. Pour in the tepid water, sunflower oil and honey. Mix together to form a dough.

3 Place the dough on a lightly floured work surface and knead for about 5 minutes, until smooth.

4 Place the dough in a greased bowl, cover and leave to prove in a warm place for 1 hour, or until doubled in size.

5 Knead in the dates and sesame seeds. Shape the dough and place in the tin.

6 Cover and stand the loaf in a warm place for an additional 30 minutes, or until springy to the touch.

7 Preheat the oven to 220°C/425°F/Gas Mark 7. Bake the loaf for 30 minutes, or until a hollow sound is heard when the bottom of the loaf is tapped.

8 Transfer the loaf to a wire rack and leave to cool completely. Serve the loaf cut into thick slices with butter or cream cheese.

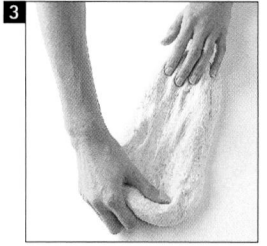

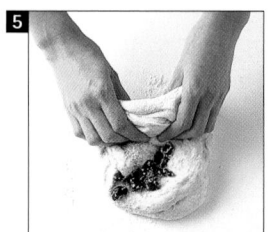

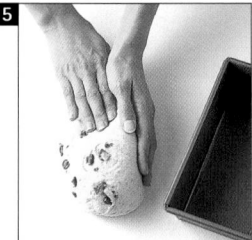

COOK'S TIP

If you cannot find a warm place, sit a bowl with the dough in it over a saucepan of warm water and cover.

Banana & Cranberry Loaf

The addition of chopped nuts, candied peel, fresh orange juice and dried cranberries makes this a rich, moist tea bread.

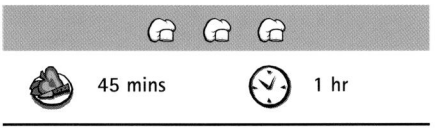

45 mins   1 hr

SERVES 8

INGREDIENTS

butter, for greasing

225 g/8 oz self-raising flour

½ tsp baking powder

125 g/4½ oz soft light brown sugar

2 bananas, mashed

50 g/1¾ oz mixed candied peel

40 g/1½ oz chopped mixed nuts

70 g/2½ oz dried cranberries

5–6 tbsp orange juice

2 eggs, beaten

150 ml/5 fl oz sunflower oil

85 g/3 oz icing sugar, sifted

grated rind of 1 orange

1 Preheat the oven to 180°C/350°F/Gas Mark 4. Grease a 900-g/2-lb loaf tin and line the base with baking paper.

2 Sift the flour and baking powder into a mixing bowl. Stir in the brown sugar, bananas, candied peel, nuts and dried cranberries.

3 Stir the orange juice, eggs and sunflower oil together until well combined. Add the mixture to the dry ingredients and mix until thoroughly blended. Spoon the mixture into the prepared loaf tin and smooth the top.

4 Bake in the preheated oven for about 1 hour, until firm to the touch or until a skewer inserted into the centre of the loaf comes out clean.

5 Turn out the loaf and set aside to cool on a wire rack.

6 Mix the icing sugar with a little water and drizzle the icing over the loaf. Sprinkle the orange rind over the top. Leave the icing to set before slicing.

COOK'S TIP
This tea bread will keep for a couple of days. Wrap it carefully and store in a cool, dry place.

Banana & Date Loaf

This fruity bread is excellent for afternoon tea or morning coffee with its moist texture and sweet flavour.

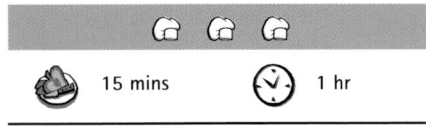

15 mins   1 hr

SERVES 6

INGREDIENTS

75 g/2¾ oz butter, cut into small pieces, plus extra for greasing

225 g/8 oz self-raising flour

60 g/2¼ oz caster sugar

115 g/4 oz stoned dried dates

2 bananas, mashed coarsely

2 eggs, beaten lightly

2 tbsp honey

1 Preheat the oven to 160°C/325°F/Gas Mark 3. Grease a 900-g/2-lb loaf tin with a little butter and line the base with baking paper.

2 Sift the flour into a mixing bowl. Rub the butter into the flour with your fingertips until the mixture resembles fine breadcrumbs.

3 Add the sugar, chopped dates, bananas, beaten eggs and honey to the dry ingredients. Mix together to form a soft dropping consistency.

4 Spoon the mixture into the prepared loaf tin, spreading it out evenly, and gently smooth the surface with the back of a knife.

5 Bake the loaf in the preheated oven for about 1 hour, or until golden brown on top and a skewer inserted into the centre of the loaf comes out clean.

6 Leave the loaf to cool in the tin before turning out and transferring to a wire rack to cool completely.

7 Serve the loaf warm or cold, cut into thick slices.

COOK'S TIP

This tea bread will keep for several days if stored in an airtight container and kept in a cool, dry place.

Date & Walnut Tea Bread

This tea bread has sticky layers of date purée running through it. It keeps well, stored in an airtight container.

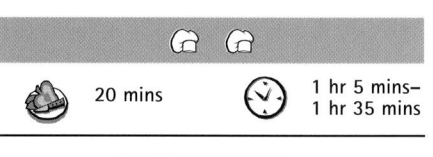

20 mins

1 hr 5 mins–
1 hr 35 mins

SERVES 10-12

INGREDIENTS

175 g/6 oz butter, plus extra for greasing

225 g/8 oz stoned dried dates, chopped into small pieces

grated rind and juice of 1 orange

50 ml/2 fl oz water

175 g/6 oz light muscovado sugar

3 eggs, beaten

85 g/3 oz self-raising wholemeal flour

85 g/3 oz self-raising white flour

55 g/2 oz chopped walnuts

8 walnut halves, to decorate

1 Preheat the oven to 160°C/325°F/Gas Mark 3. Grease and line a 900-g/2-lb loaf tin. Put the dates in a saucepan with the orange rind and juice and the water and cook for 5 minutes until you have a soft purée.

2 Put the butter and sugar in a bowl and beat together until light and fluffy. Gradually beat in the eggs, then sift in the flours and fold in with the walnuts. Spread one-third of the mixture over the base of the prepared tin and spread half the date purée over.

3 Repeat the layers, ending with the cake mixture. Arrange walnut halves down the centre of the loaf. Bake in the oven for 1-1½ hours, until well risen and firm to the touch. Leave in the tin for 10 minutes, then turn out and remove the paper and leave to stand on a wire rack to cool. Serve sliced.

COOK'S TIP
Do not use the dates sold for baking, which are rolled in sugar. They are too sweet.

Glossy Fruit Loaf

This is a rich, sweet fruit loaf, ideal for family celebrations or parties, and tastes superb with a cup of hot tea.

20 mins, plus
8 hrs 20 mins
soaking/cooling

1 hr 30 mins–
1 hr 45 mins

SERVES 10

INGREDIENTS

50 g/1¾ oz raisins

85 g/3 oz ready-to-eat dried apricots, chopped coarsely

55 g/2 oz stoned dried dates, chopped

75 ml/2½ fl oz cold black tea

115 g/4 oz butter, plus extra for greasing

115 g/4 oz soft light brown sugar

2 eggs, beaten

175 g/6 oz self-raising flour, sifted

scant 40 g/1½ oz coarsely chopped candied pineapple

85 g/3 oz glacé cherries, halved

generous 85 g/3 oz coarsely chopped Brazil nuts

TOPPING

25 g/1 oz walnut halves

25 g/1 oz Brazil nuts

50 g/1¾ oz glacé cherries, halved

2 tbsp apricot jam, sieved and warmed

1 Place the raisins, apricots and dates in a bowl, pour over the tea and leave to soak for 8 hours, or overnight. The following day, preheat the oven to 160°C/325°F/Gas Mark 3. Grease and line a 900-g/2-lb loaf tin. Beat the butter and sugar together until light and fluffy.

2 Gradually beat in the eggs, then fold in the flour alternately with the soaked fruit. Gently stir in the pineapple, cherries and chopped nuts. Turn the mixture into the prepared tin. To make the topping, arrange the walnuts, Brazil nuts and cherries on top.

3 Bake in the preheated oven for 1½–1¾ hours, or until a skewer inserted into the centre comes out clean. Leave to cool in the tin for 10 minutes, then turn out and peel off the lining paper. Transfer to a wire rack to cool completely. Warm the apricot jam and brush over the top of the cake.

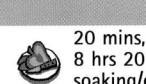

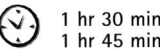

COOK'S TIP
Soaking dried fruit in cold black tea makes the fruit plump and juicy, which gives fruit bread extra flavour and moistness.

Welsh Cakes

You do not even have to turn on the oven to make these little scones. They were traditionally cooked on a flat griddle over a fire.

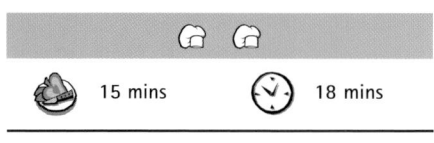

15 mins   18 mins

MAKES ABOUT 16

INGREDIENTS

280 g/10 oz self-raising flour

pinch of salt

4 tbsp lard or white vegetable fat

4 tbsp butter

85 g/3 oz golden caster sugar

75 g/2¾ oz currants

1 egg, beaten

1 tbsp milk (optional)

TO FINISH

caster sugar, for dusting

1 Sift the flour and salt into a bowl. Add the fat and butter and rub in until the mixture resembles breadcrumbs. Stir in the sugar and currants. Add the egg and a little milk, if necessary, to make a soft, but not sticky, dough.

2 On a floured work surface, roll out the dough to 5-mm/¼-inch thickness. Cut into rounds with a 6-cm/2½-inch plain or fluted biscuit cutter. Gather the trimmings, re-roll and cut out more cakes until you have used up the dough.

3 Heat a greased griddle pan or heavy-based frying pan. Cook the cakes over low heat, for about 3 minutes on each side, until golden brown. Dust generously with caster sugar and serve warm or cold.

Sticky Ginger Marmalade Loaf

Ginger marmalade gives a wonderful flavour to this moist sticky tea bread, which is very quick to prepare.

10 mins   1 hr

SERVES 10–12

INGREDIENTS

175 g/6 oz butter, softened, plus extra for greasing

125 g/4½ oz ginger marmalade

175 g/6 oz light muscovado sugar

3 eggs, beaten

225 g/8 oz self-raising flour

½ tsp baking powder

1 tsp ground ginger

100 g/3½ oz pecan nuts, chopped coarsely

1 Preheat the oven to 180°C/350°F/Gas Mark 4. Grease and line a 900-g/2-lb loaf tin. Put 1 tablespoon of the ginger marmalade in a small saucepan and set aside. Put the remaining marmalade in a bowl with the butter, sugar and eggs.

2 Sift in the flour, baking powder and ground ginger and beat together until smooth. Stir in three-quarters of the nuts. Spoon the batter into the prepared tin and smooth the top. Sprinkle with the reserved nuts and bake in the oven for 1 hour, until well risen and a skewer inserted into the centre comes out clean.

3 Leave in the tin for 10 minutes, then turn out and remove the paper. Place on a wire rack to cool. Gently heat the saucepan of reserved marmalade, then brush over the warm loaf. Serve cut in slices.

COOK'S TIP
If the loaf starts to brown too much before it is cooked, cover lightly with foil.

Banana & Chocolate Chip Loaf

Bananas make this loaf cake beautifully moist, and combining them with chocolate makes this sweet bread a favourite with children.

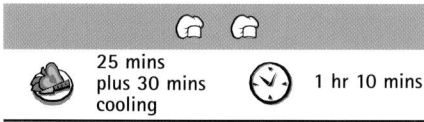

25 mins
plus 30 mins
cooling

1 hr 10 mins

SERVES 10

I N G R E D I E N T S

115 g/4 oz butter, softened, plus extra
   for greasing

175 g/6 oz plain flour

1 tsp bicarbonate of soda

pinch of salt

1 tsp ground cinnamon

175 g/6 oz golden caster sugar

2 large ripe bananas, mashed

2 eggs, beaten

5 tbsp boiling water

175 g/6 oz plain chocolate chips

TO SERVE

whipped cream

ready-made chocolate decorations

1 Preheat the oven to 160°C/325°F/Gas Mark 3. Grease and line the base and sides of a 900-g/2-lb loaf tin. Sift the flour, bicarbonate of soda, salt and cinnamon into a bowl and set aside. Place the butter and sugar in a bowl and beat together until light and fluffy.

2 Beat in the bananas and then the eggs. The batter may look curdled, but this is perfectly normal. Stir in the flour mixture alternately with the boiling water until just combined, then stir in the chocolate chips.

3 Spoon into the prepared tin and smooth the top. Bake in the preheated oven for 1 hour 10 minutes, or until well risen, golden brown and firm to the touch. Leave to cool in the tin for 30 minutes, then turn out and peel off the lining paper. Transfer to a wire rack to cool completely, then serve in slices with a little whipped cream, decorated with chocolate decorations.

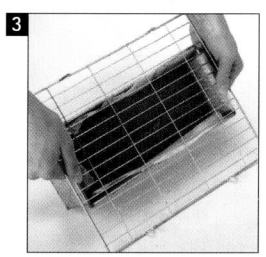

Banana & Chocolate Tea Bread

This is a good loaf to make when you have some over-ripe bananas in the fruit bowl. It will need to be eaten quickly.

10 mins   50-60 mins

SERVES 8

INGREDIENTS

115 g/4 oz butter, softened, plus extra for greasing

2 ripe bananas

85 g/3 oz golden caster sugar

2 eggs

200 g/7 oz self-raising flour

25 g/1 oz cocoa powder

1 tsp baking powder

2 tbsp milk

100 g/3½ plain chocolate chips

1 Preheat the oven to 180°C/350°F/Gas Mark 4. Grease and line a 900-g/2-lb loaf tin. Put the bananas in a large bowl and mash with a fork.

2 Add the butter, sugar and eggs and sift the flour, cocoa and baking powder. Beat vigorously until smooth, adding sufficient milk to give a thick dropping consistency. Stir in the plain chocolate chips.

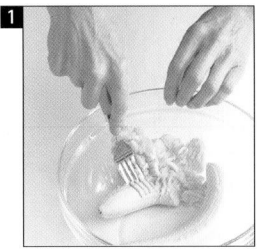
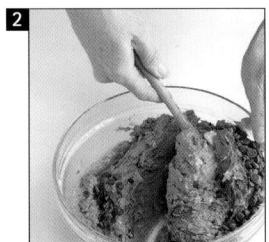

COOK'S TIP
You can mix the ingredients in a food processor, then stir in the chocolate chips by hand.

3 Spoon the mixture into the prepared tin and bake in the preheated oven for 50-60 minutes, until well risen and a skewer inserted into the centre comes out clean. Leave the tea bread in the tin for 5 minutes, then turn out on to a wire rack to cool. Serve sliced, with or without butter.

Mango Twist Bread

This is a sweet bread which has puréed mango mixed into the dough, resulting in a moist loaf with an exotic flavour.

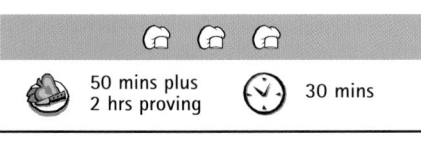

🍯 50 mins plus
2 hrs proving

🕐 30 mins

1 LOAF

INGREDIENTS

40 g/1½ oz butter, cut into small pieces, plus extra for greasing

450 g/1 lb white bread flour, plus extra for dusting

1 tsp salt

7 g/¼ oz easy-blend dried yeast

1 tsp ground ginger

50 g/1¾ oz soft light brown sugar

1 small mango, peeled, stoned and blended to a purée

225 ml/8 fl oz tepid water

2 tbsp honey

115 g/4 oz sultanas

1 egg, beaten lightly

icing sugar, for dusting

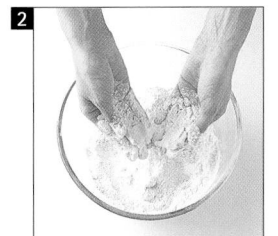

1 Grease a baking sheet with a little butter and set aside.

2 Sift the flour and salt into a large mixing bowl. Stir in the yeast, ground ginger and brown sugar. Rub in the butter with your fingertips until the mixture resembles breadcrumbs.

3 Stir in the mango purée, water and honey and mix to form a dough.

4 Place the dough on a lightly floured work surface and knead for about 5 minutes until smooth. Alternatively, use an electric mixer with a dough hook. Place the dough in a greased bowl, cover and leave to prove in a warm place for about 1 hour, until it has doubled in size.

5 Knead in the sultanas and shape the dough into 2 sausage shapes, each 25 cm/10 inches long. Carefully twist the 2 pieces together and pinch the ends to seal. Place the dough on the baking sheet, cover and leave in a warm place for an additional 40 minutes.

6 Preheat the oven to 220°C/425°F/Gas Mark 7. Brush the loaf with the egg. Bake in the oven for 30 minutes, or until golden brown. Leave to cool on a wire rack. Dust with icing sugar before serving.

COOK'S TIP
You can tell when the bread is cooked because it will sound hollow when tapped on the bottom.

Citrus Bread

This sweet loaf is flavoured with citrus fruit. It is excellent served at breakfast with a glass of freshly squeezed orange juice.

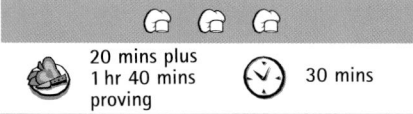

1 LOAF

INGREDIENTS

4 tbsp butter, cut into small pieces, plus extra for greasing

450 g/1 lb white bread flour, plus extra for dusting

½ tsp salt

50 g/1¾ oz caster sugar

7 g/¼ oz easy-blend dried yeast

5–6 tbsp orange juice

4 tbsp lemon juice

3–4 tbsp lime juice

150 ml/5 fl oz tepid water

1 orange

1 lemon

1 lime

2 tbsp honey

1 Lightly grease a baking sheet with a little butter.

2 Sift the flour and salt into a large mixing bowl. Stir in the sugar and yeast.

3 Rub in the butter with your fingertips until the mixture resembles breadcrumbs. Add all of the fruit juices and the water and mix to form a dough.

4 Place the dough on a lightly floured work surface and knead for 5 minutes. Alternatively, use an electric mixer with a dough hook. Place the dough in a greased bowl, cover and leave to prove in a warm place for 1 hour.

5 Meanwhile, grate the rind of the orange, lemon and lime. Knead the fruit rinds into the dough.

6 Divide the dough into 2 balls, making one slightly bigger than the other.

7 Place the larger ball on the baking sheet and set the smaller one on top.

8 Push a floured finger through the centre of the dough. Cover and leave to prove for about 40 minutes, or until springy to the touch.

9 Preheat the oven to 220°C/425°F/Gas Mark 7. Bake the loaf for 35 minutes. Transfer to a wire rack. Glaze with honey and leave to cool completely.

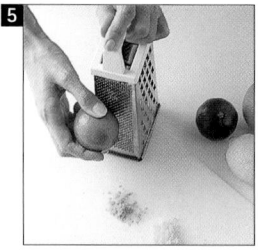

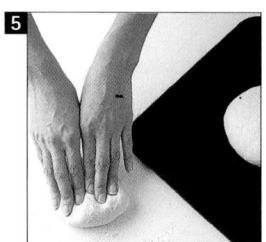

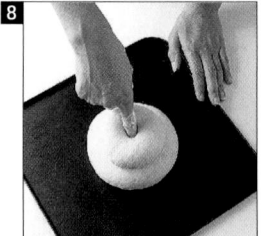

Fruit & Nut Loaf

This fruit bread may be served warm or cold, perhaps spread with a little butter, or topped with apricot jam.

30 mins plus 1 hr proving

40 mins

SERVES 4

INGREDIENTS

280 g/10 oz white bread flour, plus extra for dusting

½ tsp salt

1 tbsp margarine, plus extra for greasing

2 tbsp soft light brown sugar

115 g/4 oz sultanas

55 g/2 oz ready-to-eat dried apricots, chopped

75 g/2¾ oz chopped hazelnuts

2 tsp easy-blend dried yeast

6 tbsp orange juice

6 tbsp low-fat natural yogurt

2 tbsp sieved apricot jam

1 Sift the flour and salt into a bowl. Rub in the margarine and stir in the sugar, raisins, apricots, nuts and yeast.

2 Warm the orange juice in a saucepan but do not let it boil.

3 Stir the warm orange juice into the flour mixture with the yogurt and then bring the mixture together to form a dough.

4 Knead the dough on a lightly floured work surface for 5 minutes until smooth and elastic. Shape into a circle and place on a lightly greased baking sheet. Cover with a clean tea towel and set aside to prove in a warm place until doubled in size.

5 Preheat the oven to 220°C/425°F/Gas Mark 7. Bake the loaf for 35–40 minutes, until cooked through. Transfer to a wire rack and brush the top of the warm cake with the apricot jam. Leave the cake to cool before serving.

COOK'S TIP
To test whether yeast bread or cake is done, tap the loaf from underneath. If it sounds hollow, the bread or cake is ready.

Stollen

Stollen is a spiced German fruit bread with a marzipan filling which is traditionally served at Christmas.

🍰🍰🍰
30 mins plus 3 hrs 40 mins proving
🕐 40 mins

SERVES 10

INGREDIENTS

85 g/3 oz currants

55 g/2 oz raisins

35 g/1¼ oz chopped mixed candied peel

55 g/2 oz glacé cherries, rinsed, dried and quartered

2 tbsp dark rum

4 tbsp butter

175 ml/6 fl oz milk

3 tbsp golden caster sugar

375 g/13 oz white bread flour, plus extra for dusting

½ tsp salt

½ tsp ground nutmeg

½ tsp ground cinnamon

seeds from 3 cardamom pods

2 tsp easy-blend dried yeast

finely grated rind of 1 lemon

1 egg, beaten

40 g/1½ oz flaked almonds

oil, for greasing

175 g/6 oz marzipan

melted butter, for brushing

sifted icing sugar, for dusting

COOK'S TIP

An enriched dough such as this takes longer to prove than ordinary bread dough, so do not be tempted to put it somewhere hot to try to speed up the process.

1 Put the currants, raisins, candied peel and cherries in a bowl. Stir in the rum and set aside. Put the butter, milk and sugar in a saucepan and heat gently until the sugar has dissolved and the butter has just melted. Cool until hand-hot. Sift the flour, salt, nutmeg and cinnamon into a bowl. Crush the cardamom seeds with a pestle and mortar and add them to the flour mixture. Stir in the yeast. Make a well in the centre and stir in the milk mixture, lemon rind and beaten egg. Beat to form a soft dough.

2 Turn the dough on to a floured work surface. With floured hands, knead the dough for about 5 minutes. It will be quite sticky, so add more flour if necessary. Knead the soaked fruit and flaked almonds into the dough until just combined. Return the dough to the clean, lightly oiled bowl. Cover with clingfilm and leave in a warm place for up to 3 hours, or until doubled in size. Turn the dough on to a floured work surface and knead lightly for 1-2 minutes, then roll out to a 25-cm/10-inch square.

3 Roll the marzipan into a sausage shape slightly shorter than the length of the dough and place down the centre. Fold one side over to cover the marzipan. Repeat with the other side, overlapping in the centre. Seal the ends. Place the roll, seam-side down, on a greased baking sheet. Cover with oiled clingfilm and leave in a warm place until doubled in size. Preheat the oven to 190°C/375°F/Gas Mark 5. Bake the stollen for 40 minutes, or until it is golden and it sounds hollow when tapped underneath. Brush the hot stollen generously with melted butter and dredge heavily with icing sugar. Leave to cool on a wire rack.

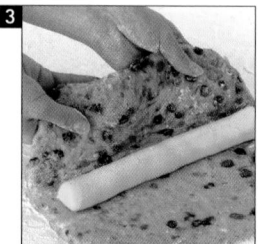

Tropical Fruit Bread

The flavours in this fruit bread will bring a touch of sunshine to your table, whatever the time of year.

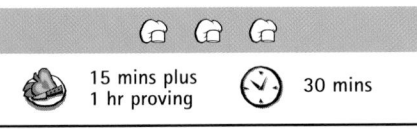

🍰 15 mins plus 1 hr proving   🕐 30 mins

SERVES 4

INGREDIENTS

2 tbsp butter, cut into small pieces, plus extra for greasing

375 g/13 oz white bread flour

25 g/1 oz bran

½ tsp salt

½ tsp ground ginger

7 g/¼ oz easy-blend dried yeast

2 tbsp soft light brown sugar

250 ml/9 fl oz tepid water

55 g/2 oz glacé pineapple, chopped finely

2 tbsp finely chopped dried mango

70 g/2½ oz grated coconut, toasted, plus extra for sprinkling

1 egg, beaten lightly

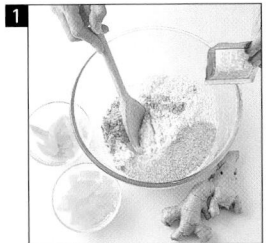
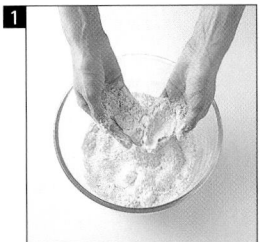

1 Grease a baking sheet. Sift the flour into a large mixing bowl. Stir in the bran, salt, ginger, yeast and sugar. Rub in the butter with your fingers, then add the water and mix to form a dough.

2 On a lightly floured work surface, knead the dough for 5–8 minutes, until smooth. Alternatively, use an electric mixer with a dough hook. Place the dough in a greased bowl, cover and leave to prove in a warm place for 30 minutes until doubled in size.

3 Knead the pineapple, mango and coconut into the dough. Shape into a circle and place on the baking sheet. Score the top with the back of a knife. Cover and set aside for an additional 30 minutes in a warm place.

4 Preheat the oven to 220°C/425°F/ Gas Mark 7. Brush the loaf with the beaten egg and sprinkle with coconut. Bake in the preheated oven for about 30 minutes, or until golden brown.

5 Set the bread aside to cool on a wire rack before serving.

COOK'S TIP
To test the bread after the second proving, gently prod the dough with your finger – it should spring back if it has proved enough.

Apple & Apricot Tea Loaf

The firm texture of this cake makes it an ideal fruity snack for picnic hampers and children's lunchboxes.

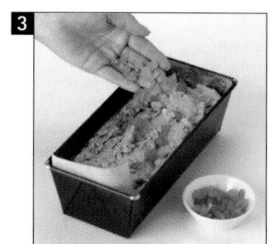

15 mins plus
10 mins cooling

55–60 mins

SERVES 10

INGREDIENTS

115 g/4 oz butter, softened, plus extra for greasing

115 g/4 oz soft light brown sugar

2 eggs, beaten

55 g/2 oz ready-to-eat dried apricots, chopped

2 eating apples, peeled and grated coarsely

2 tbsp milk

225 g/8 oz self-raising flour

1 tsp ground mixed spice

½ tsp ground cinnamon

1 Preheat the oven to 180°C/350°F/Gas Mark 4. Grease and line a 900-g/2-lb loaf tin. Place the butter and sugar in a bowl and beat until light and fluffy. Gradually beat in the eggs.

2 Reserve 1 tablespoon of the apricots, then fold the rest into the creamed mixture with the grated apples and milk. Sift in the flour, mixed spice and cinnamon and fold into the mixture.

3 Spoon into the prepared tin and sprinkle over the reserved apricots. Bake in the preheated oven for 55–60 minutes, or until risen and a skewer inserted into the centre comes out clean. Leave to cool in the tin for 10 minutes, then turn out and peel off the lining paper. Transfer to a wire rack to cool completely.

Fruit Loaf with Apple Spread

This sweet, fruity loaf is ideal served with coffee for a healthy snack.
The fruit spread can be made quickly while the cake is in the oven.

1 hr 15 mins · 2 hrs

SERVES 10

INGREDIENTS

butter, for greasing

150 g/5½ oz rolled oats

85 g/3 oz light muscovado sugar

1 tsp ground cinnamon

150 g/5½ oz sultanas

150 g/5½ oz raisins

2 tbsp malt extract

300 ml/10 fl oz unsweetened apple juice

225 g/8 oz self-raising wholemeal flour

1½ tsp baking powder

FRUIT SPREAD

300 g/10½ oz strawberries, washed and hulled

2 eating apples, cored, chopped and mixed with 1 tbsp lemon juice to prevent them browning

300 ml/10 fl oz unsweetened apple juice

TO SERVE

strawberries

apple wedges

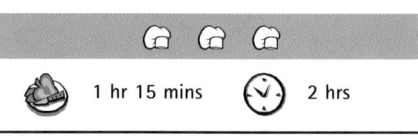

1 Grease and line a 900-g/2-lb loaf tin. Place the oats, sugar, cinnamon, sultanas, raisins and malt extract in a mixing bowl. Pour in the apple juice, stir well and set aside to soak for 30 minutes.

2 Preheat the oven to 180°C/350°F/Gas Mark 4. Sift in the flour and baking powder, adding any husks that remain in the sieve, and fold in using a metal spoon. Spoon the mixture into the tin and bake in the preheated oven for 1½ hours, until firm or until a skewer inserted into the centre of the loaf comes out clean.

3 Remove the tin from the oven and place on a wire rack to cool for about 10 minutes, then turn the loaf out on to the rack and set aside to cool completely.

4 Meanwhile, make the fruit spread. Place the strawberries and apples in a saucepan and pour in the apple juice.

Bring to the boil, cover and simmer for 30 minutes. Beat the sauce well and spoon into a clean, warmed jar. Set aside to cool, then seal, and label.

5 Serve the loaf with the fruit spread and strawberries, and apple wedges.

Spiced Chocolate Yule Bread

A delicious loaf, rich with spices, chocolate and fruit which tastes good any time of year.

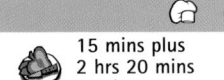

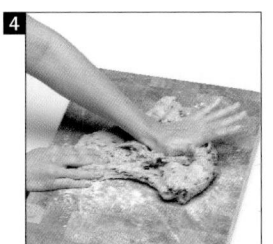
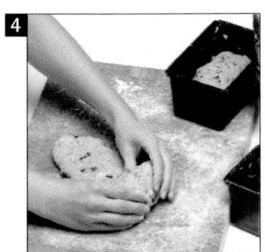

15 mins plus 2 hrs 20 mins proving

1 hr

SERVES 6

INGREDIENTS

450 g/1 lb white bread flour

pinch of salt

2 tsp each mixed spice, nutmeg and cinnamon

115 g/4 oz cold butter, diced

7 g/¼ oz easy-blend dried yeast

115 g/4 oz caster sugar

55 g/2 oz mixed candied peel

grated rind of 1 orange

150 g/5½ oz chocolate chips

1 egg

150 ml/5 fl oz milk

oil, for greasing

1 Sift the flour, salt and spices together into a large bowl and rub in the butter until the mixture resembles breadcrumbs.

2 Add the yeast, sugar, candied peel, orange rind and chocolate, then add the egg. Warm the milk until tepid and add to the mixture to form a soft dough.

3 Put the dough in a floured bowl and cover. Leave to prove in a warm place for 2 hours. Oil 2 x 450 g/1-lb loaf tins.

4 Tip the dough out of the bowl and knead it lightly on a floured board. Shape the dough and fit it into the tins. Leave to rest for 20 minutes. Preheat the oven to 180°C/350°F/Gas Mark 4.

5 Bake the loaves in the centre of the oven for 1 hour. Remove from the oven and cool in the tins.

Chocolate Bread

For the chocoholics among us, this bread is not only great fun to make, it also has a fantastic chocolate flavour.

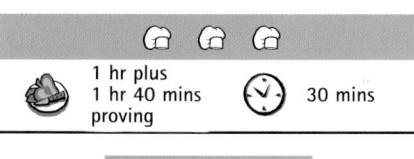

1 hr plus
1 hr 40 mins
proving

30 mins

MAKES 1 LOAF

INGREDIENTS

butter, for greasing

450 g/1 lb white bread flour

25 g/1 oz cocoa powder

1 tsp salt

7 g/¼ oz easy-blend dried yeast

2 tbsp brown sugar

1 tbsp oil, plus extra for greasing

300 ml/10 fl oz tepid water

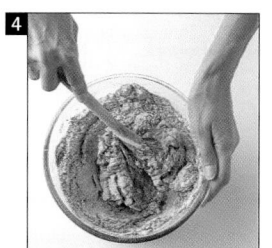
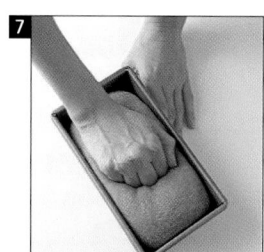

1 Lightly grease a 900-g/2-lb loaf tin with a little butter.

2 Sift the flour and cocoa into a large mixing bowl.

3 Stir in the salt, yeast and brown sugar, mixing well.

4 Pour in the oil along with the tepid water and mix the ingredients together to make a dough.

5 Place the dough on a lightly floured surface and knead for 5 minutes.

6 Place the dough in a greased bowl, cover and leave to prove in a warm place for about 1 hour, or until the dough has doubled in size.

7 Punch down the dough and shape it into a loaf. Place the dough in the prepared tin, cover and leave to prove in a warm place for an additional 30 minutes.

8 Preheat the oven to 200°C/400°F/Gas Mark 6. Bake the loaf for 25–30 minutes, or until a hollow sound is heard when the bottom of the bread is tapped. Transfer the bread to a wire rack and leave to cool completely. Cut into slices to serve.

COOK'S TIP
This bread can be sliced and spread with butter, or it can be lightly toasted.

Chocolate Fruit Bread

It is one of life's luxuries to sit down with a cup of coffee and a slice of fruit bread, especially if it's made with chocolate.

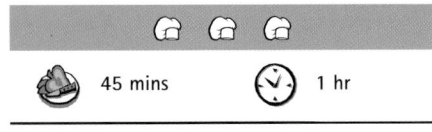

45 mins   1 hr

SERVES 4

INGREDIENTS

175 g/6 oz butter, softened, plus extra for greasing

175 g/6 oz soft light brown sugar

4 eggs, beaten lightly

225 g/8 oz plain chocolate chips

85 g/3 oz raisins

85 g/3 oz chopped walnuts

finely grated rind of 1 orange

280 g/10 oz self-raising flour

1 Preheat the oven to 160°C/325°F/Gas Mark 3. Grease a 900-g/2-lb loaf tin and line the base with baking paper.

2 Cream together the butter and sugar in a bowl until light and fluffy.

3 Gradually add the eggs, beating well after each addition. If the mixture starts to curdle, beat in 1–2 tablespoons of the flour.

4 Stir in the chocolate chips, raisins, walnuts and orange rind. Sift the flour and carefully fold it into the mixture.

VARIATIONS
Use white or milk chocolate chips instead of plain chocolate chips, or a mixture of all three, if desired. Dried cranberries instead of the raisins also work well in this recipe.

5 Spoon the mixture into the prepared loaf tin and then make a slight dip in the centre of the top with the back of a spoon.

6 Bake in the preheated oven for 1 hour, or until a fine skewer inserted into the centre of the loaf comes out clean.

7 Leave the loaf to cool in the tin for 5 minutes before carefully turning out on to a wire rack to cool completely.

8 To serve the fruit bread, cut it into thin slices.

Chocolate Orange Tea Bread

This recipe makes two delicious marble loaves; one to eat now and one to freeze for another day.

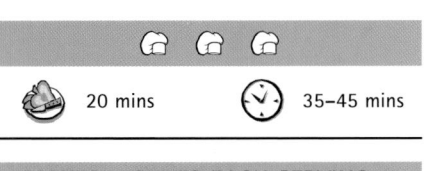

🥐 20 mins   🕐 35–45 mins

MAKES 2 CAKES EACH SERVING 6

I N G R E D I E N T S

150 g/5½ oz butter, softened, plus extra
    for greasing

75 g/2¾ oz plain chocolate,
    broken into pieces

250 g/9 oz golden caster sugar

5 large eggs, beaten

150 g/5½ oz plain flour

2 tsp baking powder

pinch of salt

grated rind of 2 oranges

1 Preheat the oven to 180°C/350°F/Gas Mark 4. Grease and line 2 x 450-g/1-lb loaf tins. Put the chocolate in a heatproof bowl set over a saucepan of gently simmering water, making sure that the base of the bowl does not touch the water. Remove from the heat once the chocolate has melted.

2 Put the butter and sugar in another bowl and beat until light and fluffy. Gradually beat in the eggs. Sift the flour, baking powder and salt into the mixture and fold in. Transfer one-third of the mixture to the melted chocolate and stir together. Stir the orange rind into the remaining mixture. Divide half the orange batter between the 2 loaf tins and spread in an even layer.

3 Drop tablespoonfuls of the chocolate mixture on top, dividing it between the 2 pans, but do not smooth it out. Add the last of the orange mixture to the 2 pans, then, using a knife, gently swirl the 2 mixtures together to give a marbled effect. Bake in the preheated oven for 35–40 minutes, until a skewer inserted into the centre of each loaf comes out clean. Leave to cool in the tins for 10 minutes, then turn out, remove the paper and cool completely on a wire rack.

COOK'S TIP
When you add the eggs, the mixture may appear to curdle. This does not matter.

Italian Chocolate Chip Bread

Serve this flavourful bread plain with butter or jam, or Italian-style with a spoonful of mascarpone cheese.

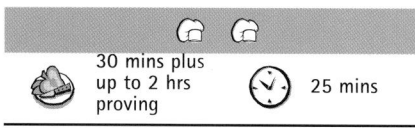

30 mins plus up to 2 hrs proving

25 mins

MAKES 1 LOAF

INGREDIENTS

1 tsp vegetable oil, for brushing

280 g/10 oz plain flour, plus extra for dusting

1 tbsp cocoa powder

pinch of salt

1 tbsp butter, unsalted for preference, plus ½ tsp extra, melted, for brushing

1 tbsp caster sugar

7 g/¼ oz easy-blend dried yeast

150 ml/5 fl oz lukewarm water

55 g/2 oz plain chocolate chips

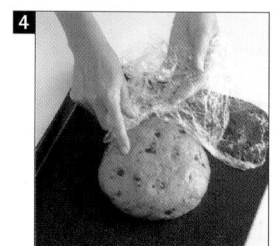

1 Brush a baking sheet with ½ teaspoon of the oil. Sift the flour, cocoa and salt into a bowl. Add the butter and rub it into the flour mixture, then stir in the sugar and yeast.

2 Gradually add the water, stirring well to mix. When the dough becomes too firm to stir with a spoon, gather it together with your hands. Turn it out on to a lightly floured work surface and knead thoroughly until smooth and elastic.

3 Knead the chocolate chips into the dough, distributing them throughout. Form into a round loaf, then place on the baking sheet, cover with oiled clingfilm and set aside in a warm place for 1½–2 hours, or until doubled in bulk.

4 Preheat the oven to 220°C/425°F/Gas Mark 7. Bake the loaf in the oven for 10 minutes. Reduce the temperature to 190°C/375°F/Gas Mark 5 and bake for an additional 15 minutes.

5 Transfer the loaf to a wire rack and brush with melted butter. Cover with a clean tea towel until cooled.

Chocolate Fruit Loaf

A very moreish loaf that smells divine while it is baking. It is best enjoyed warm.

  40 mins plus 1 hr proving　⏱ 30 mins

SERVES 10

INGREDIENTS

butter, for greasing

400 g/14 oz white bread flour, plus extra for dusting

25 g/1 oz cocoa powder

2 tbsp caster sugar

7 g/¼ oz easy-blend dried yeast

¼ tsp salt

225 ml/8 fl oz tepid water

2 tbsp butter, melted

5 tbsp coarsely chopped glacé cherries

55 g/2 oz plain chocolate chips

55 g/2 oz sultanas

75 g/2¾ oz ready-to-eat dried apricots, chopped coarsely

GLAZE

1 tbsp caster sugar

1 tbsp water

1　Lightly grease a 900-g/2-lb loaf tin. Sift the flour and cocoa into a large mixing bowl. Stir in the sugar, yeast and salt.

2　Mix together the tepid water and butter. Make a well in the centre of the dry ingredients and add the liquid. Mix well with a wooden spoon, then use your hands to bring the dough together. Turn out on to a lightly floured surface and knead for 5 minutes, until a smooth elastic dough forms. Return to a clean bowl, cover with a damp tea towel and leave to prove in a warm place for about 1 hour, or until doubled in size.

3　Turn the dough out on to a floured work surface and knead for 5 minutes. Roll out to a rectangle about 1-cm/½-inch thick and the same width as the length of the tin. Scatter the cherries, chocolate chips, sultanas and chopped apricots over the dough. Carefully roll up the dough, like a Swiss roll, enclosing the filling. Transfer to the loaf tin, cover with a damp tea towel and leave to prove for 20 minutes, or until the top of the dough is level with the top of the tin.

4　Preheat the oven to 200°C/400°F/Gas Mark 6. To make the glaze, mix together the sugar and water, then brush it over the top of the loaf. Bake in the preheated oven for 30 minutes, or until well risen. Serve.

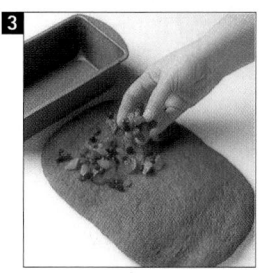

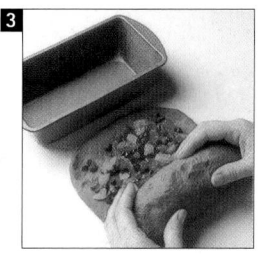

Crown Loaf

This is a rich, sweet bread combining alcohol, nuts and fruit in a decorative wreath shape. It is ideal for serving at Christmas.

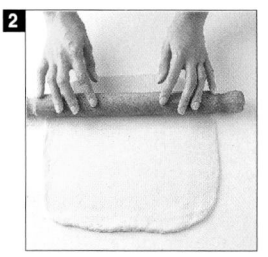
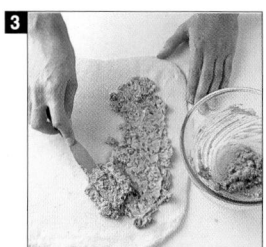
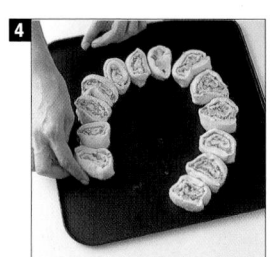

30 mins plus 1 hr 10 mins proving

30 mins

MAKES 1 LOAF

INGREDIENTS

2 tbsp butter, cut into small pieces, plus extra for greasing

225 g/8 oz white bread flour

½ tsp salt

7 g/¼ oz easy-blend dried yeast

125 ml/4 fl oz tepid milk

1 egg, beaten lightly

FILLING

4 tbsp butter, softened

50 g/1¾ oz soft light brown sugar

2 tbsp chopped hazelnuts

1 tbsp chopped stem ginger

50 g/1¾ oz mixed candied peel

1 tbsp dark rum or brandy

115 g/4 oz icing sugar

2 tbsp lemon juice

1 Grease a baking sheet. Sift the flour and salt into a bowl. Stir in the yeast. Rub in the butter with your fingertips. Add the milk and egg and mix to form a dough.

2 Place the dough in a greased bowl, cover and stand in a warm place for 40 minutes, until doubled in size. Punch down the dough lightly for 1 minute. Roll out to a rectangle about 30 x 23 cm/ 12 x 9 inches.

3 To make the filling, cream together the butter and sugar until light and fluffy. Stir in the hazelnuts, ginger, candied peel and rum or brandy. Spread the filling over the dough, leaving a 2.5-cm/1-inch border.

4 Roll up the dough, starting from one of the long edges, into a sausage shape. Cut into slices at 5-cm/2-inch intervals and place in a circle on the baking sheet with the slices just touching. Cover and stand in a warm place to prove for 30 minutes.

5 Preheat the oven to 190°C/375°F/Gas Mark 5. Bake the loaf for 20–30 minutes, or until golden. Meanwhile, mix the icing sugar with enough lemon juice to form a thin icing.

6 Leave the loaf to cool slightly before drizzling with icing. Leave the icing to set slightly before serving.

Cinnamon & Currant Loaf

This spiced tea bread is quick and easy to make. Serve it buttered and with a drizzle of honey for an afternoon snack.

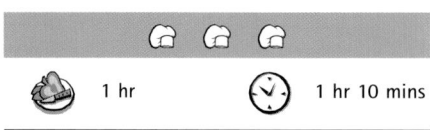

🧈 1 hr   🕐 1 hr 10 mins

SERVES 8

INGREDIENTS

175 g/6 oz butter, cut into small pieces, plus extra for greasing

350 g/12 oz plain flour

pinch of salt

1 tbsp baking powder

1 tbsp ground cinnamon

175 g/6 oz soft light brown sugar

115 g/4 oz currants

finely grated rind of 1 orange

5–6 tbsp orange juice

6 tbsp milk

2 eggs, beaten lightly

1 Preheat the oven to 180°C/350°F/Gas Mark 4. Grease a 900-g/2-lb loaf tin and line the base with baking paper.

2 Sift the flour, salt, baking powder and ground cinnamon into a bowl. Rub in the butter with your fingertips until the mixture resembles breadcrumbs.

3 Stir in the sugar, currants and orange rind. Beat the orange juice, milk and eggs together and add to the dry ingredients. Mix well together.

4 Spoon the mixture into the prepared tin. Make a slight dip in the centre of the mixture to help it rise evenly.

5 Bake in the preheated oven for about 1–1 hour 10 minutes, until a fine metal skewer inserted into the centre of the loaf comes out clean.

6 Leave the loaf to cool before turning it out of the tin. Transfer to a wire rack and leave to cool completely before slicing.

COOK'S TIP
Once you have added the liquid to the dry ingredients, work as quickly as possible, because the baking powder is activated by the liquid.

Pains au Chocolat

These croissants can be a bit fiddly to make, but the flaky pastry enclosing a fabulous rich chocolate filling makes them worth the effort.

20 mins plus
3 hrs chilling
and proving

20–25 mins

MAKES 12

INGREDIENTS

175 g/6 oz butter, softened, plus extra
for greasing

500 g/1 lb 2 oz white bread flour

½ tsp salt

7 g/¼ oz easy-blend dried yeast

2 tbsp lard or white vegetable fat

1 egg, beaten lightly

225 ml/8 fl oz tepid water

100 g/3½ oz plain chocolate,
broken into 12 squares

beaten egg, for glazing

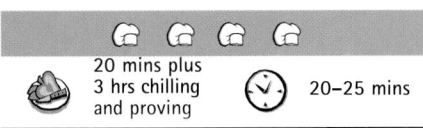

1 Lightly grease a baking sheet. Sift the flour and salt into a mixing bowl and stir in the yeast. Rub in the fat with your fingertips. Add the egg and enough of the water to mix to a soft dough. Knead for about 10 minutes to make a smooth elastic dough.

2 Roll out to form a 38 x 20-cm/15 x 8-inch rectangle. Divide the butter into 3 portions and dot one portion over two-thirds of the rectangle, leaving a small border around the edge.

3 Fold the rectangle into 3 by first folding the plain part of the dough over and then the other side. Seal the edges of the dough by pressing with a rolling pin. Give the dough a quarter turn so the sealed edges are at the top and bottom. Re-roll and fold (without adding butter), then wrap the dough and chill for 30 minutes.

4 Repeat steps 2 and 3 until all of the butter has been used, chilling the dough each time. Re-roll and fold twice more without butter. Chill for a final 30 minutes.

5 Roll out the dough to a 45 x 30-cm/18 x 12-inch rectangle, trim and halve lengthways. Cut each half into 6 rectangles and brush with beaten egg.

Place a chocolate square at one end of each rectangle and roll up to form a sausage. Press the ends together and place, seam-side down, on the baking sheet. Cover and leave to prove for 40 minutes in a warm place. Preheat the oven to 220°C/425°F/Gas Mark 7. Brush each pastry roll with egg and bake in the oven for 20–25 minutes, until golden. Cool on wire rack. Serve warm or cold.

Orange & Currant Brioches

Brioche is a light rich French bread which can be made as one large loaf or small buns. They are usually served with coffee for breakfast.

30 mins plus
1 hr 40 mins proving

15 mins

MAKES 12

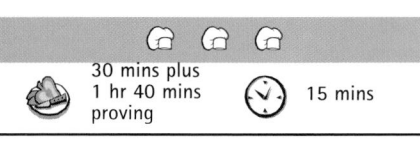
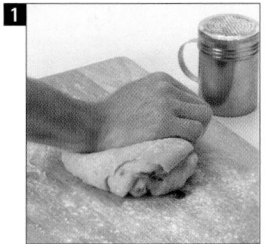

INGREDIENTS

225 g/8 oz white bread flour, plus extra for dusting

½ tsp salt

7 g/¼ oz easy-blend dried yeast

1 tbsp golden caster sugar

55 g/2 oz raisins

grated rind of 1 orange

2 tbsp tepid water

2 eggs, beaten

4 tbsp butter, melted

vegetable oil, for greasing

beaten egg, for glazing

butter, to serve

1 Butter 12 individual brioche moulds. Sift the flour and salt into a warm bowl. Add the yeast, sugar, raisins and orange rind. Make a well in the centre. Mix the water, eggs and melted butter, and add to the well. Beat vigorously to make a soft dough. Turn on to a lightly floured work surface and knead for 5 minutes until smooth and elastic. Put the dough in an oiled bowl, cover with clingfilm and leave in a warm place for 1 hour, or until doubled in size.

2 Turn out on to a lightly floured work surface, knead lightly for 1 minute, then roll into a sausage shape. Cut into 12 equal pieces. Shape three-quarters of each piece into a ball and place in the prepared moulds. With a floured finger, press a hole in the centre of each. Shape the remaining pieces of dough into a little plug and press into the holes.

3 Place the moulds on a baking sheet, cover lightly with oiled clingfilm and leave in a warm place until the dough comes almost to the top of the moulds. Preheat the oven to 220°C/425°F/Gas Mark 7. Brush the brioches with beaten egg and bake in the oven for 15 minutes, until golden brown. Serve the brioches warm with butter.

COOK'S TIP
If you do not have brioche moulds, use a muffin tin instead.

Teacakes

These popular snacks are ideal split in half and toasted, then spread with butter. A mixture of luxury dried fruit gives them a rich taste.

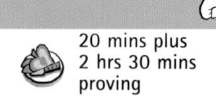

20 mins plus
2 hrs 30 mins
proving

20 mins

MAKES 12

INGREDIENTS

2 tbsp butter, cut into small pieces, plus extra for greasing

450 g/1 lb white bread flour, plus extra for dusting

7 g/¼ oz easy-blend dried yeast

50 g/1¼ oz caster sugar

1 tsp salt

300 ml/10 fl oz tepid milk

85 g/3 oz mixed dried fruit

honey, for brushing

butter, to serve

1 Grease several baking sheets with a little butter.

2 Sift the flour into a large bowl. Stir in the yeast, sugar and salt. Rub in the butter with your fingertips until the mixture resembles fine breadcrumbs. Add the milk and mix all of the ingredients together to form a soft dough.

3 Place the dough on a lightly floured work surface and knead for about 5 minutes. Alternatively, you can knead the dough with an electric mixer with a dough hook.

4 Form the dough into a ball and place in a greased bowl, cover and leave to prove in a warm place for about 1–1½ hours, or until it has doubled in size.

5 Knead the dough again for a few minutes and knead in the fruit. Divide the dough into 12 circles and place on the

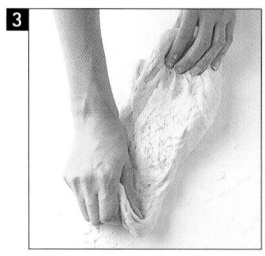 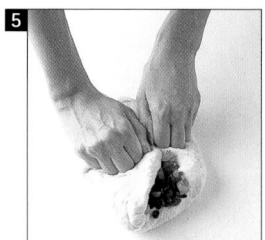 

baking sheets. Cover and leave to stand for 1 hour, or until springy to the touch.

6 Preheat the oven to 200°C/400°F/ Gas Mark 6. Bake the teacakes for 20 minutes.

7 Transfer the teacakes to a wire rack. Brush with honey while still warm. Leave to cool before serving split in half, toasted if liked, and spread with butter.

COOK'S TIP

It is important to have the milk at the right temperature: heat it until you can put your little finger into the milk and leave it there for 10 seconds without it feeling too hot.

Cinnamon Swirls

These cinnamon-flavoured buns are delicious if they are served warm a few minutes after they come out of the oven.

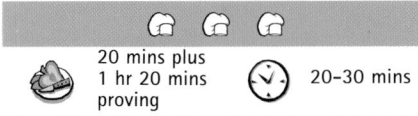

20 mins plus 1 hr 20 mins proving

20–30 mins

MAKES 12

INGREDIENTS

2 tbsp butter, cut into small pieces, plus extra for greasing

225 g/8 oz white bread flour

½ tsp salt

7 g/¼ oz easy-blend dried yeast

1 egg, beaten lightly

125 ml/4 fl oz tepid milk

2 tbsp maple syrup

FILLING

4 tbsp butter, softened

2 tsp ground cinnamon

50 g/1¾ oz soft light brown sugar

50 g/1¾ oz currants

1 Grease a 23-cm/9-inch square baking tin with a little butter.

2 Sift the flour and salt into a mixing bowl. Stir in the yeast. Rub in the butter with your fingertips until the mixture resembles breadcrumbs. Add the egg and milk and mix to form a dough.

3 Form the dough into a ball, place in a greased bowl, cover and leave to stand in a warm place for about 40 minutes, or until doubled in size.

4 Punch down the dough lightly for 1 minute, then roll out to a rectangle measuring 30 x 23 cm/12 x 9 inches.

5 To make the filling, cream together the softened butter, cinnamon and brown sugar until light and fluffy. Spread the filling evenly over the dough rectangle, leaving a 2.5-cm/1-inch border all around. Sprinkle the currants evenly over the top.

6 Roll up the dough from one of the long edges, and press down to seal. Cut the roll into 12 slices. Place them in the tin, cover and leave to stand for 30 minutes.

7 Preheat the oven to 190°C/375°F/Gas Mark 5. Bake the buns for 20–30 minutes, or until well risen. Brush with the syrup and leave to cool slightly before serving.

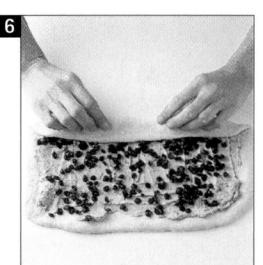

Double-Chocolate Swirls

These rich, chocolate buns are very quick to make for breakfast because the dough is prepared the night before.

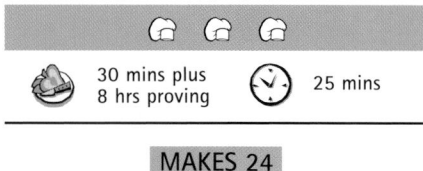

30 mins plus 8 hrs proving

25 mins

MAKES 24

INGREDIENTS

600 g/1 lb 5 oz white bread flour, plus extra for dusting

7 g/¼ oz easy-blend dried yeast

115 g/4 oz caster sugar

½ tsp salt

1 tsp ground cinnamon

85 g/3 oz unsalted butter

2 large eggs, beaten, plus 1 egg, beaten, for glazing

300 ml/10 fl oz milk

6 tbsp chocolate hazelnut spread

200 g/7 oz milk chocolate, chopped

oil, for greasing

1 Mix the flour, yeast, sugar, salt and cinnamon together in a large bowl.

2 Melt the butter and cool slightly, then whisk in the 2 eggs and milk. Pour into the flour and mix well.

3 Turn on to a floured work surface and knead for 10 minutes until smooth. Put into a large floured bowl, cover with clingfilm and put in a warm place for 8 hours, or overnight.

4 When you are ready to make the buns, take the dough from the bowl and punch down. Preheat the oven to 220°C/425°F/Gas Mark 7 and lightly oil 2 baking sheets.

5 Divide the dough into 4 pieces and roll each piece into a rectangle about 2.5-cm/1-inch thick. Spread each rectangle with the chocolate hazelnut spread and scatter with the chopped chocolate. Roll up each piece like a Swiss roll, then cut into 6 pieces. Place each swirl, cut-side down, on the baking sheets and brush each one well with the beaten egg. Bake in the preheated oven for 20 minutes and serve warm.

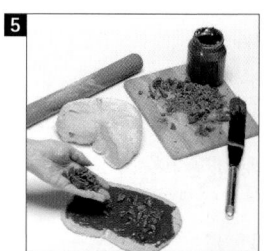

Hot Cross Buns

There is nothing more tempting than the aroma of spicy hot cross buns straight from the oven.

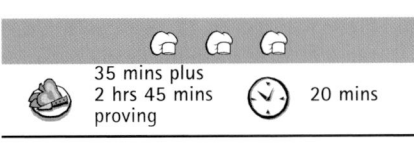

35 mins plus
2 hrs 45 mins
proving

20 mins

MAKES 12

INGREDIENTS

500 g/1 lb 2 oz white bread flour, plus extra for dusting

½ tsp salt

2 tsp ground mixed spice

1 tsp ground nutmeg

1 tsp ground cinnamon

7 g/¼ oz easy-blend dried yeast

50 g/1¾ oz golden caster sugar

finely grated rind of 1 lemon

175 g/6 oz currants

75 g/2¾ oz mixed candied peel

75 g/2¾ oz butter, melted, plus extra for greasing

1 egg

225 ml/8 fl oz tepid milk

vegetable oil, for greasing

CROSSES

50 g/1¾ oz plain flour

2 tbsp butter, cut into pieces

GLAZE

3 tbsp milk

3 tbsp golden caster sugar

1 Sift the flour, salt, mixed spice, nutmeg and cinnamon into a bowl. Stir in the yeast, sugar, lemon rind, currants and candied peel. Make a well in the centre. Mix together the melted butter, egg and milk and pour into the dry ingredients. Mix to form a soft dough, adding a little more milk if necessary. Turn the dough on to a floured work surface and knead for about 10 minutes, until the dough is smooth and elastic. Place the dough in a lightly oiled bowl, cover with clingfilm and leave in a warm place for 1½–2 hours, or until doubled in size.

2 Turn the dough on to a floured work surface and knead lightly. Divide the dough into 12 equal-sized pieces and knead each one into a ball. Place them on a greased baking sheet and flatten slightly. Cover loosely with oiled clingfilm and leave in a warm place for about 45 minutes, or until doubled in size. Preheat the oven to 220°C/425°F/Gas Mark 7.

3 To make the crosses, sift the flour into a bowl and rub in the butter. Stir in 1 tablespoon of cold water to make a dough. Divide the dough to form 24 strips, about 18 cm/7 inches long. To make the glaze, put the milk and sugar in a small saucepan and heat gently until the sugar has dissolved. Brush some of the glaze over the buns and lay the pastry strips on the buns to form crosses. Bake for 15–20 minutes, until golden. Brush with the remaining glaze and return to the oven for 1 minute. Transfer to a wire rack to cool.

Chelsea Buns

These sweet and sticky buns, with a hint of spice, are irresistible.
Perfect, served at any time of day!

30 mins plus
1 hr 45 mins
proving

30 mins

MAKES 9

INGREDIENTS

2 tbsp butter, plus extra for greasing

225 g/8 oz white bread flour, plus extra
   for dusting

½ tsp salt

7 g/¼ oz easy-blend dried yeast

1 tsp golden caster sugar

125 ml/4 fl oz tepid milk

vegetable oil, for greasing

1 egg, beaten

FILLING

55 g/2 oz light muscovado sugar

115 g/4 oz luxury mixed dried fruit

1 tsp mixed spice

4 tbsp butter, softened

GLAZE

85 g/3 oz icing sugar

1 Grease an 18-cm/7-inch square cake tin. Sift the flour and salt into a warmed bowl, stir in the yeast and sugar and rub in the butter. Make a well in the centre. In another bowl, mix together the milk and egg and pour into the dry ingredients. Beat vigorously to make a soft dough. On a floured work surface, knead the dough for 5–10 minutes, until smooth. Put the dough in an oiled bowl, cover with clingfilm and leave in a warm place for about 1 hour, or until doubled in size.

2 Turn the dough out on to a floured work surface and knead lightly for 1 minute. Roll out to a rectangle measuring 30 x 23 cm/12 x 9 inches.

To make the filling, put the sugar, dried fruit and mixed spice in a bowl and mix together. Spread the dough with the softened butter and sprinkle the fruit mixture on top. Roll up from a long side and cut into 9 pieces. Place in the prepared tin, cut-side up. Cover with oiled clingfilm and leave in a warm place for 45 minutes, until well risen.

3 Preheat the oven to 190°C/375°F/Gas Mark 5. Bake the buns in the oven for 30 minutes, until golden. Leave to cool in the tin for 10 minutes, then transfer, in one piece, to a wire rack to cool. To make the glaze, sift the icing sugar into a bowl and stir in enough water to make a thin glaze. Brush over the buns and leave to set. Pull the buns apart, to serve.

Cherry Scones

These are an alternative to traditional scones, using sweet glacé cherries which not only create colour but add a distinct flavour.

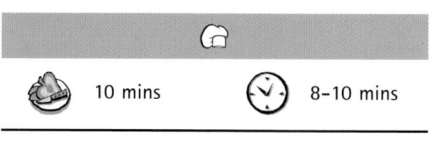

10 mins   8–10 mins

MAKES 8

INGREDIENTS

85 g/3 oz butter, cut into small pieces, plus extra for greasing

225 g/8 oz self-raising flour, plus extra for dusting

1 tbsp caster sugar

pinch of salt

3 tbsp glacé cherries, chopped

3 tbsp sultanas

1 egg, beaten lightly

3 tbsp milk

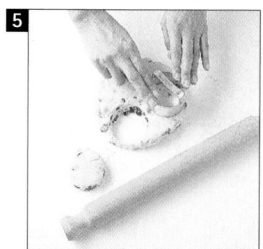

1 Preheat the oven to 220°C/425°F/Gas Mark 7. Lightly grease a baking sheet with a little butter.

2 Sift the flour, sugar and salt into a mixing bowl and rub in the butter with your fingertips until the mixture resembles breadcrumbs.

3 Stir in the glacé cherries and sultanas. Add the beaten egg.

4 Reserve 1 tablespoon of the milk for glazing, then add the remainder to the mixture. Mix well together to form a soft dough.

5 On a lightly floured work surface, roll out the dough to a thickness of 2 cm/¾ inch and cut out 8 circles, using a 5-cm/2-inch cutter.

6 Place the scones on the prepared baking sheet and brush the tops with the reserved milk.

7 Bake in the preheated oven for 8–10 minutes, or until the scones are golden brown.

8 Transfer the scones to a wire rack to cool completely, then serve them split and buttered.

COOK'S TIP
These scones will freeze very successfully, but they are best thawed and eaten within 1 month.

Molasses Scones

These scones are light and buttery like traditional scones, but the molasses give them a deliciously rich flavour.

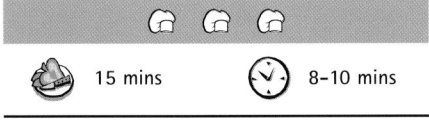

15 mins

8-10 mins

SERVES 8

INGREDIENTS

85 g/3 oz butter, cut into small pieces, plus extra for greasing

225 g/8 oz self-raising flour

1 tbsp caster sugar

salt

plain flour, for dusting

1 eating apple, peeled, cored and chopped

1 egg, beaten lightly

2 tbsp molasses

5 tbsp milk

1 Preheat the oven to 220°C/425°F/ Gas Mark 7. Lightly grease a baking sheet with a little butter.

2 Sift the flour, sugar and a pinch of salt into a mixing bowl.

3 Add the butter and rub it in with your fingertips until the mixture resembles fine breadcrumbs.

4 Add the chopped apple to the mixture and stir until thoroughly combined.

5 Mix the beaten egg, molasses and milk together in a large jug. Add to the dry ingredients and mix to form a soft dough.

6 On a lightly floured work surface, roll out the dough to a thickness of 2 cm/³/₄ inch and cut out 8 circles, using a 5-cm/2-inch cutter.

7 Arrange the scones on the prepared baking sheet and bake in the preheated oven for about 8–10 minutes.

8 Transfer the scones to a wire rack and leave to cool slightly. Serve split in half and spread with butter.

COOK'S TIP

These scones can be frozen, but are best defrosted and eaten within 1 month.

Chocolate Scones

A plain scone mixture is transformed into a chocoholic's treat by the simple addition of chocolate chips.

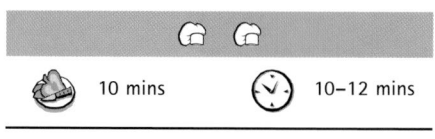   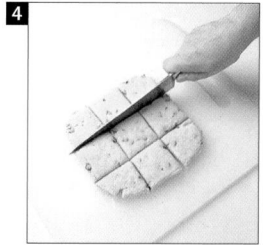

⏲ 10 mins   🕐 10–12 mins

MAKES 9

INGREDIENTS

70 g/2½ oz butter, plus extra for greasing

280 g/10 oz self-raising flour, sifted

1 tbsp caster sugar

55 g/2 oz chocolate chips

150 ml/5 fl oz milk

plain flour, for dusting

1 Preheat the oven to 220°C/425°F/Gas Mark 7. Lightly grease a baking sheet. Place the flour in a mixing bowl. Cut the butter into small pieces and rub it into the flour with your fingertips until the scone mixture resembles fine breadcrumbs.

2 Stir in the caster sugar and chocolate chips.

3 Mix in enough of the milk to form a soft dough.

4 On a lightly floured work surface, roll out the dough to form a 10 x 15-cm/ 4 x 6-inch rectangle, about 2.5 cm/1 inch thick. Cut the dough into 9 squares.

5 Place the scones spaced well apart on the prepared baking sheet.

6 Brush the tops with a little milk and bake in the preheated oven for 10–12 minutes, until risen and golden.

Buttermilk Scones

Buttermilk makes these scones extra light, and gives them a tangy flavour. Serve with whipped cream and strawberry jam.

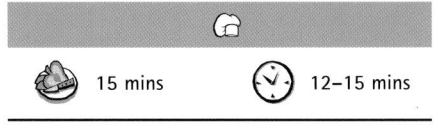

15 mins

12–15 mins

MAKES 8

INGREDIENTS

4 tbsp cold butter, cut into pieces, plus extra for greasing

300 g/10½ oz self-raising flour

1 tsp baking powder

pinch of salt

40 g/1½ oz golden caster sugar

300 ml/10 fl oz buttermilk

plain flour, for dusting

2 tbsp milk

TO SERVE

whipped cream

strawberry jam

1 Preheat the oven to 220°C/425°F/Gas Mark 7. Grease a baking sheet. Sift the flour, baking powder and salt into a bowl. Add the butter and rub in until the mixture resembles fine breadcrumbs. Add the sugar and buttermilk and quickly mix together.

2 Turn on to a floured work surface and knead lightly. Roll out to a thickness of 2.5 cm/1 inch. Using a 6-cm/2½-inch plain or fluted cutter, cut out the scones and place on the prepared baking sheet. Gather the trimmings, re-roll and cut out more scones until you have used up all the dough.

3 Brush the tops of the scones with milk. Bake in the oven for 12–15 minutes, until well risen and golden. Transfer to a wire rack to cool. Split and serve with whipped cream and strawberry jam.

COOK'S TIP
If you dip the cutter in a little flour it prevents it sticking when you cut out the scone circles.

Chinese Custard Tarts

These small custard tarts, baked in a rich, sweet pastry, are equally good served either warm or cold.

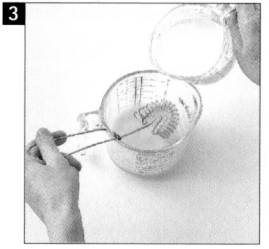
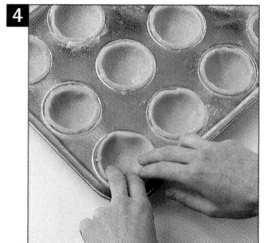
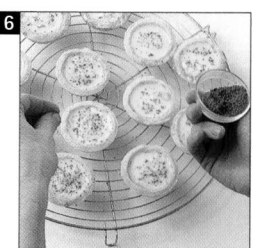

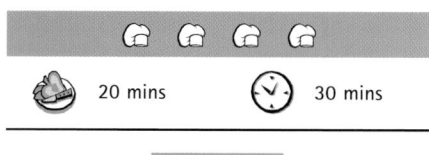 20 mins ⏱ 30 mins

MAKES 15

INGREDIENTS

PASTRY

300 g/10½ oz plain flour, plus extra for dusting

40 g/1½ oz caster sugar

5 tbsp butter, unsalted for preference

2 tbsp lard or white vegetable fat

2 tbsp water

CUSTARD

2 small eggs

55 g/2 oz caster sugar

175 ml/6 fl oz milk

½ tsp ground nutmeg, plus extra for sprinkling

cream, to serve

1 Preheat the oven to 150°C/300°F/Gas Mark 2. To make the dough, sift the flour into a bowl. Add the sugar and rub in the butter and fat with your fingertips until the mixture resembles breadcrumbs. Add the water and mix to a firm dough.

2 Transfer the dough to a lightly floured work surface and knead for 5 minutes until smooth. Cover with clingfilm and chill in the refrigerator while you are preparing the filling.

3 To make the custard, beat the eggs and sugar together. Gradually add the milk and ground nutmeg and beat until well combined.

4 Divide the dough into 15 even-sized pieces. Flatten into circles and press into shallow muffin tins.

5 Spoon the custard into the tart cases and cook in the preheated oven for 25–30 minutes.

6 Transfer the custard tarts to a wire rack, leave to cool slightly, then sprinkle with nutmeg. Serve warm or cold with a little cream.

COOK'S TIP
For extra convenience, make the dough in advance, cover and chill in the refrigerator until required.

Pine Kernel Tartlets

Pine kernels and orange rind are popular ingredients in Mediterranean dishes – here they add a twist of flavour to luscious chocolate tartlets.

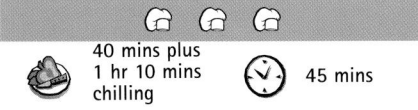

40 mins plus
1 hr 10 mins
chilling

45 mins

SERVES 8

INGREDIENTS

55 g/2 oz plain chocolate,
    broken into pieces

4 tbsp butter, unsalted for preference

140 g/5 oz plus 2 tbsp caster sugar

5 tbsp brown sugar

6 tbsp milk

3½ tbsp golden syrup

finely grated rind of 2 large oranges and
    2 tbsp freshly squeezed juice

1 tsp vanilla essence

3 large eggs, beaten lightly

115 g/4 oz pine kernels

PASTRY

225 g/8 oz plain flour

pinch of salt

75 g/2¾ oz butter

115 g/4 oz icing sugar

1 large egg, plus 2 large egg yolks

1 To make the pastry, sift the flour and salt into a bowl. Make a well in the centre and add the butter, icing sugar, whole egg and egg yolks. Using your fingertips, mix the ingredients in the well into a paste.

2 Gradually incorporate the surrounding flour to make a soft dough. Quickly and lightly knead the dough. Shape into a ball, wrap in clingfilm and chill for at least 1 hour.

3 Preheat the oven to 200°C/400°F/Gas Mark 6. Roll the pastry into 8 circles, 15 cm/6 inches across. Use to line 8 x 10-cm/4-inch loose-based tartlet tins. Line each with baking paper to fit and top with dried beans. Chill for 10 minutes.

4 Bake the tartlet cases in the preheated oven for 5 minutes. Remove the paper and beans and bake for an additional 8 minutes. Leave to cool on a wire rack. Reduce the oven temperature to 180°C/350°F/Gas Mark 4.

5 Meanwhile, put the chocolate in a saucepan over medium heat. Add the butter and stir until blended.

6 Stir in the remaining ingredients. Spoon the filling into the pastry cases on a baking sheet. Bake for 25–30 minutes, or until the tops puff up and crack and feel set. Cover with baking paper for the final 5 minutes if the cases are browning too much. Transfer to a wire rack and leave to cool for at least 15 minutes before unmoulding. Serve warm or at room temperature.

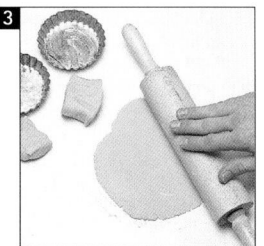

Chocolate Fruit Tartlets

Chocolate pastry trimmed with nuts makes a perfect flan case for fruit in these tasty individual tartlets. You can use fresh or canned fruit.

🕐 1 hr plus 30 mins chilling   ⏱ 20–25 mins

SERVES 4

I N G R E D I E N T S

280 g/10 oz plain flour, plus extra for dusting

3 tbsp cocoa powder

175 g/6 oz butter, cut into pieces

3 tbsp caster sugar

2–3 tbsp water

50 g/1¾ oz plain chocolate, broken into pieces

75 g/2¾ oz chopped mixed nuts, toasted

350 g/12 oz prepared fruit

3 tbsp apricot or redcurrant jam

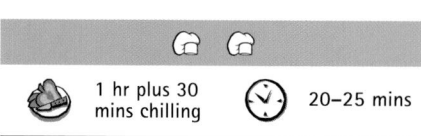
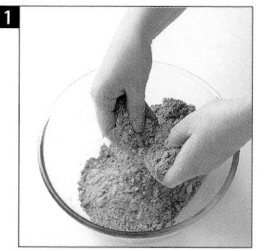

1 Sift the flour and cocoa into a mixing bowl. Rub the butter into the flour with your fingertips until the mixture resembles fine breadcrumbs.

2 Stir in the sugar. Add enough of the water to mix to a soft dough. Cover and chill for 15 minutes.

3 Preheat the oven to 190°C/375°F/Gas Mark 5. Roll out the pastry on a lightly floured work surface and use to line 4 tartlet pans, each 10 cm/4 inches across. Prick the bases with a fork and line with a little crumpled foil. Bake in the preheated oven for 10 minutes.

4 Remove the foil and bake for an additional 5–10 minutes, until the pastry is crisp. Place the tins on a wire rack to cool completely.

5 Put the chocolate in a heatproof bowl set over a saucepan of gently simmering water until melted. Spread out the chopped nuts on a plate. Remove the tartlet cases from the tins. Spread melted chocolate on the rims, then dip in the nuts. Leave the chocolate to set.

6 Arrange the fruit in the tartlet cases. Melt the apricot or redcurrant jam with the remaining 1 tablespoon water and brush it over the fruit. Chill the tartlets until required.

VARIATION

If liked, you can fill the cases with a little sweetened cream before topping with the fruit. For a chocolate-flavoured filling, blend 225 g/8 oz chocolate hazelnut spread with 5 tablespoons thick yogurt or whipped cream.

Chocolate Chip Tartlets

These little tartlets will be a big hit with the kids. Serve as a midweek supper dessert or a special treat.

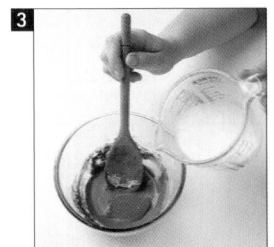

1 hr plus
10 mins chilling

20 mins

MAKES 6

INGREDIENTS

50 g/1¾ oz toasted hazelnuts

175 g/6 oz plain flour

1 tbsp icing sugar

75 g/2¾ oz soft margarine

2–3 tbsp water

FILLING

2 tbsp cornflour

1 tbsp cocoa powder

1 tbsp caster sugar

300 ml/10 fl oz semi-skimmed milk

3 tbsp chocolate hazelnut spread

2½ tbsp plain chocolate chips

2½ tbsp milk chocolate chips

2½ tbsp white chocolate chips

1 Finely chop the nuts in a food processor. Add the flour, 1 tablespoon icing sugar and the margarine. Process for a few seconds until the mixture resembles breadcrumbs. Add the water and process to form a soft dough. Cover and chill in the freezer for 10 minutes.

2 Preheat the oven to 200°C/400°F/Gas Mark 6. Roll out the dough and use it to line 6 x 10-cm/4-inch loose-based tartlet tins. Prick the base of the tartlet cases with a fork and line them with loosely crumpled foil. Bake in the preheated oven for 15 minutes. Remove the foil and bake for an additional 5 minutes, until the tartlet cases are crisp and golden. Remove from the oven and leave to cool.

3 Mix together the cornflour, cocoa and sugar with enough milk to make a smooth paste. Stir in the remaining milk. Pour into a saucepan and cook gently over a low heat, stirring until thickened. Stir in the chocolate hazelnut spread.

4 Mix together the chocolate chips and reserve a quarter. Stir half of the remaining chips into the custard. Cover with damp greaseproof paper, leave to stand until almost cold, then stir in the second half of the chocolate chips. Spoon the mixture into the pastry cases and leave to cool. Sprinkle the reserved chocolate chips over the top, to decorate.

Toffee Chocolate Puff Tarts

These crisp puff pastry tarts, with their smooth filling, are a chocolate version of the more famous Portuguese custard tarts.

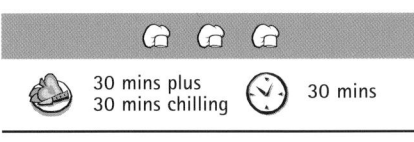

30 mins plus
30 mins chilling

30 mins

MAKES 12

INGREDIENTS

375 g/15 oz ready-rolled puff pastry

140 g/5 oz plain chocolate

300 ml/10 fl oz double cream

50 g/1¾ oz caster sugar

4 egg yolks

12 tsp ready-made toffee sauce

TO SERVE

whipped cream

cocoa powder, for dusting

1 Line the bases of a 12-hole non-stick muffin tin with discs of greaseproof paper.

2 Cut out 12 x 5 cm/2-inch circles from the edge of the pastry and cut the remainder into 12 strips. Roll the strips to half their thickness and line the sides of each hole with 1 strip. Put a disc of pastry in the base, and press well together to seal and make a tart case. Prick the bases and chill in the refrigerator for 30 minutes.

3 Preheat the oven to 200°C/400°F/Gas Mark 6. While the pastry is chilling, melt the chocolate in a heatproof bowl set over a saucepan of gently simmering water. Remove the bowl from the heat, cool slightly, then stir in the cream. Beat the sugar and egg yolks together and mix well with the melted chocolate.

4 Remove the muffin tin from the refrigerator and put a teaspoonful of toffee sauce into each tart case. Divide the chocolate mixture between the tarts and bake in the preheated oven for 20–25 minutes, turning the tray around halfway through the cooking, until just set. Cool the tarts in the tin. Remove carefully, leaving behind the greaseproof paper. Serve with whipped cream and a dusting of cocoa powder.

COOK'S TIP
Don't fill the tarts to the top because the chocolate will puff up in the oven then collapse back as it cools.

Chocolate Hazelnut Palmiers

These delicious chocolate and hazelnut biscuits are very simple to make, yet so effective. For very young children, leave out the chopped nuts.

  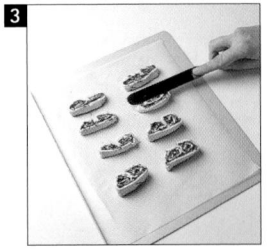

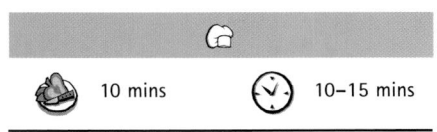

10 mins   10–15 mins

MAKES 26

INGREDIENTS

butter, for greasing

plain flour, for dusting

375 g/13 oz ready-made puff pastry

8 tbsp chocolate hazelnut spread

75 g/2¾ oz chopped toasted hazelnuts

2 tbsp caster sugar

1 Preheat the oven to 220°C/425°F/Gas Mark 7. Grease a baking sheet. On a lightly floured work surface, roll out the puff pastry to a rectangle measuring about 38 x 23 cm/15 x 9 inches.

2 Spread the chocolate hazelnut spread over the pastry using a palette knife, then scatter the hazelnuts over the top.

3 Roll up one long side of the pastry to the centre, then the other, so they meet in the centre. Where the pieces meet, dampen the edges with a little water to join them. Using a sharp knife, cut into thin slices. Place each one on the prepared baking sheet and flatten slightly with a palette knife. Sprinkle with caster sugar.

4 Bake in the preheated oven for about 10–15 minutes, until golden. Transfer to a wire rack to cool.

VARIATION

For an extra chocolate flavour, dip the palmiers in melted plain chocolate to half cover each biscuit.

Paper-Thin Fruit Pies

These extra-crisp filo pastry cases, filled with slices of fruit and glazed with apricot jam, are best served hot with low-fat custard.

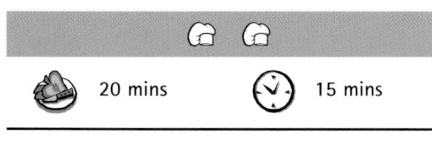

🕐 20 mins   🕐 15 mins

SERVES 4

INGREDIENTS

1 medium eating apple

1 medium ripe pear

2 tbsp lemon juice

55 g/2 oz low-fat spread

4 sheets filo pastry, defrosted if frozen

2 tbsp reduced-sugar apricot jam

1 tbsp unsweetened orange juice

1 tbsp finely chopped pistachio nuts

2 tsp icing sugar, for dusting

low-fat custard, to serve

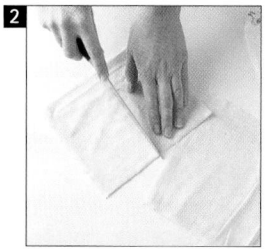

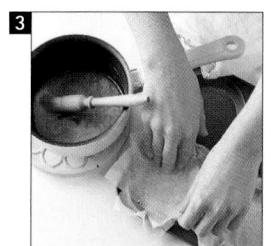

1 Preheat the oven to 200°C/400°F/Gas Mark 6. Core and thinly slice the apple and pear and immediately toss them in the lemon juice to prevent them turning brown. Gently melt the low-fat spread in a saucepan over a low heat.

2 Cut each sheet of pastry into 4 and cover with a clean, damp tea towel. Brush 4 non-stick muffin tins, measuring 10 cm/4 inches in diameter, with a little of the low-fat spread.

3 Working on each pie separately, brush 4 small sheets of pastry with low-fat spread. Press a sheet of pastry into the base of 1 pan. Arrange the other sheets of pastry on top at slightly different angles. Repeat with the other sheets of pastry to make another 3 pies.

4 Arrange the apple and pear slices alternately in the centre of each pie case and lightly crimp the edges of the pastry of each pie.

5 Stir the jam and orange juice together until smooth and brush over the fruit. Bake in the preheated oven for 12–15 minutes. Sprinkle with the pistachio nuts, dust lightly with icing sugar and serve hot from the oven with low-fat custard.

VARIATION
Other combinations of fruit are equally delicious. Try peach and apricot, raspberry and apple or pineapple and mango.

Filo Nests

Green and black grapes decorate the creamy chocolate filling in these crisp little filo pastry nests.

25 mins plus
20 mins cooling   15–18 mins

SERVES 4

INGREDIENTS

1 tbsp unsalted butter

6 sheets filo pastry

40 g/1½ oz plain chocolate, broken into pieces

115 g/4 oz ricotta cheese

16 seedless green grapes, halved

24 seedless black grapes, halved

1 Preheat the oven to 190°C/375°F/Gas Mark 5. Put the butter into a small saucepan and set over a low heat until melted. Remove from the heat. Cut each sheet of filo pastry into 4, to give 24 rectangles, each measuring about 15 x 7.5 cm/6 x 3 inches, then stack them all on top of each other. Brush 4 shallow muffin tins with melted butter. Line 1 tin with a rectangle of filo pastry, brush with melted butter, place another rectangle on top at an angle to the first and brush it with melted butter. Continue in this way, lining each tin with 6 rectangles, each brushed with melted butter. Brush the top layers with melted butter.

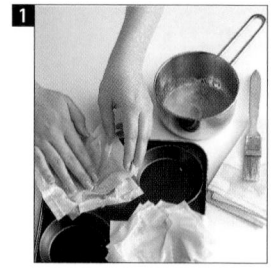

2 Bake in the preheated oven for 7–8 minutes, until golden and crisp. Remove from the oven and set aside to cool in the tins.

3 Put the chocolate in a heatproof bowl set over a saucepan of gently simmering water. Stir over a low heat until melted. Remove from the heat and cool slightly. Brush the insides of the pastry cases with about half the melted chocolate. Beat the ricotta until smooth, then beat in the remaining melted chocolate.

4 Divide the chocolate ricotta mixture between the pastry cases and arrange the grapes around the edges. Carefully lift the cases out of the tins and serve immediately.

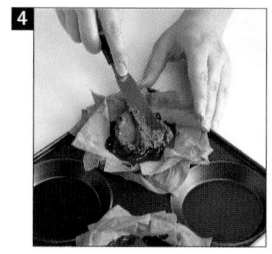

Pistachio Pastries

Pistachio nuts and rosewater give these crisp little pastries a Middle Eastern flavour. Dust with icing sugar just before serving.

20 mins   20 mins

MAKES 20

INGREDIENTS

4 tbsp butter, melted, plus extra for greasing

10 sheets filo pastry

FILLING

75 g/2¾ oz pistachio nuts, ground coarsely

50 g/1¾ oz ground hazelnuts

2 tbsp golden granulated sugar

1 tbsp rosewater

55 g/2 oz plain chocolate, grated

sifted icing sugar, to decorate

1 Preheat the oven to 180°C/350°F/Gas Mark 4. Grease 2 baking sheets. To make the filling, put the pistachio nuts and hazelnuts in a bowl with the sugar, rosewater and chocolate. Mix together. Cut each sheet of filo pastry lengthways. Pile the rectangles on top of each other and cover with a tea towel to prevent them drying out.

2 Brush a filo sheet with melted butter. Spread a teaspoon of filling along one short end. Fold the long sides in, slightly over the filling and roll up from the filling end. Place on the prepared baking sheets with the seam underneath and brush with melted butter.

3 Repeat with the remaining pastry and filling. Bake in the preheated oven for 20 minutes, or until crisp and very lightly coloured. Transfer to a wire rack to cool. Dust with sifted icing sugar before serving.

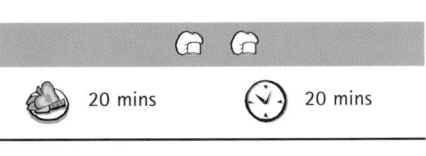

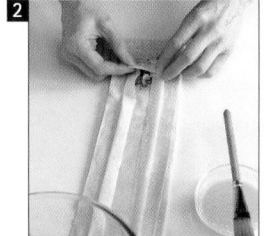

Banana & Chocolate Triangles

These crisp little parcels make a delicious snack, or could equally be enjoyed at the end of a dinner party, with coffee.

MAKES 12 SMALL TRIANGLES

15 mins   14–16 mins

INGREDIENTS

1 banana

25 g/1 oz chocolate chips

4 sheets filo pastry

4 tbsp butter, melted

CHOCOLATE SAUCE

150 ml/5 fl oz single cream

55 g/2 oz plain chocolate, broken into pieces

1 Preheat the oven to 180°C/350°F/Gas Mark 4. Peel the banana, put in a bowl and mash with a fork. Stir in the chocolate chips. Cover the filo sheets with a tea towel to prevent them drying out. Brush a filo sheet with melted butter and cut lengthways into strips 6 cm/2½ inches wide.

2 Spoon a little of the banana mixture on to the bottom end of each strip, fold the corner of the pastry over to enclose it in a triangle and continue folding along the whole length of the strip to make a triangular parcel. Place on a baking sheet with the seam underneath. Repeat with the remaining pastry and filling. Bake in the preheated oven for 10–12 minutes, until golden.

3 To make the chocolate sauce, put the cream and chocolate in a saucepan and heat gently until the chocolate has melted. Stir until smooth. Serve the pastries with the chocolate sauce.

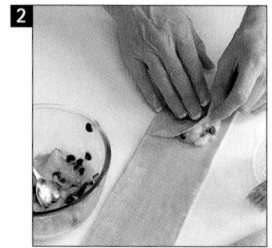
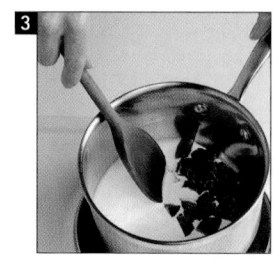

Banana Empanadas

Filo pastry makes these empanadas light and crisp on the outside, with a scrumptious, hot banana-chocolate filling.

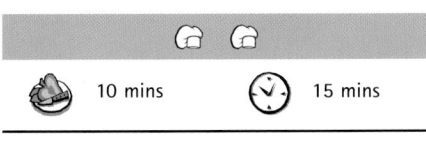

🥗 10 mins   🕐 15 mins

SERVES 4

INGREDIENTS

8 sheets filo pastry, cut into half lengthways

melted butter or vegetable oil, for brushing

2 ripe bananas

1–2 tsp sugar

juice of ½ lemon

175–200 g/6–7 oz plain chocolate, broken into small pieces

icing sugar and ground cinnamon, for dusting

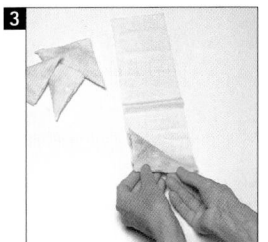
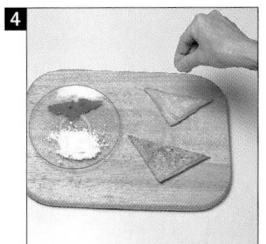

1 Preheat the oven to 190°C/375°F/Gas Mark 5. Working 1 at a time, lay a sheet of filo pastry out in front of you, and brush it with butter or oil.

2 Peel and dice and bananas and put in a bowl. Add the sugar and lemon juice and stir well to combine. Stir in the chocolate.

3 Place 1–2 teaspoons of the banana and chocolate mixture in one corner of the filo pastry, then fold over into a triangle shape to enclose the filling. Continue to fold in a triangular shape, until the pastry is completely wrapped around the filling.

COOK'S TIP
You could use ready-made puff pastry instead of filo for a more puffed-up effect.

4 Dust the parcels with icing sugar and cinnamon. Place them on a lightly greased baking sheet and continue the process with the remaining filo pastry and filling.

5 Bake in the preheated oven for about 15 minutes, or until the empanadas are golden. Remove from the oven and serve immediately. The filling is very hot, so do take care.

Banana Pies

These miniature pies require a little time to prepare, but are well worth the effort. A sweet banana filling is wrapped in pastry and baked.

🍞 45 mins plus 30 mins chilling   🕐 25 mins

SERVES 4

INGREDIENTS

PASTRY

450 g/1 lb plain flour, plus extra for dusting

5 tbsp lard or white vegetable fat

5 tbsp butter, unsalted for preference

125 ml/4 fl oz water

FILLING

2 large bananas

55 g/2 oz finely chopped ready-to-eat dried apricots

pinch of nutmeg

dash of orange juice

1 egg yolk, beaten

icing sugar, for dusting

cream or ice cream, to serve

1 To make the pastry, sift the flour into a large mixing bowl. Add the fat and butter and rub into the flour with the fingertips until the mixture resembles breadcrumbs. Gradually blend in the water to make a soft dough. Wrap in clingfilm and chill for 30 minutes.

2 Preheat the oven to 180°C/350°F/Gas Mark 4. Peel and mash the bananas in a bowl with a fork and stir in the apricots, nutmeg and orange juice, mixing well.

3 Roll the dough out on a lightly floured work surface and cut out 16 circles, each 10 cm/4 inches across.

4 Spoon a little of the banana filling on to one half of each circle and fold the dough over the filling to form semicircles. Pinch the sides together and seal by pressing the edges with the tines of a fork.

5 Arrange the pies on a non-stick baking sheet and brush them with the beaten egg yolk. Cut a small slit in each pie and cook in the preheated oven for about 25 minutes, or until golden brown.

6 Dust the banana pies with icing sugar and serve with cream or ice cream.

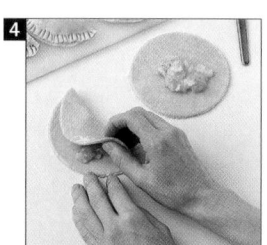

VARIATION
Use a fruit filling of your choice, such as apple or plum, as an alternative.

Rice Tartlets

These little tartlets have a soft plain chocolate ganache layer covered with creamy rice pudding for a delicious special-occasion dessert.

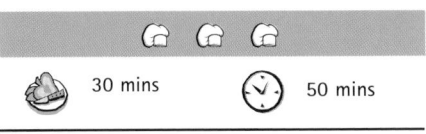

30 mins   50 mins

SERVES 6

INGREDIENTS

1 packet frozen unsweetened pastry, thawed

1.2 litres/2 pints milk

pinch of salt

100 g/3½ oz risotto or short-grain white rice

1 vanilla pod, split, seeds removed and reserved

1 tbsp cornflour

2 tbsp sugar

2–3 tbsp water

cocoa powder, for dusting

chocolate, broken into pieces, to decorate

GANACHE

200 ml/7 fl oz double cream

1 tbsp golden syrup

175 g/6 oz plain or continental plain chocolate, broken into pieces

1 tbsp butter, unsalted for preference

1 Preheat the oven to 200°C/400°F/ Gas Mark 6. Use the pastry to line 6 x 10-cm/4-inch tart tins. Fill them with dried beans and bake blind in the preheated oven for about 20 minutes, until the pastry is set and golden at the edges. Transfer to a wire rack to cool, and remove the dried beans.

2 To make the ganache, bring the cream and syrup to the boil. Remove from the heat and immediately stir in the chocolate. Continue stirring until melted and smooth, then beat in the butter until well combined. Spoon a 2.5-cm/1-inch thick layer into each tartlet. Set aside.

3 Bring the milk and salt to the boil in a saucepan. Sprinkle in the rice and bring back to the boil. Add the vanilla pod and seeds. Reduce the heat and simmer until the rice is tender and the milk creamy.

4 Blend the cornflour and sugar in a small bowl and add enough water to make a paste. Stir in a few spoonfuls of the rice mixture, then stir the cornflour mixture into the rice. Bring to the boil and cook for 1 minute until thickened. Cool the saucepan in ice-cold water, stirring occasionally, until it has thickened.

5 Spoon into the tartlets, filling each to the brim. Leave to set at room temperature. Place a little chocolate in a heatproof bowl set over a saucepan of gently simmering water until melted. To serve, dust the tartlets with cocoa and pipe or drizzle with melted chocolate.

Festive Mince Pies

Serve these seasonal pastries with spiced mulled wine or eggnog. The filling is very hot when the pies come out of the oven, so let them cool.

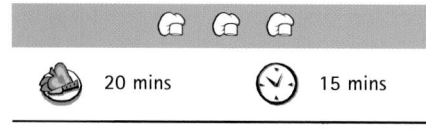

20 mins   15 mins

MAKES 12

INGREDIENTS

200 g/7oz plain flour, plus extra for dusting

100 g/3½ oz butter

25 g/1 oz icing sugar

1 egg yolk

2–3 tbsp milk

300 g/10½ oz mincemeat

1 egg, beaten, for sealing and glazing

icing sugar, to decorate

1 Preheat the oven to 180°C/350°F/Gas Mark 4. Sift the flour into a mixing bowl. Using your fingertips, rub in the butter until the mixture resembles breadcrumbs. Mix in the icing sugar and egg yolk. Stir in enough milk to form a soft dough, turn out on to a lightly floured work surface and knead lightly until smooth.

2 Shape the dough into a ball and roll out to a thickness of 1 cm/½ inch. Use fluted cutters to cut out 12 circles of 7-cm/2¾-inch diameter and 12 circles of 5-cm/2-inch diameter. Dust 12 tartlet tins with flour and line with the larger dough circles. Prick the bases with a fork, then half fill each pie with mincemeat. Brush beaten egg around the pie rims, then gently press the smaller circles of dough on top to seal. Make a small hole in the top of each one, then shape any remaining dough into Christmas trees and leaves and use them to decorate the pies. Brush with beaten egg, then bake for 15 minutes. Remove from the oven and cool on a wire rack. Dust with icing sugar and serve.

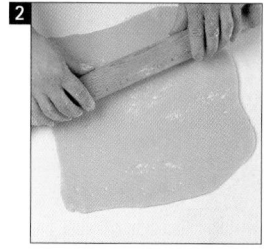
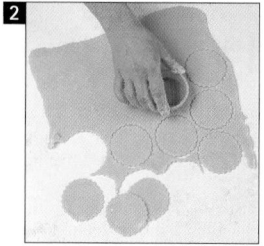

Maple Pecan Tarts

Maple syrup and pecan nuts give a wonderful flavour to the toffee filling in these little tarts. Serve on their own, or with a little whipped cream.

20 mins plus
30 mins chilling   17–23 mins

MAKES 12

INGREDIENTS

PASTRY

140 g/5 oz plain flour, plus extra for dusting

85 g/3 oz butter

55 g/2 oz golden caster sugar

2 egg yolks

FILLING

2 tbsp maple syrup

150 ml/5 fl oz double cream

115 g/4 oz golden caster sugar

pinch of cream of tartar

6 tbsp water

115 g/4 oz pecan nuts

14 pecan nut halves, to decorate

1 To make the pastry, sift the flour into a mixing bowl and rub in the butter. Add the sugar and egg yolks, and mix to form a soft dough. Wrap and chill in the refrigerator for 30 minutes. Preheat the oven to 200°C/400°F/Gas Mark 6. On a floured work surface, roll out the pastry thinly, cut out circles and use to line 12 tartlet tins. Prick the bases. Press a piece of foil into each tart case. Bake in the oven for 10–15 minutes, until light golden. Remove the foil and bake for an additional 2–3 minutes. Leave to cool on a wire rack.

2 To make the filling, mix half the maple syrup and half the cream in a bowl. Put the sugar, cream of tartar and water in a saucepan and heat gently until the sugar dissolves. Bring to the boil and boil until light golden. Remove from the heat and stir in the maple syrup and cream mixture.

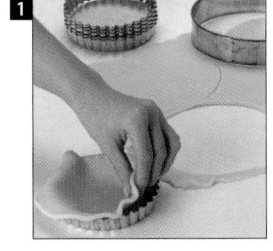

3 Return the saucepan to the heat and cook to the soft ball stage (116°C/240°F): that is, when a little of the mixture dropped into a bowl of cold water forms a soft ball. Stir in the remaining cream and leave until warm. Brush the remaining maple syrup over the edges of the tarts. Put the pecan nuts in the pastry cases and spoon in the toffee. Top each one with a pecan nut half. Leave to cool.

Sicilian Ricotta Tart

Pine kernels and candied peel are included in the filling of this Italian speciality.

30 mins   1 hr 10 mins

SERVES 6

INGREDIENTS

1 packet frozen sweetened pastry, defrosted

FILLING

250 g/8 oz ricotta cheese

2 eggs, beaten

55 g/2 oz golden caster sugar

55 g/2 oz pine kernels

55 g mixed candied peel

finely grated rind of 1 lemon

½ tsp vanilla essence

icing sugar, for dusting

1 Preheat the oven to 200°C/400°F/ Gas Mark 6. Use the pastry to line a 20-cm/8-inch flan tin. Fill with dried beans and bake blind for 20 minutes. Reduce the temperature to 180°C/350°F/Gas Mark 4.

2 Press the ricotta through a sieve into a bowl. Mix in the eggs, sugar, pine kernels, candied peel, lemon rind and vanilla essence. Pour into the pastry case.

3 Bake for 45 minutes, until set. Cool, then dust with icing sugar.

COOK'S TIP
If possible, buy whole pieces of candied peel and chop them yourself.

Cheese & Apple Tart

Chopped apples, dates and brown sugar combined with tasty cheese make this a sweet tart with a difference.

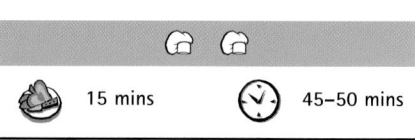

15 mins   45–50 mins

SERVES 8

INGREDIENTS

butter, for greasing

175 g/6 oz self-raising flour

1 tsp baking powder

pinch of salt

60 g/2¼ oz soft brown sugar

200 g/7 oz stoned dates, chopped

500 g/1 lb 2 oz eating apples, cored and chopped

40 g/1½ oz chopped walnuts

50 ml/2 fl oz sunflower oil

2 eggs

200 g/7 oz grated hard cheese, such as Cheddar

1 Preheat the oven to 180°C/350°F/ Gas Mark 4. Grease a 23-cm/9-inch loose-based flan tin with a little butter and line with baking paper.

2 Sift the flour, baking powder and salt into a large bowl. Stir in the brown sugar and the dates, apples and walnuts. Mix together until thoroughly combined.

3 Beat the oil and eggs together and add the mixture to the dry ingredients. Stir with a wooden spoon until well combined.

4 Spoon half of the mixture into the prepared tin and smooth the surface with the back of a spoon.

5 Sprinkle with the grated cheese, then spoon over the remaining mixture, spreading it to the edges of the tin.

6 Bake in the preheated oven for 45–50 minutes, or until golden and firm to the touch.

7 Leave the tart to cool slightly in the tin. Remove the tart from the tin and serve warm.

COOK'S TIP

This is a deliciously moist tart. Any leftovers should be stored in the refrigerator and heated to serve.

Chocolate Crumble Pie

This substantial tart has a crisp topping of nuts, chocolate and almond-flavoured amaretti biscuits.

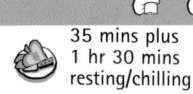

35 mins plus 1 hr 30 mins resting/chilling

35 mins

SERVES 8

INGREDIENTS

175 g/6 oz plain flour

1 tsp baking powder

115 g/4 oz unsalted butter

55 g/2 oz caster sugar

1 egg yolk

150 ml/5 fl oz double cream

150 ml/5 fl oz milk

225 g/8 oz plain chocolate, chopped

2 eggs

CRUMBLE TOPPING

115 g/4 oz soft brown sugar

75 g/3 oz toasted pecan nuts

115 g/4 oz plain chocolate

85 g/3 oz amaretti biscuits

1 tsp cocoa powder

1 To make the pastry, put the flour, baking powder, butter and sugar into a food processor and pulse to mix. Add the egg, and a little cold water if necessary, to bring the dough together. (If you don't have a food processor, sift the flour and baking powder into a large bowl and rub in the butter, stir in the sugar and add the egg and a little water to bring the dough together.) Turn the dough out, knead briefly and wrap in clingfilm. Chill in the refrigerator for 30 minutes.

2 Preheat the oven to 190°C/375°F/Gas Mark 5. Roll out the pastry and use to line a 23-cm/9-inch loose-based flan tin. Prick the base with a fork. Line with baking paper, fill with dried beans and bake blind for 15 minutes. Remove the paper and beans. Reduce the oven temperature to 180°C/350°F/Gas Mark 4.

3 In a saucepan, bring the cream and milk to the boil, remove from the heat and add the chocolate. Stir until melted and smooth. Beat the eggs and add to the chocolate mixture, mix thoroughly and pour into the case. Bake for 15 minutes, remove from the oven and leave to rest for 1 hour.

4 When you are ready to serve the tart, put the topping ingredients into the food processor and pulse to chop. (If you don't have a processor, put the sugar in a large bowl, chop the nuts and chocolate with a large knife and crush the biscuits, then add to the bowl with the cocoa and mix well.) The mixture should resemble coarse breadcrumbs. Scatter over the tart, then serve it sliced.

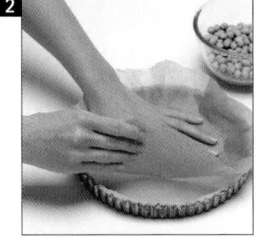

Chocolate Mousse Tart

The smooth mousse topping contrasts deliciously with the crumbly biscuit base in this elegant tart.

30 mins plus
8 hrs chilling

5 mins

SERVES 8

INGREDIENTS

85 g/3 oz digestive biscuits, crushed

85 g/3 oz amaretti biscuits, crushed

70 g/2½ oz butter, melted

TOPPING

200 g/7 oz plain chocolate

115 g/4 oz milk chocolate

3 large eggs, separated

55 g/2 oz caster sugar

3 chocolate flake bars, to decorate

1 To make the base, mix the digestive biscuits and amaretti biscuits with the butter and press well into the base of a 23-cm/9-inch springform cake tin. Chill in the refrigerator.

2 Melt the plain and milk chocolate in a heatproof bowl set over a saucepan of gently simmering water. Cool slightly, then add the egg yolks and mix well.

3 Whisk the egg whites until they form soft peaks, then add the caster sugar, and whisk until stiff.

4 Fold the chocolate into the egg whites and pour over the biscuit base. Chill in the refrigerator for 8 hours, or overnight.

5 When you are ready to serve the tart, unmould it, transfer to a serving dish and crumble the chocolate flake bars over the top.

Crème Brûlée Tarts

Serve these melt-in-the-mouth tarts with fresh fruit, such as mixed summer berries, if you wish.

 40 mins plus up to 12 hrs chilling

 25 mins

SERVES 6

INGREDIENTS

PASTRY

175 g/6 oz plain flour, plus extra for dusting

2 tbsp caster sugar

115 g/4 oz butter, cut into small pieces

1 tbsp water

FILLING

4 egg yolks

55 g/2 oz caster sugar

400 ml/14 oz double cream

1 tsp vanilla essence

demerara sugar, for sprinkling

1 To make the pastry, place the flour and sugar in a bowl and rub in the butter with your fingertips until the mixture resembles breadcrumbs. Add the water and work the mixture together until a soft dough has formed. Wrap and chill in the refrigerator for 30 minutes.

2 On a lightly floured work surface, roll out the dough to line 6 tart tins, each 10 cm/4 inches wide. Prick the base of the pastry cases with a fork and chill in the refrigerator for 20 minutes.

3 Preheat the oven to 190°C/375°F/Gas Mark 5. Line the cases with foil and dried beans. Bake blind in the oven for 15 minutes. Remove the foil and beans and cook for an additional 10 minutes, until crisp and golden. Leave to cool.

4 Meanwhile, make the filling. In a bowl, beat the egg yolks and sugar until

pale. Heat the cream and vanilla essence in a small saucepan until just below boiling point, then pour it on to the egg mixture, whisking constantly.

5 Return the mixture to a clean saucepan and bring to just below the boil, stirring constantly until thick. Do not let the mixture boil or it will curdle.

6 Leave the mixture to cool slightly, then pour it into the pastry cases. Leave to cool, then chill overnight.

7 Sprinkle the tarts with the sugar. Place under a preheated hot grill for a few minutes to caramelize. Leave to cool, then chill for 2 hours before serving.

Mini Frangipane Tartlets

These little tartlets have an unusual lime-flavoured pastry, and are filled with a delicious almond frangipane mixture.

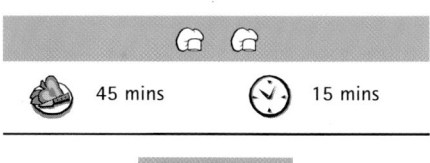

45 mins   15 mins

SERVES 12

INGREDIENTS

115 g/4 oz plain flour, plus extra
   for dusting

75 g/2¾ oz butter, softened

1 tsp grated lime rind

1 tbsp lime juice

50 g/1¾ oz caster sugar

1 egg

25 g/1 oz ground almonds

40 g/1½ oz icing sugar, sifted

½ tbsp water

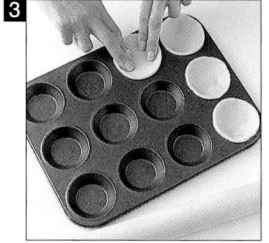

1 Preheat the oven to 200°C/400°F/Gas Mark 6. Reserve 5 teaspoons of the flour and 3 teaspoons of the butter.

2 Rub the remaining butter into the remaining flour with your fingertips until the mixture resembles fine breadcrumbs. Stir in the lime rind, followed by the lime juice, and bring the mixture together to form a soft dough.

3 On a lightly floured work surface, roll out the pastry thinly. Stamp out 12 circles, 7.5 cm/3 inches in diameter and use them to line a shallow muffin tin.

4 In a bowl, cream together the reserved butter with the caster sugar until pale and fluffy.

5 Mix in the egg, then the ground almonds and the reserved flour.

6 Divide the mixture between the pastry cases and smooth the tops.

7 Bake in the preheated oven for 15 minutes, until set and lightly golden. Remove the tartlets from the tin, place on wire racks and leave to cool completely.

8 Mix the icing sugar with the water. Drizzle a little of this icing over each tartlet and serve.

COOK'S TIP
These tartlets can be made in advance. Store them in an airtight container and decorate them just before serving.

Summer Fruit Tartlets

These small almond pastry cases filled with bright summer fruit taste as good as they look.

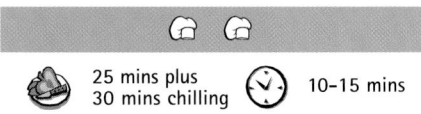

25 mins plus 30 mins chilling   10–15 mins

MAKES 12

I N G R E D I E N T S

PASTRY

200 g/7 oz plain flour

85 g/3 oz icing sugar

55 g/2 oz ground almonds

115 g/4 oz butter

1 egg yolk

1 tbsp milk

FILLING

225 g/8 oz cream cheese

icing sugar, to taste

350 g/12 oz fresh summer fruit, such as redcurrants and whitecurrants, raspberries and small strawberries

sifted icing sugar, to decorate

1 To make the pastry, sift the flour and icing sugar into a bowl. Stir in the ground almonds. Add the butter and rub in until the mixture resembles breadcrumbs. Add the egg yolk and milk and work in with a palette knife, then with fingers until the dough binds together. Wrap the dough in clingfilm and chill for 30 minutes.

VARIATION
The fruit in the tarts could be brushed with warmed redcurrant jam to make an attractive glaze.

2 Preheat the oven to 200°C/400°F/Gas Mark 6. On a floured work surface, roll out the pastry and use to line 12 deep tartlet tins or brioche moulds. Prick the bases. Press a piece of foil into each tartlet, covering the edges. Bake blind for 10–15 minutes, until light golden brown. Remove the foil and bake for an additional 2–3 minutes. Transfer to a wire rack to cool.

3 To make the filling, put the cream cheese and icing sugar in a bowl and mix together. Put a tablespoonful of filling in each pastry case and arrange the fruit on top. Dust with sifted icing sugar and serve at once.

White Chocolate Tarts

These dainty little tarts make a delicious afternoon treat, and are also wonderful for serving after dinner with coffee.

25 mins plus 1 hr 35 mins chilling

15 mins

SERVES 4

INGREDIENTS

225 g/8 oz plain flour, plus extra for dusting

2 tbsp golden caster sugar

150 g/5½ oz chilled butter, diced

2 egg yolks

2 tbsp cold water

plain chocolate curls (see page 9), to decorate

cocoa powder, to dust

FILLING

1 vanilla pod

400 ml/14 fl oz double cream

350 g/12 oz white chocolate, broken into pieces

1 Place the flour and sugar in a bowl. Add the butter and rub it in until the mixture resembles fine breadcrumbs. Place the egg yolks and water in a separate bowl and mix together. Stir into the dry ingredients and mix to form a dough. Knead for 1 minute, or until smooth. Wrap in clingfilm and leave to chill for 20 minutes.

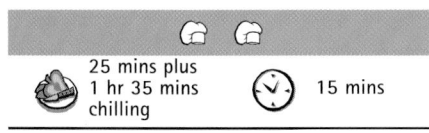

2 Preheat the oven to 200°C/400°F/Gas Mark 6. Roll out the dough on a floured work surface and use to line 12 tartlet tins. Prick the bases, cover and leave to chill for 15 minutes. Line the cases with foil and dried beans and bake for 10 minutes. Remove the beans and foil and cook for an additional 5 minutes. Leave to cool.

3 To make the filling, split the vanilla pod lengthways and scrape out the black seeds with a knife. Place the seeds in a saucepan with the cream and heat until almost boiling. Melt the chocolate in a heatproof bowl set over a saucepan of gently simmering water, then pour over the hot cream. Keep stirring until smooth. Whisk the mixture with an electric whisk until thickened and the whisk leaves a trail when lifted. Leave to chill in the refrigerator for 30 minutes, then whisk until soft peaks form. Divide the filling between the pastry cases and leave to chill for 30 minutes. Decorate with chocolate curls and dust with cocoa.

Pear Tarts

These tarts are quick to prepare because they are made with ready-made puff pastry. The finished result is rich and buttery.

35 mins plus
30 mins chilling

20 mins

SERVES 6

INGREDIENTS

250 g/9 oz frozen ready-made puff pastry, defrosted

plain flour, for dusting

2 tbsp soft brown sugar

2 tbsp butter, plus extra for brushing

1 tbsp finely chopped stem ginger

3 pears, peeled, halved and cored

1 Roll out the puff pastry on a lightly floured work surface. Cut or stamp out 6 circles, each about 10 cm/4 inches in diameter.

2 Place the circles on a large baking sheet and chill in the refrigerator for 30 minutes.

3 Cream together the brown sugar and butter in a small bowl, then stir in the chopped stem ginger.

4 Preheat the oven to 200°C/400°F/Gas Mark 6. Prick the pastry circles with a fork and spread a little of the ginger mixture on to each one.

5 Slice the pears halves lengthways, keeping them intact at the tip. Fan out the slices slightly.

6 Place a fanned-out pear half on top of each pastry circle. Make small flutes around the edge of the circles with the back of a knife blade and brush each pear half with melted butter.

7 Bake in the preheated oven for 15–20 minutes, until the pastry is well risen and golden. Leave to cool slightly before serving the tarts warm.

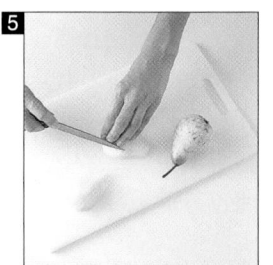

COOK'S TIP

If you prefer, serve these tarts with vanilla ice cream for a delicious dessert.

Chocolate Fudge Tart

This rich fudgy tart is sure to become a favourite, and is quick and easy to prepare using ready-made pastry.

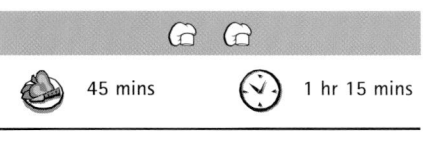

45 mins   1 hr 15 mins

SERVES 6-8

I N G R E D I E N T S

350 g/12 oz ready-made unsweetened
  pastry

plain flour, for dusting

icing sugar, for dusting

F I L L I N G

140 g/5 oz plain chocolate,
  chopped finely

175 g/6 oz butter, diced

350 g/12 oz golden granulated sugar

115 g/4 oz plain flour

½ tsp vanilla essence

6 eggs, beaten

T O   D E C O R A T E

150 ml/5 fl oz whipped cream

ground cinnamon

1 Preheat the oven to 200°C/400°F/Gas Mark 6. Roll out the pastry on a lightly floured work surface and use to line a 20-cm/8-inch deep loose-based flan tin. Prick the pastry base lightly with a fork, then line with foil and fill with dried beans. Bake in the preheated oven for 12–15 minutes, or until the pastry no longer looks raw. Remove the beans and foil and bake for an additional 10 minutes, or until the pastry is firm. Leave to cool. Reduce the oven temperature to 180°C/350°F/Gas Mark 4.

2 To make the filling, place the chocolate and butter in a heatproof bowl and set over a saucepan of gently simmering water until melted. Stir until smooth, then remove from the heat and leave to cool. Place the sugar, flour, vanilla essence and eggs in a separate bowl and whisk until well blended. Stir in the butter and chocolate mixture.

3 Pour the filling into the pastry case and bake in the oven for 50 minutes, or until the filling is just set. Transfer to a wire rack to cool completely. Dust with icing sugar before serving with a little whipped cream lightly sprinkled with ground cinnamon.

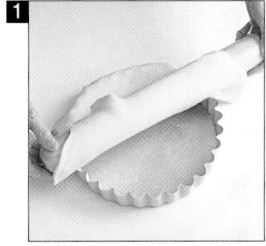

Chocolate & Chestnut Tart

This biscuit crumb case is ideal if you do not like making pastry.
Try it with whipped cream, decorated with chocolate caraque.

30 mins plus
1 hr chilling

45 mins

SERVES 8

INGREDIENTS

BISCUIT CASE

85 g/3 oz butter

250 g/9 oz gingernut biscuits, crushed

FILLING

175 g/6 oz unsweetened chestnut purée

55 g/2 oz golden caster sugar

175 g/6 oz ricotta cheese

2 eggs

100 g/3½ oz plain chocolate,
   broken into pieces

3 pieces stem ginger,
   chopped very finely

25 g/1 oz ground almonds

TO DECORATE

150 ml/5 fl oz whipping cream

chocolate caraque (see page 9)

1 Preheat the oven to 180°C/350°F/Gas Mark 4. Put the butter in a saucepan and heat gently until just melted. Stir in the crushed gingernut biscuits. Press the crumbs on to the base and up the sides of a 23-cm/9-inch loose-based flan tin. Bake in the preheated oven for 10 minutes, then set aside to cool.

2 To make the filling, put the chestnut purée and sugar in a bowl and beat until smooth. Put the ricotta cheese and eggs in another bowl and beat until smooth and combined. Put the chocolate in a heatproof bowl set over a saucepan of gently simmering water until melted. Remove the saucepan from the heat and leave to cool slightly. Carefully stir the melted chocolate into the ricotta mixture. Add the chestnut purée mixture and mix thoroughly. Stir in the ginger and ground almonds.

3 Pour the filling into the biscuit case and bake in the preheated oven for 35 minutes, until lightly set. Leave to cool, then chill thoroughly. Before serving, put the whipping cream in a bowl and whip until thick. Spread over the top of the tart and decorate with chocolate caraque.

Lemon & Chocolate Tart

In this tart, a crisp chocolate pastry case is the perfect foil for the smooth creamy lemon filling. It is the perfect end to a supper party.

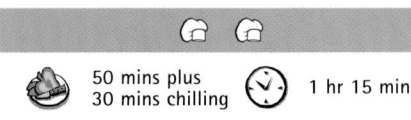

🕙 50 mins plus 30 mins chilling   🕐 1 hr 15 mins

SERVES 8

INGREDIENTS

115 g/4 oz plain flour

25 g/1 oz cocoa powder

75 g/2¾ oz butter

25 g/1 oz ground almonds

50 g/1¾ oz golden caster sugar

1 egg, beaten

chocolate curls or caraque (see page 9), to decorate

FILLING

4 eggs

1 egg yolk

200 g/7 oz golden caster sugar

150 ml/5 fl oz double cream

grated rind and juice of 2 lemons

1 Sift the flour and cocoa into a food processor. Add the butter, almonds, sugar and egg and process until the mixture forms a ball. Gather the dough together and press into a flattened ball. Place in the centre of a 22-cm/8½-inch loose-based flan tin and press evenly over the base of the pan with your fingers, then work the pastry up the sides with your thumbs. Allow any excess pastry to go over the edge. Cover and leave to chill for 30 minutes.

2 Preheat the oven to 200°C/400°F/ Gas Mark 6. Trim off the excess pastry. Prick the base lightly with a fork, then line with baking paper and fill with dried beans. Bake for 12–15 minutes, or until the pastry no longer looks raw. Remove the beans and paper, return to the oven and bake for 10 minutes, or until the pastry is firm. Leave to cool. Reduce the oven to 150°C/300°F/Gas Mark 2.

3 To make the filling, whisk the whole eggs, egg yolk and sugar together until smooth. Add the cream and whisk again, then stir in the lemon rind and juice. Pour the filling into the pastry case and bake for 50 minutes, or until just set. When the tart is cooked, remove the flan tin and leave to cool. Decorate with chocolate curls or caraque before serving.

Boston Chocolate Pie

This lighter version of the popular chocolate cream pie is made with yogurt and soured cream or crème fraîche.

🍓 25 mins   🕐 35 mins

SERVES 6

INGREDIENTS

225 g/8 oz ready-prepared pastry

225 g/8 oz plain chocolate, to make caraque (see page 9)

FILLING

3 eggs

125 g/4½ oz caster sugar

60 g/2¼ oz plain flour, plus extra for dusting

1 tbsp icing sugar

pinch of salt

1 tsp vanilla essence

400 ml/14 fl oz milk

150 ml/5 fl oz natural yogurt

150 g/5½ oz plain chocolate, broken into pieces

2 tbsp kirsch

TOPPING

150 ml/5 fl oz soured cream or crème fraîche (see page 9)

1 Preheat the oven to 200°C/400°F/Gas Mark 6. Roll out the pastry and use to line a 23-cm/9-inch loose-based flan tin. Prick the base with a fork, line with baking paper and fill with dried beans. Bake blind for about 20 minutes in the preheated oven. Remove the beans and paper and return the pastry case to the oven for an additional 5 minutes. Remove from the oven and place on a wire rack to cool.

2 Make the chocolate caraque (see page 9) and set aside.

3 To make the filling, beat the eggs and sugar until fluffy. Sift in the flour, icing sugar and salt. Stir in the vanilla essence.

4 Bring the milk and yogurt to the boil in a small saucepan and strain it over the egg mixture. Pour into a heatproof bowl set over a saucepan of gently simmering water. Stir until it coats the back of a spoon.

5 Gently heat the chocolate with the kirsch in a small saucepan until the chocolate has melted. Stir into the custard. Remove from the heat and stand the bowl in cold water. Leave it to cool.

6 Pour the chocolate mixture into the pastry case. Spread the soured cream over the chocolate and arrange the chocolate caraque on top.

Chocolate Apple Lattice Tart

This is a tempting combination of rich chocolate pastry and a cream-rich apple filling.

25 mins plus 1–1 hr 30 mins cooling/chilling

40–45 mins

SERVES 4–6

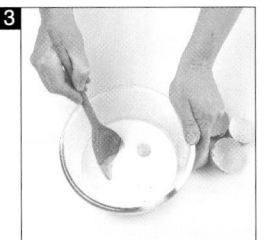  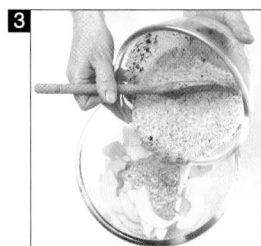

INGREDIENTS

PASTRY

200 g/7 oz plain flour, plus extra for dusting

2 tbsp cocoa powder

3 tbsp caster sugar

100 g/3½ oz unsalted butter, diced, plus extra for greasing

1–2 egg yolks, beaten

FILLING

225 g/8 oz double cream

2 eggs, beaten

1 tsp ground cinnamon

115 g/4 oz plain chocolate, grated

4 eating apples, peeled, sliced and brushed with lemon juice

3 tbsp demerara sugar

whipped cream, to serve

1 To make the pastry, sift the flour and cocoa into a bowl. Add the sugar, rub in the butter and mix well. Stir in enough egg yolk to form a dough. Form into a ball, wrap in foil and chill for 45 minutes.

2 Preheat the oven to 180°C/350°F/ Gas Mark 4. Grease a 25-cm/1-inch loose-based flan tin. Roll out the dough on a lightly floured work surface and use three-quarters of it to line the tin.

3 Beat together the cream, the eggs (reserving a little), cinnamon and chocolate. Pour this over the apples and stir in. Spoon the mixture into the tart case, then sprinkle over the demerara sugar. Roll out the remaining dough and cut into long strips, then arrange over the tart to form a lattice pattern. Brush the pastry strips with the reserved egg yolk, then bake in the oven for 40–45 minutes.

4 Remove from the oven and leave to cool to room temperature. Serve with whipped cream.

Crispy Chocolate Pie

The rich, whisky-flavoured chocolate filling makes this delicious almond-crust pie very moreish.

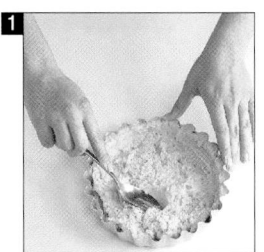

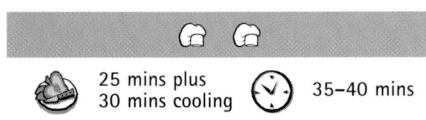

25 mins plus
30 mins cooling

35–40 mins

SERVES 6

INGREDIENTS

2 tsp butter, for greasing

2 egg whites

100 g/3½ oz ground almonds

4 tbsp ground rice

125 g/4½ oz caster sugar

¼ tsp almond essence

225 g/8 oz plain chocolate, broken into small pieces

4 egg yolks

4 tbsp icing sugar

4 tbsp whisky

4 tbsp double cream

TO DECORATE

150 ml/5 fl oz whipped cream

55 g/2 oz plain chocolate, grated

1 Preheat the oven to 160°C/325°F/Gas Mark 3. Grease a 20-cm/8-inch flan tin and line the base with baking paper. Whisk the egg whites until stiff peaks form. Gently fold in the ground almonds, ground rice, caster sugar and almond essence. Spread the mixture over the base and sides of the prepared tin. Bake in the preheated oven for 15 minutes.

2 Meanwhile, put the chocolate in a heatproof bowl set over a saucepan of gently simmering water until melted. Remove from the heat and cool slightly, then beat in the egg yolks, icing sugar, whisky and 4 tablespoons double cream until thoroughly incorporated.

3 Remove the flan tin from the oven and pour in the chocolate mixture. Cover with foil, return to the oven and bake at the same temperature for 20–25 minutes, until set. Remove from the oven and leave to cool completely.

4 Cut the pie into 6 slices. Decorate each slice with whipped cream and sprinkled grated chocolate. Serve immediately.

Chocolate & Almond Tart

This is a variation on the classic pecan pie recipe – here, almonds and chocolate are encased in a thick syrup filling.

30 mins plus 1 hr chilling

1 hr

SERVES 8

INGREDIENTS

PASTRY

175 g/6 oz plain flour, plus extra for dusting

2 tbsp caster sugar

115 g/4 oz butter, cut into small pieces

1 tbsp water

FILLING

175 g/6 oz golden syrup

4 tbsp butter

100 g/3½ oz soft brown sugar

3 eggs, beaten lightly

75 g/2¾ oz whole blanched almonds, chopped coarsely

100 g/3½ oz white chocolate, chopped coarsely

cream, to serve (optional)

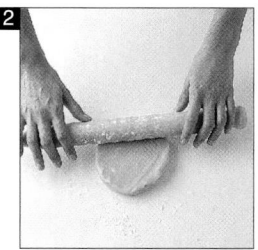

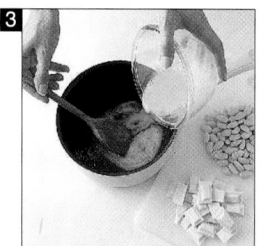

1 To make the pastry, place the flour and sugar in a mixing bowl and rub in the butter with your fingers. Add the water and work the mixture together until a soft dough has formed. Wrap and leave to chill for 30 minutes.

2 On a lightly floured work surface, roll out the dough and line a 24-cm/ 9½-inch loose-based flan tin. Prick the pastry case with the tines of a fork and leave to chill for 30 minutes. Preheat the oven to 190°C/375°F/Gas Mark 5. Line the case with foil and dried beans and bake blind in the preheated oven for 15 minutes. Remove the foil and dried beans and cook for an additional 15 minutes.

3 To make the filling, gently melt the syrup, butter and sugar together in a saucepan. Remove from the heat and leave to cool slightly. Stir in the beaten eggs, almonds and chocolate.

4 Pour the chocolate and nut filling into the prepared pastry case and cook in the oven for 30–35 minutes, or until just set. Leave to cool before removing the tart from the tin. Serve with cream, if wished.

VARIATION
You can use a mixture of white and plain chocolate for this tart, if preferred.

Chocolate Orange Tart

Chocolate and orange are flavours that were made for each other. If time is limited, just serve with plain whipped cream.

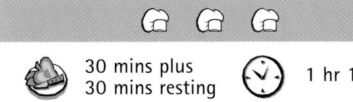

30 mins plus
30 mins resting

1 hr 10 mins

SERVES 4

INGREDIENTS

PASTRY

200 g/7 oz plain flour, plus extra
  for dusting

100 g/3½ oz butter, cut into small pieces,
  plus extra for greasing

50 g/1¾ oz icing sugar, sifted

finely grated rind of 1 orange

1 egg yolk, beaten

3 tbsp milk

FILLING

200 g/7 oz plain chocolate,
  broken into small pieces

2 eggs, separated

100 ml/3½ fl oz milk

100 g/3½ oz caster sugar

8 amaretti biscuits, crushed

ORANGE CREAM

1 tbsp orange-flavoured liqueur,
  such as Cointreau

1 tbsp finely grated orange rind

125 ml/4 fl oz double cream

finely grated orange rind, to decorate

1 To make the pastry, sift the flour into a bowl. Rub in the butter. Mix in the icing sugar, orange rind, egg yolk and milk. Knead briefly, then leave to stand for 30 minutes. Preheat the oven to 180°C/ 350°F/Gas Mark 4. Grease a 23-cm/9-inch flan tin with butter. Roll out two-thirds of the pastry to a thickness of ¼ inch/5 mm and use to line the base and sides of the flan tin.

2 To make the filling, melt the chocolate in a heatproof bowl set over a saucepan of gently simmering water. Beat in the egg yolks, then the milk. Remove from the heat. In a separate bowl, whisk the egg whites until stiff, then stir in the sugar. Fold the egg whites into the chocolate, then stir in the biscuits. Spoon

into the pastry case. Roll out the remaining pastry, cut into strips and use to form a lattice over the tart. Bake in the preheated oven for 1 hour. To make the orange cream, beat together the liqueur, orange rind and cream. Remove the tart from the oven, decorate with orange rind and serve with the orange cream.

Chocolate, Pear & Almond Tart

This attractive tart is filled with pears cooked in a chocolate and almond-flavoured sponge. It is delicious hot or cold.

 30 mins plus 10 mins freezing 35 mins

SERVES 6

I N G R E D I E N T S

85 g/3 oz margarine, plus extra for greasing

140 g/5 oz plain flour

25 g/1 oz ground almonds

about 3 tbsp water

FILLING

400 g/14 oz canned pear halves (in natural juice)

4 tbsp butter

4 tbsp caster sugar

2 eggs, beaten

100 g/3½ oz ground almonds

2 tbsp cocoa powder

few drops almond essence

icing sugar, for dusting

CHOCOLATE SAUCE

4 tbsp caster sugar

3 tbsp golden syrup

100 ml/3½ fl oz water

175 g/6 oz plain chocolate, broken into pieces

2 tbsp butter

1 Lightly grease a 20-cm/8-inch flan tin. Sift the flour into a mixing bowl and stir in the almonds. Rub in the margarine with your fingertips until the mixture resembles breadcrumbs. Add enough water to mix to a soft dough. Cover, chill in the freezer for 10 minutes, then roll out and use to line the tin. Prick the base and chill.

2 Preheat the oven to 200°C/400°F/Gas Mark 6. Meanwhile, make the filling. Drain the pears well. Beat the butter and sugar until light and fluffy. Beat in the eggs. Fold in the almonds, cocoa and almond essence. Spread the chocolate mixture in the pastry case and arrange the pears on top, pressing down lightly. Bake in the centre of the preheated oven for 30 minutes, or until the filling has risen. Leave to cool slightly and transfer to a serving dish, if wished. Dust with sugar.

3 To make the sauce, place the sugar, syrup and water in a saucepan and heat gently, stirring until the sugar dissolves. Boil gently for 1 minute. Remove from the heat, add the chocolate and butter and stir until melted. Serve with the tart.

 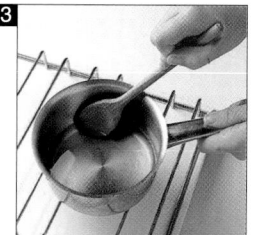 

Chocolate Pear Tart

The classic partnership of chocolate and pears appears in many forms, both hot and cold. This tart will soon become a family favourite.

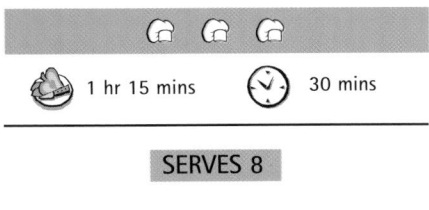

1 hr 15 mins   30 mins

SERVES 8

INGREDIENTS

PASTRY

175 g/6 oz plain flour, plus extra for dusting

pinch of salt

2 tbsp caster sugar

115 g/4 oz butter, unsalted for preference, cut into small pieces

1 egg yolk

1 tbsp lemon juice

TOPPING

115 g/4 oz plain chocolate, grated

4 pears

125 ml/4 fl oz single cream

1 egg

1 egg yolk

½ tsp almond essence

3 tbsp caster sugar

1 To make the pastry, sift the flour and salt into a mixing bowl. Add the sugar and butter and mix well in an electric mixer with a dough hook or with two forks until thoroughly incorporated. Stir in the egg yolk and the lemon juice to form a dough. Form the dough into a ball, wrap in clingfilm and chill in the refrigerator for 30 minutes.

2 Preheat the oven to 200°C/400°F/Gas Mark 6. Roll out the dough on a lightly floured work surface and use it to line a 25-cm/10-inch loose-based flan tin. Sprinkle the grated plain chocolate over the base of the pastry case. Peel the pears, cut them in half lengthways and remove the cores. Thinly slice each pear half and fan out slightly. Using a palette knife, scoop up each sliced pear half and arrange in the tart case.

3 Beat together the cream, egg, extra yolk and almond essence, and pour the mixture over the pears. Sprinkle the sugar over the tart.

4 Bake in the preheated oven for 10 minutes, then reduce the temperature to 180°C/350°F/Gas Mark 4 and bake for an additional 20 minutes, until the pears are starting to caramelize and the filling is just set. Remove from the oven and cool to room temperature before serving.

Pear Tart

Pears are a very popular fruit in Italy. In this recipe they are flavoured with almonds, cinnamon, raisins and apricot jam.

30 mins plus 1 hr chilling   50 mins

SERVES 6

INGREDIENTS

275 g/9½ oz plain flour

pinch of salt

125 g/4½ oz caster sugar

115 g/4 oz butter, cut into small pieces

1 egg

1 egg yolk

few drops vanilla essence

2–3 tsp water

sifted icing sugar, for sprinkling

FILLING

4 tbsp apricot jam

55 g/2 oz amaretti or ratafia biscuits, crumbled

850 g–1 kg/1 lb 14 oz–2 lb 4 oz pears, peeled and cored

1 tsp ground cinnamon

85 g/3 oz raisins

60 g/2¼ oz soft brown or demerara sugar

  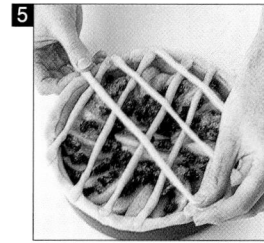

1 Sift the flour and salt on to a work surface, make a well in the centre and add the sugar, butter, egg, egg yolk, vanilla essence and most of the water.

2 Using your fingers, gradually work the flour into the other ingredients to form a smooth dough, adding more water if necessary. Alternatively, put all the ingredients into a food processor and process until smooth. Wrap in clingfilm and chill for 1 hour or until firm.

3 Preheat the oven to 200°C/400°F/Gas Mark 6. Roll out three-quarters of the dough and use to line a shallow 25-cm/ 10-inch cake tin or deep flan tin. Spread the jam over the base and sprinkle with the crushed biscuits.

4 Slice the pears very thinly. Arrange over the biscuits in the pastry case. Sprinkle with cinnamon, then with raisins and finally with brown sugar.

5 Roll out a thin sausage shape using one-third of the remaining pastry, and place around the edge of the tart. Roll the remainder into thin sausages and arrange in a lattice over the tart, 4 or 5 strips in each direction, attaching them to the strip around the edge.

6 Cook in the preheated oven for 50 minutes, until golden brown and cooked through. Leave to cool, then serve the tart warm or chilled, sprinkled with sifted icing sugar.

Pear & Cardamom Tarte Tatin

This is a variation on Tarte Tatin, the classic French upside-down apple tart. Serve warm with cream or ice cream if desired.

20 mins 35 mins

SERVES 4

INGREDIENTS

55 g/2 oz butter, softened

55 g/2 oz caster sugar

seeds from 10 cardamom pods

plain flour, for dusting

225 g/8 oz puff pastry, defrosted if frozen

3 ripe pears

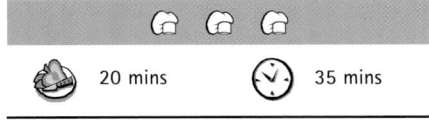
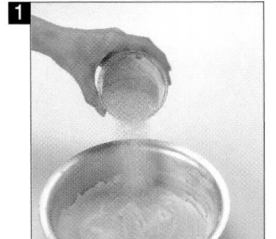

1 Preheat the oven to 220°C/425°F/Gas Mark 7. Spread the butter over the base of an 18-cm/7-inch ovenproof frying pan or heavy-based cake tin. Spread the sugar evenly over the butter and scatter the cardamom seeds over the sugar. On a floured work surface, roll out the pastry to a circle slightly larger than the frying pan. Prick the pastry lightly, place it on a plate and chill while preparing the pears.

2 Peel the pears, cut in half lengthways and cut out the cores. Arrange the pears, rounded-side down, on the butter and sugar. Set the frying pan over a medium heat until the sugar melts and starts to bubble with the butter and juice from the pears. If any areas are browning

more than others, move the frying pan, but do not stir. As soon as the sugar has caramelized remove the frying pan carefully from the heat.

3 Place the pastry on top, tucking the edges down the side of the frying pan. Transfer to the oven and bake for 25 minutes, until the pastry is well risen and golden. Leave the tart in the frying pan for 2–3 minutes, until the juices have stopped bubbling. Invert the frying pan over a plate and shake to release the tart. It may be necessary to slide a palette knife underneath the pears to loosen them. Serve the tart warm.

COOK'S TIP
Choose fairly large round pears for this tart, rather than the more elongated varieties.

Individual Apricot Tartes Tatin

These pretty little apricot tarts look and taste delicious drizzled with the chocolate sauce.

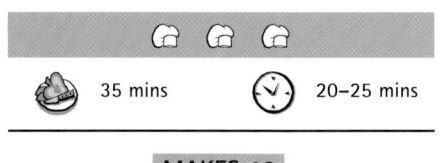
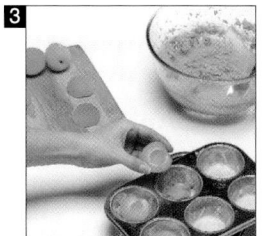

🕒 35 mins   ⏰ 20–25 mins

MAKES 12

INGREDIENTS

225 g/8 oz butter, unsalted for preference, plus extra for greasing

115 g/4 oz soft brown sugar

6 fresh apricots, halved and stoned

115 g/4 oz plain flour

pinch of salt

1 tbsp caster sugar

1 egg yolk

1 tbsp cold water

CHOCOLATE SAUCE

115 g/4 oz plain chocolate

2 tbsp butter, unsalted for preference

1 Preheat the oven to 200°C/400°F/Gas Mark 6. To make the sauce, melt the chocolate and butter together in a heatproof bowl set over a saucepan of gently simmering water and whisk until smooth. Set aside.

2 Grease 2 x 6-hole muffin tins with 1 tablespoon of butter, then line each with a disc of greaseproof paper.

3 Beat 140 g/5 oz butter with the brown sugar until very soft and divide between the holes. Place an apricot half, cut-side up, in each.

4 To make the pastry, rub in the remaining 85 g/3 oz butter to the flour and salt, then stir in the sugar. The mixture should resemble breadcrumbs. Add the egg and a little cold water, if needed, to make a dough. Knead lightly and roll out. Cut out 12 x 7.5-cm/3-inch discs and fit them over the apricot halves.

5 Bake for 15–20 minutes, until crisp and golden. Remove from the oven and leave to stand for 5 minutes. Turn out, with the apricot on top, and drizzle with the chocolate sauce to serve.

Chocolate Nut Strudel

This is an indulgent chocolate version of a classic strudel. It is delicious served with vanilla ice cream.

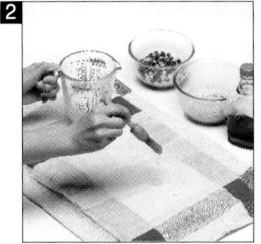

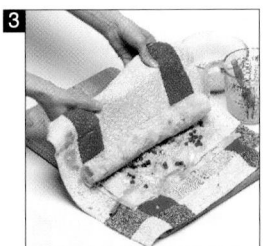

20 mins

20–25 mins

SERVES 6

INGREDIENTS

1 tbsp butter, for greasing

200 g/7 oz mixed chopped nuts

115 g/4 oz each of plain, milk and white chocolate, chopped

200 g/7 oz filo pastry

150 g/5½ oz butter, unsalted for preference

3 tbsp golden syrup

55 g/2 oz icing sugar

ice cream, to serve

1 Preheat the oven to 190°C/375°F/ Gas Mark 5. Lightly grease a baking sheet with 1 tablespoon butter. Reserve 1 tablespoon nuts. Mix the 3 types of chocolate together.

2 Place 1 sheet of filo on a clean tea towel. Melt the butter and brush the sheet of filo with butter, drizzle with a little syrup and sprinkle with some nuts and chocolate. Place another sheet of filo on top and repeat until you have used all the nuts and chocolate.

3 Use the tea towel to help you carefully roll up the strudel and place on the baking sheet, drizzle with a little more golden syrup and sprinkle with the reserved nuts. Bake for 20–25 minutes. If the nuts start to brown too much, cover the strudel with foil.

4 Sprinkle with icing sugar, slice and eat warm with ice cream.

Pear & Pecan Strudel

Crisp filo pastry is wrapped round a nutty pear filling in this easy-to-make strudel. It is delicious served warm.

15 mins   30 mins

SERVE 4

INGREDIENTS

2 ripe pears

4 tbsp butter

55 g/2 oz fresh white breadcrumbs

55 g/2 oz pecan nuts, chopped

25 g/1 oz light muscovado sugar

finely grated rind of 1 orange

100 g/3½ oz filo pastry

6 tbsp orange blossom honey

2 tbsp orange juice

sifted icing sugar, for dusting

Greek-style yogurt, to serve (optional)

1 Preheat the oven to 200°C/400°F/Gas Mark 6. Peel, core and chop the pears. Put 1 tablespoon of butter in a frying pan and gently fry the breadcrumbs until golden. Transfer the breadcrumbs to a bowl and add the pears, nuts, sugar and orange rind. Put the remaining butter in a small saucepan and heat until melted.

2 Reserve one sheet of filo pastry, keeping it well wrapped, and brush the remaining filo sheets with a little melted butter. Spoon the nut filling on to the first filo sheet, leaving a 2.5-cm/1-inch margin round the edge, and build up the strudel by placing buttered sheets on top of the first, spreading each one with nut filling as you build up the layers. Drizzle the honey and orange juice over the top.

3 Fold the short ends over the filling, then roll up, starting at a long side. Carefully lift on to a baking sheet, with the join uppermost. Brush with any remaining

melted butter and crumple the reserved sheet of filo pastry around the strudel. Bake for about 25 minutes, until golden and crisp. Dust with sifted icing sugar and serve warm with Greek-style yogurt, if liked.

COOK'S TIP

When working with filo pastry it is important to keep it covered until you are ready to use it, otherwise it will dry out very quickly.

Pecan Pie

Pecan pie is a classic recipe. Served with a spoonful of whipped cream or ice cream, this pie is the perfect finale to a special meal.

25 mins plus
30 mins chilling

1 hr 5 mins

SERVES 8

INGREDIENTS

PASTRY

225 g/8 oz plain flour

pinch of salt

115 g/4 oz butter

1 tbsp lard or white vegetable fat

55 g/2 oz golden caster sugar

6 tbsp cold milk

FILLING

3 eggs

225 g/8 oz dark muscovado sugar

1 tsp vanilla essence

pinch of salt

85 g/3 oz butter, melted

3 tbsp golden syrup

3 tbsp molasses

225 g/8 oz pecan nuts, chopped coarsely

pecan halves, to decorate

whipped cream or vanilla ice cream,
   to serve

1 To make the pastry, sift the flour and salt into a mixing bowl and rub in the butter and fat with your fingertips until the mixture resembles breadcrumbs. Work in the sugar and add the milk. Work the mixture together until a soft dough has formed. Wrap and chill in the refrigerator for 30 minutes. Preheat the oven to 200°C/400°F/Gas Mark 6. Roll out the pastry and use it to line a 23–25-cm/9–10-inch flan tin. Trim off the excess by using the rolling pin over the top of the flan tin. Line with baking paper, then fill with dried beans. Bake blind in the preheated oven for about 20 minutes. Take out of the oven and remove the paper and dried beans. Reduce the oven temperature to 180°C/350°F/Gas Mark 4 and place a baking sheet in the oven.

2 Put the eggs in a bowl and beat lightly. Beat in the sugar, vanilla essence and salt. Stir in the melted butter, syrup, molasses and chopped nuts. Pour into the pastry case and decorate with the pecan halves.

3 Place on the heated baking sheet and bake in the oven for 35-40 minutes, until the filling is set. Serve warm or at room temperature with whipped cream or vanilla ice cream.

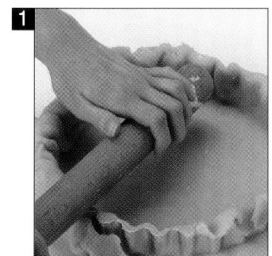

COOK'S TIP

Cover the pie with foil if the pastry is becoming too brown before the pie is cooked.

Chocolate Pecan Pie

This version of a favourite classic is packed with deliciously contrasting flavours and textures and is simply irresistible.

40 mins plus
2 hrs chilling

1 hr 15 mins

SERVES 4

I N G R E D I E N T S

PASTRY

280 g/10 oz plain flour, plus extra
    for dusting

55 g/2 oz cocoa powder

115 g/4 oz icing sugar

pinch of salt

200 g/7 oz butter, unsalted for preference,
    cut into small pieces

1 egg yolk

FILLING

85 g/3 oz plain chocolate,
    broken into pieces

350 g/12 oz shelled pecan nuts

85 g/ 3 oz butter, unsalted for preference

200 g/7 oz soft brown sugar

3 eggs

2 tbsp double cream

25 g/1 oz plain flour

1 tbsp icing sugar, for dusting

1 To make the pastry, sift the flour, cocoa, sugar and salt into a mixing bowl and make a well in the centre. Put the butter and egg yolk in the well and gradually mix in the dry ingredients. Knead lightly into a ball. Cover with clingfilm and chill in the refrigerator for 1 hour.

2 Unwrap the dough and roll it out on a lightly floured work surface. Use it to line a 25-cm/10-inch non-stick springform cake tin and prick the case with the tines of a fork. Preheat the oven to 180°C/350°F/ Gas Mark 4. Line the pastry case with baking paper and fill with dried beans. Bake blind in the preheated oven for 15 minutes. Remove from the oven, discard the beans and paper and leave to cool.

3 To make the filling, put the chocolate in a heatproof bowl set over a saucepan of gently simmering water until melted. Remove from the heat and set aside. Roughly chop 225 g/8 oz of the pecan nuts and set aside. Mix the butter with one-third of the brown sugar. Beat in the eggs, one at a time, then add the remaining brown sugar and mix well. Stir in the cream, flour, melted chocolate and chopped pecan nuts.

4 Spoon the filling into the pastry case and smooth the surface. Cut the remaining pecan nuts in half and arrange in concentric circles over the pie.

5 Bake in the preheated oven at the same temperature for 30 minutes, then remove the pie and cover the top with foil to prevent it burning. Bake for an additional 25 minutes. Remove the pie from the oven and leave to cool slightly before removing from the tin and transferring to a wire rack to cool completely. Dust with icing sugar.

Chocolate & Raspberry Tart

This is a very pretty and light white chocolate tart, swirled with raspberry sauce and served with fresh raspberries.

30 mins plus
30 mins chilling

40 mins

SERVES 6

INGREDIENTS

PASTRY

175 g/6 oz plain flour

115 g/4 oz butter, very cold

1 tbsp caster sugar

1 egg yolk

FILLING

450 g/1 lb raspberries

2 tbsp flower honey

125 g/4½ oz white chocolate

250 g/9 oz mascarpone cheese

150 ml/5 fl oz double cream

1 To make the pastry, sift the flour into a bowl and grate in the butter. Rub in until the mixture resembles breadcrumbs, then stir in the sugar, egg yolk and enough cold water to form a softish ball. Roll out to fit a 20-cm/8-inch flan tin, prick the base with a fork and chill in the refrigerator for 30 minutes.

2 Preheat the oven to 190°C/375°F/Gas Mark 5. Line the pastry with baking paper, fill with dried beans and bake blind for 15 minutes. Reduce the oven temperature to 180°C/350°F/Gas Mark 4, remove the baking paper and beans and cook for an additional 15–20 minutes. Leave the tart case to cool, then transfer from the flan tin to a serving plate.

3 Reserve a handful of raspberries, then push the rest through a sieve into a small saucepan. Mix with the honey. Boil until thick, then leave to cool completely.

4 Melt the white chocolate in a heatproof bowl set over a saucepan of gently simmering water, cool, then mix with the mascarpone. Whisk the cream until thick and mix into the mascarpone. Swirl in the raspberry sauce to give a marbled effect and spoon into the tart case. Decorate with the remaining raspberries and serve.

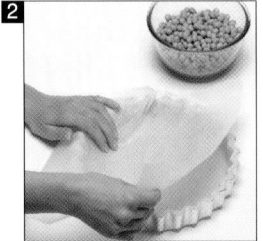

COOK'S TIP
This tart would be equally delicious made with strawberries or blueberries.

Pine Kernel Tart

This tart has a sweet filling made with creamy cheese and it is topped with pine kernels for a decorative finish and contrasting texture.

40 mins plus
1 hr chilling

1 hr 5 mins

SERVES 8

INGREDIENTS

PASTRY

175 g/6 oz plain flour, plus extra
for dusting

2 tbsp caster sugar

115 g/4 oz butter, cut into small pieces

1 tbsp water

FILLING

350 g/12 oz curd cheese

4 tbsp double cream

3 eggs

100 g/3½ oz caster sugar

grated rind of 1 orange

115 g/4 oz pine kernels

icing sugar, for dusting

1 To make the pastry, place the flour and sugar in a bowl and rub in the butter with your fingertips until the mixture resembles breadcrumbs. Add the water and work the mixture together until a soft dough has formed. Wrap and chill in the refrigerator for 30 minutes.

2 On a lightly floured work surface, roll out the dough and line a 24-cm/9½-inch loose-based flan tin. Prick the pastry with the tines of a fork and leave to chill for 30 minutes.

3 Preheat the oven to 190°C/375°F/Gas Mark 5. Line the pastry case with foil and dried beans and bake in the preheated oven for 15 minutes. Remove the foil and beans and cook the pastry case for an additional 15 minutes.

4 To make the filling, beat together the curd cheese, cream, eggs, sugar, orange rind and half of the pine kernels. Pour the filling into the pastry case and sprinkle over the remaining pine kernels.

5 Bake in the preheated oven for about 35 minutes, or until the filling is just set. Leave to cool and dust with icing sugar before serving.

VARIATION
Replace the pine kernels with flaked almonds, if you prefer.

Date & Apricot Tart

There is no need to add any extra sugar to this filling because dried fruit is naturally sweet. Serve with hot custard, if desired.

40 mins plus
30 mins chilling

50 mins

SERVES 8

INGREDIENTS

225 g/8 oz plain wholemeal flour, plus extra for dusting

75 g/2¾ oz mixed nuts, ground

115 g/4 oz margarine, cut into small pieces

4 tbsp water

175 g/6 oz dried apricots, chopped

225 g/8 oz chopped stoned dried dates

200 ml/7 fl oz unsweetened apple juice

1 tsp ground cinnamon

grated rind of 1 lemon

custard, to serve (optional)

1 Place the flour and ground nuts in a mixing bowl and rub in the margarine with your fingertips until the mixture resembles breadcrumbs. Stir in the water and bring together to form a dough. Wrap the dough in clingfilm and chill in the refrigerator for 30 minutes.

2 Meanwhile, place the apricots, dates, apple juice, cinnamon and lemon rind in a saucepan. Bring to the boil, cover and simmer over low heat for about 15 minutes, or until the fruit softens. Mash to a purée.

3 Preheat the oven to 200°C/400°F/Gas Mark 6. Reserve a small ball of pastry for making lattice strips. On a lightly floured work surface, roll out the rest of the pastry to form a circle and use to line a 23-cm/9-inch loose-based flan tin.

4 Spread the fruit filling evenly over the base of the pastry case. Roll out the reserved pastry and cut into strips

1 cm/½ inch wide. Cut the strips to fit the tart and twist them across the top of the fruit to form a decorative lattice pattern. Moisten the edges of the strips with a little water and seal them firmly around the rim of the tart.

5 Bake in the preheated oven for 25–30 minutes, until golden brown. Cut into slices and serve immediately, with custard if wished.

Plum & Almond Tart

The flavours of plums and almonds make a particularly good combination – delicious served warm with a spoonful of whipped cream.

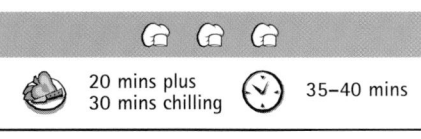 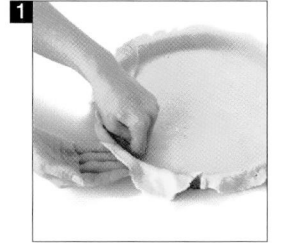 

20 mins plus
30 mins chilling

35–40 mins

SERVES 8

INGREDIENTS

PASTRY

225 g/8 oz plain flour

pinch of salt

115 g/4 oz butter

15 g/½ oz lard or white vegetable fat

55 g/2 oz golden caster sugar

6 tbsp cold milk

FILLING

1 egg

1 egg yolk

100 g/3½ oz golden caster sugar

4 tbsp butter, melted

100 g/3½ oz ground almonds

1 tbsp brandy

900 g/2 lb plums, halved and stoned

3 tbsp golden caster sugar, for sprinkling

whipped cream, to serve

1 To make the pastry, sift the flour and salt into a mixing bowl and rub in the butter and fat with your fingertips until the mixture resembles breadcrumbs. Work in the sugar and add the milk. Work until a soft dough has formed. Wrap and chill in the refrigerator for 30 minutes. Preheat the oven to 200°C/400°F/Gas Mark 6 and place a baking sheet in the oven to heat. Roll out the dough and use it to line a 23-cm/9-inch flan tin.

2 To make the filling, put the egg, the egg yolk, caster sugar, melted butter, ground almonds and brandy in a bowl and mix together. Spread the mixture in the tart case.

3 Arrange the plum halves, cut-side up, on top of the almond mixture. Fit them together tightly because they will shrink during cooking. Sprinkle with the caster sugar and bake in the preheated oven for 35–40 minutes, until the filling is set and the pastry is brown. Serve warm with whipped cream.

VARIATION
As an alternative to plums, apricots, cherries or halved and sliced pears may be used.

Chocolate Plum Tarts

The dark rich chocolate filling in these tarts contrasts beautifully with the rich red colour of the plums. Delicious served with ice cream.

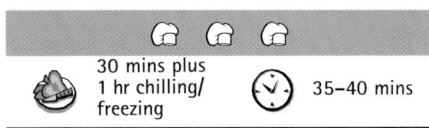

30 mins plus 1 hr chilling/ freezing

35–40 mins

MAKES 8

INGREDIENTS

250 g/9 oz plain flour

40 g/1½ oz icing sugar

pinch of salt

175 g/6 oz butter, unsalted for preference

FILLING

4 tbsp butter

140 g/5 oz plain chocolate

2 egg yolks

1 whole egg

55 g/2 oz caster sugar, plus extra for sprinkling

3 ripe plums, halved and stoned

ice cream, to serve (optional)

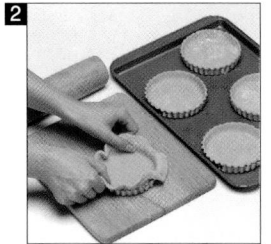

1 To make the pastry, put the flour, sugar and salt into a bowl and add the butter. Rub in until the mixture resembles breadcrumbs, then add a little cold water to bring the dough together. Cover in clingfilm and chill in the refrigerator for 30 minutes.

2 Remove the pastry from the refrigerator and cut into 8 pieces. Roll out to fit 8 x 10-cm/4-inch individual flan tins. Freeze for 30 minutes. Preheat the oven to 180°C/350°F/Gas Mark 4 and bake the tart cases for 20–25 minutes, or until they have dried out. Remove from the oven and leave to cool on a wire rack.

3 Increase the oven temperature to 190°C/375°F/Gas Mark 5. Melt the butter and chocolate for the filling in a heatproof bowl set over a saucepan of simmering water, stir and leave to cool.

4 Whisk the egg yolks, whole egg and sugar together, then add to the chocolate, mixing well. Divide between the tart cases. Thinly slice the plum halves and divide the slices between the tarts, fanning out the slices for a pretty effect. Sprinkle with a little sugar and bake for 10–15 minutes, until set.

5 Remove carefully from the tins and serve with ice cream, if desired.

Chocolate Almond Pithiviers

Pithiviers is a traditional French pastry stuffed with almond paste. This version adds chocolate for extra luxury.

🥐 15 mins plus 30 mins chilling   🕐 25 mins

SERVES 8

INGREDIENTS

125 g/4½ oz butter, unsalted for preference, softened

125 g/4½ oz caster sugar

1 egg

125 g/4½ oz ground almonds

85 g/3 oz milk chocolate, grated

250 g/9 oz ready-made puff pastry

1 egg, beaten

2 tbsp caster sugar

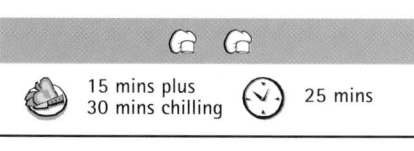

1 Cream the butter and sugar together until light and pale, then gradually add the egg, beating well between each addition. Fold in the ground almonds and the chocolate.

2 Roll out the pastry and cut 2 x 25-cm/10-inch diameter discs. Place 1 disc on a baking sheet and mound the almond mixture on top, leaving a 3-cm/1¼-inch edge. Brush the edges with beaten egg. Put the second disc on top, seal the edges and score the top with a swirl pattern. Chill for 30 minutes.

3 Preheat the oven to 200°C/400°F/Gas Mark 6. Bake the Pithiviers for 15 minutes, then reduce the oven temperature to 190°C/375°F/Gas Mark 5 for an additional 10 minutes.

4 Remove the Pithiviers from the oven and sprinkle with the sugar. Place under a preheated grill and caramelize the sugar – if your grill is really hot, this should take less than 1 minute. Slice and serve warm.

Candied Peel & Nut Tart

This very rich tart is not for the faint-hearted. Keep your portions small – even for dessert enthusiasts and those with a sweet tooth.

40 mins plus
1 hr chilling

50 mins

SERVES 8

INGREDIENTS

PASTRY

175 g/6 oz plain flour, plus extra
for dusting

2 tbsp caster sugar

115 g/4 oz butter, cut into small pieces

1 tbsp water

FILLING

85 g/3 oz butter

50 g/1¾ oz caster sugar

75 g/2¾ oz set honey

200 ml/7 fl oz double cream

1 egg, beaten

140 g/5 oz mixed nuts

150 g/5½ oz mixed candied peel

1 To make the pastry, place the flour and sugar in a bowl and rub in the butter with your fingertips until the mixture resembles breadcrumbs. Add the water and work the mixture together until a soft dough has formed. Wrap and chill in the refrigerator for 30 minutes.

2 On a lightly floured work surface, roll out the dough and line a 24-cm/9½-inch loose-based flan tin. Prick the pastry with a fork and chill in the refrigerator for 30 minutes.

3 Preheat the oven to 190°C/375°F/Gas Mark 5. Line the pastry case with foil and dried beans and bake in the oven for 15 minutes. Remove the foil and dried beans and cook for an additional 15 minutes.

4 To make the filling, melt the butter, sugar and honey in a small saucepan over a low heat. Stir in the cream and beaten egg, then add the nuts and candied peel. Cook over a low heat, stirring constantly, for 2 minutes, until the mixture is a pale golden colour.

5 Pour the filling into the pastry case and return the tart to the oven for 15–20 minutes, or until the filling is just set. Leave to cool, then serve in slices.

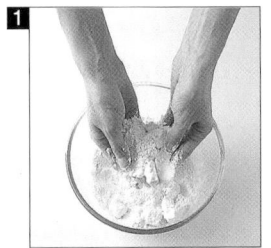
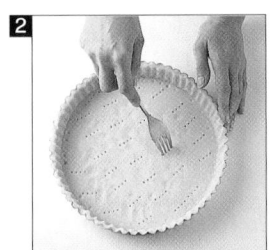

VARIATION
Substitute walnuts or pecan nuts for the mixed nuts, if you prefer.

Fruit Crumble Tart

This tart has a double helping of flavours, with a succulent fruit filling covered in a rich crumbly topping.

 20 mins plus 1 hr chilling 25 mins

SERVES 8

INGREDIENTS

PASTRY

175 g/6 oz plain flour, plus extra for greasing

2 tbsp caster sugar

115 g/4 oz butter, cut into small pieces

1 tbsp water

FILLING

200 g/7 oz raspberries

450 g/1 lb plums, halved, stoned and chopped coarsely

60 g/2¼ oz demerara sugar

TOPPING

115 g/4 oz plain flour

60 g/2¼ oz cup demerara sugar

115 g/4 oz butter, cut into small pieces

100 g/3½ oz chopped mixed nuts

1 tsp ground cinnamon

single cream, to serve

1 To make the dough, place the flour, sugar and butter in a bowl and rub in the butter with your fingertips. Add the water and work the mixture together until a soft dough has formed. Wrap and leave to chill in the refrigerator for 30 minutes.

2 Roll out the dough on a lightly floured work surface and line the base of a 24-cm/9½-inch loose-based flan tin. Prick the pastry with a fork and leave to chill for about 30 minutes.

3 Preheat the oven to 200°C/400°F/Gas Mark 6. To make the filling, toss the raspberries and plums together with the sugar and spoon into the pastry case.

4 To make the crumble topping, combine the flour, sugar and butter in a bowl. Work the butter into the flour with your fingertips until the mixture resembles coarse breadcrumbs. Stir in the nuts and ground cinnamon.

5 Sprinkle the topping over the fruit and press down gently with the back of a spoon. Bake in the preheated oven for 20–25 minutes, until the topping is golden. Serve the tart immediately with cream.

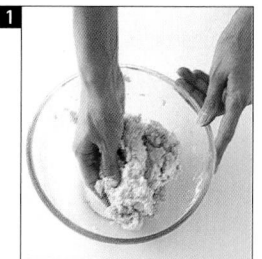

Forest Fruit Pie

This pie is brimming with fruit. Ground hazelnuts and lime rind are added to the pastry for extra flavour.

20 mins plus
30 mins resting

45 mins

SERVES 4

INGREDIENTS

250 g/9 oz blueberries

250 g/9 oz raspberries

250 g/9 oz blackberries

100 g/3½ cup caster sugar

200 g/7 oz plain flour, plus extra
for dusting

25 g/1 oz ground hazelnuts

100 g/3½ oz butter, cut into pieces, plus
extra for greasing

finely grated rind of 1 lemon

1 egg yolk, beaten

4 tbsp milk

2 tbsp icing sugar, to decorate

whipped cream, to serve

1 Put the fruit in a saucepan with 3 tablespoons of caster sugar and simmer, stirring, for 5 minutes. Remove from the heat. Sift the flour into a bowl, then add the hazelnuts. Rub in the butter, then sift in the remaining sugar. Add the lemon rind, egg yolk and 3 tablespoons of milk and mix. Turn out on to a lightly floured work surface and knead briefly. Leave to rest for 30 minutes.

2 Preheat the oven to 190°C/375°F/Gas Mark 5. Grease a 20-cm/8-inch ovenproof pie dish with butter. Roll out the pastry to a thickness of 5 mm/¼ inch and use it to line the base and sides of the dish. Spoon the fruit into the pastry case. Brush the rim with water, then roll out the remaining pastry and use it to cover the pie. Trim and crimp round the edges, then make

2 small slits in the top and decorate with 2 leaf shapes cut out from the dough trimmings. Brush all over with the remaining milk. Bake for 40 minutes. Remove from the oven, sprinkle over the icing sugar and serve with whipped cream.

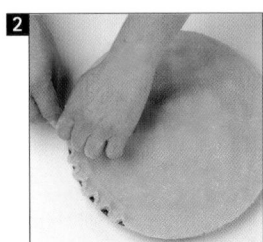

One Roll Fruit Pie

This is an easy way to make a pie – once you have rolled out the pastry and filled it with fruit, you just turn the edges in.

🥧 20 mins plus
   30 mins chilling   🕐 45 mins

SERVES 8

I N G R E D I E N T S

PASTRY

85 g/3 oz butter, cut into small pieces, plus extra for greasing

175 g/6 oz plain flour

1 tbsp water

1 egg, separated

sugar lumps, crushed, for sprinkling

FILLING

600 g/1 lb 5 oz prepared fruit (rhubarb, gooseberries, plums or damsons)

60 g/2¼ oz soft light brown sugar

1 tbsp ground ginger

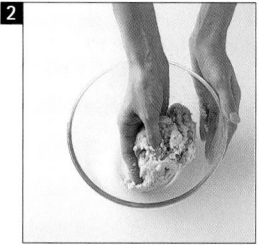

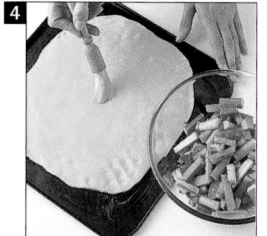

1 Grease a large baking sheet with a little butter and set aside until required.

2 To make the pastry, place the flour and butter in a mixing bowl and rub in the butter with your fingertips until the mixture resembles breadcrumbs. Add the water and work the mixture together until a soft dough has formed. Wrap and chill in the refrigerator for 30 minutes.

3 Preheat the oven to 200°C/400°F/Gas Mark 6. Roll out the chilled dough to a circle about 35 cm/14 inches in diameter.

4 Transfer the dough circle to the centre of the prepared baking sheet. Brush the dough with the egg yolk.

5 To make the filling, mix the fruit with the brown sugar and ground ginger. Pile it into the centre of the dough.

6 Turn in the edges of the dough circle all the way around. Brush the surface of the dough with the egg white and sprinkle with the crushed sugar lumps.

7 Bake in the preheated oven for 35 minutes, or until golden brown. Serve warm.

COOK'S TIP
If the pastry breaks when you are shaping it into a circle, don't panic – just patch and seal, because the overall effect of this tart is quite rough.

Chocolate Blueberry Tarts

The combination of chocolate pastry, rich filling and glistening berries makes these tarts very impressive.

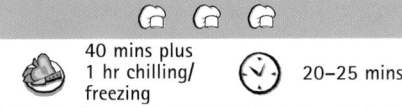

40 mins plus 1 hr chilling/freezing

20–25 mins

MAKES 10

INGREDIENTS

175 g/6 oz plain flour

40 g/1½ oz cocoa powder

55 g/2 oz caster sugar

pinch of salt

125 g/4½ oz butter

1 large egg yolk

200 g/7 oz blueberries

2 tbsp cassis

10 g/¼ oz icing sugar, sifted

FILLING

140 g/5 oz plain chocolate

225 ml/8 fl oz double cream

150 ml/5 fl oz soured cream (or crème fraîche, see page 9)

1 To make the pastry, put the flour, cocoa, sugar and salt in a food processor and pulse to mix. Add the butter, pulse again, then add the egg and a little cold water to form a dough. (If you do not have a processor put the flour, cocoa, sugar and salt in a large bowl and rub in the butter until the mixture resembles breadcrumbs. Add the egg and a little cold water to form a dough). Cover the pastry with clingfilm and chill in the refrigerator for 30 minutes.

2 Preheat the oven to 180°C/350°F/Gas mark 4. Remove the pastry from the refrigerator and roll out. Use to line 10 x 10-cm/4-inch tart cases. Freeze for 30 minutes, then bake in the oven for 15–20 minutes. Leave to cool.

3 Put the blueberries, cassis and icing sugar in a saucepan and warm through so the berries become shiny, but do not burst. Leave to cool.

4 Melt the chocolate in a heatproof bowl set over a saucepan of gently simmering water, then cool slightly. Whip the cream until stiff and fold in the soured cream and chocolate.

5 Remove the tart cases to a serving plate and divide the chocolate filling between them, smoothing the surface, then top with the blueberries.

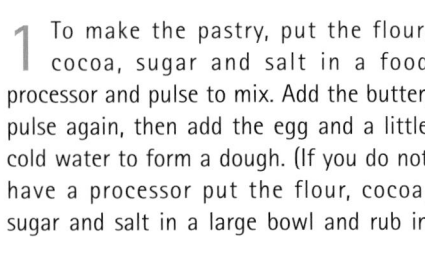

COOK'S TIP
These tarts also look pretty with a little icing sugar sifted over them just before serving.

Peach & Strawberry Tart

Peaches and strawberries make this the perfect choice for a summer lunch. Serve with a spoonful or two of whipped cream.

20 mins plus 1 hr 15 mins resting/chilling **15 mins**

SERVES 4

INGREDIENTS

PASTRY

200 g/7 oz plain flour, plus extra for dusting

100 g/3½ oz butter, cut into pieces, plus extra for greasing

50 g/1¾ oz icing sugar, sifted

finely grated rind of 1 orange

1 egg yolk, beaten

3 tbsp milk

4 tbsp strawberry jam

FILLING

175 ml/6 fl oz double cream

4 tbsp icing sugar

1 tbsp peach brandy

2 peaches, stoned and sliced

100 g/3½ oz strawberries, hulled and sliced

icing sugar, to decorate

whipped cream, to serve

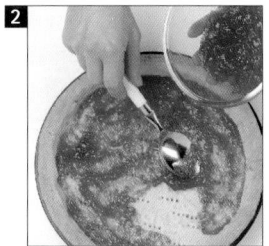

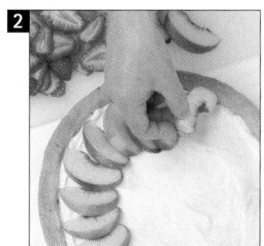

1 To make the pastry, sift the flour into a bowl. Rub in the butter, then mix in the icing sugar, orange rind, egg yolk and milk. Knead briefly, then leave for 30 minutes. Preheat the oven to 180°C/350°F/Gas Mark 4. Grease a 23-cm/9-inch flan tin with butter. Roll out the pastry to a thickness of 5 mm/¼ inch and use to line the base and sides of the tin. Prick all over with a fork, line with baking paper and fill with dried beans. Bake for 15 minutes. Remove from the oven and set aside.

2 To make the filling, put the cream into a bowl and beat in the icing sugar. Stir in the peach brandy. Spread the base of the pastry case with strawberry jam, then spoon in the cream filling. Arrange the sliced peaches and strawberries over the top, then cover with clingfilm and leave to chill for 45 minutes. Remove from the refrigerator. Dust with icing sugar and serve with whipped cream.

Apricot & Cranberry Tart

This frangipane tart, made with fresh cranberries, would be ideal for Christmas. If you wish, brush the warm tart with melted apricot jam.

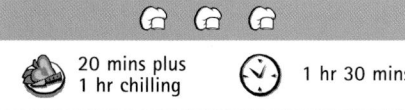

20 mins plus 1 hr chilling

1 hr 30 mins

SERVES 8

INGREDIENTS

PASTRY

175 g/6 oz plain flour

2 tbsp caster sugar

115 g/4 oz butter, cut into small pieces

1 tbsp water

FILLING

225 g/8 oz butter, unsalted for preference

200 g/7 oz caster sugar

1 egg

2 egg yolks

40 g/1½ oz plain flour, sifted

175 g/6 oz ground almonds

4 tbsp double cream

400 oz/14 oz canned apricot halves, drained

125 g/4½ oz fresh cranberries

1 To make the dough, place the flour and sugar in a bowl and rub in the butter with your fingertips until the mixture resembles breadcrumbs. Add the water and work the mixture together until a soft dough has formed. Wrap and chill in the refrigerator for 30 minutes.

2 Roll out the dough and line a 24-cm/ 9½-inch loose-bottomed flan tin. Prick the pastry with a fork and chill in the refrigerator for 30 minutes.

3 Preheat the oven to 190°C/375°F/Gas Mark 5. Line the pastry case with foil and dried beans and bake in the oven for 15 minutes. Remove the foil and dried beans and cook for an additional 10 minutes.

4 To make the filling, cream together the butter and sugar until light and fluffy. Beat in the egg and egg yolks, then stir in the flour, almonds and cream.

5 Place the apricot halves and cranberries on the base of the pastry case and spoon the filling over the top.

6 Return the tart to the oven and bake for about 1 hour, or until the topping is just set. Leave to cool slightly, then serve warm or cold.

Apple Tarte Tatin

This attractive, French upside-down apple tart is always a popular choice for a comforting dessert.

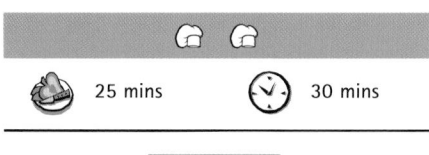

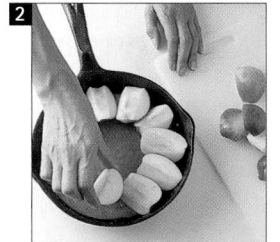
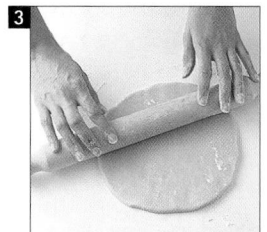
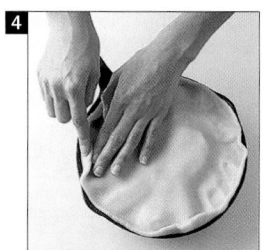

25 mins   30 mins

SERVES 8

I N G R E D I E N T S

115 g/4 oz butter

125 g/4½ oz caster sugar

4 eating apples, cored and quartered

250 g/9 oz ready-made pastry,
   thawed if frozen

plain flour, for dusting

soured cream or cream, to serve

1 Preheat the oven to 200°C/400°F/Gas Mark 6. Heat the butter and sugar in a 23-cm/8-inch ovenproof frying pan over medium heat for about 5 minutes, until the mixture starts to caramelize. Remove the frying pan from the heat.

2 Arrange the apple quarters, skin-side down, in the frying pan, taking care as the butter and sugar will be very hot. Place the frying pan back on the heat and simmer for 2 minutes.

3 Roll out the pastry on a lightly floured work surface to form a circle just a little larger than the frying pan.

4 Place the pastry over the apples, press down and carefully tuck in the edges to seal the apples under the layer of pastry.

5 Bake in the preheated oven for 20–25 minutes, until the pastry is golden. Remove from the oven and leave to cool for about 10 minutes.

6 Place a serving plate over the frying pan and, holding them firmly together, invert so that the pastry forms the bottom of the turned-out tart. Serve warm with soured cream or cream.

VARIATION
Replace the apples with pears, if you prefer. Leave the skin on the pears, cut them into quarters and then remove the core.

Traditional Apple Pie

This apple pie has a double crust and can be served either hot or cold.
The apples can be flavoured with other spices or grated citrus rind.

30 mins plus
30 mins chilling

50 mins

SERVES 6

INGREDIENTS

750 g–1 kg/1 lb 10 oz–2 lb 4 oz cooking
apples, peeled, cored and sliced

125 g/4½ oz soft light brown or caster
sugar, plus extra for sprinkling

½–1 tsp ground cinnamon, mixed spice
or ground ginger

1–2 tbsp water

PASTRY

350 g/12 oz plain flour

pinch of salt

6 tbsp butter or margarine

85 g/3 oz lard or white vegetable fat

about 6 tbsp cold water

beaten egg or milk, for glazing

1 To make the pastry, sift the flour and
salt into a mixing bowl. Add the
butter and fat and rub in with the
fingertips until the mixture resembles fine
breadcrumbs. Add the water and gather
the mixture together into a dough. Wrap
the dough and leave to chill for 30
minutes.

2 Preheat the oven to 220°C/425°F/Gas
Mark 7. Roll out almost two-thirds of
the pastry thinly and use to line a
20–23-cm/8–9-inch deep pie plate or
shallow pie tin.

3 Mix the apples with the sugar and
spice and pack into the pastry case;
the filling can come up above the rim. Add
the water if liked, particularly if the apples
are a dry variety.

4 Roll out the remaining pastry to form
a lid. Dampen the edges of the pie rim
with water and position the lid, pressing
the edges firmly together. Trim and crimp
the edges.

5 Use the trimmings to cut out leaves
or other shapes to decorate the top of
the pie, dampen and attach. Glaze the top
of the pie with beaten egg or milk, make
1–2 slits in the top and put the pie on a
baking sheet.

6 Bake in the preheated oven for
20 minutes, then reduce the
temperature to 180°C/350°F/Gas Mark 4
and cook for about 30 minutes, until the
pastry is a light golden brown. Serve hot or
cold, sprinkled with sugar.

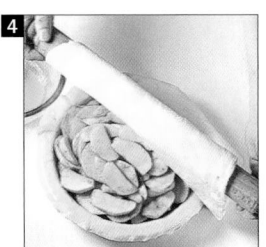

Spiced Apple Tart

Apples and spice are a classic, ever-popular combination. This tart makes a fabulous dessert, whatever the occasion.

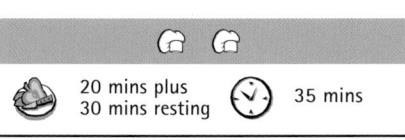

20 mins plus
30 mins resting   35 mins

SERVES 4

INGREDIENTS

PASTRY

200 g/7 oz plain flour, plus extra
    for dusting

100 g/3½ oz butter, diced, plus extra
    for greasing

50 g/1¾ oz icing sugar, sifted

finely grated rind of 1 lemon

1 egg yolk, beaten

3 tbsp milk

FILLING

3 medium cooking apples

2 tbsp lemon juice

finely grated rind of 1 lemon

150 ml/5 fl oz honey

175 g/6 oz white or wholemeal fresh
    breadcrumbs

1 tsp mixed spice

pinch of ground nutmeg

whipped cream, to serve

1 To make the pastry, sift the flour into a bowl. Rub in the butter, then mix in the icing sugar, lemon rind, egg yolk and milk. Knead briefly, then leave for 30 minutes. Preheat the oven to 200°C/400°F/Gas Mark 6. Grease a 20-cm/8-inch flan tin with butter. Roll out the pastry to a thickness of 5 mm/¼ inch and use to line the base and sides of the tin.

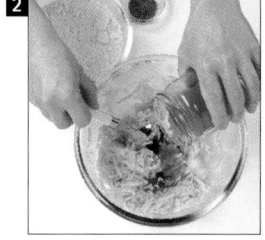

2 To make the filling, core 2 apples and grate them into a bowl. Add 1 tablespoon of lemon juice and all the lemon rind, along with the honey,

breadcrumbs and mixed spice. Mix together well. Spoon evenly into the pastry case. Core and slice the remaining apple, and use to decorate the top of the tart.

Brush the apple slices with lemon juice, then sprinkle over the nutmeg. Bake in the oven for 35 minutes, or until firm. Remove from the oven and serve with cream.

Apple & Mincemeat Tart

The fresh apple brings out the flavour of the sweet rich mincemeat and makes it a beautifully moist filling for pies and tarts.

15 mins plus 1 hr chilling

50 mins

SERVES 8

INGREDIENTS

PASTRY

175 g/6 oz plain flour, plus extra for dusting

2 tbsp caster sugar

115 g/4 oz butter, cut into small pieces

1 tbsp water

FILLING

400 g/14 oz mincemeat

3 eating apples

1 tbsp lemon juice

2 tbsp golden syrup

3 tbsp butter

1 To make the pastry, place the flour and caster sugar in a large mixing bowl and rub in the butter with your fingertips until the mixture resembles breadcrumbs.

2 Add the water and work the mixture together until a soft dough has formed. Wrap and chill in the refrigerator for 30 minutes.

3 On a lightly floured work surface, roll out the dough and line a 24-cm/9¹/₂-inch loose-bottomed flan tin. Prick the base of the tart with the tines of a fork and chill in the refrigerator for 30 minutes.

4 Preheat the oven to 190°C/375°F/Gas Mark 5. Line the pastry case with foil and dried beans. Bake the case in the preheated oven for 15 minutes. Remove the foil and beans and cook for an additional 15 minutes.

5 Core and grate the apples, then combine with the mincemeat and lemon juice. Spoon into the pastry case.

6 Melt the syrup and butter together in a small saucepan over low heat. Pour the syrup mixture over the mincemeat filling in the tart.

7 Return the tart to the oven and bake for about 20 minutes, or until firm. Serve warm.

VARIATION

Add 2 tablespoons of sherry to spice up the mincemeat, if you wish.

Custard Tart

This is a classic egg custard tart which should be served as fresh as possible for the best flavour and texture.

15 mins plus 1 hr chilling

1 hr

SERVES 8

INGREDIENTS

PASTRY

175 g/6 oz plain flour

2 tbsp caster sugar

115 g/4 oz butter, cut into small pieces

1 tbsp water

FILLING

3 eggs

150 ml/5 fl oz single cream

150 ml/5 fl oz milk

freshly grated nutmeg

whipped cream (optional), to serve

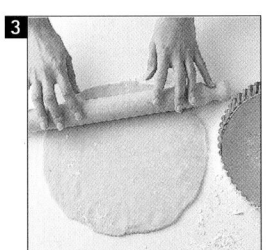

1 To make the pastry, place the flour and sugar in a mixing bowl and rub in the butter with your fingertips.

2 Add the water and mix together until a soft dough has formed. Wrap and chill in the refrigerator for about 30 minutes.

3 Roll out the dough to form a circle slightly larger than a 24-cm/9½-inch loose-bottomed flan tin.

4 Line the tin with the dough, trimming off the edges. Prick the base of the tart with the tines of a fork and chill in the refrigerator for 30 minutes.

5 Preheat the oven to 190°C/375°F/Gas Mark 5. Line the pastry case with foil and dried beans. Bake in the preheated oven for 15 minutes. Remove the foil and dried beans and bake the pastry case for an additional 15 minutes.

6 To make the filling, whisk together the eggs, cream, milk and nutmeg. Pour the filling into the prepared pastry case.

7 Return the tart to the oven and cook for an additional 25–30 minutes, or until the filling is just set. Serve with whipped cream, if wished.

COOK'S TIP

Baking the pastry case blind ensures that the finished tart has a crisp base.

Orange Tart

This is a variation of the classic lemon tart – in this recipe, fresh breadcrumbs are used to create a thicker texture.

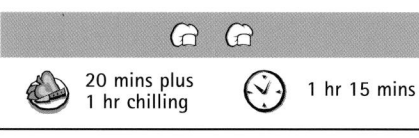

20 mins plus 1 hr chilling   1 hr 15 mins

SERVES 6–8

INGREDIENTS

PASTRY

175 g/6 oz plain flour, plus extra
   for dusting

2 tbsp caster sugar

115 g/4 oz butter, cut into small pieces

1 tbsp water

FILLING

grated rind of 2 oranges

125 ml/4 fl oz orange juice

50 g/1¾ oz fresh white breadcrumbs

2 tbsp lemon juice

150 ml/5 fl oz single cream

4 tbsp butter

50 g/1¾ oz caster sugar

2 eggs, separated

salt

whipped cream, to serve

1 To make the pastry, place the flour and sugar in a bowl and rub in the butter until the mixture resembles breadcrumbs. Add enough water to form a soft dough. Cover in clingfilm and chill in the refrigerator for 30 minutes.

2 Roll out the pastry on a lightly floured work surface to a circle and line a 24-cm/9¹/₂-inch loose-bottomed flan tin. Prick the pastry with a fork and chill in the refrigerator for 30 minutes.

3 Preheat the oven to 190°C/375°F/Gas Mark 5. Line the pastry case with foil and dried beans and bake in the oven for 15 minutes. Remove the foil and beans and cook for an additional 15 minutes.

4 To make the filling, combine the orange rind and juice with the breadcrumbs in a bowl. Stir in the lemon juice and single cream. Melt the butter and sugar in a small saucepan over low heat. Remove the saucepan from the heat, add the 2 egg yolks, a pinch of salt and the breadcrumb mixture and stir.

5 In a mixing bowl, whisk the egg whites with a pinch of salt until soft peaks form. Fold them into the egg yolk mixture.

6 Pour the filling mixture into the pastry case. Reduce the oven temperature to 160°C/325°F/Gas Mark 3 and bake for about 45 minutes, or until just set. Leave to cool slightly and serve warm with cream.

Tarte au Citron

Few desserts can be more appealing to round off a meal on a hot evening than this creamy, tangy tart.

20 mins plus 1 hr chilling   35 mins

SERVES 6–8

INGREDIENTS

grated rind of 2–3 large lemons

150 ml/5 fl oz lemon juice

100 g/3½ oz caster sugar

125 ml/4 fl oz double cream or soured cream

3 large eggs

3 large egg yolks

icing sugar, for dusting

PASTRY

175 g/6 oz plain flour, plus extra for dusting

½ tsp salt

115 g/4 oz cold unsalted butter, cut into small pieces

1 egg yolk beaten with 2 tbsp ice-cold water

1 To make the pastry, sift the flour and salt into a bowl. Using your fingertips, rub the butter into the flour until the mixture resembles fine breadcrumbs. Add the egg yolk and water and stir to form a dough. Gather the dough into a ball, cover in clingfilm and chill for at least 1 hour.

2 Preheat the oven to 200°C/400°F/Gas Mark 6. Roll out on a lightly floured work surface and use to line a 23–25-cm/9–10-inch fluted flan tin with a removable bottom. Prick the base all over with a fork and line with a sheet of baking paper and dried beans.

3 Bake in the preheated oven for 15 minutes, until the pastry looks set. Remove the paper and beans. Reduce the

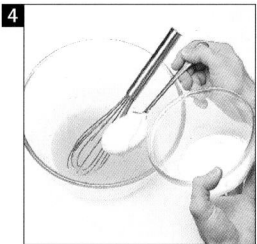

oven temperature to 190°C/375°F/Gas Mark 5.

4 Beat the lemon rind, lemon juice and sugar together until blended. Slowly beat in the cream, then beat in the eggs and yolks, one by one.

5 Set the pastry case on a baking sheet and pour in the filling. Transfer to the preheated oven and bake for 20 minutes, until the filling is set.

6 Leave to cool completely on a wire rack. Dust with icing sugar.

Lemon Meringue Pie

A combination of tangy lemon and soft meringue, this is a classic dessert which is ideal for both dinner parties or family gatherings.

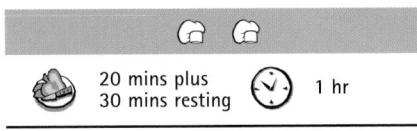

20 mins plus
30 mins resting

1 hr

SERVES 4

INGREDIENTS

PASTRY

200 g/7 oz plain flour, plus extra
    for dusting

100 g/3½ oz butter, cut into small pieces,
    plus extra for greasing

50 g/1¾ oz icing sugar, sifted

finely grated rind of 1 lemon

1 egg yolk, beaten

3 tbsp milk

FILLING

3 tbsp cornflour

300 ml/10 fl oz cold water

juice and grated rind of 2 lemons

175 g/6 oz caster sugar

2 eggs, separated

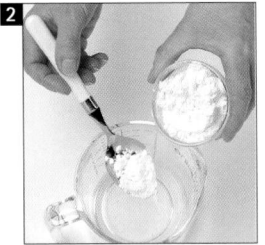

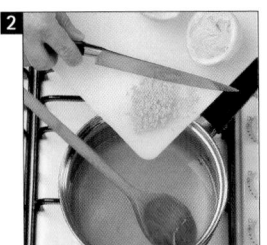

1 To make the pastry, sift the flour into a bowl. Rub in the butter. Mix in the remaining ingredients. Knead briefly on a lightly floured work surface. Leave to rest for 30 minutes. Preheat the oven to 180°C/350°F/Gas Mark 4. Grease a 20-cm/ 8-inch ovenproof pie dish with butter. Roll out the pastry to a thickness of 5 mm/ ¼ inch; use it to line the base and sides of the dish. Prick all over with the tines of a fork, line with baking paper and fill with dried beans. Bake for 15 minutes. Remove from the oven. Reduce the temperature to 150°C/300°F/Gas Mark 2.

2 To make the filling, mix the cornflour with a little water. Put the remaining water in a saucepan. Stir in the lemon juice and rind and cornflour paste. Bring to the boil, stirring. Cook for 2 minutes. Cool a little. Stir in 5 tablespoons of sugar and the egg yolks; pour into the pastry case. In a separate bowl, whisk the egg whites until stiff. Gradually whisk in the remaining sugar and spread over the pie. Bake for 40 minutes. Remove from the oven and serve.

Chocolate Meringue Pie

This pretty tart, with its three contrasting layers, is surprisingly light.
Use plain digestive biscuits if preferred.

25 mins

35 mins

SERVES 8

INGREDIENTS

250 g/9 oz chocolate digestive
 biscuits, crushed

85 g/3 oz butter, unsalted for preference,
 melted

140 g/5 oz plain chocolate, chopped

150 ml/5 fl oz double cream

115 g/4 oz mascarpone cheese

2 large eggs

2 large egg whites

pinch of salt

55 g/2 oz caster sugar

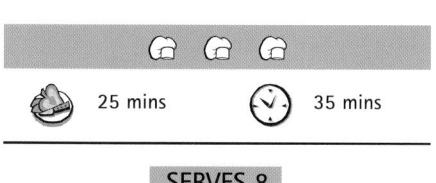

1 Preheat the oven to 160°C/325°F/Gas Mark 3. To make the biscuit base, mix the digestive biscuit crumbs and butter together and press well down into the base of a 23-cm/9-inch springform cake tin. Put the chocolate into a heatproof bowl.

2 Heat the cream to boiling point and pour it over the chocolate, stirring until the chocolate is melted and smooth. Beat the mascarpone cheese until smooth and mix in the whole eggs. Stir the mixture into the chocolate. Pour over the biscuit base and bake for 15–20 minutes, until just set.

3 Meanwhile, make the meringue. Whisk the egg whites with a pinch of salt until they form soft peaks. Gradually add the sugar, whisking between additions, until the meringue is stiff and glossy.

4 After the chocolate filling has cooked for 15–20 minutes, remove the tart from the oven and increase the oven temperature to 200°C/400°F/Gas Mark 6. Pile the meringue on top of the chocolate filling and bake for an additional 10–15 minutes, until lightly browned.

5 Remove from the oven and leave to cool. Carefully remove the springform tin and serve.

Lime & Coconut Meringue Pie

There is a Caribbean flavour to this variation on a classic lemon meringue pie. Serve it hot or cold.

30 mins plus
30 mins chilling   50 mins

SERVES 6-8

INGREDIENTS

PASTRY
175 g/6 oz plain flour

pinch of salt

4 tbsp butter

4 tbsp lard or white vegetable fat

2–3 tbsp cold water

FILLING
4 tbsp cornflour

400 ml/14 fl oz canned coconut milk

grated rind and juice of 2 limes

2 large eggs, separated

175 g/6 oz caster sugar

1 To make the pastry, place the flour and salt in a bowl and rub in the butter and fat with your fingertips until the mixture resembles breadcrumbs. Add the water and work the mixture together until a soft dough has formed. Wrap and chill in the refrigerator for 30 minutes. Preheat the oven to 180°C/350°F/Gas Mark 4. Roll out the pastry and use to line a 23-cm/9-inch flan tin. Line with baking paper and dried beans. Bake blind in the preheated oven for 15 minutes. Remove from the oven and remove the beans and discard the paper. Reduce the oven temperature to 160°C/325°F/Gas Mark 3. To make the filling, put the cornflour in a saucepan with a little of the coconut milk and stir to make a paste.

2 Stir in the rest of the coconut milk. Bring to the boil slowly, stirring constantly. Cook, stirring, for 3 minutes until thickened. Remove from the heat and add the lime rind and juice, the egg yolks and 4 tablespoons of the sugar. Pour into the pastry case.

3 Put the egg whites in a bowl and whisk until very stiff, then gradually whisk in the remaining sugar. Spread over the filling and swirl with a palette knife. Bake in the oven for 20 minutes, or until lightly browned. Serve hot or cold.

VARIATION
Add a teaspoon of coconut liqueur to the filling with the sugar in step 2, if you like.

Coconut Tart

Coconut makes the filling in this tart beautifully moist. If you buy a ready-cooked flan case, this recipe is quickly prepared.

5 mins plus 1 hr resting   40 mins

SERVES 8

INGREDIENTS

PASTRY

1 x 23-cm/9-inch ready-cooked flan case

FILLING

2 eggs

grated rind and lime of 2 lemons

200 g/7 oz golden caster sugar

375 ml/13 fl oz double cream

250 g/9 oz desiccated coconut

1 Preheat the oven to 180°C/350°F/Gas Mark 4. To make the filling, put the eggs, lemon rind and sugar in a bowl and beat together for 1 minute.

2 Gently stir in the cream, then the lemon juice and, finally, the coconut.

3 Spread the mixture into the pastry case and bake in the oven for 40 minutes, until set and golden. Leave to cool for about 1 hour to firm up. Serve at room temperature.

COOK'S TIP
This tart is particularly good served accompanied by passion fruit pulp.

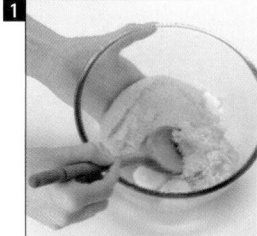  

Coconut Cream Tart

Decorate this tart with some fresh tropical fruit, such as mango or pineapple, and extra grated coconut, toasted.

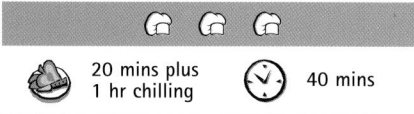

20 mins plus
1 hr chilling

40 mins

SERVES 6–8

I N G R E D I E N T S

PASTRY

175 g/6 oz plain flour, plus extra
   for dusting

2 tbsp caster sugar

115 g/4 oz butter, cut into small pieces

1 tbsp water

FILLING

425 ml/15 fl oz milk

125 g/4½ oz creamed coconut

3 egg yolks

115 g/4 oz caster sugar

50 g/1¾ oz plain flour, sifted

25 g/1 oz grated coconut

40 g/1½ oz chopped glacé pineapple

2 tbsp dark rum or pineapple juice

325 ml/11 fl oz whipping cream, whipped

1 To make the pastry, place the flour and sugar in a bowl and rub in the butter until the mixture resembles breadcrumbs. Add the water and work the mixture together until a soft dough has formed. Wrap and chill for 30 minutes.

2 On a lightly floured work surface, roll out the dough to a circle and line a 24-cm/9½-inch loose-bottomed flan tin. Prick the pastry with the tines of a fork and chill in the refrigerator for 30 minutes.

3 Preheat the oven to 190°C/375°F/Gas Mark 5. Line the pastry case with foil and dried beans. Bake in the oven for 15 minutes. Remove the foil and beans. Cook for an additional 15 minutes. Leave to cool.

4 To make the filling, bring the milk and creamed coconut to just below boiling point in a small saucepan over low heat, stirring to melt the coconut.

5 In a bowl, whisk the egg yolks with the sugar until pale and fluffy. Whisk in the flour. Pour the hot milk over the egg mixture, stirring constantly. Return the mixture to the saucepan and heat gently, stirring constantly, for about 8 minutes until thick. Leave to cool.

6 Stir the coconut, pineapple and rum or juice into the coconut cream filling. Spread the filling in the pastry case. Cover with the whipped cream and chill in the refrigerator until required.

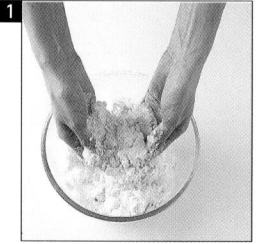

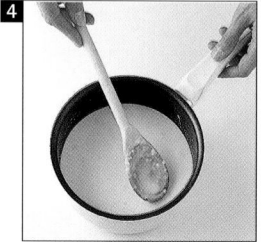

Chocolate Walnut Tart

This rich chocolate nut tart is served with a caramel sauce as an unusual alternative to cream. It makes a fantastic dinner-party dessert.

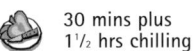 30 mins plus 1½ hrs chilling 55 mins

SERVES 12

I N G R E D I E N T S

125 g/4½ oz butter

250 g/9 oz plain flour

115 g/4 oz icing sugar

2 egg yolks

FILLING

400 ml/14 fl oz double cream

55 g/2 oz caster sugar

pinch of salt

125 g/4½ oz softened butter

400 g/14 oz plain chocolate, chopped

150 g/5½ oz chopped walnuts

CARAMEL SAUCE

115 g/4 oz soft light brown sugar

225 ml/8 fl oz maple syrup

115 g/4 oz butter

2 tbsp boiling water

1 To make the pastry, put the butter, flour and sugar in a food processor and pulse until the mixture resembles breadcrumbs, add the egg and a little cold water to bring the dough together. (If you do not have a processor, rub the butter into the flour and sugar until the mixture resembles breadcrumbs. Add the egg and a little cold water to form a dough.) Cover the pastry in clingfilm and chill in the refrigerator for 30 minutes.

2 Preheat the oven to 190°C/375°F/Gas Mark 5. Remove the pastry from the refrigerator and roll out. Use to line a 24-cm/9½-inch square flan tin and line with baking paper, fill with dried beans and bake blind for 10 minutes. Remove the paper and beans and bake for an additional 10–15 minutes, until the pastry has dried out. Remove and leave to cool.

3 Put the cream, sugar and salt into a saucepan and bring to the boil. Remove from the heat and add the butter and chocolate, stirring well to combine. Leave to cool and add the walnuts, stir well and pour into the pastry case.

Smooth the surface and chill in the refrigerator for at least 1 hour.

4 To make the caramel sauce, heat the sugar and maple syrup until the sugar has melted, remove from the heat and stir in the butter and hot water. Leave to cool.

5 Slice the tart into squares and pour a little caramel sauce over to serve.

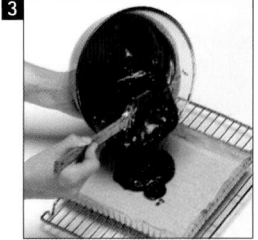

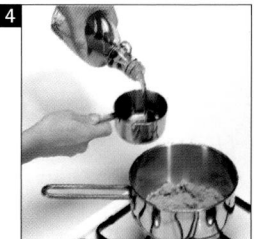

Chocolate & Coffee Tarts

These tarts have a crisp chocolate pastry and a smooth coffee filling topped with cream and a few plain chocolate sticks.

30 mins plus
30 mins chilling

45 mins

MAKES 10

INGREDIENTS

250 g/9 oz plain flour

40 g/1½ oz icing sugar

1 tsp ground cinnamon

1 tbsp cocoa powder

175 g/6 oz butter

1 egg yolk

FILLING

25 g/1 oz plain flour

pinch of salt

3 egg yolks

85 g/3 oz caster sugar

1 cup milk

2 tbsp instant coffee powder, mixed to a paste with a little boiling water

1 tbsp coffee liqueur (optional)

150 ml/5 fl oz double cream

115 g/4 oz plain chocolate

1 Put the flour, sugar, cinnamon and cocoa in a food processor and pulse to combine. Add the butter and pulse until the mixture resembles breadcrumbs, then add the egg and a little cold water to form a dough. (If you do not have a processor, sift the flour, sugar, cinnamon and cocoa into a large bowl and rub in the butter until the mixture resembles breadcrumbs, then add the egg and a little cold water to form a dough.) Cover the pastry in clingfilm and chill in the refrigerator for 30 minutes.

2 Preheat the oven to 180°C/350°F/Gas Mark 4. Remove the pastry from the refrigerator and roll out. Use to line 10 x 10-cm/4-inch tart tins. Line each tart with baking paper and dried beans and bake blind for 10 minutes. Remove the paper and beans and bake for an additional 5–10 minutes. Remove and leave to cool.

3 To make the filling, sift the flour and salt into a bowl. In a separate bowl, whisk the eggs and sugar together with an electric whisk until pale and thick. Gradually add the flour and mix well. Heat the milk to boiling point, then set aside to cool slightly. Pour the milk in a steady stream into the egg mixture, whisking constantly, add the coffee and return to the saucepan. Bring the mixture to the boil, stirring all the time and boil for 2 minutes. Pour into a clean bowl, leave to cool and stir in the liqueur (if using).

4 Whip the cream until thick. Spoon the coffee filling in to the tart cases and transfer to individual serving plates. Top with a teaspoonful of cream and, using a vegetable peeler, decorative sticks of plain chocolate.

Treacle Tart

This is an old-fashioned dessert, which still delights people time after time. It is very quick to make if you use ready-made pastry.

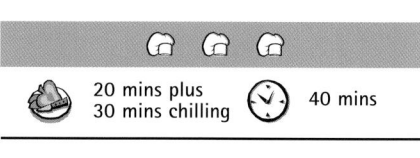

20 mins plus
30 mins chilling

40 mins

SERVES 8

INGREDIENTS

250 g/9 oz ready-made pastry, thawed if frozen

350 g/12 oz golden syrup

100 g/3½ oz fresh white breadcrumbs

125 ml/4 fl oz double cream

finely grated rind of ½ lemon or orange

2 tbsp lemon or orange juice

custard or single cream, to serve

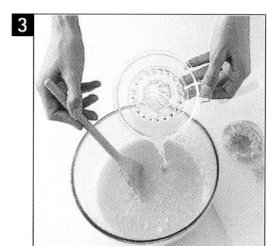

1 Roll out the pastry to line a 20-cm/8-inch loose-bottomed flan tin, reserving the trimmings. Prick the base of the pastry with a fork and leave to chill in the refrigerator for 30 minutes. Preheat the oven to 190°C/375°F/Gas Mark 5.

2 Cut out small shapes from the reserved pastry trimmings, such as hearts, leaves or stars, to decorate the top of the tart.

3 In a bowl, combine the golden syrup, breadcrumbs, double cream, grated lemon or orange rind and lemon or orange juice.

4 Pour the mixture into the pastry case and decorate the edges of the tart with the reserved pastry shapes.

5 Bake in the preheated oven for 35–40 minutes, or until the filling is just set.

6 Leave the tart to cool slightly in the tom. Turn out and serve hot or cold, with custard or single cream.

VARIATION
Use the pastry trimmings to create a lattice pattern on top of the tart, if preferred.

Treacle & Orange Tart

An irresistibly sweet combination of golden syrup and orange. It is the perfect finale to a special occasion meal.

20 mins plus
30 mins chilling

30 mins

SERVES 6

INGREDIENTS

PASTRY

115 g/4 oz plain flour, plus extra for greasing

pinch of salt

2 tbsp butter

2 tbsp lard or white vegetable fat

2 tbsp cold water

FILLING

8 tbsp golden syrup

finely grated rind of 1 orange

1 tbsp orange juice

6 tbsp fresh white breadcrumbs

1 To make the pastry, put the flour and salt in a bowl and rub in the butter and fat until the mixture resembles breadcrumbs. Add the water and work the mixture together until a soft dough has formed. Wrap and chill for 30 minutes. Preheat the oven to 190°C/375°F/Gas Mark 5. Roll out the pastry and use to line a 20-cm/8-inch flan tin. Reserve the trimmings. To make the filling, put the syrup, orange rind and juice in a saucepan and heat very gently until runny. Remove from the heat and stir in the breadcrumbs.

2 Leave for 10 minutes until the crumbs have absorbed the syrup. If the mixture looks stodgy, add a little more syrup; and if it looks thin, add some more breadcrumbs. It should have the consistency of thick honey.

3 Spread the mixture in the pastry case. Roll out the pastry trimmings and cut into narrow strips. Use to make a lattice pattern across the top of the tart. Bake in the oven for 30 minutes, or until the filling is almost set and the edge of the pastry is brown. Serve warm or cold.

COOK'S TIP

When the tart is removed from the oven, the filling should still be on the soft side if the tart is to be eaten cold, because it hardens as it cools.

Bakewell Tart

Strawberry jam topped with a delicious almond mixture make this pie very moreish. It is best served warm.

 20 mins plus 30 mins resting   40 mins

SERVES 4

INGREDIENTS

PASTRY

200 g/7 oz plain flour, plus extra for dusting

100 g/3½ oz butter, cut into small pieces, plus extra for greasing

50 g/1¾ oz icing sugar, sifted

finely grated rind of 1 lemon

1 egg yolk, beaten

3 tbsp milk

4 tbsp strawberry jam

FILLING

100 g/3½ oz butter

100 g/3½ oz soft light brown sugar

2 eggs, beaten

1 tsp almond essence

75 g/2¾ oz ground rice

3 tbsp ground almonds

3 tbsp flaked almonds, toasted

icing sugar, to decorate

1 To make the pastry, sift the flour into a bowl. Rub in the butter. Mix in the icing sugar, lemon rind, egg yolk and milk. Knead briefly on a lightly floured work surface. Leave to rest for 30 minutes.

2 Preheat the oven to 190°C/375°F/Gas Mark 5. Grease a 20-cm/8-inch ovenproof flan tin. Roll out the pastry to a thickness of 5 mm/¼ inch and use it to line the base and sides of the tin. Prick all over the base with a fork, then spread with jam.

3 To make the filling, cream together the butter and sugar until fluffy. Gradually beat in the eggs, followed by the almond essence, rice and ground almonds. Spread the mixture evenly over the jam-covered pastry, then scatter over the flaked almonds. Bake in the preheated oven for 40 minutes, until golden. Remove the tart from the oven, dust with icing sugar and serve.

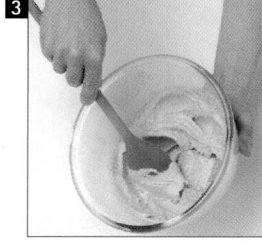

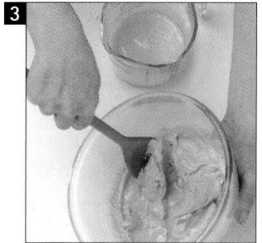

Hazelnut Cream Tarts

These elegant little tarts look particularly attractive with their sprinkling of chopped toasted hazelnuts.

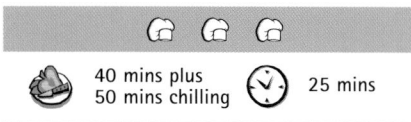

40 mins plus 50 mins chilling

25 mins

MAKES 8

INGREDIENTS

125 g/4½ oz plain flour

115 g/4 oz butter

1 tbsp icing sugar, sifted

1 small egg yolk

FILLING

3 egg yolks

60 g/2¼ oz caster sugar

3 tbsp plain flour

225 ml/8 fl oz milk

85 g/3 oz chocolate

1 tbsp honey

50 ml/2 fl oz double cream

55 g/2 oz toasted hazelnuts, chopped

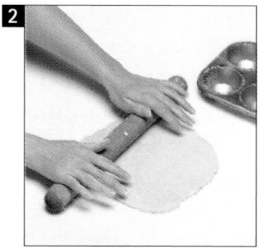

1 Place the flour, butter and icing sugar in a food processor and process until the mixture resembles breadcrumbs. Add the egg yolk and a little cold water to form a dough. (If you do not have a processor, sift the flour into a bowl and rub in the butter and sugar until the mixture resembles breadcrumbs, add the egg and a little cold water to form a dough). Cover the pastry in clingfilm and leave to chill in the refrigerator for 30 minutes.

2 Preheat the oven to 190°C/375°F/Gas Mark 5. Roll out the pastry and use it to line an 8-hole muffin tin. Chill in the refrigerator for 20 minutes. Bake for 12–15 minutes. Leave to cool in the muffin tin.

3 To make the filling, beat the egg yolks and sugar in a bowl until pale and thick, add the flour a little at a time and mix to combine. Bring the milk to the boil and pour over the eggs, whisking all the time and beat well. Pour back into a clean saucepan and bring to the boil over low heat, stirring constantly. Boil for 1 minute, then pour into a cold bowl and stir. Leave to cool, stirring occasionally.

4 Melt the chocolate with the honey in a heatproof bowl set over a saucepan of gently simmering water. When melted, remove from the heat and stir in the cream. Leave to cool.

5 Spoon the cream filling into each tart, cover with the melted chocolate, sprinkle with the nuts and transfer to a serving dish.

Chocolate Chestnut Angel Tart

Chestnut purée adds an unusual flavour to this smooth, dense tart. A pile of white chocolate caraque in the centre adds the finishing touch.

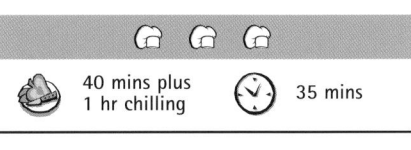

40 mins plus
1 hr chilling

35 mins

SERVES 8

INGREDIENTS

125 g/4½ oz butter

250 g/9 oz plain flour, sifted, plus extra for dusting

115 g/4 oz icing sugar

2 egg yolks, beaten

FILLING

200 g/7 oz plain chocolate

450 g/1 lb canned unsweetened chestnut purée

115 g/4 oz icing sugar

225 ml/8 fl oz double cream, whipped

140 g/5 oz white chocolate caraque (see page 9)

1 To make the pastry, rub the butter into the sifted flour and sugar and add enough egg yolk to form a dough. Cover in clingfilm and leave to chill in the refrigerator for 30 minutes.

2 Preheat the oven to 180°C/350°F/Gas Mark 4. Remove the pastry from the refrigerator and roll out. Use to line a 23-cm/9-inch loose-bottomed flan tin and prick the base with a fork. Line with baking paper, fill with dried beans and bake for 10 minutes. Remove the paper and beans and bake for an additional 10–15 minutes, until the pastry case has dried out. Remove from the oven and leave to cool.

3 Melt the plain chocolate in a heatproof bowl set over a saucepan of gently simmering water.

4 Put the chestnut purée and sugar into a large bowl and stir together until smooth. Fold in the chocolate, then the whipped cream.

5 Remove the pastry case from the flan tin on to a serving plate. Spoon the chestnut mixture into the case and chill in the refrigerator.

6 Make the caraque (see page 9) using the white chocolate. When you are ready to serve the tart, pile up the white chocolate caraque in the centre of the chestnut filling.

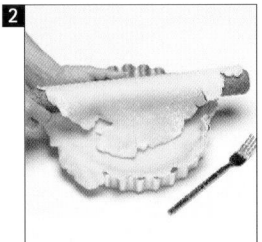

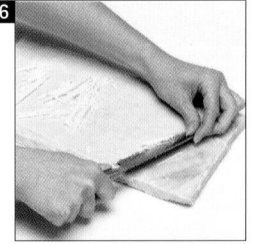

Banoffee Pie

A melt-in-the-mouth combination of toffee and bananas, topped with grated plain chocolate, this pie has become a classic.

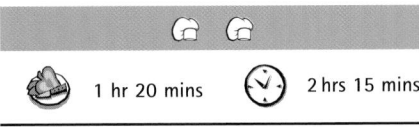

1 hr 20 mins   2 hrs 15 mins

SERVES 4

INGREDIENTS

800 ml/28 fl oz canned sweetened condensed milk

85 g/3 oz butter, melted

150 g/5½ oz digestive biscuits, crushed into crumbs

50 g/1¾ oz almonds, toasted and ground

50 g/1¾ oz hazelnuts, toasted and ground

4 ripe bananas

half a lemon

1 tsp vanilla essence

450 ml/16 fl oz double cream, whipped

75 g/2¾ oz plain chocolate, grated

1 Place the unopened cans of milk in a large saucepan and cover them with water. Bring to the boil, then reduce the heat and simmer for 2 hours, topping up the water level to keep the cans covered. Lift out the hot cans and leave to cool.

2 Preheat the oven to 180°C/350°F/Gas Mark 4. Grease a 23-cm/9-inch flan tin with butter. Put the remaining butter in a bowl and add the crushed biscuits and ground nuts. Mix together well, then press the mixture evenly into the base and sides of the flan tin. Bake for 10–12 minutes, remove from the oven and leave to cool.

3 Peel and slice the bananas and put in a bowl. Squeeze over the juice from the lemon, add the vanilla essence, and mix together. Spread the banana mixture over the biscuit crust in the tin, then spoon the contents of the cooled cans of condensed milk over the bananas. Sprinkle over 50 g/1¾ oz of the chocolate, then top with a layer of whipped cream. Scatter over the remaining chocolate and serve.

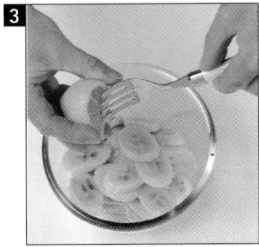

Magic Cheesecake

This superb dessert proves that you can indulge in a wonderful creamy and luxurious cheesecake and still stick to a healthy, low-fat diet.

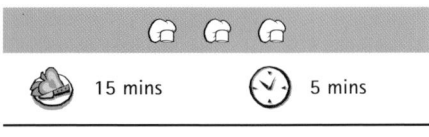

15 mins   5 mins

SERVES 6

INGREDIENTS

4 tbsp low-fat spread

6 tbsp apple juice

115 g/4 oz bran flakes

280 g/10 oz tofu or bean curd

200 ml/7 fl oz low-fat natural yogurt

1 tbsp powdered gelatine

350 g/12 oz prepared mixed fruit, such as star fruit, strawberries, kiwi fruit, papayas and blackberries

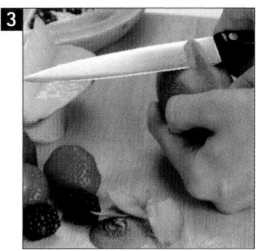

1 Using a rolling pin, crush the bran flakes in a polythene bag. Place the low-fat spread and 2 tablespoons of the apple juice in a saucepan and set over very low heat. When the spread has melted, stir in the bran flakes. Turn the mixture into a 23-cm/9-inch loose-bottomed flan tin and press down firmly with a wooden spoon or your fingertips to cover the base. Set aside.

2 Put the tofu and yogurt in a food processor and process until smooth, then scrape into a bowl. Pour the remaining apple juice into a small heatproof bowl, sprinkle the gelatine over the surface and set aside for 5 minutes to soften. Set the bowl over a saucepan of gently simmering water for 5 minutes, or until the gelatine has dissolved completely. Pour the gelatine in a steady stream into the tofu mixture, beating constantly. Spread the tofu mixture evenly over the base in the flan tin and chill in the refrigerator until set.

3 Remove the cheesecake from the tin and place on a serving plate. Peel the kiwi fruit and papayas and slice thinly, along with the strawberries and star fruit. Arrange the slices on the cheesecake, together with the blackberries.

Hot Chocolate Cheesecake

This rich cheesecake has chocolate in the pastry and in the filling. Your guests will want to come back for more.

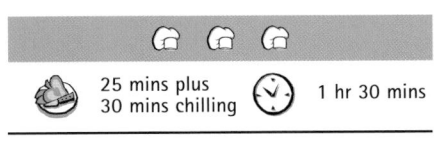

25 mins plus
30 mins chilling

1 hr 30 mins

SERVES 8–10

INGREDIENTS

PASTRY

4 tbsp butter, plus extra for greasing

150 g/5½ oz plain flour, plus extra for dusting

2 tbsp cocoa powder

2 tbsp golden caster sugar

25 g/1 oz ground almonds

1 egg yolk

FILLING

2 eggs, separated

75 g/2¾ oz golden caster sugar

350 g/12 oz cream cheese

4 tbsp ground almonds

150 ml/5 fl oz double cream

25 g/1 oz cocoa, sifted

1 tsp vanilla essence

icing sugar, for dusting

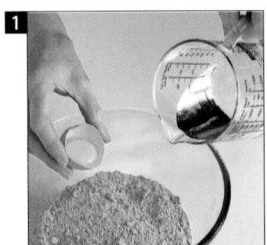

1 Grease a 20-cm/8-inch loose-bottomed cake tin. To make the pastry, sift the flour and cocoa into a bowl and rub in the butter until the mixture resembles fine breadcrumbs. Stir in the sugar and ground almonds. Add the egg yolk and sufficient water to make a soft dough.

2 Roll the pastry out on a lightly floured work surface and use to line the prepared tin. Leave to chill for 30 minutes. Preheat the oven to 160°C/325°F/Gas Mark 3. To make the filling, put the egg yolks and sugar in a large bowl and whisk until thick and pale. Whisk in the cream cheese, ground almonds, cream, cocoa and vanilla essence until well combined.

3 Put the egg whites in a large bowl and whisk until stiff but not dry. Stir a little of the egg white into the cheese mixture, then fold in the remainder. Pour into the pastry case. Bake in the oven for 1 hour 30 minutes, until well risen and just firm to the touch. Carefully remove from the tin and dust with icing sugar. Serve the cheesecake warm.

Chocolate Amaretto Cheesecake

Amaretto is an Italian almond-flavoured liqueur which complements the plain chocolate perfectly.

🌀 🌀 🌀

🍮 30 mins plus 3 hrs chilling   🕐 1 hr 10 mins

SERVES 10-12

I N G R E D I E N T S

B A S E
vegetable oil, for oiling

175 g/6 oz digestive biscuits

55 g/2 oz amaretti biscuits

85 g/3 oz butter

F I L L I N G
225 g/8 oz plain chocolate, broken into pieces

400 g/14 oz cream cheese, at room temperature

115 g/4 oz golden caster sugar

4 eggs

300 ml/10 fl oz double cream

50 ml/2 fl oz Amaretto

T O P P I N G
1 tbsp Amaretto

300 ml/10 fl oz soured cream

crushed amaretti biscuits

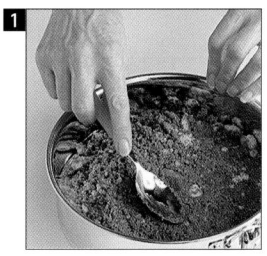

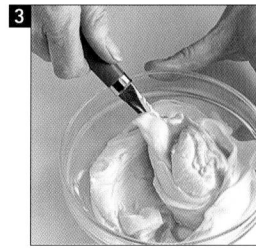

1 Line the bottom of a 23-cm/9-inch springform cake tin with foil and brush the sides of the tin with oil. Place the biscuits in a polythene bag and crush with a rolling pin. Place the butter in a saucepan and heat gently until just melted, then stir in the biscuits. Press into the base of the tin and chill for 1 hour.

2 Melt the chocolate in a heatproof bowl set over a saucepan of gently simmering water, then set aside to cool slightly. Preheat the oven to 160°C/325°F/ Gas Mark 3. To make the filling, put the cream cheese in a bowl and beat until fluffy, then add the sugar and beat until smooth. Gradually add the eggs, beating until well blended. Blend in the melted chocolate, cream and Amaretto. Pour the mixture over the biscuit case and bake in the oven for 50 minutes—1 hour, until set.

3 Leave the cheesecake in the oven with the door slightly ajar, until cold. Run a knife round the inside of the tin to loosen the cheesecake. Chill for 2 hours, then remove from the tin and place the cheesecake on a serving plate. To make the topping, stir the Amaretto into the soured cream and spread over the cheesecake. Sprinkle the crushed biscuits round the edge to decorate.

COOK'S TIP
If you do not have Amaretto, use another liqueur or brandy instead.

Irish Cream Cheesecake

This is an unbaked cheesecake, and although it uses no gelatine, its high chocolate content ensures that it sets perfectly.

45 mins plus 3 hrs chilling

5 mins

SERVES 12

INGREDIENTS

BASE

vegetable oil, for oiling

175 g/6 oz chocolate chip cookies

4 tbsp butter

FILLING

225 g/8 oz plain chocolate, broken into pieces

225 g/8 oz milk chocolate, broken into pieces

55 g/2 oz golden caster sugar

350 g/12 oz cream cheese

425 ml/15 fl oz double cream, whipped lightly

3 tbsp Baileys Irish Cream

TO SERVE

soured cream

fresh fruit

1 Line the base of a 20-cm/8-inch springform tin with foil and brush the sides with oil. Place the cookies in a polythene bag and crush with a rolling pin. Put the butter in a saucepan and heat gently until melted. Stir in the crushed cookies. Press into the base of the tin and chill for 1 hour.

2 Put the plain and milk chocolate into a heatproof bowl set over a saucepan of gently simmering water until melted. Leave to cool. Put the sugar and cream cheese in a bowl and beat together until smooth, then fold in the cream. Fold the melted chocolate into the cream cheese mixture, then stir in the Baileys Irish Cream.

3 Spoon into the prepared tin and smooth the surface. Leave to chill in the refrigerator for 2 hours, or until quite firm. Transfer to a serving plate and cut into small slices. Serve with soured cream and fresh fruit.

COOK'S TIP
Look out for miniature bottles of Baileys Irish Cream.

Chocolate Cheesecake

This cheesecake takes a little time to prepare, but is well worth the effort.
It is quite rich and is good served with a little fresh fruit.

🍰🍰🍰

🥧 1 hr 15 mins
plus 2 hrs chilling

🕐 1 hr–
1 hr 15 mins

SERVES 12

I N G R E D I E N T S

175 g/6 oz margarine, plus extra
 for greasing

100 g/3½ oz plain flour

85 g/3 oz ground almonds

85 g/3 oz molasses sugar

675 g/1 lb 8 oz firm tofu or bean curd

175 ml/6 fl oz vegetable oil

125 ml/4 fl oz orange juice

175 ml/6 fl oz brandy

6 tbsp cocoa powder, plus extra to decorate

2 tsp almond essence

TO DECORATE

icing sugar

cape gooseberries

1 Preheat the oven to 160°C/325°F/
Gas Mark 3. Lightly grease and line
the base of a 23-cm/9-inch springform
cake tin. Put the flour, ground almonds
and 1 tablespoon of the sugar in a bowl
and mix well. Rub the margarine into the
mixture to form a dough.

2 Press the dough into the base of the
tin to cover, pushing the dough right
up to the edge of the tin.

3 Coarsely chop the tofu and put into a
food processor with the vegetable
oil, orange juice, brandy, cocoa, almond
essence and remaining sugar and process
until smooth and creamy. Pour into the
pastry case and cook in the preheated
oven for about 1–1¼ hours, or until set.

4 Leave to cool in the tin for 5 minutes,
then remove from the tin and chill in
the refrigerator. Dust with icing sugar and
cocoa. Decorate with cape gooseberries
and serve.

COOK'S TIP
Cape gooseberries make an
attractive decoration for many
desserts. If you peel open the
papery husks to expose the orange
fruit, they are even brighter.

Ginger Cheesecake

Chocolate has a natural affinity with spices. Vanilla seeds and bay leaves in this recipe add an enticing flavour.

20 mins plus 3 hrs chilling

10 mins

SERVES 6–8

INGREDIENTS

175 g/6 oz gingernut biscuits

sunflower oil, for oiling

55 g/2 oz butter, unsalted for preference

400 g/14 oz good-quality continental plain chocolate

55 g/2 oz icing sugar

2 tbsp maple syrup or golden syrup

3 bay leaves

seeds from 1 vanilla pod, soaked in 4 tsp milk or dark rum

200 g/7 oz cream cheese

125 ml/4 fl oz double cream, whipped

70 g/2½ oz crystallized ginger pieces, sliced thinly, plus extra to decorate

TO SERVE

whipped cream

cocoa powder

1 To make the base, crush the gingernut biscuits in a food processor, or place them in a polythene bag, loosely seal the end and pound with a rolling pin to reduce them to crumbs. Oil a 20-cm/8-inch loose-bottomed cake tin, line the base with greaseproof paper and oil again.

2 Melt the butter, stir in the crushed biscuits, then press the mixture over the base of the tin. Refrigerate to set while you make the filling.

3 Break the chocolate into pieces and place in a large heatproof bowl set over a saucepan of gently simmering water. Add the icing sugar, syrup, bay leaves, vanilla seeds and their soaking liquid and stir until the chocolate has melted and the mixture is smooth and glossy. Remove from the heat and leave to cool, stirring occasionally. Remove and discard the bay leaves.

4 Beat in the cream cheese, then fold in the lightly whipped cream and the crystallized ginger. Pour into the saucepan, cover with clingfilm and return to the refrigerator for about 3 hours. When it is firm, carefully remove the cheesecake from the tin.

5 Decorate the cheesecake with slices of ginger and serve with cream, dusted with cocoa.

COOK'S TIP

To remove the vanilla seeds, slit the bean lengthwise and run the tip of a teaspoon or knife point down the length. You can use ¼ teaspoon vanilla extract instead of the soaked seeds for convenience, though the flavour will be less intense. You still need to add the milk or rum.

Marble Cheesecake

A dark and white chocolate cheesecake filling is marbled together to give an attractive finish to this rich and decadent dessert.

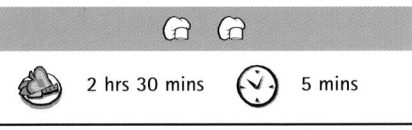

🕒 2 hrs 30 mins ⏱ 5 mins

SERVES 10

I N G R E D I E N T S

BASE

225 g/8 oz toasted oat cereal

75 g/2¾ oz toasted hazelnuts, chopped

4 tbsp butter

25 g/1 oz plain chocolate

FILLING

350 g/12 oz cream cheese

100 g/3½ oz caster sugar

200 ml/7 fl oz natural yogurt

300 ml/10 fl oz double cream

7 g/¼ oz powdered gelatine

3 tbsp water

175 g/6 oz plain chocolate, melted

175 g/6 oz white chocolate, melted

1 Place the toasted oat cereal in a polythene bag and crush with a rolling pin. Pour the crushed cereal into a mixing bowl and stir in the hazelnuts.

2 Melt the butter and chocolate together over low heat and stir into the cereal mixture, stirring until well coated.

3 Using the bottom of a glass, press the cereal mixture into the base and up the sides of a 20-cm/8-inch springform tin.

4 Beat together the cheese and sugar with a wooden spoon until smooth. Beat in the yogurt. Whip the cream until just holding its shape and fold into the mixture. Sprinkle the gelatine over the water in a heatproof bowl and leave until spongy. Place over a saucepan of hot water and stir until dissolved. Stir into the mixture.

5 Divide the mixture in half and beat the plain chocolate into one half and the white chocolate into the other half.

6 Place alternate spoonfuls of filling on the cereal base. Swirl the filling together with the tip of a knife to give a marbled effect. Decorate the top using a serrated scraper. Leave to chill for at least 2 hours, until set, before serving.

Strawberry Cheesecake

Sweet strawberries are teamed with creamy mascarpone cheese and luxurious white chocolate to make this mouthwatering cheesecake.

3 hrs   1 hr 30 mins

SERVES 8

INGREDIENTS

BASE

55 g/2 oz butter, unsalted for preference

200 g/7 oz crushed digestive biscuits

85 g/3 oz chopped walnuts

FILLING

450 g/1 lb mascarpone cheese

2 eggs, beaten

3 tbsp caster sugar

250 g/9 oz white chocolate, broken into pieces

300 g/10½ oz strawberries, hulled and quartered

TOPPING

175 g/6 oz mascarpone cheese

chocolate caraque (see page 9)

16 whole strawberries

1 Melt the butter over low heat and stir in the crushed biscuits and the nuts. Spoon the mixture into a 23-cm/9-inch springform cake tin and press evenly over the base with the back of a spoon. Set aside.

2 Preheat the oven to 150°C/300°F/Gas Mark 2. To make the filling, beat the cheese until smooth, then beat in the eggs and sugar. Put the chocolate in a heatproof bowl set over a saucepan of gently simmering water. Stir over low heat until melted and smooth. Remove from the heat and cool slightly, then stir into the cheese mixture. Finally, stir in the strawberries.

3 Spoon the mixture into the cake tin, spread out evenly and smooth the surface. Bake in the preheated oven for 1 hour, until the filling is just firm. Turn off the oven and leave the cheesecake to cool inside with the door slightly ajar until completely cold.

4 Transfer the cheesecake to a serving plate and spread the mascarpone on top. Decorate with chocolate caraque and whole strawberries.

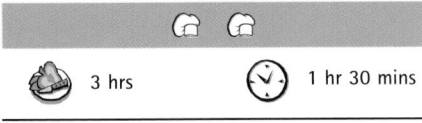

Berry Cheesecake

Use a mixture of berries, such as blueberries, blackberries, raspberries and strawberries, for a really fruity cheesecake.

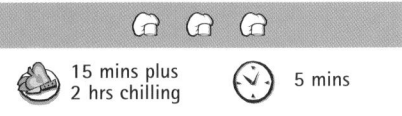

15 mins plus
2 hrs chilling

5 mins

SERVES 8

I N G R E D I E N T S

BASE

85 g/3 oz margarine

175 g/6 oz oatmeal biscuits

70 g/2½ oz desiccated coconut

TOPPING

1½ tsp powdered gelatine

150 ml/5 fl oz cold water

125 ml/4 fl oz evaporated milk

1 egg

6 tbsp soft light brown sugar

450 g/1 lb soft cream cheese

350 g/12 oz mixed berries

2 tbsp honey

1 Melt the margarine in a saucepan. Put the biscuits into a food processor and process until crushed, or crush finely with a rolling pin. Stir the crumbs into the margarine with the coconut.

2 Press the mixture evenly into a base-lined 20-cm/ 8-inch springform cake tin and set aside to chill in the refrigerator.

3 To make the topping, sprinkle the gelatine over the water in a heatproof bowl and leave until spongy. Place over a saucepan of hot water and stir until dissolved. Set aside to cool slightly.

4 Beat the milk with the egg, sugar and cream cheese until smooth. Stir in 55 g/2 oz of the berries. Add the gelatine in a thin stream, stirring constantly.

5 Spoon the mixture on to the biscuit base and return to the refrigerator to chill for 2 hours, or until set.

6 Remove the cheesecake from the tin and transfer to a serving plate. Arrange the remaining berries on top of the cheesecake and drizzle the honey over the top. Serve.

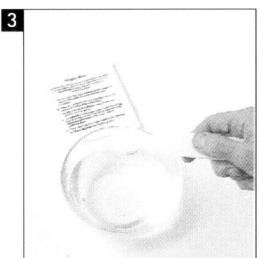

Lime Cheesecakes

These cheesecakes are flavoured with lime and mint, and set on a base of crushed digestive biscuits mixed with dark chocolate.

30 mins plus
2 hrs 30 mins
chilling

5 mins

SERVES 2

INGREDIENTS

BASE

2 tbsp butter, plus extra for greasing

25 g/1 oz continental plain chocolate

175 g/6 oz crushed digestive biscuits

FILLING

finely grated rind of 1 lime

75 g/2¾ oz sieved cottage cheese

75 g/2¾ oz low-fat cream cheese

1 fresh mint sprig, chopped very finely (optional)

1 tsp gelatine

1 tbsp lime juice

1 egg yolk

3 tbsp caster sugar

TO DECORATE

whipped cream

kiwi fruit slices

fresh mint sprigs

1 Grease 2 fluted, loose-bottomed 12-cm/4½-inch flan tins thoroughly. To make the base, melt the butter and chocolate in a heatproof bowl set over a saucepan of gently simmering water. Stir until smooth.

2 Stir the crushed biscuits evenly through the melted chocolate and then press into the bases of the flan tins, smoothing the surface. Chill until set.

3 Put the lime rind and cheeses into a bowl and beat until smooth and blended, then beat in the mint (if using).

4 Dissolve the gelatine in the lime juice in a heatproof bowl set over a saucepan of gently simmering water.

5 Beat the egg yolk and sugar together until creamy and fold into the cheese mixture, followed by the dissolved gelatine. Pour over the base and chill until set.

6 To serve, remove the cheesecakes carefully from the flan tins. Decorate with whipped cream, slices of kiwi fruit and mint sprigs.

Marbled Chocolate Cheesecake

Cheesecake is always a popular dessert, and this one, with marbled swirls of plain and white chocolate, is no exception.

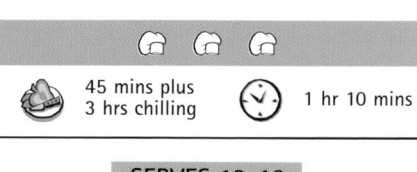

45 mins plus 3 hrs chilling

1 hr 10 mins

SERVES 10-12

INGREDIENTS

BASE

vegetable oil, for oiling

225 g/8 oz plain chocolate digestive biscuits

85 g/3 oz butter

FILLING

700 g/1 lb 9 oz cream cheese

175 g/6 oz golden caster sugar

3 tbsp plain flour

2 tsp vanilla essence

3 eggs, beaten

115 g/4 oz plain chocolate

115 g/4 oz white chocolate

1 Line the base of a 23-cm/9-inch springform cake tin with foil and brush the sides of the tin with oil. Place the biscuits in a polythene bag and crush with a rolling pin. Place the butter in a saucepan and heat gently until just melted. Stir in the crushed biscuits. Press into the base of the tin. Chill for 1 hour.

2 Preheat the oven to 160°C/325°F/Gas Mark 3. To make the filling, put the cream cheese in a bowl and beat until fluffy, then add the sugar, flour and vanilla essence and beat until smooth. Gradually add the eggs, beating until well blended. Place half the mixture in another bowl. Put the plain chocolate and white chocolate in 2 separate heatproof bowls set over 2 saucepans of gently simmering water until melted and leave to cool. Stir the plain chocolate into one bowl of cream cheese mixture and the white chocolate into the other.

3 Spoon the 2 mixtures alternately over the chilled biscuit base, then swirl with a knife to give a marbled effect. Bake in the oven for 50 minutes–1 hour, until set. Leave the cheesecake in the oven with the door slightly ajar, until cold. Run a knife round the inside of the tin to loosen the cheesecake. Chill for 2 hours before removing from the tin to serve.

COOK'S TIP
Leaving the cheesecake in the oven to cool helps to prevent it cracking.

Manhattan Cheesecake

This is a classic baked cheesecake. The combination of juicy blueberries and baked cheese is sure to impress your guests at a dinner party.

🐻 🐻 🐻

🍮 1 hr plus
8 hrs chilling

🕐 35 mins

SERVES 8-10

I N G R E D I E N T S

B A S E
vegetable oil, for brushing

85 g/3 oz butter

200 g/7 oz digestive biscuits, crushed

F I L L I N G
400 g/14 oz cream cheese

2 large eggs

140 g/5 oz caster sugar

1½ tsp vanilla essence

450 ml/16 fl oz soured cream

T O P P I N G
55 g/2 oz caster sugar

250 g/9 oz fresh blueberries

1 tsp arrowroot

1 Preheat the oven to 190°C/375°F/Gas Mark 5. Lightly brush a 20-cm/8-inch springform cake tin with oil. To make the base, melt the butter in a saucepan and stir in the crushed biscuits. Place in the tin and spread evenly over the base. To make the filling, put the cream cheese, eggs, 100 g/3½ oz of the sugar and ½ teaspoon

of the vanilla essence in a food processor and process until smooth. Pour over the biscuit base and smooth the top. Place the cheesecake on a rimmed baking sheet and bake in the oven for 20 minutes, until just set. Remove from the oven, leaving it turned on, and set aside for 20 minutes.

2 Put the soured cream, remaining sugar and vanilla essence in a bowl and mix together. Spoon over the cheesecake and return to the oven for 10 minutes. Remove from the oven and leave to cool. Chill overnight. To make the topping, put the sugar in a saucepan with 2 tablespoons of water and heat gently until the sugar has

dissolved. Increase the heat and add the blueberries. Cover and cook for a few minutes until they start to soften. Remove from the heat.

3 Put the arrowroot and 2 tablespoons of water in a small bowl and blend together. Add to the blueberries and stir until smooth. Return to low heat and cook until the juice thickens and turns translucent. Set aside to cool. One hour before serving, remove the cheesecake from the tin and place on a serving plate. Spoon the blueberries on top and return the cheesecake to the refrigerator until ready to serve.

VARIATION
As an alternative to blueberries, other fruit such as raspberries, blackcurrants or cranberries may be used in the topping.

Almond Cheesecakes

These creamy cheese desserts are so delicious that it's hard to believe that they are low in fat – a healthy and flavourful option.

15 mins plus 1 hr chilling

10 mins

SERVES 4

I N G R E D I E N T S

12 amaretti biscuits, crushed

1 egg white, beaten lightly

225 ml/8 fl oz skimmed milk cream cheese

½ tsp almond essence

½ tsp finely grated lime rind

50 g/1¾ oz ground almonds

2 tbsp caster sugar

55 g/2 oz sultanas

2 tsp powdered gelatine

2 tbsp cold water

2 tbsp lime juice

T O   D E C O R A T E

2 tbsp flaked almonds, toasted

strips of lime rind

1 Preheat the oven to 180°C/350°F/Gas Mark 4. Place the amaretti crumbs in a bowl and stir in the egg white to bind them together.

2 Put 4 non-stick cooking rings or poached egg rings, 9 cm/3½ inches across, on a baking sheet.

3 Divide the amaretti mixture into 4 equal portions and spoon it into the rings, pressing it down well. Bake in the preheated oven for about 10 minutes, until crisp. Remove from the oven and leave to cool in the rings.

4 Put the cream cheese, almond essence, lime rind, ground almonds, sugar and sultanas in a bowl and beat thoroughly until well mixed.

5 Sprinkle the gelatine over the water in a heatproof bowl and leave until spongy. Place over a saucepan of hot water and stir until dissolved, then stir in the lime juice. Fold into the cheese mixture and spoon over the amaretti bases. Smooth over the tops and chill for 1 hour, or until set.

6 Loosen the cheesecakes from the rings using a small palette knife and transfer to serving plates. Decorate with flaked almonds and strips of lime rind and serve.

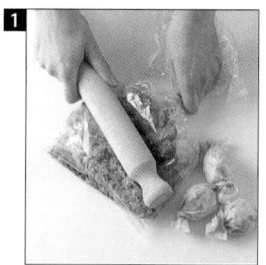

Ricotta Lemon Cheesecake

Italian bakers pride themselves on their baked ricotta cheesecakes, studded with fruit soaked in spirits.

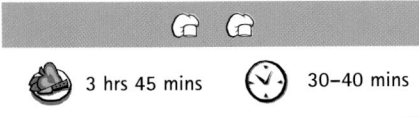

3 hrs 45 mins   30–40 mins

SERVES 6–8

INGREDIENTS

60 g/2½ oz sultanas

3 tbsp Marsala or grappa

butter, for greasing

2 tbsp semolina, plus extra for dusting

350 g/12 oz ricotta cheese, drained

3 large egg yolks, beaten

100 g/3½ oz caster sugar

3 tbsp lemon juice

2 tbsp candied orange peel, chopped finely

finely grated rind of 2 large lemons

TO DECORATE

icing sugar

fresh mint sprigs

redcurrants or berries (optional)

1 Soak the sultanas in the Marsala or grappa in a small bowl for about 30 minutes, or until the liquid has been absorbed and the fruit is swollen.

2 Preheat the oven to 180°C/350°F/Gas Mark 4. Cut out a circle of baking paper to fit the base of a loose-bottomed 20-cm/8-inch round cake tin that is about 5 cm/2 inches deep. Grease the sides and base of the tin and line the base. Lightly dust with semolina and tip out the excess.

3 Using a wooden spoon, press the ricotta cheese though a nylon sieve into a bowl. Beat in the egg yolks, sugar, semolina and lemon juice and continue beating until blended.

4 Fold in the sultanas, orange peel and lemon rind. Pour into the prepared tin and smooth the surface.

5 Bake the cheesecake in the centre of the preheated oven for 30–40 minutes, until firm to the touch and coming away slightly from the side of the tin.

6 Turn off the oven and open the door. Leave the cheesecake to cool in the turned-off oven for 2–3 hours. To serve, remove from the tin and transfer to a plate. Sift over a layer of icing sugar from at least 30 cm/12 inches above the cheesecake to dust the top and sides lightly. Decorate with mint leaves and redcurrants, if wished.

Mascarpone Cheesecake

The mascarpone gives this baked cheesecake a wonderfully tangy flavour. Ricotta cheese could be used as an alternative.

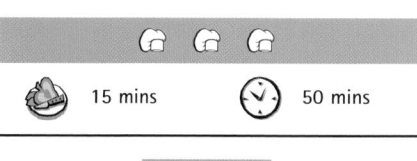

15 mins   50 mins

SERVES 8

INGREDIENTS

4 tbsp butter, unsalted for preference, plus extra for greasing

350 g/12 oz gingernut biscuit crumbs

1 tbsp chopped stem ginger

500 g/1 lb 2 oz mascarpone cheese

finely grated rind and juice of 2 lemons

100 g/3½ oz caster sugar

2 large eggs, separated

fruit coulis (see Cook's Tip), to serve

1 Preheat the oven to 180°C/350°F/Gas Mark 4. Grease and line the base of a 25-cm/10-inch springform cake tin or loose-bottomed cake tin.

2 Melt the butter in a saucepan and stir in the biscuit crumbs and chopped ginger. Use the mixture to line the tin, pressing the mixture about 5 mm/¼ inch up the sides.

3 Beat together the cheese, lemon rind and juice, sugar and egg yolks until quite smooth.

4 Whisk the egg whites until they are stiff and fold into the cheese and lemon mixture.

5 Pour the mixture into the tin and bake in the preheated oven for 35–45 minutes, until just set. Don't worry if it cracks or sinks – this is quite normal.

6 Leave the cheesecake in the tin to cool. Serve with fruit coulis (see Cook's Tip).

COOK'S TIP
Fruit coulis can be made by cooking 225 g/8 oz fruit, such as blueberries, for 5 minutes with 2 tablespoons of water. Sieve the mixture, then stir in 1 tablespoon (or more, to taste) of sifted icing sugar. Leave to cool before serving.

Pineapple Cheesecake

A delicious summer dessert, this cheesecake will have your guests coming back for another serving.

20 mins plus
4 hrs chilling

0 mins

SERVES 4

I N G R E D I E N T S

4 tbsp butter, melted, plus extra
   for greasing

115 g/4 oz digestive biscuits, crushed finely

100 g/3½ oz caster sugar

juice of 1 lemon

2 tbsp grated lemon rind

350 g/12 oz cream cheese

350 g/12 oz curd cheese

150 ml/5 fl oz double cream, whipped

400 g/14 oz canned pineapple slices,
   drained

pinch of ground nutmeg, to decorate
   (optional)

1 Grease a 20-c/8-inch loose-bottomed flan tin with butter, put the crushed biscuits in a large bowl and mix in the melted butter, then press the biscuit mixture evenly over the base.

2 Put the sugar into a separate bowl and stir in the lemon juice and half of the lemon rind. Add the cheeses and beat until thoroughly combined. Fold in the cream. Spread the cream mixture evenly over the biscuit layer. Cover with clingfilm and leave to chill in the refrigerator for at least 4 hours.

3 Remove the cheesecake from the refrigerator, turn out on to a serving platter and arrange the pineapple slices over the top. Sprinkle over a little ground nutmeg (if using). Serve immediately.

Banana Coconut Cheesecake

The exotic combination of banana and coconut goes well with chocolate.
Fresh coconut gives a better flavour than dried coconut.

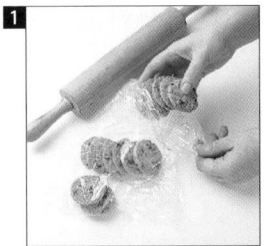

30 mins plus
2 hrs chilling   5 mins

SERVES 10

INGREDIENTS

225 g/8 oz chocolate chip cookies

4 tbsp butter

350 g/12 oz medium-fat cream cheese

60 g/2¼ oz caster sugar

50 g/1¾ oz grated fresh coconut

2 tbsp coconut-flavoured liqueur

2 ripe bananas

125 g/4½ oz plain chocolate

7 g/¼ oz powdered gelatine

3 tbsp water

150 ml/5 fl oz double cream

TO DECORATE

1 banana

lemon juice

a little plain chocolate, melted

1 Place the cookies in a polythene bag and crush with a rolling pin. Pour into a mixing bowl. Melt the butter and stir into the cookie crumbs until well coated. Firmly press the biscuit mixture into the base and up the sides of a 20-cm/8-inch springform cake tin.

2 Beat together the cream cheese and caster sugar until well combined, then beat in the grated coconut and coconut-flavoured liqueur. Mash the 2 bananas and beat them in. Melt the plain chocolate and beat in until well combined.

3 Sprinkle the gelatine over the water in a heatproof bowl and leave until spongy. Place over a saucepan of gently simmering water and stir until dissolved. Stir into the chocolate mixture. Whisk the cream until just holding its shape and stir into the chocolate mixture. Spoon over the biscuit base and leave to chill for 2 hours, until set.

4 To serve, carefully transfer to a serving plate. Slice the banana, toss in the lemon juice and arrange around the edge of the cheesecake. Drizzle with melted plain chocolate and leave to set.

COOK'S TIP
To crack the coconut, pierce 2 of the 'eyes' and drain off the liquid. Tap hard around the centre with a hammer until it cracks and lever it apart.

Hot Desserts

If you like hot desserts, you will be spoiled for choice in

this section. Light or filling, the range of exciting recipes

will bring family meals or formal gatherings to

a contented close. There are favourites such as

steamed desserts or creamy rice puddings, with

exotic twists and tempting

flavourings to stimulate your taste

buds. Fusions of East and West cuisine

come together to create unusual warm

salads and grilled fruit kebabs, hot fudgy chocolate sauces

and wobbly soufflés. Whatever you choose, you can be

sure your guests will be back for more.

Chocolate Rum Bananas

A simple and quick dessert, ideal to prepare when unexpected guests drop in. Sprinkle with ground cinnamon, if preferred.

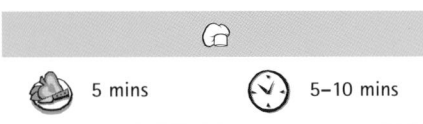

5 mins   5–10 mins

SERVES 4

I N G R E D I E N T S

1 tbsp butter, melted

225 g/8 oz plain chocolate

4 large bananas

2 tbsp dark rum

grated nutmeg, to decorate

crème fraîche (see page 9), mascarpone cheese or ice cream, to serve

1 Take 4 x 25-cm/10-inch squares of foil and brush them with butter.

2 Cut the chocolate into very small pieces. Make a careful slit lengthways in the peel of each banana, and open just wide enough to insert the chocolate. Place the chocolate pieces inside the bananas, along their lengths, then close them up.

3 Wrap each stuffed banana in a square of foil, then grill them over hot coals for about 5–10 minutes, until the chocolate has melted inside the bananas. Remove from the grill, place the bananas on individual serving plates and pour some rum into each banana. Serve at once with crème fraîche, mascarpone cheese or ice cream, topped with a little grated nutmeg.

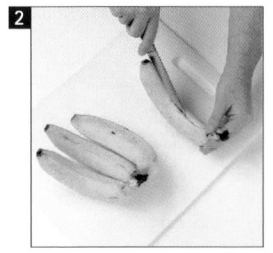

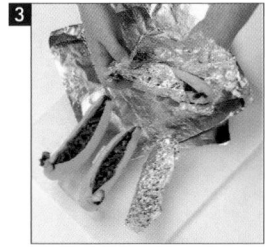

Coconut Bananas

This elaborate dessert is the perfect finale for a Chinese banquet.
Bananas are fried in a citrus-flavoured butter and served with coconut.

10 mins

10 mins

SERVES 4

INGREDIENTS

3 tbsp grated fresh coconut

55 g/2 oz butter, unsalted for preference

1 tbsp grated fresh ginger root

grated rind of 1 orange

60 g/2¼ oz caster sugar

4 tbsp fresh lime juice

6 bananas

6 tbsp orange-flavoured liqueur, such as
  Cointreau or Grand Marnier

3 tsp toasted sesame seeds

lime slices, to decorate

ice cream, to serve (optional)

1 Heat a small non-stick frying pan until hot. Add the coconut and cook, stirring constantly, for 1 minute until lightly coloured. Remove from the pan and let cool.

2 Melt the butter in a large frying pan and add the ginger, orange rind, sugar and lime juice. Mix well.

3 Peel and slice the bananas lengthways (and cut in half if they are very large). Place the bananas cut-side down in the butter mixture and cook for 1–2 minutes, or until the sauce mixture starts to become sticky. Turn the bananas to coat in the sauce.

4 Remove the bananas and place on heated serving plates. Keep warm.

5 Return the frying pan to the heat and add the orange liqueur, blending well. Ignite with a taper, let the flames die down, then pour over the bananas.

6 Sprinkle with the reserved coconut and sesame seeds and serve at once, decorated with slices of lime.

COOK'S TIP
For a very special treat
try serving this with a
flavoured ice cream such as
coconut, ginger or praline.

Barbecued Bananas

This is a very simple dessert to serve at the end of a summer barbecue. Open the parcels carefully as they will be very hot.

5 mins

10 mins

SERVES 4

INGREDIENTS

4 bananas

50 g/1¾ oz chocolate chips

12 mini marshmallows

whipped cream, to serve

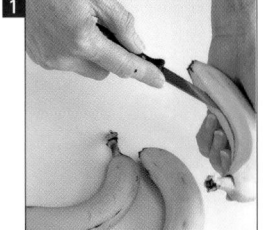

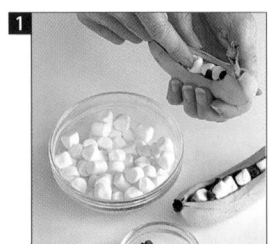

1 With a sharp knife, slit the banana skins and cut almost through the bananas. Push chocolate chips and marshmallow into the slits and wrap the bananas in foil.

2 Place the foil parcels on the barbecue and cook for 10 minutes, turning after 5 minutes.

3 Open up the parcels and serve the bananas with cream.

VARIATION
The bananas can also be baked in an oven at 220°C/425°F, Gas Mark 8 for 15–20 minutes.

Char-Cooked Pineapple

Fresh pineapple slices are cooked on the barbecue and brushed with a buttery fresh ginger and brown sugar baste. Serve immediately.

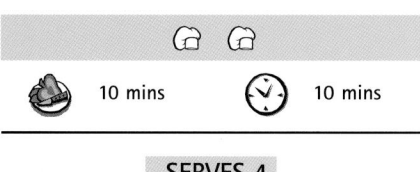

🐻 🐻

🍍 10 mins   🕐 10 mins

SERVES 4

INGREDIENTS

1 pineapple

GINGER BUTTER BASTE

125 g/4½ oz butter

85 g/3 oz light muscovado sugar

1 tsp finely grated fresh root ginger

TOPPING

225 g/8 oz mascarpone cheese

½ tsp ground cinnamon

1 tbsp light muscovado sugar

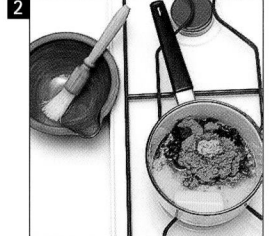

1 Prepare the pineapple by cutting off the spiky top. Peel the pineapple with a sharp knife, remove the 'eyes' and cut the flesh into thick slices.

2 To make the ginger-flavoured butter, put the butter, sugar and ginger into a small saucepan and heat gently until melted. Transfer to a heatproof bowl and keep warm at the side of the barbecue, ready for basting the fruit.

3 To prepare the topping, mix together the mascarpone cheese, cinnamon and sugar. Cover and chill until ready to serve.

4 Barbecue the pineapple slices for about 2 minutes on each side, brushing them well with the ginger butter baste.

5 Serve the char-cooked pineapple with a little extra ginger butter baste poured over. Top with a spoonful of the spiced mascarpone cheese.

VARIATION
If you prefer, substitute ½ teaspoon ground ginger for the grated root ginger. Light muscovado sugar gives the best flavour, but you can use ordinary brown sugar instead. You can make this dessert indoors by cooking the pineapple under a hot grill.

Chargrilled Fruit

Fruit is the obvious choice for a low-fat dessert, but it can be rather unexciting. Liven it up with a flavourful glaze and serve hot.

10 mins | 10 mins

SERVES 4

INGREDIENTS

4 fresh pineapple rings

4 slices mango

4 kiwi fruit, peeled and sliced

4 slices papaya

2 nectarines, peeled, stoned and halved

2 bananas, peeled and halved

6 tbsp honey

grated rind of 1 orange

grated rind of 1 lemon

2.5-cm/1-inch piece fresh root ginger, grated

1 Prepare the fruit. Combine the honey, orange and lemon rind and ginger in a small bowl. Brush the mixture over all the fruit.

2 Cook under a preheated grill for about 10 minutes, brushing with the glaze and turning frequently.

3 Divide the fruit between individual serving plates and serve immediately.

COOK'S TIP

Use a single flower honey, if possible. Try clover, acacia, orange blossom or lavender.

Grilled Fruit with Lime Butter

This delicious variation of a hot fruit salad includes wedges of tropical fruits, dusted with dark brown sugar and a pinch of spice before grilling.

15 mins plus 30 mins resting   10 mins

SERVES 4

INGREDIENTS

1 baby pineapple

1 ripe papaya

1 ripe mango

2 kiwi fruit

4 finger bananas

4 tbsp dark rum

1 tsp mixed spice

2 tbsp lime juice

4 tbsp dark muscovado sugar

LIME 'BUTTER'

55 g/2 oz low-fat spread

½ tsp finely grated lime rind

1 tbsp icing sugar

1 Quarter the pineapple, trimming away most of the leaves, and place in a shallow dish. Peel the papaya, cut it in half and scoop out the seeds. Cut the flesh into thick wedges and place in the same dish as the pineapple.

2 Peel the mango, cut either side of the smooth, central flat stone and remove the stone. Slice the flesh into thick wedges. Peel the kiwi fruit and cut in half. Peel the bananas. Add the fruit to the dish.

3 Sprinkle over the rum, mixed spice and lime juice, cover and leave at room temperature for 30 minutes, turning occasionally, to allow the flavours to develop.

4 Meanwhile, make the butter. Place the low-fat spread in a small bowl and beat in the lime rind and sugar until well mixed. Leave to chill until required.

5 Preheat the grill to hot. Drain the fruit, reserving the juices, and arrange in the grill pan. Sprinkle with the sugar and grill for 3–4 minutes, until hot, bubbling and starting to char.

6 Transfer the fruit to a serving plate and spoon over the juices. Serve with the lime butter.

VARIATION

Serve with a light sauce of 300 ml/10 fl oz tropical fruit juice thickened with 2 tsp arrowroot.

Barbecued Apples

Easy to prepare and delicious to eat, these apples will be enjoyed by both adults and children.

10 mins   10 mins

SERVES 4

INGREDIENTS

4 eating apples

3 tbsp lemon juice

3 tbsp butter

4 tsp soft light brown sugar

8 tbsp mincemeat

plain yogurt, crème fraîche (see page 9) or mascarpone cheese, to serve

1 Wash the apples, then cut them in half from top to bottom. Remove the cores and pips, then brush the cut sides of the apples with lemon juice to prevent discoloration.

2 Put the butter in a small saucepan and gently melt it over low heat. Remove from the heat, then brush the cut sides of the apples with half of the butter. Reserve the rest of the melted butter.

3 Sprinkle the apples with sugar, then transfer them to the barbecue, cut-side down, and cook over hot coals for about 5 minutes. Brush the apples with the remaining butter, then turn them over. Add 1 tablespoon of mincemeat to the centre of each apple, then cook for an additional 5 minutes, or until they are cooked to your taste.

4 Remove from the heat and transfer to serving plates. Serve at once with plain yogurt, crème fraîche or mascarpone cheese.

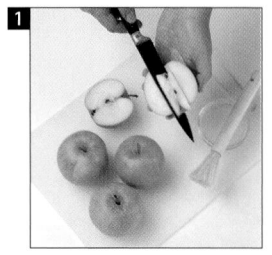
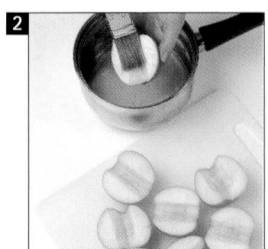

Barbecued Baked Apples

When they are wrapped in foil, apples bake to perfection on the barbecue and make a delightful finale to any meal.

🍎 15 mins 🕐 25–30 mins

SERVES 4

INGREDIENTS

4 medium cooking apples

4 tbsp chopped walnuts

4 tbsp ground almonds

2 tbsp molasses sugar

25 g/1 oz cherries, chopped

2 tbsp chopped stem ginger

1 tbsp Amaretto (optional)

2 tbsp butter

single cream or thick natural yogurt,
    to serve

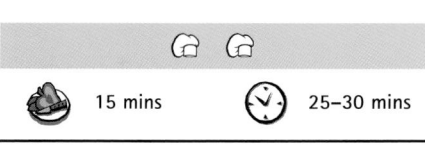

1 Core the apples and using a knife, score each around the centre to prevent the skins from splitting while they are grilling.

2 To make the filling, combine the walnuts, almonds, sugar, cherries, ginger and Amaretto (if using) in a small bowl.

3 Spoon the filling mixture into each apple, pushing it down into the hollowed-out core. Mound a little of the filling mixture on top of each apple.

4 Place each apple on a large square of double-thickness foil and generously dot all over with the butter. Wrap up the foil so that the apple is completely enclosed.

5 Barbecue the foil packages over hot coals for 25–30 minutes, or until the apples are tender.

6 Transfer the apples to warm, individual serving plates. Serve immediately with lashings of single cream or thick natural yogurt.

COOK'S TIP

If the coals are dying down, place the foil packages directly on them, raking them up around the apples. Barbecue for 25–30 minutes and serve with the cream or yogurt.

Baked Apples with Berries

This winter dessert is a classic dish. Large, fluffy apples are hollowed out and filled with spices, almonds and blackberries.

10 mins   55 mins

SERVES 4

INGREDIENTS

4 medium cooking apples

1 tbsp lemon juice

70 g/2½ oz blackberries, thawed if frozen

55 g/2 oz flaked almonds

½ tsp mixed spice

½ tsp finely grated lemon rind

2 tbsp raw brown sugar

300 ml/10 fl oz ruby port

1 cinnamon stick, broken

2 tsp cornflour blended with 2 tbsp cold water

low-fat custard, to serve

1 Preheat the oven to 200°C/400°F/Gas Mark 6. Wash and dry the apples. Using a small sharp knife, make a shallow cut through the skin around the centre of each apple – this will help the apples to cook through.

2 Core the apples, brush the centres with the lemon juice to prevent them browning and stand them in an ovenproof dish.

3 In a bowl, mix together the blackberries, almonds, mixed spice, lemon rind and sugar. Using a teaspoon, spoon the mixture into the centre of each apple.

4 Pour the port into the dish, add the cinnamon stick and bake the apples in the preheated oven for 35–40 minutes, or until tender and soft.

5 Drain the cooking juices into a saucepan and keep the apples warm.

6 Discard the cinnamon stick and add the cornflour mixture to the cooking juices. Cook over medium heat, stirring constantly, until thickened.

7 Heat the custard until piping hot. Pour the sauce over the apples and serve with the custard.

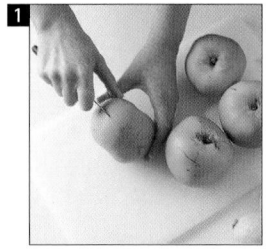
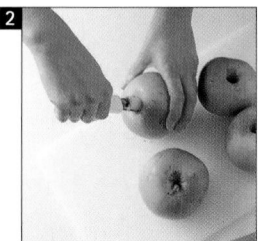

Stuffed Baked Apples

Baked apples are a family favourite, often stuffed with sultanas and brown sugar. Try this ginger-flavoured flapjack stuffing for a change.

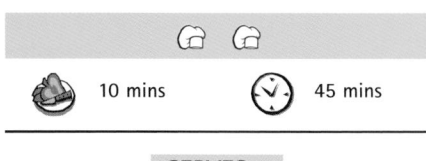

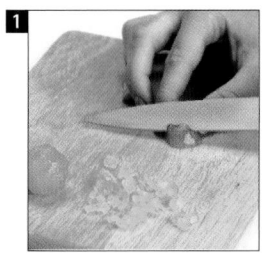

⏲ 10 mins   🕐 45 mins

SERVES 4

INGREDIENTS

1 tbsp honey

1 tbsp syrup from the stem ginger jar (see below)

4 tbsp rolled oats

75 g/2¾ oz ready-to-eat dried apricots

40 g/1½ oz blanched almonds

1 piece stem ginger, drained

4 large cooking apples

1 Preheat the oven to 180°C/350°F/Gas Mark 4. Finely chop the apricots, almonds and ginger. Put the honey and syrup in a saucepan and heat gently until the honey has melted. Stir in the oats and cook over low heat for 2 minutes. Remove the saucepan from the heat and stir in the apricots, almonds and stem ginger.

2 Core the apples, widen the tops slightly and score around the circumference of each to prevent the skins bursting during cooking. Place them in an ovenproof dish and fill the cavities with the stuffing. Pour in just enough water to come about one-third of the way up the apples.

3 Bake in the preheated oven for 40 minutes, or until tender. Serve immediately.

VARIATION
Omit the stem ginger and ginger syrup. Use 2 tablespoons of honey, substitute chopped walnuts for the almonds and add ½ teaspoon of ground cinnamon to the stuffing.

Coconut Apples

A barbecue variation on baked apples, but instead of being filled with dried fruit, they are layered with jam and desiccated coconut.

10 mins   **15–20 mins**

SERVES 4

INGREDIENTS

2 tsp butter, unsalted for preference

4 tbsp ginger and apple jam

150g/5½ oz desiccated coconut

pinch of ground cinnamon

4 cooking apples

double cream or ice cream, to serve (optional)

1 Cut 4 squares of foil, each large enough to enclose 1 apple, and lightly grease with the butter. Combine the jam and coconut in a small bowl and stir in cinnamon to taste.

2 Core the apples, but don't peel them. Cut each apple horizontally into 3 slices. Spread the mixture between the apple slices and reassemble the apples. Place 1 apple on each sheet of foil and fold up the sides to enclose securely.

3 Cook the apples on a hot barbecue for 15–20 minutes. Serve immediately, with cream or ice cream, if you like.

VARIATION
Substitute large, firm pears for the apples.

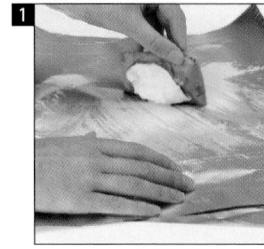

Summer Fruit Nectarines

These easily prepared nectarines taste as good as they look and will soon become a favourite for the barbecue.

5 mins

10–15 mins

SERVES 4

I N G R E D I E N T S

4 large nectarines

115 g/4 oz frozen summer fruit, such as blueberries and raspberries, thawed

3 tbsp lemon juice

3 tbsp honey

crème fraîche (see page 9), mascarpone cheese or ice cream, to serve

1 Cut out 8 x 18-cm/7-inch squares of foil. Wash the nectarines, cut them in half and remove the stones. Place each nectarine half on a square of foil.

2 Fill each nectarine half with summer fruit, then top each one with 1 teaspoon of lemon juice, then 1 teaspoon of honey.

3 Close the foil around each nectarine half to make a parcel, then barbecue them over hot coals for about 10–15 minutes, according to your taste. Remove the parcels from the barbecue, place the nectarines on serving plates and serve at once with crème fraîche, mascarpone cheese or ice cream.

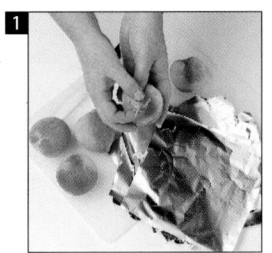

Stuffed Nectarines

This delectable combination of juicy fruit, crunchy amaretti biscuits and dark chocolate is an irresistible summer treat.

15 mins

40–45 mins

SERVES 6

INGREDIENTS

85 g/3 oz continental plain chocolate, chopped finely

115 g/4 oz amaretti biscuit crumbs

1 tsp finely grated lemon rind

1 large egg, separated

6 tbsp Amaretto

6 nectarines, halved and stoned

300 ml/10 fl oz white wine

55 g/2 oz milk chocolate, grated

whipped cream or ice cream, to serve

1 Preheat the oven to 190°C/375°F/Gas Mark 5. In a large bowl, mix together the chocolate, amaretti crumbs and lemon rind. Lightly beat the egg white and add it to the mixture with half the Amaretto. (Use the yolk in another recipe.) Using a small sharp knife, slightly enlarge the cavities in the nectarines. Add the removed nectarine flesh to the chocolate and crumb mixture and mix together well.

2 Place the nectarines, cut-side up, in an ovenproof dish just large enough to hold them in a single layer. Pile the chocolate and crumb mixture into the cavities, dividing it equally between them. Mix the wine and remaining Amaretto together and pour it into the dish around the nectarines. Bake in the preheated oven for 40–45 minutes, until the nectarines are tender. Transfer 2 nectarine halves to each individual serving plate and spoon over a little of the cooking juices. Sprinkle over the grated milk chocolate and serve immediately with a spoonful of whipped cream or ice cream.

Baked Bananas

The orange-flavoured cream can be prepared in advance, but do not make up the banana parcels until just before you need to cook them.

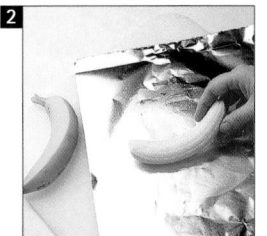
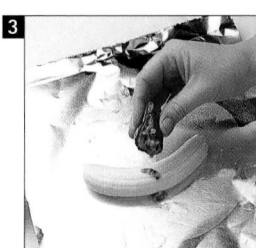

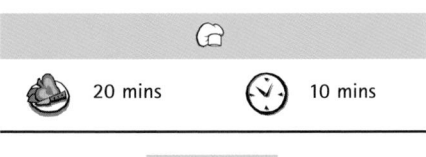

20 mins   10 mins

SERVES 4

INGREDIENTS

4 bananas

2 passion fruit

4 tbsp orange juice

4 tbsp orange-flavoured liqueur

ORANGE-FLAVOURED CREAM

150 ml/5 fl oz double cream

3 tbsp icing sugar

2 tbsp orange-flavoured liqueur

1 Preheat the oven to 180°C/350°F/Gas Mark 4. To make the orange-flavoured cream, pour the double cream into a mixing bowl and sprinkle with the icing sugar. Whisk the mixture until it is standing in soft peaks. Carefully fold in the orange-flavoured liqueur and chill in the refrigerator until required.

2 Peel the bananas and place each on a sheet of foil.

3 Cut the passion fruit in half and squeeze the juice of each half over each banana. Spoon over the orange juice and liqueur.

4 Fold the foil over the top of the bananas so that they are completely enclosed.

5 Place the parcels on a baking sheet and bake the bananas in the oven for about 10 minutes, or until they are just tender (test by inserting a cocktail stick).

6 Transfer the foil parcels to warm, individual serving plates. Open out the foil parcels at the table and then serve immediately with the chilled orange-flavoured cream.

VARIATION
Try using different-flavoured liqueurs, such as coconut liqueur, to make the cream. The results can be both delicious and exotic.

Fried Bananas

This wonderfully sticky dessert of bananas deep-fried in sesame batter will bring out the child in every member of the family.

🍳 10 mins   🕙 10 mins

SERVES 4

INGREDIENTS

125 g/4½ oz plain flour

½ tsp bicarbonate of soda

salt

2 tbsp sugar

1 egg

1 tbsp sesame seeds

4 bananas

peanut or sunflower oil, for deep-frying

2 tbsp honey, to serve

1 Sift the flour into a bowl with the bicarbonate of soda and a pinch of salt. Stir in the sugar, then whisk in the egg and 4–6 tablespoons of water to make a smooth, thin batter. Whisk in the sesame seeds.

2 Peel the bananas and halve lengthways, then cut in half across the centres. Dip the bananas in the batter to coat completely.

3 Meanwhile, heat the oil in a wok or deep, heavy-based frying pan to 180-190°C/350-375°F, or until a cube of bread browns in 30 seconds. Deep-fry the bananas, in batches, until golden brown. Remove with a slotted spoon and drain on kitchen paper. Transfer to plates and drizzle with the honey before serving.

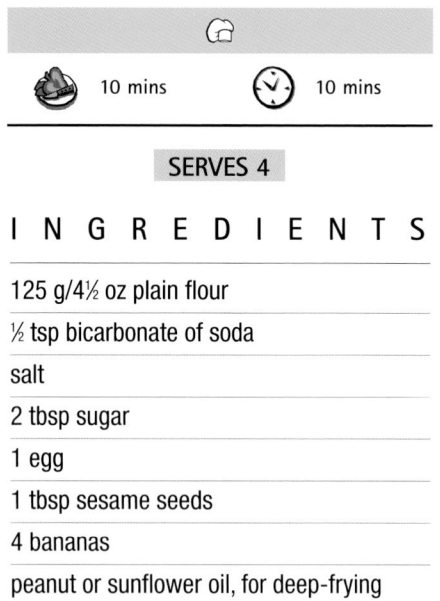

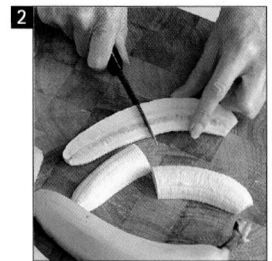

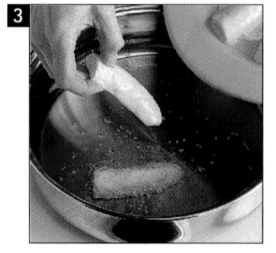

VARIATION
Fresh pineapple rings are also delicious prepared in this way.

Banana Sizzles

Bananas are particularly sweet and delicious when barbecued – and conveniently come with their own protective wrapping.

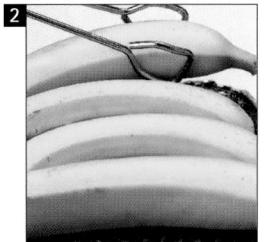
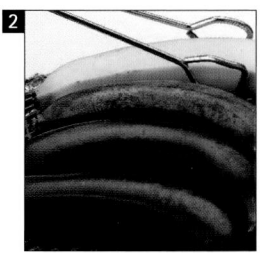

10 mins   6–8 mins

SERVES 4

I N G R E D I E N T S

3 tbsp butter, softened

2 tbsp dark rum

1 tbsp orange juice

4 tbsp dark muscovado sugar

pinch of ground cinnamon

4 bananas

1 Beat the butter with the rum, orange juice, sugar and cinnamon in a small bowl until thoroughly combined and smooth.

2 Place the bananas, without peeling, on a hot barbecue and cook, turning frequently, for 6–8 minutes, until the skins are blackened.

3 Transfer the bananas to serving plates, slit the skins and cut partially through the flesh lengthways. Divide the flavoured butter between the bananas and serve.

VARIATION
You can also cook the bananas wrapped in foil. Cut them in half lengthways without peeling. Spread the flavoured butter of the cut surfaces and reassemble the bananas. Wrap in foil parcels and cook on a medium barbecue for 5–10 minutes.

Battered Bananas

These bananas are quite irresistible, therefore it may be wise to make double quantities for weak-willed guests!

10 mins   20 mins

SERVES 4

INGREDIENTS

8 medium bananas

2 tsp lemon juice

40 g/1½ oz self-raising flour

40 g/1½ oz rice flour

1 tbsp cornflour

½ tsp ground cinnamon

1 cup water

oil, for deep-frying

4 tbsp soft light brown sugar

cream or ice cream, to serve

1 Cut the bananas into even-sized chunks and place them in a large mixing bowl.

2 Sprinkle the lemon juice over the bananas to prevent discoloration.

3 Sift the self-raising flour, rice flour, cornflour and cinnamon into a mixing bowl. Gradually stir in the water to make a thin batter.

4 Heat the oil in a preheated wok until smoking, then reduce the heat slightly.

5 Place a piece of banana on the end of a fork and carefully dip it into the batter, draining off any excess. Repeat with the remaining banana pieces.

6 Sprinkle the brown sugar on to a large plate.

7 Carefully place the banana pieces in the oil and cook for 2–3 minutes, until golden. Remove the banana pieces from the oil with a slotted spoon and roll them in the sugar.

8 Transfer the battered bananas to serving bowls and serve immediately with cream or ice cream.

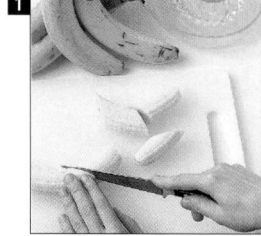

COOK'S TIP

Rice flour can be bought from wholefood stores or from Chinese supermarkets.

Peaches & Mascarpone

If you prepare these peaches in advance, all you have to do is pop them on the barbecue when you are ready to serve them.

🍳 10 mins   🕐 10 mins

SERVES 4

I N G R E D I E N T S

4 peaches

175 g/6 oz mascarpone cheese

75 g/2¾ oz pecan nuts or walnuts, chopped

1 tsp sunflower oil

4 tbsp maple syrup

1 Cut the peaches in half and remove the stones. If you are preparing this recipe in advance, press the peach halves together again and wrap them in clingfilm until required.

2 Combine the mascarpone cheese and pecan nuts or walnuts in a small bowl. Chill in the refrigerator until required.

3 Brush the peaches with a little oil and place on a rack set over medium-hot coals. Barbecue for 5–10 minutes, turning once, until hot.

4 Transfer the peaches to a serving dish and top with the mascarpone cheese mixture.

5 Drizzle the maple syrup over the peaches and mascarpone filling and serve immediately.

VARIATION

You can use nectarines instead of peaches for this recipe. Choose ripe but firm fruit which won't go soft and mushy when barbecued. Prepare the nectarines in the same way as the peaches and barbecue for 5–10 minutes.

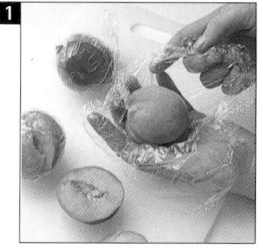

Piña Colada Pineapple

The flavours of pineapple and coconut blend as well together on the barbecue as they do in the well-known cocktail.

15 mins

25 mins

SERVES 4

INGREDIENTS

1 small pineapple

2 tbsp butter, unsalted for preference

2 tbsp molasses sugar

50 g/1¾ oz grated coconut

2 tbsp coconut-flavoured liqueur or dark rum

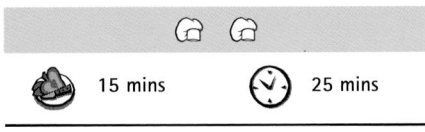

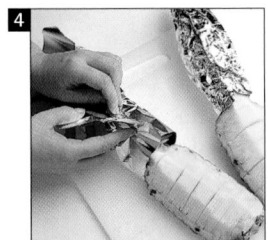

1 Using a very sharp knife, cut the pineapple into quarters and then remove the tough core from the centre, leaving the leaves attached.

2 Carefully cut the pineapple flesh away from the skin. Remove any 'eyes' with a small sharp knife. Make horizontal cuts across the flesh of the pineapple quarters.

3 Place the butter in a saucepan and heat gently until melted, stirring constantly. Brush the melted butter over the pineapple and sprinkle with the sugar.

4 Cover the pineapple leaves with foil in order to prevent them burning and transfer the pineapple quarters to a rack set over hot coals.

COOK'S TIP
Fresh coconut has the best flavour for this dish. If you prefer, however, you can use desiccated coconut.

5 Barbecue the pineapple for about 10 minutes.

6 Sprinkle the coconut over the pineapple and barbecue, cut-side up, for an additional 5–10 minutes, or until the pineapple is piping hot.

7 Transfer the pineapple to serving plates and remove the foil from the leaves. Spoon a little coconut-flavoured liqueur or rum over the pineapple and serve immediately.

Flambéed Peaches

A fabulous end to a dinner party, this is a luxurious but, at the same time, refreshing dessert.

🍰 5 mins   🕐 5 mins

SERVES 4

INGREDIENTS

3 tbsp butter, unsalted for preference

3 tbsp light muscovado sugar

4 tbsp orange juice

4 peaches, peeled, halved and stoned

2 tbsp Amaretto or peach brandy

4 tbsp flaked almonds, toasted

1 Heat the butter, sugar and orange juice in a large, heavy-based frying pan until the butter has melted and the sugar has dissolved.

2 Add the peach halves and cook for 1–2 minutes on each side until turning golden.

3 Add the Amaretto or peach brandy and leave time for it to become warm before igniting with a match or taper. When the flames have died down, transfer to a plate, sprinkle with the flaked almonds and serve.

VARIATION

Igniting the spirit burns off the alcohol and mellows the flavour. However, if you are serving this dessert to children, you can omit the Amaretto or brandy.

Poached Mixed Spice Pears

These pears are moist and delicious from being poached in an orange juice, sugar and mixed spice mixture.

5 mins   15 mins

SERVES 4

INGREDIENTS

4 large ripe pears

300 ml/10 fl oz orange juice

2 tsp mixed spice

75 g/2¾ oz raisins

2 tbsp soft light brown sugar

grated orange rind, to decorate

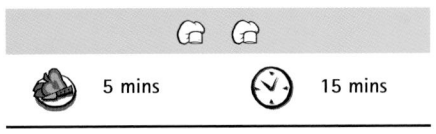
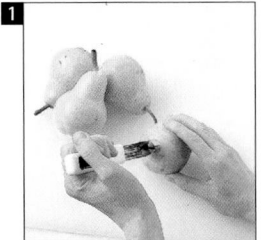

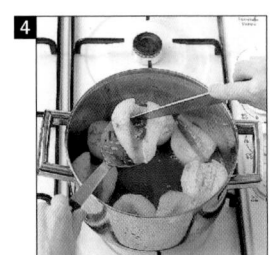

1 Using an apple corer, core the pears. Using a sharp knife, peel the pears and cut them in half.

2 Place the pear halves in a large saucepan.

3 Add the orange juice, mixed spice, raisins and sugar to the saucepan and heat gently, stirring, until the sugar has dissolved. Bring the mixture to the boil for 1 minute.

4 Reduce the heat to low and leave to simmer for about 10 minutes, or until the pears are cooked, but still fairly firm – test them by inserting the tip of a sharp knife.

COOK'S TIP

This dessert is refreshing at the end of a big meal. It can also be served cold.

5 Remove the pears from the saucepan with a slotted spoon and transfer to individual serving plates. Decorate and serve hot with the syrup.

Spiced Baked Pears

This simple, well-flavoured dessert is delightful hot, but can also be prepared in advance and served cold.

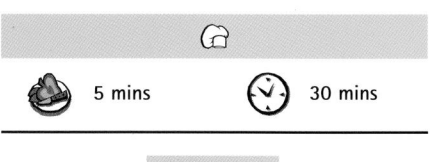

5 mins   30 mins

SERVES 4

I N G R E D I E N T S

4 large firm pears

150 ml/5 fl oz apple juice

1 cinnamon stick

4 cloves

1 bay leaf

1 Preheat the oven to 180°C/350°F/ Gas Mark 4.

2 Peel and core the pears and cut them into quarters. Place in an ovenproof dish and add the remaining ingredients.

3 Cover the dish and bake in the preheated oven for 30 minutes.

4 Serve the pears hot or cold.

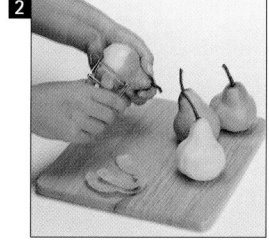

Caramelized Fruit

It is unusual to include strawberries in a chargrilled fruit salad, but they work surprising well. Choose large ripe berries and don't hull them.

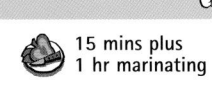

15 mins plus
1 hr marinating

5 mins

SERVES 4

INGREDIENTS

150 ml/5 fl oz medium sherry

115 g/4 oz caster sugar

1 Ogen melon, halved and seeded

4 peaches, halved and stoned

125 g/4½ oz strawberries

1 Combine the sherry and sugar in a large bowl, stirring until the sugar has dissolved.

2 Cut the melon halves into wedges and cut the flesh away from the skin. Peel the peaches (see Cook's Tip). Add the melon wedges, peach halves and strawberries to the bowl, tossing gently to coat. Cover with clingfilm and set aside to marinate for 1 hour.

3 Drain the fruit, reserving the marinade. Cook the melon and peaches on a hot barbecue for 3 minutes, then add the strawberries and cook for an additional 2 minutes. Turn the fruit and brush frequently with the reserved marinade. Serve immediately.

COOK'S TIP

To peel peaches, make a tiny nick in the skin with the point of a sharp knife. Place in a bowl and cover with boiling water. Leave for 15–30 seconds, then remove with a slotted spoon. Peel off the skin.

Pineapple Rings with Brandy

In this recipe, pineapple rings are marinated in a delicious mixture of honey and brandy, then barbecued.

15 mins plus
1 hr–1 hr 15 mins
marinating

10 mins

SERVES 4

INGREDIENTS

1 pineapple

MARINADE

2 tbsp honey

3 tbsp brandy

2 tsp lemon juice

fresh mint sprigs, to decorate

  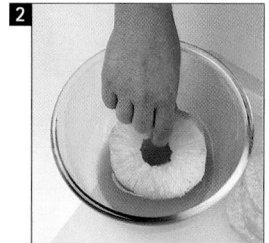

1 Peel and core the pineapple and cut into rings. For the marinade, put the honey, brandy and lemon juice into a large, non-metallic (glass or ceramic) bowl, which will not react with acid. Stir together until well combined. Put the pineapple rings into the bowl and turn them in the mixture until thoroughly coated. Cover with clingfilm, transfer to the refrigerator and leave to marinate for 1–1½ hours.

2 When the pineapple rings are thoroughly marinated, lift them out and barbecue them over hot coals for about 10 minutes, turning them frequently and basting with more marinade if necessary.

3 Remove the pineapple rings from the barbecue, arrange them on individual serving plates and decorate with fresh mint sprigs.

Totally Tropical Pineapple

The delicious aroma of fresh pineapple and dark rum as the succulent dessert is cooking will transport your imagination to a Caribbean beach.

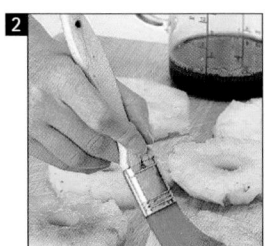

15 mins   6–8 mins

SERVES 4

INGREDIENTS

1 pineapple

3 tbsp dark rum

2 tbsp light muscovado sugar

1 tsp ground ginger

4 tbsp melted butter, unsalted for preference

1 Using a sharp knife, cut off the crown of the pineapple, then cut the fruit into 2-cm/¾-inch thick slices. Cut away the peel from each slice and flick out the 'eyes' with the point of the knife. Stamp out the cores with an apple corer or small biscuit cutter.

2 Combine the rum, sugar, ginger and butter in a jug, stirring until the sugar has dissolved. Brush the pineapple rings with the mixture.

3 Cook the pineapple rings on a hot barbecue for 3–4 minutes on each side. Serve immediately with the remaining rum mixture poured over them.

VARIATION
If you prefer, you can cut the pineapple into cubes or quarter slices and thread on metal skewers before brushing with the rum mixture and cooking.

Glazed Pineapple Slices

Pineapple slices brushed with melted butter and honey, then cooked in a griddle pan – simple but delicious. Cook on a grill, if preferred.

5 mins

5 mins

SERVES 4

INGREDIENTS

1 pineapple

85 g/3 oz honey

115 g/4 oz butter, melted

mint leaves, to decorate

SERVING SUGGESTIONS

fruit sorbet

crème fraîche (see page 9)

whipped cream

ice cream

1 Peel and core the pineapple. Cut into thick slices, about 2.5 cm/1 inch wide.

2 Preheat the griddle pan over medium heat. Meanwhile, heat the honey in a small saucepan over medium heat, until it is liquid.

3 Brush both sides of the pineapple slices with the melted butter. Place in the griddle pan and cook for 2 minutes on each side, brushing with honey before and after turning so that both sides are well coated and sticky.

4 Remove the hot pineapple slices from the griddle pan. Decorate with mint leaves and serve with a scoop of fruit sorbet, crème fraîche, whipped cream or ice cream.

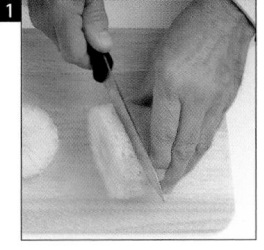

Caribbean Pineapple

Complement fresh pineapple with a fabulous dark rum and raisin chocolate sauce for a simple but special dessert.

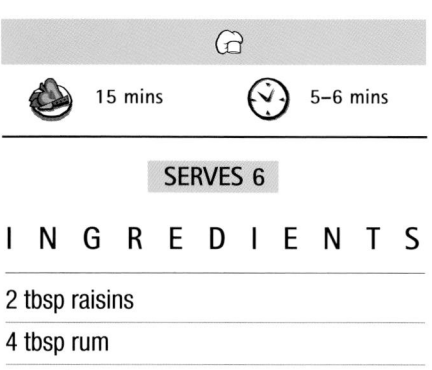

15 mins

5–6 mins

SERVES 6

INGREDIENTS

2 tbsp raisins

4 tbsp rum

175 g/6 oz good-quality plain chocolate

1 fresh pineapple

4 tbsp unsalted butter

6 tbsp golden syrup

fresh mint sprigs, to decorate

1 Place the raisins in a heatproof bowl and add the rum. Set aside to soak and plump up. Break up the chocolate into fairly small pieces.

2 Meanwhile, cut off the leafy top and the base of the pineapple. Stand the pineapple up and slice off the skin. Remove any remaining eyes with a small, sharp knife. Cut the pineapple in half lengthways and cut out the hard, woody core, then slice the flesh.

3 Arrange the pineapple slices on a baking sheet in a single layer and dot with half the butter. Cook under a preheated grill for 5–6 minutes, until just beginning to brown.

4 Meanwhile, make the sauce. Add the syrup and the remaining butter to the raisins and set the bowl over a saucepan of gently simmering water. Stir until the syrup has melted, then add the chocolate. Continue to stir until the chocolate has melted.

5 Divide the grilled pineapple between warm serving plates, spoon over the chocolate sauce, decorate with mint sprigs and serve immediately.

VARIATION
This would also work well with other fruit, such as halved nectarines, wedges of fresh mango, or peeled bananas halved lengthwise.

Fruit Parcels with Maple Syrup

Slices of juicy fruit are coated in a rich maple syrup sauce as they cook in little parcels on the barbecue.

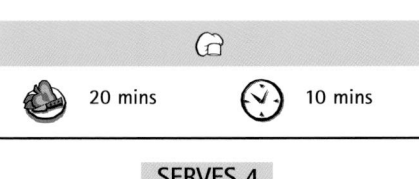
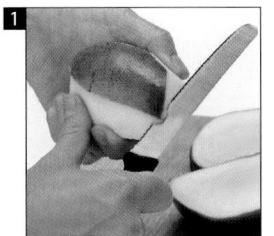

20 mins   10 mins

SERVES 4

INGREDIENTS

1 mango

1 papaya

2 bananas

2 peaches, peeled and stoned

1 Ogen melon, halved and seeded

115 g/4 oz butter, unsalted for preference, cut into pieces

4 tbsp maple syrup

pinch of ground mixed spice

1 Peel, stone and slice the mango. Halve and seed the papaya, cut into thick slices and peel off the skin. Cut out 4 large squares of foil. Peel the bananas and cut in half lengthways. Slice the peach halves. Cut the melon halves into thin wedges, then cut the flesh away from the rind. Divide the fruit between the foil squares.

2 Put the butter and maple syrup in a food processor and process until thoroughly combined and smooth. Divide the flavoured butter between the fruit parcels and sprinkle with a little mixed spice. Fold up the sides of the foil to enclose the fruit securely.

3 Cook on a medium barbecue, turning occasionally, for 10 minutes. Serve immediately.

COOK'S TIP
Look for 'pure' or '100 per cent' maple syrup. Cheaper varieties may be blended with other types of syrup.

Mexican Glazed Pumpkin

This simple dessert looks and smells wonderful and makes an unusual and tasty finale to a meal. Serve with soured cream or natural yogurt.

20 mins   10 mins

SERVES 4

INGREDIENTS

900 g/2 lb pumpkin

425 g/15 oz light muscovado sugar

1 tsp ground mixed spice

225 ml/8 fl oz water

1 Cut the pumpkin into wedges and scrape out the seeds with a spoon. Arrange the wedges in a large, flameproof casserole.

2 Combine the sugar and mixed spice in a bowl, then spoon it into the spaces between the wedges. Add the water, pouring it down the side of the casserole so that it doesn't wash away the sugar.

3 Cover and cook over low heat for 20 minutes, until the pumpkin is tender. Transfer the wedges to a serving dish and pour the sugary glaze over them. Serve immediately.

COOK'S TIP
Keep an eye on the water level while the pumpkin is cooking and top up with more hot water, if necessary.

Crunchy Ginger Apples

The flavour of ginger complements apples very well and this dessert can be quickly assembled. Serve warm with a little whipped or ice cream.

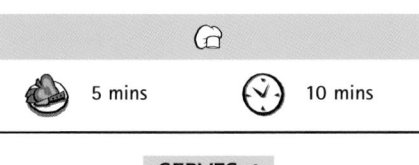

5 mins   10 mins

SERVES 4

INGREDIENTS

4 eating apples

2 tbsp lemon juice

2 tbsp butter, melted

2 tbsp raw brown sugar

4 tbsp diced stem ginger

mint leaves, to decorate

SERVING SUGGESTIONS

crème fraîche (see page 9)

whipped cream

ice cream

1 Cut the apples in half through their circumference. Carefully remove the pips and core.

2 Place the lemon juice, butter and raw sugar in 3 separate small dishes. Dip the cut side of the apples first in the lemon juice, then in the melted butter and, finally, in the sugar.

3 Preheat a griddle pan over medium heat. Add the apples, cut-side down, and cook for 5 minutes, or until the sugar caramelizes and the apple surfaces are dark. Turn and cook for an additional 5 minutes to blacken the skin. The cooked apples should still retain their crunch.

4 Arrange the apple halves in individual dishes (allowing 2 halves per serving), cut-side up, and spoon diced ginger over each half. Decorate with mint leaves and serve with a bowl of crème fraîche, whipped cream or ice cream.

Pears with Chocolate Custard

Whole pears baked in a red wine and mixed spice syrup and served with a chocolate custard sauce – wonderful!

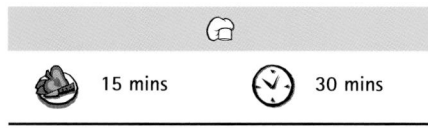

15 mins | 30 mins

SERVES 4

INGREDIENTS

4 ripe pears

1 tbsp lime juice

2 tbsp red wine

55 g/2 oz butter

4 tbsp light brown sugar

1 tsp ground mixed spice

CHOCOLATE CUSTARD

450 ml/16 fl oz milk

4 egg yolks

100 g/3½ oz caster sugar

2 tbsp grated plain chocolate

thin strips of lime rind, to decorate

1 Preheat the oven to 200°C/400°F/Gas Mark 6. Peel and core the pears, leaving them whole, then brush with lime juice. Put the pears into a small, non-stick baking tin, then pour over the wine.

2 Heat the butter, sugar and mixed spice in a small saucepan over low heat, stirring, until melted. Pour the mixture over the pears. Bake in the oven, basting occasionally, for 25 minutes, or until golden and cooked through.

3 Heat the milk until very hot. Beat the egg yolks while slowly adding the sugar until the mixture is pale and thick. Gradually add the milk, stirring constantly. Return the mixture to the saucepan and cook over medium heat, stirring constantly, until it is thickened. Add the chocolate and stir until melted.

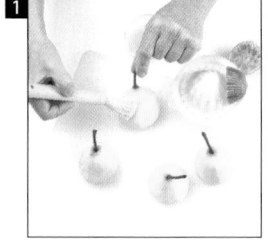

4 Divide the custard between serving dishes. Remove the pears from the oven and put a pear in the centre of each pool of custard. Decorate with strips of lime rind and serve.

Spun Sugar Pears

Whole pears are poached in a Madeira syrup in the microwave, then served with a delicate spun sugar surround.

🔔 20 mins   🕐 35 mins

SERVES 4

INGREDIENTS

150 ml/5 fl oz water

150 ml/5 fl oz Madeira

115 g/4 oz caster sugar

2 tbsp lime juice

4 ripe pears, peeled, stalks left on

fresh mint sprigs, to decorate

SPUN SUGAR

115 g/4 oz caster sugar

3 tbsp water

1 Combine the water, Madeira, sugar and lime juice in a large bowl. Cover and cook on Full Power for 3 minutes. Stir well until the sugar dissolves.

2 Peel the pears and cut a thin slice from the base of each, so that they stand upright.

3 Add the pears to the bowl, spooning the wine syrup over them. Cover and cook on Full Power for about 10 minutes, turning the pears over every few minutes, until they are tender. The cooking time may vary slightly depending on the ripeness of the pears. Set aside to cool, covered, in the syrup.

4 Remove the cooled pears from the syrup and set aside on serving plates. Cook the syrup, uncovered, on Full Power for about 15 minutes, until reduced by half and thickened slightly. Set aside for 5 minutes. Spoon the syrup over the pears.

5 To make the spun sugar, combine the sugar and water in a bowl. Cook, uncovered, on Full Power for 1½ minutes. Stir until the sugar has dissolved completely. Continue to cook on Full Power for about 5–6 minutes, or until the sugar has caramelized.

6 Wait for the bubbles to subside and set aside for 2 minutes. Dip a teaspoon in the caramel and spin the caramelized sugar around each pear in a circular motion. Serve decorated with mint.

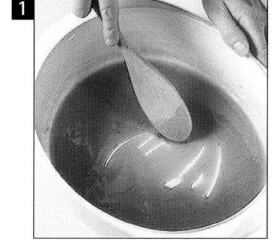

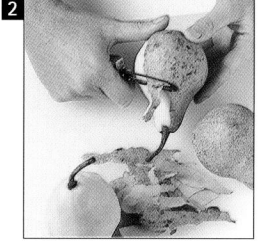

Baked Pears with Cinnamon

This simple, healthy recipe is easy to prepare and cook, but is deliciously warming. For a treat, serve hot on a pool of low-fat custard.

10 mins   25 mins

SERVES 4

INGREDIENTS

4 ripe pears

2 tbsp lemon juice

4 tbsp molasses

1 tsp ground cinnamon

4 tbsp low-fat spread

finely shredded lemon rind, to decorate

low-fat custard, to serve

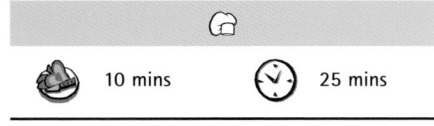

1 Preheat the oven to 200°C/ 400°F/Gas Mark 6. Core and peel the pears, then slice them in half lengthways and brush them all over with the lemon juice to prevent them discolouring. Place the pears, cored side down, in a small non-stick roasting tin.

2 Place the sugar, cinnamon and low-fat spread in a small saucepan and heat gently, stirring constantly, until the sugar has dissolved. Keep the heat very low to stop too much water evaporating from the low-fat spread as it gets hot. Spoon the mixture over the pears.

VARIATION
For alternative flavours, replace the cinnamon with ground ginger and serve the pears sprinkled with chopped stem ginger in syrup. Alternatively, use ground allspice and spoon over some warmed dark rum to serve.

3 Bake the pears in the preheated oven for 20–25 minutes, or until they are tender and golden, occasionally spooning the sugar mixture over the fruit during the cooking time.

4 To serve, heat the low-fat custard in a small saucepan over a low heat until it is piping hot and spoon a little over the surface of each of 4 warm dessert plates. Then arrange 2 pear halves on each plate.

5 Decorate the pears with a little finely shredded lemon rind and serve immediately.

Stuffed Pears

It has long been a popular practice to sprinkle strawberries with pepper to bring out their flavour. This is equally effective with pears.

20 mins

20 mins

SERVES 4

INGREDIENTS

2 tsp unsalted butter

4 firm pears

2 tbsp lemon juice

4 tbsp rosehip syrup

1 tsp green peppercorns, crushed lightly

140 g/5 oz redcurrants

4 tbsp caster sugar

ice cream, to serve

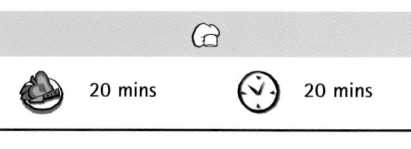

1 Cut 4 squares of foil, each large enough to enclose the pears, and grease with the butter. Halve and core the pears but do not peel. Brush the cut surfaces with lemon juice. Place 2 pear halves on each of the foil squares, brush them with the rosehip syrup and sprinkle with the pepper.

2 Put the redcurrants in a bowl and sprinkle with the sugar. Spoon the redcurrant mixture into the cavities of the pears. Fold up the sides of the foil to enclose the pears securely.

3 Cook on a hot barbecue for 20 minutes. Serve with ice cream.

VARIATION
Substitute your own favourites, such as blackcurrants or blueberries, for the redcurrants.

Stuffed Pears with Mincemeat

Pears quickly go soft and lose their shape when they are cooked, so choose fruit with good firm flesh for this recipe.

20 mins

25–30 mins

SERVES 4

INGREDIENTS

4 firm pears

1 tsp lemon juice

2 tbsp mincemeat

5 tbsp cake crumbs or 4 amaretti biscuits, crushed

1 tbsp butter

ice cream, to serve

1 Using a sharp knife, cut the pears in half. Using a teaspoon, scoop out the core and discard.

2 Brush the cut surface of each of the pear halves with a little lemon juice to prevent discolouration.

3 Mix together the mincemeat and cake crumbs, or crushed amaretti biscuits.

4 Divide the mixture between the pear halves, spooning it into a mound where the core has been removed.

5 Place 2 pear halves on a large square of double-thickness foil and generously dot all over with the butter.

6 Wrap up the foil around the pears so that they are completely enclosed.

7 Transfer the foil packets to a rack set over hot coals. Cook for 25–30 minutes, or until the pears are hot and just tender.

8 Transfer the pears to individual serving plates. Serve with 2 scoops of ice cream per serving.

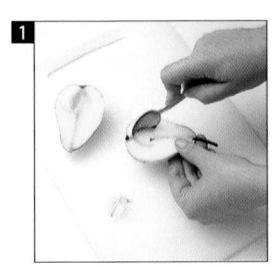

COOK'S TIP
If the coals are dying down, place the foil packets directly on to the coals and barbecue for 25–30 minutes.

Pears with Chocolate Sauce

Pears and chocolate were made for each other, and the partnership is seen at its best in this simple dessert.

20 mins

20 mins

SERVES 4

INGREDIENTS

4 pears

475 ml/16 fl oz water

140 g/5 oz golden caster sugar

10-cm/4-inch piece fresh ginger, peeled and sliced

½ cinnamon stick

squeeze of lemon juice

CHOCOLATE SAUCE

4 tbsp single cream

200 g/7 oz plain chocolate, broken into pieces

1 Peel the pears, leaving the stalks intact. Cut the base of each pear so that it sits flat. Carefully remove as much of the core as possible with a small spoon.

2 Put the water, sugar, ginger, cinnamon stick and lemon juice in a large saucepan. Bring to the boil and boil for 5 minutes. Add the pears and cook, turning occasionally, for about 15-20 minutes until softened. Place each pear on a serving plate.

3 To make the chocolate sauce, put the cream and chocolate in a heatproof bowl set over a saucepan of gently simmering water and heat until the chocolate has melted. Stir until smooth and serve with the warm pears.

COOK'S TIP
Choose pears which are ripe but still firm.

Chocolate Fudge Pears

Melt-in-the-mouth, spicy poached pears are enveloped in a wonderfully self-indulgent chocolate fudge sauce. Serve immediately.

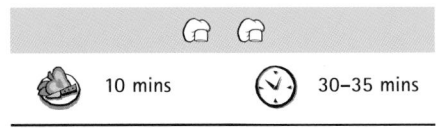

🥄 10 mins   ⏱ 30–35 mins

SERVES 4

INGREDIENTS

4 pears

1–2 tbsp lemon juice

1¼ cups water

5 tbsp caster sugar

5-cm/2-inch piece cinnamon stick

2 cloves

200 ml/7 fl oz double cream

125 ml/4 fl oz milk

170 g/6 oz light brown sugar

2 tbsp unsalted butter, diced

2 tbsp maple syrup

200 g/7 oz plain chocolate, broken
into pieces

1 Peel the pears using a swivel vegetable peeler. Carefully cut out the cores from underneath, but leave the stalks intact because they look more attractive. Brush the pears with the lemon juice to prevent discolouration.

2 Pour the water into a large, heavy-based saucepan and add the caster sugar. Stir over a low heat until the sugar has dissolved. Add the pears, cinnamon and cloves and bring to the boil. (Add a little more water if the pears are not almost covered.) Reduce the heat and simmer for 20 minutes.

3 Meanwhile, pour the cream and milk into another heavy-based saucepan and add the brown sugar, butter and maple syrup. Stir over a low heat until the sugar has dissolved and the butter has melted. Still stirring, bring to the boil and continue to boil, stirring constantly, for 5 minutes, until thick and smooth. Remove the saucepan from the heat and stir in the chocolate, a little at a time, waiting until each batch has melted before adding the next. Set aside.

4 Transfer the pears to individual serving plates using a slotted spoon and keep warm. Bring the poaching syrup back to the boil and cook until reduced. Remove and discard the cinnamon and cloves, then fold the syrup into the chocolate sauce. Pour the sauce over the pears and serve immediately.

Pears with Maple Cream

These spicy cinnamon pears are accompanied by a delicious melt-in-the-mouth maple and ricotta cream – you won't believe it's low in fat!

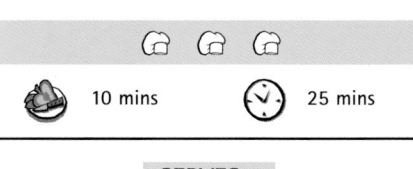

🍮 10 mins   🕐 25 mins

SERVES 4

INGREDIENTS

1 lemon

4 firm pears

300 ml/10 fl oz cider or unsweetened
apple juice

1 cinnamon stick, broken in half

fresh mint leaves to decorate

MAPLE RICOTTA CREAM

125 g/4½ oz low-fat ricotta cheese

125 g/4½ oz low-fat natural fromage frais

½ tsp ground cinnamon

½ tsp grated lemon rind

1 tbsp maple syrup

lemon rind, to decorate

1 Using a vegetable peeler, remove the rind from the lemon and place in a non-stick frying pan. Squeeze the lemon and pour into a shallow bowl.

2 Peel the pears, then halve and core them. Toss them in the lemon juice to prevent discolouration. Place in the frying pan and pour over the remaining lemon juice.

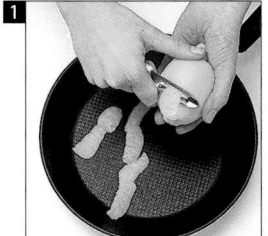

3 Add the cider or apple juice and cinnamon stick halves. Gently bring to the boil, lower the heat so the liquid just simmers and cook the pears for 10 minutes. Remove the pears using a slotted spoon. Reserve the cooking liquid. Place the pears in a warmed heatproof serving dish, cover with foil and put in a warming drawer or low oven.

4 Return the frying pan to the heat, bring to the boil, then simmer for 8–10 minutes until reduced by half. Spoon the mixture over the pears.

5 To make the maple ricotta cream, combine all the ingredients. Decorate the cream with lemon rind, and the pears with mint leaves, and serve together.

COOK'S TIP
Pears ripen quickly and can bruise easily. It's best to buy them just before you plan to cook them.

Pears Poached in Rosé Wine

This elegant dessert can be served hot or cold. The pears can be poached 2 days in advance and stored in their poaching juices in the refrigerator.

10 mins   25 mins

SERVES 6

INGREDIENTS

6 firm ripe pears

100 g/3½ oz caster sugar

2 cinnamon sticks

zest of 1 orange

2 cloves

1 bottle rosé wine

CHOCOLATE SAUCE

175 g/6 oz plain chocolate

250 g/9 oz mascarpone cheese

2 tbsp Cointreau

1 Carefully peel the pears, leaving the stalks intact.

2 Place the sugar, cinnamon sticks, orange zest, cloves and wine in a saucepan that will hold the 6 pears snugly.

3 Heat gently until the sugar has dissolved, then add the pears to the liquid and bring to a simmer. Cover and poach gently for 20 minutes. If serving them cold, let the pears cool in the liquid, then chill until required. If serving hot, leave the pears in the hot liquid while preparing the chocolate sauce.

4 To make the sauce, melt the chocolate. Beat together the mascarpone cheese and the Cointreau. Beat the mascarpone mixture into the chocolate.

5 Remove the pears from the poaching liquid and place each one on a serving plate. Add a generous spoonful of sauce beside each pear and serve the remainder of the sauce separately.

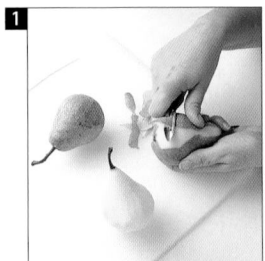

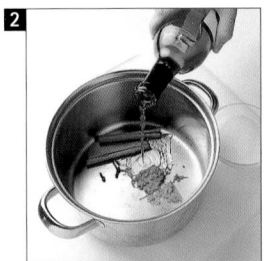

COOK'S TIP

There is no need to waste the poaching liquid. Boil it rapidly in a clean saucepan for about 10 minutes to reduce to a syrup. Use the syrup to sweeten a fresh fruit salad or spoon it over ice cream.

Baked Peaches with Liqueur

Peaches are stuffed with a nut stuffing and baked, then served with a hot honey syrup and a contrasting cold Cointreau cream. Sheer luxury.

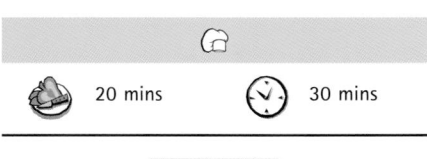

🍧 20 mins   🕐 30 mins

SERVES 4

I N G R E D I E N T S

50 g/1¾ oz shelled pistachio nuts,
    finely chopped

50 g/1¾ oz toasted hazelnuts,
    finely chopped

1 tbsp grated orange rind

1 tbsp light brown sugar

pinch of ground allspice

4 large ripe (but firm) peaches

1 tbsp unsalted butter

H O N E Y   S Y R U P

125 ml/4 fl oz water

1 tbsp honey

2 tsp freshly squeezed orange juice

140 g/5 oz caster sugar

C O I N T R E A U   C R E A M

1 tbsp finely grated orange rind

125 ml/4 fl oz double cream

1 tbsp Cointreau

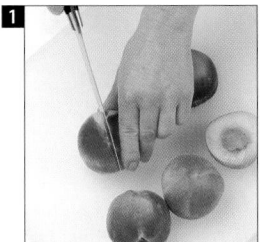

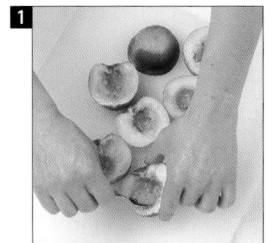

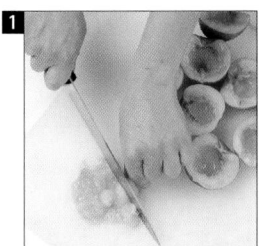

1 Preheat the oven to 180°C/350°F/Gas Mark 4. Put the nuts, orange rind, brown sugar and allspice in a mixing bowl and stir together well. Halve and stone the peaches. Remove a little more of the flesh in the centre of each peach. Chop the flesh and stir into the nut mixture. Transfer the peaches to an ovenproof dish and dot with butter. Bake in the preheated oven for 30 minutes.

2 About halfway through the cooking time, put the water, honey, orange juice and caster sugar into a saucepan and bring to the boil, stirring constantly. Reduce the heat and simmer, without stirring, for about 15 minutes.

3 To make the Cointreau cream, put the orange rind and cream in a bowl and beat together, then stir in the Cointreau. Remove the peaches from the oven and divide between serving dishes. Pour over the honey syrup and serve with the Cointreau cream.

Special Peach Melba

The elegant simplicity of this dessert makes it the perfect end to a special-occasion barbecue party.

15 mins plus
1 hr marinating

3-5 mins

SERVES 4

INGREDIENTS

2 large peaches, peeled, halved and stoned

1 tbsp light brown sugar

1 tbsp Amaretto

1 lb/450 g raspberries

115 g/4 oz icing sugar

600 ml/1 pint vanilla ice cream

1 Put the peach halves in a large shallow dish and sprinkle with the brown sugar. Pour the Amaretto over them, cover with clingfilm and set aside for 1 hour.

2 Meanwhile, using the back of a metal spoon, press the raspberries through a fine sieve set over a bowl. Discard the contents of the sieve. Stir the icing sugar into the raspberry purée. Cover the bowl with clingfilm and chill in the refrigerator until required.

3 Drain the peach halves, reserving the marinade. Cook on a hot barbecue, turning and brushing frequently with the reserved marinade, for 3-5 minutes. To serve, put 2 scoops of ice cream in each of 4 sundae glasses, top with a peach half and spoon the raspberry sauce over it.

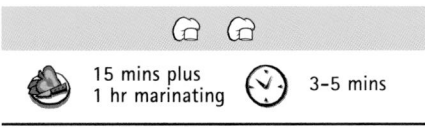

Apples in Red Wine

This simple combination of apples and raspberries cooked in red wine makes a colourful and tempting dessert.

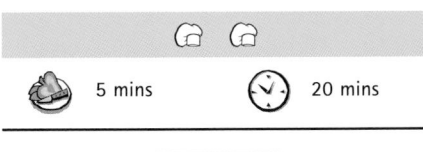

5 mins   20 mins

SERVES 4

INGREDIENTS

4 eating apples

2 tbsp lemon juice

3 tbsp low-fat spread

4 tbsp molasses

1 small orange

1 cinnamon stick, broken

150 ml/5 fl oz red wine

225 g/8 oz raspberries, hulled, defrosted if frozen

fresh mint sprigs, to decorate

1 Peel and core the apples, then cut them into thick wedges. Place the apples in a bowl and toss thoroughly in the lemon juice to prevent the fruit turning brown.

2 In a frying pan, gently melt the low-fat spread over a low heat, add the sugar and stir to form a paste.

3 Stir the apple wedges into the frying pan and cook, stirring, for 2 minutes until well coated in the sugar paste.

4 Using a vegetable peeler, pare off a few strips of orange rind. Add the orange rind to the frying pan with the cinnamon pieces. Squeeze the juice from the orange and pour into the frying pan with the red wine. Bring to the boil, then simmer for 10 minutes, stirring constantly.

5 Add the raspberries and cook for 5 minutes, until the apples are tender.

6 Discard the orange rind and cinnamon pieces. Transfer the apple and raspberry mixture to a serving plate with the wine sauce. Decorate with a sprig of fresh mint and serve hot.

VARIATION

For other fruity combinations, cook the apples with blackberries, blackcurrants, or redcurrants. You may need to add more sugar if you use currants because they are not as sweet as raspberries.

Warm Currants in Cassis

Crème de cassis is a blackcurrant liqueur which comes from France and is an excellent flavouring for fruit dishes.

10 mins   10 mins

SERVES 4

INGREDIENTS

350 g/12 oz blackcurrants

225 g/8 oz redcurrants

4 tbsp caster sugar

grated rind and juice of 1 orange

2 tsp arrowroot

2 tbsp crème de cassis

whipped cream or low-fat yogurt, to serve

1 Using a fork, strip the blackcurrants and redcurrants from their stalks and put in a saucepan.

2 Add the caster sugar and orange rind and juice and heat gently, stirring, until the sugar has dissolved. Bring to the boil and simmer gently for 5 minutes.

3 Strain the currants and place in a bowl, then return the juice to the saucepan.

4 Blend the arrowroot with a little water and mix into the juice in the saucepan. Boil the mixture until thickened.

5 Set aside to cool slightly, then stir in the crème de cassis and pour over the fruit.

6 Serve in individual dishes with whipped cream or yogurt.

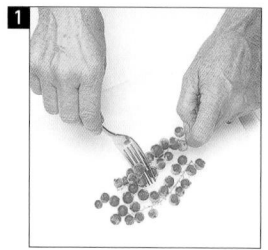

Hot Chocolate Cherries

A gloriously self-indulgent dessert, perfect for rounding off a celebration dinner party.

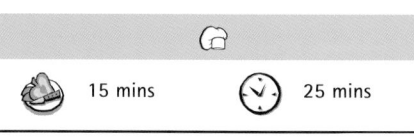

🍨 15 mins   🕐 25 mins

SERVES 4

INGREDIENTS

4 tbsp water

55 g/2 oz caster sugar

1 strip pared lemon rind

450 g/1 lb sweet black cherries, stoned

1 tbsp cocoa powder

salt

4 tbsp double cream

4 tbsp maraschino liqueur or cherry brandy

1 Put the water, sugar and lemon rind into a heavy-based saucepan and bring to the boil over a low heat, stirring constantly until the sugar has dissolved. Add the cherries and cook, stirring constantly, for 1 minute. Remove the saucepan from the heat and, using a slotted spoon, transfer the cherries to a flameproof dish. Reserve the syrup.

2 Preheat the grill to medium. Put the cocoa powder in a bowl and mix in a pinch of salt. Whisking constantly, pour in the cream in a steady stream. Remove and discard the lemon rind from the syrup, then stir in the cream mixture. Return the pan to the heat and bring to the boil, stirring constantly. Simmer over a very low heat, stirring occasionally, for 10–15 minutes, or until reduced by about half.

3 Remove from the heat, stir in the maraschino liqueur or cherry brandy and pour the sauce over the cherries. Place under the preheated grill for 2 minutes, then serve.

VARIATION
Instead of pared lemon rind, flavour the syrup with a split vanilla pod and remove it in step 2, or add ½ teaspoon vanilla essence with the liqueur or brandy in step 3.

Red Fruits with Frothy Sauce

A colourful combination of soft fruits, served with a marshmallow sauce, is an ideal dessert when summer fruits are in season.

15 mins plus 1 hr chilling

20 mins

SERVES 4

INGREDIENTS

225 g/8 oz redcurrants, trimmed, defrosted if frozen

225 g/8 oz cranberries

5 tbsp molasses sugar

200 ml/7 fl oz unsweetened apple juice

1 cinnamon stick, broken

300 g/10½ oz small strawberries, hulled and halved

SAUCE

225 g/8 oz raspberries, defrosted if frozen

2 tbsp red berry fruit cordial

100 g/3½ oz marshmallows

1 Place the redcurrants, cranberries and sugar in a saucepan. Pour in the apple juice and add the cinnamon stick. Bring the mixture to the boil and simmer gently for 10 minutes, until the fruit is soft.

2 Stir the strawberries into the fruit mixture and mix well. Transfer the mixture to a bowl, cover with clingfilm and set aside to chill in the refrigerator for about 1 hour. Remove and discard the cinnamon stick.

3 Just before serving, make the sauce. Put the raspberries and fruit cordial in a small saucepan, bring to the boil and simmer for 2–3 minutes, until the fruit just starts to soften. Stir the marshmallows into the raspberry mixture and heat through, stirring constantly, until the marshmallows start to melt.

4 Transfer the fruit salad to serving bowls. Spoon over the raspberry and marshmallow sauce and serve.

COOK'S TIP

This sauce is delicious poured over low-fat ice cream. For an extra-colourful sauce, replace the raspberries with an assortment of summer berries.

Caramelized Omelettes

This sophisticated dessert looks wonderful and tastes delicious. You will need six small individual tart rings to shape the omelettes.

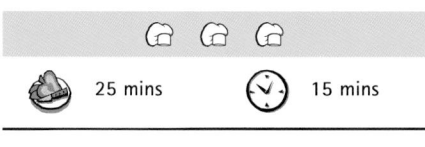

🍧 25 mins 🕐 15 mins

SERVES 6

INGREDIENTS

115 g/4 oz unsalted butter, cut into pieces, plus extra for greasing

100 g/3½ oz caster sugar, plus extra for dusting

115 g/4 oz plain chocolate

2 eggs

6 x 7.5-cm/3-inch round plain biscuits

icing sugar, for dusting

FRUIT COULIS

450 g/1 lb kiwi fruit

300 g/10½ oz caster sugar

TO DECORATE

55 g/2 oz plain chocolate

6 Cape gooseberries

1 To make the decoration, break the chocolate into pieces and melt in a heatproof bowl. Remove from the heat. Peel back the papery coverings of the Cape gooseberries and dip the fruits, 1 at a time, into the melted chocolate to half coat. Leave to set on non-stick baking paper.

2 To make the coulis, halve the kiwi fruit and scoop their contents into a blender using a teaspoon. Add about half the sugar and process to a purée, taste and gradually add more sugar, if necessary, processing again to mix. Push the purée through a metal sieve into a bowl if you want to remove the seeds, or simply scrape into a bowl. Cover and chill in the refrigerator.

3 Preheat the oven to 190°C/375°F/Gas Mark 5. Grease 6 x 7.5-cm/3-inch round small individual tart rings and dust with caster sugar. Arrange the tart rings on a baking sheet.

4 To make the omelettes, break the chocolate into pieces and melt in a heatproof bowl set over a saucepan of gently simmering water. Remove from the heat and leave to cool slightly.

5 Beat the eggs with the sugar in another heatproof bowl set over a saucepan of gently simmering water until thickened and frothy. Remove from the heat. Stir the butter into the warm chocolate, then fold into the eggs.

6 Preheat the grill to medium. Place a biscuit inside each tart ring and top with the egg mixture, filling the ring about two-thirds full. Dredge generously with icing sugar and bake for 6 minutes. Transfer to the preheated grill and cook for a few seconds to caramelize the sugar.

7 To serve, spoon a little of the fruit coulis on to each of 6 serving plates. Run a knife around the inside of each tart ring, remove the rings and carefully transfer the omelettes to the plates. Decorate with the chocolate-dipped Cape gooseberries and serve immediately.

Warm Fruit Compôte

Serve this dish of lightly cooked summer fruits with single cream or vanilla ice cream for a simple and flavourful dessert.

8–10 mins

10 mins

SERVES 4

INGREDIENTS

4 plums, halved and stoned

225 g/8 oz raspberries

225 g/8 oz strawberries, hulled and halved

2 tbsp light muscovado sugar

2 tbsp dry white wine

2 star anise

1 cinnamon stick

4 cloves

1 Put the fruit, sugar, white wine and spices in a large heavy-based saucepan and set over a low heat until the sugar has dissolved.

2 Cover tightly and simmer very gently for about 5 minutes, until the fruit is tender but still retains its shape. Do not allow the mixture to boil.

3 Remove and discard the star anise, cinnamon and cloves and serve the compôte warm.

Thai Bananas

Bananas go well with coconut, as this easy-to-make dessert shows.
Drizzle with maple syrup for a deliciously gooey treat, if liked.

10 mins   10 mins

SERVES 6

INGREDIENTS

6 slightly under-ripe bananas

350 ml/12 fl oz coconut milk

2 tbsp granulated sugar

½ tsp salt

TO DECORATE

1 tbsp toasted sesame seeds

maple syrup to drizzle

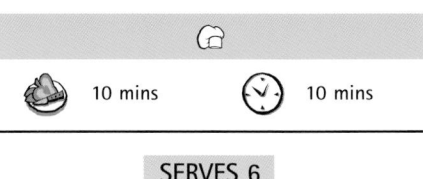

1 Peel the bananas and cut into 5-cm/2-inch lengths. Place the coconut milk, sugar and salt in a saucepan and heat gently until the sugar has dissolved. Add the banana pieces and cook gently for 5 minutes, or until the bananas are soft but not mushy.

2 Divide the mixture between 6 small bowls. Scatter the sesame seeds over, drizzle with maple syrup (if using) and serve.

Rum Bananas

Rum and bananas is a classic combination, but Cointreau partners bananas just as successfully.

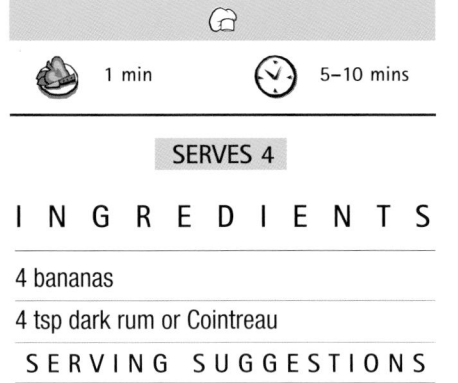

🕐 1 min   5–10 mins

SERVES 4

I N G R E D I E N T S

4 bananas

4 tsp dark rum or Cointreau

S E R V I N G   S U G G E S T I O N S

peach slices

sorbet

ice cream

double cream

crème fraîche

1 Preheat a ridged griddle pan over a high heat.

2 Place the bananas, still in their skins, on the griddle pan. Cook for 5–10 minutes, or until the skins are black, turning occasionally.

3 Remove the bananas from the griddle pan, peel and place in individual serving bowls. Pour 1 teaspoonful of rum or Cointreau over each banana and serve while still hot, with the peach slices. Top with sorbet, ice cream, double cream or crème fraîche.

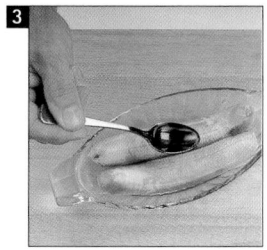

Toffee Bananas

These deep-fried banana morsels coated in sesame toffee mixture are sweet and delicious. They are best served hot.

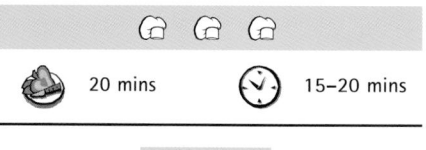

20 mins   15–20 mins

SERVES 4

INGREDIENTS

70 g/2½ oz self-raising flour

1 egg, beaten

135 ml/4½ fl oz iced water, plus an extra
   bowl of iced water for setting

4 large ripe bananas

3 tbsp lemon juice

2 tbsp rice flour

vegetable oil, for deep-frying

115 g/4 oz caster sugar

2 tbsp sesame seeds

1 Sift the flour into a bowl. Make a well in the centre, add the egg and 5 tablespoons of water and beat from the centre outwards until thoroughly mixed.

2 Peel the bananas and cut into 5-cm/2-inch pieces. Using your hands, gently shape them into balls. Brush all over with lemon juice to prevent discolouration, then roll them in rice flour until coated. Pour enough oil into a deep-fryer to cover the bananas and heat to 190°C/375°F. Coat the balls in the batter and deep-fry for about 2 minutes until golden (you may need to do this in batches). Lift them out and drain on greaseproof paper.

3 To make the toffee, put the sugar in a small saucepan over a low heat. Add 4 tablespoons of iced water and heat, stirring constantly, until the sugar dissolves. Simmer for 5 minutes, then remove from the heat and stir in the sesame seeds. Toss the banana balls in the toffee, scoop them out with a slotted spoon and drop into the bowl of iced water to set. Lift them out and divide between individual serving bowls. Serve hot.

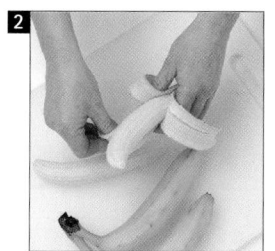
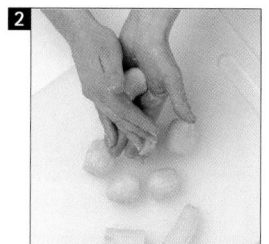
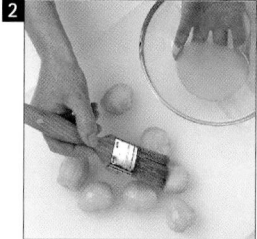

Bananas in Coconut Milk

An unusual dessert which is equally good served hot or cold, this is a classic Thai combination of fruit and vegetables.

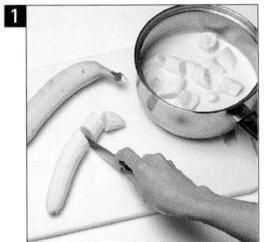

10 mins

3–5 mins

SERVES 4

INGREDIENTS

4 large bananas

350 ml/12 fl oz coconut milk

2 tbsp caster sugar

pinch of salt

½ tsp orange-flower water

1 tbsp shredded fresh mint

2 tbsp mung beans, cooked

fresh mint sprigs, to decorate

COOK'S TIP
If you prefer, the mung beans could be replaced with sliced, toasted almonds or hazelnuts.

1 Peel the bananas and cut them into short chunks. Place in a large, heavy-based saucepan with the coconut milk, caster sugar and salt. Heat gently until boiling, then simmer for 1 minute. Remove the saucepan from the heat.

2 Sprinkle the orange-flower water over, stir in the mint and spoon into a serving dish.

3 Place the mung beans in a heavy-based frying pan and cook over a high heat until turning crisp and golden, shaking the frying pan occasionally. Remove, leave to cool slightly and crush lightly with a pestle and mortar.

4 Sprinkle the toasted beans over the bananas and serve warm or cold, decorated with fresh mint sprigs.

Fruit with Chocolate Malt Dip

Use your favourite fresh fruit in season and dip the pieces in this wonderful malted chocolate mixture.

🍲 20 mins 🕐 5 mins

SERVES 4

INGREDIENTS

55 g/2 oz plain chocolate,
  broken into pieces

2 large bananas

1 tbsp malt extract

selection of fresh fruit, cut into chunks or
  slices, as necessary

1 Put the chocolate in a heatproof bowl set over a saucepan of gently simmering water. Stir over a low heat until melted. Remove from the heat and leave to cool for 10 minutes.

2 Peel and slice the bananas. Place them in a food processor and process until smooth. With the motor still running, pour the malt extract through the feed tube. Continue to process until thick and frothy and fully incorporated. With the motor still running, pour the melted chocolate through the feed tube in a slow, steady stream. Continue to process until thoroughly combined.

3 Scrape the dip into a small serving bowl and stand on a large serving plate. Arrange the fruit around the bowl and serve immediately.

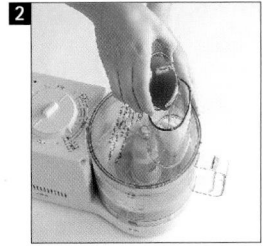
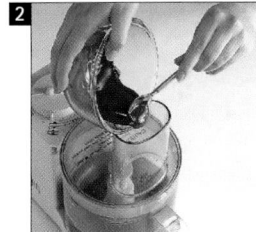

Chocolate Fondue

This is a fun dessert to serve at the end of a meal. You can prepare the fondue in advance, then just warm through before serving.

5 mins

5 mins

SERVES 4

I N G R E D I E N T S

8 oz/225 g plain chocolate

175 ml/6 fl oz double cream

2 tbsp brandy

TO SERVE

selection of fruit

white and pink marshmallows

sweet biscuits

1 Break the chocolate into small pieces and place in a small saucepan with the double cream.

2 Heat the mixture gently, stirring constantly until the chocolate has melted and blended with the cream.

3 Remove the saucepan from the heat and stir in the brandy.

4 Pour into a fondue pot or a small flameproof dish and keep warm, preferably over a small burner.

5 Serve with a selection of fruit, marshmallows and biscuits for dipping. The fruit and marshmallows can be spiked on fondue forks, wooden skewers or ordinary forks, for dipping into the chocolate fondue.

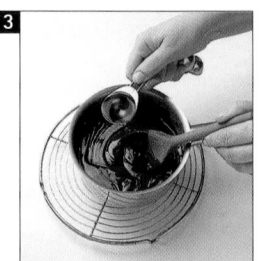

COOK'S TIP

To prepare the fruit for dipping, cut larger fruit into bite-sized pieces. Fruit that discolours, such as bananas, apples and pears, should be dipped in a little lemon juice as soon as it is cut.

Chocolate Fruit Dip

These warm, lightly grilled fruit kebabs are served with a delicious rich chocolate dipping sauce. It is best to use metal skewers.

 10 mins   5–10 mins

SERVES 4

INGREDIENTS

selection of fruit (oranges, bananas, apples, strawberries, pineapple chunks, apricots (fresh or canned), pears, kiwi fruit)

1 tbsp lemon juice

CHOCOLATE SAUCE

4 tbsp butter

50 g/1¾ oz plain chocolate, broken into small cubes

½ tbsp cocoa powder

2 tbsp golden syrup

BASTE

4 tbsp clear honey

grated zest and juice of ½ orange

1 To make the chocolate sauce, place the butter, chocolate, cocoa powder and syrup in a small saucepan. Heat gently on a stove or at the side of a barbecue grill, stirring continuously, until all of the ingredients have melted and combined.

2 To prepare the fruit, peel and core if necessary, then cut into large, bite-sized pieces or wedges as appropriate. Dip apples, pears and bananas in lemon juice to prevent discolouration. Thread the pieces of fruit on to skewers.

3 To make the baste, mix together the honey, orange zest and orange juice, heat gently if required and brush over the fruit.

4 Grill the fruit skewers over warm coals for 5–10 minutes until hot. Serve with the chocolate dipping sauce.

COOK'S TIP
If the coals are too hot, raise the rack so that it is about 15 cm/6 inches above the coals, or spread out the coals a little to reduce the heat. Do not assemble the fruit kebabs more than 1–2 hours before they are required.

Toasted Tropical Fruit

Spear some chunks of exotic tropical fruits on to kebab skewers, sear them over a barbecue and serve with this amazing chocolate dip.

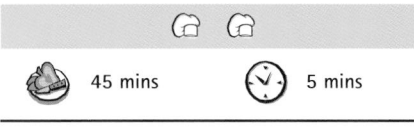

45 mins   5 mins

SERVES 4

I N G R E D I E N T S

DIP

125 g/4½ oz plain chocolate, broken into pieces

2 tbsp golden syrup

1 tbsp cocoa powder

1 tbsp cornflour

200 ml/7 fl oz cup milk

KEBABS

1 mango

1 pawpaw

2 kiwi fruit

½ small pineapple

1 large banana

2 tbsp lemon juice

150 ml/5 fl oz white rum

1 Put all the ingredients for the chocolate dip into a heavy-based saucepan. Heat over the barbecue or over a low heat on the stove, stirring constantly, until thickened and smooth. Keep warm at the edge of the barbecue.

2 Slice the mango on each side of its large flat stone. Cut the flesh into chunks, removing the peel. Halve, deseed and peel the pawpaw and cut it into chunks. Peel the kiwi fruit and slice into chunks. Peel and cut the pineapple into chunks. Peel and slice the banana and dip the pieces in the lemon juice to prevent it discolouring.

3 Thread the pieces of fruit alternately on to 4 wooden skewers. Place them in a shallow dish and pour over the rum. Set aside to soak up the flavour of the rum for at least 30 minutes, until ready to cook.

4 Cook the kebabs over the hot coals, turning frequently, for about 2 minutes, until seared. Serve, accompanied by the hot chocolate dip.

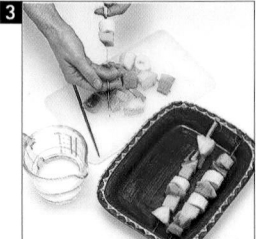

Toffee Fruit Kebabs

Serve these fruit kebabs with a sticky toffee sauce. They are perfect for autumn celebrations such as Hallowe'en.

15 mins   10 mins

SERVES 4

I N G R E D I E N T S

2 eating apples, cored and cut into wedges

2 firm pears, cored and cut into wedges

juice of ½ lemon

2 tbsp light muscovado sugar

¼ tsp ground allspice

25 g/1 oz unsalted butter, melted

S A U C E

125 g/4½ oz butter

1½ tbsp light muscovado sugar

6 tbsp double cream

1   Toss the apples and pears in the lemon juice to prevent any discolouration.

2   Mix the sugar and allspice together and sprinkle over the fruit.

3   Thread the fruit pieces on to skewers.

4   To make the toffee sauce, place the butter and sugar in a saucepan and heat, stirring gently, until the butter has melted and the sugar has dissolved.

5   Add the cream to the saucepan and bring to the boil. Boil for 1–2 minutes, then set aside to cool slightly.

6   Meanwhile, place the fruit kebabs over hot coals and barbecue for about 5 minutes, turning and basting frequently with the melted butter, until the fruit is just tender.

7   Transfer the fruit kebabs to warm serving plates and serve with the slightly cooled toffee sauce.

COOK'S TIP
Firm apples that will keep their shape are needed for this dish. Soft apples and pears will become mushy as they cook.

Fruit Skewers

These easily assembled skewers are served with delicious almond-flavoured chocolate sauce. Use other combinations of fruits if preferred.

15–20 mins | 10 mins

SERVES 4

INGREDIENTS

SKEWERS

6 tbsp brown sugar

pinch of ground allspice

8 whole strawberries, hulled

3 nectarines, stoned and cut into bite-sized chunks

400 g/14 oz canned pineapple chunks, drained

4 plums, stoned and cut into bite-sized chunks

6 tbsp butter, melted

CHOCOLATE ALMOND SAUCE

125 g/4½ oz plain chocolate, broken into small pieces

2½ tbsp butter

6 tbsp water

1 tbsp Amaretto

chopped mixed nuts, to decorate

1 Preheat the barbecue or grill to medium. Combine the sugar and allspice and spread out on a large plate. Thread the whole strawberries on to skewers, alternating with the chunks of nectarine, pineapple and plum. When the skewers are full (leave a small space at either end), brush them with melted butter and then turn them in the sugar until lightly coated. Transfer to the preheated barbecue or grill pan and cook, turning occasionally, for 8–10 minutes.

2 To make the sauce, gently melt the chocolate, butter and water together in a small saucepan, stirring constantly until smooth. Stir in the Amaretto. Remove the skewers from the heat, divide between individual plates, decorate with chopped mixed nuts and serve hot with the chocolate almond sauce.

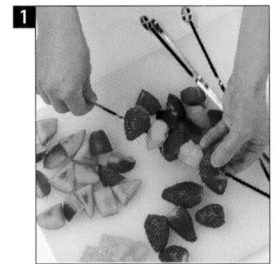

Fruit Kebabs

The sugar in which these kebabs are rolled melts to a deliciously sticky coating. If using wooden skewers, remember to presoak them.

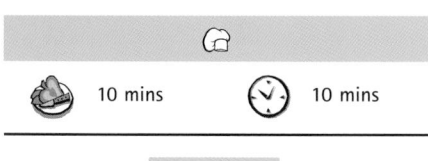

10 mins   10 mins

SERVES 4

INGREDIENTS

450 g/1 lb assorted fruit such as peaches, apricots, plums, apples, pears

4 tbsp butter, melted

2 tbsp sugar

pinch of cinnamon, optional

SERVING SUGGESTIONS

crème fraîche

natural yogurt

ice cream

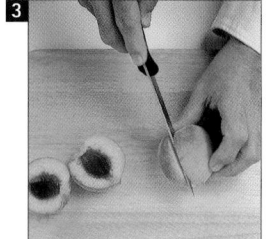
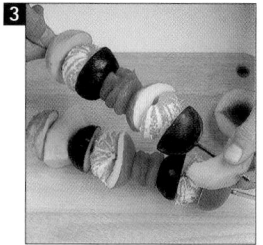
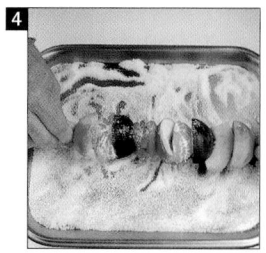

1 Select skewers that will fit comfortably on your griddle. If using wooden skewers, presoak them in water for 30 minutes to prevent them burning.

2 Preheat the griddle over a medium heat.

3 Stone the fruit as necessary, or remove cores, and cut into similar-sized pieces. Small fruit may be left whole. Arrange alternating pieces on the skewers. Brush the fruit with melted butter.

4 Spread the sugar on a plate large enough to take the skewers. Mix in the cinnamon (if using). Roll the fruit kebabs in the sugar, pressing gently to coat.

5 Cook the kebabs on the barbecue, turning occasionally. Cook for about 10 minutes, or until the sugar has melted and started to bubble. The fruit should still be firm.

6 Serve hot, with crème fraîche, natural yogurt or ice cream.

Mixed Fruit Kebabs

You can use almost any combination of firm-fleshed fruits to make these colourful, quick and easy-to-assemble kebabs.

20 mins plus
1 hr marinating

5–7 mins

SERVES 4

INGREDIENTS

2 nectarines

2 kiwi fruit, peeled

4 red plums

1 mango, peeled, halved and stoned

2 bananas, peeled and thickly sliced

8 strawberries, hulled

1 tbsp clear honey

3 tbsp Cointreau

1 Halve and stone the nectarines. Cut the nectarine halves in half again and place in a large shallow dish. Peel and quarter the kiwi fruit. Cut the plums in half and remove the stones. Cut the mango flesh into chunks and add to the dish with the kiwi fruit, plums, bananas and strawberries.

2 Mix the honey and Cointreau in a jug until blended. Pour the mixture over the fruit and toss to coat. Cover with clingfilm and set aside to marinate in the refrigerator for 1 hour.

3 Preheat the barbecue. Drain the fruit, reserving the marinade. Thread the fruit onto several presoaked wooden skewers and cook over medium hot coals, turning and brushing frequently with the reserved marinade, for 5–7 minutes, then serve.

Apple & Melon Kebabs

These fresh-tasting kebabs are ideal to serve as a light dessert to follow a barbecue. They are perfect served with vanilla ice cream.

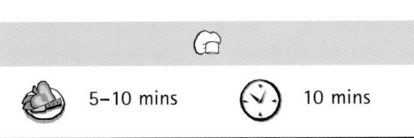

5–10 mins   10 mins

SERVES 4

INGREDIENTS

6 tbsp butter

1–2 tbsp light brown sugar

pinch of mixed spice

½ melon, such as Galia or Charentais

2 apples

1 tbsp lemon juice

natural yogurt, crème fraîche, mascarpone cheese or ice cream, to serve

1 In a small saucepan, melt the butter gently over a low heat. Stir in the brown sugar and mixed spice, then remove from the heat and pour into a large bowl.

2 Cut the melon flesh into small chunks. Wash and core the apples and cut into small chunks. Brush the fruit with lemon juice.

3 Thread the melon chunks on to skewers, alternating with pieces of apple. When the skewers are full (leave a small space at either end), transfer them to the bowl and turn them in the butter mixture until they are well coated.

4 Barbecue the kebabs over hot coals, turning them frequently, for about 10 minutes or until they are cooked to your taste. Serve with natural yogurt, crème fraîche, mascarpone cheese or ice cream.

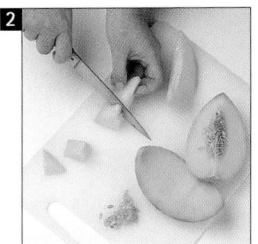

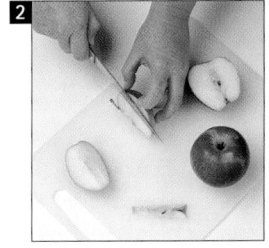

Butterscotch Melts

This delicious dessert will appeal to children of all ages. Bananas and marshmallows taste fantastic with butterscotch sauce.

5 mins

5 mins

SERVES 4

INGREDIENTS

4 bananas

4 tbsp lemon juice

225 g/8 oz marshmallows

SAUCE

125 g/4½ oz butter

125 g/4½ oz light muscovado sugar

⅓ cup golden syrup

4 tbsp hot water

1 Slice the bananas into large chunks and dip them into the lemon juice to prevent them going brown.

2 Thread the marshmallows and pieces of banana alternately on to kebab sticks or bamboo skewers, placing 2 marshmallows and 1 piece of banana on to each one.

3 To make the sauce, melt the butter, sugar and syrup together in a small saucepan. Add the hot water, stirring until blended and smooth. Do not boil or else the mixture will become toffee-like. Keep the sauce warm at the edge of the barbecue, stirring from time to time.

4 Sear the kebabs over the hot coals for 30–40 seconds, turning constantly, so that the marshmallows are just starting to brown and melt.

5 Serve the kebabs with a little of the butterscotch sauce spooned over them. (Use half of the sauce to serve 4; the remainder can be used later.)

COOK'S TIP
The warm butterscotch sauce tastes wonderful with vanilla ice cream. Make double the quantity of sauce if you plan to serve ice cream at a barbecue.

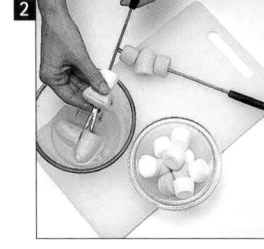

Banana Coconut Fritters

These sweet banana fritters need only a dusting of icing sugar and ground cinnamon to complete them.

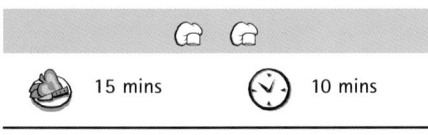

15 mins | 10 mins

SERVES 4

INGREDIENTS

75 g/2¾ oz plain flour

2 tbsp rice flour

1 tbsp caster sugar

1 egg, separated

150 ml/5 fl oz coconut milk

sunflower oil, for deep frying

4 large bananas

TO DECORATE

1 tsp icing sugar

1 tsp ground cinnamon

1 Sift the plain flour, rice flour and sugar into a bowl and make a well in the centre. Add the egg yolk and coconut milk and beat until a smooth, thick batter forms.

2 Whisk the egg white in a clean, dry, grease-free bowl until soft peaks form. Fold it into the batter lightly and evenly.

3 Heat a 6-cm/2½-inch depth of oil in a large heavy-based frying pan to 350°F/180°C, or until a cube of bread browns in 30 seconds. Cut the bananas in half crossways, then dip them quickly into the batter to coat. Drop them carefully into the hot oil and fry in batches for 2–3 minutes, until golden brown, turning once.

4 Drain well on kitchen paper. Sprinkle with icing sugar and cinnamon and serve immediately.

COOK'S TIP
If you can buy the baby finger bananas that are popular in this dish in the East, leave them whole for coating and frying.

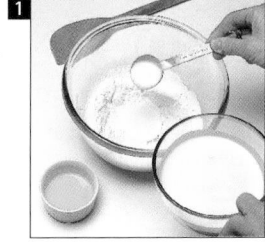

Apple Fritters

This is a popular choice for family meals, as children and adults alike love the flavour and crispness of the apple rings.

15 mins plus
30 mins resting

4–6 mins

SERVES 4

INGREDIENTS

salt

140 g/5 oz plain flour

2 egg yolks

1 egg white

1 tbsp sunflower oil

150 ml/5 fl oz milk

450 g/1 lb cooking apples

juice of 1 lemon

caster sugar, for sprinkling

115 g/4 oz unsalted butter

1 Sift the flour with a pinch of salt into a bowl. Make a well in the centre and add the egg yolks, egg white and oil. Gradually incorporate the flour into the liquid with a wooden spoon. Gradually beat in the milk and continue beating to make a smooth batter. Cover with clingfilm and set aside for 30 minutes.

2 Peel and core the apples, then cut them into rings about 5-mm/¼-inch thick. Spread them out on a plate and sprinkle with the lemon juice and caster sugar.

3 Melt the butter in a large, heavy-based frying pan. Dip the apple rings, one at a time, into the batter and then drop them into the pan. Cook for 2–3 minutes on each side, until golden brown. Transfer to a platter, sprinkle with more caster sugar and serve immediately.

COOK'S TIP
You can prepare the batter and the apples in advance. Keep the apples covered in clingfilm until you are ready to dip them into the batter.

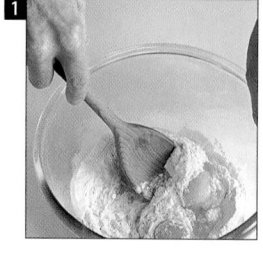  

Deep-Fried Apple Chunks

These apple fritters are coated in a light, spiced batter and deep-fried until crisp and golden. Serve warm with an unusual almond sauce.

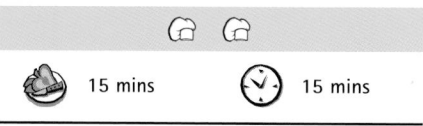

15 mins   15 mins

SERVES 4

INGREDIENTS

100 g/3½ oz plain flour

pinch of salt

½ tsp ground cinnamon

175 ml/6 fl oz warm water

4 tsp vegetable oil

2 egg whites

2 eating apples, peeled

vegetable or sunflower oil, for deep-frying

caster sugar and cinnamon, to decorate

SAUCE

150 ml/¼ pint natural yogurt

½ tsp almond essence

2 tsp clear honey

1 Sift the flour and salt together into a large mixing bowl.

2 Add the cinnamon and mix well. Stir in the warm water and vegetable oil to make a smooth batter.

3 Whisk the egg whites until stiff peaks form and fold into the batter.

4 Using a sharp knife, cut the apples into chunks and dip the pieces of apple into the batter to coat.

5 Heat the oil for deep-frying to 180°C/350°F, or until a cube of bread browns in 30 seconds. Fry the apple chunks, in batches if necessary, for about 3–4 minutes, until light golden-brown and puffy.

6 Remove the apple chunks from the oil with a slotted spoon and drain on kitchen paper. Mix together the caster sugar and cinnamon and sprinkle over the apple chunks.

7 Mix the sauce ingredients in a serving bowl and serve with the apple chunks.

Apricot & Chocolate Fritters

Despite their appearance, both Hunza apricots from Afghanistan and Kashmir and Turkish dried apricots have a wonderful flavour.

 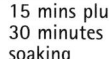

15 mins plus 30 minutes soaking

10–15 mins

SERVES 4

INGREDIENTS

175 g/6 oz dried Turkish apricots, stoned

100 g/3½ oz plain flour

3 tbsp ground almonds

3 tbsp melted unsalted butter

1 egg white

vegetable oil, for deep-frying

1 tbsp cocoa powder

3 tbsp caster sugar

WHITE SAUCE

175 g/6 oz white chocolate

4 tbsp unsalted butter

150 ml/5 fl oz double cream

3 tbsp caster sugar

2 tbsp apricot brandy

1 Place the apricots in a bowl, pour over boiling water to cover and set aside for at least 30 minutes to plump up.

2 To make the white chocolate sauce, break the chocolate into pieces and set aside. Cut the butter into pieces and place in a heavy-based saucepan with the cream and sugar. Melt over a low heat, stirring frequently, until smooth. Stir in the chocolate and continue to stir until melted and smooth. Remove from the heat, leave to cool slightly, then stir in the apricot brandy. Set aside until required.

3 Sift the flour into a bowl, add the almonds, melted butter and egg white and mix well. Gradually add 3–4 tablespoons of water, beating well until the mixture forms a smooth batter.

4 Heat the oil for deep-frying to 180°C/350°F, or until a cube of bread browns in about 45 seconds. Meanwhile, drain the apricots and pat dry with kitchen paper.

5 Dip the apricots a few at a time into the batter and carefully lower into the hot oil. Cook until they rise to the surface and are golden brown. Remove with a slotted spoon and drain on kitchen paper. Keep them warm while you cook the remaining apricots.

6 Divide the apricots between warmed serving plates. Mix together the cocoa powder and sugar in a small bowl, then sift the mixture over the fritters. Serve immediately, with the sauce at room temperature.

Chocolate & Apple Dumplings

A melt-in-the-mouth combination of tart fruit and sweet chocolate pastry, these dumplings are sensational.

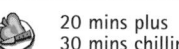

20 mins plus
30 mins chilling

35 mins

SERVES 4

INGREDIENTS

4 large cooking apples

4 tbsp mincemeat

2 tbsp chopped walnuts

1 egg, lightly beaten

crème fraîche, to serve

PASTRY

175 g/6 oz plain chocolate

70 g/2½ oz plain flour, plus extra
  for dusting

1 tsp ground cinnamon

4 tbsp butter

1 egg yolk, or 1–2 tbsp cold water

1 First, make the pastry. Break the chocolate into squares and place in a heatproof bowl. Set over a pan of gently simmering water and heat, stirring occasionally, until melted. Remove from the heat and set aside to cool slightly. Sift the flour into a bowl and stir in the cinnamon. Rub in the butter with your fingertips until the mixture resembles breadcrumbs. Make a well in the centre

and pour in the cooled chocolate and the egg yolk and mix to form a dough. Knead lightly, then form into a ball, wrap and chill in the refrigerator for 30 minutes.

2 Preheat the oven to 200°C/400°F/Gas Mark 6. Divide the pastry into 4 equal pieces and roll each out on a lightly floured work surface to a round large enough to enclose 1 apple.

3 Core the apples and place 1 apple on each pastry round. Mix together the mincemeat and chopped walnuts and spoon into the cavities of the apples.

Brush the edges of the pastry with the beaten egg, then wrap the pastry around the apples, pressing the edges together to seal.

4 Transfer the dumplings to a baking sheet and brush all over with beaten egg to glaze. Bake in the preheated oven for about 35 minutes, until golden. Serve immediately, with crème fraîche.

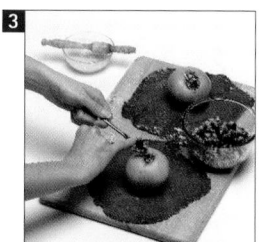

VARIATION
This recipe would also work well with pears. Omit the cinnamon from the pastry.

Chocolate Polenta Pudding

This rich dessert is delicious when served with a generous scoop of chocolate or vanilla ice cream.

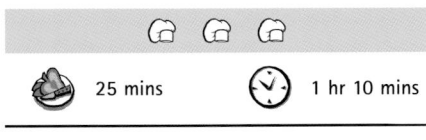

🍰 25 mins   🕐 1 hr 10 mins

SERVES 8

I N G R E D I E N T S

450 g/1 lb good quality Continental plain chocolate

115 g/4 oz chocolate hazelnut spread

115 g/4 oz sweet butter, plus extra for greasing

50 g/2 oz quick-cook polenta

300 ml/10 fl oz milk

6 egg yolks

115 g/4 oz caster or icing sugar, plus extra for dusting

8 egg whites

vanilla or chocolate ice cream, to serve

5 Whisk the egg whites until stiff, adding the sugar gradually. Gently fold the egg whites into the chocolate polenta mixture.

6 Fill the prepared soufflé dish with the mixture and bake for 45-60 minutes, until the top starts to split open. Serve hot, dusted with the remaining sugar over the top.

1 Preheat the oven to 180°C/350°F/Gas Mark 4.

2 Break the chocolate into pieces and place in a heatproof bowl set over a saucepan of gently simmering water until melted. Stir the chocolate hazelnut spread into the melted chocolate.

3 Melt the butter in a heavy-based saucepan, stir in the polenta and cook for 2–3 minutes. Stir in the milk, reduce the heat and cook, stirring constantly, over a low heat for 5–10 minutes, until thickened. Stir the chocolate mixture into the cooked polenta. Beat in the egg yolks one at a time.

4 Grease a 1-litre/1¾ pint soufflé dish with butter, then dust with caster or icing sugar and set aside.

Stuffed Pooris

Pooris are puffy Indian dumplings. They freeze well, so it pays to make a large quantity and reheat them in the oven.

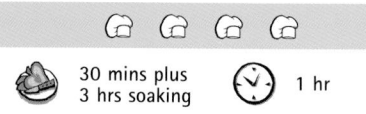

🍰 30 mins plus
3 hrs soaking

🕐 1 hr

MAKES 10

INGREDIENTS

POORIS

140 g/5 oz wholemeal flour

100 g/3½ oz plain flour, plus extra for dusting

½ tsp salt

1½ tbsp ghee, plus extra for frying

150 ml/5 fl oz milk

FILLING

8 tbsp chana dal

900 ml/1½ pints water

5 tbsp ghee

2 green cardamom pods, peeled

4 cloves

8 tbsp sugar

2 tbsp ground almonds

½ tsp saffron strands

40 g/1½ oz sultanas

3 To make the filling, soak the chana dal for at least 3 hours if time allows. Place the dal in a saucepan and add water. Bring to the boil over a medium heat until all the water has evaporated and the dal is soft enough to be mashed into a paste.

4 In a separate saucepan, heat the ghee and add the cardamom seeds and cloves. Reduce the heat, add the chana dal paste and stir for 5–7 minutes.

5 Fold in the sugar and almonds and cook, stirring, for 10 minutes. Add the saffron and sultanas and blend until thickened, stirring, for 5 minutes.

6 Spoon the filling on to one half of each pastry circle. Dampen the edges with water and fold the other half over to seal.

7 Heat the extra ghee in a frying pan and cook the filled pooris over a low heat until golden. Transfer to kitchen towels, drain and serve.

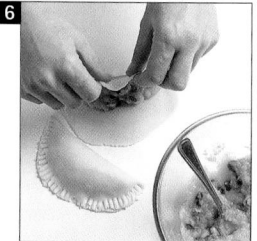

1 To make the pooris, place the wholemeal flour, plain flour and salt in a bowl and mix. Add the ghee and rub in with your fingers. Add the milk and mix to form a dough. Knead the dough for 5 minutes, cover and leave to prove for about 3 hours. Knead the dough on a floured work surface for 15 minutes.

2 Roll out the dough until it measures 25 cm/10 inches and divide into 10 portions. Roll out each of these into 12.5-cm/5-inch circles and set aside.

Apple Strudel & Cider Sauce

This light, crisp and spicy strudel, delicious either warm or cold, is served with a hot cider sauce.

🍰 15 mins 🕐 20–25 mins

SERVES 2–4

INGREDIENTS

8 crisp eating apples

1 tbsp lemon juice

115 g/4 oz sultanas

1 tsp ground cinnamon

½ tsp grated nutmeg

1 tbsp light brown sugar

6 sheets filo pastry

vegetable oil spray

SAUCE

1 tbsp cornflour

450 ml/16 fl oz dry cider

icing sugar, to serve

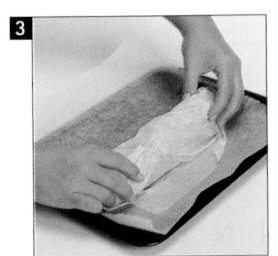

1 Preheat the oven to 190°C/375°F/ Gas Mark 5. Line a baking tray with baking parchment.

2 Peel and core the apples and chop them into 1-cm/½-inch dice. Toss the dice in a bowl, with the lemon juice, sultanas, cinnamon, nutmeg and sugar.

3 Lay out a sheet of filo pastry, spray with vegetable oil and lay a second sheet on top. Repeat with a third sheet. Spread over half the apple mixture and roll up lengthways, tucking in the ends to enclose the filling. Repeat to make a second strudel. Slide on to the baking tray, spray with oil, and bake for 15–20 minutes.

4 Blend the cornflour in a saucepan with a little dry cider until smooth. Add the remaining cider and heat gently, stirring, until the mixture boils and thickens. Serve the strudel warm or cold, dredged with icing sugar, accompanied by the cider sauce.

Fruit Parcels

If you don't have a spare barbecue, cooking fruit in a foil parcel is a good idea for dessert, as it avoids any contamination from foods cooked earlier.

15 mins | 4 mins

SERVES 4

INGREDIENTS

2 oranges

2 eating apples

juice of 1 lemon

2 pears

4 tsp muscovado sugar

1 Peel the oranges, carefully removing all the pith. Cut each horizontally into 6 slices. Core the apples, but do not peel. Cut each horizontally into 6 slices. Brush the slices with lemon juice. Peel and core the pears, then cut each of them horizontally into 6 slices. Brush the slices with lemon juice.

2 Cut out 4 large squares of foil. Divide the fruit slices equally among the squares and sprinkle each pile with 1 teaspoon of the sugar. Fold up the sides of the squares to enclose the fruit securely.

3 Cook the parcels on a medium-hot barbecue for about 4 minutes. Serve immediately.

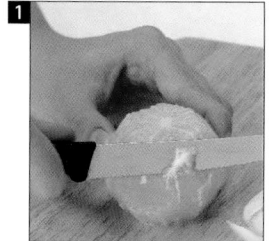
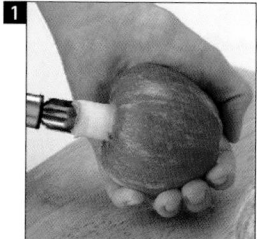

Exotic Fruit Parcels

Delicious pieces of exotic fruit are warmed through in a deliciously scented sauce to make a fabulous barbecue dessert.

10 mins plus 30 mins marinating

15–20 mins

SERVES 4

INGREDIENTS

1 papaya

1 mango

1 starfruit

1 tbsp grenadine

3 tbsp orange juice

single cream or low-fat natural yogurt, to serve

1 Cut the papaya in half, scoop out the seeds and discard them. Peel the papaya and cut the flesh into thick slices.

2 Prepare the mango by cutting it in half lengthways around the central stone and carefully twisting the fruit off the stone.

3 Score each mango half in a criss-cross pattern. Push each mango half inside out to separate the cubes and cut them away from the skin.

4 Using a sharp knife, thickly slice the starfruit.

5 Place all the fruit in a bowl and mix them together.

6 Mix the grenadine and orange juice together and pour over the fruit. Leave to marinate for at least 30 minutes.

7 Divide the fruit among 4 double-thickness squares of foil and gather up the edges to form a parcel that encloses the fruit.

8 Place the foil parcel on a rack set over warm coals and barbecue the fruit for 15–20 minutes.

9 Serve the fruit in the parcel, with the low-fat yogurt.

COOK'S TIP

Grenadine is a sweet syrup made from pomegranates. If you prefer you could use pomegranate juice instead. To extract the juice, cut the pomegranate in half and squeeze gently with a lemon squeezer – do not press too hard or the juice may become bitter.

Warm Fruit Nests

These attractive pastry shells are filled with a delicious mixture of summer berries. Serve with cream if you wish.

 15–20 mins 10 mins

SERVES 4

INGREDIENTS

2–3 tbsp lemon oil

8 sheets of filo pastry, defrosted if frozen

250 g/9 oz blueberries

250 g/9 oz raspberries

250 g/9 oz blackberries

3 tbsp caster sugar

1 tsp ground mixed spice

fresh mint sprigs, to decorate

double cream, to serve

1 Preheat the oven to 180°C/350°F/Gas Mark 4. Brush 4 small tartlet tins with oil. Cut the filo pastry into 16 squares measuring about 12 cm/ 4½ inches. Brush each square with oil and use to line the tartlet tins. Use 4 sheets in each tin, and stagger each sheet so that you have star-shaped effect. Transfer to a baking tray and bake in the preheated oven for 7–8 minutes until golden. Remove from the oven and set aside.

2 Meanwhile, warm the fruit in a saucepan with the caster sugar and mixed spice over a medium heat. Reduce the heat and simmer, stirring, for 10 minutes. Remove from the heat and drain. Using a slotted spoon, divide the warm fruit among the pastry shells. Decorate with sprigs of fresh mint and serve warm with fresh double cream.

Sweet Fruit Wontons

These sweet wontons are very adaptable and may be filled with whole, small fruits, or a spicy chopped mixture as here.

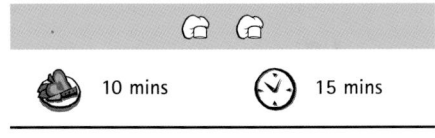

10 mins   15 mins

SERVES 4

INGREDIENTS

12 wonton wrappers

2 tsp cornflour

6 tsp cold water

oil, for deep-frying

2 tbsp clear honey

selection of fresh fruit, such as kiwi fruit, limes, oranges, mango and apples, sliced, to serve

FILLING

175 g/6 oz chopped dried, stoned dates

2 tsp brown sugar

½ tsp ground cinnamon

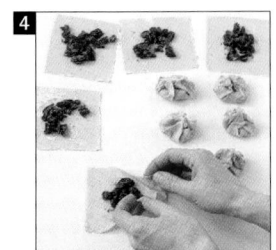

1 To make the filling, mix together the dates, sugar and cinnamon in a bowl.

2 Spread out the wonton wrappers on a chopping board and spoon a little of the filling into the centre of each wrapper.

3 Blend the cornflour and water and brush this mixture around the edges of the wrappers.

4 Fold the wrappers over the filling, bringing the edges together, then bring the 2 corners together, sealing with the cornflour mixture.

5 Heat the oil for deep-frying in a wok to 180°C/350°F or until a cube of bread browns in 30 seconds. Fry the wontons in batches for 2–3 minutes until golden. Remove the wontons from the oil with a slotted spoon and leave to drain on kitchen paper.

6 Place the honey in a bowl and stand it in warm water to soften it slightly. Drizzle the honey over the sweet fruit wontons and serve with a selection of fresh fruit.

COOK'S TIP
wonton wrappers may be found in Chinese supermarkets.

Mango Dumplings

Fresh mango and canned lychees fill these small steamed dumplings, making a really colourful and tasty treat.

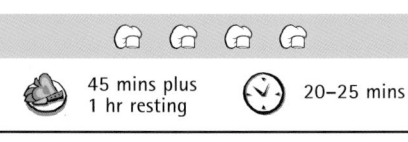

45 mins plus 1 hr resting

20–25 mins

SERVES 4

I N G R E D I E N T S

DOUGH

2 tsp baking powder

1 tbsp caster sugar

150 ml/5 fl oz water

150 ml/5 fl oz milk

400 g/14 oz plain flour, plus extra for dusting

FILLING AND SAUCE

1 small mango

100 g/3½ oz canned lychees, drained

1 tbsp ground almonds

4 tbsp orange juice

ground cinnamon, for dusting

1 To make the dough, place the baking powder and caster sugar in a large mixing bowl.

2 Mix the water and milk together and then stir this mixture into the baking powder and sugar mixture until well combined. Gradually stir in the plain flour to make a soft dough. Set the dough aside in a warm place for about 1 hour.

3 To make the filling, peel the mango and cut the flesh from the stone. Roughly chop the mango flesh and set aside half for the sauce.

4 Chop the lychees and add to half of the chopped mango, together with the ground almonds. Leave to stand for 20 minutes.

5 Meanwhile, make the sauce. Blend the reserved mango and the orange juice in a food processor until smooth. Using the back of a tablespoon, press the mixture through a sieve to make a smooth sauce.

6 Divide the dough into 16 equal pieces. Roll each piece out on a lightly floured work surface into 7.5-cm/3-inch circles.

7 Spoon a little of the mango and lychee filling on to the centre of each circle and fold the dough over the filling to make semicircles. Pinch the edges together to seal firmly.

8 Place the dumplings on a heatproof plate in a steamer, cover and steam for about 20-25 minutes or until cooked through.

9 Remove the mango dumplings from the steamer, dust with a little ground cinnamon and serve immediately with the mango sauce.

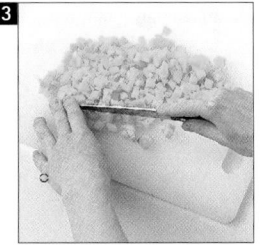

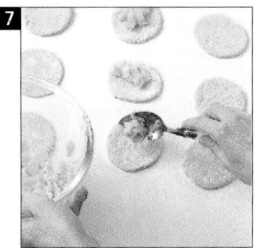

Caramel Apple Wedges

A Thai version of a Chinese dessert, these sweet caramel-covered pieces of fruit take practice to perfect, but the trick is to get the timing right.

20 mins   10 mins

SERVES 4

INGREDIENTS

140 g/5 oz rice flour

1 medium egg

125 ml/4 fl oz cold water

4 crisp eating apples

2½ tbsp sesame seeds

225 g/8 oz caster sugar

2 tbsp vegetable oil, plus extra vegetable oil for deep frying

1 Place the flour, egg and water in a bowl and whisk well until a smooth, thick batter forms.

2 Core the apples and cut each into 8 wedges. Drop into the batter and stir in the sesame seeds.

3 Place the sugar and 2 tablespoons oil in a heavy-based saucepan and heat, stirring, until the sugar dissolves completely. Continue to stir until the syrup just starts to turn pale golden. Remove from the heat but keep warm.

4 Heat the oil for frying in a wok or deep frying pan to 180°C/350°F, or until a cube of bread browns in 30 seconds. Lift the apple pieces one by one from the batter and, using chopsticks or tongs, lower into the hot oil and fry for 2–3 minutes, until golden brown and crisp.

5 Remove with a slotted spoon and dip very quickly into the sugar mixture. Dip briefly into ice water and drain on kitchen paper. Serve immediately.

COOK'S TIP
Take care not to overheat the sugar syrup or it will become difficult to handle and burn. If it starts to set before you have finished dipping the apple pieces, warm it slightly over the heat until it becomes liquid again.

Mixed Fruit Brûlées

Traditionally a rich mixture made with cream, this fruit-based version is just as tempting using low-fat smetana and fromage frais as a topping.

🕐 5 mins   🕐 5 mins

SERVES 4

INGREDIENTS

450 g/1 lb prepared assorted summer fruits, such as strawberries, raspberries, blackcurrants, redcurrants and cherries, thawed if frozen

150 ml/5 fl oz smetana

150 ml/5 fl oz low-fat natural fromage frais

1 tsp vanilla essence

4 tbsp demerara sugar

1 Preheat the grill to medium. Divide the prepared strawberries, raspberries, blackcurrants, redcurrants and cherries evenly between 4 small ramekin dishes.

2 Combine the smetana, fromage frais and vanilla essence.

3 Spoon the mixture over the fruit, to cover it completely.

4 Top each serving with 1 tablespoon of demerara sugar and place the desserts under the preheated grill until the sugar starts to caramelize. Set aside for a couple of minutes before serving.

COOK'S TIP
Look out for half-fat creams, in single and double varieties. They are good substitutes for occasional use. Alternatively, in this recipe, double the quantity of fromage frais for a lower-fat version.

Chocolate Soufflé

Served with hot chocolate custard, this is a chocoholic's dream. Do not be put off by the mystique of soufflés—this one is not difficult to make.

🍫 🍫

🍮 15 mins   🕐 50–55 mins

SERVES 4

I N G R E D I E N T S

2 tbsp butter, plus extra for greasing

100 g/3½ oz plain chocolate

300 ml/10 fl oz milk

4 large eggs, separated

1 tbsp cornflour

4 tbsp caster sugar

½ tsp vanilla essence

100 g/3½ oz plain chocolate chips

caster and icing sugar, for dusting

C H O C O L A T E   C U S T A R D

2 tbsp cornflour

1 tbsp caster sugar

450 ml/16 fl oz milk

50 g/1¾ oz plain chocolate

1 Preheat the oven to 180°C/350°F/Gas Mark 4. Grease a 900-ml/1½-pint soufflé dish and sprinkle with caster sugar. Break the chocolate into pieces.

2 Heat the milk with the butter in a saucepan until almost boiling. Mix the egg yolks, cornflour and caster sugar in a bowl and pour on some of the hot milk, whisking. Return it to the saucepan and cook gently, stirring constantly until thickened. Add the chocolate and stir until melted. Remove from the heat and stir in the vanilla essence.

3 Whisk the egg whites until soft peaks form. Fold half of the egg whites into the chocolate mixture. Fold in the rest with the chocolate chips. Pour into the dish and bake in the preheated oven for 40–45 minutes until well risen.

4 Meanwhile, make the custard. Put the cornflour and sugar in a small bowl and mix to a smooth paste with a little of the milk. Heat the remaining milk until almost boiling. Pour a little of the hot milk on to the cornflour, mix well, then pour back into the saucepan. Cook gently, stirring until thickened. Break the chocolate into pieces and add to the custard, stirring until melted.

5 Dust the soufflé with sugar and serve immediately with the chocolate custard.

Soufflé with Coffee Sabayon

Soufflés, especially chocolate ones, are not as tricky to make as is often thought. Just make sure everyone is sitting at the table when it is ready.

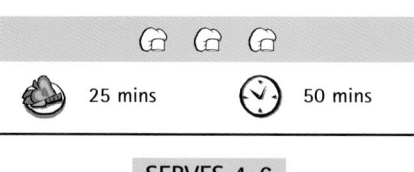
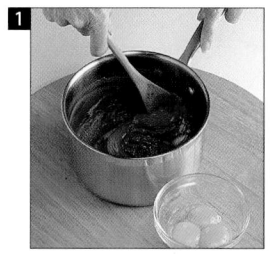

🕐 25 mins   🕐 50 mins

SERVES 4–6

INGREDIENTS

SOUFFLE

butter and a little caster sugar, for coating the dish

3 tbsp cornflour

250 ml/9 fl oz milk

115 g/4 oz plain chocolate, broken into pieces

4 eggs, separated

55 g/2 oz golden caster sugar

icing sugar, for dusting

COFFEE SABAYON

2 eggs

3 egg yolks

85 g/3 oz golden caster sugar

4 tsp instant coffee granules

2 tbsp brandy

1 Preheat the oven to 190°C/375°F/Gas Mark 5. Grease a 1-litre/1³/₄-cup soufflé dish and sprinkle with caster sugar. To make the soufflé, put the cornflour in a bowl. Add a little of the milk and stir to make a smooth paste. Pour the remaining milk into a saucepan and add the chocolate. Heat gently until the chocolate has melted. Pour the chocolate milk on to the cornflour paste, stirring. Return to the saucepan and bring to the boil, stirring constantly. Simmer gently for 1 minute. Remove from the heat and stir in the egg yolks, 1 at a time. Cover the surface closely with clingfilm and leave to cool slightly.

2 Place the egg whites in a large bowl and whisk until soft peaks start to form. Gradually whisk in the caster sugar until stiff but not dry. Stir a little of the meringue into the chocolate mixture, then carefully fold in the remainder. Pour into the prepared soufflé dish and bake in the oven for 40 minutes, until well risen and with a slight wobble when pushed.

3 Just before the soufflé is ready, make the sabayon. Put the eggs, yolks, sugar, coffee and brandy in a heavy-based saucepan. Place over a very low heat and whisk constantly until the mixture is thick and light. Dust a little icing sugar over the soufflé and serve with the sabayon.

COOK'S TIP

A prepared soufflé will keep in the refrigerator for up to 2 hours before cooking and it will still rise.

Cappuccino Soufflé Puddings

These individual light and airy soufflés are very quick to cook and just melt in the mouth. They are perfect served with vanilla ice cream.

SERVES 6

INGREDIENTS

butter, for greasing

6 tbsp whipping cream

2 tsp instant espresso coffee granules

2 tbsp Kahlúa

3 large eggs, separated, plus 1 extra white

25 g/1 oz golden caster sugar, plus extra for coating

150 g/5½ oz plain chocolate, broken into pieces

cocoa powder, for dusting

vanilla ice cream, to serve

1 Preheat the oven to 190°C/375°F/ Gas Mark 5. Grease the sides of 6 x 175-ml/6-fl oz ramekin dishes with butter and coat with caster sugar. Place on a baking tray. Place the cream in a saucepan and warm gently. Stir in the coffee until dissolved, then add the Kahlúa. Divide the mixture among the prepared ramekin dishes.

2 In a clean, greasefree bowl, whisk the egg whites until soft peaks form, then gradually whisk in the caster sugar until stiff and glossy but not dry. Put the chocolate in a heatproof bowl set over a saucepan of gently simmering water until melted. Add the egg yolks to the melted chocolate, then stir in a little of the whisked egg whites.

3 Gradually fold in the remaining egg whites. Divide the mixture between the ramekins. Cook in the preheated oven for 15 minutes until just set. Dust with cocoa powder and serve immediately with vanilla ice cream.

VARIATION
Kahlúa is a coffee liqueur, but rum or cognac could be used as an alternative.

Banana Soufflés

These elegant individual soufflés would be a good choice for a dinner party dessert, especially as they are so simple to make.

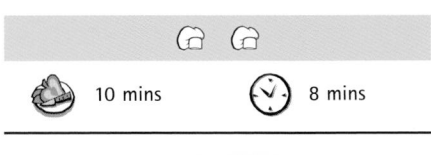

🍓 10 mins   🕐 8 mins

SERVES 4

I N G R E D I E N T S

sunflower or corn oil, for brushing

2 ripe bananas

1 tbsp lemon or lime juice

1 tbsp Malibu or coconut liqueur

4 eggs, separated

55 g/2 oz caster sugar

1 Preheat the oven to 230°C/450°F/Gas Mark 8. Lightly brush 4 x 350-ml/12-fl oz soufflé dishes with oil. Cut the bananas into 2.5-cm/1-inch lengths. Place the bananas, lemon juice and liqueur in a food processor and process to a smooth purée. Add the egg yolks and 1 teaspoon of the sugar and process briefly again to mix. Scrape into a bowl.

2 Whisk the egg whites until stiff peaks form, then whisk in the remaining sugar, 1 tablespoon at a time, until stiff and glossy. Fold 1 tablespoon of the egg whites into the banana mixture to loosen it, then gently incorporate the remainder.

3 Spoon the soufflé mixture into the dishes and make a rim with the end of a teaspoon. Place on a baking tray and bake in preheated oven for 8 minutes or until well risen and golden. Serve immediately.

COOK'S TIP

To whisk egg whites successfully, make sure that they are as fresh as possible and that they are at room temperature, rather than directly from the refrigerator. Some cooks like to add a pinch of salt or cream of tartar before they start to whisk.

Orange Soufflés

Light-as-air, these delicious little soufflés are the perfect choice for entertaining. As with all soufflés, they should be served immediately.

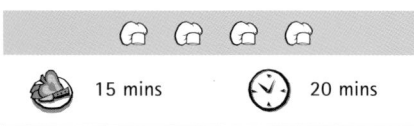

15 mins

20 mins

SERVES 6

INGREDIENTS

140 g/5 oz unsalted butter, plus 1 tbsp extra for greasing

3 tbsp caster sugar, plus 1 tbsp extra for sprinkling

175 g/6 oz plain chocolate, broken into small pieces

4 large eggs, separated

2 tbsp orange liqueur

¼ tsp cream of tartar

1 tbsp icing sugar, for dusting

Chocolate Custard (see page 570), to serve

1 Preheat the oven to 220°C/425°F/Gas Mark 7. Grease 6 ramekins and sprinkle with caster sugar to coat the bases and sides. Tip out any excess. Stand the ramekins on a baking tray.

2 Chop the butter and place in a heavy-based saucepan with the chocolate. Stir over a very low heat until melted and smooth. Remove the saucepan from the heat and cool slightly. Beat in the egg yolks, 1 at a time, and stir in the orange liqueur. Set aside, stirring occasionally.

3 Gently whisk the egg whites until they are frothy, then sprinkle in the cream of tartar and whisk rapidly until soft peaks form. Add 1 tablespoon of caster sugar and whisk rapidly again. Add the remaining caster sugar, 1 tablespoon at a time, whisking until the whites form stiff, glossy peaks. Gently stir about one-quarter of the whites into the cooled chocolate mixture, then fold the chocolate mixture into the remaining whites using a metal spoon.

4 Divide the mixture among the ramekins and bake in the preheated oven for about 10 minutes until risen and just set. Dust the soufflés with icing sugar and serve immediately, handing the custard around separately.

Chocolate Mandarin Soufflé

A perfect way to end a special-occasion meal or dinner party, this soufflé with a difference tastes and looks superb.

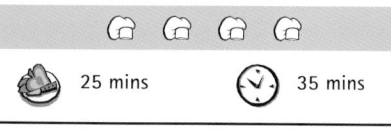

🍦 25 mins   🕐 35 mins

SERVES 4

INGREDIENTS

butter, for greasing

3 mandarins or clementines

70 g/2½ oz plain chocolate

600 ml/1 pint milk

55 g/2 oz soft brown sugar

55 g/2 oz semolina

3 eggs

6 tbsp Mandarine Napoléon liqueur

1 Grease a 1.7-litre/3-pint soufflé dish with butter. Place a baking tray in the oven and preheat to 200°C/400°F/Gas Mark 6. Grate the rind of 2 of the oranges and set aside. Pare the zest from the other orange, removing all the pith, and cut into very fine shreds. Use the fruit for another dish (see Cook's Tip). Grate the chocolate.

2 Gently heat the milk in a heavy-based saucepan. Sprinkle in the sugar and semolina and bring to the boil, stirring constantly until thickened and smooth. Remove the saucepan from the heat and set aside to cool slightly.

3 Separate the eggs, placing the whites in a greasefree bowl. Lightly beat the yolks together, then beat them into the milk mixture with grated rind, liqueur and most of the grated chocolate, reserving 2–3 teaspoons for decoration.

4 Whisk the egg whites until soft peaks form. Gently fold in about one-third of the milk mixture, then fold in the remainder. Spoon the mixture into the soufflé dish and place on the preheated baking tray. Bake for 30 minutes, until risen and just set. Sprinkle with the reserved chocolate and the shreds of orange zest and serve immediately.

COOK'S TIP
Separate the leftover mandarins or clementines into segments, removing all traces of pith. Half-dip into a bowl of melted plain chocolate and leave to set on non-stick baking parchment. Serve as petits fours with after-dinner coffee.

Choux Puffs with Chocolate

Sweet choux puffs are rarely served hot, which is a great shame because they are truly a special treat. Serve with your favourite ice cream.

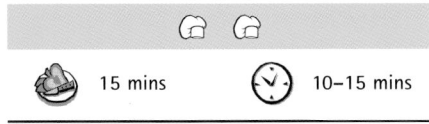

🍞 15 mins   🕐 10–15 mins

SERVES 6–8

INGREDIENTS

2 tbsp flaked almonds

125 g/4½ plain flour

70 g/2½ oz unsalted butter

225 ml/8 fl oz water

2 tsp caster sugar

4 eggs

40 g/1½ oz milk chocolate chips

sunflower oil, for deep-frying

2 bananas

icing sugar, for dusting

ice cream, to serve

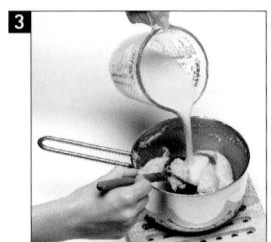

1 Spread out the almonds on a baking tray and toast under a preheated grill until golden brown. Keep an eye on them because they burn easily. Set aside to cool.

2 Sift the flour on to a sheet of greaseproof paper. Put the butter in a heavy-based saucepan, pour in the water, add the caster sugar and heat gently until the butter has melted. Increase the heat to medium and bring just to the boil. Immediately remove the saucepan from the heat and add all the flour. Mix well, then return the saucepan to a low heat and cook, stirring constantly, for about 1 minute, until the dough is smooth and comes away from the side of the saucepan. Set aside to cool slightly.

3 Beat the eggs in a jug, then gradually beat them into the dough. Continue to beat vigorously until the dough is thick and glossy, then beat in the toasted almonds and chocolate chips.

4 Heat the sunflower oil in a deep-fryer or large, heavy-based saucepan to 180°C/350°F, or until a cube of day-old bread browns in 45–60 seconds.

5 Meanwhile, peel and chop the bananas, then gently stir them into the dough. When the oil is hot, cook the choux puffs in batches. Scoop up tablespoonfuls of the dough and, using another spoon to help, drop them into the oil. Cook for 3–5 minutes, until they are puffed up, golden brown and rise to the surface of the oil. Remove, drain well on paper towels and keep warm while you cook the remaining batches.

6 Transfer to serving plates, dust with icing sugar, and serve immediately with scoops of ice cream.

COOK'S TIP

The secret to successful choux pastry is to stir, rather than beat the mixture when you add the flour and not to over-cook it. Remove the saucepan from the heat as soon as the dough comes away from the side of the saucepan.

Profiteroles

A classic dessert that never goes out of fashion. This version, with its chocolate and brandy sauce, is especially good.

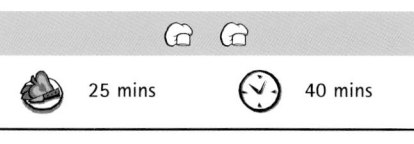

🍰 25 mins   🕐 40 mins

SERVES 4

INGREDIENTS

CHOUX PASTRY

100 g/3½ oz unsalted butter, plus extra for greasing

200 ml/7 fl oz water

100 g/3½ oz plain flour

3 eggs, beaten

CREAM FILLING

300 ml/10 fl oz double cream

3 tbsp caster sugar

1 tsp vanilla essence

CHOCOLATE AND COGNAC SAUCE

125 g/4½ oz plain chocolate, broken into small pieces

2½ tbsp butter

6 tbsp water

2 tbsp cognac

1 Preheat the oven to 200°C/400°F/Gas Mark 6. Grease a large baking tray with butter. To make the pastry, put the water and butter in a saucepan and bring to the boil. Meanwhile, sift the flour into a bowl. Remove the saucepan from the heat and add in the flour all at once, beating until smooth. Leave to cool for 5 minutes. Beat in enough of the eggs to make a soft, dropping consistency. Transfer to a piping bag fitted with a 1-cm/½-inch plain nozzle. Pipe small balls on to the baking tray. Bake for 25 minutes. Remove from the oven. Pierce the bottom of each ball with a skewer to allow steam to escape.

2 To make the filling, whip together the cream, sugar and vanilla. Cut the pastry balls almost in half horizontally, then fill each one with the cream.

3 To make the sauce, gently melt the chocolate, butter and water together in a small saucepan, stirring constantly, until smooth. Stir in the cognac. Pile the profiteroles into individual serving dishes or in a large pyramid on a raised cake stand. Pour over the sauce and serve.

Raspberry Croissants

Simple to prepare, these tasty croissants are placed on a barbecue to warm through until the chocolate melts.

🍞 10 mins 🕐 10–15 mins

SERVES 4

INGREDIENTS

4 butter croissants

4 tsp raspberry jam

75 g/2¾ oz plain chocolate

oil, for greasing

125 g/4½ oz raspberries

1 Slice the croissants in half. Spread the bottom half of each croissant with 1 teaspoon of the raspberry jam.

2 Grate or finely chop the chocolate and sprinkle over the raspberry jam.

3 Lightly grease 4 sheets of foil, brushing with a little oil.

4 Divide the raspberries equally among the croissants and replace the top half of each croissant. Place each croissant on a sheet of foil, wrapping the foil to enclose the croissant completely.

5 Place the rack 15 cm/6 inches above hot coals. Transfer the croissants to the rack and allow them to heat through for 10–15 minutes, or until the chocolate just starts to melt.

6 Remove the foil and transfer the croissants to individual serving plates. Serve hot.

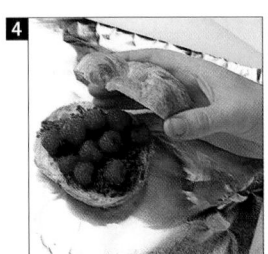

VARIATION

For a delicious chocolate and strawberry filling for the croissants, use sliced strawberries and strawberry jam instead of the raspberries.

Chocolate French Toasties

There is something very moreish about these delicious chocolate toasts, served with whipped cream and a raspberry and rum sauce.

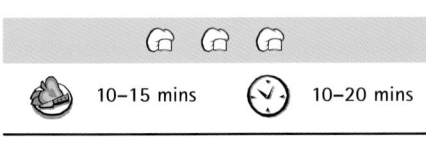

🍰 10–15 mins   🕐 10–20 mins

SERVES 4

INGREDIENTS

50 g/1¾ oz plain chocolate

150 ml/5 fl oz milk

1 egg

4 tbsp seedless raspberry jam

2 tbsp dark rum (optional)

8 thick slices white bread

butter or oil, for shallow-frying

½ tsp ground cinnamon

3 tbsp caster sugar

a little whipped cream, to serve

1 Break the chocolate into small pieces and place in a small saucepan with the milk. Heat gently, stirring, until the chocolate melts. Leave the mixture to cool slightly.

2 Beat the egg in a large mixing bowl and whisk in the chocolate milk.

3 Heat the raspberry jam gently and stir in the rum (if using). Set aside and keep warm.

4 Remove the crusts from the bread, cut into triangles, and dip each one into the chocolate mixture. Heat the butter or oil in a frying pan and shallow-fry the bread triangles for 2–3 minutes, turning once, until just crisp.

5 Mix together the cinnamon and caster sugar and sprinkle it over the toasties. Serve with the hot raspberry and rum sauce and a little whipped cream.

COOK'S TIP

Young children adore this dessert, made without the rum. Cut the bread into fingers to make it easier for them to handle.

Panettone & Strawberries

Panettone is a sweet Italian bread. It is delicious toasted, and when it is topped with mascarpone and strawberries it makes a sumptuous dessert.

5 mins plus
30 mins chilling   2 mins

SERVES 4

INGREDIENTS

250 g/8 oz strawberries

25 g/1 oz caster sugar

6 tbsp Marsala

½ tsp ground cinnamon

4 slices panettone

4 tbsp mascarpone cheese

1 Hull and slice the strawberries and place them in a large bowl. Add the sugar, Marsala and cinnamon to the strawberries.

2 Toss the strawberries in the sugar and cinnamon mixture until they are well coated. Leave to chill in the refrigerator for at least 30 minutes.

3 When ready to serve, transfer the slices of panettone to a rack set over medium hot coals. Barbecue the panettone for about 1 minute on each side or until golden brown.

4 Carefully remove the panettone from the barbecue and transfer to individual serving plates.

5 Top the panettone with the mascarpone cheese and the marinated strawberries. Serve immediately.

Strings of Gold

A delicate and elegant dessert with which to end a Chinese meal. Be sure that your jasmine flowers are untreated.

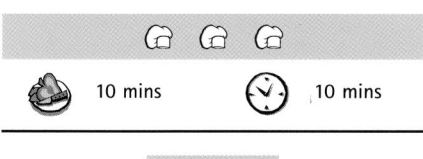

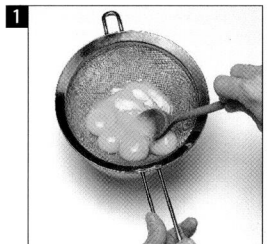

10 mins   10 mins

SERVES 4

INGREDIENTS

7 egg yolks

1 tbsp egg white

450 g/1 lb granulated sugar

200 ml/7 fl oz water

handful of scented jasmine flowers

1 Press the egg yolks and egg white through a fine sieve, then whisk together lightly.

2 Place the sugar and water in a large saucepan and heat gently until the sugar dissolves. Add the jasmine flowers, bring to the boil, and boil rapidly until a thin syrup forms. Remove the flowers with a slotted spoon.

3 Bring the syrup to simmering point. Using a piping bag with a fine nozzle, or a paper icing cone, quickly drizzle the egg mixture into the syrup in a thin steam to form loose nests or pyramid shapes.

4 As soon as the threads set, remove the nests carefully and drain well on kitchen paper. Arrange on a warmed serving dish. Garnish with fresh fruit.

COOK'S TIP
If you can't get hold of fresh, scented jasmine flowers, add a few drops of rosewater or orange-flower water to the syrup instead.

Sweet Rice

This dessert is served at banquets and celebratory meals in China, because it looks wonderful when sliced.

20 mins   1 hr 15 mins

SERVES 4

INGREDIENTS

175 g/6 oz pudding rice

2 tbsp unsalted butter, plus extra for greasing

1 tbsp caster sugar

8 dried dates, stoned and chopped

1 tbsp raisins

5 glacé cherries, halved

5 pieces angelica, chopped

5 walnut halves

125 g/4½ oz canned unsweetened chestnut purée

SYRUP

150 ml/5 fl oz water

2 tbsp orange juice

4½ tsp light brown sugar

1½ tsp cornflour

1 tbsp cold water

1 Put the rice in a saucepan, cover with cold water and bring to the boil. Reduce the heat, cover and simmer for about 15 minutes or until the water has been absorbed. Stir in the butter and caster sugar.

2 Grease a 600-ml/1½-pint pudding basin. Cover the base and side of the basin with a thin layer of the rice, pressing with the back of a spoon.

3 Mix the fruit and walnuts together and press them into the rice.

4 Spread a thicker layer of rice on top and then fill the centre with the chestnut purée. Cover with the remaining rice, pressing the top down to seal in the purée completely.

5 Cover the basin with pleated greaseproof paper and foil and secure with string. Place in a steamer or stand the basin in a saucepan and fill with hot water until it reaches halfway up the side of the basin. Cover and steam for 45 minutes. Leave to stand for 10 minutes.

6 Before serving, gently heat the water and orange juice in a small saucepan. Add the brown sugar and stir to dissolve. Bring the syrup to the boil.

7 Mix the cornflour with the cold water to form a smooth paste, then stir into the boiling syrup. Cook for 1 minute until thickened and clear.

8 Turn the pudding out on to a serving plate. Pour the syrup over the top, cut into slices and serve.

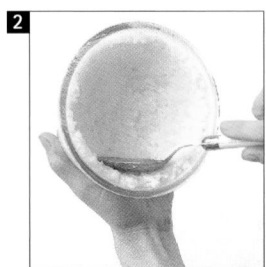

Mango with Sticky Rice

Coconut-flavoured cooked rice is served in domes with cubes of fresh mango. Serve the rice cut into diamond shapes instead, if preferred.

30 mins plus
30 mins soaking   25 mins

SERVES 4

INGREDIENTS

200 g/7 oz glutinous rice, soaked for 30 minutes in cold water

250 ml/8 fl oz coconut milk

2 tbsp caster sugar

pinch of salt

2 large ripe mangoes

1 Drain the rice and rinse thoroughly. Place in a saucepan with the coconut milk, sugar and salt. Bring to the boil and simmer, stirring occasionally, until the rice has absorbed all the coconut milk and is very soft.

2 Transfer the rice to a steamer set over a saucepan of gently simmering water. Cover and steam for 15 minutes. Leave to cool a little. Press the rice into the base of four ramekins and turn out on to individual plates to form rice domes. Alternatively, spread the rice out on a baking tray lined with foil, roll it flat with a wet rolling pin, and cut into diamond shapes.

3 Peel the mangoes and cut the flesh into cubes. To serve, pile the mango cubes around the rice domes, or arrange the rice diamonds and mango cubes on individual plates.

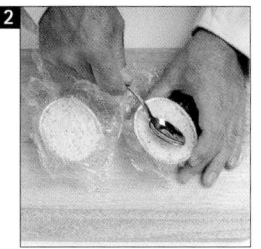
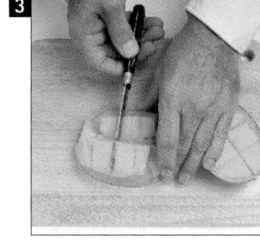

Sticky Rice Balls

Serve these sweet Chinese rice morsels as part of a dessert selection to follow a traditional Chinese banquet.

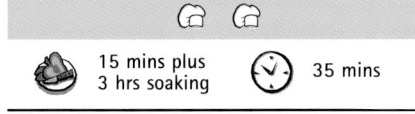

15 mins plus
3 hrs soaking

35 mins

SERVES 4

INGREDIENTS

300 g/10½oz glutinous rice

450 g/1 lb granulated sugar

300 ml/10 fl oz water

pink and green food colourings

rose petals or jasmine flowers, to decorate

1 Place the rice in a bowl and add enough cold water to cover. Leave to soak for 3 hours or overnight.

2 Drain the rice and rinse thoroughly in cold water.

3 Line the top part of a steamer with muslin and pour the rice into it. Place over boiling water, cover and steam the rice for 30 minutes. Remove and leave to cool.

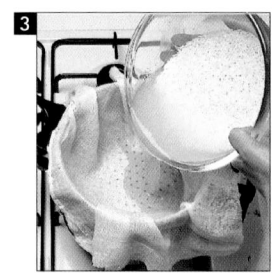

4 Heat the sugar and water gently until the sugar dissolves. Bring to the boil and boil for 4–5 minutes to reduce to a thin syrup. Remove the saucepan from the heat and set aside.

5 Divide the rice in half and colour one half pale pink, the other half pale green. Shape into small balls.

6 Using 2 forks, dip the rice balls into the syrup, drain off the excess and pile on to a dish. Scatter with rose petals or jasmine flowers.

COOK'S TIP
If you prefer, the rice can be shaped in small moulds like dariole moulds seen in the photo on the right.

Deep-Fried Sweetmeats

This is one of the most popular Indian sweetmeats. The flavour and beautiful aroma comes from rose water. Serve them hot or cold.

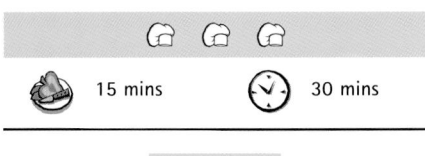

🍮 15 mins   🕐 30 mins

SERVES 8

INGREDIENTS

5 tbsp full-cream milk powder

1½ tbsp plain flour

1 tsp baking powder

1½ tbsp unsalted butter

1 medium egg

1 tsp milk to mix (if required)

10 tbsp pure or vegetable ghee

SYRUP

750 ml/1¼ pints water

8 tbsp sugar

2 green cardamom pods, peeled with seeds crushed

generous pinch of saffron strands

2 tbsp rosewater

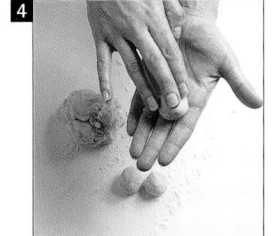

1 Place the milk powder, flour and baking powder in a large bowl.

2 Place the butter in a saucepan and heat until melted, stirring.

3 Beat the egg in a bowl. Add the melted butter and beaten egg to the dry ingredients and blend together with a fork (add the 1 teaspoon extra milk at this stage if necessary) to form a soft dough.

4 Break the dough into about 12 small pieces and shape into smooth balls.

5 Heat the ghee in a deep frying pan. Reduce the heat and start frying the dough balls, about 3–4 at a time, tossing and turning gently with a slotted spoon until a dark golden brown colour. Remove the sweetmeats from the frying pan and set aside in a deep serving bowl.

6 To make the syrup, boil the water and sugar in a saucepan for 7–10 minutes. Add the crushed cardamom seeds and saffron, and pour the syrup over the sweetmeats.

7 Pour the rosewater sparingly over the top. Leave for about 10 minutes to allow the sweetmeats to soak up some of the syrup. Serve hot or cold.

Sweet Carrot Halva

This nutritious dessert is flavoured with spices, nuts and raisins. Serve with cream.

10 mins   55 mins

SERVES 6

INGREDIENTS

750 g/1 lb 10 oz carrots, grated

700 ml/1¼ pints milk

1 cinnamon stick or piece of cassia bark (optional)

4 tbsp vegetable ghee or oil

55 g/2 oz granulated sugar

25 g/1 oz unsalted pistachio nuts, chopped

25–50 g/1–1¾ oz blanched almonds, flaked or chopped

55 g/2 oz raisins

8 whole cardamom pods, peeled and crushed

thick cream, to serve

COOK'S TIP

The quickest and easiest way to grate this quantity of carrots is by using a food processor fitted with the appropriate blade. This mixture may be prepared ahead of time and reheated in the microwave when required.

1 Put the grated carrots, milk, and cinnamon or cassia (if using), into a large, heavy-based saucepan and bring to the boil. Reduce the heat to very low and simmer, uncovered, for about 35–40 minutes, or until the mixture is thick (with no milk remaining). Stir the mixture frequently during cooking to prevent it sticking.

2 Remove and discard the cinnamon or cassia. Heat the ghee or oil in a non-stick frying pan, add the carrot mixture, and stir-fry over medium heat for about 5 minutes, or until the carrots take on a glossy sheen.

3 Add the sugar, pistachios, almonds, raisins, and crushed cardamom seeds, mix thoroughly, and continue stir-frying for an additional 3–4 minutes. Serve warm or cold, with thick cream.

Carrot Dessert

This makes an impressive dinner-party dessert. It is best served warm with cream and can be made well in advance because it freezes well.

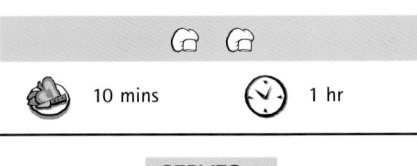

10 mins   1 hr

SERVES 6

INGREDIENTS

1.5 kg/3 lb 5 oz carrots

10 tbsp ghee

600 ml/1 pint milk

175 ml/6 fl oz evaporated milk

10 whole cardamom pods, peeled and crushed

8–10 tbsp sugar

TO DECORATE

4 tbsp chopped pistachio nuts

2 leaves varq (silver leaf), optional

1 Grate the carrots. Heat the ghee in a large, heavy-based frying pan over medium heat. Add the grated carrots and cook, stirring constantly, for about 15–20 minutes or until the moisture from the carrots has evaporated and the carrots have darkened in colour.

2 Add the milk, evaporated milk, crushed cardamom seeds, and sugar and cook, stirring constantly, for a further 30–35 minutes, until the mixture is a rich brownish-red colour.

3 Transfer the carrot mixture to a large shallow serving dish. Decorate with the pistachio nuts and varq (if using), and serve immediately.

COOK'S TIP
Pure ghee is best for this dessert because it will taste better. However, if you are trying to limit your fat intake, you can use vegetable ghee instead.

German Noodle Dessert

This rich and satisfying dessert is a traditional Jewish recipe that will quickly become popular with all the family.

10 mins   45 mins

SERVES 4

INGREDIENTS

4 tbsp butter, plus extra for greasing

175 g/6 oz ribbon egg noodles

115 g/4 oz cream cheese

225 g/8 oz cottage cheese

85 g/3 oz caster sugar

2 eggs, beaten lightly

125 ml/4 fl oz soured cream

1 tsp vanilla essence

pinch of ground cinnamon

1 tsp grated lemon rind

25 g/1 oz flaked almonds

25 g/1 oz dry white bread crumbs

icing sugar, for dusting

1 Preheat the oven to 350°F/180°C. Lightly grease an oval ovenproof dish with a little butter. Bring a large saucepan of water to the boil. Add the noodles, bring back to the boil, and cook over medium heat for 10 minutes until tender, but still firm to the bite. Drain and set aside.

2 Beat the cream cheese with the cottage cheese and caster sugar in a mixing bowl until the mixture is smooth. Add the beaten eggs, a little at a time, beating thoroughly after each addition.

3 Stir in the soured cream, vanilla essence, cinnamon and lemon rind and fold in the noodles. Transfer the mixture to the prepared ovenproof dish and smooth the surface.

4 Melt the butter in a small frying pan over a low heat. Add the almonds and cook gently, stirring constantly, for about 1–1½ minutes until they are lightly coloured. Remove the frying pan from the heat and stir the breadcrumbs into the almonds.

5 Sprinkle the almond and breadcrumb mixture evenly over the top of the pudding and bake in the preheated oven for about 35–40 minutes until just set. Dust the top with a little sifted icing sugar and serve immediately.

VARIATION
Although not authentic, you could add 3 tablespoons of raisins with the lemon rind in step 3, if desired.

Indian Vermicelli Pudding

Indian vermicelli (seviyan), which are very fine, are delicious cooked in milk and ghee. Muslims make this for a religious festival called Eid.

5 mins

20 mins

SERVES 6

INGREDIENTS

25 g/1 oz pistachio nuts (optional)

25 g/1 oz flaked almonds

3 tbsp ghee

100 g/3½ oz seviyan (Indian vermicelli)

900 ml/1½ pints milk

175 ml/6 fl oz evaporated milk

8 tbsp sugar

6 dried dates, stoned

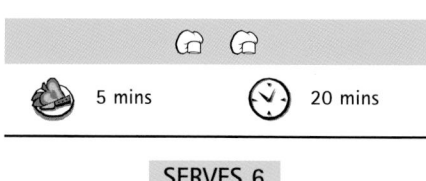

1 Soak the pistachio nuts (if using) in a bowl of water for at least 3 hours. Peel the pistachio nuts and mix them with the flaked almonds. Chop the nuts finely and set aside.

2 Melt the ghee in a large saucepan and lightly cook the seviyan. Reduce the heat immediately (the seviyan turns golden brown very quickly so be careful not to burn it), and if necessary remove the saucepan from the heat (do not worry if some bits are darker than others).

3 Add the milk to the seviyan and bring to the boil over a low heat, taking care that it does not boil over.

4 Add the evaporated milk, sugar, and dates to the mixture in the saucepan. Simmer over a low heat, uncovered, stirring occasionally, for about 10 minutes. When the mixture starts to thicken, pour the pudding into a warm serving bowl.

5 Decorate the pudding with the chopped pistachio nuts and almonds.

COOK'S TIP
You will find seviyan (Indian vermicelli) in Indian food stores. This dessert can be served warm or cold.

Sweet Potato Dessert

This unusual milky dessert is very easy to make and is equally delicious whether it is eaten hot or cold.

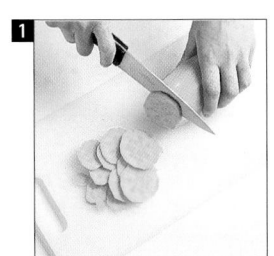
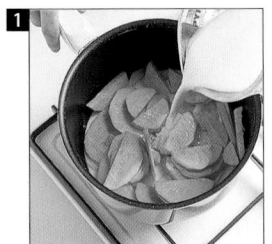

15 mins

20 mins

SERVES 4

INGREDIENTS

1 kg/2 lb 4 oz sweet potatoes

900 ml/1½ pints milk

175 g/6 oz sugar

chopped almonds, to decorate

1 Using a sharp knife, peel the sweet potatoes. Rinse them and then cut them into slices. Place in a large saucepan. Cover with 600 ml/1 pint of the milk and cook over a low heat until the sweet potato is soft enough to be mashed.

2 Remove the sweet potatoes from the heat and mash thoroughly until completely smooth. Add the sugar and the remaining milk and stir gently until completely blended together.

3 Return the saucepan to the heat and simmer the mixture until it starts to thicken (it should reach the consistency of a creamy soup).

4 Transfer to a serving dish. Decorate with almonds and serve immediately.

COOK'S TIP

Look for the sweet potatoes with a pinkish skin and yellow flesh, which give a good colour to this dessert.

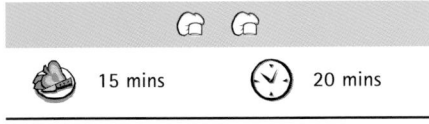

Indian Bread Pudding

This, the Indian equivalent of the English bread and butter pudding, is rather a special dessert, usually cooked for special occasions.

20 mins   25 mins

SERVES 6

I N G R E D I E N T S

6 medium slices bread

5 tbsp ghee (preferably pure)

150 g/5½ oz sugar

300 ml/10 fl oz water

3 green cardamom pods, husks removed

600 ml/1 pint milk

175 ml/6 fl oz evaporated milk or khoya (see Cook's Tip)

½ tsp saffron strands

double cream, to serve (optional)

T O D E C O R A T E

8 pistachio nuts, soaked, peeled and chopped

chopped almonds

2 leaves varq (silver leaf), optional

1 Cut the bread slices into quarters. Heat the ghee in a large, heavy-based frying pan. Add the bread slices and cook, turning once, until crisp and golden brown. Place the fried bread in the bottom of a heatproof dish and set aside.

2 To make a syrup, place the sugar, water and cardamom seeds in a saucepan and bring to the boil over a medium heat, stirring constantly, until the sugar has dissolved. Boil until thickened. Pour the syrup over the fried bread.

3 Put the milk, evaporated milk or khoya (see Cook's Tip), and the saffron in a separate saucepan and bring to the boil over a low heat. Simmer until it has halved in volume. Pour the mixture over the syrup-coated bread.

4 Decorate with the pistachio nuts, chopped almonds and varq (if using). Serve the bread pudding with cream, if liked.

COOK'S TIP
To make khoya, bring 900 ml/ 1½ pints milk to the boil in a large, heavy-based saucepan. Reduce the heat and boil, stirring occasionally, for 35–40 minutes, until reduced to a quarter of its volume and resembling a sticky dough.

Italian Bread Dessert

This deliciously rich dessert is cooked with cream and apples and is delicately flavoured with orange.

45 mins   25 mins

SERVES 4

I N G R E D I E N T S

1 tbsp butter

2 small eating apples, peeled, cored and sliced into rings

85 g/3 oz granulated sugar

2 tbsp white wine

4 thick slices bread (about 115 g/4 oz), crusts removed (day-old baguette is ideal)

300 ml/10 fl oz single cream

2 eggs, beaten

pared zest of 1 orange, cut into short, thin strips

1 Lightly grease a 1.2-litre/2-pint deep ovenproof dish with the butter.

2 Arrange the apple rings in the bottom of the dish. Sprinkle half of the sugar over the apples.

3 Pour the wine over the apples. Add the bread slices, pushing them down with your hands to flatten them slightly.

4 Mix the cream with the eggs, the remaining sugar and the orange zest and pour the mixture over the bread. Set aside to soak for 30 minutes. Preheat the oven to 180°C/350°F/Gas Mark 4.

5 Bake the pudding for 25 minutes, until golden and set. Remove from the oven, leave to cool slightly and serve warm.

Chocolate Bread Dessert

This chocolate sponge is served with hot fudge sauce, making it the most delicious way to use up bread that is slightly stale.

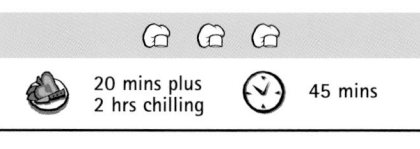

20 mins plus
2 hrs chilling

45 mins

SERVES 4

I N G R E D I E N T S

butter, for greasing

6 thick slices white bread, crusts removed

450 ml/16 fl oz milk

175 g/6 oz canned evaporated milk

2 tbsp cocoa powder

2 eggs

2 tbsp dark muscovado sugar

1 tsp vanilla essence

icing sugar, for dusting

H O T   F U D G E   S A U C E

55 g/2 oz plain chocolate, broken
into pieces

1 tbsp cocoa powder

2 tbsp golden syrup

55 g/2 oz butter or margarine

2 tbsp dark muscovado sugar

150 ml/5 fl oz milk

1 tbsp cornflour

1 Grease a shallow ovenproof dish. Cut the bread into squares and layer them in the dish.

2 Put the milk, evaporated milk and cocoa powder in a saucepan and heat gently, stirring occasionally until the mixture is tepid.

3 Whisk together the eggs, sugar and vanilla essence. Add the warm milk mixture and beat well.

4 Pour into the prepared dish, making sure that all the bread is completely covered. Cover the dish with clingfilm and chill in the refrigerator for 1–2 hours.

5 Preheat the oven to 180°C/350°F/Gas Mark 4. Bake the dessert for 35–40 minutes until set. Leave to stand for 5 minutes.

6 To make the sauce, put the chocolate, cocoa powder, syrup, butter (or margarine), sugar, milk and cornflour into a saucepan. Heat gently, stirring until smooth.

7 Dust the dessert with icing sugar and serve immediately with the hot fudge sauce.

Chocolate Marmalade Brioche

The light, buttery texture of brioche makes it the ideal basis for a rich, chocolate dessert, perfect for family meals or entertaining.

10 mins plus 1 hr soaking

1 hr 10 mins

SERVES 6

INGREDIENTS

5 tbsp unsalted butter, plus extra for greasing

300 g/10½ oz plain chocolate

6 tbsp Oxford marmalade

6 individual brioches

4 large eggs

425 ml/15 fl oz milk

425 ml/15 fl oz double cream

3 tbsp light brown sugar

1 Preheat the oven to 180°C/350°F/ Gas Mark 4. Grease a large ovenproof dish. Break the chocolate into pieces and place in a heatproof bowl with the marmalade. Melt over a saucepan of gently simmering water, stirring frequently, until melted and combined. Remove the bowl from the heat.

2 Cut the brioches in half and spread the cut sides with the chocolate and marmalade mixture, then arrange the slices evenly in the dish. Beat the eggs in a bowl, then beat in the milk and cream. Pour the mixture evenly over the brioches, pressing them down so that they are submerged. Cover the dish with clingfilm and leave to soak for up to 1 hour.

3 Uncover the dish and sprinkle the sugar evenly over the surface. Bake for 50–60 minutes, until set. Remove the dish from the oven and leave to stand for 10 minutes, then serve.

COOK'S TIP
Oxford marmalade is made from bitter Seville oranges. Alternatively, you could use grapefruit or a mixed citrus fruit marmalade, but choose one that has a bitter edge.

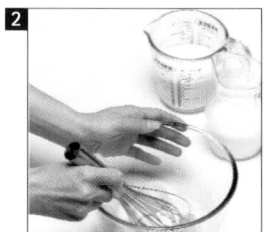

Sunday Pudding

A popular, easy-to-make chocolate and fruit pudding that is the perfect choice for a family lunch. It can be served hot or cold.

🍮 15 mins plus 1 hr soaking
🕐 45–50 mins

SERVES 4

INGREDIENTS

2–3 tbsp butter, plus extra for greasing

6 slices brown bread

400 g/14 oz canned mangoes, drained and chopped

2 tbsp chopped blanched almonds or hazelnuts

4 tbsp sultanas

1 tsp ground cinnamon

55 g/2 oz plain chocolate

2 eggs

1 tbsp caster sugar

350 ml/12 fl oz single cream

1 tsp white rum (optional)

1 Grease a medium-size ovenproof dish. Cut off and discard the crusts from the bread and generously spread 1 side of each slice with butter. Cut the slices into quarters.

2 Cover the bottom of the dish with a layer of bread, buttered side up. Spoon half the mangoes evenly over them, then sprinkle with half the nuts, half the raisins, and half the cinnamon. Cover with a second layer of bread, buttered side up and top with the remaining mangoes, nuts, sultanas and cinnamon. Cover with the remaining bread, buttered side up. Set aside.

3 Chop the chocolate, place in a heatproof bowl and set over a saucepan of gently simmering water to melt. When melted, remove the saucepan from the heat and stir until smooth.

4 Beat the eggs in another heatproof bowl, then gradually whisk in the sugar and the cream. Set the bowl over a saucepan of gently simmering water and cook, whisking constantly, until thickened and a trail is left when the whisk is dragged across the surface. Remove the bowl from the heat and whisk in the melted chocolate and rum, if using. Pour the chocolate mixture evenly over the bread. Cover and leave to soak for 1 hour.

5 Preheat the oven to 190°C/375°F/ Gas Mark 5. Bake the pudding for 40–45 minutes, until the top is crisp and golden. Leave to stand for 5 minutes before serving. Alternatively, leave to cool and serve cold.

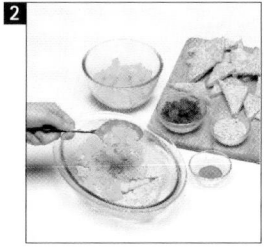

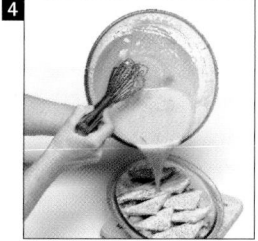

Brioche & Butter Pudding

Brioche gives this dessert a lovely rich flavour, but this recipe also works well with soft-baked batch bread.

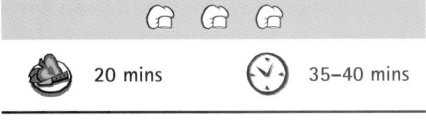

20 mins   35–40 mins

SERVES 6

INGREDIENTS

225 g/8 oz brioche

1 tbsp butter

50 g/1¾ oz plain chocolate chips

1 egg

2 egg yolks

4 tbsp caster sugar

425 ml/15 fl oz canned light
    evaporated milk

1 Preheat the oven to 180°C/350°F/ Gas Mark 4. Cut the brioche into thin slices. Lightly butter one side of each slice.

2 Place a layer of brioche, buttered side down, in the bottom of a shallow ovenproof dish. Sprinkle a few chocolate chips over the top.

3 Continue layering the brioche and chocolate chips, finishing with a layer of brioche on top.

4 Whisk together the egg, egg yolks and sugar until well combined. Heat the milk in a small saucepan until it just starts to simmer. Gradually add to the egg mixture, whisking well.

5 Pour the custard over the brioche and leave to stand for 5 minutes. Press the brioche down into the custard.

6 Place the dish in a roasting tin and fill with boiling water to come halfway up the side of the dish. Bake in the preheated oven for 30 minutes or until the custard has set. Leave the dessert to cool for about 5 minutes before serving.

VARIATION
For a double-chocolate dessert, heat the milk with 1 tablespoon of cocoa powder, stirring until well dissolved, then continue from step 4.

Bread & Butter Pudding

A traditional pudding full of fruit and spices. It is the perfect way to use up day-old bread.

50 mins   45–55 mins

SERVES 6

INGREDIENTS

10 tsp butter, softened, plus extra for greasing

200 g/7 oz white bread, sliced

2 tbsp sultanas

25 g/1 oz candied peel

600 ml/1 pint milk

4 egg yolks

5 tbsp caster sugar

½ tsp ground mixed spice

1 Preheat the oven to 200°C/400°F/Gas Mark 6. Grease a 1.2-litre/2-pint ovenproof dish.

2 Remove the crusts from the bread (optional), spread with butter and cut into quarters.

3 Arrange half of the buttered bread slices in the prepared ovenproof dish. Sprinkle half of the sultanas and candied peel over the top of the bread.

4 Place the remaining bread slices over the fruit and then sprinkle over the reserved fruit.

5 To make the custard, bring the milk almost to a boil in a saucepan. Whisk together the egg yolks and the sugar in a bowl, then pour in the warm milk.

6 Strain the warm custard through a sieve. Pour the custard over the bread slices.

7 Leave to stand for 30 minutes, then sprinkle with the mixed spice.

8 Place the ovenproof dish in a roasting tin half-filled with hot water.

9 Bake in the preheated oven for 40-45 minutes, until the pudding has just set. Serve warm.

COOK'S TIP
The pudding can be prepared in advance up to step 7 and then set aside until required.

Apple Bread & Butter Pudding

Bread and butter pudding is a great favourite. This one has added marmalade and grated apples for a really rich and unique taste.

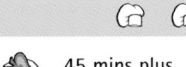 

45 mins plus
30 mins standing   1 hr

SERVES 6

INGREDIENTS

5 tbsp butter, softened

4–5 slices white or brown bread

4 tbsp chunky orange marmalade

grated zest of 1 lemon

85–125 g/3–4½ oz raisins or sultanas

40 g/1½ oz chopped mixed peel

1 tsp ground cinnamon or mixed spice

1 cooking apple, peeled, cored
   and coarsely grated

85 g/3 oz light brown sugar

3 eggs

500 ml/18 fl oz milk

2 tbsp demerara sugar

1 Use the softened butter to grease an ovenproof dish and to spread on the slices of bread, then spread the bread with the marmalade.

2 Place a layer of bread in the base of the dish and sprinkle with the lemon zest, half the raisins or sultanas, half the mixed peel, half the spice, all of the apple and half the brown sugar. Add another layer of bread, cutting it to fit the dish.

3 Sprinkle over most of the remaining raisins or sultanas and the remaining mixed peel, spice and brown sugar, scattering it evenly over the bread. Top with a final layer of bread, again cutting it to fit the dish.

4 Lightly beat together the eggs and milk and then carefully strain the mixture over the bread in the dish. If time allows, set the pudding aside to stand for 20–30 minutes. Preheat the oven to 200°C/400°F/Gas Mark 6.

5 Sprinkle the demerara sugar over the pudding and scatter the remaining raisins or sultanas on top. Cook in the preheated oven for 50–60 minutes until risen and golden brown. Serve immediately or leave to cool and then serve cold.

Panettone Pudding

This is a variation of bread and butter pudding, made with an Italian cross between a bread and a cake which is traditionally served at Christmas.

15 mins plus
1 hr soaking

40 mins

SERVES 6

I N G R E D I E N T S

3 tbsp butter, softened, plus extra
 for greasing

250 g/9 oz panettone, cut into slices

225 ml/8 fl oz milk

225 ml/8 fl oz double cream

1 vanilla pod, split

3 eggs

115 g/4 oz golden caster sugar

2 tbsp apricot jam, warmed and sieved

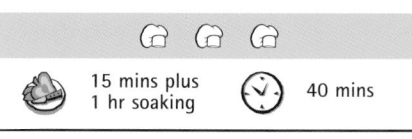

1 Preheat the oven to 160°C/325°F/Gas Mark 3. Grease an 900-ml/1½-pint shallow baking dish. Butter the slices of panettone and arrange in the dish. Put the milk, cream and vanilla pod in a saucepan and heat gently to boiling point. Put the eggs and sugar in a bowl and beat together, then pour in the milk mixture and beat together.

2 Pour the custard through a sieve over the buttered panettone. Leave to stand for 1 hour so that the panettone soaks up the custard.

3 Bake the pudding in the oven for about 40 minutes, then brush the apricot jam over the top. If the top crusts of the pudding are not crisp and golden, heat under the grill for a minute.

COOK'S TIP
The vanilla pod may
be rinsed and dried
and used again.

Spiced Steamed Pudding

Steamed puddings are irresistible on a winter's day, but the texture of this pudding is so light it can be served throughout the year.

🍲 15 mins   🕐 1 hr 30 mins

SERVES 6

I N G R E D I E N T S

125 g/4½ oz butter or margarine, plus extra for greasing

2 tbsp golden syrup, plus extra to serve

125 g/4½ oz caster or light brown sugar

2 eggs

175 g/6 oz self-raising flour

¾ tsp ground cinnamon or mixed spice

grated rind of 1 orange

1 tbsp orange juice

85 g/3 oz sultanas

5 tbsp stem ginger, finely chopped

1 eating apple, peeled, cored and coarsely grated

1   Thoroughly grease a 900-ml/1½-pint pudding basin. Put the golden syrup into the basin.

2   Cream the butter or margarine and sugar together until very light and fluffy and pale in colour. Beat in the eggs, one at a time, following each with a spoonful of the flour.

3   Sift the remaining flour with the cinnamon or mixed spice and fold into the mixture, followed by the orange rind and juice. Fold in the sultanas, then the ginger and apple.

4   Turn the mixture into the basin and level the top. Cover with a piece of pleated greased baking parchment, tucking the edges under the rim of the basin.

5   Cover with a sheet of pleated foil. Tie securely in place with string, with a piece of string tied over the top of the basin for a handle to make it easy to lift out of the saucepan.

6   Put the basin into a saucepan half filled with boiling water, cover and steam for 1½ hours, adding more boiling water to the saucepan as necessary during cooking.

7   To serve the pudding, remove the foil and baking parchment, turn the pudding on to a warm serving plate and serve immediately.

Snowdon Pudding

This old-fashioned British steamed pudding was named after the Welsh mountain, Snowdon. The story goes it was served to hungry climbers.

15 mins   2 hrs 10 mins

SERVES 6

I N G R E D I E N T S

butter, for greasing

2 tbsp chopped angelica

125 g/4½ oz raisins

115 g/4 oz fresh white breadcrumbs

25 g/1 oz rice flour

pinch of salt

115 g/4 oz plus 2 tbsp shredded suet

2 tbsp light brown sugar

grated rind of 1 large lemon

2 eggs

85 g/3 oz marmalade

3–4 tsp milk

L E M O N   S A U C E

1 tbsp cornflour

250 ml/9 fl oz plus 2 tbsp milk

grated rind and juice of 2 lemons

3 tbsp golden syrup

1 Sprinkle a well-greased 1.2-litre/ 2-pint pudding basin with the angelica and 1 tablespoon of the raisins.

2 Put the remaining raisins in a bowl with the breadcrumbs, rice flour, salt, suet, sugar and lemon rind and toss to combine. Make a well in the centre.

3 Beat the eggs and marmalade for about 1 minute until starting to lighten. Beat in 3 tablespoons of the milk, then pour into the well. Gently stir into the dry ingredients to form a soft consistency. Add more milk if necessary. Spoon into the prepared pudding basin.

4 Grease a sheet of greaseproof paper and make a pleat along the centre. Cover the bowl loosely with the paper, buttered side down and secure with string.

5 Stand the pudding basin on a wire rack in a large saucepan. Fill with enough boiling water to come three-quarters of the way up the side of the basin. Cover and steam over a low heat for about 2 hours, until the top is risen. Top up with boiling water when needed.

6 To make the lemon sauce, mix the cornflour with about 3 tablespoons of milk to form a paste. Bring the remaining milk and the lemon rind to a simmer, then whisk into the paste until blended. Return the mixture to the saucepan and simmer gently for about 3 minutes, whisking, until smooth. Stir in the lemon juice and syrup. Pour into a jug and keep warm.

7 Remove the basin from the saucepan, discard the paper and let the pudding shrink slightly before unmoulding. Serve hot with the lemon sauce.

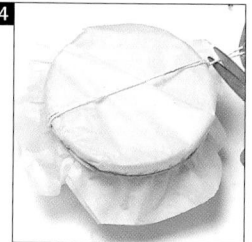

Steamed Coconut Cake

This steamed coconut cake, steeped in a syrup of lime and ginger, is typical of Thai desserts and sweets. It has a distinctly Chinese influence.

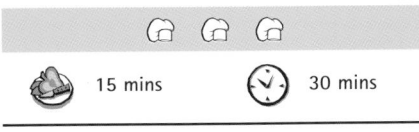

15 mins | 30 mins

SERVES 4

INGREDIENTS

2 large eggs, separated

pinch of salt

100 g/3½ oz caster sugar

75 g/2¾ oz butter, melted and cooled

5 tbsp coconut milk

150 g/5½ oz self-raising flour

½ tsp baking powder

3 tbsp desiccated coconut

4 tbsp stem ginger syrup

3 tbsp lime juice

TO DECORATE

3 pieces stem ginger, diced

curls of freshly grated coconut

fine strips of lime zest

1 Cut a 28-cm/11-inch round of baking parchment and press into an 18-cm/7-inch steamer basket to line it.

2 Whisk the egg whites with the salt until stiff. Gradually whisk in the sugar, 1 tablespoon at a time, whisking hard after each addition until the mixture forms stiff peaks.

3 Whisk in the yolks, then quickly stir in the butter and coconut milk. Sift the flour and baking powder over the mixture, then fold in lightly and evenly with a large metal spoon. Fold in the coconut.

4 Spoon the mixture into the lined steamer basket and tuck the spare paper over the top. Place the basket over boiling water, cover and steam for 30 minutes.

5 Turn the cake on to a plate, remove the paper and leave to cool slightly. Mix the ginger syrup and lime juice and spoon over the cake. Cut into squares and top with ginger, coconut and lime zest.

COOK'S TIP

Coconuts grow on tropical beaches all around the world, but probably originated in Southeast Asia, and it is here that coconut is most important in cooking.

Quick Syrup Sponge

You won't believe your eyes when you see just how quickly this light-as-air sponge pudding cooks in the microwave oven!

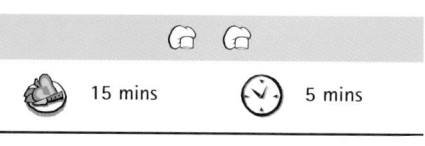

🥘 15 mins   🕐 5 mins

SERVES 4

INGREDIENTS

125 g/4½ oz butter or margarine

4 tbsp golden syrup

85 g/3 oz caster sugar

2 eggs

125 g/4½ oz self-raising flour

1 tsp baking powder

about 2 tbsp warm water

custard, to serve

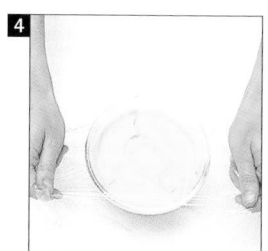

1 Grease a 1.5-litre/2½-pint pudding basin with a small amount of the butter or margarine. Spoon the syrup into the basin.

2 Cream the remaining butter or margarine with the sugar until light and fluffy. Gradually add the eggs, beating well between each addition.

3 Sift the flour and baking powder together, then fold into the creamed mixture using a large metal spoon. Add enough water to give a soft, dropping consistency. Spoon into the pudding basin and level the surface.

4 Cover with microwave-safe film, leaving a small space to let air escape. Microwave on HIGH power for 4 minutes, then remove from the microwave and leave the pudding to stand for 5 minutes, while it continues to cook.

5 Turn the pudding out on to a serving plate. Serve with custard.

COOK'S TIP
If you don't have a microwave, this pudding can be steamed. Cover with a piece of pleated baking parchment and a piece of pleated foil. Place in a saucepan, add boiling water and steam for 1½ hours.

Steamed Coffee Sponge

This sponge dessert is very light and is delicious served with a coffee or chocolate sauce.

10 mins

1 hr–
1 hr 15 mins

SERVES 4

INGREDIENTS

2 tbsp margarine

2 tbsp brown sugar

2 eggs

5½ tbsp plain flour

¾ tsp baking powder

6 tbsp milk

1 tsp coffee essence

SAUCE

300 ml/10 fl oz milk

1 tbsp brown sugar

1 tsp cocoa powder

2 tbsp cornflour

1 Lightly grease a 600-ml/1-pint pudding basin. Cream the margarine and sugar until the mixture is light and fluffy, then beat in the eggs.

2 Gradually stir in the flour and baking powder, then stir in the milk and coffee essence to make a smooth mixture.

3 Spoon the mixture into the basin and cover with a pleated piece of baking parchment, then a pleated piece of foil and tie them on securely with kitchen string.

4 Place in a steamer or large saucepan half full of boiling water. Cover and steam for 1–1¼ hours or until cooked.

5 To make the sauce, put the milk, sugar and cocoa powder in a saucepan and heat until the sugar dissolves. Blend the cornflour to a paste with 4 tablespoons of water and stir into the saucepan. Bring the sauce to the boil, stirring until thickened. Cook for 1 minute.

6 Turn the pudding out on to a warm serving plate and spoon the sauce over the top. Serve immediately.

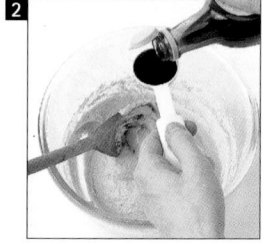

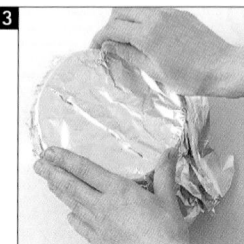

Chocolate Cranberry Sponge

The sharpness of the fruit contrasts deliciously with the sweetness of the chocolate in this wonderful, fluffy sponge pudding.

20 mins   1 hr 10 mins

SERVES 4

INGREDIENTS

4 tbsp unsalted butter, plus
  1 tsp for greasing

4 tbsp dark brown sugar, plus 2 tsp
  for sprinkling

85 g/3 oz cranberries, thawed if frozen

1 large cooking apple

2 eggs, lightly beaten

85 g/3 oz self-raising flour

3 tbsp cocoa powder

SAUCE

175 g/6 oz plain chocolate, broken
  into pieces

400 ml/14 fl oz evaporated milk

1 tsp vanilla essence

½ tsp almond essence

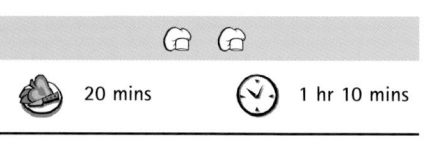

1 Grease a 1.2-litre/2-pint pudding basin, sprinkle with brown sugar to coat the side and tip out any excess. Put the cranberries in a bowl. Peel, core and dice the apple and mix with the cranberries. Put the fruit in the prepared pudding basin.

2 Place the butter, brown sugar and eggs in a large bowl. Sift in the flour and cocoa powder and beat well until thoroughly mixed. Pour the mixture into the pudding basin on top of the fruit, cover the top with foil and tie with string. Steam for about 1 hour, until risen, topping up with boiling water if necessary.

3 Meanwhile, to make the sauce, put the plain chocolate and milk in a double boiler or a heatproof bowl set over a saucepan of gently simmering water. Stir until the chocolate has melted, then remove from the heat. Whisk in the vanilla and almond essences and continue to beat until the sauce is thick and smooth.

4 To serve, remove the sponge from the heat and discard the foil. Run a palette knife around the side of the bowl, place a serving plate on top of the sponge and, holding them together, invert. Serve immediately, handing the sauce round separately in a jug.

German Chocolate Dessert

This heavenly confection from southern Germany is definitely not for those who are watching their weight.

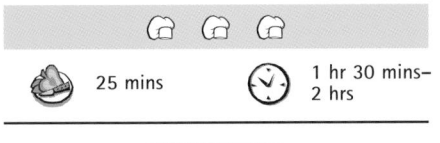

25 mins

1 hr 30 mins–2 hrs

SERVES 6

INGREDIENTS

1 tsp vegetable oil, for greasing

175 g/6 oz plain chocolate

6 slices white bread

225 ml/8 fl oz double cream

115 g/4 oz unsalted butter

175 g/6 oz caster sugar

175 g/6 oz ground almonds

½ tsp instant coffee powder

6 eggs

1 Brush a 1.2-litre/2-pint metal mould with a little vegetable oil. Break the chocolate into pieces and place in a heatproof bowl. Set over a saucepan of gently simmering water, stirring occasionally, until melted. Remove from the heat and set aside.

2 Cut off and discard the crusts from the bread and cut the slices into cubes. Place in a bowl, pour in the cream, stir well and leave to soak for 5 minutes.

3 Meanwhile, cream the butter with the sugar until fluffy, then add the bread and cream and beat until smooth and creamy. Then gradually beat in the melted chocolate, ground almonds and instant coffee. Continue to beat until smooth and thoroughly incorporated. Gradually beat in the eggs, 1 at a time.

4 Pour the mixture into the prepared mould. Cut out a round of foil about 10 cm/4 inches larger than the rim of the mould. Make a pleat in the centre of the round, place on top of the mould and tie securely in place with kitchen string.

5 Place the mould in a large saucepan and pour in enough boiling water to come about halfway up the side. Cover and steam over a low heat for 1½–2 hours, topping up the boiling water as necessary.

6 Turn off the heat and remove the mould from the saucepan. Remove and discard the foil. Run a round-bladed knife around the edge of the mould to loosen, then invert the dessert on to a warm serving plate. Serve immediately.

Austrian Chocolate Dessert

This is rather like a very rich soufflé, traditionally served with chocolate sauce and fruit bottled in brandy.

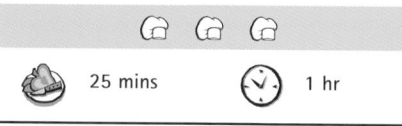

🍧 25 mins   🕐 1 hr

SERVES 8

INGREDIENTS

PUDDING

55 g/2 oz plain chocolate, broken into pieces

100 g/3½ oz butter, plus extra for greasing

85 g/3 oz caster sugar, plus extra for sprinkling

225 ml/8 fl oz milk

1 tsp vanilla essence

pinch of salt

85 g/3 oz plain flour

6 eggs, separated

icing sugar, for dusting

apricots or prunes in brandy, to serve

SAUCE

125 ml/4 fl oz water

3 tbsp sugar

175 g/6 oz dark chocolate, broken into pieces

2 tbsp unsalted butter, diced

5 tbsp single cream

½ tsp vanilla essence

1 To make the pudding, melt the chocolate in a heatproof bowl set over a saucepan of gently simmering water. Remove from the heat and leave to cool slightly. Grease a 1.75-litre/3-pint soufflé dish, sprinkle with sugar, tapping the side to coat and tipping out any excess. Preheat the oven to 160°C/325°F/Gas Mark 3.

2 Place the milk, butter, vanilla essence and salt in a large, heavy-based saucepan and bring to the boil over a low heat, stirring occasionally. Gradually stir in the flour and continue to stir until the mixture is just coming away from the side of the saucepan. Remove from the heat and stir in the melted chocolate, then stir in the egg yolks, 1 at a time.

3 Whisk the egg whites in a clean, greasefree bowl until soft peaks form, then gradually whisk in the sugar until stiff. Spoon about a quarter of the egg white into the chocolate mixture to lighten it, then gently fold in the remainder in 2 batches.

4 Spoon the mixture into the prepared dish, place in a large roasting tin, and pour in enough hot water to come halfway up the side of the dish. Bake for 50 minutes.

5 Just before serving, make the sauce. Pour the water into a saucepan, add the sugar, and bring to the boil, stirring until the sugar has dissolved. Stir in the chocolate and butter, then remove the saucepan from the heat and stir well until the mixture is smooth. Stir in the cream and vanilla essence.

6 Divide the chocolate pudding between warm serving plates and dust the top with a little icing sugar. Spoon over a little of the sauce, add 1 or 2 pieces of brandy-soaked fruit and serve immediately.

Golden Pudding

A comforting pudding, perfect for a winter's day. The golden syrup gives this delicious dessert a golden glow.

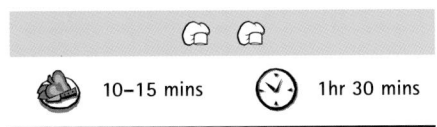

10–15 mins   1hr 30 mins

SERVES 4–6

INGREDIENTS

3 tbsp butter, plus extra for greasing

2 tbsp caster sugar

2 eggs

6 tbsp plain flour, sifted

1 tsp baking powder, sifted

6 tbsp milk

1 tsp vanilla essence

4 tbsp golden syrup

thin strips of crystallized orange peel, to decorate

hot custard, to serve

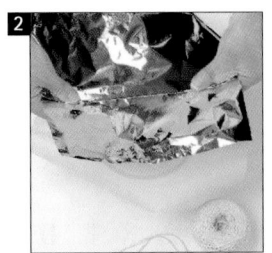

1 Lightly grease a 900-ml/1½-pint pudding basin with butter. Put the remaining butter in a large bowl with the sugar and beat until light and fluffy. Add the eggs and beat together well. Mix in the flour and baking powder, then stir in the milk and vanilla essence. Continue to stir until smooth and pale.

2 Pour the golden syrup into the pudding basin, then spoon the pudding mixture over the top. Cover with greaseproof paper, top with a piece of foil, tied on securely with string. Transfer to a large saucepan of gently simmering water that comes halfway up the side of the pudding basin. Simmer gently for about 1½ hours until cooked through, topping up the water level if necessary.

3 Lift out the pudding and leave to rest for 5 minutes, then turn it out on to a serving plate. Decorate with thin strips of crystallized orange peel and serve hot, with custard.

New Age Spotted Dick

This is a deliciously moist low-fat pudding. The sauce is in the centre of the pudding, and will spill out when the pudding is cut.

🕐 25 mins   🕐 1 hrs 15 mins

SERVES 6–8

INGREDIENTS

125 g/4½ oz raisins

125 ml/4 fl oz corn oil, plus extra
for brushing

125 g/4½ oz caster sugar

25 g/1 oz ground almonds

2 eggs, lightly beaten

175 g/6 oz self-raising flour

SAUCE

55 g/2 oz walnuts, chopped

55 g/2 oz ground almonds

300 ml/10 fl oz semi-skimmed milk

4 tbsp granulated sugar

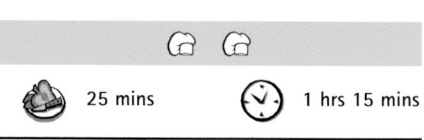 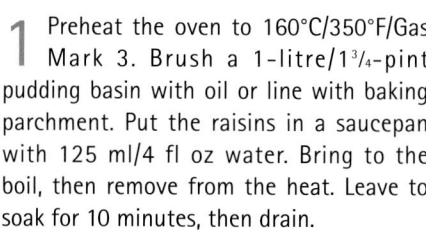 

1 Preheat the oven to 160°C/350°F/Gas Mark 3. Brush a 1-litre/1¾-pint pudding basin with oil or line with baking parchment. Put the raisins in a saucepan with 125 ml/4 fl oz water. Bring to the boil, then remove from the heat. Leave to soak for 10 minutes, then drain.

2 Whisk together the oil, sugar and ground almonds until thick and syrupy; this will need about 8 minutes of beating (on medium speed if using an electric whisk).

3 Add the eggs, 1 at a time, beating well after each addition. Combine the flour and raisins. Stir into the mixture. Put all the sauce ingredients into a saucepan. Bring to the boil, stir and simmer for 10 minutes.

4 Transfer the sponge mixture to the prepared pudding basin and pour on the hot sauce. Place on a baking sheet.

5 Bake in the preheated oven for about 1 hour. Lay a piece of baking parchment across the top if it starts to brown too fast.

6 Leave to cool for 2–3 minutes in the bowl before turning out on to a serving plate.

COOK'S TIP
Always soak raisins before baking them, as they retain their moisture nicely and you taste the flavour of them instead of biting on a dried-out raisin.

Mocha Pudding

This delectable mixture of dried and candied fruit in a coffee- and chocolate-flavoured sponge is guaranteed to warm you up on a cold day.

15 mins   2 hrs 30 mins

SERVES 4

I N G R E D I E N T S

butter, for greasing

4 egg yolks

2 egg whites

115 g/4 oz caster sugar

55 g/2 oz cocoa powder

425 ml/15 fl oz milk

150 ml/5 fl oz strong black coffee

55 g/2 oz glacé cherries, chopped

55 g/2 oz chopped walnuts

55 g/2 oz sultanas

2 tsp very finely chopped candied peel

2 tbsp Marsala

double cream or custard, to serve

1 Preheat the oven to 150°C/350°F/Gas Mark 2. Grease a medium-size ovenproof dish. Beat together the egg yolks, egg whites, sugar and cocoa powder until thoroughly combined. Beat in the milk and coffee. Stir in the glacé cherries, walnuts, sultanas, candied peel and Marsala and mix well.

2 Spoon the mixture into the dish, smoothing the top. Stand the dish in a roasting tin and pour in enough water to come about halfway up the sides of the dish. Cover the roasting tin with a sheet of lightly greased foil and tuck it in round the sides. Bake for 2½ hours, until just set

3 Discard the foil and serve the pudding immediately, with a jug of double cream or custard.

COOK'S TIP
You can also steam this pudding very gently for the same length of time. Place in a saucepan of water, keep the water gently simmering, and do not allow to boil. Top up the water as necessary.

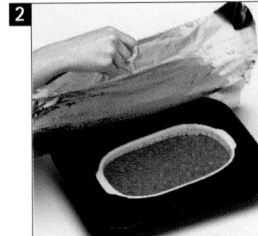

Chocolate Pecan Pudding

This traditional American recipe tastes wonderful served with an equally traditional lemon-flavoured hard sauce.

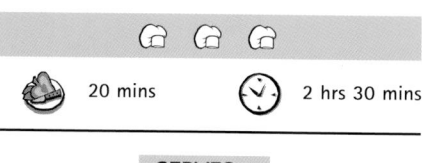

20 mins   2 hrs 30 mins

SERVES 4

INGREDIENTS

butter, for greasing

85 g/3 oz dark chocolate

85 g/3 oz white vegetable shortening

225 g/8 oz plain flour

4 tsp baking powder

pinch of salt

½ tsp ground cinnamon

½ tsp ground ginger

140 g/5 oz granulated sugar

55 g/2 oz pecan nuts, chopped

1 tbsp finely chopped stem ginger

2 eggs

150 ml/5 fl oz milk

½ tsp vanilla essence

HARD LEMON SAUCE

85 g/3 oz unsalted butter, softened

225 g/8 oz icing sugar

juice of ½ lemon

finely grated rind of 1 lemon

1 Grease a 1-litre/1¾-pint pudding basin. Break the chocolate into pieces and place in a heatproof bowl with the shortening. Melt over a saucepan of gently simmering water. When the mixture has melted, remove from the heat, then stir until smooth and set aside.

2 Cut out a round of greaseproof paper and a round of foil 10 cm/4 inches larger than the top of the basin. Grease the paper, then place on the foil round, greased side up. Make a pleat in the centre of both rounds. Sift together the flour, baking powder, salt, cinnamon and ground ginger into a bowl. Stir in the sugar, nuts and stem ginger. Beat the eggs in a bowl, then beat in the milk. Stir the egg mixture into the dry ingredients, then stir in the chocolate mixture and vanilla essence.

3 Spoon the mixture into the basin and smooth the top. Then place the paper and foil rounds together over the top of the basin, with the foil round upwards. Tie securely in place with kitchen string.

4 Place the basin in a large saucepan and pour in enough boiling water to come about halfway up the side. Cover and steam over a low heat for 2½ hours, topping up the boiling water, as necessary.

5 Meanwhile, make the sauce. Cream the butter and icing sugar in a bowl until well combined and fluffy. Gradually beat in the lemon juice and rind. Spoon into a bowl, cover and chill until required.

6 Remove the basin from the saucepan and discard the foil and paper. Run a round-bladed knife around the edge of the pudding to loosen it, then invert on to a warm serving plate. Serve immediately with the hard lemon sauce.

Christmas Pudding

This timeless, classic pudding is an essential part of the Christmas table. Make it well in advance, because it needs to chill for at least two weeks.

20 mins plus
2 hrs soaking

6 hrs

SERVES 4

INGREDIENTS

200 g/7 oz currants

200 g/7 oz raisins

200 g/7 oz sultanas

150 ml/5 fl oz sweet sherry

175 g/6 oz butter, plus extra for greasing

175 g/6 oz dark soft brown sugar

4 eggs, beaten

150 g/5½ oz self-raising flour

100 g/3½ oz fresh white or wholemeal breadcrumbs

50 g/1¾ oz blanched almonds, chopped

juice of 1 orange

grated rind of ½ orange

grated rind of ½ lemon

½ tsp ground mixed spice

holly leaves, to decorate

fresh whipped cream, to serve

1 Put the currants, raisins and sultanas in a glass bowl and pour over the sherry. Leave to soak for at least 2 hours.

2 Mix the butter and sugar in a bowl. Beat in the eggs, then fold in the flour. Stir in the soaked fruit and the remaining sherry with the breadcrumbs, almonds, orange juice and rind, lemon rind and mixed spice. Grease a large pudding basin with butter and press the mixture into it, leaving a gap of 2.5 cm/1 inch at the top. Cut a round of greaseproof paper 3 cm/1¼ inches larger than the top of the pudding basin, grease with butter, and place over the pudding. Top with 2 layers of foil, then tie on securely with kitchen string. Tie a string handle across the top of the basin to make it easier to lift out of the hot water. Place the pudding in a large saucepan of boiling water so that the water comes two-thirds of the way up the basin. Reduce the heat and simmer for 6 hours, topping up the water when necessary.

3 Remove from the heat and leave to cool. Renew the greaseproof paper and foil and refrigerate for 2–8 weeks. To reheat, steam for 2 hours as before. Decorate with holly leaves and serve with whipped cream.

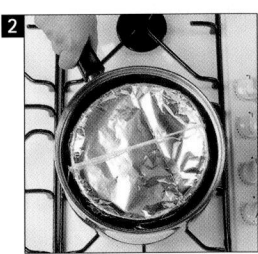

Chocolate Fudge Dessert

This dessert has a hidden surprise when cooked because it separates to give a rich chocolate sauce at the bottom of the dish.

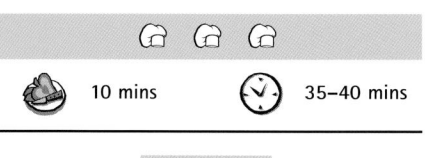

10 mins   35–40 mins

SERVES 4

INGREDIENTS

4 tbsp margarine, plus extra for greasing

6 tbsp soft light brown sugar

2 eggs, beaten

350 ml/12 fl oz milk

50 g/1¼ oz chopped walnuts

5 tbsp plain flour

2 tbsp cocoa powder

icing sugar and cocoa powder, for dusting

1 Preheat the oven to 180°C/350°F/Gas Mark 4. Lightly grease a 1-litre/1¾-pint ovenproof dish.

2 Cream together the margarine and sugar in a large mixing bowl until fluffy. Beat in the eggs.

3 Gradually stir in the milk and add the chopped walnuts.

4 Sift the flour and cocoa into the mixture and fold in gently, with a metal spoon until well mixed.

5 Spoon the mixture into the dish and cook in the preheated oven for 35–40 minutes or until the sponge is cooked.

6 Dust with icing sugar and cocoa powder and serve.

VARIATION
Add 1–2 tablespoons of brandy or dark rum to the mixture for a slightly alcoholic dessert, or 1–2 tablespoons of orange juice for a child-friendly version.

Chocolate Fudge Pudding

This fabulous steamed sponge pudding, served with a rich chocolate fudge sauce, is perfect for cold winter days.

10 mins

1 hr 40 mins–
2 hrs 10 mins

SERVES 6

INGREDIENTS

150 g/5½ oz soft margarine

150 g/5½ oz self-raising flour

150 g/5½ oz golden syrup

3 eggs

25 g/1oz cocoa powder

CHOCOLATE FUDGE SAUCE

100 g/3½ oz plain chocolate

125 ml/4 fl oz condensed milk

4 tbsp double cream

1 Lightly grease a 1.2-litre/2-pint pudding basin.

2 Place the ingredients for the sponge pudding in a separate mixing bowl and beat until well combined and smooth.

3 Spoon into the prepared basin and smooth the top. Cover with a disc of baking parchment and tie a pleated sheet of foil over the basin. Steam for 1½–2 hours, until the sponge is cooked and springy to the touch.

4 To make the sauce, break the chocolate into small pieces and place in a small saucepan with the condensed milk. Heat gently, stirring constantly, until the chocolate melts. Remove from the heat and stir in the double cream.

5 To serve, turn the pudding out on to a serving plate and pour over a little of the chocolate fudge sauce. Serve the remaining sauce separately.

Pecan Fudge Ring

Although this can be served cold as a cake, it is absolutely delicious served as a hot dessert.

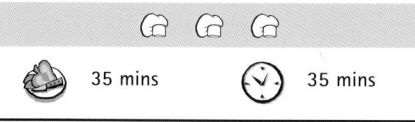

35 mins   35 mins

SERVES 6

INGREDIENTS

FUDGE SAUCE

3 tbsp butter

3 tbsp light soft brown sugar

4 tbsp golden syrup

2 tbsp milk

1 tbsp cocoa powder

40 g/1½ oz plain chocolate, broken into pieces

50 g/1¾ oz pecan nuts, finely chopped

CAKE

100 g/3½ oz soft margarine

100 g/3½ oz light soft brown sugar

125 g/4½ oz self-raising flour

2 eggs

2 tbsp milk

1 tbsp golden syrup

1 Preheat the oven to 180°C/350°F/Gas Mark 4. Lightly grease a 20-cm/8-inch ring tin.

2 To make the fudge sauce, place the butter, sugar, syrup, milk and cocoa powder in a small saucepan and heat gently, stirring until combined.

3 Add the chocolate and stir until melted, then stir in the pecan nuts. Pour into the tin and leave to cool.

4 To make the cake, place all of the ingredients in a mixing bowl and beat until smooth. Carefully spoon the cake mixture over the chocolate fudge sauce.

5 Bake in the preheated oven for 35 minutes or until the cake is springy to the touch.

6 Leave the cake to cool in the tin for 5 minutes, then turn out on to a serving dish and serve warm.

Steamed Chocolate Pudding

This is a rich pudding, perfect for chocolate lovers. Serve it with a delicious sauce flavoured with hazelnuts, brandy and dried fruit.

🍧 25 mins | 🕐 1 hr 30 mins

SERVES 4–6

INGREDIENTS

115 g/4 oz butter, softened, plus extra for greasing

115 g/4 oz light soft brown sugar

2 eggs, beaten

85 g/3 oz self-raising flour

25 g/1 oz cocoa powder

a little milk

100 g/3½ oz plain chocolate chips

SAUCE

4 tbsp butter

55 g/2 oz light soft brown sugar

3 tbsp brandy

55 g/2 oz blanched whole hazelnuts

55 g/2 oz luxury mixed dried fruit

1 Grease a 1.2-litre/2-pint pudding basin and line the bottom with a small disc of greaseproof paper. Put the butter and sugar in a mixing bowl and beat together until light and fluffy. Gradually beat in the beaten eggs. Sift the flour and cocoa powder into the mixture and fold in carefully. Add a little milk, if necessary, to make a dropping consistency. Stir in the chocolate chips.

2 Spoon the mixture into the prepared basin. Cut a large round of greaseproof paper and one of foil about 7.5 cm/3 inches larger than the top of the basin. Grease the paper and make a fold in the centre of both. Use to cover the basin, with the foil on top, and secure with kitchen string. Place the basin in a saucepan and pour in boiling water to come halfway up the basin. Cover the saucepan and simmer for 1½ hours. Check the water from time to time and top up with boiling water as necessary.

3 To make the sauce, place the butter and sugar in a small saucepan and heat gently until the sugar has dissolved and the mixture looks slightly caramelized. Add the brandy and allow to bubble for a minute. Stir in the nuts and dried fruit. Carefully invert the pudding on to a warm plate and spoon the sauce over. Serve at once.

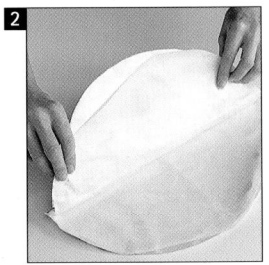

COOK'S TIP
You can make the pudding in advance. To reheat, simply put the covered basin back into a saucepan of boiling water for 20–30 minutes before serving.

Chocolate Filo Parcels

Not only do these little filo parcels look delightful, they taste superb and are sure to impress dinner-party guests.

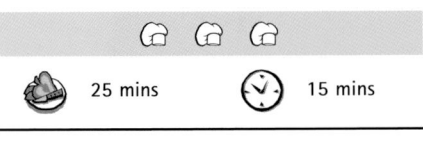

🥧 25 mins   🕐 15 mins

SERVES 6

INGREDIENTS

55 g/2 oz plain chocolate, broken
   into pieces

85 g/3 oz ground hazelnuts

1 tbsp finely chopped fresh mint

125 ml/4 fl oz sour cream

2 eating apples

9 sheets filo pastry,
   about 15 cm/6 inches square

55–85 g/2–3 oz butter, melted

icing sugar, for dusting

fresh mint sprigs, to decorate

whipping cream, to serve

1 Preheat the oven to 190°C/375°F/Gas Mark 5. Melt chocolate in a heatproof bowl set over a saucepan of gently simmering water. Remove from the heat and leave to cool slightly.

2 Mix together the hazelnuts, mint and sour cream in a bowl. Peel the apples and grate them into the bowl, then stir in the melted chocolate and mix well.

3 Cut each sheet of filo pastry into 4 squares. Keep the squares you are not using covered with a damp cloth. Brush 1 square with melted butter, place a second square on top and brush with melted butter. Place a tablespoonful of the chocolate mixture in the centre, then bring up the corners of the squares and twist together to enclose the filling completely. Continue making parcels in the same way until you have used up all the pastry and filling.

4 Brush a baking sheet with melted butter and place the parcels on it. Bake for about 10 minutes until crisp and golden. Leave to cool slightly, then dust with icing sugar. Serve with cream.

COOK'S TIP
These parcels are best served warm, rather than hot, and can also be served cold.

Saucy Chocolate Pudding

When you take this pudding out of the oven it doesn't look very impressive, but when you cut into it you find a lovely pool of sauce.

10 mins

50–60 mins

SERVES 4–6

INGREDIENTS

55 g/2 oz self-raising flour

25 g/1 oz cocoa powder

1 tsp ground cinnamon

85 g/3 oz butter, softened

115 g/4 oz golden caster sugar

1 egg

25 g/1 oz dark soft brown sugar

55 g/2 oz pecan nuts, chopped

300 ml/10 fl oz hot black coffee

icing sugar, for dusting

whipped cream, to serve

1 Preheat the oven to 160°C/325°F/Gas Mark 3. Butter a 1.2-litre/2-pint ovenproof dish. Sift the flour, cocoa powder and cinnamon into a bowl. Add the butter, 85 g/3 oz of the caster sugar and the egg and beat together thoroughly until well blended.

2 Turn into the prepared dish and sprinkle with the soft brown sugar and the pecan nuts. Pour the coffee into a large jug, stir in the remaining caster sugar and carefully pour over the pudding.

3 Bake in the preheated oven for 50–60 minutes, until firm to the touch in the centre. Dust with icing sugar and serve at once, with whipped cream.

COOK'S TIP
Take care not to open the oven for the first 40 minutes of the cooking time.

Sticky Chocolate Sponges

These rich individual desserts served with a cream sauce always look and taste impressive at the end of a meal.

20 mins   1 hr

SERVES 6

I N G R E D I E N T S

115 g/4 oz butter, softened, plus extra for greasing

150 g/5½ oz soft brown sugar

3 eggs, beaten

pinch of salt

25 g/1 oz cocoa powder

125 g/4½ oz self-raising flour

25 g/1 oz dark chocolate, finely chopped

75 g/2¾ oz white chocolate, finely chopped

S A U C E

150 ml/5 fl oz double cream

75 g/2¾ oz soft brown sugar

2 tbsp butter

1 Preheat the oven to 180°C/350°F/ Gas Mark 4. Lightly grease 6 175-ml/ 6-fl oz individual pudding basins.

2 In a bowl, cream together the butter and sugar until pale and fluffy. Beat in the eggs a little at a time, beating well after each addition.

3 Sift the salt, cocoa powder and flour into the creamed mixture and fold through the mixture. Stir in the chopped chocolate until evenly distributed throughout the mixture.

4 Divide the mixture between the prepared pudding basins. Lightly grease 6 squares of foil and use them to cover the tops of the basins. Press around the edges to seal.

5 Place the basins in a roasting tin and pour in boiling water to come halfway up the sides of the basins.

6 Bake in the preheated oven for 50 minutes or until a skewer inserted into the centre of the sponges comes out clean.

7 Remove the basins from the roasting tin and set aside while you prepare the sauce.

8 To make the sauce, put the cream, sugar and butter into a saucepan and bring to the boil over a gentle heat. Simmer gently until the sugar has completely dissolved.

9 To serve, run a knife around the edge of each sponge, then turn out on to individual plates and serve, handing the sauce around separately.

Coffee & Walnut Puddings

These little coffee puddings with a butterscotch sauce are guaranteed to delight your guests.

20 mins

30–40 mins

SERVES 6

INGREDIENTS

55 g/2 oz unsalted butter, softened, plus extra for greasing

150 g/5½ oz self-raising flour

1 tsp ground cinnamon

55 g/2 oz light soft brown sugar, sieved

2 large eggs, beaten

1 tbsp instant coffee granules dissolved in 2 tbsp boiling water

55 g/2 oz walnuts, finely chopped

SAUCE

25 g/1 oz walnuts, roughly chopped

55 g/2 oz unsalted butter

55 g/2 oz light soft brown sugar

150 ml/ 5 fl oz double cream

1 Preheat the oven to 190°C/375°F/Gas Mark 5. Grease 6 individual metal pudding basins. Sift the flour and cinnamon into a bowl. Put the butter and sugar in a bowl and beat together until light and fluffy. Gradually beat in the eggs. Add a little flour if the mixture shows signs of curdling. Fold in half of the flour then fold in the remaining flour, alternately with the coffee. Gently stir in the walnuts.

2 Divide the mixture between the prepared basins. Place a piece of buttered foil over each basin and secure with an elastic band. Stand the basins in a roasting tin and pour in boiling water to come half way up the sides of the basins. Cover the whole roasting tin with foil, folding it under the rim. Bake in the oven for 30–40 minutes until well risen and firm to the touch.

3 Meanwhile, make the sauce. Put the walnuts, butter, sugar and cream in a saucepan and heat gently, stirring. Bring to a simmer then remove from the heat. Turn the puddings out on to serving plates, spoon over the hot sauce and serve.

COOK'S TIP

This mixture could be cooked as one large pudding, in which case the mixture should be put into a pudding basin, covered and steamed for 1½ hours.

Sticky Toffee Pudding

This delicious fruit-studded pudding has a rich toffee sauce poured over it. The cold whipped cream contrasts well with the hot pudding.

10–15 mins   35–40 mins

SERVES 4

INGREDIENTS

PUDDING

75 g/2¾ oz sultanas

150 g/5½ oz stoned dates, chopped

1 tsp bicarbonate of soda

2 tbsp butter, plus extra for greasing

200 g/7 oz soft brown sugar

2 eggs

200 g/7 oz self-raising flour, sifted

grated orange zest, to decorate

whipped cream, to serve

STICKY TOFFEE SAUCE

2 tbsp butter

175 ml/6 fl oz double cream

200 g/7 oz brown sugar

1 To make the pudding, put the sultanas, dates and bicarbonate of soda in a heatproof bowl. Cover with boiling water and set aside to soak.

2 Preheat the oven to 180°C/350°F/Gas Mark 4. Grease a 20-cm/8-inch round cake tin with butter. Put the remaining butter in a separate bowl, add the sugar and mix well. Beat in the eggs then fold in the flour. Drain the soaked fruits, add to the bowl and mix well. Spoon the mixture evenly into the prepared cake tin. Transfer to the preheated oven and bake for 35–40 minutes or until a skewer inserted into the centre comes out clean.

3 About 5 minutes before the end of the cooking time, make the sauce. Melt the butter in a saucepan over a medium heat. Stir in the cream and sugar and bring to the boil, stirring constantly. Reduce the heat and simmer for 5 minutes.

4 Turn out the pudding on to a serving plate and pour over the sauce. Decorate with grated orange zest and serve with whipped cream.

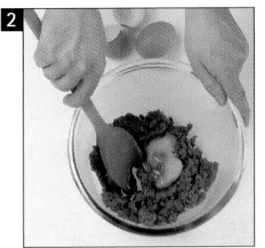

Individual Chocolate Moulds

These little puddings are served with a delicious chocolate sauce flavoured with coffee liqueur.

🍰 10–15 mins 🕐 50 mins

SERVES 4

I N G R E D I E N T S

PUDDINGS

100 g/3½ oz caster sugar

3 eggs

75 g/2¾ oz plain flour

50 g/1¾ oz cocoa powder

100 g/3½ oz unsalted butter, melted, plus extra for greasing

100 g/3½ oz plain chocolate, melted

CHOCOLATE SAUCE

2 tbsp unsalted butter

100 g/3½ oz plain chocolate

5 tbsp water

1 tbsp caster sugar

1 tbsp coffee liqueur, such as Kahlúa

coffee beans, to decorate (optional)

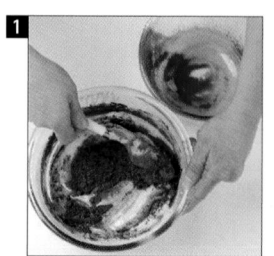

1 To make the puddings, put the sugar and eggs in a heatproof bowl and place over a saucepan of simmering water. Whisk for about 10 minutes until frothy. Remove the bowl from the heat and fold in the flour and cocoa powder. Fold in the melted butter, then the melted chocolate. Mix together well. Grease 4 small pudding basins with butter. Spoon the mixture into the pudding basins, then cover with greaseproof paper. Top with foil and secure with string. Place the puddings in a large saucepan filled with enough simmering water to come halfway up the sides of the pudding basins. Steam for about 40 minutes or until cooked through.

2 About 2–3 minutes before the end of the cooking time, make the sauce. Put the butter, chocolate, water and sugar into a small saucepan and warm over a low heat, stirring constantly, until melted together. Stir in the liqueur.

3 Remove the puddings from the heat, turn out on to serving dishes and pour over the sauce. Decorate with coffee beans, if using, and serve.

Chocolate Castles

Covered in a rich chocolate sauce, these light-as-air individual puddings are a delicious treat on a cold day.

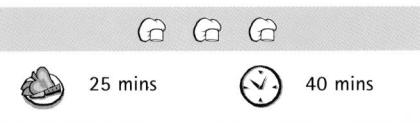

🍮 25 mins   🕙 40 mins

SERVES 4

INGREDIENTS

3 tbsp butter, plus 2 tsp extra for greasing

3 tbsp caster sugar

1 large egg, lightly beaten

85 g/3 oz self-raising flour

55 g/2 oz plain chocolate, melted

SAUCE

2 tbsp cornflour

2 tbsp cocoa powder

150 ml/5 fl oz single cream

300 ml/10 fl oz milk

1–2 tbsp dark brown sugar

1 Grease 4 dariole moulds or individual pudding basins with butter. In a mixing bowl, cream together the butter and sugar until pale and fluffy. Then gradually add the egg, beating vigorously after each addition.

2 Sift the flour into a separate bowl, then fold it into the butter mixture with a metal spoon and stir in the melted chocolate. Divide the mixture between the moulds, filling them to about two-thirds full to allow for expansion during cooking. Cover each mould with a disc of foil and tie in place with string.

3 Bring a large saucepan of water to the boil and set a steamer over it. Place the moulds in the steamer and cook for 40 minutes. Check the water level from time to time and top up with boiling water when necessary.

4 To make the sauce, put the cornflour, cocoa powder, cream and milk in a heavy-based saucepan. Bring to the boil, then lower the heat and simmer over a low heat, whisking constantly, until thick and smooth. Cook for a further 2–3 minutes, then stir in brown sugar to taste. Pour the sauce into a jug.

5 Lift the moulds out of the steamer and remove the foil. Run a knife blade around the sides of the moulds and turn out the chocolate castles on to warm individual plates. Serve immediately with the sauce in the jug.

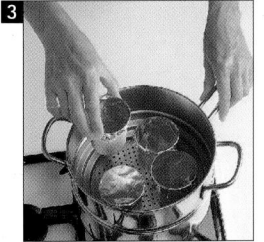

Eve's Pudding

This is a popular family dessert which has soft apples on the bottom and a light buttery sponge-cake topping.

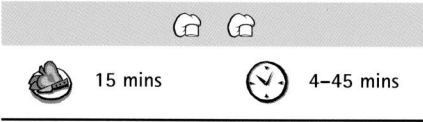

15 mins

4–45 mins

SERVES 4

INGREDIENTS

6 tbsp butter, plus extra for greasing

450 g/1 lb cooking apples, peeled, cored and sliced

85 g/3 oz granulated sugar

1 tbsp lemon juice

55 g/2 oz sultanas

85 g/3 oz caster sugar

1 egg, beaten

150 g/5½ oz self-raising flour

3 tbsp milk

25 g/1 oz flaked almonds

custard or double cream, to serve

1 Preheat the oven to 180°C/350°F/Gas Mark 4. Grease a 900-ml/1½-pint round ovenproof dish with a little butter.

2 Mix the apples with the granulated sugar, lemon juice and sultanas. Spoon the mixture into the dish.

3 In a bowl, cream the butter and caster sugar together until pale. Add the beaten egg, a little at a time. Carefully fold in the self-raising flour and stir in the milk to give a soft dropping consistency.

4 Spread the mixture over the apples and sprinkle with the flaked almonds.

5 Bake in the preheated oven for 40–45 minutes, until the sponge cake topping is golden brown.

6 Serve the pudding piping hot, accompanied by homemade custard or double cream.

COOK'S TIP
To increase the almond flavour of this pudding, add 25 g/1 oz ground almonds with the flour in step 4.

Chocolate Eve's Pudding

Eve's Pudding is traditionally made with apples; this one has raspberries and white chocolate sponge with a plain chocolate sauce.

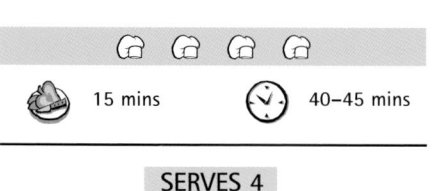

15 mins

40–45 mins

SERVES 4

INGREDIENTS

225 g/8 oz fresh or frozen raspberries

2 eating apples, peeled, cored and thickly sliced

4 tbsp seedless raspberry jam

2 tbsp port, optional

SPONGE TOPPING

4 tbsp soft margarine

4 tbsp caster sugar

75 g/2¾ oz self-raising flour, sifted

50 g/1¾ oz white chocolate, grated

1 egg

2 tbsp milk

PLAIN CHOCOLATE SAUCE

85 g/3 oz plain chocolate, broken into pieces

150 ml/5 fl oz single cream

1 Preheat the oven to 180°C/350°F/Gas Mark 4. Place the raspberries and apple slices in a shallow 1.2-litre/2-pint ovenproof dish.

2 Place the raspberry jam and port (if using) in a small saucepan and heat gently until the jam melts into the port. Pour the mixture over the fruit.

3 Place all the ingredients for the sponge topping in a large mixing bowl and beat until the mixture is smooth.

4 Spoon the sponge mixture over the fruit and level the top. Bake in the preheated oven for 40–45 minutes or until the sponge is springy to the touch.

5 To make the sauce, place the chocolate in a heavy-based saucepan with the cream. Heat gently, beating until a smooth sauce is formed. Serve warm with the pudding.

VARIATION
Use plain chocolate in the sponge and top with apricot halves, covered with peach schnapps and apricot jam.

Chocolate Sponge with Rum

A warming way to end supper on a wintry evening, this steamed sponge pudding is very easy to make.

15 mins   1 hr 20 mins

SERVES 4

INGREDIENTS

4 tbsp butter, sweet for preference, plus extra for greasing

175 g/6 oz self-raising flour, plus extra for dusting

55 g/2 oz plain chocolate

¼ tsp vanilla essence

115 g/4 oz caster sugar

2 eggs, lightly beaten

5 tbsp milk

SAUCE

300 ml/10 fl oz milk

2 tbsp cornflour

2 tbsp caster sugar

2 tbsp dark rum

1 Grease and flour a 1.2-litre/2-pint pudding basin. Put the butter, chocolate and vanilla in a heatproof bowl set over a saucepan of gently simmering water. Heat gently until the butter and sugar have melted, then remove from the heat and cool slightly. Stir the sugar into the chocolate mixture, then beat in the eggs. Sift in the flour, stir in the milk and mix well. Pour the mixture into the prepared pudding basin, cover the top with foil and tie with string. Steam the sponge for 1 hour, topping up the saucepan with more boiling water if necessary.

2 To make the sauce, pour the milk into a small saucepan set over a medium heat. Stir in the sugar until dissolved, then stir in the cornflour. Bring to the boil, stirring constantly, then reduce the heat and simmer until thickened and smooth. Remove from the heat and stir in the rum.

3 To serve, remove the sponge from the heat and discard the foil. Run a round-bladed knife around the side of the basin, place a serving plate on top of the sponge and, holding them together, invert. Serve immediately, handing the sauce around separately.

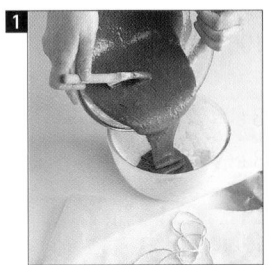

Fail-Safe Puddings

Many people don't serve hot desserts when entertaining because of lack of time or fear of failure. These little puddings are absolutely trouble free.

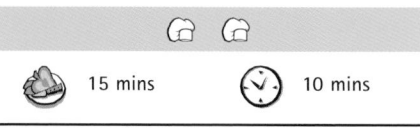

🍰 15 mins   🕙 10 mins

SERVES 6

INGREDIENTS

190 g/6½ oz unsalted butter

190 g/6½ oz plain or Continental plain chocolate, broken into pieces

3 eggs

3 egg yolks

85 g/3 oz caster sugar

1 tbsp plain flour

ORANGE SAUCE

4–5 blood oranges

2 tsp cornflour

2 tbsp water

caster sugar, to taste

1 For the sauce, squeeze the juice from the oranges, pouring it into a measuring jug until you have about 300 ml/10 fl oz. Cover with clingfilm and place in the refrigerator until required.

2 To make the puddings, put the butter and chocolate into a small heatproof bowl. Melt over a saucepan of gently simmering water, stirring occasionally. When the mixture is smooth, remove from the heat and set aside to cool slightly.

3 Whisk the eggs, egg yolks and sugar in a separate bowl until thickened and pale. Whisk in the chocolate mixture, then sift over the flour and fold in with a metal spoon. Grease 6 ramekin dishes or ovenproof moulds and divide the mixture between them. When cool, cover and place in the refrigerator until required.

4 When you are ready to cook, preheat the oven to 230°C/450°F/Gas Mark 8. Uncover the moulds and bake for 6–8 minutes until just set.

5 Meanwhile, make the orange sauce. Pour the measured orange juice into a heavy-based saucepan. Mix the cornflour with the water to a smooth paste in a small bowl, then add to the orange juice. Bring just to simmering point, stirring constantly. Remove from the heat, taste and stir in sugar, if required.

6 Invert the puddings on to 6 warm dessert plates and serve immediately. Pour the orange sauce into a jug and serve separately.

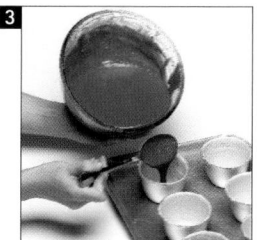

Pears & Chocolate Meringue

This will quickly become a family favourite, so keep a can of pears and a block of chocolate handy to make it whenever you like.

10 mins   45 mins

SERVES 4–6

INGREDIENTS

115 g/4 oz butter, plus extra for greasing

200 g/7 oz plain chocolate

400 g/14 oz canned pear halves, drained

4 eggs, separated

115 g/4 oz caster sugar

1 Preheat the oven to 160°C/325°F/Gas Mark 3. Grease an ovenproof dish. Place the butter in a heatproof bowl. Break up the chocolate and add it to the bowl, then melt over a saucepan of gently simmering water, stirring occasionally. Remove from the heat and set aside to cool. Slice the pears.

2 Whisk the egg yolks with the sugar until pale and thickened, then beat in the melted chocolate. Whisk the egg white in a separate greasefree bowl until stiff. Stir a spoonful of the whites into the chocolate mixture to slacken it, then fold in the remainder with a metal spoon. Fold in the sliced pears.

3 Spoon the mixture into the dish and bake for about 40 minutes, until just set and golden brown on top. Serve immediately.

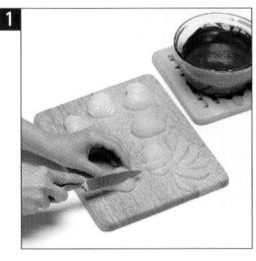

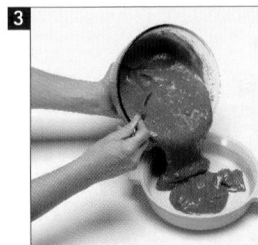

VARIATION
You could also make this meringue dessert with canned apricots or fresh peaches.

Chocolate & Nut Meringue Pie

This gloriously rich and self-indulgent dessert is best served warm, rather than hot.

 25 mins plus 30 mins chilling 40 mins

SERVES 6

INGREDIENTS

PASTRY

225 g/8 oz plain flour, plus extra for dusting

pinch of salt

140 g/5 oz butter

55 g/2 oz caster sugar

2 egg yolks

FILLING

140 g/5 oz plain chocolate

2 tbsp butter

225 g/8 oz caster sugar

2 tsp cornflour

4 egg yolks

85 g/3 oz ground hazelnuts

3 egg whites

1 To make the pastry, sift the flour with the pinch of salt into a bowl. Cream the butter and sugar together in a separate bowl until pale and fluffy. Sift over the flour, in 2 batches, and mix in, alternating with the egg yolks. Add a little cold water, a teaspoonful at a time, if necessary to make a dough.

2 Roll out the pastry on a lightly floured surface and use to line a 23-cm/9-inch flan tin. Chill for 30 minutes. Preheat the oven to 190°C/ 375°F/ Gas Mark 5.

3 Prick the base of the flan case with a fork, line with baking parchment and partly fill with dried beans. Place on a baking sheet and bake blind for10 minutes.

4 To make the filling, break the chocolate into pieces and melt in a heatproof bowl set over a saucepan of gently simmering water. Remove from the heat and leave to cool slightly.

5 Cream the butter with 6 tablespoons of the sugar until pale and fluffy. Beat in the cornflour and egg yolks, 1 at a time. Fold in the melted chocolate and the nuts.

6 Remove the dried beans and lining from the flan case and spoon in the chocolate filling. Return to the oven and bake for a further 10 minutes.

7 Whisk the egg whites in a clean, greasefree bowl until soft peaks form. Gradually whisk in the remaining sugar and continue to whisk until stiff and glossy. Spoon the meringue over the filling in the flan case, covering it completely. Return to the oven and bake for another 15 minutes, until lightly set and golden.

Chocolate Meringue Pie

Crumbly biscuit base, rich creamy chocolate filling topped with fluffy meringue – what could be more indulgent than this fabulous dessert?

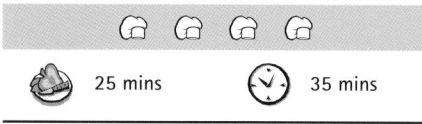
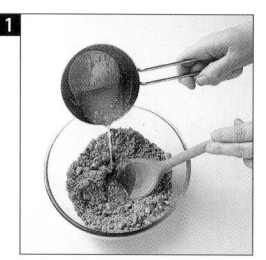

25 mins   35 mins

SERVES 6

INGREDIENTS

225 g/8 oz plain chocolate
    digestive biscuits

4 tbsp butter

FILLING

3 egg yolks

4 tbsp caster sugar

4 tbsp cornflour

600 ml/1 pint milk

100 g/3½ oz plain chocolate,
    broken into pieces

MERINGUE

2 egg whites

100 g/3½ oz caster sugar

¼ tsp vanilla essence

1 Preheat the oven to 190°C/375°F/Gas Mark 5. Place the digestive biscuits in a plastic bag and crush with a rolling pin. Put in a bowl. Melt the butter and stir into the biscuit crumbs until well mixed. Press the mixture firmly into the base and up the side of a 23-cm/9-inch flan tin or dish.

2 To make the filling, beat the egg yolks, sugar and cornflour in a large bowl until they form a smooth paste. Heat the milk in a heavy-based saucepan until almost boiling, then slowly pour it on to the egg mixture, whisking well.

3 Return the mixture to the saucepan and cook gently, whisking until it thickens. Remove from the heat. Melt the chocolate in a bowl over a saucepan of simmering water. Whisk into the egg mixture and pour into the biscuit base.

4 To make the meringue, whisk the egg whites in a large mixing bowl until soft peaks form. Gradually whisk in about two-thirds of the sugar until the mixture is stiff and glossy. Fold in the remaining sugar and vanilla essence.

5 Spread the meringue over the chocolate filling, swirling the surface with the back of a spoon to give it an attractive finish. Bake in the centre of the preheated oven for 30 minutes or until the meringue is golden. Serve the pie hot or just warm.

Chocolate Apple Pie

Easy-to-make crumbly chocolate pie dough encases a delicious apple filling studded with chocolate chips – a guaranteed family favourite.

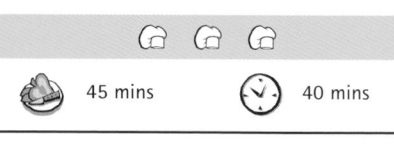

45 mins 40 mins

SERVES 6

INGREDIENTS

CHOCOLATE PASTRY

4 tbsp cocoa powder

200 g/7 oz plain flour, plus extra for dusting

100 g/3½ oz softened butter

4 tbsp caster sugar

2 egg yolks

few drops vanilla essence

cold water, for mixing

FILLING

750 g/1 lb 10 oz cooking apples

2 tbsp butter

½ tsp ground cinnamon

50 g/1¾ oz plain chocolate chips

little egg white, beaten

½ tsp caster sugar

whipped cream or vanilla ice cream, to serve

1 To make the pastry, sift the cocoa and flour into a mixing bowl and rub in the butter until the mixture resembles fine breadcrumbs. Stir in the sugar. Add the egg yolks, vanilla essence and enough water to mix to a dough.

2 Roll out the dough on a lightly floured surface and use to line a deep 20-cm/8-inch flan or cake tin. Chill for 30 minutes. Roll out any trimmings and cut out some pastry leaves to decorate the top of the pie.

3 Preheat the oven to 180°C/350°F/Gas Mark 4. Peel, core and thickly slice the apples. Place half of the apple slices in a saucepan with the butter and cinnamon and cook over a gentle heat, stirring occasionally, until the apples soften.

4 Stir in the uncooked apple slices, leave to cool slightly, then stir in the chocolate chips. Prick the base of the pastry case and pile the apple mixture into it. Arrange the pastry leaves on top. Brush the leaves with egg white and sprinkle with caster sugar.

5 Bake in the preheated oven for 35 minutes, until the pastry is crisp. Serve warm or cold, with whipped cream or vanilla ice cream.

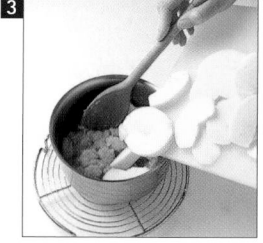

Pantry Chocolate Pudding

Just the thing for unexpected guests – a rich pudding made with storecupboard ingredients, complete with its own delicious sauce.

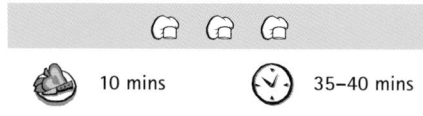

🔲 10 mins   🕐 35–40 mins

SERVES 4

INGREDIENTS

2 tbsp butter

150 ml/5 fl oz milk

140 g/5 oz self-raising flour

70 g/2½ oz cocoa powder

200 g/7 oz caster sugar

225 g/8 oz brown sugar

50 ml/2 fl oz crème de menthe (optional)

icing sugar, for dusting

1 Preheat the oven to 180°C/350°F/Gas Mark 4. Melt the butter in a small saucepan over a low heat, then combine it with the milk in a jug.

2 Sift together the flour and half the cocoa powder into a bowl, stir in the caster sugar and make a well in the centre. Gradually pour the milk mixture into the well, beating with a wooden spoon until the dry ingredients are thoroughly combined.

3 Divide the mixture evenly between 4 x 225-ml/8-fl-oz ramekins or other individual ovenproof dishes. Place on a baking sheet and set aside.

COOK'S TIP

These puddings look attractive in individual dishes and they also cook more quickly than they would in a single large dish. If there is no hurry, you could use a 1.2-litre/2-pint ovenproof dish and bake the pudding for an extra 20 minutes.

4 Sift the remaining cocoa powder into a jug and add the brown sugar. If you are going to use the liqueur, pour in 300 ml/10 fl oz boiling water; if not, pour in 350 ml/12 fl oz boiling water. Stir until the sugar has dissolved, then add the liqueur (if using), and stir until smooth.

5 Very carefully pour the cocoa mixture evenly over the tops of the puddings. Bake for 30–35 minutes until risen and just firm to the touch. Dust with a little icing sugar and serve immediately.

Queen of Puddings

This is a slightly different version of an old favourite made with the addition of orange rind and marmalade to give a delicious citrus flavour.

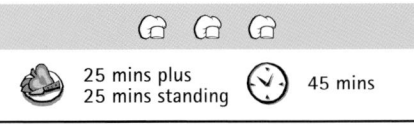

25 mins plus
25 mins standing

45 mins

SERVES 8

INGREDIENTS

2 tbsp butter, plus extra for greasing

600 ml/1 pint milk

225 g/8 oz caster sugar

finely grated rind of 1 orange

4 eggs, separated

75 g/2¾ oz fresh white breadcrumbs

salt

6 tbsp orange marmalade

1 Preheat the oven to 180°C/350°F/ Gas Mark 4. Grease a 1.5-litre/2½-pint ovenproof dish.

2 To make the custard, heat the milk in a saucepan with the butter, 50 g/ 2½ oz of the caster sugar and the grated orange rind until just warm.

3 Whisk the egg yolks in a bowl. Gradually pour the warm milk over the eggs, stirring constantly.

4 Stir the breadcrumbs into the bowl, then transfer the mixture to the prepared dish and leave to stand for about 15 minutes.

5 Bake in the preheated oven for 20–25 minutes, until the custard has just set. Remove the dish from the oven but do not turn off the oven.

6 To make the meringue, whisk the egg whites with a pinch of salt until soft peaks form. Whisk in the remaining sugar, a little at a time.

7 Spread the orange marmalade over the cooked custard. Top with the meringue, spreading it right to the edges of the dish.

8 Return the pudding to the oven and bake for another 20 minutes until the meringue is crisp and golden.

 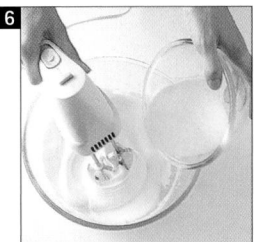 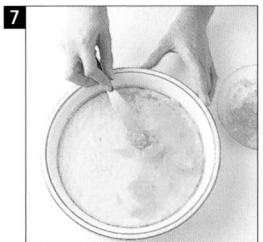

COOK'S TIP
If you prefer a crisper meringue, bake the pudding in the oven for an extra 5 minutes.

Fruity Queen of Puddings

A delicious version of a classic British dessert, made here with fresh bananas and apricot jam.

15 mins plus
15 mins standing   1 hr

SERVES 4

INGREDIENTS

115 g/4 oz fresh white breadcrumbs

600 ml/1 pint milk

3 eggs

½ tsp vanilla essence

4 tbsp caster sugar

2 bananas

1 tbsp lemon juice

3 tbsp apricot jam

1 Preheat the oven to 180°C/350°F/Gas Mark 4. Sprinkle the breadcrumbs evenly into a round 1-litre/ 1³/₄-pint ovenproof dish. Heat the milk until just tepid, then pour it over the breadcrumbs.

2 Separate 2 of the eggs and beat the yolks with the remaining whole egg. Add to the dish with the vanilla essence and half the sugar, stirring well to mix. Set aside for 10 minutes.

3 Bake in the preheated oven for 40 minutes until set. Remove the dish from the oven.

4 Slice the bananas and sprinkle with the lemon juice. Spoon the apricot jam on to the pudding and spread evenly over the surface. Arrange the banana slices on top of the apricot jam.

5 Whisk the egg whites until stiff, then add the remaining sugar. Continue whisking until the meringue is very stiff and glossy.

6 Pile the meringue on top of the pudding, return to the oven and cook for another 10–15 minutes, until the meringue is just set and golden brown. Serve immediately.

COOK'S TIP
The meringue will have a soft, marshmallowlike texture, unlike a hard meringue, which is cooked slowly for 2–3 hours until dry. Always use a greasefree whisk and bowl for whisking egg whites.

Chocolate Queen of Puddings

An old time favourite with an up-to-date twist, this dessert makes the perfect end to a special family meal.

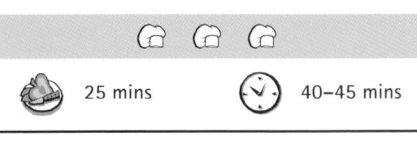

🍮 25 mins   🕐 40–45 mins

SERVES 4

INGREDIENTS

50 g/1¾ oz plain chocolate

450 ml/16 fl oz chocolate-flavoured milk

100 g/3½ oz fresh white or wholemeal breadcrumbs

125 g/4½ oz caster sugar

2 eggs, separated

4 tbsp black cherry jam

1 Preheat the oven to 180°C/350°F/Gas Mark 4. Break the chocolate into small pieces and place in a saucepan with the chocolate-flavoured milk. Heat gently, stirring until the chocolate melts. Bring almost to a boil, then remove the saucepan from the heat.

2 Place the breadcrumbs in a large mixing bowl with 25 g/1 oz of the sugar. Pour over the chocolate milk and mix well. Beat in the egg yolks.

3 Spoon into a 1.2-litres/2-pint ovenproof dish and bake in the preheated oven for 25–30 minutes or until set and firm to the touch.

4 Whisk the egg whites in a large greasefree bowl until soft peaks form. Gradually whisk in the remaining caster sugar and whisk until you have a glossy, thick meringue.

5 Spread the black cherry jam over the surface of the chocolate mixture and pile the meringue on top. Return the dish to the oven for about 15 minutes or until the meringue is crisp and golden.

VARIATION

If you prefer, add 40 g/1½ oz desiccated coconut to the breadcrumbs and omit the jam.

Ginger & Apricot Alaskas

There is no ice cream in this Alaska but a mixture of apples and apricots poached in orange juice enclosed in meringue.

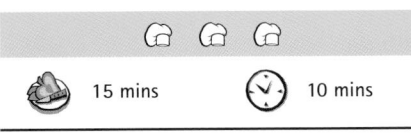

🍰 15 mins 🕐 10 mins

SERVES 2

INGREDIENTS

2 slices rich, dark ginger cake, about 2 cm/¾ inch thick

1–2 tbsp ginger wine or dark rum

1 eating apple

6 ready-to-eat dried apricots, chopped

4 tbsp orange juice or water

1 tbsp flaked almonds

2 small egg whites

100 g/3½ oz caster sugar

1 Preheat the oven to 200°C/400°F/Gas Mark 6. Place each slice of ginger cake on an ovenproof plate and sprinkle with the ginger wine or dark rum.

2 Quarter, core and slice the apple into a small saucepan. Add the chopped apricots and orange juice or water, then simmer over a low heat for about 5 minutes or until tender.

3 Stir the almonds into the fruit and spoon the mixture equally over the slices of soaked cake, piling it up in the centre.

VARIATION
A slice of vanilla, coffee or chocolate ice cream can be placed on the fruit before adding the meringue, but this must be done at the last minute and the dessert must be eaten immediately after it is removed from the oven.

4 Whisk the egg whites until very stiff and dry, then whisk in the sugar, a little at a time, making sure the meringue has become stiff again before adding any more sugar.

5 Either pipe or spread the meringue over the fruit and cake, making sure that both are completely covered.

6 Place in the preheated oven for 4–5 minutes until the meringue is golden brown. Serve hot.

Pecan & Chocolate Pie

Pecan pie is an all-time American favourite and with the addition of chocolate it is even more delicious.

   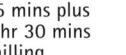

25 mins plus 1 hr 30 mins chilling

35–45 mins

SERVES 6–8

INGREDIENTS

PASTRY

175 g/6 oz plain flour, plus extra for dusting

100 g/3½ oz butter

1 tbsp golden caster sugar

1 egg yolk, beaten with 1 tbsp water

FILLING

55 g/2 oz butter

3 tbsp cocoa powder

225 ml/8 fl oz golden syrup

3 eggs

70 g/2½ oz dark soft brown sugar

175 g/6 oz shelled pecan nuts

whipped cream or cinnamon or coffee ice cream, to serve

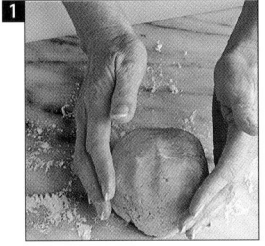  

1 To make the pastry, sift the flour into a bowl. Rub in the butter until it resembles breadcrumbs, stir in the sugar, then the beaten egg yolk. Knead lightly to form a firm dough. Cover and chill for 90 minutes. Preheat the oven to 190°C/375°F/Gas Mark 5.

2 On a lightly floured surface, roll out the pastry and use to line a 20-cm/8-inch flan tin. Put a baking sheet in the oven to get hot.

3 To make the filling, put the butter in a saucepan and heat gently until melted. Sift in the cocoa powder and add the golden syrup. Put the eggs and sugar in a bowl and beat together. Stir in the syrup mixture and the nuts. Pour the mixture into the pastry case and bake on the hot baking sheet for 35–40 minutes until the filling is just set. Allow to cool slightly and serve warm with whipped cream or cinnamon or coffee ice cream.

COOK'S TIP
Cover the pie with foil if the pastry becomes too dark.

Peach & Almond Flan

This is a very elegant and luxurious dessert that would make a grand finale to a dinner party or celebration meal.

   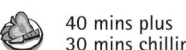

40 mins plus 30 mins chilling | 55 mins

SERVES 6

INGREDIENTS

PASTRY

115 g/4 oz plain chocolate

225 g/8 oz plain flour, plus extra for dusting

115 g/4 oz unsalted butter

4 tbsp ground almonds

few drops almond essence

1–2 tbsp cold water

FILLING

115 g/4 oz blanched almonds

55 g/2 oz caster sugar

70 g/2½ oz unsalted butter

1 egg yolk

2 egg whites

few drops almond essence

5–6 ripe peaches

4 tbsp peach jam

1 tbsp peach brandy

1 First, make the pastry. Break the chocolate into pieces and melt in a heatproof bowl over a saucepan of simmering water. Remove from the heat and leave to cool slightly. Sift the flour into a bowl and rub in the butter with your fingers until the mixture resembles breadcrumbs. Make a well in the centre and add the melted chocolate, ground almonds, almond essence and enough water to mix to a dough. Knead the dough lightly, cover and chill for 30 minutes.

2 Roll out the dough on a lightly floured surface. Use to line a 23-cm/9-inch loose-based flan tin. Chill until ready to use.

3 Preheat the oven to 190°C/375°F/Gas Mark 5 and place a baking sheet in it. Process the blanched almonds and sugar in a food processor, pulsing until finely ground. Do not over-process or they will become oily. Add the butter and process until smooth. Add the egg yolk, egg whites and almond essence and process briefly until combined.

4 Peel and halve the peaches and remove the stones. Thinly slice the peach halves crossways, keeping the slices together so the halves remain in shape.

5 Spoon the almond mixture into the flan case and level out. Using a fish slice, transfer the sliced peach halves to the flan case, then spread them out slightly like the spokes of a wheel.

6 Place on the heated baking sheet and bake for about 50 minutes, until set and golden brown. Remove from the oven and leave to cool slightly on a wire rack.

7 Meanwhile, heat the jam and brandy in a small saucepan, stirring until melted. Brush the glaze over the top of the flan and serve warm.

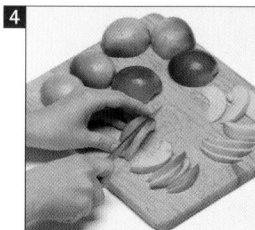

Ginger & Lemon Sponges

These little puddings are very light and make a good choice to serve at the end of a heavy meal.

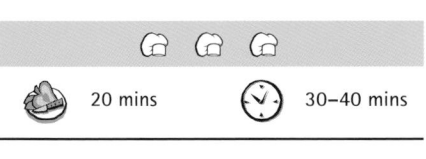
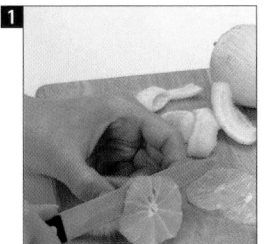

🍮 🍮 🍮

🕐 20 mins   ⏱ 30–40 mins

SERVES 8

INGREDIENTS

115 g/4 oz butter, softened, plus extra for greasing

2 lemons

85 g/3 oz drained stem ginger, chopped, plus 1 tbsp syrup from the ginger jar

2 tbsp golden syrup

175 g/6 oz self-raising flour

2 tsp ground ginger

115 g/4 oz golden caster sugar

2 eggs, beaten

3–4 tbsp milk

vanilla custard, to serve

1 Preheat the oven to 160°C/325°F/Gas Mark 3. Grease 8 individual metal pudding basins. Grate the rind from the lemons and reserve in a bowl. Remove all the pith from one of the lemons and slice the flesh into 8 thin circles. Squeeze the juice from half of the second lemon and reserve. Place the ginger syrup, golden syrup and 1 teaspoon of the lemon juice in a bowl and mix together.

2 Divide the syrup mixture between the prepared pudding basins. Place a slice of lemon in the bottom of each basin. Sift the flour and ground ginger into a bowl. Place the butter and sugar in a separate bowl and beat together until light and fluffy. Gradually beat in the eggs, then fold in the flour mixture and add enough milk to give a soft dropping consistency. Stir in the reserved grated lemon rind and the stem ginger.

3 Divide the sponge mixture among the prepared basins. Place a piece of buttered foil over each basin and secure with an elastic band. Stand the basins in a roasting tin and pour in enough boiling water to reach halfway up the sides of the basins. Cover the roasting tin with a tent of foil, folding it under the rim. Bake in the oven for 30–40 minutes or until well risen and firm to the touch. Turn the sponges out on to serving plates and serve with custard.

COOK'S TIP
When grating the rind from the lemons, be careful not to include any of the white pith, otherwise the finished dish will taste bitter.

Chocolate Rosemary Cake

This cake is good cold, but when served warm with a rosemary-flavoured custard it is even more special.

25 mins plus 30 mins infusing   **60–70 mins**

SERVES 8

INGREDIENTS

CAKE

115 g/4 oz unsalted butter, plus extra for greasing

150 g/5½ oz plain chocolate, broken into pieces

3 large eggs, separated, plus 1 extra egg white

115 g/4 oz golden caster sugar

¾ tsp cream of tartar

3 tbsp plain flour

1 tsp ground cinnamon

20 g/¾ oz ground almonds

icing sugar, for dusting

sprigs of rosemary, to decorate

CUSTARD

2 sprigs of rosemary

1 vanilla pod, split

300 ml/10 fl oz single cream

150 ml/5 fl oz milk

5 large egg yolks

40 g/1½ oz golden caster sugar

1 Preheat the oven to 180°C/350°F/Gas Mark 4. Grease and base-line a 22-cm/8½-inch round cake tin. Put the chocolate and butter in a bowl and set over a saucepan of gently simmering water until melted. Stir until smooth. Stir in the egg yolks and half the sugar. Put the egg whites and cream of tartar in a large bowl and whisk until soft peaks form. Gradually whisk in the remaining sugar until stiff but not dry. Sift the flour and cinnamon into a bowl and stir in the ground almonds. Fold into the egg white mixture, then fold this mixture into the chocolate.

2 Spoon into the prepared cake tin and stand it in a roasting tin. Pour in hot water to come halfway up the side of the cake tin. Bake in the oven for 60–70 minutes until firm to the touch in the centre. Remove from the roasting tin, cover with a clean cloth and leave for 10 minutes, before turning out and placing on a wire rack to cool slightly.

3 Meanwhile, make the custard. Put the rosemary, vanilla pod, single cream and milk in a saucepan and heat until almost boiling. Remove from the heat and leave to infuse for 30 minutes. Put the egg yolks and sugar in a bowl and beat together until thick and pale. Reheat the cream mixture and strain it on to the yolk mixture, whisking. Set the bowl over a saucepan of gently simmering water and cook, stirring constantly, until the custard thickens. Dust the cake with icing sugar and decorate with the sprigs of rosemary. Serve, cut into slices, with the warm custard.

VARIATION

As an alternative to rosemary, the custard could be flavoured with orange rind, bay leaves, brandy or a liqueur.

Chocolate Half-Pay Pudding

This variation of a traditional English dessert is warming, filling, and comforting on a cold winter's evening.

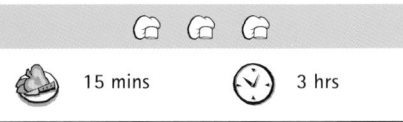

15 mins   3 hrs

SERVES 6–8

INGREDIENTS

85 g/3 oz self-raising flour

25 g/1 oz cocoa powder

pinch of salt

½ tsp ground cinnamon

115 g/4 oz fresh white breadcrumbs

115 g/4 oz shredded suet

115 g/4 oz raisins

55 g/2 oz currants

55 g/2 oz chopped candied peel

300 ml/10 fl oz milk

2 tbsp golden syrup

butter, for greasing

custard or single cream, to serve

1 Sift together the flour, cocoa powder and salt into a large bowl, add the cinnamon, breadcrumbs, suet, raisins, currants and candied peel and stir until thoroughly combined. Gradually stir in the milk and syrup until well mixed.

2 Grease a 1.2-litre/2-pint pudding basin with butter and spoon the mixture into it, smoothing the top. Cut out

a circle of greaseproof paper and a circle of foil about 10 cm/4 inches larger than the rim of the basin. Grease the paper with butter, then place on the foil circle, greased side up. Make a pleat in the centre of both circles then, still holding them together and with the foil upward, place them on top of the bowl. Tie securely in place with kitchen string.

3 Place the basin in a large saucepan and add boiling water to come about

halfway up the side of the basin. Cover and steam over a low heat for 3 hours, topping up the saucepan with more boiling water, as necessary.

4 Turn off the heat and remove the basin from the saucepan. Remove and discard the foil and greaseproof paper. Run a round-bladed knife around the edge of the pudding to loosen it, then invert on to a warm serving plate. Serve immediately with custard or cream.

COOK'S TIP
For an extra treat, put 2 tablespoons of golden syrup in the bottom of the basin before adding the mixture. When the pudding is turned out, the syrup will run down the side like a sauce.

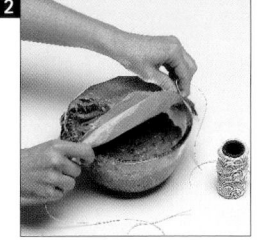

Upside-Down Cake

This recipe shows how a classic favourite can be adapted for vegans by using vegetarian margarine and oil instead of butter and eggs.

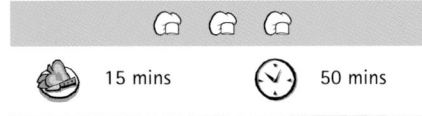

15 mins   50 mins

SERVES 6

I N G R E D I E N T S

40 g/1½ oz vegetarian margarine, cut into small pieces, plus extra for greasing

425 g/15 oz canned pineapple chunks in natural juice, drained, juice reserved

4 tsp cornflour

50 g/1¾ oz soft light brown sugar

125 ml/4 fl oz water

grated rind of 1 lemon

S P O N G E   C A K E

4 tbsp sunflower oil

60 g/2¼ oz soft light brown sugar

150 ml/5 fl oz water

175 g/6 oz plain flour

2 tsp baking powder

1 tsp ground cinnamon

1 Preheat the oven to 180°C/350°F/Gas Mark 4. Lightly grease a deep 18-cm/7-inch cake tin with a little vegetarian margarine.

2 Mix the reserved pineapple juice with the cornflour to a smooth paste. Put the paste in a saucepan with the sugar, margarine and water and stir over a low heat until the sugar has dissolved. Bring to a boil and simmer for 2–3 minutes until thickened. Leave to cool slightly.

3 To make the cake, heat the oil, sugar and water in a saucepan until the sugar has dissolved, but do not allow to boil. Remove from the heat and leave to cool. Sift the flour, baking powder and ground cinnamon into a bowl. Pour in the cooled sugar syrup and beat well to form a batter.

4 Place the pineapple chunks and lemon rind on the bottom of the prepared cake tin and spoon over 4 tablespoons of the pineapple syrup. Spoon the sponge mixture on top, smoothing the surface.

5 Bake in the preheated oven for 35–40 minutes until firm and a skewer inserted into the centre comes out clean. Invert on to a plate, leave to stand for 5 minutes, then remove the tin. Serve with the remaining syrup.

Apple Upside-Down Cake

Perfect for either a celebration meal or a more informal occasion, this cake tastes as good as it looks.

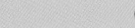

15 mins plus
15 mins cooling

45 mins

SERVES 4–6

INGREDIENTS

700 g/1 lb 9 oz apples

8 cloves

140 g/5 oz butter

250 g/9 oz caster sugar

2 eggs

25 g/1 oz flaked almonds, lightly toasted

25 g/1 oz hazelnuts, lightly toasted and ground

125 ml/4 fl oz double cream

125 ml/4 fl oz milk

½ tsp ground mixed spice

150 g/5½ oz self-raising flour

double cream, to serve

1 Preheat the oven to 180°C/350°F/Gas Mark 4. Bring a large saucepan of water to the boil. Peel and core the apples, cut into slices, then add them to the saucepan with the cloves. Lower the heat and simmer for 5 minutes, then remove from the heat. Drain well. Discard the cloves. Leave the apple to cool a little.

2 Grease a 20-cm/8-inch round cake tin with butter, then arrange the apple slices over the bottom of the tin. Sprinkle over 2 tablespoons of the sugar. In a separate bowl, cream together the remaining butter and sugar. Gradually mix in the eggs, then the nuts, cream, milk and mixed spice. Gradually add the flour, beating until the mixture is smooth.

3 Spread the mixture evenly over the apples, then bake in the preheated oven for about 40 minutes until golden or when a skewer inserted into the centre comes out clean. Remove the tin from the oven and leave to cool for 5 minutes, then turn out the cake on to a serving plate. Serve hot with double cream.

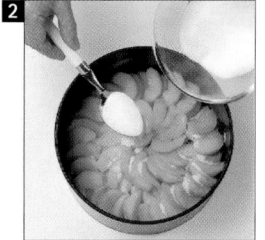

Mini Chocolate Gingers

Individually made desserts look professional and are quick to cook.
If you do not have small ovenproof bowls, use small teacups instead.

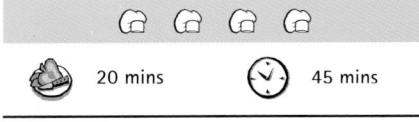

🍮 20 mins   🕐 45 mins

SERVES 4

INGREDIENTS

85 g/3 oz soft margarine, plus extra
   for greasing

100 g/3½ oz self-raising flour, sifted

100 g/3½ oz caster sugar

2 eggs

25 g/1 oz cocoa powder, sifted

25 g/1 oz plain chocolate

50 g/1¾ oz stem ginger

CHOCOLATE CUSTARD

2 egg yolks

1 tbsp caster sugar

1 tbsp cornflour

300 ml/10 fl oz milk

100 g/3½ oz plain chocolate,
   broken into pieces

icing sugar, for dusting

1 Lightly grease 4 individual metal pudding basins. Place the margarine, flour, sugar, eggs and cocoa powder in a mixing bowl and beat until well combined and smooth. Chop the chocolate and ginger and stir into the mixture.

2 Spoon the mixture into the prepared basins and smooth the tops. The mixture should three-quarters fill the basins. Cover the basins with discs of baking parchment and cover with a pleated sheet of foil. Steam for 45 minutes until the sponges are cooked and springy to the touch.

3 Meanwhile, make the custard. Beat together the egg yolks, sugar and cornflour to form a smooth paste. Heat the milk until boiling and pour over the egg mixture. Return to the saucepan and cook over a low heat, stirring until thick. Remove from the heat and beat in the chocolate. Stir until the chocolate melts.

4 Lift the mini chocolate gingers from the steamer, run a knife around the edge of the basins and turn out on to serving plates. Dust with icing sugar and drizzle chocolate custard over the top. Serve the remaining custard separately.

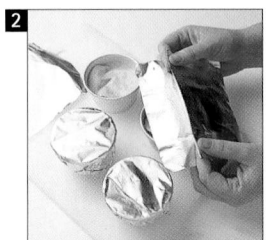

Tuscan Puddings

These baked mini ricotta puddings are delicious served warm or chilled and will keep in the refrigerator for 3–4 days.

 20 mins plus 10 mins soaking

 15 mins

SERVES 4

INGREDIENTS

1 tbsp butter

75 g/2¾ oz mixed dried fruit

250 g/9 oz ricotta cheese

3 egg yolks

50 g/1¾ oz caster sugar

1 tsp ground cinnamon

finely grated rind of 1 orange, plus longer strips of zest to decorate

crème fraîche (see page 9), to serve

1 Preheat the oven to 180°C/350°F/Gas Mark 4. Lightly grease 4 mini metal pudding basins or ramekins with the butter.

2 Put the dried fruit in a bowl and cover with warm water. Set aside to soak for 10 minutes.

3 Beat the ricotta cheese with the egg yolks in a bowl. Stir in the caster sugar, cinnamon and orange rind and mix to combine.

4 Drain the dried fruit in a sieve set over a bowl. Mix the drained fruit with the ricotta cheese mixture.

5 Spoon the mixture into the basins or ramekins and smooth the tops.

6 Bake in the preheated oven for 15 minutes. The tops should just be firm to the touch but not brown.

7 Decorate the puddings with strips of orange zest. Serve warm or chilled with a spoonful of crème fraîche, if liked.

COOK'S TIP

Crème fraîche has a slightly sour, nutty taste and is very thick. It has the same fat content as double cream and is suitable for cooking. You can use sour cream instead.

Semolina Dessert

This dish is eaten with pooris and potato curry for breakfast in northern India, but you can serve it with fresh cream as a delicious dessert.

5 mins   10 mins

SERVES 4

INGREDIENTS

6 tbsp pure ghee

3 cloves

3 cardamom pods

8 tbsp coarse semolina

½ tsp saffron

50 g/1¾ oz sultanas

10 tbsp granulated sugar

300 ml/10 fl oz water

300 ml/10 fl oz milk

cream, to serve

TO DECORATE

25 g/1 oz desiccated coconut, toasted

25 g/1 oz chopped almonds

25 g/1 oz pistachio nuts, soaked and chopped (optional)

1 Place the ghee in a saucepan and melt over a medium heat.

2 Add the cloves and whole cardamom pods to the melted butter and lower the heat, stirring to mix.

3 Add the semolina to the mixture in the saucepan and stir-fry until it turns a little darker.

4 Add the saffron, sultanas and the sugar to the semolina mixture, stirring to mix well.

5 Pour in the water and milk and stir the mixture continuously until the semolina has softened. Add a little more water if required.

6 Remove the saucepan from the heat and transfer the semolina to a warmed serving dish.

7 Decorate the semolina dessert with the toasted coconut, chopped almonds and pistachio nuts. Serve with a little cream drizzled over the top.

Baked Semolina Dessert

Succulent plums simmered in orange juice and spices complement this rich and creamy semolina dessert perfectly.

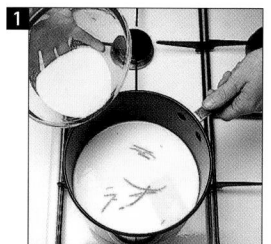

🕐 5 mins   🕐 45 mins

SERVES 4

I N G R E D I E N T S

2 tbsp butter or margarine, plus extra for greasing

600 ml/1 pint milk

finely pared zest and juice of 1 orange

55 g/2 oz semolina

pinch of grated nutmeg

2 tbsp caster sugar

1 egg, beaten

TO SERVE

small piece of butter

grated nutmeg

SPICED PLUMS

225 g/8 oz plums, halved and stoned

150 ml/5 fl oz orange juice

2 tbsp caster sugar

½ tsp ground mixed spice

1 Preheat the oven to 190°C/375°F/Gas Mark 5. Grease a 1-litre/1¾-pint ovenproof dish with a little of the butter or margarine. Put the milk, the remaining butter or margarine and orange rind into a saucepan. Sprinkle in the semolina and bring to the boil over a low heat, stirring constantly. Simmer gently for 2–3 minutes. Remove the saucepan from the heat.

2 Add the nutmeg, orange juice and sugar, stirring well. Add the egg and stir to mix.

3 Transfer the mixture to the prepared dish and bake in the preheated oven for about 30 minutes until lightly browned.

4 To make the spiced plums, put the plums, orange juice, sugar and mixed spice into a saucepan and simmer gently for about 10 minutes until the plums are just tender. Remove the saucepan from the heat and set aside to cool slightly.

5 Top the dessert with the piece of butter and a sprinkling of grated nutmegs and serve with the spiced plums.

Chocolate Almond Dessert

This is a very rich combination of light, delicate cake and glossy brandy sauce and would be a good choice for entertaining guests.

20 mins | 1 hr 5 mins

SERVES 6

INGREDIENTS

115 g/4 oz unsalted butter, plus extra for greasing

125 g/4½ oz caster sugar

85 g/3 oz plain chocolate, broken into pieces

6 eggs, separated

115 g/4 oz ground almonds

6 amaretti biscuits, crushed

BRANDY SAUCE

55 g/2 oz unsalted butter

115 g/4 oz caster sugar

115 g/4 oz plain chocolate, broken into pieces

50 ml/2 fl oz milk

2 tbsp brandy

1 Grease a 1.2-litre/2-pint pudding basin and sprinkle with 1 tablespoon of the sugar. Turn the basin to coat, then tip out any excess. Melt the chocolate in a heatproof bowl set over a saucepan of simmering water. Remove from the heat and leave to cool slightly.

2 Cream the butter and remaining sugar together until pale and fluffy, then beat in the egg yolks, 1 at a time. Beat in the melted chocolate, then fold in the ground almonds and amaretti crumbs. Put the egg whites in a clean, greasefree bowl and whisk until stiff, then fold into the chocolate mixture.

3 Spoon the mixture into the pudding basin. Cut out a circle of greaseproof paper and a circle of foil about 10 cm/

4 inches larger than the rim of the basin. Butter the paper, then place on the foil circle, greased side up. Make a pleat in the centre of both circles then, still holding them together and with the foil circle upward, place them on top of the basin. Tie securely in place with kitchen string.

4 Place the basin in a large saucepan and add boiling water to come about halfway up the side of the basin. Cover and steam over a low heat for 1 hour, adding more boiling water, as necessary.

5 Meanwhile, make the sauce. Melt the butter with the sugar in a small saucepan over a low heat, stirring constantly. Remove from the heat. Melt the chocolate in a bowl over a saucepan of simmering water. Stir in the butter mixture, then the milk and 50 ml/2 fl oz water. Remove from the heat and add the brandy.

6 Lift the basin out of the saucepan and discard the paper and foil. Invert the dessert on to a warm serving dish, pour over the sauce and serve immediately.

Ground Almonds in Milk

Traditionally served at breakfast in India, this almond-based dish is said to sharpen the mind. It is also delicious served as a dessert.

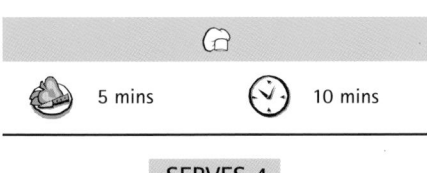

5 mins   10 mins

SERVES 4

INGREDIENTS

2 tbsp vegetable or pure ghee

4 tbsp plain flour

100 g/3½ oz ground almonds

300 ml/10 fl oz milk

55 g/2 oz sugar

fresh mint leaves, to decorate

1 Place the ghee in a small, heavy-based saucepan and melt over a gentle heat, stirring constantly so that it doesn't burn.

2 Reduce the heat and add the flour, stirring vigorously to remove any lumps. Stir in the ground almonds.

3 Gradually stir in the milk and sugar. Bring to the boil, stirring constantly. Continue cooking, stirring constantly, for 3–5 minutes or until the mixture is smooth and has the consistency of a creamy soup.

4 Transfer to a serving dish, decorate with fresh mint leaves and serve hot.

Raspberry Almond Spirals

This is the ultimate in self-indulgence – a truly delicious dessert that tastes every bit as good as it looks.

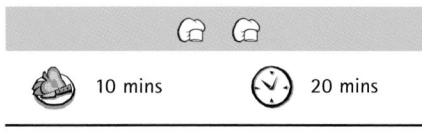

10 mins   20 mins

SERVES 4

INGREDIENTS

salt

55 g/2 oz fusilli

450 g/1 lb raspberries

2 tbsp caster sugar

1 tbsp lemon juice

25 g/1 oz flaked almonds

3 tbsp raspberry liqueur

1 Bring a large saucepan of lightly salted water to the boil. Add the fusilli and cook until tender, but still firm to the bite. Drain the fusilli thoroughly, then return to the pan and set aside to cool.

2 Using a spoon, firmly press 150 g/ 5⅓ oz of the raspberries through a sieve set over a large mixing bowl to form a smooth purée.

3 Put the raspberry purée and sugar in a small saucepan and simmer over a low heat, stirring occasionally, for 5 minutes. Stir in the lemon juice and set the sauce aside until required.

4 Add the remaining raspberries to the cooled fusilli in the saucepan and mix together well. Transfer the raspberry and fusilli mixture to a serving dish.

5 Preheat the grill to high. Spread the almonds out on a baking sheet and toast under the grill until golden brown. Remove and set aside to cool slightly.

6 Stir the raspberry liqueur into the reserved raspberry sauce and mix together well until very smooth. Pour the raspberry sauce over the fusilli, then generously sprinkle over the toasted almonds and serve.

COOK'S TIP

You could use almost any sweet, ripe berry for making this dessert. Strawberries and blackberries are especially suitable, combined with the appropriately flavoured liqueur. Alternatively, you could use a different berry mixed with the fusilli but still pour over the raspberry sauce.

Teacup Pudding

This dessert is simple to make, because everything, except the allspice, is measured in the same cup. It tastes best served with warm custard.

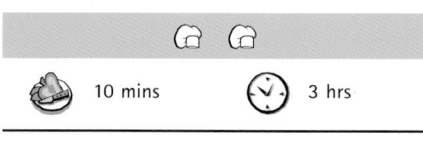

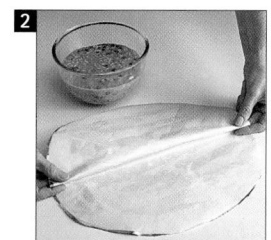

10 mins   3 hrs

SERVES 4

INGREDIENTS

butter, for greasing

1 cup self-raising flour

1 tsp mixed spice

1 cup brown sugar

1 cup shredded suet

1 cup currants

1 cup milk

custard, to serve

1 Grease a 1-litre/1³/₄-pint pudding basin with butter. Sift the flour and mixed spice into a bowl and stir in the sugar, suet and currants, then add the milk and mix thoroughly. Spoon the mixture into the prepared basin.

2 Cut out a circle of greaseproof paper and a circle of foil about 7.5 cm/ 3 inches larger than the rim of the basin. Grease the paper circle, place it on top of the foil circle, greased side up and pleat both circles across the centre. Place them over the bowl, with the foil circle upwards, and tie in place with kitchen string.

3 Place the basin on a trivet in a large saucepan and pour in enough boiling water to come halfway up the side of the basin. Alternatively, place it in a steamer over a saucepan of boiling water. Steam for 3 hours, then carefully remove the basin from the saucepan or steamer. Discard the paper and foil, turn out the pudding on to a warmed serving dish and serve with custard.

COOK'S TIP
It doesn't matter whether you use a standard measuring cup or an ordinary teacup to measure the ingredients, because the proportions remain the same.

Baked Sweet Ravioli

These unusual and scrumptious little parcels are the perfect dessert for anyone with a really sweet tooth.

1 hr 15 mins   20 mins

SERVES 4

I N G R E D I E N T S

PASTA

425 g/15 oz plain flour, plus extra
  for dusting

140 g/5 oz butter, plus extra for greasing

140 g/5 oz caster sugar

4 eggs

25 g/1 oz yeast

125 ml/4 fl oz lukewarm milk

FILLING

175 g/6 oz chestnut purée

55 g/2 oz cocoa powder

55 g/2 oz caster sugar

55 g/2 oz chopped almonds

6 amaretti biscuits, crushed

175 g/6 oz orange marmalade

1 To make the sweet pasta dough, sift the flour into a mixing bowl, then add the butter, sugar and 3 of the eggs and mix well to combine.

2 Mix together the yeast and tepid milk in a small bowl. When thoroughly combined, mix into flour mixture to form a dough.

3 Knead the dough for 20 minutes, cover with a clean cloth and set aside in a warm place for 1 hour to rise.

4 In a separate bowl, mix together the chestnut purée, cocoa powder, sugar, almonds, crushed amaretti and orange marmalade.

5 Preheat the oven to 180°C/350°F/Gas Mark 4. Grease 1 or 2 baking trays with a little butter.

6 Lightly flour the work surface. Roll out the pasta dough into a thin sheet and cut into 5 cm/2 inch circles with a plain pastry cutter.

7 Put a spoonful of filling on to each circle and then fold in half, pressing the edges to seal. Arrange on the prepared baking sheet, spacing the ravioli out.

8 Beat the remaining egg and brush all over the ravioli. Bake in the preheated oven for 20 minutes. Serve hot.

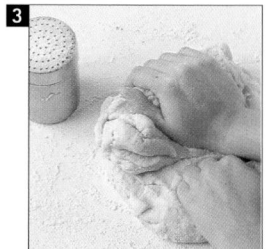

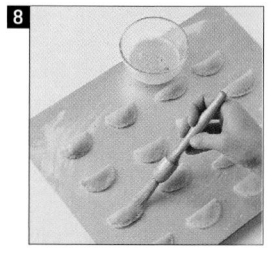

Jam Roly Poly

A classic dessert, warming and comforting, which is delicious served with plenty of hot custard.

20 mins   1 hr 30 mins

SERVES 4

INGREDIENTS

175 g/6 oz self-raising flour,
    plus extra for dusting

pinch of salt

75 g/2¾ oz shredded suet

3–4 tbsp hot water

6 tbsp raspberry jam

2 tbsp milk

butter, for greasing

raspberries, to decorate

custard, to serve

1 Put the flour and salt in a bowl and mix together well. Add the suet and then stir in enough hot water to give a light dough. Using your hands, shape the dough into a ball. Turn out the dough on to a lightly floured work surface and knead gently until smooth. Roll out into a rectangle about 28 x 23 cm/11 x 9 inches.

2 Spread the jam over the dough, leaving a border about 1 cm/½ inch all round. Brush the border with milk. Starting with the short side, roll up the dough evenly until you have one large roll.

3 Lightly grease a large piece of foil with butter, then place the dough roll in the centre. Gently close up the foil around the dough, leaving room for expansion, and seal tightly. Transfer to a steamer on top of a saucepan of boiling water. Steam for 1½ hours, keeping the water level topped up, until cooked.

4 Turn out the roly poly on to a serving platter and decorate with raspberries. Serve with hot custard.

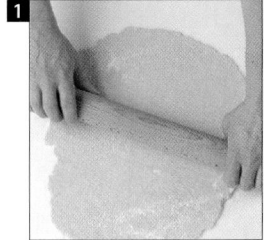

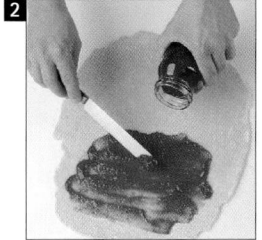

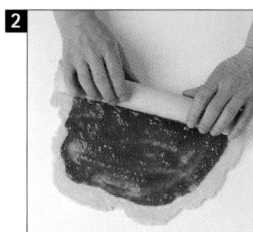

Creamy Rice Pudding

A well-made rice pudding is always popular. Even adults will come back for a second helping.

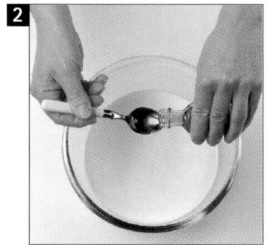

10–15 mins   2 hrs 30 mins

SERVES 4

INGREDIENTS

15 g/½ oz butter, for greasing

85 g/3 oz sultanas

5 tbsp caster sugar

90 g/3¼ oz pudding rice

1.2 litres/2 pints milk

1 tsp vanilla essence

finely grated rind of 1 large lemon

pinch of freshly grated nutmeg

chopped pistachio nuts, to decorate

1 Preheat the oven to 160°C/325°F/Gas Mark 3. Grease a 900-ml/1½-pint ovenproof dish with the butter.

2 Put the sultanas, sugar and rice into a mixing bowl, then stir in the milk and vanilla. Sprinkle over the lemon rind and grate in a pinch of nutmeg, then bake in the preheated oven for 2½ hours.

3 Remove from the oven and transfer to individual serving bowls. Decorate with chopped pistachio nuts and serve.

Indian Rice Pudding

Indian rice pudding is cooked in a saucepan over a low heat rather than in the oven like the Western version – which is also far less sweet.

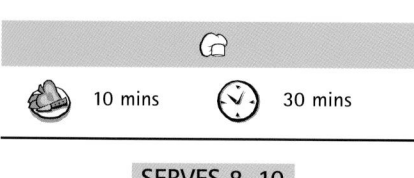

🕙 10 mins ⏲ 30 mins

SERVES 8–10

INGREDIENTS

75 g/2¾ oz basmati rice

1.2 litres/2 pints milk

100 g/3½ oz sugar

varq (edible silver leaf) or chopped pistachio nuts, to decorate

1 Rinse the rice and place in a large saucepan. Add 600 ml/1 pint of the milk and bring to the boil over a very low heat. Cook until the milk has been completely absorbed by the rice, stirring occasionally.

2 Remove the saucepan from the heat. Mash the rice, making swift, round movements in the saucepan, for at least 5 minutes until all the lumps have been removed.

3 Gradually add the remaining 600 ml/ 1 pint of milk and return the saucepan to the heat. Bring to the boil over a low heat, stirring occasionally.

4 Add the sugar and continue to cook, stirring constantly, for 7–10 minutes or until the mixture is quite thick in consistency.

5 Transfer the rice pudding to a heatproof serving bowl. Decorate with varq (silver leaf) or chopped pistachio nuts and serve on its own or with Pooris (see page 561).

VARIATION
If desired, you can substitute white or patna long-grain rice for the basmati rice, but the result won't be as good.

Basmati & Bay Leaf Pudding

Don't be put off by the bay leaves in this recipe. They add an interesting depth of flavour to the pudding.

10 mins   1 hr 10 mins

SERVES 4

INGREDIENTS

600 ml/1 pint milk

225 ml/8 fl oz single cream

4 fresh bay leaves, washed and lightly bruised

55 g/2 oz basmati or long-grain white rice

2 tbsp sultanas or raisins

55 g/2 oz sugar

grated rind of 1 orange

1 tsp vanilla essence

2 tbsp pine kernels or green pistachio nuts

sweet biscuits, to serve

1 Put the milk and cream in a medium-size heavy-based saucepan and bring to the boil over a medium heat, stirring occasionally to prevent sticking.

2 Add the bay leaves, then sprinkle in the rice. Reduce the heat to low and simmer gently for about 1 hour, stirring occasionally, until the rice is tender and the mixture is thickened and creamy.

3 Stir in the sultanas, sugar and orange rind and stir frequently until the sugar is dissolved and the fruit is plump. Remove from the heat, discard the bay leaves, and stir in the vanilla essence.

4 Meanwhile, toast the pine nuts in a small frying pan until golden.

5 Spoon the pudding into individual bowls and sprinkle with the toasted nuts. Serve warm or refrigerate to thicken and chill. Serve the biscuits separately.

VARIATION
Bay has a lovely flavour and goes well with rice but, if preferred, you can substitute a cinnamon stick, lightly crushed cardamom seeds, freshly grated nutmeg or seeds from a vanilla pod.

Baked Coconut Rice Pudding

A wonderful baked rice pudding cooked with flavoursome coconut milk and a little lime rind. Serve hot or chilled with fresh or stewed fruit.

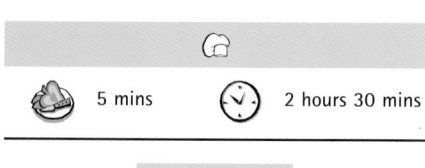

5 mins   2 hours 30 mins

SERVES 4–6

INGREDIENTS

knob of butter, plus extra for greasing

85 g/3 oz short or round-grain pudding rice

600 ml/1 pint coconut milk

300 ml/10 fl oz milk

1 large strip lime zest

55 g/2 oz caster sugar

pinch of ground star anise (optional)

fresh or stewed fruit, to serve

1 Lightly grease a 1.4-litre/2½-pint shallow ovenproof dish.

2 Mix the pudding rice with the coconut milk, milk, lime zest and caster sugar until all the ingredients are well blended.

3 Pour the rice mixture into the greased ovenproof dish and dot the surface with a little butter. Bake in the oven for about 30 minutes.

4 Remove the dish from the oven. Remove and discard the strip of lime zest from the rice pudding.

5 Stir the pudding well, add the pinch of ground star anise (if using), return to the oven, and cook for a further 1–2 hours or until almost all the milk has been absorbed and a golden brown skin has formed on the top of the pudding.

6 Cover the top of the pudding with foil if it starts to brown too much towards the end of the cooking time.

7 Serve the baked coconut rice pudding warm or chilled, if you prefer, with fresh or stewed fruit.

COOK'S TIP
As the mixture cools it thickens. If you plan to serve the rice chilled then fold in about 3 tablespoons of cream or extra coconut milk before serving, to give a thinner consistency.

Honeyed Rice Puddings

These small rice puddings are quite sweet, and have a wonderful flavour thanks to the combination of ginger, honey and cinnamon.

🍚 10 mins   🕐 50 mins

SERVES 4

INGREDIENTS

300 g/10½ oz pudding rice

2 tbsp clear honey, plus extra for drizzling

large pinch of ground cinnamon

butter, for greasing

15 ready-to-eat dried apricots, chopped

3 pieces stem ginger, drained and chopped

8 whole ready-to-eat dried apricots, to decorate

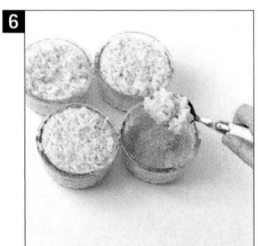

1 Put the rice in a saucepan and just cover with cold water. Bring to a boil, reduce the heat, cover and cook for about 15 minutes, or until the water has been absorbed. Stir the honey and cinnamon into the rice.

2 Lightly grease 4 x 150-ml/5-fl oz ramekin dishes.

3 Blend the chopped apricots and ginger in a food processor to make a smooth paste.

4 Divide the paste into 4 equal portions and shape each into a flat round to fit into the ramekin dishes.

5 Divide half of the rice between the ramekin dishes and place an apricot-paste round on top.

6 Cover the apricot paste with the remaining rice. Cover the ramekin dishes with greaseproof paper and foil and steam for 30 minutes or until set.

7 Remove the ramekin dishes from the steamer and leave to stand for 5 minutes.

8 Turn out the puddings on to warm serving plates and drizzle with honey. Decorate with dried apricots and serve.

COOK'S TIP

The puddings may be left to chill in their ramekin dishes in the refrigerator, then turned out and served with ice cream or cream.

Rice Pudding Brûlée

Brown sugar sprinkled over the finished rice puddings caramelizes to an irresistible brûlée topping under a hot grill.

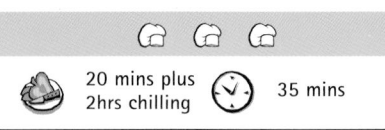

20 mins plus 2hrs chilling

35 mins

SERVES 6–8

INGREDIENTS

200 g/7 oz arborio rice

pinch of salt

1 vanilla pod, split

700 ml/1¼ pints milk

200 g/7 oz caster sugar

2 egg yolks

125 ml/4 fl oz double or whipping cream

grated rind of 1 large lemon

55 g/2 oz butter

2 tbsp brandy

light brown sugar, for glazing

1 Put the rice in a large heavy-based saucepan with a pinch of salt and add enough cold water to just cover. Bring to the boil, then reduce the heat and simmer gently for about 12 minutes until the water is absorbed.

2 Scrape the seeds from the split vanilla pod into the milk. Bring to a simmer and pour over the rice. Add the sugar and cook over a low heat, stirring, until the rice is tender and the milk thickened.

3 In a small bowl, beat the egg yolks with the cream and lemon rind. Stir in a large spoonful of the rice mixture and beat well to blend. Return the mixture to the saucepan and cook very gently until the pudding is thick and creamy. Do not allow to boil. Stir in the butter.

4 Remove from the heat, discard the vanilla pod and stir in the brandy. Spoon the mixture into 6–8 flameproof ramekins or crème brûlée pots. Allow to cool, then chill for at least 2 hours.

5 Sprinkle a very thin layer of brown sugar on top of each ramekin, to cover completely. Wipe the edge of each ramekin, as the sugar may stick and burn.

6 Place the ramekins in a small roasting tin containing about 1 cm/½ inch iced water. Place under a preheated grill, close to the heat, and grill until the sugar melts and caramelizes. Alternatively, use a small kitchen blowtorch to caramelize the sugar.

7 Allow the ramekins to cool for 2–3 minutes before serving.

Indonesian Rice Pudding

Also known as glutinous rice, sticky rice is available from Chinese supermarkets and may be black or white – the former is unpolished.

45 mins   5 mins

SERVES 4

INGREDIENTS

115 g/4 oz black sticky rice

450 ml/16 fl oz water

55 g/2 oz dark brown sugar

55 g/2 oz caster sugar

300 ml/10 fl oz coconut milk, to serve

1 Rinse the rice under cold running water, drain and place in a large saucepan. Add the measured water and bring to the boil, stirring constantly. Cover and simmer for 30 minutes.

2 Stir in the sugars and cook for a further 15 minutes. If necessary, add a little more water to prevent the rice from sticking.

3 Ladle the rice into warm bowls and serve immediately with the coconut milk. Alternatively, allow to cool and serve cold.

VARIATION

Add a small piece of bruised fresh root ginger when cooking the rice to add extra flavour. Remove and discard before serving.

Black Rice Pudding with Fruit

This sticky black rice is like congee, the traditional rice porridge eaten all over Southeast Asia for breakfast or as a base for other dishes.

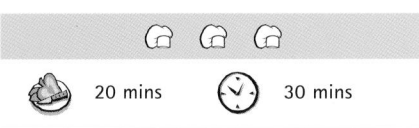

🍧 20 mins 🕑 30 mins

SERVES 6–8

INGREDIENTS

300 g/10½ oz black sticky rice

900 ml/1½ pints boiling water

1 vanilla pod, split, black seeds removed and reserved

225 g/8 oz light brown sugar

55 g/2 oz coconut powder

400 ml/14 fl oz canned thick coconut milk

2 ripe mangoes

6 passion fruit

TO DECORATE

shredded fresh coconut (optional)

fresh mint leaves

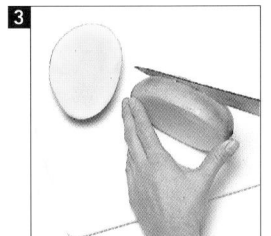

1 Put the rice in a large heavy-based saucepan and pour the boiling water over. Add the vanilla pod and seeds to the saucepan. Return to the boil, stirring once or twice. Reduce the heat to low and simmer, covered, for about 25 minutes until the rice is tender and the liquid almost totally absorbed. Do not uncover during cooking.

2 Remove from the heat and stir in the sugar, coconut powder and half the coconut milk. Stir until the sugar is dissolved. Cover and leave to stand for 10 minutes. If the rice becomes too thick, add a little more of the coconut milk or a little milk or water.

3 Cut each mango lengthways along each side of the large stone to remove the flesh. Peel the mangoes, slice thinly and arrange on a serving plate.

4 Cut the passion fruit in half crossways, scoop out the pulp and juice and spoon over the mango slices. Decorate with shredded coconut, if desired, and a few mint leaves.

5 Spoon the warm pudding into wide shallow bowls and decorate with shredded coconut and mint leaves. Drizzle some of the remaining coconut milk around the edges, if desired. Serve with the mango and passion fruit salad.

Florentine Rice Pudding

This delicious pudding is flavoured with orange and baked in the oven until puffed.

15 mins   15 mins

SERVES 6

INGREDIENTS

150 g/5½ oz long-grain rice or risotto rice

pinch of salt

1 litre/1¾ pints milk

5 eggs

400 g/14 oz sugar or 450 g/1 lb honey, or a mixture

115 g/4 oz butter, melted and cooled, plus extra for greasing

2 tbsp orange flower water or 4 tbsp orange liqueur

225 g/8 oz diced candied orange peel

225 g/8 oz orange marmalade

2–3 tbsp water

icing sugar, for dusting

1 Preheat the oven to 180°C/350°F/Gas Mark 4. Put the rice and salt in a large heavy-based saucepan. Add the milk and bring to the boil, stirring occasionally. Reduce the heat to low and simmer gently for about 25 minutes until the rice is tender and creamy. Remove from the heat.

2 Pass the cooked rice through a food mill into a large bowl. Alternatively, process in a food processor for about 30 seconds until smooth. Set aside. Stir from time to time to prevent a skin forming.

3 Meanwhile, using an electric mixer, whisk the eggs with the sugar in a large bowl for about 4 minutes until very light and fluffy. Gently fold into the rice with the melted butter. Stir in half the orange flower water, then stir in the candied orange peel.

4 Pour into a well-buttered 2-litre/ 3½-pint soufflé dish or charlotte mould. Place the dish in a roasting tin and pour in enough boiling water to come 4 cm/1½ inches up the side of the dish.

5 Bake in the preheated oven for about 25 minutes until puffed and lightly set. Transfer the dish to a wire rack to cool slightly.

6 Heat the marmalade with the water, stirring until dissolved and smooth. Stir in the remaining orange flower water and pour into a sauceboat or jug. Dust the top of the pudding with the icing sugar and serve warm with the marmalade sauce.

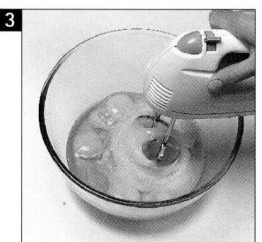

Raspberry Risotto

The combination of coconut milk, raspberry liqueur and fresh raspberries make this a memorable sweet risotto.

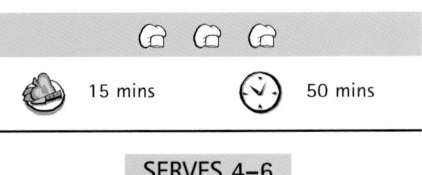

15 mins   50 mins

SERVES 4–6

INGREDIENTS

450 ml/16 fl oz milk

450 ml/16 fl oz canned unsweetened coconut milk

pinch of salt

1 vanilla pod, split

2–3 strips lemon zest

25 g/1 oz unsalted butter

125 g/4½ oz arborio rice

50 ml/2 fl oz dry white vermouth

115 g/4 oz sugar

125 ml/4 fl oz double or whipping cream

2–3 tbsp raspberry liqueur

350 g/12 oz fresh raspberries

2 tbsp good-quality raspberry jam or preserve

squeeze of lemon juice

toasted slivered almonds, to decorate (optional)

1 Heat the milk in a heavy-based saucepan with the coconut milk, salt, vanilla pod and lemon zest until bubbles start to form around the sides. Reduce the heat to low and keep the milk mixture hot, stirring occasionally.

2 Heat the butter in another large heavy-based saucepan over a medium heat until foaming. Add the rice and cook, stirring, for 2 minutes to coat well.

3 Add the vermouth; it will bubble and steam fiercely. Cook, stirring, until the wine is completely absorbed. Gradually add the hot milk, about 125 ml/4 fl oz at a time, allowing each addition to be absorbed before adding the next.

4 When half the milk has been added, stir in the sugar until dissolved. Continue stirring and adding the milk until the rice is tender, but still firm to the bite; this should take about 25 minutes. Remove from the heat and discard the vanilla pod and lemon strips. Stir in half the cream, the liqueur and half the fresh raspberries, then cover.

5 Heat the raspberry jam with the lemon juice and 1–2 tablespoons of water, stirring until melted and smooth. Remove from the heat, add the remaining raspberries and mix. Stir the remaining cream into the risotto and serve with the glazed raspberries.

Thai Rice Dessert

This Thai-style version of rice dessert is mildly spiced and creamy, with a rich custard topping. It's excellent served warm or cold.

10 mins   1–1 hr 15 mins

SERVES 4

INGREDIENTS

100 g/3½ oz short-grain rice

2 tbsp palm sugar

1 cardamom pod, split

300 ml/10 fl oz coconut milk

150 ml/5 fl oz water

3 eggs

200 ml/7 fl oz coconut cream

1½ tbsp caster sugar

sweetened coconut flakes, to decorate

fresh fruit, to serve

1 Preheat the oven to 180°C/350°F/Gas Mark 4. Place the rice and palm sugar in a saucepan. Crush the seeds from the cardamom pod using a pestle and mortar and add to the saucepan. Stir in the coconut milk and water.

2 Bring to the boil, stirring to dissolve the sugar. Lower the heat and simmer, uncovered, stirring occasionally, for about 20 minutes until the rice is tender and most of the liquid has been absorbed.

3 Spoon the rice into 4 individual ovenproof dishes and spread evenly. Place the dishes in a roasting tin with water to come about halfway up the sides.

4 Beat the eggs with the coconut cream and caster sugar and spoon over the rice. Cover with foil and bake in the preheated oven for 45–50 minutes until the custard sets.

5 Serve the rice desserts warm or cold, with fresh fruit and decorated with coconut flakes.

COOK'S TIP

Cardamom is quite a powerful spice, so if you find it too strong, it can be left out altogether or replaced with a little ground cinnamon.

Creamed Rice Pudding

This is real comfort food for cold winter days. Serve it with canned or stewed fruit or just enjoy it on its own.

🧊 5 mins   🕐 1 hr 5 mins

SERVES 4

I N G R E D I E N T S

140 g/5 oz short-grain rice

1 litre/1¾ pints milk

115 g/4 oz caster sugar

1 tsp vanilla essence

ground cinnamon, to decorate

1 Rinse the rice well under cold running water and drain. Pour the milk into a large, heavy-based saucepan, add the sugar and bring to the boil, stirring constantly.

2 Add the rice, lower the heat, cover and simmer gently, stirring occasionally, for 1 hour, until all the milk has been absorbed.

3 Stir in the vanilla essence and serve immediately, sprinkled with a light dusting of cinnamon.

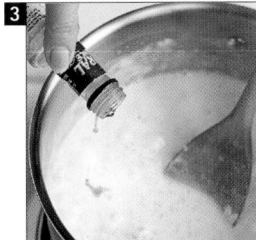

Meringue-Topped Rice Pudding

Probably Scandinavian in origin, this mouthwatering pudding is thickened with cornflour and egg yolks, making it extra rich and comforting.

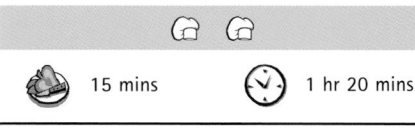

🍮 15 mins   🕐 1 hr 20 mins

SERVES 6–8

INGREDIENTS

125 ml/4 fl oz water

1.2 litres/2 pints milk

100 g/3½ oz long-grain white rice

2–3 strips of lemon zest

1 cinnamon stick

1 vanilla pod, split

115 g/4 oz sugar

3 tbsp cornflour

4 egg yolks

MERINGUE

6 egg whites

¼ tsp cream of tartar

225 g/8 oz plus 2 tbsp caster sugar

1 Preheat the oven to 150°C/300°F/ Gas Mark 2. Bring the water and 225 ml/8 fl oz of the milk to the boil in a large heavy-based saucepan. Add the rice, lemon zest, cinnamon stick and vanilla pod and reduce the heat to low. Cover and simmer for about 20 minutes, until the rice is tender and all the liquid has been absorbed. Remove the lemon zest, cinnamon stick and vanilla pod and add the remaining milk. Return to the boil.

2 Stir together the sugar and the cornflour. Stir in a little of the hot rice-milk to make a paste, then stir into the saucepan of rice. Cook, stirring constantly, until the mixture boils and thickens. Boil for 1 minute, then remove from the heat to cool slightly.

3 Beat the egg yolks until smooth. Stir a large spoonful of the hot rice mixture into the yolks, beating until well blended, then stir into the rice mixture. Pour into a 3-litre/5¼-pint baking dish.

4 To make the meringue, whisk the egg whites with the cream of tartar in a large bowl until stiff peaks form. Add the sugar, 2 tablespoons at a time, beating well after each addition, until stiff and glossy.

5 Gently spoon the meringue over the top of the rice pudding, spreading evenly. Make swirls with the back of the spoon.

6 Bake in the preheated oven for about 1 hour, until the top is golden and set. Turn off the oven, open the door, and allow the pudding to cool in the oven. Serve warm, at room temperature or cold.

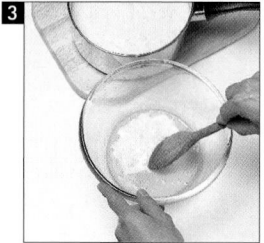

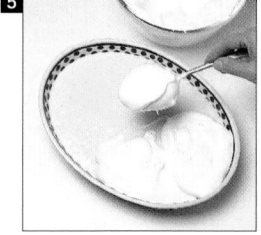

Saffron-Spiced Rice Pudding

This rich pudding is cooked in milk delicately flavoured with saffron, then mixed with dried fruit, almonds and cream before baking.

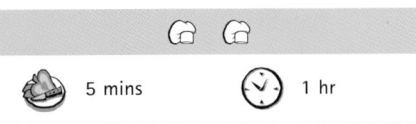

5 mins   1 hr

SERVES 4

INGREDIENTS

600 ml/1 pint creamy milk

several pinches of saffron strands, finely crushed (see Cook's Tip)

60 g/2¼ oz pudding rice

1 cinnamon stick or piece of cassia bark

40 g/1½ oz sugar

25 g/1 oz seedless raisins or sultanas

25 g/1 oz ready-to-eat dried apricots, chopped

1 egg, beaten

5 tbsp single cream

15 g/½ oz butter, diced, plus extra for greasing

15 g/½ oz flaked almonds

freshly grated nutmeg, for sprinkling

cream, to serve (optional)

1 Preheat the oven to 180°C/350°F/Gas Mark 4. Place the milk and crushed saffron in a non-stick saucepan and bring to the boil. Stir in the rice and cinnamon stick or cassia bark, lower the heat and simmer very gently, uncovered, stirring frequently, for 25 minutes until tender.

2 Remove the saucepan from the heat. Remove the cinnamon stick from the rice mixture and discard. Stir in the sugar, raisins or sultanas and apricots, then beat in the egg, cream and diced butter.

3 Transfer the mixture to a greased ovenproof pie or flan dish and sprinkle with the almonds and freshly grated nutmeg to taste. Cook in the preheated oven for 25–30 minutes until set and lightly golden. Serve hot with extra cream, if wished.

COOK'S TIP
For a slightly stronger flavour, place the saffron strands on a small piece of kitchen foil and toast them lightly under a hot grill for a few moments, then crush them between your fingers and thumb.

Sweet Saffron Rice

This is a traditional dessert, which is easy to make and looks very impressive, especially decorated with pistachio nuts and varq (silver leaf).

5 mins

35 mins

SERVES 4

INGREDIENTS

200 g/7 oz basmati rice

200 g/7 oz sugar

pinch of saffron strands

300 ml/10 fl oz water

2 tbsp vegetable ghee

3 cloves

3 cardamom pods

25 g/1 oz sultanas

TO DECORATE

few pistachio nuts (optional)

varq (silver leaf) (optional)

1 Rinse the rice twice and bring to the boil in a saucepan of water, stirring constantly. Remove the saucepan from the heat when the rice is half-cooked, drain the rice thoroughly and set aside.

2 In a separate saucepan, boil the sugar and saffron in the water, stirring constantly, until the syrup thickens. Set the syrup aside until required.

3 In another saucepan, heat the ghee, cloves and cardamom pods, stirring occasionally. Remove the saucepan from the heat.

4 Return the rice to a low heat and stir in the sultanas.

5 Pour the syrup over the rice mixture and stir to mix.

6 Pour the ghee mixture over the rice and simmer over a low heat for 10–15 minutes. Check to see whether the rice is cooked. If it is not, add a little boiling water, cover and continue to simmer until tender.

7 Serve warm, decorated with pistachio nuts and varq (silver leaf), if desired.

COOK'S TIP
Basmati rice is the 'prince of rices' and comes from the Himalayan foothills. Its name means fragrant and it has a superb texture and flavour.

Apricot Crumble

In this delicious dessert, fresh apricots flavoured with cinnamon are topped with a hazelnut crumble topping.

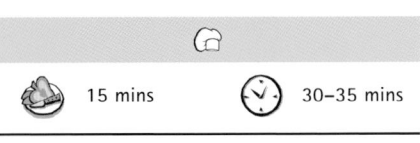

15 mins   30–35 mins

SERVES 4

INGREDIENTS

125 g/4½ oz butter, plus extra for greasing

175 g/6 oz brown sugar

500 g/1 lb 2 oz fresh apricots, stoned and sliced

1 tsp ground cinnamon

175 g/6 oz wholemeal flour

50 g/1¾ oz hazelnuts, toasted and finely chopped

fresh clotted cream, to serve

1 Preheat the oven to 200°C/400°F/Gas Mark 6. Grease a 1.2-litre/2-pint ovenproof dish with a little butter.

2 Put 3 tablespoons of the butter and 100 g/3½ oz of the sugar in a saucepan and melt together, stirring, over a low heat. Add the apricots and cinnamon, cover the saucepan and simmer for 5 minutes.

3 Meanwhile, put the flour in a bowl and rub in the remaining butter. Stir in the remaining sugar and then the hazelnuts. Remove the fruit from the heat and arrange in the bottom of the prepared dish. Sprinkle the crumble topping evenly over the fruit until it is covered all over. Transfer to the preheated oven and bake for about 25 minutes until golden. Remove from the oven and serve hot with fresh clotted cream.

Apple & Blackberry Crumble

A crumble is one of the easiest puddings to make and is always popular. It is delicious served with custard or cream.

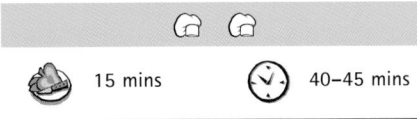

15 mins   40–45 mins

SERVES 4-6

INGREDIENTS

900 g/2 lb cooking apples

300 g/10½ oz blackberries, fresh or frozen

55 g/2 oz light muscovado sugar

1 tsp ground cinnamon

custard or single cream, to serve

CRUMBLE

85 g/3 oz self-raising flour

85 g/3 oz plain wholemeal flour

115 g/4 oz butter

55 g/2 oz demerara sugar

1 Preheat the oven to 200°C/400°F/Gas Mark 6. Peel and core the apples and cut into slices. Place in a bowl with the blackberries, sugar and cinnamon, mix well and place in an ovenproof dish.

2 To make the crumble, sift the self-raising flour into a bowl and stir in the wholemeal flour. Add the butter and rub in until the mixture resembles coarse breadcrumbs. Stir in the sugar.

3 Spread the crumble over the apple and blackberry mixture and bake in the oven for 40–45 minutes until the apples are soft and the crumble is golden brown and crisp. Serve with custard or single cream.

COOK'S TIP
When making a crumble, keep rubbing in the butter until the crumbs are quite coarse. This ensures that the crumble will be crunchy.

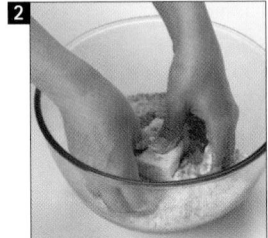

Fruit Crumble

Any fruits in season can be used in this wholesome dessert. It is suitable for vegans because it contains no dairy produce.

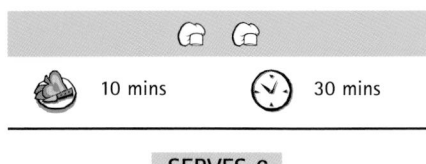

10 mins

30 mins

SERVES 6

INGREDIENTS

vegan margarine, for greasing

6 dessert pears

1 tbsp chopped stem ginger

1 tbsp molasses

2 tbsp orange juice

soy custard, to serve (optional)

CRUMBLE

175 g/6 oz all-purpose flour

85 g/3 oz vegan margarine, cut into small pieces

25 g/1 oz flaked almonds

25 g/1 oz porridge oats

85 g/3 oz soft dark brown sugar

1 Preheat the oven to 190°C/375°F/Gas Mark 5. Grease a 1-litre/1¾-pint ovenproof dish with vegan margarine.

2 Peel, core, quarter and slice the pears. In a bowl, mix together the pears, ginger, molasses and orange juice. Spoon the mixture into the prepared dish.

3 To make the crumble topping, sift the flour into a mixing bowl. Add the margarine and rub it in with your fingertips until the mixture resembles fine breadcrumbs. Stir in the flaked almonds, rolled oats and molasses sugar. Mix well until thoroughly combined.

4 Sprinkle the crumble topping evenly over the pear and ginger mixture in the dish, pressing it down gently with the back of a spoon.

5 Bake in the preheated oven for 30 minutes, until the topping is golden and the fruit tender. Serve the crumble hot, with soy custard (if using).

VARIATION
Stir 1 teaspoon of ground mixed spice into the crumble mixture in step 3 for added flavour.

Tropical Fruit Crumble

In this crumble, tropical fruits are flavoured with ginger and coconut, for something a little different and very tasty.

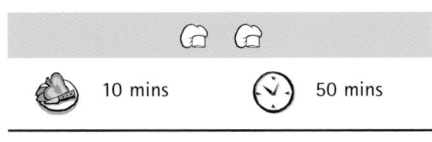

🕙 10 mins   🕐 50 mins

SERVES 4

I N G R E D I E N T S

2 mangoes, peeled and sliced

1 papaya, peeled, seeded and sliced

225 g/8 oz fresh pineapple, peeled, trimmed and cubed

1½ tsp ground ginger

100 g/3½ oz margarine

100 g/3½ oz light brown sugar

175 g/6 oz plain flour

55 g/2 oz desiccated coconut, plus extra to decorate

1 Preheat the oven to 180°C/350°F/Gas Mark 4. Place the fruit in a saucepan with ½ teaspoon of the ground ginger, 2 tablespoons of the margarine and 4 tablespoons of the sugar. Cook over a low heat for 10 minutes until the fruit softens. Spoon the fruit into the bottom of a shallow ovenproof dish.

2 Combine the flour and remaining ginger. Rub in the remaining margarine until the mixture resembles fine breadcrumbs. Stir in the remaining sugar and the coconut and spoon over the fruit to cover completely.

3 Cook the crumble in the preheated oven for about 40 minutes or until the top is golden and crisp. Decorate with a sprinkling of desiccated coconut and serve immediately.

Rhubarb & Orange Crumble

A mixture of rhubarb and apples flavoured with orange rind, brown sugar and spices and topped with a crunchy crumble topping is scrumptious.

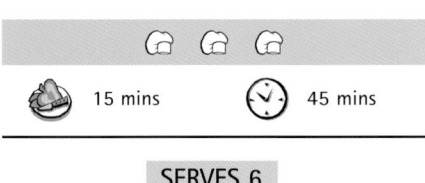

15 mins 45 mins

SERVES 6

INGREDIENTS

500 g/1 lb 2 oz rhubarb

500 g/1 lb 2 oz cooking apples

grated rind and juice of 1 orange

½–1 tsp ground cinnamon

about 85 g/3 oz light soft brown sugar

CRUMBLE

225 g/8 oz plain flour

125 g/4½ oz butter or margarine

125 g/4½ oz light soft brown sugar

40–55 g/1½–2 oz toasted chopped hazelnuts

2 tbsp demerara sugar (optional)

1 Preheat the oven to 200°C/400°F/ Gas Mark 6. Cut the rhubarb into 2.5-cm/1-inch lengths and place in a large saucepan.

2 Peel, core and slice the apples and add to the rhubarb, together with the grated orange rind and juice. Bring to the boil, lowers the heat and simmer for 2–3 minutes until the fruit softens.

3 Add the cinnamon and sugar to taste and turn the mixture into an ovenproof dish, so it is not more than two-thirds full.

4 Sift the flour into a bowl and rub in the butter or margarine until the mixture resembles fine breadcrumbs (this can be done by hand or in a food processor). Stir in the sugar, followed by the nuts.

5 Spoon the crumble mixture evenly over the fruit in the dish and lightly smooth the top. Sprinkle with demerara sugar, if liked.

6 Cook in the preheated oven for 30–40 minutes until the topping is browned. Serve hot or cold.

VARIATION
Other flavourings, such as 55 g/2 oz chopped stem ginger, can be added either to the fruit or the crumble mixture. Any fruit or mixture of fruits can be topped with crumble.

Chocolate Fruit Crumble

The addition of chocolate to a crumble topping makes it even more of a treat and is a good way of enticing children to eat a fruit dessert.

5–10 mins   40–45 mins

SERVES 4

INGREDIENTS

6 tbsp butter, plus extra for greasing

400 g/14 oz canned apricots, in natural juice

450 g/1 lb cooking apples, peeled and thickly sliced

100 g/3½ oz plain flour

50 g/1¾ oz porridge oats

4 tbsp caster sugar

55 g/2 oz plain or milk chocolate chips

1 Preheat the oven to 180°C/350°F/Gas Mark 4. Lightly grease an ovenproof dish with a little butter.

2 Drain the apricots, reserving 4 tablespoons of the juice. Place the apples and apricots in the prepared ovenproof dish with the reserved apricot juice and toss to mix.

3 Sift the flour into a mixing bowl. Cut the butter into small pieces and rub in with your fingertips until the mixture resembles fine breadcrumbs. Stir in the porridge oats, sugar and chocolate chips.

4 Sprinkle the crumble mixture over the apples and apricots and smooth the top lightly. Do not press the crumble into the fruit.

5 Bake in the preheated oven for 40–45 minutes or until the topping is golden. Serve hot or cold.

VARIATION
Other fruits can be used to make this crumble – fresh pears mixed with fresh or frozen raspberries work well. If you do not use canned fruit, add 4 tablespoons of orange juice to the fresh fruit.

Golden Baked Apple Pudding

This is a low-fat dessert, perfect for those who enjoy sweet things but are watching their weight.

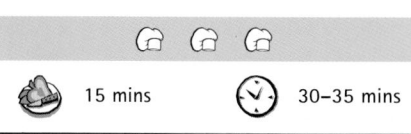

🍎 15 mins　　🕐 30–35 mins

SERVES 4

INGREDIENTS

450 g/1 lb cooking apples

1 tsp ground cinnamon

25 g/1 oz sultanas

115 g/4 oz wholemeal bread, about 4 thick slices

115 g/4 oz low-fat cottage cheese

4 tbsp light brown sugar

225 ml/8 fl oz skimmed milk

1　Preheat the oven to 220°C/425°F/Gas Mark 7.

2　Peel and core the apples and chop the flesh into 1-cm/½-inch pieces. Put the apple pieces in a bowl and toss with the cinnamon and sultanas.

3　Remove the crusts and cut the bread into 1-cm/½-inch cubes. Add to the apples with the cottage cheese and 3 tablespoons of the brown sugar and mix together. Stir in the milk.

4　Turn the mixture into an ovenproof dish and sprinkle with the remaining sugar. Bake in the oven for 30–35 minutes or until golden brown. Serve hot.

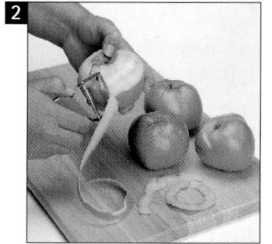

Chocolate Cherry Betty

This is a variation of the famous American dessert, apple brown betty, which is, in turn, a variation of the French apple charlotte.

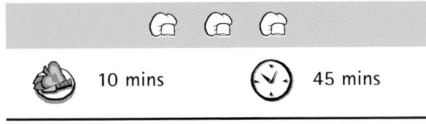

10 mins

45 mins

SERVES 4

INGREDIENTS

70 g/2½ oz butter, plus extra for greasing

175 g/6 oz chocolate cake crumbs

350 g/12 oz cherries, stoned

115 g/4 oz brown sugar

½ tsp ground cinnamon

grated rind of ½ orange

2 tbsp orange juice

5 tbsp sherry

whipped cream or custard, to serve

VARIATION
Substitute sliced peaches or nectarines for the cherries.

1 Preheat the oven to 190°C/375°F/Gas Mark 5. Grease a medium-size ovenproof dish with butter.

2 Sprinkle one-third of the cake crumbs over the bottom of the dish and dot with one-third of the butter. Arrange half the cherries evenly on top and sprinkle with half the sugar, cinnamon, orange rind and orange juice. Make another layer with half the remaining cake crumbs, dot with half the remaining butter, and top with the remaining cherries, sugar, cinnamon, orange rind and orange juice. Cover with the remaining crumbs and dot with the last of the butter.

3 Bake for 40 minutes until the cherries are tender. Remove the betty from the oven, pour the sherry over the top and return to the oven for 5 minutes. Serve hot with cream or custard.

Chocolate Apple Dessert

This light and airy dessert is surprisingly filling – just the thing to cheer you up on a cold winter's evening.

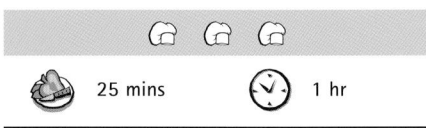

🍓 25 mins   🕐 1 hr

SERVES 4

INGREDIENTS

3 tbsp butter, plus extra for greasing

55 g/2 oz plain chocolate

175 ml/6 fl oz milk

4 tbsp plain flour

1 tbsp grated orange rind

1 tsp mixed spice

2 tbsp light muscovado sugar

2 eggs, separated

55 g/2 oz sultanas

1 large cooking apple

whipping cream, to serve

1 Preheat the oven to 160°C/325°F/Gas Mark 3. Grease a 1.2-litre/2-pint ovenproof dish. Break the chocolate into pieces and place in a saucepan with the milk. Set over a low heat and bring to just below simmering point, stirring constantly. Remove from the heat.

2 Melt 2 tablespoons of the butter in another saucepan over a low heat. When the butter is foamy, stir in the flour and cook, stirring constantly, for 1 minute. Remove the saucepan from the heat and gradually stir in the chocolate-flavoured milk. Return to the heat, add the orange rind and mixed spice and cook, stirring constantly, for 2–3 minutes until thickened and smooth.

3 Remove from the heat and stir in the muscovado sugar. Add the egg yolks, 1 at a time, beating well until thoroughly blended. Stir in the sultanas and set aside.

4 Melt the remaining butter in a heavy-based frying pan. Meanwhile peel, core and chop the apple. Add the apple to the frying pan and cook over a medium heat, stirring frequently, for 4–5 minutes, until golden. Remove from the frying pan with a slotted spoon and drain well on kitchen paper. Stir the apples into the chocolate mixture.

5 Whisk the egg whites in a clean, greasefree bowl until stiff. Stir about one-quarter into the chocolate and apple mixture to lighten it, then fold in the remainder with a metal spoon.

6 Place the prepared dish in a roasting tin. Pour the mixture into the dish and spread out evenly. Add enough hot water to the roasting tin to come about halfway up the sides of the dish. Bake for 1 hour or until just set. Remove the dish from the oven, invert on to a warm serving plate and serve immediately with cream.

Cherry Dessert with Sauce

This is a good way to use up slightly stale cake. You can use plain or chocolate cake crumbs – whichever are available.

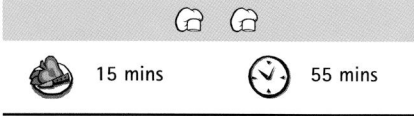

15 mins   55 mins

SERVES 6

INGREDIENTS

unsalted butter for greasing

450 g/1 lb raspberries

140 g/5 oz caster sugar

4 eggs, separated

115 g/4 oz cake crumbs

55 g/2 oz ground almonds

1 tbsp single cream

1 tbsp unsalted butter

55 g/2 oz glacé cherries, to decorate

SAUCE

175 g/6 oz plain chocolate

400 ml/14fl oz evaporated milk

½ tsp almond essence

1 Preheat the oven to 180°C/350°F/Gas Mark 4. Grease a 1.2-litre/2-pint soufflé dish. Place the raspberries in the dish and sprinkle with 55 g/2 oz of the sugar. Stir gently and set aside.

2 Whisk together the egg yolks and remaining sugar until pale and fluffy. Stir in the cake crumbs, ground almonds, cream and butter.

3 Whisk the egg whites in a clean, greasefree bowl until stiff. Stir one-quarter of the whites into the egg yolk mixture to lighten, then gently fold in the remainder. Spoon the mixture over the raspberries. Cut the glacé cherries in half and use to decorate the dessert. Bake for 50 minutes, until the top is golden brown and set.

4 Meanwhile, make the sauce. Break the chocolate into pieces and place in a heatproof bowl with the evaporated milk. Set over a saucepan of barely simmering water, stirring frequently until melted. Remove the bowl from the heat and whisk in the almond essence. Continue to whisk until thick and smooth. Serve warm with the dessert.

COOK'S TIP

You can use frozen raspberries or mixed berries, but thaw them completely first.

Plum Cobbler

This is another popular dessert which can be adapted to suit almost all types of fruit if plums are not available.

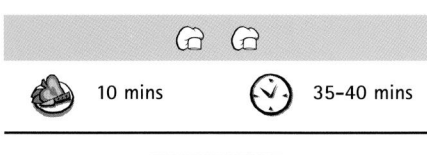

10 mins

35–40 mins

SERVES 6

I N G R E D I E N T S

butter, for greasing

1 kg/2 lb 4 oz plums, stoned and sliced

100 g/3½ oz caster sugar

1 tbsp lemon juice

250 g/9 oz plain flour

2 tsp baking powder

85 g/3 oz granulated sugar

1 egg, beaten

150 ml/5 fl oz buttermilk

85 g/3 oz butter, melted and cooled

double cream, to serve

1 Preheat the oven to 190°C/375°F/Gas Mark 5. Lightly grease a 2-litre/ 3½-pint ovenproof dish with butter.

2 In a large bowl, combine the plums, caster sugar, lemon juice and 25 g/1 oz of the plain flour.

3 Spoon the coated plums into the bottom of the prepared ovenproof dish, spreading them out evenly.

4 Sift the remaining flour, together with the baking powder, into a large bowl and add the granulated sugar. Stir well to combine.

5 Add the beaten egg, buttermilk and cooled melted butter. Mix everything gently together to form a soft dough.

6 Place tablespoonfuls of the dough on top of the fruit mixture until it is almost completely covered.

7 Bake the cobbler in the preheated oven for 35–40 minutes until the topping is golden brown and the plums are bubbling.

8 Serve the cobbler piping hot with double cream.

COOK'S TIP
If you cannot find buttermilk, try using soured cream.

Clafoutis

Although recipes for this dessert may use a variety of fruits, cherries are the classic filling in Limousin, France, where this dish originated.

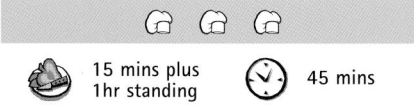

15 mins plus 1hr standing

45 mins

SERVES 4

INGREDIENTS

450 g/1 lb sweet black cherries

2 tbsp cherry brandy

1 tbsp icing sugar, plus extra for dusting

butter, for greasing

BATTER

3 tbsp plain flour

3 tbsp sugar

175 ml/6 fl oz single cream

2 eggs, lightly beaten

grated rind of ½ lemon

¼ tsp vanilla essence

1 Stone the cherries. Combine them with the cherry brandy and icing sugar in a bowl, cover with clingfilm and set aside for 1 hour.

2 Meanwhile, preheat the oven to 190°C/375°F/Gas Mark 5. Grease a shallow ovenproof dish with butter. To make the batter, sift the flour into a bowl and stir in the sugar. Gradually whisk in the cream, eggs, lemon rind and vanilla essence. Continue whisking until the batter is smooth.

3 Spoon the cherries into the dish and pour the batter over them. Bake in the preheated oven for 45 minutes until golden and set. Dust with extra icing sugar and serve warm or leave to cool to room temperature.

COOK'S TIP

Traditionally the cherries are not stoned before cooking because the stones are thought to add extra flavour to the batter.

Blackberry Clafoutis

A delicious dessert to make when blackberries are in abundance.
If blackberries are unavailable, try using currants or gooseberries.

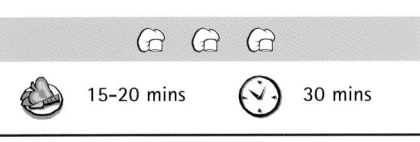

SERVES 4

I N G R E D I E N T S

butter, for greasing

450 g/1 lb blackberries

75 g/2¾ oz caster sugar, plus extra
for sprinkling

1 egg

75 g/2¾ oz brown sugar

6 tbsp butter, melted

8 tbsp milk

125 g/4½ oz self-raising flour

1 Preheat the oven to 180°C/350°F/Gas Mark 4. Lightly grease a 900-ml/1½-pint ovenproof dish with a little butter.

2 In a large mixing bowl, gently mix together the blackberries and caster sugar until well combined.

3 Transfer the blackberry and sugar mixture to the prepared ovenproof dish, spreading it out evenly.

4 Beat the egg and brown sugar in a separate mixing bowl. Stir in the melted butter and milk.

5 Sift the flour into the egg and butter mixture and fold together lightly to form a smooth batter.

6 Carefully spoon the batter over the blackberries in the ovenproof dish.

7 Bake the pudding in the preheated oven for about 25–30 minutes until the topping is firm and golden.

8 Sprinkle the pudding with a little sugar and serve hot.

Blueberry Clafoutis

A good dessert to make when blueberries are in season. Serve with single cream.

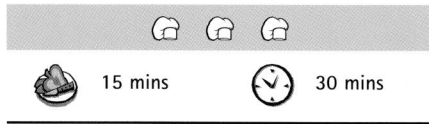

15 mins   30 mins

SERVES 4

I N G R E D I E N T S

2 tbsp butter, plus extra for greasing

125 g/4½ oz caster sugar

3 eggs

60 g/2¼ oz plain flour

250 ml/9 fl oz single cream

½ tsp ground cinnamon

450 g/1 lb blueberries

icing sugar, to decorate

single cream, to serve

1 Preheat the oven to 180°C/350°F/Gas Mark 4. Grease a 1-litre/1¾-pint ovenproof dish with butter.

2 Put the remaining butter in a bowl with the sugar and cream together until fluffy. Add the eggs and beat together well. Mix in the flour, then gradually stir in the cream followed by the cinnamon. Continue to stir until smooth.

3 Arrange the blueberries in the bottom of the prepared dish, then pour over the cream batter. Transfer to the preheated oven and bake for about 30 minutes or until puffed and golden.

4 Remove from the oven, dust lightly with icing sugar and serve with single cream.

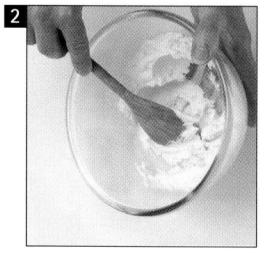

Summer Fruit Clafoutis

Serve this mouthwatering French-style fruit-in-batter dessert hot or cold with low fat yogurt.

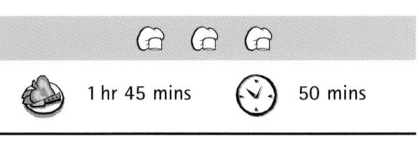

1 hr 45 mins   50 mins

SERVES 4

INGREDIENTS

500 g/1 lb 2 oz prepared fresh assorted soft fruits, such as blackberries, raspberries, strawberries, blueberries, cherries, gooseberries, redcurrants, blackcurrants

4 tbsp soft fruit liqueur such as crème de cassis, kirsch or framboise

4 tbsp skimmed milk powder

115 g/4 oz plain flour

pinch of salt

55 g/2 oz caster sugar

2 eggs, beaten

300 ml/10 fl oz skimmed milk

1 tsp vanilla essence

2 tsp caster sugar, for dusting

TO SERVE

assorted soft fruits

low-fat natural yogurt or fromage frais

1 Place the assorted fruits in a mixing bowl and spoon over the fruit liqueur. Cover and chill for 1 hour.

2 In a large bowl, combine the skimmed milk powder, flour, salt and sugar. Make a well in the centre and gradually whisk in the eggs, milk and vanilla essence, using a balloon whisk, until smooth. Transfer to a jug and set aside for 30 minutes.

3 Preheat the oven to 200°C/400°F/Gas Mark 6. Line the bottom of a 23-cm/ 9-inch round ovenproof dish with baking parchment and spoon in all the fruits and their juices.

4 Whisk the batter again and pour it over the fruits, stand the dish on a baking sheet and bake in the preheated oven for 50 minutes until firm, risen and golden brown.

5 Dust with caster sugar. Serve immediately with extra fruits and low-fat natural yogurt or fromage frais.

Cherry & Chocolate Clafoutis

Clafoutis is a classic dessert from France, typically filled with cherries.
Here it is given a new twist with the addition of unsweetened cocoa.

15 mins   50-60 mins

SERVES 6-8

INGREDIENTS

butter, for greasing

450 g/1 lb black cherries, stoned

25 g/1 oz golden granulated sugar

3 eggs

55 g/2 oz golden caster sugar

55 g/2 oz self-raising flour

2 tbsp cocoa powder

150 ml/5 fl oz double cream

300 ml/10 fl oz milk

2 tbsp kirsch (optional)

icing sugar, for dusting

cream, to serve

1 Preheat the oven to 190°C/375°F/Gas Mark 5. Lightly butter a 23-cm/9-inch square ovenproof dish. Arrange the cherries in the dish, sprinkle with the granulated sugar and set aside.

2 Put the eggs and caster sugar in a bowl and whisk together until light and frothy. Sift the flour and cocoa powder on to a plate and add, all at once, to the egg mixture. Beat in thoroughly, then whisk in the cream followed by the milk and kirsch (if using). Pour the batter over the cherries.

3 Bake in the preheated oven for 50-60 minutes until slightly risen and set in the centre. Sift icing sugar over the top and serve warm with cream.

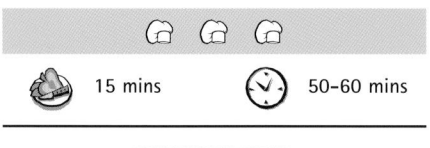

Chocolate Mirabelle Clafoutis

Mirabelles are a French variety of sweet, firm-fleshed, yellow plums, also used for making slivovitz liqueur.

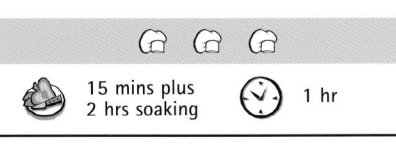

15 mins plus
2 hrs soaking

1 hr

SERVES 6

INGREDIENTS

675 g/1 lb 8 oz ripe Mirabelle plums, halved and stoned

3 tbsp slivovitz

1½ tbsp icing sugar

55 g/2 oz plain chocolate

225 ml/8 fl oz single cream

butter, for greasing

40 g/1½ oz plain flour

70 g/2½ oz caster sugar

3 eggs

grated rind of 1 lemon

pinch of grated nutmeg

1 Place the plums in a bowl and add the slivovitz and icing sugar. Mix well and set aside to soak for about 2 hours.

2 Break the chocolate into pieces and place in a small saucepan with the cream. Heat gently, stirring frequently, until the chocolate has melted. Do not allow to boil. Remove from the heat and set aside to cool.

3 Preheat the oven to 190°C/375°F/Gas Mark 5. Thoroughly grease a 25-cm/ 10-inch ovenproof dish.

4 Sift the flour into a bowl and stir in the caster sugar. Gradually whisk in the cooled chocolate-flavoured cream until smooth. Whisk in the eggs, lemon rind and nutmeg.

5 Arrange the plums on the bottom of the dish, then pour over the batter. Bake for about 55 minutes until puffed up around the edges and set in the centre. Remove from the oven and leave to cool slightly, then serve warm.

VARIATION
If Mirabelles are unavailable, use any small ripe plums. You can also substitute Amaretto liqueur for the slivovitz, if you prefer.

Chocolate & Orange Surprise

A classic combination with a twist, this rich, tangy pudding will delight and intrigue friends and family.

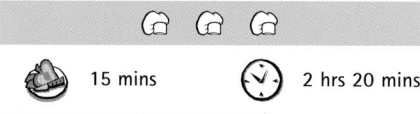

🍧 15 mins   🕐 2 hrs 20 mins

SERVES 6

INGREDIENTS

1 unwaxed, seedless orange, such as Valenciana

175 g/6 oz unsalted butter, plus extra for greasing

55 g/2 oz plain chocolate

175 g/6 oz self-raising flour

55 g/2 oz cocoa powder

175 g/6 oz light muscovado sugar

2 eggs

2 tbsp milk

85 g/3 oz caster sugar

single cream, to serve

1 Bring a saucepan of water to the boil. Add the orange, cover and boil for 20 minutes. Grease a 1.2-litre/2-pint pudding basin with butter.

2 Meanwhile, break the chocolate into pieces and place in a heatproof bowl with half the butter. Melt over a saucepan of gently simmering water, then remove from the heat and set aside to cool slightly.

3 Sift together the flour and cocoa powder into a large bowl and stir in the sugar. Make a well in the centre. Lightly beat the eggs together in a jug and pour into the well with the milk and melted chocolate mixture. Stir well to mix.

4 Spoon about half the mixture into the pudding basin and make a fairly shallow indentation with the back of the spoon. Drain the orange and, holding it with tongs, pat dry with kitchen paper, then prick all over with a fork. Place the orange in the bowl. Dice the butter and dot it over the orange, then sprinkle with the caster sugar. Spoon in the remaining chocolate mixture and level the surface.

5 Cut out a circle of greaseproof paper and a circle of foil about 10 cm/ 4 inches larger than the rim of the basin. Grease the paper with butter, then place on the foil circle, greased side up. Make a pleat in the centre of both circles, then, still holding them together and with the foil circle upwards, place them on top of the basin. Tie in place with kitchen string.

6 Place the basin in a large saucepan and pour in enough boiling water to come about halfway up the side. Cover and steam over a low heat for 2 hours, topping up the boiling water, as necessary.

7 Turn off the heat and remove the basin. Remove and discard the paper and foil. Invert the pudding on to a warmed serving dish and serve immediately, with cream.

Zabaglione

This well-known dish is really a light but rich egg mousse flavoured with Marsala or sweet sherry.

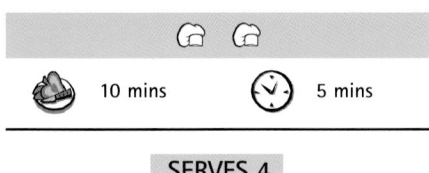

10 mins   5 mins

SERVES 4

INGREDIENTS

5 egg yolks

100 g/3½ oz caster sugar

150 ml/5 fl oz Marsala or sweet sherry

amaretti biscuits, to serve (optional)

1 Place all the egg yolks in a large mixing bowl.

2 Add the caster sugar to the egg yolks and whisk until the mixture is thick and very pale and has doubled in volume.

3 Set the bowl containing the egg yolk and sugar mixture over a saucepan of gently simmering water.

4 Add the Marsala or sherry to the egg yolk and sugar mixture and continue whisking until the foam mixture becomes warm. This process may take as long as 10 minutes.

5 Pour the mixture, which should be frothy and light, into 4 wine glasses.

6 Serve the zabaglione warm with fresh amaretti biscuits or fruit, if you wish.

Chocolate Zabaglione

As this recipe only uses a little chocolate, choose one with a minimum of 70 per cent cocoa solids for a good flavour.

10 mins · 5 mins

SERVES 4

INGREDIENTS

4 egg yolks

4 tbsp caster sugar

50 g/1¾ oz dark chocolate

125 ml/4 fl oz Marsala

cocoa powder, for dusting

amaretti biscuits, to serve (optional)

1 In a large glass heatproof mixing bowl, whisk together the egg yolks and caster sugar using an electric whisk, until you have a very pale mixture.

2 Grate the chocolate finely and fold into the egg mixture.

3 Gradually fold the Marsala into the chocolate mixture.

4 Set the mixing bowl over a saucepan of gently simmering water and set the electric whisk on the lowest speed or change to a hand-held balloon whisk. Cook gently, whisking constantly until the mixture thickens; take care not to overcook or the mixture will curdle.

5 Spoon the hot mixture into warm individual glass dishes or coffee cups and dust with cocoa powder. Serve the zabaglione as soon as possible so that it is warm, light and fluffy, with amaretti biscuits, if you wish.

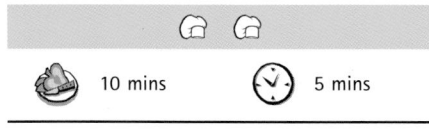

COOK'S TIP

Make the dessert just before serving because it will separate if you let it stand. If it starts to curdle, remove it from the heat immediately and place it in a bowl of cold water to stop the cooking. Whisk furiously until the mixture comes together again.

Italian Drowned Ice Cream

Vanilla ice cream topped with hot coffee makes a wonderful instant dessert. The ice cream will keep frozen for up to 3 months.

30 mins plus 2 hrs 30 mins freezing

10 mins

SERVES 4

INGREDIENTS

450 ml/16 fl oz freshly made espresso coffee

chocolate-covered coffee beans, to decorate

VANILLA ICE CREAM

1 vanilla pod

6 large egg yolks

150 g/5½ oz caster sugar or vanilla-flavoured sugar

500 ml/17 fl oz milk

225 ml/8 fl oz plus 2 tbsp double cream

1 To make the ice cream, slit the vanilla pod lengthways and scrape out the tiny brown seeds. Set aside.

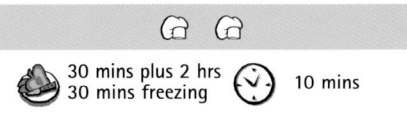

2 Put the yolks and sugar in a heatproof bowl that will sit over a saucepan of gently simmering water with plenty of room underneath so that the bottom of the bowl does not touch the hot water.. Beat the eggs and sugar together until thick and creamy.

3 Put the milk, cream, the vanilla seeds and their pods in a saucepan over a low heat and bring to a simmer. Pour the milk over the egg mixture, whisking. Pour 2.5 cm/1 inch of water into the bottom of another large saucepan. Sit the bowl on top, ensuring that the base of the bowl does not touch the water. Increase the heat to medium-high.

4 Cook the mixture, stirring constantly, until it is thick enough to coat the back of the spoon. Remove from the heat, transfer to a clean bowl and leave to cool. Remove and discard the vanilla pods.

5 Churn the mixture in an ice-cream maker, following the manufacturer's instructions. Alternatively, place it in a freezerproof container and freeze for 1 hour. Turn out into a bowl and whisk to break up the ice crystals, then return to the freezer. Repeat 4 times at 30-minute intervals.

6 Transfer the ice cream to a freezerproof bowl and smooth the top. Cover with clingfilm or foil and keep in the freezer.

7 Take out of the freezer and soften the ice cream in the refrigerator for 20 minutes before serving. Place scoops of ice cream in heatproof serving bowls. Pour over the hot coffee and sprinkle with chocolate-covered coffee beans.

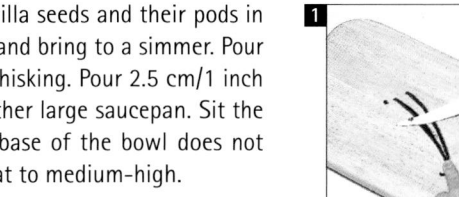

Almond Rice Custard

This traditional Turkish dessert is simply an almond milk thickened with ground rice. Serve with the traditional decoration of strawberries.

50 mins   30 mins

SERVES 6

INGREDIENTS

85 g/3 oz whole blanched almonds

1 litre/1¾ pints milk

25 g/1 oz rice flour

pinch of salt

55 g/2 oz sugar

½ tsp almond essence or 1 tbsp Amaretto

toasted flaked almonds, to decorate

350 g/12 oz fresh strawberries, sliced, sprinkled with 2 tbsp sugar, and chilled, to serve (optional)

1 Put the almonds in a food processor and process until a thick paste forms. Bring 225 ml/8 fl oz of the milk to the boil. Gradually pour into the almond paste through the feed tube of the food processor, with the machine running, until the mixture is smooth. Set aside for about 10 minutes.

2 Combine the rice flour, salt and sugar in a large bowl, then stir in about 4–5 tablespoons of the remaining milk to form a smooth paste.

3 Bring the remaining milk to the boil in a heavy-based saucepan. Pour the hot milk into the rice flour paste and stir constantly, then return the mixture to the saucepan and bring to a boil. Lower the heat and simmer for about 10 minutes until smooth and thickened. Remove from the heat.

4 Strain the almond milk through a very fine sieve into the rice custard, pressing through the almonds with the back of a spoon. Return to the heat and simmer for an additional 7–10 minutes or until the mixture becomes thick.

5 Remove from the heat and stir in the almond essence or liqueur. Cool slightly, stirring, then pour into individual bowls. Sprinkle with the almonds and serve with the strawberries, if wished. Serve immediately or chill until required.

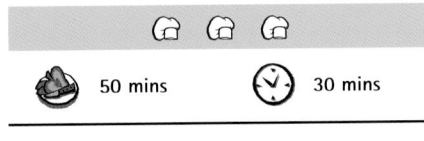

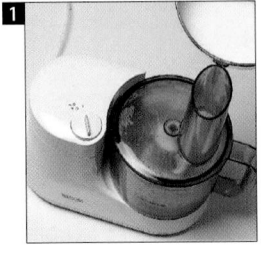

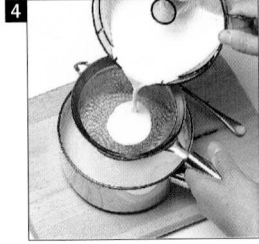

French Chocolate Sauce

This rich, warm – and alcoholic – sauce is superb with both hot and cold desserts and positively magical with ice cream.

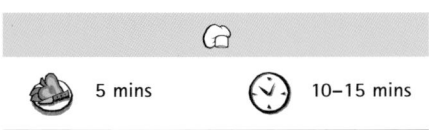

5 mins   10–15 mins

MAKES 150 ML/5 FL OZ

I N G R E D I E N T S

6 tbsp double cream

85 g/3 oz dark chocolate, broken into small pieces

2 tbsp orange liqueur

1 Bring the cream gently to the boil in a small, heavy-based saucepan over a low heat. Remove the saucepan from the heat, add the broken chocolate and stir until smooth.

2 Stir in the liqueur and serve immediately, or keep the sauce warm until required.

Glossy Chocolate Sauce

This simple sauce is a deliciously rich accompaniment to hot and cold desserts and is suitable for all the family.

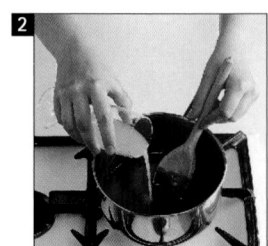

5 mins   10–15 mins

MAKES 150 ML/5 FL OZ

INGREDIENTS

115 g/4 oz caster sugar

4 tbsp water

175 g/6 oz dark chocolate, broken into pieces

25 g/1 oz unsalted butter, diced

2 tbsp orange juice

1 Put the sugar and water into a small, heavy-based saucepan set over a low heat and stir until the sugar has dissolved. Stir in the chocolate, a few pieces at a time, waiting until each batch has melted before adding the next. Stir in the butter, a few pieces at a time, waiting until each batch has been incorporated before adding the next. Do not allow the sauce to boil.

2 Stir in the orange juice and remove the saucepan from the heat. Serve immediately or keep warm until required. Alternatively, leave to cool, then transfer to a freezerproof container and freeze for up to 3 months. Thaw at room temperature before reheating to serve.

Chocolate Fudge Sauce

This creamy white chocolate sauce adds a touch of sophistication and luxury to the dinner table.

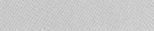

5 mins plus 15–20 mins cooling

10–15 mins

MAKES 150 ML/5 FL OZ

INGREDIENTS

150 ml/5 fl oz double cream

4 tbsp unsalted butter, cut into small pieces

3 tbsp caster sugar

175 g/6 oz white chocolate, broken into pieces

2 tbsp brandy

1 Pour the cream into the top of a double boiler or a heatproof bowl set over a saucepan of gently simmering water. Add the butter and sugar and stir until the mixture is smooth. Remove from the heat.

2 Stir in the chocolate, a few pieces at a time, waiting until each batch has melted before adding the next. Add the brandy and stir the sauce until smooth. Cool to room temperature before serving.

Cold Desserts

Dessert is not an essential part of the menu but for many

people this is the part of the meal they particularly

look forward to, and it gives you, the cook, the chance

to indulge your creative juices. Most of these cold

desserts are easy to master and represent a treat

because so many of us are too busy, or conscious of our

weight or health, to enjoy dessert at

every meal. So when you do want to

make the effort, spend a little time

on the presentation. Use chocolate

leaves or curls, fresh or crystallized fruit or flowers,

a sprig of mint or a light dusting of icing sugar – and

present your mouthwatering

creations in style.

Cannoli

No Sicilian celebration is complete without cannoli. If you can't find the moulds, use large, dried pasta tubes covered with foil, shiny-side out.

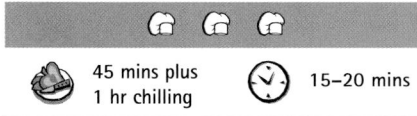

45 mins plus 1 hr chilling

15–20 mins

MAKES 20

I N G R E D I E N T S

3 tbsp lemon juice

3 tbsp water

1 large egg

250 g/9 oz plain flour

1 tbsp caster sugar

1 tsp ground mixed spice

pinch of salt

2 tbsp butter, softened

sunflower oil, for deep-frying

1 small egg white, lightly beaten

icing sugar

F I L L I N G

750 g/1 lb 10 oz ricotta cheese, drained

4 tbsp icing sugar

1 tsp vanilla essence

finely grated rind of 1 large orange

4 tbsp very finely chopped glacé fruit

50 g/1¾ oz plain chocolate, grated

pinch of ground cinnamon

2 tbsp Marsala or orange juice

1 Combine the lemon juice, water and egg. Put the flour, sugar, spice and salt in a food processor and quickly process. Add the butter, then, with the motor running, pour the egg mixture through the feed tube. Process until the mixture just forms a dough.

2 Turn the dough out on to a lightly floured work surface and knead lightly. Wrap in clingfilm and chill for at least 1 hour.

3 Meanwhile, make the filling. Beat the ricotta cheese until smooth. Sift in the icing sugar, then beat in the remaining ingredients. Cover and chill until required.

4 Roll out the dough on a floured work surface until 2 mm/¹⁄₁₆ inch thick. Using a ruler, cut out 9 × 7.5-cm/ 3½ × 3-inch pieces, re-rolling and cutting the trimmings; the dough should make about 20 pieces.

5 Heat 5 cm/2 inches oil in a heavy-based frying pan to 190°C/375°F. Roll a piece of dough around a greased cannoli mould, just overlapping the edges. Seal with egg white, pressing firmly together. Repeat with all the moulds you have. Fry 2 or 3 moulds at the same time until the cannoli are golden, crisp and bubbly.

6 Remove with a slotted spoon and drain on kitchen paper. Leave to cool, then carefully slide off the moulds. Repeat with the remaining pieces of dough.

7 Store unfilled in an airtight container for up to 2 days. Pipe in the filling no more than 30 minutes before serving to prevent the cannoli becoming soggy. Sift a light dusting of icing sugar over the top and serve.

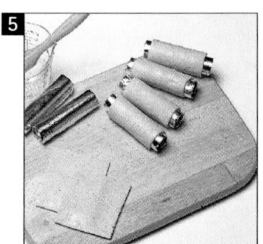

Moroccan Orange Cake

This moist cake is made with semolina and ground almonds, then soaked in a fragrant orange and cardamom syrup.

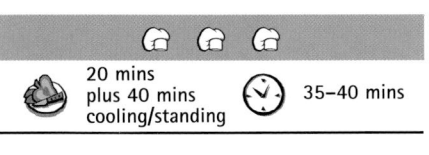

20 mins plus 40 mins cooling/standing

35–40 mins

SERVES 4

INGREDIENTS

115 g/4 oz butter, softened, plus extra for greasing

1 orange

115 g/4 oz golden caster sugar

2 eggs, beaten

175 g/6 oz semolina

115 g/4 oz ground almonds

1½ tsp baking powder

icing sugar, for dusting

strained natural yogurt, to serve

SYRUP

300 ml/10 fl oz orange juice

140 g/5 oz caster sugar

8 cardamom pods, crushed

1 Preheat the oven to 180°C/350°F/Gas Mark 4. Grease and line the bottom of a 20-cm/8-inch cake tin. Grate the rind from half the orange and cut strips of zest for decoration from the other half and set aside. Place the butter, orange rind and caster sugar in a bowl and beat together until light and fluffy. Gradually beat in the eggs. In a separate bowl, mix the semolina, ground almonds and baking powder, then fold into the creamed mixture with the juice from half the orange. Spoon into the prepared tin and bake in the preheated oven for 30–40 minutes, or until well risen and a skewer inserted into the centre comes out clean. Leave to cool in the tin for 10 minutes.

2 To make the syrup, place the orange juice, sugar and cardamom pods in a saucepan over a low heat and stir until the sugar has dissolved. Bring to the boil and simmer for 4 minutes or until syrupy.

3 Turn out the cake into a deep serving dish. Use a skewer to make holes over the surface of the warm cake. Strain the syrup into a separate bowl and spoon three-quarters of it over the cake. Leave to stand for 30 minutes. Dust the cake with icing sugar and cut into slices. Serve with the remaining syrup drizzled around, accompanied by the natural yogurt decorated with the reserved orange zest.

COOK'S TIP
Do not be tempted to rush this cake – make sure that you give the orange syrup plenty of time to soak into the sponge.

Cherry Baskets

In this dessert, cherries and cream sit in little baskets sealed with a shiny redcurrant glaze.

🍰 25 mins plus
1 hr setting   🕐 20 mins

SERVES 4

INGREDIENTS

BASKETS

3 tbsp unsalted butter, plus extra for greasing

3 tbsp caster sugar

4 tbsp golden syrup

½ tsp ground mixed spice

1 tsp almond essence

1 tbsp cherry brandy

5 tbsp plain flour

FILLING

300 g/10½ oz cherries, stoned

1 tbsp cherry brandy

150 ml/5 fl oz double cream, whipped

GLAZE

150 g/5½ oz redcurrant jelly

1 tbsp water

1 To make the baskets, put the butter, sugar and golden syrup in a saucepan and stir over a medium heat until melted. Simmer for 3 minutes, then remove from the heat. Stir in the mixed spice, almond essence, cherry brandy and flour and mix until smooth. Set aside for 10 minutes.

2 Preheat the oven to 180°C/350°F/Gas Mark 4. Grease a large baking sheet with butter. Drop enough of the mixture on the baking sheet to make 4 circles, each measuring 10 cm/4 inches in diameter. Allow plenty of space between them because they will spread during cooking. Shape the remaining mixture into 4 'handles' and arrange on the cookie sheet. Bake for 15 minutes or until golden. Remove from the oven, then mould them into basket shapes over 4 upturned cups or ramekin dishes. When shaped, release the baskets and add the handles, pressing to the basket to secure. Leave to set for 1 hour.

3 To make the filling, mix together the cherries and cherry brandy. Just before serving, spoon whipped cream into each basket and top with the cherries. To glaze, gently melt the redcurrant jelly with the water, brush it over the cherries and serve.

Almond & Pistachio Dessert

Rich and mouthwatering, this dessert can be prepared well in advance of the meal. It is best served cold.

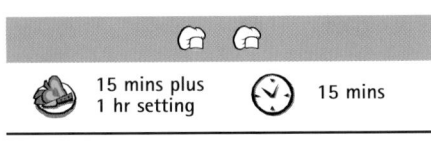

15 mins plus 1 hr setting

15 mins

SERVES 6

INGREDIENTS

75 g/2¾ oz unsalted butter

200 g/7 oz ground almonds

150 ml/5 fl oz single cream

200 g/7 oz sugar

8 almonds, chopped

10 pistachio nuts, chopped

1 Place the butter in a medium-size saucepan, preferably non-stick. Melt the butter, stirring well.

2 Add the ground almonds, cream and sugar to the melted butter in the saucepan, stirring to combine thoroughly. Lower the heat and stir constantly for 10-12 minutes, scraping the bottom of the saucepan to prevent the mixture sticking.

3 Increase the heat until the mixture turns a little darker in colour.

4 Transfer the almond mixture to a shallow serving dish and smooth the top with the back of a spoon.

5 Decorate the top of the dessert with the almonds and pistachio nuts.

6 Leave the dessert to set for about 1 hour, then cut into diamond shapes and serve cold.

COOK'S TIP

This dessert can be made in advance and stored in an airtight container in the refrigerator for several days. You could use a variety of shaped pastry cutters to cut the dessert into different shapes, if you prefer.

Pistachio Dessert

Rather an attractive-looking dessert, especially when decorated with varq (silver leaf), this is another dish that can be prepared in advance.

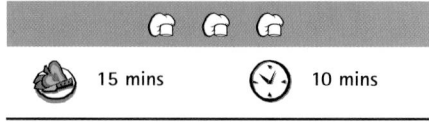

15 mins   10 mins

SERVES 6

INGREDIENTS

900 ml/1½ pints water

225 g/8 oz pistachio nuts

225 g/8 oz full-cream dried milk

500 g/1 lb 2 oz sugar

seeds of 2 cardamom pods, crushed

2 tbsp rosewater

a few strands of saffron

TO DECORATE

25 g/1 oz flaked almonds (optional)

mint leaves

1 Put about 600 ml/1 pint of the water in a saucepan and bring to the boil. Remove the saucepan from the heat and soak the pistachio nuts in this water for about 5 minutes. Drain the pistachio nuts thoroughly, then remove their skins.

2 Process the pistachio nuts in a food processor or grind them in a pestle and mortar.

3 Add the milk powder to the ground pistachio nuts and mix well.

COOK'S TIP

It is best to buy whole pistachio nuts and grind them yourself, rather than using packets of ready-ground nuts. Freshly ground nuts have the best flavour because grinding releases their natural oils.

4 To make the syrup, place the remaining water and the sugar in a saucepan and heat gently. When the liquid starts to thicken, add the cardamom seeds, rosewater and saffron.

5 Add the pistachio mixture to the syrup and cook, stirring constantly, for about 5 minutes, until the mixture thickens. Set the mixture aside to cool slightly.

6 Once cool enough to handle, roll the mixture into balls between the palms of your hands. Leave to set before serving, decorated with the flaked almonds (if using) and fresh mint leaves.

Banana Splits

A perennial favourite, all the more special when made with homemade vanilla ice cream and a rum and nut chocolate sauce.

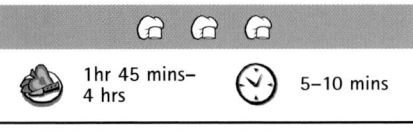

🍨 1hr 45 mins– 4 hrs   🕐 5–10 mins

SERVES 4

INGREDIENTS

4 bananas

VANILLA ICE CREAM

300 ml/10 fl oz milk

1 tsp vanilla essence

3 egg yolks

100 g/3½ oz caster sugar

300 ml/10 fl oz double cream, whipped

CHOCOLATE RUM SAUCE

125 g/4½ oz plain chocolate, broken into small pieces

2½ tbsp butter

6 tbsp water

1 tbsp dark rum

6 tbsp chopped mixed nuts, to decorate

1 To make the ice cream, heat the milk and vanilla in a saucepan until almost boiling. Beat together the egg yolks and sugar, remove the milk from the heat and stir a little into the egg mixture. Return the mixture to the saucepan and stir over a low heat until thick. Do not allow it to boil. Remove from the heat. Cool for 30 minutes, fold in the cream, then cover with clingfilm and chill for 1 hour. Transfer to an ice-cream maker and churn for 15 minutes. Alternatively, transfer to a freezerproof container and freeze for 1 hour. Take the partly frozen mixture out of the freezer, transfer it to a bowl and beat vigorously to break up any ice crystals. Put it back in the container and freeze for a further 30 minutes. Repeat twice more, freezing for 30 minutes and whisking each time. Store in the freezer.

2 To make the sauce, gently melt the chocolate, butter and water together in a small saucepan, stirring constantly. Remove from the heat. Stir in the rum.

Peel the bananas, slice them lengthways and arrange on 4 serving dishes. To serve, top with ice cream, drizzle with the sauce and decorate with chopped nuts.

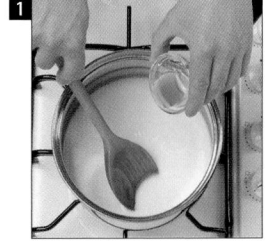

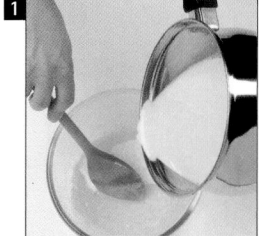

Fresh Figs & Brandy Butter

In this unusual but simple dessert, fresh figs are deliciously partnered by brandy butter.

10 mins   0 mins

SERVES 4

INGREDIENTS

115 g/4 oz butter, softened slightly

50 g/1¾ oz icing sugar

1 tbsp brandy

12 fresh figs

fresh mint leaves, to decorate

1 To make the brandy butter, put the butter and sugar in a small bowl and cream together well. Stir in the brandy.

2 Using a sharp knife, cut the figs into quarters and arrange in 4 individual serving dishes. Top each serving with the brandy butter, decorate with fresh mint leaves and serve.

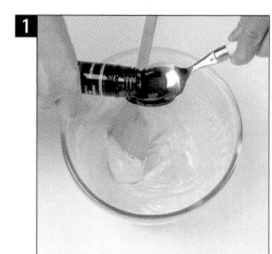

Baklava

These nut and spice pastries are sticky and delicious. Serve them with coffee or tea.

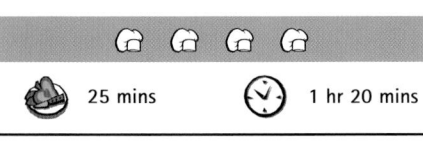

25 mins   1 hr 20 mins

MAKES 12 PIECES

INGREDIENTS

225 g/8 oz walnut halves

225 g/8 oz shelled pistachio nuts

100 g/3½ oz blanched almonds

4 tbsp pine kernels, finely chopped

finely grated rind of 2 large oranges

6 tbsp sesame seeds

1 tbsp sugar

½ tsp ground cinnamon

½ tsp mixed spice

250 g/9 oz butter, melted, plus extra for greasing

23 sheets filo pastry, thawed if frozen

SYRUP

450 g/1 lb caster sugar

450 ml/16 fl oz water

5 tbsp honey

3 cloves

2 large strips lemon zest

1 To make the filling, put the walnuts, pistachio nuts, almonds and pine kernels in a food processor and process gently, until finely chopped but not ground. Transfer the ground nuts to a bowl and stir in the orange rind, sesame seeds, sugar, cinnamon and mixed spice.

2 Grease a 25-cm/10-inch square (or similar) ovenproof dish that is 5 cm/ 2 inches deep. Preheat the oven to 160°C/ 325°F/Gas Mark 3. Cut the stacked filo sheets to size, using a ruler. Keep the sheets covered with a damp cloth. Place a sheet of filo on the bottom of the dish and brush with melted butter. Top with 7 more sheets, brushing with butter between each layer.

3 Sprinkle with a generous 150 g/5 oz of the nutty filling. Top with 3 sheets of filo, brushing each one with butter. Continue layering until you have used up all the filo and filling, ending with a top layer of 3 filo sheets. Brush with butter.

4 Using a sharp knife cut the baklava into 5-cm/2-inch squares. Brush again with butter. Bake in the preheated oven for 1 hour.

5 Meanwhile, put all the syrup ingredients in a saucepan. Slowly bring to the boil, stirring to dissolve the sugar, then simmer for 15 minutes, without stirring, until a thin syrup forms. Leave to cool.

6 Remove the baklava from the oven and pour the syrup over the top. Leave to cool in the dish, then cut out the squares to serve.

Coconut Custard Squares

This tempting dessert is especially luxurious served with a few slivers of mango or papaya on the side.

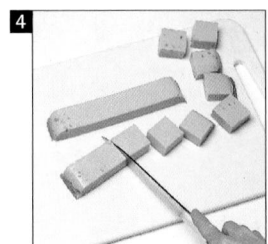

10 mins plus
30 mins cooling

30 mins

SERVES 6

INGREDIENTS

1 tsp butter, melted

6 large eggs

400 ml/14 fl oz coconut milk

150 g/5½ oz soft light brown sugar

pinch of salt

shredded fresh coconut and lime zest, to decorate

1 Preheat the oven to 180°C/350°F/Gas Mark 4. Brush the inside of a 19-cm/7½-inch square ovenproof dish or tin, about 4 cm/1½ inches deep, with the butter.

2 Beat the eggs in a large bowl and beat in the coconut milk, sugar and salt. Set the bowl over a saucepan of gently simmering water and stir with a wooden spoon for 15 minutes or until it starts to thicken. Pour into the prepared dish or tin.

3 Bake in the preheated oven for 20–25 minutes, until just set. Remove from the oven and leave to cool completely.

4 Cut the cold custard into squares and serve scattered with the shredded coconut and lime zest.

COOK'S TIP

Keep an eye on the custard as it bakes, because if it overcooks the texture will be spoiled. When it comes out of the oven it should be barely set and still slightly wobbly in the centre, then it will firm up slightly as it cools.

Coconut Cream Moulds

Smooth, creamy, and refreshing – these tempting little custards are made with an unusual combination of coconut milk, cream and eggs.

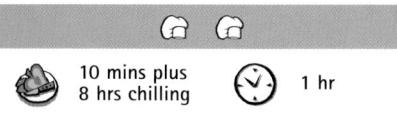

10 mins plus 8 hrs chilling

1 hr

SERVES 8

INGREDIENTS

CARAMEL

125 g/4½ oz granulated sugar

150 ml/5 fl oz water

CUSTARD

300 ml/10 fl oz water

85 g/3 oz creamed coconut, chopped

2 eggs

2 egg yolks

1½ tbsp caster sugar

300 ml/10 fl oz single cream

sliced banana or slivers of fresh pineapple

1 Have ready 8 small ovenproof dishes about 150-ml/5-fl oz capacity. To make the caramel, place the granulated sugar and water in a saucepan and heat gently to dissolve the sugar, then boil rapidly, without stirring, until the mixture turns a rich golden brown.

2 Immediately remove the saucepan from the heat and dip the bottom into a bowl of cold water to prevent the caramel cooking further. Quickly but carefully, pour the caramel into the dishes to coat their bases. Preheat the oven to 150°C/ 300°F/Gas Mark 2.

3 To make the custard, place the water in the same saucepan, add the creamed coconut and heat, stirring constantly until it dissolves. Place the eggs, egg yolks and caster sugar in a bowl and beat with a fork. Add the hot coconut milk and stir to dissolve the sugar. Stir in the cream and strain the mixture into a jug.

4 Arrange the caramel-lined dishes in a roasting tin and fill with enough cold water to come halfway up the sides of the dishes. Pour the custard mixture into the dishes, cover with greaseproof paper or foil and cook in the preheated oven for about 40 minutes or until the tops are set.

5 Remove the dishes from the roasting tin, set aside to cool, then chill overnight. To serve, run a knife around the edge of each dish and turn out on to a serving plate. Serve with slices of banana or slivers of fresh pineapple.

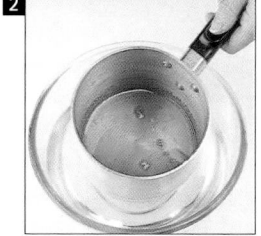

Cottage Cheese Hearts

These little moulds look very attractive when they are made in the French coeur à la crème china moulds, but you could use small ramekins instead.

50 mins

30 mins

SERVES 6

INGREDIENTS

150 g/5½ oz low-fat cottage cheese

150 ml/5 fl oz low-fat natural fromage frais

1 medium egg white

2 tbsp caster sugar

1–2 tsp vanilla essence

rose-scented geranium leaves, to decorate

SAUCE

225 g/8 oz strawberries

4 tbsp unsweetened orange juice

2–3 tsp icing sugar

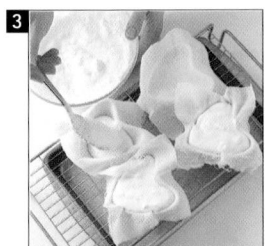

1 Line 4 heart-shaped moulds or ramekins with clean muslin. Place a sieve over a mixing bowl and, using the back of a metal spoon, press the cottage cheese through. Mix in the yogurt.

2 Whisk the egg white until stiff. Fold into the cheese mixture with the caster sugar and vanilla essence.

3 Spoon the cheese mixture into the moulds and smooth over the tops. Place on a wire rack over a tray and chill for 1 hour until firm and drained.

4 Meanwhile, make the sauce. Wash the strawberries under cold running water. Reserving a few strawberries for decoration, hull and chop the remainder. Place the strawberries in a blender or food processor with the orange juice and process until smooth. Alternatively, push through a sieve to purée. Mix with the icing sugar to taste. Cover and chill until ready to serve the sauce.

5 Remove the cheese hearts from the moulds and transfer to serving plates. Gently remove the muslin, taking care not to damage the heart shapes, decorate with strawberries and geranium leaves and serve with the sauce.

Blueberry Coeur à la Crème

This simple combination of sweetened cream, egg white and vanilla marries well with the tartness of blueberries and looks divine.

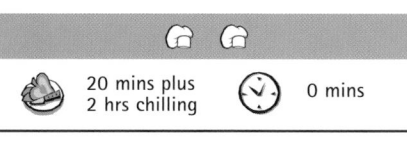

20 mins plus 2 hrs chilling   0 mins

SERVES 4

INGREDIENTS

200 g/7 oz cream cheese

200 g/7 oz crème fraîche

2 egg whites, whisked

2 tbsp caster sugar

1 tsp vanilla essence

BLUEBERRY COULIS

200 g/7 oz blueberries

juice of ½ lemon

1 tbsp icing sugar

whole blueberries, to decorate

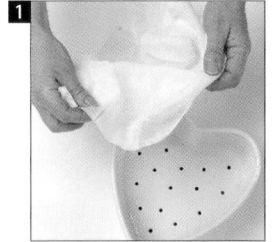
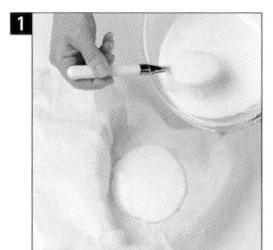
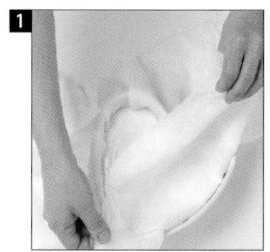

1 Put the cream cheese, crème fraîche, and egg whites into a bowl and mix well. Stir in the caster sugar and vanilla essence. Line a large coeur à la crème mould with muslin, spoon in the cheese mixture and smooth the surface. Fold the muslin over the top.

2 Place a wire rack over a tray, then place the mould on the wire rack. Transfer to the refrigerator to drain and chill for at least 2 hours.

3 To make the coulis, purée the blueberries in a food processor, then press through a sieve into a bowl. Stir in the lemon juice and icing sugar, then cover with clingfilm and chill in the refrigerator until required.

4 To serve, carefully turn out the cheese from the mould and discard the muslins. Decorate with whole blueberries and serve with the blueberry coulis.

White Chocolate Moulds

These pretty, colourful desserts are deliciously refreshing and would make a good finale to an alfresco meal.

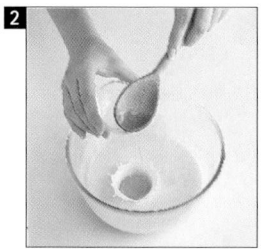

20 mins plus 4 hrs chilling

10–15 mins

SERVES 4

INGREDIENTS

125 g/4½ oz white chocolate, broken into pieces

225 ml/8 fl oz double cream

3 tbsp crème fraîche

2 eggs, separated

3 tbsp water

1½ tsp powdered gelatine

1 tsp oil, for brushing

140 g/5 oz sliced strawberries

140 g/5 oz raspberries

140 g/5 oz blackcurrants

70 g/2½ oz caster sugar

125 ml/4 fl oz crème de framboise

12 blackcurrant leaves, if available

1 Put the chocolate in a heatproof bowl set over a saucepan of gently simmering water. Stir over a low heat until melted and smooth. Remove from the heat and set aside.

2 Meanwhile, pour the cream into a saucepan and bring to just below boiling point over a low heat. Remove from the heat, then stir the cream and crème fraîche into the chocolate and cool slightly. Beat in the egg yolks, 1 at a time.

3 Pour the water into a small, heatproof bowl and sprinkle the gelatine on the surface. Leave for 2–3 minutes to soften, then set over a saucepan of gently simmering water until dissolved. Stir the gelatine into the chocolate mixture and leave until nearly set.

4 Brush the inside of 6 timbales, dariole moulds or ramekins with oil and line the bottoms with baking parchment. Whisk the egg whites until soft peaks form, then fold them into the chocolate mixture. Divide the mixture evenly between the prepared moulds and smooth the surface. Cover with clingfilm and chill in the refrigerator for 2 hours until set.

5 Put the strawberries, raspberries and blackcurrants in a bowl and sprinkle with the caster sugar. Pour in the liqueur and stir gently to mix. Cover with clingfilm and chill in the refrigerator for 2 hours.

6 To serve, run a round-bladed knife around the sides of the moulds and carefully turn out on to individual serving plates. Arrange the prepared fruit around the base of each dessert and serve immediately, decorated with blackcurrant leaves, if available.

Citrus Meringue Crush

This is an excellent way to use up leftover meringue shells and is quite simple to prepare. Serve with a spoonful of tangy fruit sauce.

20 mins plus
2 hrs chilling

10 mins

SERVES 4

I N G R E D I E N T S

8 ready-made meringue nests

300 ml/10 fl oz low-fat natural yogurt

½ tsp finely grated orange rind

½ tsp finely grated lemon rind

½ tsp finely grated lime rind

2 tbsp orange liqueur or unsweetened
   orange juice

S A U C E

55 g/2 oz kumquats

8 tbsp unsweetened orange juice

2 tbsp lemon juice

2 tbsp lime juice

2 tbsp water

2–3 tsp caster sugar

1 tsp cornflour mixed with
   1 tbsp water

T O   D E C O R A T E

sliced kumquats

strips of lime zest

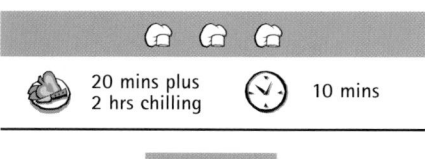
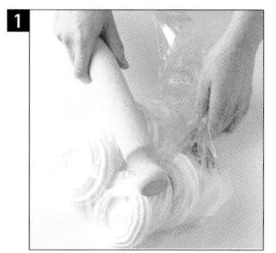

1 Place the meringues in a plastic bag and, using a rolling pin, crush into small pieces. Place in a mixing bowl. Stir in the yogurt, grated citrus rinds and the liqueur or juice. Spoon the mixture into 4 mini pudding basins and freeze for 1½–2 hours until firm.

2 To make the sauce, thinly slice the kumquats and place them in a small saucepan with the fruit juices and water. Bring gently to the boil and then simmer over a low heat for 3–4 minutes until the kumquats have softened.

3 Sweeten with sugar to taste, stir in the cornflour mixture and cook, stirring, until thickened. Pour into a small bowl, cover the surface with clingfilm, and set aside to cool – the clingfilm will help prevent a skin forming. Chill in the refrigerator until required.

4 To serve, dip the meringue basins in hot water for 5 seconds or until they loosen. Turn on to serving plates. Spoon over a little sauce, decorate with slices of kumquat and lime zest and serve.

Apricot & Orange Jellies

These bright fruity little desserts are easy to make and taste so much better than store-bought jellies. Serve them with low-fat ice cream.

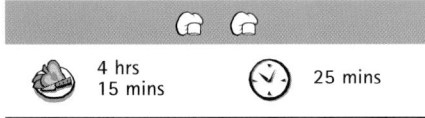

4 hrs 15 mins

25 mins

SERVES 4

INGREDIENTS

225 g/8 oz ready-to-eat dried apricots

300 ml/10 fl oz unsweetened orange juice

2 tbsp lemon juice

2–3 tsp clear honey

1 tbsp powdered gelatine

4 tbsp boiling water

CINNAMON 'CREAM'

125 g/4½ oz medium-fat ricotta cheese

125 g/4½ oz low-fat natural fromage frais (unsweetened yogurt)

1 tsp ground cinnamon, plus extra for dusting

1 tbsp honey

TO DECORATE

orange segments

sprigs of mint

1 Place the apricots in a saucepan and pour in the orange juice. Bring to the boil, cover and simmer for 15–20 minutes until plump and soft. Leave to cool for 10 minutes.

2 Transfer the apricot mixture to a blender or food processor and blend until smooth. Stir in the lemon juice and add the honey. Pour the mixture into a measuring cup and make up to 600 ml/ 1 pint with cold water.

3 Sprinkle the gelatine over the boiling water, stir to dissolve, then stir into the apricot mixture.

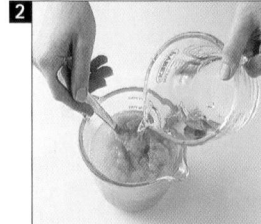
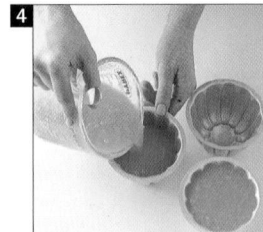

4 Pour the mixture into 4 individual moulds, each with a 150-ml/5-fl oz capacity, or 1 large 600 ml/1 pint mould. Leave to chill until set.

5 Meanwhile, make the cinnamon 'cream'. Mix all the ingredients together and place in a small serving bowl. Cover the mixture and chill until firm.

6 To turn out the jellies, dip the moulds in hot water for a few seconds and invert on to serving plates.

7 Decorate with the orange segments and mint sprigs. Serve with the cinnamon 'cream' dusted with extra cinnamon.

Orange Crème à Catalana

This Spanish dessert will please all those who favour oranges. Serve it immediately, while the caramel topping is hard.

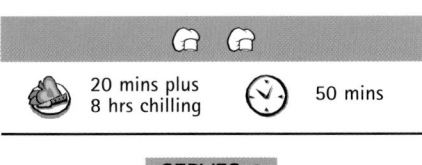

20 mins plus 8 hrs chilling   50 mins

SERVES 6

INGREDIENTS

1 litre/1¾ pints milk

finely grated rind of 6 large oranges

9 large egg yolks

200 g/7 oz caster sugar, plus extra for the topping

3 tbsp cornflour

1 Put the milk and orange rind in a saucepan over a medium-high heat. Bring to the boil, then remove from the heat, cover and leave to cool for 2 hours.

2 Return the milk to the heat and simmer for 10 minutes. Put the egg yolks and sugar in a heatproof bowl set over a saucepan of gently simmering water. Whisk until the mixture is fluffy and the sugar has dissolved.

3 Add 5 tablespoons of the flavoured milk to the cornflour, stirring until smooth. Stir into the milk. Strain the milk into the eggs, whisking until blended.

4 Rinse out the milk saucepan and put a layer of water in the bottom. Put the bowl on top of the saucepan, making sure that the bottom does not touch the water. Simmer over a medium heat, whisking, for about 20 minutes, until the custard is thick enough to coat the back of a wooden spoon. Do not allow to boil.

5 Pour into 8 x 150-ml/5-fl oz ramekins and leave to cool. Cover each with a piece of clingfilm and put in the refrigerator to chill for at least 6 hours.

6 When ready to serve, sprinkle the top of each ramekin with a layer of sugar. Use a kitchen blowtorch to melt and caramelize the sugar. Let stand for a few minutes until the caramel hardens, then serve at once. Do not return to the refrigerator or the topping will become soft.

COOK'S TIP
A kitchen blowtorch is the best way to melt the sugar quickly and guarantees a crisp topping. Blowtorches are sold at good kitchen-supply stores. Alternatively, you can melt the sugar under a preheated hot grill.

Apricot Brûlée

Serve this melt-in-the-mouth dessert with crisp-baked meringues for an extra-special occasion.

🍰 15 mins plus 2 hrs soaking/chilling ⏱ 35 mins

SERVES 4

INGREDIENTS

125 g/4½ oz dried apricots

150 ml/5 fl oz orange juice

4 egg yolks

2 tbsp caster sugar

150 ml/5 fl oz natural yogurt

150 ml/5 fl oz double cream

1 tsp vanilla essence

85 g/3 oz demerara sugar

meringues, to serve (optional)

1 Place the apricots and orange juice in a bowl and set aside to soak for at least 1 hour. Pour into a small saucepan, bring slowly to the boil and simmer for 20 minutes. Process in a blender or food processor or chop very finely and push through a sieve.

2 Beat together the egg yolks and sugar in a heatproof bowl until the mixture is light and fluffy. Place the yogurt in a small saucepan, add the cream and vanilla and bring to the boil over a low heat.

3 Pour the yogurt mixture over the eggs, beating all the time, then set the bowl over a saucepan of gently simmering water. Stir until the custard thickens. Divide the apricot mixture between 6 ramekins and carefully spoon on the custard. Cool, then chill in the refrigerator for at least 1 hour.

4 Preheat the grill. Sprinkle the demerara sugar evenly over the top of each ramekin and place under the preheated grill until the sugar caramelizes. Set aside to cool. To serve the brûlée, crack the hard caramel topping by tapping sharply with the back of a tablespoon.

Raspberry Brûlées

This dessert is quick to make and extremely enjoyable. It can be served hot or cold.

10 mins

7–8 mins

SERVES 4

INGREDIENTS

250 g/9 oz raspberries

1 tbsp lemon juice

2 tbsp raspberry jam

125 ml/4 fl oz crème fraîche

125 ml/4 fl oz double cream

1 tsp vanilla essence

6 tbsp caster sugar

whole raspberries, to decorate

1 Put the raspberries and lemon juice in a saucepan and stir over a low heat for about 5 minutes until they start to soften. Remove from the heat, stir in the jam, then divide among 4 ramekins.

2 Preheat the grill to hot. In a separate bowl, mix together the crème fraîche, cream and vanilla. Spoon it over the raspberries and smooth the surfaces. Sprinkle the sugar over the top, allowing 1½ tablespoons per ramekin. Put under the preheated grill, as close to the heat source as possible, for 2–3 minutes until the sugar caramelizes. Remove from the grill, decorate with whole raspberries and serve immediately. Alternatively, to serve chilled, leave to cool to room temperature, then cover with clingfilm and refrigerate for 3–4 hours.

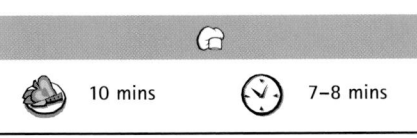

Fruit Brûlée

This is a cheat's brûlée, in that natural yogurt is used to cover a base of fruit, before being sprinkled with sugar and grilled.

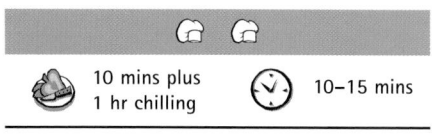

10 mins plus 1 hr chilling

10–15 mins

SERVES 4

INGREDIENTS

4 plums, stoned and sliced

2 cooking apples, peeled and sliced

2 tbsp water

1 tsp ground ginger

600 ml/1 pint Greek-style yogurt

2 tbsp icing sugar, sifted

1 tsp almond essence

85 g/3 oz demerara sugar

1 Put the plums and apples in a saucepan with the water and cook gently for 7–10 minutes, until the fruit is tender but not mushy. Set aside to cool, then stir in the ground ginger.

2 Using a slotted spoon, spoon the mixture into the bottom of a shallow heatproof serving dish.

3 Combine the yogurt, icing sugar and almond essence and spoon over the fruit to cover.

4 Preheat the grill. Sprinkle the demerara sugar over the top of the yogurt and cook under the preheated grill for 3–4 minutes or until the sugar has melted and formed a crust.

5 Set aside to chill in the refrigerator for 1 hour before serving.

Lemon & Redcurrant Brûlées

Beneath the caramelized topping is a surprise fruity sauce. Made with yogurt rather than cream, these desserts are wonderful low-fat treats.

10 mins plus 30 mins chilling · **10 mins**

SERVES 4

INGREDIENTS

1 lemon

175 g/6 oz redcurrants

3 tbsp caster sugar

600 ml/1 pint Greek-style yogurt

¼ tsp ground cinnamon

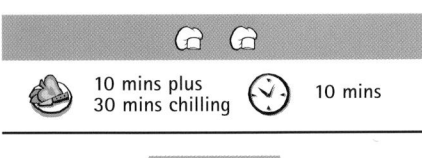
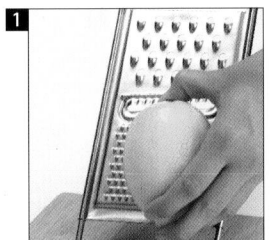

1 Grate the lemon rind. Put the redcurrants and 1 tablespoon of the sugar in a heavy-based saucepan over a low heat. Cook until the juices start to run, then remove from the heat, stir in the lemon rind and set aside.

2 Preheat the grill. Combine the yogurt and cinnamon in a bowl. Divide the redcurrants between 4 ramekins or small flameproof dishes. Top with the yogurt and sprinkle with the remaining sugar.

3 Place under the preheated grill for 4–5 minutes, or until the sugar is golden and bubbling. Chill in the refrigerator for at least 30 minutes before serving.

VARIATION
These brûlées are equally delicious made with blackcurrants, whitecurrants, bilberries or blueberries.

Rice & Banana Brûlée

Take canned creamed rice, flavour it with orange rind, stem ginger, raisins and sliced bananas and top with a brown sugar glaze.

50 mins

2–3 mins

SERVES 2

INGREDIENTS

400 g/14 oz can creamed rice

grated rind of ½ orange

2 pieces of stem ginger, finely chopped

2 tsp ginger syrup from the jar

40 g/1½ oz raisins

1–2 bananas

1–2 tsp lemon juice

4–5 tbsp demerara sugar

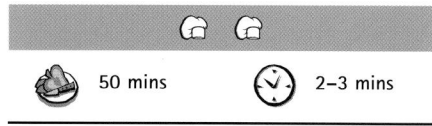

1 Empty the creamed rice into a bowl and stir in the grated orange rind, ginger, ginger syrup and raisins.

2 Cut the bananas diagonally into slices, toss in the lemon juice to prevent them from discolouring, drain and divide between 2 small flameproof dishes.

3 Spoon the rice mixture in an even layer over the bananas so that the dishes are almost full.

4 Sprinkle an even layer of sugar over the rice in each dish. Preheat the grill to medium.

COOK'S TIP
Canned creamed rice is very versatile and is delicious heated with orange segments and grated apples added. Try it served cold with grated chocolate and mixed chopped nuts stirred through it.

5 Place the dishes under the preheated grill and heat until the sugar melts, taking care the sugar does not burn.

6 Set aside to cool until the caramel sets, then chill in the refrigerator until ready to serve. Tap the caramel with the back of a spoon to break it.

Spanish Flan

This is a classic Spanish recipe which would be delicious served with a glass of sweet dessert wine.

30 mins plus 8 hrs chilling

2 hrs

SERVES 4

INGREDIENTS

butter, for greasing

175 g/6 oz plus 2 tbsp caster sugar

4 tbsp water

juice of ½ lemon

450 ml/16 fl oz milk

1 vanilla pod

2 large eggs

2 large egg yolks

TO DECORATE

redcurrants

fresh mint sprigs

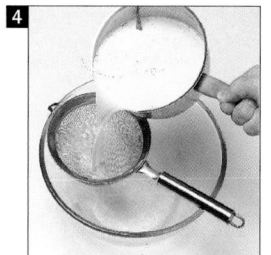

1 Lightly grease the inside of a 1.2-litre/2-pint soufflé dish. To make the caramel, put the water and 55 g/2 oz sugar in a saucepan over a medium-high heat and stir until the sugar dissolves. Then boil without stirring until the syrup becomes deep golden-brown.

2 Remove from the heat and add a few drops of lemon juice. Pour into the soufflé dish and swirl around. Set aside.

3 Pour the milk into a saucepan. Slit the vanilla pod lengthways and add it to the milk. Bring to the boil, remove from the heat and stir in the remaining sugar, until it dissolves. Set the saucepan aside. Preheat the oven to160°C/325°F/Gas Mark 3.

4 Beat the eggs and egg yolks together in a bowl. Pour the milk mixture over them, whisking. Remove the vanilla pod. Strain the egg mixture into a bowl, then transfer to the soufflé dish.

5 Place the dish in a roasting tin. Pour enough boiling water into the tin to come two-thirds up the side of the dish.

6 Bake in the preheated oven for 1¼–1½ hours, until a knife inserted into the centre comes out clean. Cool completely. Cover with clingfilm and refrigerate for at least 24 hours.

7 Run a spatula knife around the edge of the dish. Place an upturned serving plate with a rim over the top of the soufflé dish, then invert the plate and dish, giving a sharp shake halfway over. Lift off the soufflé dish and serve, decorated with the redcurrants and mint sprigs.

Coconut Cream Custard

Here is an easy, fresh-tasting dessert. Serve it with a selection of seasonal fruits.

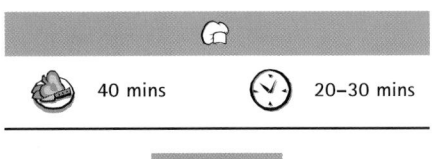

40 mins   20–30 mins

SERVES 4

INGREDIENTS

4 large eggs

115 g/4 oz caster sugar

200 ml/7 fl oz coconut cream

1 tbsp rosewater

fresh fruit, to serve

1 Preheat the oven to 180°C/350°F/ Gas Mark 4.

2 In a bowl, beat together the eggs, sugar, coconut cream and rosewater and stir until the sugar is dissolved.

3 Divide the custard between 4 ramekins. Place in a roasting tin and pour in boiling water to come halfway up the sides of the ramekins. Bake in the preheated oven for 20–30 minutes, or until set. Remove from the tin and leave to cool.

4 To turn out, run a sharp knife around the edge of each custard and turn out on to a serving dish. Serve with fresh fruit.

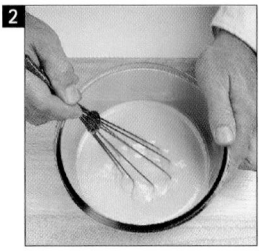

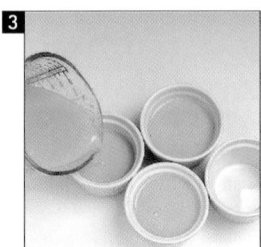

Cream Custards

These individual cream custards are flavoured with nutmeg and topped with strips of caramelized orange zest.

15 mins plus
2 hrs chilling

25 mins

SERVES 4

INGREDIENTS

450 ml/ 16 fl oz single cream

100 g/3½ oz caster sugar

1 orange

2 tsp grated nutmeg

3 large eggs, beaten

1 tbsp honey

1 tsp ground cinnamon

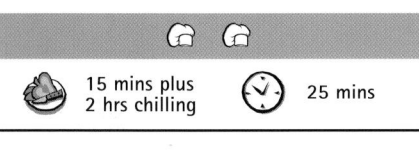

1 Place the cream and sugar in a large non-stick saucepan and heat gently, stirring until the sugar caramelizes.

2 Finely grate half of the orange rind and stir it into the saucepan with the nutmeg.

3 Add the eggs and cook over a low heat for 10–15 minutes, stirring constantly until thickened.

4 Strain the custard through a fine sieve into 4 shallow serving dishes. Set aside to chill in the refrigerator for 2 hours.

5 Meanwhile, pare the remaining orange zest with a vegetable peeler and cut it into thin strips.

6 Place the honey and cinnamon in a saucepan with the water and heat gently. Add the orange zest and cook for 2–3 minutes, stirring constantly, until the mixture has caramelized.

7 Pour the mixture into a bowl and separate out the orange strips. Leave to cool until set.

8 Once the custards have set, decorate them with the caramelized orange zest and serve.

COOK'S TIP
The cream custards will keep for 1–2 days in the refrigerator. Decorate with the caramelized orange zest just before serving.

Mung Bean Custards

Mung beans give this sweet custard an unusual texture. Serve it with a generous spoonful of crème fraîche or whipped cream.

🥔 40 mins ⏱ 50–60 mins

SERVES 6

INGREDIENTS

115 g/4 oz dried mung beans

2 eggs, beaten

175 ml/6 fl oz coconut milk

100 g/3½ oz caster sugar

1 tbsp ground rice

1 tsp ground cinnamon

butter, for greasing

TO DECORATE

ground cinnamon

crème fraîche or whipped cream

finely grated lime zest

sliced starfruit

pomegranate seeds

1 Place the beans in a saucepan with enough water to cover. Bring to the boil, then reduce the heat, and simmer for 30–40 minutes, until the beans are very tender. Drain well. Preheat the oven to 180°C/350°F/Gas Mark 4.

2 Mash the beans, then press through a strainer to make a smooth purée. Place the bean purée, eggs, coconut milk, sugar, ground rice and cinnamon in a large bowl and beat well until mixed.

3 Grease and base-line 4 x 150-ml/5-fl oz moulds or ramekin dishes and pour in the mixture. Place on a baking sheet and bake in the preheated oven for 20–25 minutes or until just set.

4 Cool the custards in the moulds or ramekins, then run a spatula around the edges to loosen, and turn out on to a serving plate. Sprinkle with cinnamon. Top with crème fraîche or whipped cream and sprinkle with lime zest. Serve with starfruit and pomegranate seeds.

COOK'S TIP

To save time, use canned mung beans. Omit step 1, drain the beans thoroughly, and continue with step 2.

Summer Pudding

Use whatever summer fruit you have available, but avoid strawberries because they do not give a good result. Stoned cherries are delicious.

 20 mins plus 8 hrs chilling   10 mins

SERVES 4–6

INGREDIENTS

1 kg/2 lb 4 oz mixed summer fruit, such as blackberries, redcurrants, blackcurrants, raspberries, loganberries and cherries

175 g/6 oz caster sugar

8 small slices white bread

low-fat fromage frais, to serve

 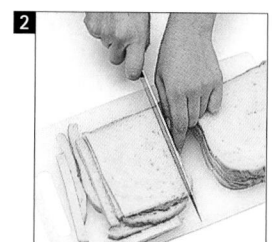 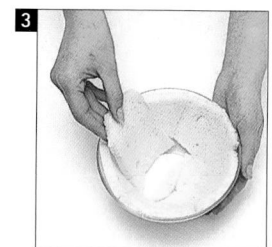

1 Stir the fruit and caster sugar together in a large saucepan, cover and bring to the boil. Simmer for 10 minutes, stirring once.

2 Cut the crusts off the bread slices.

3 Line a 1-litre/1¾-pint pudding basin with the bread, ensuring there are no gaps between the bread slices.

4 Add the fruit and as much of the cooking juices as will fit into the bread-lined basin.

5 Cover the fruit with the remaining bread slices.

6 Put the pudding basin on to a large plate or a shallow baking tray. Place a plate on top and weigh it down with cans. Leave to chill overnight in the refrigerator.

7 When ready to serve, turn the summer pudding out on to a serving plate or shallow bowl, cut into slices and serve cold with low-fat fromage frais.

COOK'S TIP
To give the pudding a more lasting set, dissolve 2 tablespoons of powdered gelatine in water and stir into the fruit mixture. This enables you to turn it out on to the serving plate a couple of hours before serving.

Banana & Ginger Cream

This lusciously rich and incredibly simple dessert is made almost entirely from pantry ingredients.

10 mins plus
30 mins chilling

2–3 mins

SERVES 6

INGREDIENTS

6 slices chocolate sponge cake

6 bananas

juice of ½ lemon

4 pieces stem ginger, chopped, plus 4 tbsp
ginger syrup from the jar

300 ml/10 fl oz double cream

3 tbsp brown sugar

1 Break up the slices of cake and put them into the bottom of a large gratin dish or 6 individual heatproof dishes. Peel and slice the bananas. Place them in a bowl, add the lemon juice and stem ginger, then toss lightly together.

2 Whisk the cream in a separate bowl until soft peaks form. Using a metal spoon, fold in the ginger syrup, then fold in the banana and ginger mixture.

3 Preheat the grill. Spread the cream mixture to cover the cake base in the gratin dish or dishes. Sprinkle the sugar over the top and flash under the preheated grill for about 2 minutes, until the sugar has melted and caramelized. Chill in the refrigerator for 30 minutes before serving.

VARIATION
For a more sophisticated flavour, substitute 4 tablespoons of Cointreau for the ginger syrup.

Rosewater Yogurt Dessert

Yogurt with Middle Eastern flavourings makes a delicious, low-fat dessert – the perfect ending to a summer meal.

25 mins plus 2–3 hrs infusing & 4 hrs chilling

10 mins

SERVES 6–8

INGREDIENTS

1 heaped tbsp green cardamom pods

150 ml/5 fl oz milk

1 tbsp caster sugar

1 kg/2 lb 4 oz natural yogurt

5 tbsp rosewater

rind of ½ lime

2 medium egg whites

pinch of salt

5 tsp powdered gelatine

3 tbsp hot water

honey, to serve

fresh fruit, to decorate

1 Remove the seeds from the cardamom pods and crush them with a pestle and mortar. Put the seeds and the milk in a saucepan and bring to the boil. Remove from the heat, cover and infuse for 2–3 hours.

2 Pour the milk through a fine sieve, retaining the cardamom seeds. Pound the seeds with the sugar.

3 In a large bowl, whisk the yogurt, milk, cardamom-sugar mix, rosewater and the lime rind together.

4 In a separate bowl, whisk the egg whites with the salt until soft peaks form. Set aside.

5 Dissolve the gelatine in the hot water. Let it cool slightly, then stir into the yogurt mixture. Fold one-third of the yogurt mixture into the egg whites, then stir it into the remaining yogurt mixture.

6 Pour the mixture into a large ring mould or soufflé dish. Cover with clingfilm and chill thoroughly in the refrigerator until set.

7 To serve, run a round-bladed knife round the edge of the mould or dish then invert it on to a serving plate. Drizzle with honey and decorate with fresh fruit.

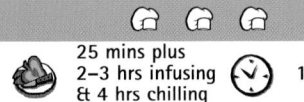

Iced Chocolate Soufflés

Individual iced soufflés look very special and they are far easier to serve than a hot one!

30 mins plus 8 hrs freezing

5 mins

SERVES 6

INGREDIENTS

100 g/3½ oz plain chocolate, broken into pieces

1 tbsp instant coffee powder

4 eggs, separated

115 g/4 oz icing sugar, sifted

225 ml/8 fl oz double cream

2 tbsp Tia Maria

white chocolate caraque, to decorate (see page 9)

1 Tie a double band of foil very tightly around 6 ramekins, to stand 2.5 cm/ 1 inch above the rim. Put the chocolate, coffee powder and 2 tablespoons of water in a small saucepan and heat very gently until melted. Leave to cool slightly.

2 Put the egg yolks and icing sugar in a bowl and whisk together, using an electric whisk, until thick and light. Whisk in the melted chocolate mixture. Put the cream and Tia Maria in a bowl and whisk until thick. Set aside.

3 In another bowl, whisk the egg whites until stiff but not dry. Stir 1 tablespoon of egg whites into the chocolate mixture, then gently fold in the remaining egg whites with the whipped cream. Pour into the prepared ramekins and freeze overnight.

4 When ready to serve, remove the foil carefully and decorate the tops of the soufflés with the white chocolate caraque.

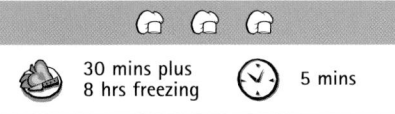

Frozen Citrus Soufflés

These delicious desserts are a refreshing way to end a meal. They can be made in advance and kept in the freezer until required.

35 mins plus
2 hrs freezing

0 mins

SERVES 4

INGREDIENTS

1 tbsp vegetarian gelatine

6 tbsp very hot water

3 eggs, separated

85 g/3 oz caster sugar

finely grated rind and juice of 1 lemon,
½ lime and ½ orange

150 ml/5 fl oz double cream

125 g/4½ oz fromage frais

thin lemon, lime and orange slices,
to decorate

1 Tie greaseproof paper collars around 4 individual soufflé dishes or ramekins or around 1 large (15-cm/6-inch diameter) soufflé dish.

2 Sprinkle the gelatine into the very hot but not boiling water, stirring well to disperse. Leave to stand for 2–3 minutes, stirring occasionally, to give a clear liquid. Leave to cool for 10–15 minutes.

3 Meanwhile, whisk the egg yolks and sugar, using a hand-held electric mixer or balloon whisk until very pale and light. Add the rind and juice from the fruits, mixing well. Stir in the cooled liquid gelatine, making sure that it is thoroughly incorporated.

4 Put the cream into a large chilled bowl and whip until it holds its shape. Stir the fromage frais and then add it to the cream, mixing it in gently. Fold the cream mixture into the citrus mixture, using a large metal spoon.

5 Using a clean whisk, beat the egg whites in a clean bowl until stiff and then gently fold them into the citrus mixture, using a metal spoon.

6 Spoon the mixture into the prepared dishes, almost to the top of their collars. Allow some room for the mixture to expand on freezing. Transfer the dishes to the freezer and open-freeze for about 2 hours until frozen.

7 Remove from the freezer 10 minutes before serving. Peel away the paper collars carefully and decorate with the slices of lemon, lime and orange.

Chocolate Ice Cream Roll

This is a family favourite – spiral slices of moist sponge cake and chocolate ice cream never fail to please.

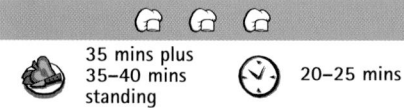

35 mins plus
35–40 mins
standing

20–25 mins

SERVES 8

INGREDIENTS

butter, for greasing

115 g/4 oz plain flour, plus extra for dusting

4 eggs

115 g/4 oz caster sugar

3 tbsp cocoa powder

icing sugar, for dusting

600 ml/1 pint chocolate ice cream

plain chocolate curls, (see page 9),
   to decorate

225 ml/8 fl oz chocolate fudge sauce,
   (see page 693), to serve

1 Line a 38 x 25-cm/15 x 10-inch Swiss roll tin with greaseproof paper. Grease the bottom and dust with flour. Put the eggs and caster sugar in a heatproof bowl set over a saucepan of simmering water. Whisk over a low heat for 5–10 minutes until the mixture is pale and fluffy. Remove from the heat and continue whisking for 10 minutes until the mixture is cool and the whisk leaves a ribbon trail when lifted. Sift the flour and cocoa powder over the surface and gently fold it in.

2 Preheat the oven to 190°C/375°F/Gas Mark 5. Pour the mixture into the prepared tin and spread out evenly with a spatula. Bake in the preheated oven for 15 minutes, until firm to the touch and starting to shrink from the sides of the tin.

3 Spread out a clean cloth and cover with a sheet of baking parchment. Lightly dust the baking parchment with icing sugar. Turn out the cake on to the baking parchment and carefully peel off the lining paper. Trim off any crusty edges. Starting from a short side, pick up the cake and the baking parchment and roll them up together. Wrap the cloth around the rolled cake and place on a wire rack to cool.

4 Remove the ice cream from the freezer and put it in the refrigerator for 15–20 minutes to soften slightly.

Remove the cloth and unroll the cake. Spread the ice cream evenly over the cake, then roll it up again, this time without the baking parchment. Wrap the cake in foil and place in the freezer.

5 Remove the cake from the freezer about 20 minutes before serving. Unwrap, place on a serving plate and dust with icing sugar. Make the chocolate quick curls and arrange them over the top. Place the cake in the refrigerator until required. Serve in slices with Chocolate Fudge Sauce.

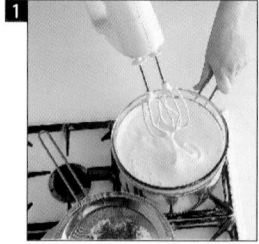

Strawberry Petits Choux

These little chocolate puffs are filled with a melting mixture of strawberry mousse and fresh fruit.

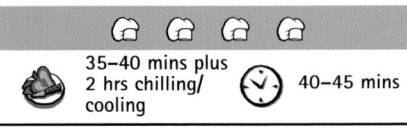

35–40 mins plus 2 hrs chilling/ cooling

40–45 mins

SERVES 6

INGREDIENTS

2 tsp powdered gelatine

2 tbsp water

350 g/12 oz strawberries

225 g/8 oz ricotta cheese

1 tbsp caster sugar

2 tsp crème de fraises de bois

PETITS CHOUX

100 g/3½ oz plain flour

2 tbsp cocoa powder

pinch of salt

6 tbsp unsalted butter

225 ml/8 fl oz water

2 eggs, plus 1 egg white

icing sugar, for dusting

1 Sprinkle the gelatine over the water in a heatproof bowl. Let it soften for 2 minutes. Place the bowl over a saucepan of simmering water and stir until the gelatine dissolves. Remove from the heat.

2 Place 225 g/8 oz of the strawberries in a blender with the ricotta, sugar and liqueur. Process until blended. Add the gelatine and process briefly. Transfer the mousse to a bowl, cover with clingfilm and chill for 1–1½ hours, until set.

3 Meanwhile, make the petits choux. Line a baking tray with baking parchment. Sift the flour, cocoa powder and salt on to a sheet of greaseproof paper. Put the butter and water into a heavy-based saucepan and heat gently until the butter has melted.

4 Preheat the oven to 220°C/425°F/Gas Mark 7. Remove the saucepan from the heat and add the flour mixture all at once, beating vigorously with a wooden spoon. Return the saucepan to the heat and continue to beat vigorously until the mixture comes away from the sides. Remove from the heat and cool slightly.

5 In a separate bowl, beat the eggs with the extra egg white, then gradually add them to the chocolate mixture, beating hard until a glossy paste forms. Drop 12 rounded tablespoonfuls of the mixture on to the prepared baking sheet and bake for 20–25 minutes, until puffed up and crisp.

6 Remove from the oven and make a slit in the side of each petit chou. Return the petits choux to the oven for 5 minutes to dry out. Transfer to a wire rack to cool.

7 Slice the remaining strawberries. Slice the petits choux in half, removing any uncooked dough from the centres and divide the set strawberry mousse between them. Add a layer of strawberry slices and replace the tops. Dust lightly with icing sugar and place in the refrigerator. Serve within 1½ hours.

Chocolate Shortcake Towers

Stacks of crisp shortcake are sandwiched with chocolate-flavoured cream and fresh raspberries and served with a fresh raspberry coulis.

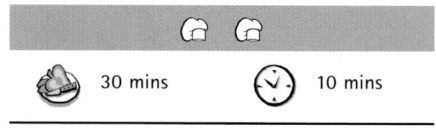

30 mins   10 mins

SERVES 6

INGREDIENTS

SHORTCAKE

225 g/8 oz butter, plus extra for greasing

75 g/2¾ light brown sugar

50 g/1¾ oz plain chocolate, grated

275 g/9½ oz plain flour, plus extra for dusting

TO FINISH

350 g/12 oz fresh raspberries

2 tbsp icing sugar

300 ml/10 fl oz double cream

3 tbsp milk

100 g/3½ oz white chocolate, melted

icing sugar, for dusting

1 Grease a baking tray and preheat the oven to 200°C/400°F/Gas Mark 6. Beat together the butter and sugar until light and fluffy. Beat in the chocolate. Mix in the flour to form a stiff dough.

2 Roll out the dough on a lightly floured surface and stamp out 18 circles, 7.5 cm/3 inches across, with a plain biscuit cutter. Place the circles on the baking tray and bake in the preheated oven for 10 minutes, until crisp and golden. Leave to cool on the baking tray.

3 To make the coulis, set aside about 100 g/3½ oz of the raspberries. Blend the remainder in a food processor with the icing sugar, then strain a sieve to remove the seeds. Chill the purée. Set aside 2 teaspoons of the cream, then whip the remainder until just holding its shape. Fold in the milk and the melted chocolate.

4 For each tower, spoon a little coulis on to a serving plate. Drop small dots of the reserved cream into the coulis around the edge of the plate and use a skewer to drag through the cream to make an attractive pattern.

5 Place a shortcake circle on the plate and spoon on a little of the chocolate cream. Add 2 or 3 raspberries and more cream, top with another shortcake, and repeat the layers. Place a third shortcake on top. Dust with icing sugar.

Chocolate Wafer Layers

Crisp delicate wafers of chocolate layered with a rich pistachio cream filling taste as impressive as they look.

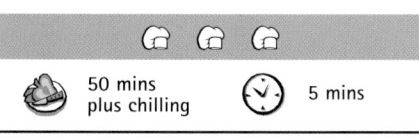

50 mins
plus chilling

5 mins

SERVES 6

INGREDIENTS

175 g/6 oz plain chocolate,
  broken into pieces

250 g/9 oz mascarpone cheese

1 tbsp caster sugar

4 tbsp Tia Maria

300 ml/10 fl oz double cream

85 g/3 oz pistachio nuts, chopped

115 g/4 oz milk chocolate, grated

1 Put the chocolate in a heatproof bowl set over a saucepan of gently simmering water until melted. Let cool. Cut 6 strips of non-stick baking parchment 6 x 26 cm/2½ x 10½ inches. Brush evenly with melted chocolate. Mark each strip with a knife every 9 cm/3½ inches. Leave in the refrigerator to set, then carefully peel the paper off the chocolate wafers.

2 Put the mascarpone cheese and sugar in a bowl and beat until smooth, then beat in the Tia Maria and cream until forming soft peaks. Fold in the pistachio nuts and grated chocolate.

3 Carefully break each chocolate strip along the marked lines to make 3 wafers, giving 18 in total. Spread a little pistachio cream over 1 wafer and top with a second. Spread cream on a third wafer and stack it, cream-side down, on top of the second wafer. Repeat to make 6 stacks. Chill until ready to serve.

COOK'S TIP
Do not overbeat the mascarpone filling or it will be difficult to spread over the chocolate wafers.

Chocolate Fingers

Tasty bread fingers flavoured with sherry and coated with chocolate and sugar are surprisingly tasty and very popular.

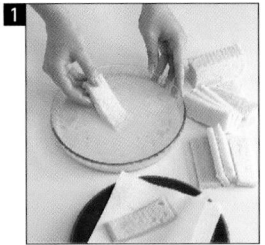

🍰 15 mins   🕐 30 mins

MAKES 24

INGREDIENTS

4 eggs, lightly beaten

600 ml/1 pint milk

5 tbsp sherry

8 slices day-old white bread,
   1-cm/½-inch thick, crusts removed

4 tbsp sunflower oil

115 g/4 oz caster sugar

225 g/8 oz dark chocolate, grated

vanilla ice cream, to serve (optional)

1 Pour the beaten eggs, milk and sherry into a shallow dish and beat lightly to mix. Cut each slice of bread lengthways into 3 fingers. Soak the bread fingers in the egg mixture until soft, then drain on kitchen paper.

2 Heat the oil in a large, heavy-based frying pan. Carefully add the bread fingers to the frying pan, in batches and cook over a medium heat for 12 minutes on each side, until golden. Using tongs, carefully transfer the fingers to kitchen paper to drain.

3 When all the fingers are cooked and thoroughly drained, roll them first in the sugar and then in the grated chocolate. Pile them on a warm serving plate and serve immediately, with ice cream if desired.

Blackberry Chocolate Flan

This richly flavoured tart looks superb and tastes wonderful – a perfect choice for a special occasion.

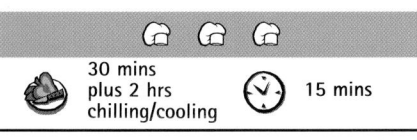

30 mins
plus 2 hrs
chilling/cooling

15 mins

SERVES 6

INGREDIENTS

280 g/10 oz plain flour, plus extra for dusting

55 g/2 oz cocoa powder

115 g/4 oz icing sugar

pinch of salt

175 g/6 oz butter, diced

1 egg yolk

675 g/1 lb 8 oz blackberries

1 tbsp lemon juice

2 tbsp caster sugar

2 tbsp crème de cassis

FILLING

300 ml/10 fl oz double cream

175 g/6 oz blackberry jam

225 g/8 oz plain chocolate, broken into pieces

25 g/1 oz unsalted butter, diced

1 First, make the pastry. Sift the flour, cocoa powder, icing sugar and salt into a mixing bowl and make a well in the centre. Put the butter and egg yolk in the well and gradually mix in the dry ingredients, using a pastry blender or two forks. Knead lightly and form into a ball. Wrap in clingfilm and chill in the refrigerator for 1 hour.

2 When chilled, unwrap the dough. Preheat the oven to 180°C/350°F/Gas Mark 4. Roll out the dough on a lightly floured work surface. Use it to line a 30 x 10-cm/12 x 4-inch rectangular flan tin and prick the pastry case with a fork. Line the base with baking parchment and fill with dried beans. Bake in the preheated oven for 15 minutes. Remove from the oven, remove the beans and baking parchment and set aside to cool.

3 To make the filling, put the cream and jam into a saucepan and bring to the boil over a low heat. Remove the saucepan from the heat and stir in the chocolate until melted and smooth. Stir in the butter until melted and smooth. Pour the mixture into the pastry case and set aside to cool.

4 Put 225 g/8 oz of the blackberries, the lemon juice and caster sugar into a food processor and process until smooth. Strain through a sieve into a bowl and stir in the crème de cassis. Set aside.

5 Remove the flan from the tin and place on a serving plate. Arrange the remaining blackberries on top and brush with a little blackberry and liqueur sauce. Serve the flan with the sauce on the side.

Banana & Mango Tart

Bananas and mangoes are a great combination of colours and flavours, especially when topped with toasted coconut chips.

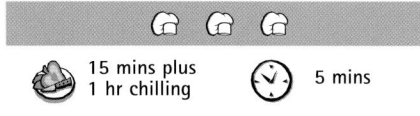

🍰 15 mins plus 1 hr chilling   🕐 5 mins

SERVES 8

INGREDIENTS

20-cm/8-inch ready-made pastry case

FILLING

2 small ripe bananas

1 mango, peeled and sliced

3½ tbsp cornflour

6 tbsp demerara sugar

300 ml/10 fl oz soy milk

150 ml/5 fl oz coconut milk

1 tsp vanilla essence

toasted coconut chips, to decorate

1 Slice the bananas and arrange half of them in the pastry case with half of the mango pieces.

2 Put the cornflour and sugar in a saucepan and mix together. Gradually, whisk in the soy milk and coconut milk until combined. Simmer over a low heat, whisking constantly for 2–3 minutes until the mixture thickens.

3 Stir in the vanilla essence, then spoon the mixture over the fruit.

4 Top with the remaining fruit and toasted coconut chips. Chill in the refrigerator for 1 hour before serving.

COOK'S TIP
Coconut chips are available in some supermarkets and most health food stores. They are worth using as they look more attractive than dry shredded coconut.

Chocolate Chiffon Pie

The nutty crust of this delectable pie contrasts with the tempting, creamy chocolate filling.

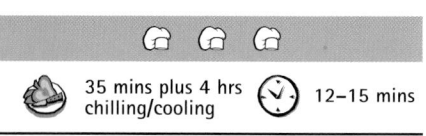

35 mins plus 4 hrs chilling/cooling

12–15 mins

SERVES 8

INGREDIENTS

140 g/5 oz shelled Brazil nuts

2 tbsp granulated sugar

2 tsp melted butter

225 ml/8 fl oz milk

2 tsp powdered gelatine

115 g/4 oz caster sugar

2 eggs, separated

225 g/8 oz plain chocolate, roughly chopped

1 tsp vanilla essence

150 ml/5 fl oz double cream

2 tbsp chopped Brazil nuts

1 Preheat the oven to 200°C/400°F/Gas Mark 6. Put the Brazil nuts into a food processor and process until finely ground. Add the granulated sugar and melted butter and process briefly to combine. Tip the mixture into a 23-cm/ 9-inch round flan tin and press it on to the base and sides with a spoon or your fingertips. Bake in the preheated oven for 8–10 minutes, until light golden brown. Set aside to cool.

2 Pour the milk into a heatproof bowl and sprinkle the gelatine over the surface. Let it soften for 2 minutes, then set over a saucepan of gently simmering water. Stir in half the caster sugar, both the egg yolks and all the chocolate. Stir constantly over a low heat for 4–5 minutes, until the gelatine has dissolved and the chocolate has melted. Remove from the heat and beat until the mixture is smooth. Stir in the vanilla essence, cover with clingfilm and chill for 45–60 minutes, until starting to set.

3 Whip the cream until it is stiff, then fold all but about 3 tablespoons into the chocolate mixture. Whisk the egg whites in another bowl until soft peaks form. Add 2 teaspoons of the remaining sugar and whisk until stiff peaks form. Fold in the remaining sugar, then fold the egg whites into the chocolate mixture. Pour the filling into the pie case and chill in the refrigerator for 3 hours, or until set. Decorate the pie with the remaining whipped cream and the chopped nuts before serving.

Chocolate Charlotte

This chocolate dessert, consisting of a rich chocolate mousse-like filling enclosed in sponge finger biscuits, is a variation of a popular classic.

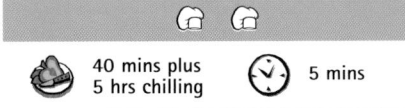

40 mins plus 5 hrs chilling

5 mins

SERVES 8

INGREDIENTS

about 22 sponge finger biscuits

4 tbsp orange liqueur

250 g/9 oz plain chocolate

150 ml/5 fl oz double cream

4 eggs

150g/5½ oz caster sugar

TO DECORATE

150 ml/5 fl oz whipping cream

2 tbsp caster sugar

½ tsp vanilla essence

plain chocolate curls (see page 9)

chocolate decorations (see page 9), optional

1 Line the bottom of a charlotte mould or a deep 18-cm/7-inch round cake tin with a piece of baking parchment.

2 Place the sponge fingers on a baking tray and sprinkle with half of the orange liqueur. Use to line the sides of the mould or tin, trimming if necessary to ensure a tight fit.

3 Put the chocolate in a heatproof bowl set over a saucepan of simmering water until melted. Remove from the heat and stir in the double cream.

4 Separate the eggs and place the whites in a large greasefree bowl. Beat the egg yolks into the chocolate mixture.

5 Whisk the egg whites until stiff peaks form, then gradually add the caster sugar, whisking until stiff and glossy. Carefully fold the egg whites into the chocolate mixture in 2 batches, taking care not to knock out all of the air. Pour into the centre of the mould. Trim the sponge fingers so that they are level with the chocolate mixture. Chill in the refrigerator for at least 5 hours.

6 To decorate, whisk the cream, sugar and vanilla essence until soft peaks form. Turn out the charlotte on to a serving dish. Pipe cream rosettes around the bottom and decorate with chocolate curls and other chocolate decorations of your choice.

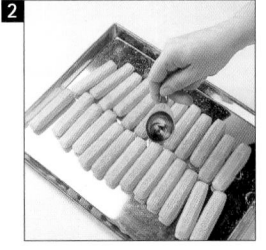

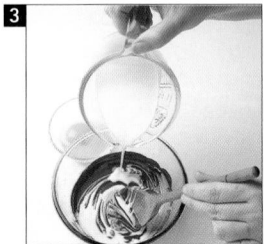

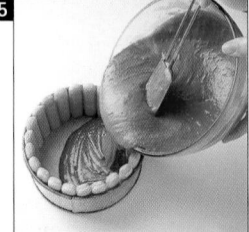

Passion Fruit Charlotte

If passion fruit are not in season, use clear apple juice for the jelly and flavour the cream filling with either vanilla or orange.

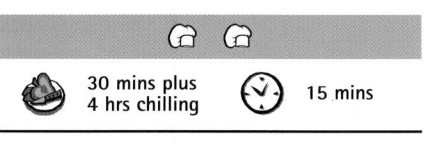

30 mins plus 4 hrs chilling   **15 mins**

SERVES 6

INGREDIENTS

300 ml/10 fl oz passion fruit juice

4 tsp powdered gelatine

2–3 fresh strawberries, sliced

225 g/8 oz fresh raspberries

20 sponge finger biscuits

2 eggs, separated

55 g/2 oz caster sugar

150 ml/5 fl oz single cream, warmed

3 passion fruit

85 g/3 oz plain chocolate

150 ml/5 fl oz double cream

1 To make the jelly, heat the fruit juice until almost boiling, remove from the heat and sprinkle in 2 teaspoons of the gelatine. Stir to dissolve, then pour a thin layer into a rinsed 1.2-litre/2-pint charlotte mould. Leave until set.

2 Dip the sliced strawberries and a few raspberries in the jelly, then arrange on top of the layer of jelly in the mould. Leave to set, then pour over half of the remaining jelly. Leave until completely set.

3 Dip each side of the sponge finger biscuits into the remaining jelly and place, sugar-side out, round the edge of the mould. Leave to chill.

4 Meanwhile, whisk the egg yolks and sugar until thick and creamy. Stir in the warm cream, then strain into a heavy-based saucepan and cook, stirring, until the mixture thickens and coats the back of a wooden spoon. Remove and cool slightly.

5 Sprinkle the remaining gelatine over 3 tablespoons of very hot water. Stir until dissolved. Cool slightly, then stir into the custard. Halve the passion fruit, and add the juice to the custard. Melt the chocolate in a heatproof bowl set over a saucepan of simmering water. Stir into the custard with the remaining raspberries.

6 Whip the cream until soft peaks form and stir two-thirds of it into the custard. Whisk the egg whites until soft peaks form and stir into the mixture. Mix lightly, then spoon into the mould. Chill for at least 4 hours, or until set.

7 To unmould, dip the base of the mould in a saucepan of very hot water for a few seconds then invert on to a serving plate. Pipe the remainder of the whipped cream between the sponge finger biscuits and around the top, then serve.

Mississippi Mud Pie

An all-time favourite with chocoholics – the 'mud' refers to the gooey, rich chocolate layer of the filling.

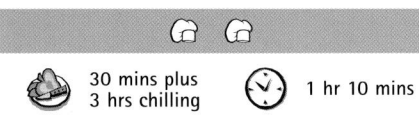

30 mins plus
3 hrs chilling

1 hr 10 mins

SERVES 8

INGREDIENTS

225 g/8 oz plain flour, plus extra for dusting

2 tbsp cocoa powder

140 g/5 oz butter

2 tbsp caster sugar

about 2 tbsp cold water

FILLING

175 g/6 oz butter

350 g/12 oz soft dark brown sugar

4 eggs, lightly beaten

4 tbsp cocoa powder, sifted

150 g/5½ oz plain chocolate

300 ml/10 fl oz single cream

1 tsp chocolate essence

TO DECORATE

425 ml/15 fl oz double cream, whipped

chocolate flakes and chocolate curls (see page 9)

1 To make the pastry, sift the flour and cocoa powder into a mixing bowl. Rub in the butter until the mixture resembles fine breadcrumbs. Stir in the sugar and enough cold water to mix to a soft dough. Chill for 15 minutes.

2 Preheat the oven to 190°C/375°F/Gas Mark 5. Roll out the dough on a lightly floured surface and use to line a 23-cm/9-inch loose-bottomed flan tin or ceramic flan dish. Line with baking parchment and baking beans. Bake blind in the preheated oven for 15 minutes. Remove the beans and parchment and cook for a further 10 minutes until crisp.

3 To make the filling, beat the butter and sugar in a bowl and gradually beat in the eggs with the cocoa powder. Melt the chocolate and beat it into the mixture with the single cream and the chocolate essence.

4 Reduce the oven temperature to 160°C/325°F/Gas Mark 3. Pour the mixture into the pastry case and bake for 45 minutes or until the filling is set.

5 Let the mud pie cool completely, then transfer the pie to a serving plate if preferred. Cover with the whipped cream and leave to chill.

6 Decorate the pie with quick chocolate curls and chocolate flakes and then chill until ready to serve.

Chocolate Freezer Cake

Hidden in a ring of chocolate sponge lies the secret of this freezer cake – a chocolate-mint ice cream. Use orange or coffee ice cream if preferred.

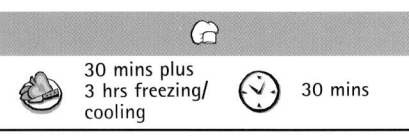

30 mins plus 3 hrs freezing/cooling

30 mins

SERVES 8

INGREDIENTS

butter, for greasing

4 eggs

175 g/6 oz caster sugar

100 g/3½ oz self-raising flour

3 tbsp cocoa powder

500 ml/17 fl oz chocolate-mint ice cream

chocolate sauce (see page 9), to serve

1 Preheat the oven to 180°C/350°F/Gas Mark 4. Lightly grease a 23-cm/9-inch ring mould. Place the eggs and sugar in a large mixing bowl. Using an electric whisk if you have one, whisk the mixture until it is very thick and a trail is left when the whisk is dragged across the surface. If using a balloon whisk, use a heatproof bowl, set over a saucepan of gently simmering water while whisking.

2 Sift the flour and cocoa powder together and fold into the egg mixture. Pour into the prepared mould and bake in the preheated oven for 30 minutes, or until springy to the touch. Leave to cool in the mould before turning out on to a wire rack to cool completely.

3 Rinse the ring mould and line with a strip of clingfilm, hanging it over the rim slightly. Carefully cut off the top 1 cm/½ inch of the cake in one slice and then set aside.

4 Return the cake to the mould. Using a spoon, scoop out the centre of the cake, leaving a shell about 1 cm/½ inch thick.

5 Remove the ice cream from the freezer and leave to stand for a few minutes, then beat with a wooden spoon until softened a little. Fill the centre of the cake with the ice cream, smoothing the top. Replace the top of the cake.

6 Cover with the overhanging clingfilm and freeze for at least 2 hours.

7 To serve, turn the cake out on to a serving dish and drizzle over some of the chocolate sauce in an attractive pattern, if you wish. Cut the cake into slices, then serve with the remaining sauce on the side.

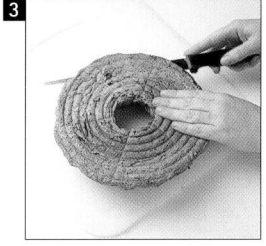

Tiramisu Layers

This is a modern version of the well-known and very traditional chocolate- and coffee-flavoured dessert from Italy.

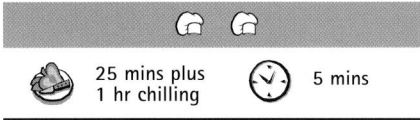

25 mins plus
1 hr chilling

5 mins

SERVES 6

INGREDIENTS

150 ml/5 fl oz double cream

400 g/14 oz mascarpone cheese

300 g/10 oz plain chocolate

400 ml/14 fl oz hot black coffee

55 g/2 oz caster sugar

6 tbsp dark rum or brandy

54 sponge finger biscuits

cocoa powder, for dusting

1 Whip the cream until it just holds its shape. Beat the mascarpone to soften slightly, then fold in the whipped cream. Melt the chocolate in a heatproof bowl set over a saucepan of simmering water, stirring occasionally. Let the chocolate cool slightly, then stir it into the mascarpone and cream mixture.

2 Mix the hot coffee and sugar in a saucepan and stir until dissolved. Leave to cool then add the dark rum. Dip the sponge finger biscuits into the mixture briefly so that they absorb some coffee and rum mixture but do not become soggy.

3 Place 3 sponge finger biscuits on 6 serving plates.

4 Spoon a layer of the chocolate, mascarpone and cream mixture over the sponge finger biscuits.

5 Place 3 more sponge finger biscuits on top of the chocolate mixture. Spread another layer of chocolate mixture and place 3 more sponge finger biscuits on top.

6 Leave to chill in the refrigerator for at least 1 hour. Dust with a little cocoa powder just before serving.

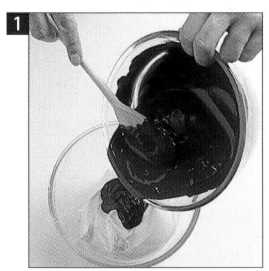

VARIATION
Try adding 55 g/2 oz chopped, toasted hazelnuts to the chocolate and mascarpone mixture in step 1, if you prefer.

Traditional Tiramisu

A favourite Italian dessert flavoured with coffee and Amaretto. You could substitute the Amaretto with brandy or Marsala.

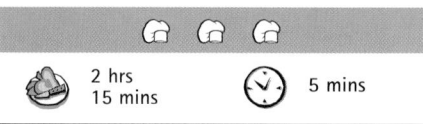

2 hrs 15 mins

5 mins

SERVES 6

I N G R E D I E N T S

20–24 sponge finger biscuits

2 tbsp cold black coffee

2 tbsp coffee essence

2 tbsp Amaretto

4 egg yolks

85 g/3 oz caster sugar

few drops vanilla essence

grated rind of ½ lemon

350 g/12 oz mascarpone cheese

2 tsp lemon juice

250 ml/9 fl oz double cream

1 tbsp milk

25 g/1 oz flaked almonds, lightly toasted

2 tbsp cocoa powder

1 tbsp icing sugar

1 Arrange half of the sponge finger biscuits in the base of a glass bowl or serving dish.

2 Combine the black coffee, coffee essence and Amaretto together and sprinkle just over half of the mixture over the sponge finger biscuits.

3 Put the egg yolks into a heatproof bowl with the sugar, vanilla and lemon rind. Stand over a saucepan of simmering water and whisk until very thick and creamy and a trail is left when the whisk is dragged across the surface.

4 Put the mascarpone cheese in a bowl with the lemon juice and beat vigorously until smooth.

5 Combine the egg and mascarpone cheese mixtures and when evenly blended pour half over the sponge finger biscuits and spread evenly.

6 Add another layer of sponge finger biscuits, sprinkle with the remaining coffee mixture and then cover with the rest of the egg and mascarpone cheese mixture. Chill for at least 2 hours and preferably longer, or overnight.

7 To serve, whip the cream and milk together until fairly stiff and spread or pipe over the dessert. Sprinkle the flaked almonds over the top, then sift on a layer of cocoa powder so the top is completely covered. Finally sift a light dusting of icing sugar over the cocoa powder.

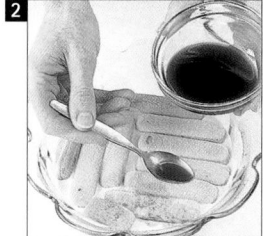

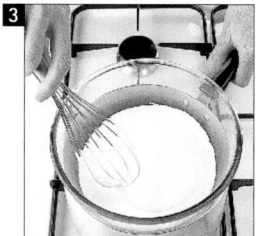

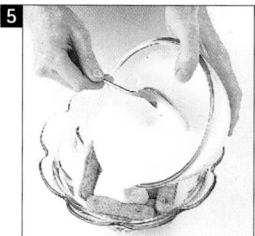

Chocolate & Cherry Tiramisu

There are now several variations on the original tiramisu theme. This one has the delectable flavours of chocolate, cherry and coffee.

 20 mins plus 2 hrs to chill   0 mins

SERVES 4

INGREDIENTS

200 ml/7 fl oz strong black coffee, cooled to room temperature

6 tbsp cherry brandy

4 trifle sponges

250 g/9 oz mascarpone cheese

300 ml/10 fl oz double cream, lightly whipped

3 tbsp icing sugar

275 g/9½ oz sweet cherries, halved and stoned

65 g/2½ oz chocolate, grated

whole cherries, to decorate

1 Pour the cooled coffee into a jug and stir in the cherry brandy. Put 2 of the sponges in the bottom of a serving dish, then pour over half of the coffee mixture.

2 Put the mascarpone cheese in a separate bowl along with the cream and sugar and mix together well. Spread half of the mascarpone mixture over the coffee-soaked trifle sponges, then top with half of the cherries. Arrange the remaining trifle sponges on top. Pour over the remaining coffee mixture and top with the remaining cherries. Finish with a layer of mascarpone. Scatter over the grated chocolate, cover with clingfilm and chill in the refrigerator for at least 2 hours.

3 Remove from the refrigerator, and serve, decorated with whole cherries.

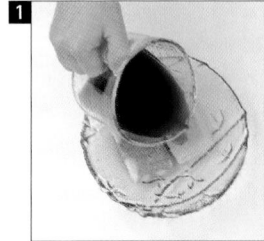

Quick Tiramisu

This quick and simple version of one of the most popular Italian desserts is ready in minutes.

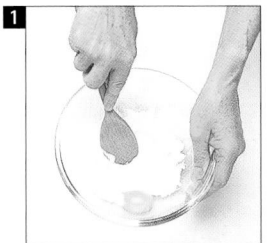

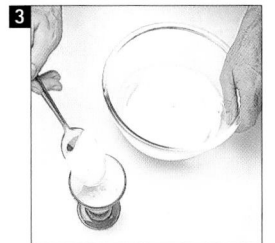

15 mins   0 mins

SERVES 4

INGREDIENTS

225 g/8 oz mascarpone or full-fat soft cheese

1 egg, separated

2 tbsp natural yogurt

2 tbsp caster sugar

2 tbsp dark rum

2 tbsp strong black coffee

8 sponge finger biscuits

2 tbsp grated plain chocolate

1 Put the mascarpone cheese in a large bowl, add the egg yolk and yogurt and beat until smooth.

2 Whisk the egg white until stiff but not dry, then whisk in the sugar and fold into the mascarpone mixture.

3 Spoon half of the mixture into 4 sundae glasses.

4 Mix together the rum and coffee in a shallow dish. Dip the sponge fingers into the rum mixture, break them in half, or into smaller pieces if necessary, and divide between the glasses.

5 Stir any remaining coffee mixture into the remaining cheese and spoon over the top.

6 Sprinkle with grated chocolate. Serve immediately or chill until required.

COOK'S TIP
Mascarpone is an Italian soft cream cheese made from cow's milk. It has a rich, silky smooth texture and a deliciously creamy flavour. It can be eaten as it is with fresh fruits or flavoured with coffee or chocolate.

Chestnut & Chocolate Terrine

Chestnut and chocolate is a classic combination, seen at its best in this layered terrine.

30 mins
plus chilling

5 mins

SERVES 6

INGREDIENTS

115 g/4 oz plain chocolate, broken into pieces

200 ml/7 fl oz double cream

1 packet rectangular plain sweet biscuits

100 ml/3½ fl oz dark rum

225 g/8 oz can sweetened chestnut purée

cocoa powder and icing sugar for dusting

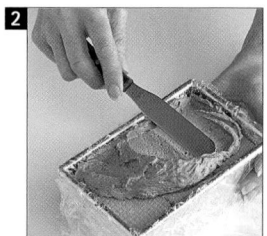

1 Line a 450-g/1-lb loaf tin with clingfilm. Put the chocolate in a heatproof bowl set over a saucepan of gently simmering water until melted. Set aside to cool. Put the cream in a bowl and whip lightly until soft peaks form. Fold in the cooled chocolate.

2 Place the rum in a shallow dish. Lightly dip 4 biscuits into the rum and arrange on the bottom of the tin. Then repeat with 4 more biscuits. Spread half the chocolate cream over the cookies. Make another layer of 8 biscuits dipped in rum and spread the chestnut purée over them, followed by another layer of biscuits. Spread the remaining chocolate cream over and top with a final layer of biscuits. Chill overnight.

3 Turn the terrine out on to a serving dish. Dust with cocoa powder then cut strips of paper and place randomly on top of the terrine and sift icing sugar over to make a pattern. Remove the paper and cut the terrine into slices with a sharp knife dipped in hot water.

COOK'S TIP

When soaking the biscuits take care not to dip them into the rum for too long, otherwise they will disintegrate.

Three Chocolate Terrine

Contrasting bands of white, milk and plain chocolate look stunning when the terrine is sliced and surrounded with orange cream.

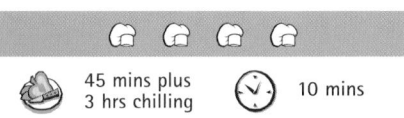

45 mins plus 3 hrs chilling

10 mins

SERVES 10-12

INGREDIENTS

3 tsp powdered gelatine

115 g/4 oz each of milk chocolate, white chocolate and plain chocolate

450 ml/16 fl oz whipping cream

6 eggs, separated

75 g/2¾ oz caster sugar

ORANGE CREAM

2 tbsp caster sugar

1 tbsp cornflour

2 egg yolks

150 ml/5 fl oz milk

150 ml/5 fl oz double cream

strips of zest from 1 orange

1 tbsp Cointreau

a little orange juice (optional)

chocolate-covered coffee beans, to decorate

1 To make the milk chocolate mousse, put 2 tablespoons water in a small heatproof bowl, sprinkle on the gelatine and leave until spongy. Then set the bowl over a saucepan of simmering water until the gelatine is dissolved. Leave to cool. Break the milk chocolate into pieces and place in a heatproof bowl set over a saucepan of simmering water until melted. Leave to cool. Put one-third of the cream in a bowl and whip until thick. Put 2 egg whites in another bowl and whisk until stiff but not dry. Put 2 egg yolks and one-third of the caster sugar in a bowl and whisk until thick and pale, then stir in the cooled melted chocolate, the gelatine and finally the cream. Gently fold in the egg whites.

2 Pour the mixture into a 1.2-litre/1¾-pint loaf tin lined with clingfilm. Put in the freezer for 20 minutes. Make the white chocolate mousse in the same way and pour over the milk chocolate layer. Freeze as before then make the plain chocolate mousse and pour on top. Chill for 2 hours or until set.

3 To make the orange cream, put the sugar, cornflour and egg yolks in a bowl and stir until smooth. Put the milk and cream in a saucepan with some of the strips of zest, reserving a few for decoration. Heat gently until almost boiling, then pour over the yolk mixture, whisking. Strain back into the saucepan and return to the heat. Heat gently, stirring until thickened. Cover the surface with clingfilm and leave to cool. Stir in the Cointreau. The cream should have a pouring consistency. If too thick, stir in a little orange juice. Turn out the terrine and cut into slices. Decorate with the chocolate-coated coffee beans and orange zest and serve with the orange cream.

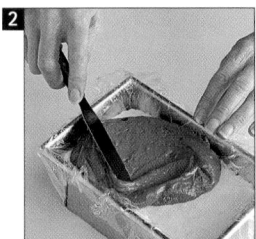

White Chocolate Terrine

This iced dessert is somewhere between a chocolate mousse and an ice cream. Serve it with a chocolate sauce or a fruit coulis and fresh fruit.

50 mins plus 8 hrs freezing

5 mins

SERVES 8

INGREDIENTS

2 tbsp granulated sugar

5 tbsp water

300 g/10½ oz white chocolate

3 eggs, separated

300 ml/10 fl oz double cream

1 Line a 450-g/1-lb loaf tin with foil or clingfilm pressing out as many creases as you can.

2 Place the granulated sugar and water in a heavy-based saucepan and heat gently, stirring until the sugar has dissolved. Bring to the boil and boil for 1–2 minutes until syrupy, then remove from the heat.

3 Break the white chocolate into small pieces and stir it into the hot syrup, continuing to stir until the chocolate has melted and combined with the syrup. Let the mixture cool slightly.

4 Beat the egg yolks into the chocolate mixture. Leave to cool completely.

5 Lightly whip the cream until it is just holding its shape, and fold it into the chocolate mixture.

6 Whisk the egg whites in a greasefree bowl until soft peaks form. Fold the whites into the chocolate mixture. Pour into the prepared loaf tin and freeze overnight.

7 To serve, remove the terrine from the freezer about 10–15 minutes before serving. Turn out of the tin and cut into slices. Serve with a fruit coulis, if liked (see Cook's Tip).

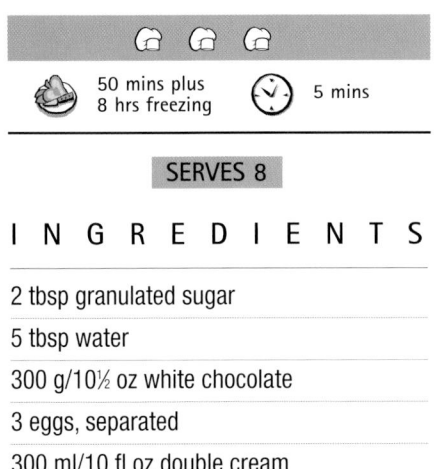

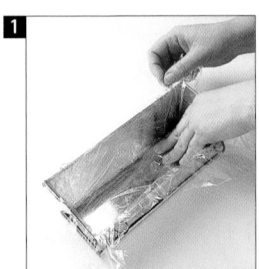

COOK'S TIP

To make a coulis, place 225 g/8 oz of soft fruit–mangoes, strawberries or raspberries are ideal–in a food processor. Add 1–2 tablespoons of icing sugar and blend to a purée. If the fruit contains seeds, push the purée through a sieve to remove them. Chill until required.

Chocolate Salami

This Italian cold chocolate 'sausage' dish gets its name from its appearance, which looks just like salami.

25 mins
plus 6–8 hrs
standing/freezing

5–7 mins

SERVES 10

INGREDIENTS

350 g/12 oz plain chocolate,
  broken into small pieces

4 tbsp Amaretto or brandy

225 g/8 oz butter, diced

2 egg yolks

24 plain sweet biscuits, such as Petit
  Beurre, roughly crushed

55 g/2 oz toasted flaked almonds, chopped

25 g/1 oz ground almonds

1 tsp vegetable oil or olive oil, for greasing

1 Put the chocolate in a heatproof bowl set over a saucepan of gently simmering water. Add the Amaretto and 2 tablespoons of the butter. Stir over a low heat until melted and smooth. Remove from the heat and cool slightly.

2 Stir in the egg yolks, then add the remaining butter, a little at a time, making sure each addition is fully incorporated before adding more. Stir in about three-quarters of the crushed biscuits and all the toasted almonds. Cover with clingfilm, then set aside for 45–60 minutes, until starting to set. Meanwhile, put the remaining crushed biscuits into a food processor and process until finely crushed. Transfer them to a bowl and stir in the ground almonds. Set aside.

3 Lightly oil a sheet of baking parchment and turn out the chocolate mixture on to it. Using a spatula, shape the mixture into a salami about 35 cm/ 14 inches long. Wrap the salami in the baking parchment and place in the freezer for 4–6 hours, until set.

4 About 1¼ hours before serving, spread out the ground almond mixture on a sheet of baking parchment.

Remove the salami from the freezer and unwrap. Roll it over the ground almond mixture until thoroughly and evenly coated. Cover with clingfilm, then set aside for 1 hour at room temperature. Cut into slices and serve.

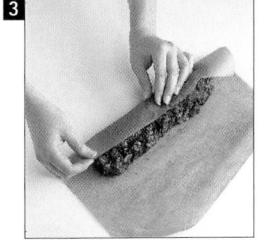

Chocolate & Almond Terrine

Full of flavour and contrasting textures, this classic Italian dessert is very quick and easy to prepare.

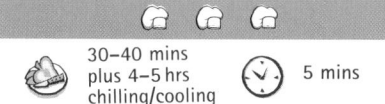

30–40 mins
plus 4–5 hrs
chilling/cooling

5 mins

SERVES 8

INGREDIENTS

vegetable oil, for brushing

225 g/8 oz plain chocolate, broken into pieces

4 tbsp dark rum

225 g/8 oz unsalted butter

115 g/4 oz caster sugar

2 eggs, separated

175 g/6 oz ground almonds

pinch of salt

115 g/4 oz crushed amaretti biscuits or macaroons

2 tbsp icing sugar

TO DECORATE

75 g/2¾ oz plain chocolate

8 cherries

8 chocolate leaves (see page 9)

1 Line a 1-kg/2-lb loaf tin with baking parchment, letting it overlap the sides. Brush with oil. Put the chocolate in a heatproof bowl set over a saucepan of simmering water. Stir over a low heat until melted. Remove the saucepan from the heat, stir in the rum and set aside to cool.

2 Cream together the butter and caster sugar until pale and fluffy, then beat in the egg yolks, one at a time. Add the ground almonds and then beat in the cooled chocolate.

3 Whisk the egg whites with a pinch of salt until stiff peaks form. Gently fold the whites into the chocolate mixture, then fold in the biscuit crumbs. Spoon the mixture into the prepared tin, spread it out evenly and smooth the top. Cover with clingfilm and chill in the refrigerator for 4–5 hours, until firm.

4 To serve, uncover the tin and run a round-bladed knife around the sides.

Dip the bottom in hot water. Place a serving plate on top of the tin, then, holding them firmly together, invert. Remove the baking parchment. Dust with the icing sugar.

5 To decorate, melt the plain chocolate as before and put spoonfuls along the top of the cake. Top with cherries and chocolate leaves.

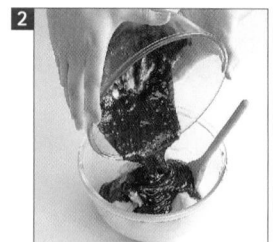

Chocolate Brownie Roulade

The addition of nuts and raisins has given this dessert extra texture, making it similar to that of chocolate brownies.

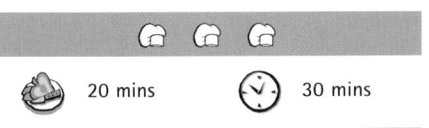

🍮 20 mins   ⏲ 30 mins

SERVES 4

INGREDIENTS

150 g/5½ oz plain chocolate, broken into pieces

3 tbsp water

175 g/6 oz caster sugar

5 eggs, separated

25 g/1 oz raisins, chopped

25 g/1 oz pecan nuts, chopped

pinch of salt

300 ml/10 fl oz double cream, lightly whipped

icing sugar, for dusting

1 Preheat the oven to 180°C/350°F/Gas Mark 4. Lightly grease a 30 x 20-cm/ 12 x 8-inch Swiss roll tin, line with baking parchment and grease the parchment.

2 Melt the chocolate with the water in a small saucepan over a low heat until the chocolate has melted. Leave to cool.

3 In a bowl, whisk the sugar and egg yolks for 2-3 minutes with a hand-held electric whisk until thick and pale.

4 Fold in the cooled chocolate, raisins and pecan nuts.

5 In a separate bowl, whisk the egg whites with the salt. Fold one-quarter of the egg whites into the chocolate mixture, then fold in the rest of the whites, working lightly and quickly.

6 Transfer the mixture to the prepared tin and bake in the preheated oven for 25 minutes until risen and just firm to the touch. Leave to cool before covering with a sheet of baking parchment and a damp clean tea towel. Leave until cold.

7 Turn the roulade out on to another piece of baking parchment dusted with icing sugar and carefully remove the lining paper.

8 Spread the cream over the roulade. Starting from a short end, roll the sponge away from you using the paper to guide you. Trim the ends of the roulade to make a neat finish and transfer to a serving plate. Leave to chill in the refrigerator until ready to serve. Dust the top with a little icing sugar before serving, if wished.

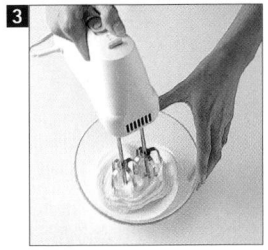

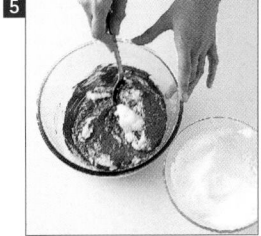

Strawberry & Almond Roulade

A light, flourless almond sponge is wrapped around a filling of strawberries and mascarpone cheese in this variation on a classic, popular dessert.

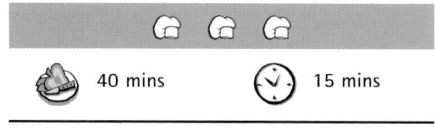

40 mins   15 mins

SERVES 4

INGREDIENTS

butter, for greasing

6 eggs

200 g/7 oz golden caster sugar

2 tsp baking powder

175 g/6 oz ground almonds

icing sugar, for dusting

FILLING

150 g/5½ oz mascarpone cheese

150 ml/5 fl oz double cream

450 g/1 lb fresh strawberries

1 Preheat the oven to 180°C/350°F/Gas Mark 4. Grease and line the bottom and sides of a 38 x 25-cm/15 x 10-inch Swiss roll tin. Separate the eggs, placing the whites in a large bowl and the yolks in a separate bowl. Add the sugar to the yolks and whisk together until pale and thick. Place the baking powder and ground almonds in a bowl and mix together. Stir into the yolk mixture, taking care not to overmix. Carefully fold in the egg whites.

2 Spread in the tin and bake in the preheated oven for 15 minutes or until firm. Cover with a clean cloth and leave to cool in the tin. To make the filling, place the mascarpone cheese and cream in a bowl and stir together to give a spreading consistency. Place half the strawberries in a separate bowl and mash. Coarsely chop the remainder and reserve. Stir the mashed strawberries into the cream.

3 Place a sheet of greaseproof paper on the work surface and dust thickly with icing sugar. Turn the cake out on to the paper and peel off the lining paper. Spread the cream over the cake and scatter the chopped strawberries over. Roll up and serve the roulade, cut into slices, within 1–2 hours of assembling.

VARIATION
Raspberries will also complement the flavour of almonds, and make a good alternative to strawberries.

Chocolate Christmas Pudding

This is a wonderful alternative for anyone who dislikes a traditional Christmas pudding, but it can be enjoyed at any time.

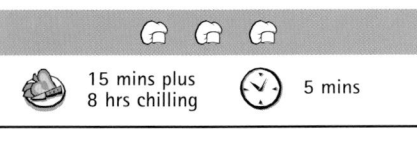

15 mins plus 8 hrs chilling

5 mins

SERVES 10

INGREDIENTS

115 g/4 oz mixed glacé fruits, chopped

55 g/2 oz raisins

grated rind of ½ orange

3 tbsp orange juice

3 tbsp single cream

350 g/12 oz plain chocolate, cut into pieces

115 g/4 oz cream cheese

115 g/4 oz amaretti biscuits, broken into rough pieces

TO SERVE

125 ml/4 fl oz whipping cream

2 tbsp Amaretto

25 g/1 oz grated plain chocolate

1 Grease a 900-ml/1½-pint pudding basin. Put the glacé fruits, raisins, orange rind and juice in a bowl and mix together. Put the single cream and chocolate into a saucepan and heat very gently until melted. Stir until smooth then stir in the fruit mixture. Leave to cool.

2 Put the cream cheese and a little of the chocolate mixture in a bowl and beat together until smooth, then stir in the remaining chocolate mixture. Stir in the amaretti biscuits. Pour into the prepared basin, cover and chill overnight.

3 To serve, turn the pudding out on to a chilled serving plate. Pour the whipping cream into a bowl and add the Amaretto. Whip lightly until slightly thickened. Pour some over the pudding and sprinkle grated chocolate on top before serving.

COOK'S TIP
Because this pudding is very rich it should be cut into thin slices. To make it easier to slice, dip a sharp knife into hot water.

Chocolate & Orange Slices

Contrasting flavours, textures and colours are combined to create this delectable masterpiece.

30–40 mins plus 3–4 hrs chilling

10 mins

SERVES 8

INGREDIENTS

2 tsp butter, for greasing

450 g/1 lb plain chocolate, broken into pieces

3 small, loose-skinned oranges, such as tangerines, mandarins or satsumas

4 egg yolks

200 ml/7 fl oz crème fraîche

2 tbsp raisins

300 ml/10 fl oz whipping cream, whipped, to serve

1 Lightly grease a 450-g/1-lb loaf tin and line it with clingfilm. Put 400 g/14 oz of the chocolate in a heatproof bowl set over a saucepan of gently simmering water. Stir over a low heat until melted. Remove from the heat and leave to cool slightly.

2 Meanwhile, peel the oranges, removing all traces of pith. Cut the zest into very thin strips. Beat the egg yolks into the chocolate, one at a time, then add most of the orange zest (reserving the rest for decoration), all the crème fraîche and raisins, and beat until thoroughly combined. Spoon the mixture into the prepared tin, cover with clingfilm and chill for 3–4 hours, until set.

3 While the chocolate mixture is chilling, put the remaining chocolate in a heatproof bowl set over a saucepan of gently simmering water until melted. Remove the saucepan from the heat and cool slightly. Meanwhile, segment the oranges. Dip each segment into the melted chocolate and spread out on a sheet of baking parchment for about 30 minutes, until set.

4 To serve, remove the tin from the refrigerator and turn out the chocolate mould. Remove the clingfilm and cut the mould into slices. Place a slice on individual serving plates and decorate with the chocolate-covered orange segments and the remaining orange zest. Serve immediately with the whipped cream.

Chocolate Rice Dessert

What could be more delicious than creamy, tender rice cooked in a rich chocolate sauce? This dessert is almost like a dense chocolate mousse.

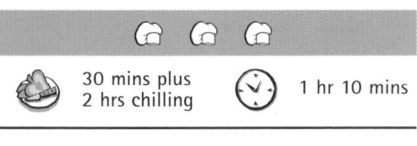

30 mins plus 2 hrs chilling

1 hr 10 mins

SERVES 8

INGREDIENTS

100 g/3½ oz long-grain white rice

pinch of salt

600 ml/1 pint milk

100 g/3½ oz caster sugar

200 g/7 oz Continental dark or plain chocolate, broken into pieces

55 g/2 oz butter, diced

1 tsp vanilla essence

2 tbsp brandy

175 ml/6 fl oz double cream

whipped cream, for piping (optional)

chocolate curls or leaves, to decorate (see page 9), optional

1 Bring a saucepan of water to the boil. Sprinkle in the rice and add the salt, then reduce the heat and simmer gently for 15–20 minutes or until the rice is just tender. Drain, rinse, then drain again.

2 Heat the milk and the sugar in a large heavy-based saucepan over a medium heat until the sugar dissolves, stirring frequently. Add the chocolate and butter and stir until they are melted and smooth.

3 Stir in the cooked rice and reduce the heat to low. Cover and simmer, stirring occasionally, for 30 minutes or until the milk is absorbed and the mixture thickened. Stir in the vanilla essence and brandy. Remove the mixture from the heat and leave it to cool to room temperature.

4 Using an electric whisk, whisk the cream until soft peaks form. Stir one heaped tablespoonful of the cream into the chocolate rice mixture to lighten it, then fold in the remaining cream.

5 Spoon the dessert into glass serving dishes, cover them and chill for about 2 hours. If wished, decorate with whipped cream and top with curls of chocolate or chocolate leaves.

VARIATION
To mould the dessert, soften 15 g/½ oz of gelatine in 4 tablespoons of cold water and heat gently until dissolved. Stir into the chocolate rice just before folding in the cream. Pour into a rinsed mould, allow to set, then unmould.

Rice Pudding with Lemon

Rice is transformed into a creamy, family-style dessert. At the height of summer, serve well chilled with a mixture of summer berries.

30 mins plus 1 hr chilling   25 mins

SERVES 4

INGREDIENTS

1 tsp cornflour

900 ml/1½ pints milk, plus an extra 2 tbsp

125 g/4½ oz short grain rice

about 2 tbsp sugar or 1 tbsp honey

finely grated rind of 1 large lemon

freshly squeezed lemon juice

55 g/2 oz shelled pistachio nuts

1 Place the cornflour in a small bowl and stir in 2 tablespoons of the milk, stirring until there are no lumps. Rinse a saucepan with cold water.

2 Place the remaining milk and the cornflour mixture in the rinsed saucepan over a medium–high heat and heat, stirring occasionally, until small bubbles form all around the edge. Do not allow to boil.

3 Stir in the rice, reduce the heat, and continue stirring for 20 minutes or until all but about 2 tablespoons of the excess liquid has evaporated and the rice is tender.

4 Remove from the heat and pour into a heatproof bowl. Stir in sugar to taste. Stir in the lemon rind, then stir in lemon juice to taste. Set the bowl aside to cool completely.

5 Tightly cover the top of the cool rice with clingfilm and chill in the refrigerator for at least 1 hour – the colder the rice is, the better it tastes with fresh fruit.

6 Meanwhile, finely chop the pistachio nuts. To serve, spoon the rice pudding into individual bowls and sprinkle with the chopped nuts.

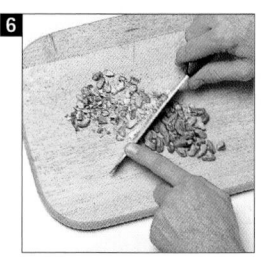

COOK'S TIP

It is important to rinse the saucepan in step 1 to prevent the milk from scorching on the sides or bottom.

Orange-Scented Rice

This delicious creamy dessert is flavoured with fresh oranges, orange-flavoured liqueur, and two kinds of ginger.

2 hrs   45 mins

SERVES 6

INGREDIENTS

140 g/5 oz round grain rice

225 ml/8 fl oz fresh orange juice

pinch of salt

500 ml/18 fl oz milk

1 vanilla pod, split

5-cm/2-inch piece of fresh root ginger, gently bruised

200 g/7 oz sugar

50 ml/2 fl oz double cream

4 tbsp orange liqueur

25 g/1 oz butter

4–6 seedless oranges

2 pieces stem ginger, thinly sliced, plus 2 tbsp ginger syrup from the jar

ground ginger, for dusting (optional)

1 Put the rice in a saucepan with the orange juice and salt. Bring to the boil, skimming off any foam. Reduce the heat and simmer for 10 minutes, stirring occasionally, until the juice is absorbed.

2 Gradually stir in the milk, add the vanilla pod and fresh root ginger and simmer for 30 minutes, stirring frequently, until the milk is absorbed and the rice is very tender. Remove from the heat. Take out the vanilla pod and fresh root ginger.

3 Stir in half the sugar, half the cream, the liqueur and butter. Continue stirring until the sugar is dissolved and the butter is melted. Set aside to cool, then stir in the remaining cream and pour into a bowl. Cover and set aside at room temperature.

4 Pare the zest from the oranges and set aside. Working over a bowl to catch the juices, remove the pith from all the oranges. Cut out the segments and drop into the bowl. Stir in the stem ginger and syrup. Chill in the refrigerator.

5 Cut the pared orange zest into thin strips and blanch for 1 minute. Drain and rinse. Bring 225 ml/8 fl oz water to the boil with the remaining sugar. Add the zest strips and simmer gently until the syrup is reduced by half. Set aside to cool.

6 Serve the rice with the chilled oranges and top with the strips of caramelized orange zest. Lightly dust with ground ginger, if liked.

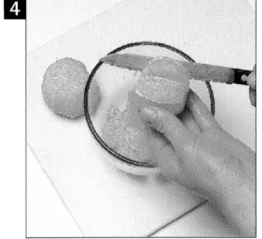

Portuguese Rice Pudding

This buttery, egg-rich rice pudding is quite irresistible, and makes a deliciously different dessert for a dinner party.

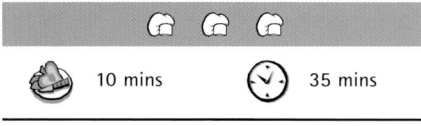

🍳 10 mins   🕐 35 mins

SERVES 6–8

INGREDIENTS

215 g/7½ oz valencia, risotto or pudding rice

pinch of salt

1 lemon

450 ml/16 fl oz milk

150 ml/5 fl oz single cream

1 cinnamon stick

6 tbsp butter

140 g/5 oz sugar (or to taste)

8 egg yolks

ground cinnamon, for dusting

TO DECORATE

fresh mint leaves

a few strawberries, hulled and sliced

1 Bring a saucepan of water to the boil. Sprinkle in the rice and salt and return to the boil, then reduce the heat and simmer for 15 minutes or until just tender. Drain the rice, rinse, then drain again.

2 Using a small sharp knife or vegetable peeler, try to peel the zest off the lemon in one piece, working round the fruit. Alternatively, peel it off in strips.

3 Place the milk and cream in a saucepan and bring to a simmer over a medium heat. Add the rice, cinnamon stick, butter and the lemon zest. Reduce the heat to low and simmer the mixture very gently for about 20 minutes, or until it becomes thick and creamy. Remove from the heat; remove and discard the cinnamon stick and the lemon zest. Stir in the sugar until it is dissolved.

4 In a large bowl, beat the egg yolks until well blended. Gradually beat in the rice mixture until smooth. Stir frequently, to prevent the eggs curdling, until slightly cooled, then pour into a bowl or 6–8 individual glasses. Dust with ground cinnamon, decorate with the mint and fruit and serve at room temperature.

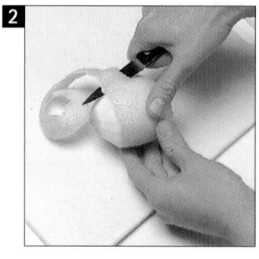

Flummery

This charming, traditional English dessert looks pretty and tastes delicious. It would be a good choice for a summer dinner party.

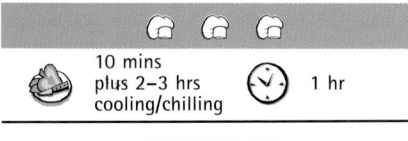

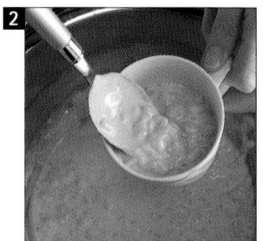

10 mins
plus 2–3 hrs
cooling/chilling

1 hr

SERVES 4

INGREDIENTS

115 g/4 oz short-grain rice

300 ml/10 fl oz milk

300 ml/10 fl oz double cream, plus extra, whipped for decoration

55 g/2 oz caster sugar

1 tbsp grated lemon rind

1 tsp ground cinnamon, plus extra for dusting

1 Wash the rice well and place in the top of a double boiler with the milk, cream, sugar, lemon rind and cinnamon. Set over a saucepan of gently simmering water, cover and cook, stirring occasionally, for 55 minutes, until most of the liquid has been absorbed and the rice is tender.

2 Remove the saucepan from the heat and transfer the rice mixture to a serving bowl or individual cups. Set aside to cool, then cover with clingfilm and chill in the refrigerator for 2–3 hours until set.

3 To serve, top the flummery with a swirl of whipped double cream, lightly dusted with ground cinnamon.

Kesari Kheer

This exotic dessert combines the flavour of cardamom, saffron and pistachio nuts. Decorate with silver leaf (varq).

40 mins   1 hr

SERVES 4–6

INGREDIENTS

2 tbsp clarified butter or pure ghee

70 g/2½ oz basmati rice, rinsed and well drained

1.5 litres/2½ pints milk

115 g/4 oz sugar (or to taste)

10–12 green cardamom pods, crushed to remove the black seeds (pods discarded)

85 g/3 oz sultanas or raisins

generous pinch saffron strands, about ½ tsp, soaked in 2–3 tbsp milk

70 g/2½ oz green pistachio nuts, lightly toasted

150 ml/5 fl oz double cream, whipped (optional)

ground cinnamon, for dusting

silver leaf (varq), to decorate (optional)

1 Melt the butter in a large, heavy-based saucepan over a medium heat. Pour in the rice and cook, stirring almost constantly, for about 6 minutes, until the rice grains are translucent and a deep golden brown.

2 Pour in the milk and bring to the boil over a high heat. Reduce the heat and simmer for about 30 minutes, stirring occasionally, until the milk has reduced by about half.

3 Add the sugar, cardamom seeds and sultanas and cook for about 20 minutes until reduced and thick. Stir in the saffron-milk mixture and simmer over a low heat until as very thick, stirring almost constantly. Remove from the heat and stir in half the pistachio nuts.

4 Place the saucepan in a large bowl of iced water and stir until cool. If using, stir in the cream, then spoon into a serving bowl and chill.

5 To serve, dust the top of the pudding with cinnamon. Sprinkle with the remaining pistachio nuts. If using, decorate with pieces of edible silver leaf.

COOK'S TIP
Edible silver leaf, called varq, is available in some Asian or Indian food stores or speciality stores.

Passion Fruit Rice

This creamy rice pudding, adapted for the microwave, is spiced with cardamom, cinnamon and bay leaf, and served with passion fruit.

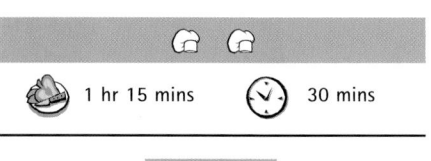

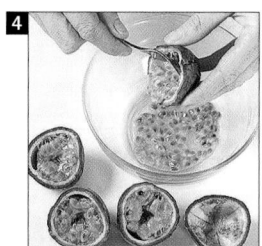

1 hr 15 mins   30 mins

SERVES 4

INGREDIENTS

175 g/6 oz jasmine fragrant rice

600 ml/1 pint milk

125 g/4½ oz caster sugar

6 cardamom pods, split open

1 dried bay leaf

1 cinnamon stick

150 ml/5 fl oz double cream, whipped

4 passion fruit

soft berry fruits, to decorate

1 Place the jasmine fragrant rice in a large bowl with the milk, caster sugar, cardamom pods, bay leaf and cinnamon stick. Cover and place in the microwave, cook on Medium power for 25–30 minutes, stirring occasionally. The rice should be just tender and have absorbed most of the milk. Add a little extra milk, if necessary.

2 Leave the rice to cool, still covered. Remove the bay leaf, cardamom husks and cinnamon stick.

3 Gently fold the cream into the cooled rice mixture.

4 Halve the passion fruits and scoop out the centres into a bowl.

5 Layer the rice with the passion fruit in 4 tall glasses, finishing with a layer of passion fruit. Leave to chill in the refrigerator for 30 minutes.

6 Decorate the passion fruit rice with berries and serve immediately.

COOK'S TIP
If you are unable to obtain passion fruit, you can use a purée of another fruit of your choice, such as kiwi fruit, raspberry or strawberry.

Tropical Fruit Rice Mould

A rice pudding with a twist. Light flakes of rice with a tang of pineapple and lime. You can serve it with any selection of your favourite fruits.

🕐 4 hrs 30 mins 🕑 25 mins

SERVES 8

INGREDIENTS

225 g/8 oz plus 2 tbsp short-grain or pudding rice, rinsed

900 ml/1½ pints skimmed milk

1 tbsp caster sugar

4 tbsp white rum with coconut or unsweetened pineapple juice

175 ml/6 fl oz low-fat natural yogurt

14 oz/400 g canned pineapple pieces in natural juice, drained and chopped

1 tsp grated lime rind

1 tbsp lime juice

1 sachet powdered gelatine dissolved in 3 tbsp very hot water

lime wedges, to decorate

mixed tropical fruits such as passion fruit, baby pineapple, papaya, mango, lime, starfruit, to serve

1 Place the rice and milk in a saucepan. Bring to the boil, then simmer gently, uncovered, for 20 minutes until the rice is soft and the milk is absorbed.

2 Stir the mixture occasionally and keep the heat low to prevent sticking. Transfer to a mixing bowl and leave to cool.

3 Stir the sugar, white rum with coconut or pineapple juice, yogurt, pineapple pieces, lime rind and juice into the rice, then fold in the gelatine mixture.

4 Rinse a 1.2-litre/2-pint non-stick ring mould with water and spoon in the rice mixture. Press down well and chill for 2 hours until firm.

5 To serve, loosen the rice from the mould with a small palette knife and invert on to a serving plate.

6 Decorate with lime wedges and fill the centre of the rice ring with assorted tropical fruits.

COOK'S TIP

Try serving this dessert with a light sauce made from 300 ml/10 fl oz tropical fruit or pineapple juice, heated gently, then thickened with 2 teaspoons arrowroot.

Riz à l'Impératrice

A sublime combination of rice, cherry-flavoured liqueur, dried fruit and cream that is certain to win compliments.

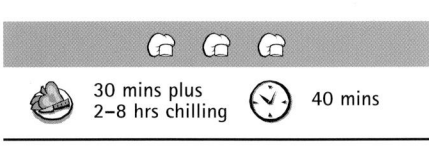

30 mins plus
2–8 hrs chilling

40 mins

SERVES 6–8

INGREDIENTS

125 ml/4 fl oz kirsch or other fruit liqueur

115 g/4 oz glacé or dried fruits, such as sour cherries, cranberries, blueberries, raisins or candied peel

115 g/4 oz long-grain white rice

pinch of salt

750 ml/1¼ pints milk

55 g/2 oz caster sugar

1 vanilla pod

1 sachet powdered gelatine

4 tbsp cold water

2 egg yolks, lightly beaten

225 ml/8 fl oz double cream, whipped until soft peaks form

4 tbsp apricot jam or preserve

glacé cherries, to decorate

fruit coulis, to serve (optional)

1 Split open the vanilla pod, scrape out the seeds and reserve. Combine 2–3 tablespoons of the kirsch with the glacé or dried fruits and set aside.

2 Bring a saucepan of water to the boil. Sprinkle in the rice and salt; simmer gently for 15 minutes or until the rice is just tender. Drain, rinse, and drain again.

3 Bring the milk and sugar to the boil in a large non-stick saucepan. Add the vanilla seeds and pod and stir in the rice. Cover, reduce the heat to low and simmer until the rice is very tender and the milk reduced by about a third. Remove from the heat and discard the vanilla pod.

4 Soften the gelatine in the water in a heatproof bowl, then heat gently over a saucepan of hot water until it is completely dissolved.

5 Add about 2 tablespoons of the hot rice to the egg yolks and whisk to blend, then beat into the rice with the dissolved gelatine, until the mixture thickens slightly. Pour into a large mixing bowl. Place the bowl in a roasting tin half-filled with iced water and stir until starting to set.

6 Fold in the soaked fruits and cream. Stir until it starts to set again, then pour into a rinsed 1.2–1.8-litre/2–3-pint mould. Smooth the surface, cover and chill for at least 2 hours or overnight.

7 Unmould the rice on to a serving plate. Heat the jam with the remaining kirsch and 2 tablespoons of water to make a smooth glaze. Brush over the top of the unmoulded rice. Decorate with the cherries and allow to stand for 15 minutes before serving with fruit coulis, if liked.

Chocolate Dairy Wraps

Light chocolate sponge is wrapped around a dairy cream filling. These individual cakes can be served for dessert, if desired.

40 mins

6–8 mins

SERVES 6

INGREDIENTS

2 eggs

4 tbsp caster sugar

6 tbsp plain flour

1½ tbsp cocoa powder

4 tbsp apricot jam

150 ml/5 fl oz double cream, whipped

icing sugar, for dusting

1 Preheat the oven to 220°C/425°F/Gas Mark 7. Line 2 baking trays with baking parchment. Whisk the eggs and sugar together until the mixture is very light and fluffy and the whisk leaves a trail when lifted.

2 Sift together the flour and cocoa powder. Using a metal spoon or a spatula, gently fold it into the eggs and sugar in a figure-of-eight movement.

3 Drop rounded tablespoonfuls of the mixture on to the lined baking trays and spread them into oval shapes, allowing room for the little sponge cakes to spread during cooking.

VARIATIONS

Fold 4 teaspoons crème de menthe or 55 g/2 oz melted chocolate into the cream for fabulous alternatives to plain cream.

4 Bake in the preheated oven for about 6–8 minutes, or until springy to the touch. Leave to cool on the baking trays.

5 When cold, slide the baking parchment with the cakes on to a damp tea towel and leave until cold. Then carefully remove the cakes from the dampened baking parchment. Spread the flat side of the cakes with apricot jam, then spoon or pipe the whipped cream down the centre of each one.

6 Fold the cakes in half and place them on a serving plate. Dust with a little icing sugar and serve.

Fruit & Fibre Layers

A good, hearty dessert, guaranteed to fill you up. Use your own favourite dried fruits in the compôte.

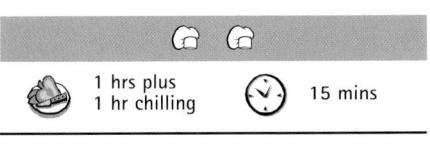

1 hrs plus
1 hr chilling

15 mins

SERVES 4

INGREDIENTS

115 g/4 oz ready-to-eat dried apricots

115 g/4 oz ready-to-eat dried prunes

115 g/4 oz ready-to-eat dried peaches

55 g/2 oz dried apple

25 g/1 oz dried cherries

450 ml/16 fl oz unsweetened apple juice

6 cardamom pods

6 cloves

1 cinnamon stick, broken

300 ml/10 fl oz low-fat natural yogurt

115 g/4 oz crunchy oat cereal

apricot slices, to decorate

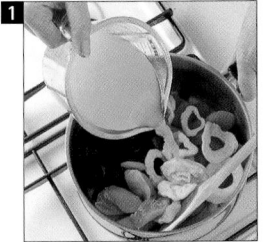

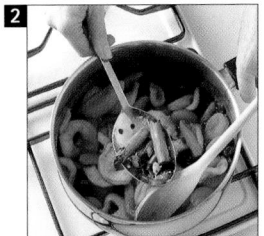

1 Place the apricots, prunes, peaches, apples and cherries in a saucepan and pour in the apple juice. Add the cardamom pods, cloves and cinnamon stick, bring to the boil and simmer for 10–15 minutes until the fruits are plump and tender.

2 Remove and discard the spices from the fruits. Remove the saucepan from the heat and set aside to cool completely, then transfer the mixture to a bowl and chill in the refrigerator for 1 hour.

3 Spoon the compôte into 4 dessert glasses, layering it alternately with yogurt and oat cereal, finishing with the oat cereal on top.

4 Decorate each dessert with slices of apricot and serve immediately.

COOK'S TIP
Check the ingredients labels of dried fruit because several types have added sugar or are rolled in sugar and this will affect the sweetness of the dish that you use them in.

Raspberry Shortcake

For this lovely summery dessert, two crisp rounds of shortbread are sandwiched together with fresh raspberries and lightly whipped cream.

40 mins   15 mins

SERVES 8

INGREDIENTS

100 g/3½ oz butter, cut into cubes, plus extra for greasing

175 g/6 oz self-raising flour

85 g/3 oz caster sugar

1 egg yolk

1 tbsp rosewater

plain flour, for dusting

600 ml/1 pint whipping cream, lightly whipped

225 g/8 oz raspberries, plus a few extra to decorate

TO DECORATE

icing sugar

1 Preheat the oven to 190°C/375°F/Gas Mark 5. Lightly grease 2 baking sheets with a little butter.

2 To make the shortcake, sift the self-raising flour into a bowl. Add the butter and rub it into the flour with your fingertips until the mixture resembles fine breadcrumbs.

3 Stir the sugar, egg yolk and rosewater into the mixture and bring together with your fingers to form a soft dough. Divide the dough in half.

4 Roll out each piece of dough to a 20-cm/8-inch round on a lightly floured work surface. Carefully lift each of them with the rolling pin on to the prepared baking sheets. Gently crimp the edges of the dough with your finger.

5 Bake in the preheated oven for 15 minutes until lightly golden. Transfer the shortcakes to a wire rack and set aside to cool completely.

6 Mix the whipped cream with the raspberries and spoon the mixture on top of 1 of the shortcakes, spreading it out evenly. Top with the other shortcake round, dust with a little icing sugar and decorate with the extra raspberries.

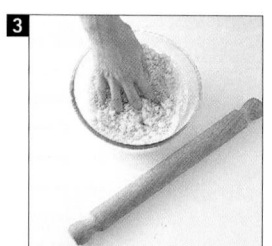

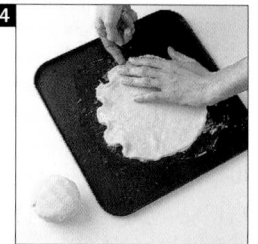

COOK'S TIP

The shortcake can be made a few days in advance and stored in an airtight container until required.

Cherry & Chocolate Meringue

A luscious, sticky chocolate meringue base smothered in cream and sticky cherries.

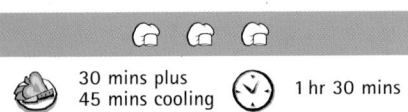

🍰 30 mins plus
45 mins cooling

🕐 1 hr 30 mins

SERVES 4

INGREDIENTS

4 large egg whites

200 g/7 oz caster sugar

1 tsp cornflour, sifted

1 tsp white wine vinegar

1 tbsp cocoa powder

140 g/5 oz plain chocolate, chopped

TOPPING

400 ml/14 fl oz double cream

25 g/1 oz icing sugar, sifted

4 tbsp maple syrup

4 tbsp unsalted butter

450 g/1 lb black cherries

plain chocolate caraque (see page 9),
   to decorate

1 Preheat the oven to 140°C/275°F/ Gas Mark 1. Line a baking sheet with baking parchment.

2 Whisk the egg whites until stiff. Gradually add the sugar, and whisk until stiff and shiny. Fold in the cornflour, vinegar, cocoa and chocolate. Spread the meringue on to the baking sheet to form a 24-cm/9¹⁄₂-inch disc. Bake for 1¹⁄₂ hours.

3 Turn off the oven and leave the meringue in the oven for 45 minutes.

4 Whisk the cream and icing sugar until stiff, then chill. Remove the stones from most of the cherries, reserving a few whole. Melt the maple syrup with the butter in a frying pan and stir in the stoned cherries to coat, then set aside to cool.

5 Make the chocolate caraque and set aside until you are ready to assemble the meringue. Peel off the paper from the meringue when cold.

6 To serve, put the meringue on a dish. Spoon the cream into the centre, pile on the cherries, using the whole ones around the edge. Top with the caraque.

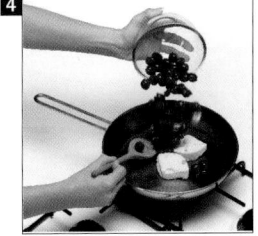

Pavlova

This fruit meringue was created for Anna Pavlova, and it looks very impressive. Use fruits of your choice to make a colourful display.

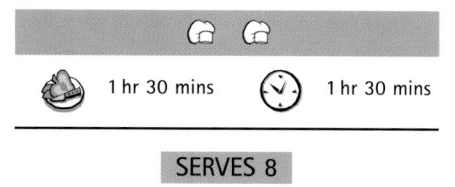

1 hr 30 mins   1 hr 30 mins

SERVES 8

INGREDIENTS

6 egg whites

½ tsp cream of tartar

225 g/8 oz caster sugar

1 tsp vanilla essence

300 ml/10 fl oz whipping cream

400 g/14 oz strawberries, hulled and halved

3 tbsp orange liqueur

fruit of your choice, to decorate

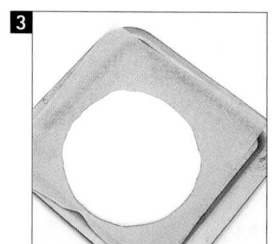
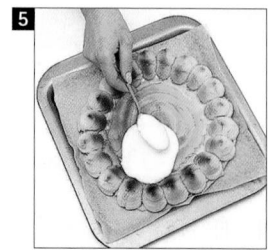

1 Preheat the oven to 140°C/275°F/Gas Mark 1 for a chewy meringue, or 110°C/225°F/Gas Mark ¼ for a drier meringue. Line a baking sheet with baking parchment and mark out a circle to fit your serving plate. The recipe makes enough meringue for a 30-cm/12-inch circle.

2 Whisk the egg whites and cream of tartar together until stiff. Gradually beat in the caster sugar and vanilla essence. Whisk well until glossy and stiff.

3 Either spoon or pipe the meringue mixture into the marked circle, in an even layer, slightly raised at the edges.

COOK'S TIP

If you like a dry meringue, you can also leave it in the oven on the lowest setting overnight. However, do not use this technique with a gas oven – but in an electric oven or solid fuel cooker it would be fine.

4 Baking the meringue depends on your preference. If you like a soft chewy meringue, bake in the preheated oven for about 1½ hours, until dry but slightly soft in the centre, or for 3 hours, until dry.

5 Before serving, whip the cream to a piping consistency and either spoon or pipe on to the meringue base, leaving a border of meringue all around the edge.

6 Stir the strawberries and liqueur together and spoon on to the cream. Decorate with fruit of your choice.

Brown Sugar Pavlovas

This simple combination of fudgy meringue topped with fromage frais and raspberries is the perfect finale to any meal.

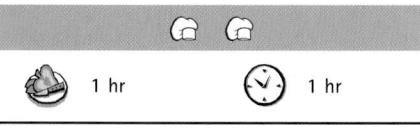
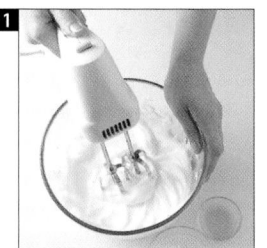

1 hr   1 hr

SERVES 4

INGREDIENTS

2 large egg whites

1 tsp cornflour

1 tsp raspberry vinegar

100 g/3½ oz light soft brown sugar, crushed free of lumps

2 tbsp redcurrant jelly

2 tbsp unsweetened orange juice

150 ml/5 fl oz low-fat fromage frais

175 g/6 oz raspberries, thawed if frozen

rose-scented geranium leaves, to decorate (optional)

1 Preheat the oven to 150°C/300°F/Gas Mark 2. Line a large baking tray with baking parchment. Whisk the egg whites until very stiff and dry. Gently fold in the cornflour and vinegar.

2 Gradually whisk in the sugar, a spoonful at a time, until the mixture is thick and glossy.

3 Divide the mixture into 4 and spoon on to the prepared baking tray, spaced well apart. Smooth each heap into a circle, about 10 cm/4 inches in diameter, and bake in the preheated oven for 40–45 minutes until crisp and light brown. Leave to cool on the baking tray.

4 Place the redcurrant jelly and orange juice in a small saucepan and heat, stirring, until melted. Leave to cool for 10 minutes.

5 Using a spatula, carefully remove each pavlova from the baking parchment and transfer to a serving plate. Top with the fromage frais and the raspberries. Glaze the fruit with the melted redcurrant and orange glaze and decorate with the rose-scented geranium leaves (if using).

COOK'S TIP
Make a large pavlova by forming the meringue into a circle, measuring 18 cm/7 inches across, on a lined baking tray, and bake it for 1 hour.

Strawberry Meringues

The combination of aromatic strawberries and rosewater with crisp caramelized sugar meringues makes this a truly irresistible dessert.

1 hr | 3 hrs 30 mins

SERVES 6

INGREDIENTS

3 egg whites

pinch of salt

175 g/6 oz soft light brown sugar, crushed

225 g/8 oz strawberries, hulled

2 tsp rosewater

150 ml/5 fl oz low-fat natural fromage frais

extra strawberries, to serve (optional)

TO DECORATE

rose petals

rose-scented geranium leaves

1 Preheat the oven to 120°C/250°F/Gas Mark ½. In a large greasefree bowl, whisk the egg whites with the salt until very stiff and dry. Gradually whisk in the sugar, a spoonful at a time, until the mixture is stiff again.

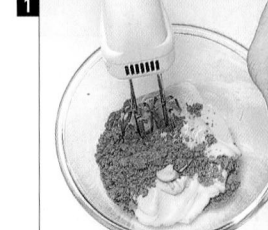

2 Line a baking sheet with baking parchment and drop 12 tablespoonfuls of the meringue mixture on to it. Bake in the preheated oven for 3–3½ hours, until completely dried out and crisp. Set aside to cool.

3 Reserve 55 g/2 oz of the strawberries. Place the remaining strawberries in a blender or food processor and blend for a few seconds until smooth.

4 Alternatively, mash the strawberries with a fork and press through a sieve to form a purée. Stir in the rosewater. Chill until required.

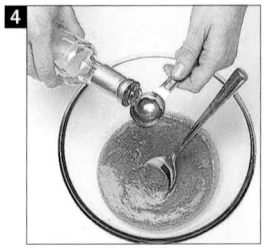

5 Slice the reserved strawberries lengthways. Sandwich the meringues together with ricotta and strawberries.

6 To serve, spoon the strawberry rose purée on to 6 serving plates and top with a meringue.

7 Decorate with rose petals and rose-scented geranium leaves, and serve with extra strawberries (if using).

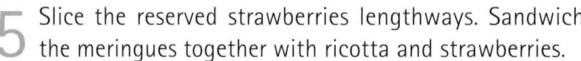

Raspberry Meringue

This meringue makes an easy yet elegant dessert, perfect for a celebration dinner.

15 mins plus
2 hrs 15 mins
cooling/chilling

30 mins

SERVES 4

INGREDIENTS

6 egg whites

250 g/9 oz caster sugar

125 g/4½ oz ground almonds

butter, for greasing

900 ml/1½ pints double cream

5 tbsp icing sugar

600 g/1 lb 5 oz raspberries

TO DECORATE

whole raspberries

fresh mint leaves

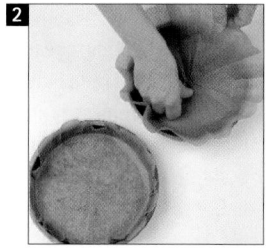

1 Preheat the oven to 150°C/300°F/Gas Mark 2. Put the egg whites into a bowl and whisk until stiff peaks form. Gradually whisk in the caster sugar, then fold in the ground almonds.

2 Grease 2 x 20-cm/8-inch sandwich tins with butter and line with baking parchment. Divide the egg mixture among the 2 tins and smooth the surfaces. Transfer to the preheated oven and bake for 30 minutes. Remove from the oven and leave to cool on a wire rack.

3 Put the cream into a bowl, add the icing sugar and whip to form soft peaks. Put one of the meringues on a cake stand or serving plate and spread over a generous layer of cream. Cover with a generous layer of raspberries and then top with the other meringue. Spread the remaining cream evenly over the top of the cake, and chill in the refrigerator for at least 2 hours.

4 Remove from the refrigerator, decorate with the remaining raspberries and fresh mint leaves and serve.

Satsuma & Pecan Pavlova

Make this spectacular dessert for the perfect way to round off a special occasion. You can make the meringue base well in advance.

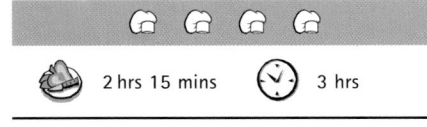

2 hrs 15 mins   3 hrs

SERVES 8

INGREDIENTS

4 egg whites

225 g/8 oz light brown sugar

300 ml/10 fl oz double or whipping cream

55 g/2 oz pecan nuts

4 satsumas, peeled

1 passion fruit or pomegranate

1 Preheat the oven to 140°C/275°F/Gas Mark 1. Line 2 baking sheets with baking parchment. Draw a 23-cm/9-inch circle on one of them.

2 Whisk the egg whites in a large greasefree bowl until stiff. Add the sugar gradually, continuing to beat until the mixture is very glossy.

3 Pipe or spoon a layer of meringue mixture on to the circle marked on the baking parchment; then pipe large rosettes or place spoonfuls on top of the meringue's outer edge. Pipe any remaining meringue mixture in tiny rosettes on the second baking sheet.

4 Bake in the preheated oven for 2–3 hours, making sure that the oven is well-ventilated by using a folded tea towel to keep the door slightly open. Remove from the oven and leave to cool completely. When cold, carefully peel off the baking parchment.

5 Whip the double or whipping cream in a large chilled bowl until thick. Spoon about one-third into a piping bag, fitted with a star nozzle. Reserve a few pecan nuts and 1 satsuma for decoration. Chop the remaining nuts and fruit and fold into the remaining cream.

6 Pile on top of the meringue base and decorate with the tiny meringue rosettes, piped cream, segments of satsuma and pecan nuts. Scoop out the seeds from the passion fruit or pomegranate with a teaspoon and sprinkle them on top.

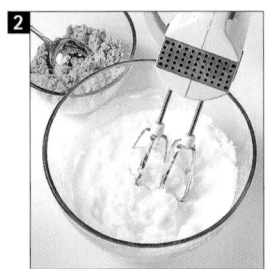

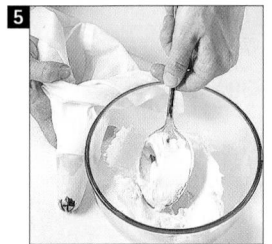

Black Forest Trifle

Try all the delightful flavours of a Black Forest gâteau in this new guise – the results are stunning.

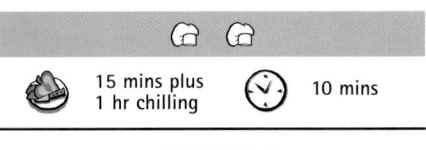

🍞 🍞

🍰 15 mins plus 1 hr chilling   🕐 10 mins

SERVES 6

INGREDIENTS

6 thin slices chocolate buttercream roll

800 g/1 lb 12 oz canned black cherries

2 tbsp kirsch

1 tbsp cornflour

2 tbsp caster sugar

425 ml/15 fl oz milk

3 egg yolks

1 egg

75 g/2¾ oz plain chocolate

300 ml/10 fl oz double cream, whipped

TO DECORATE

chocolate caraque (see page 9)

maraschino cherries (optional)

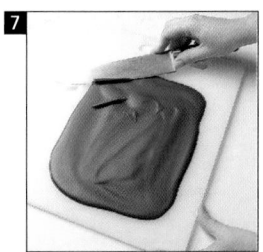

1 Place the slices of chocolate roll in the bottom of a glass serving bowl.

2 Drain the black cherries, reserving 6 tablespoons of the juice. Place the cherries and the reserved juice on top of the cake. Sprinkle with the kirsch.

3 In a heatproof bowl, mix the cornflour and caster sugar. Stir in enough milk to mix to a smooth paste. Beat in the egg yolks and the whole egg.

4 Heat the remaining milk in a small saucepan until almost boiling, then gradually pour it on to the egg mixture, whisking well until it is combined.

5 Set the bowl over a saucepan of hot water and stir over a low heat until the custard thickens. Add the chocolate and stir until melted.

6 Pour the chocolate custard over the cherries and cool. When cold, spread the cream over the custard, swirling with the back of a spoon. Chill before decorating.

7 Decorate with chocolate caraque and whole maraschino cherries (if using) before serving.

Chocolate Trifle

This is a wonderful dessert for a party and makes a change from a conventional trifle.

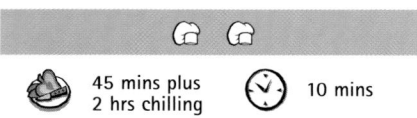

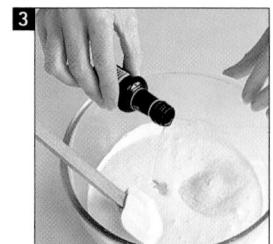

45 mins plus 2 hrs chilling

10 mins

SERVES 8

INGREDIENTS

280 g/10 oz ready-made chocolate loaf cake

3–4 tbsp seedless raspberry jam

4 tbsp Amaretto

250 g/9 oz packet frozen mixed red fruit, thawed

CHOCOLATE CUSTARD

6 egg yolks

55 g/2 oz golden caster sugar

1 tbsp cornflour

500 ml/18 fl oz milk

55 g/2 oz plain chocolate, broken into pieces

TOPPING

225 ml/8 fl oz double cream

1 tbsp golden caster sugar

½ tsp vanilla essence

ready-made chocolate truffles, to decorate

fresh fruit, such as cherries and strawberries

COOK'S TIP

Frozen packs of fruit are available in most supermarkets. Sometimes they are described as 'summer fruits' or 'fruits of the forest'. Try to find a variety that includes cherries.

1 Cut the cake into slices and make 'sandwiches' with the raspberry jam. Cut the 'sandwiches' into cubes and place in a large glass serving bowl. Sprinkle with Amaretto. Spread the fruit over the cake.

2 To make the custard, put the egg yolks and sugar in a bowl and whisk until thick and pale. Stir in the cornflour. Put the milk in a saucepan and heat until almost boiling. Pour on to the yolk mixture, stirring. Return the mixture to the saucepan and bring just to the boil, stirring constantly until it thickens. Remove from the heat and leave to cool slightly. Put the chocolate in a bowl set over a saucepan of simmering water until melted, then add to the custard. Pour over the cake and fruit. Cool, cover and chill for 2 hours to set.

3 Put the cream in a bowl and whip until soft peaks form. Beat in the sugar and vanilla. Spoon over the trifle. Decorate with truffles and chill until ready to serve.

Chocolate & Orange Trifle

The slight tartness of satsumas beautifully counterbalances the richness of this trifle, but you could use clementines if preferred.

25 mins plus 1 hr 30 mins chilling

15 mins

SERVES 6

I N G R E D I E N T S

4 trifle sponges

2 large chocolate coconut macaroons, crumbled

4 tbsp sweet sherry

8 satsumas

200 g/7 oz plain chocolate, broken into pieces

2 egg yolks

2 tbsp caster sugar

2 tbsp cornflour

200 ml/7 fl oz milk

250 g/9 oz mascarpone cheese

225 ml/8 fl oz heavy cream

TO DECORATE

marbled chocolate shapes (see page 821)

10–12 satsuma segments

1 Break up the trifle sponges and place in a large glass serving dish. Sprinkle the crumbled macaroons on top, then sprinkle with the sherry. Squeeze the juice from 2 of the satsumas and sprinkle it over the crumbled macaroons. Peel and segment the remaining satsumas and arrange them in the dish.

2 Put the chocolate in a heatproof bowl set over a saucepan of gently simmering water. Stir over a low heat until melted and smooth. Remove from the heat and leave to cool completely.

3 In a separate bowl, mix together the egg yolks, sugar and cornflour to make a smooth paste. Bring the milk to just

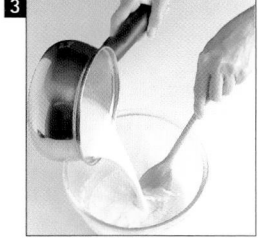

below boiling point in a small saucepan. Remove from the heat and pour it into the egg yolk mixture, stirring constantly. Return the custard to a clean saucepan and cook over low heat, stirring constantly until thickened and smooth. Return to the bowl, then stir in the cooled melted chocolate. Stir in the mascarpone cheese until thoroughly combined. Spread the

chocolate custard evenly over the satsuma segments and transfer to the refrigerator to chill for 1 hour until set.

4 Whip the cream until thick, then spread it over the top of the trifle, swirling it with the back of a spoon. Decorate with marbled chocolate shapes and satsuma segments.

Almond Trifles

Amaretti biscuits made with ground almonds have a high fat content.
Use biscuits made from apricot kernels for a lower fat content.

 15 mins plus
1 hr standing/
cooling

 0 mins

SERVES 4

INGREDIENTS

8 amaretti biscuits

4 tbsp brandy or Amaretto

225 g/8 oz raspberries

300 ml/10 fl oz low-fat custard

300 ml/10 fl oz low-fat natural
fromage frais

1 tsp almond essence

2 tbsp flaked almonds, toasted

1 tsp cocoa powder

1 Place the biscuits in a mixing bowl
and, using the end of a rolling pin,
carefully crush them into small pieces.

2 Divide the crushed biscuits between
4 serving glasses. Sprinkle over the
brandy or Amaretto and set aside for about
30 minutes to soften.

3 Top with a layer of raspberries and
spoon over enough custard just to
cover the fruit.

4 Combine the fromage frais with the
almond essence and spoon over the
custard, smoothing the surface. Chill in
the refrigerator for about 30 minutes.

5 Sprinkle with the toasted almonds
and dust with cocoa powder.
Decorate the trifles with extra fruit, if
liked, and serve immediately.

VARIATION

Try this trifle with assorted summer
fruits. If they are a frozen mix, use
them frozen so that as they thaw
the juices soak into the biscuit base
– it will taste delicious.

Sherry Trifle

This is a classic, timeless and elegant dessert which is always a dinner-party favourite.

15 mins plus 4 hrs cooling

0 mins

SERVES 4

INGREDIENTS

FRUIT LAYER

6 trifle sponges

2 tbsp strawberry jam

6 large strawberries, hulled and sliced

2 bananas, peeled and sliced

400 g/14 oz canned sliced peaches, drained

6 tbsp sherry

CUSTARD LAYER

250 ml/9 fl oz double cream

1 tsp vanilla essence

3 egg yolks

4 tbsp caster sugar

TOPPING

300 ml/10 fl oz double cream

2 tbsp caster sugar

chopped mixed nuts, to decorate

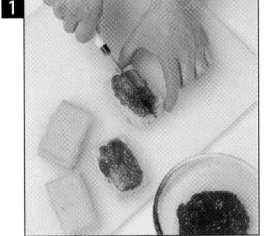
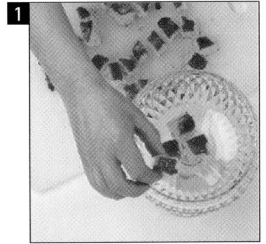
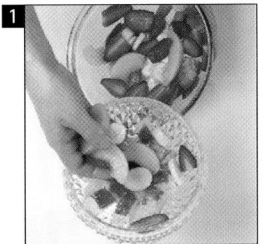

1 To make the fruit layer, spread the trifle sponges with jam and cut into bite-size pieces. Arrange them in the bottom of a large glass serving bowl or 4 serving glasses, and scatter over the strawberries, bananas and peaches. Pour over the sherry and set aside.

2 To make the custard, put the cream and vanilla into a saucepan and bring almost to the boil over a low heat. Meanwhile, put the egg yolks and sugar into a bowl and whisk together well. Remove the cream from the heat and gradually stir into the egg mixture. Return the mixture to the saucepan and warm over a low heat, stirring, until thickened. Remove the custard from the heat and leave to cool for at least 20 minutes, then pour it evenly over the fruit layer. Cover with clingfilm and chill for 2½ hours.

3 Remove the trifle from the refrigerator. Whip together the cream and sugar, then spread it evenly over the custard layer. Scatter over the chopped mixed nuts, then cover again with clingfilm and chill for a further 1½ hours. Serve chilled.

Festive Trifle

It is quite unusual to use vodka in desserts, but it works well, especially with raspberries and cherries. Substitute sherry, if you prefer.

15 mins plus
6 hrs soaking/
chilling

2–3 mins

SERVES 4

INGREDIENTS

FRUIT LAYER

100 g/3½ oz trifle sponges

225 g/8 oz raspberry jam

3–4 tbsp vodka or sherry

150 g/5½ oz frozen raspberries, thawed

400 g/14 oz mixed fruit, frozen or canned

CUSTARD LAYER

6 egg yolks

55 g/2 oz caster sugar

500 ml/17 fl oz milk

1 tsp vanilla essence

TOPPING

280 g/10 oz mascarpone cheese

1–2 tbsp caster sugar

toasted mixed nuts, chopped, to decorate

1 Spread the trifle sponges with jam, cut them into bite-size cubes and arrange in the bottom of a large glass serving bowl. Pour over the vodka or sherry and let stand for 30 minutes.

2 Combine the raspberries and other fruits and place on the sponges. Cover with clingfilm and chill for 30 minutes.

3 To make the custard, put the egg yolks and sugar into a bowl and whisk together. Pour the milk into a saucepan and warm over a low heat. Remove from the heat, stir into the egg mixture, then return it all to the saucepan and stir constantly over a low heat until thickened. Do not boil. Remove from the heat, pour into a bowl and stir in the vanilla. Cool for 1 hour. Spread the custard over the trifle, cover with clingfilm and chill for 2 hours.

4 For the topping, turn the mascarpone into a bowl and beat in sugar to taste. Spread over the trifle, then scatter over the nuts. Cover with clingfilm and chill for 2 hours before serving.

Sticky Sesame Bananas

These tasty morsels are a real treat. Pieces of banana are dipped in caramel and then sprinkled with sesame seeds.

10 mins plus 10 mins cooling   **20 mins**

SERVES 4

INGREDIENTS

4 ripe medium bananas

3 tbsp lemon juice

115 g/4 oz caster sugar

4 tbsp cold water

2 tbsp sesame seeds

150 ml/5 fl oz low-fat natural fromage frais

1 tbsp icing sugar

1 tsp vanilla essence

TO DECORATE

shredded lemon zest

shredded lime zest

1 Peel the bananas and cut into 5-cm/2-inch pieces. Place the banana pieces in a bowl, spoon over the lemon juice and stir well to coat – this will help prevent the bananas discolouring.

2 Place the sugar and water in a small saucepan and heat gently, stirring constantly, until the sugar dissolves. Bring to the boil and cook for 5–6 minutes, until the mixture turns golden brown.

3 Meanwhile, drain the bananas and blot with kitchen paper to dry. Line a baking sheet or cutting board with baking parchment and arrange the bananas, spaced well apart, on top.

4 When the caramel is ready, drizzle it over the bananas, working quickly because the caramel sets almost instantly. Sprinkle the sesame seeds over the caramelized bananas and set aside to cool for 10 minutes.

5 Combine the yogurt, icing sugar and vanilla essence.

6 Peel the bananas away from the baking parchment and arrange on serving plates.

7 Serve the fromage frais as a dip, decorated with the shredded lemon and lime zest.

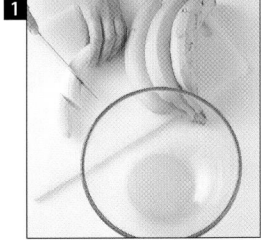

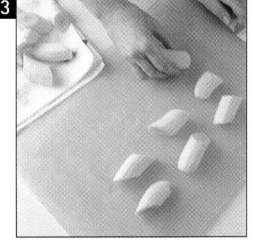

Caramelized Oranges

The secret of these oranges is to allow them to marinate in the syrup for at least 3 hours, and preferably up to 2 days, so the flavours amalgamate.

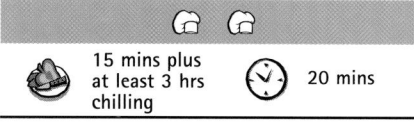

15 mins plus at least 3 hrs chilling

20 mins

SERVES 6

INGREDIENTS

6 large oranges

225 g/8 oz granulated sugar

250 ml/9 fl oz water

6 cloves (optional)

2–4 tbsp orange liqueur

1 Using a citrus zester or potato peeler, pare the zest from 2 of the oranges in narrow strips without any white pith attached. If using a potato peeler, cut the peel into very thin julienne strips.

2 Put the strips into a small saucepan and barely cover with water. Bring to the boil and simmer for 5 minutes. Drain the strips and reserve the water.

3 Cut away all the peel and white pith from the remaining oranges using a very sharp knife. Then cut each one horizontally into 4 slices. Reassemble the oranges and hold in place with wooden cocktail sticks. Stand in a heatproof dish.

4 Put the sugar and water into a heavy-based saucepan with the cloves (if using). Bring to the boil and simmer gently until the sugar has dissolved, then boil hard without stirring until the syrup thickens and starts to colour. Continue to cook until a light golden brown, then quickly remove from the heat and carefully pour in the reserved orange zest liquid.

5 Place over a gentle heat until the caramel has fully dissolved again, then remove from the heat and add the liqueur. Pour over the oranges.

6 Sprinkle the orange strips over the oranges, cover with clingfilm, and leave until cold. Chill for at least 3 hours and preferably for 24–48 hours before serving. If time allows, spoon the syrup over the oranges several times while they are marinating. Discard the cocktail sticks before serving.

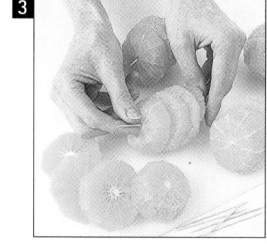

Aztec Oranges

Simplicity itself, this refreshing orange dessert is hard to beat and is the perfect follow-up to a hearty, spiced main course.

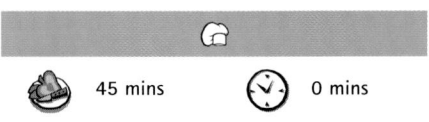

45 mins   0 mins

SERVES 4–6

INGREDIENTS

6 oranges

1 lime

2 tbsp tequila

2 tbsp orange liqueur

soft dark brown sugar, to taste

fine lime zest strips, to decorate
   (see Cook's Tip)

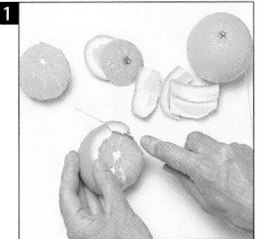
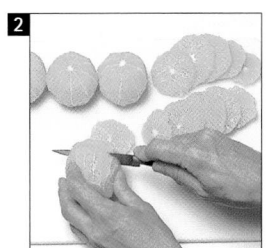

1 Using a sharp knife, cut a slice off the top and bottom of the oranges, then remove the peel and pith, cutting downward and taking care to retain the shape of the oranges.

2 Holding the oranges on their side, cut them horizontally into slices.

3 Place the oranges in a bowl. Cut the lime in half and squeeze over the oranges. Sprinkle with the tequila and liqueur, then sprinkle with sugar to taste.

4 Cover with clingfilm and chill in the refrigerator until ready to serve, then transfer to a serving dish and decorate with lime strips.

COOK'S TIP
To make the decoration, finely pare the zest from a lime using a vegetable peeler, then cut into thin strips. Blanch in boiling water for 2 minutes. Drain and rinse under cold running water. Drain again and pat dry with kitchen paper.

Minted Pears

Choose firm but ripe pears that will hold their shape when poached and leave the stalk intact after peeling for an attractive appearance.

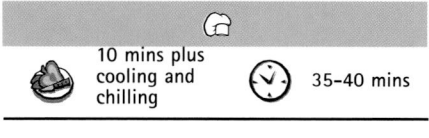

10 mins plus cooling and chilling

35–40 mins

SERVES 4

INGREDIENTS

4 large pears, peeled

4 tbsp caster sugar

4 tbsp honey

2 tbsp green crème de menthe

fresh mint sprigs, to decorate

1 Stand the pears upright in a heavy-based saucepan and add enough water to cover. Bring to the boil, reduce the heat, cover and simmer for 25–30 minutes, until tender. Pour away half the water and add the sugar to the saucepan. Simmer for a further 10 minutes.

2 Transfer the pears to a bowl using a slotted spoon. Measure 150 ml/ 5 fl oz of the cooking water. Stir in the honey and crème de menthe. Pour the syrup over the pears.

3 Set the pears aside to cool, then cover with clingfilm and chill in the refrigerator for 1–2 hours. Transfer the pears to individual serving bowls, spoon over the mint syrup and serve, decorated with fresh mint sprigs.

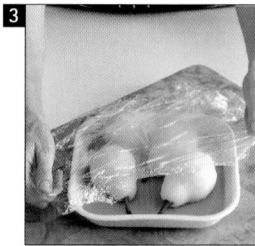

Mangoes in Syrup

A simple, fresh-tasting fruit dessert to round off a rich meal perfectly.
Serve the mango lightly chilled.

15 mins

5 mins

SERVES 4

INGREDIENTS

2 large ripe mangoes

1 lime

1 lemongrass stem, chopped

3 tbsp caster sugar

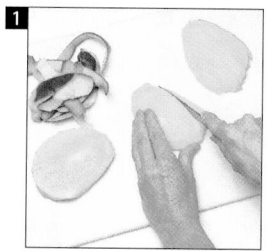

1 Peel the mangoes, then cut away the flesh from either side of the large stones. Slice the flesh into long, thin slices and arrange them in a large, chilled serving dish.

2 Remove a few shreds of the zest from the lime and reserve for decoration, then cut the lime in half and squeeze out the juice.

3 Place the lime juice in a small saucepan with the lemongrass and sugar. Heat gently, without boiling, until the sugar is completely dissolved. Remove from the heat and set aside to cool completely.

4 Strain the cooled syrup into a jug and pour evenly over the mango slices. Sprinkle with the lime zest strips, cover and chill before serving.

COOK'S TIP
To serve this dessert on a hot day, particularly if it is to stand for a while, place the dish on a bed of crushed ice to keep the fruit and syrup chilled.

Poached Peaches

Soaking the peaches overnight is an old Turkish tip to prevent the fruit becoming too soft and falling apart while they are being poached.

15 mins plus
24 hrs chilling

10 mins

SERVES 4–6

INGREDIENTS

8–12 ripe peaches

1 large lime

475 ml/16 fl oz fruity dry white wine

1 tbsp black peppercorns, lightly crushed

7.5-cm/3-inch cinnamon stick, halved

finely pared zest of 1 unwaxed lemon

100 g/3½ oz caster sugar

fresh mint sprigs, to decorate

AMARETTO-MASCARPONE CREAM

2 tbsp Amaretto

250 g/9 oz mascarpone cheese

1 Fill a large bowl with iced water. Bring a large saucepan of water to the boil. Add the peaches and cook for 1 minute. Using a slotted spoon, immediately transfer the peaches to the iced water to stop the cooking process.

2 Squeeze the juice from the lime into a bowl of water. Peel the peaches, then quarter each, and remove the stone. Drop the fruit into the lime water as it is prepared. Cover and leave to chill in the refrigerator for 24 hours.

3 Meanwhile, make the Amaretto-mascarpone cream. Stir the Amaretto into the mascarpone cheese until thoroughly incorporated, cover and chill.

4 Place the wine, peppercorns, cinnamon, lemon zest and sugar in a saucepan over a medium-high heat and stir until the sugar dissolves.

5 Boil the syrup for 2 minutes then reduce to a simmer. Remove the peaches from the refrigerator, and add them to the syrup. Poach for 2 minutes or until they are tender – they should not be falling apart.

6 Using a slotted spoon, transfer the peaches to a bowl. Bring the syrup to the boil and continue boiling until thickened and reduced to about 125 ml/4 fl oz. Pour over the peaches. Cover and chill until required. To serve, decorate with mint sprigs.

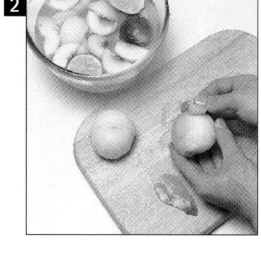

Figs with Orange Blossom

Luscious, sweet fresh figs are piled high on market stalls throughout the Mediterranean during the summer.

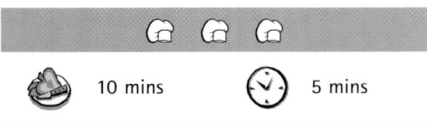

10 mins   5 mins

SERVES 4

INGREDIENTS

8 large fresh figs

4 large fresh fig leaves, rinsed and dried

ORANGE-BLOSSOM CREAM

115 g/4 oz crème fraîche, homemade (see page 9) or bought

4 tbsp orange-flower water

1 tsp orange-blossom honey

finely grated rind of ½ orange

2 tbsp flaked almonds, to decorate (optional)

1 If you are making the crème fraîche at home, start at least a day ahead (see page 9).

2 To toast the almonds for the decoration, place in a dry frying pan over a medium heat and stir until lightly browned. Take care that the almonds do not burn. Immediately tip them out of the frying pan and set aside.

3 To make the orange-blossom cream, put the crème fraîche in a small bowl and stir in 4 tablespoons of orange flower water, with the honey and the orange rind. Taste and add a little extra orange flower water if necessary, and sweeten with a little more honey, if liked.

4 To serve, cut the stems off the figs, but do not peel them. Stand the figs upright with the pointed end upward. Cut each into quarters without cutting all the way through, so you can open them out into attractive 'flowers.'

5 If you are using fig leaves, place one in the centre of each serving plate. Arrange 2 figs on top of each leaf and spoon a small amount of the orange-flavoured cream alongside them. Sprinkle the cream with the toasted flaked almonds, if desired, just before serving.

Balsamic Strawberries

Generations of Italian cooks have known that the unlikely combination of freshly ground black pepper and ripe, juicy strawberries is fantastic.

30 mins plus
4 hrs chilling

0 mins

SERVES 4–6

INGREDIENTS

450 g/1 lb fresh strawberries

2–3 tbsp balsamic vinegar

pepper

fresh mint leaves, torn, plus extra to decorate (optional)

115–175 g/4–6 oz mascarpone cheese

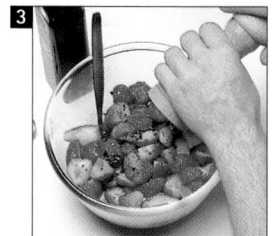

1 Wipe the strawberries with a damp cloth, rather than rinsing them, so they do not become soggy. Using a paring knife, cut off the green stalks at the top and use the tip of the knife to remove the core or hull.

2 Cut each small or medium-size strawberry in half lengthways; cut large ones into quarters. Put in a bowl.

3 Add the balsamic vinegar, allowing ½ tablespoon per person. Add several twists of ground black pepper, then gently stir together. Cover with clingfilm and chill for up to 4 hours.

COOK'S TIP

This is most enjoyable when it is made with the best-quality balsamic vinegar, one that has aged slowly and has turned thick and syrupy. Unfortunately, the genuine mixture is always expensive. Less expensive versions are artificially sweetened and coloured with caramel.

4 Just before serving, stir in torn mint leaves to taste. Spoon the mascarpone cheese into bowls and the berries on top. Decorate with a few mint leaves, if wished. Sprinkle with extra pepper to taste.

Autumn Fruit Bread Pudding

This is like a summer pudding, but it uses fruits which appear later in the year, such as apples, pears and blackberries, as a juicy filling.

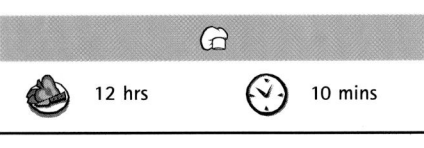

12 hrs   10 mins

SERVES 8

900 g/2 lb mixed blackberries, chopped apples, chopped pears

150 g/5½ oz soft light brown sugar

1 tsp ground cinnamon

100 ml/3½ fl oz water

225 g/8 oz white bread, thinly sliced, crusts removed

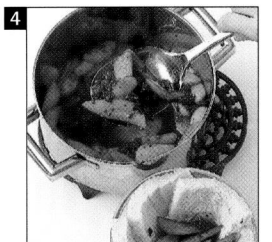

1 Place the prepared fruit in a large saucepan with the brown sugar, cinnamon and water, stir together and bring to the boil.

2 Lower the heat and simmer for 5–10 minutes so that the fruits soften but still hold their shape.

3 Meanwhile, line the base and sides of a 900-ml/1½-pint pudding basin with the bread slices, ensuring that there are no gaps between the pieces of bread.

4 Spoon the fruit into the centre of the bread-lined bowl and cover the fruit with the remaining bread.

5 Place a saucer on top of the bread and weigh it down with a 225-g/8-oz weight or a food can. Leave the pudding to chill in the refrigerator overnight.

6 Turn the pudding out on to a serving plate and serve immediately.

VARIATION
You can use thin slices of plain sponge cake instead of the sliced bread. The sponge will turn a pinkish colour from the fruit juices and the brown edges of the cake will form an attractive pattern of irregular brown lines.

Winter Desserts

An interesting alternative to the familiar and ever-popular summer dessert that uses dried fruit and a tasty malt loaf.

40 mins plus
8 hrs chilling

15 mins

SERVES 4

I N G R E D I E N T S

325 g/11½ oz fruit malt loaf

150 g/5½ oz ready-to-eat dried apricots, coarsely chopped

85 g/3 oz coarsely chopped dried apple

425 ml/ 15 fl oz orange juice

1 tsp grated orange rind, plus strips of zest to decorate

2 tbsp orange liqueur

low-fat crème fraîche (see page 9) or low-fat natural fromage frais, to serve

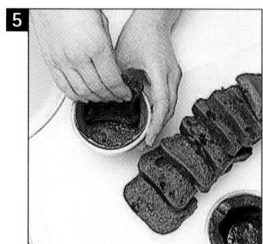

1 Cut the malt loaf into 5-mm/½-inch thick slices.

2 Place the apricots, apple and orange juice in a saucepan. Bring to the boil, then simmer for 10 minutes. Remove the fruit, using a slotted spoon, and reserve the liquid. Place the fruit in a dish and set aside to cool. Stir in the orange rind and orange liqueur.

3 Line 4 x 175-ml/6-fl-oz individual pudding basins or ramekin dishes with baking parchment.

4 Cut 4 circles from the malt-loaf slices to fit the tops of the moulds and cut the remaining slices to line them.

5 Soak the malt-loaf slices in the reserved fruit syrup, then arrange around the base and sides of the moulds. Trim away any crusts which overhang the edges. Fill the centres with the chopped

fruit, pressing down well, and place the malt-loaf circles on top.

6 Cover with baking parchment and weigh each bowl down with a 225-g/ 8-oz weight or a food can. Chill in the refrigerator overnight.

7 Remove the weight and baking parchment. Carefully turn the puddings out on to 4 serving plates. Remove the baking parchment.

8 Decorate with orange zest and serve with crème fraîche or fromage frais.

Orchard Fruits Bristol

An elegant fruit salad of poached pears and apples, oranges and strawberries in a wine and caramel syrup topped with crumbled caramel.

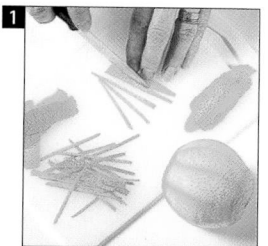

🐻 🐻 🐻 🐻

50 mins   🕐 20 mins

SERVES 4

INGREDIENTS

4 oranges

175 g/6 oz granulated sugar

4 tbsp water

150 ml/5 fl oz white wine

4 firm pears

4 eating apples

115 g/4 oz strawberries

1 Pare the zest thinly from 1 orange and cut into narrow strips. Cook in the minimum of boiling water for 3–4 minutes until tender. Drain and reserve the cooking liquid. Squeeze the juice from this and 1 other orange.

2 Lay a sheet of baking parchment on a baking sheet or cutting board.

3 Heat the sugar gently in a saucepan, stirring until it melts, then continue without stirring until it turns a pale golden brown. Pour half the caramel carefully but quickly on to the baking parchment and leave to set.

4 Add the water and squeezed orange juice immediately to the caramel left in the saucepan with 150 ml/5 fl oz of the reserved cooking liquid. Heat until it melts, then add the wine and remove the saucepan from the heat.

5 Peel, core and slice the pears and apples thickly (you can leave the apple skins on, if you prefer) and add to the caramel syrup. Bring gently to the boil and simmer for 3–4 minutes until just

starting to soften – they should still be firm in the centre. Transfer the pears and apples to a bowl.

6 Cut away the peel and pith from the remaining oranges and either ease out the segments or cut into slices, discarding any pips. Add to the other fruits. Hull the strawberries and halve,

quarter or slice thickly, depending on the size, and add to the other fruits.

7 Add the orange zest strips to the syrup and return to the boil for 1 minute, then pour over the fruits. Set aside to cool completely, then break up the caramel and sprinkle it over the fruit. Cover and chill until ready to serve.

Oranges & Strawberries

Ideal as a summery dessert, this dish can also be served as a fresh fruit dish with brunch. The oranges enhance the delicate flavour of the berries.

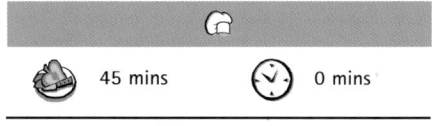

45 mins   0 mins

SERVES 4

INGREDIENTS

3 sweet oranges

225 g/8 oz strawberries

grated zest and juice of 1 lime

1–2 tbsp caster sugar

1 fresh mint sprig, to decorate

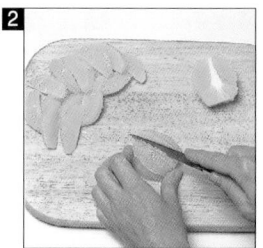

1 Using a sharp knife, cut a slice off the top and bottom of the oranges, then remove the peel and all the pith, cutting downward and taking care to retain the shape of the oranges.

2 Using a small sharp knife, cut down between the membranes of the oranges to remove the segments. Discard the membranes.

3 Hull the strawberries, pulling the leaves off with a pinching action. Cut into slices, along the length of the strawberries.

VARIATION

An optional hint of orange liqueur is delicious on this – reduce or omit the sugar. You can replace the oranges with mangoes and the strawberries with blackberries, for a dramatically coloured dessert.

4 Put the oranges and strawberries in a bowl, then sprinkle with the lime zest, lime juice and sugar. Chill in the refrigerator until ready to serve.

5 To serve, transfer to a serving bowl and decorate the dish with the fresh mint sprig.

Oranges in Spiced Caramel

This flavourful and refreshing dessert is suitable to serve at the end of dinner in summer or winter.

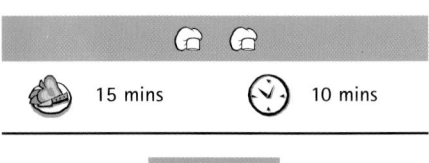

🍴 15 mins   🕐 10 mins

SERVES 4

INGREDIENTS

4 large juicy oranges

4–6 tbsp shelled pistachio nuts, chopped, to decorate

SPICED CARAMEL

250 g/9 oz caster sugar

5 black peppercorns, lightly crushed

4 cloves

1 green cardamom pod, lightly crushed

300 ml/10 fl oz water

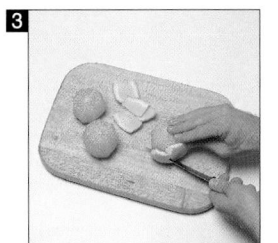
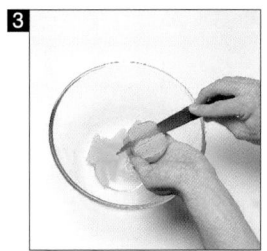

1 To make the spiced caramel, put the sugar, peppercorns, cloves, cardamom pod and 150 ml/5 fl oz of the water in a saucepan and stir over a medium heat to dissolve the sugar. When it has dissolved, increase the heat and boil, without stirring, until the syrup thickens and turns a deep caramel colour. Use a wet pastry brush to brush the syrup down from the sides of the saucepan if necessary.

2 Carefully pour in an additional 150ml/5 fl oz of the water, standing back because it will splatter. Remove from the heat and, using a long-handled wooden spoon, stir until all the caramel has dissolved. Leave to cool.

3 Remove the orange peel and pith, cutting carefully so that the oranges retain their shape. Leave the oranges whole or, working over a bowl, cut into segments, cutting the flesh away from between the membranes.

4 Pour over the caramel syrup with the spices and stir together. Cover and chill, until ready to serve. Serve the dessert in individual bowls with chopped pistachio nuts sprinkled over the tops at the last minute.

VARIATION

Turn this Spanish dessert into a Sicilian-style one by using the blood oranges that grow in great profusion on the island.

Nectarine Crunch

This incredibly easy and nutritious dessert is very popular with children, who enjoy making it themselves.

🥣 10 mins 🕐 10 mins

SERVES 4

INGREDIENTS

4 nectarines

175 g/6 oz raisin and nut crunchy oat cereal

300 ml/10 fl oz low-fat natural yogurt

2 tbsp peach jam

2 tbsp peach nectar

1 Cut the nectarines in half and remove the stones. Chop the flesh into bite-size pieces. Reserve 12–16 pieces for decoration and divide the remainder among 4 sundae glasses or individual bowls.

2 Divide the crunchy oat cereal between the glasses or bowls and top with the yogurt.

3 Combine the jam and peach nectar in a jug, stirring well to mix. Drizzle the sauce over the yogurt and decorate with the reserved nectarine pieces. Serve immediately.

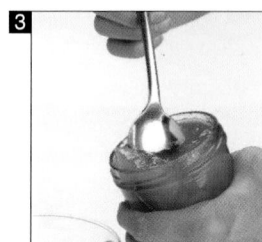

Peaches in White Wine

A very simple but incredibly pleasing dessert, which is especially good for a dinner party on a hot summer day.

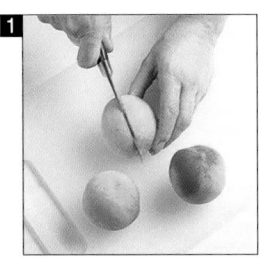
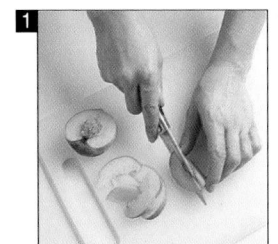
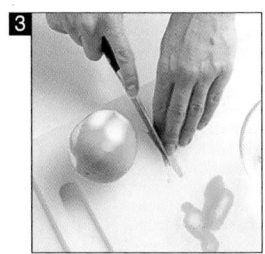

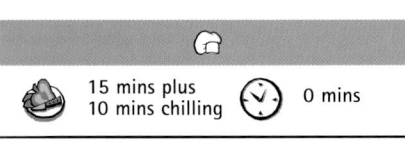

15 mins plus
10 mins chilling   0 mins

SERVES 4

I N G R E D I E N T S

4 large ripe peaches

2 tbsp icing sugar, sifted

1 orange

175 ml/6 fl oz medium or sweet white wine, chilled

1 Using a sharp knife, halve the peaches, remove the stones and discard them. Peel the peaches if you prefer. Slice the peaches into thin wedges.

2 Place the peach wedges in a glass serving bowl and sprinkle the sugar over.

3 Using a sharp knife, pare the zest from the orange. Cut the zest into matchstick-size strips, place them in a bowl of cold water and set aside.

4 Squeeze the juice from the orange and pour over the peaches, together with the wine.

5 Let the peaches marinate and chill in the refrigerator for at least 1 hour.

6 Remove the orange zest from the cold water and pat dry with kitchen paper.

7 Decorate the peaches with the strips of orange zest and serve immediately.

COOK'S TIP
There is absolutely no need to use expensive wine in this recipe, so it can be quite economical to make.

Fruit in Lemongrass Syrup

This simple tropical fruit salad with its oriental flavours makes a refreshing and exotic dessert.

15 mins plus 8 hrs chilling   15 mins

SERVES 4

INGREDIENTS

LEMONGRASS SYRUP

300 g/10½ oz caster sugar

150 ml/5 fl oz water

2 lemongrass stalks, bruised

2 kaffir lime leaves

juice of 1 lime

TROPICAL FRUIT SALAD

1 honeydew melon

1 small pineapple

1 papaya

400 g/14 oz lychees, stones removed

3 passion fruit

TO DECORATE

1 tbsp lime zest

small handful of fresh mint leaves

1 To make the syrup, place the sugar, water, lemongrass, lime leaves and lime juice in a saucepan. Heat gently until the sugar has dissolved. Bring to the boil and boil, uncovered, for 5 minutes. Leave to cool, then chill in the refrigerator overnight.

2 Cut the melon in half, then remove the seeds and scoop out the flesh with a melon baller. Place in a bowl. Peel the pineapple, then cut into quarters lengthways and remove the core. Cut into cubes and add to the melon. Peel the papaya, then remove the seeds and cut the flesh into cubes and add to the other fruit.

3 Add the lychees. Cut the passion fruit in half and scoop the pulp and seeds into the bowl of fruit. Stir to combine, then transfer to a serving bowl. Remove the lemongrass stalks and lime leaves from the syrup and pour over the fruit. Decorate with the lime zest and fresh mint leaves and serve.

Pineapple with Lime

Pineapples are sweet and fragrant and feature regularly as a dessert in Thailand, usually served very simply, as in this recipe.

15 mins plus 30 mins chilling   2 mins

SERVES 4

INGREDIENTS

1 pineapple

2 cardamom pods

1 strip lime zest, pared thinly

4 tbsp water

1 tbsp soft light brown sugar

3 tbsp lime juice

fresh mint sprigs and whipped cream, to decorate

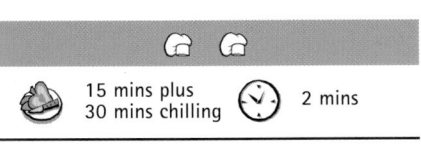

1 Using a sharp knife, cut the top and bottom from the pineapple, then cut away the peel and remove all the 'eyes' from the flesh. Cut into quarters and remove the core. Slice the pineapple flesh lengthways.

2 Crush the cardamom pods in a pestle and mortar and place in a small saucepan with the lime zest and water. Heat gently until the mixture is boiling, then simmer for 30 seconds.

3 Remove the saucepan from the heat and stir in the sugar until it has dissolved, then cover, and set aside to steep for 5 minutes.

4 Add the lime juice, stir well to mix, then strain the syrup over the pineapple. Chill for 30 minutes.

5 Arrange the pineapple on a serving dish, spoon the syrup over it and serve decorated with fresh mint sprigs and whipped cream.

COOK'S TIP
To remove the 'eyes' from pineapple, cut off the peel, then use a small sharp knife to cut a V-shaped channel down the pineapple. Cut diagonally through the lines of brown 'eyes' in the flesh, to make spiralling cuts around the fruit.

Pineapple Compôte

For a more elaborate dish, accompany the pineapple with a scoop of good-quality pineapple sorbet.

15 mins   0 mins

SERVES 4–6

INGREDIENTS

1 ripe pineapple

sugar

juice of 1 lemon

2–3 tbsp tequila or a few drops of vanilla essence

several fresh mint sprigs, leaves removed and cut into thin strips

fresh mint sprig, to decorate

1 Using a sharp knife, cut off the top and bottom of the pineapple. Place upright on a cutting board, then slice off the skin, cutting downward. Cut in half, remove the core, then cut the flesh into slices, then into chunks.

2 Put the pineapple in a bowl and sprinkle with the sugar, lemon juice and tequila or vanilla essence.

3 Toss the pineapple to coat well, then chill until ready to serve.

4 To serve, arrange on a serving plate and sprinkle with the mint strips. Decorate the dish with a mint sprig.

COOK'S TIP
Make sure you slice off the 'eyes' when removing the skin from the pineapple.

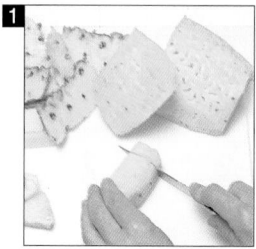

Compôte of Dried Fruit

Dried fruit, soaked in tea and orange juice, makes a fragrant compôte.
This is a good dessert and can also be served with cereal for breakfast.

25 mins
plus 24 hrs
marinading

0 mins

SERVES 4

INGREDIENTS

1 tbsp jasmine tea

300 ml/10 fl oz boiling water

55 g/2 oz dried apricots

55 g/2 oz dried apple rings

55 g/2 oz prunes

300 ml/10 fl oz fresh orange juice

1 Put the tea in a jug and pour in the boiling water. Leave to steep for 20 minutes, then strain.

2 Put the dried fruit in a serving bowl and pour the jasmine tea and orange juice over them. Cover and leave to marinate in the refrigerator for 24 hours.

3 Serve the compôte well chilled.

Fresh Fruit Compôte

Elderflower cordial is used in the syrup for this refreshing fruit compôte, giving it a delightfully summery flavour.

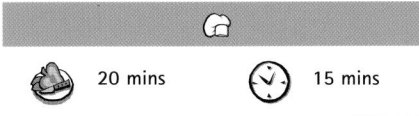

20 mins   15 mins

SERVES 4

INGREDIENTS

| 1 lemon |
| 55 g/2 oz caster sugar |
| 4 tbsp elderflower cordial |
| 300 ml/10 fl oz water |
| 4 eating apples |
| 225 g/ 8 oz blackberries |
| 2 fresh figs |

TOPPING

| 150 g/5½ oz thick natural yogurt |
| 2 tbsp clear honey |

1 Thinly pare the zest from the lemon using a vegetable peeler. Squeeze the juice. Put the lemon zest and juice into a saucepan, together with the sugar, elderflower cordial and water. Set over a low heat and simmer, uncovered, for 10 minutes.

2 Peel, core and slice the apples. Add the apples to the saucepan. Simmer gently for about 4–5 minutes, until just tender. Remove the saucepan from the heat and set aside to cool.

3 When cold, transfer the apples and syrup to a serving bowl and add the blackberries. Slice and add the figs. Stir gently to mix. Cover and chill in the refrigerator until ready to serve.

4 Spoon the yogurt into a small serving bowl and drizzle the honey over the top. Cover and chill before serving.

COOK'S TIP

Strained natural yogurt may be made from cow's or ewe's milk. The former is often strained to make it more concentrated and has a high fat content, which perfectly counterbalances the sharpness and acidity of fruit.

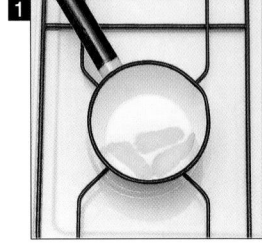

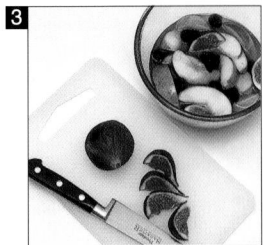

Fruit Compôte with Port

Port complements the flavour of berries very well. This delicious compôte is topped with sweetened whipped cream and grated chocolate.

15 mins plus
30 mins cooling   15 mins

SERVES 4

I N G R E D I E N T S

1 tbsp butter

200 g/7 oz blueberries

200 g/7 oz blackberries

100 g/3½ oz strawberries

6 tbsp port

3 tbsp blueberry jam

1 tbsp cornflour

1 tsp mixed spice

T O P P I N G

450 ml/16 fl oz double cream

3–4 tbsp caster sugar

grated chocolate, to decorate

1 Preheat the oven to 190°C/375°F/Gas Mark 5. Grease a baking dish with butter and add all the fruit.

2 In a bowl, mix together the port, jam, cornflour and mixed spice until blended. Pour over the fruit and mix together well. Bake in the preheated oven for 15 minutes, stirring from time to time. Remove from the oven and leave to cool to room temperature, then divide between 4 decorative serving glasses.

3 For the topping, put the cream in a mixing bowl and beat in enough sugar to taste. Spoon the mixture over the fruit, top with grated chocolate and serve.

Blueberry Compôte

Serve this easy dish with whipped cream or ice cream and biscuits. It is perfect for entertaining, as it has to be made in advance and chilled.

10 mins plus
3 hrs chilling

5 mins

SERVES 6

INGREDIENTS

675 g/1 lb 8 oz blueberries

280 g/10 oz caster sugar

1 tbsp water

2 tbsp gin

crisp biscuits, to serve

1 Place the blueberries, caster sugar and water in a heavy-based saucepan over a low heat, shaking the saucepan occasionally, until the sugar has dissolved completely. Remove the saucepan from the heat and gradually stir in the gin, then let the fruit mixture cool completely.

2 Transfer the compôte to individual dishes, cover and leave to chill in the refrigerator for 2–3 hours before serving with crisp biscuits.

VARIATION
You can substitute fresh redcurrants for the blueberries and brandy for the gin, if you prefer.

Fig & Watermelon Salad

Fruit salads are always popular and easy to prepare. Ring the changes with this summery combination that looks almost too pretty to eat.

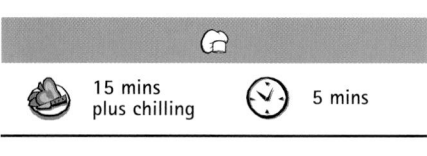

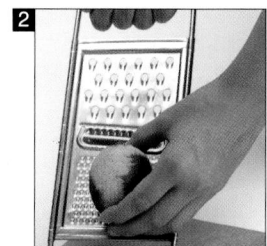

15 mins
plus chilling

5 mins

SERVES 4

INGREDIENTS

1 watermelon, weighing about
  1.5 kg/3 lb 5 oz

100 g/3½ oz seedless black grapes

4 figs

1 lime

1 orange

1 tbsp maple syrup

2 tbsp honey

4 fresh mint sprigs, to decorate (optional)

1 Cut the watermelon into quarters and discard as many seeds as possible. Cut the flesh away from the rind, then chop the flesh into 2.5-cm/1-inch cubes. Place the watermelon cubes in a bowl with the grapes. Cut each fig lengthways into 8 wedges and add to the bowl.

2 Grate the rind from the lime and orange and squeeze the juice from the orange. Mix the lime rind with the orange rind and juice, maple syrup and honey in a small saucepan. Bring to the boil over a low heat. Pour the mixture over the fruit and stir. Leave to cool. Stir again, cover and chill in the refrigerator for at least 1 hour, stirring occasionally.

3 To serve, divide the fruit salad equally among 4 glass dishes and decorate with a fresh mint sprig, if you like.

VARIATION
Add 2 pieces of finely chopped stem ginger to the fruit in step 1 and substitute 1 tablespoon of the syrup from the jar for the maple syrup.

Mango & Passion Fruit Salad

The rich mascarpone cream which accompanies this exotic fruit salad gives this Chinese dessert an Italian twist.

1 hrs 15 mins   0 mins

SERVES 4

INGREDIENTS

1 large mango

2 oranges

4 passion fruit

2 tbsp orange liqueur such as
   Grand Marnier

mint or geranium leaves, to decorate

MASCARPONE CREAM

125 g/4½ oz mascarpone cheese

1 tbsp clear honey

4 tbsp thick natural yogurt

few drops vanilla essence

1 Using a sharp knife, cut the mango in half lengthwise as close to the stone as possible. Remove the stone, using a sharp knife.

2 Peel off the mango skin, cut the flesh into slices, and place in a large bowl.

3 Peel the oranges, removing all the pith and cut into segments. Add to the bowl with any juices.

4 Halve the passion fruit, scoop out the flesh and add to the bowl with the orange liqueur. Mix together all the ingredients in the bowl.

5 Cover the bowl with clingfilm and chill in the refrigerator for 1 hour. Turn into glass serving dishes.

6 To make the mascarpone cream, blend the mascarpone cheese and honey together. Stir in the natural yogurt and vanilla essence until thoroughly blended.

7 Serve the fruit salad with the mascarpone cream, decorated with mint or geranium leaves.

COOK'S TIP

Passion fruit are ready to eat when their skins are well dimpled. They are most readily available in the summer. Substitute guava or pineapple for the passion fruit, if you prefer.

Melon & Kiwi Salad

A refreshing fruit salad, ideal to serve after a rich meal. Charentais or Cantaloupe melons are also good.

1 hr 15 mins   0 mins

SERVES 4

INGREDIENTS

½ Galia melon

2 kiwi fruit

125 g/4½ oz seedless green grapes

1 papaya, halved

3 tbsp orange liqueur such as Cointreau

1 tbsp chopped lemon verbena, lemon balm or mint

sprigs of lemon verbena, or cape gooseberries, to decorate

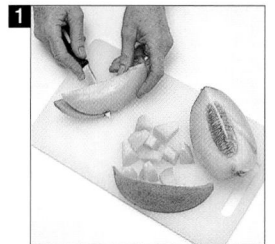
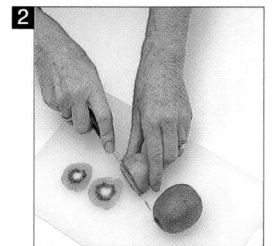

1 Remove the seeds from the melon, cut into 4 slices and cut away the skin. Cut the flesh into cubes and put into a bowl.

2 Peel the kiwi fruit and cut across into slices. Add to the melon with the green grapes.

3 Remove the seeds from the papaya and cut off the skin. Slice the flesh thickly and cut into diagonal pieces. Add to the fruit bowl and mix well.

4 Mix together the liqueur and lemon verbena, pour over the fruit, and set aside for 1 hour, stirring occasionally.

5 Spoon the fruit salad into glasses, pour over the juices, and decorate with lemon verbena sprigs or cape gooseberries.

COOK'S TIP

Lemon balm or sweet balm is a fragrant lemon-scented plant with slightly hairy serrated leaves and a pronounced lemon flavour. Lemon verbena can also be used – this has an even stronger lemon flavour and smooth, elongated leaves.

Orange & Grapefruit Salad

Sliced citrus fruits with a delicious lime and honey dressing make an unusual and refreshing dessert.

15 mins plus 2 hrs chilling

3 mins

SERVES 4

INGREDIENTS

2 grapefruit, ruby or plain

4 oranges

pared zest and juice of 1 lime

4 tbsp honey

2 tbsp warm water

1 fresh mint sprig, roughly chopped

55 g/2 oz chopped walnuts

1 Using a sharp knife, slice the top and bottom from the grapefruits, then slice away the rest of the peel and pith.

2 Cut between each segment of the grapefruit and remove the fleshy part only, discarding the membranes.

3 Using a sharp knife, slice the top and bottom from the oranges, then slice away the rest of the peel and pith.

4 Cut between each segment of the oranges to remove the fleshy part, discarding the membranes. Add the orange segments to the grapefruit.

5 Place the lime zest, 2 tablespoons lime juice, the honey and the warm water in a small bowl. Whisk with a fork to mix the dressing.

6 Pour the dressing over the segmented fruit, add the chopped mint and mix well. Set aside to chill in the refrigerator for 2 hours for the flavours to mingle.

7 Preheat the grill to medium. Place the chopped walnuts on a baking sheet. Toast lightly under the preheated grill for 2–3 minutes or until browned.

8 Sprinkle the toasted walnuts over the fruit and serve.

Aromatic Fruit Salad

The fruits in this salad are arranged attractively on serving plates with a spicy syrup spooned over.

🍧 25 mins   🕐 5 mins

SERVES 6

INGREDIENTS

40 g/1½ oz granulated sugar

150 ml/5 fl oz water

1 cinnamon stick or large piece cassia bark

4 cardamom pods, crushed

1 clove

juice of 1 orange

juice of 1 lime

½ honeydew melon

1 large wedge watermelon

2 ripe guavas

3 ripe nectarines

about 18 strawberries

toasted shredded coconut, for sprinkling

sprigs of mint or rose petals, to decorate

thick low-fat natural yogurt, to serve

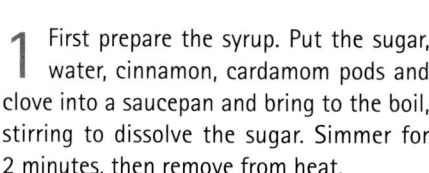   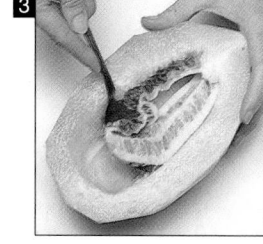

1 First prepare the syrup. Put the sugar, water, cinnamon, cardamom pods and clove into a saucepan and bring to the boil, stirring to dissolve the sugar. Simmer for 2 minutes, then remove from heat.

2 Add the orange and lime juices to the syrup and leave to cool and infuse while you prepare the fruits.

3 Peel and remove the seeds from the melons and cut the flesh into neat, regular slices.

4 Cut the guavas in half, scoop out the seeds, then peel and slice the flesh neatly.

5 Cut the nectarines into slices and hull and slice the strawberries.

6 Arrange the slices of fruit attractively on 6 serving plates.

7 Strain the cooled prepared syrup and spoon over the sliced fruits.

8 Sprinkle the fruit salad with a little toasted coconut. Decorate each serving with sprigs of mint or rose petals and serve with yogurt.

Summer Fruit Salad

A mixture of soft summer fruits in an orange-flavoured syrup with a dash of port. Serve with a spoonful of low-fat fromage frais.

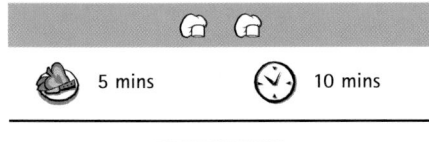

🍰 5 mins   🕐 10 mins

SERVES 6

INGREDIENTS

85 g/3 oz caster sugar

5 tbsp water

grated rind and juice of 1 small orange

250 g/9 oz redcurrants, stripped from their stalks

2 tsp arrowroot

2 tbsp port

115 g/4 oz blackberries

115 g/4 oz blueberries

115 g/4 oz strawberries

225 g/8 oz raspberries

low-fat fromage frais, to serve

1 Put the sugar, water and grated orange rind into a heavy-based saucepan and heat gently, stirring until the sugar has completely dissolved.

2 Add the redcurrants and orange juice, bring to the boil and simmer gently for 2–3 minutes.

3 Strain the fruit, reserving the syrup, and put into a bowl.

4 Blend the arrowroot with a little water. Return the syrup to the saucepan, add the arrowroot and bring to a boil, stirring constantly, until thickened.

5 Add the port and mix together well. Then pour the syrup over the redcurrants in the bowl.

6 Add the blackberries, blueberries, strawberries and raspberries. Mix the fruit together and set aside to cool until required. Serve in individual glass dishes with low-fat fromage frais.

COOK'S TIP

Although this salad is really best made with fresh fruits in season, you can achieve an acceptable result with frozen equivalents, with perhaps the exception of strawberries. You can buy frozen 'fruits of the forest', which would be ideal, in most supermarkets.

Tropical Salad

Papayas are ready to eat when they yield to gentle pressure. Serve in the shells of baby pineapples for a stunning effect.

🍲

🍋 10 mins   🕐 0 mins

SERVES 8

INGREDIENTS

1 papaya

2 tbsp fresh orange juice

3 tbsp dark rum

2 bananas

2 guavas

1 small pineapple or 2 baby pineapples

2 passion fruit

pineapple leaves, to decorate

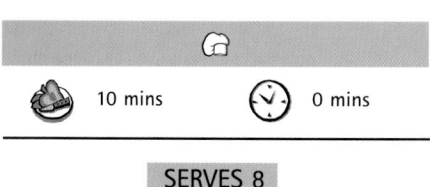

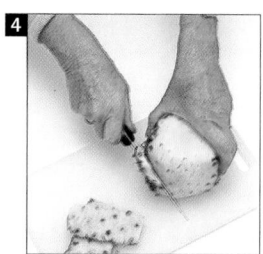

1 Cut the papaya in half and remove the seeds. Peel and slice the flesh into a bowl.

2 Pour over the orange juice together with the rum.

3 Slice the bananas, peel and slice the guavas and add both to the bowl.

4 Cut the top and base from the pineapple, then cut off the skin.

5 Slice the pineapple flesh, discard the core, cut into pieces and add to the bowl.

6 Halve the passion fruit, scoop out the flesh with a teaspoon, add to the bowl and stir well to mix.

7 Spoon the salad into glass bowls and decorate with pineapple leaves.

COOK'S TIP
Guavas have a heavenly smell when ripe – their scent will fill a whole room. They should give to gentle pressure when ripe, and their skins should be yellow. The canned varieties are very good and have a pink tinge to the flesh.

Exotic Fruit Salad

This colourful, exotic salad is infused with the delicate flavours of jasmine tea and ginger. Ideally, it should be chilled about an hour before serving.

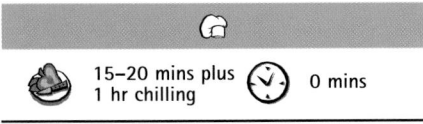

15–20 mins plus 1 hr chilling

0 mins

SERVES 6

INGREDIENTS

1 tsp jasmine tea leaves

1 tsp grated fresh root ginger

1 strip lime zest

125 ml/4 fl oz boiling water

2 tbsp caster sugar

1 papaya

1 mango

½ small pineapple

1 starfruit

2 passion fruit

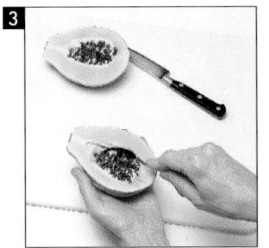

1 Place the tea leaves, ginger and lime zest in a heatproof jug and pour over the boiling water. Leave to infuse for 5 minutes, then strain the liquid.

2 Add the sugar to the liquid and stir well to dissolve. Leave the syrup to stand until it is completely cool.

3 Halve, deseed and peel the papaya. Halve the mango, remove the stone and peel. Peel and remove the core from the pineapple. Cut the fruits into regular, bite-size pieces.

4 Slice the starfruit crossways. Place all the prepared fruits in a wide serving bowl and pour over the cooled syrup. Cover the bowl with clingfilm and chill for about 1 hour.

5 Cut the passion fruit in half, scoop out the flesh and mix with the lime juice. Spoon over the salad and serve.

COOK'S TIP
Starfruit have little flavour when unripe and green, but when ripe and yellow they are sweet and fragrant. The tips of the ridges often turn brown, so run a vegetable peeler along each ridge before slicing.

Chinese Fruit Salad

The syrup for this colourful dish is filled with Chinese flavours for a refreshing and mouth-watering dessert.

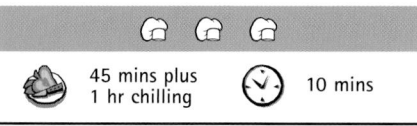

45 mins plus
1 hr chilling

10 mins

SERVES 4

INGREDIENTS

75 ml/3 fl oz Chinese rice wine or dry sherry

grated rind and juice of 1 lemon

900 ml/1¾ pints water

225 g/8 oz caster sugar

2 cloves

2.5-cm/1-inch piece cinnamon stick, bruised

1 vanilla pod

pinch of ground mixed spice

1 star anise

2.5-cm/1-inch piece of fresh root ginger, sliced

50 g/1¾ oz unsalted cashews

2 kiwi fruits

1 star fruit

115 g/4 oz strawberries

400 g/14 oz canned lychees in syrup, drained

1 piece stem ginger, drained and sliced

chopped fresh mint, to decorate

1 Put the Chinese rice wine or sherry, lemon rind and juice and water into a heavy-based saucepan.

2 Add the caster sugar, cloves, cinnamon stick, vanilla bean, mixed spice, star anise and fresh root ginger to the saucepan.

3 Heat the mixture in the saucepan gently, stirring constantly, until the sugar has dissolved and then bring to the boil. Reduce the heat and simmer for 5 minutes. Set aside to cool completely.

4 Strain the syrup, discarding the flavourings. Stir in the cashews, cover with clingfilm and chill in the refrigerator.

5 Meanwhile, prepare the fruits: halve and slice the kiwi fruit, slice the star fruit and hull and slice the strawberries.

6 Spoon the prepared fruit into a dish with the lychees and stem ginger. Stir through gently to mix.

7 Pour the syrup over the fruit, decorate with chopped mint and serve.

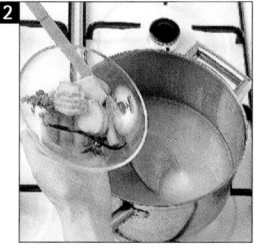

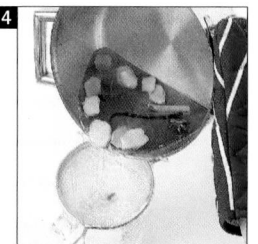

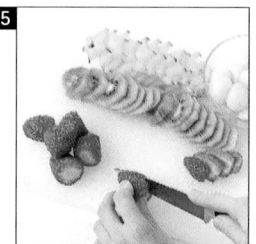

Green Fruit Salad

This delightfully refreshing fruit salad is the perfect finale for a Chinese meal. It has a lovely light syrup made with fresh mint and honey.

30 mins   15 mins

SERVES 4

INGREDIENTS

SYRUP

1 orange

150 ml/5 fl oz white wine

150 ml/5 fl oz water

4 tbsp clear honey

fresh mint sprigs

FRUIT

1 small Charentais or honeydew melon

2 green apples

2 kiwi fruit

115 g/4 oz seedless white grapes

fresh mint sprigs, to decorate

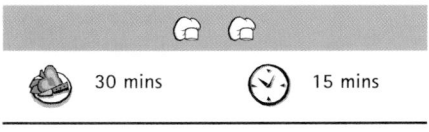
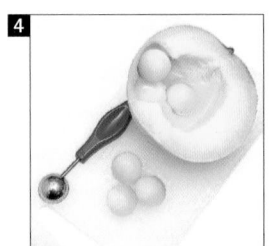

1 To make the syrup, pare the zest from the orange using a vegetable peeler.

2 Put the orange zest in a saucepan with the white wine, water and honey. Bring to the boil, then simmer gently for 10 minutes.

3 Remove the syrup from the heat. Add the mint sprigs and set aside to cool.

COOK'S TIP
Single-flower honey has a better, more individual flavour than blended honey. Acacia honey is typically Chinese, but you could also try clove, lemon blossom, lime flower or orange blossom.

4 To prepare the fruit, first slice the melon in half and scoop out the seeds. Use a melon baller or a teaspoon to make melon balls.

5 Core and chop the apples. Peel and slice the kiwi fruit.

6 Strain the cooled syrup into a serving bowl, removing and reserving the strips of orange zest but discarding the mint sprigs.

7 Add the apple, grapes, kiwi fruit and melon to the serving bowl. Stir through gently to mix.

8 Serve the fruit salad, decorated with sprigs of fresh mint and some of the reserved orange zest.

Fruit Salad & Ginger Syrup

This is a very special fruit salad made from the most exotic and colourful fruits that are soaked in a syrup made with fresh ginger and ginger wine.

30 mins plus 2–4 hrs chilling

5 mins

SERVES 4

INGREDIENTS

2.5-cm/1-inch piece fresh root ginger, peeled and chopped

55 g/2 oz caster sugar

150 ml/5fl oz water

grated rind and juice of 1 lime

4 tbsp ginger wine

1 fresh pineapple, peeled, cored and cut into bite-size pieces

2 ripe mangoes, peeled, stoned and diced

4 kiwi fruit, peeled and sliced

1 papaya, peeled, seeded and diced

2 passion fruit, halved and flesh removed

350 g/12 oz lychees, peeled and stoned

¼ fresh coconut, grated

Cape gooseberries, to decorate (optional)

coconut ice cream, to serve (optional)

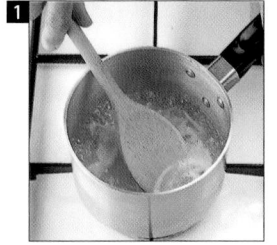
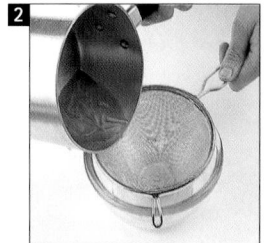

1 Place the fresh root ginger, sugar, water and lime zest and juice in a saucepan and bring slowly to a boil. Simmer for 1 minute, remove from the heat and leave to cool slightly.

2 Strain the syrup, add the ginger wine and mix well. Cool completely.

3 Place the prepared fruit in a serving bowl. Add the cold syrup and mix well. Cover and chill in the refrigerator for 2–4 hours.

4 Just before serving, add half of the grated coconut to the salad and mix well. Sprinkle the remainder on top.

5 If using Cape gooseberries to decorate the salad, peel back each calyx to form a flower. Wipe the berries clean, then arrange them around the side of the fruit salad before serving with coconut ice cream.

COOK'S TIP
Cape gooseberries are golden in colour and make a delightful decoration to many fruit-based desserts.

Creamy Fruit Parfait

On the tiny Greek island of Kythera, this luscious combination of summer fruits and yogurt is served at tavernas as well as in homes.

15 mins plus
1 hr cooling

0 mins

SERVES 4–6

INGREDIENTS

225 g/8 oz cherries

2 large peaches

2 large apricots

700 ml/1¼ pints Greek yogurt

55 g/2 oz walnut halves

2 tbsp flower-scented honey

fresh redcurrants or berries,
to decorate (optional)

1 To prepare the fruit, use a cherry or olive stoner to remove the cherry stones. Cut each cherry in half. Cut the peaches and apricots in half lengthways and remove the stones, then finely chop the flesh of all the fruit.

2 Place the finely chopped cherries, peaches and apricots in a bowl and gently stir together.

3 Spoon one-third of the yogurt into an attractive glass serving bowl. Top with half the fruit mixture.

4 Repeat with another layer of yogurt and fruit and, finally, top with the remaining yogurt.

5 Place the walnuts in a small food processor and pulse until chopped but not finely ground. Take care not to over-process. Sprinkle the walnuts over the top layer of the yogurt.

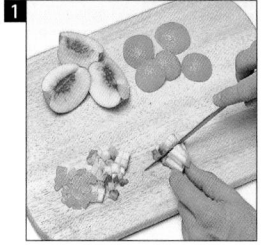

6 Drizzle the honey over the nuts and yogurt. Cover the glass bowl with clingfilm and chill in the refrigerator for at least 1 hour. Decorate the bowl with a small bunch of redcurrants (if using), just before serving.

Chocolate Hazelnut Parfait

Richly flavoured moulded ice creams make a scrumptious and attractive summertime dessert for all the family.

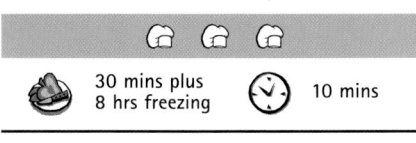

30 mins plus 8 hrs freezing

10 mins

SERVES 6

INGREDIENTS

175 g/6 oz blanched hazelnuts

175 g/6 oz plain chocolate, broken into small pieces

600 ml/1 pint double cream

3 eggs, separated

250 g/9 oz icing sugar

1 tbsp cocoa powder, for dusting

6 small fresh mint sprigs, to decorate

wafer biscuits, to serve

1 Preheat the grill to medium. Spread out the hazelnuts on a baking tray and toast under the grill for about 5 minutes, shaking the sheet from time to time, until golden all over. Set aside to cool.

2 Put the chocolate in a heatproof bowl set over a saucepan of gently simmering water. Stir over a low heat until melted, then remove from the heat and cool. Put the toasted hazelnuts in a food processor and process until finely ground.

3 Whisk the cream until it is stiff, then fold in the ground hazelnuts and set aside. Add 3 tablespoons of the sugar to the egg yolks and beat for 10 minutes until pale and thick.

4 Whisk the egg whites in a separate bowl until soft peaks form. Whisk in the remaining sugar, a little at a time, until the whites are stiff and glossy. Stir the

cooled chocolate into the egg yolk mixture, then fold in the cream and finally, fold in the egg whites. Divide the mixture among 6 freezerproof timbales or moulds, cover with clingfilm, and freeze for at least 8 hours, or overnight, until firm.

5 Transfer the frozen parfaits to the refrigerator about 10 minutes before serving to soften slightly. Turn out on to individual serving plates, dust the tops lightly with cocoa powder, decorate with mint sprigs and serve with wafers.

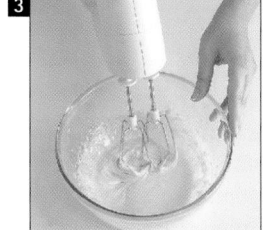

Oeufs à la Neige au Chocolat

In this dessert, poached meringues float on a richly flavoured chocolate custard like little snowballs.

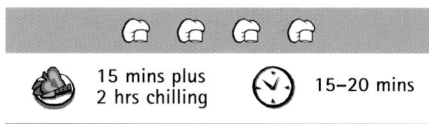

15 mins plus
2 hrs chilling

15–20 mins

SERVES 6

INGREDIENTS

600 ml/1 pint milk

1 tsp vanilla essence

175 g/6 oz caster sugar

2 egg whites

CUSTARD

4 tbsp caster sugar

3 tbsp cocoa powder, plus extra for dusting

4 egg yolks

1 Put the milk, vanilla essence and 5 tablespoons of the caster sugar into a heavy-based saucepan and stir over a low heat until the sugar has dissolved. Simmer gently.

2 Whisk the egg whites until stiff peaks form. Whisk in 2 teaspoons of the remaining sugar and continue to whisk until glossy. Gently fold in the rest of the caster sugar.

3 Drop large spoonfuls of the meringue mixture on to the simmering milk mixture and cook, stirring once, for 4–5 minutes until the meringues are firm. Remove with a slotted spoon and set aside on kitchen paper to drain. Poach the remaining meringues in the same way, then reserve the milk mixture.

4 To make the custard, mix the sugar, cocoa powder and egg yolks in a heatproof bowl. Place over gently simmering water. Gradually whisk in the reserved milk mixture and cook for 5–10 minutes, whisking constantly, until thickened. Remove from the heat and cool slightly. Divide the chocolate custard among individual serving glasses, top with the meringues and dust with cocoa. Cover with clingfilm and chill for at least 2 hours before serving.

Chocolate Marquise

This classic French dish is part way between a mousse and a parfait. It is usually chilled in a large mould, but here it is made in individual moulds.

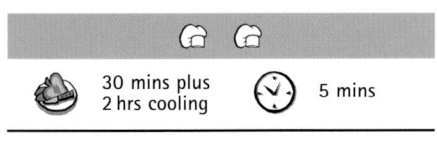

30 mins plus
2 hrs cooling

5 mins

SERVES 6

I N G R E D I E N T S

200 g/7 oz plain chocolate, broken into pieces

100 g/3½ oz butter

3 egg yolks

75 g/2¾ oz caster sugar

1 tsp chocolate essence or
1 tbsp chocolate liqueur

300 ml/10 fl oz double cream

TO SERVE

chocolate-dipped fruits

crème fraîche

cocoa powder, for dusting

1 Put the chocolate and butter in a heatproof bowl set over a saucepan of gently simmering water and stir until melted and well combined. Remove from the heat and leave to cool.

2 Place the egg yolks in a mixing bowl with the sugar and whisk until pale and fluffy. Using an electric whisk running on low speed, slowly whisk in the cool chocolate mixture. Stir in the chocolate essence or chocolate liqueur.

3 Whip the cream until just holding its shape. Fold into the chocolate mixture. Spoon into 6 small custard pots or individual metal moulds. Chill the desserts for at least 2 hours.

4 To serve, turn out the desserts on to individual serving dishes. If you have difficulty turning them out, dip each pot or mould into a bowl of warm water for a few seconds to help the marquise to slip out. Serve with chocolate-dipped fruits and crème fraîche and dust with cocoa powder.

COOK'S TIP
The slight tartness of the crème fraîche contrasts well with this very rich dessert. Dip the fruit in melted white chocolate to give a good colour contrast.

Coffee Panna Cotta

Panna cotta, which means 'cooked cream', is an Italian dessert. Here it is flavoured with coffee and served with a chocolate sauce.

🍮 25 mins plus 8 hrs chilling   🕐 5 mins

SERVES 6

INGREDIENTS

oil, for brushing

600 ml/1 pint double cream

1 vanilla pod

55 g/2 oz golden caster sugar

2 tsp instant espresso coffee powder dissolved in 4 tbsp water

2 tsp powdered gelatine

chocolate-covered coffee beans, to serve

CHOCOLATE CREAM SAUCE

55 g/2 oz plain chocolate

150 ml/5 fl oz single cream

1 Lightly brush 6 x 150 ml/5-fl oz moulds with oil. Put the cream in a saucepan. Split the vanilla pod and scrape the black seeds into the cream. Add the vanilla pod and the sugar and heat gently until almost boiling. Strain the cream into a bowl. Put the coffee into a small heatproof bowl, sprinkle on the gelatine, and leave for 5 minutes until spongy. Set the bowl over a saucepan of simmering water until the gelatine is dissolved.

2 Stir a little of the cream into the gelatine mixture, then stir the gelatine into the rest of the cream. Divide the mixture between the prepared moulds, filling them only two-thirds full, and leave to cool. Chill in the refrigerator overnight.

3 Make the chocolate cream sauce. Put the chocolate in a heatproof bowl set over a saucepan of gently simmering water until melted. Put one-quarter of the cream into a bowl and stir in the melted chocolate. Gradually stir in the remaining cream, reserving about 1 tablespoon. To serve the panna cotta, dip the base of the moulds briefly into hot water and turn out on to 6 serving plates. Pour the chocolate cream around. Dot drops of the reserved cream on to the sauce and feather them with a skewer. Decorate with chocolate-covered coffee beans and serve.

COOK'S TIP

Individual metal pudding basin-shaped moulds are ideal for this, and the panna cotta turns out more easily than from china moulds.

Chocolate Ice Cream Bombe

An ice cream bombe is a spectacular dessert to serve at a dinner party and the combination of white and plain chocolate is a winner.

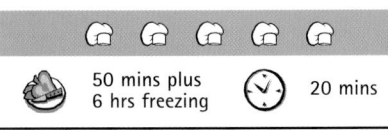

50 mins plus
6 hrs freezing

20 mins

SERVES 4

I N G R E D I E N T S

PLAIN CHOCOLATE ICE CREAM

2 eggs

2 egg yolks

115 g/4 oz golden caster sugar

300 ml/10 fl oz single cream

225 g/8 oz plain chocolate, chopped

300 ml/10 fl oz double cream

WHITE CHOCOLATE ICE CREAM

140 g/5 oz white chocolate, broken into pieces

150 ml/5 fl oz milk

55 g/2 oz golden caster sugar

300 ml/10 fl oz double cream

chocolate leaves, to decorate

1 Put a 1.5-litre/2½-pint bombe mould into the freezer and turn the freezer to its lowest setting. Place the eggs, egg yolks and sugar in a heatproof bowl and beat together until well blended. Put the single cream and chocolate in a saucepan and heat gently until the chocolate has melted, then continue to heat, stirring until almost boiling. Pour on to the egg mixture, stirring vigorously, then place the bowl over a saucepan of simmering water, making sure that the bottom of the bowl does not touch the water. Cook, stirring until the mixture coats the back of the spoon. Strain into another bowl and leave to cool. Place the double cream in a bowl and whisk until slightly thickened, then fold into the cooled chocolate mixture.

2 Either freeze in an ice-cream maker, following the manufacturer's directions, or pour the mixture into a freezerproof container, cover and freeze for 2 hours until just frozen. Spoon into a bowl and beat with a fork to break down the ice crystals. Return to the freezer until almost solid. Line the bombe mould with the chocolate ice cream and return to the freezer. Transfer from the freezer to the refrigerator 30 minutes before serving.

3 To make the white chocolate ice cream, put the chocolate and half the milk in a saucepan and heat gently until the chocolate has just melted. Remove from the heat and stir. Put the sugar and remaining milk in another saucepan and heat gently until the sugar has melted. Set aside to cool, then stir into the cooled chocolate mixture. Place the cream in a bowl and whisk until slightly thickened, then fold into the chocolate mixture. Spoon into the centre of the bombe, cover and freeze for about 4 hours, until firm. To serve, dip the mould briefly into warm water, then turn out on to a serving plate. Decorate with chocolate leaves.

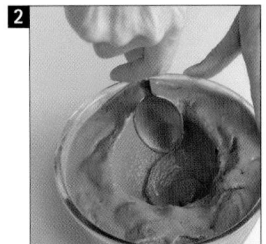

Chocolate & Orange Pots

These little pots of rich chocolate cream will satisfy the most serious chocolate lovers. Decorate with orange zest, if liked.

15 mins plus 1 hr chilling

5 mins

SERVES 8

INGREDIENTS

200 g/7 oz plain chocolate, broken into pieces

grated rind of 1 orange

300 ml/10 fl oz double cream

140 g/5 oz golden caster sugar

3 tbsp Cointreau

3 large egg whites

strips of orange zest, to decorate

crisp biscuits, to serve

1 Melt the chocolate in a heatproof bowl set over a saucepan of gently simmering water until melted. Stir in the orange rind. Put the cream in a bowl with 100 g/3½ oz of the sugar and the Cointreau and whisk until thick.

2 Put the egg whites in a clean bowl and whisk until soft peaks form, then gradually whisk in the remaining sugar until stiff but not dry. Fold the melted chocolate into the cream, then beat in a spoonful of the whisked whites. Gently fold in the remaining egg whites until thoroughly mixed.

3 Spoon the mixture into 8 small ramekin dishes or demi-tasse coffee cups. Chill for 1 hour, then decorate with strips of orange zest, before serving with crisp biscuits.

COOK'S NOTE
Chill the chocolate pots for no more than 2 hours otherwise the mixture becomes too firmly set.

Chocolate Coeur à la Crème

This classic French dessert is traditionally made in special pierced heart-shaped porcelain moulds.

15 mins plus 8 hrs standing

5 mins

SERVES 8

INGREDIENTS

225 g/8 oz ricotta cheese

55 g/2 oz icing sugar, sifted

300 ml/10 fl oz double cream

1 tsp vanilla essence

55 g/2 oz plain chocolate, grated

2 egg whites

few strawberries, halved, to decorate

RASPBERRY COULIS

225 g/8 oz raspberries

icing sugar, to taste

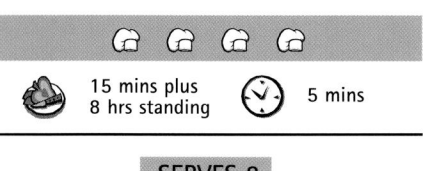

1 Line 8 individual heart-shaped moulds with muslin. Press the ricotta cheese through a sieve into a bowl. Add the icing sugar, double cream and vanilla essence and beat together thoroughly. Stir in the grated chocolate. Place the egg whites in a large bowl and whisk until stiff but not dry. Gently fold into the chocolate cheese mixture.

2 Spoon the mixture into the prepared moulds. Stand the moulds on a tray or dish and leave in the refrigerator overnight to drain. The muslin will absorb most of the liquid. To make the raspberry coulis, put the raspberries in a blender or food processor and process to a purée. Press the purée through a sieve into a bowl and add icing sugar to taste.

3 To serve, turn each coeur à la crème on to a serving plate and pour the raspberry coulis round. Decorate with halved strawberries.

COOK'S TIP
If you do not have the special heart-shaped moulds, use yogurt pots which have been pierced at the bottom. Alternatively, make one large mould by lining a sieve with cheesecloth.

Chocolate Rum Pots

Wickedly rich little chocolate pots, flavoured with a hint of dark rum, are pure indulgence on any occasion!

  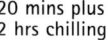

20 mins plus
2 hrs chilling

5 mins

SERVES 6

INGREDIENTS

225 g/8 oz plain chocolate

4 eggs, separated

6 tbsp caster sugar

4 tbsp dark rum

4 tbsp double cream

TO DECORATE

whipped cream

marbled chocolate shapes (see page 821)

1 Put the chocolate in a heatproof bowl set over a saucepan of gently simmering water until melted. Leave to cool slightly.

2 Whisk the egg yolks with the caster sugar in a clean bowl until very pale and fluffy.

3 Drizzle the melted chocolate into the mixture and fold in together with the rum and the double cream.

4 Whisk the egg whites in a greasefree bowl until soft peaks form. Fold the egg whites into the chocolate mixture in 2 batches. Divide the mixture among 6 individual dishes and chill in the refrigerator for at least 2 hours.

5 To serve, decorate with a little whipped cream and with marbled chocolate shapes.

COOK'S TIP

Make sure you use a perfectly clean, greasefree bowl for whisking the egg whites. They will not aerate if any grease is present as the smallest amount breaks down the bubbles in the whites, preventing them from trapping and holding air.

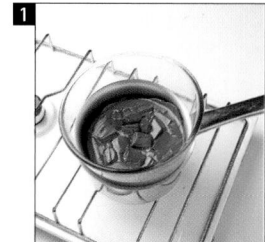  

Chocolate Hazelnut Pots

Chocoholics will adore these creamy desserts consisting of a rich baked chocolate custard with the delicious flavour of hazelnuts.

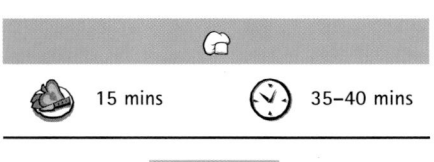

15 mins   35–40 mins

SERVES 4

I N G R E D I E N T S

2 eggs

2 egg yolks

1 tbsp caster sugar

1 tsp cornflour

600 ml/1 pint milk

85 g/3 oz plain chocolate

4 tbsp chocolate hazelnut spread

grated chocolate or quick chocolate curls

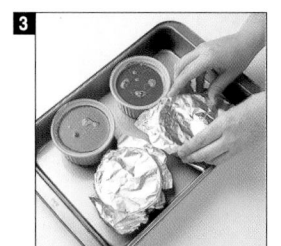

1 Preheat the oven to 160°C/325°F/Gas Mark 3. Beat together the eggs, egg yolks, caster sugar and cornflour until well combined. Heat the milk in a small saucepan until it is almost boiling.

2 Gradually pour the milk on to the eggs, whisking as you do so. Melt the chocolate and chocolate hazelnut spread in a heatproof bowl set over a saucepan of gently simmering water, then whisk the melted chocolate mixture into the eggs.

3 Pour into 4 small ovenproof dishes and cover the dishes with foil. Place them in a roasting tin. Fill the tin with boiling water until it comes halfway up the sides of the dishes.

4 Bake in the preheated oven for 35–40 minutes, until the custard is just set. Remove from the roasting tin and cool, then chill until required. Serve decorated with grated chocolate or chocolate curls.

COOK'S TIP
This dish is traditionally made in little pots called pots de crème, which are individual ovenproof dishes with a lid. Custard pots are fine. The dessert can also be made in one large dish: cook for about 1 hour, or until set.

Chocolate Cheese Pots

These super-light desserts are just the thing if you have a craving for chocolate. Serve them on their own or with a selection of fruits.

10 mins plus
30 mins chilling

0 mins

SERVES 4

INGREDIENTS

300 ml/10 fl oz low-fat natural
 fromage frais

150 ml/5 fl oz low-fat natural yogurt

2 tbsp icing sugar

4 tsp low-fat drinking chocolate powder

4 tsp cocoa powder

1 tsp vanilla essence

2 tbsp dark rum (optional)

2 egg whites

4 chocolate cake decorations

TO SERVE

pieces of kiwi fruit, orange and banana

strawberries and raspberries

1 Combine the fromage frais and low-fat yogurt in a bowl. Sift in the icing sugar, drinking chocolate powder and cocoa powder and mix well. Add the vanilla essence and rum (if using).

2 In a clean bowl, whisk the egg whites until stiff. Using a metal spoon, gently fold the egg whites into the chocolate mixture.

3 Spoon the yogurt and chocolate mixture into 4 small china dessert pots and chill in the refrigerator for about 30 minutes.

4 Decorate each chocolate cheese pot with a chocolate cake decoration and serve with an assortment of fresh fruit, such as pieces of kiwi fruit, orange, banana, strawberries and raspberries.

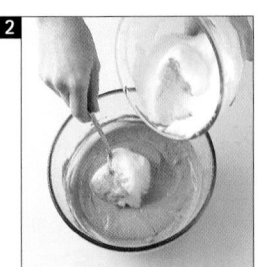

COOK'S TIP

This chocolate mixture can also be used as a cheesecake filling. Make the base out of crushed amaretti biscuits and egg white, and set the filling with 2 teaspoons of powdered gelatine dissolved in 2 tablespoons of boiling water.

Lebanese Almond Rice

This delicate rice cream is flavoured with almonds and rosewater.
If pomegranates are in season, decorate with the gorgeous pink seeds.

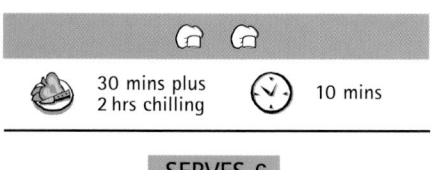

30 mins plus
2 hrs chilling   10 mins

SERVES 6

INGREDIENTS

6 tbsp rice flour

pinch of salt

700 ml/1¼ pints milk

55 g/2 oz caster sugar

85 g/3 oz ground almonds

1 tbsp rosewater

TO DECORATE

2 tbsp chopped pistachio nuts or toasted flaked almonds

pomegranate seeds (optional)

washed rose petals (optional)

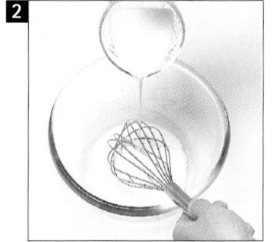
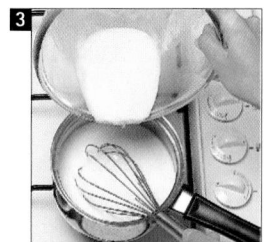

1 Put the rice flour in a bowl, stir in the salt and make a well in the centre.

2 Pour about 50 ml/2 fl oz of the milk into the well and whisk thoroughly to form a smooth paste.

3 Bring the remaining milk to the boil in a heavy-based saucepan. Whisk in the rice flour paste and the sugar and cook, stirring constantly, until the mixture thickens and bubbles. Reduce the heat and simmer gently for 5 minutes.

4 Whisk in the ground almonds until the mixture is smooth and thickened, then remove from the heat to cool slightly. Stir in the rosewater and cool completely, stirring occasionally.

5 Divide the mixture between 6 glasses or pour into a serving bowl. Chill for at least 2 hours before serving.

6 To serve, sprinkle with the pistachio nuts or almonds, pomegranate seeds and rose petals, if wished.

COOK'S TIP
For a smoother texture, this can be made without the ground almonds. Stir 2 tablespoons of cornflour into the ground rice and use a little more of the milk to make the paste. Proceed as directed, omitting the ground almonds.

Zuccotto

This famous Italian ice cream bombe is so named because its shape resembles a pumpkin, or zucca. Serve with fresh cherries, if wished.

30 mins plus
2 hrs chilling

0 mins

SERVES 4

INGREDIENTS

300 ml/10 fl oz double cream

25 g/1 oz icing sugar

55 g/ 2 oz hazelnuts, toasted

225 g/8 oz cherries, halved and stoned

55 g/2 oz plain chocolate,
    finely chopped

2 x 20-cm/8-inch round chocolate
    sponge cakes

3 tbsp brandy

2 tbsp kirsch

TO DECORATE

1 tbsp icing sugar

1 tbsp cocoa powder

fresh cherries (optional)

1 In a large bowl, whisk the cream until it is thick, then fold in the sugar, followed by the hazelnuts, cherries and chocolate. Cover with clingfilm and chill in the refrigerator until required.

2 Meanwhile, cut the sponge cakes in half horizontally and then cut the pieces to fit a 1.2-litre/2-pint bowl, so that the bottom and sides are completely lined. Reserve the remaining sponge cake. Mix together the brandy and kirsch in a small bowl and sprinkle the mixture over the sponge cake lining.

3 Remove the cream filling from the refrigerator and spoon it into the lined bowl. Cover the top with the remaining sponge cake, cut to fit. Cover with clingfilm and chill the bombe in the refrigerator for 2 hours, or until it is ready to serve.

4 For the decoration, sift the icing sugar into a bowl and the cocoa powder into another bowl. To serve, remove the bombe from the refrigerator and run a round-bladed knife around the sides to loosen it. Place a serving plate on top of the bowl and, holding them firmly together, invert. Dust opposite quarters with icing sugar and cocoa powder to make alternating sections of colour. Decorate with fresh cherries (if using).

Chocolate & Vanilla Creams

These rich, creamy desserts are completely irresistible. Decorate with chocolate shapes and serve them with crisp biscuits, if liked.

40 mins plus 1 hr chilling

5–10 mins

SERVES 4

INGREDIENTS

475 ml/ 16 fl oz double cream

6 tbsp caster sugar

1 vanilla pod

200 ml/6 fl oz crème fraîche

2 tsp powdered gelatine

3 tbsp water

50 g/1¾ oz plain chocolate

MARBLED CHOCOLATE SHAPES

little melted white chocolate

little melted plain chocolate

1 Place the cream and sugar in a saucepan and add the vanilla pod. Heat gently, stirring until the sugar has dissolved, then bring to the boil. Reduce the heat and simmer for 2–3 minutes.

2 Remove the saucepan from the heat and take out the vanilla pod. Stir in the crème fraîche.

3 Sprinkle the gelatine over the water in a small heatproof bowl and let it go spongy, then set over a saucepan of hot water and stir until dissolved. Stir into the cream mixture. Pour half of this mixture into another mixing bowl.

4 Put the plain chocolate in a heatproof bowl over a saucepan of simmering water until melted. Stir the melted chocolate into one half of the cream mixture. Pour the chocolate mixture into 4 individual glass serving dishes and chill for 15–20 minutes, until just set. While the chocolate mixture is chilling, keep the vanilla mixture at room temperature.

5 Spoon the vanilla mixture on top of the chocolate mixture and chill until the vanilla cream is set.

6 Meanwhile, make the shapes for the decoration. Spoon the melted white chocolate into a paper piping bag and snip off the tip. Spread some melted plain chocolate on a piece of baking parchment. While still soft, pipe a fine line of white chocolate in a scribble over the top. Use the tip of a cocktail stick to marble the white chocolate into the plain. When firm but not too hard, cut into shapes with a small shaped cutter or a sharp knife. Chill the shapes until firm, then use to decorate.

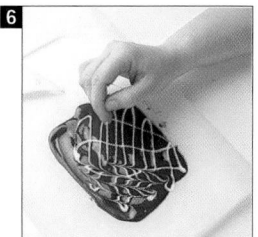

Chocolate & Pernod Creams

This unusual combination of flavours makes a sophisticated and tempting dessert to serve at a dinner party.

10 mins plus
2 hrs chilling

20 mins

SERVES 4

INGREDIENTS

55 g/2 oz plain chocolate, broken
into pieces

250 ml/8 fl oz milk

300 ml/10 fl oz double cream

2 tbsp caster sugar

1 tbsp arrowroot dissolved in 2 tbsp milk

3 tbsp Pernod

langues de chat biscuits, or chocolate-
tipped rolled wafers, to serve

1 Put the chocolate in a heatproof bowl set over a saucepan of gently simmering water. Stir over a low heat until melted. Remove the saucepan from the heat and cool slightly.

2 Pour the milk and cream into a saucepan over a low heat and bring to just below boiling point, stirring occasionally. Remove the saucepan from the heat and then set aside.

3 Beat the sugar and the arrowroot mixture into the melted chocolate. Gradually stir in the hot milk and cream mixture, then stir in the Pernod. Set the bowl over a saucepan of gently simmering water and cook, over a low heat, for 10 minutes, stirring constantly, until thick and smooth. Remove from the heat and leave to cool.

4 Pour the chocolate and Pernod mixture into 4 individual serving glasses. Cover with clingfilm and chill in the refrigerator for 2 hours before serving with langues de chat biscuits or chocolate-tipped rolled wafers, whichever you prefer.

Chocolate Mint Swirls

The classic combination of plain chocolate and mint flavours makes an attractive dessert for special occasions.

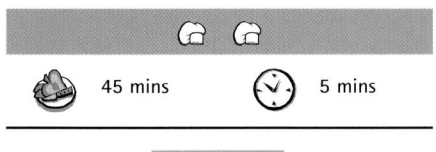

45 mins   5 mins

SERVES 6

INGREDIENTS

300 ml/10 fl oz double cream

150 g/5½ oz mascarpone cheese

2 tbsp icing sugar

1 tbsp crème de menthe

175 g/6 oz plain chocolate, broken into pieces plus extra for decorating

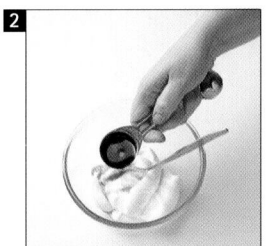

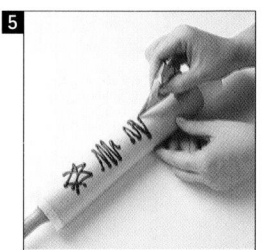

1 Place the cream in a large mixing bowl and whisk until soft peaks form.

2 Fold in the mascarpone cheese and icing sugar, then place about one-third of the mixture in a smaller bowl. Stir the crème de menthe into the smaller bowl. Put the plain chocolate in a heatproof bowl set over a saucepan of gently simmering water until melted. Stir the melted chocolate into the remaining mascarpone mixture.

3 Place alternate tablespoonfuls of the 2 mixtures into serving glasses, then swirl the mixture together to give a decorative effect. Chill until required.

4 To make the piped chocolate decorations, melt a small amount of chocolate and place in a paper piping bag.

5 Place a sheet of baking parchment on a cutting board and pipe squiggles, stars or flower shapes on to it with the melted chocolate. Alternatively, to make curved decorations, pipe decorations on to a long strip of baking parchment, then carefully place the strip over a rolling pin, securing with sticky tape. Let the chocolate set, then carefully remove from the baking parchment.

6 Decorate each dessert with the piped chocolate decorations and serve. The desserts can be decorated and then chilled, if preferred.

COOK'S TIP
Pipe the patterns freehand or draw patterns on to the baking parchment first, turn the baking parchment over and then pipe the chocolate, following the drawn outline.

Quick Chocolate Desserts

This rich creamy dessert takes hardly any time to prepare, but you will need to allow time for chilling before serving.

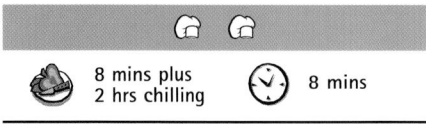

🍫 8 mins plus 2 hrs chilling 🕐 8 mins

SERVES 4

INGREDIENTS

125 ml/4 fl oz water

4 tbsp caster sugar

175 g/6 oz plain chocolate, broken into pieces

3 egg yolks

300 ml/10 fl oz double cream

sweet biscuits, to serve

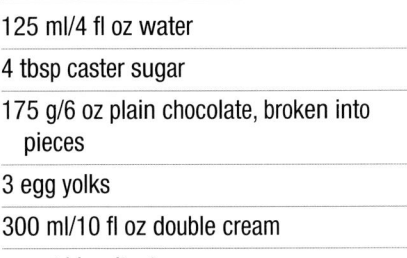

1 Pour the water into a saucepan and add the sugar. Stir over a low heat until the sugar has dissolved. Bring to the boil and continue to boil, without stirring, for 3 minutes. Remove the saucepan from the heat and leave to cool slightly.

2 Put the chocolate in a food processor and add the hot syrup. Process until the chocolate has melted, then add the egg yolks and process briefly until smooth. Finally, add the cream and process until fully incorporated.

3 Pour the mixture into 4 glasses or individual bowls, cover with clingfilm and chill in the refrigerator for 2 hours, until set. Serve with sweet biscuits.

Mocha Creams

These creamy chocolate- and coffee-flavoured desserts make a perfect end to an elegant meal. Serve with amaretti biscuits, if liked.

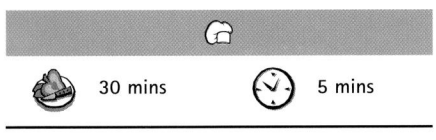

30 mins   5 mins

SERVES 4

I N G R E D I E N T S

225 g/8 oz plain chocolate

1 tbsp instant coffee powder

300 ml/10 fl oz boiling water

1 sachet powdered gelatine

3 tbsp cold water

1 tsp vanilla essence

1 tbsp Kahlúa or other coffee liqueur (optional)

300 ml/10 fl oz double cream

4 chocolate-covered coffee beans, to decorate

8 amaretti biscuits, to serve

1 Break the chocolate into small pieces and place in a saucepan with the coffee. Stir in the boiling water and heat gently, stirring until the chocolate melts.

2 Sprinkle the gelatine over the cold water, leave to go spongy, then whisk into the hot chocolate mixture to dissolve it.

3 Stir in the vanilla essence and coffee liqueur (if using). Leave to stand in a cool place until just starting to thicken, whisking from time to time.

4 Whisk the cream until soft peaks form, then reserve a little for decorating the desserts and fold the remainder into the chocolate mixture. Spoon into serving dishes and leave to set.

5 Decorate with the reserved cream and coffee beans and serve with the amaretti biscuits.

VARIATION
To add a delicious almond flavour to this dessert, replace the coffee liqueur with Amaretto.

Triple Stripe Cream

Layers of chocolate, vanilla and coffee, topped with a swirl of whipped cream, make a simple but elegant dessert for any occasion.

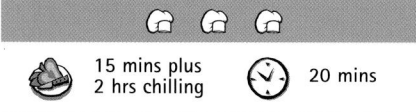

15 mins plus
2 hrs chilling

20 mins

SERVES 6

I N G R E D I E N T S

300 g/10½ oz caster sugar

6 tbsp cornflour

900 ml/1½ pints milk

3 egg yolks

6 tbsp unsalted butter, cut into pieces

1 heaped tbsp instant coffee powder

2 tsp vanilla essence

2 tbsp cocoa powder, sifted

150 ml/5 fl oz whipped cream, to decorate

1 Put 100 g/3½ oz of the caster sugar and 2 tablespoons of the cornflour in a small, heavy-based saucepan. Gradually whisk in one-third of the milk. Set the saucepan over a low heat and whisk in one of the egg yolks. Bring to the boil, whisking constantly, and boil for 1 minute. Remove the saucepan from the heat and stir in 1 tablespoon of the butter and all the coffee powder. Set aside to cool slightly, then divide between 6 wine goblets and smooth the surfaces.

2 Place 100 g/3½ oz of the remaining sugar and 2 tablespoons of the remaining cornflour in a small, heavy-based saucepan. Gradually, whisk in 300 ml/10 fl oz of the remaining milk. Set the saucepan over a low heat and whisk in one of the remaining egg yolks. Bring to the boil, whisking constantly, and boil for 1 minute. Remove the saucepan from the heat and stir in 2 tablespoons of the remaining butter and all the vanilla. Set aside to cool slightly, then divide between the goblets and smooth the surfaces.

3 Put the remaining sugar and cornstarch into a small, heavy-based saucepan. Gradually, whisk in the remaining milk. Set the saucepan over a low heat and whisk in the last egg yolk. Bring to the boil, whisking constantly, and boil for 1 minute. Remove from the heat and stir in the remaining butter and all the cocoa powder. Set the mixture aside to cool slightly, then divide among the goblets. Cover with clingfilm and chill in the refrigerator for 2 hours until set.

4 Whip the cream until thick, then pipe a swirl on top of each of the desserts. Serve immediately.

Chocolate Clouds

This unbelievably easy but delicious dessert can be made in a matter of a few minutes. Add the cream just before serving.

 50 mins plus 1 hr 30 mins chilling

 5 mins

SERVES 6

INGREDIENTS

115 g/4 oz plain chocolate, broken into pieces

4 eggs, separated

600 ml/1 pint double cream

toasted flaked almonds, to decorate

1 Put the chocolate in a heatproof bowl set over a saucepan of gently simmering water. Stir over a low heat until melted. Remove from the heat and leave to cool slightly, then beat in the egg yolks.

2 In a separate bowl, whisk the egg whites until they are stiff, then fold them into the chocolate mixture. Set aside for 30 minutes until starting to set.

3 Whip half the cream until thick, then fold 150 ml/5 fl oz of it into the chocolate mixture. Spoon half the chocolate mixture into 6 sundae glasses. Divide another 150 ml/5 fl oz of the whipped cream among the glasses in a layer over the chocolate mixture, then top with the remaining chocolate mixture. Cover with clingfilm and chill in the refrigerator for 30 minutes.

4 Just before serving, whip the remaining cream until it is thick. Pipe a swirl of cream on the top of each dessert and sprinkle with the almonds.

Chocolate Banana Sundae

A banana split in a glass! Choose the best vanilla ice cream you can find, or better still, make your own. Serve with fan wafers.

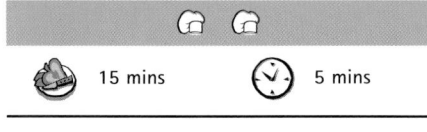

15 mins   5 mins

SERVES 4

INGREDIENTS

GLOSSY CHOCOLATE SAUCE

55 g/2 oz plain chocolate

4 tbsp golden syrup

1 tbsp butter

1 tbsp brandy or dark rum (optional)

SUNDAE

4 bananas, peeled

150 ml/5 fl oz double cream

8–12 scoops good-quality vanilla ice cream

75 g/2¾ oz flaked or chopped almonds, toasted

grated or flaked chocolate, for sprinkling

4 fan wafers, to serve

1 To make the chocolate sauce, break the chocolate into small pieces and place in a heatproof bowl with the syrup and butter. Set over a saucepan of gently simmering water until melted, stirring until well combined. Remove the bowl from the heat and stir in the brandy or rum (if using).

2 Whip the cream until just holding its shape and slice the bananas. Place a scoop of ice cream in the bottom of 4 tall sundae dishes. Top with slices of banana, some chocolate sauce, a spoonful of cream and a generous sprinkling of nuts.

3 Repeat the layers, finishing with a good dollop of cream, sprinkled with nuts and a little grated or flaked chocolate. Serve with fan wafers.

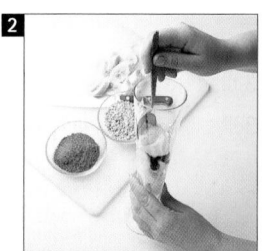

VARIATION

For a traditional banana split, halve the bananas lengthwise and place on a plate with 2 scoops of ice cream between. Top with cream and sprinkle with nuts. Serve with the glossy chocolate sauce poured over the top.

Champagne Mousse

Any dry sparkling wine made by the traditional method used for champagne can be used for this elegant dessert.

🍲 1 hr plus
2 hrs chilling

🕐 8 mins

SERVES 4

I N G R E D I E N T S

SPONGE

2 tbsp butter, melted, plus extra
for greasing

4 eggs

100 g/3½ oz caster sugar

75 g/2¾ oz self-raising flour

2 tbsp cocoa powder

MOUSSE

1 sachet powdered gelatine

3 tbsp water

300 ml/10 fl oz champagne of dry sparkling
wine

300 ml/10 fl oz double cream

2 egg whites

6 tbsp caster sugar

55 g/2 oz plain chocolate, melted, to
decorate

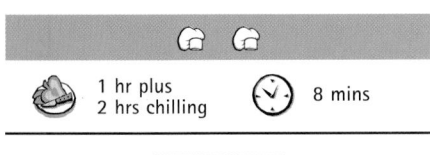

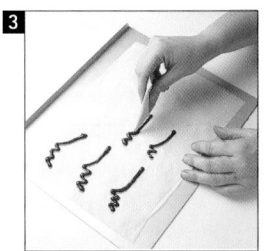

1 Preheat the oven to 200°C/400°F/ Gas Mark 6. Line a 38 x 25-cm/ 15 x 10-inch Swiss roll tin with greased baking parchment. Place the eggs and sugar in a bowl and whisk, using an electric whisk if you have one, until the mixture is very thick and a trail is left when the whisk is dragged across the surface. If using a balloon whisk, use a heatproof bowl set over a saucepan of gently simmering water while whisking. Sift the flour and cocoa powder together and fold into the egg mixture. Fold in the butter. Pour into the tin and bake in the preheated oven for 8 minutes, or until springy to the touch. Cool for 5 minutes,

then turn out on to a wire rack until cold. Meanwhile, line 4 x 10-cm/4-inch baking rings with baking parchment. Line the sides with 2.5-cm/1-inch strips of cake and the bottom with circles.

2 For the mousse, sprinkle the gelatine over the water and let it go spongy. Set the bowl over a saucepan of gently simmering water; stir until dissolved. Stir in the champagne.

3 Whip the cream until just holding its shape. Fold in the champagne mixture. Stand in a cool place until on the point of setting, stirring. Whisk the egg whites until soft peaks form, add the sugar and whisk until glossy. Fold into the setting mixture. Spoon into the sponge cases, letting the mixture go above the sponge. Chill for 2 hours. Pipe the chocolate in squiggles on a piece of baking parchment, leave them to set, then use them to decorate the mousses.

Layered Chocolate Mousse

Three layers of rich mousse give this elegant dessert extra chocolate appeal. It is a little fiddly to prepare, but well worth the extra effort.

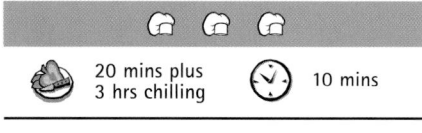

20 mins plus
3 hrs chilling

10 mins

SERVES 4

INGREDIENTS

3 eggs

1 tsp cornflour

4 tbsp caster sugar

300 ml/10 fl oz milk

1 sachet powdered gelatine

3 tbsp water

300 ml/10 fl oz double cream

75 g/2¾ oz plain chocolate, broken into pieces

75 g/2¾ oz white chocolate, broken into pieces

75 g/2¾ oz milk chocolate, broken into pieces

chocolate caraque, to decorate (see page 9)

3 Sprinkle the gelatine over the water in a small heatproof bowl and let it go spongy. Set over a saucepan of hot water and stir until dissolved. Stir into the hot custard mixture. Leave the mixture to cool.

4 Whip the cream until just holding its shape. Fold into the egg custard, then divide the mixture into 3. Put the 3 types of chocolate in separate heatproof bowls set over saucepans of gently simmering water until melted. Fold the plain chocolate into one egg custard portion. Whisk one egg white until soft peaks form and fold into the plain chocolate custard until combined. Pour into the prepared tin and smooth the top. Chill in the coldest part of the refrigerator until just set. Leave the remaining mixtures at room temperature.

5 Fold the white chocolate into another portion of the egg custard. Whisk another egg white and fold in. Pour on top of the plain chocolate layer and chill quickly. Repeat with the remaining milk chocolate and egg white. Chill for at least 2 hours, until set. To serve, carefully turn out on to a serving dish and decorate with chocolate caraque.

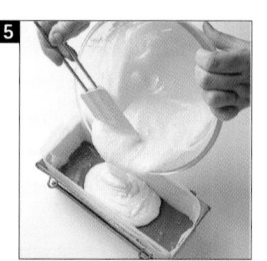

1 Line a 450-g/1-lb loaf tin with baking parchment. Separate the eggs, putting each egg white in a separate bowl. Place the egg yolks and sugar in a large mixing bowl and whisk until well combined. Place the milk in a saucepan and heat gently, stirring until almost boiling. Pour the milk on to the egg yolks, whisking.

2 Set the bowl over a saucepan of gently simmering water and cook, stirring until the mixture thickens enough to thinly coat the back of a wooden spoon.

White Chocolate Mousse

White chocolate makes a sweet and creamy mousse and fragrant rosewater adds an interesting flavour. Decorate with washed rose petals.

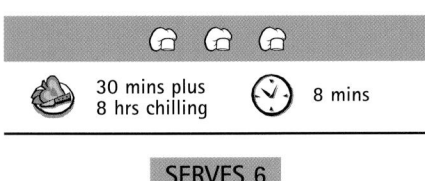
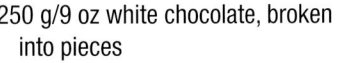

30 mins plus
8 hrs chilling

8 mins

SERVES 6

INGREDIENTS

250 g/9 oz white chocolate, broken into pieces

125 ml/4 fl oz full-cream milk

300 ml/10 fl oz double cream

1 tsp rosewater

115 g/4 oz plain chocolate, broken into pieces

washed rose petals, to decorate

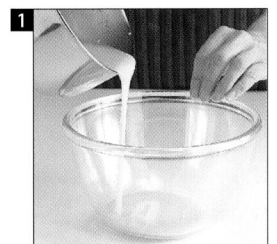

1 Put the white chocolate and milk in a saucepan and heat very gently until the chocolate has melted. Transfer to a large bowl and leave to cool.

2 Put the cream and rosewater in a bowl and whisk until soft peaks form. In a large bowl, whisk the egg whites until stiff but not dry. Fold the whipped cream into the chocolate, then fold in the egg whites. Spoon the mixture into 6 small dishes or glasses, cover with clingfilm, and chill in the refrigerator for 8 hours, or overnight, to set.

3 Put the plain chocolate in a heatproof bowl set over a saucepan of gently simmering water until melted. Leave to cool, then spread evenly over the mousses. Leave until hardened, then decorate with rose petals and serve.

Mocha Swirl Mousse

A combination of feather-light yet rich chocolate and coffee mousses, whipped and attractively presented in serving glasses or dishes.

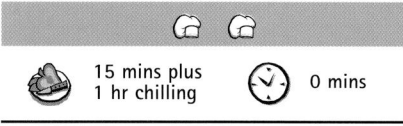

15 mins plus 1 hr chilling

0 mins

SERVES 4

INGREDIENTS

1 tbsp coffee and chicory essence

2 tsp cocoa powder, plus extra for dusting

1 tsp low-fat drinking chocolate powder

150 ml/5 fl oz low-fat crème fraîche, plus 4 tsp to serve

2 tsp powdered gelatine

2 tbsp boiling water

2 large egg whites

2 tbsp caster sugar

4 chocolate-covered coffee beans, to serve

1 Place the coffee and chicory essence in one bowl, and 2 teaspoons of cocoa powder and the drinking chocolate in another bowl. Divide the crème fraîche between the 2 bowls and mix both well.

2 Dissolve the gelatine in the boiling water and set aside. In a greasefree bowl, whisk the egg whites and sugar until stiff and divide this evenly between the 2 mixtures.

3 Divide the dissolved gelatine among the 2 mixtures. Using a large metal spoon, gently fold in until well mixed.

4 Spoon small amounts of the 2 mousses alternately into 4 serving glasses and swirl together gently. Chill for 1 hour or until set.

5 To serve, top each mousse with a teaspoon of crème fraîche, a chocolate coffee bean, and a light dusting of cocoa. Serve immediately.

COOK'S TIP

Vegetarians should not be denied this delicious chocolate dessert. Instead of gelatine, use the vegetarian equivalent, gelozone, available from health-food shops. Be sure to read the instructions on the package first, because it is prepared differently from gelatine.

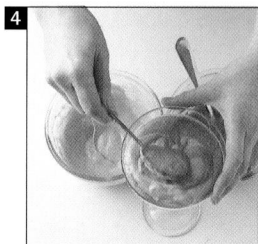

Chocolate Mousse

This is a light and fluffy mousse with a subtle hint of orange. It is wickedly delicious served with a fresh fruit sauce.

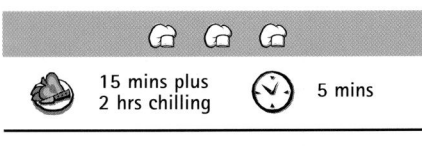

15 mins plus
2 hrs chilling

5 mins

SERVES 8

INGREDIENTS

100 g/3½ oz plain chocolate, broken into pieces

300 ml/10 fl oz natural yogurt

150 ml/5 fl oz Quark

4 tbsp caster sugar

1 tbsp orange juice

1 tbsp brandy

1½ tsp powdered gelatine, or gelozone (vegetarian gelatine)

125 ml/4 fl oz cold water

2 large egg whites

TO DECORATE

coarsely grated Continental plain and white chocolate

orange zest

1 Put the chocolate in a heatproof bowl set over a saucepan of gently simmering water until melted. Put the melted chocolate, yogurt, Quark, sugar, orange juice and brandy in a food processor or blender and process for 30 seconds. Transfer to a large bowl.

2 Sprinkle the gelatine or gelozone over the water and stir until dissolved.

3 In a saucepan, bring the gelatine or gelozone and water to a boil for 2 minutes. Cool slightly, then thoroughly stir into the chocolate mixture.

4 Whisk the egg whites until stiff peaks form and fold into the chocolate mixture using a metal spoon.

5 Line a 500-g/1-lb 2 oz loaf tin with clingfilm. Spoon the mousse into the tin. Chill in the refrigerator for 2 hours, until set. Turn the mousse out on to a serving plate, decorate with grated chocolate and orange zest, then serve.

COOK'S TIP

For a quick fruit sauce, process canned mandarin segments in natural juice in a food processor and press through a strainer. Stir in 1 tablespoon of honey and serve with the mousse.

Rich Chocolate Mousses

A serious dessert for dedicated chocolate lovers, they make a spectacular finale to any special-occasion meal.

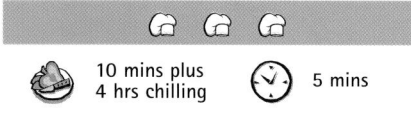

10 mins plus
4 hrs chilling

5 mins

SERVES 4

INGREDIENTS

300 g/10½ oz plain chocolate (at least 70% cocoa solids)

5 tbsp caster sugar

1½ tbsp unsalted butter

1 tbsp brandy

4 eggs, separated

cocoa powder, to decorate

1 Break the chocolate into small pieces and put it in a heatproof bowl over a saucepan of gently simmering water. Add the caster sugar and butter and melt together, stirring, until smooth. Remove from the heat, stir in the brandy, and leave to cool a little. Add the egg yolks and beat until smooth.

2 In a separate bowl, whisk the egg whites until stiff peaks form, then fold them into the chocolate mixture. Place a stainless steel cooking ring on each of 4 small serving plates, then spoon the mixture into each ring and smooth the surfaces. Transfer to the refrigerator and chill for at least 4 hours until set.

3 Remove the mousses from the refrigerator and carefully remove the cooking rings. Dust with cocoa powder and serve immediately.

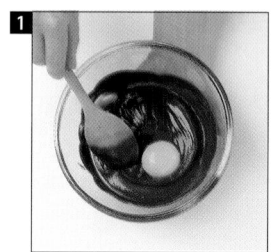

Sweet Mascarpone Mousse

A sweet cream cheese dessert that complements the tartness of fresh summer fruits rather well. Serve with amaretti biscuits, if liked.

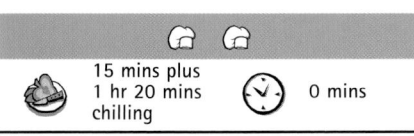

15 mins plus 1 hr 20 mins chilling

0 mins

SERVES 4

INGREDIENTS

450 g/1 lb mascarpone cheese

115 g/4 oz caster sugar

4 egg yolks

400 g/14 oz frozen summer fruits, such as raspberries and redcurrants

redcurrants, to decorate

amaretti biscuits, to serve

1 Place the mascarpone cheese in a large mixing bowl. Using a wooden spoon, beat the mascarpone cheese until smooth and creamy.

2 Stir the sugar and egg yolks into the mascarpone cheese, mixing well. Chill the mixture in the refrigerator for 1 hour.

3 Spoon a layer of the mascarpone mixture into the bottom of 4 individual serving dishes. Spoon a layer of the summer fruits on top. Repeat the layers in the same order, reserving some of the mascarpone mixture for the top.

4 Chill the mousses in the refrigerator for about 20 minutes. The fruits should still be slightly frozen.

5 Decorate the mascarpone mousses with redcurrants and serve with amaretti biscuits.

VARIATION
Try adding 3 tablespoons of your favourite liqueur to the mascarpone cheese mixture in step 1, if you prefer.

Black & White Pudding

This rich dessert is a cross between a steamed pudding and a soufflé.
It makes an extravagant treat whatever the occasion.

30 mins   45 mins

SERVES 4

INGREDIENTS

oil, for brushing

115 g/4 oz unsalted butter

115 g/4 oz golden caster sugar

½ tsp ground cardamom seeds

4 eggs, separated

115 g/4 oz plain chocolate, broken
   into pieces

1 tbsp rum

150 ml/5 fl oz double cream

55 g/2 oz crème fraîche

1 Lightly brush a 900-ml/1½-pint pudding basin with oil. Place the butter, sugar and cardamom in a bowl and beat until light and thick. Gradually beat in the egg yolks. Put the chocolate in a heatproof bowl set over a saucepan of gently simmering water until melted. Leave to cool. Stir the cooled chocolate and the rum into the egg mixture. Place the egg whites in a separate greasefree bowl and whisk until stiff. Stir 1 tablespoon of the whisked egg whites into the chocolate mixture, then carefully fold in the remainder.

2 Turn the mixture into the basin. Cover with oiled baking parchment and foil and tie securely with string. Place the basin in a large, heavy-based saucepan and pour in enough boiling water to come one-third of the way up the side of the basin. Cover and simmer for 45 minutes.

3 Leave in the basin until cold, then turn out on to a serving dish. Whip the cream and crème fraîche together and pour over the pudding to serve.

Raspberry Creams

A refreshing dessert that, as well as being delicious and simple to prepare, has the advantage of being low in fat.

10 mins plus
1 hr chilling

0 mins

SERVES 4

INGREDIENTS

400 g/14 oz raspberries

175 g/6 oz low-fat cottage cheese

3 tbsp sugar

150 ml/5 fl oz low-fat natural yogurt

icing sugar, sifted, to decorate

1 Reserving a few whole raspberries to decorate, use the back of a spoon to push the raspberries and cottage cheese through a sieve into a bowl.

2 Stir the sugar and yogurt into the raspberry mixture and stir to blend, then spoon into individual serving dishes. Chill in the refrigerator for about 1 hour.

3 Serve chilled, decorated with the reserved raspberries and dusted with sifted icing sugar.

Lime Mousse with Mango

Lime-flavoured cream moulds, served with a fresh mango and lime sauce, make a stunning dessert for any occasion.

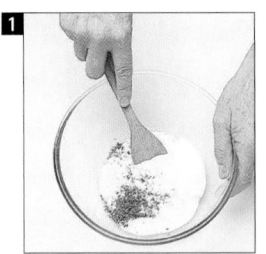

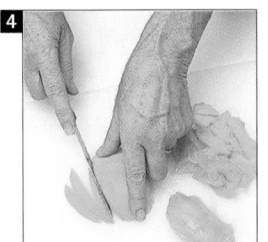

10 mins   0 mins

SERVES 4

INGREDIENTS

250 g/9 oz cream cheese

grated rind of 1 lime

1 tbsp caster sugar

125 ml/4 oz double cream

MANGO SAUCE

1 mango

juice of 1 lime

4 tsp caster sugar

TO DECORATE

4 Cape gooseberries

strips of lime zest

1 Put the cream cheese, lime rind and sugar in a bowl and mix together.

2 Whisk the double cream in a separate bowl and fold into the cream cheese.

COOK'S TIP
Cape gooseberries have a tart and mildly scented flavour and make an excellent decoration for many desserts. Peel back the papery husks to expose the bright orange fruits.

3 Line 4 decorative moulds or ramekins with cheesecloth or clingfilm and divide the mixture evenly among them. Fold the lining over the top and press down firmly.

4 To make the sauce, slice through the mango on each side of the large flat stone, then cut the flesh from the stone. Remove the skin, cut 12 thin, neat slices and set aside.

5 Chop the remaining mango and put into a food processor with the lime juice and sugar. Blend until smooth, or push the mango through a sieve, then mix with the lime juice and sugar.

6 Turn out the moulds on to serving plates. Arrange 3 slices of mango on each plate, pour some sauce around, decorate with Cape gooseberries and lime zest and serve.

Mango Mousse

This is a light, softly set and tangy mousse, which is perfect for clearing the palate after a Chinese meal of mixed flavours.

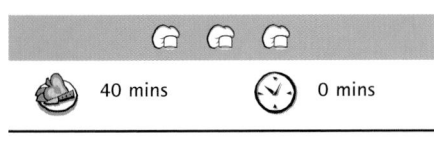

🍮 40 mins   🕐 0 mins

SERVES 4

I N G R E D I E N T S

400 g/14 oz canned mangoes in syrup

2 pieces stem ginger, chopped,
   plus extra to decorate

200 ml/7 fl oz double cream

4 tsp powdered gelatine

2 tbsp hot water

2 egg whites

1½ tbsp light soft brown sugar

lime zest, to decorate

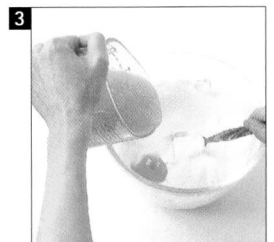

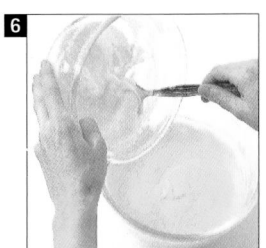

1 Drain the mangoes, reserving the syrup. Blend the mango pieces and ginger in a food processor or blender for 30 seconds, or until smooth.

2 Measure the purée and make up to 300 ml/10 fl oz with the reserved mango syrup.

3 In a separate bowl, whip the cream until soft peaks form. Fold the mango mixture into the cream until well combined.

4 Dissolve the gelatine in the hot water and leave to cool slightly.

5 Pour the gelatine into the mango mixture in a steady stream, stirring. Leave to cool in the refrigerator for 30 minutes until almost set.

6 Whisk the egg whites in a clean bowl until soft peaks form, then whisk in the sugar. Gently fold the egg whites into the mango mixture with a metal spoon.

7 Spoon the mousse into individual serving dishes, decorate with stem ginger and lime zest and serve.

COOK'S TIP
The gelatine must be stirred into the mango mixture in a gentle, steady stream to prevent it from setting in lumps when it comes into contact with the cold mixture.

Orange Syllabub

A zesty, creamy whip made from yogurt and milk with a hint of orange, served with light and luscious sweet sponge cakes.

30 mins plus
2 hrs chilling

10 mins

SERVES 4

INGREDIENTS

4 oranges

600 ml/1 pint low-fat natural yogurt

6 tbsp low-fat milk powder

4 tbsp caster sugar

1 tbsp grated orange rind

4 tbsp orange juice

2 egg whites

orange zest, to decorate

SPONGE HEARTS

2 medium eggs

85 g/3 oz caster sugar

40 g/1½ oz plain flour

40 g/1½ oz wholemeal flour

1 tbsp hot water

1 tsp icing sugar, for dusting

1 Slice off the tops and bottoms of the oranges, then the peel. Cut out the segments, removing the pith and membranes between each one. Divide the orange segments among 4 dessert glasses, then chill.

2 In a mixing bowl, combine the yogurt, milk powder, sugar, orange rind and juice. Cover and chill for 1 hour. Whisk the egg whites until stiff, then fold into the yogurt mixture. Pile on to the orange slices and chill for 1 hour. Decorate with fresh orange zest.

3 To make the sponge hearts, preheat the oven to 220°C/ 425°F/Gas Mark 7. Line a 15 x 25-cm/6 x 10-inch baking tin with baking parchment. Whisk the eggs and caster sugar until thick and pale. Sift the flours, then fold in using a large metal spoon, adding the hot water at the same time.

4 Pour into the tin and bake in the preheated oven for 9–10 minutes, until golden and firm to the touch.

5 Turn on to a sheet of baking parchment. Using a 2-inch/5-cm heart-shaped cutter, stamp out hearts. Transfer to a wire rack to cool. Lightly dust with icing sugar before serving with the syllabub.

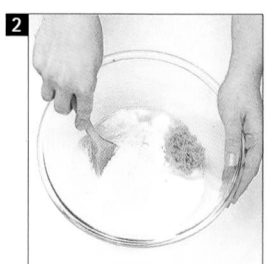

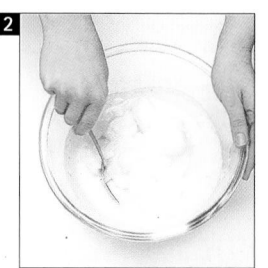

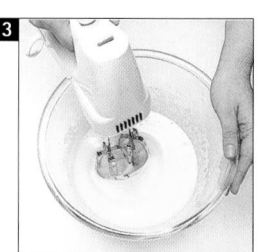

Syllabub

Wine, brandy and cream make this old-fashioned dessert wonderfully self-indulgent and it is guaranteed to impress at dinner parties.

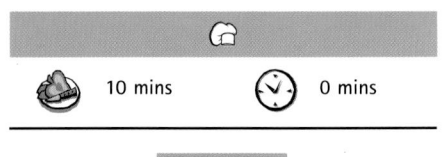

10 mins   0 mins

SERVES 6

I N G R E D I E N T S

175 ml/6 fl oz Madeira

2 tbsp brandy

grated rind of 1 lemon

125 ml/4 fl oz lemon juice

115 g/4 oz caster sugar

600 ml/1 pint double cream

10 amaretti or ratafia biscuits, crumbled

ground cinnamon and lemon slices,
   to decorate

1 Whisk the Madeira, brandy, lemon rind, lemon juice and sugar in a bowl until combined.

2 Add the cream and whisk until the mixture is thick.

3 Divide the biscuits among 6 long-stemmed glasses or sundae dishes. Fill each glass or dish with the syllabub mixture and chill until ready to serve. Dust the surface of each dessert with a little ground cinnamon and decorate with the lemon slices.

COOK'S TIP

Madeira is a fortified wine from the island of the same name. It may be dry, medium or sweet. Sweet Madeira is best for this recipe.

Lemon & Lime Syllabub

This dessert is rich but absolutely delicious. It is not, however, for the calorie-conscious because it contains a high proportion of cream.

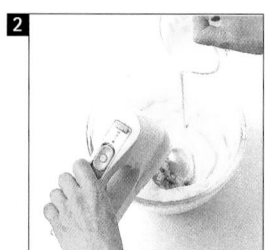
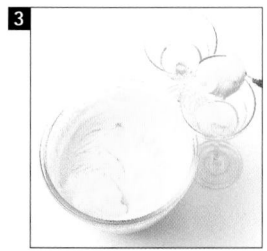

15 mins plus
4 hrs infusing/
chilling

0 mins

SERVES 4

INGREDIENTS

50 g/1¾ oz caster sugar

grated rind and juice of 1 small lemon

grated rind and juice of 1 small lime

50 ml/2 fl oz Marsala or medium sherry

300 ml/10 fl oz double cream

strips of lime and lemon zest, to decorate

1 Put the sugar, lemon rind and juice, lime rind and juice and Marsala in a bowl, mix well, and set aside to infuse for 2 hours.

2 Add the cream to the fruit juice mixture and whisk until it just holds its shape.

3 Spoon the mixture into 4 tall serving glasses and chill in the refrigerator for 2 hours.

4 Decorate with strips of lime and lemon zest and serve.

Pink Syllabub

The pretty pink colour of this dessert is achieved by adding blackcurrant liqueur to the wine and cream before whipping.

45 mins

0 mins

SERVES 2

INGREDIENTS

5 tbsp white wine

2–3 tsp blackcurrant liqueur

finely grated rind of ½ lemon or orange

1 tbsp caster sugar

200 ml/7 fl oz double cream

4 boudoir biscuits (optional)

fresh fruit, such as strawberries, raspberries or redcurrants, or pecan or walnut halves

fresh mint sprigs

1 Mix together the white wine, blackcurrant liqueur, grated lemon or orange rind and caster sugar in a bowl and set aside for at least 30 minutes.

2 Add the cream to the wine mixture and whip until the mixture has thickened enough to stand in soft peaks.

3 If you are using the boudoir biscuits, break them up roughly and divide them among 2 glasses.

4 Put the mixture into a piping bag fitted with a large star or plain nozzle and pipe it over the boudoir biscuits. Alternatively, simply pour the syllabub over the boudoir biscuits. Leave to chill until ready to serve.

5 Before serving, decorate each syllabub with slices or small pieces of fresh soft fruit or nuts and sprigs of mint.

COOK'S TIP
These syllabubs will keep in the refrigerator for 48 hours, so it is worth making more than you need, and keeping the extra for another day.

Baked Chocolate Alaska

A cool dessert that leaves the cook completely unflustered – assemble it in advance and keep it in the freezer until required.

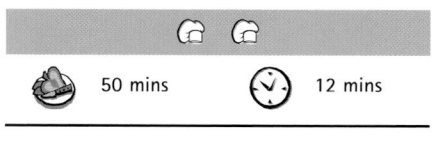

50 mins 12 mins

SERVES 4

INGREDIENTS

butter, for greasing

2 eggs

4 tbsp caster sugar

4 tbsp plain flour

2 tbsp cocoa powder

3 egg whites

150 g/5½ oz caster sugar

1 litre/1¾ good-quality chocolate ice cream

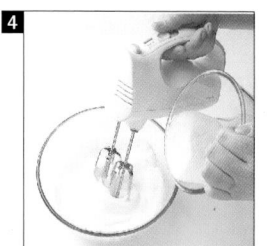

1 Preheat the oven to 220°C/425°F/ Gas Mark 7. Grease an 18-cm/7-inch round cake tin and line the base with baking parchment.

2 Whisk the eggs and the 4 tablespoons of sugar in a mixing bowl until very thick and pale. Sift the flour and cocoa powder together and carefully fold in.

3 Pour into the prepared tin and bake in the preheated oven for 7 minutes, or until springy to the touch. Transfer to a wire rack to cool completely.

COOK'S TIP

This dessert is delicious served with a blackcurrant coulis. Cook a few blackcurrants in a little orange juice until soft, blend to a purée and push through a sieve, then sweeten to taste with a little icing sugar.

4 Whisk the egg whites in a greasefree bowl until soft peaks form. Gradually add the sugar, whisking until you have a thick, glossy meringue.

5 Place the sponge on a baking tray and pile the ice cream on to the centre in a heaped dome.

6 Pipe or spread the meringue over the ice cream, making sure the ice cream is completely enclosed. (At this point the dessert can be frozen, if wished.)

7 Return it to the oven, for 5 minutes until the meringue is just golden. Serve immediately.

Apricot & Orange Fool

A simple, summery dessert that takes only minutes to make. Apricots and orange juice make a refreshing combination.

5 mins   0 mins

SERVES 4

I N G R E D I E N T S

175 g/6 oz ready-to-eat dried apricots

1 tbsp honey

225 ml/8 fl oz fresh orange juice

225 ml/8 fl oz low-fat natural yogurt

2 tsp toasted flaked almonds, to decorate

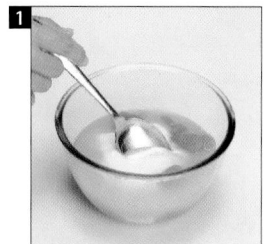

1 Put all the ingredients, except the almonds, in a bowl and mix thoroughly until smooth.

2 Serve in individual glass dishes, decorated with the toasted almonds.

Tropical Fruit Fool

Fruit fools are always popular, and this light, tangy version will be no exception. You can use your favourite fruits in this recipe.

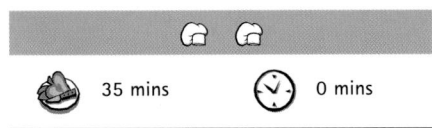

🕐 35 mins ⏱ 0 mins

SERVES 4

INGREDIENTS

1 medium ripe mango

2 kiwi fruit

1 medium banana

2 tbsp lime juice

½ tsp finely grated lime rind, plus extra strands of zest to decorate

2 egg whites

425 ml/15 fl oz canned low-fat custard

½ tsp vanilla essence

2 passion fruit

1 Peel the mango, then slice either side of the smooth, flat central stone. Roughly chop the flesh and process the fruit in a food processor or blender until smooth. Alternatively, mash with a fork.

2 Peel the kiwi fruit, chop the flesh into small pieces and place in a bowl. Peel and chop the banana and add to the bowl. Toss all of the fruit in the lime juice and rind and mix well.

3 In a greasefree bowl, whisk the egg whites until stiff and then gently fold in the custard and vanilla essence until thoroughly mixed.

4 In 4 tall glasses, alternately layer the chopped fruit, mango purée and custard mixture, finishing with the custard on top. Set aside to chill in the refrigerator for 20 minutes.

5 Halve the passion fruit, scoop out the seeds, and spoon over the fruit fools. Decorate each serving with the extra lime zest and serve.

VARIATION

Other tropical fruits to try include papaya purée, with chopped pineapple and dates, or pomegranate seeds to decorate.

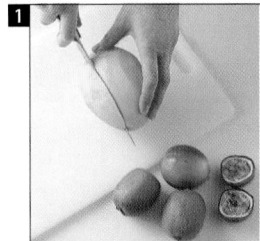
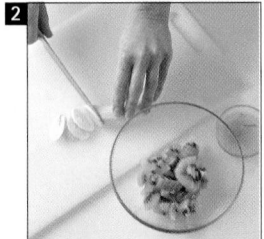
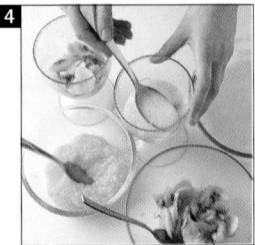

Raspberry Fool

This dish is very easy to make and can be prepared in advance and stored in the refrigerator until required.

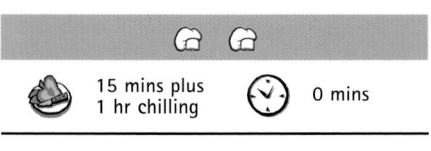

15 mins plus
1 hr chilling

0 mins

SERVES 4

INGREDIENTS

300 g/10½ oz fresh raspberries, plus extra to decorate

50 g/1¾ oz icing sugar

300 ml/10 fl oz crème fraîche, plus extra to decorate

½ tsp vanilla essence

2 egg whites

lemon balm leaves, to decorate

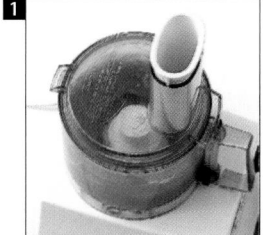

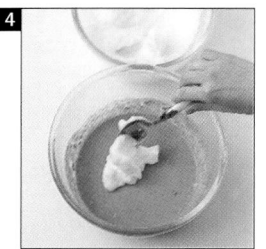

1 Put the raspberries and icing sugar in a food processor or blender and process until smooth. Alternatively, press through a sieve with the back of a spoon.

2 Reserve 1 tablespoon per portion of crème fraîche for decorating.

3 Put the vanilla essence and remaining crème fraîche in a bowl and stir in the raspberry mixture.

4 Whisk the egg whites in a separate mixing bowl until stiff peaks form. Gently fold the egg whites into the raspberry mixture using a metal spoon, until fully incorporated.

5 Spoon the raspberry fool into individual serving dishes and chill for at least 1 hour. Decorate with the reserved crème fraîche, raspberries and lemon balm leaves and serve.

COOK'S TIP
Although this dessert is best made with fresh raspberries in season, an acceptable result can be achieved with frozen raspberries, which are available from most stores.

Almond Sherbet

It is best to use whole almonds rather than ready-ground almonds for this dish because they give it a better texture.

45 mins plus
3–8 hrs 30 mins
soaking/chilling

0 mins

SERVES 2

INGREDIENTS

225 g/8 oz shelled almonds

2 tbsp sugar

300 ml/10 fl oz milk

300 ml/10 fl oz water

1 Put the almonds in a bowl, cover with water, and set aside to soak for at least 3 hours or preferably overnight.

2 Using a sharp knife, chop the almonds into small pieces. Grind to a fine paste in a food processor or in a pestle and mortar.

3 Add the sugar to the almond paste and grind once again to form a very fine paste.

4 Add the milk and water and mix thoroughly in a bowl or use a blender.

5 Transfer the almond sherbet to a large serving dish.

6 Chill the almond sherbet in the refrigerator for about 30 minutes. Stir it well just before serving.

Mocha Sorbet

This mocha sorbet makes a light and refreshing yet luxurious end to any meal. Serve with some crisp biscuits and freshly brewed coffee.

15 mins plus 9 hrs freezing/ chilling

10 mins

SERVES 6

INGREDIENTS

100 g/3½ oz cocoa powder

150 g/5 oz golden caster sugar

2 tsp instant coffee powder

475 ml/16 fl oz water

crisp biscuits, to serve

1 Sift the cocoa powder into a small, heavy-based saucepan and add the caster sugar, coffee powder and a little of the water. Using a wooden spoon, mix together to form a thin paste, then gradually stir in the remaining water. Bring the mixture to the boil over low heat and simmer gently for 8 minutes, stirring frequently.

2 Remove the saucepan from the heat and leave to cool. Transfer the mixture to a bowl, cover with clingfilm, and place in the refrigerator until well chilled. Freeze in an ice-cream maker, following the manufacturer's instructions. Alternatively, pour the mixture into a large freezerproof container, then cover and freeze for 2 hours. Remove the sorbet from the freezer and beat to break down the ice crystals. Freeze for an additional 6 hours, beating the sorbet every 2 hours.

3 Transfer the sorbet to the refrigerator 30 minutes before serving. Scoop into 6 small bowls and serve with biscuits.

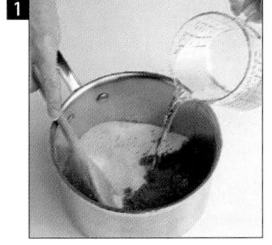
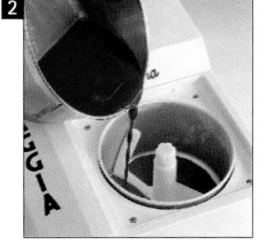
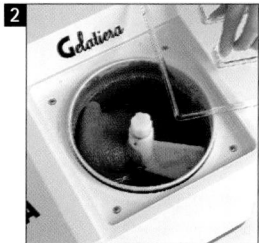

Chocolate Sorbet

This is a truly special sorbet, and it is worth buying the best possible quality Continental plain and plain chocolate for it.

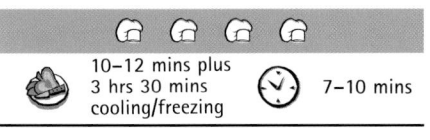

10–12 mins plus
3 hrs 30 mins
cooling/freezing

7–10 mins

SERVES 6

INGREDIENTS

5 oz/140 g Continental plain chocolate, roughly chopped

5 oz/140 g plain chocolate, roughly chopped

450 ml/16 fl oz water

200 g/7 oz caster sugar

langues de chat biscuits, to serve

1 Put both types of chocolate into a food processor and process briefly until chopped very finely.

2 Pour the water into a heavy-based saucepan and add the sugar. Stir over a medium heat to dissolve, then bring to the boil. Boil for 2 minutes, without stirring, then remove the saucepan from the heat.

3 With the motor of the food processor running, pour the hot syrup on to the chocolate. Process for about 2 minutes, until all the chocolate has melted and the mixture is smooth. Scrape down the sides of the food processor, if necessary. Strain the chocolate mixture into a freezerproof container and leave to cool.

4 When the mixture is cool, place it in the freezer for about 1 hour, until slushy but starting to become firm around the edges. Tip the mixture into the food processor again and process until smooth. Return to the container and freeze for at least 2 hours until firm.

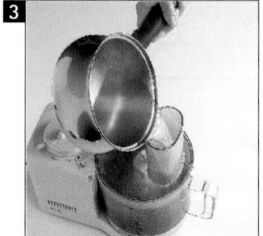
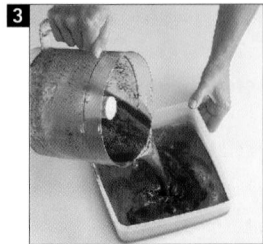

5 Remove the sorbet from the freezer about 10 minutes before serving and leave to stand at room temperature to soften slightly. Serve in scoops with langues de chat biscuits.

Chocolate Orange Sorbet

Plain chocolate encases liqueur-flavoured sorbet to provide this very elegant and sophisticated dinner party dessert.

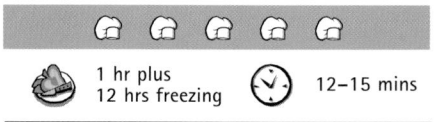

1 hr plus
12 hrs freezing

12–15 mins

SERVES 4

INGREDIENTS

2 tsp vegetable oil, for brushing

225 g/8 oz plain chocolate, broken into small pieces

1 litre/1¾ pints crushed ice

600 ml/1 pint freshly squeezed orange juice

150 ml/5 fl oz water

4 tbsp caster sugar

finely grated rind of 1 orange

juice and finely grated rind of 1 lemon

1 tsp powdered gelatine

3 tbsp orange liqueur

fresh mint leaves, to decorate

1 Brush a 900-ml/1½-pint mould with oil, drain well, then chill in the refrigerator. Put the chocolate in a heatproof bowl set over a saucepan of gently simmering water. Stir over a low heat until melted, then remove from the heat.

2 Remove the mould from the refrigerator and pour in the melted chocolate. Tip and turn the mould to coat the interior. Place the mould on a bed of crushed ice and continue tipping and turning until the chocolate has set. Return the mould to the refrigerator.

3 Reserve 3 tablespoons of the orange juice in a small, heatproof bowl. Pour the remainder into a saucepan and add the water, sugar, orange rind and lemon juice and rind. Stir over a low heat until the sugar has dissolved, then increase the heat and bring the mixture to the boil. Remove the saucepan from the heat.

4 Meanwhile, sprinkle the gelatine on the surface of the orange juice in the bowl. Set aside for 2 minutes to soften, then set over a saucepan of gently simmering water until dissolved. Stir the dissolved gelatine and the liqueur into the orange juice mixture. Pour into a freezerproof container and place in the freezer for 30 minutes, until slushy.

5 Remove the sorbet from the freezer, transfer to a bowl, and beat thoroughly to break up the ice crystals. Return it to the freezerproof container and put it back in the freezer for 1 hour. Repeat this process 3 more times.

6 Remove the sorbet from the freezer, transfer to a bowl and beat well once more. Remove the mould from the refrigerator and spoon the sorbet into it. Smooth the surface with a spatula. Put the mould in the freezer overnight.

7 Remove the mould from the freezer shortly before serving. Place a chilled serving plate on top and, holding them firmly together, invert. Decorate with fresh mint leaves and serve immediately.

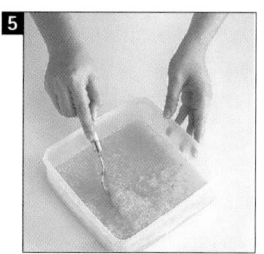

Orange Sorbet

Serve this fresh-tasting sorbet in scooped-out orange shells for a dramatic effect to impress your guests.

45 mins plus 4 hrs chilling/ freezing | 4 mins

SERVES 4

INGREDIENTS

500 ml/18 fl oz water

200 g/7 oz caster sugar

8 large oranges

2 tbsp orange liqueur

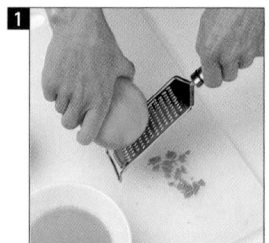

1 Heat the water and caster sugar in a saucepan over a low heat, stirring, until the sugar has dissolved, then boil without stirring for 2 minutes. Pour into a heatproof glass bowl. Cool to room temperature. While it cools, grate the rind from 2 oranges and extract the juice. Extract the juice from 2 more oranges. Mix the juice and rind in a bowl, cover with clingfilm, and set aside. Discard the squeezed oranges. When the sugar syrup has cooled, stir in the orange juice, the grated rind, and the orange liqueur. Cover with clingfilm and chill for 1 hour.

2 Transfer the orange mixture to an ice-cream maker and process for 15 minutes. Alternatively, transfer it into a freezerproof container and freeze for 1 hour. Transfer to a large bowl, beat to break up the crystals, then put it back in the freezerproof container and freeze for 30 minutes. Repeat twice more, freezing for 30 minutes and whisking each time. Cut the tops off the remaining 4 oranges. Scoop out the flesh, divide the frozen sorbet among the orange cups, and serve.

Orange & Campari Sorbet

Campari is a distinctive Italian drink made with the rind of bitter oranges. Combined with freshly squeezed orange juice it makes a cooling sorbet.

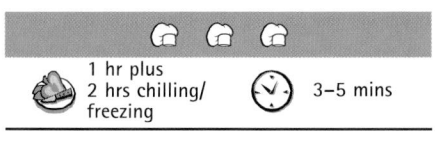

1 hr plus
2 hrs chilling/
freezing

3–5 mins

SERVES 4–6

INGREDIENTS

3–4 large oranges

225 g/8 oz caster sugar

600 ml/1 pint water

3 tbsp Campari

2 extra large egg whites

TO DECORATE

fresh mint leaves

candied citrus peel (optional)

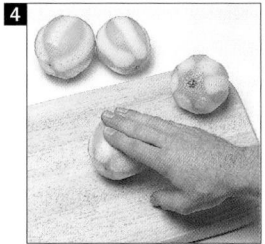

1 Working over a bowl to catch any juice, pare the zest from 3 of the oranges, without removing the bitter white pith. If some of the pith does come off with the zest, use the knife to scrape it off.

2 Put the sugar and water into a saucepan and stir over a low heat until dissolved. Increase the heat and boil for 2 minutes, without stirring. Using a wet pastry brush, brush any crystals down the side of the saucepan, if necessary.

3 Remove the saucepan from the heat and pour into a heatproof non-metallic bowl. Add the orange zest and leave the mixture to cool to room temperature.

4 Roll the pared oranges back and forth on the work surface, pressing down firmly. Cut them in half and squeeze 125 ml/4 fl oz juice. If you need more juice, squeeze the remaining orange.

5 When the syrup is cool, stir in the orange juice and Campari. Strain into a container, cover and chill for at least 30 minutes.

6 Put the mixture in an ice-cream maker and churn for 15 minutes. Alternatively, follow the instructions for Orange Sorbet (opposite). Whisk the egg whites in a clean, greasefree bowl until stiff peaks form.

7 Add the egg whites to the ice-cream maker and continue churning for 5 minutes, or according to the manufacturer's instructions. Transfer to a shallow, freezerproof container, cover and freeze for up to 2 months.

8 About 15 minutes before serving, place the ice cream in the refrigerator to soften. Scoop into bowls and serve decorated with mint leaves and candied citrus peel, if wished.

Lychees with Orange Sorbet

This dish is truly delicious! The fresh flavour of the sorbet complements the gingery lychees. Perfect for a dinner party dessert.

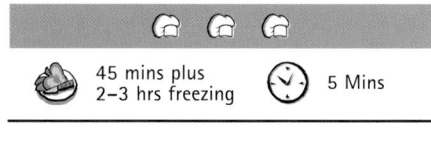

45 mins plus
2–3 hrs freezing

5 Mins

SERVES 4

INGREDIENTS

SORBET

225 g/8 oz caster sugar

425 ml/15 fl oz cold water

350 g/12 oz canned mandarins, in natural juice

2 tbsp lemon juice

STUFFED LYCHEES

425 g/15 oz canned lychees, drained

2 pieces stem ginger, drained and finely chopped

lime zest, cut into diamond shapes, to decorate

1 To make the sorbet, place the sugar and water in a saucepan and stir over a low heat until the sugar has dissolved. Bring the mixture to the boil and boil vigorously for 2–3 minutes.

2 Blend the mandarins in a food processor or blender until smooth. Press the purée through a sieve then stir into the syrup, together with the lemon juice. Set aside to cool. Once cooled, pour the mixture into a freezerproof container and freeze until set, stirring occasionally.

3 Meanwhile, drain the lychees on kitchen paper. Spoon the chopped ginger into the centre of the lychees.

4 Arrange the lychees on serving plates and serve with scoops of orange sorbet. Decorate with lime zest.

COOK'S TIP

It is best to leave the sorbet in the refrigerator for 10 minutes before serving, so that it softens slightly, so that you can scoop it to serve.

Lychee & Ginger Sorbet

A refreshing palate-cleanser after a rich meal, this sorbet couldn't be easier to make, and can be served with a fruit salad.

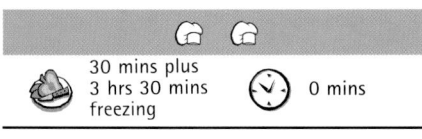

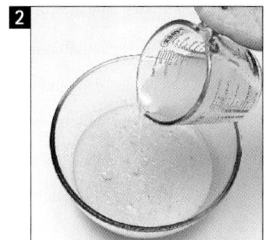
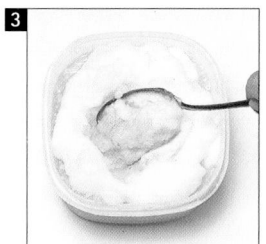

30 mins plus
3 hrs 30 mins
freezing

0 mins

SERVES 4

I N G R E D I E N T S

800 g/1 lb 12 oz canned lychees in syrup

finely grated rind of 1 lime

2 tbsp lime juice

3 tbsp stem ginger syrup from the jar

2 egg whites

TO DECORATE

starfruit slices

slivers of stem ginger

1 Drain the lychees, reserving the syrup. Place the fruits in a blender or food processor with the lime rind, juice and ginger syrup and process until completely smooth. Transfer to a mixing bowl.

2 Mix the purée thoroughly with the reserved syrup, then pour into a freezerproof container and freeze for 1–1½ hours until slushy in texture. Alternatively, use an ice-cream maker.

3 Remove from the freezer and whisk to break up the ice crystals. Whisk the egg whites in a clean, dry bowl until stiff, then quickly and lightly fold them into the lychee mixture.

4 Return to the freezer and freeze until firm. Remove from the freezer 15 minutes before serving to soften slightly. Serve the sorbet in scoops, with slices of starfruit and ginger to decorate.

COOK'S TIP
It is not recommended that raw egg whites are served to young children, pregnant women, the elderly or anyone weakened by chronic illness. The egg whites may be left out of this recipe, but you will need to whisk the sorbet a second time.

Mango & Lime Sorbet

A refreshing sorbet is the perfect way to round off a spicy Thai meal, and mangoes make a deliciously smooth-textured, velvety sorbet.

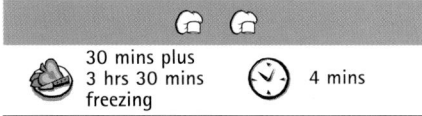

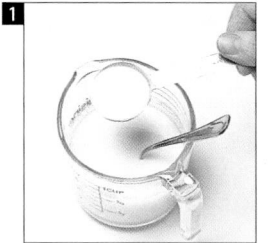

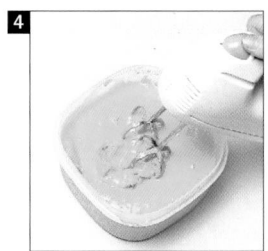

30 mins plus 3 hrs 30 mins freezing

4 mins

SERVES 4

INGREDIENTS

6 tbsp caster sugar

100 ml/3½ fl oz water

finely grated rind of 3 limes

2 tbsp coconut cream

2 large, ripe mangoes

135 ml/4½ fl oz lime juice

curls of fresh coconut, toasted, to decorate

1 Place the sugar, water and lime rind in a small saucepan and heat gently, stirring constantly, until the sugar dissolves. Boil rapidly for 2 minutes to reduce slightly, then remove from the heat and strain into a bowl or jug. Stir in the coconut cream and set aside to cool.

2 Halve the mangoes, remove the stones and peel thinly. Chop the flesh roughly and place in a food processor with the lime juice. Process to a smooth purée and transfer to a small bowl.

3 Pour the cooled syrup into the mango purée, mixing evenly. Tip into a freezerproof container and freeze for 1 hour, or until slushy in texture. Alternatively, use an ice-cream maker.

4 Remove the container from the freezer and beat with an electric whisk to break up the ice crystals. Freeze for a further hour, then remove from the freezer and vigorously beat the contents again until smooth.

5 Cover the container, return to the freezer and freeze until firm. To serve, remove from the freezer and leave to stand at room temperature for about 15 minutes to soften slightly before scooping. Sprinkle with curls of toasted coconut to serve.

COOK'S TIP
If you prefer, canned mangoes in syrup can be used to make the sorbet. Omit the sugar and water, and steep the lime rind in the syrup from the can instead.

Peach Sorbet

This is a quick, but still effective way of making a luscious frozen dessert full of intense fruit flavour. Decorate with fresh mint leaves.

10 mins plus
1 hr freezing

0 mins

SERVES 4

INGREDIENTS

3 large ripe peaches

1 tbsp lemon juice

1 tbsp honey

1 tsp Southern Comfort or peach brandy

fresh mint leaves, to decorate

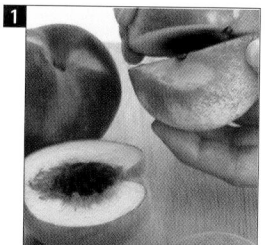

1 Cut the peaches in half, remove the stones and place in a bowl of handhot water to loosen the skins. Peel away the skins and drain the peach halves on kitchen paper towels.

2 Cut the peach halves into 2.5-cm/ 1-inch chunks and toss with the lemon juice. Spread the chunks out on a baking sheet, cover with clingfilm, and freeze until solid.

3 Remove the peaches from the freezer and place in a food processor. Process until granular, scraping down the sides from time to time.

4 Add the honey and Southern Comfort or peach brandy and process again until thoroughly combined and fairly firm in consistency. Decorate with fresh mint leaves and serve immediately or place in a freezerproof container and store in the freezer for up to 24 hours.

Peach & Banana Sorbet

An easy dish, perfect to make when peaches are in season. This sorbet is an ideal refreshing dessert to follow a barbecue.

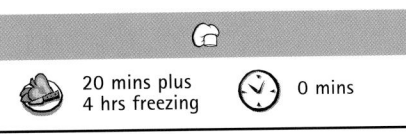

20 mins plus
4 hrs freezing

0 mins

SERVES 4

INGREDIENTS

4 large peaches

2 bananas

1 tbsp peach brandy

fresh mint leaves, to decorate

1 Peel and stone the peaches, then cut the flesh into small chunks. Arrange them in a single layer on a baking sheet. Peel and slice the bananas and arrange in a single layer on another baking sheet. Transfer the baking sheets to the freezer and freeze for 4 hours.

2 Remove the frozen peaches and bananas from the freezer and transfer to a food processor. Pour in the peach brandy and process until the mixture is smooth.

3 Scoop the sorbet into serving bowls, decorate with fresh mint leaves and serve immediately.

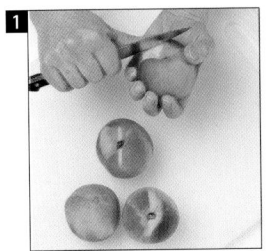

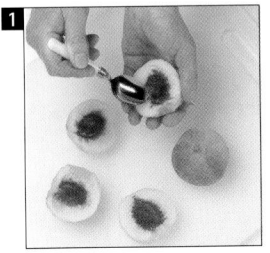

Apple & Honey Water Ice

Apples lend a refreshing tang to this quick, easy-to-make water ice.
Serve straight from the freezer on a hot summer afternoon.

10 mins plus
5–6 hrs freezing

20 mins

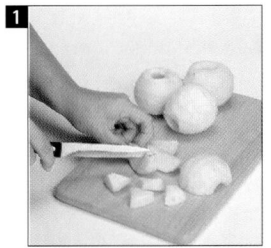

SERVES 4

I N G R E D I E N T S

4 crisp eating apples

2 tbsp lemon juice

200 ml/7 fl oz water

5 tbsp sugar

2 tbsp clear honey

apple slices, to decorate

1 Peel and core the apples and cut them into chunks. Put in a saucepan with the lemon juice and 1 tablespoon of water and heat gently for about 20 minutes, stirring frequently, until soft.

2 Meanwhile, put the sugar and the remaining water in a saucepan and heat gently, stirring, until dissolved. Bring to the boil, then boil for 2 minutes. Remove from the heat.

3 Push the apple through a sieve into a bowl. Stir in the sugar syrup and honey. Leave to stand until cold.

4 When cold, pour the mixture into a freezerproof container. Freeze, uncovered, for 2 hours until the water ice mixture starts to set. Turn the mixture into a bowl and whisk until smooth. Return to the container and freeze for a further 3–4 hours until firm.

5 Serve decorated with apple slices.

Granita

A delightful end to a meal or a refreshing way to cleanse the palate between courses, granita needs to be served very quickly.

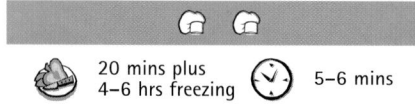

20 mins plus
4–6 hrs freezing

5–6 mins

SERVES 4

INGREDIENTS

LEMON GRANITA

3 lemons

175 ml/6 fl oz lemon juice

100 g/3½ oz caster sugar

600 ml/1 pint cold water

COFFEE GRANITA

2 tbsp instant coffee powder

2 tbsp sugar

2 tbsp hot water

600 ml/1 pint cold water

2 tbsp dark rum or brandy

1 To make the lemon granita, finely grate the lemon rind. Place the lemon rind, juice and caster sugar in a saucepan. Bring the mixture to the boil and simmer for 5–6 minutes, or until thick and syrupy. Leave to cool.

2 Once cooled, stir in the cold water and pour into a shallow freezerproof container with a lid. Freeze the granita for 4–5 hours, stirring occasionally to break up the ice. Serve as a palate cleanser between courses at a dinner party.

3 To make the coffee granita, place the coffee and sugar in a bowl and pour over the hot water, stirring constantly until dissolved.

4 Stir in the cold water and dark rum or brandy.

5 Pour the mixture into a shallow freezerproof container with a lid. Freeze the granita for at least 6 hours, stirring every 1–2 hours in order to create a grainy texture. Serve after dinner.

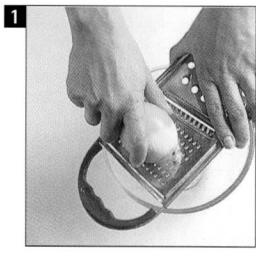

COOK'S TIP

If you would prefer a non-alcoholic version of the coffee granita, simply omit the dark rum or brandy and add extra instant coffee powder instead.

Espresso Granita

Enjoy this crunchy granita as a cooling light dessert at the end of an alfresco supper. Keeps in the freezer for up to three months.

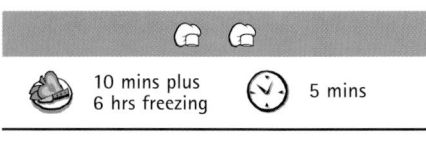

🧊 10 mins plus 6 hrs freezing   🕐 5 mins

SERVES 4–6

I N G R E D I E N T S

200 g/7 oz caster sugar

600 ml/1 pint water

½ tsp vanilla essence

600 ml/1 pint very strong espresso coffee, chilled

fresh mint, to decorate

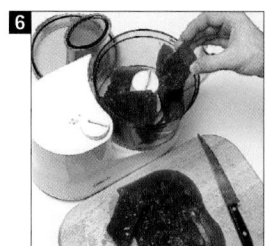

1 Put the sugar in a saucepan with the water and stir over a low heat to dissolve the sugar. Increase the heat and boil for 4 minutes, without stirring. Use a wet pastry brush to brush down any spatters on the side of the saucepan.

2 Remove the saucepan from the heat and pour the syrup into a heatproof non-metallic bowl. Sit the bowl in the kitchen sink filled with iced water to speed up the cooling process. Stir in the vanilla essence and coffee and leave to stand until completely cool.

3 Transfer to a shallow freezerproof container, cover and freeze for at least 6 hours, stirring occasionally.

4 Before serving, chill individual serving bowls in the refrigerator.

5 To serve, invert the container on to a cutting board. Rinse a cloth in very hot water, wring it out, then rub on the bottom of the container for 15 seconds. Give the container a sharp shake and the mixture should fall out.

6 Break up the granita with a knife and transfer to a food processor. Process until it becomes grainy and crunchy. Serve in the chilled bowls, decorated with mint.

COOK'S TIP
A very dark, full-flavoured espresso is the only choice for this Italian speciality. Otherwise the flavour will be marred by the freezing.

Lemon Granita

Soft and granular, this iced dessert has a sharp, zingy flavour, which is refreshing and ideal for rounding off any rich meal.

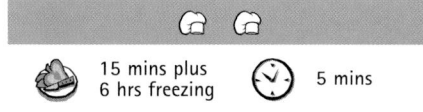

15 mins plus 6 hrs freezing

5 mins

SERVES 4–6

INGREDIENTS

4 large unwaxed lemons

100 g/3½ oz caster sugar

700 ml/1¼ pints water

fresh mint sprigs, to decorate (optional)

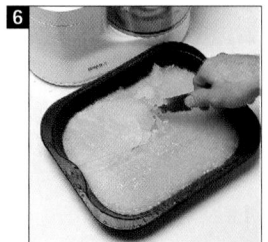

1 Pare 6 strips of zest from 1 of the lemons, then finely grate the remaining rind from the remaining lemons, being very careful not to remove any bitter white pith.

2 Roll the lemons back and forth on the work surface, pressing down firmly. Cut each in half and squeeze 125 ml/ 4 fl oz juice. Add the grated rind to the juice. Set aside.

3 Put the pared strips of lemon zest, sugar and water in a saucepan and stir over a low heat to dissolve the sugar. Increase the heat and boil for 4 minutes, without stirring. Use a wet pastry brush to brush down any spatters on the side of the saucepan. Remove from the heat, pour into a non-metallic bowl, and set aside to cool.

VARIATION

Lemon-scented herbs add a unique and unexpected flavour. Add 4 small lemon balm sprigs or 2 lemon thyme sprigs to the syrup in step 3. Remove and discard with the pared rind in step 4. Alternatively, stir ½ tablespoon of finely chopped lemon thyme into the mixture in step 4.

4 Remove the strips of zest from the syrup. Stir in the grated rind and juice. Transfer to a shallow freezerproof container, cover, and freeze for at least 6 hours, stirring occasionally.

5 Chill serving bowls 30 minutes before serving. To serve, invert the container on to a cutting board. Rinse a cloth in very hot water, wring it out, then rub on the bottom of the container for 15 seconds. Give the container a shake and the mixture should fall out.

6 Break up the granita with a knife and transfer to a food processor. Process until it becomes granular. Serve in the chilled bowls (or in scooped-out lemons). Decorate with mint sprigs, if wished.

Rose Ice

A delicately perfumed sweet granita ice, which is coarser than many ice creams. This looks very pretty on a glass dish sprinkled with rose petals.

 15 mins plus 6 hrs freezing 10 mins

SERVES 4

I N G R E D I E N T S

400 ml/14 fl oz water

2 tbsp coconut cream

4 tbsp sweetened condensed milk

2 tsp rosewater

few drops pink food colouring (optional)

pink rose petals, to decorate

1 Place the water in a small saucepan and add the coconut cream. Heat the mixture gently without boiling, stirring.

2 Remove from the heat and leave to cool. Stir in the condensed milk, rosewater and food colouring (if using).

3 Pour into a freezerproof container and freeze for 1–1½ hours, until slushy.

4 Remove from the freezer and break up the ice crystals with a fork. Return to the freezer and freeze until firm.

5 Spoon the ice roughly into a pile on a serving dish and sprinkle with rose petals to decorate.

COOK'S TIP

To prevent the ice thawing too quickly at the table, nestle the bottom of the serving dish in another dish filled with crushed ice.

Forest Fruits Granita

This is a wonderfully refreshing dessert on a hot summer day. It's more cooling and less calorie-packed than ice cream, but full of flavour.

1 hr plus
2–3 hrs freezing

5 mins

SERVES 4–6

I N G R E D I E N T S

225 g/8 oz strawberries, hulled

175 g/6 oz raspberries

175 g/6 oz blackberries

1–2 tbsp lemon juice (optional)

140 g/5 oz caster sugar

150 ml/5 fl oz water

T O   D E C O R A T E

whipped cream

fresh mint sprigs

1 Put the strawberries, raspberries and blackberries into a food processor or blender and process to a purée. Push the purée through a fine-meshed sieve into a freezerproof container to remove the seeds. Add lemon juice to taste.

2 Place the sugar and water in a small saucepan over a low heat and stir until the sugar has dissolved. Pour the syrup over the fruit purée and stir well. Set aside to cool, stirring occasionally, then cover and freeze until set.

3 Transfer the granita to the refrigerator 30 minutes before serving. Spoon the granita into glasses and serve decorated with whipped cream and mint sprigs.

VARIATION
For a really lazy granita, replace the fruit purée with 1 litre/1¾ pints fruit juice, such as orange or cranberry.

Berry Yogurt Ice

This refreshing ice makes a wonderful summer dessert after a filling meal, because it is light and cooling without the richness, or fat, of ice cream.

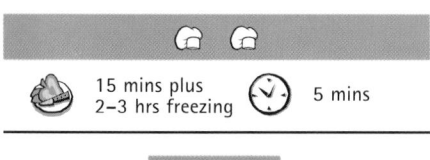

15 mins plus
2–3 hrs freezing   5 mins

SERVES 4

INGREDIENTS

125 g/4½ oz raspberries

125 g/4½ oz blackberries

125 g/4½ oz strawberries

1 large egg

175 ml/6 oz natural Greek yogurt

125 ml/4 fl oz red wine

2¼ tsp powdered gelatine

fresh berries, to decorate

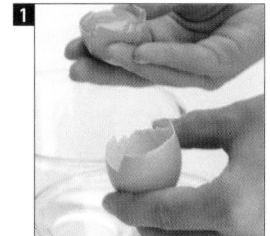

1 Put the raspberries, blackberries and strawberries in a food processor and process to a purée. Rub the purée through a sieve into a bowl to remove the seeds. Separate the egg and stir in the yolk and yogurt.

2 Pour the wine into a heatproof bowl and sprinkle the gelatine on the surface. Set aside for 5 minutes to soften, then set the bowl over a saucepan of gently simmering water until the gelatine has completely dissolved. Pour the gelatine in a steady stream into the berry purée, whisking constantly. Transfer the mixture to a freezerproof container and freeze until slushy.

3 Whisk the egg white until very stiff. Remove the berry mixture from the freezer and fold in the egg white. Return to the freezer and freeze until firm. To serve, scoop the berry yogurt ice into tall glasses and decorate with fresh berries of your choice.

VARIATION
Substitute 40 g/1¼ oz redcurrants for half the raspberries and 40 g/1¼ oz blackcurrants for half the blackberries.

Icy Fruit Blizzard

Keep a store of prepared fruit in the freezer, then whirl it up into this refreshing dessert, which is as light and healthy as it is satisfying.

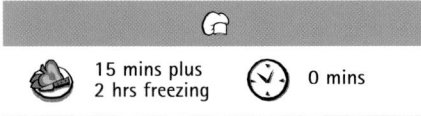
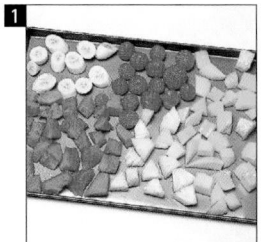

15 mins plus
2 hrs freezing

0 mins

SERVES 4

I N G R E D I E N T S

1 pineapple, peeled and cut into small pieces

1 large piece watermelon, peeled, seeded and cut into small pieces

225 g/8 oz strawberries or other berries, hulled and whole or sliced

1 mango, peach or nectarine, peeled and sliced

1 banana, peeled and sliced

orange juice

caster sugar

1 Arrange the fruit on top of 2 non stick baking sheets and freeze for at least 2 hours or until firm and icy.

2 Place 1 type of fruit in a food processor and process until it is broken up into small pieces.

3 Add a little orange juice and sugar, to taste, and continue to process until it forms a granular mixture. Repeat with the remaining fruit. Arrange in chilled bowls and serve immediately.

Rose Petal Ice Cream

This delicate ice cream is subtly flavoured with coconut and rosewater, and is guaranteed to impress guests at a dinner party.

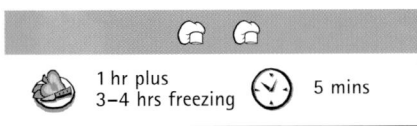

1 hr plus
3–4 hrs freezing

5 mins

SERVES 4

INGREDIENTS

300 ml/10 fl oz milk

2 tbsp coconut cream

3 egg yolks

100 g/3½ oz caster sugar

300 ml/10 fl oz double cream, whipped

1 tbsp rose water

TO DECORATE

grated fresh coconut

rose petals

1 Pour the milk into a saucepan, stir in the coconut cream and heat gently until almost boiling. In a separate bowl, beat together the egg yolks and sugar, remove the milk from the heat and stir a little into the egg mixture. Return the mixture to the saucepan and stir over a low heat until thickened and smooth. Do not let it boil. Remove from the heat and cool for 30 minutes. Add the mixture to the cream, then stir in the rosewater. Cover with clingfilm and chill for 1 hour.

2 Remove from the refrigerator. Transfer to an ice-cream maker and process for 15 minutes. Alternatively, transfer to a freezerproof container and freeze for 1 hour. Take it out of the freezer, transfer to a bowl, and beat to break up the ice crystals. Put it back in the container and freeze for 30 minutes. Repeat twice more, freezing for 30 minutes and whisking each time. Store in the freezer until required.

3 Remove from the freezer and scoop into serving dishes. Scatter over the grated coconut and rose petals and serve.

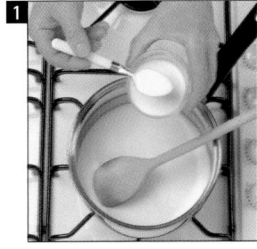

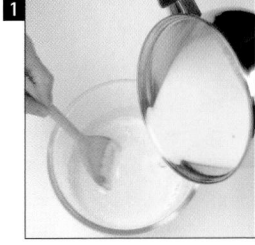

Rich Vanilla Gelato

Italy is synonymous with ice cream. This homemade version of real vanilla ice cream is absolutely delicious and so easy to make.

45 mins plus
8 hrs freezing

15 mins

SERVES 4–6

INGREDIENTS

600 ml/1 pint double cream

1 vanilla pod

pared rind of 1 lemon

4 eggs, beaten

2 egg yolks

175 g/6 oz caster sugar

1 Place the cream in a heavy-based saucepan and heat gently, whisking. Add the vanilla pod, lemon rind, eggs, and egg yolks and heat until the mixture reaches just below boiling point.

2 Reduce the heat and cook for 8–10 minutes, whisking the mixture constantly, until thickened.

3 Stir the sugar into the cream mixture, then set aside and leave to cool.

4 Strain the cream mixture through a fine sieve.

5 Slit open the vanilla pod and scoop out the tiny black seeds, then stir them into the cream.

6 Pour the mixture into a shallow freezerproof container with a lid and freeze overnight until set. Serve when required.

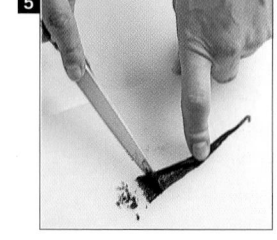

COOK'S TIP

Ice cream is one of the traditional dishes of Italy. Everyone eats it and there are numerous gelato stalls selling a wide variety of flavours, usually in a cone. It is also serve in scoops and even sliced!

Chocolate Chip Ice Cream

This marvellous frozen dessert offers the best of both worlds, delicious chocolate chip cookies and a rich dairy-flavoured ice.

45 mins plus 6 hrs freezing/chilling

5 mins

SERVES 6

I N G R E D I E N T S

300 ml/10 fl oz milk

1 vanilla pod

2 eggs

2 egg yolks

55 g/2 oz caster sugar

300 ml/10 fl oz natural yogurt

125 g/4½ oz chocolate chip cookies, broken into small pieces

1 Pour the milk into a small saucepan, add the vanilla pod and bring to the boil over a low heat. Remove from the heat, cover the saucepan and leave on one side to cool.

2 Beat the eggs and egg yolks in a heatproof bowl set over a saucepan of simmering water. Add the sugar and beat until the mixture is pale and creamy.

3 Reheat the milk to simmering point and strain it over the egg mixture. Stir constantly until the custard is thick enough to coat the back of a spoon. Remove the custard from the heat and stand the saucepan or bowl in cold water to prevent any further cooking. Wash and dry the vanilla pod for future use.

4 Stir the yogurt into the cooled custard and beat until it is well blended. When the mixture is thoroughly cold, stir in the broken biscuits.

5 Transfer the mixture to a chilled metal cake tin or freezerproof container, cover and freeze for 4 hours.

Remove from the freezer every hour, transfer to a chilled bowl and beat vigorously to prevent ice crystals forming, then return to the freezer. Alternatively, freeze the mixture in an ice-cream maker, following the manufacturer's instructions.

6 To serve the ice cream, transfer it to the main part of the refrigerator for 1 hour. Serve in scoops.

Chocolate Fudge Ice Cream

This is an ice cream which is equally popular with adults and children. For best results, transfer to the refrigerator 15 minutes before serving.

15 mins plus
5–6 hrs freezing

0 mins

SERVES 6

INGREDIENTS

4 medium ripe bananas

juice of ½ lemon

200 g/7 oz golden caster sugar

500 ml/18 fl oz whipping cream

100 g/3½ oz plain chocolate chips

100 g/3½ oz fudge, cut into small pieces

1 Peel the bananas and chop them roughly then place in a blender or food processor with the lemon juice and caster sugar. Process until well chopped, then pour in the cream and process again until well blended.

2 Either freeze in an ice-cream maker, following the manufacturer's directions, adding the chocolate chips and fudge just before the ice cream is ready, or pour the mixture into a freezerproof container, cover and freeze for 2 hours until just frozen. Spoon into a bowl and beat with a fork to break down the ice crystals. Return to the freezer for a further 2 hours, or until almost frozen.

3 Whisk again and stir in the chocolate chips and fudge. Return to the freezer until firm. Transfer from the freezer to the refrigerator for 15 minutes before serving.

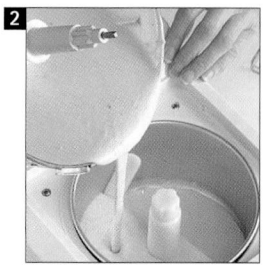

COOK'S TIP
Choose bananas which are ripe but not brown.

Chocolate Kulfi

Kulfi is a delicately spiced Indian ice cream made not with cream but milk. It is traditionally made in special tube-shaped terracotta containers.

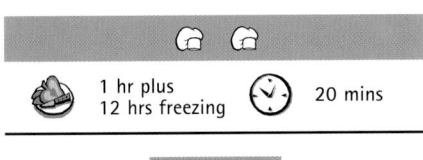
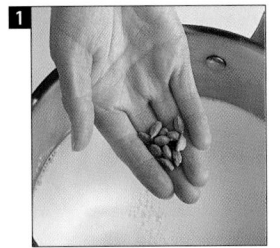

1 hr plus
12 hrs freezing

20 mins

SERVES 6

INGREDIENTS

2 litres/3½ pints full cream milk

12 whole cardamom pods

85 g/3 oz golden caster sugar

100 g/3½ oz plain chocolate

15 g/½ oz chopped blanched almonds

25 g/1 oz chopped unsalted pistachio nuts

1 Place the milk and cardamom pods in a large heavy-based saucepan. Bring to the boil, then simmer until reduced to one-third of its original amount.

2 Strain the milk into a bowl, discarding the cardamom pods, then stir in the sugar and chocolate until melted. Add the almonds and half the pistachio nuts, then set aside to cool. Pour the mixture into a freezerproof container, cover and freeze until almost firm, stirring every 30 minutes.

3 When the ice cream is almost solid, pack it into 6 yogurt pots or dariole moulds, cover with clingfilm and freeze overnight or until completely solid. To serve, dip the moulds briefly into hot water then turn out on to dessert plates. Scatter the remaining pistachio nuts over, to decorate.

COOK'S TIP
Use a wide heavy-based saucepan for reducing the milk to allow plenty of room for the milk to bubble up and to speed the evaporation.

Marbled Chocolate Ice Cream

Swirls of orange-flavoured chocolate running through the white chocolate ice cream not only look attractive but taste delicious, too.

15 mins plus 9 hrs freezing

15 mins

SERVES 6

INGREDIENTS

175 g/6 oz white chocolate

1 tsp cornflour

1 tsp vanilla essence

3 egg yolks

300 ml/10 fl oz milk

450 ml/16 fl oz double cream

115 g/4 oz orange-flavoured plain chocolate

strips of orange zest, to decorate

orange segments, to serve

1 Chop the white chocolate into small pieces. Place the cornflour, vanilla essence and egg yolks in a bowl and stir together until well blended. Pour the milk into a saucepan and bring to the boil. Pour over the yolk mixture, stirring.

2 Strain the mixture back into the saucepan and heat gently, stirring, until thickened. Remove from the heat, add the white chocolate pieces and stir until melted. Stir in the cream. Reserve 150 ml/5 fl oz of the mixture and pour the remainder into a freezerproof container. Freeze until starting to set. Melt the orange-flavoured chocolate and stir into the reserved mixture.

3 Remove the partially frozen ice cream from the freezer and beat with a fork. Place spoonfuls of the orange chocolate mixture over the ice cream and swirl with a knife to give a marbled effect. Freeze overnight until firm. Transfer the ice cream to the refrigerator 30 minutes before serving. To serve, scoop the ice cream into individual glasses and serve with the orange segments and orange zest.

VARIATION
Use mint-flavoured chocolate instead of orange chocolate.

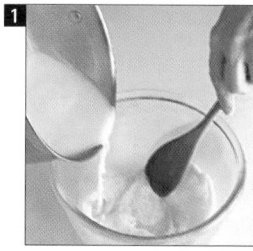

Chocolate Marshmallow Ice

Richly flavoured and with a wonderful texture, this homemade ice cream really couldn't be simpler. Store for up to a month in the freezer.

 10 mins plus
2 hrs 30 mins
cooling/freezing   5–10 mins

SERVES 4

I N G R E D I E N T S

85 g/3 oz plain chocolate, broken
  into pieces

175 g/6 oz white marshmallows

150 ml/5 fl oz milk

300 ml/10 fl oz double cream

fresh fruit to serve

1 Put the chocolate and marshmallows in a saucepan and pour in the milk. Warm gently over a very low heat until the chocolate and marshmallows have melted. Remove from the heat and leave to cool completely.

2 Whisk the cream until thick, then fold it into the cold chocolate mixture with a metal spoon. Pour into a 450-g/1-lb loaf tin and freeze for at least 2 hours, until firm. Serve with fresh fruit.

White Chocolate Ice Cream

This white chocolate ice cream is served in a biscuit cup. If desired, top with a chocolate sauce for a true chocolate addict's treat.

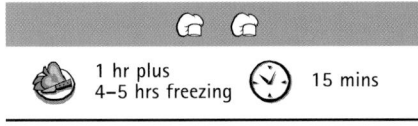

🕑 1 hr plus 4–5 hrs freezing 🕐 15 mins

SERVES 6

INGREDIENTS

ICE CREAM

1 egg

1 egg yolk

3 tbsp caster sugar

150 g/5½ oz white chocolate, broken into pieces

300 ml/10 fl oz milk

150 ml/5 fl oz double cream

BISCUIT CUPS

1 egg white

4 tbsp caster sugar

2 tbsp plain flour, sifted

2 tbsp cocoa powder, sifted

2 tbsp butter, melted

1 Place baking parchment on 2 baking trays. To make the ice cream, beat together the egg, egg yolks and sugar. Put the chocolate in a heatproof bowl with 3 tablespoons of milk and set over a saucepan of gently simmering water. Heat the milk in another saucepan until almost boiling and pour on to the eggs, whisking. Set over a saucepan of gently simmering water and stir until the mixture coats the back of a wooden spoon. Whisk in the chocolate. Cover with dampened baking parchment and leave to cool.

2 Whip the cream until just holding its shape and fold into the custard. Transfer to a freezerproof container and freeze the mixture for 1–2 hours, until frozen 2.5 cm/1 inch from the sides. Scrape into a bowl and beat again until smooth. Refreeze until firm.

3 To make the cups, preheat the oven to 200°C/400°F/Gas Mark 6. Beat the egg white and sugar together. Beat in the flour and cocoa powder, then the butter. Place 1 tablespoon of mixture on one baking sheet and spread out into a 12.5-cm/5-inch circle. Bake in the preheated oven for 4–5 minutes. Remove and mould into shape over an upturned cup. Let the biscuit cup set, then cool on a wire rack. Repeat to make 6 biscuit cups. Serve the ice cream decorated in the cups.

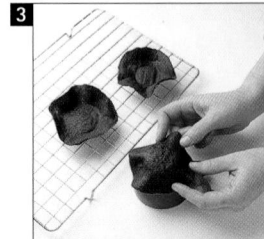

Rich Chocolate Ice Cream

This chocolate ice cream is delicious on its own or with chocolate sauce. For a special dessert, serve it in these attractive trellis cups.

🔔 45 mins plus 4–5 hrs freezing 🕐 12 mins

SERVES 6

I N G R E D I E N T S

I C E   C R E A M

1 egg

3 egg yolks

100 g/3½ oz caster sugar

300 ml/10 fl oz full cream milk

250 g/9 oz plain chocolate, broken into small pieces

300 ml/10 fl oz double cream

T R E L L I S   C U P S

100 g/3½ oz plain chocolate

1 Beat together the egg, egg yolks and caster sugar in a heatproof bowl until well combined. Heat the milk until it is almost boiling.

2 Gradually pour the hot milk on to the eggs, whisking as you do so. Set the bowl over a saucepan of gently simmering water and cook, stirring until the mixture thickens enough to thinly coat the back of a wooden spoon.

3 Add the pieces of plain chocolate to the hot custard. Stir until the chocolate has melted. Cover with a sheet of dampened baking parchment and leave to cool.

4 Whip the cream until just holding its shape, then fold into the cooled chocolate custard. Transfer to a freezerproof container and freeze for 1–2 hours, until the mixture is frozen 2.5 cm/1 inch from the sides.

5 Scrape the ice cream into a chilled bowl and beat again until smooth. Freeze until firm.

6 To make the trellis cups, invert a muffin tin and cover 6 alternate mounds with clingfilm. Melt the chocolate, place it in a paper piping bag, and snip off the end.

7 Pipe a circle around the bottom of the mound, then pipe chocolate back and forth over it to form a trellis; carefully pipe a double thickness. Pipe around the bottom again. Chill until set, then lift from the tin and remove the clingfilm. Serve the ice cream in the trellis cups.

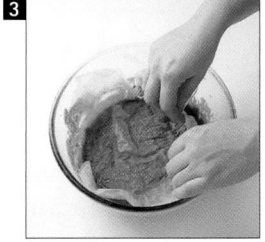

Chocolate & Honey Ice

Ice cream is always a popular summer dessert – try this rather different recipe for a change. It looks even better decorated with strawberries.

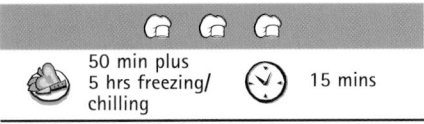

50 min plus
5 hrs freezing/
chilling

15 mins

SERVES 6

I N G R E D I E N T S

500 ml/18 fl oz milk

200 g/7 oz plain chocolate, broken
  into pieces

4 eggs, separated

85 g/3 oz caster sugar

2 tbsp honey

pinch of salt

12 strawberries, washed and hulled

1 Pour the milk into a saucepan, add 150 g/5½ oz of the chocolate and stir over a medium heat for 3–5 minutes until melted. Remove the saucepan from the heat and set aside.

2 In a separate bowl, beat the egg yolks with all but 1 tablespoon of the sugar until pale and thickened. Gradually beat in the milk mixture, a little at a time. Return the mixture to a clean saucepan and cook over a low heat, whisking constantly, until smooth and thickened. Remove from the heat and set aside to cool completely. Cover with clingfilm and chill in the refrigerator for 30 minutes.

3 Whisk the egg whites with a pinch of salt until soft peaks form. Gradually whisk in the remaining sugar and continue whisking until stiff and glossy. Remove the chocolate mixture from the refrigerator and stir in the honey, then gently fold in the egg whites.

4 Divide the mixture between 6 individual freezerproof moulds and place in the freezer for at least 4 hours, until frozen. Meanwhile, put the remaining chocolate in a heatproof bowl set over a saucepan of gently simmering water. Stir over a low heat until melted and smooth, then dip the strawberries in the melted chocolate so that they are half-coated. Place on a sheet of baking parchment to set. Transfer the ice cream to the refrigerator 10 minutes before serving. Turn out on to serving plates and decorate with the strawberries.

Coconut Ice Cream

Coconut and white chocolate combine to make a smooth creamy ice cream with an exotic flavour. Serve with tropical fruit of your choice.

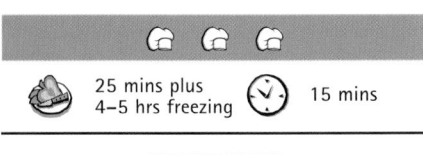

25 mins plus 4–5 hrs freezing   15 mins

SERVES 6

INGREDIENTS

2 eggs

2 egg yolks

115 g/4 oz golden caster sugar

300 ml/10 fl oz single cream

115 g/4 oz white chocolate, chopped

115 g/4 oz creamed coconut, chopped

300 ml/10 fl oz double cream

3 tbsp coconut rum

tropical fruit such as mango, pineapple, passion fruit, to serve

1 Place the eggs, egg yolks and sugar in a heatproof bowl and beat together until well blended. Put the single cream, chocolate and coconut in a saucepan and heat gently until the chocolate has melted, then continue to heat, stirring until almost boiling. Pour on to the egg mixture, stirring vigorously, then place the bowl over a saucepan of gently simmering water, making sure that the bottom of the bowl does not touch the water.

2 Cook, stirring constantly, until the mixture lightly coats the back of the spoon. Strain into another bowl and leave to cool. Place the double cream and coconut rum in a bowl and whisk until slightly thickened, then fold into the cooled chocolate mixture.

3 Either freeze in an ice-cream maker, following the manufacturer's directions, or pour the mixture into a freezerproof container, cover and freeze for 2 hours, until just frozen. Spoon into a bowl and beat with a fork to break down the ice crystals. Return to the freezer until firm. Transfer from the freezer to the refrigerator 30 minutes before serving. Serve with tropical fruit.

VARIATION
As an alternative to serving this ice cream with fruit, it is also delicious served with a plain chocolate sauce.

Mint-Chocolate Gelato

Rich, creamy gelati, or ice creams, are one of the great Italian culinary contributions to the world. This version is made with fresh mint.

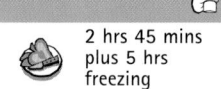

2 hrs 45 mins plus 5 hrs freezing

20 mins

SERVES 4

INGREDIENTS

6 large eggs

150 g/5½ oz caster sugar

300 ml/10 fl oz milk

150 ml/5 fl oz double cream

large handful fresh mint leaves, rinsed and dried

2 drops green food colouring (optional)

55 g/2 oz plain chocolate, finely chopped

1 Put the eggs and sugar in a heatproof bowl that will sit over a saucepan with plenty of room underneath. Using an electric whisk, beat the eggs and sugar together until thick and creamy.

2 Put the milk and cream in the saucepan and bring to a simmer, where small bubbles appear all around the edge, stirring. Pour on to the eggs, whisking constantly. Rinse the saucepan and put 2.5 cm/1 inch water in the bottom. Place the bowl on top, making sure the bottom does not touch the water. Turn the heat to medium–high.

3 Transfer the mixture to a saucepan and cook the mixture, stirring constantly, until it is thick enough to coat the back of the spoon and leave a mark when you pull your finger across it.

4 Tear the mint leaves and stir them into the custard. Remove the custard from the heat. Leave to cool, then cover and set aside to infuse for at least 2 hours, chilling for the last 30 minutes.

5 Strain the mixture through a small nylon sieve to remove the pieces of mint. Stir in the food colouring (if using). Transfer to a freezerproof container and freeze the mixture for 1–2 hours, until frozen 2.5 cm/1 inch from the sides.

6 Scrape into a bowl and beat again until smooth. Stir in the chocolate pieces, smooth the top and cover with clingfilm or foil. Freeze until set, for up to 3 months. Soften in the refrigerator for 20 minutes before serving.

Coffee Ice Cream

This wonderful Italian-style dessert tastes as if it is full of double cream. In fact, it is made with ricotta and low-fat natural yogurt.

1 hr plus
6 hrs freezing

0 mins

SERVES 6

INGREDIENTS

25 g/1 oz plain chocolate

225 g/8 oz ricotta cheese

5 tbsp low-fat natural yogurt

85 g/3 oz caster sugar

175 ml/6 fl oz strong black coffee, chilled

½ tsp ground cinnamon

dash of vanilla essence

chocolate curls, to decorate (see page 9)

1 Grate the chocolate. Put the ricotta cheese, yogurt and sugar in a food processor and process until smooth. Scrape into a bowl and beat in the remaining ingredients.

2 Spoon the mixture into a freezerproof container and freeze for 1½ hours, or until slushy. Remove from the freezer, turn into a bowl and beat vigorously. Return to the container and freeze again for 1½ hours.

3 Repeat this beating and freezing process twice more, then return to the freezer for 15 minutes before serving in scoops. Alternatively, store in the freezer until 15 minutes before serving, then transfer to the refrigerator to soften slightly. Decorate with chocolate curls and serve.

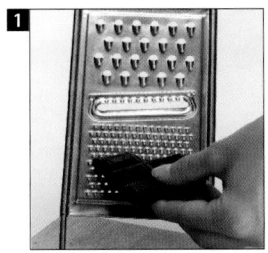

VARIATION
Omit the cinnamon and vanilla essence and substitute 40 g/1½ oz grated mint chocolate for the plain chocolate.

Coconut & Ginger Ice Cream

Coconut and ginger are very compatible flavours. Serve with a few lychees and a little ginger syrup drizzled over.

20 mins plus
6–8 hrs freezing   10 mins

SERVES 4

INGREDIENTS

400 ml/14 fl oz coconut milk

225 ml/8 fl oz whipping cream

4 egg yolks

5 tbsp caster sugar

4 tbsp ginger syrup from the jar

6 pieces stem ginger, drained and finely chopped

2 tbsp lime juice

fresh mint sprigs, to decorate

TO SERVE

lychees

ginger syrup from the jar

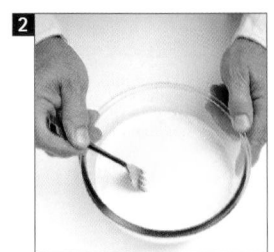

1 Place the coconut milk and cream in a medium-size saucepan. Heat gently until just starting to simmer. Remove from the heat.

2 In a large bowl, beat together the egg yolks, sugar, and ginger syrup until pale and creamy. Slowly pour in the hot milk mixture, while stirring. Return to the saucepan and heat gently, stirring constantly, until the mixture thickens and coats the back of a spoon. Remove from the heat and leave to cool. Stir in the ginger and lime juice.

3 Transfer the mixture to a freezerproof container. Cover and freeze for 2–3 hours, or until just frozen. Spoon into a bowl and mash with a fork or whisk to break down any ice crystals. Return the mixture to the container and freeze for a further 2 hours. Mash once more, then freeze for 2–3 hours, or until firm. Transfer from the freezer to the refrigerator 20–30 minutes before serving. Decorate with mint sprigs and serve with lychees and a little ginger syrup drizzled over.

Brown Bread Ice Cream

Although it sounds unusual, this yogurt-based recipe is delicious.
It contains no cream and is ideal for a low-fat diet.

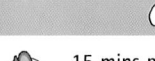

15 mins plus
2 hrs freezing   5 mins

SERVES 4

INGREDIENTS

175 g/6 oz fresh wholemeal breadcrumbs

25 g/1 oz finely chopped walnuts

55 g/2 oz caster sugar

½ tsp ground nutmeg

1 tsp finely grated orange rind

450 ml/16 fl oz low-fat natural yogurt

2 large egg whites

TO DECORATE

walnut halves

orange slices

fresh mint sprigs

1 Preheat the grill to medium. Mix together the breadcrumbs, walnuts, and sugar and spread over a sheet of foil in the grill pan.

2 Toast, stirring frequently, for 5 minutes until crisp and evenly browned. (Take care that the sugar does not burn.) Remove from the heat and leave to cool.

3 When cool, transfer to a mixing bowl and mix in the nutmeg, orange rind and yogurt. In another bowl, whisk the egg whites until stiff. Gently fold into the breadcrumb mixture, using a metal spoon.

4 Spoon the mixture into 4 mini pudding basins, smoothing the surface, and freeze for 1½–2 hours, until firm.

5 To serve, hold the bottoms of the basins in hot water for a few seconds, then turn on to serving plates.

6 Serve immediately, decorated with the walnuts, oranges and fresh mint.

COOK'S TIP

If you don't have mini pudding basins, use ramekins or teacups or, if you prefer, use one large bowl. Alternatively, spoon the mixture into a large freezerproof container to freeze and serve the ice cream in scoops.

Lavender Ice Cream

Lavender is a herb that works very well in cooking. You can store this deliciously fragrant ice cream in the freezer for up to three months.

2 hrs 45 mins plus 6–8 hrs freezing

15 mins

SERVES 6–8

INGREDIENTS

flowers from 10–12 large fresh lavender sprigs, plus extra to decorate

6 large egg yolks

140 g/5 oz caster sugar, or lavender sugar (see Cook's Tip)

450 ml/16 fl oz milk

225 ml/8 fl oz double cream

1 tsp vanilla essence

1 Strip the small flowers from the lavender stems, without any brown or green bits. Place them in a small sieve and rinse, then pat dry with kitchen paper. Set aside.

2 Put the egg yolks and sugar in a heatproof bowl that will sit over a saucepan with plenty of room underneath. Using an electric whisk, whisk the eggs and sugar together until they are thick.

3 Put the milk, cream and vanilla in a saucepan over a low heat and bring to a simmer, stirring. Pour the hot milk over the egg mixture, whisking constantly. Rinse the saucepan and place 2.5 cm/1 inch water in the bottom. Place the bowl on top, making sure that the bottom does not touch the water. Turn the heat to medium-high.

4 Cook the mixture, stirring, until it is thick enough to coat the back of a spoon.

5 Remove the custard from the heat and stir in the flowers. Cool, then cover and set aside to infuse for 2 hours, chilling for the last 30 minutes. Strain the mixture through a nylon sieve to remove the flowers.

6 Churn in an ice-cream maker, following the manufacturer's instructions. Alternatively, freeze and whisk as in step 3 of Coconut & Ginger Ice Cream (see page 880).

7 Transfer to a freezerproof bowl, smooth the top and cover with clingfilm or foil. Freeze for up to 3 months. Soften in the refrigerator for 20 minutes before serving. Decorate with fresh lavender flowers.

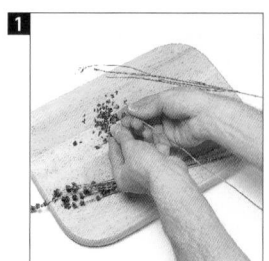

COOK'S TIP

To make lavender sugar, put 350 g/12 oz sugar and 125 g/ 4½ oz lavender flowers in a food processor. Process until blended, then leave in a sealed container for 10 days. Sift out the flower pieces. Store the sugar in a sealed jar.

Easy Mango Ice Cream

Mangoes make excellent ice cream. Add sugar to taste, because some of the sweetness will be lost during the freezing process.

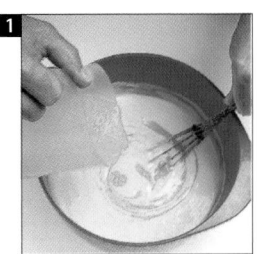

10 mins plus
6–8 hrs freezing   0 mins

SERVES 4

I N G R E D I E N T S

150 ml/5 fl oz whipping cream

600 ml/1 pint ready-made traditional custard

flesh of 2 ripe mangoes, puréed

icing sugar, to taste

passion fruit seeds, to serve

1 Whip the cream lightly. In a large bowl, mix together the custard, cream and mango purée.

2 Taste for sweetness and, if necessary, add icing sugar to taste, remembering that when frozen, the mixture will taste less sweet.

3 Transfer the mixture to a freezerproof container. Cover and freeze for 2–3 hours, or until just frozen. Spoon into a bowl and mash with a fork or whisk to break down any ice crystals. Return the mixture to the container and freeze for a further 2 hours. Mash once more, then freeze for 2–3 hours, or until firm.

4 Transfer from the freezer to the refrigerator 20–30 minutes before serving. Serve with the passion fruit seeds.

Brandy & Orange Ice Cream

The brandy adds a subtle depth of flavour to this orange ice cream. You may use other fruits of your choice, if you prefer.

45 mins plus
3–4 hrs chilling/
freezing

5 mins

SERVES 4

INGREDIENTS

4 egg yolks

100 g/3½ oz caster sugar

200 ml/7 fl oz milk

250 ml/9 fl oz double cream

3 tbsp orange juice

3 tbsp brandy

1 tbsp finely grated orange rind

TO DECORATE

star fruit, sliced finely

pieces of crystallized orange peel

1 Beat the egg yolks and sugar together in a heatproof bowl until fluffy. Put the milk, cream, orange juice, brandy and grated orange rind into a large saucepan and bring to the boil. Remove from the heat and whisk into the beaten egg yolks. Return the mixture to the saucepan and cook, stirring constantly, over a very low heat until thickened. Do not let it reach a simmer. Remove from the heat, transfer to a bowl, and cool. Cover with clingfilm and chill for 1 hour.

2 Transfer the mixture to an ice-cream maker and process for 15 minutes. Alternatively, put the mixture in a freezerproof container and freeze for 1 hour. Transfer to a bowl and beat to break up the ice crystals, then put it back in the freezerproof container and freeze for 30 minutes. Repeat twice more, freezing for 30 minutes and whisking each time. Freeze until ready to serve.

3 To serve, soften in the refrigerator for 20 minutes beforehand. Scoop into serving dishes, and decorate with star fruit slices and crystallized orange peel. Serve immediately.

Candied Fruit Ice Cream

This ice cream looks very effective made in a large pudding bowl, then turned out on to a serving plate to be sliced in front of your guests.

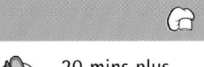

20 mins plus 4–5 hrs freezing   0 mins

SERVES 4

INGREDIENTS

75 g/2¾ oz sultanas

75 g/2¾ oz raisins

6 tbsp Amaretto

4 eggs, separated

100 g/3½ oz caster sugar

600 ml/1 pint double cream

100 g/3½ oz glacé cherries

50 g/1¾ oz crystallized citrus peel

70 g/2½ oz blanched almonds, chopped

lemon zest, to decorate

1 Put the sultanas and raisins in a bowl and pour over 4 tablespoons of Amaretto. Cover with clingfilm and leave to soak.

2 Beat the egg yolks and sugar together in a heatproof bowl until fluffy. In a separate bowl, whisk together the cream and remaining Amaretto, then whisk the mixture into the beaten egg yolks. In a separate bowl, whisk the egg whites until stiff peaks form, then fold into the cream mixture along with the soaked fruit, cherries, crystallized citrus peel and chopped almonds.

3 Transfer the mixture to a large pudding basin, cover and freeze for 4–5 hours, until set. To serve, dip the pudding basin in hot water to loosen the ice cream, then turn it out on to a serving plate. Decorate with lemon zest and serve immediately.

Ice Cream Sauces

Serve plain vanilla or chocolate ice cream with one or more of these delicious sauces on the side.

15–20 mins   5–10 mins

SERVES 6

INGREDIENTS

vanilla or chocolate ice cream, to serve

BERRY SAUCE

225 g/8 oz berries, such as blackberries or raspberries

2 tbsp water

2–3 tbsp caster sugar

2 tbsp fruit liqueur, such as crème de cassis or crème de framboise

MOCHA SAUCE

150 ml/5 fl oz double cream

4 tbsp unsalted butter

55 g/2 oz soft light brown sugar

175 g/6 oz plain chocolate, broken into pieces

2 tbsp dark rum (optional)

PORT SAUCE

350 ml/12 fl oz ruby port

2 tsp cornflour

1 For the berry sauce, put all the ingredients into a small, heavy-based saucepan and heat gently, until the sugar has dissolved and the fruit juices run. Purée with a hand-held blender or in a food processor, then push through a sieve into a serving bowl to remove the seeds. Add more sugar if necessary and serve warm or cold.

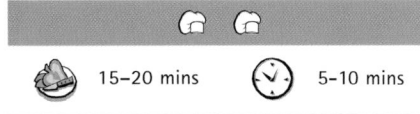

2 For the mocha sauce, pour the cream into a heatproof bowl and add the butter and sugar. Set over a saucepan of gently simmering water and cook, stirring constantly, until smooth. Remove from the heat and set aside to cool slightly. Stir in the chocolate and continue stirring until it has melted. Stir in the rum (if using), then leave the sauce to cool to room temperature before serving.

3 For the port sauce, combine 4 tablespoons of the port with the cornflour to make a smooth paste. Pour the remainder of the port into a saucepan and bring to the boil. Stir in the cornflour paste and cook, stirring constantly, for about 1 minute, until thickened. Remove from the heat and set aside to cool. Pour into a bowl, cover and chill in the refrigerator.

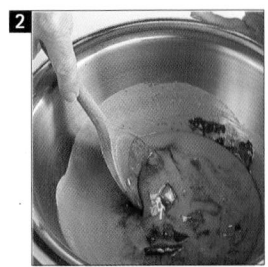

4 Serve scoops of ice cream with a little of the 3 sauces on the side. Serve the remaining sauce in jugs.

Italian Rice Ice Cream

In this ice cream, pudding rice is flavoured with honey and lemon curd. Decorate with angelica for an elegant dinner-party dessert.

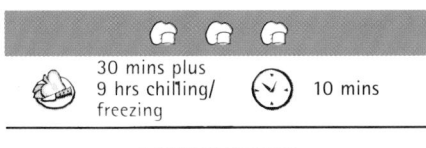

30 mins plus 9 hrs chilling/ freezing

10 mins

SERVES 4–6

INGREDIENTS

100 g/3½ oz pudding rice

500 ml/18 fl oz milk

85 g/3 oz sugar

85 g/3 oz good-quality clear honey

1 tsp vanilla essence

½ tsp lemon essence

175 g/6 oz good-quality lemon curd

500 ml/18 fl oz double or whipping cream

grated rind and juice of 1 large lemon

lemon slices and angelica to decorate

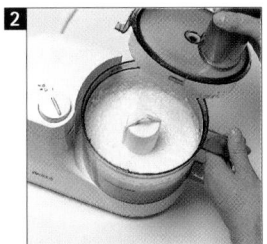

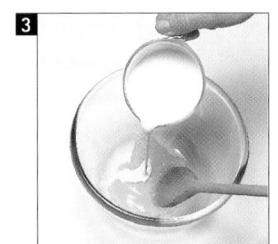

1 Put the rice and milk in a large, heavy-based saucepan and bring to a gentle simmer, stirring occasionally. Do not allow to boil. Reduce the heat to low, cover and simmer very gently for about 10 minutes, stirring occasionally, until the rice is just tender and the liquid absorbed.

2 Remove from the heat and stir in the sugar, honey and vanilla and lemon essence, stirring until the sugar has dissolved. Pour into a food processor and pulse 3 or 4 times. The mixture should be thick and creamy but not completely smooth.

3 Put the lemon curd in a bowl and gradually beat in about 225 ml/8 fl oz of the cream. Stir in the rice mixture with the lemon rind and juice until blended. Lightly whip the remaining cream until it just starts to hold its shape, then fold into the lemon-rice mixture. Chill.

4 Stir the rice mixture and pour into an ice-cream maker. Churn according to the manufacturers' instructions for 15–20 minutes. Transfer to a freezerproof container and freeze for 6–8 hours, or overnight. Transfer to the refrigerator about 1 hour before serving. Serve scoops of the ice cream in individual glasses, decorated with twists of lemon slices and pieces of angelica.

COOK'S TIP
If you do not have an ice-cream maker, transfer the chilled rice mixture to a freezerproof container. Freeze for 1 hour until slightly slushy, then whisk to break up any crystals; refreeze. Repeat twice more.

Ricotta Ice Cream

The ricotta cheese adds a creamy flavour, while the nuts add a crunchy texture. This ice cream needs to be chilled in the freezer overnight.

20 mins plus 8 hrs freezing

0 mins

SERVES 6

INGREDIENTS

50 g/1¾ oz pistachio nuts

50 g/1¾ oz walnuts or pecans

50 g/1¾ oz toasted chopped hazelnuts

grated rind of 1 orange

grated rind of 1 lemon

2 tbsp chopped stem ginger

2 tbsp glacé cherries

40 g/1½ oz ready-to-eat dried apricots

40 g/1½ oz raisins

450 g/1 lb ricotta cheese

2 tbsp maraschino, Amaretto or brandy

1 tsp vanilla essence

4 egg yolks

100 g/3½ oz caster sugar

TO DECORATE

whipped cream

few glacé cherries, pistachio nuts,
  or mint leaves

1 Coarsely chop the pistachio nuts and walnuts and mix with the toasted hazelnuts, orange rind and lemon rind.

2 Finely chop the stem ginger, glacé cherries, apricots and raisins and add them to the bowl.

3 Stir the ricotta cheese evenly through the fruit mixture, then beat in the liqueur and vanilla essence.

4 Put the egg yolks and sugar in a bowl and whisk hard until very thick and creamy. Use an electric whisk if you have

one, otherwise whisk over a saucepan of gently simmering water to speed up the process. Leave to cool if necessary.

5 Carefully fold the ricotta mixture evenly through the beaten eggs and sugar until smooth.

6 Line an 18 x 12-cm/7 x 5-inch loaf tin with a double layer of clingfilm or baking parchment. Pour in the ricotta mixture, smooth the top, cover with more clingfilm or baking parchment and freeze until firm – at least overnight.

7 To serve, remove the ice cream from the tin and peel off the lining.

8 Transfer the ice cream to a serving dish and decorate with whipped cream, glacé cherries, pistachio nuts and mint leaves. Serve in slices.

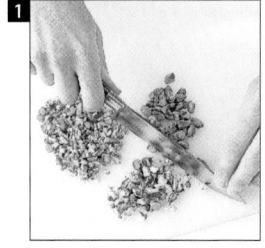

Cardamom Cream Horns

A crisp chocolate biscuit cone encloses a fabulous cardamom-and-ginger-flavoured cream, making this an unusual dessert.

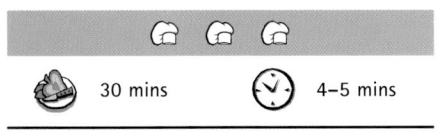
30 mins

4–5 mins

SERVES 6

INGREDIENTS

2 tbsp unsalted butter, melted, plus extra for greasing

1 egg white

4 tbsp caster sugar

2 tbsp plain flour

2 tbsp cocoa powder

50 g/1¾ oz plain chocolate

CARDAMOM CREAM

150 ml/5 fl oz double cream

1 tbsp icing sugar

¼ tsp ground cardamom

pinch of ground ginger

25 g/1 oz stem ginger, chopped finely

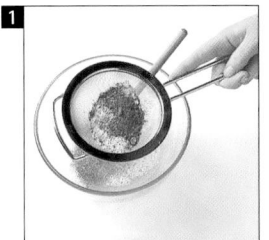
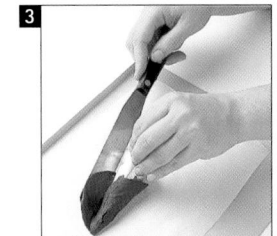
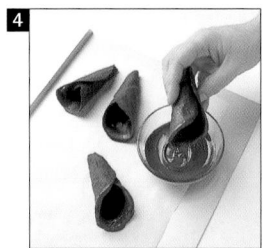

1 Preheat the oven to 200°C/400°F/Gas Mark 6. Place a sheet of baking parchment on 2 baking trays. Lightly grease 6 cream horn moulds. To make the horns, beat the egg white and sugar in a mixing bowl until well mixed. Sift the flour and cocoa powder together, then beat into the egg followed by the melted butter.

2 Place 1 tablespoon of the mixture on to 1 baking tray and spread out to form a 12.5-cm/5-inch circle. Bake in the preheated oven for 4–5 minutes.

3 Working quickly, remove the biscuits with a spatula and wrap around the cream horn mould to form a cone. Leave the cone to set, then remove from the mould. Repeat with the remaining mixture to make 6 cones.

4 Melt the chocolate and dip the open edges of the horn in the chocolate. Place on a piece of baking parchment and leave the chocolate to set.

5 To make the cardamom cream, place the cream in a bowl and sift the icing sugar and ground spices over the surface. Whisk the cream until soft peaks form. Fold in the chopped ginger and use to fill the chocolate cones.

Zuccherini

Italians, especially Sicilians and Sardinians, are famous for having a sweet tooth – and for their superb desserts, such as this one.

30 mins plus
8 hrs 30 mins
chilling   10 mins

SERVES 6

INGREDIENTS

175 g/6 oz plain chocolate, broken into pieces

10 amaretti biscuits, crushed

MOUSSE

55 g/2 oz plain chocolate, broken into pieces

1 tbsp cold strong black coffee

2 eggs, separated

2 tsp orange liqueur

TO DECORATE

150 ml/5 fl oz double cream

6 chocolate-covered coffee beans

2 tbsp cocoa powder

1 To make the chocolate cups, put the 175 g/6 oz of plain chocolate in a heatproof bowl set over a saucepan of gently simmering water. Stir until melted and smooth, but not too runny, then remove from the heat. Coat the inside of 12 double paper cake cases with the chocolate, using a small brush. Stand them on a plate and chill for at least 8 hours, or overnight in the refrigerator.

2 To make the mousse, put the chocolate and coffee in a heatproof bowl set over a saucepan of gently simmering water. Stir over a low heat until the chocolate has melted and the mixture is smooth, then remove from the heat. Leave to cool slightly, then stir in the egg yolks and orange liqueur.

3 Whisk the egg whites in a separate bowl until stiff peaks form. Fold the whites into the chocolate mixture with a metal spoon, then set aside to cool.

4 Remove the chocolate cups from the refrigerator and carefully peel off the paper cases. Divide the crushed amaretti biscuits equally among the chocolate cups and top with the chocolate mousse. Return to the refrigerator for at least 30 minutes. Just before serving, whip the cream and pipe a star on the top of each chocolate cup. Decorate half of the zuccherini with the chocolate-covered coffee beans and dust the other half with cocoa powder.

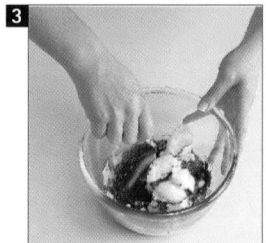

Raspberry Chocolate Boxes

Mocha mousse, fresh raspberries and light sponge cake, all presented in neat little chocolate boxes – almost too good to eat.

50 mins plus 3 hrs chilling/ cooling

45–55 mins

SERVES 12

INGREDIENTS

200 g/7 oz plain chocolate, broken into pieces

1½ tsp cold, strong black coffee

1 egg yolk

1½ tsp Kahlúa or other coffee liqueur

2 egg whites

200 g/7 oz raspberries

SPONGE CAKE

2 tsp butter, for greasing

1 egg, plus 1 egg white

4 tbsp caster sugar

5 tbsp plain flour

1 To make the mocha mousse, melt 55 g/2 oz of the chocolate in a heatproof bowl set over a saucepan of gently simmering water. Add the coffee and stir over a low heat until smooth, then remove from the heat and cool slightly. Stir in the egg yolk and the coffee liqueur.

2 Whisk the egg whites in a separate bowl until stiff peaks form. Fold into the chocolate mixture, cover with clingfilm and chill for 2 hours, until set.

3 For the sponge cake, lightly grease a 20-cm/8-inch square cake tin and line the bottom with baking parchment. Put the egg and extra white with the sugar in a heatproof bowl set over a saucepan of gently simmering water. Whisk over a low heat for 5–10 minutes, until pale and thick. Remove from the heat and continue

whisking for 10 minutes until cold and a trail is left when the whisk is dragged across the surface.

4 Preheat the oven to 180°C/350°F/Gas Mark 4. Sift the flour over the egg mixture and gently fold it in. Pour the mixture into the prepared tin and spread evenly. Bake in the preheated oven for 20–25 minutes, until firm to the touch. Turn out on to a wire rack to cool, then invert the cake, leaving the baking parchment in place.

5 To make the chocolate boxes, grease a 30 x 23-cm/12 x 9-inch Swiss roll tin and line with greaseproof paper. Place the remaining chocolate in a heatproof bowl set over a saucepan of simmering water. Stir over a low heat until melted,

but not too runny. Pour into the pan and spread evenly with a spatula. Leave in a cool place for about 30 minutes, until set.

6 Turn out the set chocolate on to parchment paper on a work surface. Cut it into 36 rectangles, measuring 7.5 x 2.5 cm/ 3 x 1 inches. Cut 12 of these rectangles in half to make 24 rectangles measuring 4 x 2.5 cm/1½ x 1 inches.

7 Trim the edges off the sponge cake, then cut it into 12 slices, measuring 7.5 x 3 cm/3 x 1¼ inches. Spread a little of the mocha mousse along the sides of each sponge rectangle and press 2 long and 2 short chocolate rectangles on to the sides to make boxes. Divide the remaining mousse among the boxes and top with raspberries. Chill until ready to serve.

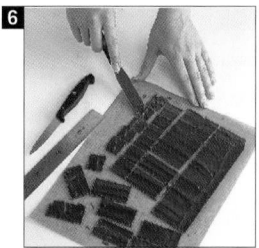

Mini Chocolate Tartlets

Small tartlet cases are filled with a rich chocolate cream to serve as dessert or petits fours. Use individual tartlet tins to make the cases.

20 mins plus
15 mins chilling

15 mins

SERVES 18

INGREDIENTS

225 g/8 oz plain flour, plus extra for dusting

75 g/2¾ oz butter

1 tbsp caster sugar

about 1 tbsp water

FILLING

100 g/3½ oz full-fat soft cheese

2 tbsp caster sugar

1 small egg, beaten lightly

50 g/1¾ oz plain chocolate

TO DECORATE

90 ml/3 fl oz double cream

plain chocolate curls (see page 9)

cocoa powder, for dusting

1 Sift the flour into a mixing bowl. Cut the butter into small pieces and rub in with your fingertips until the mixture resembles fine breadcrumbs. Stir in the sugar. Add enough water to mix to a soft dough, then cover with clingfilm and chill for 15 minutes.

2 Preheat the oven to 190°C/375°F/Gas Mark 5. Roll out the dough on a lightly floured work surface and use to line 18 mini tartlet tins or mini muffin tins. Prick the tartlet cases with a toothpick.

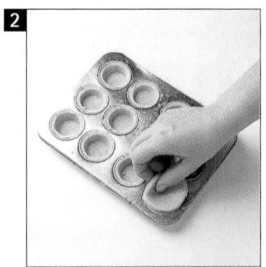

3 Beat together the full-fat soft cheese and the sugar. Beat in the egg. Melt the chocolate and beat it into the mixture. Spoon into the tartlet cases and bake in the preheated oven for 15 minutes, until the dough is crisp and the filling set. Place the tins on a wire rack to cool completely.

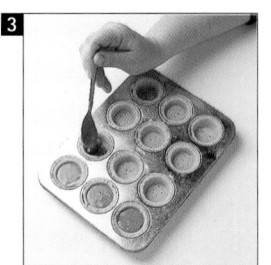

4 Chill the tartlets. Whip the cream until it is just holding its shape. Place in a piping bag fitted with a star nozzle. Pipe rosettes of cream on top of the tartlets. Decorate with chocolate curls and dust with cocoa.

COOK'S TIP
The tartlets can be made up to 3 days ahead. Decorate on the day of serving, preferably no more than 4 hours in advance.

Pineapple Chocolate Rings

These pretty little fruit desserts make a perfect end to a summertime supper, but can also be served with mid-morning coffee.

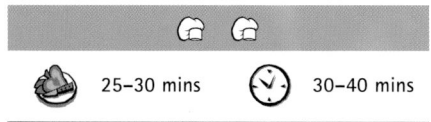

🍰 25–30 mins   ⏱ 30–40 mins

SERVES 10

INGREDIENTS

175 g/6 oz unsalted butter

4 tbsp caster sugar

175 g/6 oz plain flour, plus extra
  for dusting

3 tbsp ground almonds

½ tsp almond essence

200 g/7 oz plain chocolate, broken into
  small pieces

10 canned pineapple rings, drained and
  juice reserved

10 maraschino cherries

1 tsp cornflour

1 Line a baking tray with baking parchment. Cream 115 g/4 oz of the butter with all the sugar until pale and fluffy. Sift in the flour, add the ground almonds and almond essence and knead the mixture thoroughly until it forms a soft dough.

2 Preheat the oven to 190°C/375°F/Gas Mark 5. Turn out the dough on to a lightly floured chopping board and roll out to 5-mm/¼-inch thick. Stamp out 20 rounds with a 7.5-cm/3-inch round cutter and place them on the prepared baking tray. Prick the surface of each almond circle with a fork, then bake in the preheated oven for 20 minutes, until lightly browned. Using a spatula, transfer the rounds to a wire rack to cool.

3 Place the remaining butter and the chocolate in a heatproof bowl set over a saucepan of gently simmering water. Stir over a low heat until melted and smooth. Remove from the heat. Sandwich the almond rounds together in pairs, while still moist, with the chocolate mixture spread between them. Place a pineapple ring on top of each pair of rounds before the chocolate sets and place a cherry in the centre of each ring.

4 Put 4 tablespoons of the reserved can juice into a small saucepan and stir in the cornflour. Bring to the boil over a medium heat, stirring constantly, and cook for 5–7 minutes until thickened. Remove the saucepan from the heat and leave to cool to room temperature. Brush the glaze over the pineapple rings and leave for 10 minutes to set before serving.

Honey & Nut Nests

Pistachio nuts and honey are combined with crisp cooked angel hair pasta in this unusual, delicious and charming dessert.

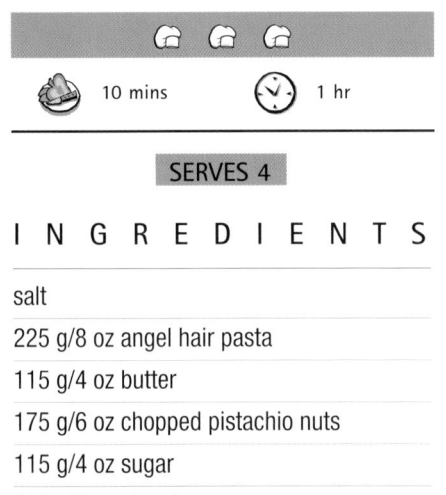

10 mins   1 hr

SERVES 4

INGREDIENTS

salt

225 g/8 oz angel hair pasta

115 g/4 oz butter

175 g/6 oz chopped pistachio nuts

115 g/4 oz sugar

115 g/4 oz clear honey

150 ml/5 fl oz water

2 tsp lemon juice

Greek-style yogurt, to serve

1 Preheat the oven to 180°C/350°F/Gas Mark 4. Bring a large saucepan of lightly salted water to the boil. Add the angel hair pasta, bring back to the boil and cook for 8–10 minutes, or until tender, but still firm to the bite. Drain the pasta and return to the saucepan. Add the butter and toss to coat the pasta thoroughly. Leave to cool.

2 Arrange 4 small tart or cooking rings on a baking tray. Divide the angel hair pasta into 8 equal quantities and spoon 4 of them into the rings. Press down lightly. Top the pasta with half of the nuts, then add the remaining pasta.

3 Bake in the preheated oven for 45 minutes or until golden brown.

4 Meanwhile, put the sugar, honey and water in a saucepan and bring to the boil over a low heat, stirring constantly until the sugar has dissolved completely. Simmer for 10 minutes, add the lemon juice and simmer for a further 5 minutes.

5 Using a spatula, carefully transfer the angel hair nests to a serving dish. Pour over the honey syrup, sprinkle over the remaining nuts, and set aside to cool before serving at room temperature. Serve the yogurt separately.

COOK'S TIP

Angel hair pasta is also known as *capelli d'angelo*. Long and very fine, it is usually sold in small bunches that already resemble nests.

Banana Cream Profiteroles

Chocolate profiteroles are a popular choice. In this recipe they are filled with a delicious banana-flavoured cream – the perfect combination!

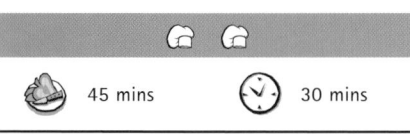

45 mins   30 mins

SERVES 4

INGREDIENTS

DOUGH

5 tbsp butter, plus extra for greasing

150 ml/5 fl oz water, plus extra for sprinkling

85 g/3 oz strong plain flour, sifted

2 eggs

CHOCOLATE SAUCE

100 g /3½ oz plain chocolate, broken into pieces

2 tbsp water

4 tbsp icing sugar

2 tbsp butter, sweet for preference

FILLING

300 ml/10 fl oz double cream

1 banana, peeled

2 tbsp icing sugar

2 tbsp crème de banane

1 Preheat the oven to 220°C/425°F/Gas Mark 7. Lightly grease a baking tray and sprinkle with a little water. To make the dough, place the water in a saucepan. Cut the butter into small pieces and add to the saucepan. Heat gently until the butter melts, then bring to a rolling boil. Remove the saucepan from the heat and add the flour in one go, beating well until the mixture leaves the sides of the saucepan and forms a ball. Leave to cool slightly, then gradually beat in the eggs to form a smooth, glossy mixture. Spoon the paste into a large piping bag fitted with a 1-cm/½-inch plain nozzle.

2 Pipe about 18 small balls of the paste on to the baking tray, allowing enough room for them to expand during cooking. Bake in the preheated oven for 15–20 minutes, until crisp and golden. Remove from the oven and make a small slit in each one for steam to escape. Cool on a wire rack.

3 To make the sauce, place all the ingredients in a heatproof bowl, set over a saucepan of gently simmering water and heat until combined to make a smooth sauce, stirring constantly.

4 To make the filling, whip the cream until soft peaks form. Mash the banana with the sugar and liqueur. Fold into the cream. Place in a piping bag fitted with a 1-cm/½-inch plain nozzle and pipe into the profiteroles. Serve with the sauce poured over.

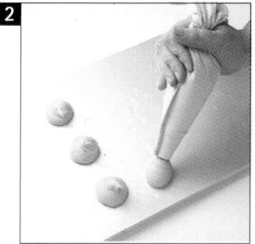

Petits Fours, Sweets & Drinks

Here are some delightful ways to round off a meal, or

the day. There are mini bites such as Almond & Chocolate

Tuiles and Churros to appreciate with afternoon tea;

petits fours, such as Mini Minted Meringues and Praline &

Coffee Truffles to offer after dinner;

and fudge and toffee recipes which

make a welcome gift or enjoyable treat.

There are also extravagant cocktails,

including Krechma, Mona Lisa, and Chocolate Cake

Cocktail; decadent smoothies and shakes using spices, mint

and mocha; and hot chocolate drinks

with cream and brandy.

Dried Fruit Petits Fours

Irresistibly sweet and unbelievably tempting, these fruity little chocolates can be served with coffee at the end of a dinner party.

20–25 mins plus
30 mins setting

5 mins

MAKES 30

INGREDIENTS

175 g/6 oz ready-to-eat dried apricots

175 g/6 oz ready-to-eat dried figs

115 g/4 oz ready-to-eat dried dates

85 g/3 oz roughly chopped walnuts

3 tbsp finely chopped candied orange peel

3 tbsp apricot brandy,
    plus extra for moistening

icing sugar, for dusting

115 g/4 oz milk chocolate,
    broken into pieces

4 tbsp chopped toasted hazelnuts

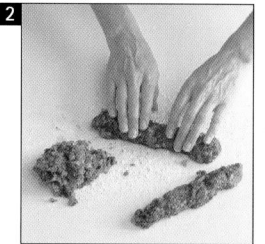
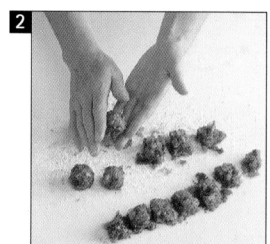

1 Chop the dried fruits by hand or in a food processor. Place the chopped fruits in a bowl and add the walnuts, candied peel and apricot brandy. Mix well.

2 Gather the mixture together and turn out on to a work surface lightly dusted with icing sugar. Divide the mixture into 3 pieces and form each piece into a roll about 20 cm/8 inches long, then cut each roll into slices about 2 cm/ ³/₄ inch thick. Moisten your hands with a little apricot brandy and roll each slice into a ball between your palms.

3 Place the chocolate in a heatproof bowl set over a saucepan of gently simmering water. Stir over a low heat until melted. Remove from the heat and cool slightly. Spear each fruit ball with a fork or skewer and dip it in the melted chocolate to coat it. Place on a sheet of baking parchment and sprinkle the hazelnuts on top. Leave for 30 minutes or until set.

Chocolate Almond Petits Fours

These rich little petits fours are the perfect partner to serve with coffee after dinner. For the best results, use good-quality chocolate.

25 mins   5 mins

MAKES 15

INGREDIENTS

40 g/1½ oz ground almonds

85 g/3 oz granulated sugar

5 tsp cocoa powder

1 egg white

8 blanched almonds, halved

55 g/2 oz plain chocolate, broken into pieces

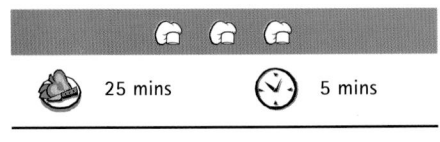

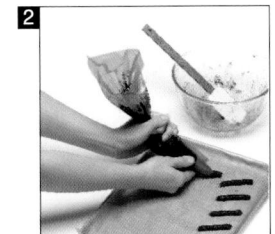
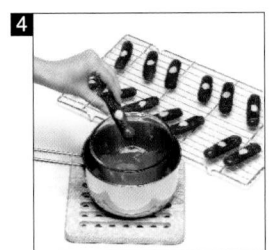

1 Preheat the oven to 190°C/375°F/Gas Mark 5. Line a baking tray with baking parchment. Put the ground almonds, sugar and cocoa powder in a bowl and mix well together. Add the egg white and mix to form a firm mixture.

2 Fill a piping bag, fitted with a small plain nozzle, with the mixture and pipe 5-cm/2-inch lengths, spaced well apart, on to the prepared baking tray. Place an almond half on top of each.

3 Bake in the oven for about 5 minutes, until firm. Transfer to a wire rack and leave to cool.

4 When the petits fours are cold, melt the chocolate in a heatproof bowl set over a saucepan of gently simmering water. Dip each end of the petits fours into the melted chocolate, then leave on the wire rack to set.

COOK'S TIP
You could use the remaining egg yolk from this recipe to make Chocolate Cherry Cups on page 967.

Chocolate Fruit & Nut Balls

These chocolate balls, packed with dried fruit and nuts, become favourites with all who try them. Serve in paper sweet cases if preferred.

20 mins plus
2 hrs chilling

5 mins

MAKES 20

INGREDIENTS

115 g/4 oz sultanas

115 g/4 oz raisins

115 g/4 oz blanched almonds

grated rind of 1 orange

225 g/8 oz plain chocolate, broken
  into pieces

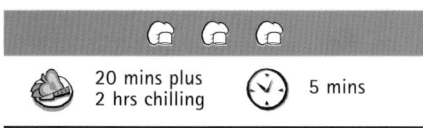

1 Line a baking tray with baking parchment. Put the sultanas, raisins, almonds, and orange rind in a food processor and chop very finely.

2 Take a heaped teaspoonful of the mixture at a time and roll into a ball. Place on the prepared baking tray. Continue until you have used up the remaining mixture. Chill in the refrigerator for about 2 hours, until firm.

3 Melt the chocolate in a heatproof bowl set over a saucepan of gently simmering water. Using a dipping ring or 2 forks, carefully dip each ball into the melted chocolate. Lift it out quickly, letting any excess chocolate drain against the side of the bowl, and place on the prepared baking tray. Leave to set.

4 When the chocolate balls have set, place in paper sweet cases.

Chocolate & Honey Fudge

Honey not only flavours the fudge but also gives it a smooth, soft texture. Pieces of fudge make an ideal gift packed in a pretty box.

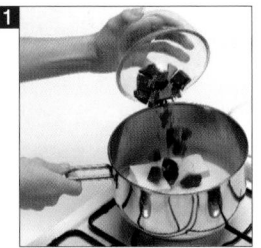

35–40 mins

15–20 mins

MAKES ABOUT 64 PIECES

INGREDIENTS

115 g/4 oz unsalted butter, plus extra for greasing

115 g/4 oz Continental plain chocolate, broken into pieces

450 g/1lb granulated sugar

175 ml/6 fl oz canned evaporated milk

115 g/4 oz honey

1 Grease an 18-cm/7-inch shallow square tin or a 20 x 15-cm/8 x 6-inch shallow tin. Put all the ingredients into a large, heavy-based saucepan and heat gently, stirring all the time, until the chocolate and butter have melted and the sugar has dissolved.

2 Bring to the boil and boil for about 10–15 minutes, stirring occasionally, until a little of the mixture, when dropped into a small bowl of cold water, forms a soft ball when rolled between the fingers.

3 Remove the saucepan from the heat and leave to cool for 5 minutes, then beat the mixture vigorously with a wooden spoon, until it becomes thick, creamy and grainy.

4 Immediately pour the mixture into the prepared tin, leave to cool, then mark into small squares. When the fudge is cold and set, cut up the squares with a sharp knife.

COOK'S TIP
It is better to use unsalted butter in the mixture, rather than salted, as it has less tendency to burn.

Chocolate & Peppermint Fudge

The addition of peppermint gives this chocolate fudge a deliciously fresh flavour. This fudge is perfect for eating at any time of the day.

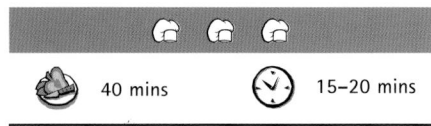

40 mins   15–20 mins

MAKES ABOUT 64 PIECES

INGREDIENTS

115 g/4 oz butter, plus extra for greasing

175 ml/6 fl oz canned evaporated milk

2 tbsp milk

675 g/1 lb 8oz granulated sugar

150 g/5½ oz Continental plain chocolate, broken into pieces

1 tsp peppermint oil

1 Grease an 18-cm/7-inch shallow square tin or a 20 x 15-cm/8 x 6-inch shallow tin. Pour the evaporated milk and milk into a large, heavy-based saucepan and add the sugar, butter and chocolate. Heat gently, stirring all the time, until the sugar has dissolved and the butter and chocolate have melted.

2 Bring to the boil and boil for about 10–15 minutes, stirring occasionally, until a little of the mixture, when dropped into a small bowl of cold water, forms a soft ball when rolled between the fingers.

COOK'S TIP

For a superior flavour, use extract of peppermint rather than peppermint flavouring.

3 Remove the saucepan from the heat and leave to cool for 5 minutes, then add the peppermint oil. Beat the mixture vigorously with a wooden spoon until thick, creamy and grainy.

4 Immediately pour the mixture into the prepared tin, leave to cool, then mark into squares. When the fudge is cold and set, cut up the squares using a sharp knife.

Ginger Chocolate Fudge

The combination of the hot ginger flavour and sweet chocolate flavour in this fudge is a great success. Leave to cool completely before serving.

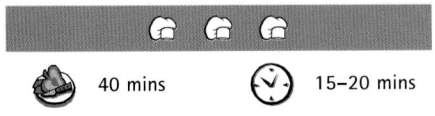

🔔 40 mins 🕐 15–20 mins

MAKES 49 PIECES

INGREDIENTS

115 g/4 oz butter, plus extra for greasing

6 pieces stem ginger

300 ml/10 fl oz milk

150 g/5½ oz plain chocolate, broken into pieces

450 g/1 lb granulated sugar

1 Grease an 18-cm/7-inch shallow square tin or a 20 x 15-cm/8 x 6-inch shallow tin. Dry the syrup off the pieces of stem ginger on kitchen paper, then chop finely.

2 Pour the milk into a large, heavy-based saucepan and add the chocolate, butter and sugar. Heat gently, stirring all the time, until the chocolate and butter have melted and the sugar has completely dissolved.

3 Bring to the boil and boil for about 10–15 minutes, stirring occasionally, until a little of the mixture, when dropped into a small bowl of cold water, forms a soft ball when rolled between the fingers.

4 Remove the saucepan from the heat and stir in the chopped ginger. Leave to cool for 5 minutes, then beat the mixture vigorously with a wooden spoon, until thick, creamy and grainy.

5 Immediately pour the mixture into the prepared tin, leave to cool, then mark into small squares. Leave the fudge until cold and set, then cut up the squares with a sharp knife.

COOK'S TIP
Dipping the knife in hot water makes the fudge much easier to cut.

Light & Dark Fudge

Creamy white fudge and dark fudge, flavoured with cocoa powder
for an intense chocolate flavour, are swirled together for a stunning effect.

35 mins   15–20 mins

MAKES ABOUT 64 PIECES

I N G R E D I E N T S

115 g/4 oz butter, plus extra for greasing

300 ml/10 fl oz milk

800 g/1 lb 12 oz granulated sugar

½ tsp vanilla essence

2 tbsp cocoa powder

1 Grease an 18-cm/7-inch shallow square tin or a 20 x 15-cm/8 x 6-inch shallow tin. Pour the milk into a large, heavy-based saucepan. Add the sugar and butter and heat gently, stirring all the time, until the sugar has dissolved and the butter has melted.

2 Bring to the boil and boil for about 10–15 minutes, stirring occasionally, until a little of the mixture, when dropped into a small bowl of cold water, forms a soft ball when rolled between the fingers.

3 Remove the saucepan from the heat and carefully pour half the mixture into a clean saucepan. Stir in the vanilla essence. Sift the cocoa powder into the remaining mixture, then beat the mixture vigorously with a wooden spoon, until thick, creamy and grainy.

4 Immediately swirl the mixture over the bottom of the prepared tin, leaving gaps. Beat the vanilla mixture vigorously until thick, creamy and grainy, then pour into the gaps in the tin.

5 Leave the fudge to cool, then mark into squares. When cold and set, cut up the squares with a sharp knife.

COOK'S TIP
It is important to use a heavy-based saucepan to help prevent the fudge from sticking to the bottom.

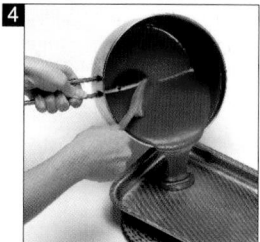

Pecan Mocha Fudge

This recipe makes plenty of delicious fudge for eating yourself, for sharing, and for giving away as presents to your family and friends!

15 mins plus 2 hrs setting

15–20 mins

MAKES ABOUT 108 PIECES

INGREDIENTS

250 g/9 oz butter, plus extra for greasing

300 ml/10 fl oz milk

1 kg/2 lb 4 oz golden granulated sugar

2 tbsp instant coffee granules

2 tbsp cocoa powder

2 tbsp golden syrup

400 g/14 oz canned condensed milk

70 g/2½ oz shelled pecans, chopped

1 Grease a 30 x 23-cm/12 x 9-inch Swiss roll tin. Place the milk, sugar and butter in a large saucepan. Stir over gentle heat until the sugar has dissolved. Stir in the coffee granules, cocoa powder, syrup and condensed milk.

2 Bring to the boil and boil steadily, whisking constantly, for 10 minutes, or until a temperature of 116°C/241°F is reached on a sugar thermometer, or a small amount of the mixture forms a soft ball when dropped into cold water.

3 Leave to cool for 5 minutes, then beat vigorously with a wooden spoon until the mixture starts to thicken. Stir in the nuts. Continue beating until the mixture takes on a fudge-like consistency. Quickly pour into the prepared tin and leave in a cool place to set. Cut the fudge into squares to serve.

COOK'S TIP
To test the temperature of the fudge accurately, it is best to use a sugar thermometer. These are available from specialist kitchen shops.

Fruit & Nut Fudge

Chocolate, nuts and dried fruit – the perfect combination – are all found in this simple-to-make fudge. Cut into even-size squares to serve.

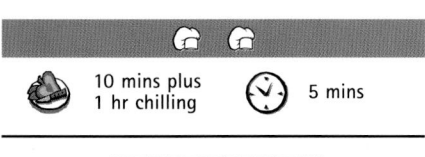

10 mins plus
1 hr chilling

5 mins

MAKES 36 PIECES

INGREDIENTS

250 g/9 oz plain chocolate, broken into pieces

2 tbsp butter, plus extra for greasing

4 tbsp evaporated milk

450 g/1 lb icing sugar, sifted

50 g/1¾ oz roughly chopped hazelnuts

50 g/1¾ oz sultanas

1 Lightly grease a 20-cm/8-inch square cake tin.

2 Put the chocolate in a heatproof bowl with the butter and evaporated milk and set over a saucepan of gently simmering water. Stir until the chocolate and butter have melted and the mixture is well blended.

3 Remove the bowl from the heat and gradually beat in the icing sugar. Stir the hazelnuts and sultanas into the mixture. Press the fudge into the prepared tin and smooth the top. Chill until firm.

4 Tip the fudge out on to a chopping board and cut into squares. Chill in the refrigerator until required.

VARIATION
Vary the nuts used in this recipe; try making the fudge with almonds, Brazil nuts, walnuts or pecans.

Chocolate Marshmallow Fudge

This fudge is not made by the traditional method of boiling because the addition of marshmallows gives the mixture its fudge-like texture.

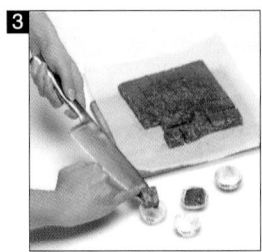

15 mins plus
1–2 hrs setting

5 mins

MAKES 49 PIECES

INGREDIENTS

115 g/4 oz Continental plain chocolate, broken into pieces

70 g/2½ oz butter, plus extra for greasing

200 g/7 oz white mini marshmallows

2 tsp water

115 g/4 oz blanched almonds, roughly chopped

1 Grease an 18-cm/7-inch shallow square tin or a 20 x 15-cm/8 x 6-inch shallow tin. Melt the chocolate in a heatproof bowl over a saucepan of simmering water. Put the marshmallows, butter, and water in a large, heavy-based saucepan and heat gently, stirring frequently, until melted.

2 Remove the saucepan from the heat and pour the chocolate into the mixture. Add the almonds and stir until well mixed.

3 Pour the mixture into the prepared tin and leave to cool for 1–2 hours, until set. Then cut into squares with a sharp knife. To serve, place each piece of fudge in a small paper sweet case.

COOK'S TIP
You could use large marshmallows for this recipe, cut into small pieces. The best way of doing this is to use wet scissors.

Mocha Fudge

Chocolate and coffee are a classic combination and in this fudge recipe the chocolate is made deeper in flavour by the addition of the coffee.

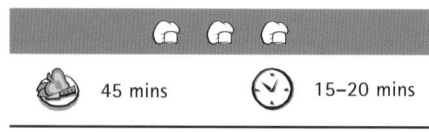

45 mins   15–20 mins

MAKES 49 PIECES

INGREDIENTS

115 g/4 oz butter, plus extra for greasing

300 ml/10 fl oz milk

115 g/4 oz Continental plain chocolate, broken into pieces

800 g/1 lb 12 oz granulated sugar

2 tbsp instant coffee granules

1 Grease an 18-cm/7-inch shallow square tin or a 20 x 15-cm/8 x 6-inch shallow tin. Pour the milk into a large, heavy-based saucepan and add all the remaining ingredients. Heat gently, stirring all the time, until the chocolate and butter have melted and the sugar and coffee have dissolved.

2 Bring to the boil and boil for about 10–15 minutes, stirring occasionally, until a little of the mixture, when dropped into a bowl of cold water, forms a soft ball when rolled between the fingers.

3 Remove the saucepan from the heat and leave to cool for 5 minutes, then beat the mixture vigorously with a wooden spoon until it becomes thick, creamy and grainy.

4 Immediately pour the mixture into the prepared tin, leave to cool, then mark into squares. When the fudge is cold and set, cut up the squares with a sharp knife dipped in hot water.

Easy Chocolate Fudge

This is the easiest fudge to make – for a really rich flavour, use a good plain chocolate with a high cocoa content, at least 70 per cent.

10 mins plus
1 hr setting

5 mins

MAKES 64 PIECES

INGREDIENTS

75 g/2¾ oz unsalted butter, plus extra
  for greasing

500 g/1 lb 2 oz plain chocolate

400 ml/14 fl oz condensed milk

½ tsp vanilla essence

1 Lightly grease a 20-cm/8-inch square cake tin.

2 Break the chocolate into pieces and place in a large saucepan with the butter and condensed milk.

3 Heat gently, stirring until the chocolate and butter melts and the mixture is smooth. Do not allow to boil.

4 Remove from the heat. Beat in the vanilla essence, then beat the mixture for a few minutes until thickened. Pour it into the prepared pan and smooth the top.

5 Chill the mixture in the refrigerator until firm.

6 Tip the fudge out on to a chopping board and cut into squares to serve.

Microwave Chocolate Fudge

This cheat's fudge takes only minutes to make. If there is any left after serving, then store in an airtight container for several days.

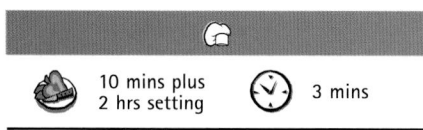

10 mins plus
2 hrs setting

3 mins

MAKES 49 PIECES

INGREDIENTS

sunflower oil, for oiling

115 g/4 oz plain chocolate, broken into pieces

40 g/1½ oz unsalted butter

450 g/1 lb icing sugar, sifted

2 tbsp milk

50 g/1½ oz chopped walnuts

1 Lightly oil an 18-cm/7-inch shallow square baking tin.

2 Place the chocolate in a large bowl. Cut the butter into pieces and add to the bowl. Add the icing sugar and milk.

3 Heat in the microwave, on Full Power, for 3 minutes or until the chocolate and butter have melted. Beat until smooth.

4 Stir in the nuts and pour the mixture into the prepared tin. Smooth the top and leave to stand in a cool place until set. Cut into squares.

COOK'S TIP

To make this fudge without a microwave, melt all the ingredients in a saucepan and bring to the boil, stirring constantly. Cook for 1 minute, then proceed as in the recipe.

Chocolate Creams

These soft, creamy sweets are quick and simple to make, and ideal if the children want to be involved. Perfect served with a cup of coffee or tea.

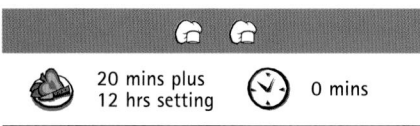

20 mins plus 12 hrs setting   0 mins

MAKES ABOUT 30

INGREDIENTS

200 g/7 oz plain chocolate, broken into pieces

2 tbsp single cream

225 g/8 oz icing sugar

drinking chocolate powder, for dusting

1 Line a baking tray with baking parchment. Melt 55 g/2 oz of the chocolate in a large heatproof bowl set over a saucepan of gently simmering water. Stir in the cream and remove the bowl from the heat.

2 Sift the icing sugar into the melted chocolate then, using a fork, mix well together. Knead to form a firm, smooth, pliable mixture.

3 Lightly dust a work counter with drinking chocolate powder, turn out the mixture, and roll out to 5-mm/¼-inch thickness, then cut into rounds, using a 2.5-cm/1-inch plain round cutter.

4 Transfer to the prepared baking tray and leave to stand for about 12 hours, or overnight, until set and dry.

5 When the chocolate creams have set, line a baking tray with baking parchment. Melt the remaining chocolate in a heatproof bowl set over a saucepan of gently simmering water. Using 2 forks, carefully dip each chocolate cream into the melted chocolate. Lift it out quickly, letting any excess chocolate drain against the side of the bowl, and place on the prepared baking tray. Leave to set.

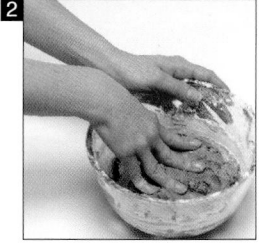

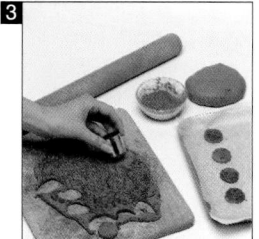

Coffee Creams

Coffee-flavoured fondant is extra special when coated with plain chocolate. Serve with a cappuccino or hot chocolate for a real treat.

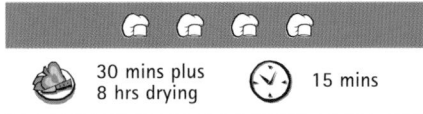

30 mins plus 8 hrs drying

15 mins

MAKES 20

INGREDIENTS

450 g/1 lb granulated sugar

150 ml/5 fl oz water

pinch of cream of tartar

3 tbsp single cream

½ tsp coffee essence

85 g/3 oz Continental plain chocolate, for coating

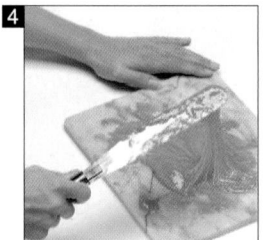
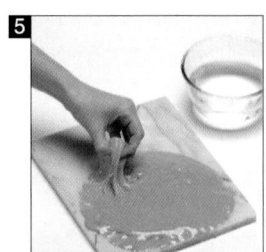

1 Put the sugar and water in a heavy-based saucepan and heat gently until the sugar has dissolved. Bring to the boil and add the cream of tartar.

2 Boil until the syrup registers 116°C/240°F on a sugar thermometer, or until a few drops of syrup form a soft ball when dropped into a bowl of cold water. Stir the syrup into the cream.

3 Sprinkle a little water on a chopping board. Pour the syrup on to the chopping board and leave to cool for a few minutes until a skin forms around the edges.

4 Collect the syrup together with a spatula. Turn the mixture, working it backward and forward in a figure-of-eight movement, until it becomes opaque and grainy, then knead in the coffee essence.

5 Pull off walnut-size pieces of fondant. Roll each piece into a ball, then press to flatten slightly. Leave to dry for 8 hours, or overnight, on a baking tray lined with non-stick baking parchment.

6 Break the chocolate into pieces and place in a heatproof bowl set over a saucepan of gently simmering water until melted. Dip one end of each coffee cream into the melted chocolate to half-coat. Leave on the baking parchment to dry.

Nutty Chocolate Clusters

Nuts and crisp biscuits encased in chocolate make these little nuggets rich, chocolatey and quite irresistible at any time of the day!

| | 30 mins plus 1 hr chilling | | 5 mins |

MAKES 30

INGREDIENTS

175 g/6 oz white chocolate, broken into pieces

100 g/3½ oz digestive biscuits

100 g/3½ oz chopped macadamia nuts or Brazil nuts

25 g/1 oz stem ginger, chopped (optional)

175 g/6 oz plain chocolate, broken into pieces

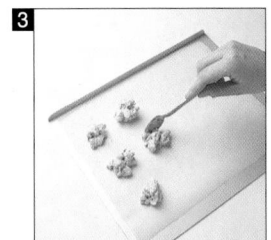

1 Line a baking tray with a sheet of baking parchment. Put the white chocolate in a large heatproof bowl set over a saucepan of gently simmering water and stir until melted.

2 Break the digestive biscuits into small pieces. Stir the crumbs into the melted chocolate with the chopped nuts and stem ginger (if using).

3 Place heaped teaspoons of the mixture on the prepared baking tray.

4 Chill the mixture until set, then remove from the baking parchment.

5 Melt the plain chocolate (see step 1) and let it cool slightly. Dip the clusters into the melted chocolate, allowing the excess drip back into the bowl. Return the clusters to the baking tray and chill in the refrigerator until set.

COOK'S TIP
Macadamia and Brazil nuts are both rich and high in fat, which makes them particularly popular for confectionery, but other nuts can be used if preferred.

Chocolate-Covered Brazil Nuts

In a box of chocolates these are often a favourite, yet they are surprisingly easy to make at home and are perfect for serving after dinner.

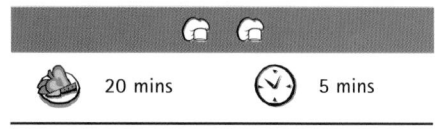

20 mins   5 mins

MAKES ABOUT 28

INGREDIENTS

200 g/7 oz plain or milk chocolate, broken into pieces

200 g/7 oz shelled Brazil nuts

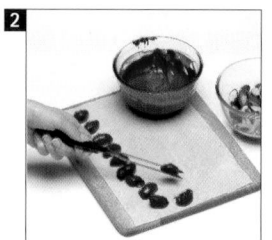
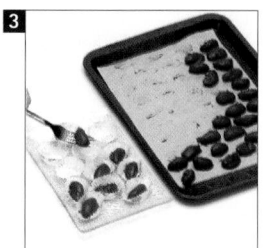

1 Line a baking tray with baking parchment. Break the chocolate into pieces and place in a heatproof bowl set over a saucepan of gently simmering water. Remove from the heat.

2 Using a fork, carefully dip and turn each Brazil nut into the melted chocolate. Lift it out quickly, letting any excess chocolate drain against the side of the bowl, and place on the baking tray. Leave to set.

3 When the chocolate has set, put the Brazil nuts into paper sweet cases.

VARIATIONS
Other nuts that can be coated in the same way include walnuts, macadamia nuts and blanched almonds.

Chocolate Almonds

These sweets look very elegant served in gold and silver foil cases. Alternatively, use paper sweet cases or place in an attractive dish.

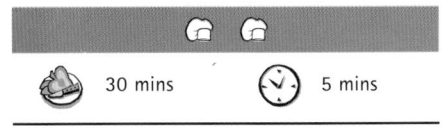

🍰 30 mins   🕐 5 mins

MAKES 32

INGREDIENTS

225 g/8 oz icing sugar, plus extra
   for dusting

55 g/2 oz cocoa powder

1 tbsp milk

55 g/2 oz butter

55 g/2 oz whole blanched almonds

115 g/4 oz plain chocolate

1 Sift the icing sugar and cocoa powder into a bowl.

2 Place the milk and butter in a small saucepan and heat together until the butter has melted. Add to the icing sugar mixture and beat to a stiff paste.

3 Turn the paste on to a work surface and dust your hands with icing sugar. Roll the mixture into a thick rope. Cut into 32 pieces and shape each piece into an oval. Top each oval with an almond.

4 Break the chocolate into pieces and place in a heatproof bowl with 1 tablespoon of water. Set over a saucepan of gently simmering water until melted. Dip one side of each oval in chocolate and leave on a wire rack to set.

Chocolate Pralines

These heavenly chocolates, packed with crunchy almond praline, are wonderful served with a chocolate dessert such as a mousse or soufflé.

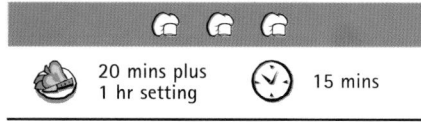

20 mins plus
1 hr setting

15 mins

MAKES 49

INGREDIENTS

sunflower oil, for brushing

150 g/5½ oz granulated sugar

3 tbsp water

75 g/2¾ oz blanched almonds

200 g/7 oz Continental plain chocolate

1 Brush a baking tray with oil. Put the sugar and water in a saucepan and heat gently, stirring, until the sugar has dissolved, then allow to bubble gently, without stirring, for 6–10 minutes, until lightly golden brown.

2 Remove the saucepan from the heat and stir in the almonds. Immediately pour the mixture on to the prepared baking tray and spread out evenly. Leave to stand in a cool place for about 1 hour, until cold and hardened.

3 When the praline has hardened, crush it into tiny pieces in a food processor or in a plastic bag with a hammer.

4 Break the chocolate into pieces and place in a heatproof bowl set over a pan of gently simmering water. Add the crushed praline and mix together to form a stiff paste. Turn into an 18-cm/ 7-inch shallow square tin and leave to set.

5 When the chocolate praline has set, cut into squares to serve.

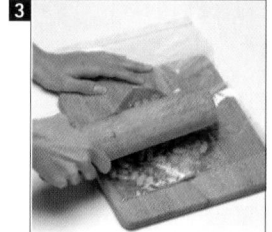

VARIATIONS
Instead of almonds, other nuts could be used such as blanched hazelnuts or pistachios.

Chocolate Marzipans

These delightful little morsels make the perfect gift, if you can resist eating them all yourself! Store in an airtight container.

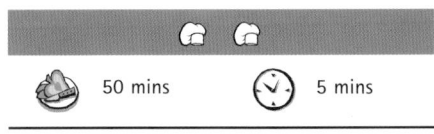

50 mins   5 mins

MAKES 30

INGREDIENTS

450 g/1 lb marzipan

25 g/1 oz very finely chopped glacé cherries

25 g/1 oz stem ginger, very finely chopped

icing sugar, for dusting

50 g/1¾ oz ready-to-eat dried apricots, very finely chopped

350 g/12 oz plain chocolate, broken into pieces

25 g/1 oz white chocolate, broken into pieces

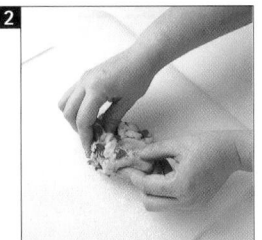

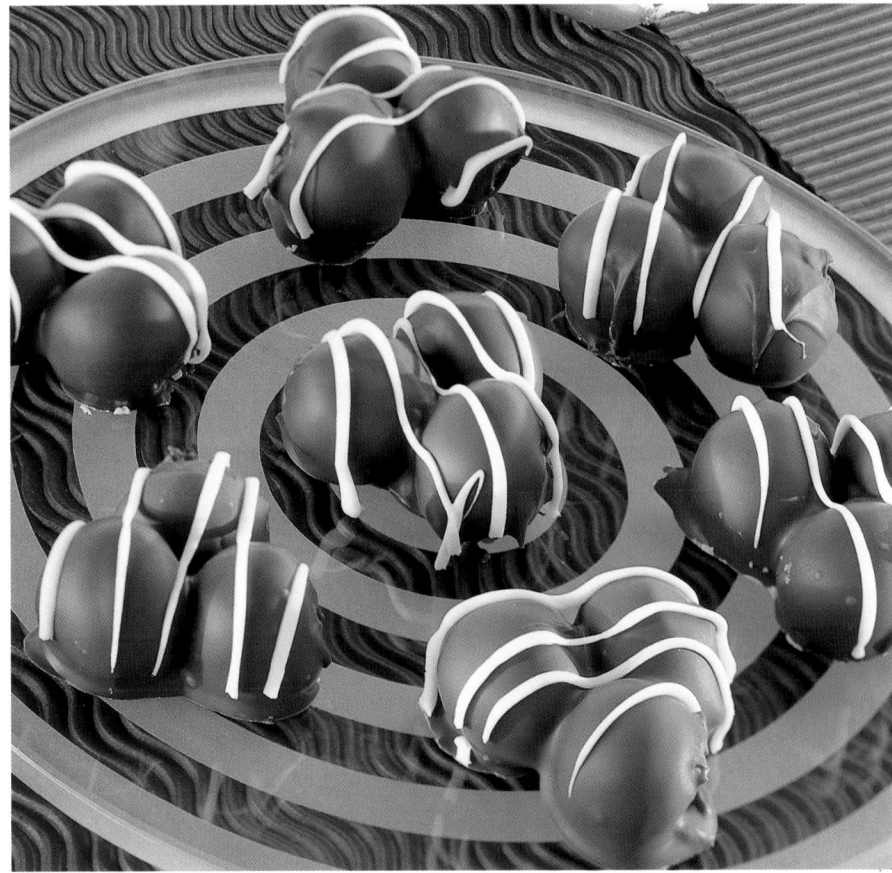

1 Line a baking tray with baking parchment. Divide the marzipan into 3 balls and knead each ball to soften it.

2 Work the glacé cherries into one portion of the marzipan by kneading on a work surface lightly dusted with icing sugar.

3 Do the same with the stem ginger and another portion of the marzipan, and then the apricots and the third portion of marzipan.

4 Form each flavoured portion of marzipan into small balls, keeping the different flavours separate.

5 Put the plain chocolate in a heatproof bowl and set over a saucepan of gently simmering water. Stir until melted. Dip one of each flavour of marzipan ball into the chocolate by spiking each one with a cocktail stick. Let any excess chocolate drip into the bowl.

6 Place the balls in clusters of the 3 flavours on the baking tray. Repeat with the remaining balls. Chill until set.

7 Melt the white chocolate (see step 5) and drizzle a little over the tops of each cluster of marzipan balls. Chill until hardened, then remove from the baking parchment.

VARIATIONS
Coat the marzipan balls in white or milk chocolate and drizzle with plain chocolate if you prefer.

Chocolate Raisin Clusters

These delicious chocolate raisin clusters are very simple to prepare and perfect for children to make on a rainy day.

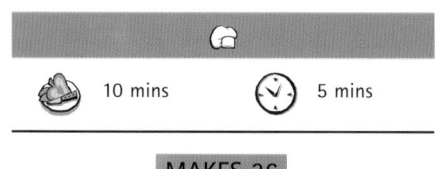   

10 mins   5 mins

MAKES 36

INGREDIENTS

225 g/8 oz plain chocolate, broken into pieces

225 g/8 oz raisins

1 Line a baking tray with baking parchment. Melt the chocolate in a heatproof bowl set over a pan of gently simmering water.

2 Stir the raisins into the melted chocolate until well coated. Leave to cool slightly, then drop heaped teaspoonfuls of the mixture on to the prepared baking tray. Leave until cold.

3 When the chocolate raisin clusters have set, place in paper sweet cases.

VARIATION
Sultanas could be used instead of seedless raisins.

Almond Balls

The crunchy, nutty texture comes as a pleasant surprise in these balls of rich chocolate. They are ideal for serving after dinner with coffee.

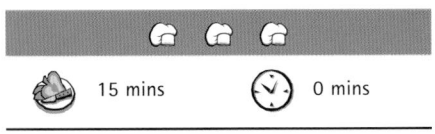

🐾 15 mins   🕐 0 mins

MAKES 20

INGREDIENTS

150 g/5½ oz plain chocolate

55 g/2 oz finely chopped almonds

115 g/4 oz icing sugar

3 tbsp single cream

1 Finely grate the chocolate. Put 115 g/ 4 oz of the chocolate into a bowl and spread the remaining chocolate evenly on to a plate.

2 Add the almonds to the chocolate in the bowl, then sift in the icing sugar. Stir together and add enough cream to form a firm mixture.

3 Take a heaped teaspoonful of the mixture at a time and roll into a ball. Continue until you have used up all the mixture. Drop each ball on to the plate of grated chocolate.

4 Roll the balls in the grated chocolate on the plate, to coat them. Place the balls in paper sweet cases.

VARIATIONS
Other nuts, such as hazelnuts or macadamia nuts, could replace the almonds.

Chocolate Cherries

These cherry and marzipan sweets are easy to make. Serve as petits fours at the end of a meal or as an indulgent nibble at any time of day.

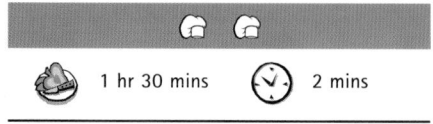

1 hr 30 mins   2 mins

MAKES 24

INGREDIENTS

12 glacé cherries

2 tbsp dark rum or brandy

250 g/9 oz marzipan

125 g/4½ oz plain chocolate,
  broken into pieces

milk, plain or white chocolate, to decorate
  (optional)

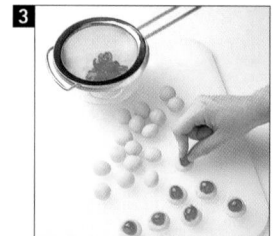

1 Line a baking tray with a sheet of baking parchment.

2 Cut the cherries in half and place in a small bowl. Add the rum or brandy and stir to coat. Leave the cherries to soak for at least 1 hour, stirring occasionally.

3 Divide the marzipan into 24 pieces and roll each piece into a ball. Press half a cherry into the top of each marzipan ball.

4 Put the chocolate in a heatproof bowl and set over a saucepan of gently simmering water. Stir until all the chocolate has melted.

VARIATION
Flatten the marzipan and use it to mould around the cherries to cover them, then dip in the chocolate as above.

5 Dip each sweet into the melted chocolate using a cocktail stick, letting the excess to drip back into the bowl. Place the coated cherries on the baking parchment and chill until set.

6 If liked, melt a little extra chocolate and drizzle it over the top of the coated cherries. Leave to set.

Mini Florentines

Serve these delicious biscuits at the end of a meal with coffee or arrange in a shallow presentation box for an attractive gift.

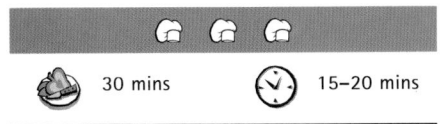
30 mins   15–20 mins

MAKES 40

INGREDIENTS

6 tbsp butter, plus extra for greasing

plain flour, for dusting

75 g/2¾ oz caster sugar

2 tbsp sultanas or raisins

2 tbsp chopped glacé cherries

2 tbsp chopped stem ginger

25 g/1 oz sunflower seeds

100 g/3½ oz flaked almonds

2 tbsp double cream

175 g/6 oz plain or milk chocolate, broken into pieces

1 Preheat the oven to 180°C/350°F/Gas Mark 4. Grease and flour 2 baking trays or line with baking parchment.

2 Place the butter in a small saucepan and heat gently until melted. Add the sugar, stir until dissolved, then bring the mixture to the boil. Remove from the heat and stir in the golden raisins or raisins, cherries, ginger, sunflower seeds and almonds. Mix well, then beat in the cream.

3 Place small teaspoons of the fruit and nut mixture on to the prepared baking trays, allowing plenty of room for the mixture to spread during baking. Bake in the preheated oven for 10–12 minutes, or until light golden in colour.

4 Remove from the oven and, while still hot, use a circular biscuit cutter to pull in the edges to form perfect circles. Leave to cool and go crisp before removing from the baking trays.

5 Put the chocolate in a heatproof bowl set over a saucepan of gently simmering water and stir until melted. Spread most of the chocolate on to a sheet of baking parchment. When the chocolate is on the point of setting, place the biscuits flat-side down on the chocolate and let it harden completely.

6 Cut around the florentines and remove from the baking parchment. Spread a little more chocolate on the coated side of the florentines and use a fork to mark waves in the chocolate. Leave to set. Arrange the florentines on a plate (or in a presentation box for a gift) with alternate sides facing upwards. Keep cool.

Italian Chocolate Truffles

These tasty morsels are flavoured with almonds and chocolate, and are simplicity itself to make. Serve with coffee for the perfect end to a meal.

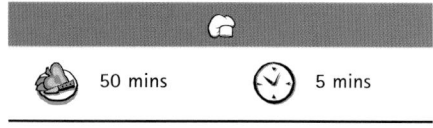

50 mins **5 mins**

MAKES 24

INGREDIENTS

175 g/6 oz plain chocolate, broken into pieces

2 tbsp Amaretto or orange liqueur

3 tbsp unsalted butter

4 tbsp icing sugar

50 g/1¾ oz ground almonds

50 g/1¾ oz grated chocolate

1 Melt the plain chocolate with the Amaretto or orange liqueur in a heatproof bowl set over a saucepan of gently simmering water, stirring until well combined.

2 Add the butter and stir until it has melted. Stir in the icing sugar and the ground almonds.

3 Leave the mixture in a cool place until firm enough to roll into 24 balls.

4 Place the grated chocolate on a plate and roll the truffles in the chocolate to coat them.

5 Place the truffles in paper sweet cases and chill.

VARIATION
The Amaretto gives these truffles an authentic Italian flavour. The original Amaretto di Saronno comes from Saronno in Italy.

White Chocolate Truffles

These delicious creamy white truffles will testify to the fact that there is nothing quite as nice as homemade chocolates.

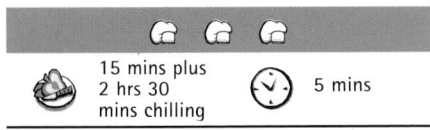

15 mins plus
2 hrs 30
mins chilling

5 mins

MAKES 20

INGREDIENTS

2 tbsp unsalted butter

5 tbsp double cream

225 g/8 oz good-quality Swiss white chocolate

1 tbsp orange liqueur (optional)

100 g/3½ oz white chocolate, broken into pieces, for coating

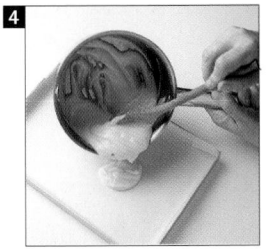
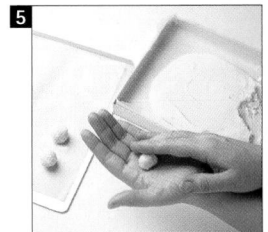
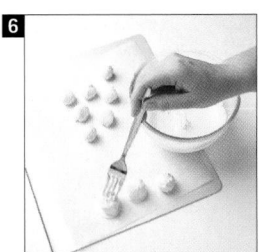

1 Line a Swiss roll tin with baking parchment.

2 Place the butter and cream in a small saucepan and bring slowly to the boil, stirring constantly. Boil for 1 minute, then remove from the heat.

3 Add the chocolate to the cream. Stir until melted, then beat in the liqueur (if using).

4 Pour into the prepared tin and chill for about 2 hours until firm.

5 Break off pieces of the mixture and roll them into balls. Chill for an additional 30 minutes before finishing the truffles.

6 To finish, put the white chocolate in a heatproof bowl set over a saucepan of gently simmering water until melted. Dip the balls in the chocolate, letting the excess drip back into the bowl. Place on non-stick baking parchment, swirl the chocolate with the tines of a fork, and let it harden.

COOK'S TIP
The truffle mixture needs to be firm but not too hard to roll. If the mixture is too hard, leave it to stand at room temperature for a few minutes to soften slightly. During rolling the mixture will become sticky, but will reharden in the refrigerator before coating.

Chocolate Orange Truffles

These rich orange-flavoured truffles make a delicious change from the more usual liqueur-flavoured truffles. Serve in paper sweet cases.

2 hrs 30 mins   0 mins

MAKES 36

INGREDIENTS

115 g/4 oz Continental plain chocolate, broken into pieces

55 g/2 oz butter

2 egg yolks

finely grated rind of 1 small orange

1 tbsp orange juice

25 g/1 oz cake crumbs

25 g/1 oz ground almonds

225 g/8 oz icing sugar

chocolate vermicelli, for coating

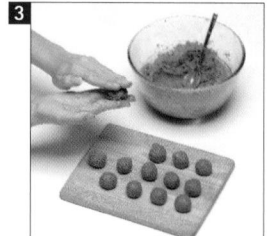

1 Put the chocolate and butter in heatproof bowl set over a saucepan of gently simmering water until melted. Remove from the heat, add the egg yolks, and mix well together.

2 Add the orange rind and juice, cake crumbs, and almonds. Sift in the icing sugar, then beat together until well mixed. Leave to cool for about 2 hours until the mixture is firm.

VARIATION
The truffles can be coated in drinking chocolate powder as an alternative to the chocolate vermicelli.

3 Take a teaspoonful of the mixture at a time and roll into a ball between your hands. Continue until you have used up the remaining mixture.

4 Spread the chocolate vermicelli on to a plate, then roll the truffles in the chocolate vermicelli to coat them. Place the truffles in paper sweet cases.

Chocolate Chestnut Truffles

Christmas is the time for eating chestnuts so make a batch of these for a festive treat. Use a package of cooked whole chestnuts for this recipe.

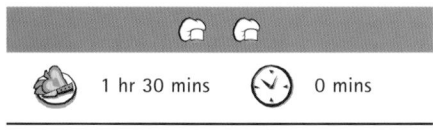

1 hr 30 mins   0 mins

MAKES 24

INGREDIENTS

85 g/3 oz Continental plain chocolate, broken into pieces

40 g/1½ oz butter

7 oz/200 g cooked whole chestnuts

50 g/1¾ oz caster sugar

1 tsp vanilla essence

25 g/1 oz ground almonds, for coating

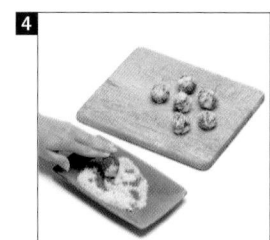

1 Place the chocolate and the butter in a heatproof bowl set over a saucepan of gently simmering water and heat gently until melted. Remove from the heat and let cool. Meanwhile, mash the chestnuts.

2 Whisk together the butter and the sugar until pale and fluffy. Add the mashed chestnuts and vanilla essence and mix well together. Stir in the cooled chocolate until combined. Chill the mixture in the refrigerator for about 1 hour until firm.

3 Take a heaped teaspoonful of the mixture at a time and roll into a ball between your hands. Continue until you have used up the remaining mixture.

4 Spread out the ground almonds on a plate, then roll the truffles in the ground almonds to coat them. Place the truffles in paper sweet cases.

COOK'S TIP
If you find it difficult to mash the chestnuts, soften them in a microwave for 1 minute. If wished, 55 g/2 oz chopped almonds can be added to the mixture.

Chocolate Liqueurs

These tasty chocolate cups are filled with a delicious liqueur-flavoured filling. Use your favourite liqueur to flavour the cream.

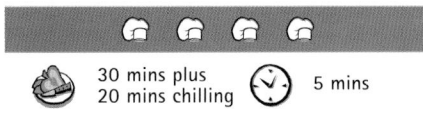

30 mins plus
20 mins chilling

5 mins

MAKES 20

INGREDIENTS

100 g/3½ oz plain chocolate, broken into pieces

20 glacé cherries

20 hazelnuts or macadamia nuts

150 ml/5 fl oz double cream

2 tbsp icing sugar

4 tbsp liqueur

TO FINISH

50 g/1¾ oz plain chocolate, melted

little white chocolate, melted, or white chocolate curls (see page 9), or extra nuts and cherries

1 Line a baking tray with a sheet of baking parchment. Put the plain chocolate in a heatproof bowl and set over a saucepan of gently simmering water. Stir until melted. Spoon the chocolate into 40 paper sweet cases, spreading up the sides with a spoon or brush. Place upside down on the baking tray and leave to set.

2 Carefully peel away the paper cases. Place a cherry or nut in each cup.

3 To make the filling, place the double cream in a mixing bowl and sift the icing sugar on top. Whisk the cream until it is just holding its shape, then whisk in the liqueur.

4 Place the cream in a piping bag fitted with a 1-cm/½-inch plain nozzle and pipe a little into each chocolate case. Leave to chill for 20 minutes.

5 To finish, spoon a little of the melted chocolate over the cream to cover it, then pipe melted white chocolate on top, swirling it into the plain chocolate with a cocktail stick. Leave the liqueurs to harden. Alternatively, cover the cream with melted plain chocolate and decorate with white chocolate curls before setting, or place a small piece of nut or cherry on top of the cream, then cover with plain chocolate.

COOK'S TIP
paper sweet cases can vary in size. Use the smallest you can find for this recipe.

Rocky Road Bites

Young children will love these chewy bites. You can vary the ingredients and use different nuts and dried fruit according to taste.

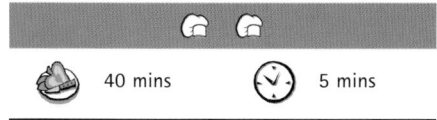

🍰 40 mins 🕐 5 mins

MAKES 20

INGREDIENTS

FILLING

125 g/4½ oz milk chocolate, broken into pieces

50 g/1½ oz mini multicoloured marshmallows

25 g/1 oz chopped walnuts

25 g/1 oz ready-to-eat dried apricots, chopped

1 Line a baking tray with baking parchment and set aside.

2 Put the milk chocolate in a large heatproof bowl. Set the bowl over a saucepan of gently simmering water and stir until the chocolate has melted.

3 Stir in the marshmallows, walnuts and apricots, and toss in the melted chocolate until well covered.

4 Put heaped teaspoonfuls of the mixture on the prepared baking tray.

5 Let the sweets chill in the refrigerator until set.

VARIATION
Light, fluffy marshmallows are available in white or pastel colours. If you cannot find mini marshmallows, use large ones and snip them into smaller pieces with wet kitchen scissors before mixing them into the melted chocolate in step 3.

6 Once set, carefully remove the sweets from the baking parchment.

7 The chewy bites can be placed in paper sweet cases to serve, if desired.

Chocolate Popcorn

Children love popcorn, even more so when coated in chocolate.
Make sure that it is cool enough to eat before serving.

15 mins   15 mins

MAKES ABOUT 250 G/9 OZ

INGREDIENTS

3 tbsp sunflower oil

70 g/2½ oz popcorn

25 g/1 oz butter

55 g/2 oz light soft brown sugar

2 tbsp golden syrup

1 tbsp milk

55 g/2 oz plain chocolate chips

1 Preheat the oven to 150°C/300°F/Gas Mark 2. Heat the oil in a large, heavy-based saucepan. Add the popcorn, cover the saucepan, and cook, shaking the saucepan vigorously and frequently, for about 2 minutes, until the popping stops. Turn into a large bowl.

2 Put the butter, sugar, golden syrup and milk in a saucepan and heat gently until the butter has melted. Bring to the boil, without stirring, and boil for 2 minutes. Remove from the heat, add the chocolate chips, and stir until melted.

3 Pour the chocolate mixture over the popcorn and toss together until evenly coated. Spread the mixture on to a large baking tray.

4 Bake the popcorn in the oven for about 15 minutes, until crisp. Leave to cool before serving.

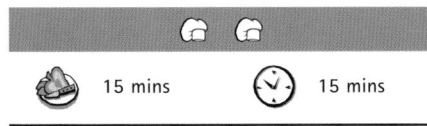

Italian Amaretti Slices

Serve these delicious traditional almond-flavoured chocolate slices with coffee, at the end of an Italian meal.

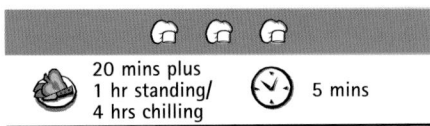

20 mins plus
1 hr standing/
4 hrs chilling

5 mins

MAKES 28–30 SLICES

INGREDIENTS

115 g/4 oz Continental plain chocolate, broken into pieces

85 g/3 oz butter

1 tbsp Amaretto or brandy

25 g/1 oz toasted blanched almonds

225 g/8 oz amaretti biscuits

1 Place the chocolate, butter and Amaretto in a saucepan and heat gently. Stir occasionally until it has all melted and mixed together. Remove from the heat.

2 Put the almonds in a food processor and chop finely. Stir into the chocolate mixture.

3 Put the amaretti biscuits in the food processor and chop finely. Reserve 2 tablespoons of the crumbs. Add the remaining crumbs to the chocolate mixture and mix well together. Leave to stand in a cool place for about 1 hour until firm.

4 When the mixture is firm, turn out on to a sheet of greaseproof paper and shape into a sausage shape measuring about 23 cm/9 inch long. Wrap in the greaseproof paper and chill in the refrigerator for at least 4 hours or overnight, until solid.

5 Unwrap the sausage and dust with the reserved crumbs until coated, then cut into slices.

COOK'S TIP
If you are unable to buy ready-toasted almonds, toast blanched almonds under the grill for 2–3 minutes, shaking frequently. Other nuts can be used, such as hazelnuts or walnuts if preferred.

Chocolate & Pistachio Truffles

These wickedly rich truffles add a touch of decadence at the end of a light meal. Use other types of nuts, such as almonds, if preferred.

30 mins plus 8 hrs chilling

5 mins

MAKES 26–30

INGREDIENTS

100 g/3½ oz white chocolate, broken into pieces

1 tbsp butter

75 ml/2½ fl oz double cream

25 g/1 oz shelled unsalted pistachios, finely chopped

icing sugar, for dusting

1 Put the chocolate, butter and cream in a heatproof bowl set over a saucepan of gently simmering water and heat, without stirring, until the chocolate has melted. Stir gently and add the nuts.

2 Remove the bowl from the heat. Leave to cool, then cover and chill overnight in the refrigerator. Line a baking tray with baking parchment.

3 Take teaspoonfuls of mixture and roll them into balls. Place them on the baking tray and chill until firm. Just before serving, roll the truffles in icing sugar.

COOK'S TIP
The truffles look best if they are quite rough, rather than being rolled into smooth balls.

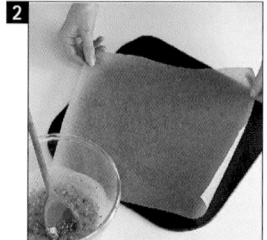

Rum Truffles

Truffles are always popular. They make a fabulous gift or, served with coffee, they are a perfect end to a special-occasion meal.

15 mins plus
30 mins chilling

5 mins

MAKES 20

INGREDIENTS

150 g/5½ oz plain chocolate, broken into pieces

small knob of butter

2 tbsp dark rum

50 g/1¾ oz desiccated coconut

100 g/3½ oz cake crumbs

6 tbsp icing sugar

2 tbsp cocoa powder

1 Put the chocolate in a heatproof bowl with the butter. Set the bowl over a saucepan of gently simmering water, stirring until melted and combined.

2 Remove from the heat and beat in the rum. Stir in the desiccated coconut, cake crumbs and two-thirds of the icing sugar. Beat until combined. Add a little extra rum if the mixture is stiff.

3 Roll the mixture into small balls and place them on a sheet of baking parchment. Chill until firm.

4 Sift the remaining icing sugar on to a large plate. Sift the cocoa powder on to another plate. Roll half of the truffles in the icing sugar until coated and roll the remaining truffles in the cocoa powder.

5 Chill the truffles in the refrigerator until ready to serve.

VARIATIONS
Make the truffles with white chocolate and replace the rum with coconut liqueur or milk if you prefer. Roll them in cocoa powder or dip in melted milk chocolate.

Irish Cream Truffles

Truffles are quickly and easily made and are the ideal gift for chocoholics. They look particularly attractive arranged in alternate colours.

35 mins plus
8 hrs chilling   5–10 mins

MAKES ABOUT 24

INGREDIENTS

150 ml/5 fl oz double cream

225 g/8 oz plain chocolate, broken into pieces

2 tbsp butter

3 tbsp Bailey's Irish cream

FOR COATING

115 g/4 oz white chocolate, broken into pieces

115 g/4 oz plain chocolate, broken into pieces

1 Put the cream in a saucepan and heat without boiling. Remove from the heat and stir in the chocolate and butter. Leave for 2 minutes, then stir until melted and smooth. Stir in the liqueur. Pour the mixture into a bowl and leave to stand until cool. Cover and leave to chill in the refrigerator overnight, until firm.

2 Line a baking tray with baking parchment. Take teaspoonfuls of mixture and roll them into balls. Place them on the baking tray and chill again until firm. Put the white chocolate in a heatproof bowl set over a saucepan of gently simmering water until melted. Leave to cool a little.

3 Coat half the truffles by spearing on thin skewers and dipping in the white chocolate. Leave on non-stick baking parchment to set. Melt the plain chocolate in the same way and coat the remaining truffles. Store in the refrigerator in an airtight container, separated by layers of greaseproof paper, for up to 1 week.

COOK'S TIP
It is essential that the best-quality chocolate is used in this recipe.

Peanut Butter Truffles

Peanut butter combined with apricots and walnuts gives these truffles a wonderful flavour. Store in the refrigerator for several days.

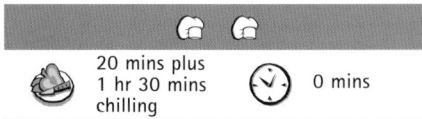

20 mins plus
1 hr 30 mins
chilling

0 mins

MAKES 24

INGREDIENTS

115 g/4 oz icing sugar

115 g/4 oz ready-to-eat dried apricots, roughly chopped

115 g/4 oz walnut pieces, finely chopped

225 g/8 oz smooth peanut butter

115 g/4 oz plain chocolate

grated chocolate, to decorate

 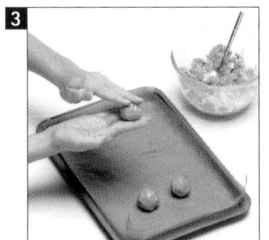 

1 Line a baking tray with non-stick baking parchment.

2 Sift the icing sugar into a bowl. Add the apricots, walnuts and peanut butter. Stir together thoroughly to make a chunky mixture.

3 Shape teaspoonfuls of the mixture into walnut-size balls and arrange on the prepared baking tray. Chill in the refrigerator for 1 hour.

4 Break the chocolate into pieces and place in a heatproof bowl set over a saucepan of gently simmering water until melted. Using a fork, dip the truffles into the melted chocolate and set them on the baking parchment. Sprinkle with grated chocolate, then chill until firm.

Chocolate & Pistachio Biscotti

These crunchy biscuits from northern Italy are traditionally dunked in dessert wine, but they are just as good dipped into coffee or tea!

25 mins   40–45 mins

MAKES 48

I N G R E D I E N T S

225 g/8 oz plain flour, plus extra for dusting

1 tsp bicarbonate of soda

pinch of salt

100 g/3½ oz golden caster sugar

55 g/2 oz ground almonds

2 eggs

85 g/3 oz plain chocolate, melted

55 g/2 oz shelled pistachio nuts, roughly chopped

1 egg white, beaten lightly

1 Preheat the oven to 190°C/375°F/Gas Mark 5. Line 2 baking trays with non-stick baking parchment.

2 Sift the flour, bicarbonate of soda and salt into a bowl. Stir in the caster sugar and ground almonds. Make a well in the centre and break in the eggs. Stir from the centre to form a rough dough.

3 Stir the melted chocolate into the dough. Turn out on to a floured cutting board and knead until well blended, then work in the chopped pistachio nuts.

4 Divide the dough into 3 equal pieces and roll each one into a sausage shape 2.5 cm/1 inch in diameter. Place them on 1 of the prepared baking trays, allowing room for the biscotti to spread during cooking. Brush with beaten egg white. Bake in the preheated oven for 20 minutes.

5 Remove from the oven and leave for 5 minutes to cool and firm up. Reduce the oven temperature to 140°C/275°F/Gas Mark 1. Using a serrated knife, cut the biscotti at an angle into 1-cm/½-inch thick slices. Arrange the slices on the baking trays and return to the oven for 20–25 minutes, turning once. Cool on wire racks.

Collettes

A creamy, orange-flavoured chocolate filling in little white chocolate cups makes a wonderful treat for any occasion.

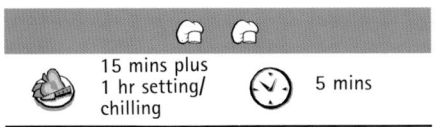

15 mins plus 1 hr setting/ chilling

5 mins

MAKES 20

INGREDIENTS

100 g/3½ oz white chocolate, broken into pieces

FILLING

150 g/5½ oz orange-flavoured plain chocolate, broken into pieces

150 ml/5 fl oz double cream

2 tbsp icing sugar

1 Line a baking tray with baking parchment. Put the white chocolate in a heatproof bowl and set over a saucepan of gently simmering water. Stir until melted. Spoon the melted chocolate into 20 paper sweet cases, spreading up the sides with a small spoon or brush. Place upside down on the prepared baking tray and leave to set.

2 When set, carefully peel away the paper cases.

3 To make the filling, melt the orange-flavoured chocolate and place in a mixing bowl with the double cream and the icing sugar. Beat until smooth. Chill until the mixture becomes firm enough to pipe, stirring occasionally.

4 Place the filling in a piping bag fitted with a star nozzle and pipe a little into each paper sweet case. Chill in the refrigerator until required.

COOK'S TIP
If the chocolate cups do not hold their shape well, use 2 cases to make a double-thickness mould. Foil cases are firmer, so use these if you can find them.

Pastel Chocolate Cups

Packed in a box, these delicately coloured chocolate cups make an attractive gift. Store in the refrigerator for up to a week.

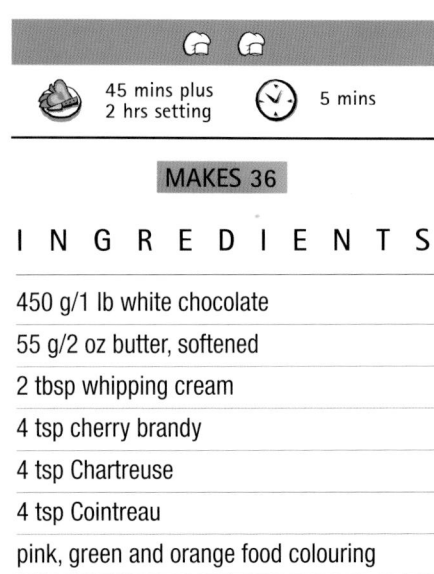

45 mins plus 2 hrs setting

5 mins

MAKES 36

INGREDIENTS

450 g/1 lb white chocolate

55 g/2 oz butter, softened

2 tbsp whipping cream

4 tsp cherry brandy

4 tsp Chartreuse

4 tsp Cointreau

pink, green and orange food colouring

1 Place the chocolate in a heatproof bowl set over a saucepan of gently simmering water until melted.

2 Arrange 36 foil petit-four cases on a tray and spoon a little chocolate into each case. Using a fine brush, coat the inside of each case with chocolate. Leave to set.

3 Add the softened butter and cream to the remaining chocolate and stir until smooth. Divide the mixture between 3 bowls.

4 Add the cherry brandy to one bowl, Chartreuse to another and Cointreau to the third. Colour the mixtures pink, pale green and pale orange respectively.

5 When the chocolate mixtures are set to a soft peaking consistency place each in a separate piping bag fitted with a small star nozzle. Pipe swirls of each colour into 12 chocolate cases. Leave to set.

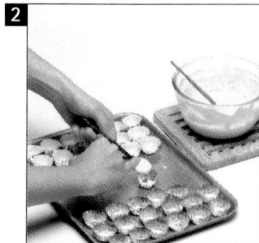

COOK'S TIP
Buy miniature liqueur bottles for this recipe.

Chocolate Mascarpone Cups

Mascarpone – the velvety smooth Italian cheese – makes a rich, creamy filling for these tasty chocolates. Dust with cocoa just before serving.

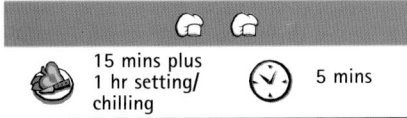

15 mins plus 1 hr setting/ chilling

5 mins

MAKES 20

INGREDIENTS

100 g/3½ oz plain chocolate, broken into pieces

FILLING

100 g/3½ oz milk or plain chocolate, broken into pieces

200 g/7 oz mascarpone cheese

¼ tsp vanilla essence

cocoa powder, for dusting

1 Line a baking tray with baking parchment. Put the plain chocolate in a heatproof bowl and set over a saucepan of gently simmering water. Stir until melted. Spoon the chocolate into 20 paper sweet cases, and spread up the sides with a spoon or brush. Place upside down on the baking tray and leave to set.

2 When set, carefully peel away the paper cases.

3 To make the filling, melt the milk or plain chocolate (see step 1). Put the mascarpone in a bowl and beat in the vanilla essence and melted chocolate until well combined. Let the mixture chill, beating occasionally until firm enough to pipe.

4 Put the mascarpone filling in a piping bag fitted with a star nozzle and pipe the mixture into the cups. Decorate with a dusting of cocoa powder.

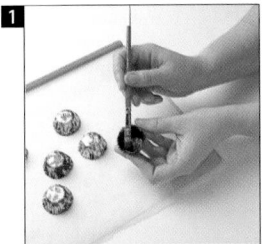

VARIATION

Mascarpone is a rich Italian soft cheese made from fresh cream, so it has a high fat content. Its delicate flavour blends well with chocolate.

Double Chocolate Truffles

Marzipan, honey, and plain and milk chocolate are combined into little morsels of sheer delight. They are perfect for serving with coffee.

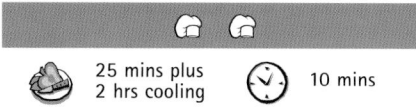
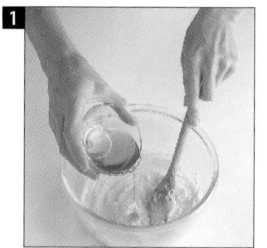

25 mins plus 2 hrs cooling

10 mins

MAKES 60

INGREDIENTS

175 g/6 oz unsalted butter

100 g/3½ oz grated marzipan

4 tbsp clear honey

½ tsp vanilla essence

200 g/7 oz plain chocolate, broken into pieces

350 g/12 oz milk chocolate, broken into pieces

1 Line 2 baking trays with baking parchment. Beat together the butter and marzipan until thoroughly combined and fluffy. Stir in the honey, a little at a time, then stir in the vanilla.

2 Place the plain chocolate and 200 g/7 oz of the milk chocolate in a heatproof bowl set over a saucepan of gently simmering water. Stir over a low heat until melted and smooth. Remove from the heat and leave to cool slightly.

3 Stir the melted chocolate into the marzipan mixture, then spoon the chocolate and marzipan mixture into a piping bag fitted with a large plain nozzle and pipe small balls on to the prepared baking trays. Leave to cool and set.

4 Put the remaining milk chocolate in a heatproof bowl set over a saucepan of gently simmering water. Stir over low heat until melted, then remove from the heat. Dip the truffles, 1 at a time, in the melted chocolate to coat them, then texture some of them with a fork. Place on the baking trays to cool and set.

Mocha Truffles

Continental plain chocolate and coffee are the perfect combination.
Serve these delicious truffles with coffee at the end of a meal.

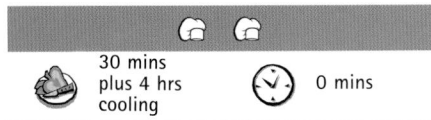

30 mins
plus 4 hrs
cooling

0 mins

MAKES 35

INGREDIENTS

2 tbsp instant coffee granules

2 tbsp boiling water

350 g/12 oz Continental plain chocolate

175 g/6 oz butter

3 tbsp double cream

2 tbsp cocoa powder, for coating

1 In a heatproof bowl, dissolve the coffee in the boiling water. Break the chocolate into pieces and add to the bowl. Set the bowl over a saucepan of gently simmering water until melted.

2 Remove the bowl from the heat and gradually beat in the butter, then stir in the cream. Let the mixture cool for at least 4 hours or overnight until the mixture is firm.

3 Take a heaped teaspoonful of the mixture at a time and roll into a ball between your hands. Continue until you have used up the remaining mixture.

4 Spread the cocoa powder on to a plate, then roll the truffles in the cocoa powder to coat them. Place the truffles in paper sweet cases.

VARIATION
For a different effect, roll the truffles in ground almonds.

Praline & Coffee Truffles

Made with chocolate, praline, coffee, brandy, and cream, these rich truffles are pure indulgence and will surely impress your guests!

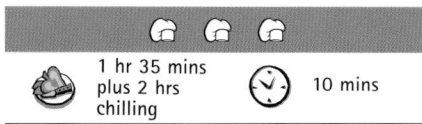

1 hr 35 mins
plus 2 hrs
chilling

10 mins

MAKES 40

INGREDIENTS

sunflower oil, for brushing

70 g/2½ oz granulated sugar

2 tbsp water

40 g/1½ oz blanched almonds

350 g/12 oz Continental plain chocolate

125 ml/4 fl oz strong black coffee

1 tbsp brandy

115 g/4 oz butter

3 tbsp double cream

1 tbsp cocoa powder

1 tbsp icing sugar

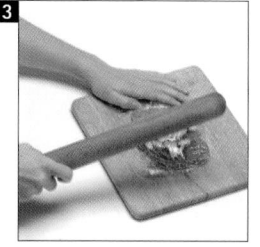

1 Brush a baking tray with oil. Put the sugar and water in a saucepan and heat gently, stirring, until the sugar has dissolved, then allow to bubble gently, without stirring, for 6–10 minutes, until lightly golden brown.

2 Remove the saucepan from the heat and stir in the almonds. Immediately pour the mixture on to the baking tray and spread out evenly. Leave in a cool place for about 1 hour, until cold and hardened.

3 When the praline has hardened, crush it to a fine powder in a food processor or in a plastic bag with a hammer.

4 Break the chocolate into small even-size pieces and place, with the coffee and brandy, in a heatproof bowl set over a saucepan of gently simmering water until melted. Remove the saucepan from the heat and let the mixture cool slightly.

5 Gradually add the butter to the chocolate mixture, then leave to cool, until a trail is left on the surface when lifted with a spoon.

6 Add the crushed praline and cream to the cooled chocolate mixture and stir together. Chill for about 2 hours, or until the chocolate mixture is firm.

7 Take a teaspoonful of the mixture at a time and roll into a ball between your hands. Continue until you have used up all the mixture.

8 Spread the cocoa powder and icing sugar on 2 separate plates, then roll half the truffles in the cocoa powder and half in the icing sugar to coat them. Place the truffles in paper sweet cases.

Candied Citrus Peel

Strips of chocolate-covered candied citrus peel make a refreshing change from candy or chocolates with after-dinner coffee.

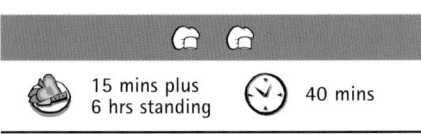

🍮 15 mins plus 6 hrs standing ⏱ 40 mins

MAKES 60–80 PIECES

INGREDIENTS

1 large unwaxed, thick-skinned orange

1 large unwaxed, thick-skinned lemon

1 large unwaxed, thick-skinned lime

600 g/1 lb 5 oz caster sugar

300 ml/10 fl oz water

125 g/4½ oz best-quality plain chocolate, chopped (optional)

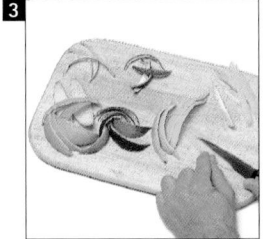

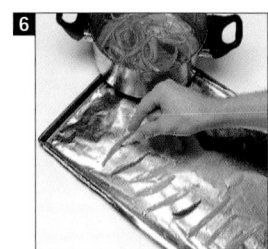

1 Cut the orange into quarters lengthways and squeeze the juice into a cup to drink, or use in another recipe. Cut each quarter in half lengthways to make 8 pieces in all.

2 Cut the fruit and pith away from the zest. If any of the pith remains on the rind, lay the knife almost flat on the white side of the rind and gently 'saw' backwards and forwards to slice it off because it will make the rind taste bitter.

3 Repeat with the lemon and lime, only cutting the lime into quarters. Cut each piece into 3–4 strips to make 60–80 strips in total. Place the strips in a saucepan of water and boil for 30 seconds. Drain.

4 Dissolve the sugar in the water in a saucepan over medium heat, stirring. Increase the heat and bring to the boil, without stirring. When the syrup becomes clear, turn the heat to its lowest setting.

5 Add the citrus strips, using a wooden spoon to push them in without stirring. Simmer in the syrup for 30 minutes, without stirring. Turn off the heat and set aside for at least 6 hours until completely cool.

6 Line a baking tray with foil. Skim off the thin crust on top of the syrup without stirring. Remove the citrus strips, one by one, from the syrup, shaking off any excess. Place the strips on the foil to cool.

7 Put the chocolate in a heatproof bowl set over a saucepan of gently simmering water until melted. Working with 1 piece of candied peel at a time, dip the peel halfway into the chocolate. Drizzle a little melted chocolate over some of the strips. Return to the foil and leave to set. Store in an airtight container.

Rum & Chocolate Cups

Use firm foil sweet cases, rather than paper ones, to make the chocolate cups, because they offer extra support. Use brandy if preferred.

40 mins plus 1 hr 45 mins chilling

10–15 mins

MAKES 12

I N G R E D I E N T S

55 g/2 oz plain chocolate, broken into pieces

12 toasted hazelnuts

F I L L I N G

115 g/4 oz plain chocolate, broken into pieces

1 tbsp dark rum

4 tbsp mascarpone cheese

1 To make the chocolate cups, place the chocolate in a heatproof bowl set over a saucepan of gently simmering water. Stir over a low heat until the chocolate is just melted but not too runny, then remove from the heat. Spoon about $\frac{1}{2}$ teaspoon of melted chocolate into a foil sweet case and brush it over the base and up the sides. Coat 11 more foil cases in the same way and leave to set for 30 minutes. Chill in the refrigerator for 15 minutes. If necessary, reheat the chocolate in the heatproof bowl to melt it again, then coat the foil cases with a second, slightly thinner coating. Let the cases chill in the refrigerator for an additional 30 minutes.

2 Meanwhile, make the filling. Place the chocolate in a heatproof bowl set over a saucepan of gently simmering water. Stir over a low heat until melted, then remove from the heat. Leave to cool slightly, then stir in the rum and beat in the mascarpone cheese until fully incorporated and smooth. Leave to cool completely, stirring occasionally.

3 Spoon the filling into a piping bag fitted with a 1-cm/$\frac{1}{2}$-inch star nozzle. If preferred, carefully peel away the foil cases from the chocolate cups. Pipe the filling into the cups and top each one with a toasted hazelnut.

Chocolate-Dipped Prunes

A much underrated dried fruit, prunes make delicious and very attractive after-dinner treats, especially if dipped in white chocolate.

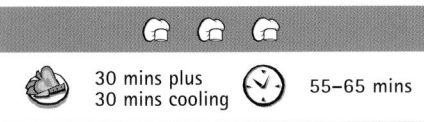

30 mins plus
30 mins cooling   55–65 mins

MAKES 24

INGREDIENTS

225 ml/8 fl oz water

125 ml/4½ fl oz granulated sugar

2 cinnamon sticks,
   each 7.5 cm/3 inches long

1 vanilla pod

450 g/1 lb whole prunes

75 g/2¾ oz leftover sponge cake

85 g/3 oz ground toasted walnuts

5 tbsp slivovitz or brandy

½ tsp vanilla essence

100 g/3½ oz white chocolate,
   broken into pieces

1 Pour the water into a saucepan, add the sugar, and stir over a low heat until the sugar has dissolved. Add the cinnamon sticks and vanilla pod, increase the heat and bring to the boil. Then reduce the heat and simmer for 5 minutes.

2 Add the prunes, bring back to the boil, and simmer for 5 minutes. Lift out 24 large, well-shaped prunes with a slotted spoon and set aside to cool. Simmer the remaining prunes for 30–40 minutes until very tender. Meanwhile, slit the 24 reserved prunes and remove the stones, leaving a neat cavity for the filling.

3 Drain the soft-cooked prunes and discard the syrup. Remove the stones and place the prunes in a food processor with the sponge cake, ground walnuts, slivovitz or brandy and vanilla. Process to a smooth paste. Divide the filling among the reserved prunes, carefully pressing it into the cavities and gently reshaping the prunes around it.

4 Put the chocolate in a heatproof bowl set over a saucepan of gently simmering water. Stir over a low heat until melted, then remove from the heat. Dip each prune into the melted chocolate to half-coat, then spoon the remaining chocolate into a piping bag fitted with a fine nozzle. Pipe thin lines over the tops of the prunes, then place them on a sheet of baking parchment until set.

Brazil Nut Brittle

Chunks of fudge, white chocolate and Brazil nuts are embedded in plain chocolate. Serve with coffee at the end of a meal.

10 mins   20 mins

MAKES 20 PIECES

INGREDIENTS

oil, for brushing

350 g/12 oz plain chocolate, broken into pieces

100 g/3½ oz shelled Brazil nuts, chopped

175 g/6 oz white chocolate, roughly chopped

175 g/6 oz fudge, roughly chopped

1 Brush the bottom of a 20-cm/8-inch square cake tin with oil and line with baking parchment. Put half the plain chocolate in a heatproof bowl and set over a saucepan of gently simmering water. Stir until melted, then spread in the prepared tin.

2 Sprinkle with the chopped Brazil nuts, white chocolate and fudge. Melt the remaining plain chocolate pieces (see step 1) and pour over the top.

3 Let the brittle set, then break up into jagged pieces using the tip of a strong knife.

COOK'S TIP

Put the brittle on a serving plate or in an airtight container and keep, covered, in a cool place. Alternatively, you can store it in the refrigerator for up to 3 days.

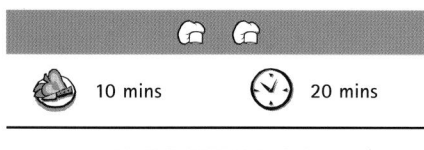

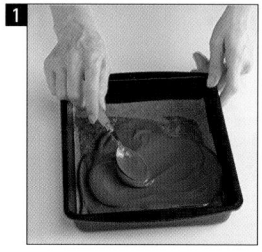

Chocolate & Rum Tartlets

These tiny tarts filled with a delicious concoction of chocolate and rum then topped with a white frosting are very popular in France.

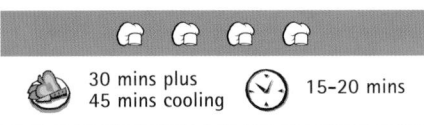

30 mins plus
45 mins cooling

15–20 mins

MAKES 18-20

INGREDIENTS

PASTRY

55 g/2 oz butter

55 g/2 oz caster sugar

1 egg yolk

115 g/4 oz plain flour, plus extra
for dusting

FILLING

85 g/3 oz plain chocolate

1 tbsp unsalted butter

2 tbsp light cream

2 tsp dark rum

FROSTING

175 g/6 oz icing sugar

vanilla essence

chocolate curls (see page 9),
to decorate

1 Preheat the oven to 190°C/375°F/Gas Mark 5.

2 Make the pastry. Beat together the butter and sugar in a bowl until light and fluffy. Gradually beat in the egg yolk. Sift the flour into the bowl and work into the mixture.

3 Turn the dough on to a floured chopping board and roll out quite thinly. Use to line 18–20 tiny tartlet tins with a capacity of about 1 tablespoon. Prick the bases. Bake in the oven for 10–15 minutes, until crisp and very lightly browned. Leave to cool in the tin for 2 minutes, then transfer to a wire rack.

4 Make the filling. Place the chocolate, butter and cream in a saucepan and heat very gently, stirring, until melted and combined. Remove from the heat and stir in the rum. Leave to cool completely, beating occasionally until thick. Divide among the tartlet cases.

5 Make the frosting. Sift the icing sugar into a bowl. Stir in a few drops of vanilla essence and enough cold water to make a thick glacé frosting. Spoon the frosting over the chocolate mixture and decorate with a chocolate curls. Leave on one side to set.

Chocolate Coconut Squares

Chocolate and coconut are a perennially favourite combination. These squares are perfect served with coffee or tea at any time of the day.

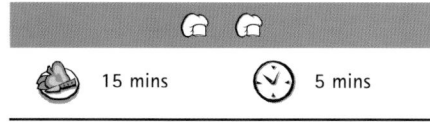

🍬 15 mins   🕐 5 mins

MAKES 49 PIECES

INGREDIENTS

100 g/3½ oz Continental plain chocolate

150 ml/5 fl oz milk

450 g/1 lb granulated sugar

115 g/4 oz desiccated coconut

2 tsp cocoa powder

1 Rinse out an 18-cm/7-inch shallow square tin with cold water. Break the chocolate into pieces and place in a heatproof bowl set over a saucepan of gently simmering water until melted. Remove from the heat.

2 Pour the milk into a saucepan and add the sugar. Heat gently, stirring, until the sugar dissolves, then bring to the boil and boil gently for about 5 minutes, until a little of the mixture, when dropped into a bowl of cold water, forms a soft ball when rolled between the fingers.

3 Remove the saucepan from the heat and stir in the melted chocolate. Beat vigorously until the mixture is thick and creamy, then immediately pour into the prepared tin.

4 Leave the mixture until half set, then mark into squares. Cut when cold and firm. Mix the coconut and cocoa powder on a plate. Roll the fudge cubes in the mixture to coat them, pressing gently to make sure the coconut sticks firmly to all sides.

Strawberry Shortbread Hearts

It is very easy to become addicted to this combination of buttery chocolate shortbread, fresh strawberries and cream!

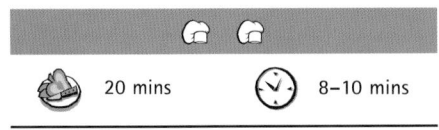

20 mins

8–10 mins

MAKES 20

INGREDIENTS

70 g/2½ oz plain flour, plus extra for dusting

1 tbsp cocoa powder

55 g/2 oz butter

25 g/1 oz golden caster sugar

125 ml/4 fl oz double cream

2 tbsp caster sugar

10 strawberries, halved

2 tsp icing sugar, for dusting

1 Preheat the oven to 180°C/350°F/Gas Mark 4.

2 Sift the flour and cocoa powder into a food processor and add the butter and caster sugar. Process until the mixture forms a ball.

3 Transfer the dough to floured work surface and roll out to a thickness of 5 mm/¼ inch. Using a 6-cm/2½-inch heart-shaped cutter, cut out 20 biscuits and place on a baking tray.

4 Bake the biscuits in the preheated oven for 8–10 minutes until firm. Transfer to a wire rack to cool.

5 In a bowl, whip together the cream and sugar until soft peaks form. Transfer to a piping bag fitted with a large star nozzle and pipe 3 rosettes of cream on to each biscuit. Place half a strawberry in the middle of each one.

6 Dust the tops with icing sugar just before serving.

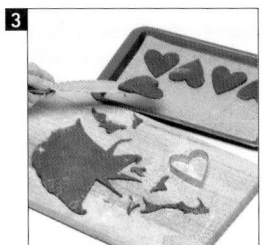

Chocolate Peppermint Creams

Peppermint creams are a great favourite and the addition of a chocolate coating makes them even more popular. Serve at the end of a meal.

20 mins plus
24 hrs setting

0 mins

MAKES 40

I N G R E D I E N T S

1 egg white

225 g/8 oz icing sugar, plus extra
for dusting

few drops peppermint oil

200 g/7 oz plain chocolate, broken
into pieces

1 Line a baking tray with baking parchment. Whisk the egg white until stiff. Gradually sift in the icing sugar and mix together to form a firm, pliable mixture. Add the peppermint oil to taste and mix well together.

2 Dust a chopping board with icing sugar, turn out the mixture, and knead for 2–3 minutes. Roll out to a thickness of 5 mm/¼ inch then cut into circles using a 2.5-cm/1-inch round cutter.

3 Transfer to the prepared baking tray and leave for about 24 hours, or overnight, until set and dry.

4 Melt the chocolate in a heatproof bowl set over a saucepan of gently simmering water. When the peppermints have set carefully dip each peppermint into the melted chocolate using 2 forks.

Lift it out quickly, letting any excess chocolate drain against the side of the bowl, and place on the prepared baking tray. Leave to set.

COOK'S TIP

Peppermint oil has a very strong flavour, so must be added sparingly. To do this, dip the end of a skewer into the bottle and shake off the drops one by one. Peppermint oil is far superior to peppermint flavouring, but if you do use peppermint flavouring, you will need to add about ½ teaspoon to this recipe.

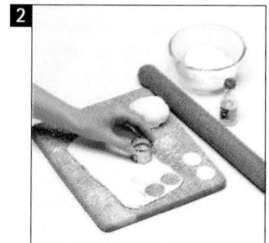

Mint Chocolate Crisps

Crushed mints give these thin chocolates a crisp texture. These little sweets are a real treat at any time of the day.

🍴 15 mins plus 30 mins chilling ⏱ 10 mins

MAKES 20

INGREDIENTS

1 packet extra-strong mints

115 g/4 oz milk chocolate

55 g/2 oz plain chocolate

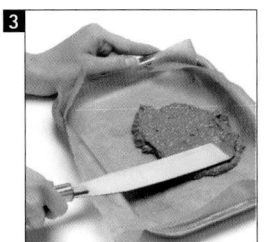

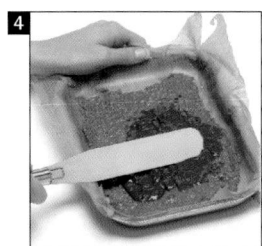

1 Line a baking tray with non-stick baking parchment.

2 Place the mints in a plastic bag and, using a rolling pin, crush them to a coarse powder.

3 Break the milk chocolate in pieces and place in a heatproof bowl set over a saucepan of gently simmering water until melted. Stir the crushed mints into the melted chocolate. Using a round-bladed knife, spread the mixture on the prepared baking tray to a rectangle measuring 23 x 18 cm/9 x 7 inches. Chill the mixture for 10 minutes or until almost set.

4 Melt the plain chocolate in the same way as the milk chocolate, then spread in a very thin layer over the chocolate-mint mixture. Chill in the refrigerator until set.

5 Trim the edges, then warm a knife in hot water and cut into 20 squares.

Mini Mint Meringues

Serve these tiny mint-flavoured meringues with after-dinner coffee.
If there are any left, keep in the refrigerator for several days.

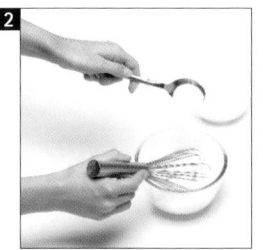

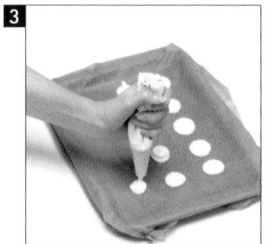

40 mins   1 hr

MAKES 45

INGREDIENTS

1 egg white

55 g/2 oz caster sugar

¼ tsp peppermint essence

115 g/4 oz plain chocolate

1 Preheat the oven to 140°C/275°F/Gas Mark 1. Line 2 baking trays with non-stick baking parchment.

2 Place the egg white in a bowl and whisk until stiff. Gradually whisk in the sugar, then whisk in the peppermint essence.

3 Spoon the mixture into a piping bag fitted with a 5-mm/¼-inch plain nozzle. Pipe 45 small circles, about 2.5 cm/1 inch in diameter on to the prepared baking trays. Cook in the oven for 1 hour, until firm and easy to lift.

4 Break the chocolate into small pieces and place in a heatproof bowl set over a saucepan of gently simmering water until melted.

5 Dip the meringues into the melted chocolate. Remove with a fork, shaking gently and transfer to a wire rack to set.

Ginger & Chocolate Meringues

Chocolate, ginger, and meringue: a winning, melt-in-the-mouth combination. They are best assembled just before serving.

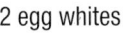 30 mins  1 hr

MAKES 20

INGREDIENTS

2 egg whites

115 g/4 oz caster sugar

55 g/2 oz plain chocolate, grated

FILLING

150 ml/5 fl oz double cream

2 tsp syrup from the stem ginger jar

2 pieces stem ginger, finely chopped

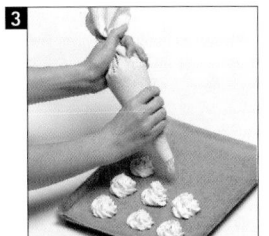

1 Preheat the oven to 120°C/250°F/Gas Mark ½. Line 2 baking trays with non-stick baking parchment.

2 Place the egg whites in a bowl and whisk until stiff. Gradually whisk in the sugar. Fold in the grated chocolate.

3 Spoon the mixture into a piping bag fitted with a large star nozzle and pipe 40 meringue rosettes on to the prepared baking trays. Bake in the oven for 1 hour, or until crisp and dry. Cool completely before removing from the baking tray.

4 Make the filling. Whip the cream until thick, stir in the ginger syrup, then add the chopped stem ginger. Use the filling to sandwich the meringues together in pairs.

Mocha Coconut Clusters

These little clusters are the perfect sweets for coconut lovers, with the addition of chocolate and coffee to give them their mocha flavour.

15 mins

5 mins

MAKES 30

INGREDIENTS

115 g/4 oz milk chocolate, broken into pieces

2 tbsp butter

1 tsp instant coffee powder

55 g/2 oz desiccated coconut

1 Line 2–3 baking trays with baking parchment. Melt the chocolate and butter in a heatproof bowl set over a saucepan of gently simmering water. Remove from the heat.

2 Stir the coffee granules into the chocolate until dissolved, then stir in the coconut.

3 Place heaped teaspoonfuls of the mixture on to the prepared baking trays and leave to set. Serve the clusters in paper sweet cases.

COOK'S TIP

If you wish, toast the coconut before you add it to the mixture, to bring out its full flavour. To do this, put it in a large dry skillet and heat gently, stirring constantly, until golden brown.

Chocolate Eggs

Who can resist a chocolate egg? Certainly not when they are packed with praline. Wrapped in foil, these eggs make great gifts at Easter.

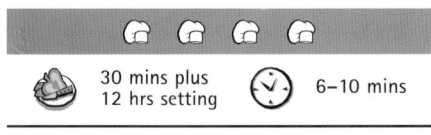

🍴 30 mins plus 12 hrs setting   🕐 6–10 mins

MAKES 4

INGREDIENTS

sunflower oil, for brushing

70 g/2½ oz granulated sugar

2 tbsp water

40 g/1½ oz blanched almonds

4 large eggs

225 g/8 oz plain or milk chocolate, broken into pieces

2 tbsp double cream

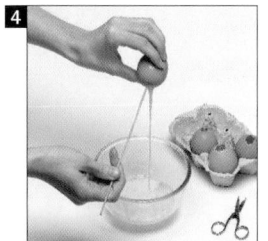

1 Brush a baking tray with oil. Put the sugar and water in a saucepan and heat gently, stirring, until the sugar has dissolved, then leave to bubble gently, without stirring, for 6–10 minutes, until lightly golden brown.

2 Remove the saucepan from the heat and stir in the almonds. Immediately pour the mixture on to the baking tray and spread out evenly. Leave in a cool place for about 1 hour until cold.

3 When the praline has hardened, finely crush it to a powder in a food processor or place it in a plastic bag and crush with a hammer.

4 Using a pin, pierce a hole in the pointed end of each egg. Using small scissors, carefully enlarge the hole to about 1 cm/½ inch in diameter.

5 Using a skewer or cocktail stick, burst the egg yolk, then shake the raw egg into a bowl. (Use the eggs in another recipe.) Carefully pour running water into the shells, then shake out until clean.

Turn the shells upside down and leave to dry for 30 minutes on kitchen paper.

6 When the egg shells are dry, melt the chocolate in a heatproof bowl set over a saucepan of gently simmering water. Remove from the heat and stir in the praline and cream.

7 Fill a piping bag, fitted with a small plain nozzle, with the mixture and pipe into the egg shells. Leave to stand for up to 12 hours until set.

8 When set, carefully crack the eggs and peel off the shells, then wrap each egg in coloured foil.

Cocochoc Pyramids

This is a traditional favourite. In this recipe, coconut ice is deliciously dipped in melted chocolate to make a two-tone treat.

35 mins, plus 90–150 mins setting/standing   15–25 mins

MAKES 12

INGREDIENTS

150 ml/5 fl oz water

450 g/1 lb granulated sugar

pinch of cream of tartar

115 g/4 oz desiccated coconut

1 tbsp double cream

few drops of yellow food colouring

85 g/3 oz plain chocolate,
    broken into pieces

1 Pour the water into a heavy-based saucepan, add the sugar and stir over a low heat until the sugar has dissolved. Stir in a pinch of cream of tartar and bring to the boil. Boil steadily, without stirring, until the temperature reaches 119°C/238°F on a sugar thermometer. If you do not have a sugar thermometer, test the syrup frequently by dropping a small quantity into a bowl of cold water. If the mixture can be rolled between your finger and thumb to make a soft ball, it is ready.

2 Remove the saucepan from the heat and beat in the coconut and cream. Continue to beat for 5–10 minutes until the mixture becomes cloudy. Beat in a few drops of yellow food colouring, then leave to cool. When cool enough to handle, take small pieces of the mixture and form them into pyramids. Place on a sheet of baking parchment and leave to harden.

3 Put the chocolate in a heatproof bowl set over a saucepan of gently simmering water. Stir over a low heat until melted, then remove from the heat. Dip the bottom of the pyramids into the melted chocolate and leave to set.

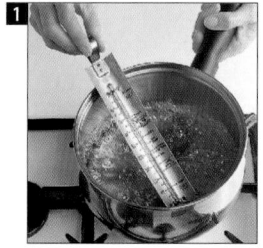

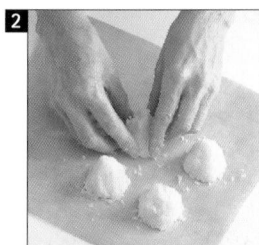

Mini Chocolate Cones

These unusual cone-shaped mint-cream chocolates make a change from the more usual cup shape, and are perfect for an after-dinner chocolate.

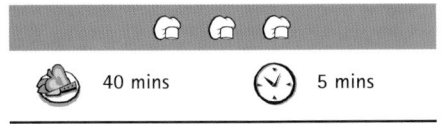

40 mins   5 mins

MAKES 10

INGREDIENTS

75 g/2¾ oz plain chocolate,
   broken into pieces

100 ml/3½ fl oz double cream

1 tbsp icing sugar

1 tbsp crème de menthe

chocolate-covered coffee beans,
   to decorate (optional)

1 Cut 10 circles, 7.5 cm/3 inches across, out of baking parchment. Shape each circle into a cone shape and secure with sticky tape.

2 Put the chocolate in a heatproof bowl and set over a saucepan of gently simmering water. Stir until melted. Using a small brush, coat the inside of each cone with the melted chocolate. Chill to set.

3 Brush a second layer of chocolate on the inside of the cones and chill until set. Carefully peel away the paper.

4 Place the double cream, icing sugar and crème de menthe in a mixing bowl and whip until just holding its shape. Place in a piping bag fitted with a star nozzle and pipe the mixture into the chocolate cones.

5 Decorate the cones with chocolate-covered coffee beans (if using) and chill in the refrigerator until required.

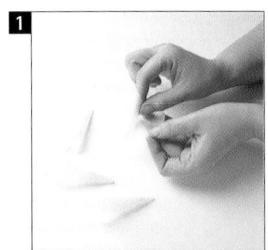

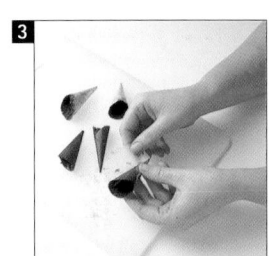

COOK'S TIP
The chocolate cones can be made in advance and kept in the refrigerator for up to 1 week. Do not fill them more than 2 hours before you are going to serve them.

Chocolate Puff Fingers

Using ready-made puff pastry and chocolate hazelnut spread, making these crisp fingers could not be easier.

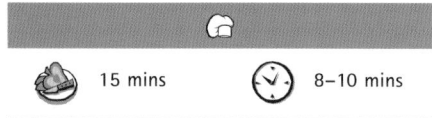

15 mins   8–10 mins

MAKES 30

INGREDIENTS

1 packet ready-rolled puff pastry, thawed if frozen

2 tbsp chocolate and hazelnut spread

icing sugar, to decorate

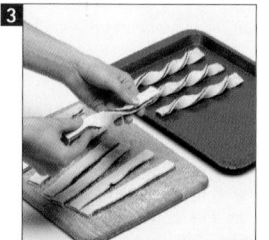

1 Preheat the oven to 220°C/425°F/Gas Mark 7.

2 Cut the puff pastry in half. Spread the chocolate hazelnut spread over one half and place the other half on top.

3 Cut into 30 strips. Twist each strip, arrange on a baking tray, and bake in the oven for 8–10 minutes until browned and crisp. Transfer to a wire rack to cool.

4 When the fingers are cold, dust with sifted icing sugar.

Chocolate Toffee

This is traditional toffee, with the addition of chocolate. It looks very attractive in paper or foil sweet cases.

10 mins

20–25 mins

MAKES 36

INGREDIENTS

115 g/4 oz butter, plus extra for greasing

450 g/1 lb golden granulated sugar

150 ml/5 fl oz water

2 tbsp golden syrup

115 g/4 oz plain chocolate, broken into pieces

1 Grease a shallow 18-cm/7-inch square cake tin.

2 Put the sugar, butter, water and golden syrup in a large, heavy-based saucepan. Stir over a low heat until the sugar has dissolved.

3 Bring slowly to the boil and cook, for 10–15 minutes, without stirring, until the temperature reaches 120°C/250°F. If you do not have a sugar thermometer, test the toffee by dropping a small amount into cold water. It is ready when it reaches the soft crack stage: that is when it separates into threads that are brittle.

4 Remove the saucepan from the heat and stir in the chocolate. Stir gently until melted, then pour immediately into the prepared tin.

5 When the toffee is starting to set, mark into squares with a sharp knife. Leave to set, then cut into squares when completely cold.

Walnut & Chocolate Fingers

Filo pastry makes a lovely crisp shell round the nutty chocolate filling. Try to find the best-quality plain chocolate available.

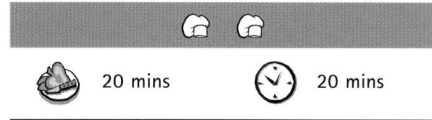

🍰 20 mins   🕐 20 mins

MAKES 20

INGREDIENTS

55 g/2 oz unsalted butter, melted, plus extra for greasing

5 large sheets filo pastry

1 tbsp icing sugar, for dusting

FILLING

115 g/4 oz walnut pieces, coarsely ground

25 g/1 oz golden granulated sugar

½ teaspoon ground cinnamon

55 g/2 oz plain chocolate, grated

1 Preheat the oven to 160°C/325°F/Gas Mark 3. Grease 2 baking trays.

2 Make the filling. In a bowl, mix together the walnuts, granulated sugar, cinnamon and grated chocolate.

3 Cut each sheet of filo pastry into 4 rectangles measuring 23 x 18 cm/ 9 x 7 inches. Pile on top of each other and cover with a tea towel to prevent drying out.

4 Brush a filo rectangle with melted butter. Spread a teaspoon of filling along one short end. Fold the long sides in, slightly over the filling. Roll up from the end with the filling.

5 Place on the prepared baking tray with the seam underneath and brush with melted butter. Repeat with the remaining pastry and filling. Bake in the oven for 20 minutes, or until very lightly coloured.

6 Transfer to a wire rack to cool. Dust the walnut and chocolate fingers with icing sugar before serving.

VARIATIONS
Substitute ground almonds, or chopped pistachios or pine nuts, for the walnuts.

Almond & Chocolate Tuiles

These little biscuits are very crisp and extremely moreish! Try them with vanilla ice cream. Make sure that they are completely cold before serving.

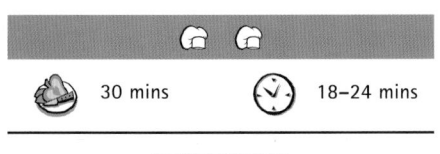

30 mins   18–24 mins

MAKES 36

INGREDIENTS

55 g/2 oz unsalted butter, melted and cooled, plus extra for greasing

2 egg whites

115 g/4 oz golden caster sugar

40 g/1½ oz plain flour

2 tbsp unsweetened cocoa

25 g/1 oz flaked almonds

1 Preheat the oven to 180°C/350°F/Gas Mark 4. Grease 4 baking trays.

2 Put the egg whites and caster sugar in a bowl and whisk together with a fork until the mixture is frothy. Sift the flour and cocoa powder over the egg whites. Add the flaked almonds and mix with a fork. Add the melted butter and mix together thoroughly.

3 Drop 20 half teaspoons of the mixture on to the prepared baking trays, allowing room for the biscuits to spread during cooking. Using a round-bladed knife, spread each one out slightly.

4 Bake in the oven, 1 sheet at a time, for 6–8 minutes, until the edges feel firm.

5 Lift the biscuits off carefully with a round-bladed knife and place on a wooden rolling pin while still warm. Leave for 2 minutes until set into a curved shape. Transfer to a wire rack to cool completely. Store in an airtight container.

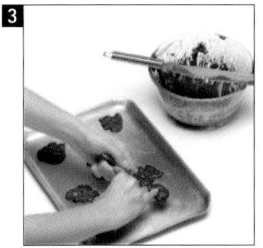

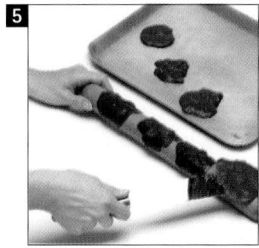

Praline & Sesame Sweets

The addition of sesame seeds gives these praline sweets an exotic flavour.
Serve with your favourite liqueur or spirit for a special treat.

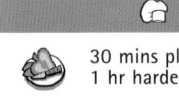

30 mins plus
1 hr hardening

15 mins

MAKES 20–24

INGREDIENTS

sunflower oil, for brushing

115 g/4 oz golden caster sugar

115 g/4 oz whole unblanched almonds

1 tbsp sesame seeds, toasted

55 g/2 oz plain chocolate

1 Brush a large baking tray with oil. Put the sugar and almonds in a heavy-based saucepan and heat very gently until the sugar has dissolved.

2 Cook gently until the almonds start to pop and turn brown and the caramel is a rich brown colour, shaking the saucepan so the almonds are well coated.

3 Pour in the sesame seeds and shake the saucepan to mix. Pour on to the prepared baking tray and leave to harden.

4 Break the chocolate into pieces and place in a heatproof bowl set over a saucepan of gently simmering water until melted. Break the praline into large pieces and half-dip in the warm melted chocolate. Shake off the excess and place on non-stick baking parchment to set.

COOK'S TIP

If the praline is not going to be used immediately it should be completely coated in chocolate, otherwise it will become sticky.

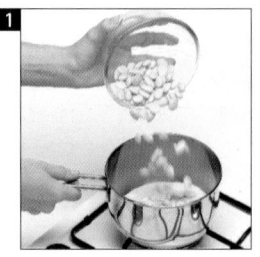

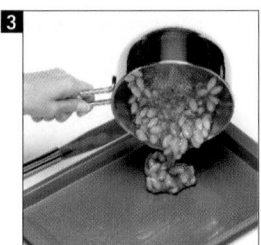

Sesame Bites

These delicious, little deep-fried treats are crisp on the outside and melt-in-the mouth on the inside. Excellent served warm.

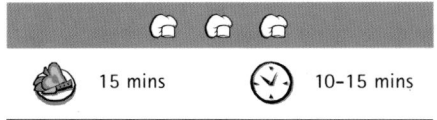

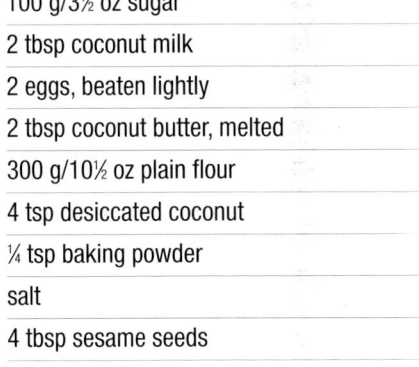

15 mins   10-15 mins

MAKES 10

I N G R E D I E N T S

100 g/3½ oz sugar

2 tbsp coconut milk

2 eggs, beaten lightly

2 tbsp coconut butter, melted

300 g/10½ oz plain flour

4 tsp desiccated coconut

¼ tsp baking powder

salt

4 tbsp sesame seeds

sunflower oil, for deep-frying

1 Combine the sugar, coconut milk, eggs and coconut butter in a bowl. Combine the flour, desiccated coconut, baking powder and a pinch of salt in another bowl, then stir the flour mixture into the egg mixture. Knead lightly until smooth.

2 Form the mixture into small balls with your hands or using 2 teaspoons. Spread out the sesame seeds on a plate and roll the balls in them to coat.

3 Half fill a wok or deep, heavy-based frying pan or saucepan with oil and heat to 180-190°C/350-375°F or until a cube of bread browns in 30 seconds. Add the sesame bites, in batches and deep-fry until golden brown. Remove with a slotted spoon and drain well on kitchen paper. Serve warm.

Bunuelo Stars

Tortillas, cut into star shapes, deep-fried and sprinkled with cinnamon and sugar, are simply delicious served with chocolate or vanilla ice cream.

5–10 mins 15 mins

SERVES 4

INGREDIENTS

4 flour tortillas

3 tbsp ground cinnamon

6–8 tbsp sugar

vegetable oil, for frying

chocolate ice cream, to serve

fine strips of orange zest, to decorate

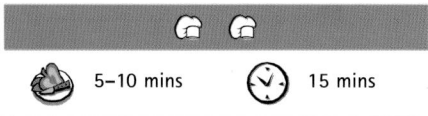

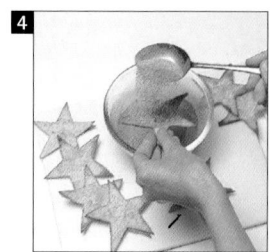

1 Using a sharp knife or kitchen scissors cut each tortilla into star shapes.

2 Mix the cinnamon and sugar together and set aside.

3 Heat the oil in a shallow, wide frying pan until it is hot enough to brown a cube of bread in 30 seconds. Working one at a time, fry the star-shaped tortillas until one side is golden, then turn over and cook until golden on the other side. Remove from the hot oil with a slotted spoon and drain on kitchen paper.

4 Sprinkle generously with the cinnamon and sugar mixture. Serve with chocolate ice cream, sprinkled with strips of orange zest.

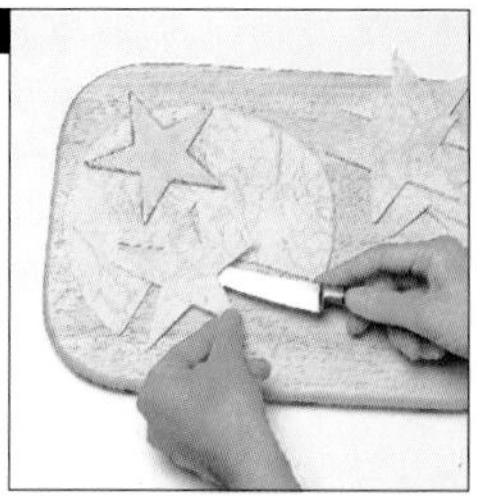

COOK'S TIP

These star-shaped bunuelos make an attractive decoration for an ice cream sundae with Mexican flavours, caramel, cinnamon, coffee and chocolate.

Pistachio & Chocolate Halva

The word 'halva' is derived from the Arabic word *hulw* meaning sweet.
For best results, try to find unsalted pistachio nuts for this recipe.

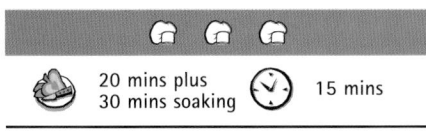

20 mins plus
30 mins soaking   15 mins

MAKES 25 SQUARES

INGREDIENTS

175 g/6 oz shelled pistachio nuts

250 ml/8 fl oz boiling water

2 tbsp milk

115 g/4 oz golden caster sugar

25 g/1 oz butter

55 g/2 oz plain chocolate, broken into small
  pieces

1 Put the pistachios in a bowl. Pour over the boiling water and leave to soak for 30 minutes. Grease and base-line an 18-cm/7-inch square tin.

2 Drain the pistachio nuts thoroughly and place in a blender or food processor. Add the milk and process until finely chopped. Stir in the sugar.

3 Heat a large, non-stick skillet and add the butter. Melt over low heat and add the nut mixture. Cook for 15 minutes, stirring constantly, until the mixture is very thick.

4 Stir in the chocolate and leave to melt. Mix together, then spoon the mixture into the prepared tin and spread evenly. Leave to cool and set completely, then cut into 25 squares. Store in the refrigerator for up to 2 weeks.

Noisettes

These classic petits fours consist of a hazelnut paste encased in chocolate, then topped with a chocolate-covered hazelnut.

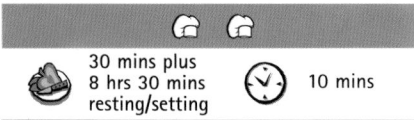

30 mins plus
8 hrs 30 mins
resting/setting

10 mins

MAKES 25

INGREDIENTS

225 g/8 oz plain chocolate, broken into pieces

115 g/4 oz blanched hazelnuts

115 g/4 oz caster sugar

1 tbsp water

icing sugar, for dusting

1 Line 2 baking trays with baking parchment. Melt 85 g/3 oz of the chocolate in a heatproof bowl set over a saucepan of gently simmering water. Remove from the heat.

2 Using 2 forks, carefully dip 25 hazelnuts, one at a time, into the melted chocolate. Lift out quickly, letting any excess chocolate drain against the side of the bowl and place on a prepared baking tray. Leave to set.

3 Put the remaining hazelnuts in a food processor and chop until finely ground. Add to the bowl with the remaining melted chocolate, then add the caster sugar and water and mix to form a firm paste. Leave to rest in the refrigerator for 30 minutes.

4 Lightly dust a chopping board with icing sugar, turn out the mixture, and knead for 2–3 minutes. Using your fingers, flatten the paste to a 1-cm/¹⁄₂-inch thickness, then cut into circles, using a 2.5-cm/1-inch plain round cutter. Place on a prepared baking tray and leave overnight, until set.

5 Melt the remaining 140 g/5 oz of the chocolate in a heatproof bowl set over a saucepan of gently simmering water. Remove from the heat. Using 2 forks, carefully dip the hazelnut circles, one at a time, into the melted chocolate then place on the baking tray.

6 Place a chocolate-covered hazelnut on top of each hazelnut circle and leave to set. Serve in paper sweet cases.

COOK'S TIP

If you are unable to buy ready-blanched hazelnuts, you can remove the skins yourself. Spread them on a sheet of foil and lightly toast under a grill, turning them frequently, then rub in a clean tea towel to remove the skins.

Walnut Cups

If walnuts are your favourite nut, you will adore the filling of these petits fours. If not, simply choose one of the variations suggested below.

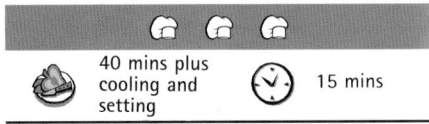

40 mins plus cooling and setting

15 mins

MAKES 14

INGREDIENTS

280 g/10 oz plain chocolate, broken into pieces

40 g/1½ oz walnut pieces

3 tbsp granulated sugar

2 tsp water

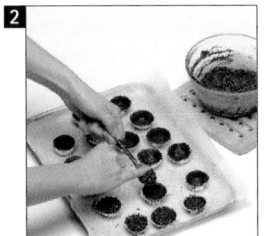

1 Line a baking tray with baking parchment and place 14 double-thickness paper sweet cases on it.

2 Melt 115 g/4 oz of the chocolate in a heatproof bowl set over a saucepan of gently simmering water. Spoon the melted chocolate into the prepared sweet cases, spreading up the sides with a small brush. Place on the baking tray and leave to set.

3 Put 35 g/1¼ oz of the walnuts in a food processor and mix until finely ground. Put the sugar and water in a small, heavy-based saucepan and heat gently, stirring constantly, until the sugar has dissolved. Bring to the boil and boil for 2 minutes. Remove from the heat and stir in the ground walnuts.

4 Melt a further 115 g/4 oz of the chocolate, then stir into the walnut mixture. Leave to cool.

5 Spoon the walnut filling equally into the chocolate cups and smooth the surface. Leave in a cool place to set.

6 Melt the remaining 55 g/2 oz of the chocolate, then pour over the cups to cover the surface completely. Leave to cool, then top each cup with a small sprinkling of the remaining walnuts. Leave to set.

7 When the chocolate cups have set, carefully peel away the paper sweet cases and place in clean cases.

VARIATIONS
If preferred use almonds, hazelnuts, or macadamia nuts instead of the walnuts.

Chocolate Orange Cups

Orange-flavoured chocolate plus grated orange rind gives the filling in these chocolate cups an intense flavour. Serve at the end of a meal.

40 mins
plus 2 hrs
setting

15 mins

MAKES 24

INGREDIENTS

250 g/9 oz orange-flavoured plain chocolate

1 egg yolk

1 tbsp unsalted butter

finely grated rind of 1 small orange, plus extra for decorating

100 ml/3½ fl oz cup whipping cream, whipped

1 Break half the chocolate into pieces and place in a heatproof bowl set over a saucepan of gently simmering water until melted. Leave to cool.

2 Arrange 24 paper sweet cases on a tray and spoon a little chocolate into each case. Using a fine brush, coat the inside of each case with chocolate. Leave to set. Make a small tear in each paper case, then carefully peel off.

3 Meanwhile, in a bowl set over a saucepan of gently simmering water, warm the remaining chocolate until almost melted. Add the egg yolk and stir until thickened. Remove from the heat and stir in the butter and orange rind. Set aside to cool to room temperature.

4 Fold the cream into the chocolate mixture and spoon into a piping bag fitted with a star nozzle. Pipe the filling into each chocolate case. Leave to set. Decorate with a little orange rind and serve.

Chocolate Cherry Cups

These look very professional yet are incredibly easy to prepare. They look particularly attractive if placed in paper sweet cases.

30 mins plus 2 hrs marinating/ setting

10 mins

MAKES 16

INGREDIENTS

115 g/4 oz glacé cherries, chopped

1 tbsp brandy

225 g/8 oz plain chocolate, broken into pieces

1 egg yolk

2 tsp icing sugar

1 Line a baking tray with baking parchment and place 16 double-thickness paper sweet cases on it. Put the cherries and brandy in a bowl and leave to marinate for about 1 hour.

2 Meanwhile, melt 125 g/4½ oz of the chocolate in a heatproof bowl set over a saucepan of gently simmering water. Spoon the melted chocolate into the prepared candy cases, spreading up the sides with a small brush. Place on the baking tray and leave to set.

3 When set, carefully peel away the paper cases and place the cups in clean cases. Drain the cherries, reserving the brandy, then put the cherries in the chocolate cases.

4 Melt the remaining chocolate, then remove from the heat and leave to cool slightly. Add the egg yolk and reserved brandy and mix well together. Sift in the icing sugar, then stir together.

5 Fill a piping bag, fitted with a star nozzle, with the chocolate mixture and pipe into the chocolate cups.

COOK'S TIP
Should the chocolate cases crack as you are removing them from the paper cases, you can patch them up by brushing on a little extra melted chocolate.

Chocolate Ice Cream Bites

These miniature chocolate-covered ice creams are irresistible at the end of a meal. Use your favourite ice cream flavour.

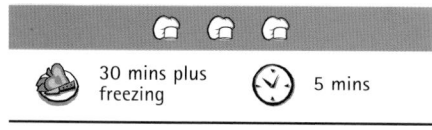

30 mins plus freezing

5 mins

SERVES 6

INGREDIENTS

600 ml/1 pint good-quality ice cream

200 g/7 oz plain chocolate

2 tbsp unsalted butter

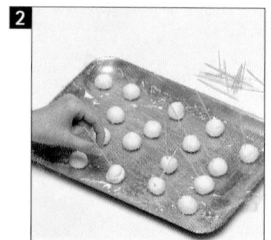
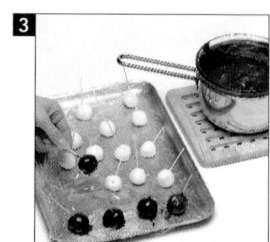

1 Line a baking tray with clingfilm.

2 Using a melon baller, scoop out balls of ice cream and place them on the prepared baking tray. Alternatively, cut the ice cream into bite-size cubes. Stick a cocktail stick in each piece and return to the freezer until very hard.

3 Place the chocolate and the butter in a heatproof bowl set over a saucepan of gently simmering water until melted. Quickly dip the frozen ice cream balls into the warm chocolate and return to the freezer. Keep them there until ready to serve.

Chocolate & Prune Balls

Children enjoy making these sweets if an adult helps with melting the syrup and butter. Coat the balls with cocoa powder if preferred.

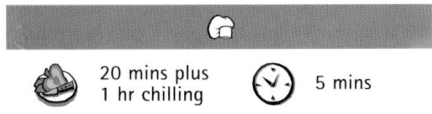

20 mins plus 1 hr chilling

5 mins

MAKES 20

INGREDIENTS

115 g/4 oz butter

3 tbsp golden syrup

115 g/4 oz plain chocolate

85 g/3 oz ready-to-eat dried prunes, chopped

175 g/6 oz muesli

drinking chocolate powder, for coating

1 Put the butter and golden syrup in a heavy-based saucepan and heat gently until melted. Remove the saucepan from the heat.

2 Break the chocolate into pieces and add to the saucepan. Leave to melt, then beat together until smooth. Stir in the prunes and muesli and mix thoroughly. Leave to cool, then chill in the refrigerator for 1 hour.

3 Take teaspoonfuls of the mixture and roll into balls. Roll the chocolate balls in the drinking chocolate powder, then place in paper sweet cases and return to the refrigerator until firm.

Apricot & Almond Clusters

These delicious little morsels are extremely quick and easy to make. They will quickly become a firm favourite with children.

10 mins
plus setting

4–5 mins

MAKES 24–28

INGREDIENTS

115 g/4 oz plain chocolate, broken into pieces

2 tbsp clear honey

115 g/4 oz ready-to-eat dried apricots, chopped

55 g/2 oz blanched almonds, chopped

1 Put the chocolate and honey in a heatproof bowl set over a saucepan of gently simmering water and stir until melted and smooth.

2 Stir in the apricots and almonds.

3 Drop teaspoonfuls of the mixture into paper sweet cases. Leave to set.

COOK'S TIP

These would be an easy sweets for children to make, if they had some help with melting the chocolate.

Chocolate Caramel Turtles

This traditional South American sweet consists of clumps of pecan nuts with a chocolate caramel coating. Use other types of nuts if preferred.

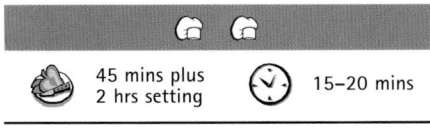

🕐 45 mins plus 2 hrs setting   🕐 15–20 mins

MAKES 15

INGREDIENTS

sunflower oil, for brushing

250 ml/9 fl oz double cream

175 g/6 oz golden syrup

25 g/1 oz butter

225 g/8 oz granulated sugar

3 tbsp soft light brown sugar

140 g/5 oz pecan nuts

175 g/6 oz plain chocolate, broken into pieces

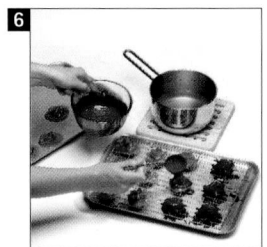

1 Oil a baking tray. Put the cream, golden syrup, butter, granulated and brown sugar in a heavy-based saucepan and heat gently, stirring until the butter has melted and the sugars have dissolved.

2 Bring to the boil and boil for about 15–20 minutes, stirring frequently, until a little of the mixture, when dropped into a cup of cold water, forms a soft ball when rolled between the fingers.

3 Remove the saucepan from the heat and leave to cool for 2–3 minutes, then gently stir in the nuts until coated in the caramel.

4 Using an oiled tablespoon, drop spoonfuls of the mixture, well apart, on to the prepared baking tray. Leave until cold and set.

5 When set, transfer to a wire rack and set the rack over the baking tray. Melt the chocolate in a heatproof bowl set over a saucepan of gently simmering water, then set aside to cool slightly.

6 Using a tablespoon, spoon the melted chocolate over the turtles to coat them completely. Return the chocolate on the baking tray to the heatproof bowl, reheat if necessary, and use to cover all the turtles. Leave for about 2 hours, until set.

Chocolate Squares

These are extremely simple to make yet, when packed into paper or foil sweet cases, they look very elegant.

10 mins

4–5 mins

MAKES 64

INGREDIENTS

115 g/4 oz butter, plus extra for greasing

55 g/2 oz caster sugar

115 g/4 oz cocoa powder

115 g/4 oz drinking chocolate powder

1 Grease an 18-cm/7-inch shallow square tin or a 20 x 15-cm/8 x 6-inch shallow tin. Melt the butter in a saucepan. Remove from the heat and stir in the sugar.

2 Sift the cocoa powder and drinking chocolate powder into the butter mixture, then beat vigorously together until smooth.

3 Turn the mixture into the prepared tin and leave until cold and set. When the chocolate has set, cut into squares using a sharp knife.

Chocolate Coated Toffee

Real, old-fashioned toffee is delicious on its own, but coated in chocolate it becomes truly irresistible. Store in an airtight container for a few days.

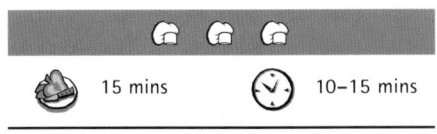

🍬 15 mins   🕐 10–15 mins

MAKES ABOUT 60

INGREDIENTS

sunflower oil, for brushing

225 g/8 oz butter

350 g/12 oz granulated sugar

pinch of cream of tartar

200 g/7 oz plain chocolate chips

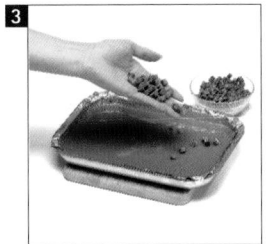

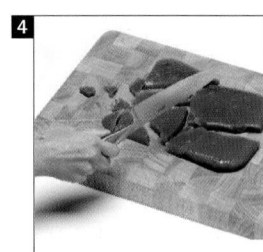

1 Invert a 23-cm/9-inch square cake tin and mould a piece of foil over the bottom and sides, then use the foil to line the tin. Brush the foil generously with oil. Put the butter, sugar, and cream of tartar in a large, heavy-based saucepan and heat gently, stirring constantly, until the butter has melted and the sugar has dissolved.

2 Bring the mixture to the boil, then cover the saucepan and leave for 2 minutes. Uncover the saucepan and boil for about 10–15 minutes, until a little of the mixture, when dropped into a cup of cold water, separates into threads that are hard and brittle.

3 Carefully pour the mixture into the prepared tin and leave for 1 minute. Sprinkle the chocolate chips evenly over the top and leave for 2–3 minutes, until starting to melt then, using the tines of a fork, swirl the chocolate over the top. Leave until hard and set.

4 When hard, using the foil to lift the toffee, remove from the tin and place on a board. Using the back of a heavy knife or a small hammer, break the toffee into pieces.

Torrone Molle

This is an Italian speciality, which is a wickedly rich mixture of plain chocolate, nuts, brandy and plain biscuits.

20 mins plus
8 hrs chilling

20 mins

MAKES 24 PIECES

INGREDIENTS

sunflower oil, for brushing

175 g/6 oz butter, softened

175 g/6 oz plain chocolate, melted

55 g/2 oz walnuts, roughly ground

55 g/2 oz blanched almonds, roughly ground

55 g/2 oz hazelnuts, roughly ground

115 g/4 oz golden caster sugar

3 tbsp water

1 tbsp brandy

175 g/6 oz plain biscuits, such as Petit Beurre, broken into small pieces

1 Oil a 28 x 20-cm/11 x 8-inch Swiss roll tin. Put the butter in a bowl and set aside. Put the chocolate in a heatproof bowl set over a saucepan of gently simmering water until melted, then beat with the butter until smooth. Stir in the ground walnuts, almonds and hazelnuts. Put the sugar and water in a saucepan and heat until the sugar has dissolved.

2 Boil steadily until the mixture reaches the soft ball stage (116°C/240°F on a sugar thermometer). To test, drop a spoonful of the mixture into cold water. A soft ball should form. Leave to cool for a few minutes, then beat vigorously and pour into the chocolate mixture, stirring until smooth.

3 Stir the brandy, then the biscuit pieces into the mixture. Turn into the prepared tin and press to flatten. Cover and chill overnight. Remove from the refrigerator just before serving and cut into diamond shapes.

COOK'S TIP
If you are grinding the nuts yourself in a food processor, take care not to over-process them or they will become oily.

Churros

These delicious Spanish morsels are an excellent choice with a cup of coffee as a mid-morning treat. They are best served hot.

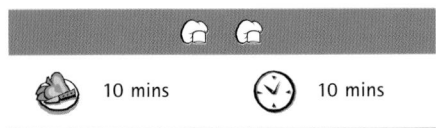

🍲 10 mins 🕐 10 mins

MAKES 4

INGREDIENTS

225 ml/8 fl oz water

grated rind of 1 lemon

85 g/3 oz butter

⅛ tsp salt

140 g/5 oz plain flour

¼ tsp ground cinnamon, plus extra for dusting

½–1 tsp vanilla essence

3 eggs

olive oil, for frying

about 5 tbsp sugar

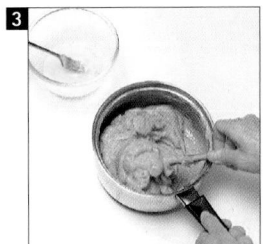

1 Place the water with the lemon rind in a heavy-based saucepan. Bring to the boil, add the butter and salt and cook for a few moments until the butter melts.

2 Add the flour all at once, with the cinnamon and vanilla, then remove the saucepan from the heat and stir rapidly until it forms the consistency of mashed potatoes.

3 Beat in the eggs, one at a time, using a wooden spoon; if you have difficulty incorporating the eggs to a smooth mixture, use a potato masher, then when it is mixed, return to a wooden spoon and mix until smooth.

4 Heat 2.5 cm/1 inch of oil in a deep frying pan until it is hot enough to brown a cube of bread in 30 seconds.

5 Place the batter in a piping bag with a wide star nozzle, then squeeze out 12.5-cm/5-inch lengths directly into the hot oil, making sure that the churros are about 7.5–10 cm/3–4 inches apart, as they will puff up as they cook. You may need to fry them in 2 or 3 batches.

6 Cook the churros in the hot oil for about 2 minutes on each side, until they are golden brown. Remove with a slotted spoon and drain on kitchen paper.

7 Dust generously with sugar and sprinkle with cinnamon to taste. Serve either hot or at room temperature.

Mini Cinnamon Muffins

To enjoy them at their best, serve these chocolate and spice muffins warm from the oven. They are particularly good served for breakfast.

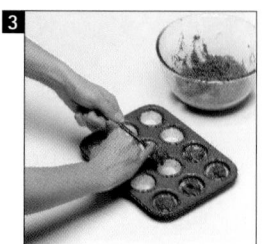

10 mins plus
5 mins cooling

15–20 mins

MAKES 20

INGREDIENTS

140 g/5 oz self-raising flour

1 tsp baking powder

2 tbsp cocoa powder

½ tsp ground cinnamon

55 g/2 oz light brown sugar

1 small egg, lightly beaten

150 ml/5 fl oz milk

4 tbsp butter, melted

1 Preheat the oven to 200°C/400°F/Gas Mark 6. Line 20 mini muffin cups with mini muffin paper cases.

2 Sift the flour, baking powder, cocoa powder and cinnamon into a bowl. Stir in the sugar. Mix together the egg, milk and melted butter.

3 Pour the egg mixture on to the dry ingredients and mix briefly. The mixture should be lumpy. Divide the mixture between the paper cases.

4 Bake in the oven for 15–20 minutes, until risen and the top springs back when lightly touched with a finger. Transfer the muffins to a wire rack to cool for 5 minutes, then serve warm.

Ginger Thins

Thin discs of chocolate studded with chopped stem ginger are the perfect accompaniment to after-dinner coffee.

15 mins plus setting

5 mins

MAKES 18–20

INGREDIENTS

200 g/7 oz plain chocolate

finely grated rind of 1 orange

3 pieces stem ginger, chopped-

1 Line a baking tray with non-stick baking parchment.

2 Break the chocolate into pieces and set over a saucepan of gently simmering water until melted. Stir the grated rind into the melted chocolate.

3 Place scant teaspoonfuls of chocolate on the prepared baking tray and spread them out with the back of the spoon to form thin discs.

4 Scatter the chopped ginger over the chocolate discs and leave to set.

Sopaipillas

These little, deep-fried puffs are popular sweet snacks in Mexico. You can serve them with honey, syrup or sprinkled with sugar and cinnamon.

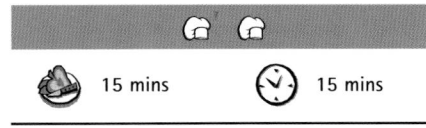

15 mins   15 mins

SERVES 6

INGREDIENTS

280 g/10 oz plain flour, plus extra for dusting

1 tbsp baking powder

salt

2 tbsp margarine, cut into pieces

175 ml/6 fl oz water

sunflower oil, for deep-frying

TO SERVE

85 g/3 oz caster sugar

1 tbsp ground cinnamon

1 Sift the flour, baking powder and a pinch of salt into a bowl. Add the margarine and rub it in with your fingertips until the mixture resembles breadcrumbs. Gradually stir in the water to form a soft dough.

2 Turn out the dough on to a floured surface and knead gently until smooth. Roll out to a large, thin rectangle, then cut into 7.5-cm/3-inch squares.

3 Heat the oil in a large, deep frying pan to 180–190°C/350–375°F or until a cube of bread browns in 30 seconds. Add the dough squares, a few at a time, and cook until puffed up and golden. Turn over and cook on the other side. Remove with a slotted spoon and drain on kitchen paper. Combine the sugar and cinnamon. Serve the sopaipillas warm, sprinkled with the sugar and cinnamon mixture.

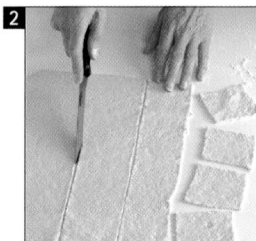

COOK'S TIP

Make sure the oil heats up again after you have cooked one batch before adding the next.

Chocolate Boxes

Guests will think you have spent hours creating these little boxes, but a few tricks (such as ready-made cake) make them quick to put together.

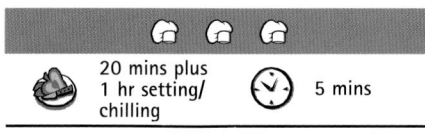

20 mins plus 1 hr setting/ chilling

5 mins

SERVES 4

INGREDIENTS

225 g/8 oz plain chocolate, broken into pieces

about 225 g/8 oz ready-made plain or chocolate sponge cake

2 tbsp apricot jam

150 ml/5 fl oz double cream

1 tbsp maple syrup

55 g/2 oz prepared fresh fruit, such as small strawberries, raspberries, kiwi fruit, cherries or redcurrants

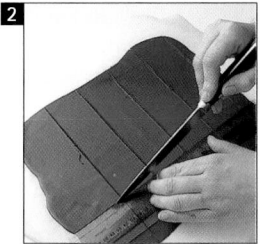

1 Melt the plain chocolate and spread it evenly over a large sheet of baking parchment with a spatula. Leave to harden in a cool place.

2 When just set, cut the chocolate into 16 x 5-cm/2-inch squares and remove from the baking parchment. Make sure that your hands are cool and handle the chocolate as little as possible.

3 Cut the cake into 2 cubes, 5 cm/ 2 inches across, then cut each cube in half. Warm the apricot jam and brush it over the sides of the cake. Carefully press a chocolate square on to each side of the cake to make 4 chocolate boxes with cake at the bottom. Chill in the refrigerator for 20 minutes.

4 Whip the double cream with the maple syrup until just holding its shape. Spoon or pipe a little of the mixture into each chocolate box.

5 Decorate the top of each box with the prepared fruit. If liked, the fruit can be partially dipped in melted chocolate and allowed to harden before being placed on top of the boxes.

COOK'S TIP
For the best results, keep the boxes well chilled and fill and decorate them just before you are ready to serve them.

Christmas Tree Decorations

Ribbon loops are sandwiched between chocolate shapes so that they can be hung on the Christmas tree.

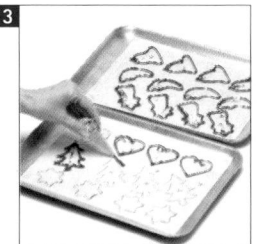

40 mins plus 1 hr setting

5 mins

MAKES 20

I N G R E D I E N T S

175 g/6 oz plain chocolate, broken into pieces

175 g/6 oz milk chocolate, broken into pieces

silver balls (optional)

coloured ribbon

1 On non-stick baking parchment, draw around Christmas biscuit cutters, such as stars and Christmas trees. Turn the paper over and place on a baking tray.

2 Melt the plain and milk chocolate in 2 separate heatproof bowls set over saucepans of gently simmering water.

3 Half fill 2 greaseproof paper piping bags with melted plain chocolate. Snip a small point off one bag and pipe a fine outline of chocolate, following the drawn shapes. Snip a larger point off the end of the second piping bag and pipe chocolate into the shapes to give an over-filled and rounded appearance. Repeat with the milk chocolate. If liked, decorate with silver balls. Leave to set hard.

4 Carefully peel off the paper. Cut the ribbon into short lengths to make loops. Sandwich matching chocolate shapes together with the remaining melted chocolate, placing the ribbon loops in between. Leave to set hard before hanging on the Christmas tree.

Chocolate Baskets

Chocolate-covered brandy snap baskets make perfect containers for a strawberry and cream filling delicately flavoured with raspberry liqueur.

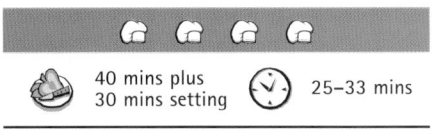

🍰 40 mins plus
30 mins setting

🕐 25–33 mins

MAKES 20

INGREDIENTS

55 g/2 oz unsalted butter

55 g/2 oz demerara sugar

2 tbsp golden syrup

55 g/2 oz plain flour, sifted

175 g/6 oz plain chocolate, broken into pieces

FILLING

225 ml/8 fl oz double cream

2 tbsp crème de framboise

115 g/4 oz small strawberries

1 Preheat the oven to 180°C/350°F/Gas Mark 4.

2 Put the butter, demerara sugar and golden syrup in a saucepan and heat gently until the butter has melted and the sugar has dissolved. Leave to cool slightly, then beat in the flour.

3 Place 20 half teaspoonfuls of the mixture on 4 baking trays, allowing room for the biscuits to spread during cooking, and press out with wet fingertips into 6-cm/2½-inch circles. Bake in the oven, 1 sheet at a time, for 5–7 minutes, until golden.

4 Leave to cool slightly, then remove with a round-bladed knife and invert over the bottom of an inverted tartlet tin or small glass. Mould the biscuits to give a wavy edge. Leave for a few minutes to set, then remove carefully. If the biscuits become too brittle to handle, return to the oven for 30 seconds to soften.

5 Put the chocolate in a heatproof bowl set over a saucepan of gently simmering water until melted. Put a spoonful of melted chocolate inside one of the baskets and rotate to coat the inside, using the back of a teaspoon to help. Repeat with the remaining chocolate and baskets. Leave to set.

6 Make the filling. Whip the cream and framboise together in a bowl until thick. Slice the strawberries and set aside 20 slices for decoration. Fold the rest into the cream and spoon into the baskets. Decorate with the sliced strawberries.

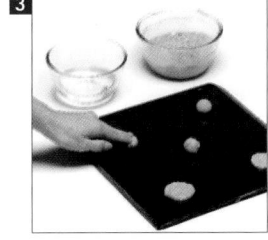

Real Hot Chocolate

You will never go back to commercial drinking chocolate powder once you have tasted this! Decorate with whipped cream for a real treat.

5 mins

5 mins

SERVES 1-2

INGREDIENTS

40 g/1½ oz plain chocolate,
  broken into pieces

300 ml/10 fl oz milk

2 tbsp whipped cream and drinking
  chocolate powder, to decorate

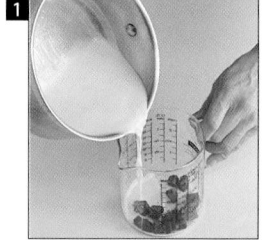
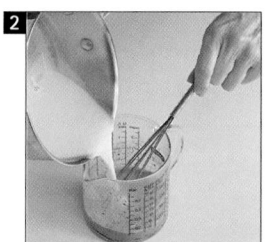

1 Put the chocolate into a large jug. Put the milk in a saucepan and bring to the boil. Pour about a quarter of the milk on to the chocolate and leave until the chocolate has softened.

2 Whisk until smooth. Return the remaining milk to the heat and bring back to the boil. Pour on to the chocolate, whisking constantly.

3 Pour into warmed mugs and top with whipped cream dusted with drinking chocolate powder.

COOK'S TIP
Chocolate powder for dusting on cappuccinos is available in supermarkets alongside the coffee.

Hot Chocolate Drinks

Rich and soothing, a hot chocolate drink in the evening can be just what you need to help ease away the stresses of the day.

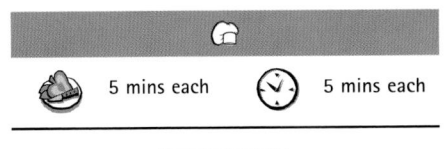

5 mins each   5 mins each

SERVES 2

INGREDIENTS

SPICY HOT CHOCOLATE

600 ml/1 pint milk

1 tsp mixed spice

100 g/3½ oz plain chocolate, broken into pieces

4 cinnamon sticks

100 ml/3½ fl oz double cream, lightly whipped

HOT CHOCOLATE & ORANGE TODDY

75 g/2½ oz orange-flavoured plain chocolate

600 ml/1 pint milk

3 tbsp dark rum

2 tbsp double cream

grated nutmeg

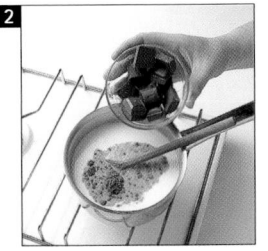

1 To make Spicy Hot Chocolate, pour the milk into a saucepan. Add the mixed spice.

2 Add the plain chocolate to the milk. Heat over a low heat until the milk is just boiling, stirring all the time to prevent the milk burning on the bottom.

3 Place 2 cinnamon sticks in 2 cups and pour in the hot chocolate. Top with the whipped double cream and serve.

4 To make Hot Chocolate & Orange Toddy, put the orange-flavoured chocolate in a saucepan with the milk. Heat the mixture over a low heat until just boiling, stirring constantly.

5 Remove the saucepan from the heat and stir in the dark rum. Pour into cups or heatproof glasses.

6 Pour the cream over the back of a spoon or swirl on to the top so that it sits on top of the hot chocolate. Sprinkle with grated nutmeg and serve at once.

COOK'S TIP

Using a cinnamon stick as a stirrer will give any hot chocolate drink a sweet, pungent flavour of cinnamon without overpowering the flavour of the chocolate.

White Heat

It is unusual to make a hot drink with white chocolate, but this winter warmer demonstrates that it works extremely well.

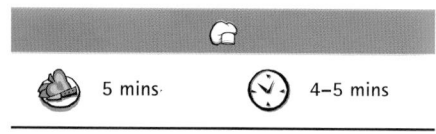

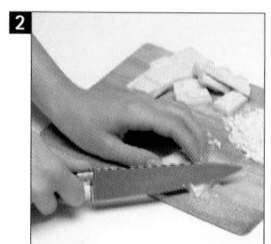

5 mins · 4–5 mins

SERVES 4

INGREDIENTS

4 tbsp double cream

1.7 litres/3 pints milk

175 g/6 oz white chocolate

2 tsp instant coffee

2 tsp brandy

1 tsp grated nutmeg

1 Whisk the double cream with an electric whisk until thickened. Set aside.

2 Pour the milk into a small saucepan and bring to just below boiling point, then remove from the heat. Meanwhile, finely chop the chocolate.

3 Whisk the chocolate, instant coffee and brandy into the milk and continue to whisk until the chocolate has melted and the mixture is smooth.

4 Pour the mixture into 4 warmed glasses or mugs. Top each with a spoonful of whipped cream, sprinkle with the nutmeg, and serve immediately.

VARIATIONS

Substitute another spirit for the brandy, if you prefer. Try whisky, crème de menthe or Grand Marnier.

Spiced Hot Chocolate

Plain chocolate and spices complement each other perfectly. Use a little ground cinnamon instead of mixed spice if preferred.

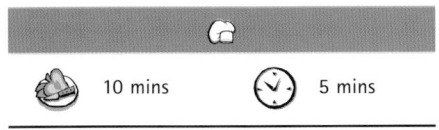

10 mins 5 mins

·SERVES 4

INGREDIENTS

900 ml/1½ pints milk

7 oz/200 g plain chocolate, broken into pieces (preferably one that contains at least 70 percent cocoa solids)

2 tsp sugar

1 tsp ground mixed spice

TO DECORATE

cocoa powder

grated white chocolate

1 Put the milk, chocolate, sugar and mixed spice in a saucepan over a medium heat. Whisk, stirring constantly, until the chocolate has melted and the mixture is simmering but not boiling.

2 Remove from the heat and pour into heatproof glasses. Sprinkle over some cocoa powder and grated white chocolate and serve immediately.

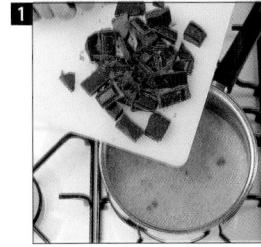
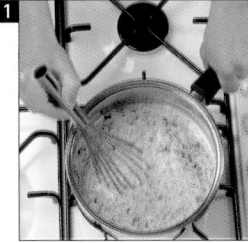

Chocolate Eggnog

The perfect pick-me-up on a cold winter's night, this delicious drink will get the taste buds tingling. Use brandy or whisky if preferred.

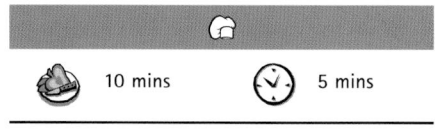

10 mins   5 mins

SERVES 4

INGREDIENTS

8 egg yolks

200 g/7 oz sugar

1 litre/1¾ pints milk

225 g/8 oz plain chocolate, grated

150 ml/5 fl oz dark rum

1 Beat the egg yolks with the sugar until thickened.

2 Pour the milk into a large saucepan, add the grated chocolate and bring to the boil. Remove from the heat and gradually beat in the egg yolk mixture. Stir in the rum, pour into heatproof glasses and serve immediately.

Hot Brandy Chocolate

Brandy and chocolate have a natural affinity, as this richly flavoured drink amply demonstrates. For pure indulgence top with whipped cream.

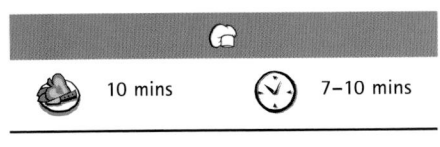

10 mins   7–10 mins

SERVES 4

I N G R E D I E N T S

1 litre/1¾ pints milk

115 g/4 oz plain chocolate, broken into pieces

2 tbsp sugar

5 tbsp brandy

6 tbsp whipped cream, to decorate

4 tsp cocoa powder, for sprinkling

1 Pour the milk into a saucepan and bring to the boil, then remove from the heat. Place the chocolate in a small saucepan and add 2 tablespoons of the hot milk. Stir over a low heat until the chocolate has melted. Stir the chocolate mixture into the remaining milk and add the sugar.

2 Stir in the brandy and pour into 4 heatproof glasses. Top each with a swirl of whipped cream and sprinkle with a little sifted cocoa powder.

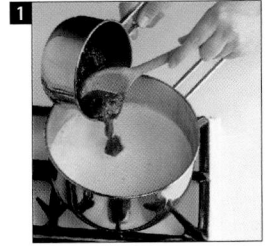
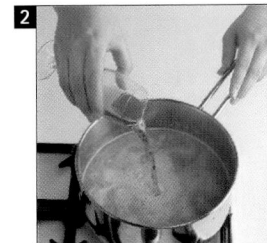

Café Mocha

This is sheer indulgence for coffee and chocolate lovers alike: the perfect nightcap. Use chocolate ice cream if preferred.

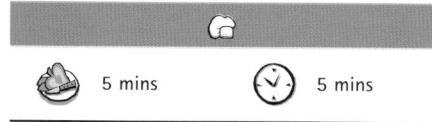
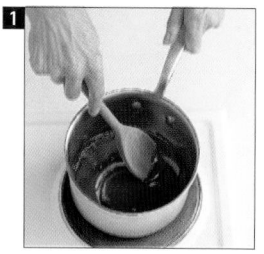

5 mins   5 mins

SERVES 2

INGREDIENTS

55 g/2 oz plain chocolate

2 tbsp water

2 tbsp golden caster sugar

225 ml/8 fl oz milk

125 ml/4 fl oz strong freshly made black coffee

2 scoops coffee ice cream

2 tbsp whipped cream, to decorate

1 Put the chocolate, water and sugar in a saucepan and heat gently until melted. Stir until smooth. Reserve a little of the chocolate sauce for decoration.

2 Stir the milk into the chocolate sauce. Divide the coffee among 2 warmed glasses and pour the chocolate mixture on the top.

3 Add the ice cream and drizzle the reserved chocolate sauce over.

Nutty Hot Chocolate

A cup of hot chocolate at bedtime will never be the same again after you have tasted this fabulous concoction.

15 mins

8 mins

SERVES 4

INGREDIENTS

70 g/2½ oz caster sugar

2 tbsp blanched almonds, coarsely chopped

55 g/2 oz cocoa powder

1 litre/1¾ pints milk

3 tbsp Amaretto

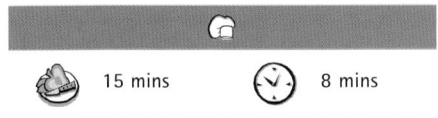
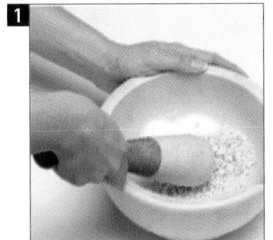

1 Grind 1 tablespoon of the sugar and the almonds with a pestle and mortar, or pulse briefly in a food processor.

2 Place the remaining sugar and the cocoa powder in a small bowl and add 3 tablespoons of the milk. Mix to a smooth paste.

3 Bring the remaining milk to the boil and whisk in the cocoa paste until thoroughly combined. Pour 225 ml/8 fl oz of the mixture into another saucepan and whisk in the almond mixture. Whisk over a low heat for 2 minutes, then return to the main saucepan. Remove the saucepan from the heat.

4 Stir in the Amaretto and pour the mixture into warmed glasses. Serve immediately.

COOK'S TIP
Be careful not to over-grind or over-process the almonds or they will become oily.

Hot Chocolate Float

It isn't only children who love the sensational combination of hot chocolate, whipped cream and coconut ice cream.

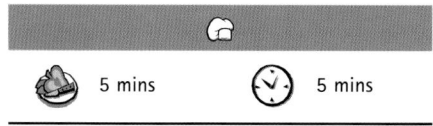

🍮 5 mins   🕐 5 mins

SERVES 4

INGREDIENTS

450 ml/16 fl oz milk

225 g/8 oz plain chocolate

2 tbsp caster sugar

8 scoops coconut ice cream

8 scoops plain chocolate ice cream

whipped cream, to decorate

1 Pour the milk into a saucepan. Break the chocolate into small pieces and add to the saucepan with the sugar. Stir over a low heat until the chocolate has melted, the sugar has dissolved and the mixture is smooth. Remove the saucepan from the heat.

2 Put 1 scoop of coconut ice cream into each of 4 heatproof glasses, top with a scoop of chocolate ice cream, then repeat the layers.

3 Pour the chocolate-flavoured milk into the glasses, top with whipped cream and serve immediately.

VARIATION

For a richer-tasting drink, substitute Continental plain chocolate for the plain chocolate.

Marshmallow Float

Children love this drink – let them choose which colour marshmallows they want to add. Find the best-quality chocolate for a good flavour.

5 mins   5 mins

SERVES 4

INGREDIENTS

225 g/8 oz plain chocolate, broken into pieces

900 ml/1½ pints milk

3 tbsp caster sugar

8 marshmallows

1 Finely chop the chocolate with a knife or in a food processor. Do not over-process or the chocolate will melt.

2 Pour the milk into a saucepan and bring to just below boiling point. Remove the saucepan from the heat and whisk in the sugar and the chocolate.

3 Pour into warmed mugs or heatproof glasses, top with a marshmallow or two and serve immediately.

COOK'S TIP

For an attractive finish, save 1 tablespoon of chopped chocolate to sprinkle over the marshmallows on top of the chocolate.

Alhambra Royale

This stylish version of hot chocolate is one to serve with a real flourish for a special occasion. Flame the glasses, one at a time.

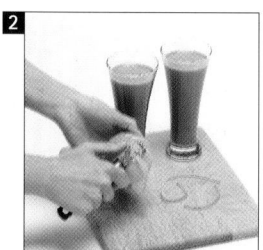

5 mins

10 mins

SERVES 4

INGREDIENTS

450 ml/16 fl oz milk

225 g/8 oz plain chocolate, broken into pieces

2 tbsp caster sugar

4 wide strips orange zest

175 ml/6 fl oz brandy

whipped cream, to decorate

1 Pour the milk into a saucepan. Add the chocolate and the sugar. Stir over a low heat until the chocolate has melted, the sugar dissolved and the mixture is smooth. Remove the saucepan from the heat.

2 Fill 1 heatproof glass almost full with the hot chocolate. Twist a strip of orange zest over it, then drop the zest into the glass.

3 Heat one-quarter of the brandy in a ladle over a saucepan of simmering water. When hot, carefully ignite it and ladle the flaming brandy into the glass. Stir well and top with a spoonful of whipped cream. Repeat to make 3 more glasses. Serve immediately.

VARIATION

For an Alhambra Mocha, stir 4 teaspoons of instant coffee powder into the hot chocolate milk until completely dissolved before pouring into the glasses.

Cinnamon Mocha

This drink is equally delicious hot or cold. It looks particularly attractive served in tall heatproof glasses.

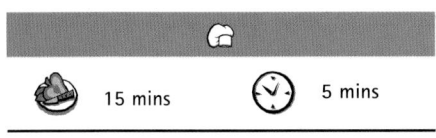

15 mins 5 mins

SERVES 6

INGREDIENTS

250 g/9 oz milk chocolate, broken into pieces

175 ml/6 fl oz single cream

1 litre/1¾ pints freshly brewed coffee

1 tsp ground cinnamon

whipped cream, to decorate

1 Put the chocolate in a large heatproof bowl set over a saucepan of gently simmering water. Add the light cream and stir until the chocolate has melted and the mixture is smooth.

2 Pour in the coffee, add the cinnamon, and whisk until foamy. If serving hot, pour into heatproof glasses or mugs, top with cream, and serve immediately. If serving cold, remove the bowl from the heat and let cool, then chill in the refrigerator until required.

VARIATIONS
You could also serve this with a scoop of chocolate ice cream or marshmallows.

Hot Ginger Chocolate

The combination of chocolate and stem ginger is a classic one, but it is not often found in drinks, although it works extremely well.

5 mins

10 mins

SERVES 4

INGREDIENTS

225 g/8 oz plain chocolate, broken into pieces

900 ml/1½ pints milk

4 tbsp syrup from a jar of stem ginger

4 tbsp double cream

1 Put the chocolate in a heatproof bowl set over a saucepan of gently simmering water until it melts. Remove from the heat.

2 Heat the milk in a saucepan until just below boiling point, then remove the saucepan from the heat. Stir in the melted chocolate and ginger syrup.

3 Pour into 4 mugs or heatproof glasses and float the cream on top. Serve immediately.

COOK'S TIP
To float cream on top of a drink, hold a spoon, round-side upward, against the rim of the mug or glass. Gently pour the cream over the back of the spoon so that it floats on the surface of the drink.

Viennese Chocolate

The perfect antidote to the winter blues, this rich drink is warming and wonderfully self-indulgent. Sprinkle with grated chocolate if wished.

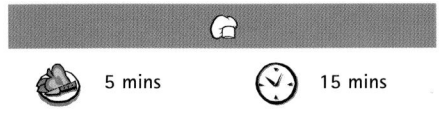

5 mins | 15 mins

SERVES 6

INGREDIENTS

5 tbsp double cream

2 tbsp icing sugar

few drops vanilla essence

200 g/7 oz plain chocolate, broken into pieces

1 litre/1¾ pints milk

1 tbsp caster sugar

1 Whisk the double cream until soft peaks form, then whisk in the icing sugar and vanilla. Set aside.

2 Put the chocolate in a heatproof bowl with 225 ml/8 fl oz of the milk. Set over a saucepan of gently simmering water until the chocolate melts, stirring occasionally.

3 Pour the remaining milk into a saucepan, add the caster sugar and heat gently. Add the chocolate and milk mixture as soon as the chocolate has melted and whisk constantly over the heat for 5 minutes until frothy.

4 Pour into warmed cups, top with the whipped cream mixture and serve immediately.

VARIATION
If you like, you can add 1–2 tablespoons of dark rum for an extra luxurious treat.

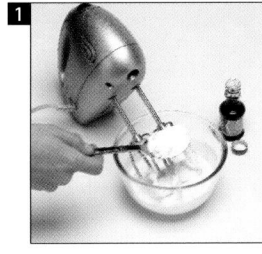

Mexican Chocolate Corn

If you can obtain Mexican chocolate, it is worth doing so, but otherwise use any good-quality, plain chocolate.

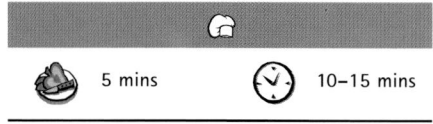
5 mins 10–15 mins

SERVES 6

INGREDIENTS

750 ml/1¼ pints water

55 g/2 oz tortilla flour

5-cm/2-inch piece cinnamon stick

750 ml/1¼ pints milk

85 g/3 oz plain chocolate, grated

sugar, to taste

1 Pour the water into a large saucepan, stir in the tortilla flour and add the cinnamon stick. Stir over a low heat for about 10–15 minutes, until thickened and smooth. Gradually stir in the milk, then beat in 85 g/3 oz of the grated chocolate, a little at a time, until melted and fully incorporated. Remove and discard the cinnamon stick.

2 Remove the saucepan from the heat and carefully ladle the mixture into heatproof glasses. Sweeten to taste with sugar and sprinkle the remaining grated chocolate on top.

Mexicana

Chocolate, coffee and rum make this a drink to really lift the spirits.
Sprinkle the tops with cocoa or grated plain chocolate if preferred.

5 mins   0 mins

SERVES 2

INGREDIENTS

25 g/1 oz plain chocolate

300 ml/10 fl oz hot black coffee

sugar

1 tbsp dark rum

TO DECORATE

2 tbsp whipped cream

ground coffee, for sprinkling

1 Put the chocolate, coffee and sugar in a blender and process until well blended.

2 Briefly blend in the rum and pour into 2 heatproof glasses.

3 Top with whipped cream and sprinkle with a little ground coffee.

Cold Chocolate Drinks

These delicious chocolate summer drinks are perfect for making a chocoholic's summer day! Use vanilla ice cream if preferred.

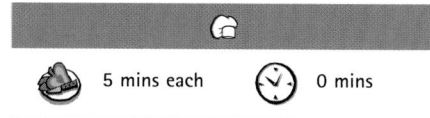

🧊 5 mins each   🕐 0 mins

SERVES 2

INGREDIENTS

CHOCOLATE MILKSHAKE

450 ml/16 fl oz ice-cold milk

3 tbsp drinking chocolate powder

3 scoops chocolate ice cream

cocoa powder, for dusting (optional)

CHOCOLATE ICE CREAM SODA

5 tbsp Glossy Chocolate Sauce (see page 692)

soda water

2 scoops chocolate ice cream

double cream, whipped

plain or milk chocolate, grated

1 To make the Chocolate Milkshake, pour half of the milk into a blender.

2 Add the drinking chocolate powder to the blender and 1 scoop of the chocolate ice cream. Blend until frothy and well mixed. Stir in the remaining milk.

3 Place the remaining 2 scoops of chocolate ice cream in 2 serving glasses and carefully pour the chocolate milk over the ice cream.

4 Sprinkle a little cocoa (if using) over the top of each drink and serve.

5 To make the Chocolate Ice Cream Soda, divide the Glossy Chocolate Sauce among 2 glasses. (You could also use a ready-made chocolate dessert sauce.)

6 Add a little soda water to each glass and stir to combine. Place a scoop of ice cream in each glass and top up with more soda water.

7 Place a dollop of whipped double cream on the top, if liked, and sprinkle with a little grated plain or milk chocolate to serve.

COOK'S TIP

Served in a tall glass, a milk shake or an ice cream soda makes a scrumptious snack in a drink. Serve with straws, if wished.

Quick Chocolate Milkshake

This is a great way to encourage children to drink milk, although adults will also enjoy this refreshing drink, especially on a hot summer's day.

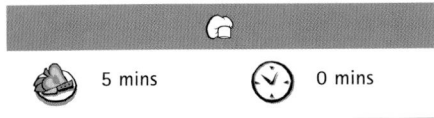

5 mins   0 mins

SERVES 2

I N G R E D I E N T S

6 rounded tbsp vanilla ice cream

4 tbsp drinking chocolate

300 ml/10 fl oz milk

1 chocolate flake bar, roughly crushed

ground cinnamon, for dusting

1 Place the vanilla ice cream, drinking chocolate and milk in a blender or food processor.

2 Process the mixture for 30 seconds, then pour into 2 tall serving glasses.

3 Sprinkle with the flake, add a light dusting of cinnamon and serve with straws, if you like.

VARIATION
For a more chocolatey milkshake, use chocolate ice cream instead of vanilla, and decorate the top with a light dusting of cocoa powder.

Iced Coffee & Chocolate Crush

Coffee, chocolate and peppermint make a wonderful combination. Serve in tall glasses and decorate with fresh mint sprigs.

🔥 5 mins   🕐 0 mins

SERVES 2

INGREDIENTS

400 ml/14 fl oz milk

175 ml/6 fl oz coffee syrup

125 ml/4 fl oz peppermint syrup

1 tbsp chopped fresh mint leaves

4 ice cubes

TO DECORATE

grated chocolate

fresh mint sprigs

1 Pour the milk, coffee syrup and peppermint syrup into a food processor and process gently until combined.

2 Add the mint and ice cubes and process until a slushy consistency has been reached.

3 Pour the mixture into glasses. Scatter over the grated chocolate, decorate with sprigs of fresh mint and serve.

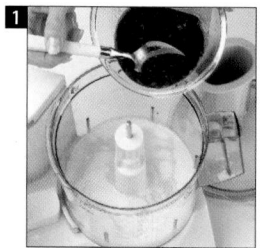
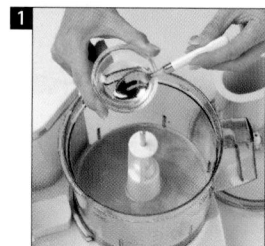

Mocha Float

This is deliciously refreshing on a hot summer's day and can double as dessert after an informal al fresco meal.

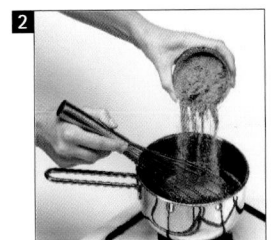

5 mins plus chilling

6 mins

SERVES 4

I N G R E D I E N T S

300 ml/10 fl oz water

225 g/8 oz sugar

55 g/2 oz cocoa powder, plus extra for dusting

2 tsp instant coffee powder

1.2 litres/2 pints ice-cold milk

4 scoops vanilla ice cream

4 cinnamon sticks

1 Pour the water into a saucepan and add the sugar. Stir over a low heat until the sugar has completely dissolved, bring to the boil, then boil without stirring for 3 minutes.

2 Whisk in the cocoa powder and instant coffee and remove the saucepan from the heat. Leave to cool, then chill in the refrigerator.

3 Measure about 6 tablespoons of the chocolate syrup into each of 4 glasses. Top with ice-cold milk. Add a scoop of ice cream. Break the cinnamon sticks in half and lay two halves crossed over on top of each glass. Dust lightly with cocoa powder and serve immediately.

Mocha Cream

Coffee and chocolate make perfect partners. You can prepare this drink stronger or sweeter according to your own particular taste.

15 mins

0 mins

SERVES 2

INGREDIENTS

175 ml/6 fl oz milk

4 tbsp single cream

1 tbsp soft brown sugar

2 tbsp cocoa powder

1 tbsp coffee syrup or instant coffee powder

6 ice cubes

TO DECORATE

whipped cream

grated chocolate

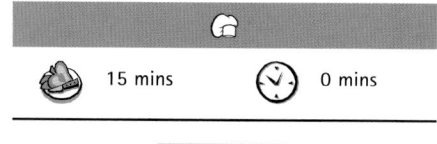
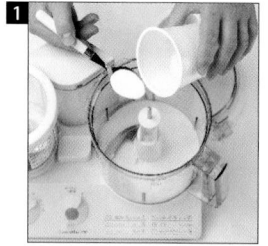

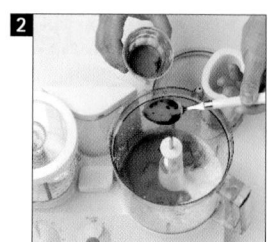

1 Put the milk, cream and sugar into a food processor and process gently until combined.

2 Add the cocoa powder and coffee syrup or powder and process well, then add the ice cubes and process again until smooth.

3 Pour the mixture into glasses. Top with whipped cream, sprinkle over the grated chocolate and serve.

Cool Minty Chocolate

This is a great non-alcoholic choice for an outdoor brunch party and also a good alternative for those who don't like coffee.

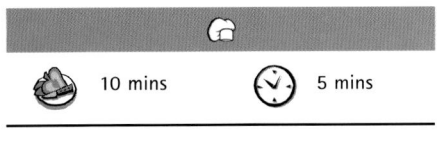

10 mins   5 mins

SERVES 4

I N G R E D I E N T S

600 ml/1 pint ice-cold milk

6 tbsp drinking chocolate powder

200 g/7 oz single cream

1 tsp peppermint essence

6 scoops chocolate-mint ice cream

fresh mint sprigs, to decorate

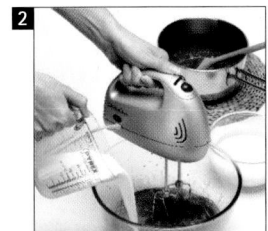

1 Pour half the milk into a small saucepan and stir in the drinking chocolate powder. Heat gently, stirring constantly, until just below boiling point and the mixture is smooth. Remove the saucepan from the heat.

2 Pour the chocolate-flavoured milk into a large, chilled bowl and whisk in the remaining milk. Whisk in the cream and peppermint essence and continue to whisk until cold.

3 Pour the mixture into 6 glasses, top each with a scoop of ice cream, decorate with a mint sprig and serve immediately.

VARIATIONS

Substitute natural yogurt for the cream. Omit the peppermint essence and mint sprigs and add 4 tablespoons of lime cordial with the yogurt. Serve with scoops of chocolate or vanilla ice cream.

Chocolate & Almond Float

Drinking chocolate powder, which is already sweetened and dissolves easily, is a very quick and easy way to make both hot and cold drinks.

🍲 10 mins 🕐 0 mins

SERVES 4

I N G R E D I E N T S

8 tsp drinking chocolate powder

3 tbsp boiling water

1 tsp almond essence, or to taste

700 ml/1¾ pints ice-cold milk

4 scoops chocolate-chip ice cream

1 Put the drinking chocolate powder into a bowl, add the boiling water and stir to a smooth paste.

2 Whisk in the almond essence and milk and continue to whisk until cold and thoroughly mixed. Taste and add more almond essence if liked.

3 Pour into 4 glass, top with a scoop of chocolate-chip ice cream and serve.

VARIATION
Substitute 4 teaspoons of maple syrup for the almond essence and top with popcorn instead of ice cream.

Egg Cream

It is difficult to know why this 'mocktail' is called egg cream, since it contains no eggs. However, it does resemble eggnog in texture.

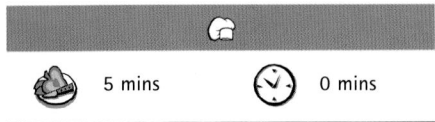

5 mins   0 mins

SERVES 2

I N G R E D I E N T S

50 ml/2 fl oz chocolate syrup

225 ml/8 fl oz oz ice-cold milk

soda water

1 Divide the chocolate syrup equally between 2 glasses. Stir in the milk until thoroughly combined.

2 Top up with soda water and stir until foamy. Serve immediately.

COOK'S TIP
Many syrups, fruit-flavoured as well as chocolate-flavoured, are ideal for making milkshakes and cocktails. They are available from large supermarkets.

Wonderful Town

A non-alcoholic cocktail, which is popular with both adults and children. This drink is fabulous to serve at a barbecue party.

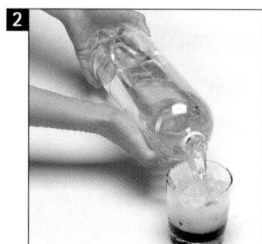

🍴 5 mins   🕐 0 mins

SERVES 4

INGREDIENTS

50 ml/2 fl oz chocolate syrup

125 ml/4 fl oz peppermint syrup

ice cubes

sparkling mineral water

TO DECORATE

fresh mint sprigs

grated chocolate

1 Divide the chocolate syrup and peppermint syrup equally among 4 medium tumblers or whisky glasses and mix well.

2 Fill the glasses with ice cubes, then top up with mineral water. Decorate with mint sprigs and grated chocolate and serve immediately.

VARIATION

For an alcoholic version of this cocktail, substitute clear crème de menthe for the peppermint syrup.

Barbary Coast

You will need a cocktail shaker to make this potent mixture. To ensure that it is properly mixed, make only one cocktail at a time.

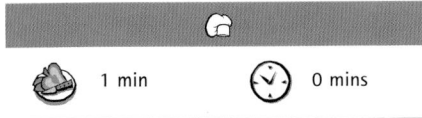

1 min   0 mins

SERVES 1

INGREDIENTS

cracked ice

1 tbsp white crème de cacao

2 tbsp white rum

1 tbsp Scotch whisky

1 tbsp gin

1 tbsp single cream

1 Half-fill a cocktail shaker with cracked ice, then pour in the crème de cacao, rum, whisky, gin and cream.

2 Replace the top and shake vigorously for 10–20 seconds. Strain into a chilled cocktail glass and serve immediately.

COOK'S TIP

If you are planning to serve cocktails frequently, it is worth buying a bar measure. A double measure usually has a 1½-tablespoon capacity at one end – a single – and slightly more than a 2-tablespoon capacity at the other end.

Chocolate Cocktail

It is drinking chocolate powder rather than a chocolate-flavoured liqueur that gives this cocktail its flavour. It's still quite potent, though.

1 min   0 mins

SERVES 1

INGREDIENTS

cracked ice

1½ tbsp maraschino

1½ tbsp yellow Chartreuse

1 tsp drinking chocolate powder

1 egg

1 Half-fill a cocktail shaker with cracked ice. Pour in the maraschino and Chartreuse and add the drinking chocolate powder and egg.

2 Replace the top and shake vigorously for 10–20 seconds. Strain into a chilled cocktail glass and serve immediately.

COOK'S TIP
If you like, frost the rim of the glass before serving. Brush the rim with a little egg white, then dip into a saucer of caster sugar to coat. Leave to dry.

Bushwhacker

This cocktail is based on Bailey's Irish Cream, an extremely popular chocolate-flavoured liqueur made with Irish whiskey and double cream.

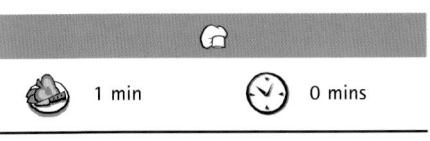

🧊 1 min   🕐 0 mins

SERVES 1

INGREDIENTS

cracked ice

ice cubes

1½ tbsp Bailey's Irish Cream

½ tbsp Tia Maria

1½ tbsp white rum

1½ tbsp Amaretto

175 ml/6 fl oz single cream

slice of lemon

1 Half-fill a cocktail shaker with cracked ice and half-fill a tumbler with ice cubes. Pour in the Bailey's, Tia Maria, rum and amaretto, then add the cream.

2 Replace the top and shake vigorously for 10–20 seconds, then strain into the tumbler, decorate with a slice of lemon and serve immediately.

VARIATION

For a Bushranger, half-fill a cocktail shaker with cracked ice, add a dash of Angostura bitters, pour in 50 ml/ 2 fl oz white rum and 1½ tablespoons of Dubonnet and shake for 10–20 seconds. Strain into a chilled glass and decorate with a slice of lemon.

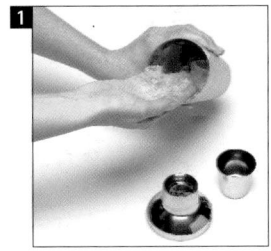

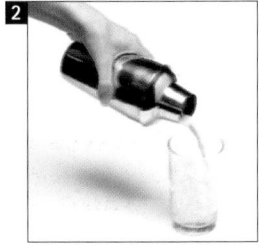

Tropical Cocktail

Crème de cacao, a chocolate-flavoured liqueur from France, varies in colour from pale cream to deep brown and in degrees of sweetness.

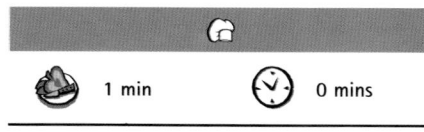

🕐 1 min   🕐 0 mins

SERVES 1

INGREDIENTS

cracked ice

dash of Angostura bitters

4 tbsp white crème de cacao

1½ tbsp maraschino

1 tbsp dry vermouth

1–2 maraschino cherries, to decorate

1 Half-fill a cocktail shaker with cracked ice and add a dash of Angostura bitters. Pour in the crème de cacao, maraschino and vermouth.

2 Replace the top and shake vigorously for 10–20 seconds. Strain into a chilled cocktail glass. Spear 1–2 maraschino cherries with a cocktail stick, add to the glass and serve immediately.

VARIATION
You can add a dash of orange bitters as well as the Angostura bitters to the cracked ice if you like.

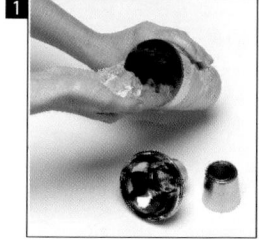

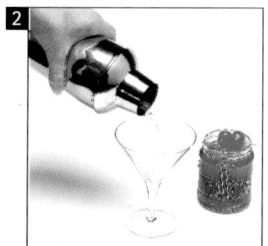

Macaroon

This cocktail, a mixture of chocolate and almond flavours, was no doubt named after the popular biscuit. Chill the cocktail glass before using.

1 min   0 mins

SERVES 1

I N G R E D I E N T S

cracked ice

1½ tbsp crème de cacao

1½ tbsp Amaretto

135 ml/4½ fl oz vodka

thin slice of orange, to decorate

1 Half-fill a cocktail shaker with cracked ice. Pour in the crème de cacao, amaretto, and vodka.

2 Replace the top and shake vigorously for 10–20 seconds. Strain into a chilled cocktail glass, decorate with a thin slice of orange, and serve immediately.

VARIATION
Moon Landing is a similar cocktail. Substitute Bailey's Irish Cream for the crème de cacao, use only 1½ tablespoons of vodka, and add 1½ tablespoons of Tia Maria. Shake and serve as above.

Krechma

The innocent appearance and smooth taste of this cocktail can deceive you into believing that it is far less potent than it actually is.

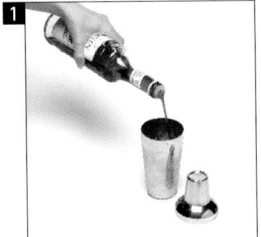

1 min | 0 mins

SERVES 1

INGREDIENTS

cracked ice

1–2 dashes grenadine

50 ml/2 fl oz crème de cacao

50 ml/2 fl oz vodka

1½ tbsp freshly squeezed lemon juice

1 Half-fill a cocktail shaker with cracked ice and add 1–2 dashes of grenadine. Pour in the crème de cacao, vodka, and lemon juice.

2 Replace the top and shake vigorously for 10–20 seconds. Strain into a chilled cocktail glass and serve immediately.

COOK'S TIP
Grenadine is a non-alcoholic syrup flavoured with pomegranate juice. It is used both for colouring and flavouring alcoholic and non-alcoholic drinks.

Irish Charlie

As fans of James Bond will be aware, some cocktails are indeed stirred, not shaken. The trick is to stir just long enough to chill, as well as mix.

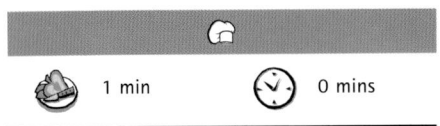

🧊 1 min   🕐 0 mins

SERVES 1

INGREDIENTS

ice cubes

1½ tbsp Bailey's Irish Cream

1½ tbsp white crème de menthe

fresh mint sprigs, to decorate

1 Place a few ice cubes in a large glass or jug. Pour in the Bailey's and crème de menthe.

2 Using a long, metal spoon, stir vigorously for 20 seconds. Strain into a chilled cocktail glass, decorate with the mint sprig and serve immediately.

COOK'S TIP
Cocktails are almost always strained into the glass, either through a small separate strainer or the integral strainer of a cocktail shaker, to avoid including the ice. This is because as the ice melts, it dilutes the cocktail and spoils the flavour.

Mocha Mint

This tastes just like a liquid version of a rich chocolate, coffee and mint mousse and has the same creamy texture. Perfect for a special occasion.

1 min   0 mins

SERVES 1

INGREDIENTS

cracked ice

1½ tbsp white crème de cacao

1½ tbsp Kahlúa

1½ tbsp white crème de menthe

slice of orange zest, to decorate

1 Half-fill a cocktail shaker with cracked ice. Pour in the crème de cacao, Kahlúa and crème de menthe.

2 Replace the top and shake vigorously for 10–20 seconds. Strain into a chilled cocktail glass, decorate with a slice of orange zest and serve immediately.

COOK'S TIP
Kahlúa is a coffee-flavoured liqueur from Mexico. It is slightly sweeter than Tia Maria, the other leading brand.

Mona Lisa

Guaranteed to give you an enigmatic smile as you sip, this cocktail is traditionally served in a glass frosted with lemon juice and sugar.

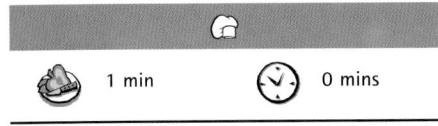

🕐 1 min   ⏰ 0 mins

SERVES 1

INGREDIENTS

1 lemon wedge

icing sugar or caster sugar, for frosting

ice cubes

4½ tbsp dark crème de cacao

1½ tbsp Noilly Prat or other dry vermouth

1 Rub the rim of the glass with the lemon wedge, then dip in a saucer of icing or caster sugar to frost.

2 Place a few ice cubes in a jug or large glass. Pour in the crème de cacao and vermouth.

3 Using a long metal spoon, stir vigorously for 20 seconds, then strain into a cocktail glass and serve immediately.

VARIATION

For a Duchamp's Mona Lisa, substitute Lillet for the Noilly Prat. Lillet is quite like vermouth in that it is a herb-flavoured apéritif made from wine fortified with brandy, in this case Armagnac.

Princess Mary

This is a creamy cocktail for the truly sweet-toothed. Adjust the quantity of sugar according to your personal taste.

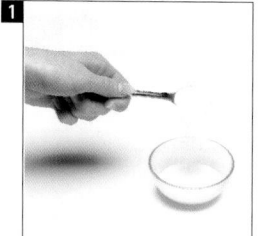

🍶 3 mins 🕐 0 mins

SERVES 1

INGREDIENTS

1½ tbsp single cream

1–2 tsp caster sugar

cracked ice

1½ tbsp white crème de cacao

1½ tbsp gin

grated plain chocolate, to decorate

1 Pour the cream into a small bowl and stir in caster sugar to taste. Half fill a cocktail shaker with cracked ice. Add the sweetened cream and pour in the crème de cacao and gin.

2 Replace the top and shake vigorously for 10–20 seconds. Strain into a chilled cocktail glass, sprinkle with grated chocolate and serve immediately.

VARIATION

For a Queen Mary, shake together the cracked ice, crème de cacao and gin, then float the cream on top and sprinkle with grated chocolate.

Panama Cocktail

Like many cocktails based on chocolate-flavoured liqueurs, this one is enriched by the addition of cream. Serve in a tall glass if liked.

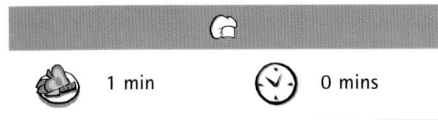

1 min   0 mins

SERVES 1

INGREDIENTS

cracked ice

1½ tbsp white crème de cacao

50 ml/2 fl oz brandy

4½ tbsp single cream

freshly grated nutmeg, to decorate

1 Half-fill a cocktail shaker with cracked ice. Pour in the crème de cacao, brandy and cream.

2 Replace the top and shake vigorously for 10–20 seconds. Strain into a chilled cocktail glass, sprinkle with freshly grated nutmeg and serve immediately.

COOK'S TIP

This is very similar to the well-known Brandy Alexander, which is made with dark crème de cacao and brandy.

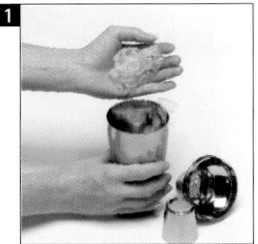

New York Knickerbocker

This is such a richly flavoured and substantial cocktail, it's almost a milkshake – but one that's strictly for adults. A great drink for a party.

🖐 1 min   🕐 0 mins

SERVES 1

INGREDIENTS

cracked ice

dash of grenadine

50 ml/2 fl oz white crème de cacao

1½ tbsp crème de banane

1½ tbsp Cointreau

4 tbsp single cream

banana slices, to decorate (optional)

1 Half-fill a cocktail shaker with cracked ice and add a dash of grenadine. Pour in the crème de cacao, crème de banane, Cointreau and cream.

2 Replace the top and shake vigorously for 10–20 seconds. Strain into a chilled cocktail glass, decorate with the banana slices and serve immediately.

VARIATION

For a much simpler version, shake 1½ tablespoons of crème de cacao and 1½ tablespoons of crème de banane with ice, strain and serve.

Chocolate Cake Cocktail

You will need a steady hand to achieve the attractive layered effect of this cocktail. Chill all the ingredients well before you start.

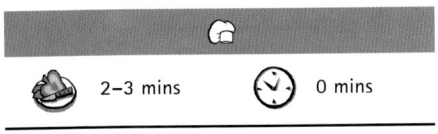

2–3 mins   0 mins

SERVES 1

INGREDIENTS

1½ tbsp dark crème de cacao, chilled

1½ tbsp brandy, chilled

1½ tbsp double cream, chilled

1 Pour the crème de cacao into a chilled liqueur glass or other small glass. When it is still, carefully spoon the brandy on top. Finally, spoon on the cream. Serve immediately.

VARIATION
If you have a steady hand you can make 2 additional layers. Spoon in 1½ tablespoons of Bailey's Irish Cream before adding the crème de cacao and 1½ tablespoons of Kahlúa before adding the cream.

Savoy Hotel

This is said to be named in honour of the eponymous London hotel, where the cocktail bar has been very creative over the decades.

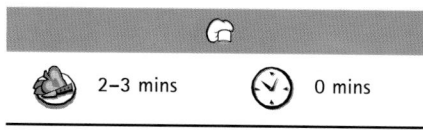

2–3 mins   0 mins

SERVES 1

INGREDIENTS

1½ tbsp dark crème de cacao, chilled

1½ tbsp Bénédictine, chilled

1½ tbsp brandy, chilled

1 Pour the crème de cacao into a chilled liqueur glass or other small glass. When it is still, carefully spoon the Bénédictine on top. Finally, spoon on the brandy. Serve immediately.

COOK'S TIP

Many cocktails that form layers in the glass have been inspired by the original Pousse-Café, which features 6 differently coloured ingredients poured in layers. A small, straight-sided glass, known as a pousse-café glass, is the best one to use for this sort of cocktail.

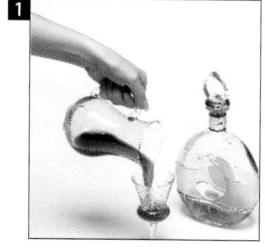

Velvet Hammer

This smooth cocktail seems innocuous, so it is extremely tempting to have several – that's where the hammer comes in.

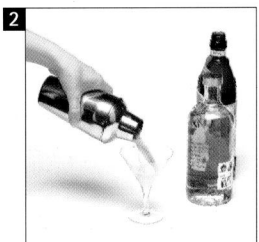

1 min   0 mins

SERVES 1

INGREDIENTS

crushed ice

5 tbsp vodka

1½ tbsp dark crème de cacao

1½ tbsp single cream

1 Half-fill a cocktail shaker with cracked ice. Pour in the vodka, crème de cacao and cream.

2 Replace the top and shake vigorously for 10–20 seconds. Strain into a chilled cocktail glass and serve immediately.

COOK'S TIP
Opinion is divided about decorating cocktails, although some classics are always served in the same way. If you want to add a decoration, choose something that complements the flavour of the drink.

index